Custom Version for the University of Houston - Third Edition

AMERICA AND ITS PEOPLES

A Mosaic in the Making

Volume II - from 1865

James Kirby Martin   Randy Roberts   Steven Mintz
Linda O. McMurry   James H. Jones

Containing Material From

America and Its Peoples: A Mosaic in the Making, Volume 2-to 1865, Fifth Edition
by James Kirby Martin, Randy Roberts, Steven Mintz,
Linda O. McMurry, James H. Jones

PEARSON
Custom
Publishing

PEARSON
Longman

Cover photograph courtesy of Comstock Images.

Taken from:

America and Its Peoples, Fifth Edition, Volume 2—from 1865
by James Kirby Martin, Randy Roberts, Steven Mintz, Linda O. McMurry, and James H. Jones
Copyright © 2003 by James Kirby Martin, Randy Roberts, Steven Mintz, Linda O. McMurry, and James H. Jones
Published by Longman, Inc.
A Pearson Education Company
New York, New York 10036

This special edition published in cooperation with Pearson Custom Publishing.

Printed in the United States of America

10 9 8 7 6 5 4 3 2 1

ISBN 0-536-86092-0

2004300083

LW

Please visit our web site at *www.pearsoncustom.com*

PEARSON CUSTOM PUBLISHING
75 Arlington Street, Suite 300, Boston, MA 02116
A Pearson Education Company

BRIEF CONTENTS

DETAILED CONTENTS

22 THE UNITED STATES AND WORLD WAR I   612

23 MODERN TIMES, 1920–1929   642

MAPS

TABLES AND FIGURES

FEATURES

PREFACE

Americans are of two minds about history. Popular history fascinates us. Many of Hollywood's most popular films—from *Birth of a Nation* to *Gangs of New York*—draw on history for their themes, characters, and drama. Nothing better underscores this fascination with history than the fact that more Americans visit historical sites and museums like Colonial Williamsburg or the National Museum of American History each year than attend major league baseball games.

Academic history is far less popular, however. "Boring" and "irrelevant" are adjectives often appended to the word *history*. At the high school level, history requirements have increasingly been replaced by courses in social studies. At colleges and universities, the number of history majors and enrollment in history courses has fallen at an alarming rate.

A disturbingly large number of students are ignorant about the most basic facts of our country's past. A recent survey of high school seniors showed that just two thirds of them knew that the Great Depression occurred during the twentieth century or that Germany and Japan were America's adversaries in World War II. A history report card issued by the U.S. Department of Education reported that 57 percent of high school seniors could not perform even "at the bottom of the achievement ladder" and that only 1 percent were advanced or superior.

Historical illiteracy is not a victimless crime. Time travel broadens our perspective just as physical travel does. Historical perspective is essential if we are to learn from the mistakes of the past and not repeat them. History reveals the debt we owe to past generations and reminds us that progress is not inevitable, but is the product of past decisions, choices, and struggles.

We have designed *America and Its Peoples* to convey American history's excitement and drama. The story that we tell is fraught with conflict, suspense, and controversy, and we have sought to recapture this excitement by writing a book built around vivid character sketches, colorful anecdotes, a strong narrative pulse, and a wide-angle view that allows us to examine such subjects as crime, disease, private life, and sports.

A history textbook, in our view, need not be dull, humorless, or lifeless. Rather, it should bring the past back to life in all of its complexity, underscoring history's relevance to our daily lives. The issues addressed in this book—colonialism, revolution, the origins of racial prejudice, the costs and benefits of industrialization and urbanization—are anything but trivial. They remain very much a part of the human story today.

Nor do we think that a textbook should insulate readers from controversy. One of history's greatest benefits is that it allows us to second guess the decisions and choices made in the past, to reassess the meaning of past events, and to reevaluate real-life heroes and villains. History, we believe, is the ideal laboratory for critical thinking. By engaging the past, we can assess the roles of individuals and of social forces in producing historical transformations and learn to evaluate conflicting interpretations of people and events. This textbook demonstrates that history is an arena of debate and contention as exciting as any other.

Each generation must produce a history that addresses the concerns of its own time. In writing *America and Its Peoples,* we have sought to fashion a history of the United States that speaks to the realities of a changing America. Today, the United States is the most ethnically diverse nation in the world. Over the past four centuries, 45 million people arrived in the United States from Africa, Asia, Latin America, and Europe. In *America and Its Peoples,* we recount the histories of the diverse ethnic, religious, and racial groups that have come to make up our society and underscore the pivotal role that ethnicity, race, and religion have played in our nation's social, cultural, and political development. From its earliest settlement, America has been a multicultural society, and by placing ethnicity, race, gender, and class at the very heart of our narrative, we have sought to present a new perspective on how our multifaceted culture and politics functioned through time.

Contemporary American society perceives itself as beset by unprecedented problems—of ethnic and racial tension, economic stagnation and inequality, crime, family upheaval, and environmental degradation. In *America and Its Peoples,* we have made a special point of uncovering the historical roots of the problems confronting American society today. One of history's values is that it can show how previous generations confronted the controversial issues of their times, allowing us to assess their achievements as well as their failures.

Americans are an optimistic, forward-looking people who, in the course of everyday life, care little about the past. More than two centuries ago, Thomas Jefferson gave pointed expression to this attitude when he declared "the earth belongs to the living and not the dead." But as the novelist William Faulkner once observed, "the past is never dead. It's not even past." We are convinced that the very worst forms of bigotry, fanaticism, and racism are ultimately grounded in historical ignorance and mythology. History reminds us that our values, our identities, and our most pressing social problems are rooted in our historical experience. Thus, in writing this book, we have not sought simply to create an encyclopedic compendium of names, dates, events, and concepts; we have conceived of U.S. history as a dramatic story: a story involving contention, struggle, compromise, and, above all, conflicting visions of the nation's dominant values.

Today, many Americans are wary about the future and uneasy about the state of their society. In *American and Its Peoples,* we have written a textbook that emphasizes historical contingency—the idea that different decisions and choices in the past would have created a very different world today. Ours is a history that emphasizes the importance of personal choice and collective action; a history that stresses peoples' capacity to shape their own destiny. We believe that this is an inspiring historical lesson with profound implications for the nation's future.

APPROACH AND THEMES

Written by scholars who regularly teach the introductory U.S. history survey, *America and Its Peoples* brings history to life through the stories of the women and men who have shaped our history as a people. Highly sensitive to students' needs and interests, the authors place ethnicity, race, and gender at the core of the historical narrative. Carefully balancing cultural, diplomatic, economic, military, political, religious, and social history, the authors pay special attention to the clash of ideas and peoples that has shaped American history. This fifth edition contains up-to-date coverage of the controversial presidential election of 2000, the terrorist attacks of September 11, 2001, and the presidency of George W. Bush.

America and Its Peoples thoroughly treats the history of *all* Americans, providing extensive coverage of women, African Americans, Asian Americans, Hispanic Americans, and Native Americans. It offers exceptionally complete coverage of the areas that were originally colonized by Spain, to meet the special needs of students who live in the Sunbelt. Concisely and vividly written, the textbook contains a wealth of special features designed to stimulate student interest in history and reinforce student learning.

FEATURES

America and Its Peoples, Fifth Edition, includes a wealth of features and pedagogical aids designed to engage students' interest and enhance their learning:

- *Chapter-opening outlines* help students prepare for their study of the chapter by listing the main topics and subtopics to be discussed.
- *Chapter-opening vignettes* capture students' interest through the story of an individual or a specific event. Set-off paragraphs at the end of the vignette succinctly introduce chapter themes and explain how the vignette relates to or exemplifies the chapter's themes and topics.
- *"The American Mosaic" essays* offer an in-depth examination of some aspect of such high-interest topics as crime, medicine, sports and other leisure-time activities, the experience of combat, and the reshaping of private life.
- *"The People Speak"* These excerpts from primary sources introduce students to critical documents in American history and allow them to hear the people of the past speak in their own voices. Brief introductions provide the historical context for each document.
- *Key Terms* In each chapter, key terms are highlighted in boldface type to alert students to the principal concepts and events discussed in the chapter. A page-referenced list of the key terms at the end of each chapter helps students review the main ideas and events covered in the chapter.
- *Battlefield Maps* Five watercolor maps offer close examination of some of the key battles in America's wars. An essay accompanying each battlefield map describes the battle in detail and explores its historical significance.
- *"Road to War" Tables* These specialized chronologies summarize the key events that led up to the declaration of each of America's wars, summarizing for students the background for these pivotal events in U.S. history.

- *Review Questions* End-of-the-chapter review questions allow students to examine how well they have absorbed the chapter content and invite them to think critically about the issues discussed in the chapter. The review questions can be used to spark class discussions or for written assignments.
- *Comprehensive Reference Resources* Reference material at the end of each chapter includes both print and media resources. Print resources are a selective list of scholarly works that provide additional depth and insight on the chapter content and novels that illuminate the era covered in the chapter; media resources include films, videos, and documentaries related to the chapter content and an annotated list of Web sites identifying for students sources of additional information that can be easily accessed online.
- *Glossary* An expanded glossary at the end of the book provides definitions for the key terms in each chapter. Each glossary term is page referenced so that students can easily locate discussion of the term in its historical context.

NEW TO THIS EDITION

- *Chapter 32* This new chapter offers a full account of the presidency of Bill Clinton, the disputed presidential election of 2000, the terrorist attacks of September 11, 2001, the presidency of George W. Bush, the globalization of the American economy, and the increasing diversity of the U.S. population.
- *New chapter-opening vignettes* New vignettes on Prudence Crandall (Chapter 11), the 1893 World's Columbian Exposition in Chicago (Chapter 17), and Muhammad Ali (Chapter 29) use the stories of these individuals and events to bring to life the era covered in the chapter—the age of reform, the age of industrialization and the rise of big business, and the struggle for civil rights and the liberation movements of the 1960s, respectively.
- *New "The People Speak" document excerpts.* This edition of *America and Its Peoples* contains several new primary source excerpts, among them John Winthrop, "A Model of Christian Charity" (Chapter 2); documents on the Trail of Tears (Chapter 11) and the Irish potato famine (Chapter 13); Senator William Alfred Peffer, "The Mission of the Populist Party" (Chapter 19); the Watergate tapes (Chapter 31); and international

reactions to the terrorist attacks of September 11, 2001 (Chapter 32).
- *New "The American Mosaic" essays* Two new American Mosaic essays—New Powers in the South and West (Chapter 30) and Terrorism in Historical Perspective (Chapter 32)—discuss the new immigration of the late twentieth century and the language, history, and acts of terrorism from ancient Rome to the present day.
- *Chapter Summary and Key Points* This new pedagogical device aids student understanding of the chapter by recalling chapter themes and recapping major events, topics, and concepts covered in the chapter.
- *People You Should Know* At the end of each chapter is a list of the prominent individuals discussed in the chapter, reminding students of the major players involved in the events covered in the chapter.
- *New maps* Fourteen new maps have been added in the fifth edition to provide geographical context for text discussions. Among these new maps are Ratification of the Constitution (Chapter 6), Territorial Growth to 1853 (Chapter 13), African American Population Distribution in 1890 (Chapter 19), World War I Casualties (Chapter 22), Events of the Civil Rights Movement (Chapter 29), and McDonald's Around the World (Chapter 32).

SUPPLEMENTS

A comprehensive and up-to-date supplements package accompanies *America and Its Peoples*.

For Qualified College Adopters

Companion Website (*www.ablongman.com/martin*) The instructor section of the Website includes the instructor's manual, teaching links, and PowerPoint presentations with the maps, graphs, and charts from the text.

Course Management Longman offers an American history course in CourseCompass™, Blackboard, and WebCT. These courses include primary sources, atlas maps, and map exercises. Ask your Longman representative for more details.

Digital Media Archive CD-ROM Free to qualified college adopters, this CD-ROM contains hundreds of images and maps and dozens of interactive maps and video clips.

Instructor's Manual This resource, prepared by Austin Allen of the University of Houston–Downtown, contains a synopsis, sample discussion questions, lecture supplements, and instructional flowcharts for each chapter.

Test Bank Written by Marc Maltby of Owensboro Community College, the test bank contains multiple choice, true/false, and essay test items. The questions are keyed to topic, cognitive type, and relevant text page.

TestGen-EQ Computerized Testing System This flexible, easy-to-master computerized test bank on a dual-platform CD includes all the test items in the printed test bank. The software allows instructors to select specific questions, edit existing questions, and add their own items to create exams. Tests can be printed in several different fonts and formats and can include figures, such as graphs and tables.

Text Map Transparencies A set of 40 four-color transparencies from the maps and figures in *America and Its Peoples*.

Comprehensive American History Transparency Set This vast collection of American history transparencies is a necessary teaching aid. It includes over 200 maps covering social trends, wars, elections, immigrations, and demographics. Included is a set of reproducible map exercises.

Discovering American History Through Maps and Views Transparency Set Created by Gerald Danzer of the University of Illinois at Chicago, the recipient of the AHA's 1990 James Harvey Robinson Prize for his work in the development of map transparencies, this set of 140 four-color acetates is a unique instructional tool. It contains an introduction on teaching history through maps and a detailed commentary on each transparency. The collection includes cartographic and pictorial maps, views and photos, urban plans, building diagrams, and works of art.

Video Lecture Launchers Prepared by Mark Newman of the University of Illinois at Chicago, these video lecture launchers (each two to five minutes in duration) cover key issues in American history from 1877 to the present. The launchers are accompanied by an instructor's manual.

"This Is America" Immigration Video Produced by the American Museum of Immigration, this video tells the story of American immigrants. By showing how the richness of our culture is due to the contributions of millions of immigrant Americans, the videos make the point that America's strength lies in the ethnically and culturally diverse backgrounds of its citizens.

For Students

Companion Website (*www.ablongman.com/martin*) Students will find summaries, practice test questions, Web links, and flashcards for every chapter.

Study Guide This two-volume study guide, prepared by Karen Guenther of Mansfield University, is designed to provide students with a comprehensive review of the text material and to encourage application and critical analysis of the material. Each chapter contains an overview, learning objectives, important glossary terms, and multiple choice and essay questions.

Longman American History Atlas This four-color reference tool and visual guide to American history includes almost 100 maps and covers the full scope of history. Atlas overhead transparencies are available to adopters.

Mapping American History: Student Activities Created by Gerald Danzer of the University of Illinois at Chicago, this workbook may be used in conjunction with *Discovering American History Through Maps and Views* and is designed to teach students to interpret and analyze cartographic materials as historical documents.

Mapping America: A Guide to Historical Geography, Second Edition This two-volume workbook by Ken Weatherbie of Del Mar College presents the basic geography of the United States and helps students place the history of the United States into spatial perspective. *Available free to college adopters when bundled with the book.*

Research Navigator Guide This guidebook includes exercises and tips on how to use the Internet. It also includes an access code for Research Navigator™—the easiest way for students to start a research assignment or research paper. Research Navigator™ is composed of three exclusive databases of credible and reliable source material, including EBSCO's ContentSelect™ Academic Journal Database, New York Times Search by Subject Archive, and "Best of the Web" Link Library. This comprehensive site also includes a detailed help section.

America Through the Eyes of Its People, Second Edition This comprehensive anthology makes primary sources widely available in an inexpensive format, balancing social and political history and providing up-to-date narrative material. The documents reflect the rich and varied tapestry of American life. *Free to qualified college adopters when bundled with the book.*

Sources of the African-American Past, Second Edition Edited by Roy Finkenbine of the University of Detroit at Mercy, this collection of primary sources covers themes in the African American experience from the West African background to the present. Balanced between political and social history, the documents offer a vivid snapshot of the lives of African Americans in different historical periods. The collection includes documents representing women and different regions of the United States. *Available to qualified college adopters at a reduced price when bundled with the text.*

Women and the National Experience, Second Edition Edited by Ellen Skinner of Pace University, this primary source reader contains both classic and unusual documents describing the history of women in the United States. The documents provide dramatic evidence that outspoken women attained a public voice and participated in the development of national events and policies long before they could vote. Chronologically organized and balanced between social and political history, this reader offers a striking picture of the lives of women across American history. *Available to qualified college adopters at a reduced price when bundled with the text.*

Reading the American West Edited by Mitchel Roth of Sam Houston State University, this primary source reader uses letters, diary excerpts, speeches, interviews, and newspaper articles to let students experience how historians research and how history is written. Every document is accompanied by a contextual headnote and study questions. The book is divided into chapters with extensive introductions. *Available to qualified college adopters at a reduced price when bundled with the text.*

Library of American Biography Series Each of these interpretive biographies focuses on a figure whose actions and ideas significantly influenced the course of American history and national life. At the same time, each biography relates the life of its subject to the broader themes and developments of the era. Brief and inexpensive, they are ideal for any U.S.

history course. *Available to qualified college adopters at a discounted price when bundled with the book.*

A Short Guide to Writing About History, Fourth Edition Written by Richard Marius of Harvard University and Melvin E. Page of Eastern Tennessee University, this engaging and practical text helps students get beyond merely compiling dates and facts. This guide teaches them how to incorporate their own ideas into their papers and to tell a story about history that interests them and their peers. Covering both brief essays and the documented resource paper, the text explores the writing and research processes, as well as different modes of historical writing including argument, and concludes with guidelines for improving style.

Constructing the American Past, Fourth Edition Compiled and edited by Elliot Gorn and Randy Roberts of Purdue University along with Terry Bilhartz of Sam Houston State University, this two-volume popular reader consists of a wide variety of primary sources grouped around central themes in American history. Each chapter focuses on a particular problem in American history, providing students with several points of view from which to examine the historical evidence. Introductions and study questions prompt students to participate in interpreting the past and challenge them to understand the problems in relation to the big picture of American history.

American Experiences: Readings in American History. Fifth Edition This two-volume collection of secondary source readings, compiled and edited by Randy Roberts of Purdue University and James Olson of Sam Houston State University, contains articles that emphasize social history in order to illuminate important aspects of America's past. *American Experiences* addresses the complexity and richness of the nation's past by focusing on the people themselves—how they coped with, adjusted to, or rebelled against America. The readings examine people as they worked and played, fought and loved, lived and died.

Penguin Books

The partnership between Penguin-Putnam USA and Longman Publishers offers qualified college adopters a discount on many titles when bundled with any Longman survey. Penguin titles include *Narrative of the Life of Frederick Douglass* by Frederick Douglass; *Benjamin Franklin: The Autobiography & Other Writings*, L. Jesse Lemisch (Editor); *The Jungle* by Upton Sinclair; and *Uncle Tom's Cabin* by Harriet Beecher Stowe.

ACKNOWLEDGMENTS

Any textbook project is very much a team effort. Here we acknowledge with gratitude the assistance of the many talented historians who have served as reviewers and whose valuable critiques have greatly strengthened the fifth edition of *America and Its Peoples*.

Robert Carriker, *University of Louisiana at Lafayette*
Karen Guenther, *Mansfield University*
David M. Head, *John Tyler Community College*
James R. Hedtke, *Cabrini College*
Douglas E. Kupel, *Gateway Community College*
James M. McCaffrey, *University of Houston–Downtown*
Robert E. McCarthy, *Providence College*
Kenneth T. Osborne, *Metropolitan College, Roger Williams University*
Susan A. Strauss, *Santa Fe Community College*
Jerry K. Sweeney, *South Dakota State University*
Lynn Yerby, *Cypress College*

This book also owes much to the many conscientious historians who reviewed previous editions and offered valuable suggestions that led to many improvements in the text. We acknowledge with gratitude the contributions of the following:

Joe S. Anderson, *Azusa Pacific University*
Elizabeth Reilly Ansnes, *San Jose State University*
Larry Balsamo, *Western Illinois University*
James Banks, *Cuyahoga Community College*
Lois W. Banner, *University of Southern California*
Robert A. Becker, *Louisiana State University*
Delmar L. Beene, *Glendale Community College*
Surendra Bhana, *University of Kansas*
Nancy Bowen, *Del Mar College*
Blanche Brick, *Blinn College*
Larry Burke, *Dodge City Community Junior College*
Frank L. Byrne, *Kent State University*
Colin G. Calloway, *University of Wyoming*
Albert Camarillo, *Stanford University*
Ballard Campbell, *Northeastern University*
Clayborne Carson, *Stanford University*
Jay Caughtry, *University of Nevada at Las Vegas*
Raymond W. Champagne, Jr., *University of Scranton*
Paul G. E. Clemens, *Rutgers University*
Kenton Clymer, *University of Texas at El Paso*
Berry Craig, *Paducah Community College*
John P. Crevelli, *Santa Rosa Junior College*
Shannon J. Doyle, *University of Houston*
Thelma Epstein, *DeAnza College*
John Findlay, *University of Washington*
Roy E. Finkenbine, *University of Detroit*
Mark S. Foster, *University of Colorado at Denver*
Ronald H. Fritze, *Lamar University*

David Glassberg, *University of Massachusetts*
James P. Gormly, *Washington and Jefferson College*
Elliott Gorn, *Purdue University*
Neil Hamilton, *Brevard Community College*
Sam W. Haynes, *University of Texas at Arlington*
Nancy Hewitt, *Rutgers University*
J. David Hoeveler, *University of Wisconsin at Milwaukee*
Steven R. Hoffbeck, *Minot State University*
Melissa M. Hovsepian, *University of St. Thomas, Texas*
Alphine W. Jefferson, *Southern Methodist University*
David R. Johnson, *University of Texas at San Antonio*
Ellen K. Johnson, *Northern Virginia Community College*
Deborah M. Jones, *Bristol Community College*
Kathleen Kennedy, *Western Washington University*
Sterling J. Kernek, *Western Illinois University*
Stuart E. Knee, *College of Charleston*
George W. Knepper, *University of Akron*
Tim Koerner, *Oakland Community College*
Lee Bruce Kress, *Rowan University*
Barbara E. Lacey, *Saint Joseph College*
Steven F. Lawson, *Rutgers University*
Irene Ledesma, *University of Texas–Pan American*
Barbara LeUnes, *Blinn College*
Thomas Lewis, *Mount Senario College*
Terrence Lindell, *Wartburg College*
Ann E. Liston, *Fort Hays State University*
James McMillan, *Arizona State University*
Myron Marty, *Drake University*
M. Catherine Miller, *Texas Tech University*
Otis Miller, *Belleville Area College*
William Howard Moore, *University of Wyoming*
Peter Myers, *Palo Alto College*
Daniel Nelson, *University of Akron*
Mark Newell, *Ramapo College*
Roger L. Nichols, *University of Arizona*
Barbara J. Oberlander, *Santa Fe Community College*
Michael Perman, *University of Illinois at Chicago*
Peter L. Petersen, *West Texas A&M University*
Paula Petrik, *University of Maine*
Robert Pierce, *Foothill College*
George Rable, *Anderson College*
Max Reichard, *Delgado Junior College*
Leonard R. Riforgiato, *Pennsylvania State University, Shenango Valley Campus*
Marilyn Rinehart, *North Harris County College*
Jon H. Roberts, *University of Wisconsin at Stevens Point*
Randall Rosenberg, *University of Northern Alabama*
James G. Ryan, *Texas A&M University at Galveston*
David P. Shriver, *Cuyahoga Community College*
Jason H. Silverman, *Winthrop University*
John Ray Skates, *University of Southern Mississippi*
Sheila Skemp, *University of Mississippi*

Kathryn Kish Sklar, *State University of New York at Binghamton*
Larry Steck, *Lake Michigan College*
Robert Striplin, *American River College*
Alan Taylor, *Boston University*
Jason Tetzloff, *Defiance College*
Gary E. Thompson, *Tulsa Junior College*
Jose Torres, *Mesa Community College*
Philip Vaughn, *Rose State College*
Peter H. Wang, *Cabrillo Community College*
Eddie Weller, *San Jacinto College South*
Larry Wilson, *San Jacinto College Central*
Valdenia Winn, *Kansas City Kansas Community College*
Bill Worley, *Sterling College*
Eli Zaretsky, *University of Missouri*

Each author has received invaluable assistance from friends, colleagues, and family. James Kirby Martin thanks Don R. Gerlach, Joseph T. Glatthaar, Irene Guenther, Karen Guenther, Katie Harrison, J. Kent McGaughy, David M. Oshinsky, Cathy Patterson, Jeffrey T. Sammons, Halt T. Shelton, and Karen Martin, whose talents as an editor and critic are too often overlooked. Randy Roberts thanks Terry Bilhartz, Aram Goudsouzian, James S. Olson, and Joan Randall. Steven Mintz thanks Susan Kellogg for her encouragement, support, and counsel. Linda O. McMurry thanks Joseph P. Hobbs, John David Smith, Richard McMurry, and William C. Harris. James H. Jones thanks Kimberley Weathers for her assistance in revising the fifth edition. All of the authors thank Gerard F. McCauley, whose infectious enthusiasm for this project has never wavered. And above all else, we wish to thank our students to whom we have dedicated this book.

The Authors

ABOUT THE AUTHORS

James Kirby Martin holds the rank of Distinguished University Professor of History at the University of Houston. He received his Ph.D. in history from the University of Wisconsin, Madison. His areas of special interest include early American history, including the era of the American Revolution, American military history through the years of the Civil War, and the history of such social-behavioral issues as drinking and smoking in America. He is the author, co-author, or editor of eleven books, including *Men in Rebellion* (1973), *In the Course of Human Events* (1979), *A Respectable Army: The Military Origins of the Republic* (1982), and *Drinking in America* (1982, revised edition 1987). His most recent book, *Benedict Arnold, Revolutionary Hero: An American Warrior Reconsidered* (1997), was the recipient of the Homer D. Babbidge, Jr. Award and was named by the *Los Angeles Times* to its list of the best 100 books published that year. Martin has served as general editor of the *American Social Experience* series, New York University Press. His many interests also include the study of ordinary persons and the ways in which their lives have shaped the course of American historical development. His capacity to present these lives in meaningful historical contexts helps explain why his students consistently rank him among the very best teachers in the department.

Randy Roberts earned his Ph.D. degree from Louisiana State University. His areas of special interest include modern U.S. history and popular culture in America. He is a faculty member at Purdue University, where he has won the Murphy Award for outstanding undergraduate teaching, the School of Liberal Arts Teacher of the Year award, and the Society of Professional Journalists Teacher of the Year award. The books on which he is author or co-author include *Jack Dempsey: The Manassa Mauler* (1979, expanded edition, 1984), *Papa Jack: Jack Johnson and the Era of White Hopes* (1983), *Heavy Justice:* The State of Indiana *v.* Michael G. Tyson (1994), *My Lai: A Brief History with Documents* (1998), *John Wayne: American* (1995), *Where the Domino Fell: America in Vietnam, 1945–1990* (1990, revised edition 1996), *Winning Is the Only Thing: Sports in America Since 1945* (1989), *A Line in the Sand: The Alamo in Blood and Memory* (2001), and *Pittsburgh Sports: Stories from the Steel City* (2000), among others. Roberts serves as the co-editor of the Sports and Society series, University of Illinois Press, and is on the editorial board of the *Journal of Sports History.* In addition, he has made frequent appearances on television and been involved in numerous documentaries.

Steven Mintz is the John and Rebecca Moores Professor of History and director of the American Cultures Program at the University of Houston. A leading authority on the history of the family as well as a noted expert on slavery, social reform, and the history of film, his books include *The Boisterous Sea of Liberty* (with David Brion Davis, 1998), *Moralists & Modernizers: America's Pre–Civil War Reformers* (1995), *Domestic Revolutions: A Social History of American Family Life* (with Susan Kellogg, 1989), and *A Prison of Expectations: The Family in Victorian Culture* (1983). A pioneer in the application of new computer technologies in history, he moderates a scholarly discussion list on the history of slavery and has served as Vice President for Teaching of H-Net: Humanities and Social Sciences Online. He is also the recipient of two "Teaching American History" grants from the U.S. Department of Education.

Linda O. McMurry is an emeritus professor of history at North Carolina State University, specializing in African American history. Her interest in personal perspectives and experiences of history has led her to write three biographies: *To Keep the Waters Troubled: The Life of Ida B. Wells* (1998), *Recorder of the Black Experience: A Biography of Monroe Nathan Work* (1985), and *George Washington Carver: Scientist and Symbol* (1981). Both the Wells and Carver biographies are listed in the *New York Review of Books Readers' Catalog* of the best books in print. A recipient of a Rockefeller Foundation Humanities fellowship, McMurry has been active as a consultant and lecturer on topics relating to the black experience in America, appearing on such programs as NPR's "Morning Edition" and C-SPAN's "Booknotes." In 1999, she won both the top teaching and research awards from her college. Although she is retired from full-time teaching, she continues to work with graduate students and plans to return to the classroom on a part-time basis.

James H. Jones earned his Ph.D. degree at Indiana University. His areas of specialization include modern U.S. history, the history of medical ethics and medicine, and the history of sexual behavior. Jones has been a member of the advisory board of the Arkansas Center for Oral and Visual History, a senior fellow of the National Endowment for the Humanities, a Kennedy fellow at Harvard University, a senior research fellow at the Kennedy Institute of Ethics, Georgetown University, and a Rockefeller fellow at the University of Texas Medical Branch, Galveston. His published works include *Bad Blood: The Tuskegee Syphilis Experiment, A Tragedy of Race and Medicine* (1981), revised edition (1993), which was named to the *New York Times Book Review* list of best books of 1981 and received the Arthur Viseltear prize for the Best Book in Public Health History. His most recent publication, *Alfred C. Kinsey: A Public/Private Life* (1997), was a finalist for both the Pulitzer Prize in biography and the Penn Center Award. Recently retired from teaching, Jones is now living in Santa Fe, New Mexico, where he devotes all his time to research and writing.

AMERICA
AND ITS
PEOPLES

A MOSAIC IN THE MAKING

16 The Nation Reconstructed: North, South, and the West, 1865–1877

THOMAS PINCKNEY CONFRONTS HIS FORMER SLAVES

As Thomas Pinckney approached El Dorado, his plantation on the Santee River in South Carolina, he felt a quiver of apprehension. Pinckney, a captain in the defeated Confederate army, had stayed the night with neighbors before going to reclaim his land. "Your negroes sacked your house," they reported, "stripped it of furniture, bric-a-brac, heirlooms, and divided these among themselves. They got it in their heads that the property of whites belongs to them." Pinckney remembered the days when his return home had been greeted with slaves' chants of "Howdy do, Master! Howdy do, Boss!" Now he was welcomed with an eerie silence. He did not even see any of his former slaves until he went into the house. There, a single servant seemed genuinely glad to see him, but she pleaded ignorance as to the whereabouts of any others. He lingered about the house until after the dinner hour. Still no one appeared, so he informed the servant that he would return in the morning and expected to see all his former slaves.

On his ride back the next day, Pinckney nostalgically recalled his days as a small boy when the slaves had seemed happy to see him as he accompanied his mother on her Saturday afternoon rounds. He could not believe he had any reason to fear his "own people" whom he "could only remember as respectful, happy and affectionate." He probably mistook their previous displays of submissiveness as expressions of a genuine affection that would not be altered by freedom. Yet he was armed this time, and after summoning his former slaves, he quickly noticed that they too were armed. Their sullen faces reflected their defiant spirits.

Pinckney told them, "Men, I know you are free. I do not wish to interfere with your freedom. But I want my old hands to work my lands for me. I will pay wages." They remained silent as he gave further reassurances. Finally one responded, "O yes, we gwi wuk! We gwi wuk fuh ourse'ves. We ain' gwi wuk fuh no white man." Pinckney was confused and asked how they expected to support themselves and where they would go. They quickly informed him that they intended to stay and work "right here on de lan' whar we wuz bo'n an' whar belongs tuh us." One former slave, dressed in a Union army uniform, stood beside his cabin, brought his rifle down with a crash, and declared, "I'd like tuh see any man put me outer dis house."

This 1865 illustration by Thomas Nast illustrates the optimism that came with emancipation and contrasts the opportunities of freedom with the horrors of slavery.

Pinckney had no intention of allowing the former slaves to work the land for themselves. He joined with his neighbors in an appeal to the Union commander at Charleston, who sent a company of troops and addressed the blacks himself. They still refused to work under his terms, so Pinckney decided to "starve" them into submission. He denied them access to food and supplies. Soon his head plowman begged food for his hungry family, claiming he wanted to work, "But de other niggers dee won' let me wuk." Pinckney held firm, and the man returned several days later saying, "Cap'n, I come tuh ax you tuh lemme wuk fuh you, suh." Pinckney pointed him to the plow and let him draw his rations. Slowly, his other former slaves drifted back to work. "They had suffered," he later recalled, "and their ex-master had suffered with them."

All over the South this scenario was acted out with variations, as former masters and former slaves sought to define their new relationships. Whites tried to keep the blacks a dependent labor source; African Americans struggled to win as much independence as possible. Frequently Union officials were called upon to arbitrate; the North had a stake in the final outcome. At the same time the other sections of the nation faced similar problems of determining the status of heterogeneous populations whose interests were sometimes in conflict with the majority. The war had

reaped a costly harvest of death and hostility, but at the same time it accelerated the modernization of the economy and society. Western expansion forced Americans to deal with the often hostile presence of the Plains Indians; the resumption of large-scale immigration raised issues of how to adapt to an increasingly pluralistic society made up of many different ethnic and religious groups. More and more the resolution of conflicting interests became necessary: farmer versus industrialist, whites versus blacks, Republicans versus Democrats, Indians versus settlers, North versus South, management versus labor, immigrant versus native born, men versus women, one branch of government versus another. Complicating these issues were unresolved questions about federal authority, widespread racial prejudice in both North and South, and strongly held beliefs in the sanctity of property rights.

Reconstruction offered an opportunity to balance conflicting interests with justice and fairness. In the end, however, the government was unwilling to establish ongoing programs and permanent mechanisms to protect the rights of minorities. As on Pinckney's plantation, economic power usually became the determining factor in establishing relationships. Northerners were distracted by issues related to industrialization and Westerners by conflicts with the Plains Indians. Authorities sacrificed the interests of both African Americans and the Indians of the West to the goals of national unity and economic growth. Yet in the ashes of failure were left two cornerstones on which the future could be built—the Fourteenth and Fifteenth amendments to the Constitution.

POSTWAR CONDITIONS AND ISSUES

General William T. Sherman proclaimed, "War is all hell." Undoubtedly it was for most soldiers and civilians caught up in the actual throes of battle and for the families of the 360,000 Union and 258,000 Confederate soldiers who would never return home. The costs of war, however, were not borne equally. Many segments of the North's economy were stimulated by wartime demands, and with the once powerful southern planters no longer there, Congress enacted programs to aid industrial growth. Virtually exempt from the devastation of the battlefield, the North built railroads and industries and increased agricultural production at the same time that torn-up southern rails were twisted around trees, southern factories were put to the torch, and southern farmland lay choked with weeds.

In 1865 Southerners were still reeling from the bitter legacy of total war. General Philip Sheridan announced that after his troops had finished in the Shenandoah Valley even a crow would have to carry rations to fly over the area. One year after the war, Carl Schurz noted that along the path of Sherman's march the countryside still "looked for many miles like a broad black streak of ruin and desolation." Much of what was not destroyed was confiscated, and emancipation divested Southerners of another $2 billion to $4 billion in assets. The decline of southern wealth has been estimated at more than 40 percent during the four years of war.

The War's Impact on Individuals

Returning soldiers and their wives had to reconstruct relationships disrupted by separation—and the assumption of control by the women on farms and plantations. War widows envied them that adjustment. While the homeless wandered, one plantation mistress moaned, "I have not one human being in the wide world to whom I can say 'do this for me.'" Another noted, "I have never even so much as washed out a pocket handkerchief with my own hands, and now I have to do all my work." Southerners worried about how to meet their obligations; Confederate currency and bonds were worthless except as collectors' items—and even as collectors' items, they were too plentiful to have much value. One planter remarked dryly that his new son "promises to suit the times, having remarkably large hands as if he might one day be able to hold plough handles." Many white Southerners, rich and poor, suffered a self-

induced paranoia. They imagined the end of slavery would bring a nightmare of black revenge, rape, and pillage unless whites retained social control.

For four million former slaves, emancipation had come piecemeal, following the course of the northern armies. It was not finalized until the ratification of the Thirteenth Amendment in December 1865. Most slaves waited patiently for the day of freedom, continuing to work the plantations but speaking up more boldly. Sometimes the Yankees came, proclaimed them free, and then left them to the mercy of their masters. Most, therefore, reacted cautiously to test the limits of their new freedom.

Many African Americans had to leave their plantations, at least for a short time, to feel liberated. A few were confused as to the meaning of freedom and thought they would never have to work again. Soon, most learned they had gained everything—and nothing. As **Frederick Douglass,** the famous black abolitionist, noted, the freedman "was free from the individual master but a slave of society. He had neither money, property, nor friends."

The wartime plight of homeless and hungry blacks as well as whites impelled Congress to take unprecedented action, establishing on March 3, 1865, the Bureau of Refugees, Freedmen, and Abandoned Lands (**Freedmen's Bureau**), within the War Department. The bureau was to provide "such issues of provisions, clothing, and fuel" as were needed to relieve "destitute and suffering refugees and their wives and children." It was a massive task. The bureau issued 22 million in rations between 1865 and 1870. Never before had the national government assumed responsibility for relief. Feeding and clothing the population had not been deemed its proper function. Considered drastic action, warranted only by civil war, the bureau was supposed to operate for just a year, but was extended for five years.

Under Commissioner **Oliver O. Howard,** the bureau had its own courts to deal with land and labor disputes. Agents in every state provided rations and medical supplies and helped to negotiate labor contracts between former slaves and landowners. The quality of the service rendered to the former slaves depended on the ability and motivation of the individual agents. One of the most lasting benefits of the bureau was the schools it established. During and after the war, African Americans of all ages flocked to schools to taste the previously forbidden fruit of education. The former slaves shrewdly recognized the keys to the planters' power—land, literacy, and the vote. The white South had legally denied all three to African Americans in slavery, and now many former slaves were determined to have them all.

Some former bondsmen had a firmer grasp of reality than their "liberators." Southern whites had

Day of Jubilo: Slaves Confront Emancipation

Rooted in Africa, the oral tradition became one of the tools slaves used to maintain a sense of self-worth. Each generation heard the same stories, and storytelling did not die with slavery. The day that slaves first learned of their emancipation remained vivid in their own minds and later in those of their descendants. The great-grandchildren of a strong-willed woman named Caddy relished the family account of her first taste of freedom:

> Caddy threw down that hoe, she marched herself up to the big house, then she looked around and found the mistress. She went over to the mistress, she flipped up her dress and told the white woman to do some thing. She said it mean and ugly. This is what she said: *Kiss my ass!*

Caddy's reaction was not typical. There was no typical response. Reminiscences of what was called the "Day of Jubilo" formed a tapestry as varied as the range of personality. Some, however, seem to have occurred more frequently than others. Many former slaves echoed one man's description of his and his mother's action when their master announced their emancipation: "Jes like tarpins or turtles after 'mancipation. Jes stick our heads out to see how the land lays."

Caution was a shrewd and realistic response. One of the survival lessons in slavery had been not to trust whites too much. This had been reinforced during the war when Union troops moved through regions proclaiming emancipation only to depart, leaving blacks at the mercy of local whites. One elderly slave described the aftermath to a Union correspondent. "Why, the day after you left, they jist had us all out in a row and told us they was going to shoot us, and they did hang two of us; and Mr. Pierce, the overseer, knocked one with a fence rail and he died the next day. Oh, Master! we seen stars in de day time."

Environment played a role in slaves' reactions to the Day of Jubilo. Urban slaves frequently enjoyed more freedom than plantation slaves. Even before emancipation such black social institutions as schools and churches emerged in many cities. When those cities were liberated, organized celebrations occurred quickly. In Charleston 4000 black men and women paraded before some 10,000 spectators. Two black women sat in one mule-drawn cart while a mock auctioneer shouted, "How much am I offered?" In the next cart a black-draped coffin was inscribed with the words "Slavery Is Dead." Four days after the fall of Richmond blacks there held a mass rally of some 1500 people in the First African Church.

Knowledge of their freedom came in many forms to the slaves. Rural slaves were less likely to enjoy the benefits of freedom as early as urban slaves. Many heard of the Emancipation Proclamation through the slave grapevine or from Union soldiers long before its words became reality for them. Masters sometimes took advantage of the isolation of their plantations to keep their slaves in ignorance or to make freedom seem vague and frightening. Their ploys usually failed, but learned patterns of deference made some former slaves unwilling to challenge their former masters. Months after emancipation one North Carolina slave continued to work without compensation, explaining to a northern correspondent, "No, sir; my mistress never said anything to me that I was to have wages, nor yet that I was free; nor I never said anything to her. Ye see I left it to her honor to talk to me about it, because I was afraid she'd say I was insultin' to her and presumin', so I wouldn't speak first. She ha'n't spoke yet." There were, however, limits to his patience; he intended to ask her for wages at Christmas.

Numerous blacks described the exuberance they felt. One elderly Virginia man went to the barn, jumped from one stack of straw to another, and "screamed and screamed!" A Texan remembered, "We all felt like horses" and "everybody went wild." Other blacks recalled how slave songs and spirituals were updated, and "purty soon ev'ybody fo' miles around was singin' freedom songs."

Quite a few slaves learned of freedom when a Union officer or Freedmen's Bureau agent read them the Emancipation Proclamation—often over the objections of the master. "Dat one time," Sarah Ford declared, "Massa Charley can't open he mouth, 'cause de captain tell him to shut up, dat he'd do the talkin'." Some masters, however, still sought to have the

called for him." Education was the key for others. "If I nebber does do nothing more while I live," a Mississippi freedman vowed, "I shall give my children a chance to go to school, for I considers education next best ting to liberty."

Most came to a good understanding of the benefits and limits of their new status. One explained, "Why, sar, all I made before was Miss Pinckney's, but all I make now is my own." Another noted, "You could change places and work for different men." One newly freed slave wrote his brother, "I's mighty well pleased tu git my eatin' by de 'sweat o' my face, an all I ax o' ole masser's tu jes' keep he hands off o' de Lawd Almighty's property, fur *dat's me*." A new sense of dignity was cherished by many. An elderly South Carolina freedman rejoiced, "Don't hab me feelins hurt now. Used to hab me feelins hurt all de times. But don't hab em hurt now, no more." Charlie Barbour exulted over one thing: "I won't wake up some mornin' fer fin' dat my mammy or some ob de rest of my family am done sold." Most agreed with Margrett Millin's answer when she was asked decades later whether she had liked slavery or freedom better. "Well, it's dis way. In slavery I owns nothin'. In freedom I's own de home and raise de family. All dat cause me worryment and in slavery I has no worryment, but I takes de freedom."

last word. A Louisiana planter's wife announced immediately after the Union officer departed, "Ten years from today I'll have you all back 'gain."

Fear did not leave all slaves as soon as their bondage was lifted. Jenny Proctor of Alabama recalled that her fellow slaves were stunned by the news. "We didn' hardly know what he means. We jes' sort of huddle 'round together like scared rabbits, but after we knowed what he mean, didn' many of us go, 'cause we didn' know where to of went." James Lucas, a former slave of Jefferson Davis, explained, "folks dat ain' never been free don' rightly know de *feel* of bein' free. Dey don' know de meanin' of it."

Former slaves quickly learned that one could not eat or wear freedom.

"Dis livin' on liberty," one declared, "is lak young folks livin' on love after they gits married. It just don't work." They searched for the real meaning of liberty in numerous ways. Some followed the advice of a black Florida preacher, "You ain't none 'o you, gwinter feel rale free till you shakes de dus ob de Ole Plantashun offen you feet," and moved. Others declared their independence by legalizing their marriages and taking new names or publicly using surnames they had secretly adopted while in slavery. "We had a real sho' nuff weddin' wid a preacher," one recalled. "Dat cost a dollar." When encouraged to take his old master's surname, a black man declared, "Him's nothing to me now. I don't belong to he no longer, an' I don't see no use in being

long claimed to "know our Negroes" better than outsiders could. Ironically, this was proven false, but the reverse *was* true. Ex-slaves knew their ex-masters very well. One freedman pleaded, "Gib us our own land and we can take care ourselves; but widout land, de ole massas can hire us or starve us, as dey please." The events on Pinckney's plantation proved the wisdom of that statement.

Later generations have laughed at the widespread rumor among former slaves that they were to receive "forty acres and a mule" from the government, but the rumor did have some basis. During the war, General Sherman was plagued with swarms of former slaves following his army, and in January 1865 he issued **Special Field Order 15** setting aside a strip of abandoned coastal lands from Charleston, South Carolina, to Jacksonville, Florida, for the exclusive use of former slaves. African Americans were to be given "possessory titles" to 40-acre lots. Three months later, the bill establishing the Freedmen's Bureau gave the agency control of thousands of acres of abandoned and confiscated lands to be rented to "loyal refugees and freedmen" in 40-acre plots for three-year periods with an option to buy at a later date. By June 1865, 40,000 African Americans were cultivating land. In the Sea Islands and elsewhere, they proved they could be successful independent farmers. Yet land reform was not a popular cause among whites. Although a few congressmen continued to advocate land confiscation and redistribution, the dream of "forty acres and a mule" was a casualty of the battle for control of Reconstruction when Andrew Johnson's pardons returned most confiscated lands. Indeed, the issue of economic security for the former slaves was obscured by other questions that seemed more important to whites.

Unresolved Issues

At war's end some issues had been settled, but at a terrible cost. As historian David Potter noted, "slavery was dead, secession was dead, and six hundred thousand men were dead." A host of new problems had arisen from the nature of civil war and the results of that war as well as the usual postwar dislocations. Many questions remained that shaped Reconstruction.

The first of these concerned the status of the former slaves. They were indeed free, but were they citizens? The **Dred Scott decision** (1857) had denied citizenship to all African Americans. Even if it were decided that they were citizens, what rights were conferred by that citizenship? Would they be segregated as free blacks in the antebellum North had often been? Also, citizenship did not automatically confer suffrage; women were proof of that. Were the freedmen to be given the ballot? These weighty matters were complicated by racial prejudice as well as constitutional and partisan questions.

The Constitution had been severely tested by civil war, and many felt it had been twisted by the desire to save the Union. Once the emergency was over, how were constitutional balance and limits to be restored? Except during the terms of a few strong presidents, Congress had been the most powerful branch of government during the nation's first 70 years. Lincoln had assumed unprecedented powers, and Congress was determined to regain its ascendancy. The ensuing battle directly influenced Reconstruction policies and their implementation.

Secession was dead, but what about states' rights? Almost everyone agreed that a division of power between the national and state governments was crucial to the maintenance of freedom. The fear of centralized tyranny remained strong. There was reluctance to enlarge federal power into areas traditionally controlled by the states, even though action in some of those areas was essential to craft the kind of peace many desired. Hesitation to reduce states' rights produced timid and compromised solutions to such issues as suffrage.

Another constitutional question concerned the status of the former Confederate states and how they were to be readmitted to the Union. There was no constitutional provision for failed secession, and many people debated whether the South had actually left the Union or not. The query reflected self-interest rather than an intellectual inquiry. Ironically, Southerners and their Democratic sympathizers now argued that the states had never legally separated from the rest of the nation, thus denying validity to the Confederacy in order to quickly regain their place in the Union. Extremists on the other side—**Radical Republicans**—insisted that the South had reverted to the status of conquered territory, forfeiting all rights as states. Under territorial governments, Representative Thaddeus Stevens declared, Southerners could "learn the principles of freedom and eat the fruit of foul rebellion." Others, including Lincoln, believed that the Confederate states had remained in the Union but had forfeited their rights. This constitutional hair-splitting grew out of the power struggle between the executive and legislative branches to determine which had the power to readmit the states and on what terms.

Influencing all these issues were partisan politics. Although not provided for in the Constitution, political parties had played a major role in the evolving American government. The road to war had disrupted the existing party structure—killing the Whig party, dividing the Democratic party, and creating the Republican party. The first truly sectional party, the Republican party had very few adherents in the

South. Its continued existence was dubious in the face of the probable reunion of the northern and southern wings of the Democratic party. Paradoxically, the political power of the South, and in turn the Democratic party, was increased by the abolition of slavery. As slaves, only three-fifths of African Americans had been counted for representation; with the end of slavery, all African Americans would be counted. Thus the Republican party's perceived need to make itself a national party also colored the course of Reconstruction.

PRESIDENTIAL RECONSTRUCTION

Early in the conflict, questions regarding the reconstruction of the nation were secondary to winning the war—without victory there would be no nation to reconstruct. Nonetheless, Lincoln had to take some action as Union forces pushed into the South. Authority had to be imposed in the reclaimed territory, so the president named military governors for Tennessee, Arkansas, and Louisiana in 1862 after federal armies occupied most of those states. He also began formulating plans for civilian government for those states and future Confederate areas as they came under the control of Union forces. The result was a Proclamation of Amnesty and Reconstruction issued in December 1863 on the constitutional basis of the president's power to pardon.

Lincoln's Plan

Called the **10 percent plan,** Lincoln's provisions were incredibly lenient. Rebels could receive presidential pardon by merely swearing their future allegiance to the Union and their acceptance of the end of slavery. In other words, former Confederates were not required to say they were sorry—only to promise they would be good in the future. A few people were excluded from pardons, such as Confederate military and civilian officers. After only 10 percent of the number who had voted in 1860 had taken the oath, a state could form a civilian government. When such states produced a constitution outlawing slavery, Lincoln promised to recognize them as reconstructed. He did not demand any provisions for protecting black rights or allowing black suffrage.

Tennessee, Arkansas, and Louisiana met Lincoln's requirements and soon learned they had only cleared the first barrier in what became a long obstacle course. Radical Republicans, such as Representative **Thaddeus Stevens** of Pennsylvania and Senator **Charles Sumner** of Massachusetts, were outraged by the president's generosity. They thought the provi-

sions did not adequately punish Confederate treason, restructure southern society, protect the rights of African Americans, or aid the Republican party. The Radicals were in a minority, but many moderate Republicans were also dismayed by Lincoln's leniency, and shared the Radical view that Reconstruction was a congressional, not a presidential, function. As a result Congress recognized neither the three states' elected congressmen nor their electoral votes in the 1864 election.

After denying the president's right to reconstruct the nation, Congress drew up a plan for reconstruction: the **Wade-Davis Bill.** Its terms were much more stringent. A majority, rather than 10 percent, of each states' voters had to declare their allegiance in order to form a government. Only those taking "ironclad" oaths of their past Union loyalty were allowed to participate in the making of new state constitutions. Barely a handful of high-ranking Confederates, however, were to be permanently barred from political participation. The only additional requirement imposed by Congress was the repudiation of the Confederate debt; Northerners did not want Confederate bondholders to benefit from their "investment in treason" at a cost to loyal taxpayers. Congress would determine when a state had met these requirements.

Constitutional collision was postponed by Lincoln's pocket veto of the bill and his assassination on April 14, 1865. While most of the nation mourned, some Radicals rejoiced at the results of John Wilkes Booth's action. Lincoln had been a formidable opponent and had articulated his position on the South in his second inaugural address. Calling for "malice toward none" and "charity for all," he proposed to "bind the nation's wounds" and achieve "a just and lasting peace." His successor, **Andrew Johnson,** on the other hand, had announced, "Treason is a crime, and crime must be punished." Johnson was a Tennessee Democrat and Unionist; he had been the only Southerner to remain in the Senate after his state seceded. Placed on the 1864 Republican "Union" ticket as a gesture of unity, Johnson's political affiliation was less than clear, but some considered him a weaker opponent than Lincoln. Radical Senator Benjamin Wade proclaimed, "By the gods there will be no trouble now in running this government."

Radicals found comfort in, but miscalculated, Johnson's hatred of the planters. He hated them for their aristocratic domination of the South, not for their slaveholding. Born of humble origins in Raleigh, North Carolina, and illiterate until adulthood, Johnson entered politics in Tennessee as a successful tailor. A champion of the people, he called the planters a "cheap purse-proud set . . . not half as good as the man who earns his bread by the sweat of his brow." Favoring free public education and a

North Carolina–born Andrew Johnson, a former governor of Tennessee and a U.S. senator from that state, was the only senator from a seceding state to remain loyal to the Union. In 1862 Lincoln appointed him military governor of Tennessee, and in 1864 Johnson was selected as Lincoln's running mate.

homestead act, Johnson was elected mayor, congressman, governor, and senator, before being appointed military governor of Tennessee and then becoming vice president. Although he shared the Radicals' hatred and distrust of the planters, he was a firm believer in black inferiority and did not support the Radical aim of black legal equality. He also advocated strict adherence to the Constitution and strongly supported states' rights.

Johnson's Plan

In the end Johnson did not reverse Lincoln's lenient policy. Congress was not in session when Johnson became president so he had about eight months to pursue policies without congressional interference. He issued his own proclamation of amnesty in May 1865 that excluded everyone with taxable property worth more than $20,000. Closing one door, he opened another by providing for personal presiden-

tial pardons for excluded individuals. By year's end he had issued about 13,000 pardons in response to 15,000 requests. The most important aspect of the pardons was Johnson's claim that they restored all rights, including property rights. Thus many former slaves with crops in the ground suddenly found their masters back in charge—a disillusioning first taste of freedom that foreclosed further attempts at widespread land redistribution.

Johnson's amnesty proclamation did not immediately end the Radicals' honeymoon period with him, but his other proclamation issued on the same day caused deep concern. In it, he announced plans for the reconstruction of North Carolina—a plan that would set the pattern for all southern states. A native Unionist was named provisional governor with the power to call a constitutional convention elected by loyal voters. Omitting Lincoln's 10 percent provision, Johnson did eventually require ratification of the Thirteenth Amendment, repudiation of Confederate debts, and state constitutional provisions abolishing slavery and renouncing secession. He also recommended limited black suffrage, primarily to stave off congressional attempts to give the vote to all black males.

Although more stringent than Lincoln's plan, Johnson's plan fell short of the Radicals' hopes. Many moderates might have accepted it if the South had complied with the letter and the spirit of Johnson's proposals. Instead, Southerners seemed determined to ignore their defeat, even to make light of it. The state governments, for the most part, met the minimum requirements (Mississippi and South Carolina refused to repudiate the debt and Mississippi declined to ratify the Thirteenth Amendment). Their apparent acceptance, however, grew out of a belief that very little had actually changed, and Southerners proceeded to show almost total disregard for northern sensibilities. Presenting themselves, like prodigal sons, for admission to Congress were four Confederate generals and six Confederate cabinet officials. As the crowning indignity, Confederate Vice President Alexander H. Stephens was also elected. Most Northerners were not exceedingly vindictive. Still the North did expect some sign of change and hoped for some indication of repentance by the former rebels.

Black Codes in the South

At the very least, Northerners expected adherence to the abolition of slavery, and the South was blatantly forging new forms of bondage. African Americans were to be technically free, but Southern whites expected them to work and live as they had before emancipation. To accomplish this, the new state governments enacted a series of laws known as the **Black Codes.** This legislation granted certain rights denied to slaves. Freedmen had the right to marry, own property, sue and be sued, and testify in court. Complex legalisms, however, often took away what was apparently given. Black Codes in all states prohibited racial intermarriage. Some forbade freedmen to own certain types of property, such as alcoholic beverages and firearms. Most so tightly restricted black legal rights that they were practically nonexistent. Black Codes imposed curfews on African Americans, segregated them, and outlawed their right to congregate in large groups.

The Black Codes did more than merely provide means of racial control; they also sought to fashion a labor system as close to slavery as possible. Some required that African Americans obtain special licenses for any job except agricultural labor or domestic service. Most mandated the signing of yearly labor contracts, which sometimes required African Americans to call the landowner "master" and allowed withholding wages for minor infractions. To accomplish the same objective, Mississippi prohibited black ownership or even rental of land. Mandatory apprenticeship programs took children away from their parents, and vagrancy laws allowed authorities to arrest blacks "wandering or strolling about in idleness" and use them on chain gangs or rent them out to planters for as long as a year.

When laws failed, some southern whites resorted to violence. In Memphis, whites resented the presence of black troops at nearby Fort Pickering. A local paper asserted "the negro can do the country more good in the cotton field than in the camp" and chastised "the dirty, fanatical, nigger-loving Radicals of this city." In May 1866 a street brawl erupted between white policemen and recently discharged black soldiers. That night, after the soldiers had returned to the fort, white mobs attacked the black section of the city, with the encouragement of the police and local officials, one of whom urged the mob to "go ahead and kill the last damned one of the nigger race." The reign of terror lasted over 40 hours and left 46 blacks and 2 whites dead. This and other outbreaks of violence disgusted northern voters.

Most Northerners would not have insisted on black equality or suffrage, but the South had regressed too far. Some Black Codes were even identical to the old slave codes, with the word negro substituted for slave. At the same time, reports of white violence against blacks filtered back to Washington. It is no wonder that upon finally reconvening in December 1865, Congress refused to seat the representatives and senators from the former Confederate states and instead proceeded to investigate conditions in the South.

CONGRESSIONAL RECONSTRUCTION

To discover what was really happening in the South, Congress established the **Joint Committee on Reconstruction,** which conducted inquiries and interviews that provided graphic and chilling examples of white repression and brutality toward African Americans. Prior to the committee's final report, even moderates were convinced that action was necessary. In early 1866 Congress passed a bill to extend the life of the Freedmen's Bureau. The bill also granted the agency new powers to establish special courts for disputes concerning former slaves and to promote black education. Johnson vetoed it, claiming that the bureau was constitutional only in wartime conditions. Now,

Southern whites frequently vented their frustration on blacks. Following a Radical Republican meeting in New Orleans on July 30, 1866, rioting erupted; 37 blacks and 3 white sympathizers were killed in the fighting. This cartoon shows Andrew Johnson looking with apparent approval at the violence. The crown illustrates disapproval of Johnson's "tyrannical" actions.

he claimed, the country had returned "to a state of peace and industry."

At first Johnson prevailed; his veto was not overridden. Then he made a mistake. In an impromptu speech on Washington's birthday, Johnson launched into a bitter attack on the Joint Committee on Reconstruction. Even moderates were offended. In mid-March 1866 Congress passed the Civil Rights Act. It declared that "all persons born in the United States and not subject to any foreign power, excluding Indians not taxed," were citizens and entitled to "full and equal benefit of all laws." Congress was responding to the Black Codes, but Johnson deemed the bill both unconstitutional and unwise. He vetoed it. This time, however, Congress overrode the veto. It then passed a slightly revised Freedmen's Bureau bill in July and enacted it over Johnson's veto. Even though the South had ignored much of Johnson's advice, such as granting limited suffrage to blacks, he stubbornly held to his conviction that reconstruction was complete and labeled his congressional opponents as "traitors."

His language did not create a climate of cooperation. Congress was concerned about the constitutional questions he raised and his challenge to congressional authority. To protect its handiwork and establish an alternate program of reconstruction, it drafted the **Fourteenth Amendment.** Undoubtedly the most significant legacy of Reconstruction, the first article of the amendment defined citizenship and its basic rights. Every person born in the United States and subject to its jurisdiction is declared a citizen. It also forbids any state from abridging "the privileges and immunities" of citizenship, from depriving any person of "due process of law," and from denying citizens the "equal protection of the laws." Although 100 years passed before its provisions were enforced as intended, the amendment has been interpreted to mean that states as well as the federal government are bound by the Bill of Rights—an important constitutional change that paved the way for the civil rights decisions and laws of the twentieth century.

The remaining sections of the amendment spelled out Congress's minimum demands for postwar change and was the South's last chance for a lenient peace. A creation of the congressional moderates, the amendment did not require black suffrage but reduced the "basis of representation" proportionately for those states not allowing it. Former Confederate leaders were also barred from holding office unless pardoned by Congress—not the president. Thus Congress repudiated Johnson's power to control Reconstruction. Finally, neither Confederate war debts nor compensation to former slaveholders were ever to be paid. The amendment, which passed Congress in June 1866, was then sent to the states for ratification.

TABLE 16.1
Reconstruction Amendments, 1865–1870

Amendment	Main Provisions	Congressional Passage (2/3 majority in each house required)	Ratification Process (3/4 of all states including ex-Confederate states required)
Thirteenth	Slavery prohibited in United States	January 1865	December 1865 (27 states, including 8 southern states)
Fourteenth	1. National citizenship 2. State representation in Congress reduced proportionally to number of voters disfranchised 3. Former Confederate leaders denied right to hold office 4. Only Congress could pardon former Confederates	June 1866	Rejected by 12 southern and border states, February 1867 Radicals make readmission of southern states hinge on ratification Ratified July 1868
Fifteenth	Denial of franchise because of race, color, or past servitude explicitly prohibited	February 1869	Ratification required for readmission of Virginia, Texas, Mississippi, Georgia Ratified March 1870

"Radical" Reconstruction

Everyone assumed that the 1866 congressional elections would be a referendum on the Fourteenth Amendment and that their position would prevail. At President Johnson's urging, all former Confederate states but Tennessee refused to ratify it. In the end the Republicans won overwhelming victories, which they interpreted as a mandate for congressional reconstruction. The election results along with the South's intransigence finally gave the Radicals an upper hand. In 1867 Congress passed the **Military Reconstruction Act** that raised the price of readmission. The act declared all existing "Johnson governments," except Tennessee's, void and divided the South into five military districts headed by military governors granted broad powers to govern. Delegates to new constitutional conventions were to be elected by all qualified voters—a group that by congressional stipulation included black males and excluded former Confederate leaders. Following the ratification of a new state constitution providing for black suffrage, elections were to be held and the state would be required to ratify the Fourteenth Amendment. When that amendment became part of the Constitution and Congress approved the new state constitutions, the states would be granted representation in Congress once again.

Obviously, Johnson was not pleased with the congressional plan; he vetoed it, only to see his veto overridden. Nevertheless, as commander in chief he reluctantly appointed military governors, and by the end of 1867 elections had been held in every state except Texas. Because many white Southerners boycotted the elections, the South came under the control of Republicans supported by Union forces. To many in the North, however, Southerners had brought more radical measures upon themselves by their inflexibility. As the *Nation* declared in 1867,

> Six years ago, the North would have rejoiced to accept any mild restrictions upon the spread of slavery as a final settlement. Four years ago, it would have accepted peace on the basis of gradual emancipation. Two years ago, it would have been content with emancipation and equal civil rights for the colored people without the extension of suffrage. One year ago, a slight extension of the suffrage would have satisfied it.

Congress realized the plan it had enacted was unprecedented and subject to challenge by the other two branches of government. To check Johnson's power to disrupt, Congress took two other actions on the same day it passed the Military Reconstruction Act. The Command of the Army Act limited presidential military power. The **Tenure of Office Act**

Reconstruction and Redemption

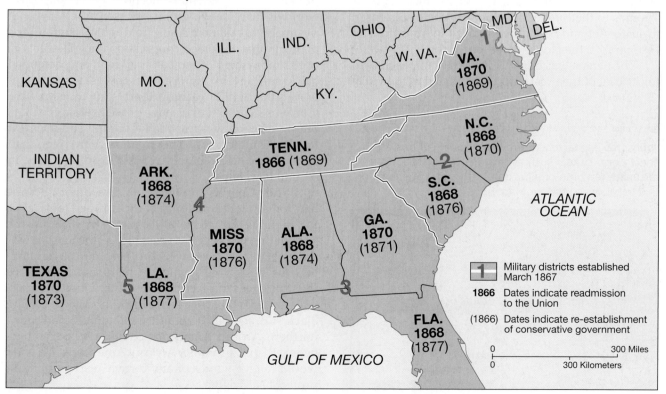

required Senate consent for the removal of any official whose appointment had required the Senate's confirmation. It was meant in part to protect Secretary of War **Edwin M. Stanton,** who supported the Radicals. Both acts represented the Radicals' anger toward Johnson.

The Supreme Court had also shown its willingness to challenge Reconstruction actions in two important cases of 1866. In *Ex parte Milligan* the justices struck down the conviction of a civilian by a military tribunal in an area where civil courts were operating. Another decision ruled as void a state law barring former Confederates from certain professions on the basis that the act was *ex post facto*. Nevertheless, other decisions reflected a hesitation to tackle some of the thornier issues of Reconstruction. Important cases were pending, and Congress acted in March 1868 to limit the court's power to review cases. Because the congressional action was clearly constitutional, the Supreme Court acquiesced and in *Texas v. White* (1869) even acknowledged congressional power to reframe state governments.

President Johnson was not so accommodating. He sought to sabotage military reconstruction by continuing to pardon former Confederates, removing military commanders who were Radical sympathizers, and naming former Confederates to federal positions. Congress was angry but could not find adequate grounds for impeachment. Johnson did not attempt to mend fences. After an unsuccessful attempt to replace Secretary of War Stanton with Ulysses S. Grant, on February 21 he named Lorenzo Thomas to the cabinet position. Stanton also refused to surrender and barricaded himself in his office. On February 24, the House voted impeachment.

The Senate was given 11 articles of impeachment for its trial of the president. Eight related to the violation of the Tenure of Office Act and another to a violation of the Command of the Army Act. These articles were merely the pretext for impeachment. Only the last two reflected the real reasons for congressional action. Those articles accused Johnson of "inflammatory and scandalous harangues" against Congress and of "unlawfully devising and contriving" to obstruct congressional will. The heated and bitter trial lasted from March 5 to May 26. Johnson did not attend, but his lawyers made a good legal case that he had not technically violated the Tenure of Office Act since Stanton had been appointed by Lincoln. They tried to keep the trial focused on indictable offenses. Radical prosecutors continued to argue that Johnson had committed "high crimes and misdemeanors," but they also asserted that a president could be removed for political reasons, even without being found legally guilty of crimes. Thus Congress asserted the power to remove a president for disagreeing with it.

The vote for conviction fell one short of the required two-thirds majority, when seven Republicans broke ranks and voted against conviction. This set the precedent that a president must be guilty of serious misdeeds to be removed from office. The outcome was a political blow to the Radicals, costing them some support. The action, however, did make Johnson more cooperative for the last months of his presidency.

Black Suffrage

In the 1868 presidential election, the Republicans won with **Ulysses S. Grant,** whose Civil War victories made his name a household word. He ran on a platform that endorsed congressional reconstruction, urged repayment of the national debt, and defended black suffrage in the South as necessary but supported the right of each northern state to restrict the vote. His slogan, "Let us have peace," was appealing, but his election was less than a ringing endorsement for Radical policies. The military hero who had seemed invincible barely won the popular vote in several key states.

While Charles Sumner and a few other Radicals had long favored national black suffrage, only after the Republicans' electoral close call in 1868 did the bulk of the party begin to consider a suffrage amendment. Many were swayed by the political certainty that the black vote would be theirs and might give them the margin of victory in future close elections. Others were embarrassed by the hypocrisy of forcing black suffrage on the South while only 7 percent of northern African Americans could vote. Still others believed that granting African Americans the vote would relieve whites of any further responsibility to protect black rights.

Johnson's impeachment drew crowds of curious spectators. Tickets such as this one were issued to a fortunate few. The original date of March 13, shown on this ticket, was reset to March 23.

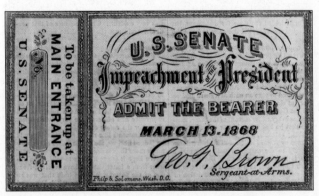

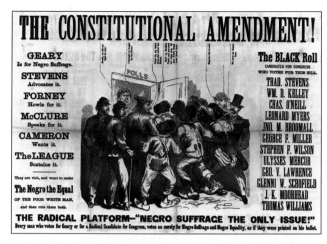

Many Northerners were opposed to the Fifteenth Amendment. Highly racist posters, such as this one from Pennsylvania, were used against politicians who supported the amendment.

Suffrage supporters faced many objections to such an amendment. One was based on the lack of popular support. At that time only seven northern states granted blacks the right to vote, and since 1865, referendum proposals for black suffrage in eight states had been voted down. In fact, only in Iowa and Minnesota (both containing minuscule black populations) had voters supported the extension of the vote. The amendment was so unpopular that, ironically, it could never have won adoption without its ratification by the southern states, where black suffrage already existed.

A more serious challenge was the question of whether Congress could legislate suffrage at all. Before Reconstruction the national government had never taken any action regarding the right to vote; suffrage had been considered not a right but a privilege which only the states could confer. The Radical answer was that the Constitution expressly declared that "the United States shall guarantee to every State in this Union a republican form of government." Charles Sumner further asserted that "anything for human rights is constitutional" and that black rights could only be protected by black votes.

Senator George Vickers sarcastically asked: "Does not the doctrine of human rights asserted by the senator apply as well to females as to males?" Although he was "no advocate for woman suffrage," he noted that "if the Congress of the United States had been composed exclusively of women we should have had no civil war. We might have had a war of words, but that would have been all." When one senator did propose female suffrage, a colleague informed him that "to extend the right of suffrage to negroes in this country I think is necessary for their protection; but to extend the right of suffrage to women is not necessary."

Some women, such as Elizabeth Cady Stanton and **Susan B. Anthony,** did not want to rely upon their fathers, brothers, or husbands to protect their rights. As leaders of the Women's Loyal League, both had worked hard for the adoption of the Thirteenth Amendment, only to be rewarded by inclusion of the word *male* in the Fourteenth Amendment of the Constitution—the first time that word appears. Some women, such as Lucy Stone of the American Woman Suffrage Association, accepted the plea of long-time woman suffrage supporter Frederick Douglass that it was the "Negro's hour," and worked for ratification. Anthony, however, vowed "[I will] cut off this right arm of mine before I will ever work for or demand the ballot for the Negro and not the woman." Such differences played a role in splitting the women's movement in 1869 between those working for a national suffrage amendment and those who concentrated their efforts on the state level. Anthony and Stanton founded the National Woman Suffrage Association to battle for a constitutional amendment and other feminist reforms. Others became disillusioned with that approach and established the American Woman Suffrage Association, which focused on obtaining suffrage on a state-by-state basis.

Actually, women did not lose much by not being included in the **Fifteenth Amendment.** To meet the various objections, compromise was necessary. The resulting amendment did not grant the vote to anyone. It merely stated that the vote could not be denied "on account of race, color, or previous condition of servitude." Suffrage was still essentially to be controlled by the states, and other bases of exclusion were not deemed unconstitutional. These loopholes would eventually allow white Southerners to make a mockery of the amendment.

Although congressional reconstruction was labeled "Radical," compromise had instead produced another essentially moderate plan. What Congress did *not* do is as important as what it did. It did not even guarantee the right to vote. There was only one execution for war crimes and only Jefferson Davis was imprisoned for more than a few months. For all but a handful, former Confederates were not permanently barred from voting or holding office. By 1872 only about 200 were still denied the right to hold office. Most local southern governments were undisturbed. Land as well as rights were restored to former rebels, eliminating the possibility of extensive land redistribution. Most areas that had traditionally been the states' domain remained so, free from federal meddling. For example, no requirements were placed on the states to provide any education to former slaves. The only attempt by the national government to meet the basic needs of its citizens was the temporary Freedmen's Bureau—justified only as an emergency measure. The limited nature of Reconstruction doomed it as an opportunity to provide means for the protection of minority rights.

Such congressional moderation reflected the spirit of the age. Enduring beliefs in the need for strict construction of the Constitution and in states' rights presented formidable barriers to truly radical changes. Property rights were considered sacrosanct—even for "traitors." Cherished ideals of self-reliance and the conviction that a person determined his or her own destiny led many to support **Horace Greeley**'s call to "break up our Freedmen's Bureaus and all manner of coddling devices and let the negroes take care of themselves." Few agreed with Charles Sterns who argued that even a hog could not root without a snout—that there could be no equality of opportunity where one group had long been allowed an unfair advantage. Many instead sided with an editorialist for the *New York Herald* who wrote of the bill to extend the life of the Freedmen's Bureau: "The bill ought to be called an act to support the negroes in idleness by the honest labor of white people, or an act to establish a gigantic and corrupt political machine for the benefit of the radical faction and a swarm of officeholders." Clearly the idea of affirmative action or even equal opportunity had less support then than it did 100 years later.

Tainting every action was the widespread conviction that African Americans were not equal to whites. Many Northerners were more concerned with keeping blacks in the South than with abstract black rights. In 1866, for example, New York Senator Roscoe Conkling catered to the northern fear of black immigration while calling for support of the Fourteenth Amendment:

> Four years ago mobs were raised, passions were aroused, votes were given, upon the idea that emancipated negroes were to burst in hordes upon the North. We then said, give them liberty and rights in the South, and they will stay there and never come into a cold climate. We say so still, and we want them let alone, and that is one thing that this part of the amendment is for.

Even Radical Representative George Julian admitted to his Indiana constituents, "the real trouble is that we hate the negro. It is not his ignorance that offends us, but his color."

The plan for Reconstruction evolved fitfully, buffeted first one way and then another by the forces of the many issues unresolved at war's end. If permanent changes were very limited, nonetheless precedents had been set for later action, and for a brief

time congressional reconstruction brought about the most democratic governments the South had ever seen—or would see for another hundred years.

RECONSTRUCTION IN THE SOUTH

Any dictated peace would probably have been unpalatable to Southern whites. They were especially leery of any action that seemed to threaten white supremacy—whether or not that was the intended result. Even before the war, suspicion greeted every Northern move. Southerners continued to see a radical abolitionist behind every bush.

Most Southerners criticized and condemned the Freedmen's Bureau from its first day to its last. Many believed its agents were partial to African Americans. As one Mississippi planter declared, "The negro is a sacred animal. The Yankees are about negroes like the Egyptians were about cats." Actually there was a great diversity in the background and goals of bureau agents. Some were idealistic young New Englanders who, like the Yankee schoolmarms, came south to aid in the transition to freedom. Others were army officers whose first priority was to maintain order—often by siding with the landowners. All were overworked, underpaid, and under pressure.

The results of bureau actions were mixed in regard to conditions for African Americans. The agents helped to negotiate labor contracts that African Americans were forced to sign to obtain rations. Frequently the wages were well below the rate at which slaves had been hired out by their owners before the war. While it should be remembered that money was

Freed persons realized that education was a key to real freedom and flocked to schools opened by the Freedmen's Bureau, the American Missionary Association, and other groups.

scarce at the time, these contracts helped to keep African Americans on the farm—someone else's farm. On the other hand, between 1865 and 1869 the bureau issued over 21 million rations, of which about 5 million went to whites. Thus it showed that the government could establish and administer a massive relief program, as it would again do during the depression of the 1930s. The bureau also operated more than 40 hospitals, opened hundreds of schools, and accomplished the Herculean task of resettling some 30,000 people displaced by the war.

Carpetbaggers, Scalawags, and Black Republicans

Until Congressional Reconstruction, Southern governments were largely unchanged. Afterwards, however, Republican officeholders joined bureau agents in directing the course of Reconstruction. Despised by many whites, these men, depending on their origins, were derisively labeled "carpetbaggers," "scalawags," and "nigrahs." Opponents considered all three groups despicable creatures whose "black and tan" governments were tyrannizing native whites, while engaged in an orgy of corruption. Myths created about Southern Republicans lingered long after the restoration of Democratic party rule.

Northerners who came to the South during or after the war and became engaged in politics were called **carpetbaggers.** According to their critics, they arrived with a few meager belongings in their carpetbags, which would expand to hold ill-gotten gains from looting an already devastated South. Probably what most infuriated whites was the carpetbaggers' willingness to cooperate with African Americans. Calling them "a kind of political dry-nurse for the negro population," native whites accused the carpetbaggers of cynically exploiting former slaves for their own gain. Many agreed with the charge that the carpetbaggers were standing "right in the public eye, stealing and plundering, many of them with both arms around negroes, and their hands in their rear pockets, seeing if they cannot pick a paltry dollar out of them."

White Southerners who voted for Republicans were labeled **scalawags.** The term, said to be derived from Scalloway, "a district in the Shetland Islands where small, runty cattle and horses were bred," had been used previously as a "synonym for scamp, loafer, or rascal." Thus southern white Republicans were depicted as people "paying no taxes, riding poor horses, wearing dirty shirts, and having no use for soap." Such men were said to have "sold themselves for office" and become a "subservient tool and accomplice" of the carpetbaggers.

Most detested by white Southerners were the black Republicans. Having long characterized African Americans as inferior creatures dependent on white management for survival, Southerners loathed the prospect of blacks in authority. They feared that the former slaves would exact payment for their years of bondage. Democrats also knew that racism was their best rallying cry to regain power. Thus Reconstruction governments were denounced for "Ethiopian minstrelsy, Ham radicalism in all its glory." Whites claimed ignorant freedmen, incapable of managing their own affairs, were allowed to run the affairs of state with disastrous results.

Such legends persisted for a long time, despite contrary facts. Southern whites had determined even before Reconstruction began that it would be "the most galling tyranny and most stupendous system of organized robbery that is to be met with in history." The truth was, as W. E. B. Du Bois later wrote, "There is one thing that the white South feared more than negro dishonesty, ignorance, and incompetency, and that was negro honesty, knowledge, and efficiency." To a surprising degree they got what they most feared.

Black voters were generally as fit to vote as the millions of illiterate whites enfranchised by Jacksonian democracy. Black officials as a group were as qualified as their white counterparts. In South Carolina two-thirds of them were literate, and in all states most of the acknowledged leaders were well educated and articulate. They usually had been members of the northern or southern free black elite or part of the slave aristocracy of skilled artisans and household slaves. Hiram Revels, a U.S. senator from Mississippi, was the son of free blacks who had sent him to college in the North. James Walker Hood, the presiding officer of the North Carolina constitutional convention of 1867, was a black carpetbagger from Pennsylvania who came to the state as an African Methodist Episcopal Zion missionary. Some, such as Francis Cardoza of South Carolina, were the privileged mulatto sons of white planters. Cardoza had been educated in Scottish and English universities. During Reconstruction 14 such men served in the U.S. House of Representatives and 2 in the Senate. By 1901, 6 others were elected to the House, before southern black political power was effectively demolished.

Even if black Republicans had been incompetent, they could hardly be held responsible for the perceived abuses of so-called black reconstruction. Only in South Carolina did African Americans have a majority of the delegates to the constitutional convention provided for by the Reconstruction Acts. Neither did they dominate the new governments; only for a two-year period in South Carolina did blacks control both houses of the legislature. None were elected governor, although P. B. S. Pinchback, the lieutenant governor of Louisiana, did serve as acting governor for a short time. When the vote was restored to ex-

African Americans participated in politics at all levels. This poster shows Senators Blanche K. Bruce and Hiram Revels flanking Frederick Douglass, who was appointed to several important positions, including Minister Resident and Counsel General to Haiti, Recorder of Deeds, and U.S. Marshall.

Confederates, African Americans comprised only one-third of the voters of the South, and only in two states did they have a majority.

Actually, carpetbaggers dominated most Republican governments to an extent not warranted by their numbers. They accounted for less than 1 percent of the party's voters but held a third of the offices. Their power was especially obvious in the higher offices. Over half of the South's Republican governors and almost half of the Republican congressmen and senators were former Northerners. Although some carpetbaggers did resemble their stereotypes, most did not. Many had come south before black enfranchisement and could not have predicted political futures based on black votes. Most were Union veterans whose wartime exposure to the region convinced them that they could make a good living there without having to shovel snow. Some brought with them much needed capital for investment in their new home. A few came with a sense of mission to educate blacks and reform southern society.

Obviously, if African Americans constituted only a third of the population and carpetbaggers less than 1 percent, those two groups had to depend on the votes of a sizable number of native white Southerners to obtain office in some regions of the South. Those men came from diverse backgrounds. Some scalawags were members of the old elite of bankers, merchants, industrialists, and even some planters who, as former Whigs, favored the "Whiggish" economic policies of the Republican party and hoped to control and use the black vote for their own pur-

poses. On discovering their inability to dominate the Republican governments, most of these soon drifted into alliance with the Democrats. The majority of southern white Republican voters were yeomen farmers and poor whites from areas where slavery had been unimportant. They had long resented planter domination and had opposed secession.

To win their vote the Republicans appealed to class interests. In Georgia they proclaimed, "Poor White men of Georgia: Be a Man! Let the Slaveholding aristocracy no longer rule you. Vote for a constitution which educates your children free of charge; relieves the poor debtor from his rich creditor; allows a liberal homestead for your families; and more than all, places you on a level with those who used to boast that for every slave they were entitled to three-fifths of a vote in congressional representation." Many accepted such arguments and joined African Americans to put Republicans into office. The coalition, however, was always shaky, given the racism of poor whites. The scalawags actually represented a swing vote that finally swung toward the Democratic party of white supremacy later in the 1870s.

Character of Republican Rule

While the coalition lasted, the Republican governments became the most democratic that the South had ever had. More people could vote for more offices, all remaining property requirements for voting and office holding were dropped, representation was made fairer through reapportionment, and more offices became elective rather than appointive. Salaries for public officials made it possible to serve without being wealthy. Most important, universal male suffrage was enacted with the support of black legislators. Ironically, by refusing to deny southern whites what had been denied to them—the vote—African Americans sowed the seeds of their own destruction.

The Republican state constitutions, which brought the South firmly into the mainstream of national reform, often remained in effect years after the end of Reconstruction. Legislatures abolished automatic imprisonment for debt and reduced the use of the death penalty. More institutions for the care of the indigent, orphans, mentally ill, deaf, and blind were established. Tax structures were overhauled, reducing head taxes and increasing property taxes to relieve somewhat poorer taxpayers. At the same time, southern railroads, harbors, and bridges were rebuilt.

Reforms also affected the status of women, increasing their rights in the possession of property and divorce. Although giving women legal control of their property was mainly intended to protect the families of their debt-ridden husbands, African Americans in particular pushed for more radical changes. When William Whipper's motion to give South Carolina women the vote did not receive a second, he declared:

> However frivolous you may think it, I know the time will come when every man and woman in this country will have the right to vote. I acknowledge the superiority of woman. There are large numbers of the sex

who have an intelligence more than equal to our own. Is it right or just to deprive these intelligent beings of the privileges which we enjoy? The time will come when you will have to meet this question. It will continue to be agitated until it must ultimately triumph.

The area in which black legislators had the most success was laying the foundations for public education. Antebellum provisions for public schools below the Mason-Dixon line were meager to nonexistent. In every state African Americans were among the main proponents of state-supported schools, but most accepted segregated facilities as necessary compromises. Some black parents did not even desire integration; they believed their children could not flourish in environments tainted by white supremacy. By 1877 some 600,000 blacks were in schools, but only the University of South Carolina and the public schools of New Orleans were integrated.

As desirable as many of the new social services were, they required money and money was scarce. Railroads and bridges also needed to be rebuilt. The necessary tax increases were bound to be unpopular, as were soaring state debts. Both were blamed on corruption, with some justification. Louisiana governor Henry C. Warmouth netted some $100,000 in a year in which his salary was only $8000. A drunken South Carolina governor signed an issue of state bonds for a woman in a burlesque show. One black man was paid $9000 to repair a bridge with an original cost of only $500. Contracts for rebuilding and expanding railroads, subsidies to industries, and bureaucracies for administering social services offered generous opportunities for graft and bribery. When these occurred, southern whites loudly proclaimed that they knew it would happen if shifty former slaves were given the keys to the till.

Actually, although African Americans received a large share of the blame, they received little of the profit. A smaller percentage of blacks than whites were involved in the scandals. Also the corruption that the Democrats denounced at every turn was rather meager compared with the shenanigans of such contemporary northern Democratic regimes as the Boss Tweed Ring of New York. There seemed to be an orgy of national corruption that infected both parties. Indeed, in the South a Democratic state treasurer who came to office after Reconstruction deserves the dubious distinction of being the largest embezzler of the era.

The "tyranny" that so distressed southern whites did not include wholesale disfranchisement or confiscation of their lands. In fact, the demands of most African Americans were quite reasonable and moderate. Their goals were expressed by the declarations of the many postwar black conventions, such as a

African Americans eagerly participated in politics when allowed. As depicted in this sketch of the 1867 election in the nation's capital, they served as polling place judges and lined up as early as 2 A.M. to vote.

Virginia one in 1865 that declared, "All we ask is an *equal chance* with the white *traitors* varnished and japanned with the oath of amnesty."

Black and White Economic and Social Adaptation

Just as the former slaves on Thomas Pinckney's plantation had learned, blacks everywhere soon realized that the economic power of whites had diminished little. If anything, land became more concentrated in the hands of a few. In one Alabama county, the richest 10 percent of landowners increased their share of landed wealth from 55 to 63 percent between 1860 and 1870. Some African Americans, usually through hard work and incredible sacrifice, were able to obtain land. The percentage of blacks owning property increased from less than 1 to 20 percent. Indeed, African Americans seemed to fare better than poor whites. One observer noted, "The negro, bad as his condition is, seems to me, on the whole, to accommodate himself more easily than the white to the change of situation." The truth of his assertion is reflected in the fact that the percentage of whites owning land dropped from 80 to 67 percent. Increasingly, poor blacks and whites became agricultural laborers on someone else's land.

The black landless farmers, like the slaves before them, were not mere pawns. If they could not control their destinies, at least they could shape them. As one northern observer wrote, "They have a mine of strategy to which the planter sooner or later yields." Through strikes and work slowdowns, African Americans resisted contract and wage labor because working in gangs under white supervision smacked too much of slavery. When they could not own land, they preferred to rent it, but the few who had the cash to do so found few southern whites would risk the wrath of their neighbors by breaking the taboo against renting to blacks.

Sharecropping emerged both as a result of blacks' desire for autonomy and whites' lack of cash. Landowners gave blacks as well as poor whites a plot of land to work in return for a share of the crops. Freedom from white supervision was so desirable to former slaves that they sometimes hitched mule teams to their old slave cabins and carried them off to their assigned acres. To put distance between themselves and slavery, many black men would not allow their wives and children to work in the fields.

Sharecropping at first seemed to be a good bargain for African Americans because they frequently negotiated their way to a half-share of the crops. Their portion of the profits from southern agriculture, including all provisions, rose from 22 percent under

slavery to 56 percent by the end of Reconstruction. Moreover, they were making more for working less. Fewer family members worked and black men labored shorter hours; as a group African Americans worked one-third fewer hours than under slavery. Per capita black income increased quickly after the war to about one-half that of whites, but then it stagnated.

Sharecropping later proved to be disastrous for most blacks and poor whites. They needed more than land to farm; they also required seeds, fertilizers, and provisions to live on until they harvested their crops. To obtain these they often borrowed against their share of the crops. Falling crop prices, high credit rates, and sometimes cheating by creditors left many to harvest a growing burden of debt with each crop. In many states, when the Democrats regained power, laws favoring creditors were passed. These led to debt peonage for many sharecroppers.

If most former slaves did not win economic freedom, they benefited from freedom in other ways. It was no longer illegal to learn to read and write, and African Americans pursued education with much zeal. Many even paid as much as 10 percent of their limited incomes for tuition. They began to learn the fundamentals, and a growing number also sought higher education. Between 1860 and 1880 over 1000 African Americans earned college degrees. Some went north to college, but most went to 1 of the 13 southern colleges established by the American Missionary Association or by black and white churches with the assistance of the Freedmen's Bureau. Such schools as Howard and Fisk were a permanent legacy of Reconstruction.

African Americans were also able to enjoy and expand their rich cultural heritage. Religion was a central focus for most, just as it had been in slavery. Withdrawing from white congregations with segregated pews and self-serving sermons on the duty of servants to their masters, blacks everywhere established separate black churches. The membership in such antebellum denominations as the African Methodist Episcopal soared. In essence, black Christians declared their religious independence, and their churches became centers of political and social activities as well as religious ones. As one carpetbagger noted, "The colored preachers are *the great power* in controlling and uniting the colored vote." The churches also functioned as vehicles for self-help and sources of entertainment.

Most African Americans desired racial intermingling no more than whites. Many could not feel free until they had removed themselves and their children as far as possible from white arrogance. They created separate congregations and acquiesced to segregated schooling. Nevertheless, they did not want to be publicly humiliated by such measures as separate railroad cars. They frequently used their limited political power to protect civil rights through clauses in state constitutions and legislation, as well as by appeals for the enforcement of national laws. Consequently, black Southerners did enjoy the use of public facilities to a greater degree than they would during the 75 years following Reconstruction.

The very changes that gave African Americans hope during Reconstruction distressed poor whites. Black political equality rankled them, but much more serious was their own declining economic status. As their landownership declined, more whites became dependent on sharecropping and low-wage jobs, primarily in the textile industry. Even these meager opportunities were eagerly greeted; as one North Carolina preacher proclaimed, "Next to God, what this town needs is a cotton mill." Economic competition between poor whites and blacks was keen, but their common plight also favored cooperation based on class interest. The economic pressures applied by the white elite frequently hurt both groups as well as middle-class yeomen farmers, and for brief periods during Reconstruction they warily united in politics. Invariably, however, these attempts were shattered by upper-class appeals to white supremacy and racial unity.

Ironically, although poor whites were perceived by nearly everyone as the group most hostile to blacks, the two shared many aspects of a rich southern cultural heritage. Both groups developed colorful dialects. For each, aesthetic expression was based on utility—reflecting their need to use wisely what little they had. Their quilts were not merely functional but often quite beautiful. In religion and recreation, their experiences were similar. At camp meetings and revivals, poor whites practiced a highly emotional religion, just as many black Southerners did. Both groups spun yarns and sang songs that reflected the perils of their existence and provided folk heroes. They also shared many superstitions as well as useful folk remedies. Race, however, was a potent wedge between them that upper-class whites frequently exploited for their own political and economic goals.

Planters no longer dominated the white elite; sharecropping turned them and others into absentee landlords. The sons of the old privileged families joined the growing ranks of lawyers, railroad entrepreneurs, bankers, industrialists, and merchants. In some ways, the upper and middle classes began to merge, but in many places the old elite and their sons still enjoyed a degree of deference and political leadership. Their hostility toward African Americans was not as intense, largely because they possessed means of control. When their control slipped, however, they also became ranting racists.

So strongly were all southern whites imbued with a belief in white superiority that most could not imagine total black equality. A Freedmen's Bureau agent reported in 1866 that "a very respectable old citizen . . . swore that, if he could not thrash a negro who insulted him, he would leave the country." White attitudes toward blacks were as irrational as they were generalized. Most whites exempted the blacks they knew from such generalizations. As an Alabama planter declared in 1865, "If all were like some of mine I wouldn't say anything. They're as intelligent and well behaved as anybody. But I can't stand free niggers anyhow!"

Violent White Resistance

Large numbers of whites engaged in massive resistance to Reconstruction. Unlike the resistance of southern blacks 100 years later, however, this brand of resistance was not passive but very aggressive. In 1866, some bored young men in Pulaski, Tennessee, organized a social club with all the trappings of fraternal orders—secret rituals, costumes, and practical jokes. They soon learned that their antics intimidated African Americans; thenceforth the **Ku Klux Klan** grew into a terrorist organization, copied all over the South under various names. A historian of the Klan asserts that it "whipped, shot, hanged, robbed, raped, and otherwise outraged Negroes and Republicans

This 1874 cartoon by Thomas Nast illustrates northern concern about southern violence and disillusionment about Reconstruction. It contrasts sharply with Nast's highly optimistic 1865 illustration of emancipation on page 422.

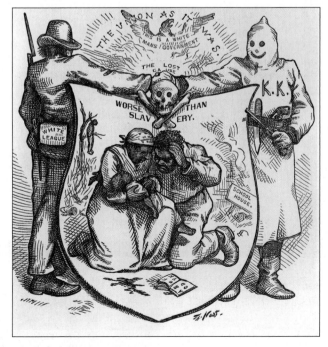

THE PEOPLE SPEAK

Testimony Against the Klan

The terrorism committed by the Ku Klux Klan is documented in the published proceedings of the Joint Committee on Reconstruction. Here Daniel H. Smith of Mississippi tells of his narrow escape from a lynching in his testimony before the committee.

Question. Have you ever been attacked by disguised men?

Answer. Yes, sir.

Question. You may state the particulars to the committee.

Answer. After I came here in 1866, and was near Brooksville, a gentleman up there named Elm tried to hire my wife, and told me he would give me a school on the place, if I would let my wife go and wait on him. When I mentioned it to her she was not willing to go there. I would not try to force her there, and he fell out with me about it. After he fell out with me about it, he met me, and asked me what sort of way I had done, and cursed me. I told him I thought I done my duty; that my wife was not willing to go. He told me he generally made negroes like me do as he wanted them to do; he didn't ask no negro what they did; he generally made them do it; and a good many words passed between us. I told him I thought I had done my duty. He threatened to kill me a time or two up there if I did not do it. When I was coming from Brooksville one night, I saw two men up here in the road before me, with white sheets around them. They lit off of horses and told me to stop. They knowed I was going to Brooksville; they always knew it; for I was teaching a colored school near Brooksville, and always went to Brooksville Saturday evening, and sometimes it was after night before I returned home. In returning back I saw two people with sheets around them, and when they ordered me to stop I did so, and they got down and asked if that was Daniel Smith. I told them it was not, it was Alleck Billips. He was a man that resembles me very much, and was about my height, and, it being dark, they could not tell whether it was me or not, and I don't think they had taken very particular notice of my features and face. They drew a rope out, and said if it had been Daniel H. Smith they aimed to hang him with that rope that night. Then they went on and asked me if I had been a good negro to my master Charley; that was Charley Sherrod. I told them I had been very good and obedient to him, and got away from them that night by telling them that falsehood. The year after

that, or a shorter time than a year, I moved away from there down here to where I am now. . .

Question. What is the feeling among the whites, so far as you have conversed with them or heard an expression of opinion in relation to colored suffrage or negroes voting?

Answer. Well, sir, they do not believe in it. . . . Out in the part of the county where I live I have known a great many of them to tell the colored people, so as to disappoint them, that there was no election—that it had all been given over. A great many ignorant people would think the employer knew, and that he told them the truth. They would deprive them in that way of their votes. And, again, they would tell them to take their wagons, and go to such a place, and haul so and so away from there. They would manage in all such ways to keep the black people away. Since I have been in the State they came to me and asked me when the election was, and I would tell them. I do not believe, sir, that the generality, the majority of the white people that were around in the neighborhood, generally appreciated me very much on account of my being a negro. I have heard them speak so very bitterly, though I have always behaved myself to them and been very obedient, and never put myself in the way to create any disturbance in any way. . . .

Question. Do the white people here favor the colored people buying lands and having homes?

Answer. No, sir. . . . [T]hey say that if you suffer the colored people here to own land they cannot get any laborers then, for where a colored man owns a piece of land, as many as can do so will go to their own land, and that will defeat them from getting labor.

Question. So that the white owners of the soil you think are generally opposed to your people becoming owners of land?

Answer. Yes, sir; or stocks [livestock] in any way; they don't believe in that. I have known a great many people that have lost their stock. Sometimes the employers would go out and shoot the stock down, if they found them in the wrong place. They did not tell them who killed them.

Testimony of Daniel H. Smith, Macon, Mississippi, November 7, 1871, in U.S. Congress. *Testimony Taken by the Joint Select Committee to Inquire into the Condition of Affairs in the Late Insurrectionary States.* Government Printing Office, Washington, D.C., Vol. II, pp. 570–573, 574, 1872.

across the South in the name of preserving white civilization." Led by former confederate officer Nathan Bedford Forrest, a major goal of the Klan was to intimidate Republican voters and restore Democrats to office. In South Carolina, when blacks working for a scalawag began to vote, Klansmen visited the plantation and "whipped every nigger man they could lay their hands on." The group's increasing lawlessness alarmed many people and led to congressional action. The Klan was broken up by three Enforcement Acts (1870–1871) that gave the president the right to suspend habeas corpus against "armed combinations" interfering with any citizen's right to vote. In 1871 Grant did so in nine South Carolina counties. Disbanding the Klan, however, did little to decrease southern violence or the activities of similar terrorist groups.

Some black Southerners were probably never allowed to vote freely. At the peak of Reconstruction, fewer than 30,000 federal troops were stationed in the entire South—hardly enough to protect the rights of 4.5 million African Americans. As troops were being withdrawn, Democrats sought to regain control of their states. They made appeals to white supremacy and charged the Republicans with corruption. Without secret ballots, landowners could threaten sharecroppers with eviction for "improper" voting. In addition to economic intimidation, violence against African Americans escalated in most states as the Democrats increased their political power. When victory seemed close, Democrats justified any means to the desired end that they called "redemption." A South Carolina Democratic campaign plan in 1876 urged, "Never threaten a man individually. If he deserves to be threatened, the necessities of the times require that he should die. A dead Radical is very harmless." One Democratic candidate for governor in Louisiana proclaimed, "We shall carry the next election if we have to ride saddle-deep in blood to do it." In six heavily black counties in Mississippi such tactics proved highly successful—reducing Republican votes from more than 14,000 in 1873 to only 723 in 1876. Beginning with Virginia and Tennessee in 1869, by 1876 all but three states—Louisiana, Florida, and South Carolina—had Democratic **Redeemer governments.** The final collapse of Reconstruction became official the following year with the withdrawal of federal troops from the three unredeemed states.

RECONSTRUCTION IN THE NORTH AND WEST

In the end, the South could be said to have lost the war but won the peace. After 1877 Southern whites found little resistance to their efforts to forge new institutions to replace both the economic benefits and racial control of slavery. By 1910 they had devised a system of legalized repression that gave whites many of the benefits of slavery without all the responsibilities. Surely this was not what the North had envisioned after Appomattox. How did it happen? Much of the answer is found in events occurring in the North and West.

Northern Shifts in Attitudes

The basic cause for the decline of Reconstruction can be seen in an 1874 conversation between two northern Republicans during which one declared that the people were "tired out with this wornout cry of 'Southern Outrages!!!' Hard times and heavy taxes make them wish the . . . 'everlasting nigger' were in [hell] or Africa. . . . It is amazing the change that has taken place in the last two years in the public sentiment." A shifting political climate, economic hard times, increasing preoccupation with other issues, and continued racism combined to make most Northerners wash their hands of the responsibility for the protection of black rights.

Although his slogan "Let us have peace" was appealing, Ulysses S. Grant proved to be a poor choice for the presidency. Not only was he politically inexperienced, but he also lacked a taste for politics. Haunted by a fear of failure and socially insecure, Grant was too easily influenced by men of wealth and prestige. He made some dismal appointments and remained loyal to individuals who did not merit his trust. The result was a series of scandals. Grant was not personally involved, but his close association with the perpetrators blemished both his and his party's image. The first major scandal surfaced in 1872; it involved **Credit Mobilier,** a dummy construction company used to milk money from railroad investors in order to line the pockets of a few insiders, including Vice President Schuyler Colfax and a number of other prominent Republicans. Later, bribes and kickback schemes surfaced that involved Indian trading posts, post office contracts, and commissions for tax collection. Such revelations as well as the corruption in some southern Republican governments did little to enhance the public image of the party, and Democrats were quick to make corruption a major issue in both the North and the South.

Although by the 1872 presidential election, there had only been a hint of scandal, some Republicans were disenchanted. In that election the Republican party was split; a number, calling themselves Liberal Republicans, formed a separate party. They supported their own candidate, *New York Tribune* editor Horace Greeley, rather than Grant. Among Greeley's campaign pledges was a more moderate southern policy. Even with the Democrats also nominating Greeley, Grant easily won reelection, but the fear of disgruntled Republicans merging with Democrats remained. By 1874 Republicans were becoming aware that the black vote would not save them. That year Democrats captured the House and gained in the Senate, following further revelations of Republican corruption.

At least as detrimental to Republican political fortunes was a depression that followed the **Panic of 1873,** which was caused by overinvestment in railroads and risky financial deals. Lasting six years, it was the most serious economic downturn the nation had yet experienced. Whatever their cause, depressions usually result in "voting the rascals out." Democratic fortunes were bound to rise as the people's fell. Yet economic distress had an even wider impact on Reconstruction. People's attention became focused on their pocketbooks rather than on abstract ideals of equality and justice.

Actually, the Panic of 1873 merely brought into clearer focus the vast changes occurring in the North during Reconstruction. The South had never had the undivided attention of the rest of the nation. Such events as the completion of the first transcontinental railroad in 1869 often overshadowed reports of "Southern outrages." The United States was experiencing the growing pains of economic modernization and western expansion. The Republican platform of 1860 had called for legislation favoring both of these as well as stopping the expansion of slavery. Comprised of diverse interest groups, the party went through a battle for its soul during Reconstruction. For a while the small abolitionist faction had gained some ascendancy due to postwar developments. By

the late 1870s, however, the Republican party had forsaken its reformist past to become a protector of privilege rather than a guarantor of basic rights. In effect, Republicans and Democrats joined hands in conservative support of railroad and industrial interests.

Western Expansion, Racism, and Native Americans

The major reason for the decline of Reconstruction was the pervasive belief in white supremacy. There could be little determination to secure equal rights for those who were considered unequal in all other respects. Reconstruction became a failed opportunity to resolve justly the status of one minority, and the climate of racism almost ensured failure for others as well. Western expansion not only diverted attention from Reconstruction but also raised the question of what was to be done about the Plains Indians. They, too, were considered inferior to whites. William H. Seward, who later became secretary of state, spoke for most white Americans when in 1860 he described blacks as "a foreign and feeble element like the Indians, incapable of assimilation." Indeed, while Reconstruction at first offered hope to African Americans, for Native Americans hope was fading.

In the end, African Americans were oppressed; Native Americans were exterminated or separated into shrinking reservations. From the white viewpoint the reason was obvious. As a so-called scientific treatise of the 1850s explained, "The *Barbarous* races of America . . . although nearly as low in intellect as the Negro races, are essentially untameable. Not merely have all attempts to civilize them failed, but also every endeavor to enslave them." Because most Africans,

Black troops, known as "buffalo soldiers," fought in the western campaigns to subdue the Plains Indians. African Americans often sought unsuccessfully to prove their loyalty and win respect and rights through military service.

like Europeans, depended on agriculture rather than hunting, they adapted more easily to agricultural slavery. Black labor was valuable, if controlled; Native Americans were merely barriers to expansion.

Cultural Differences

When settlers first began moving onto the Great Plains, they encountered about 250,000 Plains Indians and 13 million buffalo. Some groups, including the Zuni, Hopi, Navaho, and Pawnee, were fairly settled and depended on gardening and farming. Others, such as the Sioux, Apache, and Cheyenne, however, were nomadic hunters who followed the buffalo herds over vast tracts of land. These herds played a crucial role in most Plains Indians' culture—providing almost all the basic necessities. Indians ate the buffalo meat, made clothing and teepees out of the hides, used the fats for cosmetics, fashioned the bones into tools, made thread from the sinews, and even burned dried buffalo droppings as fuel. To settlers, however, the buffalo were barriers to western expansion. The herds interfered with construction, knocked over telegraph poles and fences, and could derail trains during stampedes.

Other cultural differences caused misunderstandings between settlers and Native Americans. Among Anglo-Americans, capitalism fostered competition and frontier living promoted individualism. On the other hand, Plains Indians lived in tribes based on kinship ties. As members of an extended family that included distant cousins, Indians were taught to place the welfare of the group over the interests of the individual. The emphasis within a tribe was on cooperation rather than competition. Some tribes might be richer than other tribes, but there was seldom a large gap between the rich and the poor within a tribe.

Power as well as wealth was usually shared. Tribes were loosely structured rather than tightly organized. Chiefs seldom had much individual power. The Cheyenne, for example, had a council of 44 to advise the chief. Instead of having a lot of political power, chiefs were generally religious and ceremonial leaders. Anglo-Americans did not always understand their limited power. Whites incorrectly believed that an individual Indian could make decisions and sign agreements that would be considered legal by their fellow Indians.

Another major cultural difference between the newly arriving settlers and the Plains Indians was their attitudes toward the land. Most Native Americans had no concept of private property. Chief Joseph of the Nez Percé eloquently expressed the view: "The earth was created by the assistance of the sun, and it should be left as it was. . . . The country was made without lines of demarcation, and it is no man's business to divide it."

Native Americans refused to draw property lines and borders because of how they viewed the place of people in the world. Whites tended to see land, plants, and animals as resources to be exploited. Native Americans, on the other hand, stressed the unity of all life—and its holiness.

Most of the Plains Indians believed that land could be utilized but never owned. The idea of owning land was as absurd as owning the air people breathed. To some, the sacredness of the land made farming against their religion. Chief Somohalla of the Wanapaun explained why his people refused to farm. "You ask me to plow the ground! Shall I take a knife and tear my mother's bosom? . . . You ask me to cut grass and make hay and sell it, and be rich like white men! But how dare I cut off my mother's hair?"

Indians had great reverence for all land. In addition, some particular pieces of land were considered especially sacred or holy. Certain bodies of water were seen as sources of healing and sites for worship. Some areas were burial grounds, where the spirits of ancestors were believed to reside. White settlers had little understanding of or respect for such Indian sentiments. The results could be tragic where interests collided.

From the white viewpoint, the most significant characteristic of many of the Plains Indian tribes, such as the Cheyenne, Sioux, and Arapaho, was their ability as mounted warriors. Using horses introduced by the Spanish, they had resisted white encroachment for two centuries. Most had no desire for assimilation; they merely wanted to be left alone. "If the Indians had tried to make the whites live like them," one Sioux declared, "the whites would have resisted, and it was the same way with the Indians."

Although some tribes could coexist peacefully with settlers, the nomadic tribes had a way of life that was incompatible with miners, railroad developers, cattle ranchers, and farmers. To Anglo-Americans the Indians were barriers to expansion. They agreed with Theodore Roosevelt that the West was not meant to be "kept as nothing but a game reserve for squalid savages." Thus U.S. Indian policy focused on getting more territory for white settlement. Prior to Reconstruction this was done by signing treaties that divided land between Native Americans and settlers and restricted the movement of each on the lands of the other. Frequently Indian consent was fraudulently obtained, and white respect for Indian land depended on how desirable it was for settlement. As the removal of the Southern Cherokees to Oklahoma had shown in the 1830s, compatibility of cultures did not protect Native Americans from the greed of whites.

During the Civil War, Sioux, Cheyenne, and Arapaho braves rejected the land cessions made by their chiefs. Violence against settlers erupted as frontier troop strength was reduced to fight the Confederacy. The war also provided an excuse to nullify previous

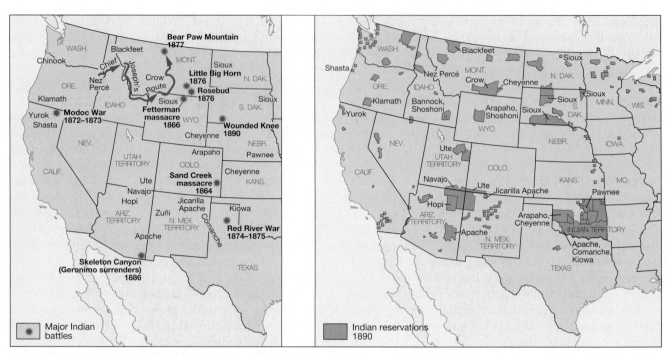

Indian Battles and Reservations

treaties and pledges with the Native Americans resettled in Oklahoma under Andrew Jackson's Indian removal policy. Some did support the Confederacy, but all suffered the consequences of Confederate defeat. Settlers moved into the most desirable land, pushing the Indians farther south and west. Some Native Americans began to resist.

Confrontation and Annihilation By the close of the Civil War, Indian hostility had escalated, especially after an 1864 massacre. The territorial governor of Colorado persuaded most of the warring Cheyennes and Arapahos to come to Fort Lyon on Sand Creek, promising them protection. Colonel J. M. Chivington's militia, however, attacked an Indian camp flying a white flag and the American flag and killed hundreds of Native American men, women, and children. The following year Congress established a committee to investigate the causes of conflict. Its final report in 1867 led to the creation of an **Indian Peace Commission** charged with negotiating settlements. At two conferences in 1867 and 1868, Indian chiefs were asked to restrict their tribes to reservations in the undesirable lands of Oklahoma and the Black Hills of the Dakotas in return for supplies and assistance from the government.

Most Indians did not consider the offer very generous. Some acquiesced and others resisted, but in the end federal authorities subdued or killed them all. Several factors made their resistance unsuccessful. Railroads had penetrated the West, bringing in both settlers and federal troops more rapidly. Most important, however, was the destruction of the buffalo herds. Just as modern Americans would be helpless without oil or electricity, the Plains Indians' culture could not survive the near extinction of the buffalo by professional and sport hunters. In 1872 the Indian commissioner accurately forecasted that in a few years the "most powerful and hostile bands of today" would be "reduced to the condition of suppliants for charity."

In 1876, the final year of Reconstruction, Lieutenant Colonel George A. Custer's defeat at Little Bighorn called attention to the "Indian problem." The stage was set for this confrontation with Chief Sitting Bull's Sioux warriors and their Cheyenne allies two years earlier when gold was discovered in the Black Hills. The territory suddenly became tempting, and miners began pouring into the lands guaranteed to the Indians only five years before. "The white man is in the Black Hills just like maggots," one Indian lamented.

Despite Sitting Bull's victory, the die had been cast during Reconstruction. All that remained were "mopping up" exercises. Federal authorities solved the Indian problem by reducing the number of Native Americans to a level that posed no threat. Still, white Americans would not leave the Indians alone to practice their religion and culture. The last major bloody confrontation occurred during the cold December of 1890 on the Pine Ridge Reservation (Sioux) in South Dakota. Poorly fed and supplied on the reservation, dissatisfied with their present, and longing for the

A Native American watercolor rendering of the Battle of Little Bighorn depicts its aftermath. As Sitting Bull and others stand watching, Sioux and Cheyenne warriors ride horseback over the corpses of Custer (*left center*) and his troops.

glories of their past, members of the Teton Sioux took up the **Ghost Dance,** a ritual that promised the faithful the mystical disappearance of the whites and the return of their lands. An inept government agent overreacted, calling in troops to suppress the Ghost Dance and arrest the Sioux leader Sitting Bull, whom the government considered the focal point of Indian resistance. When Indian police killed Sitting Bull, some Sioux took up arms and left the reservation. Near Wounded Knee Creek, U.S. soldiers, armed with rapid-fire Hotchkiss guns, attempted to disarm the Indians. When one Indian resisted, soldiers opened fire, killing more than 300 men, women, and children. The **Battle of Wounded Knee,** which resembled more a slaughter than a battle, ended the violent era of Indian and white relations.

Ethnocide and Assimilation By the time of Wounded Knee, the U.S. government had adopted a policy that emphasized ethnocide rather than genocide. An assault on tribalism, ethnocide—the calculated destruction of a culture—was an attempt by white Americans to force Native Americans to assimilate into their culture. Although not as bloody as the Indian wars, ethnocide was even more destructive to Native American societies.

At the heart of this new policy was the destruction of the reservation system. Reservations encour-

aged tribal unity, and, as such, distinctiveness from white American society. Congress believed that the solution was to treat Indians less like members of individual tribes and more like autonomous individuals. As a first step, in 1871 Congress had ruled that no Indian tribe "shall be acknowledged or recognized as an independent nation, tribe or power, with whom

This photograph, showing the mass burial of the victims after the massacre at Wounded Knee, illustrates the callous disregard of the value of Native American lives.

the United States may contract by treaty." Then in an attempt to destroy Indian culture, in 1887 Congress passed the **Dawes Severalty Act,** which authorized the president to divide tribal lands and redistribute the lands among tribal members, giving 160 acres to each head of a family and lesser amounts to bachelors, women, and children. Although the plots would be held in trust for 25 years to prevent Indians from immediately selling the land, the object of the legislation was to make Indians individual landowners. In addition, all Native Americans receiving land grants were also made citizens of the United States.

Henry Lauren Dawes, a senator from Massachusetts, was motivated by what he believed were the best interests of the Native Americans. Like other reformers, he believed that the most effective solution to the Indian problem was to assimilate Indians into mainstream white American culture. To this end, other reformers opened Indian schools to teach Indian children to be mechanics and farmers and to train them for citizenship. Richard Pratt, an army officer who founded the Carlisle Indian Industrial School in Pennsylvania in 1879, maintained that the fastest and surest way to assimilate Indians was to remove Indian children from reservations and send them to boarding schools in the East. By 1905 there were 25 boarding schools patterned after Carlisle. The schools emphasized ruthless assimilation. The "Rules for Indian Schools" called for compulsory observation of the Christian Sabbath, all formal and casual conversation in English, and instruction in "the sports and games enjoyed by white youth, such as baseball, hopscotch, croquet, marbles, bean bags, dominoes, checkers." Even more boarding schools were established on reservations to serve the same ends. What surprised reformers the most, however, was the failure of these schools to break tribal loyalties or destroy Indian culture.

While the reformers opened schools, Congress continued its efforts to break up the reservations. The Curtis Act of 1898 ended tribal sovereignty in Indian Territory, voiding tribal control of mineral rights, abolishing tribal laws and courts, and imposing the laws and courts of the United States on the Indians. The Dead Indian Act (1902) permitted Indians to sell allotted lands they had inherited, thereby circumventing the 25-year trust period imposed by the Dawes Act. Four years later, Congress continued its assault on the trust period with the Burke Act, which eliminated the trust period altogether and allowed the secretary of the interior to decide when Indians were competent to manage their own affairs. Finally, in 1924 Congress enacted the Snyder Act, which granted all Indians born in the United States full citizenship. As far as Congress was concerned, the United States had now assimilated its true natives.

TABLE 16.2	
Native Americans and the Federal Government Following the Civil War	
1864	Sand Creek Massacre
1867	Creation of the Indian Peace Commission
1876	Battle of Little Big Horn
1887	Dawes Severalty Act
1890	Ghost Dance and Wounded Knee
1898	Curtis Act
1902	Dead Indian Act
1906	Burke Act
1924	Snyder Act

Reformers believed that these acts would end the tribal system and lead to assimilation. The legislation, however, served only the land interests of white Americans. By 1932 the allotment program had taken 90 million acres of land away from tribal control. Far from being assimilated, Indians saw their own culture attacked and partially destroyed, while at the same time they were never fully accepted into the dominant American culture.

Final Retreat from Reconstruction

The exact nature of the Native Americans' status, like that of African Americans, was determined after Reconstruction was over. The treatment of both, as well as of immigrants, would be justified by the increasingly virulent racism of whites, which was given "scientific" support by the scholars of the late nineteenth century. The patriotism engendered by the 1876 centennial of the Declaration of Independence also fostered a desire for unity among white Americans at the expense of nonwhites.

By 1876, fewer Americans championed black rights than had at the close of the war. Neither could Northerners who believed that the only good Indian was a dead Indian condemn southern whites for their treatment of African Americans. Some of the old abolitionist Radicals had grown tired of what had become a protracted and complex problem. They therefore justified their withdrawal from the fight by the failures of some southern Reconstruction governments. Those least likely to do so, such as Thaddeus Stevens and Charles Sumner, were dead. Until his death in 1874, Sumner had struggled to get Congress to pass a civil rights act that would spell out more specifically the guarantees of the Fourteenth Amendment. He proposed that segregation of all public facilities, including schools, be declared illegal and the right of African Americans to serve on juries specified. After his death, in part as a tribute to him but mostly as one provision of a larger political bargain, Congress en-

This 1877 cartoon shows President Hayes as a railroad conductor ushering two Louisiana carpetbaggers out of the state.

acted the **Civil Rights Act of 1875.** The act did not include Sumner's clause on schools and did not provide any means of enforcement. For African Americans it was a paper victory that marked an end of national action on their behalf. Never effectively enforced, the act was rendered totally impotent by Supreme Court decisions of the late nineteenth century.

By 1876 all the elements were present for a national retreat on Reconstruction: the distraction of economic distress, a deep desire for unity among whites, the respectability of racism, a frustrated weariness with black problems by former allies, a growing conservatism on economic and social issues, a changing political climate featuring a resurgence of the Democratic party, and finally a general public disgust with the failure of Reconstruction. The presidential election of that year sealed the fate of Reconstruction and brought about an official end to it.

Corruption was a major issue in the 1876 election and the Democrats chose **Samuel J. Tilden,** a New Yorker whose claim to fame was breaking up the notorious Boss Tweed Ring. The Republicans nominated **Rutherford B. Hayes,** a man who had offended few—largely by doing little. Although Hayes had been elected governor of Ohio three times, to one observer he was "a third rate nonentity, whose only recommendation is that he is obnoxious to no one." As would become typical of most elections during the decades following Reconstruction, the campaign did not focus on any burning issues. The Democrats

ran against Republican corruption. The Republicans ran against Democratic violence in the South. "Our strong ground," Hayes wrote, "is the dread of a solid South, *rebel rule,* etc., etc. . . . It leads people away from 'hard times'; which is our deadliest foe."

The election itself was so riddled with corruption and violence that no one can ever know what would have happened in a fair election. One thing is certain. The Democrats gained strength. Tilden won the popular vote and led Hayes in undisputed electoral votes 184 to 165. However, 185 votes were needed for election, and 20 votes were disputed—19 of them from Louisiana, Florida, and South Carolina. They were the only southern states still under Republican rule with the backing of federal troops. In each, rival election boards sent in different returns.

With no constitutional provision for such an occurrence, the Republican Senate and Democratic House established a special commission to decide which returns were valid. The 15-member Electoral Commission had 5 members each from the House, the Senate, and the Supreme Court. At first it was evenly divided with 7 Republicans and 7 Democrats; politically independent Supreme Court Justice David Davis was the swing vote. Illinois Democrats then made a mistake and selected Davis as their senator. Thus, a Republican justice was appointed to replace him on the Electoral Commission, which proceeded to vote along party lines, 8 to 7, to give all the

Election of 1876

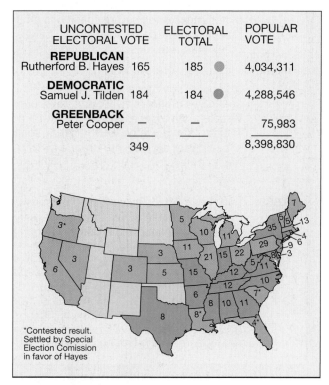

UNCONTESTED ELECTORAL VOTE	ELECTORAL TOTAL	POPULAR VOTE
REPUBLICAN Rutherford B. Hayes 165	185 ●	4,034,311
DEMOCRATIC Samuel J. Tilden 184	184 ●	4,288,546
GREENBACK Peter Cooper —	—	75,983
349		8,398,830

*Contested result. Settled by Special Election Comission in favor of Hayes

disputed votes to Hayes. Democrats were outraged, and a constitutional crisis seemed in the making if a united Democratic front in the House voted to reject the commission's findings.

A series of agreements between Hayes's advisors and southern Democratic congressmen averted the crisis. In what came to be called the **Compromise of 1877,** Hayes agreed to support federal aid for southern internal improvements, especially a transcontinental railroad. He also promised to appoint a southern Democrat to his cabinet and to allow southern Democrats a say in the allocation of federal offices in their region. Most important, however, was his pledge to remove the remaining federal troops from the South. In return southern Democrats promised to protect black rights and to support the findings of the Electoral Commission. On March 2, the House voted to accept the report and declare Hayes the presidential winner by an electoral vote of 185 to 184. After taking office, Hayes removed the troops, and

the remaining Republican governments in the South soon collapsed.

Scholars once considered the Compromise of 1877 an important factor in the end of Reconstruction. Actually, its role was more symbolic than real; it merely buried the corpse. The battle for the Republican party's soul had been lost by its abolitionist faction well before the election of 1876. The Democratic party had never sought to extend or protect blacks' rights. The Supreme Court began to interpret the Fourteenth and Fifteenth amendments very narrowly, stripping them of their strength. Thus African Americans were left with a small number of allies, and one by one many of their rights were lost during the next four decades.

CONCLUSION

As the Civil War ended, many unresolved issues remained. The most crucial involved the status of the former slaves and of the former Confederate states.

CHRONOLOGY OF KEY EVENTS

1863   Lincoln proclaims 10 percent plan for Reconstruction, which requires states to abolish slavery and have 10 percent of the citizens who had voted in the 1860 election subscribe to an oath to support the Constitution and the Union

1864   Lincoln vetoes Wade-Davis Bill on grounds that it imposes too severe conditions on the readmission of the seceded states; Sand Creek Massacre of Indians in Colorado

1865   Congress establishes Freedmen's Bureau to aid former slaves and refugees; Confederate army surrenders at Appomattox; John Wilkes Booth assassinates Lincoln at Ford's Theater in Washington, D.C.; Andrew Johnson becomes seventeenth president; Thirteenth Amendment is ratified, abolishing slavery

1866   Civil Rights Act provides that all persons born in the United States are citizens and possess equal legal and property rights; Fourteenth Amendment is proposed

1867   Reconstruction Act, passed over Johnson's veto, divides the South into five military districts, each governed by an army general. It requires each state to adopt a constitution disqualifying former Confederate officials from holding office, to grant black citizens

the right to vote, and to ratify the Fourteenth Amendment

1868   House of Representatives impeaches President Johnson; he escapes conviction in the Senate by one vote; Fourteenth Amendment is ratified, guaranteeing citizenship to black Americans; Indian peace conference leads to establishment of reservations in Oklahoma and the Black Hills of the Dakotas; Ulysses S. Grant is elected eighteenth president

1870   Fifteenth Amendment is ratified, outlawing exclusion from the vote on the basis of race

1870– 1871   Ku Klux Klan Acts are passed, which outlaw use of force to prevent people from voting and authorize use of federal troops to enforce the laws; Tweed Ring in New York City is exposed

1872   Credit Mobilier scandal is exposed

1876   Custer is defeated at Little Bighorn; disputed presidential election between Tilden and Hayes

1877   Electoral Commission awards disputed ballots to Republican Rutherford B. Hayes, who becomes nineteenth president

Last Stand at Little Big Horn. One of the most frequently depicted and least understood moments in American history is covered in this *American Experience* tape from PBS.

Geronimo and the Apache Resistance. An account of the battles of Geronimo and the Apaches from PBS.

Birth of a Nation. 1915 movie classic that gives a one-sided, southern view of Reconstruction and illustrates the popular myths about that era.

Dances with Wolves. 1990 movie with Kevin Costner that chronicles the interactions between Civil War hero Lt. John Dunbar and the peaceful Lakota Sioux.

KEY TERMS

Freedmen's Bureau (p. 423)

Special Field Order 15 (p. 426)

Dred Scott decision (p. 426)

Radical Republicans (p. 426)

Ten percent plan (p. 427)

Wade-Davis Bill (p. 427)

Black Codes (p. 428)

Joint Committee on Reconstruction (p. 429)

Fourteenth Amendment (p. 430)

Military Reconstruction Act (p. 431)

Tenure of Office Act (p. 431)

Fifteenth Amendment (p. 433)

Carpetbaggers (p. 435)

Scalawags (p. 435)

Sharecropping (p. 438)

Ku Klux Klan (p. 439)

Redeemer governments (p. 441)

Credit Mobilier (p. 441)

Panic of 1873 (p. 442)

Indian Peace Commission (p. 444)

Ghost Dance (p. 445)

Battle of Wounded Knee (p. 445)

Dawes Severalty Act (p. 446)

Civil Rights Act of 1875 (p. 447)

Compromise of 1877 (p. 448)

PEOPLE YOU SHOULD KNOW

Frederick Douglass (p. 423)

Oliver O. Howard (p. 423)

Thaddeus Stevens (p. 427)

Charles Sumner (p. 427)

Andrew Johnson (p. 427)

Edwin M. Stanton (p. 432)

Ulysses S. Grant (p. 432)

Susan B. Anthony (p. 433)

Horace Greeley (p. 434)

Samuel J. Tilden (p. 447)

Rutherford B. Hayes (p. 447)

REVIEW QUESTIONS

1. How were the Civil War and Reconstruction's impacts on black and white Southerners interrelated, and how did the impacts affect the actions of each group?

2. To what extent were white Southerners responsible for what they considered to be the harsh conditions of congressional Reconstruction?

3. Just how radical was Radical Reconstruction?

4. What factors led to the decline of Reconstruction?

5. How were white Americans' treatments of African Americans and Native Americans similar, and how did the treatment of each group differ?

17 Emergence as an Economic Power

WHITE CITY: THE WORLD'S COLUMBIAN EXPOSITION

On May 1, 1893, the World's Columbian Exposition opened in Chicago, Illinois. Fairgoers were awestruck by 633 acres of buildings, artificial lagoons, and exotic exhibits. At the center of the fair was the Court of Honor—a grouping of buildings around a large reflecting pool with an elaborate fountain and a gigantic gilded statue of the Republic. All the buildings were white, their classically styled cornices rising to heights of 60 feet. The result was breathtaking. One visitor wrote his parents, "Sell the cookstove if necessary and come. You must see the fair." Many did. Total admissions were over 27 million during the 179 days of the fair, meaning an estimated 25 percent of all Americans had visited the exposition.

Soon dubbed the "White City," the Court of Honor included buildings honoring Mines and Mining; Transportation; Electricity; Agriculture; Machinery; and Manufactures and Liberal Arts. Three years earlier Congress selected Chicago as the site for "celebrating the 400th anniversary of the discovery of America by Christopher Columbus, by holding an international exhibition of arts, industries, manufactures, and the products of the soil, mine, and sea." The overall effect of the fair was not so much to celebrate Columbus's discovery as to display to the world the emerging economic and technological dominance of the United States. An English visitor noted, "Perhaps the portion of the World's Exposition which America is far ahead of all in competition is the Palace of Electricity; here she is seen in her natural splendor, eclipsing by her dazzling light every other nation."

Electricity was the most tangible evidence of the American inventiveness that would reshape the world. In Chicago people who had never seen a light bulb before witnessed Thomas Edison's 82-foot Tower of Light with over 18,000 bulbs. They also saw the first movable sidewalk, elevated railroad, seismograph, and Edison's early version of motion pictures. One exhibit showed a house equipped with newly invented electrical appliances, including a sewing machine, stove, and iron. Some people viewed as science fiction the claim: "There will be no occasion for lighting a match in [future homes] for any purpose whatsoever." Many who had been fearful of electricity became converts. It became an icon for technological progress.

The Columbian Exposition sought in part to reassure people bewildered by rapid economic changes. One of those was the rise of mass marketing and

The Columbian Exposition of 1893 in Chicago celebrated the enormous technological progress of the late nineteenth century. In the Palace of Electricity many visitors saw their first electric lamp.

advertising. Both were transforming Americans into consumers rather than producers. The exposition was a huge success largely because its Department of Publicity and Promotion mailed out 2000 to 3000 packages every day. Scarcely a railroad station in America or Europe lacked a flyer touting the fair. In the Manufactures and Liberal Arts Building companies could display and sell their products alongside musical instruments belonging to famous composers Wolfgang Mozart and Sebastian Bach. Paired with classical architecture and music, consumerism was made to seem respectable. Brand new products, such as Cracker Jacks, Aunt Jemima Syrup, Pabst Beer, carbonated sodas, and Juicy Fruit gum, competed for prizes that companies could use to lure new customers.

By copying old European architecture, the fair managers sought to create feelings of stability and order during what was actually a very chaotic time in America. By the 1890s forces of economic change had swept through all sections and all segments of the economy. The profound alterations of the social order that resulted touched virtually every aspect of life. The natures of work and marketing were drastically transformed, affecting all social relationships. The transitions from rural to urban life, from self-employment to wage labor, from hand craftsmanship to mass produced goods, and from local economies to a national one were all creating dislocations and economic instability. Indeed the year the fair opened, the nation suffered a financial panic, which grew into a major economic depression with high unemployment and bank failures. Workers sought to organize to combat wage cuts and unsafe working conditions in the new economic order, which was one change company owners did not embrace. Among the guests of honor at the fair's dedication ceremonies was the military commander responsible for repressing a labor strike at the Homestead plant of Andrew Carnegie's steel company in 1892.

From the beginning, the Columbian Exposition was a joint venture of business and government. Inspired by the success of the 1876 Centennial Exhibition in Philadelphia, several cities had vied for the honor of hosting the 1893 fair. Congress selected Chicago because its business leaders raised $5 million in stock for the venture and agreed to raise $5 million more. Selling shares in corporations became the major way of raising money to build factories and start companies. Shareholders expected to make money from their investment, and investors in the fair were not disappointed. The exposition returned a $1 million profit to its 30,000 subscribers. To do so required abandoning to some extent the initial educational vision of the fair: "It'll be as good as a college course to spend a week there."

A strip of land called Midway Plaisance was intended to be an ethnological study of the various cultures of the world. Instead it became the site of the brand new Ferris Wheel, which cost twice as much to ride as the fair admission price. Around it was what one visitor described as "probably the greatest collection of 'fakes' the world has ever seen." Watching the 'hoochy-kootchy' belly dancer named Little Egypt was great entertainment but not at all enlightening about Egypt. Socialist writer Edmund Bellamy complained that the "underlying motive of the whole [Exposition], under the sham of patriotism is business, advertising with a view to individual money-making." Few people cared, however, as they marveled at feats of technology and celebrated American success.

uccess was undeniable. After the Civil War, the United States moved out of the ranks of second-rate industrial powers and became the leader. By 1900 its manufacturing output exceeded the combined totals of Great Britain, France, and Germany. The speed with which this happened seems more suited to fairy tales than reality. As Andrew Carnegie exclaimed in 1886, "The old nations of the earth creep on at a snail's pace; the Republic thunders past with the rush of an express."

Many yardsticks supported his assertion. Between 1870 and 1914 U.S. railroad mileage increased from 53,000 to 250,000—more than the combined railroad mileage of the rest of the world. Almost every sector of the economy grew in multiples of two or more from the 1860s to 1900. Land under agricultural production doubled; the gross national product was six times larger; the amount of manufactured goods per person tripled.

This phenomenal growth had resulted from the foundations laid by antebellum industrial development, the abundance of the land and its people, technological breakthroughs, and a favorable business climate—ideologically, financially, legally, and politically. The rapidity of change first produced chaotic conditions, which eventually led to new managerial styles and finally to economic consolidation. Farmers, miners, and ranchers in the West and South also confronted changes wrought by technology and an increasingly national and international market. Workers struggled to adapt their new status as wage laborers in jobs often requiring less skill and more discipline. The Columbian Exposition supplied a needed illusion of order and stability, even though its impressive building fronts were not carved from

marble but instead molded of temporary plaster and torn down at the fair's conclusion.

AMERICA: LAND OF PLENTY

In 1847 Walt Whitman boasted, "Yankeedoodledom is going ahead with the resistless energy of a sixty-five-hundred-horse-power steam engine. . . . Let the Old World wag on under its cumbersome load of form and conservatism; we are of a newer, fresher race and land. And all we have to say is, to point to fifty years hence and say, 'Let those laugh who win.'" By 1897 Americans were laughing. Their victory was facilitated by the abundance of the nation's new land, new people, and new ideas. Western expansion, increasing immigration, and numerous inventions ushered in a new era.

Mineral and Geographic Possibilities

It wasn't until the nineteenth century that Americans began to realize the vast wealth that their territorial expansion had brought. Most spectacular was the discovery of gold in California in the 1840s. That discovery sparked frenzied prospecting all through the West. Each new discovery led to "rushes," creating mining towns almost overnight. Between 1850 and the 1880s thousands of men and women of almost every ethnic background helped create makeshift social institutions whenever and wherever strikes were made.

Wherever it moved, the mining frontier tended to follow the same pattern. Adventurous optimists would search for the elusive glint of precious metals. After living weeks or months at subsistence level, many would go home poorer. Although a few did strike it rich, inexpensive and inefficient mining methods quickly exhausted the more easily obtainable supplies of precious metals. Extracting ore from beneath the ground and in veins of quartz was expensive. It required large amounts of capital best raised by mining syndicates. Frequently financed by eastern and European investors, these syndicates bought prospectors' claims for a fraction of their value.

As mining became an organized business, its focus moved to less exotic but more useful minerals such as copper, lead, talc, zinc, and quartz. These fed the growing demands of eastern industries. By the 1880s mining no longer represented easy riches for pioneering individuals; it had become an integrated part of the nation's modern industrial economy.

Emerging basic industries such as steel and petroleum, and those producing electric power, depended on large supplies of various minerals. New processing techniques to produce steel led to increased demand for iron. Copper became a key resource in such new fields as oil refining, electrical generation and conduction, and telephone communications. A shift from waterwheels to coal-burning steam engines sparked a spectacular rise in coal mining.

Even more dramatic was the rise in the importance of petroleum. Many people were aware of large oil reserves in Pennsylvania because it seeped into streams and springs. Early demand was mainly for making patent medicines of dubious value. Encouraged by reports of its potential use as a lighting source and lubricating oil, Pennsylvania businessman George Bissell funded the first drilling efforts. In 1859 his employee Edwin L. Drake tapped the first oil well, in Titusville, Pennsylvania. Commonly labeled "Drake's folly," the well marked the beginning of another new industry. Oil was indeed needed to lubricate the increasing number of machine parts, and in the 1870s about 20 million barrels were being produced annually. John D. Rockefeller and others built refineries to refine the oil into kerosene, which was used as a popular form of illumination, displacing candles before kerosene itself was replaced by electricity.

The growing demand led to the search for "liquid gold" in the Southwest. In 1901 a well at Spindletop, Texas, shot a 160-foot stream of oil into the air. New sources of oil led to the development of the gasoline engine in the twentieth century, exemplifying how abundant natural resources and technology often interacted—each shaping the evolution of the other.

Technological Change

Seldom has technology so dramatically transformed so much of people's lives in a single generation. Bewildering as the changes sometimes were in the late nineteenth century, the public generally welcomed new inventions with wide-eyed wonder and nationalistic pride. Many public events were like mass rituals to the new god of technology. Parades and thanksgiving services as well as the ringing of the Liberty Bell greeted the completion of the first transcontinental railway at Promontory Point, Utah, in May 1869. Awed sightseers crammed expositions celebrating "progress." At the 1876 Philadelphia Centennial Exposition, visitors saw for the first time the Corliss engine, bicycles, the typewriter, the elevator, the telephone, and even the "floor covering of the future"—linoleum. By the time of the Chicago fair in 1893, the Corliss engine was obsolete, and many of the miracles of 1876 were commonplace "necessities." The impact of new inventions was enormous. Only 276 inventions were recorded during the Patent Office's first decade, but 22,000 patents were issued in the single year of 1893.

Technological change during the era affected the lives of individuals far more than any political or philosophical development. Offices became mechanized with the invention of the typewriter in 1867 and the development of a practical adding machine in 1888. As clerical work became more necessary and required less skill, it became classed as women's work with lower pay scales. Electric streetcars profoundly changed the character of urban development by accelerating the move to the suburbs.

Innovations in communication unified a collection of island communities into a nation. The completion of a telegraphic cable across the Atlantic in 1866 increased the nation's links with the rest of the world. New inventions in printing made popular newspapers with wide circulations a reality—along with mass advertising. Photographic advances culminated in **George Eastman**'s Kodak handheld camera in 1888. However, few, if any, inventions rivaled the impact of **Alexander Graham Bell**'s 1876 "toy." Telephones rapidly became necessities—more than 1.5 million were installed by 1900.

The new inventions increasingly relied on cheap and efficient sources of electricity. The names of **Thomas Edison** and **George Westinghouse** stand above the rest in this area. Edison began his career peddling candy and newspapers on trains, but he soon became a telegrapher and invented various improvements to telegraphy. The success of his ideas

On November 26, 1876, Alexander Graham Bell used this box telephone to transmit sound between Cambridge and Salem, Massachusetts.

In his Menlo Park, New Jersey, laboratory, Thomas Edison, who eventually obtained over 1000 patents, aimed at practicality in his inventions. He is shown listening to his phonograph in 1888.

convinced him to go into the "invention business." Establishing a research lab at Menlo Park, New Jersey, in 1876, he promised to produce "a minor invention every ten days and a big thing every six months or so." In 1877 he invented the phonograph and in 1879 the incandescent light bulb, as well as hundreds of other devices over the years, such as a better telephone, the dictaphone, the mimeograph, the dynamo, motion pictures, and an electric distribution for lighting transmission. With backing from banker J. P. Morgan, he created the first electric company in 1882 in New York City, and formed the Edison General Electric Company in 1888 to produce light bulbs.

Edison's only serious mistake was his choice of direct electrical current, which limited the range of transmission to a radius of about two miles. George Westinghouse developed an alternating current system in 1886 that soon supplanted direct current, forcing even Edison's companies to make the switch. Westinghouse also acquired and improved an electric motor that had been invented by Croatian immigrant Nikola Tesla in 1888.

An Expanding Railroad Network

Americans developed a love-hate relationship with the railroads. The same locomotive that inspired Walt Whitman's rhapsody to its "fierce throated beauty" was described by Frank Norris in 1901 as "the leviathan, with tentacles of steel clutching into the soil, the soulless Force, the iron-hearted Power, the Master, the Colossus, the Octopus." Despite differing visions, no one doubted the importance of the railroads. They played a crucial role in forging a new society, transforming a continent of isolated communities into a unified nation with an interdependent economy. Rails brought raw materials to population centers, making possible large factories that mass-produced goods. Those goods were then shipped to national markets over the same rails.

Early railroads were strictly local affairs, however. Although there were already 35,000 miles of rails by 1865, few lines linked up in any rational way. Having 11 different rail gauges meant that both goods and passengers had to be unloaded from one set of cars and reloaded onto another set—sometimes at a depot on the opposite side of town. Between New York and Chicago, for example, cargo had to be unloaded and reloaded as many as six times.

Unlike many European rail systems, American railroads grew with little advance planning or government regulation, sprouting like weeds in populous areas where immediate profits could be made. While too many railroads served some sections in the East, prior to 1869 there were no transcontinental lines linking the East and West coasts due to the high cost of construction. Large amounts of capital were required in the East but a return on the investment came quickly. In the West railroads often preceded settlement and, therefore, demand for their lines. Transcontinental routes were needed, however, and land grants became the solution. Contemporary and later analysts have questioned the size of those grants, but they undoubtedly had the desired effect. By the turn of the century there were five transcontinental routes.

At the same time, after some fierce competitive battles, a few eastern railroad companies gained control of many of the local lines. When the dust settled,

FIGURE 17.1
Railroad Construction, 1861–1920

By 1865 there were 35,000 miles of railroad, but few lines connected in any logical way to provide direct routes from one location to another.
Source: U.S. Bureau of the Census, 1975.

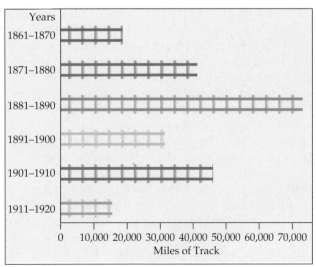

there were four main trunklines in the Northeast and five in the Southeast. The average track length of a railroad grew from a mere 100 miles in 1865 to over 1000 miles two decades later. Gauges were also standardized, and a more efficient rail system emerged.

CREATING A FAVORABLE CLIMATE: THE ROLE OF IDEOLOGY, POLITICS, AND FINANCE

An abundant harvest requires good soil, favorable climatic conditions, and adequate fertilization. Materials and machinery were the "seeds" of industrialization, but the bountiful economic harvest of the late nineteenth century depended first on the "good soil" of popular support fostered by intellectual and cultural justifications. Favorable government policies created a desirable "climate," while legal and financial developments provided the needed "fertilizer." The combination produced not only more but also larger industries.

Social Darwinism and the Gospel of Wealth

Expanding economic opportunities fostered cutthroat competition from which fewer and fewer winners emerged. The road to wealth taken by the new captains of industry was strewn with ruined competitors and broken labor movements. Ruthlessness not only seemed to become increasingly necessary, it was also transformed into a virtue by the twin ideologies of **social Darwinism** and the "gospel of wealth."

For industrialists like **Andrew Carnegie,** the writings of social Darwinists **Herbert Spencer** and William Graham Sumner helped relieve unwelcome guilt. "I remember that light came as in a flood and all was clear," Carnegie noted, after reading Spencer's writings. Spencer and his followers applied the biological concepts of Charles Darwin to the workings of society. Natural selection allowed the fittest individuals to survive and flourish in the marketplace. Survival of the fittest supposedly enriched not only the winners but also society as a whole. Human evolution would produce what Spencer called "the ultimate and inevitable development of the ideal man" through a culling process.

According to the social Darwinists, poverty and slums were as inevitable as the concentration of wealth. Spencer pleaded that "there should not be a forcible burdening of the superior for the support of the inferior." His disciple Sumner declared, "If we do not like the survival of the fittest, we have only one possible alternative, and that is the survival of the

unfittest." Both argued that governmental or charitable intervention to improve the conditions of the poor interfered with the functioning of natural law and prolonged the life of "defective gene pools" to the detriment of society as a whole.

The so-called fittest naturally greeted "scientific" endorsement of their elite positions with eagerness. John D. Rockefeller told his Baptist Sunday school class, "The growth of large business is merely the survival of the fittest. This is not an evil tendency in Business. It is merely the working out of a law of nature and a law of God." Some who found the ruthlessness of social Darwinism unpalatable sought their justification in religious rationales. Since colonial times, the Protestant work ethic had denounced idleness and viewed success as evidence of being among the "elect"—God's chosen people. Building upon this base, apologists constructed the **gospel of wealth**.

Some simply and boldly announced God's sanction of their wealth: Rockefeller asserted, "God gave

This 1901 cartoon shows Andrew Carnegie giving away "millions for the public good." It illustrates Carnegie's belief in the responsibilities of wealth.

THE PEOPLE SPEAK

The Gospel of Wealth

The religious support for wealth is illustrated by Russell Conwell, a lawyer and Baptist minister. This is one version of the "Acres of Diamonds" speech that Conwell gave approximately 6000 times between 1861 and 1925.

Money is power, and you ought to be reasonably ambitious to have it. You ought because you can do more good with it than you could without it. Money printed your Bible, money builds your churches, money sends your missionaries, and money pays your preachers, and you would not have many of them, either, if you did not pay them. I am always willing that my church should raise my salary, because the church that pays the largest salary always raises it the easiest. You never knew an exception to it in your life. The man who gets the largest salary can do the most good with the power that is furnished to him. Of course he can if his spirit be right to use it for what it is given to him.

I say, then, you ought to have money. If you can honestly attain unto riches in Philadelphia, it is your Christian and godly duty to do so. It is an awful mistake of these pious people to think you must be awfully poor in order to be pious.

Some men say, "Don't you sympathize with the poor people?" Of course I do, or else I would not have been lecturing these years. I won't give in but what I sympathize with the poor, but the number of poor who are to be sympathized with is very small. To sympathize with a man whom God has punished for his sins, thus to help him when God would still continue a just punishment, is to do wrong, no doubt about it, and we do that more than we help those who are deserving. While we should sympathize with God's poor—that is, those who cannot help themselves—let us remember there is not a poor person in the United States who was not made poor by his own shortcomings, or by the shortcomings of some one else. It is all wrong to be poor anyhow. Let us give in to that argument and pass that to one side.

Source: Russell H. Conwell, *Acres of Diamonds*, 1915, pp. 17–22, Harper & Brothers, New York.

me my riches." Carnegie produced a written, logically argued rationale: "Not evil, but good, has come to the race," he wrote, "from the accumulation of wealth by those who have the ability and energy that produces it." The masses would waste any extra income "on the indulgence of appetite." "Wealth, passing through the hands of the few," Carnegie wrote, "can be a much more potent force for the elevation of our race than if it had been distributed in small sums to the people themselves." In other words, the "fittest" could best decide what other people needed. In Carnegie's case, he took that responsibility seriously, distributing over $300 million to such philanthropic causes as the founding of libraries and the Carnegie Foundation.

Among the most effective apologists for the wealthy were religious leaders of the era. In 1901 Bishop William Lawrence, for example, proclaimed, "Godliness is in league with riches." Not only did the elite deserve their riches, but the poor were responsible for their low status. The eminent preacher Henry Ward Beecher argued that "no man suffers from poverty unless it be more than his fault—unless it be his sin."

Thus, according to both scientific and religious thought, the maldistribution of wealth was not only inevitable but also desirable. Probably more important, though, was the support for this idea provided by popular culture. *McGuffey's Readers* stressed the virtue of hard work and its inevitable rewards. Novelist Horatio Alger penned many stories in which the heroes rose from poverty to comfortable middle-class status through a combination of diligence and good luck. Popular literature reinforced the idea that success always came to those who deserved it, in America, the land of opportunity.

Laissez-Faire in Theory and Practice

The prevailing economic theory also lent respectability to greed and to the idea that government should not intervene in the economy. In 1776 Adam Smith presented arguments in *The Wealth of Nations* that would long be used to explain the workings of a free economy and to prescribe government's role in that economy. Smith asserted that the market was directed and controlled by an "invisible hand" composed of a multitude of individual choices. If government did not meddle, competition would naturally lead to the production of desired goods and services at reasonable prices—the natural laws of supply and demand. In short, if everyone were free to act according to self-interest, the resulting economy would be best suited to meet society's needs.

Popular culture at the turn of the century reinforced the American dream. In the Horatio Alger stories, the hero always escapes poverty through hard work and good fortune and joins the middle class.

Acceptance of the "invisible hand" of supply-and-demand economic theory naturally led to a policy called **laissez-faire.** Government was to leave the economy alone and not disrupt the operation of these natural forces. Business leaders naturally endorsed the theory's rejection of governmental regulation, yet they saw no contradiction in asking for government aid and subsidies to foster industrialization. And to a large extent the industrialists got what they wanted—a laissez-faire policy that left them alone, except to help. Ironically, this distortion of theory helped produce an economy where business consolidation wreaked havoc upon the very competition needed for natural regulation of the economy.

Business freedom of action boggles the modern mind. No laws protected the consumer from adulterated foods, spurious claims for ineffective or even dangerous patent medicines, the sale of stock in nonexistent companies, or unsafe and overpriced

transportation services. No national regulating agency of any kind existed prior to the establishment of the Interstate Commerce Commission in 1887. The proclamation "Let the buyer beware" asked people to make decisions and choices without enough information to protect their interests.

While denying support and protection to consumers or workers, government at all levels aided businesspeople. Alexander Hamilton's vision of an industrializing nation fostered by favorable governmental action, which had never entirely died, was rejuvenated by the Republican party. In 1860 the party pledged to enact higher tariffs, to subsidize the completion of a transcontinental railroad, and to establish a stable national banking system. The Republican victory undoubtedly helped create a favorable environment for rapid industrialization. There was no sharp break with the past, however, nor did business gain a great victory over agriculture. The pattern of governmental aid to business was, as one historian has

This drawing illustrates the dangers of unregulated patent medicines, and the unpopularity of trusts.

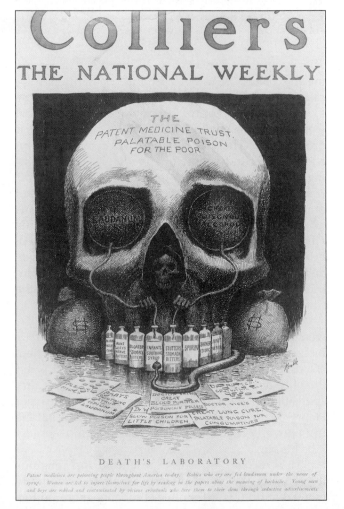

noted, "like certain kinds of embroidery . . . boldly visible but not of simple design." No form of aid was without antebellum precedents and most had wide public support. Both the motives behind many actions and their results were mixed. At the same time, agriculture was far from unrepresented and powerless, as can be seen by the passage of the Homestead and Morrill Land Grant Acts, which provided free land to settlers and financed agricultural education.

Another government aid to business was the tariff. Tariffs had a long history. At first, such American industries as steel needed to be protected from European competition to survive. Yet even after Carnegie greatly reduced the cost of steel production, the tariff remained. Without foreign competition, businesspeople were able to make higher profits by charging higher prices, which consumers came to resent. Tariffs were nevertheless widely viewed as serving the national interest by fostering economic independence.

Additional forms of subsidy were also meant to serve the public good. Dwarfing all others were the land grants to railroads. During the 1860s Congress granted 20 square miles of public land in alternating sections to the Union Pacific and Central Pacific railroads for each mile of track laid by the two railroads, to spur completion of a transcontinental route. Only the scale of these grants was new—railroads had already received nearly 20 million acres of federal land prior to the war. By the time the grants ended, railroad developers had received a total of 130 million acres of federal land and some 51 million acres of state land. Congress gave all those acres to a handful of people—creating some of America's wealthiest families. In return the government paid only half-fare to move troops and supplies, the value of the remaining land increased, and the uniting of the East and West aided the entire economy.

Business also benefited from favorable labor and financial legislation and low-interest loans. Individuals exploited these policies for personal gain, and the results were not uniformly positive. Although never unlimited or unrestricted, aid to business enjoyed wide public support at first. Indeed, nationalism and patriotism accompanied the process of industrialization. Many Americans took pride in the nation's growing economic power. When John D. Rockefeller explained his business activities by saying, "I wanted to participate in the work of making our country great," his words fell on sympathetic ears. Only after the problems of industrialization became more apparent did the public begin to cry "foul."

Corporations and Capital Formation

Although corporations were certainly not new, changes dating from the Jacksonian period paved the way for their postwar domination of the economy. Businesspeople had once been required to apply to a state legislature for a charter; by the 1830s they could incorporate on their own, provided they met certain standards. Following the Civil War, courts also began to affirm the principle of limited liability. Previously, bankruptcy could bring not only the loss of one's investment but also seizure of personal property by creditors. A corporation's liability eventually became limited to its assets—making investment a safer and more desirable venture. One knew just how much could be lost.

In *Santa Clara County v. The Southern Pacific Railroad* (1886) the Supreme Court perverted the Fourteenth Amendment by ruling that a corporation was a legal "person" and therefore entitled to all the protections granted by the amendment, such as equal protection of the law. Corporations were also eventually granted the "right" to "reasonable" profits—to be determined by the courts, not the state.

Corporations not only received "equal protection," they became privileged "persons." Real human beings whose rights were protected by the Constitution were also held responsible for illegal activities. There were no handcuffs or jail cells large enough for "corporate persons." Punishing individuals for corporate crimes was difficult because corporate directors were considered to be merely employees of the company. A popular saying noted that a corporation had "neither a soul to be damned nor a body to be kicked." Such advantages helped spur the growth of corporations—by 1904 almost 70 percent of all manufacturing employees worked for corporations.

Perhaps the greatest advantage of corporations was their ability to raise large amounts of capital. The expansion of industry in the late nineteenth century required big infusions of money. Farmers needed new machinery to increase productivity; manufacturers needed new plants to utilize the latest technology; cities needed new construction to service the needs of the urban population.

From where was all this money to come? Some, of course, was generated by the rising gross national product—the total value of goods and services produced in one year—which grew from $225 per person in 1870 to nearly $500 in 1900. New technology increased productivity and put "extra" money into the hands of middle- and upper-class people—money not required to meet physical needs. Many chose to use the extra money, or capital, to make more money by investing it.

Increasing amounts of capital were invested in manufacturing partly because investment bankers such as **J. P. Morgan** marketed corporate stocks and bonds. Foreign investment was also important; by 1900 Europeans had $3.4 billion invested in the

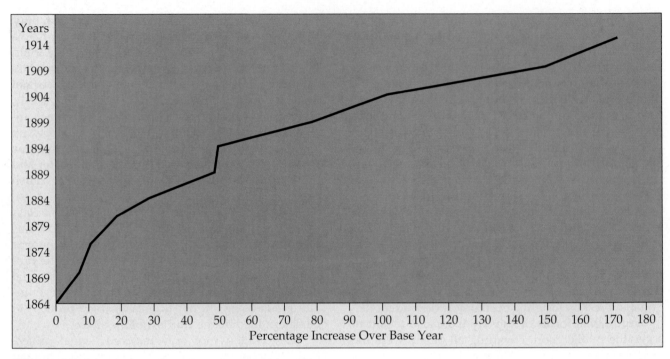

FIGURE 17.2
Index of U.S. Manufacturing Production, 1864–1914

United States, which represented approximately one-third of the almost $10 billion invested in manufacturing. This was indeed rich fertilizer for growth.

The net result of the favorable conditions of the late nineteenth century was the industrial supremacy of the United States. Vast mineral wealth, technological breakthroughs, growth of railroads, popular support, beneficial government policies, liberal corporation laws, and the availability of capital fostered this transformation and Americans reveled in it. At first these favorable conditions worked like overfertilized land—too many plants were produced for the available space and resources. This overgrowth created chaos until such entrepreneurs as Andrew Carnegie found ways to prune away their rivals.

THE RISE OF BIG BUSINESS

"You might as well endeavor to stay the formation of clouds, the falling of rains, the flowing of streams, as to attempt . . . to prevent the organization of industry." These words of John D. Rockefeller's attorney described what he considered to be the inevitable domination of entire industries by large corporations. The impact of the consolidation of industry was enormous. As companies grew larger, new management styles and more white-collar workers were needed. Mass production increased—profoundly

changing the nature of work for industrial laborers. Giant corporations thus amassed great power over production, people, and politics.

Controlling Competition

Most business leaders did not really advocate free enterprise fueled by competition. To them competition meant chaos, and they sought to eliminate it. J. P. Morgan, one historian wrote, "did not really believe in the free enterprise system, and like most ardent socialists, he hated the waste, duplication, and clutter of unrestrained competition."

As America's first big business, the railroad industry was also the first to confront the problems of competition. In some regions too many companies were after the same traffic. Some railroads desperately wooed shippers by giving lower rates for bulk shipments and long hauls. They also gave **rebates**—secret kickbacks below their published prices—to some preferred customers. They then sought to make up for that lost revenue by overcharging smaller shippers.

Such tactics did not solve the railroads' problems, however, especially when rate wars broke out. In the 1870s some railroad managers tried cooperation as a cure for competition. They formed **pools**, regional federations to divide traffic equitably and to raise rates to increase profits. Pools were not legally enforceable, however, and greed frequently doomed many.

For the railroads, consolidation—often through ruthless tactics—rather than cooperation became the key to controlling competition. The former shipping magnate Cornelius Vanderbilt gained control of the New York Central Railroad in 1867 by buying two key lines that connected with it. He then refused to accept any rail cars going to or from the Central. In response to criticism Vanderbilt replied, "Can't I do what I want with my own?" Elsewhere other buyouts and mergers eventually reduced the number of competitors—especially after the economic depressions of the 1870s and 1890s.

Like the railroads, the oil industry suffered from the proliferation of small companies and dramatically fluctuating prices. **John D. Rockefeller,** founder of the Standard Oil Company, lamented that "the butcher, the baker, and the candlestick maker began to refine oil." Rockefeller first tried a combination of pooling and rebates to deal with this problem. In 1872 he organized the South Improvement Company—a combine of oil refiners and railroad directors aimed at dividing the oil carriage trade between the railroads. In return for a guaranteed share of the shipments, Rockefeller convinced the railroads to give rebates. Eventually Rockefeller was able to obtain rebates not only on the oil he shipped but also on the shipments of his competitors. Thus Rockefeller could undersell his competitors, whom he often bought out during times of economic depression.

Although such techniques allowed Rockefeller to ultimately control 90 percent of the oil business, legal problems arose from Standard Oil's far-flung holdings. His solution was the **trust.** In 1882 he convinced the major stockholders in a number of refineries to surrender their stock to a board of nine trustees. In return the stockholders received trust certificates that entitled them to a share of the joint profits of all the refineries. Because pools had no legal standing, they could be manipulated by some members to the detriment of other members. In a trust, however,

After a period of intense competition in the railroad industry, a few rail barons consolidated lines often by using unscrupulous methods, seemingly to carve up the nation at will, as illustrated by this cartoon.

competitive actions were of no benefit. Everyone shared all losses and gains. Soon trusts began popping up throughout the economy.

Andrew Carnegie disliked pools and trusts, but he found other ways to gain a competitive edge. One of these was **vertical integration**—buying the sources of his raw materials (iron ore and coke) and later many of the transportation facilities needed to distribute his product. He thus was able to bring down his costs and control his supply and shipping costs, resulting in lower final product prices.

The key to Carnegie's success was his ability to cut costs without lowering quality. He used such traditional measures as wage cuts and increased hours for workers, but he also constantly explored new methods of increasing productivity. When told that a plant had broken all records the previous week, he replied, "Congratulations! Why not do it every week?" He did not focus only on short-term profits but was willing to invest in expensive new technology to lower long-term costs of production. He reportedly opened one board meeting with the question, "Well, what shall we throw away this year?"

Carnegie often boasted that he knew almost nothing about making steel—he hired experts to do that. He did know how to run a company and make

money. By effectively using all the economies of scale available to large firms, Carnegie was able to undersell and destroy most of the steel companies that had sprung up in response to the increased demand from railroads and industry. He also was a master at exploiting downturns in business cycles. Most of his acquisitions were made during economic depressions, when prices were lower. Although competitors and labor movements suffered from Carnegie's actions, the result was better steel at cheaper prices. And cheap steel aided the expansion of the railroads and the rise of other industries.

Of course, Carnegie was well paid for providing these benefits—receiving around $350 million dollars when he sold Carnegie Steel to J. P. Morgan. That sale led to the formation of the United States Steel Corporation and illustrates another factor in consolidation: bankers. Morgan and other bankers often stepped in during economic panics to reorganize bankrupt companies. They chewed up failing companies and railroads and spat them out as single supercorporations. U.S. Steel was capitalized at $1.4 billion, a figure three times larger than the annual budget of the U.S. government. The result was a more orderly economy and increased production, but at the price of centralizing vast economic power into the hands of a few

FIGURE 17.3
Iron, Steel, and Coal Production, 1870–1900

Source: Carl N. Degler, *The Age of Economic Revolution.* Copyright © 1977 by Scott, Foresman and Co.

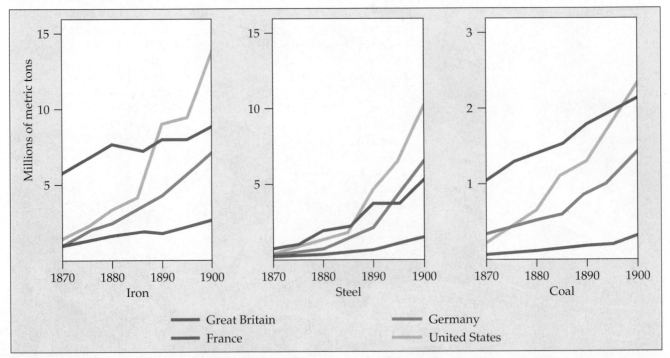

unelected individuals. One wit quipped when U.S. Steel was formed: "God created the world in 4004 B.C. and J. P. Morgan reorganized it in 1901."

New Managerial Styles and an Expanding Middle Class

Consolidation into giant corporations created the need for new management techniques, and again the railroads pioneered. As railroad companies grew larger, their activities covered hundreds of miles and employed thousands of workers. Safety and market conditions required that the entire system operate as a single unit under a tight schedule, which caused managerial problems. In the beginning, as one railroad expert wrote, "management had been personal and autocratic; the superintendent, a man gifted with energy and clearness of perception, molded the property to his own will. But as the properties grew, he found himself unable to give his personal attention to everything. Undaunted, he sought to do everything and do it well. He ended by doing nothing."

Railroad management thus required a division of responsibilities and a level of coordination previously unknown in business. Erie Railroad employee Daniel McCallum created the first organizational table for an American company in the 1850s. It had a chain of command moving from local train agents to the president and board of directors, and responsibilities were divided on a functional basis, with top management separate from daily operations. Since railroads also needed better accounting procedures to keep track of the monies collected and paid out, management and accounting of funds became the function of the controller's office.

Other large businesses began to adopt the accounting methods, hierarchical administrative structures, and divisions of responsibilities pioneered by the railroads. "Middle management" was thus created to coordinate the operations of far-flung local plants and bring reports to top executives. Big businesses were now run by bureaucracies staffed by white-collar workers, who had no role in founding the companies they served but who began to work their way up the bureaucratic ladder.

A profound consequence of the new economic order was the expansion of the middle class. Corporations needed accountants, middle managers, clerical workers, and sales representatives. Urban growth created demands for professionals, shopkeepers, and government employees. Between the Civil War and the 1890s the average earnings of the middle class rose nearly 30 percent. By 1900 more than a third of urban families owned their homes. The middle class

clearly derived benefits from and had a stake in the new economic order.

Mass Marketing, Assembly Lines, and Mass Production

Both the urban population boom and the transportation revolution created markets unparalleled in vastness and accessibility. But such markets would not have inevitably led to mass production and mass marketing without the public's acceptance of standardized goods. Several factors made Americans more receptive than Europeans to such goods. Class distinctions, although not absent, were more blurred and became increasingly so with the availability of ready-made clothing. Also, physical mobility broke down many of the local loyalties so prevalent in Europe. These factors created opportunities that modern mass advertising was quick to exploit. Nowhere were changes greater than in the food industry.

Food processors originally only produced limited quantities for nearby markets. When transportation advances widened distribution areas, producers used wholesale merchants and agents to sell their goods to the public. Then the communication revolution transformed the marketing of consumer goods. Manufacturers could now peddle their wares directly to the consumer. Rather than selling nonperishable foods by the barrel to wholesalers, they now packaged them in smaller containers of standard size and weight. By 1900, they were spending $90 million annually to convince Americans of the advantages of specific brand names—modern advertising had embarked on its unending quest to shape public tastes.

Meanwhile the same drastic transformation was taking place in the meatpacking business. The railroads again played a key role by opening up the grazing ranges of the Great Plains. Because of its rail network, Chicago quickly became the major funnel through which cattle were distributed from West to East. Cattle were shipped from its Union Stock Yards to slaughterhouses on the outskirts of eastern cities. The meat was then distributed through local butchers to city residents.

A major problem was stock deterioration during long train journeys. Until the advent of the refrigerated car, the only alternative was pickling or curing meat—processes that had made Chicago the pork-packing center but were not as well suited to beef.

Gustavus Swift, a Boston cattle buyer who had moved to Chicago, hired an engineer to design a refrigerated train car for safely shipping fresh meat long distances, with the first successful shipment in 1877. Swift also recognized the possibilities of centralized slaughtering, one of which was using all waste products (horns into buttons, hooves into glue, for example) and thus increasing profits. Eventually he formed glue, fertilizer, soap, and glycerin factories. People said that he used every part of the pig except the squeal.

Swift also pioneered assembly-line mass production. He subdivided the slaughtering and packing process into numerous distinct jobs as carcasses moved along on overhead conveyor belts. There was little wasted motion, and, as one of Swift's superintendents noted, "If you need to turn out a little more, you speed up the conveyor a little and the men speed up to keep pace."

The Power of Bigness

The creation of the gigantic U.S. Steel Corporation was not an isolated occurrence. By 1904 a single firm in each of 50 different industries accounted for 60 percent or more of the total output in that industry. The transition from local, independently owned shops and factories to giant national corporations with impersonal boards of directors dramatically altered the work and leisure time of the American people. For individuals the transition was often painful, and the economy experienced a frightening cycle of boom and bust. Periodic depressions rocked the nation, causing widespread unemployment and business failures.

Big business also created a class of millionaires who flaunted ostentatious homes and lavish lifestyles. For example, during the 1897 depression Mr. and Mrs. Bradley Martin gave a costume ball to which they invited most of the richest people in New York. The Waldorf-Astoria Hotel was redecorated to resemble the palace at Versailles in France. The hostess was dressed as Mary, Queen of Scots, and wore an enormous ruby necklace that had once adorned Queen Marie Antoinette. One guest came in a $10,000 suit of armor inlaid with gold. Those few hours of entertainment cost the Martins $369,000.

In 1890 about 11 million of the 12.5 million families in the United States averaged less than $380 a year in income, so it is obvious that all did not share equally in the economic expansion of the era. Wealth had always been concentrated and industrialization only continued the trend. In 1890 the bulk of wealth was concentrated in less than 10 percent of the population, while 0.03 percent of the population controlled 20 percent of the wealth. Many people resented or envied the lifestyles such wealth provided, and they feared the power it produced.

Government and organized labor remained relatively small while big business grew. Business leaders wielded enormous power over many phases of American life. Some of their actions benefited the nation but were taken in a high-handed manner. For example, to simplify schedules, in 1883 railroad owners established four time zones—without consulting any branch of government. And some of the freewheeling railroad barons only aggravated the fears such arbitrary power raised. Vanderbilt once remarked, "What do I care about the law? Hain't I got the power?" Another time a member of the Pennsylvania legislature reportedly said, "Mr. Speaker, I move we adjourn unless the Pennsylvania Railroad has some more business to conduct."

Because the emergence of gigantic trusts concentrated economic power into relatively few hands, many people feared the political power of big business, seen in this cartoon of the giant Rockefeller exclaiming, "What a funny little government."

This portrait of the family of William Astor illustrates the lavish lifestyle of the rich. Their parties were especially ostentatious—at one, guests smoked cigarettes rolled in one hundred dollar bills after drinking coffee.

Varieties of Economic Change in the West and South

Although most industrialization occurred in the Northeast, all regions of the country experienced profound changes as a national, interdependent economy emerged. Some of the forces feeding the growth of industry also fueled agricultural expansion. Rural population kept growing, although not as rapidly as urban population. Even as the number of farms and farmers more than doubled, farmers became a minority of the population. Most of the new farmers were in the West, where new settlers competed with existing populations to exploit the region's economic potential. Demand by urban dwellers for food sparked a farming revolution made possible by mechanization and scientific agriculture. For a variety of reasons, the South failed to keep pace with the rest of the nation. Despite numerous efforts to forge a "New South," the region's economy failed to keep pace with the rest of the nation.

Western Expansion and Exploitation

Confrontations between miners—the first actors in the drama of western expansion—and Native Americans foreshadowed the eventual expulsion of the American Indians from land that had been "given" to them "forever." But "forever" lasted only until the white men realized the region's true value. From then on, competition for resources among a diverse number of populations marked the history and culture of the West, creating a distinctly American mo-saic. Anglo-Americans came to dominate western economic development, but their lives and how they worked were shaped by earlier Native American and Hispanic societies as well as by African American and Asian immigrants.

In addition to mineral wealth, the region had two other plentiful resources: grass and cattle. Western ranching was born. At first, ranching did not require much capital. Both the cows and grass were free. By 1860, there were some five million head of wild Texas longhorn, descendants of cattle imported by Spanish colonists. They replaced the buffalo that were being hunted to virtual extinction. Although cattle were so plentiful that they were considered almost worthless in the West, steers sold for $30 to $50 a head in Chicago. All that was needed was a way to get them there. **Joseph G. McCoy** realized the potential for profit and established the first "cowtown" at Abilene, Kansas, where he built stock pens and loading chutes. Cowboys would "drive" cattle there for shipment by rail to Chicago. Other cowtowns arose as some six million head of cattle were driven to such sites between 1866 and 1888.

Since longhorns were not easily captured or herded on foot, settlers used methods of the Mexican vaquero, the predecessor of the American cowboy. Herding cattle while mounted on horses was hard, dirty work. One participant wrote, "It was tiresome grimy business for the attendant punchers, who travelled over in a cloud of dust, and heard little but the constant chorus from the crackling of hoofs and ankle joints, from the bellows, lows, and bleats of the trudging animals." Romantic stories both glorified and whitened the cowboys, at least one-third of whom were Mexicans and African Americans. The heyday of the working cowboy was brief, however, for ranching, like mining, soon turned into a more organized business.

Profits from a successful drive were very good— about 40 percent. Such figures naturally attracted eastern investors, and soon the use of long cattle drives declined as other ways of producing profit were found. The lean, rangy longhorns, better suited to enduring the long drive than to producing choice, juicy steaks, became even less desirable after traveling long distances. As the rail network expanded into Texas, ranchers switched to breeding the longhorns with superior imported stock to improve the quality of the beef.

Cattle breeders, who needed large tracts of grassland for grazing, usually just appropriated land from the public domain. During this open-range era, high profits attracted even more investors. Eventually the ranchers joined other segments of the economy that were outproducing demand. Beef prices dropped

Joseph A. Glidden's invention of barbed wire provoked range wars between cattlemen and farmers.

from $30 to $10 a head in 1885 and 1886. Poorer producers fell victim to the low prices, challenges to their land claims from sheepherders and farmers, and bad weather. A winter of terrible blizzards following the scorching summer of 1886 led to the deaths of 90 percent of western cattle.

Battles for supremacy between economic competitors in the West provoked sometimes bloody confrontations. By the 1890s these skirmishes had largely ended, leading some to claim that the "Wild West" was tamed. Those ranchers who remained established legal title to their grazing lands, surrounded them with barbed wire, and practiced scientific breeding and feeding of their stock. The forces of economic consolidation had now reached ranching—making it another business requiring large amounts of capital.

The post–Civil War development of the West initiated a pattern of federal intervention in the management of land and resources to an extent unknown in other regions. Laissez-faire economics was never practiced in the West. As elsewhere, government intervention at first helped some more than others. Large tracts of public lands were given away or sold cheaply. Laws were enacted to promote socially de-

sirable goals, but all had large loopholes that were exploited by cattlemen and land speculators.

The Homestead Act, meant to promote settlement, gave 160 free acres to those who would cultivate it for five years. The Desert Land Act granted 640 acres at $1.25 an acre to anyone who would irrigate the land. The Timber Culture Act, based on the theory that trees increased rainfall, awarded 160 acres to anyone who would plant trees on a quarter of the land. Cattlemen and speculators fraudulently claimed to have met the terms of the grants or hired dummy entrymen to stake claims for them—a bucket of water was sometimes the only basis for claims of irrigation. Lumber barons in California, Nevada, Oregon, and Washington similarly used other land-granting laws, such as the Timber and Stone Act of 1878, which allowed people to buy 160-acre plots "unfit for cultivation" and "valuable chiefly for timber" at an incredibly low $2.50 an acre. Thus, much of the newly discovered wealth of the West ended up in the hands of a few winners in the great land lottery.

Before they were transformed into capital-intensive businesses, mining, cattle, and lumber operations offered some quick, easy riches. Farming, however, required more patience to make any profit. By the time farmers arrived in the new West, much of the best land had already been appropriated, although most of the 274 million acres distributed under the terms of the Homestead Act were eventually purchased from speculators and cattlemen by bona fide settlers. Other farmers bought land from the railroads, which was promoting settlement to increase traffic in isolated areas. Railroad companies often provided easy credit terms and extolled western opportunities in flyers and speeches.

Many farming pioneers soon learned that railroad propaganda sometimes overstated the promise of the West. When they arrived, they discovered not only a shortage of wood and water but also an overabundance of severe weather, insects, and social isolation. The houses they built of "bricks" cut from thick prairie sod were functional but bleak. At first, many farmers managed only to eke out a bare subsistence. Eventually, however, western farmers were caught up in the dramatic forces of change that had already transformed other sectors of the economy.

The Changing Nature of Farming

By the time Congress passed the Homestead Act in 1862, most of the arable land east of the Mississippi was already taken. The established farmers of the old Northeast adapted fairly well to the changing economy and were generally prosperous. Most did not try to compete with the new wheat and corn areas of the West. Instead they turned their efforts to supplying the rapidly growing urban areas with fresh vegetables, dairy products, poultry, and pigs. They also profited from rising land values by selling extra acres

to residential and industrial developers at high prices. Although they may not have liked all the changes, most received a reasonable share of the fruits of economic expansion. The same could not be said for many farmers in the West and South.

The challenges of farming were much greater in the West. New agricultural techniques and adaptations to the environment were required. The scarcity of trees not only dictated the building of sod houses but also made the cost of fencing prohibitive. Until the development of barbed wire in 1874, crops were not easily protected from the millions of roaming cattle.

A more serious problem was the lack of water. Farmers came to believe they had found solutions by using new varieties of seed, pumping water from far below the ground surface with windmills, and using cultivation techniques known as dry farming. In reality their success had resulted mainly from abnormally wet summers in the 1870s, as they learned when climate conditions returned to normal. During the good times, however, optimism flourished. As one Kansas official noted: "Most of us crossed the Mississippi with no money but with a vast wealth of hope and courage. Haste to get rich has made us borrowers, and the borrowing has made booms, and the booms have made men wild, and Kansas became a vast asylum covering 50,000 square miles." Then came the droughts. By 1900 two-thirds of the homesteaders had failed, and farmers returned east with signs saying, "In God We Trusted; in Kansas We Busted." Westerners learned earlier than many Americans that the environment can't always be conquered.

In the South, the Civil War had crippled agriculture. Wartime devastation destroyed half the region's farm equipment and killed one-third of its draft animals. The death of slavery also ended the plantation

Because of the scarcity of trees on the Plains, both black and white settlers built homes with "bricks" of sod. With walls 2 to 3 feet thick, the houses were cozy and provided solid protection from the elements. But thick walls also made for gloomy interiors.

The Wild West

At 6 P.M. on April 5, 1892, a mysterious train, its shades tightly drawn, pulled out of Cheyenne, Wyoming, the state capital, bound for Casper, 200 miles to the northwest. Aboard the train were 46 vigilantes heavily armed with an impressive array of weapons including army rifles, dynamite, and strychnine. The train had been chartered by Wyoming's cattle kings. The vigilantes' mission: kill Johnson County settlers suspected of cattle rustling.

For more than two decades, the cattlemen had accused homesteaders of land grabbing and cattle theft. Juries refused to convict the small stockmen, so the cattle barons responded by taking the law into their own hands. In one incident, on the night of July 20, 1889, ten cattlemen captured two homesteaders and hanged them from a stunted pine tree. Altogether six or seven suspected rustlers were shot or hanged. Despite lynchings and shootings, the rustling continued. In the summer of 1891, the cattle barons decided to launch an armed invasion of Johnson County and kill the most notorious rustlers. The Wyoming Stock Growers' Association, asked to provide names of suspected rustlers, compiled a list of 70 purported cattle thieves. The invasion was scheduled for the following spring.

On Saturday, April 9, 1892, the vigilantes killed two suspected rustlers at K C Ranch near the southern edge of Johnson County. Word quickly spread to Buffalo, Wyoming, the county seat, 46 miles to the north.

There, 200 small stockmen formed a posse to avenge the murders. They caught up with the vigilantes at the T A Ranch, 14 miles south of Buffalo, and surrounded them.

Before they could be captured, however, the cavalry rode to the rescue early on Wednesday, April 13. Wyoming's acting governor and the state's senators had sent frantic telegrams to President Benjamin Harrison declaring that a state of insurrection existed in Johnson County and asking that the U.S. cavalry be sent in to quell the disturbances. The invaders, who included several federal marshals and state officials, were escorted out of Johnson County. Although they were charged with first-degree murder, the charges were later dropped. The Johnson County war was over.

Today it is commonly assumed that the roots of violence in American society lie in our frontier heritage of violence and lawlessness. According to popular mythology—disseminated by dime novels, pulp newspapers, and television and movie westerns— the frontier was a lawless land populated by violent men: outlaws, stagecoach robbers, gunslingers, vigilantes, claim jumpers, cattle rustlers, horse thieves, Indian fighters, border ruffians, and mule skinners.

But how violent was the Wild West? Certain forms of violence and lawlessness were indeed common: warfare between Native Americans and whites, attacks on Chinese and Mexican minorities, vigilantism, rowdyism, drunkenness, opium addiction, gambling, vigilante executions, stagecoach robberies, and gunfights. Racially motivated acts of brutality represented the ugliest side of frontier

violence. In 1871, in one of the most gruesome incidents, ranchers in California's Sacramento Valley tracked 30 Digger Indians into a cave and shot them, saving the children for last because they "could not bear to kill them with [a] 56-calibre Spencer rifle. 'It tore them up so bad.'" Instead, the children were shot with a 38-calibre Smith and Wesson revolver.

Chinese immigrants faced particular hostility. In Los Angeles, on October 24, 1871, a white mob stormed the city's Chinatown district and murdered between 20 and 25 Chinese men and women. In Rock Springs, Wyoming Territory, on September 2, 1885, a heavily armed white mob attacked the town's Chinatown, set fire to the coal miners' shacks, and shot at fleeing workers, killing 50, 10 percent of the town's Chinese population. A few days later, in Seattle, Washington Territory, a mob killed Chinese hop pickers asleep in their tents. In November, a Tacoma mob routed Chinese immigrants out of their dwellings, loaded them into wagons, and dumped them outside of town.

African Americans and Hispanics also encountered frontier violence. At least 373 black freedmen were lynched or murdered in 40 Texas counties between June 1865 and June 1868. In California, some 15,000 Mexican, Chilean, and Peruvian gold hunters were driven out of the gold fields by threats of lynching, branding, whipping, and ear cropping. Said one white miner: "Give 'em a fair jury trial and rope 'em with all the majesty of the law."

The lack of courts of law and police forces in the West gave rise to frontier committees of vigilance— extralegal committees organized to suppress and summarily punish

$5,000 REWARD

JESSE JAMES
For Train Robbery

Notify AUTHORITIES
LIBERTY, MISSOURI

between 1868, when he was 15, and 1878, when he was finally captured. Frank and Jesse James, America's most renowned bank and train robbers, staged at least 26 daring robberies between 1866 and 1881 in Missouri, taking in half a million dollars. Black Bart (born Charles E. Boles) robbed 27 stagecoaches in 28 attempts in California between 1875 and 1882, using an empty shotgun as his only weapon. Most popular accounts of Western banditry, however, appear to be grossly exaggerated and romanticized. Bat Masterson, who, according to legend, killed 30 men in gunfights, actually killed only 3. Billy the Kid, who supposedly killed 1 man for each of his 21 years of life, also apparently killed only 3.

Kansas's cattle towns, legend holds, witnessed a killing every night. But in fact in Abilene, Caldwell, Dodge City, Ellsworth, and Wichita, a grand total of 45 homicides took place during a 15-year span, 1.5 homicides per cattle trading season, never exceeding five in one year. In Deadwood, South Dakota, where Wild Bill Hickok was shot in the back while playing poker in 1876, only 4 homicides—and no lynchings—took place in the town's most violent year. And in Tombstone, Arizona, the "town too tough to die" and the site of the shoot-out at the OK Corral (where Marshall Virgil Earp, his brothers Wyatt and Morgan, and gambler Doc Holliday, hurled the Clanton brothers "into eternity in the duration of a moment") only 5 men were killed during the city's deadliest year.

Despite the omnipresence of rifles, knives, and revolvers and the prevalence of saloons, gambling houses, and bordellos, rape, robbery, and burglary were relatively rare. "We could go to sleep in our cabins," wrote one miner, "with our bag of gold dust under our pillows minus locks, bolts or bars, and feel a sense of absolute security."

murderers, counterfeiters, corrupt government officials, and horse and cattle thieves. In the single year of 1855 in California, 47 people were executed by mobs, 9 by legal tribunals, and 10 by sheriffs or police officers. Between 1865 and 1890, 27 vigilante movements that arose in Texas pursued outlaws like John Wesley Hardin. A final wave of vigilantism originated in rural southern Indiana in 1887. Known as the White Cap movement, local rural committees flogged drunks, prostitutes, and men who failed to support their families.

The most notorious perpetrators of frontier violence were the outlaws and gunmen, like Belle Starr, Billy the Kid, Black Bart, Frank and Jesse James, John Wesley Hardin, the Younger brothers, Butch Cassidy and the Sundance Kid, and the Dalton Gang, who held up stagecoaches and trains, robbed banks, and stole horses and cattle. Hardin and the Jameses—who ironically were the sons of ministers—as well as the Younger brothers learned outlaw strategy as Confederate guerrillas during the Civil War. Hardin, who was probably the most prolific murderer, killed over 20 men

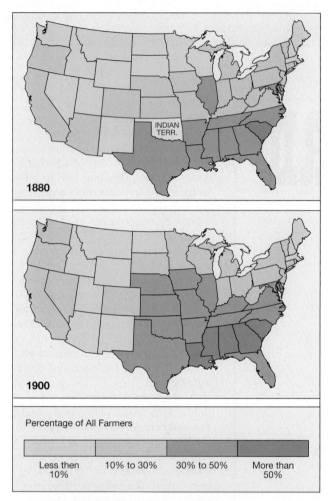

1880

1900

Percentage of All Farmers

| Less then 10% | 10% to 30% | 30% to 50% | More than 50% |

Rise of Tenancy

Most farmers agreed with a farm journal's assertion: "Agriculture, like all other business, is better for its subdivision, each one growing that which is best suited for his soil, climate, and market." Specialization became apparent in the decline of subsistence farming and the growing importance of cash crops, although general farming continued. Outside of the South, small gardens and stock raising usually supplemented cash crops. In Dixie, however, cotton reigned supreme, and landowners and merchants often forced tenant farmers to plant all available acres with cotton.

Technology revolutionized agriculture as inventions increased productivity on the farms as dramatically as they had in factories. After the mechanization of wheat farming, the time required to farm one acre dropped from 61 to 3 hours, and the per acre cost of production fell from $3.65 to $0.66. Machines entered every phase of agriculture, and farmers began to learn "scientific agriculture" at land-grant colleges that Congress had established under the Morrill Land Grant Act of 1862. Researchers at agricultural experiment stations (funded by the **Hatch Act of 1887**) explored ways to increase production and found new uses for overabundant crops. Farmers were not opposed to all government aid to the economy.

Mechanization brought economies of scale to agriculture, but they were not as easily exploitable. Although some bonanza farmers in the Dakotas cultivated 100,000 acres and more, the average farm remained at 150 acres. The farms of the West were usually much larger than average because dry-farming techniques produced low yields per acre. To succeed, then, western farmers needed more acres and more machines to work those acres; both cost money. Thus, like businesspeople, farmers needed access to capital. Unable to sell shares in their enterprise, most obtained personal loans using their land, machinery, and crops as collateral. As production increased, however, prices fell; to counteract lower profits farmers further expanded production in a self-defeating downward spiral. Mortgage indebtedness grew two and a half times faster than agricultural wealth.

One solution to overproduction was to expand markets, which required cheap and reliable transportation facilities. Railroads, therefore, had as much impact in agriculture as in industry. Instead of selling surplus food to the local cobbler, American farmers fed distant urban masses at home and abroad; 20 percent of agricultural production was exported. Thus farmers' profits now hinged on many factors beyond their control—such as the size of harvests in Argentina. Marketing became a key to success. One farm editor declared: "The work of farming is only half done when the crop is out of the ground."

system. The number of farms doubled from 1860 to 1880, but the number of landowners remained the same. The size of the average farm dropped by more than half, as **sharecropping** and tenancy rose. At the very time the rest of the economy was consolidating, southern agriculture was marching off in the opposite, less efficient direction. A shortage of cash forced southern farmers to borrow against future crops. Crop liens and high credit costs kept many black and white farmers trapped in a cycle of debt and poverty.

Although many Plains and southern farmers were losers in the changing economy, both winners and losers were playing essentially the same game—the commercialization of farming. As in manufacturing, the elements of change were specialization, new technology, mechanization, expanded markets, heavier capital investment, and reliance on interstate transportation. At first many changes were wholeheartedly embraced by farmers.

This 1895 picture of a threshing machine with a steam engine illustrates the increasing mechanization of farming. The picture was made to celebrate the first traction engine in Cavalier County, North Dakota.

Most farmers at first celebrated their status as businesspeople. Agricultural expansion initially was as dramatic as that of industry, but then farmers began to lose ground. In 1860 farmers owned 50 percent of the nation's wealth and received 30 percent of the national income. By 1910 those figures had dropped to 20 and 18 percent, respectively, and farmers were becoming a minority of the population. When they realized that they could not adapt as well as industrialists to the new economic order, farmers began to assert the superiority of rural culture. However, their functions were far removed from that of the independent, self-sufficient yeoman farmer.

The New South

Like the farmers, many Southerners wholeheartedly endorsed the new economic order at first. Some even saw the South's salvation in the destruction of slavery, proclaiming the emergence of a **New South. Henry W. Grady,** editor of the *Atlanta Constitution,* wrote and traveled extensively to proclaim the region's unlimited opportunities. Grady envisioned three major changes from the Old South: diversified farming, industrialization, and racial accommodation and cooperation. To win support for these changes, New South spokesmen linked the new order to the virtues of romanticized versions of the Old South and the "lost cause" of the Confederacy. Confederate heroes were named to boards of directors and appeals to southern nationalism were made. The

defeated South was encouraged to take up a new battle—for industrial supremacy. As one historian wrote, the "romance of the past was used to underwrite the materialism of the present."

At the Cotton States Exposition of 1895 in Atlanta, an African American spokesman for the New South emerged. **Booker T. Washington,** principal of Tuskegee Normal and Industrial Institute in Macon County, Alabama, was asked by the exposition's white organizers to give an address. His speech, known as the **Atlanta Compromise,** rivaled those of Grady in its optimistic appraisal of southern potential. It also outlined a basis for racial cooperation. If whites would allow African Americans educational and economic opportunity, Washington promised that blacks "will buy your surplus land, make blossom the waste places in your fields, and run your factories." He urged African Americans to make themselves economically indispensable to whites and forego agitation for political and social rights. Their economic importance would bring them white acceptance—and the rights they desired.

Washington practiced what he preached. Tuskegee was a model New South institution, focusing on industrial education and promoting diversified farming. It boasted the only all-black agricultural experiment station. George Washington Carver, its director of agricultural research, advocated the utilization of undeveloped southern resources and sought to expand markets for such crops as peanuts and sweet potatoes.

Booker T. Washington's close ties to business and political leaders are illustrated by this photo of Washington with (*from left to right*) Robert C. Ogden, President William Taft, and Andrew Carnegie.

The New South optimism was based on some dramatic changes in the region. Railroad development increased faster than in the nation at large. The textile, timber, and tobacco industries boomed. Birmingham grew into a major producer of raw steel, and by 1890 southern steel and iron made up almost 20 percent of the national total. Southern agriculture was also recovering—by the 1870s cotton production exceeded prewar records.

The tobacco and textile industries especially seemed to bring the dream of industrialization to life. Both were based on major southern crops. In the 1880s, **James B. Duke** introduced the cigarette industry to the region, following a path similar to that of other captains of industry. Duke was a North Carolina tobacco grower when in 1881 he encountered a machine that rolled cigarettes. He bought the patent and proceeded to change American tastes to suit his purposes. Previously, most tobacco users either chewed the weed or smoked pipes or cigars. Duke enclosed "trading cards," featuring pictures and stories of popular heroes, in packs of cigarettes to advertise his various brands. At the same time he was buying out competitors. In 1890 he created a trust through which he controlled 150 companies in an almost perfect monopoly until 1911, when federal antitrust actions disbanded the trust.

Though entirely homegrown, Duke's enterprise had no distinctly southern characteristics. The same was not true of the textile industry. Its development was flavored with a kind of regional revivalism and paternalism. A good example was the founding of Salisbury Cotton Mills. In 1887 the town of Salisbury, North Carolina, had done little to recover from the war. It was poor, dirty, and full of saloons. Then a lean, intense Tennessee preacher named Mr. Pearson came to town and set up a big tent, and preached that Salisbury needed to go to work. Idleness had bred corruption; building a cotton mill was the most Christian act his hearers could perform. The result was Salisbury Cotton Mills.

The evangelical appeal of the cotton mill crusade tended to create a myth that the mills were mainly built and run to aid the lower classes. The creation of **mill towns** helped to promote the image of mill owners as "fathers" to their employees. The company built houses, stores, schools, and even churches for the workers. In reality, many mill owners proved not to be such good fathers. By local custom African Americans were excluded from the textile mills. Mill workers tended to be poor whites; often an entire family worked an average of 12 hours a day. Wages were as low as 50 cents a day and were usually not paid in cash, but in "trade checks." The trade checks were accepted as rent for company houses or used to buy goods in company stores. Some merchants and landlords would not accept the checks at face value. So some mill workers never saw any cash. They merely turned their trade checks back over to the mill owners in return for supplies and housing. The result was high profits that caused the textile boom in the South—the number of mills grew from 161 in 1880 to 400 in 1900.

Despite all these signs of progress, major obstacles prevented the South's economy from keeping pace with that of the rest of the nation. Southern agriculture remained trapped in the inefficient sharecropping system and in single-crop agriculture. By

1880 the South was not growing enough food to feed its people. Poor nutrition thus added bad health and disease to the region's problems.

The persistent ideology of white supremacy not only doomed Booker T. Washington's vision of African American advancement but also helped keep the South mired in poverty. Race relations actually worsened in the 1890s as white Southerners struggled to keep black Southerners "in their place" (see Chapter 19). In 1896 the Supreme Court ruled in *Plessy v. Ferguson* that separate accommodations for African Americans did not violate the Fourteenth Amendment if the facilities were substantially equal in quality. The effect was to legalize segregation—a disaster for both black and white Southerners. Accommodations were never really equal, and African Americans suffered from inferior schools and services. At the same time, keeping most of the black third of the southern population in ignorance and poverty depressed wage scales and the tax base needed to support public education and other services.

Another key to the South's relative poverty was its shortage of capital. Reliance on slavery and cotton had enriched the Old South but helped impoverish the New South. While the North was using its capital to build canals, railroads, cities, and factories, the South used its profits to buy more slaves. Emancipation meant the loss of about $4 billion, and the Civil War brought devastation. Before the war the South had seen little reason to use its capital to build factories and cities. After the war, it no longer had the capital to do those things.

Southerners sought to attract outside investment by means of industrial expositions and hundreds of publications and speeches, as well as by tax exemptions and land grants. In the late nineteenth century, northern dollars did flow south, replacing Sherman's armies. However, the use of northern capital in most industries also meant that the profits went to Northerners as well. A good example of how this worked is what happened to the timber industry. In the postwar era, over 60 percent of the nation's forests were located in the South. A growing demand for lumber to build cities thus made timber the region's leading industry and number one employer. Yet in the end, the South was probably left poorer rather than richer by the exploitation of its timber.

Corrupt state governments allowed Northerners and foreigners to obtain vast tracts of timberland at prices far below their actual value. Temporary logging camps were set up and manned mainly by low-paid African American workers, who were, in the words of one visitor, "single, homeless, and possessionless." Once an area was stripped of its trees, the camp moved on to a new one. The overcutting of southern forests destroyed many of them and created erosion and flooding problems. Most of the timber was turned into raw lumber at sawmills and sold to northern factories to be made into finished products. Only in North Carolina did a significant furniture industry develop. The South therefore remained in a colonial economic position by selling unfinished raw materials, such as lumber, at low prices to the North to be converted into manufactured goods, goods that it had to buy at prices higher than it had received for the raw materials.

For all the above reasons the South's progress did not alter its position at the bottom of the economic ladder. Although its share of national manufacturing doubled between 1880 and 1920, it rose only to 10 percent of the total—roughly the same percentage it had at the start of the Civil War. Per capita income increased 21 percent, but fell from 60 percent of that of the North in 1860 to 40 percent in 1900. As in the West, the South's reliance on northern capital kept the majority of profits going elsewhere. By the late 1880s farmers in both regions, however, would unite to oppose the changes brought by industrial capitalism.

WORKING IN INDUSTRIAL AMERICA

In the post–Civil War era, perhaps no group experienced more changes than the working class. Factories sprang up near or in cities, whose populations were being swelled by rural immigrants from both abroad and the farmlands of America. City life and factory work profoundly changed the lives of these new arrivals. For many the transition was extremely painful; they were being asked to transform radically their visions of themselves and their places in the world.

The Conditions of Work

Was it worth it? Was the price paid for industrialization worth the benefits native-born and immigrant labor received? This is not a simple question to answer. In fact, each laborer might have answered it differently, since wages played an important role in a laborer's attitude. In general, wages rose and prices fell during the late nineteenth and early twentieth centuries. Exactly how much is a question of heated historical debate. One economic historian estimated that when adjusted for changes in the price level, real annual earnings increased from approximately $300 in 1860 to more than $425 in 1890. Other historians believe those estimates are overly optimistic, contending that wages tended to stagnate, especially in

This cartoon illustrates the public's perception of the failure of wages to keep up with the increasing cost of living.

$6-per-month, two-room, crowded but neat tenement apartment. During the year, he spent only $80 on food, mainly bread, salted meat, and coffee. His income was barely enough to allow his family to maintain a minimal standard of living. His existence was precarious: strikes, layoffs, sickness, or injury could easily throw him and his family into abject poverty.

The second miner worked full time in 1883 and earned $420. He had a wife and four children, three of whom were also miners and who brought home an additional $1000. They all lived comfortably in their own six-room house perched on an acre of land. They ate well, spending $900 a year on food—steak, butter, potatoes, bacon, and coffee comprised a typical breakfast. They bought books and enjoyed a full leisure life.

In many working-class families, fathers and sons, mothers and daughters—and often aunts, uncles, and grandparents—all contributed to the family economy. Carroll D. Wright in the U.S. Census of 1880 warned, "the factory system necessitates the employment of women and children to an injurious extent, and consequently its tendency is to destroy family life and ties and domestic habits, and ultimately the home." In truth, however, the opposite was probably true. Economically, families worked as a single entity; the desires of any individual often had to be sacrificed for the good of the family. Far from destroying the family, working for the family economy often strengthened it.

During the first decade of the twentieth century, social workers conducted numerous studies to determine how much money was needed to sustain a typical working-class existence for a year. Estimates for New York City ranged between $800 and $876 for a family of four, $505 for a single man, and $466 for a

A family economy was an important part of survival in America in this time period. This family earned extra money by arranging artificial flowers at home.

the large textile industries. All, however, admit that the pace of wages and earnings lagged well behind the spectacular growth in the American economy.

Even with modest improvements in wages, laborers continually battled poverty. More often than not, the prosperity of a family depended on how many members of that family worked. Carroll D. Wright, chief of the Massachusetts Bureau of the Statistics of Labor, expressed the matter plainly in 1882: "A family of workers can always live well, but the man with a family of small children to support, unless his wife works also, has a small chance of living properly." The material quality of life often depended more on circumstances than on occupation or wages.

Take, for example, two hardworking union coal miners who earned $1.50 a day and were studied in 1883 by the Illinois Bureau of Labor Statistics. The first worked only 30 weeks in 1883, and his total income was $250. He lived with his wife and five children in a

working woman. Many of New York's laborers fell painfully below the recommended minimum, and single women lived particularly difficult lives. In New York women earned about half as much as men—the majority made less than $300 per year. One woman worker described her meager existence: "I didn't live, I simply existed. I couldn't live that [which] you could call living. . . . It took me months and months to save up money to buy a dress or a pair of shoes. . . . I had the hardest struggle I ever had in my life."

Conditions for African Americans, Asians, and Mexicans in America were even worse. They were given the most exhausting and dangerous work, paid the least, and fired first during hard economic times. For a black sharecropper farming a patch of worked-over soil in Mississippi, or a Chinese miner carrying nitroglycerin down a hole in a Colorado mountain, or a Mexican working on a Texas ranch, $300 per year would have seemed a kingly sum.

There were clear divisions among workers. At the top were the highly skilled laborers. Mostly English-speaking, generally Protestant, and almost exclusively white, they were paid well, had good job security, and considered themselves elite craftsmen. Below them were the semiskilled and unskilled workers, most of whom were immigrants from southern and eastern Europe, spoke halting if any English, and were Catholics or Jews. They lacked job security and had to struggle for a decent existence. At the bottom were the nonwhite and women workers, usually semi- and unskilled, for whom even a decent existence was normally out of reach.

Hours of work varied widely. Long hours were not new—farm workers and artisans often labored from sunup to sundown. The tempo and quality of their labor was different, however. During summer months and harvest season, the work was intense, but it slowed down during the shorter days of winter. There was always time for fishing, horse racing, visiting, and tavern-going. Preindustrial workshops similarly mixed work with fellowship. If the workdays were long, they were also sociable. As they worked, laborers talked, joked, laughed, and even drank.

Nor was time measured out in teaspoons. Punctuality was not the golden virtue it became during industrialization. In the early nineteenth century, household clocks were rare and many of them possessed only a single hand. Cheap, mass-produced pocket watches did not become readily available until the Civil War. Certainly the idea of punching a time clock was alien to the preindustrial worker, who might think in terms of hours but not minutes.

Preindustrial labor, then, was done in a more relaxed atmosphere. This is not meant to romanticize it. Farm work and shop labor could be hard and dangerous, but there were not sharp lines between labor and leisure. Gambling, storytelling, singing, debating, and drinking formed a crucial part of the workday. Thrift, regularity, sobriety, orderliness, punctuality—hallmarks of an industrial society—were virtues not rigorously observed.

The new concept of time changed not only how people worked but also how they regarded the worker. The most prominent feature of nineteenth- and early-twentieth-century New England mill towns was the giant factory bell towers. Before clocks and watches, the bell towers served a utilitarian function. They told the laborers when to get out of bed, be at work, eat lunch, and go home. The importance of time was literally drilled home in a brochure prepared by the International Harvester Corporation to teach Polish laborers the English language. "Lesson One" read:

> I hear the whistle. I must hurry.
> I hear the five minute whistle.
> It is time to go into the shop.
> I take my check from the gate board and hang it on the department board.
> I change my clothes and get ready to work.
> The starting whistle blows.
> I eat my lunch.
> It is forbidden to eat until then.
> The whistle blows at five minutes of starting time.
> I get ready to go to work.
> I work until the whistle blows to quit.
> I leave my place nice and clean.
> I put all my clothes in the locker.
> I must go home.

The lesson also perfectly describes the ideal industrial worker: punctual, hardworking, clean, and sober.

Given this new standard of work and time demanded by factory owners, laborers were reluctant to work the preindustrial dawn-to-dusk workday. In 1889 hundreds of trade unionists paraded through the streets of Worcester, Massachusetts, behind a banner that stated their goal. "Eight Hours for Work, Eight Hours for Rest, Eight Hours for What We Will." A popular song of the day captured the ideal.

> We mean to make things over;
> We're tired of toil for naught;
> We may have enough to live on,
> But never an hour for thought.
> We want to feel the sunshine,
> We want to smell the flowers;
> We are sure that God has willed it,
> And we mean to have eight hours.

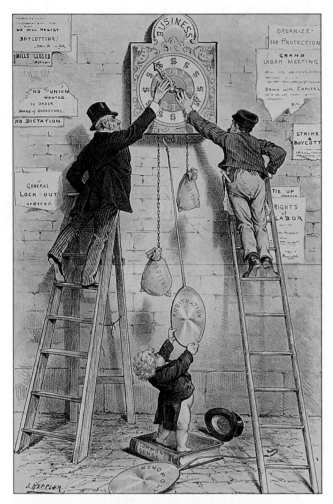

Factory owners demanded standards of work, behavior, and punctuality that left the industrial worker little leisure time or energy. Workers campaigned unsuccessfully for an eight-hour workday during the late nineteenth century.

roasting coffee beans, grinding whole spices and sugar, and cooking meals. By 1900 the typical housewife worked six hours a day on just two tasks: meal preparation and cleaning—in addition to the time she already spent on other household tasks.

Worker Discontent

Although workers complained regularly about wages and hours, they were equally disturbed by several other aspects of industrialization. The late-nineteenth-century industries differed from the preindustrial workshop in four important areas: size, discipline, mechanization, and displacement of skill. The huge new factories, employing hundreds or even thousands of laborers, needed an organized, disciplined workforce. Workers were carefully regulated to ensure maximum productivity. Work itself became formalized and structured, and several levels of bureaucrats separating the owner from workers emerged. There was an incredible boom in productivity, and the informal preindustrial workshop, with its handful of employees, was an inevitable casualty.

Mechanization also caused an erosion of certain skilled trades. Newly invented machines performed tasks previously done by skilled artisans. For example, once a single tailor took a piece of cloth, cut it, fashioned it, and sewed it into a pair of pants; by 1859 a Cincinnati clothing factory had divided the process into 17 different semiskilled jobs. This replacement of highly skilled by semiskilled workers was characteristic of the factory system. By the end of the century, it appeared to many observers that *all* work was being mechanized and moving toward a factory mode. Even farmers followed the mechanization march. By the early 1880s, one Dakota Territory wheat farm—or "food factory" as a critic called it—stretched over 30,000 acres, used 20 reapers and 30 steam-powered threshers, and employed 1000 field hands. Workers did not know their bosses, but this impersonality was offset by a remarkable increase in output.

In the long run, industrialization brought much to many. From a worker's perspective, however, industrialization was often an inhumane process. Factory labor tended to be monotonous, and machines made work more dangerous. Industrial accidents were alarmingly common—careless or tired workers sacrificed fingers, hands, arms, and sometimes even lives. Frequent production speedups increased the chances of injury. In one year at Armour's meatpacking plant in Chicago, 22,381 workers were injured or became ill. Conditions were much the same at Swift's meatpacking plant.

To make matters even worse, owners concerned with production quotas and cost efficiency often as-

The reality, however, fell far short of this ideal. It is difficult to generalize about hours since they varied considerably from occupation to occupation. In 1890, for example, bakers averaged over 65 hours a week, steelworkers over 66, and canners nearly 77. Even as late as 1920, skilled workers still averaged 50.4 hours a week and the unskilled 53.7 hours. Before the 1930s, workers regarded an 8-hour day or even a 10-hour day as an unattainable dream.

The new ideals of industrial America created even more work for women. The increased emphasis on cleanliness led to a demand for tidier homes. As a result, women now devoted more time to cleaning, dusting, and scrubbing. New washable cotton fabrics increased the amount of laundering. And more varied diets meant women spent more time plucking feathers from chickens, soaking and blanching hams,

Workers at Swift's meatpacking plant wield huge cleavers as they impassively go about their tasks. A slip of the cleaver could mean the loss of a limb or even a life.

sumed an uncaring attitude toward their laborers. Many were indeed insensitive. One factory manager even proclaimed: "I regard my people as I regard my machinery. So long as they can do my work for what I choose to pay them, I keep them, getting out of them all I can. What they do or how they fare outside my walls I don't know, nor do I consider it my business to know. They must look out for themselves as I do myself."

Where once it was workers who determined their production and work pace, factory managers with stopwatches now made laborers account for their time by seconds. Workers particularly resented scientific time-motion experts who strove to get the maximum production out of every laborer. **Frederick W. Taylor,** the father of "scientific management," believed that his ideas benefited labor as well as management. Instead, his aim "to induce men to act as nearly like machines as possible" promoted monotony and displaced workers—especially skilled ones.

Workers did not passively accept industrialization and the changes it caused. They resisted change at almost every step and they had formidable weapons at their disposal. On one level, resistance entailed a simple, individual decision not to change completely. Despite demanding a steady, dependable workforce, factory managers were plagued by chronic absenteeism. Immigrant workers refused to labor on religious holidays, and in some towns factories had to shut down on the day the circus arrived. Across America, heavy drinking on Sunday led to "blue Monday," a euphemism for absenteeism.

Another form of individual protest was quitting. Most industrial workers changed jobs at least every three years, and in many industries the annual turnover rate was over 100 percent. Some quit because they were bored, "forced to work too hard," or because they were struck by spring wanderlust and simply wanted to move on. Others quit because of severe discipline, unsafe working conditions, or low wages. This compulsive quitting was a clear indication that perhaps 20 percent of the workforce never came to terms with industrialization.

Workers were similarly quick to take collective action. The late nineteenth century witnessed the most sustained and violent industrial conflict in the nation's history. Strikes were as common as political corruption during the period—the Bureau of Labor Statistics estimated that 9668 strikes and lockouts occurred between 1881 and 1890. Although most of these conflicts were relatively peaceful, some were so violent that citizens across the nation feared that America was moving toward another revolution.

Early Labor Violence

An early, violent conflict occurred in the anthracite coal region of eastern Pennsylvania. During the depression of the mid-1870s, mine owners agreed to cut wages and increase workloads in the mines. This sort of oppression was nothing new to the Irish, and they responded much as they had in the old country of Ireland. While the Workingmen's Benevolent Association (WBA) battled owners at the negotiating table, the Ancient Order of Hibernians, a secret fraternal society of Irish immigrants, and its inner circle, the **Molly Maguires,** waged a violent guerrilla war in the coalfields in 1877. They disrupted the operation of several mines and attacked a handful of mining officials.

The mine owners infiltrated the group with a secret agent, James McParlan, who agreed to inform on his fellow Irishmen for the Pinkerton agency. While McParlan was gathering information, the WBA went on strike. Disorder and violence followed. Through the local press, management convinced much of the community that there was a direct link between the WBA, the Mollies, and the bloodshed. The tactic worked and the strike was broken. A short time later, McParlan's testimony was used to destroy both the Mollies and the WBA. Altogether, 20 Mollies were convicted and executed after sensational trials. It was a scenario that industrialists would use again and again. Their greatest weapon against strikers was the community's fear of violence.

The same depression that convulsed the Pennsylvania coalfields shook the rest of the country. To keep from going under, many businessmen cut rates and attempted to recoup their losses by reducing labor costs. This was true especially in the highly competitive railroad business. Workers, most often unskilled, suffered repeated wage cuts. Workingmen, one railroad worker declared in 1877, "know what it is to bring up a family on ninety cents a day, to live on beans and cornmeal week in and week out, to run in debt at the stores until you cannot get trusted any longer, to see the wife breaking down under privation and distress, and the children growing up sharp and fierce like wolves day after day because they don't get enough to eat." That knowledge drove many workers to desperate lengths.

During the dog days of mid-July 1877, the Baltimore and Ohio Railroad (B&O) announced its third consecutive 10 percent wage cut. Angry, frustrated, hot, and hungry railroad workers along the line, led by the new Trainmen's Union, went on strike. When trouble followed, B&O workers seized an important junction at Martinsburg, West Virginia. The state militia and local sheriffs sympathized with the workers but could not end the strike. President Rutherford B. Hayes sent in federal troops to protect an army of strikebreakers.

From Martinsburg the strike spread. Railroad workers walked off their jobs, and trains sat unused. The strike paralyzed transportation in the Midwest and much of the industrial Northeast. Violence and destruction seemed to be everywhere. In Baltimore the state militia shot into a mob and killed ten persons; in Pittsburgh rioters burned 2000 freight cars, looted stores, and torched railroad buildings; in Buffalo, Chicago, and Indianapolis, workers and police engaged in bloody battles.

When local police and state militiamen failed to control the situation, President Hayes ordered more federal troops in to do the job. Eventually, superior force restored peace and the trains started rolling again, but not before more than a hundred strikers were killed. Like most spontaneous strikes, the **Great Strike of 1877** failed. But the anger it revealed frightened America. Although some authorities labeled the disturbances as the work of communist agitators, more thoughtful observers knew workers had legitimate grievances. For owners and workers alike, the

The Great Railroad Strike, 1877

During the spontaneous uprising that followed the railroad strike of 1877 two-thirds of the nation's track was paralyzed for two weeks and millions of dollars worth of railroad property was destroyed.

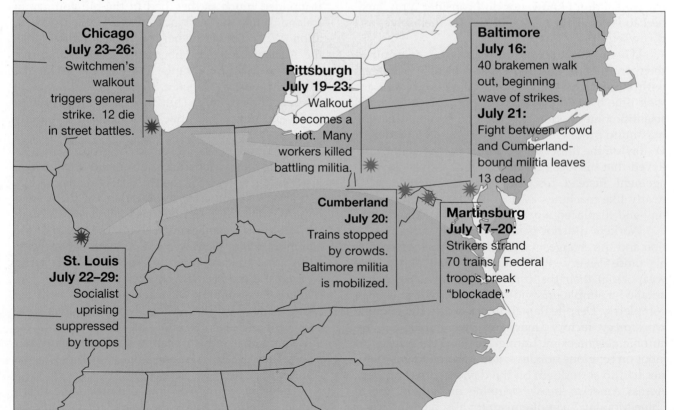

Chicago July 23–26: Switchmen's walkout triggers general strike. 12 die in street battles.

St. Louis July 22–29: Socialist uprising suppressed by troops

Pittsburgh July 19–23: Walkout becomes a riot. Many workers killed battling militia.

Cumberland July 20: Trains stopped by crowds. Baltimore militia is mobilized.

Baltimore July 16: 40 brakemen walk out, beginning wave of strikes. **July 21:** Fight between crowd and Cumberland-bound militia leaves 13 dead.

Martinsburg July 17–20: Strikers strand 70 trains. Federal troops break "blockade."

strike was a lesson. Owners learned that workers were not merely passive partners in the industrial process. Labor learned that when pressed, the federal government was not neutral—it would side with capital.

At the same time, economic consolidation increased the power of industrialists such as Carnegie, Rockefeller, and Swift. The power of industrialists can be seen in the **Haymarket Square riot** of 1886. In 1885, skilled molders at McCormick Harvester Machine Company in Chicago won a 15 percent pay increase after a strike. Reacting angrily to the union's activities, McCormick introduced pneumatic molders that could be run by unskilled workers. The skilled workers went on strike again in 1886, but with different results. The combination of McCormick's forces and local police ensured the safety of an army of strikebreakers and the plant's output continued until the strike was broken.

Tempers, however, remained high, and violence resulted. In May, after the strike ended, police and workers clashed once again, and a number of laborers were killed and wounded. Disturbed by the violence used by police in defense of industrialists' positions, August Spies, a Chicago anarchist and labor agitator who edited the radical newspaper *Arbeiter Zeitung,* called for a protest meeting in Haymarket Square, a location that could hold 20,000 persons. On the evening of May 4, a small and generally unenthusiastic crowd of about 3000 labor supporters gathered in the rain. The speeches were dull and the listeners were peaceful. But as the meeting was breaking up, local police unexpectedly charged the crowd. Then somebody—to this day no one knows who—threw a bomb into the melee, killing both police and protesters. Surrounded by a fog of confusion and anger, the police opened fire, shooting protesters and even, accidentally, each other.

Industrialists, city officials, ministers, and the local press convinced a bewildered public that the bombing was a prelude to anarchistic revolution. Police arrested eight local radicals, including Spies, and charged them with conspiracy. Despite no real evidence against them, the eight were tried and convicted, and seven were sentenced to be hanged. One man committed suicide in his cell and three were eventually pardoned, but Spies and three others were executed. For radicals, labor agitators, and unionists, the message was clear: Police and public opinion were on the side of the industrialists.

The excessive violence of the Molly Maguires, the Great Strike of 1877, and the Haymarket Square riot were not necessarily typical of disputes between labor and management. Although labor violence continued in the 1890s, with such dramatic episodes

The famous Haymarket Square riot of 1886 began as a peaceful protest meeting. The arrest and conviction of eight local radicals without any real evidence against them sent a message to workers: police and public opinion side with the industrialists.

as the Homestead strike and the Pullman strike (see Chapter 19), late-nineteenth-century labor disputes often were settled peacefully. In most cases, however, management was the winner. Only in small towns, where prolabor and anti-industrial sentiment knew no class lines, did labor battle management on anything approaching even terms.

Unorganized and Organized Labor

Historians have used the term *robber barons* to characterize late-nineteenth-century industrialists. Whether "robber" is accurate or not is debatable, but "baron" is a fitting description. They controlled their industries as medieval barons ruled their fiefs. Their word was usually final, and such a modern concept as democracy did not find a sympathetic environment inside factory walls. A Pennsylvania coal miner described the situation accurately: "They find monopolies as strong as government itself. They find capital as rigid as absolute monarchy. They find their so-called independence a myth, and that their subjection to power is as complete as when their forefathers were part and parcel of the baronial estate."

In the last third of the nineteenth century, labor was unable to form an organization powerful enough to deal with capital on equal terms. Before 1900, most unions were weak, with goals that were often out of touch with the changing American economy. In addition, the labor force itself was divided along ethnic, racial, gender, and craft lines. During this period, however, labor attempted to overcome its own divisions and fumble its way toward a clearer vision of what were its own best interests.

Before the 1870s most American unions were locally rooted, craft-based organizations. They were geared to the small workshop of Jacksonian America, not to the large modern factory. The first union to attempt to organize all workers was the short-lived **National Labor Union** (NLU), founded in Baltimore in 1866. Besides shorter work hours and higher wages, the NLU supported the rights of women and African Americans, monetary reform, and worker-owned industries. As one of their leaders said, the "only way by which the toiling masses can protect themselves against the unjust claims and soul-crushing tyranny of capital" was for "themselves to become capitalists." Rich in ideas and solutions, the NLU was poor in organization and finances, and it died during the depression of the mid-1870s.

The NLU's mission was taken up by the Noble and Holy Order of the **Knights of Labor.** Begun in 1869 as a secret fraternal order as well as a union, the Knights remained small and unimportant until 1878 when it went public. Led by **Terence V. Powderly,** a machinist and former mayor of Scranton, Pennsylvania, in 1881 the Knights opened its membership not only to "any person working for wages but to anyone who had at any time worked for wages." The Knights excluded only bankers, lawyers, liquor dealers, speculators, and stockbrokers, whom they viewed as money manipulators and exploiters.

Complete worker solidarity was the Knights' goal. "An injury to one is an injury to all," they proclaimed. They welcomed and spoke for all laborers—women and men, black and white, immigrant and native, unskilled and skilled. Like the NLU, the Knights rejected industrial capitalism and favored cooperatively owned industries. "The aim of the Knights of Labor," Powderly emphasized, "is to make each man his own employer." Although critics at the time labeled the Knights "wild-eyed, utopian visionaries," they are best understood in the context of exploited workers searching for a less exploitive alternative to industrial capitalism. If their statements were extreme, their suffering was real.

An able leader, Powderly called for reforms of the currency system, the abolition of child labor, regulation of trusts and monopolies, an end to alien contract labor networks, and government ownership of public utilities. By nature a diplomatic, good-natured man, he favored peaceful arbitration of labor disputes and opposed strikes. He also opposed the formation of narrow trade unions, instead advocating that skilled workers should assist the unskilled. Harmony and fellowship ultimately dominated his vision of America's future. Consensus, not conflict, was his goal.

The Knights' rhetoric found receptive listeners among American workers, and membership rolls grew during the early 1880s. Then came 1884, the beginning of what labor historians have called "the great upheaval." Strikes erupted in the coalfields of Pennsylvania and Ohio and the railroad yards of Missouri and Illinois. The labor conflicts continued into 1885 and 1886. Labor won some, but by no means all, of the strikes. Although its role was small, the Knights were associated with several important labor victories. By mid-1886 perhaps 750,000 workers had joined the Knights.

From that high point, however, the Knights declined rapidly. From the start, they could not weld together their diverse rank and file. Administrative and organizational problems surfaced, and Powderly's relatively conservative leadership was opposed by more radical members, who fully accepted strikes and conflict. The Haymarket Square bombing in 1886 branded all unions as un-American and violent in the public mind. By 1893, when Powderly was driven from office, the Knights' membership had declined alarmingly. Weakened and divided, it failed to survive the depression of the mid-1890s.

Unlike the NLU and the Knights, the **American Federation of Labor** (AFL) did not aspire to remake society. Its leaders accepted industrial capitalism and rejected partisan politics and the dreams of radical visionaries. Instead they concentrated on practical, reachable goals—higher wages, shorter workdays, and improved working conditions. Most importantly, they only recruited skilled laborers, recognizing that easily replaceable unskilled workers were in a poor position to negotiate with employers.

Formed in 1886 by the coming together of skilled-trade unions, the AFL was led ably by **Samuel Gompers,** a Jewish immigrant from England who had been the president of a New York cigar makers' union. Like many cigar makers, Gompers was well, if informally, educated. Cigar rolling was a quiet job, and the rollers often employed one of their number as a reader. As a boy Gompers not only learned a skill, but he absorbed the leading political, economic, and literary ideas of his day. "In fact," Gompers later wrote, "these [readings and] discussions in the shops were more like public debating societies . . . 'labor forums.'"

As the head of the AFL for almost 40 years, Gompers used his considerable "moral power" and organizational ability to fight for *achievable* goals. American laborers were divided over religious, racial, ethnic, gender, and political issues, but they all desired higher wages, more leisure time, and greater liberty. Working out of his 8 × 10 foot office, and using tomato boxes for filing cases, Gompers battled for those unifying issues. He focused on the world around him, not on the best of all possible worlds.

Once effectively organized, he maintained, labor could deal with capital on equal terms.

Gompers's approach toward working with capital and organizing labor proved successful in the long run. Before 1900, however, the AFL was not more successful than the Knights or the NLU. In fact, workers benefited little from unions before the turn of the century. Fewer than 5 percent of American workers joined trade unions, and the major areas of industrial growth were the least unionized. Nevertheless, the experimentation during the late

nineteenth century taught workers a valuable lesson: To combat the power of capital, labor needed equal power. During the twentieth century labor would move closer to that power.

CONCLUSION

In one generation the United States became the economic colossus of the world. After a heated period of intense competition, mergers forged supercorpora-

CHRONOLOGY OF KEY EVENTS

1856 Bessemer steelmaking process is invented.

1859 Edwin Drake drills the first commercial oil well in Titusville, Pennsylvania.

1861 Morrill Tariff Act is passed; first of a series of high protective tariffs.

1862 Homestead Act gives 160 acres of free public land to those who will cultivate it for five years; Morrill Land Grant Act establishes many technical and agricultural colleges.

1866 National Labor Union is founded in Baltimore; Cyrus W. Field lays the first successful transatlantic telegraph cable.

1869 First transcontinental railroad is completed on May 10.

1870 John D. Rockefeller founds Standard Oil Company.

1873 Timber Culture Act awards 160 acres of public land to anyone who will plant trees on a quarter of the land.

1876 Alexander Graham Bell invents the telephone.

1877 Thomas Edison invents the phonograph; Desert Land Act grants 640 acres at $1.25 per acre to anyone who will irrigate the land; Great Strike paralyzes railroad transportation from Midwest and most of Northeast; 20 Molly Maguires are convicted and executed for terrorism in Pennsylvania coalfields.

1879 Edison invents the incandescent light bulb.

1883 Railroad companies divide country into time zones.

1885 George Westinghouse introduces alternating current for transmitting electricity.

1886 *Santa Clara County v. Southern Pacific Railroad* decision rules that a corporation is a legal entity entitled to constitutional protection; Haymarket Square riot erupts in Chicago; Samuel Gompers founds American Federation of Labor in Columbus, Ohio.

1888 George Eastman produces the first handheld camera.

1892 Steelworkers at Carnegie Steel Company in Homestead, Pennsylvania, strike to protest decrease in wages and increase in production demands.

1894 Strike by American Railway Union members against Pullman Company to protest wage cuts and high rents in company-owned housing leads to nationwide boycott of Pullman cars.

1895 Booker T. Washington's "Atlanta Compromise" speech advocates that African Americans focus on achieving economic success as a basis for social and political equality.

1896 *Plessy v. Ferguson* decision rules that the principle of "separate but equal" does not deprive African Americans of civil rights guaranteed under the Fourteenth Amendment.

1901 Andrew Carnegie sells his steel company for almost $500 million to a group that is forming U.S. Steel.

tions that controlled the majority of their industries. This economic expansion and consolidation provided many benefits. In some cases people were able to buy superior goods at cheaper prices. (As Edwin Atkinson noted in 1886, "Did Vanderbilt keep any of you down by saving you two dollars and seventy-five cents on a barrel of flour, while he was making fourteen cents?") And social mobility did increase. Although some skilled artisans slipped downward on the social ladder, upward mobility rates usually doubled the downward rates. Of course not all shared equally. Few duplicated Andrew Carnegie's transition from rags to riches.

Average annual incomes rose steadily for almost all classes of workers, although wage increases rarely equaled the rising cost of living. Nevertheless, most families' standard of living improved because more members of the family worked for wages. Items that had been considered luxuries soon became viewed as necessities.

Individuals, however, paid huge social costs for these advances. Some paid a disproportionate share. Patterns of working and living changed dramatically. Many workers' new status imperiled their independence. Personal relationships were being replaced by impersonal, contractual arrangements. Workers confronted the changes, and some sought to organize themselves to offset the overwhelming advantages enjoyed by management. In short, all of the late nineteenth century is the story of profound transformation as well as an adaptation and adjustment to a new social and economic order.

Chapter Summary and Key Points

Between 1865 and 1900 the United States was transformed from a largely rural nation to one of the leading industrial powers in the world. In this chapter you read about the technological transformations of the era; the legal, financial, and cultural factors that encouraged rapid industrialization; business consolidation; the growth of new management techniques; and the impact of and response to these changes on the part of American workers.

- The late nineteenth century saw the creation of a modern industrial economy.

- A national transportation and communication network was created, the corporation became the dominant form of business organization, and a managerial revolution transformed business operations.

- Long hours and hazardous working conditions led many workers to attempt to form labor unions despite strong opposition from industrialists and the courts.

Suggestions for Further Reading

Walter Licht, *Industrializing America: The Nineteenth Century* (1995). Presents an up-to-date interpretation of the growth of industry and its consequences for American workers.

David Montgomery, *The Fall of the House of Labor: The Workplace, The State, and American Labor Activism, 1865–1925* (1987). Examines labor's responses to the growth of industry.

Carroll W. Pursell, *The Machine in America: A Social History of Technology* (1995). Provides a thorough examination of the growth of mechanization in U.S. industry.

Ronald Takaki, *A Different Mirror: The Making of Multicultural America* (1993). Retells American history from the perspective of ethnic and minority groups.

Alan Trachtenberg, *The Incorporation of America: Culture and Society in the Gilded Age* (1982). Explores intellectual and artistic responses to late-nineteenth-century industrialization.

Richard White, *"It's Your Misfortune and None of My Own": A History of the American West* (1991). Stresses the federal government's role in western development.

Novels

Willa Cather, *My Antonia* (1918).

David Anthony Durham, *Gabriel's Story* (2001).

William Dean Howells, *The Rise of Silas Lapham* (1885).

Larry McMurtry, *Lonesome Dove* (1985).

James Michener, *Centennial* (1975).

Frank Norris, *The Octopus* (1901).

Booth Tarkington, *The Magnificent Ambersons* (1918).

Mark Twain, *Roughing It* (1872).

Walter Van Tillburg Clark, *The Oxbow Incident* (1940).

Media Resources
Web Sites
The Centennial Exhibition, Philadelphia, 1876
http://libwww.library.phila.gov/CenCol/
A good source on the first of the world's fairs held in the United States.

World's Columbian Exposition: Idea, Experience, Aftermath
http://xroads.virginia.edu/~MA96/WCE/title.html
Web site developed as a hypertext thesis at the University of Virginia containing great pictures and quotes from observers.

Interactive Guide to the World's Columbian Exposition
http://users.vnet.net/schulman/Columbian/columbian.html
An easily accessible compilation of information about the fair, including many interesting statistics.

The Wright Stuff
http://www.pbs.org/wgbh/amex/wright/
A companion Web site to an *American Experience* television program, it includes a short movie of a reenactment of the fight as well as audio interviews.

The Wizard of Photography
http://www.pbs.org/wgbh/amex/eastman/
Companion site to PBS film about George Eastman that includes a gallery of Eastman Kodak ads and a timeline history of photography.

The Telephone
http://www.pbs.org/wgbh/amex/telephone/
Another PBS companion site, it includes a photo gallery of telephones through the years and an interactive timeline of American technology, beginning with Ben Franklin's lightning rod.

Alexander Graham Bell Family Papers at the Library of Congress
http://memory.loc.gov/ammem/bellhtml/bellhome.html
This site contains papers from 1862 to 1939 and includes a chronology, images, selected documents, and interpretive essays about Bell.

Inventing Entertainment: The Motion Pictures and Sound Recordings of the Edison Companies
http://memory.loc.gov/ammem/edhtml/edhome.html
A Library of Congress Web site that provides access to both audio and video recordings made by the Edison companies.

The Rockefellers
http://www.pbs.org/wgbh/amex/rockefellers/
A PBS companion site that examines the history and legacy of the Rockefeller family, it includes a number of special features, such as a game that allows students to attempt to corner a market.

Lighting a Revolution
http://www.americanhistory.si.edu/lighting/index.htm
Smithsonian Web site that explores the history of lighting and its impact.

Emergence of Advertising in America
http://memory.loc.gov/ammem/award98/ncdhtml/eaahome.html

Drawn from holdings at Duke University, contains numerous examples of advertising in this era.

Touring Turn-of- the-Century America, Photographs from the Detroit Publishing Company, 1880–1920
http://lcweb2.loc.gov/ammem/detroit/dethome.html
Searchable database of photos in the American Memory site of the Library of Congress.

The Inflation Calculator
http://www.westegg.com/inflation/
A very useful device for understanding the significance of the dollar figures given in this chapter. For example, in terms of the value of dollars in the year 2000, Carnegie's price for his company of $480 million equals almost $10 billion dollars, while a worker's income of $500 a year equates to less than $10,000.

The Richest Man in the World: Andrew Carnegie
http://www.pbs.org/wgbh/pages/amex/carnegie
This *American Experience*/PBS site provides images and text about Carnegie's life and activities.

John D. Rockefeller and the Standard Oil Company
http://www.micheloud.com/FXM/SO/
This study with accompanying images by François Micheloud tells of the rise of Rockefeller and his mammoth company.

National Refinery Company
http://www.enarco.com/
This positive history of the company reflects the industrial changes of late-nineteenth-century America.

New Perspectives on the West
http://www.pbs.org/weta/thewest/
A great companion Web site to the Ken Burns eight-part documentary on the history of the West.

The American West
http://thewest.harpweek.com/
Searchable database drawn from illustrations from *Harper's Weekly* (1857–1916) relating to the American West.

Prairie Settlement: Nebraska Photos and Family Letters, 1862–1912
http://memory.loc.gov/ammem/award98/nbhihtml/pshome.html
A Library of Congress searchable database of correspondence and pictures relating to the settlement of Nebraska from 1862 to 1912.

History of the American West, 1860–1920
http://memory.loc.gov/ammem/award97/codhtml/hawphome.html
Over 30,000 photographs from the holdings of the Denver Public Library.

Voices of the American South
http://memory.loc.gov/ammem/award97/ncuhtml/
fpnashome.html
First-person narratives of the American South from 1860 to 1920 drawn from the holdings of the University of North Carolina at Chapel Hill.

The Northern Great Plains, 1880–1920: Photographs from the Fred Hultstrand and F. A. Pazandak Photograph Collections
http://memory.loc.gov/ammem/award97/ndfahtml/
ngphome.html
This American Memory site from the Library of Congress contains "two collections from the Institute for Regional Studies at North Dakota State University" with "900 photographs of rural and small town life at the turn of the century." Included are "images of sod homes and the people who built them; images of farms and the machinery that made them prosper; and images of one-room schools and the children that were educated in them."

"California as I Saw It": First-Person Narratives of California's Early Years, 1849–1900
http://memory.loc.gov/ammem/cbhtml/cbhome.html
This site is a part of the American Memory Series and contains "full text and illustrations of 190 works documenting the formative era of California's history through eyewitness accounts." It covers the gold rush, the interaction of various groups, and the settling of the region.

Home on the Range/Cowboy Heritage
http://history.cc.ukans.edu/heritage/old_west/cowboy
.html
This site tells the history of cattle trails and towns like Dodge City with useful text, links, documents, and maps.

Heroes and Villains in Kansas
http://www.ukans.edu/carrie/kancoll/galhero.htm
The Kansas Collection Gallery of both famous and little-known people who made up the history of the state.

Labor-Management Conflict in American History
http://www.history.ohio-state.edu/projects/laborconflict/
A collection of materials about six major labor strikes or confrontations between 1886 and 1905.

The Samuel Gompers Papers: A Documentary History of the American Working Class
http://www.inform.umd.edu/ARHU/Depts/History/
Gompers/web1.html
A Web site maintained by the University of Maryland in conjunction with the eight-volume published papers of the American labor movement.

Americans at Work, Americans at Leisure, Motion Pictures, 1894–1915
http://memory.loc.gov/ammem/awlhtml/
Library of Congress site that includes 150 digitized motion pictures made of work, school, and leisure activities of Americans originally recorded from 1894 to 1915.

The Drama of Haymarket
http://www.chicagohistory.org/dramas/index.htm
A multimedia source about this violent confrontation that occurred in Chicago in 1886.

Anarchist Archive at Pitzer University
http://www.pitzer.edu/~dward/Anarchist_Archives/
archivehome.html
This archive includes classic anarchist texts, especially information and graphics for the Haymarket Riot.

Films and Videos

Money on the Land. Part of the 1973 Alistair Cooke *America* series on BBC, it examines the economic changes at the turn of the century.

1877, Grand Army of Starvation. A segment of the American Social History Project, *Who Built America,* it relates the events of the great railroad strikes in 1877.

The Iron Road. An *American Experience* video, it details the expansion of the railroads after the Civil War.

The Wizard of Photography. A PBS video about the life and times of George Eastman.

The Telephone. American Experience documentary regarding the development of Alexander Graham Bell's telephone.

Mr. Sears' Catalogue. PBS video examining the Sears catalogue as a reflection of American culture and consumerism.

The Grandest Enterprise Under God. Video 5 of Ken Burn's *The West* about building the transcontinental railroad.

The Geography of Hope. Video 7 of Ken Burn's *The West* about black migration west, Teddy Roosevelt, and Buffalo Bill.

KEY TERMS

Social Darwinism   (p. 458)

Gospel of wealth   (p. 458)

Laissez-faire   (p. 460)

Rebates   (p. 462)

Pools   (p. 462)

Trust   (p. 463)

Vertical integration   (p. 464)

Sharecropping   (p. 472)

Hatch Act of 1887   (p. 472)

New South   (p. 473)

Atlanta Compromise   (p. 473)

Mill towns   (p. 474)

Plessy v. Ferguson   (p. 475)

Molly Maguires   (p. 479)

Great Strike of 1877   (p. 480)

Haymarket Square riot   (p. 481)

National Labor Union   (p. 482)

Knights of Labor   (p. 482)

American Federation of Labor   (p. 482)

James B. Duke   (p. 474)

Frederick W. Taylor   (p. 479)

Terence V. Powderly   (p. 482)

Samuel Gompers   (p. 482)

PEOPLE YOU SHOULD KNOW

George Eastman   (p. 456)

Alexander Graham Bell   (p. 456)

Thomas Edison   (p. 456)

George Westinghouse   (p. 456)

Andrew Carnegie   (p. 458)

Herbert Spencer   (p. 458)

J. P. Morgan   (p. 461)

John D. Rockefeller   (p. 463)

Joseph G. McCoy   (p. 467)

Henry W. Grady   (p. 473)

Booker T. Washington   (p. 473)

REVIEW QUESTIONS

1. What factors aided the rapid expansion of American industry in the late nineteenth century?
2. How did scholarship and popular culture support the concentration of wealth?
3. What led to the consolidation of business, and how did the rise of big business change marketing and manufacturing techniques?
4. What impact did national economic trends have in the South and West?
5. How did the nature of work change, and what were workers' responses to those changes?

18 The Rise of an Urban Society and City People

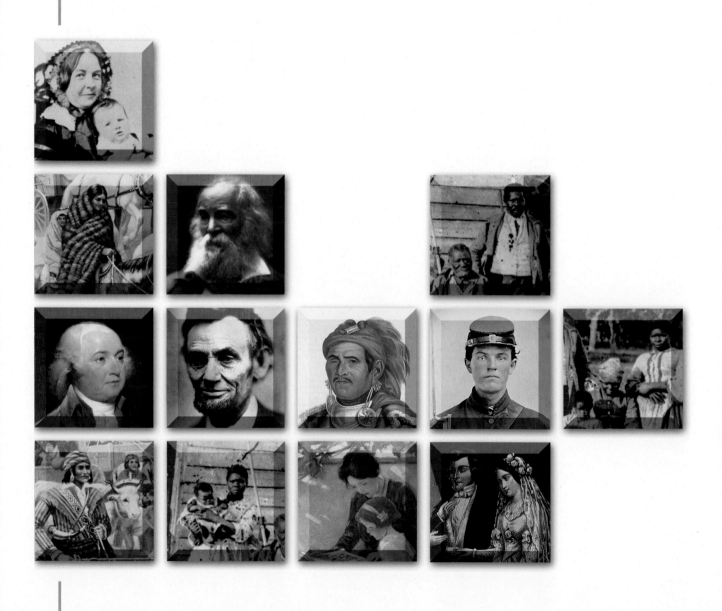

LIZZIE BORDEN: VICTORIAN WOMAN AND MURDERER

Andrew Borden had, as the old Scotch saying goes, short arms and long pockets. He was cheap not because he had to be frugal but because he hated to spend money. He had dedicated his entire life to making and saving money, and tales of his unethical and parsimonious business behavior were legendary in his hometown of Fall River, Massachusetts. Local gossips maintained that as an undertaker he cut off the feet of corpses so that he could fit them into undersized coffins that he had purchased at a very good price. Andrew, however, was not interested in rumors or the opinions of other people; he was more concerned with his own rising fortunes. By 1892 he had amassed over half a million dollars, he controlled the Fall River Union Savings Bank, and he served as the director of the Globe Yard Mill Company, the First National Bank, the Troy Cotton and Manufacturing Company, and the Merchants Manufacturing Company.

Andrew was rich, but he did not live like a wealthy man. Instead of living alongside the other prosperous Fall River citizens in the elite neighborhood known as the Hill, Andrew resided in an area near the business district called the Flats. He liked to save time as well as money, and from the Flats he could conveniently walk to work. For his daughters Lizzie and Emma, whose eyes and dreams focused on the Hill, life in the Flats was an intolerable embarrassment. Their house was a grim, boxlike structure lacking both comfort and privacy. Since Andrew believed that running water on each floor was a wasteful luxury, the only washing facilities were a cold-water faucet in the kitchen and a laundry room water tap in the cellar. Also in the cellar was the only toilet in the house. To make matters worse, the house was not connected to the Fall River gas main. Andrew preferred to use kerosene to light his house. Although it did not provide as good light or burn as cleanly as gas, it was less expensive. To save even more money, he and his family frequently sat in the dark.

The Borden home was far from happy. Lizzie and Emma, ages 32 and 42 in 1892, strongly disliked their stepmother Abby and resented Andrew's penny-pinching ways. Lizzie especially felt alienated from the world around her. Although Fall River was the largest cotton-manufacturing town in America, it offered few opportunities for the unmarried daughter of a prosperous man. Society expected a

Preconceived notions of Victorian womanhood saved Lizzie Borden from being convicted of murdering her father and stepmother.

woman of Lizzie's social position to marry, and while she waited for a proper suitor, her only respectable social outlets were church and community service. So Lizzie taught a Sunday School class and was active in the Woman's Christian Temperance Union, the Ladies' Fruit and Flower Mission, and other organizations. She kept herself busy, but she was not happy.

In August 1892, strange things started to happen in the Borden home—after Lizzie and Emma learned that Andrew had secretly changed his will. Abby became violently ill. In time so did the Borden maid Bridget Sullivan and Andrew himself. Abby told a neighborhood doctor that she had been poisoned, but Andrew refused to listen to her wild ideas. Shortly thereafter, Lizzie went shopping for prussic acid, a deadly poison, that she said she needed to clean her sealskin cape. When a Fall River druggist refused her request, she left the store in an agitated state. Later in the day, she told a friend that she feared an unknown enemy of her father's was after him. "I'm afraid somebody will do something," she said.

On August 4, 1892, Bridget awoke early and ill, but she still managed to prepare a large breakfast of johnnycakes, fresh-baked bread, ginger and oatmeal cookies with raisins, and some three-day-old mutton and hot mutton soup. After eating a hearty meal, Andrew left for work. Bridget also left to do some work outside. This left Abby and Lizzie in the house alone. Then somebody did something very grisly. As Abby was bent over making the bed in the guest room, someone moved into the room unobserved and killed her with an ax.

Andrew came home for lunch earlier than usual. He asked Lizzie where Abby was, and she said she did not know. Unconcerned, Andrew, who was not feeling well, lay down on the parlor sofa for a nap. He never awoke. Like Abby, he was slaughtered by someone with an ax. Lizzie "discovered" his body, still lying on the sofa. She called Bridget, who had taken the back stairs to her attic room: "Come down quick; father's dead; somebody came in and killed him."

Experts have examined and reexamined the crime, and most have reached the same conclusion: Lizzie killed her father and stepmother. In fact, Lizzie was tried for the gruesome murders. Despite a preponderance of evidence, however, an all-male jury found her not guilty, a verdict arrived at without debate or disagreement. A woman of Lizzie's social position, they affirmed, simply could not have committed such a terrible crime.

Even before the trial began, newspaper and magazine writers had judged Lizzie innocent for the same reason. As historian Kathryn Allamong Jacob, an expert on the case, noted, "Americans were certain that well-brought-up daughters could not commit murder with a hatchet on sunny summery mornings." Criminal women, they believed, originated in the lower classes and even looked evil. A criminologist writing in the *North American Review* commented, "[The female criminal] has coarse black hair and a good deal of it. . . . She has often a long face, a receding forehead, overjutting brows, prominent cheek bones, an exaggerated frontal angle as seen in monkeys and savage races, and nearly always square jaws." They did not look like round-faced Lizzie and did not belong to the Ladies' Fruit and Flower Mission.

Jurors and editorialists alike judged **Lizzie Borden** according to their preconceived notions of Victorian womanhood. They believed that such a woman was gentle, docile, and physically frail, short on analytical ability but long on nurturing instincts. "Women," wrote an editorialist for *Scribner's*, "are merely large babies. They are shortsighted, frivolous and occupy an intermediate stage between children and men." Too uncoordinated and weak to accurately swing an ax and too gentle and unintelligent to coldly plan a double murder, a woman of Lizzie's background simply had to be innocent because of her basic innocence.

Even as Lizzie was being tried and found innocent, Victorian notions were being challenged elsewhere. In the larger cities of America, a new culture based on freedoms, not restraints, was taking form. Anything was possible, or at least so some people claimed. Immigrants could become millionaires and women could vote and hold office. Rigid Victorian concepts crumbled under the weight of new ideas, but the price of the new freedoms was high. In both the cities and the culture that flourished within them, a new order had to be constructed out of the chaos of freedom.

THE NEW IMMIGRANTS

On October 28, 1886, President Grover Cleveland traveled to New York Harbor to watch the unveiling of the Statue of Liberty. A gift from France, Frederic Auguste Bartholdi's grand statue was meant to symbolize solidarity between the two republics, but for Americans and incoming immigrants, it was a simple symbol of welcome, the statue's torch lighting the path to a better future.

In popular theory, the promise of America exerted a powerful pull on Europe and Asia. The United States stood for political freedom, social mobility, and economic opportunity. Since the first settlers landed in Jamestown, millions of immigrants had responded to the American magnet. At no time was immigration as great as in the late nineteenth and early twentieth centuries. Between 1860 and 1890, more than 10 million immigrants arrived on America's shores; between 1890 and 1920 over 15 million more arrived.

Seen in a worldwide context, however, the United States' pull was less powerful than Europe's push. Almost every European country—from Ireland in the northwest to Greece in the southeast—experienced a dramatic population increase during the nineteenth century. Advances in medicine and public health standards reduced infant mortality rates and increased life expectancies, but available land and food supplies did not increase to meet the new population demands. Twenty or so years later, when the "baby boomers" reached maturity, emigration increased sharply. (The United States was not the only country to lure immigrants from Europe—millions more emigrated to Australia, New Zealand, South Africa, Canada, Brazil, Argentina, and other underpopulated areas of the globe.)

Historians have divided immigration to the United States into two categories: old and new. The source of the "old" immigration was for the most part northern and western Europe—England, Ireland, France, Germany, and Scandinavia. Immigrants were mostly Protestants (except for the Irish Catholics) and always white; a majority were literate and had lived under constitutional forms of government. Assimilation for them was relatively easy. But this pattern fundamentally changed beginning in the 1880s. The next wave of immigration came from eastern and southern Europe—Greeks, Poles, Russians, Italians, Slavs, Turks. These people found assimilation more difficult; politically, religiously, and culturally, they differed greatly from both the earlier immigrants and native-born Americans.

More than geography differentiated the new immigrants. Their reasons for leaving Europe, their visions of America, and their settlement patterns in the United States varied dramatically. Conditions in southern and eastern Europe were right for the push to America at this time.

With the abolition of serfdom, peasants were free to emigrate; and with the rise in population, young men faced job, land, and food shortages. Railroads and steamships made travel faster and less expensive. During the 1880s, British and German steamships carried immigrants across the Atlantic for as little as $8, and by the turn of the century the trip took only five and a half days.

"Birds of Passage"

Essentially there were two types of immigrants— permanent immigrants and migrant workers. The people in the second group, often called **birds of passage,** never intended to make the United States their home. Unable to earn a livelihood in their home countries, they came to America, worked and saved, and then returned home. Most were young men in their teens and twenties. They left behind their parents, young wives, and children, indications that their absence would not be too long. Before 1900, an estimated 78 percent of Italian immigrants and 95 percent of Greek immigrants were men. Many traveled to America in the early spring, worked until late fall, and returned to the warmer climates of their southern European homes for the winter. Some fully intended to return home, but for one reason or

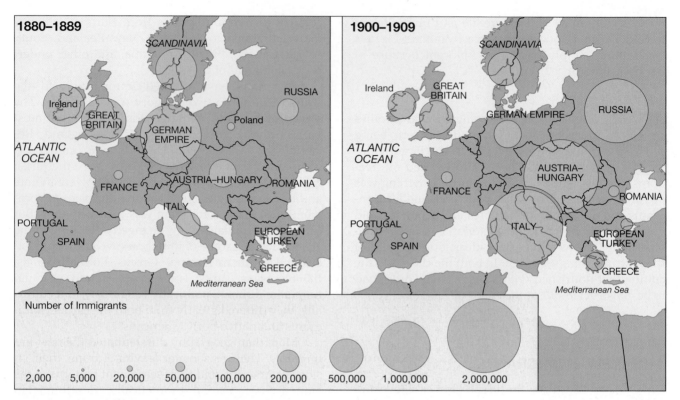

Immigration, 1880–1889 and 1900–1909

The source of old immigration was primarily northern and western Europe—England, Ireland, Germany, and Scandinavia. By the 1890's a wave of new immigrants began to arrive from eastern and southern Europe.

another—love, hardship, early death—did not. Overall, 20 to 30 percent of all immigrants did return home.

Italian immigration patterns are a good example of the activity of the birds of passage. Beginning in the 1870s, Italian birthrates rose and mortality rates fell. Population pressure became severe, especially in *Il Mezzogiorno,* the southern and poorest provinces of Italy. The central government, dominated by northerners and concerned only with northern interests, seemed unconcerned about the impoverished southern provinces. Heavily taxed and hurt by high protective tariffs on northern industrial goods, Italians in southern Italy sank deeper into poverty.

Then even nature joined the opposition. Natural disasters rocked southern Italy during the first decade of the twentieth century. Earthquakes caused untold devastation in the provinces of Basilicata and Calabria. Vesuvius erupted and buried a town near Naples. Then Etna erupted. The cruelest blow came in 1908 when an earthquake and tidal wave swept through the Strait of Messina between Sicily and the Italian mainland and killed hundreds of thousands of people.

The jobs that Italian men sought reflected their attitude toward America. They did not look for careers; occupations that provided opportunity for upward economic mobility were alien to them. Unlike most earlier immigrants, they did not want to farm in America or even own land, both of which implied a permanence that did not figure in their plans. Instead, Italians headed for the cities, where labor was needed and wages were relatively good. Particularly attracted to heavy construction jobs, they supplied the muscle that dug tunnels and canals, laid railroad tracks, and constructed bridges and roads. Expecting their stay in America to be short, they lived as inexpensively as possible under conditions that native-born families considered intolerable.

While they received good wages, they seldom forgot their homes in Italy. One nostalgic Italian admitted, "Doctor, we brought to America only our brains and our arms. Our hearts stayed there in the little house in the beautiful fields of our Italy." For women, adjustment to America was even more difficult. They often wore black clothing, an old-country practice that symbolized self-sacrifice, misery, and determination.

The same feelings of loneliness and alienation were also felt by many Chinese immigrants in the United States. Beginning in the mid-1860s, they emigrated to America to work building the Central Pacific railroad, and when that project was completed they sought jobs in western mining towns and cities. Normally only men emigrated, and they lived frugally and sent much of their wages to their families back in China. Their dream was almost always to return home, not to forge a new life in America.

Italians and Chinese were not the only birds of passage. The same forces that had initiated their flight—population pressure, unemployment, hunger, and the breakdown of agrarian societies—sent Greeks, Slavs, Japanese, Mexicans, French Canadians, and inhabitants of scores of other nations to the United States. Seeking neither permanent homes nor citizenship, they desired only an opportunity to work for a living, hoping to save enough money to return to a better life in the country of their birth. Always the land *they* coveted was some distant home, not in the United States.

In Search of a New Home

In contrast to the birds of passage were the **permanent immigrants,** for whom America offered political and religious freedom as well as economic opportunity. The promise of America was especially appealing to members of ethnic and religious minorities who were persecuted, abused, and despised in their homelands. Germans from Slavic countries, Greeks from Romania, Serbs from Hungary, Turks from Bulgaria, Poles from Russia—for these men and women home held few warm associations.

Czarist Russia, for example, was notoriously and historically inhospitable to many minorities. In 1907, 250,000 "Russians" emigrated from Russia. But who were these Russians? More than 115,000 were Jews, and another 73,000 were Poles. Others were Finns, Germans, and Lithuanians. Only a small percentage were of Russian ethnic stock.

The Jews were the prototypical new immigrants; they fled nearly unbearable hardships. Millions of Jews had maintained a relatively stable communal life in Poland until the eighteenth century when Russia, Prussia, and Austria conquered and divided the country. Most of the Polish Jews lived under Russian rule, and the quality of their lives took an immediate and drastic downward turn. Russian authorities drove Jews out of commerce and forced them into an area known as the **Pale of Settlement,** home to over 90 percent of Russian Jews. There they toiled as farmers on the poor soil of the steppes or earned a living

Hester Street on New York City's Lower East Side, in a photograph from 1907, was home to thousands of Jewish immigrants from Russia and eastern Europe. The immigrants crowded into the tenements lining the street, which bustled with peddlers and pedestrians.

as artisans or craftsmen in impoverished villages. There, too, Russian officials burned their books, disrupted their religious practices, and occasionally even broke up their families.

Starting in 1881, when the liberal Russian Czar Alexander II was assassinated, conditions for Jews in Russia went rapidly from bad to worse to intolerable. Laws restricted Jewish businesses, prevented Jewish landownership, and limited Jewish education. Pogroms, legally sanctioned mob attacks against Jews, killed and injured thousands. Sometimes at the whim of authorities, Russian Cossacks burned Jewish houses and destroyed Jewish possessions.

For Jews, then, emigration offered a chance for a far better life than that in the Pale of Settlement. Dr. George M. Price, one of the several million Jews who left Russia for America during the late nineteenth century, expressed the feelings of these immigrants for their homeland. In his diary he wrote: "Sympathy for Russia? How ironical it sounds! Am I not despised? Am I not urged to leave? Do I not hear the word zhid (Jew) constantly? Can I even think that some consider me a human capable of thinking and feeling like others? Do I not rise daily with the fear lest the hungry mob attack me? . . . It is impossible . . . that a Jew should regret leaving Russia." Compared to Russia, the United States seemed like heaven to Price.

Because these Jewish immigrants came to the United States to stay, their form of immigration differed substantially from that of the generally young, male birds of passage. Jews, like other permanent immigrants, tended to come to America in family units, men and women, young and old. They brought their life savings and most valuable possessions with them, never expecting to see again what they left behind. The move to America thus was financially and physically taxing, and once in America, whole families had more expenses than the young male birds of passage.

Since America was now their home, Jewish men looked for jobs that offered future opportunities rather than simply work for wages. They were not drawn to unskilled labor in the steel mills and mines or even in construction. Many Jews had skills, for the uncertain life of the Russian Pale had taught them not to depend on land or commerce. In the Pale a Jew's greatest possession was the ability to do something that could not be taken away, a skilled craft. First in the Pale and then in America, Jews were tailors and seamstresses, cigar makers and toy makers, tanners and butchers, carpenters, joiners, roofers, and masons, coppersmiths and blacksmiths. They had the knowledge and ability to perform the thousands of skilled tasks needed in an urban environment.

NATIVISM: THE ANTI-IMMIGRANT REACTION

Native-born citizens and new immigrants confronted each other in America's cities. Tensions often ran high, as seen in the 1891 Hennessy case. A feud between gangs on the New Orleans docks had turned violent, and Joe and Pete Provenzano were arrested and tried for attempting to massacre the rival gang. The trial took a sensational turn when **David Hennessy,** the New Orleans superintendent of police, asserted that he had evidence that a secret Sicilian organization known as the Mafia was involved in the affair. Shortly after Hennessy made his bold charges, he was gunned down by five armed men. Before he died, Hennessy was heard to say, "The dagos shot me."

The crime raised a hue and cry against Sicilians. Local police, urged on by Mayor Joseph Shakespeare to "arrest every Italian you come across, if necessary," arrested scores. Eleven Sicilians were brought to trial, but a jury failed to convict them. A local mob promptly took matters into its own hands and shot or clubbed to death nine suspects and hanged the other two. As far as most natives of New Orleans were concerned, justice had been done.

Many other Americans seemed to agree. Editorial writers praised the mob action and damned the vile "un-American" Italians. Across the country anti-

Italian rhetoric became ugly, and wild rumors ricocheted like bullets. Some said that the Italian fleet was headed toward America's east coast; others claimed that uniformed Italians were going through military drills in the streets of New York City. One thing was clear, noted an editorial writer in the *Review of Reviews:* Congress had to pass immigration legislation to keep out "the refuse of the murderbreeds of Southern Europe."

Although the Hennessy case soon faded from the front pages of American newspapers, the emotions it generated and revealed were very real. Native-born Americans harbored deep suspicion of and resentment toward immigrants, especially those from Asia and southern and eastern Europe. American industrialists saw in the immigrants a bottomless pool of dependable, inexpensive labor, but other Americans saw something far different and much less promising. Workers saw competition. Protestants saw Catholics and Jews. Educators saw illiterate hordes. Politicians saw peasants, unfamiliar with the workings of republicanism, democracy, and constitutionalism, and—even worse—perhaps contaminated by a belief in socialism, communism, or anarchism. Social Darwinists saw a mass of dark-skinned, thick-browed, bent-backed people who were far "below" northern and western Europeans on the evolutionary ladder. In short, native-born Americans, heirs of a different culture, religion, and complexion, saw something alien and inferior, perhaps even dangerous, in these new immigrants.

They reacted accordingly. They posted signs: "No Jews or Dogs Allowed." They called the Chinese "coolies," and the Mexicans "bean heads." Overall, they created an atmosphere of hostility that too often spilled over into open violence. In 1891 in a New Jersey mill town, 500 tending boys in a glassworks rioted when the management hired 14 young Russian Jews. During an 1895 labor conflict in the southern Colorado coal fields, American miners killed 6 Italians. When Slavic coal miners went on strike in 1897 in eastern Pennsylvania, local citizens massacred 21 Polish and Hungarian workers. On the West Coast, Chinese workers were subject to regular and vicious attacks. Especially during economic hard times, native-born Americans lashed out against the new immigrants.

Sources of Conflict

Nativism, as this anti-immigrant backlash was called, took many forms. Racial nativism, the subject of thousands of books and articles, is the best remembered. Using such criteria as complexion, size of cranium, length of forehead, and slope of shoulders, university professors such as Wisconsin's Edward Alsworth Ross and popular writers such as Madison Grant judged the immigrants from southern and eastern Europe as inferior to most native-born Americans. University professors and scientists gave credibility to such theories of innate racial and ethnic inferiority, and popular writers readily accepted the stereotypes. **Jacob Riis,** a Danish immigrant who became an urban reformer in America and wrote the popular book *How the Other Half Lives* (1890), characterized Italians as "born gamblers" who lived destitute and disorderly lives, Chinese as secretive and addicted to every vice, and Jews as "enslaved" by their pursuit of gold as well as living amidst filth.

Religious differences reinforced ethnic variations. Overwhelmingly Catholic and Jewish, the new immigrants challenged the Protestant orthodoxy in America. Anti-Catholicism, noted a leading student of nativism, "blossomed spectacularly" during the late nineteenth century. Many Americans regarded the pope as the Antichrist and Catholics as his evil minions. And it was widely believed that the authoritarian bent of the Catholic mind made it incompatible with democratic institutions.

Native-born Americans viewed Jews with even greater suspicion, attributing the characteristics of Shakespeare's Shylock to Jews as a whole. "Money is their God," wrote Jacob Riis. Other writers commented that Jews were tactless, tasteless, and pushy. Eventually many social clubs, country clubs, hotels, and universities excluded Jews, arguing that money alone could not purchase respectability.

The **Leo Frank** case painfully demonstrated the ubiquitous anti-Semitism in American society. Frank, a Cornell University graduate and a son of a wealthy New York merchant, managed an Atlanta pencil factory. In 1914 one of the factory hands, Mary Phagan, was found murdered on the premises. Frank was tried and convicted on flimsy evidence, but the case soon became an international cause célèbre. After reviewing the case, the governor of Georgia commuted Frank's death sentence to life imprisonment. The decision outraged native Georgia whites. They boycotted Jewish merchants and clamored for Frank's blood. Finally, a group of citizens from Mary Phagan's hometown took Leo Frank from a state prison, transported him 175 miles across the state, and coldly hanged him. As news of the hanging spread, people gathered to gaze at the sight and shout "Now we've got you! We've got you now!" In the 1980s, new evidence in the Phagan case proved Frank innocent, and Georgia's Board of Pardons granted him a

posthumous pardon. But dispassionate justice was scarce in the weeks after Frank's death.

Orators used the Frank case as an object lesson. Tom Watson, the fiery Georgia politician, warned listeners: "From all over the world, the Children of Israel are flocking to this country, and plans are on foot to move them from Europe *en masse* . . . to empty upon our shores the very scum and dregs of the *Parasite Race*." Watson believed that Congress should stop the flow of immigrants before America was flooded by the waves of eastern and southern Europeans.

Many congressmen agreed. They too harbored strong suspicions that every boat that docked at Ellis Island contained a swarm of socialists, communists, and anarchists prepared to foment revolution. As unfounded as their fears were, they could always point to isolated cases of radicalism among immigrants. They drew attention, for example, to Leon Czolgosz, born only months after his eastern European parents arrived in America. After embracing anarchism, Czolgosz shot and killed President William McKinley on September 6, 1901.

Most Americans resented the new immigrants, however, for purely economic reasons. American workers, particularly the unskilled, believed that im-

This political cartoon depicts the 1882 Chinese Exclusion Act, which barred Chinese laborers from entering the United States for ten years.

migrants depressed wages by their willingness to "work cheap." An iron worker complained: "Immigrants work for almost nothing and seem to be able to live on wind—something which I cannot do." Even skilled workers maintained that the birds-of-passage immigrants were unwilling to support any union efforts to improve working conditions in America. Samuel Gompers, himself an immigrant and head of the American Federation of Labor, believed that the immigrants from eastern and southern Europe and from Asia were ignorant, unskilled, and unassimilable. Calling for strong restrictive legislation, he said, "Some way must be found to safeguard America."

In the 1890s, a terrible depression disrupted the normal economic and social course of America, and the new immigrants became a convenient scapegoat for the nation's myriad ills. People elevated racial prejudice and rumors to universal truths. Native-born Americans blamed crime on Italians and prostitution on the Chinese; they claimed that the social ills of America's expanding cities—corruption, poor sanitation, violence, crime, disease, pollution—were the fault of the new immigrants. And they looked to the federal government for relief and protection.

Closing the Golden Door

The first immigrants attacked were those who were the most different from native-born Americans—the Chinese. The more than 160,000 Chinese who entered the United States between 1868 and 1882 laid down railroad tracks and mined for gold, silver, and coal. Unlike native-born Americans and most members of other immigrant groups, they did not consider cooking, washing, and ironing as "women's work," and in these areas they were particularly successful. Perhaps too successful.

"Americans are not all bad," noted Lee Chew, a Chinese immigrant, "nor are they wicked wizards. Still . . . their treatment of us is outrageous."

During the depression of the mid-1870s the Chinese came under increasingly bitter and violent attack. Labor and political leaders, especially in California, demanded an end to Chinese immigration. But the provisions of the Burlingame Treaty (1868) with China encouraged the Chinese to immigrate to America and establish citizenship.

Eventually Congress responded to the pressure for restriction. In 1880, China gave the United States Congress the right "to regulate, limit or suspend," though not to prohibit, the immigration of Chinese workers to the United States. The **golden door** quickly slammed shut. The **Chinese Exclusion Act** of

1882 suspended Chinese immigration for ten years and drastically restricted the rights of the Chinese already in the United States. In 1892 Congress extended the act for another ten years, and then in 1902 extended it indefinitely.

The legislation established a precedent for the future exclusion of other immigrants. By the 1890s most Americans agreed that the country should restrict "undesirable" immigrants. But how, for example, could Congress close America's door to southern and eastern Europeans while still leaving it open for northern and western Europeans? Politicians came up with the idea of **literacy testing.** As early as the late 1880s economist Edward W. Bemis proposed that the United States exclude all male adults who could not read and write their own language. He maintained that such a law would effectively stop the flow of eastern and southern Europeans into America. The idea soon had the backing of the influential Republican Senator Henry Cabot Lodge of Massachusetts and the equally important Immigration Restriction League.

In 1896 Lodge pushed through Congress a literacy test bill that would have excluded any adult immigrant unable to read 40 words in his own language. Lodge's timing was poor. The bill reached the desk of Democratic President Grover Cleveland two days before his second term expired. Cleveland promptly vetoed the measure, suggesting that the bill tested prior opportunities and that America stood for open opportunities.

Cleveland's veto neither ended the demand for restrictive legislation nor killed the idea of a literacy test. Subsequent presidents William Howard Taft and Woodrow Wilson also vetoed similar pieces of legislation. In 1917, on the eve of America's entry into World War I, Wilson vetoed a literacy test bill on the grounds that it was "not a test of character, of quality, or of personal fitness." Congress nevertheless passed the act over Wilson's veto.

World War I made even chillier the already cold climate for immigrants from southern and eastern Europe. Those born in the polyglot Austro-Hungarian empire were now considered the enemy, and others were watched with deep suspicion. This was especially true after the 1917 Bolshevik Revolution in Russia. Once again American authorities regarded Jews from Russia as potential revolutionaries. Responding to this fear, in 1918 and 1920 Congress passed legislation to exclude or deport anarchists and other "dangerous radicals."

The generation-long battle over restriction was to end with a clear victory for nativism. In the early 1920s Congress discovered its own solution: the quota system. The **Emergency Quota Act** (1921) limited immigration according to a nation-based quota system—no more than 3 percent of any given nationality in America in 1910 could annually immigrate to the United States. In 1924 the **National Origins Act** lowered the quota to 2 percent of each nationality residing in America in 1890. By using 1890 as the base year, the act was clearly aimed at restricting eastern and southern Europeans, for there were far fewer of the new immigrants in America in 1890 than in 1910. Although in 1927 the base year was changed to 1920, the National Origins Act had achieved its desired result. America's doors were no longer fully open to eastern and southern Europeans, and were completely closed to Asians. An important era in American history had ended.

Despite the prejudice against them, immigrants contributed greatly to the growth of industrial America. They and their fellow workers—native-born white and black Americans—built the railroads that crisscrossed the country; mined the gold and silver that made other men rich; and labored in the oilfields, steel mills, coal pits, packing plants, and factories that made such names as Rockefeller, Carnegie, Swift, and Westinghouse famous. Without these men and their companions, there would have been no industrialization. In the process they made the United States an ethnically rich nation, as well as helped to transform the country into an increasingly urban nation.

NEW CITIES AND NEW PROBLEMS

The physical layout of the mid-nineteenth-century city was strikingly different from its twentieth-century counterpart. In an age before reliable mass transportation, when only the rich could afford carriages, the majority of city dwellers walked to and from work. Even America's largest cities—New York, Philadelphia, and Boston—were thus compact and crowded, their sizes limited to about a two-mile radius from center city, or the distance a person could walk in half an hour.

Inside the cities, houses, businesses, and factories were strewn about willy-nilly. Tightly packed near the waterfront were shops, banks, warehouses, and business offices, and not far away were the residences of the people who owned those enterprises or worked in them. There was little residential segregation. The rich may have occupied the finest houses in the center city, but the poor lived in the alleys and dirty streets close by. People dealt with people in a congested, highly personalized world. Rich and

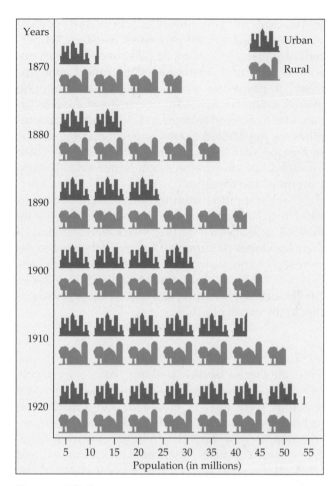

FIGURE 18.1
Urban and Rural Population, 1870–1920

Immigrants and native-born migrants from rural areas contributed to the urban population explosion in this 50-year span.

poor, native-born and immigrant, black and white—they all walked along the same streets and worked in the same area.

During the last third of the century, however, booming industrialization and immigration shattered this arrangement. Factories and cities worked in tandem to reach their full potential. In 1860, before America's industrial surge, 20 percent of the population lived in cities. By 1900 almost 40 percent of the population lived in cities or towns, and that figure climbed to over 50 percent in 1920. The numbers of large cities (those with a population of over 100,000) increased at an even faster rate. In 1860, America had only 9 large cities; in 1900 there were 38; in 1920, 68.

Immigrant and native sources fueled the urban explosion. Most of the late-nineteenth-century immigrants came from rural communities, but they settled in America's industrial heartland. In 1920, 87 percent of Irish immigrants, 89 percent of Russians, 84 percent of Italians and Poles, 80 percent of Hungarians, and 75 percent of Austrians, British, and Canadians lived in cities. For every industrial worker who moved to the countryside, 20 farmers moved to urban America. As in Europe and Asia, rural opportunities in the United States were dwindling at the same time that the population was growing. Thus, for each farm son who became a farm owner, 10 farm sons moved to the cities.

Black migration from the rural South to the urban North further expanded the labor pool in the industrial cities. Slowly at first, blacks left the land of their bondages determined to forge a better life for themselves and their families in the northern cities. Between 1897 and 1920 almost one million African Americans left the South, and 85 percent of those settled in the urban North.

City Technology

Even the largest of the "walking" cities was unprepared to meet the demands the newcomers placed on it. Cities were already crowded, and construction technology was not yet sufficiently advanced to accommodate new arrivals. In time, however, engineers and scientists discovered ways to expand cities. Horizontal and vertical growth changed the skyline and living conditions of urban America during the half-century after 1870.

Better transportation facilities solved the most basic limitation of the walking city, although at first only the wealthy and those with some money benefited. As early as the 1830s, the horse-drawn omnibus could carry 12 to 20 passengers along a fixed route for between 6 and 12 cents. Faster than walking, it was also expensive, certainly beyond the means of an unskilled laborer who earned less than $1 a day. Similarly the commuter railroads, which also dated back to the 1830s and 1840s and cost between 12 and 25 cents to ride, served only the wealthier classes. Constructed and owned by entrepreneurs, omnibuses and commuter railways existed only for the comfort of people who could pay.

The horse railway expanded the city for the middle-class urbanites, white-collar workers, and skilled workers. For 5 cents, these horse-drawn omnibuses carried passengers over steel rails at a speed of 6 to 8 miles per hour. In southern and border towns, mules, which tended to live longer, pulled the omnibuses. By the 1880s, over 300 American cities and towns had constructed horsecar lines, which significantly expanded the size of cities. Now a person could live 5 miles from his or her place of work and still be there in less than an hour. The age of walking was almost over.

The horsecar was not always as safe or as comfortable as its developers planned. Travelers complained about pickpockets, tobacco juice, and overcrowding. Entrepreneurial conductors sometimes packed 80 persons into a car designed for 25 and used underfed, overworked horses that struggled day after day until they dropped from exhaustion and were left to die. Drivers worked long hours for little pay and sat exposed to the weather in the front or rear of the cars. In the winter, cold winds whipped their faces and froze their fingers around the reins. One hardened streetcar conductor remarked, "I feel that I could almost digest cobblestones."

For hillier cities like San Francisco and Pittsburgh, the cable car, introduced during the 1870s, proved a blessing for humans and horses alike. Utilizing steam power, cable cars were faster and cleaner than horse-drawn transportation. Even relatively flat cities such as Kansas City and Chicago installed cable cars. Because it was pulled by a moving underground cable, engineers believed it would be the public transportation of the future—but its problems were considerable. Expensive to install and quick to break down, the cable car soon gave way to the **electric trolley,** which was cheaper to run and more dependable.

In 1888, former naval engineer Frank Sprague converted the horsecar network of Richmond, Virginia, to electricity. Employing electrical current in overhead wires, these trolleys could operate in stop-and-go traffic and travel at average speeds of 10 to 12 miles per hour. American cities quickly climbed aboard the electric bandwagon. By 1902, 97 percent of urban transit mileage had been electrified, and trolleys connected not only city with suburb but also city with city. By 1920 a person could travel from Boston to New York entirely by trolleys known as interurbans.

Called "one of the most rapidly accepted innovations in the history of technology," trolleys were not without their problems: overhead wires gave cities a weblike appearance; in winter the electric wires snapped from the cold and created dangerous situations; and they sometimes frightened horses, thus aggravating traffic problems. By the 1890s, the mixture of horsecars, cable cars, and trolleys jostling each other and pedestrians on city streets created immense traffic jams. English science fiction writer H. G. Wells found Chicago streets in 1906 "simply chaotic—one hoarse cry for discipline."

Engineers searching for other solutions to clogged streets designed electric-powered elevated railway lines and underground subways. Each

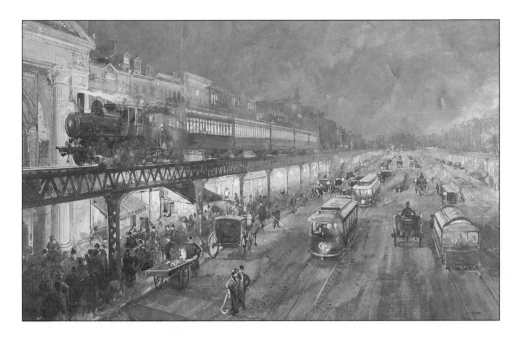

This watercolor of New York City's Bowery at night by W. Louis Sonntag, Jr. shows how steam, steel, and electricity played a major part in transforming cities.

helped ease mass transportation. The Chicago "el" (elevated railway) and the New York City subway satisfied the urban traffic engineers and even occasionally stirred the souls of artists. W. Louis Sonntag, Jr.'s beautiful watercolor captured New York City's Bowery in 1896, in which, illuminated by electric lights, an electric el and trolley pass in the night.

Mass transportation allowed cities to spread miles beyond their cores, but steel and glass permitted cities to reach for the sky. At midcentury, church spires still dominated the urban skyline. Few buildings were higher than five stories. But that would change, as a real-estate columnist wrote in the *Chicago Tribune* in 1888: "Chicago has thus far had but three directions, north, south, and west, but there are indications now that a fourth is to be added and that it is to cut a larger figure in the coming decade than all the others. The new direction is zenithward. Since water hems in the business center on three sides and a nexus of railroads on the south, Chicago must grow upward."

Architects could not design buildings much higher than ten stories, using traditional brick-and-masonry construction. In 1885 New York architect William LeBaron Jenney solved this problem by using light masonry over an iron and steel skeleton. Although only ten stories high, his Home Insurance Building in Chicago was the first true **skyscraper** in history. Materials like steel, light masonry, and eventually glass revolutionized building construction, and the use of electric elevators made tall buildings functional.

Skyscrapers changed the profile of American cities as surely as industrialism altered the American landscape. Returning to America from Europe in 1906, novelist Henry James observed "the multitudinous skyscrapers standing up to the view . . . like extravagant pins in a cushion already overplanted, and stuck in as in the dark, anywhere and anyhow." What disturbed James's sensibilities excited most Americans. The skyscraper symbolized American possibilities. Businesspeople and industrialists even used skyscrapers to glorify their own accomplishments. In 1913, President Woodrow Wilson pressed the button that lit up the Woolworth Building. At 792 feet, it was the largest building in America, a monument to five-and-ten-cents king Frank Woolworth. This hauntingly beautiful structure, which freely adapted aspects of Gothic and Moorish construction, truly was "the Cathedral of Commerce."

The Segregated City

With the outward and upward growth of cities came an end to the more personal walking city. Mass transportation freed the upper and middle classes from having to live in the city core. Voicing their decision with their feet, they scampered for the **streetcar suburbs,** where, popular theory held, the water was purer, the trees fuller, and the air fresher. They commuted to work and no longer mixed daily with their economic inferiors.

The working class moved into the areas and even houses deserted by wealthier families. In New

York City the large stately brownstone homes that had served the upper classes were divided into small apartments that satisfied the new demand for inexpensive housing. Of course, the houses had not been designed to be used as multiunit apartments, and there were numerous problems. Heatless, sunless, and poorly ventilated rooms became increasingly common.

Ethnic groups and races, like economic classes, tended to stake out particular neighborhoods in the new larger cities, and real-estate brokers and landlords restricted blacks and immigrants to specific areas. Black ghettos emerged in the major northern cities for the first time. And in Chicago, New York, Boston, and Philadelphia, English became a foreign language in ethnic neighborhoods, which reproduced in their finer details Old World conditions. Familiar faces, foods, churches, and speech patterns comforted lonely immigrants.

Since members of the ethnic working class were too poor for even moderately priced mass transit, they tended to settle close to their places of work. In New York City, Jews and Italians lived within walking distance of the Lower East Side garment factories. In Chicago, the Poles and Lithuanians who worked in the meatpacking industry awoke in the morning and went to sleep at night hearing the sounds of dying animals and smelling the stench of the stockyards.

Just as new residential trends separated rich and poor, prices for real estate in the central business district shot up at an incredible rate, sometimes as much as 1000 percent a decade in the late nineteenth century. Only businesses and industries could afford the new prices, so the central cities were turned over to high-income businesses, banks, warehouses, railroad terminals, and the recently developed department stores. It became an area where money was made, not where people lived.

The Problems of Growth

By the 1890s, British observers despaired over what had become of the once small American cities. The uncontrolled growth, they suggested, had created ugliness on an almost unprecedented scale. English traveler Charles Philips Trevelyan graphically described the horrors of industrial Pittsburgh:

> A cloud of smoke hangs over it by day. The glow of scores of furnaces light the river banks by night. It stands at the junction of two great rivers, the Monongahela which flows down in a turbid yellowish stream, and the Allegheny which is blackish. . . . All

nations are jumbled up here, the poor living in tenement dens or wooden shanties thrown up or dumped down with little reference to roads or situation, whenever a new house is wanted. It is the most chaotic city, and as yet there is no public spirit or public consciousness to make conditions healthy or decent.

Numerous American observers echoed Trevelyan's observations. American cities were unprepared for the incredible growth they experienced during the late nineteenth century. Housing, clean water, competent police, and adequate public services were all in short supply. Health standards were low everywhere and scientists had barely begun to study the problems and diseases created by crowded urban conditions. To make matters worse, the people who moved to the cities usually came from rural areas and were not familiar with city life.

Crime plagued rich and poor. Pickpockets, robbers, con artists, and violent gangs roamed the streets and alleyways of American cities. Urban police forces had been established in the 1830s and 1840s. In the 1850s, police forces wore uniforms and badges and carried clubs and revolvers but still could not control or seriously curtail urban crime. In fact, during this earlier period, police were often expected to clean streets, inspect boilers, or run poorhouses as well as prevent crime and maintain public order. In addition, police often took bribes from saloonkeepers and streetwalkers to overlook illegal activities and even intimidated voters on election day. They owed their loyalty to the political boss who appointed them, not to some abstract public. Not until the end of the century would attempts to bring professionalism and civil service reform to police departments be successful.

Housing presented an even more pressing problem. Immigrants disembarking at the ports of entry and farmers arriving by train needed places to live, which created both opportunities and problems. The building industry was one of the great urban boom industries, and its leaders largely determined the shape and profile of the modern city. Equipped with a lofty disregard for public opinion, like other businesspeople they worked in an essentially unregulated economic world and were bent on maximizing their profits.

When it came to urban housing, money talked. In large cities from New York to San Francisco the rich built stately homes with high ceilings, European furnishings, and spacious rooms. Even the apartments of the upper classes were designed and constructed by gifted architects and artisans. The beautiful Dakota Apartments, Central Park West at

Seventy-second Street, still stands as one of the architectural triumphs of the period.

On the other hand, undermaintained tenements—built to minimal codes but designed to cram the largest number of people into the smallest amount of space—greeted urban newcomers without money. Like skyscrapers, the tenements made use of vertical space by piling family upon family into small, poorly lit, badly ventilated apartments. By 1900 portions of the Jewish Tenth Ward in New York City's Lower East Side had reached population density levels of 500,000 people per one square mile and as many as one person per square foot of land in the most crowded areas. To be in the land of tenements, noted writer William Dean Howells, "is to inhale the stenches of the neglected streets, and to catch the yet fouler and dreadfuller poverty-smell which breathes from the open doorways. . . . It is to see the work-worn look of mothers, the squalor of the babies, the haggish ugliness of the old women, and the slovenly frowziness of the young girls."

Dumbbell tenements—with a dumbbell-shaped indentation in the middle to allow better ventilation—were the most notorious examples of exploitative urban housing. Although they conformed to the Tenement Reform Law of 1879, which required all rooms to have access to light and air, they made maximum use of standard 25- by 100-foot urban lots. Although the problems inherent in the dumbbell tenement were obvious from the first, the design was not outlawed in New York until 1901. Their use, in fact, spread east to Boston and west to Cincinnati and Cleveland.

Street conditions, unlike housing, were more democratic in that they plagued rich and poor alike. People dumped trash and horses unloaded their own pollution onto dirty city thoroughfares. Spring rains turned the streets into fetid quagmires, and winter freezes left them with hard deep ruts. Well into the 1870s, pigs roamed the streets of most cities, rooting for food in the garbage and further polluting the environment. When trolleys began to replace horses as the primary form of urban transportation, editorialists predicted that air pollution would soon come to an end. As late as 1900, however, there were still 150,000 horses in New York City, each producing between 20 and 30 pounds of manure a day.

Waste not dumped onto the streets often found its way into the rivers that flowed through the major cities or into the harbors that bordered them. By the turn of the century, 13 million gallons of sewage were emptied each day into the Delaware River, the major source for Philadelphia's drinking water. Even more polluted was Pittsburgh's Golden Triangle, where

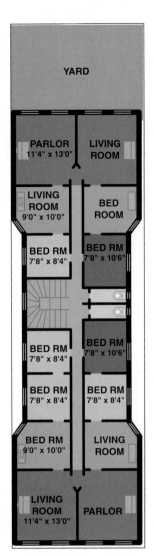

FIGURE 18.2

This 1879 dumbbell floor plan was meant to provide four apartments to a floor. However, a whole family might live in each room. Crowded, unsanitary conditions contributed to the spread of tuberculosis, the chief cause of death in the United States until 1909.

the Allegheny and Monongahela rivers meet to form the Ohio River. It could have just as aptly been dubbed the black triangle for all the industrial waste poured into it.

The establishment of dump sites did little to solve the terrible garbage problem. The Reverend Hugh Miller Thompson described the conditions in a New Orleans dump to a meeting of the American Public Health Association in 1879: "Thither were brought the dead dogs and cats, the kitchen garbage and the like, and duly dumped. This festering rotten mess was picked over by rag-pickers and wallowed over by pigs, pigs and humans contesting for a living in it, and as the heaps increased, the odors increased also, and the mass lay corrupting under a tropical sun, dispersing the pestilential fumes where the winds carried them."

The overcrowded housing, polluted streets and rivers, and uncollected garbage contributed to the

THE PEOPLE SPEAK

How the Other Half Lives

The Danish immigrant Jacob Riis began his journalistic career as a police reporter for the *New York Tribune,* where he learned to capture the colorful details of urban life and evoke emotional responses from his readers. Increasingly a social activist, Riis expanded a series of lectures, a collection of photographs, and a long article in *Scribner's Magazine* into his 1890 book *How the Other Half Lives.* This passage on New York City tenement life during the summer vividly illustrates the unfortunate combination of poverty, heat, and teeming, squalid conditions.

> With the first hot nights in June police dispatches, that record the killing of men and women by rolling off roofs and windowsills while asleep, announce that the time of greatest suffering among the poor is at hand. It is in hot weather, when life indoors is well-nigh unbearable with cooking, sleeping, and working, all crowded into the small rooms together, that the tenement expands, reckless of all restraint. Then a strange and picturesque life moves upon the flat roofs. In the day and early evening mothers air their babies there, the boys fly their kites from the housetop, undismayed by police regulations, and the young men and girls court and pass the growler. In the stifling July nights, when the big barracks are like fiery furnaces, their very walls giving out absorbed heat, men and women lie in restless, sweltering rows, panting for air and sleep. Then every truck in the street, every crowded fire escape, becomes a bedroom, infinitely preferable to any the house affords. A cooling shower on such a night is hailed as a heaven-sent blessing in a hundred thousand homes.
>
> Life in the tenements in July and August spells death to an army of little ones whom the doctor's skill is powerless to save. When the white badge of mourning flutters from every second door, sleepless mothers walk the streets in the gray of the early dawn, trying to stir a cooling breeze to fan the brow of the sick baby. There is no sadder sight than this patient devotion striving against fearfully hopeless odds. Fifty "summer doctors," especially trained for this work, are then sent into the tenements by the Board of Health, with free advice and medicine for the poor. Devoted women follow in their track with care and nursing for the sick. Fresh-air excursions run daily out of New York on land and water; but despite all efforts the gravediggers in Calvary work overtime, and little coffins are stacked mountains high on the deck of the Charity Commissioners' boat when it makes its semi-weekly trips to the city cemetery.

Source: Jacob A. Riis, *How the Other Half Lives: Studies among the Tenements of New York, 1890,* pp. 109–110 (reprinted 1970) Belknap Press. Reprinted by permission of Harvard University Press.

---

notoriously unhealthy urban environment. Unfortunately, advances in medicine and public health to cope with the consequences of such problems lagged behind technological and industrial progress. Diseases ranging from yellow fever and smallpox to diphtheria and typhoid claimed thousands of victims. In 1878 a yellow fever epidemic moved along the Mississippi River—5150 people died in Memphis, another 3977 in New Orleans. Known as the American Plague, the disease struck without warning and often led to a rapid, painful death. Walter Reed's discovery in 1900 that the disease was carried by the *Aedes aegypti* mosquito led to a cure for this dreaded scourge.

The smallpox virus proved more persistent. Although not as deadly as yellow fever, it struck more people and left millions of pockmarked faces. Like diphtheria and scarlet fever, smallpox flourished in the overcrowded and garbage-strewn cities. During the late nineteenth century, health wardens were un-successful in limiting the diseases, mostly because they were party hacks who owed their jobs to political loyalty rather than knowledge of public health.

Death, suffering, and massive inconvenience eventually prodded city officials to move toward a more systematic approach to their problems. Trained experts slowly replaced political appointees. Remarkable progress came in the 1880s with the development of the germ theory, which linked contagious disease to environmental conditions.

Health officials and urban engineers vigorously attacked the sewage and water problems. Discussing the importance of a good sewer system, one Baltimore engineer noted in 1907 that Paris is "the center of all that is best in art, literature, science, and architecture, and is both clean and beautiful. In the evolution of this ideal attainment, its sewers took at least a leading part." Without good sewers and clean drinking water, urban civilization was almost a contradiction of terms. Cities replaced cesspools and backyard privies with modern sewer systems, and most large cities turned to filtration and chlorination to assure a supply of pure water.

From Private City to Public City

In the areas of housing, pure water, and clean streets, the battle lines in most cities were drawn between individual profits and public need. Individual entrepreneurs had shaped the modern American city. They laid the horsecar and trolley lines; constructed the skyscrapers, apartments, and tenements; and provided water for the growing urban population. They worked, planned, and invested, fully expecting to earn huge profits. Because their pocketbooks came before their civic responsibilities, they provided good housing and services for only those city dwellers who could pay for it.

Historians have called this type of city the "private city." Using the profit motive to determine urban growth created numerous problems. It led to waste and inefficiency, for example competing trolley lines, where promoters could turn a profit; and such inconveniences as poorly cleaned streets, from which little money was to be made. But most important, it was contrary to **planned urban growth.** Urban entrepreneurs, generally unconcerned about the city as a whole, regarded parks as uneconomic use of real estate and battled against the idea of zoning. In the end, they contributed to the ugliness and problems of Pittsburgh, New York, Chicago, and other American cities.

By the turn of the century, however, urban engineers and other experts began calling for planned urban growth and more concern for city services. Advocates of the "public city," their aim was efficient, clean, healthy cities where rich and poor could enjoy a decent standard of life. Most urban planning advocates were college-educated professionals who brought knowledge, administrative expertise, and a taste for bureaucracy to government service. After 1900 they would increasingly dominate the quest for better services and more public responsibility, but in many cities their voices were heard too late. The scars of the private city remained on the urban landscape.

CITY CULTURE

It was almost like magic. At 3:00 P.M. on September 4, 1882, Thomas Edison's chief electrician threw the switch at the inventor's Pearl Street station in New York City. Four hundred electric lights went on. For the first time Wall Street buildings were illuminated by the brightest and clearest of all artificial lighting. "It was not until 7 o'clock, when it began to be dark that the electric light made itself known and showed how bright and steady it was," commented a *New York Times* reporter. In the *Times* offices, where 52 Edison lights illuminated the night, "it seemed almost like writing by daylight." Just as trolleys spelled the end for the horsecar, electric lights eventually replaced gaslights, candles, and kerosene and oil lamps.

Night Life and Day Life

Electricity soon bathed America's leading cities in white light, making night day. In the rural regions life revolved around the sun. Farmers awoke with the sun, labored during the daylight hours, and went to sleep soon after the sun disappeared over the horizon. Although one's labor changed depending on the season, the order of one's day was changeless. In cities and industries, however, night became more than just a time to rest. Labor and leisure soon claimed their share of the night.

Nighttime labor proved a plague for the working class, but nighttime leisure animated the lives of the wealthy. For Broadway's "fast set," the real fun began after the theaters closed. They moved down the Great White Way, stopping at an exclusive restaurant for a late-night dinner, dining on shrimp Mornay, beef marguery, canape of crab meat, bisque de crème, and other such exotic dishes. Lorenzo Delmonico, the Swiss immigrant who founded New York's most famous restaurant, popularized ices and green vegetables and made meals that rivaled the best in Paris. Eating became a refined pleasure, not just a physical necessity.

Not only did city dwellers consume different types of food, the middle and upper classes consumed more of everything. This shift in consumption patterns signaled a break with the past. The traditional Victorian ethos emphasized production and values—thrift, self-control, delayed gratification, and hard work—that encouraged production. But with industrial success came a general fear of overproduction. Increasingly, advertisers and economic advisors in various ways attempted to transform Americans from "savers" to "spenders." They told people to abandon the traditional laissez-faire economic thinking (which viewed scarcity as an inevitable and fundamental fact of life) and to give in to their desire for luxury.

This new attitude was fostered in large American cities by department stores and hotels. John Wanamaker in Philadelphia, Marshall Field in Chicago, and Rowland H. Macy in New York opened department stores that catered to and pampered the middle and upper classes by offering an unequaled range of products and quality service. The architecture and interior decoration of the department stores, with their grand entrances, marble staircases, chandeliers, stained glass, plush carpets, and wood paneling, inspired extravagance. Spending came easily when the shopper was made to feel like royalty. Grand hotels like the Waldorf Astoria in New York and the Palmer House in Chicago provided the same luxury. The austerity doctrines of the early nineteenth century were easily forgotten amidst such splendor.

It is difficult to imagine the impression electric lights, fruit salads, department stores, and grand hotels made on the people who lived in or visited American cities. They underscored a style of life clearly different from what existed in rural America. City life presented a strange new world that produced in American writers, painters, and musicians feelings of excitement and revulsion. This ambivalence formed the basis of a new urban culture, which combined the energies and experiences of all city people—black and white, male and female, immigrant and native-born.

From the Genteel Tradition to Realism and Naturalism

Frank Norris was born in Chicago, grew up in San Francisco, and lived for a time in Paris. Restlessly moving about the world looking for action, he traveled to Cuba to report on the Spanish-American War, and to South Africa to chronicle the Boer War. In his journalism and novels, he told the truth, feeding his readers bloody slices of the real world. He battled "false views of life, false characters, false sentiments, false morality, false history, false philosophy, false emotions, false heroism." Shortly before he died at 32 of appendicitis in 1902, he boasted, "I never truckled. I never took off the hat to fashion and held it out for pennies. I told them the truth. They liked it or they didn't like it. What had that to do with me? I told them the truth."

The truth. How literature had changed from the previous generation! At the end of the Civil War, American literary tradition had little to do with harsh truth. Controlled by a literary aristocracy in Boston, literature conformed to the "genteel tradition." Great writers endeavored to reinforce morality, not portray reality. Real life was too sordid, corrupt, and mean; far too coarse, violent, and vulgar. James Russell Lowell spoke for other genteel writers when he commented that no man should describe any activity that would make his wife or daughter blush. Sex, violence, and passion were taboo.

Samuel Langhorne Clemens, better known as Mark Twain, wrote humorous and insightful novels about problems in nineteenth-century America.

Out of rural America came the first challenge to this genteel tradition. Local colorists like Bret Harte, who set his stories in the rough mining camps of the West, emphasized regional differences and used regional dialects to capture the flavor of rural America. Local colorists emphasized, however, humor and innocence, rather than pressing social issues.

Mark Twain, whose real name was **Samuel Langhorne Clemens,** was the only one to transcend the genre. Like a local colorist, he used regional dialects, humor, and sentimentality, but he also explored the darker impulses of human nature. His classic, *The Adventures of Huckleberry Finn* (1884), exposed the greed, violence, corruption, alcoholism, and racism in American society. As Huck and runaway slave Jim travel down the Mississippi River toward freedom, they encounter a society based on a perversion of Christian ethics. Nowhere is Twain more insightful than when he deals with American racism. In one scene, Huck invents a story about a riverboat explosion. A woman asks if anyone was injured. "No'm," Huck responds. "Killed a nigger." Relieved, she replies, "Well, it's lucky; because sometimes people do get hurt."

The impact of industrialism and city life on the American character did not much interest Twain. It did, however, fascinate most of the other great writers of his generation. Equipped with camera eyes and critical minds, they wanted to show American life in all its harsh and sordid reality. The realism movement soon replaced the genteel sentimentality of the previous generation. Defined by its leader William Dean Howells as "the truthful treatment of material," realism depicted average individuals dealing with concrete ethical choices in realistic circumstances. Even style became secondary. "Who cares for a fine style," Norris wrote in 1899. "Tell your yarn and let your style go to the devil. We don't want literature, we want life."

As realism matured in the largely unregulated and highly competitive cities, it turned into the more pessimistic **naturalism,** which was influenced by the writings of Charles Darwin, Karl Marx, and Sigmund Freud. The individual was seen as a helpless victim in a world in which biological, social, and psychological forces determined his or her fate. Naturalists were particularly interested in the effect of the uncaring forces of industrialization and urbanization on people's lives.

Describing the Urban Jungle

The premier naturalistic writer was **Theodore Dreiser.** Unlike most earlier American novelists, he was not Protestant, Anglo-Saxon, or respectable middle-class. His German-Catholic immigrant father's life was the flip side of the American success story. After a promising beginning, the family slid deeper and deeper into poverty. Dreiser knew what it was like to subsist on potatoes and fried mush, and all his life he dreaded winter, which reminded him of his most painful days of poverty. Sympathetic to those who suffered similarly, he wrote, "Any form of distress—a wretched, down-at-heels neighborhood, a poor farm, an asylum, a jail, or an individual or group of individuals anywhere that seemed to be lacking in the means of subsistence or to be devoid of the normal comforts of life—was sufficient to set up in me thoughts and emotions, which had a close kinship to actual and severe physical pain."

Dreiser left his home in Indiana at 16 and went to Chicago, where he became first a journalist and then a novelist. Unlike better-educated writers, Dreiser had no genteel tradition to shed or rebel against. With his plodding style and atrocious English, Dreiser lacked every writing tool except genius. His first novel, *Sister Carrie* (1900), unflinchingly describes the effect of modern urban society on the lives of one woman and one man. Carrie travels to Chicago from the countryside in search of happiness, which she equates with material possessions, but she discovers only poverty, exploitation, and hardship. The likable, friendly Carrie sinks ever deeper into physical and moral despair.

Like Dreiser, Stephen Crane was also interested in the effects of poverty and urban life on individual character. In his first novel, *Maggie: A Girl of the Streets* (1893), a girl raised in a New York City slum loses, in rapid order, her innocence, her virginity, and her life. It was not a story of a character being rewarded or punished—Maggie was an honest, cheerful person—but rather being a victim of her environment. Poverty determined Maggie's, and later Carrie's, fate.

Naturalistic writers challenged the traditional idea that individuals had the power to control their own destinies. The cherished frontier ideal of rugged individualism seemed poor protection against the forces of urban poverty and industrial exploitation. Carrie was no match for the sweatshop owner, and Maggie's innocence was merely a target in her environment. Neither book was a blueprint for reform, but they did suggest a pressing need for change.

Painting Urban Reality

Unlike Europe, America did not have proud literary, artistic, or musical traditions—no Parthenon, no Rembrandt, no Beethoven. America's asset was land, thousands of square miles of wild land. "American scenery," wrote the artist Thomas Cole, "has features, and glorious ones, unknown to Europe. The most distinctive, and perhaps the most impressive, characteristic of American scenery is its wildness."

American artists shared with American writers and social critics a general aesthetic and philosophical dislike of the city. As Americans moved west, artists continued to focus on the landscape. Albert Bierstadt exaggerated the drama of the Rocky Mountains, but his pictures thrilled eastern and western Americans alike. Even the great, late-nineteenth-century realists—Winslow Homer, Thomas Eakins, and John LaFarge—harbored a suspicion, if not an outright fear, of the city. To be sure, Eakins's work demonstrated a profound respect for the machine, but his admiration did not extend to the city.

By the end of the century, however, the varied urban landscape began to intrigue artists. Steel bridges; colorful immigrant costumes; smoke-filled, congested streets; clashing boxers; washed clothes hanging between tenements; pigeons soaring over flat apartment roofs—each demonstrated the every-day beauty of the city. The energy, conflict, and power of the city seemed to explode with artistic possibilities. When a critic noted that the fighters' faces in George Bellows's *Stag at Starkey's* were hidden, Bellows replied, "Who cares what a prize fighter looks like. It's his muscles that count."

Appropriately enough, the center of this new movement was New York City. The leader of what came to be called the **Ashcan School,** because of its focus on the seamy side of urban living, was **Robert Henri,** an artistic and political radical. Skyscrapers thrilled him, and he saw beauty in the most squalid slum. He was joined by other artists who shared his love of city life and political radicalism. Generally impressionistic in style, the paintings used unmixed primary colors and quick brush strokes to produce a general impression of a scene. But they were more concerned with content than technique. As George Luks sneered at a critic, "Technique, did you say? My slats! Say, listen, you—it's in you or it isn't. Who taught Shakespeare technique? Guts! Guts! Life! Life! That's my technique."

Like Theodore Dreiser, who admired the Ashcan School, Henri and his followers used their talent to show problems in the growing cities. Bellows's *Cliff Dwellers* portrayed teeming life but also overcrowded tenement conditions; *Steaming Streets* underscored the problems of urban traffic. And George Luks's *Hester Street* illuminated the excitement but also the packed conditions of the Jewish section of Lower New York.

Maturing along with the Ashcan painters was a second school of artists who also drew inspiration from the urban landscape. Labeled modernists, they championed the pure freedom of nonrepresentational abstract painting. Their intellectual leader was Alfred Stieglitz, whose studio at 291 Fifth Avenue in New York was used to exhibit the modernist paintings. The modernists were also drawn to the conflict and power of the city. Painter John Marin observed, "I see great forces at work, great movements, the large buildings and the small buildings, the warring of the great and the small. . . . I can hear the sound of their strife, and there is great music being played."

In 1913 the Ashcanners and the modernists participated in the most important art exhibition in

John Sloan's *Sunday, Women Drying Their Hair,* 1912, is an urban portrait typical of the Ashcan School. The school got its name because the artists preferred to paint the unglamorous, everday aspects of city life.

American history. Held at the Sixty-ninth Regiment Armory in New York City, the show also included works by Cézanne, Van Gogh, Picasso, Marcel Duchamp, Georges Braque, and Juan Gris, the leaders of the European postimpressionists. The Armory Show drew some sharp criticism; Duchamp's cubist *Nude Descending a Staircase,* for example, was called "an explosion in a shingle factory." Other critics and collectors maintained that the exhibition marked a new age for American art. "The members of this association have shown you that American artists—young American artists, that is—do not dread . . . the ideas or the culture of Europe," noted leading collector John Quinn. "This exhibition will be epoch-making." Its most important result was to fuse European and American art movements. It further signaled the ascendancy of the modernists, who would dominate the next generation of American art.

The Sounds of the City

Before the nineteenth century, music critics regarded American music as decidely inferior to European music; America had produced no great classical composers in the European tradition. Modern American music, uninfluenced by those traditions, was from the very first the language of the oppressed. American blacks adapted the rhythms and melodies of Africa to meet American conditions. Out of the marriage came the work songs of Mississippi slaves, the street cries of Charleston fish and fruit vendors, and spirituals, deeply emotional religious songs. Unlike European music, which was based on a 12-note scale, African music centered on rhythmic complexity with notes that did not conform to the standard scale. Repetition, call and response, and strong beat became the hallmarks of African American music.

The two music traditions, African and European, existed independently in the United States until the 1890s. But when Jim Crow laws legally and forcefully separated the races in New Orleans, it had unexpected results for American music. Before the 1890s wealthy half-white, half-black Creoles who followed European musical traditions lived in the affluent downtown section of New Orleans. Segregation, however, forced them uptown, where the poorer blacks who followed African musical traditions lived. Although the two groups did not mix socially, they did forge a new musical style—**jazz.**

This musical form, based on improvisation within a structured band format, used both the African and European traditions. Such early New Orleans jazz bands as Buddy Bolden's Classic Jazz Band and Joe "King" Oliver's Creole Jazz Band pioneered the style. Bolden had grown up in the uptown region, where Baptist churches stood next to voodoo parlors and music provided the background for prayer, work, and play. His powerful, moody musical grace mesmerized audiences. But his music came from the soul of a troubled man. Plagued by syphilis and alcoholism, in 1907 he went berserk during a street parade and spent the rest of his life in a mental hospital.

In **Storyville,** the New Orleans red-light district, the jazz musicians, freed from manual labor during the day, honed their musical skills and explored the possibilities of their instruments. Charlie "Sweet Lovin'" Galloway, Ferdinand "Jelly Roll" Morton, Robert "Baby" Dodds, Bunk Johnson, Sidney Bechet, Alphonse Picou, and especially Louis Armstrong, entertained Storyville customers.

Storyville became a mecca for jazz musicians and a hotbed of raucous city culture. Alphonse Picou recalled the days before Storyville was officially closed with fond nostalgia: "Those were happy days, man, happy days. Buy a keg of beer for one dollar and a bag of food for another. . . . Talking 'bout wild and wooly! There were two thousand registered girls and must have been ten thousand unregistered. And all crazy about clarinet blowers."

Ragtime and the blues also flourished in Storyville. Tony Jackson, Scott Joplin, and Jelly Roll Morton played ragtime, a syncopated piano style that needed only one performer and was as popular as café and bordello entertainment. Joplin, a Texas-born African American who had formal musical training, wrote several scores of popular rags, and his "Maple Leaf Rag" (1899) probably sold a million copies in sheet music form. Morton also advanced ragtime, developing the piano swing beat. Blues musicians—mostly African Americans from the Mississippi delta region raised outside of European music traditions—performed in cheap saloons and expressed the pain of life in a hostile world.

During World War I, government officials closed Storyville, charging it was a health hazard. As the houses of prostitution closed their doors, the talented black musicians headed north—to St. Louis, Chicago, Memphis, Kansas City, and New York. They continued to play jazz and it continued to evolve. White musicians, trained in the European tradition, also contributed to this new American musical form. Bix Beiderbecke from Davenport, Iowa, for example, who formed a Chicago-based jazz band, used more instruments, replaced the African banjo with the guitar, and moved away from improvisation.

The larger jazz bands that dominated music during the next generation were an outgrowth of the New Orleans sound, the result of the mixture of European and African musical traditions. It could only have happened in the fertile atmosphere of the cities, where old and new, black and white, immigrant and native-born combined to create new literary, artistic, and musical forms.

Jazz combined European and African musical styles into a new musical form. Here King Oliver's Creole Jazz Band poses for a rare picture.

Entertaining the Multitudes

City sports, like city music, were loud and raucous. They moved to the beat of the trolley cars, steel wheels on steel tracks, not horses' hooves on dusty farm roads. Before the urbanization of the late nineteenth century, American sports and games tended to be informal and participant-oriented. Rules varied from region to region, and few people even considered the standardization of rules desirable. By 1900 this cozy informality had all but disappeared. Entertainment became a major industry, and specialized performers competed for the right to entertain the multitudes.

The emergence of commercialized entertainment was the result of changes in both American technology and values. Transportation improvements allowed professional entertainers and sports teams to move across America more easily and cheaply, and technological advances in the popular press, telegraph, and telephone allowed the results of games and entertainment news to quickly spread throughout the country. Also the Victorian notion that entertainment was somehow suspect began to decline. Drawing on Puritan criticisms of play and recreation and a Republican ideology that was hostile to luxury, hedonism, and extravagance, the Victorians had tended to associate theaters, dance halls, circuses, and organized sports with such vices as gambling, swearing, drinking, and immoral sexual behavior. Popular entertainments were judged guilty by association.

In the second half of the nineteenth century, however, these prejudices were challenged. Members of the Victorian counterculture revered play, gratification, and revelry more than the virtues of hard work, punctuality, delayed gratification, and self-control. At first, members of the counterculture tended to be immigrants and bachelors. Irish, German, and eastern and southern European immigrants brought with them a culture at odds with Victorian notions of work and play. In addition, immigrants tended to marry later than native-born Americans; even at midcentury 40 percent of men between the ages of 25 and 35 were unmarried. These men thus formed a "bachelor subculture" that revolved around saloons, gambling halls, racetracks, boxing rings, billiard rooms, and cockpits. As the Victorian economic and social order began to crumble toward the end of the century, upper-class and then middle-class Americans became interested in the activities of the bachelor subculture. The result: a new attitude toward sports and leisure.

Of Fields and Cities

"Baseball," wrote Mark Twain, "is the very symbol, the outward and visible expression of the drive and push and struggle of the raging, tearing, booming nineteenth century." Baseball captured the bustle and hustle of city life. More than any other sport of the period, baseball was an urban game. All of the early professional teams were located in cities and most of the paid players were products of the cities.

The mythology of the sport, however, still lingers—that Abner Doubleday "invented" baseball in 1839, when he laid out the first baseball diamond in the pastoral village of Cooperstown, New York. In fact, however, if anyone can be said to have invented a sport that actually evolved, it was Alexander J. Cartwright, Jr., a New York City stationery-bookstore owner who in 1845 set down the first written rules for the game.

The symbols of the game also recalled America's rural past. Unlike most modern sports, no clock governed the pace of a baseball game. In crowded, dirty cities, baseball was played on open, grassy fields with such bucolic names as Sportsman Park, Ebbets Field, and the Polo Grounds. (Yankee Stadium, opened in 1923, was the first baseball enclosure to veer from the rural tradition.) The field even had fences and bullpens, and the game was played during the planting and harvesting seasons of spring, summer, and fall.

If the symbols and mythology of baseball were rural, the game itself was very urban. Team managers, like their industrialist counterparts, preached the values of hard work, punctuality, thrift, sobriety, and self-control to their players. Baseball, they emphasized, was like modern life, ruthlessly competitive and demanding sacrifice for the "good of the team." As Mr. Clayton, a character in an 1891 baseball novel, explained, "We can't work and we can't play, we can't learn and we can't make money without getting some of other people's help." Like modern corporate society, then, modern sports reinforced the idea of teamwork.

During the last third of the nineteenth century, as men like Rockefeller and Carnegie struggled to bring order to their industrial empires, modern baseball took form. Rules were standardized, for one thing. In the early years of baseball, a base runner could be thrown out by hitting him with the ball as he ran between the bases. Organizers outlawed such violent relics of the past. Then owners attempted to make the sport suitable for the urban middle class. They banned the spitball, arranged games to fit the urban professionals' schedules, fined players for using profanity, and encouraged women to attend the games.

Most important, the owners formed competitive professional leagues centered in the industrial cities of America. In 1869 Harry Wright took his all-professional **Cincinnati Red Stockings** on a barnstorming tour. Traveling on the recently completed transcontinental railroad, they played teams from New York City to San Francisco and compiled a record of 57 wins, no losses, and 1 tie. In one year the team traveled 11,877 miles by rail, stage, and boat, and entertained more than 200,000 spectators.

The Cincinnati club taught the rest of America, as one journalist commented, that "steady, temperate habits and constant training are all conditions precedent to all first class professional organizations." It also demonstrated to entrepreneurs that there was money to be made in professional sports. In 1876 William A. Hulbert and several associates formed the National League, which was organized around owners and clubs, not players. In business terms, the league was a loosely organized cartel designed to eliminate competition among franchises for players. League officials eventually devised the "reserve clause," which effectively bound a player to the team that held the rights to him and further undermined his ability to negotiate for higher salary. Although the National League was known as a "rich man's" league because it charged a 50-cent admission price, it was certainly not a rich player's league.

In 1890 the players revolted and formed the Players' League. Headed by lawyer and star player John Montgomery Ward, the Players' League was an experiment in workers' control of an industry. In words similar to those used by workers in industry, the players' "manifesto" of 1889 claimed, "There was a time when the [National] League stood for integrity and fair dealing. Today it stands for dollars and cents. . . . Players have been bought, sold, and exchanged, as though they were sheep, instead of American citizens . . ." Although lofty in ideals, the Players' League was badly managed and lasted only one year.

With its failure, the National League increased its control over professional baseball. It either crushed rival leagues or absorbed them. In 1903, for example, after a short business war the National League entered into a partnership with the American League. The only losers were the players, whose salaries decreased with the absence of competition. Nevertheless, the sport's popularity soared. By 1909, when President William Howard Taft established the practice of the president opening each season by throwing out the first ball, baseball had become the national pastime.

"I Can Lick Any Sonofabitch in the House"

Only boxing rivaled baseball in popularity during the late nineteenth century. Like baseball, boxing began as a largely unstructured sport, but by 1900 entrepreneurs had reorganized the activity into a profitable business. Although it remained illegal in most parts of America, it produced some of the first national sports heroes.

Bare-knuckle boxing, the forerunner of modern boxing, was a brutal, bloody sport. Two men fought bare-fisted until one could not continue. A round lasted until one of the men knocked or threw down his opponent. At that point both men rested for 30 seconds and then started to fight again. Fights could and often did last over 100 rounds and as long as 7 or 8 hours. After such a fight it took months for the fighters to recover.

Boxers, unlike baseball players, were often from poor immigrant families. Irish-Americans dominated the sport during the late nineteenth century, and they used boxing as a means of social mobility. Such men as John Morrissey, James C. Heenan, and John L. Sullivan became national legends during the period. Morrissey, for instance, was born in Ireland, lived in poverty in Troy, New York, gained fame as a prizefighter, and eventually became a leading New York gambler and politician. By the time he died, he had served two terms in Congress and made a fortune.

The Great John L. (**John L. Sullivan**), however, eclipsed Morrissey in popularity. He became the best-known American athlete of the nineteenth century. "Excepting General Grant," one newspaperman wrote, "no American has received such ovations as Sullivan." Born in Boston of Irish immigrant parents, Sullivan was a loud, boastful man who loved to fight. He often walked into a saloon and claimed he could outfight and outdrink "any sonofabitch in the house." After he won the bare-knuckle world heavyweight title in 1882, tales of his punching power and his unrestrained attacks on Victorian morality spread across the country.

During the 1880s, Sullivan watched his sport move toward greater respectability. Boxing, like baseball, underwent a series of reforms. The traditional challenge system of arranging fights was replaced by modern promotional techniques pioneered by New Orleans athletic clubs. Fighters deserted bare-fisted combat and started wearing gloves. Most important of all, professional boxers adopted the **Marquis of Queensberry Rules,** which standardized a round at three minutes, allowed a one-minute rest period between rounds, and outlawed all wrestling throws and

College Football Wars

Although the year was 1905, the story is hauntingly familiar: colleges, football, corruption. Henry Beach Needham in an article in *McClure's* charged that college football had become a professional endeavor, that players were paid performers who cared little for their studies. One example was James J. Hogan, Yale's team captain and star player who knew how to make the most out of an "amateur" sport. At the age of 27, he agreed to play football for Yale. In return, Yale paid his tuition, gave him a $100-a-year scholarship, housed him in rooms at its most luxurious dormitory, and fed him at the University Club. In addition, Hogan and two other players received all the profits from the sale of game programs; Hogan was also appointed the American Tobacco Company's agent in New Haven and received a commission on every package of cigarettes sold in the area. Finally, after each season—but during the school term—Hogan was given a ten-day vacation trip to Cuba.

Hogan was by no means unique. In an age of unregulated football competition, it was each school for itself, each player for himself. Money talked and school spirit was for the students in the stands. Players were more mercenaries than students; their loyalty was constantly on the auction block. Andrew Smith demonstrated this principle in 1902. On October 4, Smith played an exceptional game for Pennsylvania State University against a powerhouse Penn team. The next

Monday he had transferred schools and was practicing with Penn, a college that had also "drafted" players from Middlebury, Colorado College, Lafayette, and Peddie. Lafayette College had little cause for complaint. Fielding H. Yost, who coached the University of Michigan for three decades, was an undergraduate at West Virginia at that time. During one season, an undefeated Lafayette "hired" Yost to play against the also unbeaten Penn. After the game, Yost "transferred" back to West Virginia.

Critics charged that football was undermining the very ethics that college professors were laboring to instill into students. As early as 1893, E. L. Godkin, editor of the influential *The Nation*, noted that the leading colleges were losing their educational orientation and becoming "huge training grounds for young gladiators, around whom as many spectators roar as roared in the Flavian amphitheatre." More than a decade later, Charles W. Eliot, president of Harvard, complained bitterly that each fall undergraduates at his university seemed totally obsessed by football, talking about or thinking about little else. Godkin and Eliot found an unlikely kindred spirit in John S. Mosby, who had led the Confederate Mosby's Raiders during the Civil War. Although he had been suspended from the University of Virginia in 1853 for shooting a fellow student, Mosby continued to think of the school as his alma mater. In 1909 the old Raider wrote, after a tragic accident there, "I do not think football should be tolerated where the youth of the country are supposed to be taught literature, science and humanity. The game seems to overshadow everything else at the University."

By the turn of the century, the number of athletes killed or injured in football games had reached an alarming level. In 1909 Virginia halfback Archer Christian died shortly after being injured in a game against Georgetown. Mosby asked, "I believe that cock-fighting is unlawful in Virginia: Why should better care be taken of a game chicken than a school boy?"

Other critics pondered the same question—during the 1909 season 30 boys were killed and 216 seriously injured in football games. The most publicized death of that season was Army's captain Eugene Byrne. He was fatally injured in a game against Harvard. The event was so shocking that the game was immediately halted, and the Army-Navy game of that year was canceled. Byrne was buried with full military honors, while thousands mourned his senseless death and questioned the place of college football in American society.

The nature of football emphasized brutality and violence. Today the team with the ball has four plays to make a 10-yard first down, but during the late-nineteenth and early-twentieth centuries the offensive team had three plays to make a 5-yard first down, and passing was severely restricted, both by the rules and by tradition. As a result, coaches emphasized "mass plays" that directed the maximum amount of force against one isolated player or point on the field. The flying wedge was the most notorious mass play. It entailed players grouping themselves in a V formation and starting to run before the ball was put into play. At the last moment the ball was snapped and passed to a player within the wall of the wedge. The wedge of runners then crashed into

their stationary opponents. Given that equipment was crude—players often played without helmets and no helmet had a facemask—this use of a massed brute force injured hundreds of players each year.

If such plays were not bad enough, referees rarely enforced rules against slugging, kicking, and piling on. Victory was the supreme object; and any method seemed justified in the pursuit of that goal. One Princeton player confessed to a reporter that he and his teammates were coached to eliminate dangerous opponents during the early minutes of a game. A writer for *The Nation* believed this ruthless drive for victory illustrated a fundamental American characteristic: "The spirit of the American youth, as of the American man, is to win, 'to get there,' by fair means or foul; and the lack of moral scruple which pervades the struggles of the business world meets with temptations equally irresistible in the miniature contests of the football field."

By the end of the particularly brutal 1905 season many educators, journalists, and politicians had decided that college football served no educational good and did considerable harm. Professor Shailer Mathews of Chicago's Divinity School labeled football "a social obsession—a boy-killing, education-prostituting, gladiatorial sport." President Theodore Roosevelt stepped in and tried to clean up the game, and officials altered the rules of the sport, but a number of universities chose to drop football from their athletic programs. Columbia, Union, Northwestern, Stanford, and the University of California led the abolitionist movement.

Critics continued to level charges of brutality, commercialism, and corruption against football between 1905 and 1910. The 1905 rules had not lessened the violence, and deaths continued to shock concerned Americans. In 1910 the rules of football were once again altered. In the most important change, the forward pass as we know

it today was legalized. Although football conservatives continued for several years to ignore the new offensive weapon, the pass came into its own in 1913. That year a highly regarded Army team filled an open date in its schedule with a small Indiana school called Notre Dame. During the game Notre Dame quarterback Charley Dorais threw perfectly timed passes to his favorite end Knute Rockne. The result was a 35–13 upset by the Irish of Notre Dame. By the end of the season other teams had adopted the new tactic and passes filled the autumn air. The age of the mass play was over.

Passing made football even more exciting, and after 1913 criticism of the sport generated little support. Continuing scandals over brutality, commercialism, and corruption led more to attacks on individual schools than against football as a college sport. Indeed, by 1917 football reigned unrivaled as college's supreme sport and public spectacle.

holds. The new rules also replaced the fight to the finish with a fight to a decision over a specified number of rounds. Although the new rules did not reduce the violence, they did provide for more orderly bouts.

With the advent of the Queensberry Rules, the factory system effectively invaded boxing. Just as workers lost control of the pace of work, fighters no longer could determine the pace of the action. Under the old rules prizefighters could tacitly agree to slow down the action in order to catch their breath or simply exchange boasts and oaths. Now a bell and a referee told them when to fight and when to rest.

John L. Sullivan won the last bare-knuckle championship contest. In 1889 he defeated Jake Kilrain in a fight held near Richburg, Mississippi. It was an illegal fight, but it attracted spectators from all social classes. Bat Masterson, the gunfighter and gambler, served as timekeeper, and he was joined at ringside by wealthy sons of southern aristocrats, gamblers, and sporting men of every variety. The fight lasted for 75 rounds, and both boxers drank whiskey between rounds. After winning the epic fight, Sullivan gained even greater fame.

In 1892 Sullivan lost the title to **James J. Corbett** in a legal gloved contest fought in New Orleans. Nicknamed "Gentleman Jim," Corbett's scientific boxing style and smooth manners outside the ring demonstrated that boxing had gained some respectability. In fact, by the 1890s boxing was no longer a working-class sport. Like baseball, it had become an organized, structured, and profitable business. All that was left of the older sport was the legend of the Great John L.—the boisterous, crude, lovable, man-child. As he told future novelist Theodore Dreiser shortly after the Corbett fight: "I'm ex-champion of the world, defeated by that little dude from California, but I'm still John L. Sullivan—ain't that right. Haw! Haw! They can't take that away from me, can they? Haw! Haw! Have some more champagne, boy."

The Excluded Americans

Although promoters talked about the democratic nature of sports, this was far from the case. To be sure, a number of Irish and German men—often immigrants or sons of immigrants—prospered in professional sports, but far more Americans were excluded from the world of sports.

In large cities the lines between social classes tended to blur, much to the discomfort of the wealthy who struggled to separate themselves from the hoi polloi. The rich moved to the suburbs and employed other methods of residential segregation to isolate themselves. Another tactic to protect their exclusive status was to allow their children only to marry within their narrow group of acquaintances. They also used sports and athletic clubs to set themselves apart. "Gentlemen and ladies," as they styled themselves, they only wanted to compete against opponents of similar dress, speech, education, and wealth.

One way to exclude the masses was to engage in sports that only the very rich could play. Yachting and polo, for example, demanded nearly unlimited free time, expensive equipment, and a retinue of hired helpers.

In 1884 the New York Yacht Club was founded, quickly gaining as members a "succession of gentlemen ranking high in the social and financial circles" in the city. By the 1890s every major eastern seaboard city had its exclusive yacht club, and each summer the richest yacht owners sailed their splendid vessels to Newport, Rhode Island, the most exclusive of the summer colonies.

Athletic clubs devoted to track and field, golf, and tennis were similarly exclusive. The members of Shinnecock Hills, one of the oldest golf clubs in America, prided themselves not only on the beauty of their course but on their social standing. Such exclusive clubs also had elaborate social calendars filled with dress balls and formal dinners. When sporting events were scheduled, participation and even the privilege of watching were normally on an invitation-only basis.

Wealthy patrons also advocated the code of amateurism to separate the greedy professionals—who often came from the poorer classes—from more prosperous athletes who participated in a sport simply for the love of the game. The constitution of the British Amateur Rowing Association, for example, included in their definition of amateur one who had never "been employed in or about boats, or in manual labour, for money or wages"; and who was not "by trade or employment for wages a mechanic, artisan or labourer, or engaged in any menial duty." The revival of the Olympic Games in 1896 strengthened the amateur code. (When it was discovered, for example, that Jim Thorpe, an Oklahoma Indian who had attended the Carlisle Indian School and who won the decathlon and the pentathlon in the 1912 Stockholm Games, had played baseball for a minor league professional team during the summer of 1909, the International Olympic Committee stripped him of his medals.)

Although **amateurism** was a subtle attack on the working class, sports leaders moved more forcefully against African Americans. During the 1870s and 1880s, blacks and whites competed against each other on a fairly regular basis. A number of blacks even rose to become world champions. Marshall W. "Major" Taylor was hailed as the "Fastest Bicycle Rider in the World"; Isaac Murphy rode to three Kentucky Derby victories; and George Dixon and other blacks won boxing titles. During the 1890s, however, most sports became segregated.

Jim Crow laws came to boxing during this period. John L. Sullivan steadfastly refused to fight African American boxers. In 1892 he issued his famous challenge to fight all contenders: "In this challenge I include all fighters—first come, first served—who are white. I will not fight a Negro. I never have and I never shall." True to his word, the Boston Strong Boy never did. The same year, lightweight champion George Dixon administered a terrible beating to white challenger Jack Skelly in New Orleans. After the fight, the editor of the *New Orleans Times-Democrat* wrote that it was "a mistake to match a negro and a white man, a mistake to bring the two races together on any terms of equality, even in the prize ring." After 1892 the number of "mixed bouts" declined rapidly.

Organized baseball also excluded African Americans during the 1890s. Several owners integrated their professional baseball teams during the 1880s, but the trend toward segregation that led to the landmark court case, *Plessy v. Ferguson* (1896), overtook baseball. In 1889 baseball's *Sporting News* announced that "race prejudice exists in professional baseball ranks to a marked degree, and the unfortunate son of Africa who makes his living as a member of a team of white professionals has a rocky road to travel." The observation was accurate. By 1892 major league baseball was all white, to remain so until Jackie Robinson broke the "color barrier" in 1946.

Cultural expectations and stereotypes also limited the development of women athletes. Scientists spoke confidently about women's "arrested evolution." Compared to men, women were considered weak and uncoordinated, athletically retarded because of their narrow sloping shoulders, broad hips, underdeveloped muscles, and short arms and legs. Women might ride a bicycle or gently swing a croquet mallet, but men ridiculed women who were interested in serious competitive athletics. The **cult of domesticity,** which idealized women as nurturers and maintained that women's proper sphere was the home, also militated against female participation in competitive sports.

Even during the 1890s, when the tall, commanding Gibson Girl was the physical ideal and women were becoming more interested in sports and exercise, women's athletics developed along different lines than men's. Male and female physical educators decided that women's sports should be noncom-petitive, promote women's physical and mental qualities, and make them more attractive to men. They also believed that sports and exercise would sublimate female sexual drives. As renowned physical educator Dudley A. Sargent noted: "No one seems to realize that there is a time in the life of a girl when it is better for her and for the community to be something of a boy rather than too much of a girl."

But tomboyish behavior had to stop short of abrasive competition. Lucille Eaton Hill, director of physical training at Wellesley College, urged women to "avoid the evils which are so apparent . . . in the conduct of athletics for men." She and other female physical educators encouraged widespread participation rather than narrow specialization. Spectator and professional sports were left to the men. It was not until 1924 that women were allowed to compete in Olympic track and field events, and even then on a limited basis.

From Central Park to Coney Island

Like sports, parks changed to satisfy new urban demands. Uneasy about the urban environment, mid-nineteenth-century park designers saw in parks an antidote for the tensions and anxieties caused by city living. **Frederick Law Olmsted,** the most famous park architect, believed cities destroyed community ties and fostered ruthless competition. He designed Central Park to serve as a rural retreat in the midst of New York City. Surrounded by trees, streams, and ponds, city dwellers would be moved toward greater sociability. "No one who has closely observed the conduct of the people who visit [Central] Park," Olmsted declared, "can doubt that it exercises a distinctly harmonizing and refining influence upon the most unfortunate and most lawless classes of the city—an influence favorable to courtesy, self-control, and temperance." But Olmsted was occasionally upset by the behavior of a "certain class" of visitors who believed "that all trees, shrubs, fruit and flowers are common property" and who refused to behave according to Olmsted's ideal.

Other leaders of Victorian culture shared Olmsted's vision. They believed that culture and leisure activities should smooth the rough edges of the urban masses. They built parks, libraries, and museums. Both the Metropolitan Museum of Art in New York and the Museum of Fine Arts in Boston opened in 1870. Visitors to these repositories of culture were expected to behave in an orderly, respectful manner. Museum officials frowned upon laughing, talking, coughing, shouting, and loud demonstrations of enthusiasm.

Many urbanites, however, wanted more excitement than the quiet world of Central Park and the new museums. This was clearly seen at the World's Columbian Exposition of 1893 in Chicago. The most popular area of the World's Fair was the Midway, the center of commercial amusements. Visitors eagerly rode the Ferris wheel, frequented the "40 Ladies from 40 Nations" exhibition, and watched "Little Egypt" perform her exotic dances. Parks and entertainment that amused, not soothed, attracted the most people.

Entrepreneurs were quick to recognize and satisfy the public's desire for entertainment. During the 1890s a series of popular amusement parks opened in Coney Island, New York. Unlike Central Park, which was constructed as a rural retreat, the Coney Island parks glorified the sense of adventure and excitement of the cities, and offered exotic, dreamland landscapes; wonderful, novel machines; and a free and loose social environment. Men could remove their coats and ties, and both sexes could enjoy a rare personal freedom. As one immigrant claimed, for the young, "privacy could be had only in public."

Coney Island also exemplified new values. If Central Park reinforced self-control, sobriety, and delayed gratification, Coney Island stressed the emerging consumer-oriented values of extravagance, gaiety, abandon, revelry, and instant gratification. It attracted working-class Americans who longed for at least a taste of the "good life." A person might never own a mansion in Newport, but for a few dimes he could experience the exotic pleasures of Luna Park or Dreamland Park.

Even the rides in the amusement parks were designed to create illusions and break down reality. Mirrors distorted people's images, and rides threw them off balance. At Luna Park, the Witching Waves simulated the bobbing of a ship in high seas, and the Tickler featured spinning circular cars that threw riders together. "Such rides," wrote a student of Coney Island, "served in effect as powerful hallucinogens, altering visitors' perceptions and transforming their consciousness, dispelling everyday concerns in the intense sensations of the present moment. They allowed customers the exhilaration of whirlwind activity without physical exertion, of thrilling drama without imaginative effort."

The Magic of the Flickering Image

Coney Island showed workers that machines could liberate as well as enslave. The motion picture industry, in turn, offered a less expensive, more convenient escape. During the early twentieth century the **motion picture** developed into a major popular culture form, one that reflected the hopes and ambitions, fears and anxieties of an urban people.

In 1887 when Thomas Edison moved his research laboratory from Menlo Park to Orange, New Jersey, he gave **William K. L. Dickson,** one of his leading inventors, the task of developing a motion picture ap-

Coney Island provided a temporary escape from the pressures of urban life. Its sense of informality and sheer excitement attracted people of every class.

paratus. Edison envisioned a machine "that should do for the eye what the phonograph did for the ear." Working closely with Edison, Dickson developed the Edison kinetophonograph, a machine capable of showing film in synchronization with a phonograph record. The idea of talking pictures, however, was not as popular as the moving pictures themselves. Further refinements by Edison and other inventors made silent moving pictures a commercial reality.

The first movies, as the new form was soon called, presented brief vaudeville turns or glimpses of everyday life. Such titles as *Fred Ott's Sneeze, Chinese Laundry, The Gaiety Girls Dancing, Dentist Scene,* and *Highland Dance* tell the full content of each 3- or 4-minute film. Filmmakers soon began to experiment with such techniques as editing and intercutting separate "shots" to form a dramatic narrative. In 1903 Edwin S. Porter's *The Great Train Robbery,* the first western and the first film to exploit the violence of armed robbery, fully demonstrated the commercial possibilities of the movie. The 12-minute film mesmerized audiences.

During the early twentieth century, movies developed a strong following in ethnic, working-class neighborhoods. Local entrepreneurs converted stores and saloons into nickelodeons and introduced immigrants to a silent world of promise, inexpensive and short escapes from the grimmer realities of urban life. Describing the experience of visiting a nickelodeon, Abraham Cahan, editor of the *Jewish Daily Forward,* wrote in 1906: "People must be entertained and five cents is little to pay. A movie lasts half an hour. If it isn't too busy you can see it several times. They open in the afternoon and customers, mostly men and women, eat fruit and have a good time." In addition, since the movies were silent, knowledge of English was not required for enjoyment.

Ministers, politicians, and other guardians of traditional Victorian morality were quick to criticize the new form of entertainment. Their fears were summarized by Nebraska's superintendent of schools Joseph R. Fulk. Movies, he said, "engendered idleness and cultivated careless spending" at the "expense of earnest and persistent work." Worse yet, they stirred "primitive passions," encouraged "daydreaming," and fostered "too much familiarity between boys and girls." Soon local boards of censorship formed to protect innocent boys and girls, and some not so innocent men and women, from being corrupted by movies.

In the cities, censorship movements ultimately failed. Attempts by white, native-born American entrepreneurs to control the new industry similarly failed. Ironically, while films were beginning to attract middle-class audiences, control of the industry began to shift to immigrant entrepreneurs, most of whom were Jews from eastern Europe who proved better able than native-born businessmen to develop the possibilities of the medium. The immigrants emerged from a culture that valued laughter, cooperation, and entertainment, which allowed them to make movies that appealed to Americans.

They were committed to giving the people what they wanted, not to the traditional Victorian code of morality. As Samuel Goldwyn, one of the best immigrant filmmakers, observed, "If the audience don't like a picture, they have a good reason. The public is never wrong. I don't go for all this thing that when I have a failure, it is because the audience doesn't have the taste or education, or isn't sensitive enough. The public pays the money. It wants to be entertained. That's all I know." Film moguls started producing feature-length films and moved the industry from the East Coast to sunny Hollywood, where they could shoot outdoors and, incidentally, escape union difficulties. While such "stars" as Charlie Chaplin, Douglas Fairbanks, and Mary Pickford captured the hearts of America, producers such as Adolph Zukor, William Fox, Louis B. Mayer, Carl Laemmle, and Harry Warner forged a multimillion-dollar industry.

The Agony of Painless Escape

At the same time as popular culture was exploring the theme of mechanized instant gratification, however, Americans were seeking escape in other, more ominous forms. Like the whirring machines at Coney Island and the flickering images on the silent silver screen, the mindless escape of narcotics attracted millions of Americans. During the late nineteenth and early twentieth centuries, as the nation underwent the trauma of industrialization and urbanization, Americans took drugs in unprecedented amounts. Apologists blamed this development on the Civil War, claiming that soldiers became addicted to morphine after using it as a painkiller. Yet France, Germany, Great Britain, Russia, and Italy also fought wars in the second half of the nineteenth century, and their drug addiction rates were far below those of the United States.

Part of the problem was that before 1915 there were few restrictions on the importation and use of **opium,** its derivatives, and **cocaine.** Physicians routinely prescribed opiates for a wide range of ailments, and patent medicine manufacturers used morphine, laudanum, cocaine, or heroin in their concoctions. William Hammond, former surgeon general of the army, swore by cocaine and drank a glass of a cocaine drink with each meal. The Hay Fever Association officially recommended cocaine as an effective remedy. Coca-Cola used cocaine as one of its secret ingredients, and the Parke-Davis Company produced coca-leaf cigarettes, cheroots, and a Coca Cordial. Vin Mariani, a wine product containing cocaine and endorsed by Pope Leo XIII, was advertised as "a perfectly safe and reliable diffusable stimulant and tonic; a powerful aid to digestion and assimilation; admirably adapted for children, invalids, and convalescents."

By the late 1890s cocaine's harmful effects had become obvious. Journalists and government officials linked it to urban crime and racial unrest in the South. Eventually, angry citizens and the federal and state governments launched the first great American crusade against cocaine. It culminated with the Harrison Anti-Narcotic Act in 1914, which controlled the distribution of opiates and cocaine; but drug addiction remained a problem in cities well into the 1920s.

Robert Louis Stevenson's *Dr. Jekyll and Mr. Hyde,* which he wrote while under the influence of cocaine, described the dangers of challenging society's standards and altering one's personality, but in America's cities a new culture had taken shape. Advocates of this culture opposed Victorian restraints, glorified the

CHRONOLOGY OF KEY EVENTS

1869 First professional baseball team, the Cincinnati Red Stockings, begins a barnstorming tour of America

1870 The Metropolitan Museum of Art in New York and the Museum of Fine Arts in Boston open

1871 Great Chicago fire claims 300 lives, destroys 17,500 buildings, and leaves 100,000 people homeless

1873 Cable car is introduced in San Francisco

1878 Yellow fever epidemic causes 5150 deaths in Memphis and 3977 in New Orleans

1879 New York City adopts Tenement Reform Law, requiring all rooms to have access to light and air

1882 Chinese Exclusion Act suspends Chinese immigration for ten years; extended in 1892 and 1902; electric lighting comes into widespread use for the first time in New York City

1884 Mark Twain's *The Adventures of Huckleberry Finn* is published

1885 William LeBaron Jenney erects the Home Insurance Building in Chicago, the first true skyscraper

1886 Statue of Liberty is unveiled

1887 W. K. L. Dickson and Thomas Edison develop motion pictures

1888 Richmond, Virginia, introduces the electric-power trolley

1892 James J. Corbett wins heavyweight boxing title from John L. Sullivan; Stephen Crane publishes his first novel, *Maggie: A Girl of the Streets*

1896 President Cleveland vetoes literacy requirement for adult immigrants

1899 Scott Joplin composes "Maple Leaf Rag"

1900 Theodore Dreiser publishes his first novel, *Sister Carrie*

1903 Edwin S. Porter's *The Great Train Robbery* is the first American film to tell a story

1912 Jim Thorpe, an Oklahoma Indian, wins the decathlon and pentathlon at the 1912 Olympic Games in Stockholm

1913 Artists from the Ashcan and modernist schools participate in the Armory Show in New York City

1914 Harrison Anti-Narcotic Act controls the distribution of opiates and cocaine

1921 Emergency Quota Act provides that no more than 3 percent of a nationality already in America in 1910 could immigrate annually to the United States

1924 National Origins Act lowers the immigration quota to 2 percent of each nationality already residing in the United States in 1890

freedoms of urban life, and at the same time worried about the implications of a liberated lifestyle. Social, as well as economic, freedom came with a price. By the 1890s many Americans believed that some new form of regulation was needed to check the social and economic freedom unleashed in urban America.

CONCLUSION

On January 17, 1906, Marshall Field, the dry-goods merchant and founder of the large Chicago department store that bears his name, died. "The first as well as the richest citizen" in Chicago, noted the *New York Sun*, Field left his children over $140 million. Americans questioned how one man could accumulate such a fortune. "No man could earn a million dollars honestly," said politician William Jennings Bryan. Another critic suggested that Field's fortune was made at the expense of his more than 10,000 employees, 95 percent of whom earned $12 a week or less: "The female sewing-machine operators, who make the clothes which are sold in the Field establishment, get $6.75 per week. . . . The makers of socks and stockings are paid: finishers, $4.75 per week of fifty-nine working hours . . . knitters, $4.75 per week of fifty-nine and one-half working hours."

Most Americans, however, focused more on what Field offered shoppers than what he paid his employees. Marshall Field, A. T. Stewart, Rowland H. Macy, John Wanamaker—their very names conjured visions of miles and miles of consumer goods. These men brought order to shopping and emphasized standardization of products. In their department stores in New York, Chicago, and Philadelphia, customers could purchase ready-made clothes, jewelry, toys, sheet music, cutlery, and a wide range of other products. Serving urban markets and satisfying urban desires, they also provided a safe haven for urban shoppers. Inside one of the great department stores, consumers were isolated from the garbage in the streets, the filth in the air, and the sounds of traffic and commerce that dominated the outside world. They chose not to think about the workers who made the goods they purchased.

The orderly world of the department store and the chaotic one of the streets were both products of the urban entrepreneurs who fashioned the modern cities. In pursuit of profits they were capable of producing dazzling monuments to commerce and terrible tributes to greed. The same spirit that built the Woolworth Building and the Dakota Apartments also constructed dumbbell tenements, but by 1900, their days of absolute dominance were numbered.

Although they would remain a vital part of American capitalism, in the future they would be rivaled by governmental planners—people who wanted to extend the smooth, efficient order of the department store to the outside streets.

The emergence of the great cities changed American life, and more than just economically. Eventually they came to dominate the American imagination. In the cities, the clash of ideas and beliefs, of peoples and traditions created an exciting, new heterogeneous culture. The result was evident at places such as Coney Island and at the Armory Show; it was visible in many of the movies, and it was audible at a New Orleans jazz café. As the nineteenth century drew to a close, a new culture was clearly emerging. It would add a new element to the new century.

CHAPTER SUMMARY AND KEY POINTS

In this chapter you read about the changing nature of the American city. You learned about the new immigrants who arrived from eastern and southern Europe; the anti-immigrant reaction; the expansion of cities horizontally and vertically; the problems caused by urban growth; the depiction of cities in art and literature; and the changing nature of urban life, including the emergence of new forms of urban entertainment.

- Cities expanded rapidly in the late nineteenth century. Immigration and the growth of industry contributed to urban growth.

- The emergence of large cities transformed American life. Large cities produced a vibrant, heterogeneous culture. They also were the source of new social and political problems.

- Cities provided new forms of entertainment and excitement.

SUGGESTIONS FOR FURTHER READING

Lois W. Banner, *American Beauty* (1983). Charts changing standards of beauty in America.

John Bodnar, *The Transplanted: A History of Immigrants in Urban America* (1985). Rejects an older interpretation that viewed immigrants as peasants whose cultures were uprooted in the course of migration.

Roger Daniels, *Coming to America: A History of Immigration and Ethnicity in American Life* (1990). Offers a thorough history of immigrants to the United States.

Leonard Dinnerstein, *The Leo Frank Case* (1968). Case history of anti-Semitism and violence in America.

Caroline Golab, *Immigrant Destinations* (1977). Study of immigrant work in industrial America.

John F. Kasson, *Amusing the Millions: Coney Island at the Turn of the Century* (1978). Uses Coney Island to illustrate changes in American values from agrarian, to industrial, to consumption.

Lawrence W. Levine, *Highbrow/Lowbrow: The Emergence of Cultural Hierarchy in America* (1988). Demonstrates that popular culture can be fascinating without being trivialized.

Kerby A. Miller, *Emigrants and Exiles: Ireland and the Irish Exodus to North America* (1985). First-rate study of why many Irish left Ireland and how they were received in America.

Robert H. Wiebe, *The Search for Order, 1870–1920* (1967). Classic synthesis of major historical trends in turn-of-the-century America.

Novels

Kate Chopin, *The Awakening* (1899).

Stephen Crane, *Maggie: A Girl of the Streets* (1893).

Theodore Dreiser, *Sister Carrie* (1900).

Jack Finney, *Time and Again* (1970).

Eric Rolff Greenberg, *The Celebrant* (1983).

William Dean Howells, *The Hazard of New Fortunes* (1890).

Frank Norris, *McTeague* (1899).

Mark Twain, *The Gilded Age* (1873).

Edith Wharton, *The Age of Innocence* (1920).

Owen Wister, *The Virginian: A Horseman of the Plains* (1902).

MEDIA RESOURCES

Web Sites

A Short History of American Labor
http://www.unionweb.org/history.htm
This brief essay is adapted from AFL-CIO *American Federationist*, March 1981.

American Labor History
http://www.geocities.com/CollegePark/Quad/6460/AmLabHist/index.html
This site takes a general look at the history of labor in America.

Samuel Gompers Papers at the University of Maryland
http://www.inform.umd.edu/HIST/Gompers/web1.html
This site includes information about the papers project but also has a photo gallery, selected documents, and a brief history of the first president of the American Federation of Labor.

Columbian Exposition of 1893
http://xroads.virginia.edu/~MA96/WCE/title.html
This site has a virtual tour of the fair along with contemporary reactions and modern analysis.

Films and Videos

The Godfather, Part II (1974). Highlights the clash between older Italian values and newer American ones.

The Great Train Robbery (1903). One of the first great American films, it shows Americans' fascination with violence and the West.

Greed (1924). Erich von Stroheim film version of Frank Norris's *McTeague*.

Ragtime (1981). The film version of E. L. Doctorow's novel of Ragtime America.

The Shootist (1976). John Wayne's last film explores the death of the mythic West.

KEY TERMS

Birds of passage   (p. 491)

Permanent immigrants   (p. 493)

Pale of Settlement   (p. 493)

Nativism   (p. 494)

Golden door   (p. 496)

Chinese Exclusion Act   (p. 496)

Literacy testing   (p. 496)

Emergency Quota Act   (p. 497)

National Origins Act   (p. 497)

Electric trolley   (p. 498)

Skyscraper   (p. 499)

Streetcar suburbs   (p. 499)

Dumbbell tenements   (p. 501)

Planned urban growth   (p. 503)

Naturalism   (p. 505)

Ashcan School   (p. 506)

Jazz   (p. 507)

Storyville   (p. 507)

Cincinnati Red Stockings   (p. 509)

Bare-knuckle boxing   (p. 509)

Marquis of Queensbury Rules   (p. 509)

Amateurism   (p. 512)

Cult of domesticity   (p. 513)

Coney Island   (p. 514)

Motion pictures   (p. 514)

Opium and cocaine   (p. 515)

PEOPLE YOU SHOULD KNOW

Lizzie Borden   (p. 490)

David Hennessy   (p. 494)

Jacob Riis   (p. 495)

Leo Frank   (p. 495)

Frank Norris   (p. 504)

Samuel Langhorne Clemens   (p. 504)

Theodore Dreiser   (p. 505)

Robert Henri   (p. 506)

John L. Sullivan   (p. 509)

James J. Corbett   (p. 512)

Frederick Law Olmsted   (p. 513)

William K. L. Dickson   (p. 514)

REVIEW QUESTIONS

1. How did the "new immigrants" of the late nineteenth and early twentieth century differ from previous immigrants to America?

2. What was nativism? What forms did it take? Why did so many native-born Americans embrace it?

3. What problems plagued the growing American city? Why?

4. How did literature, art, and music reflect both the social tensions and possibilities of the new American cities?

5. Were new entertainment choices in sports, parks, and movies a tightening of the new industrial order, a release from it, or both?

19 End-of-the-Century Crisis

THE ELECTION OF 1896: "FREE SILVER" VS. THE GOLD STANDARD

On July 9, 1896, **William Jennings Bryan** rose to speak to the delegates at the Democratic National Convention in Chicago. "I thought I had never seen a handsomer man," a reporter wrote, "young, tall, powerfully built, clear-eyed, with a mane of black hair which he occasionally thrust back with his hand." Thirty-six-year-old Bryan was the son of a circuit court judge who was a Baptist deacon; his mother was a devout Methodist. Bryan, elected to Congress from Nebraska in 1890, was thus steeped in both religion and politics from an early age.

As the cry for **free silver** swept the rural areas of the West and South, Bryan took up the cause. "I don't know anything about free silver," he admitted. "The people of Nebraska are for free silver and I am for free silver. I will look up the arguments later." In the 1890s the slogan referred to expanding the amount of money in circulation by coining more silver dollars. Farmers believed that such inflation of the currency would raise crop prices and alleviate their heavy debt burdens. Many rural residents felt the national government had not been responsive to their needs—that both political parties had been captured by industrialists, railroad owners, and bankers. In 1896 silver was a symbol for popular grievances—it represented rural values, the common people, and a growing discontent with northeastern political domination.

By the time of the Democratic convention the Republicans had nominated **William McKinley** and adopted a platform calling for the gold standard (or currency backed entirely by gold supplies in the federal treasury). The Democrats were divided between the "silverites" and the "Gold Democrats," monetary conservatives who supported President Grover Cleveland. Control of the party by Northeasterners was being challenged by southern and western delegates when Bryan finally rose to speak.

Called "the Great Commoner," Bryan voiced the frustrations of farmers with the failure of traditional politicians to meet their needs. "We have petitioned," he cried, "and our petitions have been scorned; we have entreated, and our entreaties have been disregarded; we have begged, and they have mocked when our calamity came. We beg no longer; we entreat no more; we petition no more. We defy them!"

In the 1896 election, William Jennings Bryan (above) launched a grueling campaign tour. William McKinley, on the other hand, campaigned from his own front porch in carefully orchestrated rallies, as seen in the photo (right) of his home.

He enthralled the crowd from the beginning, but his closing words created pandemonium. "We will answer the demand for a gold standard," he roared, "by saying to them: 'You shall not press down upon the brow of labor this crown of thorns, you shall not crucify mankind upon a cross of gold.'" Closing with his arms outstretched as if he were nailed to a cross, he won the Democratic nomination and cinched the victory of the party's silverites.

Cleveland supporters were unwilling to accept Bryan's "foul pit of repudiation, socialism, [and] anarchy," and one declared "I am a Democrat still—very still." Because many party regulars deserted him and nearly half the Democratic newspapers opposed him, Bryan was able to raise only the meager sum of about $500,000. Low on funds he took his campaign directly to the people, appealing to sectional and class animosities: "Probably the only passage in the Bible read by some financiers is that about the wise men of the East. They seem to think that wise men have been coming from that direction ever since."

Bryan relied on his oratorical genius and electrifying charisma rather than money. Between August and November he traveled more than 18,000 miles, visiting 27 states and giving 600 speeches. His youth

sustained him as he made his own travel arrangements, bought his own tickets, carried his own bags, rode in public cars, and walked from train stations to hotels late at night. He was often called upon to give unscheduled speeches—when one Indiana crowd awakened him, he spoke in his nightshirt.

With a Republican campaign fund of more than $3.5 million, McKinley had no need to follow Bryan's course. "I might just as well put up a trapeze in my front lawn and compete with some professional athlete as to go out speaking against Bryan," he said. Between June and November, McKinley left his home in Canton, Ohio, for only three days. Railroads provided cheap excursion rates to Canton, so every day except Sunday, crowds of up to 50,000 thronged to McKinley's lawn, from where he conducted his "front porch" campaign. The gatherings were hardly spontaneous, however. His staff organized the groups by occupation or interest, screened each delegation's remarks, and planned each event in detail, right down to brass bands and banners.

In contrast to Bryan's speeches, McKinley's were calm and dispassionate, stressing national unity rather than division. "We are all dependent on each other, no matter what our occupation may be," he declared. "All of us want good times, good wages, good markets; and then we want good money always." From his front porch he addressed some 750,000 people from 30 states. The Republicans also spent more for printing than Bryan raised for his entire campaign. By the campaign's end Republicans had sent 200 million pamphlets in several languages to 15 million voters, and some 250 paid speakers toured 27 states.

On election day Bryan and his wife rose at 6:30 A.M. and voted at a local fire station in Omaha, Nebraska. He then gave seven speeches in his hometown before collapsing, exhausted, in bed that evening. McKinley walked to his polling place and stood in line to vote. He then returned home to wait for the returns—his lawn and porch in worse shape than he was. All over the nation politicians and just plain people waited to find out which man and party would preside over the dawning of the twentieth century.

he 1896 election occurred near the end of a decade of turbulence that saw violence toward the labor movement, rising racial tensions, militancy among farmers, and discontent among the unemployed—all of which had intensified after a major depression began in 1893. The social fabric seemed to be unraveling, which is why this election was considered so important. For the first time since the 1870s voters were given a clear choice between two very different candidates and platforms.

Following Reconstruction, national politics were colorful but not very significant. No important policy differences separated the two major parties at the national level; the campaigns revolved around personalities, gimmicks, emotional slogans, and local issues. As elections were trivialized, they became a major source of entertainment, and voters turned out in record numbers. For its triumph of style over substance in politics as well as culture the era is known as the **Gilded Age,** a term taken from the title of a novel by Mark Twain and Charles Dudley Warner. By 1890 both the Democratic and Republican parties had lost touch with the sentiments of large blocks of voters—especially those in the West and South. The losers in the great national race toward economic modernization began to question its assumptions. They raised their voices in the 1890s but, unable to unite around a workable agenda, they failed to win many battles at that time. The issues they raised, however, appeared regularly on political agendas in the twentieth century.

EQUILIBRIUM AND INERTIA: THE NATIONAL POLITICAL SCENE

American politics have often seemed odd to Europeans. Never was this more true than in the closing decades of the nineteenth century. Commenting on American politics in his 1898 book, *The American Commonwealth,* Lord James Bryce wrote that "neither party has any principles, any distinctive tenets. Both have traditions. Both claim to have tendencies. Both have certainly war cries, organizations, interests enlisted in their support. But those interests are in the main interests of getting or keeping the patronage of government. . . . All has been lost, except office or the hope of it."

Patronage, or the granting of political favors and offices, became more important than issues to the two major parties for many reasons. In close elections the parties had to be careful not to alienate potential supporters. Most people also believed in limited government. Political parties were therefore organized more to win offices than to govern. The result was a failure by government to deal effectively with the enormous changes wrought by industrialization and urbanization.

Divided Power: The Parties and the Federal Government

Both the Democratic and Republican parties emerged from Reconstruction with sizable and stable constituencies. For the 20 years between 1876 and 1896 they shared a rare equality of political power. Elections were so close that until 1896 no president won office with a majority of the popular vote; the average popular vote margin was 1.5 percent. Two (Hayes and Harrison) even entered the presidency without a plurality. Republicans occupied the White House for 12 years, Democrats for 8. During only three two-year periods did the same party control the presidency and both houses of Congress—Democrats once and Republicans twice. Most of the time Congress itself was split, with Democrats generally taking the House and the Republicans the Senate. Very few seats shifted parties in any given election.

The party division of Congress inevitably weakened the presidents of the era. None was elected to consecutive terms. Calling them "the lost Americans," one observer noted that "their gravely vacant and bewhiskered faces mixed, melted, swam together" in the public mind. Lord Bryce claimed none of them "would have been remembered had he not been President." To be fair, all were competent men, most with considerable public service, and some with distinguished war records. One reason they were so forgettable was the era's concept of the presidency. Many agreed with Cleveland's assertion that the office "was essentially executive in nature." "I did not come here to legislate," he said. Presidents were only supposed to implement efficiently and honestly laws passed by Congress—occasionally vetoing ill-advised legislation. Even though these presidents did turn back many of the encroachments on presidential authority that began in Andrew Johnson's term, none considered it his duty to propose legislation.

Some found the office frustrating. After James Garfield moved from leadership roles in the House of Representatives to the presidency, he lamented, "I have heretofore been treating of the fundamental principles of government, and here I am considering all day whether A or B should be appointed to this or that office." Even representatives and senators were frequently frustrated, however, because congressional action was often stalemated. In the House, outdated and complex rules hampered action. Party discipline was practically impotent in both houses, and since neither controlled both houses for more than a two-year term, there was little possibility of formulating and enacting any coherent legislative program.

The lack of legislative action did not seem a serious problem at the start of the Gilded Age. Most people rejected the idea of an activist government—widely accepted doctrines of laissez-faire and Social Darwinism limited what people expected of government. The Social Darwinist William Graham Sumner once proclaimed that government had "at bottom . . . two chief things . . . with which to deal. They are the property of men and the honor of women. These it has to defend against crime." Both parties basically accepted a narrow vision of federal responsibility. When vetoing a small appropriation for drought relief in Texas, Democrat Cleveland asserted that "though the people support the Government, the Government should not support the people."

Such antigovernment sentiment tended to increase the power of the judicial branch. Many saw the courts as a bastion against governmental interference in the economy, and the courts certainly fulfilled that role. On the basis of the Fourteenth Amendment, judges were especially active in striking down state laws regulating business. The courts narrowly interpreted the Constitution on federal authority—ruling that the power to tax did not extend to personal incomes and that the power to regulate interstate commerce applied only to trade, not manufacturing. Congress indirectly gave judges more power by enacting vague laws that relied upon the courts for both definition and enforcement.

Subtle Differences: The Bases of Party Loyalty

One consequence of the equality of power shared by the Democrats and Republicans was the reluctance of either party to chance losing voters by taking clear positions on most contemporary issues. This reluctance may also have been based on the memories of the divisive 1860 election and its devastating impact on party and national unity. In addition, there was widespread agreement on many issues. Few members of either party questioned the pace or cost of industrialization; neither saw any need for federal action to regulate the economy. When a Democratic president replaced a Republican one in 1893, one of Andrew Carnegie's managers wrote the industrialist, "I cannot see that our interests are going to be affected one way or another by the change in administration." Business leaders had so little to fear from either party that they contributed generously to both.

Until 1896 the parties did share numerous similarities. Both were led by wealthy men but still tried to appeal to wage earners and farmers as well as merchants and manufacturers. Most members of both parties believed in protective tariffs and "sound currency." Both rejected economic radicalism and activist programs to aid workers. Presidents of both parties sent federal troops to break up strikes.

Ironically, for all their similarities the parties evoked fierce loyalty from a heterogeneous mix of people. One reason party platforms were so innocuous as to be interchangeable is that both parties were composed of factions and coalitions of "strange bedfellows." Because of its past abolitionist connections the Republican party retained the support of many activist reformers, idealists, and African Americans. Yet most Republicans came from established, "old stock" families. The more wealth a man had, the more likely he was to vote Republican. The party therefore was a curious combination of "insiders" and "outsiders."

The Democrats were even more mixed. The party's constituents sometimes seemed united mainly by opposition to the Republicans on various grounds. One Republican leader complained, "The Republican party does things, the Democratic party criticizes; the Republican party achieves, the Democratic party finds fault." Several generations later humorist Will Rogers quipped, "I don't belong to an organized party; I'm a Democrat." His words were certainly true of the Democratic party of the Gilded Age. The party contained such disparate elements as southern whites, immigrants, Catholics, and Jews.

For historical and cultural reasons, party loyalty was frequently determined by the three factors of region, religion, and ethnic origin. The regional factor was most evident in the support white Southerners gave to the Democratic party. To vote for the party of abolition and Reconstruction was considered treason and a threat to white supremacy. Republicans could count on heavy support from New England for the opposite reasons. To New Englanders, the Democrats were members of the party of traitorous rebellion against the Union. With little hope of winning southern white votes, Union loyalty was one issue the Republicans did not need to tiptoe around. They frequently "waved the bloody shirt," reminding Northerners that the Democrats had caused the Civil War. In 1876 one Republican declared, "Every man that tried to destroy this nation was a Democrat. . . . Soldiers, every scar you have on your heroic bodies was given to you by a Democrat."

For various reasons immigrants had long gravitated toward the Democratic party. Many were members of the poorest classes, which traditionally voted Democratic. In the 1850s anti-immigration Know Nothing party members joined the Republican ranks, reinforcing immigrants' ties to the Democrat party. Most of the "new immigrants" of the Gilded Age settled in cities controlled by Democratic political machines that won immigrants' loyalty by meeting their needs. As immigration swelled, increasing Democratic strength, Republicans became more and more restrictionist. In fact, immigration policy was one of the very few substantive issues on which the parties took clearly different stands.

Religious affiliations also helped determine party loyalty—partly because of the positions on immigration. Many of the late-nineteenth-century immigrants were Catholics and Jews who were suspicious of the Protestant-dominated Republican party. There were also fundamental differences in the religious orientation of most Republicans and Democrats. Republicans tended to belong to *pietistic* sects that based salvation on good works and moral behavior. Democrats, on the other hand, leaned toward *ritualistic* religions that emphasized faith and observance of church rituals above adherence to strict codes of moral conduct.

Pietistic Republicans frequently sought to legislate morality, supporting prohibition of alcohol and enforcement of Sunday blue laws, which barred various activities on the Sabbath—including baseball. Many Democrats did not believe that personal morality could or should be a matter of state concern. A Chicago Democrat explained, "A Republican is a man who wants you t' go t' church every Sunday. A Democrat says if a man wants t' have a glass of beer on Sunday he can have it."

The roots and constituencies of the parties thus created differences in their outlooks. The Republicans became the "party of morality," the Democrats the "party of personal liberty." Democrats not only rejected government interference in their personal life; in the nineteenth century, they were also more suspicious of government action of any sort. Some quoted Democrat Albert Gallatin's dictum: "We are never doing as well as when we are doing nothing."

Because of their mixed constituencies, however, the differences and divisions *within* parties were as great, and sometimes greater, than those between the parties. Democrats could count on the South for all its electoral votes, but southern Democrats frequently broke party ranks when voting on legislation. They sometimes voted with western Republicans on acts favorable to farmers. They were, however, fundamentally conservative men of Whiggish tendencies who usually voted with northern Republicans on financial and economic issues, as well as on immigration restriction. In a bizarre political arrangement, southern Democrats also voted with northern Republicans at times in order to receive a share of the patronage.

The Republicans were even more deeply divided into factions. One group, led by Roscoe Conkling, was labeled the **Stalwarts.** Followers of James G. Blaine of Maine were called **Half-breeds.** The only significant item of dispute between the two was who would receive the numerous jobs the president could make appointments to. Because the distribution of patronage was a prime function of both parties of the era, the division was bitter. When Conkling was asked if he intended to campaign for Blaine for president in 1884, he snapped that he did not engage in criminal activities.

One faction of the Republican party, however, did have some ideological basis. It was composed of reformers whose primary concern was honest and effective government. They had bolted the party in 1872 because of the corruption of the Grant regime, and they bolted again in 1884, supporting Democratic candidate Grover Cleveland for president. Party regulars ridiculed them, calling them "goo-goos" for their idealistic good government crusade. They were finally labeled **Mugwumps**—a joke that asserted they had their "mugs" on one side of the fence and their "wumps" on the other.

The divisions in the Republican party reflected the fact that the politicians of the day were less concerned with issues and ideology than with winning office and distributing patronage. Lord Bryce observed that American politicians could be differentiated from European ones by the fact "that their whole time is frequently given to political work, that many of them draw an income from politics . . . that . . . they are proficient in the acts of popular oratory, of electioneering, and of party management."

The Business of Politics: Party Organization

Gilded Age politicians were very serious about their careers. They worked hard at both "party management" and "electioneering." The result was the largest voter turnout in the nation's history. In the elections from 1860 to 1900 an average of 78 percent of eligible voters cast ballots. Outside of the South (where African Americans were increasingly pre-

Gimmicks in Gilded Age political campaigns, such as this Bryan donkey, stirred public interest, resulting in the highest voter turnouts in the nation's history.

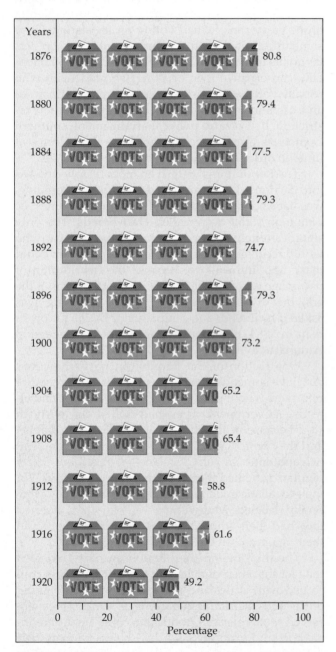

FIGURE 19.1
Voter Participation in Presidential Elections, 1876–1920

vented from voting and where the Democratic nomination determined the general election), the turnout sometimes reached 90 percent.

There was one main difference in Republican and Democratic party organization. Republicans generally depended on strong state organizations, while Democrats tended to rely on urban political machines to win and control votes. Since city governmental structures did not keep pace with the huge population increases, political machines based on ward captains provided many of the services for which government would later be held responsible. This machine also helped immigrants and rural migrants adjust to city life. One ward boss noted: "There's got to be in every ward somebody that any bloke can come to—no matter what he's done—and get help. Help, you understand, none of your law and justice, but help." Politicians took their pay in votes from the people, bribes from legal and illegal businesses, and graft from contractors. The system worked so well that the Democrats usually carried the big cities.

For both parties, recruiting and maintaining party voters was a game for professionals. Republicans in Pennsylvania compiled a list of 800,000 voters with notations as to their reliability as party loyalists. Politics was a rough and sometimes corrupt game. Conkling warned: "Parties are not built by deportment, or by ladies' magazines, or by gush." In 1888 when newly elected Benjamin Harrison proclaimed, "Providence has given us the victory," Republican party boss Matt Quay snorted, "Providence hadn't a damn thing to do with it." Quay then added that Harrison "would never know how close a number of men were impelled to approach the gates of the penitentiary to make him president." Electoral corruption was not limited to one party. In the same year a Mississippi Democrat admitted: "It is no secret that there has not been a full vote and a fair count in Mississippi since 1875, that we have been preserving the ascendancy of white people by revolutionary methods. In other words, we have been stuffing ballot boxes, committing perjury, and here and there in the state carrying the elections by fraud and violence."

Gilded Age politics was not dull. One could almost claim that the business of politics was entertainment. One observer remarked, "What the theatre is to the French, or the bull fight . . . to the Spanish . . . [election campaigns] and the ballot box are to *our* people." The drama of emotional tent meetings rivaled circuses, and the pageantry of parades provided excitement. Almost everyone got caught up in the elections, frequently displaying such paraphernalia as buttons, handkerchiefs, hats, banners, and posters emblazoned with their party's symbol or slogan. In 1888 one tobacco company enclosed in its packages pictures similar to baseball cards of the 25 presidential hopefuls. Politics was undoubtedly a prime form of mass entertainment.

Many politicians surely must have enjoyed their status as "media stars" and folk heroes. For some whose ethnic or class backgrounds closed conventional doors of opportunity, politics provided a vehicle of upward social mobility, similar to professional entertainment and athletics or trade union leadership. Yet politics as a vocation offered other rewards. Elected and appointed officials not only received salaries but many also openly accepted gifts from lobbyists and free passes from railroads. They sometimes used their governmental status to promote their private interests. James G. Blaine of Maine expressed no qualms about accepting stock concessions from an Arkansas railroad that he had aided in getting a federal land grant. One quip claimed that the United States had the best Congress money could buy.

The Struggle for Inclusion: Women and Politics

Politics could be a rough and dirty business—one many considered inappropriate for women. Increasingly women disagreed. After an 1869 split in the suffrage movement, the National Woman Suffrage Association (NWSA), led by Elizabeth Cady Stanton and Susan B. Anthony, fought for the vote on the national level through the courts and a proposed con-

stitutional amendment. At the same time the American Woman Suffrage Association (AWSA), headed by Lucy Stone and Julia Ward Howe, sought victories at the state level.

Up to the point in 1890 when the groups merged to form the **National American Woman Suffrage Association** (NAWSA), the victories of both groups had been limited. NWSA lost an 1874 Supreme Court decision in a suit filed by Virginia Minor against a St. Louis registrar for denying her the right to vote. The Court ruled that citizenship did not automatically confer the vote and that suffrage could be denied to specific groups, such as criminals, the insane, and women. In 1878 Anthony did succeed in getting a constitutional amendment introduced into the Senate that stated that "the right to vote shall not be denied or abridged by the United States or by any state on account of sex." It continued to be submitted for the next 18 years, but it was usually killed in committee and only rarely reached the Senate floor.

There was more success on the state and local level. By 1890 19 states allowed women to vote on school issues, and 3 states extended women the franchise on tax and bond issues. Referenda were held in 11 states, but only the territory of Wyoming had granted women full political equality. After 3 states—

In 1869 Wyoming became the first territory to allow women to vote in all territorial elections. It later refused to enter the Union without women's suffrage.

Colorado, Utah, and Idaho—adopted women's suffrage during the 1890s, the movement seemed to lose steam. As male resistance mounted, no other state acted on the issue until 1910. Many men agreed with a Texas senator that "equal suffrage is a repudiation of manhood."

STYLE OVER SUBSTANCE: GOVERNMENT IN THE GILDED AGE, 1877–1892

Politics provided great entertainment, but there were always people who wanted more. Local political activity was often considerably more vibrant than the political inertia at the national level. Many problems were first tackled on the city, county, and state levels before becoming a part of the national agenda. Such issues as the currency and tariffs could only be solved at the national level, but others, such as demands for clean government, were undertaken at all levels. On the whole, the states responded more vigorously than the national government to the problems created by economic changes—only to have the Supreme Court sometimes tie their hands. Out of frustration, people began to look to Washington for solutions, but the presidents and Congress responded timidly. National elections still focused mainly on trivial issues. When backed to the wall, Congress would enact laws to quiet popular cries for action, but such laws were often limited in scope and unenforceable.

Hayes and the "Money Question"

After the disputed election of 1876 almost created a constitutional crisis, the presidency was snatched from Democrat Samuel J. Tilden and given to **Rutherford B. Hayes.** A series of bargains was needed for the acceptance of the 8 to 7 vote of the electoral commission that named Hayes president. His administration was thus from the start tainted with snide references to him as "His Fraudulence" and "Old 8 to 7." He was actually honest and competent, and did much to establish the Republican party as the "party of morality" after the corruption of the Grant regime. His wife also helped to link Republicans with morality by her refusal to serve strong drinks—earning her the label of "Lemonade Lucy."

In this Greenback party cartoon from the 1870s, a gold-nosed government octopus puts a stranglehold on U.S. farmers, laborers, and small businesses. The Greenbackers wanted to distribute more money to more of the American people and opposed specie (gold) payments on bonds.

One guest at a White House party remarked in disgust that "the water flowed like champagne."

Hayes is now probably best remembered for removing the remaining federal troops from the South—marking the end of Reconstruction. At the time, however, economics rather than race relations occupied the public's mind. Hayes came into office more than three years into an economic depression that began with the panic of 1873. That depression raised the "money question," which continued to crop up for more than two decades.

At the root of this issue—as complex as it was heated—was a long period of deflation following the Civil War. Price levels dropped because the production of goods was growing faster than the supply of money. Farmers are not necessarily hurt by a general deflation if all prices fall equally and the farmers' debt levels are low. Wheat, corn, and cotton prices, however, declined more than other prices in the late nineteenth century, and farmers had also borrowed heavily to expand production. They were thus caught in a debt squeeze—their mortgage payments remained high while the prices they received fell. For example, a farmer who borrowed $1000 with a 25-year mortgage to buy a farm in 1868 had to produce over twice as much cotton to make the mortgage payment in 1888. The farmer received virtually nothing for doubled efforts, but the creditor received not only interest for the use of the money but also an additional bonanza—dollars now worth twice as much as those lent.

Debtors in all occupations began blaming their problems on deflation and saw inflation of the currency as the cure—for them it was a moral issue, a question of justice. One way to inflate currency was to increase the number of legal tender paper "greenbacks" first issued during the war. Supporters of that solution organized the **Greenback party** in 1874. Instead, two years before Hayes entered the White House, Congress enacted the **Resumption Act of 1875** to eliminate paper money not backed by gold or silver.

After the Resumption Act, some inflationists turned their attention to silver. The nation had been on a bimetallic standard since the 1790s. The dollar was based on both gold and silver, and for years dollars were coined at a **16 to 1** mint ratio—16 times as much silver as gold. By the 1870s this ratio did not reflect the market prices of the metals. Silver prices got so high that producers sold it on the open market rather than take it to the mint to be coined. Unable to buy silver at that ratio, Congress passed the **Coinage Act of 1873,** which halted the minting of silver dollars.

Soon after, the discovery of large deposits of silver drove prices down again. Then it was in the interest of both silver miners and inflationists to return to the coining of silver at 16 to 1. The two groups formed a large lobby that wrested minor concessions from Congress. The Bland-Allison Act of 1878 required the government to buy between $2 and $4 million worth of silver each month. Like much of the legislation of the Gilded Age, the Bland-Allison Act proved to be a cosmetic answer to popular demands. It neither raised silver prices nor inflated the currency significantly. Inflationists remained unhappy, and the Greenback party nominated former Union general **James B. Weaver** of Iowa for president in the 1880 election.

Garfield, Arthur, and the Patronage Issue

As in earlier elections neither of the two major parties focused on substantial issues in the 1880 election, but instead relied on slogans and gimmicks to win votes. The battle for the Republican nomination was between the Half-breed and Stalwart factions. After Hayes refused to run for a second term in 1880, Stalwarts hoped to run Grant again, but the Republican convention became deadlocked. On the thirty-sixth ballot the party picked **James A. Garfield,** a veteran but relatively unknown Ohio congressman. To conciliate the Stalwarts, **Chester A. Arthur,** a Conkling henchman, became the vice presidential nominee.

The Democrats nominated an even more obscure figure, General Winfield Scott Hancock, whose only claim to fame was being a hero of the Battle of Gettysburg. He was described as "a good man weighing 250 pounds." Garfield was also bland, but he had the advantage of a log cabin birth and a brief career on a canal towpath—giving rise to a popular Republican campaign slogan: "From the towpath to the White House." The 1880 election was one of the closest of the century in popular vote. Garfield received a mere 39,000-vote plurality out of almost 10 million ballots cast. Greenback nominee Weaver came in a distant third, gaining only 3.4 percent of the popular vote.

Returning prosperity and a tragic event focused attention on the issue of patronage, overshadowing the currency question. Four months after Garfield's inauguration he was shot twice by a deranged office-seeker, Charles Guiteau, who exclaimed, "I am a Stalwart. Arthur is now President of the United States." A native of Vermont, Arthur attended Union College, became an abolitionist lawyer, and then held a series of appointed offices. Considered by many to be a party hack, Arthur surprised them by becoming a champion of governmental reform.

The Mugwumps and others had become increasingly concerned with corruption in government. In the 1873 novel that gave the era its label of the Gilded Age, Mark Twain and Charles Dudley Warner wrote, "The present era of indelible rottenness is not Democratic, it is not Republican, it is national. Politics are not going to cure more ulcers like these, nor the decaying body they fester upon." Because of the pervasiveness of the corruption, some saw no way out. "All being corrupt together," E. L. Godkin, editor of *The Nation,* wrote, "what is the use of investigating each other?"

Some reformers believed that one answer to the problem of corruption was the reformation of the **spoils system** of patronage. Since the early 1800s government jobs had been considered the "spoils" of political victory, to be awarded to loyal party workers regardless of their qualifications. Between 1865 and 1891 problems grew as federal positions tripled from 53,000 to 166,000. Indeed, presidents of the era spent much of their time making some 100,000 appointments—most of which were in the postal service. That number of jobs provided incentives to precinct and ward bosses to get out the vote, but such inventions as the typewriter began to make it necessary for government workers to have skills other than getting people to vote.

After Garfield's assassination, Congress finally took action. With the support and encouragement of President Arthur, Congress enacted the **Pendleton Act** in 1883, which outlawed political contributions by appointed officeholders. It also established competitive examinations for federal positions to be given by the **Civil Service Commission.** The rather timid act only applied to about 10 percent of government employees, and some self-serving motives contributed to its passage. Since it was to apply only to future appointees and protected incumbents, the Democrats called it "a bill to perpetuate in office the Republicans who now control the patronage of the Government." In the same manner, every president elected after its enactment increased the number of positions protected from political removal—usually to prevent his appointees from being removed. The political system thus was becoming modernized, but some questioned whether it was being improved.

Cleveland, the Railroads, and Tariffs

By the time of the 1884 election, Arthur's actions had won more favor from the public than from his party. The Republicans bypassed him and nominated James G. Blaine, who was far from bland. He was so handsome and charismatic that a colleague's wife once remarked, "Had he been a woman, people would have rushed off to send expensive flowers." Indeed, Blaine had almost all the qualities of a successful presiden-

tial candidate: a phenomenal memory for names and faces, eloquent oratory, and a quick wit. He was, however, tainted politically. While in Congress he had become very rich without any visible means of outside income. Letters circulated that implied Blaine was up for sale to the railroads. He was more than the Mugwumps could stomach; they could not support him.

Realizing the potential advantage of a Mugwump defection, the Democrats selected **Grover Cleveland,** a reform governor of New York. Neither physically attractive nor charismatic, he did have one appealing quality. He was honest. As one supporter explained, "We love him for the enemies he has made." Cleveland and Blaine did not disagree on the major issues, so their campaign revolved around personalities and became one of the most scurrilous in the nation's history.

Blaine's tainted past was obvious fodder for the Democrats' campaign. At torchlit rallies Democrats chanted: "Blaine! Blaine! James G. Blaine! Continental liar from the state of Maine!" Unable to find a shred of evidence to challenge Cleveland's honesty, Republicans publicized a more personal scandal. Cleveland, a bachelor, had supported an illegitimate child since 1874, even though his paternity was questionable. Thus Republicans countered Democratic chants with "Ma! Ma! Where's my pa? Going to the White House? Ha! Ha! Ha!" In the end Cleveland's victory may have been due to an indiscretion by a Blaine supporter, who had labeled the Democrats as the party of "rum, Romanism, and rebellion." Even

In this cartoon, Grover Cleveland's alleged illegitimate child is used to impugn "Grover the Good's" well-known political integrity.

though Blaine's mother was Catholic, Democrats were able to rally Catholic voters to win key states.

The major legislation of Cleveland's first presidency resulted from public pressure and court actions. The power and discriminatory rates of the railroads frightened and angered many Americans, and actions to regulate the railroads had started at the state level. Beginning with the establishment in 1869 of a regulatory commission in Massachusetts, by 1880 there were railroad commissions in 14 states. Farmers and their allies, especially in the Midwest, got stronger legislation enacted that set maximum rates and charges within their states.

The railroad men naturally attacked these laws through the courts. At first they lost. In the 1877 *Munn v. Illinois* decision, the Supreme Court ruled that when "private property is affected with a public interest it . . . must submit to be controlled by the public for the common good." Nevertheless, states had difficulty regulating railroads chartered by other states and doing business across state lines. Then in the 1886 *Wabash, St. Louis & Pacific Railway Company v. Illinois* case the Supreme Court took away the rights of states to even try by ruling that only Congress had the right to regulate interstate commerce.

Pressure began to build for federal action, and Congress finally responded to the demands by passing the Interstate Commerce Act, which Grover Cleveland signed into law in February 1887. It prohibited pools, rebates, and rate discriminations; provided that all charges by the railroads should be "reasonable and just"; and established the **Interstate Commerce Commission** (ICC). Although significant as the first federal regulatory agency, the commission's power was woefully limited. It could investigate charges against the railroads and issue "cease and desist" orders, but these could only be enforced by the courts.

Conservative courts soon nullified 90 percent of the commission's orders; between 1887 and 1905 the Supreme Court decided against the ICC in 15 of 16 cases. By 1892 railroad attorney Richard S. Olney wrote, "The Commission, as its functions have now been limited by the Courts, is, or can be made of great use to the railroads. It satisfies the popular clamor for a government supervision of railroads, at the same time that such supervision is almost entirely nominal." One railroad executive admitted, "There is not a road in the country that can be accused of living up to the rules of the Interstate Commerce Commission."

The Interstate Commerce Act temporarily satisfied "popular clamor" without alienating railroad owners, so it did not become a partisan issue for either party. However, during Cleveland's term, a major issue on which Democrats and Republicans actually differed emerged: the tariff. Although both parties supported these taxes on imports to raise revenue and to protect American products from being undersold by foreign competitors, the difference lay in how high these tariffs should be. Regardless of party, congressmen voted their constituents' interests, which made few of them consistent on the issue. "I am a protectionist for every interest which I am sent here by my constituents to protect," one Democratic senator explained.

Like most Democrats, Cleveland had long been less enthusiastic about high tariffs than Republicans. While in office he found that existing tariff rates were producing treasury surpluses that were tempting congressmen to propose programs and appropriations that he considered dangerous expansions of federal activities. A moralistic man, Cleveland was deeply opposed to governmental involvement in the economy and social issues. He thus became an advocate of tariff reduction. In 1887, at his urging, the Democratic House enacted moderate reductions, but the Republican Senate blocked the bill. Cleveland then proceeded to make the tariff a focus of his reelection bid in 1888.

Harrison and Big Business

In 1888 the Democrats renominated Cleveland and wrote tariff reduction into their platform. The Republicans chose **Benjamin Harrison** and cheerfully picked up the gauntlet—denouncing Cleveland's "free trade" as unpatriotic. They also promised generous pensions to veterans. Voters at last were given some choice on a real issue. The result was a viciously corrupt and close election. Harrison's campaign chairman, Matt Quay, proceeded to "put the manufacturers of Pennsylvania under the fire and fry all the fat out of them." He asked them to make large contributions to the Republican party as insurance against lowered tariff rates. When Cleveland lost, many blamed his defeat on his taking too clear a stand on an issue. Republicans erroneously interpreted his narrow defeat as a mandate for protectionism. Congress then enacted the McKinley Tariff Act, which raised average duties to the highest level yet, but the Republicans misread public sentiment. The McKinley Tariff Act was very unpopular.

Both high tariffs and trusts were becoming distasteful to many Americans. Popular demand for legislative action against trusts had been growing during the 1880s. Again action started on the state level; 15 southern and western states had passed antitrust legislation by the mid-1880s. Of course, companies simply incorporated in more sympathetic states. The laws were ineffective and likely to be overturned by federal courts, but they did reflect popular distaste for the monopolies. Congress responded to these rumblings by enacting the **Sherman Antitrust Act** in 1890. On the surface it seemed to doom the trusts, prohibiting any "contract, combination in the form of trust or otherwise, or conspiracy in restraint of trade or commerce." As with the Interstate Commerce Act, appearances were deceiving. One senator explained that Congress had wanted to pass "some bill headed 'A bill to Punish Trusts' with which to go to the country" to aid their reelection.

Until 1901 the act was virtually unenforced—the Justice Department had instituted only 14 suits and failed to get convictions in most of them. The Supreme Court also emasculated the law in *United States v. E. C. Knight Co.* (1895), ruling that it applied to commerce but not manufacturing. Thus, the subject of that suit, a sugar trust controlling 98 percent of the industry, was not held in violation. Indeed, the only effective use made of the act in its first decade was as a tool to break up labor strikes by court injunctions.

In 1890 popular pressure also led to further action on the currency question. Following the Bland-Allison Act of 1878, the money supply continued to grow too slowly for the expanding economy. By 1890 pressure to coin more silver was growing. Congress responded with the **Sherman Silver Purchase Act,** which required the government to buy 4.5 million ounces of silver each month at the unrealistic ratio of 16 to 1. Paper money to pay for the purchases was redeemable in gold or silver, keeping the inflationary impact minimal. The act was a compromise that satisfied no one; the silver issue grew more heated in the 1890s.

Legislative Activity on Minority Rights and Social Issues

To African Americans the Republicans remained the party of black rights, but after the election of 1876 the party did less and less to earn that label. By 1890, however, increasing southern assaults on African American voting rights finally moved some Republicans to action. Senator Henry Cabot Lodge and others drafted the Lodge bill, a federal elections bill that sought to protect voter registration and guarantee fair congressional elections by establishing mechanisms to investigate charges of voting fraud and to deal with disputed elections.

Southern white response was rapid and bitter. The *Florida Times-Union* charged: "The gleam of federal bayonets will again be seen in the South." Northern Democrats lent their support to southern outrage. Cleveland exclaimed, "It is a dark blow at the freedom of the ballot." Although in 1890 Republicans controlled both houses of Congress, they finally

bartered away the Lodge election bill to gain support for the McKinley Tariff Act. Protection of manufacturers was more important to them than the protection of African Americans.

In that same year Republicans also let the Blair education bill die. This bill would have provided federal aid to schools, mostly African American, that did not get a fair share of local and state funds. The Blair bill marked the last glimpse of the party's dying abolitionist roots as well as the loss of party idealism. The Fifty-first Congress wanted to alleviate treasury surpluses to protect tariffs, but in the end the only group to receive substantial aid was Union Army veterans, who were voted pensions by the so-called Billion-Dollar Congress in 1890.

Other measures of the era affected minorities—but usually in a negative way. Southern white Democrats enacted discriminatory legislation against African Americans at the local and state level. A movement for immigration restriction, usually initiated by Republicans, led to the Chinese Exclusion Act of 1882 and other legislation that banned certain categories of immigrants and gave the federal government control of overseas immigration. The 1887 Dawes Act attacked the roots of American Indian culture by trying to make Native Americans homesteading farmers, which resulted, unintentionally, in making them dependent wards of the state.

Although most social issues received short shrift at the federal level, some received passionate attention at the local and state level. The two main ones—education and prohibition—were essentially Republican issues. An Iowa Republican slogan called for "a school house on every hill, and no saloon in the valley." Many people were alarmed by the increased use of alcohol—annual consumption of beer rose from 1.6 to 6.9 gallons per capita from 1850 to 1880. Republicans moved beyond the educational focus of the temperance movement to attempt to make drinking alcohol a crime. They also sought to increase compulsory school attendance, but these efforts were often linked to moves to undermine parochial schools and schools that taught immigrants in their native tongues. In most areas these Republican actions backfired, losing more voters than they gained. For example, Republicans had once predicted "Iowa will go Democratic when Hell goes Methodist," but in 1890 the state fell to their opponents.

By 1890 very little effective national legislation had been adopted to deal with the problems of a pluralistic society experiencing rapid social and economic change. Resulting partly from a political equilibrium that bred inertia, concepts of the limited nature of governmental responsibility also did not

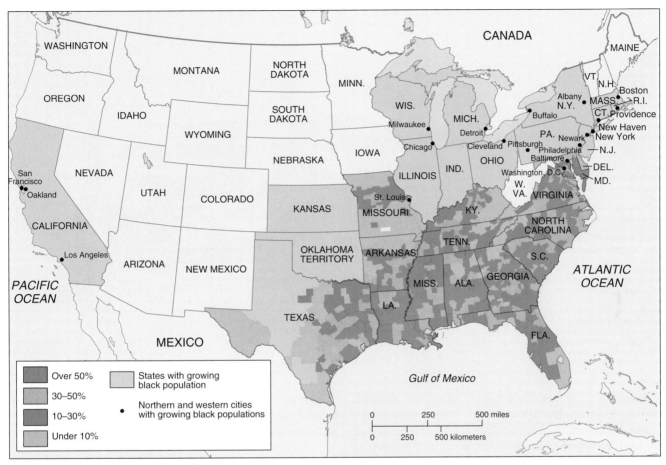

African American Population Distribution in the South, 1890

provide impetus for action. Public demands for change were nevertheless growing. No group challenged the status quo more than the farmers.

REVOLT OF THE WEST AND SOUTH

Cries for change naturally came from the losers in the new economic order, and among the greatest losers were American farmers. Their failure to thrive in the expanding economy convinced many that the cards had been stacked against them. After seeking various other solutions to their problems, farmers turned to politics—taking up Populist leader Mary E. Lease's cry "to raise less corn and more hell." Their success was limited, but they did lead the first American mass movement to reject social Darwinism and laissez-faire. They also promoted the "radical" idea that "it is the duty of government to protect the weak, because the strong are able to protect themselves." Some even questioned the basic tenets of industrial capitalism.

Grievances: Real and Imagined

In 1887 North Carolina editor Leonidas L. Polk summed up the views of many farmers: "There is something radically wrong in our industrial system. There is a screw loose. . . . The railroads have never been so prosperous, and yet agriculture languishes. The banks have never done a better . . . business, and yet agriculture languishes. Manufacturing enterprises never made more money, . . . and yet agriculture languishes. Towns and cities flourish and 'boom,' . . . and yet agriculture languishes."

The basic cause of the farmers' problems was the decline of agricultural prices—primarily because of overproduction. Farmers had a hard time believing, however, that they were producing too much. Kansas governor Lorenzo Dow Lewelling wondered how "there were hungry people . . . because there was too much bread" and "so many . . . poorly clad . . . because there was too much cloth."

Overproduction was an abstract, invisible enemy, so many farmers sought more tangible, personal villains such as the railroads, bankers, and

By the late 1880s many farmers were already suffering from severe economic dislocation. In this 1890 cartoon the West and the South are shown feeding the country, shown as a cow, while the East milks it for the benefit of factories, Wall Street, tariffs, and the National Bank.

monopolists. As "Sockless" Jerry Simpson claimed: "It is a struggle between the robbers and the robbed." Farmers believed they were being robbed by high freight and credit costs, an unfair burden of taxation, middlemen who exploited their marketing problems, and an inadequate currency.

Although there was no conspiracy by the "monopolists" to fleece the farmers, there was a germ of truth in farmers' grievances. Freight rates were higher for western farmers because of the long distances to markets and the scattered and seasonal nature of grain shipments. Although these farmers generally paid the same interest rates as Easterners, they were more dependent on mortgages to finance their operations than were the corporations, who could market stocks and bonds to raise needed capital. Southern farmers also had to pay dearly, through higher credit prices for goods obtained by crop liens. Large debts increased farmers' marketing problems. All the crops in a region were usually harvested at the same time, and farmers had to sell them immediately to pay off loans. Middlemen took advantage of the glutted markets—buying the crops at low prices and selling them when prices rose. Sometimes their profit margin was greater than that of the farmer who had gotten up before dawn every day and worked long hours to produce the goods. The unfairness of this galled farmers, living as they did isolated from the excitement and modern conveniences of the city. (The isolation was especially hard on the women, who were, as one writer noted, "not much better than

slaves. It is a weary, monotonous round of cooking and washing and mending and as a result the insane asylum is 1/3d filled with wives of farmers.")

Governmental policy seemed to hurt more than help. Property taxes hit farmers hard because they had a lot of land but little income. The tariffs affected most farmers both by raising the prices they paid for goods and by making it harder for them to sell their crops on the international market. The deflationary policy of the federal government especially hurt because of the farmers' great indebtedness. Every economic downturn brought a wave of farm foreclosures and frustration. Thousands of dreams died slowly, as one Kansas farmer's letter reveals.

> At the age of 52 years, after a long life of toil, economy and self-denial, I find myself and family virtually paupers. With hundreds of cattle, hundreds of hogs, scores of good horses, and a farm that rewarded the toil of our hands with 16,000 bushels of golden corn, we are poorer by many dollars than we were years ago. What once seemed a neat little fortune and a house of refuge for our declining years . . . has been rendered valueless.

The Farmers Organize

In this age of economic consolidation farmers realized early the need to unite and cooperate. Unfortunately they were never able to do so as effectively as the industrialists and railroad magnates because of greater geographic separation and their frontier-bred

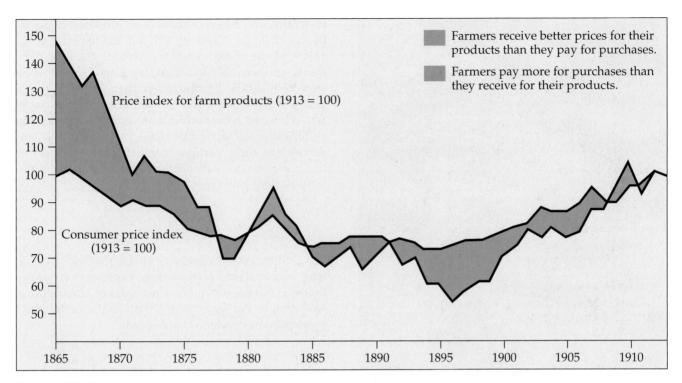

FIGURE 19.2
Price Indexes for Consumer and Farm Products, 1865–1913

individualism. A national farm organization, the **Patrons of Husbandry,** was founded in 1867 by Oliver Kelley. This U.S. Department of Agriculture employee's action illustrated that the federal government was not totally insensitive to farm problems. Local groups, called granges, sponsored lectures, dances, and picnics, fulfilling a deep hunger for social interaction, and membership in the organization grew to more than one million by 1874.

The Grangers, as they were called, soon moved beyond their social functions to address the economic grievances of the farmers. Focusing their actions on railroad regulation, they were responsible for numerous state laws that established railroad commissions to oversee and regulate railroad operations. Grangers also viewed cooperatives as one solution to the problem of high prices paid *by* farmers and the low prices paid *to* farmers. Cooperatives were formed to purchase in bulk directly from manufacturers, eliminating retail markups. In some places granges established cooperative banks, grain elevators, cotton gins, insurance companies, processing plants, and even plants to manufacture farm implements. Sales cooperatives aimed at increasing crop prices by joint marketing.

Granger victories and successes were generally short-lived and limited. The Supreme Court nullified the Granger laws that regulated railroads in the

Wabash case of 1886. Most cooperatives were short on capital and skilled management and were hampered by the continued individualism of many farmers. They were no match for the unrelenting attacks by private business. In the late 1870s the granges began to decline, reverting to rural social clubs, but continued to operate some cooperative stores.

Economic grievances remained, and farmers' organizational efforts shifted to the **Alliance movement.** Milton George, the editor of the Chicago-based *Western Rural*, organized a northwestern Alliance in 1880. Never very effective, by the late 1880s it was mainly a paper organization. The Alliance movement in the South was more radical and more successful. Started in 1877 as a frontier farmers' club in Lampasas County, Texas, it grew into the Grand State Alliance in 1879. Beginning in 1886, under the new leadership of Dr. Charles W. Macune, the southern Alliance spread rapidly by organizing new locals and absorbing existing farm groups in the South and other regions. At the same time a separate Colored Alliance was established. By 1890 the southern Alliance was a national organization with about 1.5 million members—with an additional 1 million members in its African American affiliate.

Like the Grangers, Alliancemen sought to establish cooperatives, mostly without long-term success. They also conducted wider social and educational

This lithograph illustrates the breadth of Grange activities with panels depicting musicals, sewing bees, courtships, dances, and care for the aged.

programs and boasted about 1000 affiliated newspapers. Self-help, however, proved inadequate, so in 1890 they turned to political action. In the 1890 elections southern Alliancemen tried to capture their state Democratic parties rather than supplant them. Because Northwest and Great Plains farmers were not burdened with such intense party loyalty or the complication of the racial issue, they established independent third parties. Regardless of the form of the organization, Alliancemen sought political solutions to their problems.

The Agrarian Agenda

The demands of the farmers mixed rhetoric, radicalism, and realism. Their words expressed an anger that was flaring white-hot after years of smouldering resentment. No one voiced that anger better than Kansas homesteader Mary E. Lease.

> Wall Street owns the country. It is no longer a government of the people, by the people and for the people, but a government of Wall Street, by Wall Street and for Wall Street. The great common people of this country are slaves, and monopoly is the master. The West and South are bound and prostrate before the manufacturing East. . . . Our laws are the output of a system which clothes rascals in robes and honesty in rags. The parties lie to us and the political speakers mislead us.

The roots of the Alliance movement go back to this house in Lampasas, Texas, where in 1877 farmers founded a local Alliance, which rapidly expanded through the state and then the South.

Farmers' words rang with a rejection of aspects of capitalism that in retrospect seems radical. Their rhetoric divided the nation into "haves" and "have-nots." "There are but two sides," one manifesto proclaimed. "On the one side are the allied hosts of monopolies, the money power, great trusts and railroad corporations. . . . On the other are the farmers, laborers, merchants and all the people who produce wealth. . . . Between those two there is no middle ground." To farmers, government either stood by idly or actively aided the monopolists as the "fruits of the toil of millions are stolen to build up colossal fortunes for a few."

Their rhetoric earned scorn from critics, who labeled the leaders "hayseed socialists." To be fair, there were some unsavory aspects to the movement: A few agrarians espoused simplistic and often anti-Semitic conspiracy theories, and some flamboyant demagogues—such as "Pitchfork Ben" Tillman of South Carolina—exploited rural anger for personal political ambitions. With a mixture of contempt and fear, critics called the rural reformers "crackpot radicals."

By Gilded Age standards the farmers' demands *were* radical—even though most were adopted in the twentieth century. Their most socialistic ideas called for government ownership and operation of the railroads and the telegraph and telephone, although they did not desire state ownership of all productive property. As landowners, farmers rejected socialism, but some did believe that these transportation and communication facilities were "natural monopolies" that could only be run efficiently under centralized management and were, besides, too important to the public welfare to be in the hands of private monopolies for profit.

The remainder of the agrarian political agenda reflected a realistic and moderate response to the farmers' problems. To ease their credit crisis they advocated an inflated, more flexible currency and the subtreasury plan. Considered by the Alliancemen to be the keystone of their program, subtreasuries (federal warehouses) were to be constructed as places where farmers could store their crops and receive treasury notes amounting to 80 percent of the crops' market value. Relieved from the pressure to sell immediately, farmers could wait for prices to rise to sell their crops and then pay back their subtreasury advances plus small interest and storage fees. Farmers saw the plan as a solution to the twin evils of the crop lien and depressed prices at harvest time. To finance government programs farmers called for a graduated income tax based upon the ability to pay.

Farmers believed that many of their ailments could be relieved by a more responsive, activist government. They therefore proposed political changes to "restore the government of the Republic to the hands of 'the plain people,' with which class it originated." Among the proposed changes were initiative and referendum, direct primaries, the direct election of United States senators, and the use of a secret ballot.

Initiative and **referendum** would allow people to propose legislation through petitions and enact laws by popular vote—thereby bypassing the state legislatures that seemed unwilling to act on their grievances. Direct primaries would let "the people" vote on political party candidates rather than having party leaders pick the candidates. In the same manner, people would directly elect senators instead of allowing state legislatures to select them. All of these proposals were intended to give citizens more control over their government. To make those changes effective a secret ballot was needed to protect voters from economic intimidation by employers and creditors or physical intimidation by threats of violence.

Although the farmers did not address the fundamental problem of overproduction, adoption of the agrarian demands could have relieved somewhat the agricultural distress fueling their anger. Thus it was that farmers became increasingly involved in political organization.

Emergence of the Populist Party

In 1890 Alliancemen entered politics in the West and the South with remarkable success. Under independent party banners, western Alliancemen elected a governor in Kansas, gained control of four state legislatures, and elected U.S. senators from Kansas and Nebraska. Working through the existing Democratic state parties, southern Alliancemen elected 4 governors, 44 congressmen, and several senators.

Western Alliancemen interpreted this success as a mandate to establish a national third party. At a May 1891 meeting in Cincinnati they failed to convince the southern Alliancemen to join them. By 1892, however, the Southerners were disillusioned with Alliance-backed Democrats who failed to support the subtreasury system. Overcoming their apprehension of third parties, the Alliances joined hands in St. Louis to create the **Populist (or People's) party.** In July 1892 the Populist party's national convention in Omaha drafted a platform and gave its presidential nomination to James B. Weaver, the former Union general who had been the Greenback party nominee in 1880. To symbolize the unity of the party they nominated former Confederate officer James G. Field for vice president. The Populist platform included all the agrarian agenda: the subtreasury plan; an income tax;

TABLE 19.1
Chronology of American Farm Movements

1860	941 agricultural societies exist in the United States
1867	Patrons of Husbandry (National Grange) is organized
1871	National Grange sanctions cooperative enterprise
1877	Southern Farmer's Alliance movement begins in Texas
1880	Northwestern Alliance begins but fails to grow
1886	Dr. Charles W. Macune begins to expand the southern Alliance into a national one
1890	Alliance turns to political action in congressional and state elections
1892	Populist party forms in St. Louis

free coinage of silver to inflate the currency; government ownership of railroads, telephone, and telegraph; and the political reforms intended to restore government to "the hands of the people."

Most Populists were small-scale farmers in the South and West whose farms were minimally mechanized. Most relied on a single cash crop, had unsatisfactory access to credit, and lived in social isolation some distance from towns and railroads. In other words, their existence was marginal in all respects. The majority owned some land, but sizable numbers of sharecroppers and tenant farmers joined the party. Prosperous, large-scale, diversified farmers found little appeal in the party's platforms or activities.

Because the Populists realized the need to broaden the base of their constituency, the Omaha platform also included planks to appeal to urban workers. They advocated an eight-hour day, immigration restriction, and the abolition of the Pinkerton system that supplied strikebreakers to management. One plank promised "fair and liberal" pensions to veterans. In the South some Populists, such as **Tom Watson** of Georgia, sought to woo African American voters. "You are kept apart," he told audiences of black and white farmers, "that you may be separately fleeced of your earnings. You are made to hate each other because upon that hatred is rested the keystone of the arch of financial despotism which enslaves you both."

The Populists conducted colorful campaigns, which one Nebraska Democrat called a blend of "the French Revolution and a western religious revival."

Their anger fostered a revolutionary spirit that appealed to large numbers of farmers. In 1892 Weaver became the first third-party candidate to win over one million votes. He carried Kansas, Colorado, Idaho, and Nevada for a total of 22 electoral votes. Populist strength in such mining states as Colorado reflected the appeal to silver miners of the party's demand for inflation by means of the free and unlimited coinage of silver at 16 to 1. On the other hand, the Populists failed to carry a single southern state, largely because of voting fraud, Democratic cries of white supremacy, and economic intimidation of many African American voters. Nevertheless, it was a remarkable showing for a new party, revealing the extent of popular discontent. The next year brought the **Panic of 1893,** which produced even more discontent and gave the Populists great hopes for the election of 1896.

DEPRESSION AND TURBULENCE IN THE 1890S

Social harmony became somewhat strained in the late 1880s with such violent episodes as the Haymarket Square riot of 1886. Economic "losers," mainly workers and farmers, were already becoming restless. The depression following the Panic of 1893 intensified their suffering. Naturally, turbulence increased, setting the stage for an attempt to unite the losers in a quest for political power in the election of 1896.

The Roots and Results of the Depression

While the Populists made their bid for office in the election of 1892, the two major parties were involved in a rerun of the 1888 election. Once again Cleveland and Harrison faced each other over the issue of the tariff. The presence of the unpopular McKinley Tariff Act created a different outcome, and Cleveland entered the White House—just in time for the Panic of 1893.

The depression started in Europe and spread to the United States as overseas buyers reduced their purchases of American goods as well as their American investments. Their unloading of some $300 million of investments caused American gold to leave the country to pay for these securities. Thus supplies of currency dropped, which led to rapidly falling prices. There had also been serious overexpansion of the economy, especially in railroad construction. Confidence faltered, the stock market crashed, and banks failed.

THE PEOPLE SPEAK

Senator William Alfred Peffer, "The Mission of the Populist Party"

William Peffer of Kansas was the first Populist elected to Congress in 1890. Having served as both a teacher and an editor before running for office, he used his skills in this 1893 article to set forth the major goals of his party. It demonstrates how the Populists viewed themselves as keepers of the promises of the founding fathers.

The Populist Party is an organized demand that the functions of government shall be exercised only for the mutual benefit of all the people. It asserts that government is useful only to the extent that it serves to advance the common weal. Believing that the public good is paramount to private interests, it protests against the delegation of sovereign powers to private agencies. Its motto is: "Equal rights to all; special privileges to none." Its creed is written in a single line of the Declaration of Independence—"All men are created equal." Devoted to the objects for which the constitution of the United States was adopted, it proposes to "form a more perfect union" by cultivating a national sentiment among the people; to "insure domestic tranquility" by securing to every man and woman what they earn; to "establish justice" by procuring an equitable distribution of the products and profits of labor; to "provide for the common defence" by interesting every citizen in the ownership of his home; to "promote the general welfare" by abolishing class legislation and limiting the government to its proper functions; and to "secure the blessings of liberty to ourselves and our posterity" by protecting the producing masses against the spoliation of speculators and usurers.

The Populist claims that the mission of his party is to emancipate labor. He believes that men are not only created equal, but that they are equally entitled to the use of natural resources in procuring means of subsistence and comfort. He believes that an equitable distribution of the products and profits of labor is essential to the highest form of civilization; that taxation should only be for public purposes, and that all moneys raised by taxes should go into the public treasury; that public needs should be supplied by public agencies, and that the people should be served equally and alike.

The party believes in popular government. Its demands may be summarized fairly to be

1. An exclusively national currency in amount amply sufficient for all the uses for which money is needed by the people, to consist of gold and silver coined on equal terms, and government paper, each and all legal tender in payment of debts of whatever nature or amount, receivable for taxes and all public dues.
2. That rates of interest for the use of money be reduced to the level of average net profits in productive industries.
3. That the means of public transportation be brought under public control, to the end that carriage shall not cost more than it is reasonably worth, and that charges may be made uniform.
4. That large private land-holdings be discouraged by law.

It is charged against Populists that they favor paternalism in government. This is an error. They only demand that public functions shall be exercised by public agents, and that sovereign powers shall not be delegated to private persons or corporations having only private interests to serve. They would popularize government to the end that it may accomplish the work for which it was established to serve the people, all the people, not only a few.

If it be paternalism to require the government to look after any of the private interests of the people, why do we not drive from our grounds as a tramp the postman who delivers our mail? If it be paternalism to bring our transportation business under public control, why do we not repeal the inter-State commerce law and restore the carrying trade to private citizens from whose rapacity the people were partially released some years ago? If it be paternalism to establish government agencies to supply currency to the people, what means the national bank act whose title reads: "An act to provide a national currency secured by a pledge of United States bonds, and to provide for the circulation and redemption thereof ?"

Originally appeared in *North American Review*, December 1893.

During the depression that followed, unemployment reached 20 percent of the workforce, farm prices dropped to new lows; and farm foreclosures reached new highs. Sharp wage cuts and massive layoffs took place in virtually every industry. Historian Henry Adams lamented, "Men died like flies under the strain, and Boston grew suddenly old, haggard, and thin." Still opposed to direct federal aid, President Cleveland responded to the suffering by repealing the Sherman Silver Purchase Act and selling lucrative federal bonds to a banking syndicate headed by J. P. Morgan in an effort to protect the nation's gold reserves.

The Democrats did act on their campaign issue, passing the Wilson-Gorman Tariff Act that reduced rates by 10 percent. Reformers were disappointed with the moderate cuts but were appeased by a provision placing a 2 percent tax on incomes. That provision, however, was declared unconstitutional in *Pollock* v. *The Farmer's Loan and Trust Co.* in 1895. In the face of massive suffering, many people wanted the government to do more.

Expressions of Worker Discontent

Violence had begun to escalate in labor-management relations in the late 1880s and continued into the 1890s. One episode of worker discontent was the **Homestead strike.** In 1892 Andrew Carnegie and the Amalgamated Association of Iron and Steel Workers clashed at Carnegie's Homestead plant outside of Pittsburgh. In an effort to crush the union, Carnegie had slashed wages and—expecting a confrontation—had fortified his steel mills, hired strikebreakers, and employed the Pinkerton Agency to protect them. This done, Carnegie departed for Scotland on a fishing trip and left his manager, Henry Clay Frick, to do battle with the union.

On July 5, strikers and Pinkerton agents fought their first battle. Smoke from cannons, rifles, dynamite, and burning oil filled the hot summer air. Ten men were killed and another 70 were wounded, as the strikers won the first engagement. When Frick appealed to the governor of Pennsylvania for help, the governor dispatched 8000 militiamen to Homestead "to protect law and order"—a phrase normally synonymous with defense of industrialists' property.

The fighting continued until late July when an anarchist from Chicago named Alexander Berkman took matters into his own hands. He went to Frick's office, shot the manager twice, and stabbed him seven times before being subdued. Frick lived and police arrested Berkman. Although Berkman had no connection with the steel union, the local and national press linked unionism with radicalism. Shortly afterward, strikebreakers went to work—the union was defeated and destroyed by the powerful forces of capital, government, and press.

The governor of Pennsylvania called up the militia to control striking workers from Carnegie's Homestead steel plant after they used guns and dynamite to try to keep Pinkerton guards from approaching the plant on barges from a nearby river.

During the depression, employers frequently cut wages to preserve profits, causing such strikes as the **Pullman strike.** In 1894, the workers in the Pullman plant at Chicago had their wages reduced several times while their rent for company-owned housing remained the same. When management refused to negotiate with the union, members of the American Railway Union (ARU) refused to handle any cars made in the Pullman plant. The boycott totally disrupted railroad traffic in the Midwest. Railroad executives appealed to Illinois governor John Altgeld for help, but the liberal politician refused to interfere. The executives then turned to U.S. Attorney General Richard Olney, a former railroad corporation lawyer. Olney and President Cleveland responded quickly, using the excuse of protecting the mails to come to the aid of the railroad managers. Over Altgeld's protest, the government sent 2000 troops to the Chicago area, and a federal court issued a blanket injunction that virtually ordered union leaders to discontinue the strike. When ARU president **Eugene V. Debs** defied the injunction, he was imprisoned. Only after federal troops arrived did violence occur. Within two days, bitter fighting had broken out, railcars were burned, and over $340,000 worth of damage had been done to railroad property. Force—absolute, final, and federal—crushed the Pullman strike. Such unified repressive force drove some workers to the political left.

Prior to 1894, the badly divided Socialist Labor party, led by the abrasive Daniel DeLeon, had a minuscule membership. After the Pullman strike Eugene V. Debs emerged from prison a socialist and

Businessman Jacob S. Coxey is shown from his jail cell after being arrested for leading his army of unemployed workers into Washington, D.C. in 1894.

Eugene V. Debs was the Socialist Party of America's presidential nominee four times. Here Debs addresses a crowd of railroad workers during one of his campaigns.

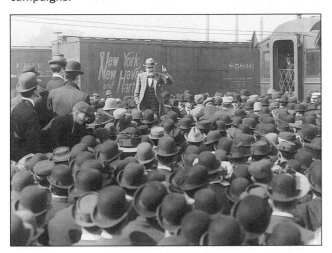

made socialism more respectable. Born in Indiana in 1855, the balding Debs had the common touch and delivered with a Hoosier twang a version of socialism based on distinctly American values. The movement thus acquired a fiery and effective orator. "Many of you think you are competing," Debs would declare. "Against whom? Against Rockefeller? About as I would if I had a wheelbarrow and competed with the Santa Fe [railroad]." Around the nucleus of his personality the larger and stronger Socialist Party of America began to form and directly challenge unrestrained capitalism.

The mass suffering during the depression also provoked some to ask the federal government to provide work for the unemployed. **Jacob S. Coxey,** a short, quiet Ohio businessman, was one who advocated putting men to work on the roads. They were to be paid by the printing of $500 million in legal tender paper money, which would also help to inflate the currency. He organized the Army of the Commonwealth of Christ to march to Washington and demand action. When about 500 of the marchers straggled into the capital on May 1, 1894, their leader was arrested for walking on the grass. Federal authorities beat and arrested his "troops." Although **Coxey's army** fell far short of his dream of a demonstration of 400,000 jobless workers, their actions did get the attention of the public. Forty-three newspaper reporters accompanied them, reporting almost every detail of the march. One journalist quipped, "Never in the annals of insurrection has so small a company of soldiers been accompanied by such a phalanx of recording angels."

Deteriorating Race Relations

The turbulent 1890s was also one of the worst decades of racial violence in the nation's history. It stemmed from class as well as race conflict. The Populist leader Tom Watson was right when he told black and white farmers that the Democrats were using race as a wedge to keep them apart.

Although the Populists failed to unite blacks and whites on the basis of class interests, the attempt led to considerable bloodshed. Whites shed white blood, but more frequently they spilled black blood. Lynching became a tool for controlling both black votes and actions. Under the pretext of "maintaining law and order," vigilante mobs hanged, mutilated, and burned African Americans in increasing numbers. During the 1890s an average of two to three black Southerners were lynched each week.

It is probably not coincidental that attempts to limit African American voting began in earnest precisely at the time that farmer unrest arose. Mississippi led the way in finding ways to skirt the Fifteenth Amendment. Without mentioning "race, color, or previous condition of servitude," the 1890 Mississippi constitution established poll taxes, literacy tests, and residency requirements, all aimed at reducing black voting. A key element of the literacy tests was the requirement that voters be able to explain what they read to the satisfaction of the voter registrars—African Americans found registrars extremely hard to satisfy. The Supreme Court displayed its disregard for black rights by upholding the so-called **Mississippi Plan** in *Williams v. Mississippi*, and other states soon adopted similar measures. Later, to woo lower-class white voters, grandfather clauses were added—providing exemptions from these requirements based on voting eligibility prior to the Reconstruction Acts. These clauses applied to all adult white males and to no African Americans.

Once whites stripped away black political power, other black rights toppled. With no need to cater to African American voters, whites soon began to pass discriminatory legislation. Most wanted to use segregation as a means of racial control, but the Fourteenth Amendment raised constitutional questions. The Supreme Court removed that barrier. After several rulings that limited constitutional protection of black rights, in the 1896 *Plessy v. Ferguson* decision the Court finally ruled that public accommodations for blacks could be "separate but equal." With segregation now legalized, for the next two decades southern states frantically passed legislation—known as "Jim Crow" laws—to make legal the separation of the races. When the frenzy stopped, some states had even passed laws prohibiting interracial checker playing and requiring textbooks used in black schools to be stored in separate rooms from those used in white schools.

Segregation and the exclusion of African Americans from public facilities had long existed in a haphazard way based on custom. As this informal and inconsistent arrangement was converted into a legalized system of repression, violence erupted, and no one stepped in to protect African Americans. The popularity of Booker T. Washington's 1895 "Atlanta

Ida B. Wells (*standing*) comforts the family of her friend Thomas Moss, who was lynched mainly for opening a grocery in competition with a white-owned one. His lynching help to launch Wells's crusade against lynching.

Compromise," with its plea for racial cooperation, is easily understandable under the conditions it was delivered. Both whites and blacks were eager to find a way out of the bloodshed. More militant black voices, however, such as that of Memphis newspaper editor **Ida B. Wells,** insisted on federal action to prevent lynching.

Fissures seemed to be opening up along a number of the seams in American society. The turbulence was enough to provoke the Democratic party to respond to popular demands for economic relief and political reform in 1896, creating a dilemma for the Populists.

The Tide Turns: The Election of 1896

After the Republicans nominated William McKinley and the Democrats chose William Jennings Bryan, the Populists were left with an impossible choice. When Bryan and the Democrats endorsed silver, the Populists had their thunder stolen. They had hoped to ride silver to power because of the growing popularity of the issue. William H. Harvey's pro-silver book *Coin's Financial School* had become a bestseller in 1894. Instead of picking up silverite bolters from the major parties as they had expected to do, the Populists were now faced with a real problem. To nominate someone else would split the silver votes and ensure a victory for McKinley. Yet to nominate Bryan meant a loss of their identity and momentum.

Many Populists argued fervently against "fusion" with the Democrats, who focused almost exclusively on silver at the expense of the rest of the Populist demands. Watson and others viewed the

In this 1896 cartoon, free silver is shown as the candle killing off the politicians drawn to it. In the end the adoption of free silver by the Democrats set the stage for the destruction of the Populist party.

obsession with silver as "a trap, a pitfall, a snare, a menace, a fraud, a crime against common sense and common honesty." In the end Populists bit the bullet and nominated Bryan for president but chose Tom Watson for vice president rather than the Democratic choice, Arthur Sewall.

"God's in his Heaven, all's right with the world!" Republican campaign manager Mark Hanna wired McKinley when he learned of the Republican victory. McKinley carried the popular vote 7.1 million to 6.5 million and the electoral votes 271 to 176. The defeat of Bryan and the silver forces brought an end to political equilibrium. Millions of Democrats left their party, and the Republican party became the majority party. Republicans then won the presidency in seven of the nine contests between 1896 and 1928, and controlled both houses of Congress 17 of the next 20 sessions. One basic reason for the Republican victory of 1896 was the bad luck of the Democrats to be in power when the depression came. Republicans gleefully noted in 1894, "We were told in the old times that the rich were getting richer and the poor were getting poorer. To cure that imaginary ailment our political opponents have brought on a time when everybody is getting poorer."

Election of 1896

ELECTORAL VOTE BY STATE		POPULAR VOTE
REPUBLICAN William McKinley	271	7,104,779
DEMOCRATIC William J. Bryan	176	6,502,925
	447	13,607,704

"Rise Brothers!": The Black Response to Jim Crow

African Americans had long struggled against white prejudice and repression. During Reconstruction constant vigilance was needed to protect and expand newly won rights. Some efforts were in vain, but a few successes had helped curb the growth of segregation. For example, African Americans in Savannah, Georgia, succeeded in desegregating their city's streetcar system in 1872 by boarding the so-called white cars, threatening legal action, and boycotting the Jim Crow cars. Beginning in the 1890s, however, a rising tide of virulent white racism eventually confounded black attempts to resist being made into second-class citizens. With a new determination white Southerners stripped African Americans of their voting rights, passed segregation laws, and lynched those who refused to cooperate.

Once whites had won the battle and the smoke had cleared from the battlefields, the mythology of African American submission and acceptance began to prevail. Booker T. Washington became a symbol of black cooperation and accommodation. Selected passages of his 1895 Atlanta address, the "Atlanta Compromise," were heralded as the "will of blacks." Other voices were ignored. Few quoted the words of John Hope, a professor at a black college in Nashville, the next year. Hope exhorted African Americans:

Rise, Brothers! Come let us possess this land. Never say "Let well enough alone." Cease to console yourself with adages that numb the moral sense. Be discontented. Be dissatisfied. . . . Be restless as the tempestuous billows on the boundless sea. Let your dissatisfaction break mountain-high against the walls of prejudice and swamp it to the very foundation. Then we shall not have to plead for justice nor on bended knee crave mercy; for we shall be men. Then and not until then will liberty in its highest sense be the boast of our Republic!

Many African Americans responded to the new wave of discrimination by employing every available tactic to protest the loss of their rights. Before disfranchisement was completed, black officeholders made impassioned speeches and lobbied their white colleagues to oppose discriminatory legislation. Activists organized local "Negro rights," "Emancipation," and "Colored uplift" groups that wrote strongly worded resolutions and organized petition drives. Individuals and groups launched legal challenges in the courts. Some tested the new laws by breaking them. Protest meetings were held. Boycotts of newly segregated facilities occurred in New Orleans, Savannah, Jacksonville, Richmond, and other southern cities. The black press often fearlessly attacked white actions; a Bay Minette, Alabama, paper counseled: "The best remedy for lynching is a good Winchester rifle." Finally, a few engaged in the ultimate protest—armed resistance.

Two very different examples illustrate the nature and results of African American protest at the turn of the century. The first, a Savannah streetcar boycott in 1906, had many similarities to the Montgomery bus boycott of 1955—the main exception being the outcome. The second, the story of Robert Charles, demonstrates that this early civil rights movement had its share of martyrs.

At the beginning of the twentieth century both whites and blacks of Savannah were proud that their city had been immune to the lynching virus. In 1906 it was also one of the few southern cities without a single Jim Crow law on its books. Race relations were better than average, though not ideal. Of the city's 72,000 residents, 54 percent were African American, but the white minority exercised a firm, if benevolent, control. There were only three black public officials, and they held positions allotted to blacks by law. Nevertheless, the black community had spawned a leadership class that commanded some respect from the white establishment and enjoyed a measure of political clout. They had thus been able to turn back all previous attempts to enact segregation.

The year 1906, however, brought increased racial tension throughout the South, with several outbreaks of violence, including those in Brownsville, Texas, and in Georgia where the bitter gubernatorial campaign of Hoke Smith aroused white prejudice. Savannah whites began to urge city leaders to get into the "new order of things" and exclude African Americans from both politics and social contact with whites. On September 12, 1906, the city adopted a law that required separate seating in streetcars and empowered the police to arrest anyone sitting in the wrong place.

The African American elite—leading ministers, physicians, and businessmen—had already formed a committee to lobby against the ordinance. Once the law was passed, they immediately organized a boycott. In the churches, ministers urged compliance with the boycott and the black *Savannah Tribune* declared: "Let us walk! walk! and save some nickels. . . . Do not trample on your pride by being 'jim crowed.' Walk!" Black hackmen reduced their fares for boycotters from 25 cents to 10 cents. One group attempted to form the United Transportation Company to compete with white lines. Those rich enough to own wagons drove themselves and friends to town.

Many who could get no other transportation heeded the words of their leaders and walked. It was reported that the mayor's secretary had given his maid carfare to bring two large suitcases from his home to city hall. When she arrived late and soaked with perspiration, he discovered that she had followed her minis-

ter's advice and refused to ride the streetcar. The local white paper noted that trolley after trolley went by with the back seats vacant. The boycott was almost total.

City authorities responded much as Montgomery authorities did in 1955. They cracked down on unlicensed hacks and harassed licensed ones. African Americans remained firm for some time—even after it became apparent that the boycott was not going to change white minds. As late as May 1908, two years after the start of the boycott, the streetcar line admitted that no more than 80 percent of blacks had returned to the cars. Without action by the federal government, even economic loss could not persuade whites to abandon segregation.

Savannah blacks suffered inconvenience to protest the infringement of their rights, but Robert Charles paid a much higher price. A quiet, intense young man in his twenties who worked at odd jobs, he supported black emigration to Africa as a response to white prejudice in the South. He read a lot and collected weapons but broke no laws. One night in July of 1900 he sat on a front porch in New Orleans talking quietly with a friend. Near midnight three police officers arrived with drawn pistols and flailing billy clubs to arrest him.

Charles responded to the attempted arrest by drawing his own gun and shooting one of the officers. Wounded himself, he then fled—not to safety but to rearm with a rifle. Charles then moved from one hiding place to another, leaving a trail of five dead police officers and a dozen wounded ones. A mob of over a thousand whites joined police in the manhunt, frequently firing indiscriminately into the African American community. Finally surrounded, Charles was burned out of his hiding place and immediately riddled with bullets. As was customary, the mob

then badly mutilated the body. They killed the man but not the spirit. African American newspaper woman Ida Wells-Barnett investigated the incident and ended her report with the words: "The white people of this county may charge that he was a desperado, but to the people of his own race Robert Charles will always be regarded as the 'hero of New Orleans.'" Later, his willingness to fight police brutality with retaliatory violence would be renewed by the Black Panthers in the 1960s.

Even heroic actions failed to protect African Americans' rights from the onslaught of discrimination at the dawn of the new century. Nevertheless these men and women added to the heritage of protest that would reap rewards a half-century later—when the media were more sympathetic and the federal government finally decided that it was in the national interest to protect the rights of all citizens.

CHRONOLOGY OF KEY EVENTS

1867 The Grangers, first national farmers' organization, is founded

1873 "Crime of '73": Coinage Act declares that gold alone would be minted to back paper money

1877 Southern Farmers' Alliance is founded in Texas; *Munn v. Illinois* upholds the constitutionality of state regulation of railroads

1878 Bland-Allison Act requires the U.S. Treasury to buy $2 to $4 million of silver a month in order to inflate the currency

1881 President James A. Garfield mortally wounded at a Washington, D.C., train station; Chester Arthur becomes twenty-first president

1883 Pendleton Act classifies approximately 15,000 federal jobs as civil service positions to be awarded only after a competitive examination

1886 *Wabash, St. Louis, & Pacific Railway Company v. Illinois* reverses *Munn v. Illinois* and states that only Congress can regulate commerce between states

1887 Congress establishes the Interstate Commerce Commission, the first federal regulatory commission, to regulate railroads

1890 National Woman Suffrage Association and American Woman Suffrage Association merge to form the National American Woman Suffrage Association; Congress passes Sherman Antitrust Act, forbidding restraints on trade; Sherman Silver Purchase Act increases amount of silver that had to be purchased annually and allows the Treasury to issue paper money based on silver; Mississippi becomes first southern state to adopt poll taxes, literacy tests, and residency requirements to restrict African American voting

1892 Populist party is formed and receives over a million votes in presidential race; violent Homestead, Pennsylvania, steel strike erupts

1893 Severe economic depression begins

1894 Pullman workers strike; Coxey's army marches on Washington, D.C., to protest unemployment and to urge a public works program to relieve unemployment

1895 *United States v. E. C. Knight Co.* weakens Sherman Antitrust Act by stating that law does not apply to companies that operate exclusively in one state; *Pollock v. Farmer's Loan and Trust Co.* declares a federal income tax unconstitutional

1896 *Plessy v. Ferguson* decision rules that the principle of "separate but equal" does not deprive blacks of civil rights guaranteed under the Fourteenth Amendment; Republican William McKinley defeats Democrat William Jennings Bryan to become the twenty-fifth president

1900 Gold Standard Act places the nation on the gold standard

The Populists, of course, suffered the most from the election results: Their party disappeared. The attempt to unite farmers and labor, blacks and whites, failed. Like the Socialists and other radicals, the Populists were never able to recruit organized labor in order to forge a broadly based working-class movement. American Federation of Labor president Samuel Gompers and other labor leaders argued that farmers were capitalists, not wage earners, and that their goals were not compatible with labor's interests. For example, the inflation that farmers wanted would raise food prices to the detriment of workers already living close to the margin. In the South race proved to be more important than class, and many disillusioned white Populists such as Tom Watson became anti-black activists following their defeat. They joined gladly with the Democrats to curtail African American suffrage. The Democrats had stirred up the issue of racism to defeat the Populists and then were unable to put the genie back into the bottle. In many states they were replaced by less elitist, bigoted demagogues.

Americans had come to a turning point in 1896 and chose the conservative path. The Republican administration quickly raised duties with the Dingley Tariff Act of 1897. Three years later the Gold Standard Act officially put the nation on the gold standard by requiring all money to be redeemable in gold. Ironically, new discoveries of gold and more efficient extracting methods brought the inflation that farmers had sought from silver. Prosperity began to return, and the Republicans could point with pride to their slogan, "The Full Dinner Pail." That prosperity sapped the strength of the agrarian movement as rising farm prices eased farmers' economic distress. And such inventions and services as the telephone and rural free delivery of mail decreased farmers' isolation—especially after mail-order catalogs began to arrive from Montgomery Ward's and Sears, Roebuck.

CONCLUSION

After Reconstruction, national politics entertained the masses and voter turnout reached all-time highs. At the same time, the emerging problems of industrialization challenged the traditional roles of state and federal governments. The failure of either major party to dominate the federal government created some degree of political inertia. Competing for voters, the parties differed little in their laissez-faire support of business or their primary concern with the spoils of office. Most people supported the government's nonintervention in the economy and society until problems escalated for farmers, workers, and minorities. State and local governments made efforts to solve emerging problems, but many ills seemed to require federal action. Political inertia in Washington bred crisis after crisis as problems remained unresolved.

Finally, in the West and South a challenge to unrestrained capitalism arose from the losers in the race toward industrialism and economic expansion. Led by disgruntled farmers, the Populist party sought to unite large segments of the American population on the basis of class interest. In 1896 the Democratic party responded by nominating William Jennings Bryan. As a result, the presidential election of that year provided a real choice for American voters. The victory of conservative William McKinley brought about the death of populism, but many of the problems the farmers addressed in the 1890s continued into the twentieth century. Time vindicated the farmers' demands. A large number of their rejected solutions were adopted in the first two decades of the new century, and most of their remaining agenda was enacted in modified form during the New Deal of the 1930s.

CHAPTER SUMMARY AND KEY POINTS

The 1880s and 1890s were years of turbulence. In this chapter you read about Gilded Age politics; disputes over currency, tariffs, patronage, and railroads; the

problems facing the nation's farmers; farmers' efforts to organize; and the critical election of 1896.

- An era of intense political partisanship, the Gilded Age was also an era of reform. The Pendleton Act sought to curb government corruption by requiring applicants for certain governmental jobs to take a competitive examination. The Interstate Commerce Act sought to end discrimination by railroads against small shippers, and the Sherman Antitrust Act outlawed business monopolies. Most of these acts had little impact at the time but established agencies that later became more effective.

- These were turbulent years that saw labor violence, rising racial tension, militancy among farmers, and discontent among the unemployed.

- These years also saw the rise of the Populist crusade. Burdened by heavy debts and falling farm prices, many farmers joined the Populist party, which called for an increase in the amount of money in circulation, government assistance to help farmers repay loans, tariff reductions, and a graduated income tax.

SUGGESTIONS FOR FURTHER READING

Ed Ayers, *The Promise of the New South: Life After Reconstruction* (1992). Provides a thorough examination of diverse aspects of southern culture following Reconstruction.

Sean Dennis Cashman, *America in the Gilded Age: From the Death of Lincoln to the Rise of Theodore Roosevelt,* 3rd ed. (1993). A thorough account of politics and society during the late nineteenth century.

Lawrence Goodwyn, *Democratic Promise: The Populist Moment in America* (1976). An interpretation that focuses on the Populists' attempt to expand democracy.

William F. Holmes, ed., *American Populism* (1994). Comprehensive collection of significant interpretations of the Populist movement.

Michael Kazin, *The Populist Persuasion: An American History* (1995). Analyzes the various functions that Populism has served in American politics.

Robert C. McMath, *American Populism: A Social History, 1877–1898* (1993). Presents an up-to-date account of Populism and its supporters.

Novels

Edward Bellamy, *Looking Backward* (1888).

Willa Cather, *My Antonia* (1918).

Frank Norris, *The Octopus* (1901).

MEDIA RESOURCES

Web Sites

Not For Ourselves Alone: The Story of Elizabeth Cady Stanton and Susan B. Anthony
http://www.pbs.org/stantonanthony/index.html
Web site companion to PBS series that includes essays, documents, and other resources relating to women's rights.

American President: Presidential History Resources
http://www.americanpresident.org/presidentialresources.htm
Contains a biography of each president along with a photo gallery and document texts.

1896: The Presidential Campaign Cartoons and Commentary
http://iberia.vassar.edu/1896/1896home.html
A great collection of documents, photos, and cartoons about this pivotal election as well as informative essays about the events and individuals of the era.

William Jennings Bryan: Resources
http://www.mission.lib.tx.us/exhibits/bryan/resource.htm
Pictures, cartoons, and documents relating to Bryan.

Cartoons of the Gilded Age and Progressive Era
http://www.cohums.ohio-state.edu/history/projects/USCartoons/GAPECartoons.htm
Grouped by category sites; contains numerous political cartoons of the era.

Jump Jim Crow, Or What Difference Did Emancipation Make?
http://www.lib.berkeley.edu/~ljones/Jimcrow/index.html
A collection of images, songs, and stories relating to the rise of segregation; also includes texts of segregation laws and a glossary.

The American 1890s, A Chronology
http://www.bgsu.edu/departments/acs/1890s/america.html
A detailed, annotated chronology with links provided by Bowling Green State University

Labor-Management Conflict in American History
http://www.history.ohio-state.edu/projects/laborconflict/
Provides documents and photos about several of the more important labor strikes at the turn of the century, including the Homestead Strike of 1892.

The Era of William McKinley
http://www.history.ohio-state.edu/projects/mckinley/default.htm
Contains valuable materials about McKinley and his age before and during his presidency.

Black History at Harpweek
http://blackhistory.harpweek.com/

Drawn from the pages of *Harper's Weekly,* this Web site includes pictures, articles, cartoons, and other resources.

Diary and Letters of Rutherford B. Hayes
http://www.ohiohistory.org/onlinedoc/hayes/index.cfm
The Rutherford B. Hayes Presidential Center in Fremont, Ohio, maintains this searchable database of 3000 pages of Hayes's writings before and after his presidency.

Turn of the Century Exhibits
http://memorialhall.mass.edu/turns/index.jsp
Multimedia exhibit that includes the years 1880–1920 with a heavy emphasis on social history.

1896: The Grand Realignment
http://jefferson.village.virginia.edu/seminar/unit8/home.htm
This University of Virginia site contains biographical information, images, cartoons, and related links about the pivotal 1896 election.

The Grange Connection
http://www.grange.org/
Official Web site of the Grange; contains some historical background.

Touring Turn-of-the-Century America, Photographs from the Detroit Publishing Company, 1880–1920
http://lcweb2.loc.gov/ammem/detroit/dethome.html
Searchable database of photos in American Memory site at the Library of Congress that illumine life during this era.

Women and Social Movements in the United States, 1775–2000
http://www.binghamton.edu/womhist/index.html
Includes a number of exhibits searchable by dates or topics about the role of women in reform movements, including the Populists.

Jim Crow Museum of Racist Memorabilia
http://www.ferris.edu/jimcrow/
Documents the pervasive racism in American culture in words and pictures.

Prairie Settlement: Nebraska Photos and Family Letters, 1862–1912
http://memory.loc.gov/ammem/award98/nbhihtml/pshome.html
Searchable database that provides information about life on the prairie.

The Last Days of a President: Films of William McKinley and the Pan-American Exposition, 1901
http://memory.loc.gov/ammem/papr/mckhome.html
Twenty-eight films from Library of Congress holdings including McKinley's second inauguration, the exposition, and McKinley's funeral.

Voices of the American South
http://memory.loc.gov/ammem/award97/ncuhtml/
fpnashome.html
First-person narratives of the American South, 1860–1920, drawn from the holdings of the University of North Carolina at Chapel Hill.

African American Perspectives: Pamphlets from the Daniel A. P. Murray Collection, 1818–1907
http://memory.loc.gov/ammem/aap/aaphome.html
Includes writings of famous African Americans including Frederick Douglass, Booker T. Washington, and Ida B. Wells-Barnett.

The Era of William McKinley
http://www.history.ohio-state.edu/projects/McKinley/
Contains photos, cartoons, and documents from all of McKinley's career as well as short biographies of other important figures of the era.

Presidential Elections, 1860–1884
http://elections.harpweek.com/
Drawn from the pages of *Harper's Weekly*, it contains writings and cartoons for each presidential election, including the victories of Hayes, Garfield, and Cleveland.

Films and Videos

Insanity on Trial. An *American Experience* film about the trial of Charles Guiteau, who assassinated James Garfield.

The Rise and Fall of Jim Crow. A fall 2002 four-part series from PBS that examines the origins of segregation and discrimination as well as its decline.

Ida B. Wells: A Passion for Justice. A biographical sketch of this fiery activist from the *American Experience* biography series.

Eugene V. Debs and the American Movement. A Cambridge Documentary film that examines the role of Debs in the Socialist party.

KEY TERMS

Free silver   (p. 521)

Gilded Age   (p. 523)

Stalwarts and Half-breeds   (p. 525)

Mugwumps   (p. 525)

National American Woman Suffrage Association   (p. 527)

Greenback party   (p. 529)

Resumption Act of 1875   (p. 529)

16 to 1   (p. 529)

Coinage Act of 1873   (p. 529)

Spoils system   (p. 530)

Pendleton Act   (p. 530)

Civil Service Commission   (p. 530)

Interstate Commerce Commission   (p. 531)

Sherman Antitrust Act   (p. 532)

Sherman Silver Purchase Act   (p. 532)

Patrons of Husbandry   (p. 535)

Alliance movement   (p. 535)

Initiative   (p. 537)

Referendum   (p. 537)

Populist (or People's) Party   (p. 537)

Panic of 1893   (p. 538)

Homestead strike   (p. 540)

Pullman strike   (p. 541)

Coxey's army   (p. 542)

Mississippi Plan   (p. 542)

PEOPLE YOU SHOULD KNOW

William Jennings Bryan   (p. 521)

William McKinley   (p. 521)

Rutherford B. Hayes   (p. 528)

James B. Weaver   (p. 529)

James A. Garfield   (p. 529)

Chester A. Arthur   (p. 529)

Grover Cleveland   (p. 530)

Benjamin Harrison   (p. 531)

Tom Watson   (p. 538)

Eugene V. Debs   (p. 541)

Jacob S. Coxey   (p. 541)

Ida B. Wells   (p. 543)

REVIEW QUESTIONS

1. What roles did the two major political parties play in the late nineteenth century?

2. How did events shape political concerns during the Gilded Age?

3. Why and how did the farmers and workers revolt?

4. How did conditions for African Americans deteriorate at the end of the century?

20 Imperial America, 1870–1900

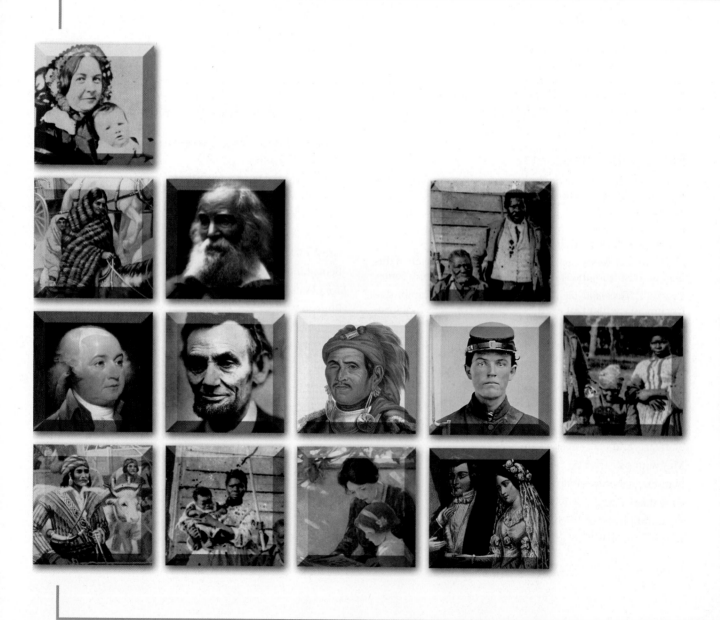

PRESIDENT GRANT'S DREAMS OF EXPANSION

Dreams of expansion came easily to Americans during the nineteenth century. For most of the century they expanded westward, moving into Texas and Kansas, pushing across the Great Plains, and occupying California and the Pacific Northwest. But they did not restrict their dreams to the millions of acres between Mexico and Canada. They cast covetous eyes toward Central America and the islands of the Caribbean and the Pacific. Plans to annex Nicaragua, Cuba, Santo Domingo, the Virgin Islands, Hawaii, and Samoa fired politicians' imaginations. Before the Civil War, the debate over slavery blocked these larger expansionist efforts. Once the Union was preserved, however, expansionists returned to their plans with revived energy and enthusiasm.

President Ulysses S. Grant had a pet expansionist project of his own—the **Dominican Republic,** the eastern two-thirds of the Caribbean island of Santo Domingo. The island was rich in mineral resources, possessed an important natural harbor, and its inhabitants were eager to buy American products. Most importantly for Grant, who was ever mindful of America's race problem, the Dominicans were black. The island could serve as a frontier for black Americans, a retreat from Ku Klux Klan harassment.

With so much to gain, Grant put his full political weight behind annexation. His conduct was less than presidential. First, he sent his personal secretary and close friend Orville Babcock to Santo Domingo on a "fact-finding" mission. Unimpressed by the islanders, Babcock reported: "The people are indolent and ignorant. The best class of people are the American Negroes who have come here from time to time." But Babcock was convinced that the Dominican Republic was a commercial and strategic prize worthy of annexation. What was more, **Buenaventura Baez,** the unscrupulous president of the republic, was eager to sell his country. With the money he would make from the transaction, Baez hoped to establish residence in Paris or Madrid, because, as Babcock noted, the Dominican Republic was "a dull country."

Unrest around him added fuel to Baez's willingness to sell. Both neighboring Haiti and a strong force of Dominican rebels threatened his government. So difficult was Baez's position that Babcock had to order a United States Navy ship to

Elected president in 1868, Ulysses S. Grant showed little aptitude for the office. When Senate Foreign Relations Committee Chairman Charles Sumner spearheaded the defeat of the treaty to annex the Dominican Republic, Grant retaliated by orchestrating Sumner's removal as chairman of the committee.

protect the Baez government during the annexation negotiations, which were completed in the late fall of 1869. The promise of American dollars had convinced Baez that his country should belong to the United States.

Grant was pleased. The treaty of annexation, however, would have to be ratified by the Senate, a body more difficult to satisfy than Baez's government. Grant decided to forgo presidential protocol and personally visit **Charles Sumner,** the chairman of the Senate Foreign Relations Committee. On the evening of January 2, 1870, Grant called at Sumner's Washington home on Lafayette Park. Sumner recalled later that Grant was drunk at the time. Drunk or sober, Grant was certainly in earnest. He energetically discussed the need to annex the Dominican Republic. Sumner listened, then replied: "Mr. President, I am an Administration man, and whatever you do will always find in me the most careful and candid consideration." Grant departed, believing he had won Sumner's full support. In fact, he had only won the powerful Massachusetts senator's "candid consideration."

After consideration and considerable investigation, Sumner decided that the entire annexation scheme was distasteful. He was disturbed by Babcock's and Baez's unethical financial dealings and was enraged that the United States Navy had been used to keep the Dominican president in power. Sumner was not a man to mince words. Labeled "probably the most intolerant man that American history has ever known," he accused Grant of being "a colossus of ignorance." By a vote of 5 to 2, the Foreign Relations Committee voiced its disapproval of the treaty of annexation.

Grant was furious. His son later recalled, "I never saw Father so grimly angry." Known for his bulldog tenacity during the Civil War, Grant was not about to quit. He hinted that if the United States did not take the Dominican Republic, one of the European powers would; he even reported the results of a rigged plebiscite in which the Dominicans supposedly supported annexation by the suspiciously lopsided vote of 15,169 to 11. Grant's efforts failed. On June 30, 1870, the Senate rejected the treaty. Defining America's duty toward the island, Sumner said, "Our duty is as plain as the Ten Commandments. Kindness, beneficence, assistance, aid, help, protection, all that is implied in good neighborhood, these we must give freely, bountifully, but their independence is as sacred to them as is ours to us."

The failed attempt to annex the Dominican Republic is important for the themes it underscored. It demonstrated both the desire for expansion by the president and his advisers and the power of Congress in foreign affairs. For the remainder of the century the scenario would be repeated again and again, often with differing results. Gradually presidents wrested more control over foreign affairs from Congress. And Congress, for its part, accepted a more expansionist foreign policy. As presidents and Congress found common ground, America expanded outward into the Caribbean and the Pacific, although the expansion took different forms. Sometimes the United States annexed countries outright; other times it was content to exercise less forceful control over nominally independent countries. The results were the same. The United States ultimately acquired an overseas empire and expanded its influence over the Western Hemisphere.

CONGRESSIONAL CONTROL AND THE REDUCTION OF AMERICAN POWER

In 1869, when Grant took office, congressmen and other Americans held the State Department and the diplomatic service in low esteem. No majestic building housed the State Department—it was headquartered in a former orphan asylum. Nor was the post of secretary of state as great a prize as it had been. Once regarded as a stepping-stone to the presidency, politicians increasingly viewed the post as a reward for outstanding party men or the refuge for defeated presidential aspirants. Even the diplomats themselves did not escape criticism. One newspaper editor said the diplomatic service was too often used as "gilt edged pigeon holes for filing away Americans, more or less illustrious, who are no longer particularly wanted at home."

Trimming the State Department

The irreverent treatment of the State Department reflected a congressional and national mood. Concerns over the currency, civil service reform, Reconstruction, taxation, the tariff, Indian fighting, and railroad building dwarfed interest in foreign affairs. During the 1870s and 1880s, when a powerful Congress largely dictated foreign policy, the spirit of Washington's Farewell Address and the Monroe Doctrine guided the country. Washington had counseled America to steer clear of foreign entanglements and Monroe had made isolationism from Europe a national obsession. Separated from a powerful Europe by the cold North Atlantic, Congress saw no reason to spend time or money on the State Department or foreign affairs.

Using its control over the budget as a sword, Congress trimmed the State Department to the bone. In 1869, Congress allowed the State Department a paltry 31 clerks; by 1881 presidential efforts had succeeded in raising that number to a still inadequate 50. Politicians who considered the foreign service "a nursery of snobs" viewed diplomats as an expensive, nearly useless luxury. A few reformers even advocated the abolition of the foreign service. They argued that two oceans protected America and that international lawyers could be hired to handle serious international crises.

Reducing the Military

The sword that trimmed the State Department was also used to pare the United States army and navy. When the Civil War ended and peace returned, Congress quickly reduced the country's military might, making the United States a weaker country. In 1865 the United States had the largest and perhaps the most powerful navy in the world, with 971 vessels. To be sure, it was a ragtag navy, composed of just about any vessel that would float, ranging from the powerful *Monitor*-class ironclads to modest yachts. Within nine months of Appomattox, the fleet had been reduced to 29.

As Congress watched unconcerned, the navy declined intellectually as well. To begin with, there were far too many officers. Although after the post–Civil War reductions the United States navy was less than one-tenth as large as Great Britain's, it contained over half as many officers. With promotions based strictly upon length of service, any officer who lived long enough could become an admiral. This system of promotion almost guaranteed poor leadership. The world's best navies converted to steel and steam, but U.S. naval leaders remained tied to wood and sails. The U.S. navy quickly became a joke. In 1881 authorities claimed, with some justification, that a single modern ship of the Chilean navy could destroy the entire United States fleet.

The power and effectiveness of the army were similarly reduced. On May 23, 1865, with the Civil War just ended, Union bluecoats marched down Pennsylvania Avenue in a victory parade. There were over 100,000 soldiers. It took an hour for General Meade's cavalry to pass the reviewing stand. "Marching twelve abreast, the general's infantry consumed another five hours." The next day thousands of General Sherman's men repeated the performance, marching briskly "like the lords of the world!"

The sight would not be repeated for over 50 years. Demobilization occurred quickly and haphazardly. In May 1865 the army contained 1,034,064 volunteers; by November 1866 only 11,043 remained in uniform. Eventually Congress slashed the number of even the regular troops. By the end of Reconstruction, Congress had reduced the army to a distant echo of its former self. In 1876 maximum strength stood at 27,442 troops.

Certainly, in 1876 the United States did not need an active foreign service and a powerful army and navy to secure its borders. No countries threatened America. Geography defended the United States, and the European balance of power discouraged European designs on any part of the Western Hemisphere. At the same time, the relative weakness of America's foreign service, army, and navy discouraged the United States from attempting to extend its influence beyond its own borders. All in all, most congressmen were entirely happy with the situation.

Seward's Dream

Not everyone in government agreed with congressional leadership in foreign affairs. Regularly during the 1860s and 1870s, presidents or their secretaries of state called for a more forceful, expansionist foreign policy. **William Henry Seward** of New York, who served as secretary of state for Lincoln and Johnson, was such a man. A cold and vain man with a weak

Political opponents of Secretary of State William Seward ridiculed his plan to purchase Alaska from Russia, referring to the territory as "Seward's Icebox" and "Seward's Folly." A massive propaganda campaign and the alleged buying of votes by Edouard de Stoeckl, the Russian minister to the United States who negotiated the annexation plan with Seward, overcame the opposition, and the Senate ratified the treaty of annexation on April 9, 1867.

chin and a prominent nose, Seward dreamed of an American empire that would dominate the Pacific and Caribbean basins. During his term as secretary of state, he advocated a vigorous expansionism. He negotiated with Denmark to purchase the Danish West Indies (Virgin Islands), with Russia to buy Alaska, and with Santo Domingo for the Dominican harbor of Samana Bay. In addition, his plan for an American empire encompassed Haiti, Cuba, Iceland, Greenland, Honduras's Tigre Island, and Hawaii.

Congress, not sharing Seward's vision, balked. During Seward's term, America did acquire the Midway Islands in the middle of the Pacific Ocean, but few Americans even noticed the addition. The purchase of Alaska in 1867 drew more comments, most of them negative. Congressmen grumbled over the treaty. Some senators claimed that $7.2 million was too much money for a frozen wasteland that only Eskimos and seals could love. Others cracked jokes about "Johnson's Polar Bear Garden" and "Frigidia." But in the end the Senate, influenced by a few well-placed bribes, reluctantly ratified the treaty.

Articulate and aggressive anti-imperialists blocked the remainder of Seward's dreams. During the late 1860s and the 1870s congressional power was at high tide. Seward and President Andrew Johnson were no match for Sumner and Thaddeus Stevens and their colleagues in Congress. Congressmen consistently found other issues more pressing than foreign affairs. Some pushed for money to enact a fair Reconstruction policy. Others freely gave money to railroad construction companies and Union veterans, such gifts contributing significantly to their reelection. But they drew America's purse strings tight when confronted with most expansionist schemes.

THE SPIRIT OF AMERICAN GREATNESS

Although Congress was reluctant to endorse expansionist schemes, during the last third of the nineteenth century many other citizens had become convinced that the United States had to adopt a more aggressive and forceful foreign policy. Their reasons varied. Some believed expansion would be good for American business. Others felt America had a duty to spread its way of life to less fortunate countries. Still others maintained that economic and strategic security required that the country acquire overseas bases. Behind all the arguments, however, rested a common assumption: The United States was a great and important country, and it should start acting the part.

American Exceptionalism

For many Americans it started with God's plan. The idea of **American exceptionalism**—that the nation houses God's chosen people—has deep roots in the country's history. Puritan concepts of "a city upon a hill" mixed easily with talk of the greatness of republicanism and democracy and the manifest destiny of America. The teachings of **Social Darwinism** added "scientific proof" to the concept of American exceptionalism. With such Darwinian phrases as "natural

THE PEOPLE SPEAK

March of the Flag

Few American leaders articulated the nation's expansionist impulse as clearly or unapologetically as Indiana Senator Albert J. Beveridge. His "March of the Flag" speech, first delivered in Indianapolis' Tomlinson Hall in September 1898, argued that Americans possessed a unique responsibility for their less "civilized" neighbors.

In this campaign, the question is larger than a party question. It is an American question. It is a world question. Shall the American people continue their march toward the commercial supremacy of the world? Shall free institutions broaden their blessed reign as the children of liberty wax in strength, until the empire of our principles is established over the hearts of all mankind? . . .

The Opposition tells us that we ought not to govern a people without their consent. I answer, The rule of liberty that all just government derives its authority from the consent of the governed, applies only to those who are capable of self-government. We govern the Indians without their consent, we govern our territories without their consent, we govern our children without their consent. How do they know that our government would be without their consent? Would not the people of the Philippines prefer the just, humane, civilizing government of this Republic to the savage, bloody rule of pillage and extortion from which we have rescued them?

And, regardless of this formula of words made only for enlightened, self-governing people, do we owe no duty to the world? Shall we turn these peoples back to the reeking hands from which we have taken them? Shall we abandon them, with Germany, England, and Japan hungering for them? Shall we save them from those nations, to give them a self-rule of tragedy? . . .

Will you say by your vote that American ability to govern has decayed; that a century's experience in self-rule has failed of a result? Will you affirm by your vote that you are an infidel to American power and practical sense? Or will you say that ours is the blood of government; ours the heart of dominion; ours the brain and genius of administration? Will you remember that we do but what our fathers did—we but pitch the tents of liberty farther westward, farther southward—we only continue the march of the flag?

Source: Albert J. Beveridge, "The March of the Flag" (printed in the *Indianapolis Journal,* September 17, 1898. *The Meaning of the Times,* 1908). Bobbs-Merrill, Indianopolis.

---

selection" and "survival of the fittest," American intellectuals praised the course of American history. Charles Darwin himself noted that "the wonderful progress of the United States, as well as the character of the people, are the results of natural selection; the more energetic, restless, and courageous men from all parts of Europe have emigrated during the last ten or twelve generations to that great country."

Such ideas found a warm reception in America. There was, however, a dark side to American exceptionalism, and too many Americans were quick to endorse it: If white Anglo-Saxon Americans were biologically superior, then other races and other nations had to be inferior. During the late nineteenth century, such Social Darwinists as Herbert Spencer in England and John Fiske in the United States helped make racism intellectually acceptable. Catering to Anglo-Saxon audiences, social Darwinists advanced pseudoscientific theories to "prove" the superiority of Anglo-Saxons.

From the idea of superiority to the acceptance of domination was a short step. If Americans were God's and Darwin's chosen people, why shouldn't they dominate and uplift less fortunate countries and peoples? This was the question that advocates of a more aggressive American foreign policy asked their audiences. Senator Albert J. Beveridge of Indiana spoke for many Americans when he told Congress:

God has not been preparing the English-speaking and Teutonic peoples for a thousand years for nothing but vain and idle self-admiration. No! He has not made us the master organizers of the world to establish a system where chaos reigns. . . . He has given us the spirit of progress to overwhelm the forces of reaction throughout the earth. He has made us adept in government that we may administer government among savage and senile peoples.

Sense of Duty

Religious leaders also noted the duty that American exceptionalism implied. Talk of the **"white man's burden"** and the duty of "advanced" peoples was rife during the period. Protestant missionaries carried their faith and beliefs to the far corners of the world, but the benefits of their message extended well beyond preaching salvation and saving souls. They also extolled the virtues of American civilization, which included everything from democracy and rule by law to sanitation, material progress, sewing machines, and cotton underwear. Defining good and bad, progress and savagery by American standards, they attempted to alter native customs and beliefs to conform to a single American model.

Popular writer and religious leader Reverend Josiah Strong voiced what other missionaries and true believers acted upon. In 1885 Strong published *Our Country: Its Possible Future and Present Crisis,* a book that quickly sold 170,000 copies and was translated into dozens of languages. "The Anglo-Saxon," Strong wrote, "is the representative of two great ideas . . . civil liberty [and] a pure *spiritual* Christianity." These two ideas, he added, are destined to elevate all mankind, and "the Anglo-Saxon . . . is divinely commissioned to be . . . his brother's keeper." He firmly believed that it was America's destiny and duty to expand and spread its influence. Quoting the Bible while speaking to Anglo-Saxon Americans, he intoned, "Prepare ye the way of the Lord!"

Search for Markets

Strong's message was not lost on the business leaders of America. They fully agreed that missionaries should preach the benefits of American material progress as well as the glories of the Protestant faith. Looking south toward Latin America and west toward Asia, American businesspeople and farmers saw vast virgin markets for their industrial and agricultural surpluses as well as endless sources of raw materials. Sensing that American markets, filled with low-paid workers, offered few new opportunities, they entertained fabulous visions of hungry Latin Americans and shoeless Chinese.

By the late nineteenth century, the United States was the leading industrial and agricultural country in the world, but domestic consumption did not keep pace with the galloping production. In addition, throughout the period the government pursued tight-money policies, and laborers' real income only modestly grew. The result was a boom-and-bust economy: spectacular growth and severe depressions. In fact, in the 25 years after 1873, the country suffered through three depressions: 1873 to 1878, 1882 to 1885, and 1893 to 1897.

During depression years, foreign trade seemed a necessity. Depressions meant farm foreclosures and industrial unemployment, problems that led to social unrest. The Grange and Populist movements, the two largest agrarian revolts, originated in cotton and wheat areas during depression years. And such labor confrontations as the violent railroad strikes of 1877, Chicago's Haymarket riot of 1886, and the Pullman strike of 1894 occurred during lean economic times. For many Americans the issue was simple: The United States had to acquire foreign markets or face economic hardship and revolution at home. As one industrial spokesman put it: The time has come for the United States to pursue "an intelligent and spirited foreign policy," one in which the government would "see to it" that the country had adequate foreign markets. If force proved necessary, then so be it.

The State Department was in full agreement. William Henry Seward and Hamilton Fish, Johnson's and Grant's secretaries of state, believed firmly that America needed new markets. Seward called the potentially bottomless markets of Asia "the prize," and he wanted the United States to acquire islands in the Pacific as stepping-stones toward that prize. He similarly believed that the United States should extend its economic control to include Canada and Latin America. Hamilton Fish agreed with the hoarsevoiced, cigar-chewing Seward. Although, like Seward, he had to contend with a cautious, isolationist Congress, Fish made several important strides toward the Asia markets. During his term as secretary of state, the United States signed treaties and established more formal relations with Hawaii and Samoa, two Pacific island groups that would later become part of the American empire.

During the late 1870s and 1880s, economic hard times quickened the search for new markets. Rutherford B. Hayes's secretary of state William Evarts valued a good story; he once told a British minister that George Washington had been able to throw a dollar across the Rappahannock River because a dollar went farther in those days. Evarts also valued dollars, and he felt Americans needed far more of them. As secretary of state, he worked toward an American commercial empire. He hoped that unexploited Asian and Latin American markets would guarantee continual economic growth and social tranquility for all Americans.

James G. Blaine and Frederick T. Frelinghuysen, who served as secretaries of state for James Garfield and Chester Arthur, concentrated their efforts on Latin American markets. Blaine later recounted that during his short stay in the State Department in 1881 he followed two principles: "first, to bring about peace . . . ; second, to cultivate such friendly commercial relations with all American countries as would lead to a large increase in the export trade of the United States." When Blaine was forced out of office after Garfield's assassination, Frelinghuysen continued his policies. He successfully negotiated bilateral reciprocity treaties with many Latin American countries, which lowered tariffs and thus stimulated trade between the United States and Latin America.

By the mid-1880s, expansion efforts combined with economic and social problems at home convinced Congress to reevaluate its isolationist policies. The West was settled, the Native Americans defeated, the Union reconstructed, and the railroads built. It was now time to look at our oceans not as defensive barriers but as paths toward new markets and increased prosperity. There was one final problem: America's navy and merchant marine seemed woefully unfit for the challenge.

The New Navy

British writer and wit Oscar Wilde was close to the truth when he had one of his fictional characters reply to an American woman who complained that her country had no ruins and no curiosities: "No ruins! No curiosities! You have your Navy and your manners!" By 1880 the United States Navy was a sad joke.

If America hoped to compete for world markets, it had to upgrade its navy. During the 1880s and early 1890s advocates of a **New Navy** moved Congress to action. The transformation from a "heterogeneous collection of naval trash" to a great navy occurred in two stages. The face-lift began in 1883, during the administration of Chester A. Arthur. Prodded by the president, Congress passed an act providing for three small cruisers and a dispatch boat, the beginning of the famous White Squadron. More vessels soon followed. Under the direction of President Grover Cleveland and his able secretary of the navy, William Whitney, the White Squadron grew in size, and naval bureaucracy and fleet personnel improved.

By 1890 great gains had been made, but there were still serious problems. The White Squadron was not a world-class navy. Its ships were lightly armored, fast cruisers, ideal for hit-and-run missions but inadequate for any major naval engagement. While Britain and Germany were building large, heavily armored battleships capable of bombarding and damaging coastal cities, the United States continued to think of naval warfare in terms of commerce raiding.

Benjamin F. Tracy, Benjamin Harrison's secretary of war, was determined to change American naval thinking. Tracy had a very modern view of what defense entailed. To adequately defend America's interests, Tracy called for ships that could "raise blockades" and attack an enemy's coast, "for a war, though defensive in principle, may be conducted most effectively by being offensive in its operations." In fact, Tracy maintained that proper defense might even include shooting first: "The nation that is ready to strike the first blow will gain an advantage which its antagonist can never offset." Such a first-strike definition of defense meant one thing: The United States needed to build modern, armored battleships. Tracy wanted two battleship fleets, one for the Atlantic and another for the Pacific.

Tracy's program was endorsed in Congress by such "Big Navy" advocates as Senator Eugene Hale of Maine and Representative Henry Cabot Lodge of Massachusetts. They found Congress in the mood to

In 1907, President Theodore Roosevelt, in order to demonstrate U.S. naval strength, sent 16 battleships on an around-the-world voyage. Painted white, the ships became known as the Great White Fleet.

act. As one senator said, "You can not negotiate without a gun." In 1890, Congress appropriated money for the construction of three first-class battleships and a heavy cruiser. It was the beginning of a new, very much offensive navy for the United States. Reviewing his accomplishments in 1891, Tracy boasted: "The sea will be the future seat of empire. And we shall rule it as certainly as the sun doth rise."

Talk of empire, navy, trade, and national greatness came together in 1890 in the publication of a monumentally important book, *The Influence of Sea Power upon History,* by Captain Alfred Thayer Mahan. Mahan, who was attached to the Naval War College, was more comfortable around books than on ships. Although he had served throughout the world, he had the look, temperament, and inclinations of a college don. His masterpiece set forward the simple thesis that naval power was the key to national greatness. Taking Greece, Rome, and England as examples, he attempted to demonstrate that countries rise to world power through expanding their foreign commerce and protecting that commerce with a strong navy. Without a powerful navy, Mahan emphasized, a nation can never enjoy full prosperity and security. Without a strong navy, in short, no nation could ever hope to be a world power.

Large Policy

Mahan's writings and Tracy's proposal were applauded by American politicians and businesspeople who felt it was time for the United States to assume the rights and responsibilities of world-power status. These were important citizens—men of wealth, education, and influence. Some like Whitelaw Reid, editor of the *New York Tribune,* helped shape public opinion through their editorials. Others like Henry Cabot Lodge, Theodore Roosevelt, Albert J. Beveridge, and John Hay were powerful politicians and administrators. They were vocal nationalists who believed that the United States was destined to be the greatest of world powers. Increasingly after 1890, these and other men of like mind dominated and shaped America's foreign policy.

These expansionists often shared common experiences and beliefs. Most were prosperous Republicans from old-line American families, and most had traveled abroad widely. Anglo-Saxon by heritage, they tended to be ardent Anglophiles, full of praise for Great Britain's imperial efforts. They believed that the United States should join "Mother England" in administering to the "uncivilized" corners of the globe. As Beveridge noted, without the work of An-

glo-Saxons "the world would relapse into barbarism and night. . . . We are trustees of the world's progress, guardians of its righteous place."

Lodge and other expansionists called for a bold foreign policy, what they called the **large policy.** They advocated the construction of a canal through Central America to allow American ships to move between the Atlantic and Pacific oceans more rapidly. To protect the canal, the United States would have to exert control over Cuba and the other strategically located Caribbean islands. Next, America would have to acquire coaling stations and naval bases across the Pacific. Secure bases in Hawaii, Guam, Wake Island, and the Philippines would allow the United States to exploit the seemingly limitless Asian market. Finally, a powerful navy would have to protect the entire American empire.

In the end, then, all of their plans were rooted in the theme of a strong navy. Like his friend Mahan, Lodge was a student of history. "It is the sea power which is essential to the greatness of every splendid people," he said. It had enabled Rome to crush the Carthaginians, England to defeat Napoleon, and the North to win the Civil War. Without the power of a strong navy, Lodge believed that America could never experience real peace and security: "All the peace the world has ever had has been obtained by fighting, and all the peace that any nation . . . can ever have, is by readiness to fight if attacked." For Lodge as for Tracy, thoughts of peace and war often ran together and appeared in the same sentences.

THE EMERGENCE OF AGGRESSION IN AMERICAN FOREIGN POLICY

"To be prepared for war is the most effectual means to promote peace," said Theodore Roosevelt. The more such politicians talked about peace, the closer war seemed. It is not coincidental that the United States launched a more belligerent foreign policy at the same time it was building and launching more powerful ships. The two developments originated from the same source: a ready acceptance of force as the final arbiter of international disputes. Before the turn of the century, the acceptance of force would lead to the Spanish-American War of 1898; between 1885 and 1897, during the presidencies of Benjamin Harrison and Grover Cleveland, the same attitudes almost caused several other wars. The Spanish-American War was not an aberrant event. Rather it was the result of a more aggressive American foreign policy, one aimed at acquiring both world respect and an empire.

Confronting the Germans in Samoa

Changing American attitudes toward foreign policy first became apparent in relation to **Samoa,** a group of 14 South Pacific volcanic islands with splendid natural harbors. In 1872 an American negotiated a treaty with a tribal chief to grant the United States rights to a naval station at Pago Pago. Although an antiexpansionist Senate took no action on the treaty, expansionists kept trying. In 1878 the Senate did ratify a similar treaty, which formally committed the United States to Samoa. Unfortunately for the United States, German Chancellor Otto von Bismarck had also decided that Samoa should belong to Germany. As a result of the intricacies of European politics, England sided with the "iron chancellor." President Cleveland and his secretary of state, Thomas F. Bayard, firmly disagreed with the Europeans. Germany and the United States were set on a collision course.

When a conference between the three countries held in Washington in 1887 failed to solve the problem, war seemed closer still. Neither Germany nor the United States had much money invested in the islands, but both felt their national pride was at stake. "We must show sharp teeth," remarked Bismarck. Cleveland, for his part, dispatched three warships to Samoa. Nature, however, had the most powerful weapon. On the morning of March 16, 1889, a typhoon swept across Samoa, destroying both American and German warships anchored in Apia harbor.

The violent winds seemed to calm the ruffled emotions of the United States and Germany. "Men and nations," wrote the *New York World*, "must bow before the decrees of nature." The same year as the typhoon, Germany, the United States, and England met for another conference, this one in Berlin. Without consulting the Samoans, they decided to partition the islands. Everyone seemed satisfied—except the Samoans, who were deprived of their independence and saddled with an unpopular king. The plan lasted until 1899, when Germany and the United States ended the facade of Samoan independence and officially made colonies of the islands. The United States was granted Tutuila, with the harbor of Pago Pago, and several smaller islands. Many expansionists believed that America's aggressive stand against Germany had paid handsome dividends.

Teaching Chile a Lesson

American expansionists had something to gain from their confrontation with Germany over Samoa. Pago Pago was, after all, "the most perfectly landlocked harbor that exists in the Pacific Ocean." It was an ideal coaling station for ships running between San Francisco and Australia. American troubles with Chile, however, are more difficult to understand. Trade and strategic policy played only small roles. More than anything else, touchy pride and jingoism pushed the United States toward war with Chile.

Had people not died, the background to the confrontation would have been amusing. In 1891 a revolutionary faction, which the United States had opposed, gained control of the Chilean government and initiated a foreign policy that was unfriendly toward America. Shortly thereafter, on October 16, 1891, an American cruiser, the **Baltimore,** anchored off the coast of Chile. About 100 members of its crew were sent ashore on leave at Valparaiso. Some sailors retired to the local True Blue Saloon. An officer who arrived on the scene later said that the men had gone ashore "for the purpose of getting drunk" and that by evening they were "probably drunk, properly drunk." As the men left the saloon, a riot broke out. An angry, anti-American mob attacked the sailors, killing 2 and injuring 16. To make matters worse, the Chilean police, who had done nothing to halt the fighting, carried the surviving Americans off to jail.

It was an unfortunate affair, and the United States loudly protested, demanding a formal apology and "prompt and full reparation." The Chilean government refused. President Harrison, a former Union general who prided himself on his patriotism and was easily swayed by jingoism, threatened to break off diplomatic relations—a serious step toward war—unless the United States received an immediate apology. When Secretary of State James G. Blaine tried to counsel moderation, Harrison angrily replied, "Mr. Secretary, that insult was to the uniform of United States sailors."

Public opinion sided with Harrison. The *New York Sun* commented that "we must teach men who will henceforth be called snarling whelps of the Pacific that we cannot be snapped at with impunity." Angry young Theodore Roosevelt insisted, "For two nickels he would declare war himself . . . and wage it sole." Finally the Chilean government backed down, apologizing for the attack on the sailors and paying a $75,000 indemnity.

The threat of force had again carried the day. Advocates of the New Navy and aggressively nationalistic Americans cheered Harrison's actions. Few Americans heeded Edwin L. Godkin, editor of *The Nation*, who wrote, "Navy officers dream of war and talk and lecture about it incessantly. The Senate debates are filled with predictions of impending war and with talk of preparing for it at once. . . . Most truculent and bloodthirsty of all, jingo editors keep up a din day after day about the way we could cripple one country's fleet and destroy another's commerce, and fill heads of boys and silly men with the idea that war is the normal state of a civilized country."

Plucking the Hawaiian Pear

Throughout the late nineteenth century, Hawaii figured prominently in American foreign policy planning. Earlier in the century, the islands had been a favorite place for American missionaries. Many went to Hawaii to spread Christianity and ended up settling and raising their families in the tropical paradise. More important still was the islands' location. Not only were they ideally situated along the trade routes to Asia, but they offered a perfect site for protecting the Pacific sea lanes to the American west coast and to the potential locations of an isthmus canal. In Hawaii, missionary, economic, and strategic concerns met in complete harmony.

By the mid-1880s, Congress was willing to accept expansionists' dreams for Hawaii. A treaty between Hawaii and the United States, ratified in 1887, set aside Pearl Harbor for the exclusive use of the American navy. By that time the islands were already economically tied to the United States. An 1875 treaty had allowed Hawaiians to sell their sugar in the United States duty-free, giving them a two-cents-per-pound advantage over other foreign producers. The legislation encouraged American speculators to invest in Hawaiian sugar and to import Chinese and Japanese laborers to the islands to work on the large plantations. The investments returned incredibly high dividends, and for a time business boomed.

Problems arose suddenly in 1890. The **McKinley Tariff Act** removed all tariffs on foreign sugar and protected domestic sugar producers by awarding American sugar a bounty of two cents per pound. Hawaiian sugar prices plummeted. The American minister in Honolulu estimated that the McKinley Tariff cost Hawaiian producers $12 million. And in 1891 the government of the islands changed. **Queen Liliuokalani** ascended the throne. A poet and a composer interested in humanitarian work, she nevertheless initiated a strongly anti-American policy. She wanted to purge American influences in Hawaii and disfranchise all white men except those married to native women.

The white population in Hawaii reacted quickly. On January 17, 1893, three days after the queen dismissed the legislature and proclaimed a new constitution, white islanders overthrew her government. Supported by American officials, sailors, and

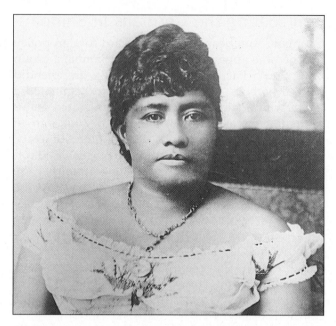

Queen Liliuokalani assumed the Hawaiian throne in 1891. Strongly nationalistic, she sought to purge white influence from Hawaii. She was overthrown by white islanders with the aid of American sailors and marines.

marines, the revolution was fast, almost bloodless, and successful. Foreign minister John L. Stevens then proclaimed Hawaii an American protectorate and wired his superiors in Washington that "the Hawaiian pear is now fully ripe, and this is the golden hour for the United States to pluck it."

The Harrison administration, due to leave office on March 4, negotiated a treaty of annexation with "indecent haste" and sent it to the Senate for ratification. Public sentiment cheered Harrison's actions. But before the Senate could ratify the treaty, Cleveland took office. An anti-imperialist, Cleveland had grave misgivings about the revolution, America's reaction, and the treaty. Five days after his inauguration, he recalled the treaty from the Senate and sent a special agent, James H. Blount of Georgia, to Hawaii to investigate the entire affair. After a careful investigation, Blount reported to Cleveland that the majority of native Hawaiians opposed annexation and that on moral and legal grounds the treaty was unjustified. Cleveland accepted Blount's report and killed the treaty.

The controversy, however, was not over. A white American minority continued to govern Hawaii. To correct the situation, Cleveland sent another representative, Albert S. Willis, to Hawaii to convince the new government to step down and allow Queen Liliuokalani to return to the throne. Willis failed in his mission. "Queen Lil" refused to promise full amnesty for the revolutionaries if she were returned to power. "My decision would be," she said, "as the law directs, that such persons should be beheaded." In addition, newly elected President Sanford B. Dole, head of a large Hawaiian pineapple corporation, refused to leave office. In the end, Cleveland washed his hands of the entire matter, and the revolutionaries proclaimed an independent Hawaiian republic on July 4, 1894. Four years and three days later, during the Spanish-American War, the United States finally annexed Hawaii.

Facing Down the British

Potentially the most serious conflict America faced during the 1890s originated in a dispute over a strip of land in a South American jungle. Venezuela and British Guiana shared a common border, but both claimed land the other side said was theirs. For almost 50 years this dispute remained peacefully unsettled, until the discovery of gold in the region in the 1880s increased the importance of the issue. It was a rich deposit—the largest nugget ever discovered, 509 ounces, was found there—and both Britain and Venezuela wanted it. In response to Venezuelan requests for help, the United States several times offered to arbitrate the matter, and each time Britain refused the offer.

By June 1895 Cleveland and his new secretary of state, Richard Olney, two short-tempered men, had decided that Britain's actions violated the spirit, if not the letter, of the Monroe Doctrine. (Ever since a cancer operation had left him with an artificial jaw of vulcanized rubber, Cleveland had been irritable.) Olney, who had persuaded Cleveland to use federal troops to put down the Pullman strike in Chicago the year before, was a man of strong ideas who did not shrink from the use of force. In a strongly worded message to Great Britain, Olney demanded that Britain submit the dispute to arbitration, hinting that the United States might intervene militarily if its wishes were not honored.

Lord Salisbury, Britain's prime minister, foreign secretary, and consummate aristocrat, did not reply to Olney's note for four months; he then answered, in effect, that the dispute did not involve either the United States or the Monroe Doctrine and would America kindly mind its own business. Olney was furious. Americans throughout the country felt insulted. When Cleveland read the message he became "mad clean through." In a special message to Congress, he asked for funds to establish a commission to determine the actual Venezuelan boundary. He also insisted that he would use force if necessary to maintain that boundary against any aggressors. Both houses of Congress unanimously approved Cleveland's request. The excitement of war was in the air.

The violence of America's reaction surprised Salisbury and British officials. England, increasingly involved in a conflict in South Africa, certainly did not want war. Salisbury reversed his position and allowed a commission to arbitrate the dispute. In the end, the arbitral tribunal gave Britain most of the land it claimed.

America, however, felt it was the real winner. Cleveland had faced the British lion and won. The Monroe Doctrine and American prestige soared to new heights. More important for the future, Cleveland's actions, coupled with his handling of the Hawaiian revolution, significantly increased the power of the president over foreign affairs. Future presidents would not soon relinquish that control.

THE WAR FOR EMPIRE

During the Venezuela crisis many Americans seemed to invite and look forward to the prospect of war. Theodore Roosevelt, who was determined to atone for the failure of his father to fight in the Civil War and to be the first in war even if he were the last in peace, wrote: "Let the fight come if it must; I don't care whether our sea coast cities are bombarded or not; we would take Canada." For Roosevelt, war would be an ennobling experience. It would test and validate American greatness. "All the great masterful races," Roosevelt wrote, "have been fighting races; and the minute that a race loses the hard fighting virtues, then . . . it has lost its proud right to stand as the equal of the best."

The Spirit of the 1890s

Throughout the 1890s other Americans echoed Roosevelt's war cries. Viewed as a whole, it was a decade of strident nationalism and aggressive posturing. It was also a troubled and violent decade. Racked by the depression of 1893, frustrated by the problems created by monopolies and overproduction, and plagued by internal strife, Americans turned on each other, often with violent results. Strikes in Pullman, Illinois, and Homestead, Pennsylvania, saw laborers battle federal and state authorities. Populist protest dramatized the widening gulf between city and country, rich and poor. Anarchists and socialists talked about the need for violent solutions to complex problems.

American heroes of all stripes reflected this aggressive mood. In saloons across the country, heavyweight boxing champion John L. Sullivan defiantly boasted, "I can lick any sonofabitch in the house." In the parlors of the wealthy, Roosevelt stressed, "Cowardice in a race, as in an individual, is the unpardonable sin." Between Sullivan and Roosevelt, and the Americans that admired both men, was a bond forged by the love of violence and power.

This attitude led to the glorification of war and jingoistic nationalism. During the mid-1890s a remarkable interest in Napoleon gripped the nation—between 1894 and 1896, 28 books were written about the Corsican general. In public schools throughout the country, administrators instituted daily flag salutes and made the recitation of the new pledge of allegiance mandatory. Even the popular music of the day had a particularly martial quality. Such marches as John Philip Sousa's "Stars and Stripes Forever" (1897) captured the aggressive, patriotic, and boisterous mood of the country.

As the disputes with Germany, Chile, and Great Britain demonstrated, neither the American people nor its leaders feared war. The horrors of the Civil War were dying with the generation that had known them. A younger generation of men, filled with romantic conceptions of battle and heroism, now openly sought a war of their own. Some Washington politicians even began to view war as a way to unite the country, to quell the protests of angry farmers and laborers.

The Cuban Revolution

Oftentimes the mood of a nation governs the reaction to and interpretation of events. Such was the case with America's attitude toward the **Cuban Revolution.** In 1895, while Sousa was writing energetic marches and Americans were cheering new boxing heroes, an independence revolt broke out in Cuba. It was not the first time the Cubans took up arms in pursuit of independence. During the Ten Years' War (1868–1878) Cuban patriots had unsuccessfully fought for independence from their Spanish rulers. The war was bloody and violent, and Cubans actively sought American support; but the United States, guided by a policy of isolationism, steered clear.

By 1895, however, cautious isolationism was out of step with the country's aggressive tempo. From the start of this revolution, Americans expressed far more than casual interest in the rebellion. American business had invested over $50 million in Cuba and the annual trade between the two countries totaled almost $100 million. Once the revolution started, insurgents burned crops in the fields, and the trade between Cuba and the United States slowed to a trickle. Overall, however, economics played a relatively unimportant role in forming America's attitude toward the revolution.

Humanitarianism was a far more important factor. In Cuba's valiant fight, Americans saw a reenactment of their own war for independence. The resourceful Cubans made sure that Americans stayed well supplied with stories of Spanish atrocities and Cuban heroism. The Cuban junta—central revolutionary committee—established bases in New York City and Tampa, Florida, and daily provided American newspapers with stories aimed at sympathetic American hearts.

Not all the stories were false. The Cuban—and Spanish—suffering was real enough. Unable to defeat the Spanish army in the field, Cuban revolutionaries resorted to guerilla tactics. They burned sugarcane fields and blew up mills. They destroyed railroad tracks and bridges. They vowed to win their independence or destroy Cuba in the process. Supported by the populace, the guerillas succeeded in turning Cuba into an economic and military nightmare for Spanish officials.

In 1896 Spain sent **Governor-General Valeriano Weyler y Nicolau** to Cuba to crush the rebellion. A man of ruthless clarity, he understood the nature of guerilla warfare. Guerrillas could not be defeated by conventional engagements. Their generals did not imitate the tactics of Napoleon; they were not concerned with flanking maneuvers and cavalry charges. Their weapons were patience and endurance and popular support. Weyler knew this, and he decided to fight the guerrillas on their own terms.

His first plan was to rob the guerrillas of their base of support, the rural villages and the sympathetic peasants. He divided the island into military districts and relocated Cubans into guarded camps. He forced over a half million Cubans from their homes and crowded them into shabbily constructed and unsanitary camps. The food was bad, the water worse. Disease spread with frightful speed and horrifying results. Perhaps 200,000 Cubans died in the camps as Weyler earned the sobriquet "the Butcher." After inspecting the camps, Senator Renfield Proctor of Vermont reported on the plight of the Cuban people to Congress: "Torn from their homes, with foul earth, foul air, foul water, and foul food or none, what wonder that one-half have died and that one-quarter of the living are so diseased that they cannot be saved? . . . Little children are still walking about with arms and chest terribly emaciated, eyes swollen, and abdomens bloated to three times the natural size."

The Yellow Press

In the United States reports of the suffering Cuban masses filled the front pages of newspapers. In New York City, **William Randolph Hearst**'s *New York Journal* and **Joseph Pulitzer**'s *New York World* used the junta's lurid stories as ammunition in a newspaper war. Newspaper reporters freely engaged in **yellow journalism,** exaggerating already sad and inhumane conditions. Most stories had a sensational twist. One particularly incendiary drawing by Frederic Remington, the famous western artist sent to Cuba by Hearst, pictured three leering Spanish officials searching a nude Cuban woman. Hearst ran the picture five columns wide on the second page of the *Journal,* and the edition sold close to one million copies, the largest newspaper run in history until then. Neither the picture nor the story, however, mentioned that Spanish women—not men—conducted the search, although men had conducted other such searches. Such coverage biased American opinion against Spain. It also sold newspapers. When Hearst bought the *Journal* in 1895 it had a daily circulation of 77,000 copies; by the summer of 1898 sales had increased to over 1.5 million daily.

"Yellow journalism" and the more sober coverage of the standard press persuaded many Americans to call for U.S. intervention in the Cuban Revolution. Grover Cleveland, however, was not easily moved by newspaper reports. His administration wanted to protect American interests in Cuba but was dead set against any sort of military intervention in the conflict. Without recognizing the revolutionaries, he worked to convince Spain to grant "home rule." But when he left office in early 1897, the revolution in Cuba was raging as violently as ever. Cleveland passed the Cuban problem to his successor William McKinley. Like Cleveland, McKinley deplored war. He had fought bravely in the Civil War, and he knew the horrors of war firsthand. Before he would even consider military intervention, McKinley was determined to exhaust every peaceful alternative.

McKinley displayed strength and patience. As many influential Americans called for U.S. intervention, McKinley worked diplomatically to end the fighting. Rather than inflame public opinion, he attempted to remove the issue from public debate. In his inaugural address, for example, he did not even mention Cuba. For a time it appeared that his efforts

This *New York Journal* sketch by Frederic Remington of Spanish officials searching a Cuban woman on an American steamer shocked the nation. Such "yellow journalism," or exaggeration of the facts, played an important role in persuading Americans to call for intervention in the Cuban Revolution.

would succeed. In October 1897 a new government in Spain moved toward granting more autonomy to Cuba. It removed Weyler and promised to end his hated reconcentration program. Spain, said McKinley, was following "honorable paths." Patience and cool heads, he hoped, would carry the day.

Spain moved with glacial slowness. Some of its reforms were half-hearted, others were merely designed to calm American emotions. In Cuba the bloodshed continued. As Spanish officials and Cuban revolutionaries ignored or denounced Spain's "honorable paths," pressure on McKinley to take stronger action mounted. In May 1897 he dispatched his trusted political friend William J. Calhoun of Ohio to Cuba to provide him with an independent report on the conditions on the island. Calhoun's report confirmed the grim picture presented in American newspapers. "The country outside of the military posts was practically depopulated," Calhoun noted. "I did not see a house, a man, woman or child; a horse, mule or cow, not even a dog; I did not see a sign of life, except an occasional vulture or buzzard sailing through the air. The country was wrapped in the stillness of death and the silence of desolation." By January of 1898 the president looked as defeated as his diplomatic efforts. He had to take drugs to sleep, his skin was pasty, and his dark eyes seemed to be sinking farther back into his head. Two events in February would end any hope of a diplomatic solution and lead to the Spanish-American War.

William Randolph Hearst had often told his reporters: "Don't wait for things to turn up. Turn them up!" He did just that in early February 1898. With the help of the Cuban junta, Hearst acquired a private letter from Enrique Dupuy de Lôme, the Spanish minister in the United States, to a Spanish friend of his in Cuba. The letter contained de Lôme's unguarded and undiplomatic opinion of McKinley. Reprinted on the front page of the *Journal* on February 9, 1898, Hearst labeled the letter: "Worst insult to the United States in Its History." De Lôme called McKinley "weak and a bidder for the admiration of the crowd." He accused the American president of being a hypocrite and a "would-be politician." Even worse, de Lôme suggested that Spain's new peace policy was mere sham and propaganda.

The letter infuriated the American public. As one leader rejoiced to the delight of the Cuban junta, "The de Lôme letter is a great thing for us."

Less than a week later a second event rocked America. On the still evening of February 15, an explosion ripped apart the *Maine,* a U.S. battleship anchored in Havana harbor. The ship quickly sank, killing over 250 officers and men. An 1898 investigation ruled that an external explosion had sunk the *Maine.* A 1976 study, however, blamed the sinking on an internal explosion. In truth, no one knows the who, how, and why answers. Americans at the time, however, were not in an impartial or philosophical mood. They blamed Spain. One diplomatic historian commented, "'**Remember the *Maine!***' became a national watch word. . . . In a Broadway bar a man raised his glass and said solemnly, 'Gentlemen, remember the *Maine!*' Through the streets of American cities went the cry, 'Remember the *Maine!* To Hell with Spain!'"

The sinking of the *Maine* was one of the major events leading to the Spanish-American War. It is still uncertain who or what caused the explosion that sank the ship.

War was in the air, and it is doubtful if McKinley or any other president could have long preserved peace. Congress was ready for war. On March 6, McKinley told a leading congressman, "I must have money to get ready for war." Congress responded on March 8 by passing the "Fifty Million Bill" (the amount of McKinley's request) without a single dissenting vote. Although McKinley continued to work for a diplomatic solution to the crisis, his efforts lacked his earlier energy and optimism. By early April, diplomacy had reached its end.

On April 11, an exhausted McKinley sent a virtual war message to Congress. He asked for authority to use force to end the Cuban war. His message mixed talk of commerce with lofty humanitarianism. America must take up the "cause of humanity," he wrote, and stop the "very serious injury to the commerce, trade, and business of our people, and the wanton destruction of property."

On April 19 Congress officially acted. It proclaimed Cuba's independence, called for Spain's evacuation, and authorized McKinley to use the army and navy to achieve those ends. In the Teller Amendment, Congress added that the United States had no intention of annexing Cuba for itself. For some Americans it was a great and noble decision. Senator Albert Beveridge, one of the great speakers of his day, intoned: "At last, God's hour has struck. The American people go forth in a warfare holier than liberty—holy as humanity." For the men and boys who would have to fight the battles, the war would soon seem considerably less noble.

The Spanish-American War

There is no simple explanation for the **Spanish-American War.** Economics and imperial ambitions certainly played a part, but no more so than did humanitarianism and selfless concern for the suffering of others. McKinley tried to find a peaceful solution, but he failed. The unpredictability of events and the mood of the nation were more powerful than the president.

In theory America had prepared for war with Spain. In 1897 the Navy Department had drawn up contingency plans for a war against Spain for the liberation of Cuba. It had envisioned a war centered mainly in the Caribbean, but the navy had plans to attack the **Philippine Islands,** which belonged to Spain, and even the coast of Spain, if necessary. In the Caribbean, the plan was to blockade Cuba and assist an army invasion of the island. On paper, neatly written and soundly reasoned, America was well prepared for a war that seemed more of a military exercise than a deadly struggle.

In reality, the military was not physically ready for war. The process of mobilizing troops was chaotic and the training given volunteers was inadequate. In addition, the army faced severe supply shortages, with volunteers suffering the most. They were herded into camps, often without such basic equipment as tents and mess kits. Long before they ever faced enemy guns or even saw Cuba, they battled wet uniforms, bad food, and deadly sanitary conditions. Far more volunteers died in stateside camps than were killed by Spanish bullets.

For African American troops, regular and volunteers, racism aggravated already difficult conditions. They too were plagued by spoiled beef, thick wool uniforms, and unsanitary conditions. Also, since most of the large camps were located in the South—in places such as Tampa, New Orleans, Mobile, and Chickamauga Park, Tennessee—they had to battle Jim Crow laws and other forms of racial hostility. They saw signs that proclaimed "Dogs and niggers not allowed" and were pelted by rocks. Once in the camps, they were given the lowest military assignments. George W. Prioleau, a black chaplain, could not help but wonder: "Is America any better than Spain?"

While the agony of mobilization was taking place, the navy moved into action. During the tense weeks before the United States went to war against Spain, Theodore Roosevelt, then acting secretary of the navy, joyfully followed McKinley's orders and wired his friend **Commodore George Dewey,** leader of America's Asiatic Squadron: "KEEP FULL OF COAL, IN THE EVENT OF DECLARATION OF WAR [WITH] SPAIN, YOUR DUTY WILL BE TO SEE THAT THE SPANISH SQUADRON DOES NOT LEAVE THE ASIATIC COAST, AND THEN OFFENSIVE OPERATIONS IN PHILIPPINE ISLANDS." Dewey had been anxiously waiting just that order.

At the break of light on the morning of May 1, 1898, he struck. In a few hours of fighting, he destroyed Spain's Asiatic fleet in the **Battle of Manila Bay.** It was a stunning victory. Only one American died, from heat prostration manning a ship's overworked boiler. "You have made a name for the nation, and the Navy, and yourself," Roosevelt wrote Dewey. Americans rejoiced in the quick victory. Newspapers were filled with stories of American heroics. One not-very-accomplished poet captured the public mood:

> Oh, dewey was the morning
> Upon the first of May,
> And Dewey was the Admiral,
> Down in Manila Bay.
> And dewey were the Spaniard's eyes,
> Them orbs of black and blue;
> And dew we feel discouraged?
> I do not think we dew.

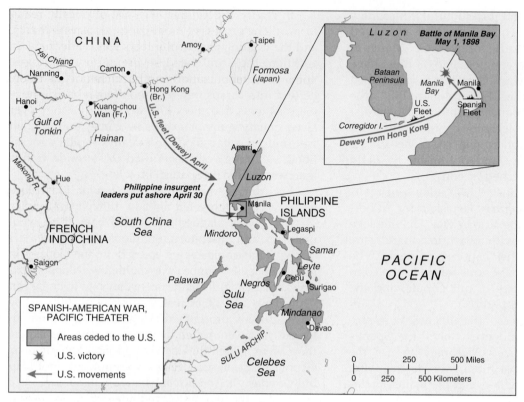

Spanish-American War, Pacific Theater

Not every victory came so easily. Closer to home, in the Caribbean theater, the war was much more prosaic. The main Spanish forces in Cuba controlled the strategically important Santiago Bay. To defeat the Spanish would require the combined efforts of the army and the navy. With this in mind, McKinley ordered Major General William R. Shafter, commander of the 5th Corps, from Tampa to Santiago. The trip to Cuba set the tone for the entire expedition. Delays, confused orders, and other problems slowed the process. Some 17,000 American troops were forced to spend 19 days on crowded transports, sweating in their woolen uniforms, eating unappetizing travel rations, and thinking about what lay ahead. Finally, toward the end of June, and with the help of Cuban rebels, American troops landed at the ports of Daiquiri and Siboney.

From there they moved toward Santiago. The distance was not great—Santiago Bay was only about 15 miles from the coastal town of Siboney. But the road to Santiago was little more than a rutted, dirt trail. When it rained, wagons became mired in the mud, streams swelled and made fording treacherous, and the troops suffered in the jungle humidity. Slowly the army moved forward, more concerned with broken wagons and tropical diseases than Spanish soldiers.

On July 1, American soldiers learned firsthand the horrors of battle. Between the American position and Santiago were Spanish troops in the tiny hamlet of El Caney and along the San Juan Heights, a ridge to the east of Santiago. From the first, American plans broke down in the face of stiff Spanish opposition. There were no romantic charges, no idealized warfare. The American troops that struggled up Kettle and San Juan hills moved very slowly and suffered alarming casualties. Although outnumbered more than ten to one, Spanish soldiers made U.S. troops pay for every foot they advanced. After America finally secured the enemy positions, correspondent Richard H. Davis wrote, "Another such victory as that of July 1 and our troops must retreat."

General Shafter was frankly worried and even considered retreat. Grossly overweight and gout-ridden, Shafter had neither the disposition nor the ability to lead an energetic campaign. Fortunately for him, Spain's forces in Cuba were even less ready to fight. In Santiago, Spanish soldiers faced shortages of food, water, and ammunition. On July 3, the Spanish squadron tried to break an American blockade and force its way out of Santiago Bay. The act was a suicidal move. American guns destroyed the Spanish fleet and killed some 500 Spanish sailors. Only one American died in the decisive engagement. When his men

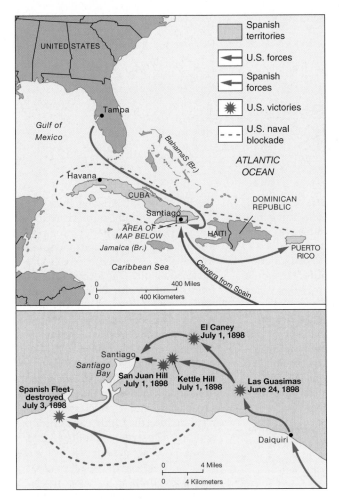

Spanish-American War, Cuban Theater

For America, it had been a short, successful war. Spanish bullets killed only 379 Americans, the smallest number in any of America's declared wars. Disease and other problems cost over 5000 more lives. If the army's mobilization had been chaotic, its troops had performed heroically under fire. And the navy, which took most of the credit for winning the war, demonstrated the wisdom of its planners. Finally, the war served to bring the North and South closer together as the two sections fought alongside each other rather than against each other. All in all, many Americans agreed with U.S. Ambassador to England John Hay that it had been a "splendid little war."

There was nothing little about the consequences of the war. With the Spanish-American War the United States became an imperial power. The war also increased America's appetite for overseas territories. The McKinley administration used the war to annex Hawaii and part of Samoa. In addition, at the Paris Peace Conference the United States wrested the Philippines, Puerto Rico, and Guam from Spain. Although the United States paid Spain $20 million for the Philippines, there was no question that Spain was forced to negotiate under duress. These new imperial possessions gave the United States strategic bases in the Caribbean and along the trade routes to Asia.

Freeing Cuba

Many Americans favored the annexation of Cuba. In the land grab that ended the war, the idealism of the Teller Amendment and the war's beginning was all but forgotten. When the war ended, U.S. troops stayed in Cuba, and the country was ruled by an American-run military government. Particularly under General Leonard Wood, the military government helped Cuba recover from its terrible conflict with Spain. Wood restored the Cuban economy and promoted reforms in the legal system, education, sanitation, and health care. Neither Wood nor McKinley, however, was willing to grant Cuba its immediate independence. In his annual message of December 1898, McKinley noted that American troops would stay in Cuba until "complete tranquility" and a "stable government" existed on the island.

The United States finally recognized Cuban independence in 1903. But it was a limited independence. According to the **Platt Amendment** to the Army Appropriation Bill of 1901, Cuba could exercise self-government, but it could sign no treaties that might limit its independence. The amendment also gave the United States the right to maintain two naval bases on Cuba. Should, in the judgment of the United States, Cuban independence ever be threatened, the Platt Amendment authorized the United

broke out in a yell of joy, Captain Philip of the *Texas* said, "Don't cheer, men, the poor devils are dying."

Little fighting remained. On July 17 the leading Spanish general in Cuba surrendered to Shafter. Timid in war, Shafter was petty in victory. He refused to permit any naval officers to sign the capitulation document, nor would he allow any Cubans to participate in the surrender negotiations and ceremonies. It was a sad moment. The Cubans who had fought so long and bravely for their independence were denied the glory of their success.

Before the full Spanish surrender, the United States extended its influence in the Caribbean. In late July, General Nelson A. Miles invaded Puerto Rico, Spain's other Caribbean colony. Without any serious resistance, U.S. forces took the island. Finally, on August 12, Spain surrendered, granting Cuban independence and ceding Puerto Rico and Guam to the United States. Both countries agreed to settle the fate of the Philippines at a postwar peace conference to be held in Paris.

Theodore Roosevelt and the Rough Riders

Aboard the *Yucatan,* anchored off the coast of Cuba, Theodore Roosevelt (TR) received the news on the evening of June 21, 1898. He and his men, a volunteer cavalry regiment dubbed the **Rough Riders,** had received their orders to disembark from the safety of the ship and join the fighting ashore. It was a welcomed invitation, celebrated with cheers, war dances, songs, boasts, and toasts. "To the Officers—may they get killed, wounded or promoted," urged one toast that captured the mood aboard the ship.

Roosevelt and many men of his generation looked forward to war, greedily anticipating the chance to prove their mettle in battle. They had been raised on stories of the Civil War, stories that over the years had taken on the golden gloss of time. Tales of Shiloh, Chancellorsville, Antietam, and Gettysburg; of Robert E. Lee, Ulysses S. Grant, and Stonewall Jackson; of battles won and causes lost had fired their imaginations. The Spanish-American War was their chance to experience firsthand what they had long only heard about from their fathers' and uncles' lips.

Few men wanted the war more than Roosevelt. Son of a wealthy New York family, he was competitive by nature and enjoyed all physical sports. He also loved history, writing books about American wars and heroic deeds. And for Roosevelt there was perhaps even a deeper motivation. During the Civil War his father, the man he admired above everyone else, had hired a substitute soldier to

serve for him. Thousands of other wealthy men had done the same, but for Theodore such a course was unmanly. During a war, he believed, able-bodied men should be in a uniform, not dressed in mufti. He would not repeat his father's mistake. When the Spanish-American War was declared, TR quickly resigned his post as assistant secretary of the navy and joined the fray. In his own mind, he could do nothing else. In *The Rough Riders,* his memoirs of the war, he quoted a poem by Bret Harte, whose last verse was:

> "But when won the coming battle,
> What of profit springs therefrom?
> What if conquest, subjugation,
> Even greater ills become?"
> But the drum
> Answered, "Come!"

And come Roosevelt did.

The men who followed him were kindred spirits. They were rough riders, the men who with Roosevelt formed the First United States Volunteer Cavalry regiment. Some were Ivy Leaguers from Harvard, Yale, and Princeton who belonged to the most exclusive clubs in Boston and New York City. Many had been college athletes, stars in football, tennis, and track and field, men for whom war was a grand playing field. Others were Westerners—cowboys, hunters, frontier sheriffs, Indian fighters, Texas Rangers, prospectors—"a splendid set of men," wrote Roosevelt, "tall and sinewy, with resolute, weather-beaten faces, and eyes that looked a man straight in the face without flinching." Such men were accustomed to riding horses, shooting rifles, and living off the land.

Bucky O'Neill was something of a Rough Rider ideal. Indian fighter and

sheriff of Prescott, Arizona, Bucky could shoot with the hunters, exchange stories with the prospectors, and philosophize with the college graduates. Roosevelt once overheard Bucky and Dr. Robb Church, the former Princeton football player who served as the surgeon for the Rough Riders, "discussing Aryan word roots together, and then sliding off into a review of the novels of Balzac, and a discussion as to how far Balzac could be said to be the founder of the modern realistic school of fiction." Once when Bucky and Roosevelt were leaning on the ship's railing searching the Caribbean sky for the Southern Cross, the old Indian fighter asked, "Who would not risk his life for a star?" TR agreed that great risk was part of greatness.

Brimming with enthusiasm, perhaps a bit innocent in their naiveté, the Rough Riders viewed Cuba as a land of stars, a place to win great honors or die in the pursuit. Like many of his men, TR believed "that the nearing future held . . . many chances of death, of honor and renown." And he was ready. Dressed in a Brooks Brothers uniform made especially for him and with several extra pairs of spectacles sewn in the lining of his Rough Rider hat, Roosevelt prepared to meet his destiny.

In a land of beauty, death often came swiftly. As the Rough Riders and other soldiers moved inland toward Santiago, snipers fired on them. The high-speed Mauser bullets seemed to come out of nowhere, making a *z-z-z-z-eu* as they moved through the air or a loud *chug* as they hit flesh. Since the Spanish snipers used smokeless gunpowder, no puffs of smoke betrayed their positions.

On their first day in Cuba, the Rough Riders experienced the "blood,

sweat, and tears" of warfare. Dr. Church looked "like a kid who had gotten his hands and arms into a bucket of thick red paint." Some men died, and others, dying, lay where they had been shot. The reality of war strikes different men differently. It horrifies some, terrifies others, and enrages still others. Sheer exhilaration was the best way to describe Roosevelt's response to the death and danger. Even sniper fire could not keep TR from jumping up and down with excitement.

On July 1, 1898, the Rough Riders faced their sternest task. Moving from the coast toward Santiago along the Camino Real, the main arm of the U.S. forces encountered an entrenched enemy. Spread out along the San Juan Heights, Spanish forces commanded a splendid position. As American troops emerged from a stretch of jungle, they found themselves in a dangerous position. Once again the sky seemed to be raining Mauser bullets and shrapnel. Clearly, the Heights had to be taken. Each hour of delay meant more American casualties.

The Rough Riders were deployed to the right to prepare to assault Kettle Hill. Once in position, they faced an agonizing wait for orders to charge. Most soldiers hunched behind cover. Bucky O'Neill, however, casually strolled up and down in front of his troops, chain-smoked cigarettes, and shouted encouragement. A sergeant implored him to take cover. "Sergeant," Bucky remarked, "the Spanish bullet isn't made that will kill me." Hardly had he finished the statement when a Mauser bullet ripped into his mouth and burst out of the back of his head. Even before he fell, Roosevelt wrote, Bucky's "wild and gallant soul had gone out into the darkness."

Finally the orders came. On foot the Rough Riders moved up Kettle Hill toward the Spanish guns. It was a slow, painful, heroic charge. Bullets, sounding "like the ripping of a silk dress," cut down a number of Roosevelt's men. But unable to stop the push of the American forces, the Spanish gave way, leaving their fortified positions and running for safety.

From the heights of Kettle Hill, Roosevelt watched another U.S. attack on nearby San Juan Hill. Once again feeling the wolf rising in his heart, he led his men toward the new objective. Again the fighting was difficult. Again the Spanish gave way. By the end of the day, American forces had taken the San Juan Heights. Before them was Santiago and victory. "The great day of my life," as TR called it, was over.

"Another such victory like that of July 1," wrote Richard Harding Davis, "and our troops must retreat." Indeed, casualties ran high, and the Rough Riders suffered the heaviest losses. But the fighting helped to break the Spanish resistance. It was the last really difficult day of fighting in the war. Perhaps more importantly, the day made Roosevelt a national hero. Aided by his ability at self-promotion, TR used the event as a political stepping-stone. "I would rather have led the charge," he later wrote, "than served three terms in the U.S. Senate."

States to intervene in Cuba's internal and external affairs. The amendment was also written into the 1901 Cuban constitution. In short, for Cuba, independence had the look and feel of an American protectorate.

The Imperial Debate

Compared to the Philippines, Cuba was a minor problem. McKinley's decision to annex the Philippines pleased some Americans and angered many more. Businessmen who dreamed of the rich Asian markets applauded McKinley's decision. Naval strategists similarly believed it was a wise move. They argued that if the United States failed to take the Philippines, then Germany, Japan or England probably would. Finally, Protestant missionaries favored annexation to facilitate their efforts to Christianize the Filipinos. That the Filipinos already favored Roman Catholicism did not seem to dampen the fervor of the Protestant missionaries.

Opposed to the annexation of the Philippines was a heterogeneous group of Americans who called themselves anti-imperialists. The group included such notable Americans as agrarian leader William Jennings Bryan, steel magnate Andrew Carnegie, labor organizer Samuel Gompers, writers Mark Twain and William Dean Howells, reformers Lincoln Steffens and Jane Addams, university presidents Charles W. Eliot of Harvard and David Starr Jordan of Stanford, and politicians George Frisbie Hoar of Massachusetts and "Pitchfork Ben" Tillman of South Carolina.

Their reasons for being anti-imperialist were as varied as their occupations and backgrounds. Some were high-minded idealists who believed that the Filipinos had the right to govern themselves. Others had more selfish reasons. Samuel Gompers, for example, feared that annexation would lead to an influx of Filipino workers into the United States and hurt the American labor movement. Still others op-

American Empire

With the Treaty of Paris, the United States gained an expanded colonial empire that included Puerto Rico, Alaska, Hawaii, parts of the Samoan islands, Guam, the Philippines, and a chain of Pacific islands.

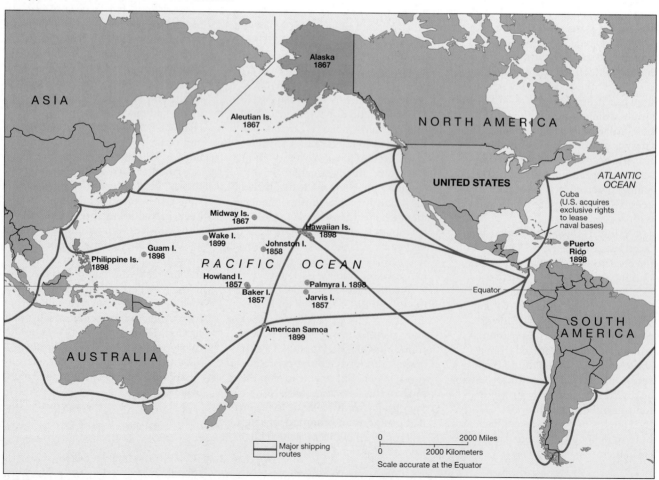

posed annexation for base racial grounds. The annexation of "dependencies inhabited by ignorant and inferior races," noted *The Nation* editor E. L. Godkin, could only lead to renewed racial problems.

During early 1899 the imperial debate raged on. Journalists editorialized, speakers pontificated, and humorists detailed the absurdities of both sides. Mark Twain asked, "Shall we . . . go on conferring our Christianity upon the peoples that sit in darkness, or shall we give those poor things a rest?" Twain's thoughtful questions about all the uproar changed very few opinions. Even Andrew Carnegie's offer to write a personal check for $20 million to buy the independence of the Philippines failed to end the debate. Ultimately, imperialists and anti-imperialists had different visions for America, and no bridge could span the gulf between.

The issue was settled on February 6, 1899, when the Senate voted on the Treaty of Paris. Strained tempers were evident in the tense atmosphere. Imperialist Senator Henry Cabot Lodge called the treaty fight the "closest, most bitter, and most exciting I have ever known, or ever expect to see in the Senate." For a time it appeared that the imperialists would not be able to muster the two-thirds majority needed to ratify the treaty. Anti-imperialist and titular leader of the Democratic party William Jennings Bryan ironically saved the imperialist cause. Not wanting to prolong the war by rejecting the treaty, he urged Democratic anti-imperialists to vote for ratification. By the close vote of 57 to 27 the Senate ratified the treaty. Undoubtedly Bryan hoped to use the issue of Philippine independence to capture the presidency in 1900, but it was not to be. With ratification of the treaty, the issue lost its sense of urgency and Americans grew tired of the debate.

The War to Crush Filipino Independence

Filipino independence, however, was not an abstract debate in the Philippines. Imperialist arguments about duty, destiny, defense, and dollars were lost on independence-minded Filipinos, led by Emilio Aguinaldo, who had fought bravely against the Spanish both before and after Dewey arrived in Manila. They had battled for their own independence, not to replace Spain with the United States as their colonial master. When it was clear that the United States did not have Filipino interests at heart, Aguinaldo and his followers resumed their fight for independence. Like the Cubans, the Filipinos held dear the cause of freedom. Like the Spanish, the United States was not willing to grant that freedom.

Between 1899 and 1902 American troops and Filipino revolutionaries fought an ugly and destructive colonial war. Mark Twain's *The War Prayer* captured the mood of the fighting: "O Lord our God, help us to tear their soldiers to bloody shreds with our shells . . . , blast their hopes, blight their lives, protract their bitter pilgrimage." American soldiers faced a difficult task. Some did not know what they were fighting for, whose interests they were defending, or what rights they were protecting. Others regarded the Filipinos as subhuman. They referred to them as "niggers" and "gugus," and they regarded the notion of Philippine independence as a joke.

African American troops fighting to destroy Filipino freedom faced an even greater and more painful dilemma. Many black soldiers readily identified with Filipino aspirations. Some white officers even suspected, as journalist Stephen Bonsel noted in 1902, that "the negro soldiers were in closer sympathy with the aims of the native populations than they were with those of their white leaders and the policy of the United States." Although the majority of black troops professionally followed the orders of their white officers, an unusually large number deserted. Bonsel suggested that, unlike white deserters, blacks left the army "for the purpose of joining the insurgents," with whose struggle they identified.

For black and white soldiers alike, however, the actual fighting was bloody and frustrating. After suffering serious losses in conventional fighting, Aguinaldo turned to guerrilla warfare. His forces fought only when victory was certain, usually ambushing small patrols. They burned bridges, destroyed railroads, sniped, and sabotaged. They filled pits with sharpened stakes and tortured prisoners. Some American captives had their ears cut off, and many Filipinos who supported the United States were hacked to death with bolos or buried alive. Aguinaldo's hope was that eventually the game would not be worth the prize, and that the American president would call his troops home.

McKinley was not about to do any such thing, and American troops proved just as vicious as the Filipino insurgents. Atrocities committed by American soldiers became alarmingly common. Americans used the "water cure" to obtain information. This entailed forcing a prisoner to drink gallons of water and then emptying his stomach quickly with a kick or a punch. In one especially violent campaign General Jacob H. Smith ordered his subordinates to take no prisoners: "I wish you to kill and burn . . . the more you kill and burn the better it will please me. I want all persons killed who are capable of bearing arms in actual hostilities against the United States." In the last category he included any male 10 years or older.

In another campaign, American leaders used the same tactics that had made the Spanish General Weyler infamous in Cuba. They tried to destroy the

American soldiers stand guard over captured Filipino guerrillas in 1899. Expansionism raised questions of whether the native peoples of acquired lands had the same rights as American citizens.

guerrilla base by herding more than 300,000 civilians into concentration zones. Death, disease, starvation, and suffering increased in the concentration centers. "Suburbs of hell" one American commander called them. Industrialist and anti-imperialist Andrew Carnegie seethed to a U.S. peace commissioner in the Philippines, "You seem to have about finished your work of civilizing the Filipinos. About 8000 of them have been completely civilized and sent to Heaven."

Although the fighting continued, Aguinaldo faced serious difficulties. Most of his leaders came from the upper classes, and they had little interest in bettering the lives of poorer Filipinos, a fact that hurt recruitment. Looking for a political solution, Aguinaldo hoped that Bryan would defeat McKinley for the presidency in 1900 and thereby install an anti-imperialist in the White House. The November election dashed Aguinaldo's hopes. Five months later American troops captured the Filipino leader. This, coupled with American reform efforts designed to improve transportation, education, and public health in the Philippines, doomed the Philippine independence movement. By July 4, 1902, the American victory was complete. However, approximately 4200 Americans and over 20,000 Filipino soldiers had died. Perhaps another 200,000 Filipino civilians died of famine, disease, and war-related incidents. The United States paid Spain $20 million for the Philippines, which it had won control of after the cease-fire. But it cost another $400 million to crush the Philippine independence movement.

Keeping the Doors Open

The struggle against the Filipinos led to congressional investigations and shocked many Americans. Political and business leaders, however, continued to

believe that the Philippines were worth the fight because the islands were of strategic importance both as a military base and a stepping-stone toward the Asian markets. Yet policy-makers understood the popular mood; they knew that the American public would be hostile to any U.S. military venture into Asia *just* to support trade.

To prevent other countries from carving up China, in 1899 Secretary of State John Hay issued an **Open Door note.** Hay believed that imperial competition in China was dangerous and economically inefficient. It stimulated costly anticolonial resistance and rebellion and gave no incentive to European countries to improve their economic efficiency. Hay's Open Door note was an attempt to prevent further European partitioning of the Manchu empire and to protect the principle of open trade in China. Under the terms of the Open Door policy, all countries active in China would respect each other's trading rights by imposing no discriminating duties and closing no ports within their spheres of influence. Although most European countries expressed little interest in Hay's Open Door policy—which, after all, benefited the United States the most—in 1900 Hay announced that the European powers had accepted his proposal.

The Chinese themselves had other plans. In the late spring of 1900 a group of Chinese nationalists, known as Boxers, besieged the Legation Quarter in Peking, calling for the expulsion or death of all westerners in China. The Boxers, whose Chinese name better translates as "Righteous and Harmonious Fists," were a quasi-religious organization that believed deeply in magic and maintained that all its members were impervious to western bullets. As a joint European and American rescue force proved, bullets could and would kill Boxers. By late

CHRONOLOGY OF KEY EVENTS

1867 Russia sells Alaska to the United States for $7.2 million, or less than 2 cents an acre

1870 Senate rejects President Grant's attempt to annex the Dominican Republic

1889 Britain, Germany, and the United States agree to share control of Samoa

1890 Captain Alfred Thayer Mahan's *The Influence of Sea Power upon History* asserts that naval power is the key to national greatness

1893 Americans organize the overthrow of Queen Liliuokalani of Hawaii and, with the help of U.S. marines, set up a new government

1895 Venezuela border dispute; Cuban revolt against Spain intensifies

1898 The battleship *Maine* explodes in Havana harbor; Spanish-American War begins; Dewey sinks Spanish fleet in Manila Bay;

Battle of San Juan Hill; destruction of Spanish fleet in Santiago harbor ends Spanish resistance in Cuba; U.S. annexes Hawaii

1899 Aguinaldo leads a rebellion against the United States to win Philippine independence; John Hay, McKinley's secretary of state, issues an Open Door note to prevent further partitioning of China by European powers and to protect the principle of free trade

1900 Boxer Rebellion, a Chinese nationalist revolt against foreigners, erupts

1901 Platt Amendment gives the United States the right to maintain two naval stations on Cuba and to send troops to the island to preserve order

1902 United States finally crushes Philippine revolt

---

summer, 1900, westernizers had crushed the Boxer Rebellion.

Additional troops in China threatened Hay's Open Door policy. On July 3, 1900, during the tensest moment of the Boxer Rebellion, he issued a second Open Door note, calling on all western powers to preserve "Chinese territorial and administrative entity" and uphold "the principle of equal and impartial trade with all parts of the Chinese Empire." Once again, few European countries paid attention to Hay's Open Door policy. Mutual distrust and the fear of provoking a general European war—more than any American plan—prevented the major European powers from dismembering China. Out of Hay's Open Door policy notes came the idea, held mostly in America, that the United States was China's protector. It was another example of the increasingly active role the United States had taken in world affairs.

CONCLUSION

Thirty-two years separated the inauguration of Ulysses S. Grant and the assassination of William McKinley, but during that generation, America and the presidency changed radically. Part of the change

can be attributed to growth—industry boomed, the population swelled, agricultural production increased. The growth was also psychological. During those years many Americans achieved a new sense of confidence, and their vision broadened. After 250 years of looking westward across America's seemingly limitless acres of land, they began to look toward the oceans and consider the possibilities of a new form of expansion. Talk of world power, world outlook, and world responsibilities colored their rhetoric.

This outward thrust was accompanied and enhanced by the growth of presidential power. Grant worked hard for the annexation of the Dominican Republic, but Congress blocked his efforts. By the turn of the century, however, Congress clearly expected the president to lead the nation in the area of foreign affairs. Harrison, Cleveland, and McKinley, as well as their advisers, firmly guided America's foreign affairs. Although the presidents pursued different policies, they agreed that America should have a greater influence in world affairs. None questioned the fundamental fact that the United States was and should be a world power.

Many questions, nevertheless, remained unanswered. What were the rights of a world power? What were its responsibilities? What were its duties?

Neither Harrison, Cleveland, nor McKinley gained much experience in running a colonial administration. The limits and possibilities of American power had yet to be defined and explored. The next three presidents—Roosevelt, Taft, and Wilson—would help define how America would use its new power.

CHAPTER SUMMARY AND KEY POINTS

At the end of the nineteenth century, the United States emerged as a world power. In this chapter you read about the country's lack of concern with foreign affairs prior to the 1880s; the reasons why the United States adopted a more aggressive foreign policy; the growing willingness of the United States to threaten force to resolve international disputes; and the causes, military history, and consequences of the Spanish-American War.

- In 1898 and 1899, the United States annexed Hawaii and acquired the Philippines, Puerto Rico, parts of the Samoan islands, and other Pacific islands.

- Expansion raised the fateful question of whether the newly annexed peoples would receive the rights of American citizens.

- The Spanish-American War and the acquisition of the Philippines represented both an extension of earlier expansionist impulses and a sharp departure from assumptions that had guided American foreign policy in the past. For the first time, the United States made a major strategic commitment in the Far East, acquired territory never intended for statehood, and committed itself to police actions and intervention in the Caribbean and Central America.

SUGGESTIONS FOR FURTHER READING

Michael Hunt, *Ideology and U.S. Foreign Policy* (1987). Examines the issue of race in American imperialism.

Gerald F. Linderman, *The Mirror of War: American Society and the Spanish-American War* (1974). Relates patterns of war to patterns in American culture.

Stuart C. Miller, *"Benevolent Assimilation": The American Conquest of the Philippines, 1899–1903* (1982). Classic study of war in the Philippines.

H. Wayne Morgan, *America's Road to Empire* (1967). Short but interesting history of the origins of the American war with Spain.

David F. Trask, *The War with Spain in 1898* (1981). Most detailed study of the Spanish-American War.

William A. Williams, *The Tragedy of American Diplomacy,* 2d ed. (1972). Pioneering but controversial study of economic motives in American imperialism.

Novels

James Michener, *Hawaii* (1959).

Gore Vidal, *Empire* (1987).

MEDIA RESOURCES

Web Sites

William McKinley and the Spanish-American War
http://www.history.ohio-state.edu/projects/mckinley/SpanAmWar.htm
Part of Ohio State University's site about William McKinley, this part highlights the Spanish-American War with an essay and photos.

Sentenaryo/Centennial: The Philippine Revolution and Philippine-American War
http://www.boondocksnet.com/centennial/index.html
Jim Zwick organizes primary documents, images, and essays focusing upon the Philippines and American involvement.

Anti-Imperialism in the United States, 1898–1935
http://www.boondocksnet.com/ail98–35.html
Jim Zwick edits this extensive site, collating a large number of primary documents about anti-imperialism in America.

Photos of the Philippine-American War
http://www.msstate.edu/Archives/History/USA/filipino/filipino.html
The Philippine-American war is one of the least discussed military engagements in American history. Many tactics employed then were later used in the Vietnam war.

Imperialism Web Page
http://www.smplanet.com/imperialism/toc.html
Focusing on the period around the turn of the century, this site puts much information about American imperialism in one place.

Films and Videos

Citizen Kane (1941). Orson Welles' classic film and thinly fictionalized life of William Randolph Hearst.

The Hawaiians (1970). A sequel to *Hawaii* (1966), this film, also based on the James Michener novel, deals with Hawaii at the end of the nineteenth century.

The Rough Riders (1997). An attempt to recreate Theodore Roosevelt's military experience in Cuba during the Spanish-American War.

The Wind and the Lion (1975). John Milius' tale of adventure and romance in turn-of-the-century Morocco. Based rather loosely on the diplomatic conflict between the United States and Morocco.

KEY TERMS

Dominican Republic   (p. 551)

American exceptionalism   (p. 554)

Social Darwinism   (p. 554)

"White man's burden"   (p. 555)

New Navy   (p. 557)

The Influence of Seapower upon History   (p. 558)

Large policy   (p. 558)

Samoa   (p. 559)

Baltimore   (p. 559)

McKinley Tariff Act   (p. 560)

Cuban Revolution (of 1895)   (p. 562)

Yellow journalism   (p. 563)

"Remember the *Maine!*"   (p. 564)

Spanish-American War   (p. 565)

Philippine Islands   (p. 565)

Battle of Manila Bay   (p. 565)

Platt Amendment   (p. 567)

Rough Riders   (p. 568)

Open Door note   (p. 572)

PEOPLE YOU SHOULD KNOW

Buenaventura Baez   (p. 551)

Charles Sumner   (p. 552)

William Henry Seward   (p. 553)

Benjamin F. Tracy   (p. 557)

Queen Liliuokalani   (p. 560)

Lord Salisbury   (p. 561)

Governor-General Valeriano Weyler y Nicolau   (p. 562)

William Randolph Hearst   (p. 563)

Joseph Pulitzer   (p. 563)

Commodore George Dewey   (p. 565)

REVIEW QUESTIONS

1. How did Congress discourage overseas expansion following the Civil War?

2. What factors drove Americans to pursue an expansionist foreign policy?

3. Why did the American government take an aggressive imperial stance in areas like Samoa, Chile, Hawaii, and Venezuela?

4. Why did the United States government decide to fight the Spanish-American War?

5. How did the Spanish-American War affect Americans? Cubans? Filipinos?

21 The Progressive Struggle, 1900–1917

THEODORE ROOSEVELT AND THE COAL MINERS' STRIKE OF 1902

Times had changed by 1902 when George F. Baer declared "anthracite mining is business and not a religious, sentimental or academic proposition." Those tough-minded words might have won public approval at an earlier time, but many believed that Baer, spokesperson for mine owners in Pennsylvania, was merely being pigheaded. His words were in response to a request by **John Mitchell** of the United Mine Workers (UMW) for arbitration of a labor dispute. There was an unusual amount of support for the coal miners' position. Exposés had increased popular awareness of miserable working conditions, and the union's demands seemed reasonable: a 9-hour day, recognition of the union, a 10 to 20 percent increase in wages, and a fair weighing of the coal mined. Mitchell repeatedly stated the miners' willingness to accept arbitration, both before and after 50,000 miners walked out of the pits in May 1902.

Skillfully led, the coal miners stood firm month after month. By September, coal reserves were running short and prices were rising. With winter approaching, empty coal bins began multiplying, even in schools and hospitals. Baer remained stubborn. "The rights and interests of the laboring man," he declared, "will be protected and cared for—not by the labor agitators, but by the Christian men to whom God in his infinite wisdom has given the control of property interests in this country." This proclamation of the gospel of wealth fell on deaf ears. Newspaper after newspaper expressed disgust with the mine owners, and some tentatively suggested government ownership of the mines.

On October 3, President **Theodore Roosevelt,** temporarily in a wheelchair as a result of an accident, presided over a conference at the White House. Attending were Mitchell, Baer, Attorney General Philander C. Knox, and other labor leaders and mine operators. Baer was not in a mood to be cooperative. "We object to being called here to meet a criminal," he told a reporter, "even by the President of the United States." Refusing to speak directly to Mitchell, Baer urged Roosevelt to prosecute UMW leaders under the Sherman Antitrust Act and to use federal troops to break the strike, just as Cleveland had done in the 1894 Pullman strike. While Mitchell "behaved like a gentleman" according to Roosevelt, Baer was obstinate, concluding one diatribe against unions by calling "free government . . . a contemptible failure if it can only protect the lives and property and secure comfort of the people by compromise with violators of law and instigators of violence and crime."

Irritated with Baer, Roosevelt declared, "If it wasn't for the high office I hold I would have taken him by the seat of the breeches and the nape of the neck and chucked him out of that window." When the owners returned to Pennsylvania, they took actions that indicated they might use force to break the strike. Roosevelt's response was to begin preparations to send 10,000 federal troops to take over and operate the mines. This action jolted opponents of state socialism, who induced banker J. P. Morgan to get involved. Serving as a broker, Morgan was able to patch together a compromise under which the miners returned to work and Roosevelt appointed a commission to arbitrate the dispute.

The commission and its findings illustrate a number of aspects of the turn-of-the-century reforms labeled "progressivism." Originally, the commission was to consist of an army engineer, a mining engineer, a businessperson "familiar with the coal industry," a federal judge, and an "eminent sociologist"—reflecting a progressive tendency to call upon "experts" to conduct public affairs. Its composition was also decidedly probusiness, and even the addition of two other members and the appointment of a labor leader as the "eminent sociologist" did not redress this imbalance. As a result, its findings were essentially conservative: a 10 percent wage increase and reduction of working hours to 8 a day for a handful of miners and to 9 for most. The union did not receive recognition, and the traditional manner of weighing coal was continued. The commission also suggested a 10 percent increase in the price of coal. Business influence on other progressive responses to social problems generally produced similar moderate solutions that frequently brought industrialists as many benefits as losses.

evertheless, Roosevelt's actions did add some new rules to the game. For the first time, a president did not give knee-jerk support to business. Government became not merely a champion of the status quo but

President Theodore Roosevelt, surrounded here by coal miners after their 1902 strike, set a precedent by threatening the use of force against management rather than labor.

also an arbiter of change. Demands from the middle class and from workers motivated this retreat from laissez-faire. By 1902 many middle-class citizens had rejected management's heavy-handed tactics, which had often ended in chaos and conflict. They sought a more orderly, stable, and just society through government intervention. Workers also began to flex their political muscles, electing sympathetic mayors in a number of cities. Like the coal miners, Americans of all classes were learning the limits of individualism and the benefits of joining together in organizations to accomplish their goals. National leaders such as Roosevelt began to recognize the need for change in order to preserve stable government and the capitalistic system. Roosevelt justified his actions in 1902 as a way to save "big propertied men . . . from the dreadful punishment which their folly would have brought upon them." He stood, he declared, "between them and socialistic action." For a variety of motives, a plethora of legislation was enacted—sometimes with unintended results.

THE PROGRESSIVE IMPULSE

Americans exalted progress as a basic characteristic of their nation's distinctiveness. Technology was reshaping the human environment in dramatic ways. The pace of change was dizzying. Then in the late 1890s, people seemed to stop, catch their breath, and look around at their brave, new world. Much filled them with pride, but some of what they saw seemed outmoded or disruptive. Problems, however, appeared eminently solvable. Modern minds were explaining and harnessing natural forces. Could they not also understand and control human behavior? Could they not eliminate conflict and bring harmony to competing interests through some simple adjustments in the system? Americans increasingly answered "yes" and called themselves "progressives." Many agreed with Thomas Edison's observation, "We've stumbled along for awhile, trying to run a new civilization in old ways, but we've got to start to make this world over."

America in 1901

The twentieth century opened with a rerun of the 1896 election between William Jennings Bryan and William McKinley. Although the outcome was the same, much was different. "I have never known a Presidential campaign so quiet," Senator Henry Cabot Lodge noted. By 1900 the crises of the 1890s had largely passed. Prosperity had returned and was shared by many. The nation also reveled in its new-found international power following the Spanish-American War. The social fabric seemed to be on the mend, but memories of the depression still haunted Americans, and society's blemishes appeared more and more intolerable to many.

As the nation reached adulthood, a number of ugly moles and warts had indeed come to the surface. Unequal distribution of wealth and income persisted. One percent of American families possessed nearly seven-eighths of its wealth. Four-fifths of Americans lived on a subsistence level, while a handful lived in incredible opulence. In 1900, Andrew Carnegie's income was $23 million; the average working man earned $500. The wealth of a few was increased by the exploitation of women and children. To feed their families women worked for wages as low as $6 a week. The sacrifice of the country's young to the god of economic growth was alarming. One reporter undertook to do a child's job in the mines for one day and wrote, "I tried to pick out the pieces of slate from the hurrying stream of coal, often missing them; my hands were bruised and cut within a few minutes; I was covered from head to foot with coal dust, and for many hours afterwards I was expectorating some of the small particles of anthracite I had swallowed."

Working conditions were equally horrifying in other industries, and for many Americans housing conditions were as bad or worse. One investigator described a Chicago neighborhood, remarking on the "filthy and rotten tenements, the dingy courts and tumble-down sheds, the foul stables and dilapidated outhouses, the broken sewer pipes, the piles of garbage fairly alive with diseased odors." At the same time the Vanderbilts summered in a "cottage" of 70 rooms, and wealthy men partied in shirts with diamond buttons.

The middle class did not experience either extreme. Its members did have their economic grievances, however. Prosperity increased the cost of living by 35 percent in less than a decade, while many middle-class incomes remained fairly stable. Such people were not poor, but they believed they were not getting a fair share of the prosperity. Many came to blame the monopolies and watched with alarm as trusts, proving to be immune from the Sherman Act, proliferated rapidly. Nearly three-fourths of all trusts in 1904 had been created since 1898. Decreasing competition seemed to threaten America's status as the land of opportunity.

People came to believe that they had to find political solutions to the nation's problems. To achieve that goal they had to wrest government from the

Breaker boys employed by the mines worked in dirty, dismal, and dangerous surroundings that robbed them of their childhood. Conditions were much the same in textile mills, where young girls were often employed.

hands of a few and return it to the "people." The great democratic experiment seemed to have run awry. Wealthy industrialists bought state and federal legislators; urban political machines paid for votes with money from bribes; southern elections had become both bloody and corrupt.

Most problems were not new in 1901; neither were the proposed solutions. What came to be called progressivism was rooted in the Gilded Age. Whereas reform had been a sideshow earlier, it now became a national preoccupation. Progressivism was more broadly based and enjoyed greater appeal than any previous reform movement. The regional differences of the North, South, and West shaped reformers' concerns but not their intensity. The entire nation had experienced war or depression, never reform. One reason it did so now was the diversity and pervasiveness of the voices calling for change.

Voices for Change

By 1900, Americans had done nothing less than reinterpret their understanding of their world. Under the old, classical interpretation, the universe was governed by absolute and unchangeable law. There was divine logic to all and truth was universal—the same

at all times and in all places. Humanity's chore was to discover these truths, not to devise new ones. Under this vision, public policy should be aligned with natural laws; to attempt to change the course of those laws through man-made law was to court disaster. Such logic justified the concentration of wealth as well as the lack of governmental regulation of business and assistance to the poor and weak.

Social Darwinism, laissez-faire economics, and the gospel of wealth never enjoyed total acceptance. Throughout the Gilded Age, challenges and alternative visions chipped away at their bases of support. The earlier challengers, however, offered either rather radical or simplistic alternatives. In 1879 Henry George wrote *Progress and Poverty*. As the title implies, he early recognized the unequal distribution of the fruits of economic growth. His solution was a "single tax" on the "unearned increment" of land values. He wanted to tax those who benefited from land speculation and rising property values without producing anything. In essence he attacked the premise of capitalism that said that one could use money to make more money without providing other goods or services. In *Looking Backward* (1888) Edward Bellamy provided a glimpse of a utopian society based upon a state-controlled economy propelled by cooperation rather than competition. Such writings profoundly influenced the Populists, the Socialists, and many who called themselves progressive.

Although critics dismissed the likes of George as crackpots, some respectable voices arose from the worlds of arts and literature, academia, the law, organized religion, and journalism. Realist writers described the world as it was, not as it should be. Instead of romantic heroes battling for abstract ideals, their characters were ordinary people dealing with concrete problems. The naturalists portrayed the powerlessness of the individual against the uncaring forces of urbanization and industrialization. Artists of the Ashcan school painted urban scenes teeming with problems as well as life. Art and literature thus became mirrors of social concerns (see Chapter 18).

A revolution was also taking place in the academic world. Two important changes were the democratization of higher education and the revolt against formalism. From 1870 to 1910 the number of colleges and universities nearly doubled, and their enrollment grew from 52,000 in 1870 to 600,000 in 1920. Higher education became less elitist, white, religious, and male, as women came to account for 47.3 percent of students in 1920 and African American enrollment grew to over 20,000. Increasingly, their professors came from the middle class as well. Such students and teachers had little interest in supporting the status quo.

Also undermining the status quo was the revolt against formalism. Previous academics had sought to explain the world by formulating abstract, universal

These women in a physics class illustrate the growing presence of women in college during the Progressive Era.

theories. The new scholars, especially in the emerging social sciences, turned this approach on its head. They began instead by collecting concrete data. In field after field that data did not support the so-called natural laws propounded by their predecessors. Knowledge, philosopher and educator John Dewey proclaimed, was "no longer an immobile solid; it has been liquefied."

Theories had prescribed limits to human action; facts became weapons for change. Classical economists asserted earlier that self-interested economic decisions by individuals in a freely competitive economy would naturally regulate markets through the laws of supply and demand. The new economists, calling themselves **institutional economists,** conducted field research to learn how the economy actually worked. Their findings challenged the laissez-faire doctrines of the classicists on two levels: (1) that free competition existed and (2) that human decisions were based on purely economic motivations. To continue policies based on competition was absurd, they argued, in an economy dominated by monopolies. In *Theory of the Leisure Class* (1899) and *The Instinct of Workmanship* (1914), economist Thorstein Veblen demonstrated the power of noneconomic motives. For example, vanity prompted the newly rich to indulge in "conspicuous consumption" well beyond their economic needs. For many economists "natural laws" were, in the words of Richard T. Ely, "used as a tool in the hands of the greedy."

A group of sociologists, calling themselves **Reform Darwinists,** rejected Spencer's Social Darwinism as another tool of exploitation. They accepted evolutionary principles and the influence of environment but denied that people were merely pawns manipulated by natural forces. Human intelligence was an active force that could control and change the environment, especially when people worked together. A leading Reform Darwinist, Lester Frank Ward, proclaimed, "The individual has reigned long enough. The day has come for society to take its affairs into its own hands and shape its own destinies." Ward called for "rational planning" and "social engineering" in his *Dynamic Sociology* (1883).

Legal scholars joined the assault on formalism in both books and court decisions. During the Gilded Age, courts had read laissez-faire principles into their interpretation of the Constitution. Decisions striking down regulatory and reform legislation invoked such abstract principles as the sanctity of property rights and contracts. In theory all such rights were equal before the law; reality was a different matter. For example, in *Lochner v. New York* (1905) the Supreme Court struck down a New York law limiting bakers' working hours. The law, the court ruled, violated the bakers' rights to bargain freely and to make contracts. Most workers, however, had no real power to bargain, and maintaining that myth merely increased management's already overwhelming advantage.

A new breed of jurists challenged laissez-faire justice. Dean Roscoe Pound of the Harvard Law School advocated "sociological jurisprudence," calling for "the adjustment of principles and doctrines to the human conditions they are to govern rather than assumed first principles." Supreme Court Justice Oliver Wendell Holmes, Jr., rejected the idea that laws had ever been the logical result of pure, universal principles. He argued that laws should be based on "the felt necessities of the time." Lawyer Louis D. Brandeis successfully argued these ideas in 1908. That year the Supreme Court upheld a law in *Muller v. Oregon* that set a ten-hour workday for women working in Oregon laundries, primarily because social research documented the damage done to women's health by long hours of work.

As Americans began to reject absolute truths and universal principles, the question remained of how to determine right from wrong and good from bad. Philosopher William James with his doctrine of **pragmatism** provided an answer. "The ultimate test for us of what a truth means," he wrote, "is the conduct it dictates or inspires." Inherited ideas and principles needed scientific scrutiny before being accepted as guides to social development. As a distinctly American philosophy, pragmatism found many adherents. One of them, John Dewey, applied its principles to education. Requiring rote memorization of a static body of facts, he believed, did not meet the needs of individuals in a dynamic, changing environment. Instead, education should be based on experience to prepare students to assume personally fulfilling roles in society. In schools modeled after Dewey's Laboratory School at the University of Chicago, students engaged in activities that taught problem solving by doing rather than reading.

The literary and intellectual currents of the era helped to set the stage for reform by combining optimism, idealism, and a tough-minded practicality. Yet the educated elite were probably reflecting rather than shaping public opinion. Priests and preachers influenced far more people than professors. The impact of organized religion on progressivism was profound. It was no coincidence that Teddy Roosevelt's supporters marched around the hall singing "Onward Christian Soldiers" at the 1912 convention.

The confrontation between the church and the city produced the **Social Gospel** movement. Urban clergymen saw ravaged bodies that needed to be healed

In 1889 Jane Addams founded Hull House, a social settlement in Chicago. A social gospeler, Addams turned to Christian ideals to solve social problems.

before souls could be saved. As a young Baptist minister in the dismal New York neighborhood "Hell's Kitchen," Walter Rauschenbusch described the poor coming to his church for aid. "They wore down our threshold, and they wore away our hearts . . . one could hear human virtue cracking and crunching all around." Following the lead of William Graham Taylor at the Chicago Theological Seminary, theology schools added courses in Christian sociology to teach "the application of our common Christianity to . . . social conditions." Social Gospelers used the tools of scientific inquiry to root out and solve human problems in order to usher in the "Kingdom of God on Earth." Many settlement house workers, such as **Jane Addams,** sought to put their faith into action for "the joy of finding the Christ that lieth in man, but which no man can unfold save in fellowship." The Social Gospelers advocated a kind of sacred humanism.

Progressivism was dominated by, but not limited to, Protestantism. The 1891 encyclical, *Rerum Novarum,* by Pope Leo XIII, inspired such Catholic priests as Father John A. Ryan to declare that "a small number of very rich men have been able to lay upon the masses of people a yoke little better than slavery itself" and that "no practical solution of this question will ever be found without the assistance of the church." Such Catholics as Alfred E. Smith and

Robert F. Wagner became prominent progressive politicians. Others such as Jewish lawyer Louis Brandeis illustrated that the reform sentiment was not exclusively Christian.

The Muckrakers

A final spark that ignited public interest in reform was popular journalism. The expansion of education and cities provided a mass audience for low-priced magazines. Such journals as *Collier's* and *McClure's* sold for only 10 cents and could only succeed if large numbers of people bought them. Their editors quickly rediscovered people's fascination with evil. Investigative reporters peered beneath all sorts of rocks and brought to light corruption in almost every facet of society. Their vivid, indignant accounts sold magazines but appalled some of the elite. Theodore Roosevelt compared the writers to the character in John Bunyan's *The Pilgrim's Progress,* who was too engrossed in raking muck to look up and accept a celestial crown. Thus these chroniclers came to be called **muckrakers.**

Most of their exposés came out serially in magazines; others were published as books, but all titillated the public. John Spargo wrote on child labor, "Statistics cannot express the withering of child lips in the poisoned air of factories; the tired strained look of child eyes that never dance to the glad music of souls tuned to Nature's symphonies." David Graham Phillips argued, "The United States Senate is a

larger factor than your labor and intelligence, you average American, in determining your income. And the Senate is a traitor to you!" State legislatures were little better, as was shown by journalist William Allen White's investigation in Missouri. "The legislature met biennially, and enacted such laws as the corporations paid for and such as were necessary to fool the people." In *Following the Color Line* journalist and author Ray Stannard Baker exhorted, "Whether we like it or not the whole nation . . . is tied by unbreakable bonds to its Negroes, its Chinamen, its slum-dwellers, its thieves, its murderers, its prostitutes. We cannot elevate ourselves by driving them back either with hatred, violence or neglect; but only by bringing them forward: by service." **Ida Tarbell** called Standard Oil "one of the most gigantic and dangerous conspiracies ever attempted." In similar, stirring words Lincoln Steffens denounced urban politics in *The Shame of the Cities,* and the socialist Upton Sinclair described the horrifying conditions in the meat-packing industry in *The Jungle.*

One might believe these men and women were cynical mudslingers, but that was not how they saw themselves: "We muckraked," said Baker, "not because we hated our world, but because we loved it. We were not hopeless, we were not cynical, we were not bitter." The public sometimes missed the intended message. Sinclair's goal in *The Jungle* was a socialist critique of the exploitation of labor in the meatpacking industry, but as he ruefully noted, "I aimed at the nation's heart and hit it in the stomach." After a few years, muckraking tended to degenerate into sloppy research and wild, unsubstantiated charges. Yet the publishers of the more than 2000 muckraking books and articles who aimed at the nation's pocketbooks hit a number of Americans in the heart.

PROGRESSIVES IN ACTION

Voices of change echoed a genuine transformation of popular sentiment. Americans of all classes began calling themselves "progressives" and sought to reform whichever social evil captured their attention. Most believed problems could be legislated away; their typical response to injustice or sin was "there ought to be a law." At the same time they rejected the individualism of Social Darwinism and believed that progress would come through cooperation rather than competition. Thus they organized themselves by droves into groups that shared their own particular vision of human progress.

The diversity of new organizations reflected the breadth of reform activity. Indeed, so varied were the

Ida Tarbell became one of the most influential muckrakers after the 1904 publication of her *History of the Standard Oil Company.*

The White Plague

During the Progressive Era, the rise of scientific ways of thinking cleared the way for reformers and health officers to launch a campaign against the disease most identified with industrialization—tuberculosis (TB). During the nineteenth century, TB was aptly called "the Captain of All the Men of Death." It killed more people and caused more sickness than any other disease in the Western world. Its very name conjures up images of fetid sweatshops and sulfurous mills where long working hours and physical exhaustion broke the health of men, women, and children; of urban slums and overcrowded tenements rotten with disease; and, finally, of emaciated, ghostlike wretches, feverish with infection, gasping for breath, coughing up mouthfuls of blood, and staring hollow-eyed into space waiting for death.

In a sense, TB mirrors the complexity of the industrial revolution, for just as the transformation of the economy was multifaceted, TB is not one but many diseases. TB is merely the generic name for a host of infections caused by tubercle bacilli, isolated in 1882 by Robert Koch, the famous German scientist. The most common (and most feared) form of TB is pulmonary tuberculosis, a chronic, debilitating disease of the lungs; it can kill its victims in a few months but usually requires several years to complete the task. Other common forms of the disease include meningeal TB, which produces an inflammation of the membranes surrounding the brain; TB of the spine, which causes a hunchback deformity of the spine; lupus, TB of the skin; and miliary TB, a generalized infection that occurs when the tubercle bacilli are distributed by the bloodstream throughout the body, producing small nodules on most organs.

Because the term *tuberculosis* did not appear in print until around 1840, most Americans knew the disease as *consumption,* which seemed the perfect metaphor because victims of the disease gradually wasted away from debilitating fever, weight loss, night sweats, chronic cough, and copious sputum containing toward the end the bright red blood spots that denoted advanced pulmonary tuberculosis.

In less polite society, consumptives were called *lungers,* a term of derision. Throughout the nineteenth century, many people associated TB with poverty and attached a social stigma to the disease. Others believed that TB was caused by some hereditary defect; for them, the perplexing problem was why the disease hit some families harder than others. In Ralph Waldo Emerson's family, for example, he and three of his brothers suffered from the disease, while his fellow transcendentalist, Henry David Thoreau, lost his father, a sister, and a grandfather to TB before dying from the disease himself.

Paradoxically, despite its dreadful symptoms and terrifying ability to wipe out entire families, TB was romanticized on both sides of the Atlantic. For many writers, it became a metaphor for comparing decay in nature to disease in man. Thus Thoreau, upon seeing the first splashes of red in the green maple leaves of autumn, could write in 1852 in his *Journal Intime:* "Decay and disease are often beautiful, like . . . the hectic glow of consumption."

In fact, the Age of Romanticism's much heralded "doom and gloom" may have derived at least in part from the sadness and melancholy caused by the deaths of loved ones from TB—especially the death of young adults, for whom the disease had a special affinity. John Keats, the quintessential romantic poet, succumbed to TB at 26; Emily Brontë, author of the powerful *Wuthering Heights,* was cut down tragically at 30. The novels of the day, Charles Dickens's *David Copperfield,* for one, are positively littered with the corpses of people killed in the bloom of youth by the "white plague."

The disease also broke its share of hearts in the theater and at the opera. Alexander Dumas lamented the death from TB of a beautiful heroine in *La Dame aux Camelias,* which in its English translation became the play, *Camille, or the Fate of a Coquette,* later adapted by Verdi for the opera as *La Traviata.* An identical fate befell the heroine in the play, *La Bohème,* which inspired Puccini's opera of the same name.

Under the spell of this heartwrenching romanticism, writers, poets, and artists created a new and profoundly twisted ideal of feminine beauty: the dying angel, smitten by consumption, whose physical appeal was somehow enhanced by her malady. One gravely ill woman confided to her diary, "I cough continually! But

 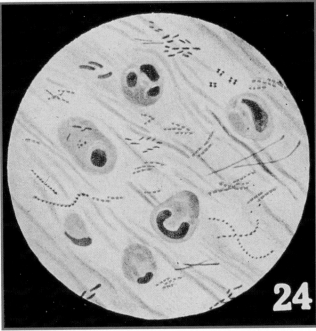

for a wonder, far from making me look ugly, this gives me an air of languor that is very becoming." As depicted by writers, the dying female consumptive was, to her fingertips, an exquisitely fragile creature, the very embodiment of both the romantic and the Victorian ideal of frail feminine beauty. Her languid pallor was rendered even more pale by the generous application of whitening powders; and her slender body, with its swanlike neck and elongated limbs, was adorned in thin, sheer white clothing of cotton or linen, giving her an ethereal quality, as a spirit not quite of this earth.

Numerous artists struggled to capture this image on canvas, including Gabriel Rossetti of the Pre-Raphaelite school, who idealized tall, slender women "with cadaverous bodies and sensual mouths." Reducing this image to a word portrait, Henry James described Janet Burden, one of the leading Pre-Raphaelite models, as "strange, pale, livid, gaunt, silent, and yet in a manner graceful and picturesque." To another observer the same woman looked "as if she had walked out of an Egyptian tomb at Luxor."

As the nineteenth century drew to a close, however, the romantic view of life gradually lost its hold on the public's imagination. Instead of celebrating TB, writers, joined by health reformers, saw TB through the lens of realism. They linked the disease to poverty, unsafe working conditions, overcrowded housing, poor diet, and the failure of government to safeguard the public's health. Rather than glorifying consumptives, this change in attitude depicted them as the victims of a cruel, punishing illness. TB was no longer something to spark the artistic imagination; it was now a microbial insult to mankind and an indictment against the society that tolerated it.

aims of people calling themselves progressive that to call progressivism a single movement is a mistake. The only unity lay in the idea that people could improve society. Most progressives, however, were middle-class moderates who abhorred radical solutions. Motivated by a fear and hatred of class conflict, such progressives sought to save the capitalists from their own excesses and thereby salvage the system. Their goal was an orderly and harmonious society.

The Drive to Organize

Organizing was a major activity at the turn of the century. Such professional groups as the American Medical Association (AMA) and the American Historical Association emerged in their modern form. These groups reflected the rise of a new professionalism that helped to create a body of "experts" who aided progressives wanting to impose order and efficiency on social institutions. The organizations themselves also acted to bring change. The AMA was reorganized in 1901, and by 1910 its membership had increased from 8400 to more than 70,000. Its major goal was to improve professional standards. Governments assisted by enacting laws that required licenses to practice medicine. In 1910 a Carnegie Foundation study recommended minimum standards for medical education. Widespread acceptance of its report closed dozens of marginal medical schools, several of which trained minority doctors. Professionalization thus reduced the number of practitioners. Although this did help weed out incompetents, it also increased the incomes of the remaining practitioners and often reduced minority participation. Order, stability, and improved standards came at the cost of decreased opportunity for some.

Given the religious bent of progressive thought, a number of church-related organizations also arose. One of the most important was the Federal Council of Churches of Christ in America. Founded in 1908, it was an interdenominational group that advocated safer working conditions, the abolition of child labor, shorter workweeks, higher wages, workmen's compensation, old-age pensions, and "the most equitable division of the products of industry that can ultimately be devised."

To a large extent, middle-class women led in the organization of reform. Technology and domestic help lessened the burdens of running a home for these women, but a stigma remained on paid employment. Women's clubs provided an outlet for the energies and abilities of many competent and educated women. Local organizations flourished and in 1890 joined to form the General Federation of Women's Clubs. In the next two decades, reform groups founded and led mainly by women sprang up.

The majority of activist, middle-class women became involved in movements closely linked to their assigned social roles as guardians of morality and nurturers of the family. Many worked through such religious groups as the Young Women's Christian Association. Numerous others joined in a resurgence of prohibitionism. The **Woman's Christian Temperance Union (WCTU),** led by Frances Willard, revived a flagging prohibition movement and by 1898 had 10,000 local branches. It was assisted by the Anti-Saloon League (organized in 1893) and such church organizations as the Temperance Society of the Methodist Episcopal Church.

Some of the prohibitionists were Protestant fundamentalists who considered the consumption of alcohol a sin; others were concerned with its social impact. Urban reformers constantly saw the consequences of alcohol abuse in domestic violence, accidents, and pauperism. Alcohol was the root of so many social problems that to ignore it was like "bailing water out of a tub with the tap turned on; letting the . . . liquor traffic run full blast while we limply stood around and picked up the wreckage." The physically devastating effects of alcoholism were reported by the AMA. Many in the Anti-Saloon League were also dismayed by the part played by drinking establishments in machine politics.

The idea of legislating morality for the good of society spilled over into the sexual sphere. A major area of concern was prostitution, and its opponents had a variety of motivations. Some stressed its role in the spread of venereal disease; others deplored the exploitation of women and the double standard that allowed only men sexual freedom. For some it was morally wrong; to others it was just one more social evil—a product of environment rather than original sin. Many linked it with immigration, as they did alcohol abuse. The crusade against this age-old problem had deep roots, but at the turn of the century it followed a typically progressive path. Muckraking journalists enraged the public with lurid accounts of "white slavery" rings that kidnapped young women and forced them into prostitution. The next step was to pressure local governments to establish commissions to study the issue. Most reports stressed the economic roots. One prostitute asked an investigator, "Do you suppose I am going back to earn five or six dollars a week in a factory, when I can earn that amount any night and often much more?"

Some people believed prostitution was merely a symptom of a larger disease, and they became **purity crusaders.** Dr. Will K. Kellogg wrote, "The exorbitant demands of the sexual appetites encountered among civilized people are not the result of a normal instinct, but are due to the incitements of an abnormally stimulating diet, including alcohol, the seduction of prurient literature and so-called art, and the temptations of impure associations." After a national Purity Congress in 1895, the purity crusaders lobbied not only for the prohibition of alcohol and prostitution but also for such things as censorship and the regulation of narcotics.

Progressive social reform had two aims: control and justice. Women were deeply involved in social justice as well as control movements like prohibition. Middle-class women had long dominated humanitarian work, but during the 1890s their work took on a new aggressiveness. Women came to believe that aid to the poor was an inadequate response to society's ills; they wanted to attack the causes of poverty. They sought to improve wages and working conditions, especially for women, and to protect children from exploitation. To this end, they started several organizations. The National Consumers League, led by former Illinois factory inspector Florence Kelly, lobbied for protective legislation for women and children as well as better working and living conditions for all. Kelly became a leading advocate of child labor laws and was joined in this cause by Alabama clergyman Edgar Gardner Murphy, who proposed the formation of the National Child Labor Committee in 1904. Like most progressives, child labor reformers gathered data and photographs to document horrors for legislators at the local, state, and finally federal level.

African American women were among the most active of the reformers. The growing black middle class produced increasing numbers of educated women. Unlike their white counterparts, most engaged in paid employment. More than financial need alleviated the stigma of employment for African American women. They were expected to play a larger role in society. Journalist Lucy Wilmot Smith explained that although the white woman "has had to contest with her brother every inch of the ground for recognition; the Negro man, having had his sister by his side on plantations and in rice swamps, keeps her there, now that he moves in other spheres." In addition to working, black women engaged in reform. Ida B. Wells (later Wells-Barnett) launched an antilynching campaign that resulted in the expulsion of both her and her newspaper, the *Free Speech*, from Memphis, Tennessee, in 1893. In 1895 she joined with other clubwomen to form what became the National Association of Colored Women.

Some reformers were not content to be merely advocates for the poor and the weak; they wanted to become directly involved with such people to edu-

cate and organize them to help themselves. Here again middle-class women played a key role. Foremost among such activities was the **settlement house movement.** Following the lead of Jane Addams of Hull House in Chicago, many young college-educated women moved into slum neighborhoods to live and work with those they sought to help. "From the first," Addams wrote, "it seemed understood that we were ready to perform the humblest neighborhood services. We were asked to wash the newborn babies, and to prepare the dead for burial, to nurse the sick, and to 'mind the children.'"

More than unselfishness motivated such women. One worker confessed that settlement houses gratified her "thirst to know how the other half lives." Some educated women wanted more freedom than marriage and part-time volunteer work seemed to offer. One appeal of settlement work was that men did not control it. A result was a growing social feminism that cut across class lines. An example was the founding of the National Women's Trade Union League in 1905. Through it, wealthy supporters organized women workers, joined their strikes, and trained leaders.

At first such activity seemed to draw attention away from the suffrage movement. Women's roles in progressive reforms, however, did eventually convince many people that women not only deserved the right to vote but also that their political participation would be socially beneficial. Jane Addams asserted, "If women have in any sense been responsible for the

Alarmed by the unhealthy child-care practices of many immigrants, visiting nurses went to immigrant homes to teach such things as the proper bathing of babies.

Susan B. Anthony, a founder of the National Woman Suffrage Association in 1869 and vice president and president of the National American Woman Suffrage Association from 1890 to 1900, fought for women's right to vote on the national level through an amendment to the U.S. Constitution. The Nineteenth Amendment (sometimes called the Anthony Amendment) guaranteeing woman suffrage was adopted in 1920, fourteen years after Anthony's death.

gentler side of life which softens and blurs some of its harsher conditions may they not have a duty to perform in our American cities?" Arguments based on women's "special role," however, cut both ways. In articles with such titles as "Famed Biologist's Warning on the Peril in Votes to Women," writers charged that voting was so "unnatural" for women that preg-

nant women would miscarry and nursing mothers' milk would cease to flow. As during the fight for ratification of the Equal Rights Amendment in the 1970s, not all opponents were male. Mrs. A. J. George of the National Association Opposed to Woman Suffrage declared, "The Woman-suffrage movement is an imitation-of-man movement, and as such, merits the condemnation of every normal man and woman."

In the face of such opposition, suffragists began to escalate their demands for the vote. Many became convinced that only national action would be effective. Thus the National American Woman Suffrage Association, led by Carrie Chapman Catt after 1915, began a broad-based campaign for an amendment to the U.S. Constitution. More militant women followed the young Quaker, Alice Paul, who founded the National Woman's party in 1914. She preferred the tactics of British suffragists who had picketed, gone on hunger strikes, and actively confronted both politicians and police.

Another group in the social justice movement sought to improve relations between blacks and whites. White Southerners had continued to devise forms of racial control to replace slavery. Their solution became a three-legged stool: legal segregation, disfranchisement, and violence. From the beginning, African Americans resisted white efforts to suppress them. In city after city, they utilized every tool and tactic that would prove successful in the 1960s. They marched, they lobbied legislative bodies, they petitioned, they challenged discriminatory legislation in courts, and they boycotted segregated streetcars. Under the leadership of Booker T. Washington, they also tried conciliation. Nothing stemmed the rising tide of racism.

As conditions worsened, Washington seemed to grow even more accommodating, at least in public. His influence with white politicians and philan-

Women employed a variety of tactics in their fight for the vote. Here women picket the White House, adorned with banners indicating their college alma maters, which also demonstrates the impact of the democratization of education.

THE PEOPLE SPEAK

An Account of the Proceedings of the Trial of Susan B. Anthony

From the inception of the women's rights movement, suffragists had argued for the right of women to vote, using all available tactics. This transcription of the 1872 trial of **Susan B. Anthony** for illegally attempting to register to vote demonstrates one of those methods—court challenges to the constitutionality of prohibiting woman suffrage. At the conclusion of the trial, Anthony was found guilty and required to pay a fine of $100 plus court costs.

> The only alleged ground of illegality of the defendant's vote is that she is a woman. If the same act has been done by her brother under the same circumstances, the act would have been not only innocent, but honorable and laudable; but having been done by a woman it is said to be a crime. The crime therefore consists not in the act done, but in the simple fact that the person doing it was a woman and not a man. I believe this is the first instance in which a woman has been arraigned in a criminal court, merely on account of her sex.

Women have the same interest that men have in the establishment and maintenance of good government; they are to the same extent as men bound to obey the laws; they suffer to the same extent by bad laws, and profit to the same extent by good laws; and upon principles of equal justice, as it would seem, should be allowed equally with men, to express their preference in the choice of lawmakers and rulers. But however that may be, no greater *absurdity*, to use no harsher term, could be presented, than that of rewarding men and punishing women, for the same act, *without giving to women any voice in the question which should be rewarded, and which punished.*

I am aware, however, that we are here to be governed by the Constitution and laws as they are, and that if the defendant has been guilty of violating the law, she must submit to the penalty, however unjust or absurd the law may be. But courts are not required to so interpret laws or constitutions as to produce absurdity or injustice, so long as they are open to a more reasonable interpretation. . . .

Source: Votes for Women: Selections from the National American Woman Suffrage Association Collection, 1848–1926. Jean H. Baker, ed. (New York: Oxford University Press, 2002).

thropists as well as his control of much of the black press gave him incredible power, which he used ruthlessly on occasion. Behind the scenes, he supported protest activities, using code names and secret funds. Educated African Americans, however, became increasingly disenchanted with his public performance. They also resented his suppression of dissent by fellow blacks. The so-called anti-Bookerite radicals found their spokesperson in **W. E. B. Du Bois.** Unlike Washington, who had been born into slavery and educated at an industrial school, Du Bois was born to free parents in Massachusetts and became the first African American to receive a doctorate from Harvard.

Gifted with staggering intellectual brilliance, Du Bois expressed the frustrations and dreams of his fellow blacks in *The Souls of Black Folks* (1903). Of being black in America, he wrote, "one ever feels his twoness—an American, a Negro, two souls, two thoughts, two unreconciled strivings, two warring ideals in one dark body." In that book he also penned a polite but devastating critique of Washington's leadership. He objected to Washington's failure to recognize the importance of the vote, his emphasis on industrial education at the expense of higher education, his reluctance to criticize as well as praise white actions, and his willingness to give up previously won rights.

Relations between the two men deteriorated steadily after 1903, even though immediate methods rather than ultimate goals separated them. Both wanted the full acceptance of African Americans as first-class citizens. To Washington, the best route was self-help and educating the masses. To these ends, he made Tuskegee Institute into an impressive institution staffed entirely by blacks. Du Bois, on the other hand, was more integrationist and believed the key to black advancement was in cultivating what he called the "Talented Tenth." To him, more of the limited education funds should go to train the ablest 10 percent of African Americans for leadership through liberal arts and professional schooling. Although most African Americans saw value in both approaches, the dispute became bitter and divisive.

In 1905 Du Bois joined William Monroe Trotter in forming the **Niagara movement,** an organization devoted to two main objectives: opposition to Washington's leadership and demands for "full manhood

W. E. B. Du Bois, shown here in the editorial offices of *The Crisis* at the New York headquarters of the NAACP, was at first the only African American to hold a significant office in the organization.

rights." Only about 50 educated African Americans—mainly Northerners—joined, and the movement struggled to exist in the face of unrelenting sabotage by Washington. It played an important role, however, in convincing northern white progressives that an alternative to Washington was desirable. When a white mob in Springfield, Illinois, went on a rampage against African Americans, concerned whites joined with Du Bois and Ida B. Wells-Barnett to found the **National Association for the Advancement of Colored People (NAACP)** in 1909. At first the group was led and dominated by whites; Du Bois was the only African American to hold a responsible position, as editor of its journal *The Crisis*. The organization became more black over time, but the focus of its activities remained essentially the same: education and propaganda, court challenges to discrimination, and lobbying for such legislation as a federal antilynching law.

The drive to organize pervaded all of society, creating such diverse groups as the Boy Scouts of America (1910), the Rotary Club (1915), the National Collegiate Athletic Association (1906), the National Birth Control League (1915), and even the Aero Club of America (1905) to popularize "ballooning as a sport, especially among the more wealthy class." Americans came to believe in cooperative efforts to reach goals. In unprecedented numbers they also began to look to government for answers—starting at the city level and moving up to Washington.

Urban Beginnings

Progressivism was a response to emerging problems and first confronted the most visible ones, many of which were found in the cities. Incredibly rapid increases in urban populations outpaced the ability of "small-town" governments to meet the challenges. Political machines provided needed services but came under attack in the 1890s as inefficient and corrupt. Middle- and upper-class reformers demanded that governments operate "on a strict business basis" and be run "not by partisans, [n]either Republican nor Democratic, but by men who are skilled in business management and social service."

Urban reformers' victories included the secret ballot and voter registration in some cities. Then in 1900, a model for efficient, nonpartisan city government emerged from the chaos created when a devastating hurricane killed more than 6000 people in Galveston, Texas. Local government broke down and the state legislature appointed a five-man commission to run the city. The idea had spread to over 400 cities by World War I. A refinement was added in 1913, when in the wake of a disastrous flood, the government of Dayton, Ohio, hired a city manager to run the city on a day-to-day basis.

The cost of efficiency was decreased democracy. Indeed, some urban reformers were openly antidemocratic. One wrote in 1901, "Ignorance should be excluded from control. City business should be carried on by trained experts selected on some other principle than popular suffrage." The ward system, under which aldermen were elected by district, was seen as a problem because, as a Chicago businessman noted in 1911, "Men of successful experience and ability large enough to do justice to public affairs will seldom live and bring up families in the poorer wards." The reformers naively sought to take politics out of government, but by "politics" they often meant the voice of people not like themselves. Nevertheless, these goals contradicted broader support for democracy, and by 1914 most city commissioners were required to run for election—although often in at-large elections rather than by district.

Middle-class progressives sometimes found their will thwarted by lower-class voters. Breaking up urban machines often destroyed the informal welfare networks that met the needs of the poor. When that happened, the poor rejected the new efficiency. In 1901, the Tammany Hall machine recaptured New York with the campaign slogan "To hell with reform." Poor immigrants did not accept that their ignorance and "foreign ways" were at the root of urban problems. "It is not so much the under crust," one declared, "as the upper crust that endangers the interests of the people."

In a number of cities, voters elected mayors who sympathized with working-class desires. Tom L. Johnson, elected mayor of Cleveland in 1901, rejected efforts to impose middle-class morality on the poor. "I am not trying to enforce Christianity," he proclaimed, "only make it possible." To this end he expanded social services and brought about the public ownership of the waterworks, gas and electric utilities, and public transportation, thereby reducing their costs to the poor. After his election in 1899, Mayor Samuel "Golden Rule" Jones sought to establish the "Cooperative Commonwealth, the Kingdom of Heaven on Earth," in Toledo, Ohio. Until his death in 1904, he worked to provide free kindergartens, free playgrounds, free golf courses, and free concerts. He also reformed the police department, substituting light canes for the heavy clubs carried by patrolmen and prohibiting the jailing of people without charges. He made some powerful enemies and once declared, "Everyone is against me but the people." Most urban liberals depended on working-class voters.

The move toward public ownership of utilities was most avidly supported by the Socialists, who showed growing strength on the local level. In 1910 a Socialist was elected mayor of Milwaukee, and in the next year 70 other Socialists were elected in towns and cities across the nation. By 1912 about 1000 held offices in 33 states and 160 cities. Their rising power, however, helped trigger a backlash by middle-class voters, who favored regulatory commissions rather than public ownership of utilities.

Urban progressivism was obviously not a coherent, unified movement. Different groups at different times succeeded in different cities. Social services were cut to lower business taxes in some cities and expanded in others. In most cities the evils of overcrowded, unhealthy tenements were attacked with varying degrees of success with such measures as building codes. By the turn of the century, however, more and more people began to look to the states to solve problems.

Reform Reaches the State Level

Regardless of their objectives, many urban reformers eventually dabbled in state politics. The city had little power and the federal government seemed too remote. Thus the states became major battlegrounds for reform. The form and leadership of state progressivism were as diverse and complex as urban progressivism. In the South, most progressives worked through the Democratic party; in the Midwest and on the Pacific Coast, progressives captured the Republican party. In the industrial Northeast, progressives emerged in both major parties, but the Democrats were the more successful. In some cases progressive governors, such as Al Smith of New York, were the products of urban machines that embraced reform to hold onto their electorates. Others, such as **Robert La Follette** of Wisconsin, were Republican regulars who bypassed party leaders to ride

Robert La Follette, shown here in Cumberland, Wisconsin, in 1897, was known for progressive reforms as governor of and U.S. senator from Wisconsin.

reform to power. In the South, reform governors were elected by startlingly diverse constituencies. In Mississippi, small-town lawyer and editor James K. Vardaman was elected by poor white farmers, the "redneck" vote. In Georgia, the urban middle class was the main support of Hoke Smith, publisher of the *Atlanta Journal.*

State progressives pursued four major goals: (1) providing "direct democracy," (2) protecting the public by regulating the economy, (3) increasing state services, and (4) establishing social control. One progressive creed was dramatically stated by writer and journalist William Allen White: "The voice of the people is indeed the will of God." By World War I many states had adopted political procedures designed to give the people a more direct say in running the government. An initiative allowed voters to propose legislative changes, usually by petition; a referendum gave the public a mechanism for voting directly on controversial legislation; recall provided a way to remove elected officials. Many states also established direct primaries. Other states adopted measures to cleanse electoral procedures, including the secret ballot, voter registration, and corrupt practices legislation. The drive for direct democracy culminated in the Seventeenth Amendment to the Constitution (1913), which substituted the popular election of senators for their election by state legislatures.

The victories of women suffragists at the state level also expanded democracy—especially in the West. In that region the relatively barren environment and the frontier conditions endured by early settlers caused husbands and wives to work together as partners to survive. The Anglo conflict with existing Hispanic and Native American cultures may have also fostered a unity that created more equality. At any rate, Washington state gave women the vote in 1910. California did so the next year, and four other western states had followed suit by 1916. That year Jeannette Rankin was elected to Congress from Montana. These victories encouraged efforts to obtain a constitutional amendment allowing women to vote.

Progressive actions by states to protect the public and regulate the economy took many forms. In the West the emphasis was on regulating railroads and utilities, reflecting the region's Populist heritage. The region was also especially vulnerable to rate discrimination because of its remoteness and the long distances to markets. Legislatures created commissions to regulate the rates charged by both railroads and utilities. At the same time, taxes on corporations were increased. For example, after La Follette's election as governor of Wisconsin in 1900, state revenues from taxes on railroads grew from $1.9 million to $3.4 million.

In the industrialized states, workmen's compensation became a major goal. Horror stories about industrial accidents had long abounded, and muckrakers further inflamed the public. Then in 1911 a major tragedy chilled the hearts of Americans. A fire broke out at the **Triangle Shirtwaist Company** in New York just 30 minutes before closing time. The doors were locked to prevent workers from leaving early, and many fire escape ladders were either broken or missing. By the time the flames were doused, 147 workers, mainly women and girls, had lost their lives—47 had jumped to their deaths, littering the street with bodies. The Triangle fire was the worst example of escalating industrial accidents. The only recourse for most maimed workers or their widowed spouses was to sue the company, which for many was not a realistic option. Some workers did get large settlements, however, which represented an unpredictable cost to businesses. Gradually, the idea of mandatory insurance grew in popularity, with the support of many factory owners. Between 1910 and 1916, 32 states enacted **workmen's compensation laws.**

The work of the **National Child Labor Committee** and other organizations moved states to legislate protection for women and children. Progressives gathered evidence of the harm done to both by long working hours and unsafe, unhealthy conditions. State action was necessary, they argued, for two reasons: Women and children could not protect themselves and the nation's future depended on the health of both. By 1916, 32 states had laws regulating the hours worked by women and children, 11 had specified minimum wages for women, and every state regulated child labor in some manner. Other protective legislation included building and sanitary codes, which benefited all workers.

A number of states also expanded social services. Because of lobbying by settlement house workers, by 1914 some 20 states had provided mother's pensions to widows or abandoned wives with dependent children. The sums paid were meager, however, ranging from $2 to $15 a month for the first child and lesser amounts for the rest. Funding for education also in-

The Triangle Shirtwaist Company fire killed 147 workers, who left behind grieving relatives and friends. It raised awareness of dangerous working conditions.

creased. A major area of reform was the expansion of compulsory education to the high school level. Support often came from businesses, which saw public education as a means of preparing individuals for life in an industrial society. As a result, very few public schools were modeled on John Dewey's progressive educational doctrines. Instead of promoting personal development, education, in the industrialists' minds, should inculcate discipline and punctuality. Hence school bells trained one for factory whistles and letter grades taught the value of individual initiative. Governments also made school organization more businesslike, with increased power given to school superintendents and principals, who were expected to be trained in management techniques.

The flip side of state social justice legislation was increased efforts at social control. Prohibitionists won many victories in the states, especially in the South. That region provided fertile soil for prohibitionists because of the strength of Protestant fundamentalism and the so-called race problem. One southern prohibitionist argued that African Americans were "a child race in the South, and if drunkenness causes three-fourths of the crime ascribed to it, whiskey must be taken out of the Negro's hands," and that it was the duty "of the stronger race to forego its own personal liberty for the protection of the weaker race." Between 1907 and 1909 Georgia, Mississippi, North Carolina, Tennessee, and Alabama adopted state prohibition; 14 other states had joined them by 1916.

The move toward social control infected all regions. Between 1907 and 1917, 16 states passed laws authorizing sterilization of various categories of allegedly unfit individuals. Social control measures were usually directed at minorities, so the South naturally offered the most extreme examples, but California progressives excluded Asians almost as ruthlessly. Southern whites trumpeted segregation as a reform, and they had the approval of many northern progressives. Even race relations muckraker Ray Stannard Baker wrote, "As for the Jim Crow laws in the South, many of them, at least, are at present necessary to avoid clashes between the ignorant of both races." Segregation was often enacted under progressive governors—a paradox only if the general progressive tendency toward social control is ignored.

In most ways, southern progressivism was for whites only. Increased school funding was common, but the bulk went to educating white children. The discrepancies between the amounts spent accelerated, making even more of a lie of the *Plessy v. Ferguson* (1896) formula of "separate but equal" facilities. In 1919 southern states spent an average of $12.16 per white student and $3.29 per black student. Racism remained a potent force. As governor of Mis-

sissippi from 1903 to 1907, James K. Vardaman pursued progressive reforms in such areas as convict-lease (a system by which states rented out their prisoners to private interests to provide a cheap labor source), school funding, and railroad regulation. At the same time he defended lynching, saying "we would be justified in slaughtering every Ethiopian on earth to preserve unsullied the honor of one Caucasian home."

The legacy of progressivism in the states was mixed, as were the motives of reformers. Regardless of their goals, most came to look to the federal government for help. One reformer expressed their frustration. "When I was in the city council . . . fighting for a shorter work day, [my opponents] told me to go to the legislature; now [my fellow legislators] tell me to go to Congress for a national law. When I get there and demand it, they will tell me to go to hell."

PROGRESSIVISM MOVES TO THE NATIONAL LEVEL

When McKinley was reelected in 1900, few expected a national reform leader, and but for a quirk of fate they would have been right. As the 1900 Republican convention rolled around, party leaders realized they had a problem. Theodore Roosevelt had become a national hero in the wake of the Spanish-American War, but he had angered party regulars by supporting regulatory legislation as governor of New York. When they decided to "bury" Roosevelt in the vice presidency, presidential adviser and politician Mark Hanna warned, "Don't you realize that there's only one life between that madman and the White House?" On September 6, 1901, anarchist Leon Czolgosz shot McKinley. Eight days later that one life was gone, and Roosevelt was president. It was not immediately apparent, however, that he would usher in reform. Many remembered that during the Pullman strike Roosevelt had suggested shooting the strikers. Most therefore did not expect the action he took in the 1902 coal strike. That year, however, became the first in a decade and a half of snowballing reform that would result in a massive amount of legislation and four constitutional amendments by 1920.

Roosevelt and New Attitudes Toward Government Power

Roosevelt became the most forceful president since Abraham Lincoln, but few men have looked or sounded less presidential. He was short, nearsighted, beaver-toothed, and talked in a high-pitched voice. A frail, asthmatic child, he seemed intent on proving his manliness. His life became a robust adventure of sports, hunting, and camping. Once he took a foreign diplomat skinny-dipping in the Potomac. His exuberance, vitality, and wit captivated most Americans. They called him "Teddy" and named a stuffed bear after him. To understand him, an observer declared, one had to remember "the president is really only six years old." He was not a simple man, however. His hobbies included writing history books, and he displayed a keen intellect that he had honed at Harvard.

Born into an aristocratic Dutch family in New York, Roosevelt rejected a leisurely life for the rough and tumble world of politics, which his friends declared was an occupation for saloonkeepers and such. He replied that he "intended to be one of the governing class." His privileged background made him an unlikely candidate for a reformer, yet he ended up making reform both fun and respectable. He saw himself as a conservative but declared, "The only true conservative is the man who resolutely sets his face toward the future." The conservatives of his time, however, rejected his call for change and continued to insist on laissez-faire policies and limited government.

Roosevelt, on the other hand, shared two progressive sentiments. One was that government should be efficiently run by able, competent people. The other was that industrialization had created the need for expanded governmental action. "A simple and poor society," he observed, "can exist as a democracy on the basis of sheer individualism. But a rich and complex society cannot so exist." As a result of these two sentiments, Roosevelt reorganized and revitalized the executive branch, modernized the army command structure and the consular service, and pursued the federal regulation of the economy that characterized twentieth-century America.

Although he was later remembered more for his "trust-busting" and "Square Deal," Roosevelt considered conservation his greatest domestic accomplishment. It was the topic of his first presidential address. "We are prone to think of the resources of this country as inexhaustible, this is not so," he later warned Congress. Roosevelt used presidential power to add almost 150 million acres to national forests and to preserve valuable coal and water sites for national development. With his ally, Chief Forester **Gifford Pinchot,** he sponsored a National Conservation Congress in 1908. Roosevelt's actions won both praise and condemnation.

The conservation movement, then as well as later, divided into two camps. Naturalist John Muir and the Sierra Club (formed in 1892) wanted to preserve the scenic beauty and biological diversity of the West.

Most businesspeople and Westerners wanted government action only to promote orderly economic exploitation of resources. In 1902 they supported the Newlands Reclamation Act, which began many years of federally sponsored irrigation and reclamation projects (for details of this and other federal legislation see Table 21.1). Furious, however, about the withdrawal from sale of so many acres of federal land, they led a move to limit presidential authority to do so. Western and business influences usually prevailed in such disputes. For the West a scarcity of water was the main ecological problem, and its solution was a regional priority. In 1913 the city of San Francisco won a dispute over a dam that had flooded one of the most beautiful areas of Yosemite National Park in order to solve the city's water shortage.

Some businesspeople already disliked Roosevelt for his conservation policies, but he aggravated others with two actions in 1902. The first was his handling of the coal strike, which served notice that the government could no longer be counted on to come automatically to the aid of management in labor disputes. The second was a suit against Northern Securities Company under the Sherman Antitrust Act. Roosevelt's trust-busting was an answer to progressive prayers. Antimonopoly was a strong component of progressivism. Most agreed with Louis Brandeis that "if the Lord had intended things to be big, he would have made men bigger—in brains and character." Antitrust action had not been undertaken on a large scale in the cities and states only because federal action seemed necessary.

Northern Securities, a highly unpopular combination of northwestern railroad systems engineered by such heavyweights as James J. Hill and J. P. Morgan, was a wise choice for action. Its unpopularity reflected the West's concern for railroad regulation. The suit infuriated Hill, who complained, "It seems hard that we should be compelled to fight for our lives against the political adventurers who have never done anything but pose and draw a salary." In 1904 the Supreme Court ordered the company's dissolution. That same year, in a case against the major meatpackers, the Court also reversed the *E. C. Knight* ruling that exempted manufacturing from federal antitrust law.

The rulings pleased Roosevelt, who rejected the Court's earlier narrow, strict interpretations of the Constitution. Instead, he believed that the Constitution "must be interpreted not as a straight-jacket . . . but as an instrument designed for the life and healthy growth of the Nation." In his desire to expand federal power, he was once credited with asking "What's the Constitution between friends?" Yet Roosevelt was not a complete convert to trust-busting.

Theodore Roosevelt is shown here campaigning in New Castle, Wyoming, as the Republican candidate in 1903. The cartoon on the right illustrates his idea for breaking up only those trusts he believed were not in the public interest.

"This is an age of combination," he wrote, "and any effort to prevent all combination will be not only useless, but in the end vicious." At the same time he believed "of all the forms of tyranny the least attractive and the most vulgar is the tyranny of mere wealth." Thus he attacked trusts that abused their power and left alone trusts that acted responsibly. He preferred to negotiate differences, and to do so he established in 1904 a Bureau of Corporations within the Department of Commerce and Labor, created the year before.

Campaigning on the promise to provide a "Square Deal" to all Americans, Roosevelt easily defeated Democratic candidate Alton B. Parker in the 1904 presidential election. Now elected in his own right, he launched into expanding the regulatory power of the federal government. His top priority, over the objections of conservative Republican senators, was to control effectively the railroads by expanding the power of the Interstate Commerce Commission (ICC). Although the Elkins Act, passed in 1903, had already eliminated rebates, Roosevelt wanted to go further and give the ICC the power to set rates. Through shrewd political maneuvering he got this with the Hepburn Act of 1906, although he had to give up his demand for limited court review of rate decisions.

Without federal regulation, meat packers exploited workers and allowed rats and other contaminants to be processed with meat in making sausages.

The publication of Upton Sinclair's *The Jungle* in that same year caused a consumer uproar for regulation of the food and drug industries. A chemist in the Agriculture Department, Harvey W. Wiley had long been analyzing food products for chemical adulteration by testing additives on volunteers known as the "Poison Squad." His data were supplemented by an investigation of the meatpacking industry ordered by Roosevelt, which proved the truth of Sinclair's charges of filth and contamination. As a result, Congress passed the Pure Food and Drug Act and the Meat Inspection Act on the same day in 1906. By 1908 Roosevelt had left his indelible mark on the nation and decided not to run for reelection. He cast his support to **William Howard Taft,** who easily defeated William Jennings Bryan, the Democratic nominee and loser for the third time. Roosevelt then retired and went to hunt lions in Africa, a move that led J. P. Morgan to toast "Health to the Lions."

Taft and Quiet Progressivism

William Howard Taft brought to the presidency a distinguished record of public service. An Ohio lawyer, he had served as a federal judge, the first civil governor of the Philippines, and secretary of war. He did not, however, look presidential; he weighed more than 350 pounds, which led to rumors that a special bathtub was to be installed in the White House. Unlike his predecessor, he was far from charismatic and indeed quite shy. Legalistic and precise, he was neither a fiery writer nor speaker. In short, he was incapable of rallying public support for any cause, and reformers were especially skeptical about him. As a judge he had been called the "injunction standard bearer" by labor leaders. When soldiers shot into the crowd at the Haymarket riot, he confided, "they have only killed six as yet. This is hardly enough to make an impression."

Taft was indeed more conservative than Roosevelt, especially in his view of governmental power. "The lesson must be learned," he argued, "that there is only a limited zone within which legislation and governments can accomplish good." Further, he declared, "We can, by passing laws which cannot be enforced, destroy that respect for laws . . . which has been the strength of people of English descent everywhere." On the other hand, his respect for the law extended to the Sherman Act. "We are going to enforce that law or die in the attempt," he promised, and his administration prosecuted far more cases than Roosevelt's had.

In his own quiet way Taft was as sympathetic to reform as Roosevelt. He supported the eight-hour workday and favored legislation to improve mine

safety. He also urged passage of the Mann-Elkins Act of 1910 to increase the power of the ICC. The Sixteenth and Seventeenth Amendments were initiated under his presidency. Purity crusaders also won a victory in 1910 with the passage of the Mann Act against prostitution.

Nevertheless, Taft was not forceful enough to effectively overcome the growing divisions within the Republican party. The conservatives, led by powerful Senator Nelson W. Aldrich of Rhode Island, were determined to draw the line against further reform. At the same time, progressive Republicans such as Robert La Follette of Wisconsin and George Norris of Nebraska were growing rebellious. Conflict came on several fronts. One was the tariff. In his campaign Taft had promised a lower tariff, but in the end he accepted the much compromised Payne-Aldrich Tariff. While placing many nonessential items on the duty-free list, it actually raised some key duties. It disappointed reformers immensely. Listing such duty-free items as silkworm eggs, canary birdseed, hog bristle, leeches, and skeletons, the political humorist Finley Peter Dunne had his fictional bartender, Mr. Dooley, proclaim, "The new tariff puts these familyer commodyties within the reach iv all." Taft had suffered a defeat but foolishly did not admit it. He called the tariff the "best" ever passed. In reality he backed down on his pledges because he believed the president should not interfere unduly with the legislative branch. And he simply had an accommodating per-

Groomed for the presidency by his predecessor and easily elected to the office in 1908, William Howard Taft found his presidential duties onerous. Here, he participates in an activity he found far more enjoyable.

sonality. One Republican griped, "The trouble with Taft is that if he were Pope he would think it necessary to appoint a few Protestant Cardinals."

Caught in the middle of several conflicts, Taft eventually alienated the progressive wing of his party as well as Teddy Roosevelt. He first supported and then abandoned party insurgents who challenged the power of conservative Speaker of the House "Uncle Joe" Cannon of Illinois. Later, when Gifford Pinchot protested a sale of public lands by Secretary of the Interior Richard A. Ballinger, Taft fired Pinchot from his position as chief of the Forest Service, which infuriated both conservationists and Roosevelt. The latter was also irritated by Taft's antitrust prosecutions. He believed that a case had been pursued against U.S. Steel to embarrass him: The investigation exposed a deal Roosevelt had made with J. P. Morgan in 1907 in return for the banker's aid in stemming a financial panic.

By 1912 progressive Republicans were ready to bolt the party if Taft were renominated, and Roosevelt declared his intention to run. The fight for the nomination became bitter. Taft called Roosevelt's supporters "political emotionalists or neurotics." Roosevelt labeled Taft's people as "men of cold heart and narrow mind, who believe we can find safety in dull timidity and dull inaction." As president, Taft was able to control the convention. The defeated Roosevelt walked out with his supporters and formed a third party, known as the **Progressive (Bull Moose) party.**

Many leading reformers attended the Progressive convention, which often resembled a religious revival, with hymn singing and marches. Its platform endorsed such wide-ranging reforms as abolition of child labor; federal old-age, accident, and unemployment insurance programs; an eight-hour workday; and women's suffrage. At Roosevelt's request, however, a plank supporting equality for African Americans was deleted. Calling the major parties "husks with no real soul," he accepted the third party's nomination.

With the Republicans divided, Democratic chances of recapturing the White House increased. A former Republican senator lamented that his party's only unanswered question was "Which corpse gets the most flowers?" The scent of victory led to a hard fight for the Democratic nomination, which New Jersey's progressive governor, Woodrow Wilson, won on the forty-sixth ballot. The Socialist party nominated Eugene V. Debs, making it a four-way race.

As soon became apparent, the real battle was between Wilson and Roosevelt. It was marked by an unusually high level of debate over the proper role of government in a modern, industrialized society. Wilson declared, "What this country needs above everything else is a body of laws which will look after the men who are on the make rather than the men who are already made." Labeling his program **New Freedom,** his aim was the restoration of competition and his tool was to be trust-busting.

Roosevelt, on the other hand, believed that big business was not necessarily bad, but he proclaimed, "Somehow or other we shall have to work out methods of controlling the big corporations without paralyzing the energies of the business community." His answer was **New Nationalism**—the expansion of federal regulatory activities to control rather than dismantle the trusts. Big government would offset the power of big business. Their rhetoric differed sharply, but in their presidencies both Roosevelt and Wilson practiced a little of both "New Nationalism" and "New Freedom."

The split in the Republican party enabled the Democrats to capture not only the White House but also the Senate. Democrats also consolidated their control of the House, so Wilson entered the presidency with his party solidly in power. Nevertheless, Wilson did not receive a majority of the popular vote. He got 6.3 million votes, Roosevelt 4.1 million, Taft 3.5 million, and Debs nearly 1 million. In the electoral college, however, Wilson won an impressive 435 votes to Roosevelt's 88 and a mere 8 for Taft.

Election of 1912

Woodrow Wilson did not receive a majority of the popular vote, but the split in the Republican party gave him the majority of the votes in the electoral college.

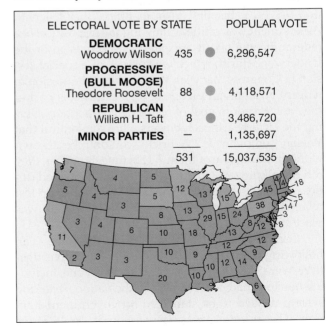

ELECTORAL VOTE BY STATE		POPULAR VOTE
DEMOCRATIC Woodrow Wilson	435	6,296,547
PROGRESSIVE (BULL MOOSE) Theodore Roosevelt	88	4,118,571
REPUBLICAN William H. Taft	8	3,486,720
MINOR PARTIES	—	1,135,697
	531	15,037,535

Wilson and Moral Progressivism

As the third progressive-era president, **Woodrow Wilson** differed from his predecessors in both appearance and leadership style. He looked very much like the moralistic professor he was. The son and grandson of Presbyterian ministers, Wilson was raised in the South and practiced law in Atlanta before receiving his doctorate from Johns Hopkins University in Baltimore. His book *Congressional Government* was published in 1895, and he became president of Princeton University in 1902 before being elected governor of New Jersey. His religion was an important factor in his personality. "My life would not be worth living," he declared, "if it were not for the driving power of religion."

Wilson was not the kind of man whom people named stuffed animals after or gave nicknames. His self-righteousness was not endearing. One politician noted that when Wilson "said something to me . . . I didn't know whether God or him was talking." Although much less charismatic, Wilson did resemble Roosevelt in being a better speaker than Taft and in his view of the role of the president. Roosevelt had called the presidency a "bully pulpit," and Wilson agreed that the president should be the "political leader of the nation" because "his is the only national voice in politics." Unlike Taft, he argued that the president must be "as much concerned with the guidance of legislation as with the just and orderly execution of the laws."

Wilson's activism coincided with growing demands for further reform. Investigations and amendments launched earlier came to fruition during his presidency. The result was an outpouring of legislation. In 1913, his first year in office, the Sixteenth Amendment was ratified, allowing the imposition of a federal income tax. It appeared as a provision of the Underwood Tariff, which was passed in a special session of Congress that year. Wilson called the session to redeem a campaign pledge to lower duties as part of the New Freedom goal of restoring competition. During the tariff hearings, lobbyists were so plentiful that Wilson complained, "A brick wouldn't be thrown without hitting one of them." This time, however, they did not all prevail. Congress significantly lowered duties for the first time since the Civil War. To recoup lost revenues, a graduated tax of from 1 to 6 percent was placed on personal incomes of $3000 and over.

Congress passed banking reform the same year. Following the panic of 1907, congressional investigations were launched into its causes. Everyone, including bankers, had come to believe the nation's banking system needed to be stabilized by governmental action. The question was *how* to do it. Wall Street wanted a centralized system owned and controlled

A distinguished professor, Woodrow Wilson brought both competence and a grim moral determination to the presidency.

by bankers. Others wanted a more decentralized system owned or controlled by the government. The Federal Reserve Act of 1913 was a compromise. It established the **Federal Reserve System** of 12 regional banks owned by bankers but under the control of a presidentially appointed Federal Reserve Board.

Prohibitionists won their first national victory with the Webb-Kenyon Act of 1913, which increased the power of states to enforce their own prohibition laws. The next year those concerned with the large amounts of narcotics in patent medicines rejoiced over the passage of the Harrison Anti-Narcotic Act. It required a doctor's prescription for the sale of any drug on a list of controlled substances. In 1914 Congress took action to deal with monopolies and to regulate business. In September it established the Federal Trade Commission to replace the Bureau of Corporations. The five-person body was charged with investigating alleged violations of antitrust law and could issue cease and desist orders against corporations found guilty of unfair trade practices. The next month the Clayton Antitrust Act sought to close some of the loopholes of the Sherman Act and limit court actions against labor unions.

At that point Wilson believed he had accomplished his agenda. He was not a supporter of further labor legislation or farm-credit plans. A firm opponent of paternalism, he said, "The old adage that

God takes care of those who take care of themselves is not gone out of date. No federal legislation can change that thing. The minute you are taken care of by the government you are wards, not independent men." As the election of 1916 approached, however, progressives reminded Wilson of the importance of the farm and labor vote. Legislation to win those votes soon followed. Farmers were given the Federal Farm Loan Act and federal supplemental funding for agricultural specialists in each county; labor leaders got the Keating-Owen Child Labor Act; railroad workers got the Adamson Act to limit their work hours; and federal employees got the Workman's Compensation Act. Progressives were also pleased by Wilson's appointment of Louis Brandeis to the Supreme Court. All of these actions helped ensure Wilson's victory over the Republican nominee Charles Evans Hughes in 1916.

PROGRESSIVISM IN THE INTERNATIONAL ARENA

Many progressives did not believe that progress was limited by national boundaries. In their eyes, human beings had the capacity to create a more just and orderly society both at home and abroad. The progressive spirit was optimistic, and progressive victories on the home front expanded Americans' confidence in their ability to solve problems—even on the international level. This confidence was further bolstered by the nation's economic growth and victory in the Spanish-American War.

Everyone agreed that by 1900, America's status in the world had changed. How to respond to those changes was the question. Just as people differed over what alterations, if any, were required in domestic policies, various visions of a new American foreign policy also emerged. For some, progressivism simply redefined and reinvigorated the old ideas of manifest destiny. The United States would solve its problems at home and then remake the world in its own image. Such a new world order would also open up new markets for America's industrial and agricultural surpluses. Other progressives believed that democratic principles required that all people, even foreigners, be free to determine their own destinies. Order and justice were two progressive goals that sometimes conflicted, and that conflict was also apparent in the international arena.

Big Stick Diplomacy

Theodore Roosevelt's foreign policy reflected the same vigor he displayed in everything else he did.

His "macho" foreign policy emerged from his belief that a man's mission was to "work, fight, and breed." He believed progress and order could benefit the world as well as the nation. He also asserted that Congress was "not well fitted for the shaping of foreign policy" and expanded presidential power in the conduct of diplomacy. It was his destiny to deal with the legacies of increased power and influence from the Spanish-American War. Order having been restored in Cuba and the Philippines by 1903, Roosevelt launched the United States into the role of policeman. His doctrine was to "speak softly and carry a big stick," but he really only lived up to the second half of the slogan.

Possession of the Philippines caused concern over turbulent Asian politics. Most alarming was the emergence of Japan as a power after its unexpected victories in the Russo-Japanese War (1904–1905). Often playing the role of arbiter at home, Roosevelt now shifted his arena and mediated an end to the war at a Portsmouth, New Hampshire, conference in August 1905—an action that won him a Nobel Peace Prize. Japan remained a formidable rival, however, and agreements were later reached to respect each other's Asian interests. In the Pacific, Roosevelt displayed his **big stick diplomacy** by sending a fleet of 16 battleships, called the "Great White Fleet," on a 1907 to 1909 around-the-world tour with conspicuous stops in the Pacific, including Japan. His intent was to intimidate the Japanese, but he failed to halt their growing power.

Within the Western Hemisphere, Roosevelt was even less reluctant to threaten or use force. In 1906 he responded to Cuban demonstrations against the Platt Amendment and insurrection by sending in marines, who stayed until 1909. "I am doing my best," he declared, "to persuade the Cubans that if only they will be good, they will be happy. I am seeking the very minimum of interference necessary to make them good." The marines could be very persuasive.

Progress and strategic considerations also demanded that a canal in Central America link the Atlantic and Pacific Oceans. Roosevelt was determined to make it happen. There were two possible routes: one through Nicaragua and one across the Panamanian isthmus, which belonged to Colombia. A French company had made a start in Panama, but it ran out of funds and was reorganized as the New Panama Canal Company. The new company's major asset was its concession from Colombia that extended to 1904.

Three commissions appointed to determine the route recommended Nicaragua, primarily because the New Panama Canal Company demanded $190 million for its rights, property, and previous work. The company's stockholders, however, were mainly Americans and frantic to convince Congress to

This 1903 cartoon shows Roosevelt dumping dirt from the Panama Canal on the capitol of Colombia, illustrating how he rode roughshod over the Colombians to get the canal built.

choose the Panamanian route. They dropped their demand to $40 million, contributed profusely to campaign funds, and hired a full-time lobbyist— Philippe Bunau-Varilla, the French chief engineer of the original company. In June 1902, Congress authorized efforts to secure the rights to a Panamanian canal. The Hay-Herrán Treaty provided the United States with rights to a 6-mile-wide zone in return for a $10 million payment to Colombia and an annual rental fee of $250,000. As in America, ratification required the consent of the Colombian senate, which in August 1903 rejected the treaty unanimously. Its motive was probably to delay the treaty until 1904, when the New Panama Canal Company's concession expired and Colombia might receive some of the $40 million originally earmarked for the company.

Roosevelt was furious. "The blackmailers of Bogota," he roared, should not be allowed "permanently to bar one of the future highways of civilization." He drafted a message to Congress proposing to take the canal zone by force but never delivered it. A different solution was found; Bunau-Varilla engineered a Panamanian revolution by providing people with a national constitution, flag, and anthem as well as assurances that the United States would not let their revolt fail. He was right. Most Colombian troops were prevented from even getting to the so-called revolution by the USS *Nashville*. Three days after its start, Roosevelt recognized the independence

of the Republic of Panama. U.S. Secretary of State John Hay and the French citizen Bunau-Varilla, who had demanded to be made ambassador to the United States, then quickly drafted the **Hay–Bunau-Varilla Treaty** with essentially the same terms as the Hay-Herrán Treaty—only now the payment went to the rebels, not Colombia.

American actions enraged people all over the world. At first Roosevelt denied any part in the revolution, but he eventually admitted, "I took the Canal Zone and let Congress debate; and while the debate goes on the Canal does also." In 1914, the canal, a monument to both progress and Yankee imperialism, was completed. It was a big investment, one that required protection from foreign military vessels.

At the same time, Latin American countries sometimes fell behind in debt payments to such European powers as Britain and Germany. As a result those two nations blockaded Venezuela in 1902 to 1903. A year later, Roosevelt announced that the United States would assume the responsibility of seeing that the nations of the Caribbean behaved themselves and paid their debts. European intervention, therefore, would not be necessary. Known as the Roosevelt Corollary to the Monroe Doctrine, this policy justified U.S. intervention in such places as the Dominican Republic, Nicaragua, and Haiti. Roosevelt's big stick diplomacy established America as

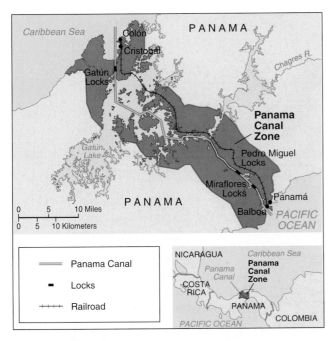

Panama Canal

The Panama Canal provided a strategic shipping and military link between the Atlantic and the Pacific Oceans.

the "police of the Western Hemisphere"—a role that would last long into the twentieth century.

Dollar Diplomacy

Before becoming president, William Howard Taft had served as governor-general in the Philippines and as Roosevelt's troubleshooter in Cuba. These experiences had convinced Taft of two principles. The first was the need for order and stability; the second was the limited capacity of armed force for solving problems. He also realized that the United States had a new source of power—its economic clout. From 1898 to 1909, American overseas investments had risen from about $800 million to more than $2.5 billion.

Called **dollar diplomacy,** Taft's approach was to use dollars instead of bullets to ensure stability and order. He wanted American capital to replace European capital in Latin America in order to increase U.S. influence there. When British bondholders wanted to collect their debts from Honduras in 1909, Taft asked American financiers to assume the debt. In 1910 he convinced New York bankers to take over the assets of the National Bank of Haiti. When needed, however, Taft also wielded a big stick. He refused to recognize a revolution in Nicaragua until the leaders agreed to accept American credits to pay off British debts and sent marines to punctuate his point.

Missionary Diplomacy

As in domestic policies, Woodrow Wilson's foreign policy differed more in style than substance from his predecessors. Wilson's moralism did not stop at national boundaries. Indeed his sermonistic foreign policy has sometimes been called **missionary diplomacy.** His gospel was American-style democracy. "When properly directed," he declared, "there is no people not fitted for self-government." That direction was to come from the United States. He spoke of "releasing the intelligence of America for the service of mankind" and proclaimed "every nation needs to be drawn into the tutelage of America."

The rhetoric was different from his predecessors, but the results were the same. Renouncing both big stick and dollar diplomacy, Wilson nevertheless used similar measures to maintain stability and order in the Caribbean. He sent marines to the Dominican Republic and Haiti and kept them in Nicaragua. His interventionism ran into more trouble in Mexico, where the overthrow of long-time dictator Porfirio Díaz in 1911 began a cycle of revolution.

General Porfirio Díaz ruled Mexico with an iron hand from the early 1870s to 1910. As dictator, he brought order to his nation and opened Mexico to foreign investors. Under his protective hand a flood of foreign businesspeople rushed in to tap Mexico's rich mineral wealth, build railroads, and exploit the agricultural sector of its economy. On the eve of World War I, Americans valued their holdings in Mexico at $1 billion. Yet only a handful of wealthy Mexicans benefited from their nation's economic development. The political stability Díaz brought to Mexico came at the expense of individual liberties. He crushed political opposition and turned a deaf ear to pleas for land reform.

In 1910, his opponents revolted and to the world's amazement Díaz proved to be a paper tiger. Unable to extinguish a series of small revolts that sprang up across Mexico, he fled the country. Mexico's new leader was Francisco I. Madero, an idealist who championed the middle class's aspirations for democracy and the peasant class's demands for land reform. Madero had hardly settled into the presidency before new revolts broke out, plunging Mexico into chaos. On February 22, 1913, less than two weeks before William Howard Taft's term as president ended, Madero and his vice president were assassinated by federal troops under the command of General Victoriano Huerta, who immediately proclaimed himself Mexico's new ruler. Despite the urgent recommendations of his ambassador to Mexico, President Taft did not extend diplomatic recognition to Huerta's government, leaving the issue to be resolved by Wilson.

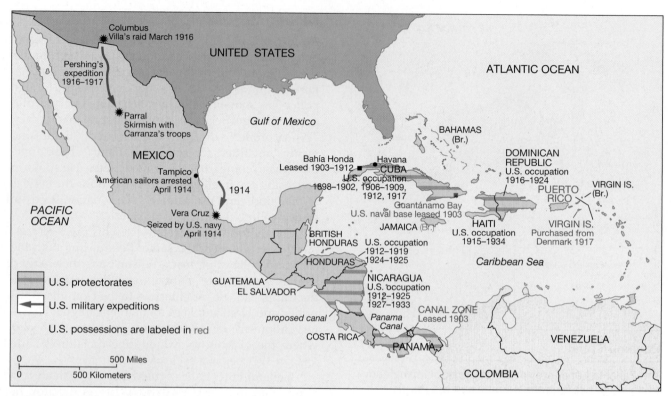

American Interventions in the Caribbean

Early in the twentieth century, the United States took it upon itself to police the Western Hemisphere and often took action when it judged Latin American countries were not running their affairs properly.

President Wilson refused to recognize Huerta's government, calling it a "government of butchers." Wilson regarded Mexico's new strongman as a murderer and a usurper, a ruler who symbolized all that was wrong with Latin American governments. Wilson believed that diplomatic recognition implied moral approval, and he could never sanction a government that had seized power by substituting bullets for ballots. He wrote one diplomat, "The United States intends not merely to force Huerta from power but to exert every influence it can to secure Mexico a better government under which all contracts and business concessions will be safer than they have ever been." Americans considered protection of contracts and concessions very important— American businesses controlled 75 percent of Mexico's mines, 60 percent of its oil, and 70 percent of its rubber.

Huerta's claims to power were shaky. Following Madero's assassination, several political factions in Mexico revolted against Huerta. Emiliano Zapata led an army against federal troops in Morelos, a mountainous state in southern Mexico. In the north, Venustiano Carranza, the governor of Coahuila, de-

clared himself the first chief of the Constitutionalist forces and won the allegiance of several powerful regional leaders, including Pancho Villa, Alvaro Obregón, and Pablo González.

Because Huerta was not able to defeat his opponents in battle, his claim to controlling Mexico was suspect; and his apparent weakness only strengthened President Wilson's decision to withhold diplomatic recognition. American policy was designed to aid Huerta's opponents, particularly Carranza, who appealed strongly to Wilson as a tool for restoring democracy to Mexico. As Wilson confided to a British diplomat, "I am going to teach the South American republics to elect good men."

However noble his ambition, Wilson allowed his animus against Huerta to trigger an American invasion of Mexico. In April 1914, Mexican officials arrested several American sailors in Tampico, a seaport on Mexico's east coast; detained a mail courier; and delayed an official Department of State dispatch. Wilson used these minor incidents to precipitate a showdown with Huerta's government—less than two weeks later American troops invaded the port city of Veracruz. At least 200 Mexicans died in the fighting

In 1916 General John Pershing led U.S. troops deep into Mexico in pursuit of Pancho Villa. This military action almost brought war with Mexico.

that followed and another 300 were wounded, most of them noncombatant civilians. American troops remained in Veracruz for six months.

None of Mexico's warring factions approved the invasion and subsequent occupation of Veracruz. In fact, no issue has produced more bitterness in Mexico against the United States—not even the Mexican-American War. To Mexicans their defeat in the 1840s inflicted a serious wound to their national pride, but they saw the war as a lesson in power politics. Manifest destiny was a harsh policy, but Mexicans could understand the motives from which it sprang. Americans wanted American land, and they took it. What made the invasion of Veracruz so galling was that President Wilson clothed American aggression, in the words of one historian, "with the sanctimonious raiment of idealism." Because he insisted his acts were moral, Wilson "aroused both the hatred and the scorn of the Mexicans—hatred over the invasion but a deep scorn for what they saw as his hypocrisy."

In one sense, Wilson got what he wanted in Mexico. Huerta's government collapsed in 1915, and Carranza became the new president. In the larger sense, however, the United States was the big loser. Mexicans deeply resented Wilson's arrogant assumption that he had the right to intervene in their internal affairs. Even after Huerta was overthrown, civil war continued between Carranza's government forces and rebels led by Pancho Villa. In an attempt to draw America into the fracas, Villa launched a raid into New Mexico in March 1916. The tactic worked. Wilson sent an expedition led by General John Pershing to capture Villa. American troops failed to find him,

but soon were 300 miles deep into Mexican territory by January 1917 and on the brink of war with Carranza's government. By then, however, America was being drawn into World War I, and Wilson decided to withdraw the troops. Although Wilson eventually got the kind of government he wanted for Mexico, Mexicans continued to believe that their government was their business and deeply resented the American intervention.

American involvement in World War I diverted attention from more than Mexico. Domestic reform took a backseat to "making the world safe for democracy." Yet war always brings changes on the home front. The nation shifted gears, but progressivism did not entirely die. Indeed prohibitionists, woman suffragists, and immigration restrictionists won their greatest victories in the wake of war.

PROGRESSIVE ACCOMPLISHMENTS, PROGRESSIVE FAILURES

The twentieth century began with great optimism about the power of human beings to shape their destinies. Progress, people believed, could be legislated. Efficient, noncorrupt government could provide order and stability, promote social justice, and improve personal morals. Groups organized to promote their goals, and more and more of them began to win their objectives. In the 1920s, however, some began to realize that legislation had not always had its desired effect, that not everyone had benefited equally, and that change had been far from radical.

TABLE 21.1

Progressive Era Legislation and Amendments

Year	Act	Provisions
1902	Newlands Reclamation	Set aside proceeds from the sale of federal land for irrigation and reclamation projects
1903	Elkins	Outlawed rebates to favored shippers; federal courts could issue injunctions to stop rate discrimination
1906	Pure Food and Drug	Made it a crime to sell adulterated foods or medicine; required correct labeling of the contents of certain substances
1906	Meat Inspection	Required governmental approval of sanitary conditions in meatpacking plants; prohibited use of dangerous chemicals or preservatives; government paid inspection costs
1906	Hepburn	Gave ICC the power to set railroad rates, subject to court review
1909	Payne-Aldrich Tariff	Raised most tariff rates, while reducing or eliminating the rates for very few products
1910	Mann-Elkins	Extended jurisdiction of the ICC to telephone and telegraph companies; gave ICC further power to suspend rate increases; rulings were still subject to court review
1910	Mann	Outlawed the transportation of women across state lines for "immoral purposes"
1913	Sixteenth Amendment	Gave Congress the right to impose an income tax
1913	Seventeenth Amendment	Provided for the direct election of senators by the people rather than by state legislatures
1913	Underwood-Simmons Tariff	Substantially reduced tariff rates; levied an income tax rising from 1 percent on incomes over $4000 to 4 percent on incomes over $10,000
1913	Federal Reserve	Reformed the banking and currency system; created 12 regional banks that were privately owned but responsible to the Federal Reserve Board, which was appointed by the president; the Board had the ability to regulate the amount of currency (federal reserve notes) through its transactions with the regional banks
1914	Federal Trade Commission	Created FTC, composed of 5 members, to oversee business transactions; could publicize infractions and issue cease and desist orders, which were subject to court review
1914	Clayton Antitrust	Outlawed unfair business practices that reduced competition; held company officials liable for actions; specifically exempted farm and labor groups from its provisions; limited the use of court injunctions against strikers
1914	Harrison Anti-Narcotic	Listed "controlled substances" that could only be sold with a doctor's prescription; required manufacturers to keep records of the manufacture and sale of such substances
1916	Federal Farm Loan	Provided farmers with cheap credit through 12 farm loan boards
1916	Keating-Owen	Outlawed the sale of goods made by children from interstate commerce
1916	Adamson	Provided for an eight-hour workday for workers on interstate railroads
1916	Workman's Compensation	Established a workmen's compensation system for federal employees

The Impact of Legislation

Measured by direct results most progressive reforms proved disappointing. In some cases unintended consequences actually worked against the intended goals of laws. This often occurs when ideals confront reality. Solving one problem frequently creates another. Nevertheless, progressives established important precedents that opened doors to later, more effective reform.

Attempts to promote direct democracy were among the least effective. Direct election of senators did not seem to alter the kinds of people elected. Initiative, referendum, and recall were rarely used, and then not by people in general. The expense and organization needed for petition drives were beyond the reach of any but well-financed pressure groups. An unintended result of democratization was to increase the power of urban machines. Bosses may have had to work a little harder, but most were still able to dominate primaries as well as elections. The move toward popular voting increased the political power of populous cities and the machines that controlled them. The greatest failing of the movement was a dramatic drop in voter participation. Nevertheless, in some states, such as Wisconsin, government did become more responsive to public needs, and urban machines often adopted reform measures to maintain power.

Other kinds of urban reforms had varying results. In some, government did indeed become more efficiently and economically run. The competency and honesty of officials generally increased. An occasional consequence, however, was decreased social services in less affluent neighborhoods. This was more likely to happen where the commissioner-manager system was adopted—usually in midsize cities without a tradition of machine politics. In other cities municipally owned utilities lowered rates, providing some real relief for the poor.

Attempts to regulate the railroads on either the state or national level rarely produced dramatic benefits for the general public. The chief advocates and beneficiaries of railroad regulation were frequently large shipping interests that did not share lower costs with consumers. With the Hepburn Act, Roosevelt did accomplish his primary goal of giving the ICC the power to set rates. The provision allowing court review of its decisions, however, made the act more significant as a precedent for expanded governmental power than as an immediate solution to problems. The courts ruled in favor of the railroads in most rate disputes.

Antimonopoly actions also did not always produce the intended results. For example, the breakups of Standard Oil and the American Tobacco Company did not increase competition or lower prices. Perhaps the only legislation to fulfill the promise of New Freedom was the Underwood Tariff, and it was reversed by the tariff legislation of the 1920s. The Clayton Antitrust Act was widely, and correctly, considered too vague for effective enforcement. The general counsel of the American Anti-Boycott Association analyzed the provision to exempt labor organizations from antitrust legislation; he declared that the law "makes few changes in existing law as relating to labor unions, injunctions and contempts of court, and those are of slight practical importance." Later court decisions proved his assessment accurate.

The Federal Trade Commission (FTC) did not become an aggressive watchdog either. One of Wilson's cabinet members reported that the president viewed it as "a counsellor and friend to the business world," rather than as a "policeman to wield a club over the head of the business community." His appointments were fairly probusiness, and appointments made in the 1920s were even more so. In the end, the FTC proved beneficial to big business by protecting firms from unexpected suits and by outlawing some "unfair trade practices," many of which had promoted competition at the expense of stability. On the other hand, the FTC was also an important precedent for the regulation of business.

Proclaimed victories for labor frequently turned out to be more symbolic than real. In the arbitration of the 1902 coal strike, for example, what the United Mine Workers did not receive is very significant: The union did not win recognition. As the 1920s would show, organized labor did not emerge from the progressive era any stronger. Yet symbolism can be important. The precedent that the government would not automatically support the demands of management was later built upon during the New Deal of the 1930s.

Some labor legislation did bring benefits but also produced unintended results. Child labor laws in combination with compulsory education legislation decreased the number of children from ages 10 to 15 who were working for wages, from 1 in 5 in 1900 to 1 in 20 by 1930. During those same years, the number of students enrolled in secondary education increased by 800 percent. Both were desirable results, but in the short run at least, it was a mixed blessing for the poor. The incomes of a family's children were often crucial to its welfare, and no alternatives were provided. As one historian noted, "Child labor laws treated the symptoms and made the disease—poverty—worse." Much the same can be said about limits imposed on women's working hours. Laws establishing minimum wages for women helped somewhat to offset earning losses resulting from child labor legislation. In any event, laws such as the Child Labor Act were declared unconstitutional in the 1920s.

Workmen's compensation laws were an improvement over existing procedures but were not an unqualified victory of labor over management. Indeed, businesspeople eventually welcomed the relief from the growing number of suits instituted by hungry lawyers on a contingency-fee basis. By agreeing to take a percentage of any damage awards and to charge no fee for lost cases, attorneys made it possible for poor workers to take legal action. The award schedule in most compensation plans provided far below what some lawyers had been winning in court. Workers, however, were guaranteed at least some compensation. For the industrialists, a predictable premium replaced the uncertainty of court actions, decreasing risks and increasing stability in the cost of doing business.

The establishment of the Federal Reserve System also enhanced order and stability. Everyone benefited from the maintenance of cash reserves for emergencies, a more flexible currency, and national check-clearing facilities. The banking system became more resistant to panics but, as 1929 would prove, not immune to them. Wall Street was not a big loser here. Three of the five seats on the Federal Reserve Board went to large bankers, and the New York Federal Reserve bank quickly came to dominate the system. The new system, in other words, was a significant improvement, but far from a radical change.

From the consumer's point of view, the Pure Food and Drug Act and the Meat Inspection Act were great victories. After the advent of mass production and mass marketing, only federal action could provide adequate protection from adulteration of the nation's foodstuffs. Unintended beneficiaries, however, were the large drug and meatpacking companies, which could more easily afford the increased expenses of meeting required production standards. The effect was thus anticompetitive. Lobbying by the big meatpackers also affected the final form of the legislation. Their victories included government payment of inspection costs and the deletion of the requirement to date canned meat. Like much progressive legislation, the final act did provide protection for consumers, but in a way agreeable to big business. Swift, one of the largest meatpackers, even endorsed its passage in an advertisement declaring, "It is a wise law."

Other progressive legislation left mixed legacies. Roosevelt's conservation measures prevented wanton squandering of resources but also aided the larger lumber companies. Morality legislation made undesirable activities illegal but at the same time more profitable for organized crime. It also fostered widespread disrespect for the law. With a maximum rate of 6 percent, the income tax did little to redistribute the huge fortunes of such men as J. P. Morgan but did establish an important tool for later use. A significant precedent was set by the Adamson Act, through which the federal government first dabbled in wage and hour legislation. Many other progressive reforms were illusory or short-lived. In the 1920s, lax enforcement and hostile court decisions reversed many of them. Nevertheless, laissez-faire had suffered an irreversible blow. That was a major accomplishment and perhaps as much as many progressives wanted.

Winners and Losers

Before the era ended, people from almost every class and occupation had sought to take advantage of the climate of change to promote their interests. Obviously not all were equally successful. Few were unqualified winners or losers, but some gained far more than others, and some lost more than they gained. Clearly, large corporations were among the biggest winners. One historian labeled the movement "the triumph of conservatism." Given the basic moderation of all three presidents and most congressmen, as well as the resources and influence of big business, this may have been inevitable. It was not, however, the original intention of all legislation. To label most progressives as conservative is a gross mistake. They rejected the strict laissez-faire principles of nineteenth-century conservatives and embraced a vision of a more activist government.

Other winners included members of the growing body of middle-class technocrats. At all levels of government the search for orderly, efficient management created new job opportunities for engineers, health professionals, trained managers, and other experts. Reforms that diminished the influence of political parties also increased the power of special-interest groups working for particular social and economic goals. Consumers of all classes shared benefits from government regulation.

In general most of the winners were white, urban, Protestant, and middle class. This was true even though working-class ethnic groups won victories in some cities and states. They and small businesspeople were among those who both lost and gained. African Americans came closest to being unqualified losers. For them, the only lasting advances came from establishing organizations. The NAACP survived to become an important force later in the century, and self-help organizations provided aid to many. Other victories were mainly token; the defeats were concrete.

In the South, and often in the North as well, African Americans were clearly losers on the local level. At the same time black relations with the federal government also deteriorated. Of the three presidents, Roosevelt was the most sympathetic. In 1901, he invited Booker T. Washington to dine at the White House, consulted with him on some southern appointments, and named a few African Americans to federal positions. His actions hardly reflected an acceptance of black equality, however. He believed, "as a race and in the mass they are altogether inferior to whites." One of his speeches to Congress seemed to condone lynching. Most disturbing to African Americans was his handling of an incident

Theodore Roosevelt gave the appearance of supporting African Americans when he invited Booker T. Washington to the White House, but like many white leaders, he did not promote equality between blacks and whites.

in Brownsville, Texas, in 1906. There, white towns-people and black soldiers met in a shoot-out. No one could determine exactly what had happened, but that did not deter Roosevelt from ordering dishonorable discharges for 167 black soldiers without court-martial.

When Taft became president, he approved of southern disfranchisement and appointed white-supremacist Republicans to federal jobs. These actions by the two Republican presidents convinced some African Americans, including W. E. B. Du Bois, to support Wilson in 1912. That was a mistake. The influence of Wilson's southern upbringing and advisers became apparent when he allowed his cabinet to segregate federal employees and to demote black officeholders, especially those "who boss white girls." Jim Crow moved to Washington, and Wilson's defense of these actions indicated the blindness and paternalism of many white progressives on race:

> It is true that the segregation of the colored employees in the several departments was begun upon the initiative and at the suggestion of the heads of departments, but as much in the interest of the negroes as for any other reason, with the approval of some of the most influential negroes I know, and with the idea that the

friction, or rather the discontent and uneasiness, which had prevailed in many departments would thereby be removed. It is as far as possible from being a movement against the negroes. I believe it to be in their interest.

It seems that white progressives often seemed to feel they knew the best interests of those not like them, at home and abroad.

CONCLUSION

At the start of the new century, Americans confronted the urban squalor, poverty, powerful monopolies, corrupt and inefficient government, disorder, and despair that had accompanied rapid industrialization and urbanization. They were determined to do something to achieve more social justice and stability. Numerous solutions were proposed and victories won. In the end, however, Americans rejected radicalism and ignored major problems.

Once again the nation resolutely refused to come to terms with its ethnic and cultural diversity. Rather than protect minorities, most actions infringed on

CHRONOLOGY OF KEY EVENTS

1879   Henry George's *Progress and Poverty* proposes a tax on land as a means of controlling illegitimate profits

1888   Edward Bellamy's *Looking Backward* depicts a utopian society guided by cooperation rather than competition

1889   Jane Addams founds Hull House

1901   President William McKinley is assassinated; Theodore Roosevelt becomes the twenty-sixth president

1902   Oregon, South Dakota, and Utah become first states to adopt initiative and recall; Roosevelt threatens to use troops to run coal mines when owners refuse to negotiate; Roosevelt charges Northern Securities with violating the Sherman Antitrust Act, and in 1904, the U.S. Supreme Court orders the company's breakup

1903   In *The Souls of Black Folks,* W. E. B. Du Bois attacks Booker T. Washington for abandoning the goal of equal rights; Wisconsin becomes the first state to adopt primary elections; Elkins Act bars railroad rebates

1904   Lincoln Steffens's *Shame of the Cities* exposes corruption in city government; United States obtains right to build the Panama Canal; announcement of Roosevelt Corollary to the Monroe Doctrine, asserting the right of the United States to exercise international police power in the Caribbean

1905   Roosevelt helps negotiate an end to a war between Russia and Japan, and wins a Nobel Peace Prize for his efforts

1906   Upton Sinclair's *The Jungle* exposes unsanitary conditions in the meatpacking industry; Meat Inspection Act enforces health and sanitary standards in meatpacking industry; Pure Food and Drug Act prohibits the use of harmful additives and misleading advertisements of drugs; Hepburn Act gives the Interstate Commerce Commission the right to set maximum freight rates

1907   Roosevelt dispatches 16 battleships (the Great White Fleet) on an around-the-world cruise

1908   Staunton, Virginia, hires the first city manager

1909   National Association for the Advancement of Colored People (NAACP) is founded to protect the rights of black Americans

1910   Mann-Elkins Act allows Interstate Commerce Commission to regulate railroad rates even without complaints from shippers

1912–   Twelve states adopt minimum wage laws
1917   for women; 30 states adopt workmen's compensation insurance (industrial accident insurance)

1912   Roosevelt and his supporters launch the Progressive (Bull Moose) party; Democrat Woodrow Wilson is elected the twenty-eighth president

1913   Sixteenth Amendment gives Congress the power to levy an income tax; Underwood-Simmons Tariff substantially lowers duties on imports and imposes a graduated income tax; Seventeenth Amendment requires direct election of senators; Federal Reserve System is created to supervise banking system and regulate money supply

1914   Federal Trade Commission is established to preserve economic competition by preventing unfair business practices; Clayton Antitrust Act prohibits interlocking corporate directorates and predatory pricing policies; U.S. Navy captures Mexican port of Veracruz

1915   U.S. marines are dispatched to Haiti

1916   U.S. troops enter Mexico to search for Pancho Villa; U.S. marines are sent to Dominican Republic

1919   Eighteenth Amendment prohibits manufacture and sale of liquor

1920   Nineteenth Amendment grants women the right to vote

their personal liberties and sought to control rather than accommodate their differences. Women won some victories, but the majority of Americans did not accept the radical feminists' vision of true equality. Socialists' dreams of a peaceful, democratic redistribution of the country's wealth fell on deaf ears. In the end, there was no significant change in the distribution of either wealth or power. The United States had weeded and tidied up its social garden, not replanted it. Although that garden produced bitter fruit for some people, many Americans benefited. Also, the vigor and diversity of progressive actions brought to light many problems and provided later generations with a body of experience in dealing with them.

Chapter Summary and Key Points

In this chapter you read about the sources of the progressive movement; progressivism at the municipal, state, and national levels; and the influence of progressive ideas upon foreign policy.

- Progressivism is an umbrella label for a wide range of economic, political, social, and moral reforms.

- Drawing support from the urban, college-educated middle class, progressive reformers sought to eliminate corruption in government, regulate business practices, address health hazards, improve working conditions, and give the public more direct control over government through direct primaries to nominate candidates for public office, direct election of senators, the initiative, referendum, and recall, and women's suffrage.

- At the local level, many progressives sought to suppress red-light districts, expand high schools, construct playgrounds, and replace corrupt urban political machines with more efficient systems of municipal government.

- At the state level, progressives enacted minimum wage laws for women workers, instituted industrial accident insurance, restricted child labor, and improved factory regulation.

- At the national level, Congress passed laws establishing federal regulation of the meatpacking, drug, and railroad industries, and strengthened antitrust laws. It also lowered the tariff, established federal control over the banking system, and enacted legislation to improve working conditions.

- Four constitutional amendments were adopted during the Progressive Era, which authorized an income tax, provided for the direct election of senators, extended the vote to women, and prohibited the manufacture and sale of alcoholic beverages.

Suggestions for Further Reading

John Whiteclay Chambers, *The Tyranny of Change: America in the Progressive Era, 1890–1920,* 2nd ed. (1992). Offers a thorough and up-to-date history of progressivism.

John Milton Cooper, *The Warrior and the Priest: Woodrow Wilson and Theodore Roosevelt* (1983). Examines the lives, philosophies, and actions of the key progressive presidents.

Morton Keller, *Regulating a New Society: Public Policy and Social Change in America, 1900–1933* (1994). Assesses government responses to the social problems of the early twentieth century.

James T. Kloppenberg, *Uncertain Victory: Social Democracy and Progressivism in European and American Thought, 1870–1920* (1986). Places the major thinkers of the Progressive Era in comparative perspective.

Martin J. Sklar, *The Corporate Reconstruction of American Capitalism, 1890–1916: The Market, the Law and Politics* (1988). Analyzes relationships between business and government during the Progressive Era.

Novels

Upton Sinclair, *The Jungle* (1906).

E. T. Doctorow, *Ragtime* (1975).

Stephen Crane, *Maggie: A Girl of the Streets* (1893).

Media Resources
Web Sites

The American Experience: America 1900
http://www.pbs.org/wgbh/pages/amex/1900/
This site is the companion site to the PBS documentary. It includes audio clips of respected historians on the economics, politics, and culture of 1900, a primary source database, a timeline of the year, downloadable software to compile your family tree, and other materials.

Turn of the Century Exhibits
http://memorialhall.mass.edu/turns/index.jsp
Covering the period 1880–1920, this site has a searchable database of resources as well as interactive activities.

The Anthracite Coal Strike, 1902
http://www.history.ohio-state.edu/projects/coal/1902AnthraciteStrike/
Site maintained by Ohio State University with pictures, cartoons, essays, and documents about this pivotal strike.

Jane Addams, Mother of the World
http://www.swarthmore.edu/Library/peace/Exhibits/
jane.addams/addams.index.htm
Swarthmore maintains this site with resources about Addams and the settlement house movement.

Women and Social Movements in the United States, 1775–2000
http://www.binghamton.edu/womhist/index.html
Includes a number of exhibits searchable by dates or topics about the role of women in reform.

Not For Ourselves Alone: The Story of Elizabeth Cady Stanton and Susan B. Anthony
http://www.pbs.org/stantonanthony/index.html
This Web site companion to the PBS series includes essays, documents, and other resources relating to women's rights.

The Evolution of the Conservation Movement, 1850–1920
http://memory.loc.gov/ammem/amrvhtml/conshome
.html
This American Memory site brings together scores of primary sources and photographs about "the historical formation and cultural foundations of the movement to conserve and protect America's natural heritage."

The Triangle Shirtwaist Factory Fire, March 25, 1911
http://www.ilr.cornell.edu/trianglefire/
The Kheel Center for Labor-Management Documentation and Archives at Cornell University put together this excellent site composed of oral histories, cartoons, images, and essays.

Labor-Management Conflict in American History
http://www.history.ohio-state.edu/projects/laborconflict/
This site at Ohio State University includes primary accounts of some of the major events in the history of labor-management conflict in the late nineteenth and early twentieth centuries.

The Samuel Gompers Papers: A Documentary History of the American Working Class
http://www.inform.umd.edu/ARHU/Depts/History/
Gompers/web1.html
A companion Web site to the published papers of this labor leader, it includes a biography, timeline, photos, and quotes by Gompers categorized by topic.

An American Factory: The Westinghouse Works, 1904
http://lcweb2.loc.gov/ammem/papr/west/westhome
.html
Part of the American Memory Project at the Library of Congress, this site provides a glimpse inside a turn-of-the-century factory.

"Votes for Women" Suffrage Pictures, 1850–1920
http://memory.loc.gov/ammem/vfwhtml/vfwhome.html
A great collection of photographs in a searchable database from the Library of Congress.

Votes for Women
http://memory.loc.gov/ammem/naw/nawshome.html
A selection from the National American Woman Suffrage Association papers of 167 books, pamphlets, and artifacts.

African American Women Writers of the 19th Century
http://digital.nypl.org/schomburg/writers_aa19/
The New York Public Library's Schomburg Center for Research in Black Culture maintains this site that contains a large number of digital texts by African American women of the nineteenth century.

Touring Turn-of-the-Century America: Photographs from the Detroit Publishing Company, 1880–1920
http://memory.loc.gov/ammem/detroit/dethome.html
This Library of Congress collection has thousands of photographs from turn-of-the-century America.

History Place: Child Labor in America, 1908–1912
http://www.historyplace.com/unitedstates/childlabor/
index.html
This collection provides pictures taken by Lewis W. Hines of child laborers, organized by category.

1912 Competing Visions for America
http://1912.history.ohio-state.edu/
This Ohio State University site explores the election of 1912 with documents, photos, and essays.

Jim Crow Museum of Racist Memorabilia
http://www.ferris.edu/jimcrow/
Documents the pervasive racism in American culture in words and pictures.

Theodore Roosevelt: His Life and Times on Film
http://lcweb2.loc.gov/ammem/trfhtml/
An assortment of film clips from the Library of Congress.

The Theodore Roosevelt Association
http://www.theodoreroosevelt.org/
This official site contains biographical and research information about this famous American.

African American Odyssey
http://memory.loc.gov/ammem/aaohtml/aohome.html
This Library of Congress site provides access to pictures, documents, rare books, films, and recordings regarding the black experience in America.

POTUS: Presidents of the United States
http://www.ipl.org/div/potus/
A good site for pictures and documents about any president.

Woodrow Wilson
http://www.pbs.org/wgbh/amex/wilson/
PBS companion Web site to its film biography; includes documents, photos, and essays about key figures and events.

Films and Videos

Heaven Will Protect the Working Girl. An American Social History Project, *Who Built America* video regarding women in the labor force.

Battle for Wilderness. American Experience video about the wilderness protection movement focusing on the 1906 battle over the building of a dam in Yosemite National Park.

The Hunt for Pancho Villa. An *American Experience* video documenting the 1916 raid into Mexico by General John Pershing that almost led to war.

America 1900. Four-part video covering most of the issues facing the nation at the turn of the century.

KEY TERMS

Institutional economists   (p. 581)

Reform Darwinists   (p. 581)

Muller v. Oregon   (p. 582)

Pragmatism   (p. 582)

Social Gospel   (p. 582)

Muckrakers   (p. 583)

Woman's Christian Temperance Union (WCTU)   (p. 586)

Purity crusaders   (p. 586)

Settlement house movement   (p. 587)

Niagara movement   (p. 589)

National Association for the Advancement of Colored People (NAACP)   (p. 590)

Triangle Shirtwaist Company   (p. 592)

Workmen's compensation laws   (p. 592)

National Child Labor Committee   (p. 592)

Plessy v. Ferguson   (p. 593)

Progressive (Bull Moose) party   (p. 597)

New Freedom   (p. 597)

New Nationalism   (p. 597)

Federal Reserve System   (p. 598)

Big stick diplomacy   (p. 599)

Hay–Bunau-Varilla Treaty   (p. 600)

Dollar diplomacy   (p. 601)

Missionary diplomacy   (p. 601)

PEOPLE YOU SHOULD KNOW

John Mitchell   (p. 577)

Theodore Roosevelt   (p. 577)

Jane Addams   (p. 582)

Ida Tarbell   (p. 583)

Susan B. Anthony   (p. 589)

W. E. B. Du Bois   (p. 589)

Robert La Follette   (p. 591)

Gifford Pinchot   (p. 594)

William Howard Taft   (p. 596)

Woodrow Wilson   (p. 598)

REVIEW QUESTIONS

1. What factors led to an increased spirit of reform at the turn of the century?

2. Who were the "progressives," and how did they respond to the problems they perceived?

3. What was the impact of presidential leadership on the course of progressivism?

4. How did the "progressive spirit" influence foreign affairs?

5. Who were the winners and losers of progressivism? Why?

22 The United States and World War I

RANDOLPH BOURNE ARGUES AGAINST WAR

Disillusioned writers of the 1920s honored **Randolph Silliman Bourne** as "the intellectual hero of World War I," yet his appearance was anything but heroic. Theodore Dreiser called Bourne "as frightening a dwarf as I had ever seen." An unusually messy forceps delivery crushed one side of Bourne's skull at birth, leaving him with a misshapen ear, a partially paralyzed face, and a mouth permanently askew in a horrible grimace. Then, when he was four, an attack of spinal tuberculosis twisted his frame and left him a hunchback dwarf.

Bourne's brain, however, was razor sharp. He started reading at the age of two, and by the time he entered school, he had finished entire books, including the Bible. A brilliant student, Bourne attended Columbia University where he studied under Franz Boaz, the father of cultural anthropology; John Dewey, the famed educator and apostle of pragmatism; and Charles A. Beard, the historian who stressed the economic motives of the founding fathers.

Bourne left college on the eve of World War I determined to become a writer. Drawn by the intense intellectual ferment of the day, he settled in New York's Greenwich Village, where self-styled literary radicals had declared war on the smugness and optimism of American culture. Bourne's interests ranged wide and far but he made his reputation as a critic of America's entrance into World War I.

Bourne loathed President Woodrow Wilson, but he directed his choicest barbs at fellow intellectuals who supported Wilson's policies. In effect, he accused them of not doing their job as thinkers—of not subjecting the president's high-sounding rhetoric to the fierce scrutiny required to sharpen public debate. Instead of questioning Wilson's policies, they had betrayed their duty by "opening the sluices and flooding the public with the sewage of the war spirit."

Bourne refused to endow the war with lofty purposes. In his judgment, World War I was not a struggle to make the world safe for democracy; it was nothing more than "frenzied mutual suicide." To those who argued that this war would be different, that this war could somehow be converted into an instrument of progress and democracy, Bourne replied that World War I would unleash "all the evils that are organically bound up with it." America's allies would reject Wilson's call for a "peace without victory," Bourne cautioned, because "war determines its own end—

Randolph Bourne, a pacifist, spoke out strongly against World War I and the prowar sentiment surrounding U.S. entry into the fighting. He warned that the war would lead to the disillusionment of youth, a heightening of nativist and racial prejudice, an end to reform, and the likelihood of further international instability. Many of his predictions proved to be true.

ponentially, making it "the inexorable arbiter and determinant of men's businesses and attitudes and opinions." The individual would lose every conflict with the state. "It will be coercion from above that will do the trick rather than patriotism from below," he warned.

Most alarming of all, the war would kill reform by diverting public attention from the unfinished work of progressivism. It would "leave the country spiritually impoverished because of the draining away of sentiment into the channels of war."

A few days after the armistice was signed in 1918, Bourne died, a victim of the influenza epidemic that killed 500,000 Americans that winter—five times the number that died in World War I. Although he had no visible impact on Wilson's administration, Bourne raised important questions about the relationship between the individual and the state during wartime, and many of his fears proved prophetic. In the end, the United States had little choice but to enter the conflict on the side of the Allies, but the war itself was a terrible human tragedy. World War I did not make "the world safe for democracy" or serve as the "war to end all wars" as President Wilson promised. Rather, World War I sowed the seeds of World War II.

THE ROAD TO WAR

World War I killed more people—more than 9 million soldiers, sailors, and flyers and another 5 million civilians—involved more countries—28—and cost more money—$186 billion in direct costs and another $151 billion in indirect costs—than any previous war in history. It was the first war in which parties used airplanes, tanks, long-range artillery, submarines, and poison gas. It left at least 7 million men permanently disabled.

World War I probably had more far-reaching consequences than any other preceding war. Politically, it resulted in the downfall of four monarchies—in Russia in 1917, in Austria-Hungary and Germany in 1918, and in Turkey in 1922. It contributed to the Bolshevik rise to power in Russia in 1917 and the triumph of fascism in Italy in 1922.

Economically, the war severely disrupted European economies and allowed the United States to become the world's leading creditor and industrial power. The war also had vast social consequences, including the mass murder of Armenians in Turkey and an influenza panepidemic that killed over 25 million people worldwide.

victory." Eschewing a just peace, they would try to win the war and "then grab what they can."

On the home front, warned Bourne, there would be "clumsily levied taxes and the robberies of imperfectly controlled private enterprises," the suppression of civil liberties, and the growth of big government. "War is the health of the State," he declared in one of his most famous lines. "It automatically sets in motion throughout society those irresistible forces for uniformity, for passionate cooperation with the Government in coercing into obedience the minority groups and individuals which lack the larger herd sense."

Like many of his contemporaries, Bourne feared the state. During wartime the state's power grew ex-

Archduke Francis Ferdinand and his wife Sophie, leave the Senate House in Sarajevo on June 28, 1914. Five minutes after this photograph was taken, the nineteen-year-old Serbian nationalist Gavrilo Princip assassinated them both, triggering World War I. Within weeks of the assassination, Germany, Turkey, Italy, and Austria-Hungary were at war with Britain, France, and Russia.

The event that triggered World War I was the assassination of Archduke Francis Ferdinand, the heir to the Austro-Hungarian throne. On June 28, 1914, Gavrilo Princip, a Serbian nationalist, assassinated the archduke while Ferdinand and his wife were riding through Sarajevo, the provincial capital of Bosnia in the Balkans. The assassination provoked outrage in Austria-Hungary, which wanted to punish Serbia for the assassination and intimidate other minority groups whose independence struggles threatened the empire's stability.

A complicated system of military alliances transformed the Balkan crisis into a full-scale European war. After consulting with its ally Germany, Austria-Hungary sent Serbia an ultimatum. Serbia accepted most of Austria-Hungary's demands and agreed to mediate the rest, but Austria-Hungary was unwilling to compromise and on July 28, declared war on Serbia. Meanwhile, Russia, vowing to defend Serbia if it was attacked, began to mobilize, while France, in turn, promised to support Russia. Germany demanded that Russia halt its military buildup; Russia refused. Germany responded by declaring war on Russia on August 1, and on France two days later.

World War I caught most people by surprise. Lulled by a century of peace, many observers had come to regard armed conflict as an anachronism, a dead relic rendered unthinkable by human progress. Convinced that the major powers had advanced too far morally and materially to fight, these optimists believed that nation-states would settle disputes

European Alliances and Battlefronts

through diplomacy. By the end of the century, peace societies abounded on both sides of the Atlantic, nurturing visions of a world without war, and the Hague Conferences of 1899 and 1907 seemed to bear out these hopes by codifying international law in order to establish procedures for the peaceful resolution of conflict. World War I shattered these dreams, demonstrating that death and destruction had not yet been banished from human affairs.

The Guns of August

Faced by Russia to the east and France to the west, Germany believed that its only hope for victory was to strike first. The German military plan, originally devised by General Alfred von Schlieffen in 1905, called for a small force to defend Germany's eastern border, while a much larger German army raced across Belgium into France.

Germany's plan involved a violation of international law. Belgium was a neutral country, and Britain was committed to its defense. Thus, a German invasion was certain to bring Britain into the war. Germany asked for permission to move its troops through Belgium, but King Albert, the country's monarch, refused, saying "Belgium is a nation, not a road." Germany decided to press ahead anyway; its forces invaded Belgium on August 3.

The German military strategy worked better on paper than it did in practice. While fierce resistance by 200,000 Belgian soldiers did not stop the German advance, it did give Britain and France time to mobilize their forces. Meanwhile, Russia mobilized faster than expected, forcing Germany to divert 100,000 troops to the eastern front. German hopes for a quick victory were dashed at the first battle of the Marne in September 1914, when a retreating French army launched a powerful counterattack, assisted by 6000 troops transported to the front by 1200 Parisian taxicabs.

World War I Casualties

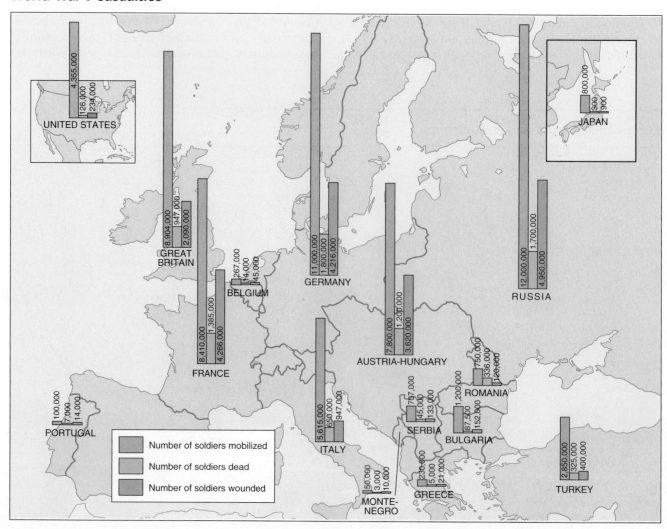

TABLE 22.1 Road to War: World War I		
1914	Archduke Francis Ferdinand assassinated	After the murder of the Crown Prince of Austria, Austria-Hungary declares war on Serbia; other war declarations follow; real war erupts when Germany invades Belgium.
	American neutrality	President Woodrow Wilson urges Americans to be "impartial in thought as well as action."
1915	Submarine warfare	President Wilson warns Germany that he will hold it responsible for the loss of American lives and property resulting from submarine warfare.
	Lusitania sunk	A British passenger liner is sunk without warning by a German submarine; 128 Americans are among the 1198 fatalities.
1917	U.S.-German relations chill	President Wilson breaks diplomatic relations with Germany, citing the resumption of unrestricted submarine warfare.
	The Zimmermann telegram	Sent from the German foreign minister to the German ambassador in Mexico, it proposes that Mexico enter the war in return for Arizona, New Mexico, and Texas.
	Merchant ships armed	President Wilson authorizes the arming of American merchant ships.
	Declaration of war	President Wilson asks Congress to declare war, stating that "the world must be made safe for democracy."

After the **Allies** halted Germany's massive offensive through France and Belgium at the Marne River, the Great War bogged down into trench warfare and a ghastly stalemate ensued. Congealed lines of men, stretching from the English Channel to the Swiss border, formed an unmovable battlefront across northern France. Four million troops burrowed into trenches that were 6 to 8 feet deep and wide enough for two men to pass, and which stretched for 450 miles. The soldiers of both sides, ravaged by tuberculosis and plagued with lice and rats, stared at each other across barren expanses called "no man's land," fighting pitched battles over narrow strips of blood-soaked earth.

To end the stalemate, Germany introduced several military innovations in 1915, but none proved decisive. Germany dispatched submarines to prevent merchant ships from reaching Britain; it added poison chlorine gas to its military arsenal at the second battle of Ypres in northern France; and it dropped incendiary bombs over London from a zeppelin. Other innovations that distinguished World War I from previous conflicts were airplanes, tanks, and hand grenades. But it was the machine gun that did most of the killing. The grim cycle repeated itself countless times: officers cried "Attack!"; men rose in waves; and the opposing forces opened fire with machine guns, spewing out death at the rate of eight bullets per second. When the war ended, Germany had lost 1,800,000 men; Russia, 1,700,000; France, 1,385,000; Austria-Hungary, 1,200,000; and Great Britain, 947,000.

In a fateful attempt to break the deadlock, German forces adopted a new objective in 1916: to kill so many French soldiers that France would be forced to sue for peace. The German plan was to attack the French city of Verdun, a psychologically important town in northeastern France, and bleed the French dry. The battle, the war's longest, lasted from February 21, 1916 through July, and engaged 2 million soldiers. When it ended, Verdun had become a symbol of wartime futility. France had suffered 315,000 casualties, Germany 280,000. The town was destroyed, but the front had not moved.

With fighting on the western front deadlocked, action spread to other arenas. A British soldier and writer named T. E. Lawrence (better known as "Lawrence of Arabia"), organized revolts against the Ottoman territories in Syria, Palestine, Iraq, and the Arabian peninsula. With Germany preoccupied in Europe, Japanese and British commonwealth forces seized German islands in the Pacific, while British forces conquered German colonies in Africa.

The military stalemate produced political turmoil across Europe. On Easter Monday, 1916, some 1500 Irish Catholics seized buildings in Dublin and declared Ireland an independent republic. Fighting raged for a week before British forces suppressed the rebellion. British reprisals created great sympathy for the rebels. In 1919, renewed fighting broke out between British forces and supporters of Irish independence.

In Czarist Russia, wartime casualties, popular discontent, and shortages of food, fuel, and housing touched off revolution and civil war. In March 1917 strikes and food riots erupted in the Russian capital of Petrograd. Soldiers called in to quell the strikes joined the uprising; and on March 15, Czar Nicholas II abdicated. The czarist regime was replaced by a succession of weak provisional governments which tried to keep Russia in World War I. On November 7 communist Bolsheviks led by **Vladimir I. Lenin** overthrew the provisional government, promising "Peace to the army, land to the peasants, ownership of the factories to the workers."

In 1917, after two and a half years of fighting, 5 million troops were dead and the western front remained deadlocked. This was the situation that awaited the United States in 1917.

American Neutrality

Like the combatants, Americans did not see the war coming. Most felt relieved when President Woodrow Wilson issued an official declaration of neutrality on August 4, 1914. Many citizens did not believe their nation's interest and security hinged on the war's outcome. Mindful of the wisdom embodied in Washington's Farewell Address, steeped in a long tradition of isolation from Europe's wars, and shielded from the hostilities by the Atlantic Ocean, they hoped to escape the insanity.

Two weeks after the official declaration of **neutrality** Wilson asked his countrymen to remain impartial "in thought as well as in action." Yet the president himself could not meet this standard. Privately, his sympathies lay with the Allies, especially Great Britain, whose culture and government he had long admired. Moreover, with the notable exception of **William Jennings Bryan,** his first secretary of state, Wilson's closest advisers all favored Great Britain. Robert Lansing, who succeeded Bryan as secretary of state; Walter Hines Page, ambassador to the Court of St. James; and Colonel Edward House, Wilson's alter ego, pushed the president to side with England and her Allies. Yet Wilson saw the war's causes as complicated and obscure; simple prudence dictated that the United States avoid taking sides.

Internal divisions underscored the wisdom of neutrality. Wilson knew his countrymen felt deeply divided over the war. Ties of language and culture prompted many Americans to side with the Allies, and, as the war progressed, the British adeptly ex-

ploited these bonds with anti-German propaganda. After the German invasion of neutral Belgium, for example, British propagandists depicted the Germans as sadistic brutes who committed atrocities against civilians. Yet the **Central Powers** had their sympathizers, too. Approximately one-third of the nation, 32 million people, were either foreign-born or the children of immigrants, and the roots of more than 10 million of these were the nations of the Central Powers. Furthermore, millions of Irish Americans sided with the Central Powers because they hated the English.

Domestic politics reinforced Wilson's determination to remain neutral. In 1914 the United States stood at the end of two decades of bitter social and political debate. Labor unrest, corporate growth, trust-busting, and the arrival of 12 million new immigrants since the turn of the century had opened deep fissures in American society. As Wilson struggled to correct these problems through legislation, he feared his domestic program would be endangered if neutrality failed. "Every reform we have won will be lost if we go into this war," declared Wilson in 1914.

Allied Violations of Neutrality

Because German armies held the edge in the land war, Great Britain had no choice but to press its naval superiority. Like Thomas Jefferson and James Madison a century earlier, President Wilson confronted a Great Britain bent upon ruling the waves, and no less than his predecessors in the White House, Wilson fought to protect neutral rights. During the early part of the war, British efforts to control the seas repeatedly posed threats to Anglo-American relations.

Immediately after war erupted, the British navy attempted to blockade Europe. In February 1915 British ships mined the North Sea and started seizing American vessels bound for neutral countries, often without offering compensation. The British captured not only war material but also noncontraband items, including food and cotton, bound for neutral nations such as Holland for reshipment to Germany. In 1916 Britain blacklisted some 87 American companies accused of trading with Germany and censored the mail coming from Europe to the United States.

These actions, coupled with England's ruthless suppression of the Irish Rebellion in 1916, infuriated Wilson. In retaliation, the State Department bombarded England with a flurry of firm protests. These objections were consistently undermined, however, by **Walter Hines Page,** the pro-British American ambassador at the Court of St. James. On one occasion, for example, Page delivered a long dispatch to Sir Edward Grey, the British foreign secretary, and declared: "I have now read the dispatch but I do not agree with it; let us consider how it should be answered." Although the British interpreted Wilson's ardent defense of neutral rights as petty, legalistic quibbling, they realized they could not push Wilson too far, since they needed American trade to survive.

Wilson could have ended the controversy over neutral rights by clamping an embargo on trade with the belligerents, but he refused to take this action because wartime trade was stimulating the American economy. The United States had been in a recession when Wilson entered office in 1913, and the war had quadrupled its exports to the Allied nations.

The huge volume of trade quickly exhausted the Allies' cash reserves, forcing them to ask the United States for credit. Secretary of State William Jennings Bryan, a near pacifist and the only member of Wilson's cabinet who supported strict neutrality, opposed their requests. After hesitating several months, Wilson agreed in October 1915 to permit loans to belligerents, a decision that favored Great Britain and France far more than Germany. By 1917 American loans to the Allies had soared to $2.25 billion; loans to Germany stood at a paltry $27 million. The United States became a creditor nation for the first time, giving Americans a strong economic interest in an Allied victory.

Submarine Warfare

Given Britain's overwhelming naval superiority, Germany decided to rely on a new weapon, the submarine, and on February 4, 1915, Germany proclaimed a "war zone" around the British Isles. Henceforth, they declared, all enemy merchant ships that entered the zone would be torpedoed without warning, and neutral ships would not be guaranteed safe passage. Germany was bluffing. It had only four submarines in the area, but Germany intended to use the threat of **submarine warfare** to terrorize and intimidate its enemies until it could build enough ships to enforce its threats.

A new development in naval technology, the submarine posed serious challenges to international law. The law required ships that attacked other vessels on the high seas to warn their intended victims, allow time for passengers to reach lifeboats, and then rescue survivors after the sinking. Moreover, merchant vessels suspected of transporting contraband had to be "visited and searched" before being attacked. A silent assassin whose effectiveness depended on the element of surprise, the submarine had to strike from below the surface in violation of international law.

Wilson's approach to foreign affairs was both legalistic and moralistic. He expected nation-states to behave like gentlemen; and, above all, that meant living up to the letter of international law and respecting the rights of every nation. To Wilson, German sub-

Crew on the deck of a German World War I submarine at sea. The German U-boat (*Unterseeboot*) violated the international law that required a warship to warn a passenger or merchant vessel before it attacked. The U-boat struck silently and without warning.

marines were committing criminal acts. In contrast to British violations of American neutrality, which merely resulted in property losses, submarine warfare threatened to kill innocent civilians. In unusually blunt language, he warned Berlin that it would be held "strictly accountable" for American lives lost to submarine attacks. While international law did not guarantee the safety of neutrals who traveled on belligerent ships, Wilson acted as though it did.

On March 28, 1915, a German submarine torpedoed the *Falaba*, a British liner, killing 104 passengers, including one American. "PIRACY," "SHOCKING BLOODTHIRSTINESS," "BARBARISM RUN MAD," screamed the American press in banner headlines. Wilson was furious, but Secretary of State Bryan reminded the president of numerous British violations of American neutrality in her attempt to blockade Germany.

On May 1, the German embassy took out ads in New York newspapers warning Americans not to travel on Allied ships. Undeterred, 197 Americans sailed for the British Isles on board the **Lusitania,** the queen of the British-owned Cunard fleet. On May 7, 1915, a German submarine torpedoed the *Lusitania* off the coast of Ireland. The ship sank in 18 minutes, killing 1198 persons, 128 of them Americans. The public was shocked and outraged. It did not seem to matter that the *Lusitania* (like the *Falaba*) was transporting munitions in her hull and had secret orders to ram submarines on sight.

In a sharply worded dispatch, Wilson ordered Germany to apologize for the sinking, compensate the victims, and pledge to stop attacking merchant ships. When Berlin equivocated, Wilson sent a second *Lusitania* note repeating his demands. This time

The First Day of the Somme

During the American Civil War Richard J. Gatling hoped to become wealthy by selling the Union army his hand-cranked precursor to the machine gun, the Gatling gun. It could unleash up to 200 rounds a minute, as compared to the 2 to 3 rounds a minute from a rifled musket being loaded and fired by a well-trained soldier. Gatling considered his weapon "providential," the ultimate device, he wrote to Abraham Lincoln, for "crushing the rebellion." After the war Gatling even spoke of social benefits. His gun would ease the pain and suffering of war. Only one soldier would be needed "to do as much battle duty as a hundred" because of its "rapidity of fire." His weapon would "supersede the necessity of large armies, and consequently exposure to battle and disease would be greatly diminished."

Hiram Maxim, another inventor, offered a major improvement to Gatling's weapon in 1884 when he demonstrated a mechanism that would permit the gun to fire automatically, simply by depressing the trigger—the modern rapid-firing machine gun was born. Because of such technological breakthroughs, water-cooled machine guns capable of shooting 600 rounds a minute were commonplace in the arsenal of weapons used by the armies engaged in World War I. The Maxim guns, as they were generically known, could spray an area with bullets and easily destroy companies of soldiers trained well enough to fire their breechloading rifles only 15 times a minute. The machine gun proved to be an effective killing weapon.

More sophisticated weapons did not, as Richard Gatling had assured his customers, result in any reduction in the size of wartime armies. During Europe's Age of Industrialization the major powers built up ever-larger military forces, as if only huge masses of troops could defeat the enhanced firepower of new weapons such as the machine gun.

When the armies of Europe first collided in August 1914 after Germany's penetration through Belgium, a stark reality became clear. Firepower, both in the form of small arms and large artillery, was so overwhelming that neither side could defeat the other without virtual annihilation. What emerged were opposing lines of trenches along what was called the western front, running without interruption south from the North Sea all the way through France to the border of Switzerland. For the next three years combat became a horrible contest in which one side or the other periodically tried to break through these trench lines.

The Battle of the Somme was in many ways typical of trench warfare. Up until June 1916 this sector in northeastern France was inactive. German divisions had been present since September 1914 and had constructed three defensive lines of trenches running back from "no man's land," an area some 500 to 1000 yards wide on the other side of which were trenches manned by the Allies—the British to the north and the French to the south of the Somme River. Because of a fearsome struggle occurring far to the south at Verdun, the Allied high command, after preliminary planning, decided in May 1916 to mount a massive offensive in the Somme sector.

If German lines could be permanently ruptured, then it would be possible to roll up enemy divisions on their flanks. German soldiers would face surrender or retreat, thus breaking the military deadlock in favor of the Allies. To breech the German trenches in coordinated fashion along a stretch of 50 miles involved detailed planning, considering the thousands of troops and massive firepower that the Allies faced. Further, surprise attacks were impossible. German artillery and machine-gun operators could obliterate waves of soldiers trying to cross no man's land, even before they reached the barbed wire placed in front of the German trenches. The alternative was to prepare the way with an extended artillery bombardment.

The Battle of the Somme was launched with a seven-day cannonade. During the last week of June some 50,000 British artillerists fired 2,960,000 rounds at the German trenches. By evening of the second day, wrote an observer, "some sectors of the German front line were already unrecognizable and had become crater fields." The next day the British started releasing clouds of chlorine gas, hoping that it would seep down into dugouts 20 or more feet belowground where German soldiers were at that moment living, surviving, and listening carefully for the climactic fury of the bombardment, a sure sign that the infantry assault was to begin.

At 6:30 A.M., on July 1, 1916, one hour before infantry troops were to advance, the cannonade reached "an intensity as yet unparalleled . . . along the whole front." German soldiers noticed the difference and knew that the moment of reckoning was near. The whole course of the battle would depend on their ability to get back aboveground, set up their machine guns, and begin firing before enemy infantry overran them. It was a moment for which they had repeatedly trained.

As zero hour approached, thousands of British and French soldiers made final preparations in their trenches. Their assignment was to secure control of the second German line by the end of the day. Soon they would climb up scaling ladders and jump over the top, then listen for the sounds of whistles from their platoon leaders to guide them across no man's land. Most found themselves "sweating at zero hour," supposedly from "nervous excitement." Many had attended church services the previous day. Explained one British soldier, "I placed my body in God's keeping, and I am going into battle with His

name on my lips." Everyone received a warm breakfast and a healthy ration of rum to settle their jittery nerves.

Promptly at 7:30 A.M., the race began. "Over the top" went hundreds of thousands of British and French troops. Up out of their dugouts came German soldiers. In most areas the Germans were ready with time to spare. Their machine gun and artillery fire cut a third of the British battalions to shreds before they reached what remained of the first German trenches.

British soldiers who survived witnessed unbelievable sights. One watched as "two men suddenly rose into the air vertically, 15 feet perhaps," as a German shell hit the ground ahead of him. "They rose and fell with the easy, graceful poise of acrobats," he noted, as they died. Another saw men "falling forward," stating that it was "some time before I realized they were hit." In one company only three soldiers made it to the German barbed wire. Their leader, a lieutenant, looked around in amazement and said: "God, God, where's the rest of the boys?"

Hardly over the top, a British sergeant heard the "patter, patter" of

German machine guns. "By the time I'd gone another ten yards," he explained, "there seemed to be only a few men left around me; by the time I had gone twenty yards, I seemed to be on my own. Then I was hit myself." This sergeant was among the fortunate. In some sectors, British soldiers who evaded machine-gun fire and reached the other side "were burned to death by [German] flame throwers."

From the British perspective, the fighting went poorly that day. By evening they had not captured the German second line, but they had suffered 60,000 casualties, including 21,000 dead. By comparison, the Germans, who got most of their machine guns up and operating, experienced only 6000 casualties.

The battle, however, had just begun. It would rage in fits and starts until November 18, 1916, when the Allies decided that a breakthrough in the Somme sector was not attainable. By that time the British had suffered 420,000 casualties, the French an estimated 200,000. No one knows exactly how many soldiers the Germans lost, but a fair guess would be in the 500,000 to 600,000 range. Yet virtually no ground had been lost or gained by either side.

It is not surprising, then, that the Allies rejoiced when the Americans finally entered the war. They needed more than loans and war goods to achieve total victory. Field Marshal Joseph Joffre, the former French commander in chief, said it all when he arrived in the United States after Congress declared war in April 1917. Declared Joffe with his usual bluntness: "We want men, men, men."

the Germans met him halfway, expressing regret over the *Lusitania* and agreeing to pay an indemnity. However, the imperial government refused to stop sinking merchant ships without warning, explaining that Germany's survival depended on full use of the submarine.

Convinced that Wilson's policies would lead to war, Bryan resigned from the cabinet to protest what he saw as a dangerous tilt toward Great Britain in American policy. For his part, Wilson knew that the issue of submarine warfare had not been resolved. "I can't keep the country out of war," he admitted privately. "Any little German lieutenant can put us into war at any time by some calculated outrage."

Events soon showed how right he was. On March 24, 1916, a German submarine attacked the *Sussex*, an unarmed French passenger ship, killing more than 80 and severely wounding 7 Americans. Wilson threatened to sever diplomatic relations unless Germany promised to stop sinking all merchant and passenger ships without warning. Anxious to keep the United States neutral, Berlin agreed. The so-called **Sussex pledge** reduced tensions between the United States and Germany for the remainder of 1916, but the fragile peace depended solely on German restraint.

Preparedness Campaign

As the submarine threatened to draw the United States into the fighting, the American people and their leaders debated whether or not to make ready for war. Initially, Wilson's policy toward preparedness was cautious. In December 1914 he told Congress, "We never have had, and while we retain our present principles and ideals we never shall have, a large standing army."

Many Americans saw the issue differently. Wilson increasingly found himself assailed by prominent and highly vocal critics who insisted that the best way to preserve peace was to prepare for war. The pugnacious Theodore Roosevelt called the president "the popular pacifist hero," while another critic growled that the Germans were "standing by their torpedoes, the British by their guns, and Wilson by strict accountability." As Tin Pan Alley produced songs with titles such as "I Did Not Raise My Boy to Be a Coward," the National Security League, headed by General Leonard Wood, organized volunteer military training programs across the country.

Yet Wilson also felt pressured by groups opposed to war. Socialists such as Eugene V. Debs dismissed the war as a struggle for assets among capitalist nations. Radicals such as anarchist Emma Goldman and "Big Bill" Haywood, head of the Industrial Workers of the World, shared this view and advocated violent resistance to preparedness. Liberal reformers such as Randolph Bourne feared that war would destroy the spirit of progressivism. Most troubling of all, Wilson had to worry about opposition from within his own party. Speaking for the peace Democrats, former Secretary of State William Jennings Bryan warned that a preparedness campaign would transform the United States into "a vast armory with skull and crossbones above the door."

In the end, Wilson shifted ground and threw his support behind a moderate preparedness program. Throughout January and February 1916, he stumped the country demanding a military force powerful enough to protect the nation's honor. In June 1916, Congress increased the army from 90,000 to 175,000 men, and a few months later appropriated more than $500 million for new ships. Though of small importance militarily, both acts drew fire from those who predicted that armaments would lead to war.

At the height of the preparedness controversy, Wilson had to beat back a serious challenge to his control of American foreign policy. During the early months of 1916, Congress considered separate resolutions sponsored by Senator Thomas Gore of Oklahoma and Representative Jeff McLemore of Texas. Fearing that Wilson's defense of neutral rights would draw the United States into the conflict, the Gore and McLemore resolutions sought to prevent future incidents by prohibiting Americans from traveling on ships owned by belligerent nations and by prohibiting American vessels or neutral vessels from transporting American citizens and contraband "at one and the same time." Both resolutions enjoyed strong support in Congress, and for a while their passage appeared inevitable, but Wilson threw his power and prestige into a furious attack on both measures, insisting that if the United States accepted any abridgment of neutral rights "many other humiliations would follow." In the end, Congress accepted his argument and the Gore and McLemore resolutions went down in defeat.

The Election of 1916

Despite his own support for military preparedness, Wilson decided to make peace the key issue in his bid for reelection in 1916. The Republicans chose Charles Evans Hughes, a former governor of New York and a Supreme Court justice who had earned a solid reputation as a liberal. His nomination demonstrated the GOP's determination to regain progressive support and avoid the split that had put Wilson in the White House four years earlier. Wilson labeled the Republicans "the party of war" and charged that Hughes's election would plunge the United States into Europe's madness. "He kept us out of war" became the Democrats' rallying cry.

The race was extremely close. On election eve the *New York Times* and the *New York World* both awarded victory to Hughes, who went to bed believing he had won. He ran well in traditional Republican strongholds such as the Midwest (he won Illinois, Indiana, and Michigan) and the large eastern states. However, Wilson won in the electoral college by a vote of 277 to 254, with a popular vote margin of 9.1 million to Hughes's 8.5 million.

A careful analysis of Wilson's victory reveals that the Democrats won because they managed to fuse progressivism with the cause of peace. Wilson carried the Solid South, Ohio, Maryland, and New Hampshire, but he owed his victory to voters west of the Mississippi River, where he took every state except Oregon, Iowa, South Dakota, and Minnesota. This was the section of the country where peace sentiment ran highest and the opposition to preparedness was strongest.

The End of Neutrality

Interpreting his reelection as a vote for peace, Wilson attempted to mediate an end to the war. In 1917, Wilson urged both sides to embrace his call for **"peace without victory,"** but neither welcomed his overtures. Randolph Bourne was right. Above all else, the belligerents wanted victory.

Any hope for a negotiated settlement ended when Germany announced that after February 1, 1917, all vessels caught in the war zone, neutral or belligerent, armed or unarmed, would be sunk without warning. Driven to desperation by the British blockade and unable to break the impasse on land, Germany had decided to risk everything on a furious U-boat campaign designed to starve Britain into submission. The German high command expected the United States to declare war in retaliation, but they believed their submarines could deliver a knockout blow before America could mobilize.

Members of his cabinet pressed Wilson to declare war, but he broke diplomatic relations instead. Though critics accused the president of shaking first his fist and then his finger, Wilson refused to budge, largely because he viewed war as a defeat for reason. For weeks he seemed indecisive and confused, unable to accept the fact that "strict accountability" demanded war once the Germans started sinking American ships.

The **Zimmermann telegram** snapped Wilson out of his daze. In January, British cryptographers had intercepted a secret message from Arthur Zimmermann, the German foreign minister, to the German ambassador to Mexico, proposing an alliance between Germany and Mexico in the event Germany went to war with the United States. Germany promised to help Mexico recover the territory it had lost in the 1840s, roughly the present-day states of Texas, New Mexico, California, and Arizona. The British revealed the scheme to Wilson in late February, hoping to draw the United States into the war.

The Zimmermann telegram convinced Wilson and millions of Americans that Germany would stop at nothing to satisfy her ambitions—goals that posed a serious danger to America's rights and security. Late in February, Wilson asked Congress for permission to arm American merchant ships. The House approved, but 11 pacifists in the Senate filibustered against the bill. Dismissing his Senate opponents as "a little band of willful men, representing no opinion but their own," Wilson issued an executive order on March 12, arming merchant ships and instructing them to shoot submarines on sight.

At this critical juncture, with the United States and Germany virtually at war, the Russian Revolution erupted. Suddenly, the czar's government was swept away, and in its place stood the provisional government of a Russian Republic, complete with a representative parliament. Given his penchant for framing issues in moral terms, Wilson could now view the Allies in a new light: With the only autocratic regime among the Allies transformed overnight into a fledgling democracy, the war truly seemed to pit the forces of democracy against the forces of despotism.

Pale and solemn, Wilson delivered his war message to Congress on April 2. The United States "had no quarrel with the German people," he insisted, but their "military masters" had to be defeated in order to make the world "safe for democracy." The next day the Senate approved the war resolution, 82 to 6; the House followed on April 6, 373 to 50. The president signed the declaration on April 7, 1917, and America was at war.

For more than two years Wilson had worked frantically to keep the United States at peace: why did he now lead the nation to war? True, cultural ties with Great Britain predisposed the United States to favor the Allies, and enormous volumes of trade and loans strengthened those ties. Yet cultural bonds and money did not decide the issue. Wilson, reluctantly, drew the sword, because he concluded that German submarines violated international law and made a mockery of America's long-standing commitment to freedom of the seas. His strong defense of neutral rights left him no choice but to declare war once Germany resumed its attacks on American ships.

One additional factor carried great weight for Wilson—his desire to help shape the peace. By entering the war, the United States would be guaranteed a place at the peace table. "I hate this war," an anguished Wilson confided to one of his aides, "and the only thing I care about on earth is the peace I am going to make at the end of it."

THE PEOPLE SPEAK

Woodrow Wilson, Address to Congress (1917)

When World War I erupted in Europe during his first term as President, Woodrow Wilson vowed to remain neutral. Despite his promises of peace in the election of 1916, President Wilson finally bowed to mounting pressures, particularly German submarine attacks on Americans, to enter World War I. The following is an excerpt from his impassioned address to Congress asking them to declare war on Germany in April 1917.

I have called the Congress into extraordinary session because there are serious, very serious choices of policy to be made, and made immediately, which it was neither right nor constitutionally permissible that I should assume the responsibility of making.

On the third of February last I officially laid before you the extraordinary announcement of the Imperial German Government that on and after the first day of February it was its purpose to put aside all restraints of law or of humanity and use its submarines to sink every vessel that sought to approach either the ports of Great Britain and Ireland or the western coasts of Europe or any of the ports controlled by the enemies of Germany within the Mediterranean . . .

I was for a little while unable to believe that such things would in fact be done by any government that had hitherto subscribed to the humane practices of civilized nations. International law had its origin in the attempt to set up some law which would be respected and observed upon the seas, where no nation had right of dominion and where lay the free highways of the world. . . . The minimum of right the German Gov-

ernment has swept aside under the plea of retaliation and necessity and because it had no weapons which it could use at sea except these which it is impossible to employ as it is employing them without throwing to the winds all scruples of humanity or of respect for all understandings that were supposed to underlie the intercourse of the world. I am not now thinking of the loss of property involved, immense and serious as that is, but only of the wanton and wholesale destruction of the lives of non-combatants, men, women, and children, engaged in pursuits which have always, even in the darkest periods of modern history, been deemed innocent and legitimate. Property can be paid for; the lives of peaceful and innocent people cannot be. The present German submarine warfare against commerce is a warfare against mankind.

It is a war against all nations. American ships have been sunk, American lives taken, in ways which it has stirred us very deeply to learn of, but the ships and people of other neutral and friendly nations have been sunk and overwhelmed in the waters in the same way. There has been no discrimination. The challenge is to all mankind. Each nation must decide for itself how it will meet it. The choice we make for ourselves must be made with a moderation of counsel and a temperateness of judgement befitting our character and our motives as a nation. We must put excited feeling away. Our motive will not be revenge or the victorious assertion of the physical might of the nation, but only the vindication of right, of human right, of which we are only a single champion. . . .

With a profound sense of the solemn and even tragical character of the step I am taking and of the grave responsibilities which it involves, but in unhesitating obedience to what I deem my constitutional

---

Most Americans supported Wilson's call to arms. John Dewey, the famed educator, spoke for progressives when he described war as an ugly reality that had to be converted into an instrument for benefiting mankind. Randolph Bourne disagreed. "If the war is too strong for you to prevent," he asked pointedly, "how is it going to be weak enough for you to control and mold to your liberal purposes?"

AMERICAN INDUSTRY GOES TO WAR

The United States entered the Great War unprepared. Americans had no idea of what the war would ask of them as a society. Decisions had to be made about mobilization, but the public had not yet formed a consensus on the proper role of government in society, especially during wartime. As a re-

sult, Wilson hesitated to place the economy on a wartime footing by decree. Instead, he tried to create a system of economic incentives that would encourage Americans to support the war in a spirit of voluntary cooperation.

Voluntarism

It took nearly a year to organize an effective war administration. Wilson established a **war cabinet** with six key boards, conferring broad power on the central government. The War Industries Board (WIB), organized early in 1918 under the leadership of **Bernard M. Baruch,** a Wall Street financier, assumed the task of managing the economy by fixing prices, setting priorities, and reducing waste. To increase production, the WIB appealed to the profit motive, permitting earnings to triple during the war.

duty, I advise that the Congress declare the recent course of the Imperial German Government to be in fact nothing less than war against the government and people of the United States; that it formally accept the status of belligerent which has thus been thrust upon it; and that it take immediate steps not only to put the country in a more thorough state of defense but also to exert all its power and employ all its resources to bring the Government of the German Empire to terms and end the war. . . .

We have no quarrel with the German people. We have no feeling towards them but of sympathy and friendship. It was not upon their impulse that their government acted in entering this war. It was not with their previous knowledge or approval. It was a war determined upon as wars used to be determined upon in the old, unhappy days when peoples were nowhere consulted by their rulers and wars were provoked and waged in the interest of dynasties or of little groups of ambitious men who were accustomed to use their fellow men as pawns and tools. . . .

We are accepting this challenge of hostile purpose because we know that in such a Government, following such methods, we can never have a friend; and that in the presence of its organized power, always lying in wait to accomplish we know not what purpose, there can be no assured security for the democratic Governments of the world. We are now about to accept gauge force of the nation to check and nullify its pretensions and its power. We are glad, now that we see the facts with no veil of false pretense about them, to fight thus for the ultimate peace of the world and for the liberation of its peoples, the German peoples included: for the rights of nations great and small and the privilege of men everywhere to choose their way of life and of obedience. The world must be made safe for democracy. Its peace must be planted upon the tested foundations of political liberty. We have no selfish ends to serve. We desire no conquest, no dominion. We seek no indemnities for ourselves, no material compensations for the sacrifices we shall freely make. We are but one of the champions of the rights of mankind. We shall be satisfied when those rights have been made as secure as the faith and the freedom of nations can make them. . . .

It is a distressing and oppressive duty, Gentlemen of the Congress, which I have performed in thus addressing you. There are, it may be, many months of fiery trial and sacrifice ahead of us. It is a fearful thing to lead this great peaceful people into war, into the most terrible and disastrous of all wars, civilization itself seeming to be in the balance. But the right is more precious than peace, and we shall fight for the things which we have always carried nearest our hearts,—for democracy, for the right of those who submit to authority to have a voice in their own Governments, for the rights and liberties of small nations, for a universal dominion of right by such a concert of free peoples as shall bring peace and safety to all nations and make the world itself at last free. To such a task we can dedicate our lives and our fortunes, everything that we have, with the pride of those who know that the day has come when America is privileged to spend her blood and her might for the principles that gave her birth and happiness and the peace which she has treasured. God helping her, she can do no other.

Source: New York Times, April 3, 1917.

The Fuel Administration, the War Trade Board, the Shipping Board, and the U.S. Railroad Administration adopted similar policies. Under the slogan "Mine More Coal," the Fuel Administration increased production by two-fifths and conserved supplies through voluntary "lightless nights" and "gasless Sundays." By spending $500 million on new equipment and repairs, offering large profits to railroads and high wages to workers, the Railroad Administration established an efficient rail system under national control.

"Hooverizing"

Agricultural production came under the jurisdiction of the Food Administration headed by Herbert Hoover, a mining engineer and self-made millionaire who had served with distinction as director of relief operations in Belgium. Appealing to the spirit of patriotism, he preached "the gospel of the clean plate." Americans **Hooverized** with wheatless Mondays and Wednesdays, meatless Tuesdays, and porkless Thursdays and Saturdays.

No foe of profits, Hoover set farm prices at high levels to encourage production. He stabilized the grain market by guaranteeing farmers a minimum price, and purchased raw sugar and then sold it to refineries at a fixed rate. The policies worked. Overall, real farm incomes rose 30 percent during the war, food production increased by one-quarter, domestic food consumption fell, and America's food shipments to the Allies tripled.

Peace with Labor

The government also made concessions to labor. Wilson addressed the American Federation of Labor (AFL) convention in November 1917, the first time a

Wilson's administration opposed militant labor unions like the Industrial Workers of the World (IWW), shown here striking against Oliver Steel in Pennsylvania.

president had so honored the trade union movement. Important policy shifts followed. Gradually, Wilson recognized labor's right to organize and engage in collective bargaining, and he sanctioned other key demands, including the eight-hour workday. To settle labor disputes, Wilson created the National War Labor Board (WLB). Though it lacked legal authority, the WLB had the president's backing and a commitment from industry and labor to accept its decisions.

While Wilson embraced the AFL, his administration opposed the militant **Industrial Workers of the World** (IWW, also called "Wobblies"). From the textile mills of New England to the logging camps of the Pacific Northwest and steel companies in between, the Wobblies demanded higher wages and better working conditions, and they went out on strike to win them. Because the Wobblies frequently employed the rhetoric of class warfare to dramatize their demands, their strikes frightened many Americans who feared social revolution. Businessmen played upon these fears to demand suppression of the so-called radical unions.

The AFL shrewdly separated its union from these more militant workers, pledging not to strike for the duration of the war. The AFL supported the war and joined the administration's attack on socialist critics. In return, the AFL won a voice in homefront policy. Union men occupied seats in wartime agencies, where they pushed for the eight-hour workday and staved off pressure from employers bent on preserving the open shop. Real income of manufacturing workers and coal miners rose by one-fifth between 1914 and 1918, hours were reduced (by

1919 half the labor force had achieved a 48-hour workweek), and AFL membership jumped from 2.7 million in 1916 to 4 million in 1919.

Financing the War

By 1920 the war had cost the nation $33.5 billion—33 times the federal government's revenues in 1916. Conservatives favored a regressive tax policy: consumption taxes, borrowing, and, if necessary, a slight increase in income taxes. Reformers and radicals demanded a progressive tax policy: inheritance and excess profits taxes coupled with higher income taxes. Wilson walked the middle ground, but the heaviest burdens fell on the wealthy, through taxes on large incomes, corporate profits, and estates.

World War I brought an important change in the sources of federal tax revenues. Before the war nearly three-quarters of federal revenues had come from excise and customs taxes. After the war, America's tax structure shifted from taxing consumption to taxing wealth, proof that progressives had won an important victory in the struggle to make upper-income groups pay a large share of the cost of government. On the tax issue Randolph Bourne was wrong.

THE AMERICAN PUBLIC GOES TO WAR

Although Wilson preferred to rely on voluntary efforts rather than mandated government interference, federal powers were greatly expanded during World

War I. Wilson's decision to substitute voluntarism for statutory controls on industry placed the burden of supporting the war on the profit motive and the public's sense of patriotism. This policy avoided a clash between Wilson and industry that would have resulted from strict government control over the economy, but it did so at a huge cost to civil liberties.

Selling the War

Throughout the war the government directed its coercion at people rather than industries, largely through the **Committee on Public Information** (CPI). Ably led by George W. Creel, the CPI created America's first propaganda agency. Creel immediately drafted a voluntary censorship agreement with newspapers to keep sensitive military information out of print. The CPI hired hundreds of musicians, writers, and artists to stage a patriotic campaign, sponsored 75,000 speakers who delivered four-minute war pep talks in vaudeville and movie theaters across the country, and got movie stars to sell war bonds.

Indeed, the CPI found a powerful ally in Hollywood. Quick to perceive the link between patriotism and profits, studio moguls cranked out scores of crude propaganda films with titles such as *The Prussian Cur, The Claws of the Hun,* and *To Hell with the Kaiser,* which reduced World War I to a conflict between good and evil, Allied heroes and Central Powers villains. Songwriters did their best to foster patriotism by pumping out a series of catchy tunes with titles like "Keep the Home Fires Burning" and "Over There."

Popular culture reflected the CPI's influence. Suddenly, dissent meant treason, Germans devolved into Huns, and all German Americans spied for the fatherland. At its best the CPI may have sold war bonds, discouraged war stoppages, and convinced the public to support the war; at its worst the CPI fostered a witch-hunt.

In the name of patriotism, musicians no longer played Bach and Beethoven, and schools stopped teaching the German language. Americans renamed sauerkraut "liberty cabbage"; dachshunds, "liberty hounds"; and German measles, "liberty measles." More alarming, vigilante groups attacked anyone suspected of being unpatriotic. Workers who refused to buy war bonds often suffered harsh retribution, and attacks on labor protesters were nothing short of brutal.

The legal system backed the suppression. German Americans became favored victims of mob violence. In one appalling instance, Robert Paul Praeger, a baker from Colinsville, Illinois, was lynched. Before the mob hanged him, they let him write a last note, which read: "Dear Parents, I must this day the fourth of April 1918 die. Please dear parents pray for me." A jury acquitted the lynch mob in less than half an hour, while a band played patriotic songs in the courthouse.

Political Repression

The government fueled the hysteria. In June 1917 Congress passed the **Espionage Act,** which gave postal officials the authority to ban newspapers and magazines from the mails and threatened individuals convicted of obstructing the draft with $10,000 fines and 20 years in jail. Congress passed the **Sedition Act** of 1918, which made it a federal offense to use "disloyal, profane, scurrilous, or abusive language" about the Constitution, the government, the American uniform, or the flag. The government prosecuted over 2100 people under these acts. Randolph Bourne's prediction that civil rights would fall victim to the power of the state rang true.

Political dissenters bore the brunt of the repression. Eugene V. Debs, who urged socialists to resist militarism, went to prison for nearly three years.

Hollywood and Tin Pan Alley did their parts to encourage patriotism by putting out a multitude of war films and a large number of music pieces like the one shown here.

Another Socialist, Kate Richards O'Hare served a year in prison for stating that the women of the United States were "nothing more nor less than brood sows, to raise children to get into the army and be made into fertilizer."

Labor radicals offered another ready target for attack. In July 1917 in Cochise County, Arizona, armed men, under the direction of a local sheriff, rounded up 1186 strikers at the Phelps Dodge copper mine. They placed these workers, many of Mexican descent, on railroad cattle cars without food or water, and left them in the New Mexico desert, 180 miles away. The *Los Angeles Times* editorialized: "The citizens of Cochise County have written a lesson that the whole of America would do well to copy."

The IWW never recovered from government attacks during World War I. In September 1917 the Justice Department staged massive raids on IWW officers, arresting 169 of its veteran leaders. The administration's purpose was, as one attorney put it, "very largely to put the IWW out of business."

The Supreme Court later approved the attacks on civil liberties. **Oliver Wendell Holmes,** the court's leading champion of civil liberties, upheld the Espionage Act in *Schenck v. United States* (1919), ruling that the conviction of Charles T. Schenck for distributing leaflets urging draftees to oppose the war did not violate Schenck's free speech rights. Holmes delivered the famous "clear and present danger" doctrine, which held that there are circumstances (like "a man

falsely shouting fire in a theater") that pose such a threat to public order that First Amendment protections do not apply. In *U.S. v. Debs* (1919), the court, with Holmes's support, again approved the Espionage Act, upholding the conviction of Eugene Debs, the Socialist Party leader, who opposed the war. In a third case, *Abrams v. United States* (1919), Holmes reversed himself, returning to his support for "free trade in ideas," but he was outvoted seven to two. The American Civil Liberties Union (ACLU) was founded during World War I to defend the First Amendment.

World War I did not *cause* repression, it merely intensified old fears. Many Americans clung to the image of the United States as a strong, isolated country, inhabited by old stock, white, middle-class Protestants. Their vision no longer reflected reality, but the war offered them a chance to lash out at those who had changed America. Immigrants, radical labor organizers, socialists, anarchists, Communists, and critics of any kind became victims of intolerance.

Wartime Reform

The war hysteria bred a curious alliance between superpatriots and old-style reformers. Prohibitionists had little difficulty turning World War I to their advantage. They had been winning victories at the state level since the middle of the nineteenth century, but they did not enjoy any success at the federal level until 1917 when Congress prohibited the use of grain

During the war, many women took jobs previously held by men. Here a group of women assemble an automobile in a factory.

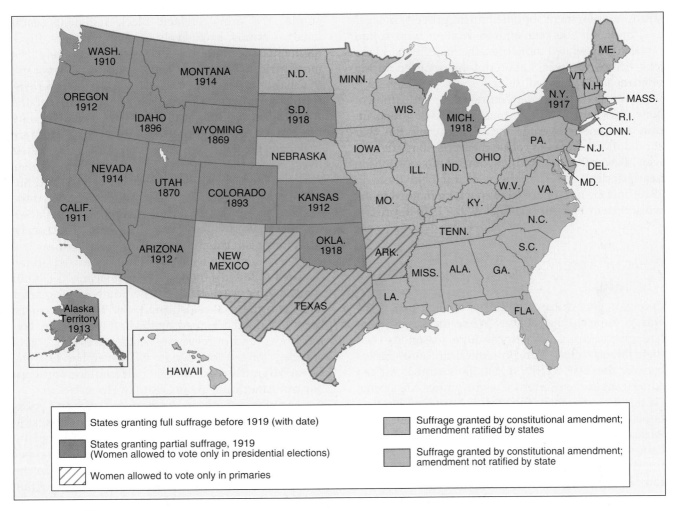

States granting full suffrage before 1919 (with date)

States granting partial suffrage, 1919
(Women allowed to vote only in presidential elections)

Women allowed to vote only in primaries

Suffrage granted by constitutional amendment;
amendment ratified by states

Suffrage granted by constitutional amendment;
amendment not ratified by state

Woman Suffrage

for the production of alcoholic beverages, insisting that foodstuffs must be used to feed America's soldiers and Allies. Prohibitionists joined the anti-German craze, warning that German Americans controlled the nation's breweries. Congress passed the **Eighteenth Amendment** in 1917 and the final state ratified the amendment two months after the armistice. The Volstead Act, which banned the manufacture, transportation, and sale of alcoholic beverages, took effect in 1920.

Like prohibition, women's suffrage benefited from the emergency atmosphere of World War I. Although radical suffragists, led by Alice Paul of the National Women's Party, refused to back the war as long as women could not vote, most women's organizations supported the war effort. Wilson appointed suffragists Carrie Chapman Catt and Anna Howard Shaw as directors of the Women's Committee of the Council of National Defense. Thousands of women joined the Red Cross and the American Women's Hospital Service and served overseas as nurses, physicians, clerks, and ambulance drivers. Thou-

sands more enlisted after the army established the Army Corps of Nurses in 1918.

Suffragists demanded the vote in return for their support of the war. Wilson had long opposed women's suffrage, but political reality ultimately forced his hand. Most western states had granted women the vote before he entered the White House. When Illinois fell in line in 1914, followed by Rhode Island and New York in 1917, pressure started building for national action. Alice Paul pressed the issue by organizing around-the-clock picketing in front of the White House. Determined to prevent women's suffrage from becoming a political issue in the congressional elections of 1918, Wilson told the Senate that the vote for women "is vital to the winning of the war." In 1919, shortly after the armistice, Congress passed the Nineteenth Amendment, granting women the right to vote. Ratification followed in the summer of 1920.

Apart from voting rights, World War I brought few permanent changes for women. Women had hoped the war would open new jobs for them. Instead, employment opportunities proved meager and brief. Of the one million women who found work in war-related industries, the majority had held jobs before the war. Labor unions opposed hiring women and tolerated their presence solely as a wartime necessity. As the Central Federated Union of New York put it: "The same patriotism which induced women to enter industry during the war should induce them to vacate their positions after the war." Fewer than half of the women who took jobs in heavy industry during the war still held them in 1919, and the number of women who remained in the workforce in 1920 dropped below the 1910 figures.

African Americans and the Great Migration

Like women, African Americans wanted to use the war to improve their status. While the government had given African Americans little reason to shed their blood, most African American newspapers backed the war. W. E. B. Du Bois urged African Americans to "close ranks" with whites, declaring, "If this is our country, then this is our war." Du Bois hoped that by demonstrating patriotism and bravery, African Americans could win public respect and earn better treatment after the war.

At first military leaders denied African Americans even the right to fight for their country. When the National Association for the Advancement of Colored People (NAACP) and other African American organizations protested, however, the army agreed to compromise. Following the Civil War ex-

ample, the army created black regiments commanded almost exclusively by white officers. Black regiments committed to battle fought bravely, but most African American soldiers in Europe never got the chance to prove their valor. Instead, they were assigned to move supplies. While two-thirds of the American Expeditionary Force saw combat, only one-fifth of African American troops did so. Even so, 14.4 percent of African American soldiers lost their lives, compared with 6.3 percent of white soldiers. African American soldiers faced segregation and humiliation. When the war ended, they were denied the right to march in the victory parade down Paris's Champs-Elysées boulevard, even though Africans from European colonies were permitted to do so.

Back home the record was equally mixed. In the decades following the Civil War a steady trickle of African Americans had left the South to search for jobs in northern cities. During World War I the trickle became a flood. Plagued by the boll weevil, low cotton prices, and unrelenting white repression, sharecroppers longed for change. By November 1918 the **Great Migration** had brought half a million southern African Americans to the "Land of Hope."

Many found jobs in northern factories and packing houses. The labor force in Chicago's packing houses had been 97 percent white in 1901, but by 1918 they employed 10,000 African Americans—over 20 percent of the workforce. The labor force in the northern steel industry had been virtually all white in 1900, but by 1920 African Americans held 10 percent of those jobs. Still, regardless of the industry, discrimination forced many to the bottom of the ladder, where they took over the menial, backbreaking

African American artist Jacob Lawrence commemorated the Great Migration of blacks from the rural South to the industrial cities of the North during the early decades of the twentieth century in his epic *Migration Series*, a series of sixty small paintings completed in 1941. Shown here is Panel 32, entitled "The railroad stations in the South were crowded with northbound travelers."

jobs that had been vacated by Slavic and Italian workers, the prior most recent wave of immigrants.

The Great Migration angered many Southerners. The price of cotton tripled during the war. Southern planters, fearing the loss of their labor force, resorted to intimidation and mob violence to stop the exodus. Like their ancestors who had taken the underground railroad to freedom, many African Americans who moved to the North during World War I had to travel under cover of darkness.

Northern whites opposed the Great Migration, too. Manufacturers welcomed the cheap labor (especially as strikebreakers), but most Northerners felt threatened by the newcomers. Middle-class whites feared changes in the racial composition of their society, while immigrants resented the competition for jobs and housing. Increasingly, Northerners turned to segregation, discrimination, and violence; and African Americans, hoping for a better life in the North, fought back. Race riots erupted in 26 cities in 1917, with the most serious violence occurring in East St. Louis, where at least 39 African Americans died in the fighting.

Clearly, World War I meant different things to different groups: for the administration, a test of the limits of voluntarism; for businessmen and technocrats, a chance to pull the levers of government; for nativists and superpatriots, an excuse to lash out at "undesirable" elements; for radicals and dissenters, repression and hardship; for manufacturers and farmers, high profits; for reformers, victories on women's suffrage and prohibition; for trade unions, the right to organize for better pay; and for African Americans, a chance to escape from southern poverty.

THE WAR FRONT

The United States entered World War I without a large army or the ships to transport one to Europe. Six weeks before Congress declared war, the army had not even drafted plans to organize a large military force. At first confident the Allies were winning, Wilson hoped to limit America's contribution to supplies, financial credit, and moral support. In truth, the Allies were ready to collapse. The French army was in the throes of mutiny. Soldiers were tired of suicidal assaults ordered by inept generals, and the submarine offensive had reduced Britain to a six-week supply of food.

The War at Sea

With the Allies ready to collapse due to huge casualties, low morale, and dwindling food supplies, Wilson ordered the United States Navy to act immediately. American ships relieved the British of patrolling the Western Hemisphere while another portion of the fleet steamed to the north Atlantic to combat the submarine menace. Six destroyers reached Ireland on May 4; 35 ships had arrived by July; and 343 ships were patrolling the seas surrounding England by the war's end.

To cut down losses of merchant ships, which in April alone totaled 881,027 tons, the Americans proposed a convoy system—using warships to escort merchant ships to Great Britain. By December the convoy system had cut losses in half.

Raising an Army

Wilson's choice to lead the American Expeditionary Force (AEF) was **Major General John J. "Black Jack" Pershing.** Despite urgent requests from Allied commanders, Pershing refused to send raw recruits to the front, and he rejected demands that American units be integrated into British and French regiments. Instead, Pershing insisted on keeping American troops as independent units under his command. To bolster Allied morale while the army trained, the War Department hurriedly dispatched the First Division to France, where it marched through Paris on July 4, 1917, to the cheers of thousands.

A bitter debate erupted over how to raise the troops. Despite heavy pressure from Theodore Roosevelt and others who favored a volunteer army, Wilson insisted on **conscription,** and Congress passed the Selective Service Act on May 18, 1917. More than 23 million men registered during World War I, and 2,810,296 draftees served in the armed forces.

To assign soldiers to the right military tasks, the army launched an ambitious program of psychological testing. "If the Army machine is to work smoothly and efficiently," declared **Robert M. Yerkes,** the man who presided over the effort, "it is as important to fit the job to the man as to fit the ammunition to the gun." Yerkes saw the war as an opportunity to establish the academic legitimacy of psychology by providing a vital service to the nation.

Though the tests supposedly measured native intelligence, in reality they favored men with the most schooling, and thus reinforced the class structure of American society. Native-born whites, who possessed academic skills, achieved the highest scores, while recent immigrants consistently scored lowest.

Apart from selecting officers, the army made little use of the test data. Ordinary soldiers were not assigned tasks on the basis of test scores. After the war, however, Yerkes boldly proclaimed that mental testing had "helped to win the war." All it really accomplished was to sell the public on the idea of mental testing and lay the groundwork for a thriving peacetime industry. After the war, numerous businesses adopted mental tests to screen personnel, and many colleges began requiring them for admission. Few legacies of the war had a more lasting or widespread impact on American society.

The Defeat of Germany

As the American army trained, the situation in Europe deteriorated. Mutiny within the French army was spreading (ten divisions were now in revolt); the eastern front dissolved in March when the Bolsheviks, who had seized power in Russia in November, accepted Germany's peace terms; and German and Austrian forces all but routed the Italian armies. In fact, by late 1917 the war had come down to a race between American mobilization and Germany's war machine.

On March 21, 1918, the Germans launched a massive offensive on the western front in the Valley of the Somme in France. For a time, it looked as though the Germans would succeed. Badly bloodied, the Allied forces lost ground. But with German troops barely 50 miles from Paris, Marshal Ferdinand Foch, the leader of the French army, assumed command of the Allied forces. Foch's troops, aided by 85,000 American soldiers, launched a furious counteroffensive, hitting the Germans hard in a series of bloody assaults. By the end of October the German army had been pushed back to the Belgian border.

During the final months of fighting, American troops hit Europe like a tidal wave. In June 279,000 American soldiers crossed the Atlantic; in July over 300,000; in August, 286,000. All told, 1.5 million American troops arrived in Europe during the last six months of the war.

Fresh and battle-ready, Pershing's forces made the crucial difference in the war. Germany had enjoyed numerical superiority when American troops first arrived, but by the end of the war the Allies could field 600,000 more men than the Germans. Buoyed by the fresh manpower, the Allies pressed their advantage. Their furious offensive in the summer of 1918 broke the opposition, and within a few months the Central Powers faced certain defeat. The Austro-Hungarian empire asked for peace; Turkey and Bulgaria stopped fighting; and Germany requested an armistice. In a direct slap at the kaiser, Wilson announced that he would negotiate only with a democratic regime in Germany. When the military leaders and the kaiser wavered, a brief revolution forced the kaiser to abdicate, and a civilian regime assumed control of the government.

Germany's new government immediately accepted the armistice and agreed to negotiate a treaty. At 11:00 A.M., November 11, 1918, the guns stopped.

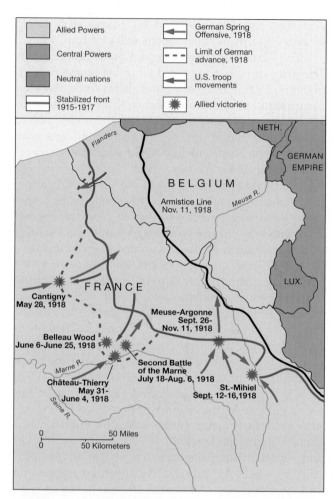

United States Participation on the Western Front

Throughout the Western world, crowds filled the streets to celebrate peace.

SOCIAL UNREST AFTER THE WAR

Peace did not restore stability to the United States. Jubilation over the armistice quickly dissolved into fear, unleashing the forces of conformity, vigilantism, and repression. Attacks centered on African Americans, organized labor, and political dissidents—the very groups old-stock citizens blamed for the changes in American society that they found most threatening. The Wilson administration led the attacks or did nothing to stop them, as government officials found new enemies at home to replace those abroad. Echoing Bourne's earlier warnings, Frederick Howe, the commissioner of immigration under President Wilson, later confided: "I became distrustful of the state. It seemed to want to hurt people; it showed no concern for innocence; it aggrandized itself and protected its powers by unscrupulous means."

Mounting Racial Tension

Race relations deteriorated badly after the war, as tensions rose in the North because of competition for jobs and housing. In the South, whites felt threatened by the return of 400,000 African American veterans, many of whom had been trained in the use of firearms, even if they had not seen actual combat. Moreover, many of the veterans had served in France, where they were treated as equals, and southern whites feared they would demand the same treatment at home. Determined to keep African Americans down, southern whites instituted a reign of terror. In 1919, 10 African American veterans were lynched (several still in uniform); 14 were burned at the stake. All told, 70 lynchings occurred in the first year of peace.

As the heat of summer brought tensions to a boil, race riots broke out in 25 cities. The worst violence erupted on a Chicago beach where 17-year-old Eugene Williams strayed into waters claimed by whites. A rock-throwing mob kept him from reaching shore, and Williams drowned. Fighting broke out when police refused to arrest his killers. Thirteen days of street violence followed, leaving 38 dead, 578 injured, and 1000 families homeless. Racial injustice remained a defining feature of American life throughout the Progressive Era, despite American efforts abroad to make the world "safe for democracy."

Labor Unrest and the Red Scare

Labor was another trouble spot. Most workers had demonstrated their patriotism by not striking during the war, but the armistice ended their truce with management. High inflation, job competition from returning veterans, and government policies all contributed to labor's discontent. Of the three, inflation hit workers the hardest. Food prices more than doubled between 1915 and 1920; clothing costs more than tripled. Wilson had made peace with trade unions only as a wartime necessity. After the fighting stopped, he removed wartime controls on industry, and business leaders closed ranks to roll back wartime concessions to workers.

The first strike came four days after the armistice, when textile workers in New York walked out for a 15-percent wage hike and a 44-hour workweek. To the surprise of most observers, the workers won. Many more strikes occurred in the months that followed. Strikers ranged from clothing workers to actors. By the end of 1919 more than 4 million workers (a staggering 20 percent of the workforce) had staged over 3600 strikes nationwide.

The strikes, however, left the labor movement in shambles. Well-established unions affiliated with the AFL came through the turmoil in good shape, but unions made up of unskilled workers in the mass production industries, such as the United Mine Workers or the steelworkers, went down for the count. The message was clear: without government backing, organized labor could not win against the united strength of antiunion employers.

The strikes frightened middle- and upper-class Americans, who feared the country might be swept by revolution. The government made matters worse by blaming the strikes on Communists. In 1919, Russian Bolsheviks called for socialists and workers in Europe and the United States to seize their governments and join the worldwide revolution. When Communist revolts erupted in eastern Europe, Americans braced themselves for trouble at home.

A bomb scare brought public fears to a head. On the eve of May 1 (May Day), 1919, authorities discovered 20 bombs in the mail of prominent capitalists, including John D. Rockefeller and J. P. Morgan, Jr., as well as government officials like Supreme Court justice Oliver Wendell Holmes. A month later, bombs exploded in eight American cities. Anarchists were probably responsible, but the public blamed the Communists.

Fear sparked by the labor unrest, Communism, and the bombings plunged the United States into the **Red Scare.** Every threat to national security, real or imagined, fed the public's anxiety. In Washington, D.C., in May 1919, a man who refused to stand during the Star Spangled Banner at a victory pageant was shot by an enraged sailor while the crowd cheered; in Hammond, Indiana, in February 1919, a jury took two minutes to acquit a man who had killed an immigrant for yelling "To Hell with the United States."

Vigilantism flourished as juries across the country acquitted individuals accused of violent acts against Communists. In the Washington lumber town of Centralia, American Legionnaires stormed the IWW office on Armistice Day. Four attackers died in the fight, and townspeople lynched an IWW member in reprisal. Federal officials then moved to break the IWW's back by prosecuting 165 Wobblie leaders, who received prison sentences of up to 25 years.

Congress joined the attack on radicalism. In May 1919 the House refused to seat **Victor Berger,** a Milwaukee Socialist, after he was convicted of sedition. The House again denied him his seat following a special election in December 1919. Not until his re-election in 1922, after the government had dropped its charges, did Congress seat him.

Attorney General **A. Mitchell Palmer** led the attack on radicalism. Determined to become president in 1920, Palmer hoped to ride a wave of public hysteria against radicalism into the White House. To root out sedition, he created a General Intelligence Division (the precursor of the Federal Bureau of Investigation) in the Justice Department under the direction of **J. Edgar Hoover.** Hoover collected the names of thousands of known or suspected Communists and made plans for a coordinated government attack on their headquarters.

In November 1919 Palmer struck with lightning speed at radicals in 12 cities. The raids netted 250 arrests, a small taste of what was to follow. A second series of raids in 33 cities came in January. This time Palmer's men arrested more than 4000 alleged Communists, many of whom were jailed without bond, beaten, and denied food and water for days. Local authorities freed most of them in a few weeks, except for 600 aliens, who were deported.

Palmer insisted he was ridding the country of the "moral perverts and hysterical neurasthenic women who abound in communism." To cooler heads, however, his tactics gave off the unmistakable odor of a police state. Suddenly on the defensive, Palmer tried to rally public support by predicting a second wave of terrorist attacks on May Day, 1920. Federal troops went on alert, and police braced themselves in cities across the country, but May Day came and went without incident. Suddenly Palmer looked more like dead

wood than presidential timber. His bid for the White House fizzled, and the Red Scare faded into memory.

THE TREATY OF VERSAILLES

Long before the war's military outcome became clear, the Allies started planning for peace, signing secret treaties and plotting harsh peace terms for Germany. Their schemes made a mockery of Wilson's call for "peace without victory." Wilson felt a punitive treaty would sow the seeds of future wars. He repeatedly elaborated his ideas on the interdependence of democracy, free trade, and liberty, and on January 8, 1918, he unveiled the **Fourteen Points,** his personal peace formula.

The Fourteen Points

Among other things, Wilson called for "open covenants openly arrived at," freedom of the seas, free trade, arms reduction, and self-determination. Other points demanded partial or full independence for minorities and a recognition of the rise of nationalist sentiments. The fourteenth point, which Wilson considered the heart of his plan, called for a **League of Nations,** an international organization to promote

---

TABLE 22.2
Woodrow Wilson's Fourteen Points, 1918: Success and Failure in Implementation

1. Open covenants of peace openly arrived at	Not fulfilled
2. Absolute freedom of navigation upon the seas in peace and war	Not fulfilled
3. Removal of all economic barriers to the equality of trade among nations	Not fulfilled
4. Reduction of armaments to the level needed only for domestic safety	Not fulfilled
5. Impartial adjustment of colonial claims	Not fulfilled
6. Evacuation of all Russian territory; Russia to be welcomed into the society of free nations	Not fulfilled
7. Evacuation and restoration of Belgium	**Fulfilled**
8. Evacuation and restoration of all French lands; return of Alsace-Lorraine to France	**Fulfilled**
9. Readjustment of Italy's frontiers along lines of Italian nationality	Compromised
10. Self-determination for the former subjects of the Austro-Hungarian Empire	Compromised
11. Evacuation of Romania, Serbia, and Montenegro; free access to the sea for Serbia	Compromised
12. Self-determination for the former subjects of the Ottoman empire; secure sovereignty for Turkish portion	Compromised
13. Establishment of an independent Poland, with free and secure access to the sea	**Fulfilled**
14. Establishment of a League of Nations affording mutual guarantees of independence and territorial integrity	Not fulfilled

Source: Data from G. M. Gathorne-Hardy, *The Fourteen Points and the Treaty of Versailles,* Oxford Pamphlets on World Affairs, no. 6, 1939); and Thomas G. Paterson et al., *American Foreign Policy, A History Since 1900,* 2nd ed., Vol. 2, pp. 282–293.

world peace by guaranteeing the territorial integrity of all nations.

Economically, the Fourteen Points projected Wilson's vision of liberal capitalism onto a world stage. His call for freedom of the seas and free trade was designed to protect free-market capitalism from monopolistic restrictions and open huge markets to booming American industries. Self-determination would offer independence to Europe's minorities and thereby delight millions of recent immigrants back in the United States, most of whom were drifting into the Democratic party. The League of Nations would enable the world to police aggression and spare the United States that responsibility.

When the tide of war turned in favor of the Allies in 1918, peace forces within Germany agreed to surrender on the basis of the Fourteen Points. They overthrew the kaiser's regime, paving the way for Wilson to make good on his promise of peace without victory.

Wilson's personal prestige peaked with the armistice. Europeans saw him as the moral leader of the Western democracies, and his authority rested not only on words but on might. Economically, the United States was now the most powerful nation on earth. It had been spared the devastation of war; its economy was booming; and its armed forces, in sharp contrast to Europe's exhausted armies, had barely geared up for battle.

Yet Wilson proved to be his own worst enemy in marshaling support for his peace plans. His first mistake was in asking voters to support Democratic candidates at the polls in 1918 if they wished him to continue as their "unembarrassed spokesman." His request offended the Republicans who had faithfully supported the administration throughout the war. When voters gave Republicans a narrow majority (primarily reflecting local issues), Wilson looked as if he had lost a national referendum on his leadership.

The American Peace Commission's composition further alienated Congress. Wilson elected to take personal responsibility for negotiating the peace, a role no previous president had assumed. In addition, he named only one Republican to the five-man commission; the other three men were loyal Democrats. The failure to include a prominent Republican senator, such as Henry Cabot Lodge of Massachusetts, the newly elected chairman of the powerful Senate Committee on Foreign Relations, was a serious tactical error. The treaty had to be approved by two-thirds of the Senate, and Republicans picked up five new Senate seats in the congressional elections of 1918, giving them a two-vote majority.

Discord Among the Victors

The delegates, who arrived in Europe early in January 1919, confronted three basic issues: territory, reparations, and future security. On each of these issues, Wilson and the Allies disagreed. Early in the war the Allies had decided to divide Germany's territorial possessions among themselves, but the Fourteen Points called for self-determination. Devastated by the war, the Allies (especially France) wanted to saddle Germany with huge reparations to pay for the war. The Fourteen Points rejected punishment, arguing it would only lead to future wars. On the issue of

Four of the five chief negotiators at the Paris Peace Conference charged with the task of drawing up the peace agreement following World War I were, seated from left in front row, Vittorio Orlando of Italy, David Lloyd George of Great Britain, Georges Clemenceau of France, and Woodrow Wilson of the United States. Missing from the picture is the fifth negotiator, Nobuaki Makino of Japan.

security, France wanted Germany dismembered while the other Allies favored treaties and alliances.

Only five nations played an important role in the proceedings (the Allies refused to allow Russia's Communist government to participate). Prime Minister David Lloyd George of Great Britain proved to be Wilson's staunchest ally, yet he also defended Britain's colonial ambitions and insisted on reparations. Premier Georges Clemenceau of France was determined to break up the German empire and bleed the German people dry in order to rebuild France. He wryly remarked, "God gave us the Ten Commandments and we broke them. Wilson gave us his Fourteen Points—we shall see."

Premier Vittorio Orlando of Italy was bent on pressing Italy's territorial ambitions in the Tyrol and on the Adriatic. When Wilson refused to sanction Italy's sovereignty over the largely Yugoslav population near Fiume, Orlando stormed out of the peace conference in disgust. The final important negotiator was Count Nobuaki Makino, the spokesman for Japan, who demanded control over German interests in the Far East. He also insisted upon a statement of racial equality in the League of Nations charter—a demand the Allies rejected.

The Russians were conspicuous by their absence at Versailles. Allied leaders, furious at the Bolsheviks for negotiating a separate peace with Germany at Brest-Litovsk in March 1918, refused to assign V. I. Lenin's "Red" government a place at the peace conference. Indeed, the Allies had earlier decided to intervene militarily in the Russian Revolution, and even as their spokesmen met in Versailles, Allied armies were fighting in Russia on the side of the "White," or anti-Communist, forces.

Personally, Wilson despised the Bolsheviks, and, in keeping with his response to Huerta's regime in Mexico, he refused to extend diplomatic recognition to Lenin's government. Moreover, much as he had with Mexico, Wilson did not stop to ponder how Russians would react to finding American soldiers on their soil. To help rescue Czech troops trapped by the Germans in northern Russia, Wilson sent 5000 American soldiers to the Soviet Union in 1918, where they joined British troops. The following year Wilson sent 9000 American troops to Siberia to help evacuate Czech troops through Vladivostok. Wilson hoped American troops in Russia would save the Czechs and discourage any Japanese designs on Siberia. In addition, he wanted this show of force to bolster the anti-Communist forces in Russia by weakening the Bolsheviks' claims to power. Consequently, the United States dragged its feet and did not withdraw its last troops from Russia until 1920.

The Bolsheviks deeply resented these heavy-handed efforts to undermine their regime. Yet the in-vasion of Russian soil by American troops was not the only reason for the intense hatred that developed between Lenin and Wilson. As the architect of the Bolshevik Revolution, Lenin emerged as Wilson's chief rival for world leadership. Where Wilson offered liberal democracy and limited social change, Lenin championed communism, social revolution, and swift changes. Wilson was determined to see his vision of the future, not Lenin's, carry the day at Versailles.

To achieve any treaty at all, Wilson had to compromise. Though he fought gallantly, he could not overcome the combined strength of his opponents. In the end he tried to scale down their demands and pinned his hopes on the League of Nations. Under the territorial compromise, the Allies gained control of Germany's colonies as "mandates" under the League of Nation's supervision. Japan acquired Germany's Pacific islands under mandate and assumed Germany's economic interest in China's Shantung peninsula. In eastern Europe, the delegates created the nation states of Poland, Yugoslavia, Czechoslovakia, Estonia, Latvia, Lithuania, and Finland. Europe's political map for the first time roughly resembled its linguistic and cultural map.

Security proved more difficult to negotiate. Over the misgivings of most delegates, Wilson insisted on making the League of Nations an integral part of the final treaty. Dubious that any international organization could protect its borders, France demanded a buffer zone. To satisfy Clemenceau, the delegates

Europe After World War I

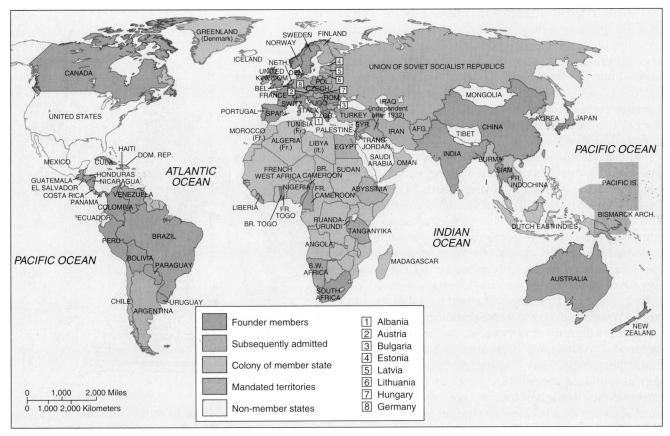

The League of Nations

gave France control over Alsace-Lorraine for 10 years and placed the coal-rich Saar Basin under the League of Nations for 15 years. After Wilson and Lloyd George both signed security treaties guaranteeing these arrangements, France grudgingly agreed to join the League of Nations.

Despite promises of a just peace, the treaty imposed a harsh settlement on Germany, saddling the country with a $34-billion reparations bill, far more than Germany could pay. In addition, Germany lost territories that contained German Alsace-Lorraine to France, the Saar Basin to a League protectorate, a corridor containing the port of Danzig to Poland, and Upper Silesia to Czechoslovakia. Moreover, under the terms of the war guilt clause in the reparations bill, Germany accepted the blame for World War I, agreed to dismantle its war machine, and pledged not to rearm in the future. Germany felt betrayed. Clearly, this was not a peace based upon the Fourteen Points. Rather, it brought to life Bourne's prediction of victors who "grab what they can."

Wilson derived no joy from the **Treaty of Versailles.** He accepted the treaty's territorial and punitive provisions in order to ensure the adoption of the League of Nations, which he hoped would secure world peace and eventually redress the treaty's inequities. The League consisted of a general assembly that included all member states and an executive council composed of the United States, Great Britain, France, Italy, Japan, and four other states to be elected by the assembly. But the heart of the League was clearly Article 10, which pledged all members "to respect and uphold the territorial integrity and independence of all members of the League." It embodied Wilson's dream of an international organization that would keep the peace by giving all nations (large and small) equality and protection.

The Struggle for Ratification

Wilson knew the treaty faced stiff opposition back home. In February 1919, 39 Senate Republicans had signed a petition warning they would not approve the League in its present form. To court domestic support, Wilson persuaded the delegates in Europe to acknowledge the Monroe Doctrine, omit domestic issues from the League's purview, and permit member states to withdraw after two years' notice. Though he worked to include provisions the Senate wanted, Wilson refused to separate the League from the treaty.

Senate opposition broke into three groups. The first, 14 "irreconcilables," were staunch isolationists who opposed the League of Nations in any form. Though their attack was broad-based, they concentrated their fire on Article 10, which called for the mutual protection of the territorial integrity of all member states. Critics charged that the article gave the League the authority to commit American troops to foreign military actions.

Henry Cabot Lodge of Massachusetts spoke for the second group of critics, the "strong reservationists." Parodying Wilson's "Fourteen Points," Lodge offered 14 amendments, called the "Lodge" reservations. The most important decreed that the United States "assumes no obligation" to protect the independence or territorial boundaries of any other nation, or to send American troops for such purposes unless Congress should so order. Lodge and his followers were basically in favor of the treaty and could have been won over if Wilson had agreed to their modifications.

The third group of opponents, the "limited reservationists," could have been assuaged by relatively minor alterations. They approached international affairs as cautious nationalists, favoring an independent foreign policy as the best tool for protecting American interests. With their backing and the support of Senate Democrats, the treaty would have passed easily.

As Wilson sailed back to the United States, polls suggested that most Americans favored the League in some form. All he had to do was compromise and the treaty would pass. Instead, Wilson descended on Washington in July itching for a fight. Dismissing his opponents as "blind and little provincial people," he declared that the "Senate must take its medicine." His use of a medical metaphor was telling, for Wilson's health had seriously deteriorated under the strain of the war.

Fearing Senate debate had eroded popular support for the treaty, Wilson decided to take his case directly to the people. Against his doctor's advice, he launched a nationwide tour in September 1919, covering 8000 miles in 33 days and delivering 32 major addresses. Totally exhausted, Wilson collapsed on September 25 in Pueblo, Colorado. Four days after returning to Washington, he suffered a severe stroke that paralyzed the left side of his body. Unable to work, he did not meet with his cabinet for more than six months. Since the law made no provision for removing an incapacitated president, Wilson's second wife, Edith Bolling Wilson, assisted by a few close aides, ran the government, operating under a cloak of silence about the president's condition.

As the Senate vote on the treaty drew near, Wilson remained intransigent, telling his wife: "Better a thousand times to go down fighting than to dip your colors to dishonorable compromise." He ordered all

The refusal of the Senate to ratify the Treaty of Versailles and join the League of Nations is satirized in this political cartoon.

Democrats to vote against the treaty if it contained any changes. On November 19, the Senate defeated the revised version of the treaty, 55 to 39; a few minutes later the Senate defeated the treaty without changes, 39 to 53.

The Senate's failure to reach a compromise must be blamed on Wilson. When the treaty's supporters tried again in March, many of the Democrats disobeyed the president and voted for a revised version. But 23 Democrats followed Wilson's orders, and the treaty fell 7 votes short of adoption. It would be wrong, however, to interpret the treaty's defeat as an endorsement of isolationism. In essence, the Senate rejected both isolationism and Wilsonian internationalism in favor of preserving a nationalistic foreign policy that would allow the United States to act independently.

The Election of 1920

Unable to accept defeat, Wilson decided to make the election of 1920 a "solemn referendum" on the League: the election of a Democrat would signify approval of the treaty; a Republican victory would mean the treaty's death. At best the president's proposal offered a dubious test of the public's support for the treaty. National elections rarely turn on a single issue.

When the Democratic convention met in San Francisco, the delegates ignored Wilson's pathetic anglings for a third term and nominated Governor James M. Cox of Ohio. To round out the ticket, they selected the assistant secretary of the navy, Franklin D. Roosevelt, for vice president, largely to capitalize on the magic Roosevelt name. The Republicans nominated Senator Warren G. Harding of Ohio. A stalwart party regular on domestic issues, Harding had voted for the Treaty of Versailles with the Lodge reservations.

While Cox barnstormed the country, campaigning unequivocally for the League of Nations and the Treaty of Versailles, Harding waffled on the issue. Tired of foreign crusades, the people wanted to repudiate Wilson's ardent internationalism, and they did just that, giving Harding 61 percent of the popular vote. (Eugene V. Debs, the Socialist candidate, won 919,799 votes, even though he was then serving a prison term for opposing American involvement in the war.) In the electoral college, Harding trounced Cox 404 to 127.

Wilson's fragile coalition of 1916 had collapsed. Many Democrats, disillusioned by the costs of the war, either stayed at home or switched parties. Angered by the Treaty of Versailles, ethnic Americans (Germans, Italians, and the Irish in particular) abandoned the Democrats in droves. Western states and the Midwest went Republican as well, for despite their wartime prosperity, many farmers believed that Wilson's agricultural policies had favored cotton growers in the South over grain producers of the Midwest. The Solid South remained a bastion of Democratic strength, but it did not have nearly enough votes to elect a president.

Harding interpreted his victory as a mandate to reject the League. America never joined the League of Nations, opening the way for those who later blamed the United States for the rise of fascism in Italy and Nazism in Germany. Critics, including a number of later historians, went so far as to claim that America's failure to join the League caused World War II. Instead of peace without victory, the war's main legacy turned out to be bitterness and suspicion.

CONCLUSION

World War I made Randolph Bourne a prophet. The changes in American life between 1914 and 1919 bore out his fear that war obliterates idealism and brings out the dark side of the human spirit. World War I accelerated social and economic changes, expanded the power of the federal government, and unleashed extraordinary fears that led to attacks on labor unions, African Americans, immigrants, Socialists, and Communists. Similar confusion gripped America's foreign policy. The United States emerged from the Great War as the premier economic power on earth, with global interests requiring protection. Tired and disillusioned, Americans attempted to flee their responsibilities rather than make global political commitments commensurate with their new economic interests.

The result was an upsurge in isolationist sentiment in the United States during the 1920s and 1930s

CHRONOLOGY OF KEY EVENTS

1914 World War I begins in Europe

1915 U.S. marines are dispatched to Haiti; German submarine sinks the British passenger ship *Lusitania*, killing 1198 passengers, including 128 Americans

1916 Germany promises to suspend unannounced submarine attacks in *Sussex* pledge

1917 Germany resumes submarine attacks; Zimmermann telegram, secret note to German ambassador in Mexico, proposing Mexico and Japan join Central Powers if the United States enters the war in Europe; United States enters the war; Espionage Act passed, imposing fines and jail sentences for aiding the enemy or obstructing recruit-

ment; Russian Revolution begins; War Industries Board is created to coordinate industrial production

1918 Wilson's Fourteen Points outline a plan for peace; National War Labor Board is created to arbitrate disputes between labor and management; Sedition Act passes, punishing any expression of disloyalty to the American government or flag; Germany surrenders

1919 Treaty of Versailles ends World War I

1920 In raids authorized by Attorney General Palmer many suspected Communists are arrested; Senate rejects Treaty of Versailles; Nineteenth Amendment grants women the right to vote; Republican Warren Harding is elected twenty-ninth president

that made it very difficult for America's leaders to respond strongly to the rise of despotic governments in Europe and the Far East. The Great War did not make the world "safe for democracy." It left humankind a legacy of bitterness, hatred, and suspicion, creating rich soil for the seeds of future conflicts.

In 1920, however, most Americans felt too tired and too disillusioned to give much thought to the future. Harding's promise of a return to "normalcy" struck a responsive chord. Millions of Americans thought he meant resurrecting rural villages and a small farm economy, restoring Anglo-Protestant culture, and forgetting about the rest of the world. The 1920s proved they were in for a surprise.

CHAPTER SUMMARY AND KEY POINTS

World War I killed more people—9 million combatants and 5 million civilians—and cost more money—$186 billion in direct costs and another $151 billion in indirect costs—than any previous war in history. In this chapter, you read about the war's causes; the reasons why the United States intervened in the conflict; how American industry and the military were mobilized for war, wartime propaganda and political repression; and the social changes and social unrest produced by the war.

- Triggered by the assassination of Archduke Franz Ferdinand, the heir to the throne of the Austro-Hungarian empire, World War I began in August 1914 when Germany invaded Belgium and France.

- Politically, World War I resulted in the downfall of four empires and contributed to the Bolshevik rise to power in Russia in 1917 and the triumph of fascism in Italy in 1922.

- The war allowed the United States to become the world's leading creditor and industrial power.

- The consequences of World War I included the mass murder of Armenians in Turkey and an influenza panepidemic that killed over 25 million people worldwide.

- Several events led to U.S. intervention in World War I: the sinking of the *Lusitania*, a British passenger liner; unrestricted German submarine warfare; and the Zimmermann note, which revealed a German plot to provoke Mexico to war against the United States.

- Millions of American men were drafted and Congress created a War Industries Board to coordinate production and a National War Labor Board to unify labor policy.

- The Treaty of Versailles deprived Germany of territory and forced it to pay reparations. President Wilson agreed to the treaty because it provided for establishment of a League of Nations, but he was unable to persuade the Senate to ratify the treaty.

SUGGESTIONS FOR FURTHER READING

Lloyd Ambrosus, *Woodrow Wilson and the American Diplomatic Tradition* (1988). Presents a comprehensive account of American diplomacy during and after the war.

Modris Eksteins, *Rites of Spring: The Great War and the Birth of the Modern Age* (1989). A look at the lasting impact of World War I on American society.

Robert H. Ferrell, *Woodrow Wilson and World War I, 1917–1921*, (1985). Study of President Wilson's approach and reaction to World War I.

Martin Gilbert, *The First World War* (1994). Discusses the conflict's causes and fighting.

Lewis L. Gould, *Reform and Regulation: American Politics from Roosevelt to Wilson* (1996). A look at the national politics from the Progressive Era to World War I through the presidencies of Theodore Roosevelt and Woodrow Wilson.

David M. Kennedy, *Over Here: The First World War and American Society* (1980). Examines the war's impact on the homefront.

Kathleen Kennedy, *Disloyal Mothers and Scurrilous Citizens: Women and Subversion During World War I.* (1999). Study of the repressive policies of the World War I era in relation to women's role in protesting American involvement in the war.

Michael J. Lyons, *World War I* (1994). Offers a comprehensive account of the conflict.

Herbert F. Margulies, *The Mild Reservations and the League of Nations Controversy in the Senate* (1989). Explores the reasons the Senate rejected American membership in the League of Nations.

Arthur Walworth, *Wilson and His Peacemakers: American Diplomacy at the Paris Peace Conference* (1986). Examines the contentious debates surrounding the Treaty of Versailles.

Novels

Erich Maria Remarque, *All Quiet on the Western Front* (1930).

Ernest Hemingway, *A Farewell to Arms* (1927).

MEDIA RESOURCES

Web Sites

Bill Haywood Trial (1907)
http://www.law.umkc.edu/faculty/projects/ftrials/haywood/haywood.htm

This site contains images, chronology, and court and official documents maintained by Dr. Doug Linder at University of Missouri–Kansas City Law School.

World War I Document Archive
http://www.lib.byu.edu/~rdh/wwi/
This archive contains sources about World War I in general, not just America's involvement.

The Great Influenza Epidemic
http://www.pbs.org/wgbh/pages/amex/influenza/
This PBS site reveals the impact of the flu epidemic of 1918.

Documents from the Women's Liberation Movement
http://scriptorium.lib.duke.edu/wlm/
Primary documents on-line from the Special Collections Library at Duke University provide firsthand information about the women's liberation movement.

The Women's Suffrage Movement
http://www.rochester.edu/SBA/hisindx.html
This site includes a chronology, important texts relating to women's suffrage, and biographical information on Susan B. Anthony and Elizabeth Cady Stanton.

World War One: Trenches on the Web
http://www.worldwar1.com/index.html
This site provides a mass of data concerning the prosecution of the world's first global war.

The Great Migration in Chicago
http://lcweb.loc.gov/exhibits/african/afam011.html
This site looks at the black experience in the Great Migration through the lens of one prominent destination.

National Geographic and the *Titanic*
http://www.nationalgeographic.com/society/ngo/explorer/titanic/movie.html
This site offers historical perspective and balanced coverage of this tragic event.

Films and Videos

World War I. A&E Home Video. Documentary narrated by Richard Karn.

World War I. CBS (1994) Documentary narrated by Robert Ryan.

World War I and the Shaping of the Twentieth Century (1997). PBS. Documentary of World War I and its impact on the rest of the century.

KEY TERMS

Allies   (p. 617)
Neutrality   (p. 618)
Central Powers   (p. 618)

Submarine warfare   (p. 619)
Lusitania   (p. 619)
Sussex pledge   (p. 622)
Peace without victory   (p. 623)
Zimmermann telegram   (p. 623)
War cabinet   (p. 624)
Hooverizing   (p. 625)
Industrial Workers of the World   (p. 626)
Committee on Public Information   (p. 627)
Espionage Act   (p. 627)
Sedition Act   (p. 627)
Eighteenth Amendment   (p. 629)
Great Migration   (p. 630)
Conscription   (p. 631)
Red Scare   (p. 633)
Fourteen Points   (p. 634)
League of Nations   (p. 634)
Treaty of Versailles   (p. 637)

PEOPLE YOU SHOULD KNOW

Randolph Silliman Bourne   (p. 613)
Vladimir I. Lenin   (p. 618)
William Jennings Bryan   (p. 618)
Walter Hines Page   (p. 618)
Bernard M. Baruch   (p. 624)
Oliver Wendell Holmes   (p. 628)
Major General John J. "Black Jack" Pershing   (p. 631)
Robert M. Yerkes   (p. 631)
Victor Berger   (p. 633)
A. Mitchell Palmer   (p. 633)
J. Edgar Hoover   (p. 634)

REVIEW QUESTIONS

1. Could the United States have avoided entering the war?
2. Did World War I propaganda serve as a mobilizing or a suppressing force for Americans?
3. How did President Wilson ensure the participation of American industry in World War I?
4. How did World War I differ from previous wars?
5. Why did the end of World War I bring tension to the homefront?
6. Was Congress justified in rejecting the League of Nations?

23 Modern Times, 1920–1929

MARGARET SANGER, BIRTH CONTROL PIONEER

In 1898 the Physicians Club of Chicago held a symposium on "sexual hygiene" to give its members some practical tips on marriage counseling. To those married women who wanted information on birth control, Chicago physicians were to offer this advice: "Get a divorce and vacate the position for some other woman, who is able and willing to fulfill all a wife's duties as well as to enjoy her privileges."

Most Americans shared this view. To the male custodians of morality, birth control challenged patriarchy. It would lead to sexual promiscuity and an epidemic of venereal diseases, they charged, and weaken the family by raising the divorce rate. Many women condemned birth control just as soundly. Taught from childhood to embrace the cult of domesticity, they accepted childbearing as their "biological duty" and rejected birth control as immoral and radical.

Yet by 1950 most Americans regarded birth control as a public virtue rather than a private vice. The person most responsible for this amazing transformation was Margaret Sanger, a tireless crusader who possessed an iron will and the soul of a firebrand. Sanger's mother, Margaret Higgins, bore 11 children, all weighing ten pounds or more; Michael Higgins, her father, worked as a stonecutter. Her mother died of pulmonary tuberculosis at 43; her father lived to 84. For the rest of her life, Sanger blamed her mother's suffering on the absence of effective family planning.

An unhappy marriage also pushed Sanger toward reform work. While still in nursing school, she married William Sanger, an architect and would-be artist. After bearing three children in rapid succession, Sanger overcame her own struggle with tuberculosis, finished school, and began a nursing career. Feeling trapped by married life and determined to achieve her own identity, Margaret plunged into New York's labor movement.

Convinced that large families placed a terrible economic burden on poor people, Sanger came to regard family planning as the most important issue of her day because it could make abortion, as well as unwanted babies, unnecessary. When male labor leaders refused to add contraception to their reform agenda, Sanger left the labor movement, resolving to make birth control her life's work.

From 1914 to 1937 Sanger campaigned to make birth control morally acceptable. She built a network of clinics where women could get accurate information

Margaret Sanger, a nurse who had watched many women suffer from unwanted births and die from illegal abortions, was one of the founders of the modern American birth control movement. After spending a year studying medical literature and learning about contraceptives, Sanger began publishing the journal *The Woman Rebel*.

about contraception and obtain inexpensive, reliable birth control devices. After World War II she helped organize the international planned parenthood movement and played a major role in the development of "the pill." Through her birth control work, Margaret Sanger probably had a greater influence on the world than any other American woman of her day.

Sanger played a major role in the transition to modern times. By promoting birth control, she helped alter American sexual behavior, redefine women's role in society, and redistributed power within the family. But the birth control movement represented just one symptom of a society in flux, one in which urban growth, ethnic diversity, and economic development set the stage for controversy.

The 1920s was a decade of exciting social changes and deep cultural conflicts. The most obvious signs of change were the growth of cities, with their huge ethnic populations; the rise of a consumer-oriented economy, evident in the spread of cars, electricity, and a host of new appliances; and the spread of mass entertainment, such as spectator sports, radio, and the movies. But a deeper transformation was also under way, a "revolution in morals and manners." Sexual mores and gender roles underwent dramatic shifts.

For many Americans, these changes represented a liberation from the restrictions of the country's Victorian past. But for others, especially those who lived in the more rural and provincial parts of the country, morals seemed to be decaying and the United States seemed to be changing in undesirable ways. The result was a thinly veiled "cultural civil war," in which a pluralistic society clashed bitterly over such issues as foreign immigration, evolution, and race.

Wets battled drys, Darwinists ridiculed fundamentalists, nativists denounced the "new immigrants," and rural folks decried the dubious morals of city dwellers. None of these disputes was new. Each was a continuing, if sharpening, controversy that had been building for decades. At bottom, these conflicts were the unavoidable growing pains of a nation struggling to come to grips with cultural pluralism and changing values.

THE EMERGENCE OF MODERN AMERICA

Americans in the 1920s were the first to wear ready-made, exact-sized clothing, the first to play electric phonographs or use electric vacuum cleaners or listen to commercial radio broadcasts or drink fresh orange juice year round. In countless ways, large and small, American life was transformed during the 1920s, at least in the nation's growing towns and cities, where the majority of Americans now lived. Cigarettes, cosmetics, and synthetic fabrics such as rayon became staples of American life. Public opinion polling, sex education, newspaper gossip columns, illuminated billboards, commercial airplane flights—all were novelties during the 1920s. In that decade, the United States became a modern consumer society.

Urban Growth

For more than four decades, the Empire State Building was the largest building in the world, rising 102 stories above New York City's Fifth Avenue. The 1454-foot-high building cost nearly $41 million to erect, but when it was finished in 1930, it stood half-empty—a symbol of a decade's broken dreams.

All across America, urban skylines were transformed. Urban growth drove up land values and reshaped the skyline of America's cities, especially in central business districts, where office space more than doubled during the 1920s. Skyrocketing land prices forced architects to build "up" instead of "out," launching the first great era of skyscrapers. By 1929, the United States had 377 buildings with more than 20 stories.

According to the census of 1920 more Americans dwelled in cities than in the country. For the first time in its history, the United States became a predominantly urban society. Most urbanites lived in small towns and cities, but a surprising number resided in rapidly growing large cities, like Chicago, of 50,000 or more.

America's cities attracted large numbers of new immigrants from southern and eastern Europe. These immigrants poured into the industrial cities of the Northeast and Midwest, filling them with new sights, sounds, and smells that many old-stock Americans found offensive. World War I briefly stopped the flow of immigrants, but after the armistice another 3.2 million immigrants poured into the United States before the country restricted entry.

Growth of Chicago

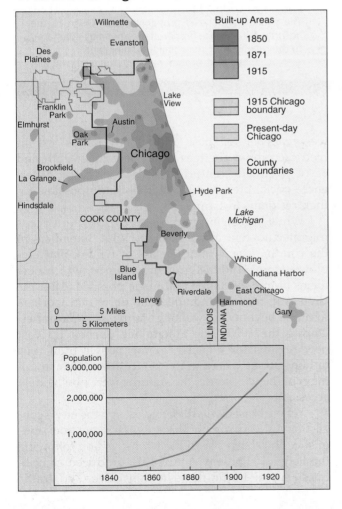

African American Population, 1910 and 1950

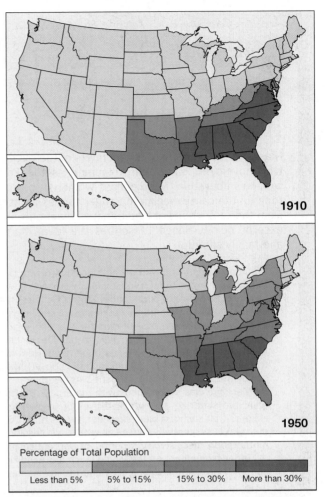

The racial composition of the nation's cities also underwent a decisive change. In 1910, urban areas outside the South were overwhelmingly white; three out of every four African Americans lived on farms and nine out of ten lived in the South. World War I changed that profile. Hoping to escape tenant farming, sharecropping, and peonage, 1.5 million southern African Americans moved to cities in the 1920s. Some went to southern cities, but most settled in major northern metropolises such as New York, Philadelphia, Cleveland, and Chicago. During the 1910s and 1920s, Chicago's African American population grew 148 percent, Cleveland's by 307 percent, Detroit's by 611 percent.

During this massive movement of people, competition for available housing became a major source of friction. In city after city, whites closed ranks against African Americans, blocking access to white neighborhoods. Cities passed municipal residential segregation ordinances; white realtors refused to show houses in white areas to African Americans; and white property owners formed "neighborhood

THE PEOPLE SPEAK

Margaret Sanger, "Happiness in Marriage" (1926)

Margaret Sanger, one of the founders of the birth control movement, saw family planning as the key to women's liberation. Middle-class women in particular took up the cause, seeing in Sanger's ideas an escape from the restrictions of traditional womanhood. In the excerpt below, Sanger describes the ideal marriage and family situation.

We must recognize that the whole position of womanhood has changed today. Not so many years ago it was assumed to be a just and natural state of affairs that marriage was considered as nothing but a preliminary to motherhood. A girl passed from the guardianship of her father or nearest male relative to that of her husband. She had no will, no wishes of her own. Hers not to question, but merely to fulfil duties imposed upon her by the man into whose care she was given.

Marriage was synonymous with maternity. But the pain, the suffering, the wrecked lives of women and children that such a system caused, show us that it did not work successfully. Like all other professions, motherhood must serve its period of apprenticeship.

Today women are on the whole much more individual. They possess as strong likes and dislikes as men. They live more and more on the plane of social equality with men. They are better companions. We should be glad that there is more enjoyable companionship and real friendship between men and women.

This very fact it is true, complicates the marriage relation, and at the same time ennobles. Marriage no longer means the slavish subservience of the woman to the will of the man. It means, instead, the union of two strong and highly individualized natures. Their first problem is to find out just what the terms of this partnership are to be. Understanding full and complete cannot come all at once, in one revealing flash. It takes time to arrive at a full and sympathetic understanding of each other, and mutually to arrange lives to increase this understanding. Out of the mutual adjustments, harmony must grow and discords gradually disappear.

These results cannot be obtained if the problem of parenthood is thrust upon the young husband and wife before they are spiritually and economically prepared to meet it. For naturally the coming of the first baby means that all other problems must be thrust aside. That baby is a great fact, a reality that must be met. Preparations must be made for its coming. The layette must be prepared. The doctor must be consulted. The health of the wife may need consideration. The young mother will probably prefer to go to the hospital. All of these preparations are small compared to the regime after the coming of the infant.

Now there is a proper moment for every human

---

improvement associations," largely in order to keep African Americans out. After the Supreme Court declared municipal resident segregation ordinances unconstitutional in 1917, whites resorted to the **restrictive covenant,** a formal deed restriction that bound white property owners in a given neighborhood to sell only to whites. Those who broke such agreements could be sued by "damaged" neighbors. Not until 1948 did the Supreme Court strike down restrictive covenants. Zoning laws offered an even more subtle way of segregating cities. Originally designed to keep businesses and industry out of residential neighborhoods, zoning restrictions had become the tool of choice for segregating people on the basis of wealth by the 1930s.

Racial animosity, restrictive covenants, and zoning restrictions confined African Americans to certain neighborhoods. The decade following World War I saw the development of scores of American cities within cities. The largest was Harlem, in upper Manhattan; 200,000 African Americans lived in a neighborhood that had been virtually all white fifteen years before. These "black metropolises" resembled the ethnic ghettoes of the late nineteenth and early twentieth centuries, with one major difference—racial prejudice made it all but impossible for their residents to escape.

While a growing number of African Americans migrated to central cities, many white members of the country's new middle class of white-collar employees moved to fast-growing suburbs, which new forms of transportation had made possible. After the Civil War, trolleys and streetcars permitted workers to move beyond the walking radius of the factories. During the 1920s, the automobile opened up vast new regions for housing, giving people numerous options about where to live. Once the exclusive domain of the well-to-do, the suburbs were now widely accessible.

Yet optimists who hoped to escape the city's congestion by moving to the suburbs were too optimistic. The sharp rise in road construction following the Federal Highway Act of 1916 produced complicated lateral traffic flows within cities, and traffic

activity, a proper season for every step in self-development. The period for cementing the bond of love is no exception to this great truth. For only by the full and glorious living through these years of early marriage are the foundations of an enduring and happy married life rendered possible. By this period the woman attains a spiritual freedom. Her womanhood has a chance to bloom. She wins a mastery over her destiny; she acquires self-reliance, poise, strength, a youthful maturity. She abolishes fear. Incidentally, few of us realize, since the world keeps no repugnance by young mothers who are the victims of undesired maternity. Nor has science yet determined the possibilities of a generation conceived and born of conscious desire.

In the wife who has lived through a happy marriage, for whom the bonds of passionate love have been fully cemented, maternal desire is intensified and matured. Motherhood becomes for such a woman not a penalty or a punishment, but the road by which she travels onward toward completely rounded self-development. Motherhood thus helps her toward the unfolding and realization of her higher nature.

Her children are not mere accidents, the outcome of chance. When motherhood is a mere accident, as so often it is in the early years of careless or reckless marriages, a constant fear of pregnancy may poison the days and nights of the young mother. Her marriage is thus converted into a tragedy. Motherhood becomes for her a horror instead of a joyfully fulfilled function.

Instead of being a self-determined and self-directing love, everything is henceforward determined by the sweet tyranny of the child. I have known of several young mothers, despite a great love for the child, to rebel against this intolerable situation. Vaguely feeling that this new maternity has rendered them unattractive to their husbands, slaves to a deadly routine of bottles, baths and washing, they have revolted. I know of innumerable marriages which have been wrecked by premature parenthood.

Love has ever been blighted by the coming of children before the real foundations of marriage have been established. Quite aside from the injustice done to the child who has been brought accidentally into the world, this lamentable fact sinks into insignificance when compared to the injustice inflicted by chance upon the young couple, and the irreparable blow to their love occasioned by premature or involuntary parenthood.

For these reasons, in order that harmonious and happy marriage may be established as the foundation for happy homes and the advent of healthy and desired children, premature parenthood must be avoided. Birth Control is the instrument by which this universal problem may be solved.

Source: Margaret Sanger, *Happiness in Marriage,* 1926. Reprinted by permission.

congestion got worse. City planners counterattacked with traffic circles, synchronized stoplights, and divided dual highways, but nothing could free motorists from rush hour and holiday traffic jams.

The Rise of a Consumer Economy

Two automotive titans—**Henry Ford** and Alfred Sloan—symbolized the profound transformations that took place in American industry during the 1910s and 1920s. In 1913, the 50-year-old Ford revolutionized American manufacturing by introducing the automated assembly line. By using conveyor belts to bring automobile parts to workers, he reduced the assembly time for a Ford car from 12½ hours in 1912 to just 1½ hours in 1914. Declining production costs allowed Ford to cut prices—six times between 1921 and 1925, reducing a new Ford's cost to just $290. This was less than three months wages for an average American worker, and it made cars affordable for the average family. To lower employee turnover and raise productivity, Ford also introduced a minimum daily wage of $5 in 1914—twice what most workers earned—and shortened the workday from nine hours to eight. Twelve years later, Ford reduced his workweek from six days to five. Ford demonstrated the logic of mass production: expanded production allows manufacturers to reduce costs and therefore increase the number of products sold, and higher wages allow workers to buy more products.

Alfred Sloan, the president of General Motors from 1923 to 1941, built his company into the world's largest automaker not by refining the production process but by adopting new approaches to advertising and marketing. Sloan summed up his philosophy with these blunt words: "The primary object of the corporation was to make money, not just make cars." Unlike Ford, a farmer's son who wanted to produce an inexpensive, functional vehicle with few frills, Sloan was convinced that Americans were willing to pay extra for luxury and prestige. He advertised his cars as symbols of wealth and status, and in 1927 introduced the yearly model change, to convince motorists to trade in old models for newer ones with flashier styling. He also developed a series of divisions that were differentiated by status, price, and level of luxury, with Chevrolets less expensive than Buicks or Cadillacs. To make his cars affordable, he set up the nation's first national consumer credit agency in 1919. If Henry Ford demonstrated the efficacy of mass production, Sloan revealed the importance of merchandising in a modern consumer society.

Cars were the symbol of the new consumer society that emerged in the 1920s. In 1919, there were just 6.7 million cars on American roads. By 1929, there were more than 27 million—nearly one car for every household in the United States. With car manufacturers and banks encouraging the public to buy the car of their dreams on credit, the American love affair with the car truly began. A quarter of all American families purchased a car in 1929. About 60 percent bought it on credit, often paying interest rates of 30 percent or more.

Cars revolutionized the American way of life. Enthusiasts claimed the automobile promoted family togetherness through evening rides, picnics, and weekend excursions. Critics decried squabbles between parents and teenagers over use of the automobile, and an apparent decline in church attendance resulting from Sunday outings. Worst of all, charged critics, automobiles gave young people freedom and privacy, serving as "portable bedrooms" that couples could take anywhere.

The automobile also transformed the American landscape, quickly obliterating all traces of the horse and buggy past. During the 1920s, the country doubled its system of roads and highways. The nation spent over $2 billion annually building and maintaining roads; by 1929 there were 852,000 miles of roads in the United States, compared to just 369,000 in 1920. The car also brought with it pollution, congestion, and nearly 30,000 traffic deaths a year.

The automobile industry provided an enormous stimulus for the national economy. By 1929, the industry produced 12.7 percent of all manufacturing output, and employed 1 out of every 12 workers. Automobiles in turn stimulated the growth of steel, glass, and rubber industries, along with gasoline stations, motor lodges, campgrounds, and the hotdog stands that dotted the nation's roadways.

Other emblems of the consumer economy were the telephone and electricity. As more and more of America's homes received electricity, new appliances followed—refrigerators, washing machines, vacuum cleaners, and toasters quickly took hold. Advertisers claimed that "labor-saving" appliances would ease the sheer physical drudgery of housework, but they did not shorten the average housewife's workweek. Women now had to do more because standards of cleanliness kept rising. Sheets had to be changed weekly; the house had to be vacuumed daily. In short, social pressure expanded household chores to keep pace with the new technology. Far from liberating women, appliances imposed new standards and pressures.

Ready-to-wear clothing was another important innovation in America's expanding consumer economy. During World War I, the federal government defined standard clothing sizes to help the nation's garment industry meet the demand for military uniforms. Standard sizes meant that it was now possible to mass-produce ready-to-wear clothing. Since there was no copyright on clothing designs until the 1950s, garment manufacturers could pirate European fashions and reproduce them using less expensive fabrics.

Even the public's eating habits underwent far-reaching shifts, as Americans began to consume fewer starches (like bread and potatoes) and more fruit and sugar. But the most striking development was the shift toward processed foods. Important innovations in food processing occurred during World War I, as manufacturers learned how to efficiently

This 1926 ad for Campbell's vegetable soup notes how the food processing company has not only provided a rich and hearty soup but also saved the homemaker the time it would have taken to prepare the soup's 32 ingredients.

can and freeze foods. Processed foods saved homemakers enormous amounts of time in peeling, grinding, and cutting.

Accompanying the rise of new consumer-oriented businesses were profound shifts in the ways that business operated. To stimulate sales and increase profits, businesses expanded advertising, offered installment credit, and created the nation's first regional and national chains.

The nation's first million-dollar advertising campaign was for Uneeda Biscuits and its patented waterproof box, demonstrating the power of advertising. During the 1920s, advertising agencies hired psychologists to design the first campaigns. They touted products by building up name-brand identification, creating memorable slogans, manipulating endorsements by doctors or celebrities, and appealing to consumers' hunger for prestige and status. By 1929, American companies were spending $3 billion annually to advertise their products, five times more than in 1914.

The use of installment credit soared during the 1920s. Banks offered the country's first home mortgages, while manufacturers of everything from cars to irons allowed consumers to pay "on time." About 60 percent of all furniture and 75 percent of all radios were purchased on the installment plan. In contrast to a Victorian society that had placed a high premium on thrift and saving, the new consumer society emphasized spending and borrowing.

A fundamental shift took place in the American economy during the 1920s. The nation's families spent a declining proportion of their income on necessities—food, clothing, and utilities—and an increasing share on appliances, recreation, and a host of new consumer products. As a result, older industries, such as textiles, railroads, and steel, declined, while newer industries, such as appliances, automobiles, aviation, chemicals, entertainment, and processed foods, surged ahead rapidly.

During the 1920s, the chain-store movement revolutionized retailing. Chains like Woolworths, five-and-dime stores, multiplied across the country. Besides drugstore and cigar-store chains, there were also interlocking networks of banks and utility companies. These banks and utilities played a critical role in promoting the financial speculation of the late 1920s that would become one of the causes of the Great Depression.

THE FORMATION OF MODERN AMERICAN CULTURE

Many of the defining features of modern American culture emerged during the 1920s. The best-seller, the book club, the record chart, the radio, the talking picture, and spectator sports all became popular forms of mass entertainment. But the primary reason the 1920s stand out as one of the most important periods in American cultural history is because the decade produced a generation of artists, musicians, and writers who were among the most innovative and creative in the country's history.

Mass Entertainment

Of all the new appliances to enter the nation's homes during the 1920s, none had a more revolutionary impact than radio. Sales soared from $60 million in 1922 to $426 million in 1929. The first commercial radio station began broadcasting in 1919, and during the 1920s, the nation's airwaves were filled with musical variety shows and comedies.

Radio drew the nation together by bringing news, entertainment, and advertisements to more than ten million households. Radio blunted regional differences and imposed similar tastes and lifestyles. No other media had the power to create heroes and villains so quickly; when **Charles Lindbergh** became the first person to fly nonstop across the Atlantic from New York to Paris in 1928, the radio brought his incredible feat into American homes, transforming him into a celebrity overnight.

Radio also brought the nation decidedly unheroic images. The nation's most popular radio show, *"Amos 'n Andy,"* which first aired in 1926 on Chicago's WMAQ, spread vicious racial stereotypes into homes whose white occupants knew little about African Americans. Other minorities fared no better. The Italian gangster and the tightfisted Jew became stock characters in radio programming.

The phonograph was not far behind the radio in importance. The 1920s saw the record player enter American life in full force. Piano sales sagged as phonograph production rose from just 190,000 in 1923 to 5 million in 1929.

The popularity of jazz, blues, and "hillbilly" music fueled the phonograph boom. Novelist F. Scott Fitzgerald called the 1920s the **"Jazz Age"**—and the decade was truly jazz's golden age. Duke Ellington wrote the first extended jazz compositions; Louis Armstrong popularized "scat" (singing of nonsense syllables); Fletcher Henderson pioneered big band jazz; and trumpeter Jimmy McPartland and clarinetist Benny Goodman popularized the Chicago school of improvisation.

The blues craze erupted in 1920, when a black singer named Mamie Smith released a recording called "Crazy Blues." The record became a sensation, selling 75,000 copies in a month and a million copies in seven months. Recordings by Ma Rainey, the "Mother of the Blues," and Bessie Smith, the "Empress of the Blues," brought the blues, with its poignant and defiant reaction to life's sorrows, to a vast audience.

"Hillbilly" music broke into mass culture in 1923, when a Georgia singer named "Fiddlin' John" Carson sold 500,000 copies of his recordings. "Country" music's appeal was not limited to the rural South or West; city people, too, listened to country songs, reflecting a deep nostalgia for a simpler past.

The single most significant new instrument of mass entertainment was the movies. Movie attendance soared, from 50 million patrons a week in 1920 to 90 million weekly in 1929. Americans spent 83 cents of every entertainment dollar going to the movies—and three-fourths of the population went to a movie theater every week.

During the late teens and 1920s, the film industry took on its modern form. In cinema's earliest days, the film industry was based in the nation's theatrical center—New York. By the 1920s, the industry had relocated to Hollywood, drawn by cheap land and labor, the ready accessibility of varied scenery, and a climate ideal for year-round filming. Each year, Hollywood released nearly 700 movies, dominating worldwide film production. By 1926, Hollywood had captured 95 percent of the British and 70 percent of the French markets.

A small group of companies consolidated their control over the film industry and created the "studio system" that would dominate film production for the next thirty years. Paramount, 20th-Century Fox, MGM, and other studios owned their own production facilities, ran their own worldwide distribution networks, and controlled theater chains committed to showing their companies' products. In addition, they kept certain actors, directors, and screenwriters under contract.

The popularity of the movies soared as films increasingly featured glamour, sophistication, and sex appeal. New kinds of movie stars appeared: the mysterious sex goddess, personified by Greta Garbo; the passionate hot-blooded lover, epitomized by Rudolph Valentino; and the flapper, with her bobbed hair and skimpy skirts. New film genres also debuted, including swashbuckling adventures, sophisticated comedies, and tales of flaming youth and the new sexual freedom. Americans flocked to see Hollywood spectacles such as Cecil B. DeMille's *Ten Commandments* (1923) with its "cast of thousands" and dazzling special effects.

Like radio, movies created a new popular culture, with common speech, dress, behavior, and heroes. And like radio, Hollywood did its share to reinforce

The Temptress, Greta Garbo's second American film, told the story of a woman who toyed with men's affections and in the process drove them to disgrace, murder, and suicide. The movie reinforced Garbo's image as a beautiful and mysterious woman, but it was her next film, *Flesh and the Devil*, co-starring John Gilbert, that established her as a screen legend.

racial stereotypes by denigrating minority groups. The radio, the electric phonograph, and the silver screen all molded and mirrored mass culture.

Spectator Sports

Spectator sports attracted vast audiences in the 1920s. The country yearned for heroes in an increasingly impersonal, bureaucratic society, and sports, as well as the film industry, provided them. Prize fighters like Jack Dempsey became national idols. Team sports flourished, but Americans focused on individual superstars, people whose talents or personalities made them appear larger than life. Knute Rockne and his "Four Horsemen" at Notre Dame spurred interest in college football, and professional football began during the 1920s. In 1925, Harold "Red" Grange, the "Galloping Ghost" halfback for the University of Illinois, attracted 68,000 fans to a professional football game at Brooklyn's Polo Grounds.

Baseball drew even bigger crowds than football. The decade began with the sport mired in scandal. In 1920, three members of the Chicago White Sox told a grand jury that they and five other players had thrown the 1919 World Series. As a result of the **"Black Sox" scandal,** eight players were banished from the sport. But baseball soon regained its popularity, thanks to **George Herman ("Babe") Ruth,** the sport's undisputed superstar. Up until the 1920s Ty Cobb's defensive brand of baseball, with its emphasis on base hits and stolen bases, had dominated the sport. Ruth transformed baseball into the game of the home-run hitter. In 1921, the New York Yankee slugger hit 59 home runs—more than any other team combined. In 1927, the "Sultan of Swat" hit 60.

Low-Brow and Middle-Brow Culture

"It was a characteristic of the Jazz Age," novelist F. Scott Fitzgerald wrote, "that it had no interest in politics at all." What, then, were Americans interested in? Entertainment was Fitzgerald's answer. Parlor games like Mah Jong and crossword puzzles became enormously popular during the 1920s. Americans hit golf balls, played tennis, and bowled. Dance crazes like the fox trot, the Charleston, and the jitterbug swept the country.

New kinds of pulp fiction found a wide audience. Edgar Rice Burroughs' *Tarzan of the Apes* became a runaway bestseller. For readers who felt concerned about urbanization and industrialization, the adventures of the lone white man in "dark Africa" revived the spirit of frontier individualism. Zane Grey's novels, such as *Riders of the Purple Sage,* enjoyed even greater popularity, with their tried but true formula of

romance, action, and a moralistic struggle between good and evil, all in a western setting.

Other readers wanted to be titillated, as evidenced by the boom in "confession magazines." Urban values, liberated women, and Hollywood films had all relaxed Victorian standards. Confession magazines rushed to fill the vacuum, purveying stories of romantic success and failure, divorce, fantasy, and adultery. Writers survived the censors' cut by placing moral tags at the end of their stories, in which readers were advised to avoid similar mistakes in their own lives.

Readers too embarrassed to pick up a copy of *True Romance* could read more urbane magazines such as *The New Yorker* or *Vanity Fair,* which offered entertainment, amusement, and gossip to those with more sophisticated tastes. They could also join the Book-of-the-Month Club or the Literary Guild, both of which were founded during the decade.

The Avant-Garde

Few decades have produced as many great works of art, music, or literature as the 1920s. At the decade's beginning, American culture stood in Europe's shadow. By the decade's end, Americans were leaders in the struggle to liberate the arts from older canons of taste, form, and style. It was during the twenties that Eugene O'Neill, the country's most talented dramatist, wrote his greatest plays, and that William Faulkner, Ernest Hemingway, F. Scott Fitzgerald, and Thomas Wolfe published their first novels.

American poets of the 1920s—such as Hart Crane, e.e. cummings, Countee Cullen, Langston Hughes, Edna St. Vincent Millay, and Wallace Stevens—experimented with new styles of punctuation, rhyming, and form. Likewise, artists like Charles Demuth, Georgia O'Keeffe, and Joseph Stella challenged the dominant realist tradition in American art and pioneered nonrepresentational and expressionist art forms.

The 1920s marked America's entry into the world of serious music. It witnessed the founding of fifty symphony orchestras and three of the country's most prominent music conservatories—Julliard, Eastman, and Curtis. The decade also produced America's first great classical composers—including Aaron Copland and Charles Ives—and George Gershwin created a new musical form by integrating jazz into symphonic and orchestral music.

World War I had left many American intellectuals and artists disillusioned and alienated. Neither Wilsonian idealism nor Progressive reformism appealed to America's postwar writers and thinkers, who believed that the crusade to end war and to make the world safe for democracy had been a senseless mistake.

Charles Demuth, *The Figure 5 in Gold*, 1928. Demuth based this painting on a poem by his friend, the novelist, essayist, poet, and playwright William Carlos Williams. Tributes to Williams are visible in the painting: "BILL" at the upper left, "Carlo(s)" on the right and at the bottom the initials of both the artist (C.D.) and the poet (W.C.W.).

During the 1920s, many of the nation's leading writers exposed the shallowness and narrow-mindedness of American life. The United States was a nation awash in materialism and devoid of spiritual vitality, a "wasteland," wrote the poet T. S. Eliot, inhabited by "hollow men." No author offered a more scathing attack on middle-class boorishness and smugness than Sinclair Lewis, who in 1930 became the first American to win the Nobel Prize for Literature. In *Main Street* (1920) and *Babbitt* (1922) he satirized the narrow-minded complacency and dullness of small-town America, while in *Elmer Gantry* (1922) he exposed religious hypocrisy and bigotry.

As the editor of *Mercury* magazine, H. L. Mencken wrote hundreds of essays mocking practically every aspect of American life. Calling the South a "gargantuan paradise of the fourth rate," and the middle class the "booboisie," Mencken directed his choicest barbs at reformers, whom he blamed for the bloodshed of World War I and the gangsters of the 1920s. "If I am convinced of anything," he snarled, "it is that Doing Good is in bad taste."

The writer Gertrude Stein defined an important group of American intellectuals when she told Ernest Hemingway in 1921, "You are all a lost generation." Stein was referring to the expatriate novelists and artists who had participated in the Great War only to emerge from the conflict convinced that it was an exercise in futility. In their novels, F. Scott Fitzgerald and Hemingway foreshadowed a philosophy now known as **existentialism**—which maintains that life has no transcendent purpose and that each individual must salvage personal meaning from the void. Hemingway's fiction lionized toughness and "manly virtues" as a counterpoint to the softness of American life. In *The Sun Also Rises* (1926) and *A Farewell to Arms* (1929) he emphasized meaningless death and the importance of facing stoically the absurdities of the universe. In the conclusion of *The Great Gatsby* (1925), Fitzgerald gave pointed expression to an existentialist outlook: "so we beat on, boats against the current, borne back ceaselessly into the past."

The Sex Debate

"If all girls at the Yale prom were laid end to end, I wouldn't be surprised," sighed Dorothy Parker, the official wit of New York's smart set. Parker's quip captured the public's perception that America's morals had taken a nosedive. Practically every newspaper featured articles on prostitution, venereal disease, sex education, birth control, and the rising divorce rate.

City life nurtured new sexual attitudes. With its crowded anonymity, urban culture eroded sexual inhibitions by relaxing community restraints on individual behavior. Cities also promoted secular, consumer values, and city people seemed to tolerate, if not welcome, many forms of diversity.

While cities provided the ideal environment for liberalized sexual values, **Sigmund Freud** provided the ideal psychology. A Vienna physician, Freud revolutionized academic and popular thinking about human behavior by arguing that unconscious sexual anxieties cause much of human behavior. Freud also explained that sexual desires and fears develop in infancy and stay with people throughout their lives. During the 1920s, Freud's theories about the sexual unconscious were widely debated by physicians, academics, advice columnists, women's magazine writers, and preachers.

The image of the **flapper**—the liberated woman who bobbed her hair, painted her lips, raised her hemline, and danced the Charleston—personified the public's anxiety about the decline of traditional morality. In the 1950s **Alfred C. Kinsey**, a sex researcher at Indiana University, found that women born after 1900 were twice as likely to have had premarital sex as their mothers, with the most pronounced changes occurring in the generation reaching maturity in the early 1920s.

Sexual permissiveness had eroded Victorian values, but the "new woman" posed less of a challenge to traditional morality than her critics feared. Far from being promiscuous, her sexual experience before marriage was generally limited to one or two partners, one of whom she married. In practice, this narrowed the gap between men and women and moved society toward a single standard of morality. Instead of turning to prostitutes, men made love with their sweethearts, who in many instances became their wives.

THE CLASH OF CULTURES

The 1920s was a decade of intense cultural conflict. No longer a nation of farms and villages, the United States had become a nation of factories and cities. The Protestant culture of rural America was being undermined by the secular values of an urban society. Country against city, native against immigrant, Protestant against Catholic and Jew, fundamentalist against liberal, conservative against progressive, wet against dry—bitter confrontations erupted as the United States underwent a colossal identity crisis as it struggled to come to terms with secular values and cultural pluralism. The chief battlegrounds in this "cultural civil war" were gender, immigration, prohibition, and the teaching of evolution in public schools.

The New Woman

In 1920, after 72 years of struggle, American women received the right to vote with the passing of the **Nineteenth Amendment.** Reformers talked about female voters uniting to clean up politics, improve society, and end discrimination.

At first, male politicians moved aggressively to court the women's vote, passing legislation guaranteeing women's right to serve on juries and hold public office. Congress also passed legislation to set up a national system of women's and infant's health care clinics as well as a constitutional amendment prohibiting child labor, a measure supported by many women's groups.

But the early momentum quickly dissipated, as the women's movement divided from within and faced growing hostility from without. The major issue that split feminists during the 1920s was a proposed **Equal Rights Amendment** to the Constitution outlawing discrimination based on sex. The issue pitted the interests of professional women against those of working-class women, many of whom feared that the amendment would prohibit "protective legislation" that stipulated the minimum wages and maximum work hours of female workers.

The women's movement also faced mounting external opposition. During the Red Scare following World War I, the War Department issued the "Spider Web" chart that linked feminist groups to foreign radicalism. Many feminist goals went down to defeat in the mid-1920s. The Supreme Court struck down a minimum wage law for women workers, while Congress failed to fund the system of health care clinics.

Women also did not win new opportunities in the workplace. Although the American workforce included eight million women in 1920, more than half were African American or foreign-born. Domestic service remained the largest occupation, followed by secretarial work, typing, and clerking—all low-paying jobs. The American Federation of Labor (AFL) remained openly hostile to women because it did not want females competing for men's jobs. Female professionals, too, made little progress. They consistently received less pay than their male counterparts. Moreover, they were concentrated in traditionally "female" occupations such as teaching and nursing.

FIGURE 23.1
Women in the Workforce, 1900–1940

Although the number of women in the workplace rose from 1900 to 1940, they were mostly concentrated in only a few fields.

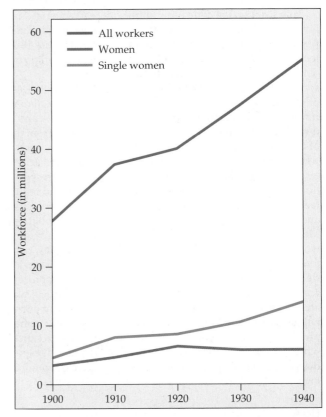

The Sexual Revolution of the Early 1900s

During the 1800s, public sexual attitudes in the United States were rooted in a moral code known as "civilized sexual morality." This sexual code condemned public discussion of sexual matters, held that sexual relations outside marriage were the blackest of sins, and declared that the only legitimate purpose of sexual relations was reproduction. Foreign travelers were invariably struck by Americans' sexual prudery. In the United States, they reported, a chicken breast was called a bosom and a piano leg was called a limb and was covered with lace trousers.

This strict sexual code drew support from a large medical literature that declared that any violation of the tenets of civilized morality would be detrimental to a person's health. Respected physicians insisted that loss of semen through masturbation or excessive sexual intercourse would produce "urinary difficulties, disorders of the genital organs, spinal diseases, weakness of the brain, loss of memory, epilepsy, insanity, apoplexy, abortions, premature births, and extreme feebleness, morbid predispositions, and an early death of offspring." Medical authorities also warned that women were too frail physically and too sensitive spiritually to engage in frequent intercourse and that "the majority of women (happily for them) are not very much troubled with sexual feelings of any kind." Above all, physicians warned that individuals who had sexual relations outside of marriage ran a high risk of contracting incurable venereal diseases.

The Victorian sexual code was a public ideal, not an accurate description of reality. Prostitution flourished in turn-of-the-century America. Every large city had at least one red-light district. In New York, there was the Tenderloin; in Chicago, the Levee; in New Orleans, Storyville; in San Francisco, the Barbary Coast. Early-twentieth-century vice commissions estimated that there were "not less" than a quarter of a million prostitutes in the country. In Chicago, an estimated quarter of the city's males visited prostitutes annually, and paid them $15 million a year. Pornography was also widespread.

Nor were nineteenth-century women necessarily the prudish, asexual, sexually ignorant figures popularized in Victorian mythology. An early sexual survey of the attitudes of 45 well-educated women, mainly born before 1870, reported that most enjoyed intercourse and experienced orgasm.

Nevertheless, the values of civilized sexual morality dominated polite society and received strong public backing from the broad-based crusade to suppress vice. A "purity crusade" had arisen in the 1860s and 1870s in response to proposals to legalize and regulate prostitution. In almost every major city in the country, former abolitionists like William Lloyd Garrison, feminists like Susan B. Anthony, temperance advocates, and ministers joined forces to defeat legalized prostitution. Prostitution, they argued, was a menace "to the chastity of our women and the sanctity of the home." It exploited poor women to satisfy male lust and endangered respectable women, who were often infected with syphilis and gonorrhea by their husbands.

In later years, the purity forces broadened their aims. In addition to fighting prostitution, they also sought to protect the family by outlawing abortion, restricting the sale of alcohol, stamping out pornography, censoring nudity in the arts, enforcing the Sabbath through enactment of "blue laws," suppressing the use of narcotics, and stopping the flow of birth control information through the mails.

The self-appointed leader of the purity forces was a staunch crusader named Anthony Comstock. Born on a farm in New Canaan, Connecticut, Comstock, as a youth, had been so upset by an impulse to masturbate that he feared he might be driven to commit suicide. While serving with a Connecticut regiment in the Civil War he had been appalled by the pornographic French postcards circulated among soldiers. After the war he moved to New York, where he became active in the Young Men's Christian Association, and was shocked by the prevalence of prostitutes and of vendors selling obscene books.

In 1873, Comstock persuaded Congress to pass a federal law banning from the mails "every obscene, lewd, lascivious or filthy book, pamphlet, paper, letter, writing, print or other publication of an indecent character." Comstock was then appointed special agent of the Post Office and made responsible for arresting those who used the mail in violation of the law. "Morals, not art or literature," was Comstock's motto. He took credit for hounding 16 persons to their deaths.

By 1910, Comstock and the purity forces had achieved many of their legislative goals. They had successfully pushed for state laws to restrict divorce; raised the age of consent for sexual intercourse (from 7, in some

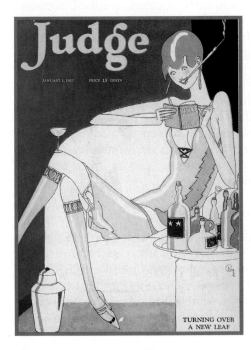

Judge

JANUARY 1, 1927   PRICE 15 CENTS

TURNING OVER
A NEW LEAF

states, to 18); imposed tests for venereal disease prior to marriage; and criminalized abortion. The purity crusaders also won passage of a federal statute that defined the mailing of birth control information a felony.

The years just before World War I witnessed a series of sharp challenges to the nineteenth-century code of sexual purity. Radical new ideas about marriage were publicized and debated. Swedish feminist Ellen Key preached a scheme of "unwed motherhood"; Edith Ellis, wife of British sex researcher Havelock Ellis, advocated trial marriage and "semi-detached marriage" in which each spouse occupied a separate domicile; still others advocated "serial marriage" and easier divorce. Greenwich Village bohemians and political radicals advocated, and to some extent practiced, free love. Psychologists, including Havelock Ellis, G. Stanley Hall, and Sigmund Freud, attacked the notion that women lacked sexual impulses.

Sexual conduct was also changing rapidly. The first scientific sex surveys indicated that women who came to maturity after the turn of the century were much more likely than their mothers to engage in sex before marriage and outside it. Women who were born around 1900 were two to three times as likely to have premarital intercourse compared to women born before 1900. They were also more likely to experience orgasm. Among men, premarital sexual experience did not increase, but it occurred less often with prostitutes and more frequently with other women.

Public alarm over the changes occurring in American sexual experience culminated in the first decade of the 1900s in an explosion of concern over "white slavery"—prostitution—and the "black plague"—venereal disease. Many lurid books appeared—with such titles as *The Traffic in Souls, The House of Bondage,* and *The Shame of a Great Nation*—that explained how innocent young girls were seduced by panderers and, through the use of a chloroformed cloth, a hypodermic needle, or a drugged drink, forced into prostitution. Congress attacked the problem of "white slavery" in 1910 by adopting the Mann Act, which made it a crime to transport women across state lines for immoral purposes. During World War I, Congress provided states with federal funds to set up facilities to detain and rehabilitate women apprehended as prostitutes. Fifteen thousand women were detained during the war. Sex was becoming a subject of open public debate and direct government involvement.

During the 1920s, the drift toward sexual liberalization continued. Journalists wrote in bewilderment about a new social phenomenon, the flapper, the independent, assertive, pleasure-hungry, young woman, "making love lightly, boldly, and promiscuously." Systematic sex surveys showed that the incidence of premarital intercourse was continuing to rise and that an increasing number of young women had slept with men other than their future husbands. Half of the women born in the first decade of the twentieth century and two-thirds of those born in the second decade had engaged in intercourse before marriage. Meanwhile, contraceptive practices were also changing dramatically. Instead of relying heavily on douching or coitus interruptus as a form of birth control, younger women were using the more effective and less disruptive diaphragm.

This growing sexual permissiveness evoked a sharp reaction. Purity forces renewed their crusade to discourage indecent styles of dancing, immodest dress, and impure books and films. Religious journals denounced popular dance styles as "impure, polluting, corrupting, debasing, destroying spirituality, [and] increasing carnality." A bill was introduced in the Utah state legislature to fine and imprison women who wore, on the streets, skirts "higher than three inches above the ankle." In the Ohio legislature it was proposed that cleavage be limited to two inches and that the sale of any "garment which unduly displays or accentuates the lines of the female figure" be prohibited. Four states and many cities established censorship boards to review films, and many other cities broke up red-light districts and required licenses for dance halls. But despite these efforts, a sexual revolution had begun that has continued to this day.

Prohibition

Prohibition exposed deep fissures in American society. The issue turned on the class, ethnic, and religious makeup of individual communities.

At first prohibition's apparent success muted its critics. Distilleries and breweries shut down, saloons locked their doors, arrests for drunkenness declined, and alcohol-related deaths all but disappeared. Compliance, however, had less to do with piety and public support than the law of supply and demand: since illegal liquor remained in short supply, its price rose beyond the average worker's means.

Private enterprise filled the void. Smugglers supplied wealthy imbibers, but the less affluent had to rely on small-time operators who produced for local consumption. Much of this liquor ran the gamut from swill to poison. Hundreds, perhaps thousands, died from drinking these illegal concoctions.

Neither federal nor state authorities had enough funds to enforce prohibition. New York's mayor estimated that it would require a police force of 250,000 to enforce prohibition—and another 250,000 to police the police. In fact, only about 2200 agents across the country enforced the law. Lax enforcement, coupled with huge profits, enticed organized crime to enter bootlegging. Long a fixture of urban life, with gambling and prostitution as its base, organized crime had operated on a small, local scale. Liquor, however, demanded production plants, distribution networks, and sales forces. Bootlegging turned into a gold mine for organized crime. By the late 1920s liquor sales generated revenue in excess of $2 billion annually. Chicago's Al Capone had a gross income of $60 million in 1927.

From the outset, cynics had insisted that prohibition could not be enforced. They were right. Particularly in large cities, people openly defied the law. In New York City, 7000 arrests for liquor law violations resulted in 17 convictions. On more than one occasion journalists saw President Warren G. Harding's bootlegger deliver cases of liquor to the White House in broad daylight.

In 1923 New York became the first state to repeal its enforcement law, and by 1930 six more states had followed suit. Others remained firmly committed to prohibition. After a presidential commission reported prohibition could not be enforced, Congress finally repealed it in 1933, making liquor control a state and local matter.

The campaign to outlaw cigarette smoking was closely allied to the prohibition movement. Opposition to tobacco was not new. During the nineteenth century the antitobacco campaign remained an appendage of the temperance movement. After the introduction of machine-made cigarettes in the 1880s, however, opponents concentrated their fire specifically on the "little white slavers."

As early as the Civil War, a few cities had banned smoking in restaurants, theaters, public buildings, trolleys, and railway cars. After antismokers organized the **National Anti-Cigarette League** in 1903, scores of prominent leaders joined the crusade. By 1923, 14 states had outlawed the sale of cigarettes, prompting calls for a constitutional amendment for national prohibition. By the end of the decade, however, every state had repealed its law against cigarette sales. A national consensus had not formed against tobacco, and the tobacco industry opposed every effort to restrict the sale of their products throughout the nation.

The Scopes Trial

During the late nineteenth century, Charles Darwin's theory of evolution produced a momentous split within the ranks of American Protestantism. Earlier in the century, virtually all American Protestant denominations were united in the belief that the findings of science confirmed the teachings of religion. But Darwin's theory shattered that consensus. Religious liberals argued that religion had to accommodate to the teachings of modern science. Religious fundamentalists sought to preserve the basic tenets of Protestant faith against liberal criticisms.

The split between religious liberals and fundamentalists widened in the early twentieth century. A religious revival in Topeka, Kansas, in 1901, marked the beginning of Pentecostalism, a movement that emphasizes the spiritual gifts conferred by the Holy Spirit, including the ability to "speak in tongues" (an unknown, but divinely inspired language) and the power of prayer to heal the sick. By arguing that the Biblical age of miracles had not ended, Pentecostals directly challenged the ideas of religious modernists. *The Fundamentals*, 12 volumes by anonymous authors published between 1910 and 1915, argued that there were certain Christian doctrines that must be accepted without question, including the infallibility of the Bible, the authenticity of the miracles described in the Scriptures, and the virgin birth of Jesus Christ. Although the fundamentalist and Pentecostal movements began in the North, they attained their greatest support in the South.

During the 1920s, conflict erupted between fundamentalists and liberals over the teaching of evolution in public schools, a clash that culminated in the celebrated **Scopes "Monkey Trial."** In 1925 the Tennessee legislature passed a bill that prohibited the teaching of evolution in public schools. Immediately afterwards, a 24-year-old science teacher, John Scopes, from Dayton, Tennessee, provoked a test case by declaring publicly that he taught biology from an evolutionary standpoint.

Scopes was brought to trial in the summer of 1925. William Jennings Bryan, rural America's defender of the faith, agreed to join the team of prosecutors, and **Clarence Darrow,** the celebrated trial lawyer and self-proclaimed agnostic, volunteered his services to defend Scopes.

The trial opened on July 10, 1925. As "Holy Rollers" from the surrounding regions held revivals and religious zealots exhorted people to read their Bibles, huge crowds poured into Dayton to watch Bryan and Darrow do combat. Near the end of testimony the defense surprised everyone by asking Bryan to take the stand as an expert witness on the Bible. His simple, direct answers to Darrow's sarcastic questions revealed an unshakable faith in the literal truth of the Bible. Bryan insisted "it is better to trust in the Rock of Ages than to know the ages of rocks."

The outcome was never in doubt. Scopes admitted he had broken the law. He was convicted and fined $100. (Tennessee's supreme court later rescinded the fine on a technicality.) What gave the trial its drama was the clash between Bryan and Darrow and the opposite images of America they represented. Bryan, who died five days after the trial ended, left the courtroom believing he had carried the day. His opponents, however, thought he had been humiliated and they proclaimed the Scopes trial a victory for academic freedom. In the end, the Scopes trial merely illustrated how little tolerance secular and fundamentalist groups had for each other.

Xenophobia and Restricting Immigration

Cultural fears unleashed a new wave of nativism in the 1920s. Organized labor, bent upon protecting high wages, resented competition from cheap labor; staunch nativists and superpatriots warned that foreign influences would corrupt the American character; and assorted businessmen denounced immigrants as dangerous radicals.

To protect the United States these groups demanded drastic changes in the nation's immigration policy. Congress passed the **National Origins Act of 1924,** establishing an annual immigration quota of 2 percent of each national group counted in the 1890 census, and barring Asians entirely. Since southern and eastern Europeans did not begin arriving in large numbers until the turn of the century, the law

Many people felt that Italian-born, self-admitted anarchists Sacco and Vanzetti, shown here in handcuffs in a painting by Ben Shahn, were persecuted for their immigrant status and radical views rather than for any real crime. Their trial became an important symbol in the fight for civil liberties and brought about violent protest in America and abroad.

gave western and northern Europeans a big edge over the "new immigrants."

Hostility to immigrants also surfaced in the **Sacco and Vanzetti case.** On April 15, 1920, two unidentified gunmen robbed a payroll messenger from a shoe factory in South Braintree, Massachusetts, killing a paymaster and a guard. Two Italian immigrants, Nicola Sacco and Bartolomeo Vanzetti, both avowed anarchists, were arrested and charged with the crime. Although the state failed to prove its case, prosecutors succeeded in parading before the jury the radical political views of both men. On July 14, 1921, Sacco and Vanzetti were convicted and sentenced to death.

The trial and conviction brought a storm of protest from Italian Americans, liberals, and civil rights advocates. Despite lengthy appeals, the conviction was upheld, and Sacco and Vanzetti, asserting their innocence to the end, went to the electric chair on August 23, 1927.

The Ku Klux Klan

Fear of political radicals and ethnic minorities found its most strident voice during the 1920s in the rebirth of the **Ku Klux Klan.** The secret organization, led by Colonel William Joseph Simmons, stood for "100 percent pure Americanism" and limited its membership to white, native-born Protestants. Membership remained modest until Simmons hired two advertising

The Ku Klux Klan exploited postwar confusion and fear of things "un-American." Although the Klan had originally flourished in small, rural towns across the South, during the 1920s it spread to working-class and middle-class neighborhoods of large cities, where people felt threatened by the influx of African American and immigrant workers.

specialists, Edward Young Clarke and Elizabeth Tyler, to market the Klan nationwide.

Clarke and Tyler hired an army of organizers to canvass the country selling memberships in the Klan. Working on commission and molding their pitch to match their clientele, the salesmen enjoyed astounding success. By 1921 the Klan had become a national organization with over 90,000 paying members; by 1925 it claimed a membership of five million. The Klan was strongest in the South, but it had a large following in the Southeast, the Far West, and the Midwest. Its natural habitat was not the countryside, but middling towns and small cities as well as larger cities like Chicago and Detroit. Most members were not "poor white trash," but members of the lower middle class from old-stock, respectable families.

In the mid-1920s the Klan was a political force to reckon with. It influenced the election of several governors and members of state legislatures. The Klan also sought to intimidate individuals, using night ridings, cross burnings, tar and featherings, public beatings, and lynching as forms of coercion. The Klan did not limit its wrath to ethnic and religious "offenders," but also lashed out against wife-beaters, drunkards, bootleggers, gamblers—anyone who violated time-honored standards of morality.

In the end poor leadership and the absence of a political program destroyed the Klan. Once they attained office, Klan-supported officials offered no constructive legislation. Even more damaging, several Klan leaders became involved in sex scandals, and several more were indicted for corruption. By 1930 the white sheets and cross burnings had vanished from public view, only to return again a few

decades later when the civil rights movement challenged white supremacy.

African American Protests

Many African Americans believed that the sacrifices of African American soldiers during World War I would be repaid when the war was over. It was not to be. The federal government denied African American soldiers the right to participate in the victory march down Paris's Champs-Elysées boulevard. In the 25 race riots that took place in 1919, 10 of the 70 African American victims were veterans of World War I.

African Americans did not respond passively to these outrages. Already, in the 1910s, they had stepped up their protests against discrimination. Closely identified with Booker T. Washington's conciliatory approach to race relations, the **National Urban League,** organized in 1911 by social workers, white philanthropists, and conservative African American leaders, concentrated on finding jobs for urban African Americans. Despite the nation's postwar prosperity, African Americans made scant progress on the job front during the 1920s.

Leaving economic issues to the Urban League, the **National Association for the Advancement of Colored People (NAACP),** formed in 1909, concentrated on civil rights and legal action. The NAACP won important Supreme Court decisions against the grandfather clause (1915) and restrictive covenants (1917). The NAACP also fought school segregation in northern cities during the 1920s, and lobbied hard, though unsuccessfully, for a federal antilynching bill. Though progress on these fronts was not made until after World War II, the NAACP became the nation's leading civil rights organization.

African American radicals dismissed the Urban League and the NAACP as too conservative. **A. Philip Randolph,** the editor of the Socialist monthly the *Messenger* called for a "New Negro" who would meet violence with violence to end discrimination and achieve racial equality. Randolph urged African American workers to seek admission to trade unions.

No black leader was more successful in touching the aspirations and needs of the mass of African Americans than **Marcus Garvey.** A flamboyant and charismatic figure from Jamaica, Garvey rejected integration and preached racial pride and self-help. He declared that Jesus Christ and Mary were black and he exhorted his followers to glorify their African heritage and revel in the beauty of their skin.

In 1917 Garvey moved to New York, where he organized the American branch of the Universal Negro Improvement Association (UNIA), the first mass movement in African American history. Convinced that African Americans would never achieve full equality in the United States, Garvey called on blacks to regard Africa as their homeland. By the mid-1920s, Garvey's organization had 700 branches in 38 states and the West Indies and published a newspaper with as many as 200,000 subscribers. The UNIA operated grocery stores, laundries, restaurants, printing plants, clothing factories, and a steamship line.

In the mid-1920s, Garvey was charged with mail fraud, jailed, and finally deported. Still, the "Black Moses" left behind a rich legacy. At a time when magazines and newspapers overflowed with advertisements for hair straighteners and skin lightening cosmetics, Garvey's message of racial pride struck a responsive chord in many African Americans.

The Harlem Renaissance

The movement for African American pride found its cultural expression in the **Harlem Renaissance**—the first self-conscious literary and artistic movement in African American history.

For over three decades, African Americans had shown increasing interest in African American history and folk culture. As early as the 1890s, W.E.B. Du Bois, Harvard's first African American Ph.D., began to trace African American culture in the United States to its African roots; Fisk University's Jubilee Singers introduced Negro spirituals to the general public;

and the American Negro Academy, organized in 1897, promoted African American literature, arts, music, and history. A growing spirit of racial pride was evident, as a group of talented writers, including Charles Chestnutt, Paul Lawrence Dunbar, and James Weldon Johnson, explored life in African American communities; as the first Negro dolls appeared; and as all-Negro towns were founded in Whitesboro, New Jersey, and Allensworth, California.

Signs of growing racial consciousness proliferated during the 1910s. Fifty new African American newspapers and magazines appeared in that decade, bringing the total to 500. The Associated Negro Press, the first national African American press agency, was founded in 1919. In 1915, Carter Woodson, a Harvard Ph.D., founded the first permanent Negro historical association—the Association for the Study of Negro Life and History—and began publication of the *Journal of Negro History.*

During the 1920s, Harlem, in upper Manhattan, became the capital of black America, attracting African American intellectuals and artists from across the country and the Caribbean as well. Soon, the Harlem Renaissance was in full bloom. The poet Countee Cullen eloquently expressed black artists' long-suppressed desire to have their voices heard: "Yet do I marvel at a curious thing: To make a poet black, and bid him sing!"

Many of the greatest works of the Harlem Renaissance sought to recover links with African and

Artist Archibald Motley, Jr., one of the black painters of the 1920s Harlem Renaissance, celebrated the energy and excitement of the era there in *Black Belt* (1934). Motley, who was born in New Orleans and raised in Chicago, trained at the Art Institute of Chicago. He said he believed art to be governed by "personality, intensity and sympathy" and it is these qualities that enliven his works, such as this dynamic urban scene.

folk traditions. In "The Negro Speaks of Rivers," the poet Langston Hughes reaffirmed his ties to an African past: "I looked upon the Nile and raised the pyramids above it." In "Cane" (1923), Jean Toomer—the grandson of P. B. S. Pinchback, who served briefly as governor of Louisiana during Reconstruction—blended realism and mysticism, poetry and prose, to describe the world of the black peasantry in Georgia and in the ghetto of Washington, D.C.

A fierce racial consciousness and a powerful sense of racial pride animated the literature of the Harlem Renaissance. The West Indian–born poet Claude McKay expressed the new spirit of defiance and protest with militant words: "If we must die—oh let us nobly die . . . dying, but fighting back!"

The Republican Restoration

The Republican party dominated American politics in the 1920s. When Republican leaders promised to restore prosperity, most Americans embraced the conservative rhetoric, hoping to find in politics the stability they found lacking in their culture. Talk about trust-busting and regulating big business gave way in New Era politics to calls for a partnership between government and industry, one that would promote the interests of American corporations at home and abroad.

Handsome Harding

By and large the presidents of the New Era were mediocre figures. Senator Warren G. Harding of Ohio, who led off the decade, suited the times perfectly. Handsome enough to be a movie star, he not only looked great, but promised voters what they wanted: a return to "normalcy." He appeared to be a moderate, responsible leader who would avoid extremes and guide the country into a decade of prosperity.

Harding, a fun-loving man who liked to play poker, drink whiskey, and shoot the breeze with old pals, left government to his cabinet members and to the Supreme Court. Political conservatives all, they equated the people's interests with those of big business, championing American business interests abroad, denouncing government regulation, and slashing taxes on the rich.

Business leaders had contributed $8 million to the GOP's campaign chest in 1920; in return they expected the federal government to roll back the gains organized labor had made during World War I. They were not disappointed. Under the leadership of Chief Justice William Howard Taft, the Court took a narrow view of federal power, assigning the responsibility for protecting individual citizens to the states.

During the 1920s the Court outlawed picketing, overturned national child labor laws, and abolished minimum wage laws for women.

The decade's most capable figure was Herbert Hoover, secretary of commerce under both Harding and his successor, Calvin Coolidge. A successful engineer, Hoover abhorred destructive competition and waste in the economy, which he proposed to eliminate through "**associationism.**" Hoover called for voluntary trade associations to foster cooperation in industry and agriculture through commissions, trade practice controls, and ethical standards. By 1929 more than 2000 trade associations were busily at work implementing Hoover's vision of a stable and prosperous economy. No other Harding appointment matched Hoover's talent and vision.

In fact, several of Harding's appointees proved to be disasters. Harding found it difficult to say "no" to old friends and cronies, members of the so-called **Ohio Gang,** when they asked for government jobs. In the end this motley assortment of political hacks and hangers-on plunged his administration into disgrace, as major scandals involving bribes and kickbacks erupted in the Justice Department and in the Veterans Bureau. Shortly after these disclosures, Harding died of a cerebral embolism, on August 2, 1923. Immediately after his death, more misdeeds came to light. In the infamous **Teapot Dome scandal,** Secretary of the Interior Albert B. Fall was convicted of accepting $360,000 in bribes in exchange for leasing drilling rights on federal naval oil reserves, the first cabinet member in American history convicted for crimes in office. Attorney General Harry Daugherty, accused of accepting payoffs for selling German chemical patents controlled by the Alien Property Office, was forced to resign in disgrace.

Silent Cal

The election of 1924 symbolized, in a variety of ways, the tensions and concerns of the 1920s. Despite the Harding scandals, President Calvin Coolidge remained extremely popular, largely because of the nation's prosperity. Deeply divided over such issues as immigration, prohibition, and the Ku Klux Klan, the Democrats balloted 103 times before nominating a compromise candidate, John W. Davis, a Wall Street attorney.

A coalition of labor leaders, social workers, and former progressives bolted both major parties and formed the Progressive party, which nominated Wisconsin Senator Robert La Follette for president. Their platform called for government ownership of natural resources, abolition of child labor, elimination of monopolies, and increased taxes on the rich. In the end, no issue could match the GOP's prosperity crusade. Coolidge won the election by a comfortable margin.

Coolidge was a stern-faced, tight-lipped New Englander. Born in Plymouth Notch, Vermont, where five generations of Coolidges had worked the same family farm, he epitomized the rural values threatened by immigration, urbanization, and industrialization. As governor of Massachusetts, Coolidge had crushed a police strike in Boston in 1919 by calling out the National Guard, prompting the Republicans to give him the number two slot on their ticket in 1920.

Coolidge had no desire to be a strong president in the tradition of a Teddy Roosevelt or a Woodrow Wilson. A firm believer in the wisdom of inactivity, Coolidge slept ten hours a night, napped every afternoon, and seldom worked more than four hours a day. A staunch conservative, Coolidge was positively consumed by his reverence for the corporate elite. Government, he believed, should do everything in its power to promote business interests. While Coolidge set the tone for his administration, he left it to his cabinet members, the courts, and Congress to devise strategies for consummating the marriage between business and government.

The Twilight of Progressivism

The government's tilt toward business signaled a retreat from progressivism. With the Democrats in disarray and Teddy Roosevelt's wing of the GOP all but dead, conservative Republicans were riding high. Still, the reform impulse did not disappear entirely during the 1920s. A small band of beleaguered reformers, led by Robert La Follette of Wisconsin and George Norris of Nebraska, kept progressivism alive in Congress, where they worked for farm relief, child labor laws, and regulation of wages and working hours for women.

In keeping with their historic pattern, progressives had better luck at the state and local level than at the federal level, where they ran into stiff opposition from Congress or from Coolidge himself. Social workers and women's groups spearheaded campaigns that sponsored a broad range of welfare legislation. By 1930, 43 states had passed laws providing assistance to women with dependent children, and 34 states had adopted workers' compensation laws. Under the leadership of Governor Alfred Smith, New York granted women a 40-hour workweek and instituted the nation's first public housing program.

Welfare opponents counterattacked, arguing labor reforms would increase production costs and leave states that passed welfare legislation at a competitive disadvantage with states without such laws. Asked to choose between social welfare programs and jobs, Congress, along with most states, opted for jobs.

The Election of 1928

After Coolidge announced his retirement from politics in 1928, the Republicans nominated Herbert Hoover, while the Democrats turned to **Alfred E. Smith.** Since both parties adopted nearly identical platforms, the election turned on personalities and images. Few elections have pitted opponents who better defined the two faces of America—one rural, the other urban.

A native of Iowa, Hoover depicted himself as a simple farmboy who, through hard work and pluck, had grown up to become wealthy and famous. Orphaned as a boy and cared for by a variety of relatives, Hoover worked his way through Stanford University, earning a degree in mining engineering. Brilliant and hard-working, he was a millionaire 12 years after landing his first engineering job. As a self-made man, Hoover presented a portrait of a safe, reassuring world.

Yet Hoover was also a spokesman for the future. He thought the federal government had a responsibility to coordinate the competing interests of a modern economy. He accepted the reality of industrialization, technology, governmental activism, and global markets, and in contrast to Harding and Coolidge, Hoover believed the president should lead the nation. According to Hoover, technology and expertise would make economic prosperity a permanent feature of American life.

The son of immigrants, Smith was an Irish Catholic from Hell's Kitchen in New York City. He had started public life with nothing and had climbed the political ladder as a faithful son of the New York Democratic machine. Smith also represented the future, not so much in terms of science, technology, and organization, but in terms of cultural pluralism and urbanization. America's future lay with her cities, and the cities contained large groups of ethnic Americans struggling for acceptance and their share of the good life.

Aided by prosperity, Hoover coasted to an easy victory. Smith was hurt by his failure to bridge the North-South, urban-rural split in the Democratic party; by anti-Catholic sentiment; and by his opposition to prohibition. Yet even in defeat, Smith's campaign revealed the most significant political change of the 1920s—the growing power of urban and ethnic voters and the shrinking influence of the rural element within the Democratic party.

Herbert Hoover's election marked the climax of New Era politics. As president he advocated total cooperation between government and business. Optimistic businesspeople, bankers, and stockbrokers applauded Hoover's promises, predicting a future of prosperity and progress. Ironically, the stock market crashed before their cheers had stopped echoing.

THE GREAT CRASH

Few people ever see their name enter the English language, but Charles Ponzi did. A **"Ponzi scheme"** has become synonymous with wild speculation. In September 1919, Ponzi was a 42-year-old former vegetable dealer with just $150 to his name. He promised to return $15 to anyone who lent him $10 for 90 days. His plan, he explained, was to buy foreign currencies at low prices and sell them at higher prices. After newspapers reported his scheme, dollars began to pour in—$1 million a week.

It was too good to be true. Ponzi took in $15 million in eight months—and less than $200,000 was ever returned to investors.

Speculative Manias

Ponzi symbolized the "get-rich-quick" mentality that infected the public during the 1920s. A vivid example was the Florida land boom. During the 1920s, sun-worshiping Northerners discovered Florida's warm winter climate and its sun-drenched beaches. Could there be a safer investment? Real estate promoters—including the former presidential candidate William Jennings Bryan—offered seafront lots to investors for 10 percent down. Investors snapped up the properties—much of which turned out to be swamp and scrub land. Prices skyrocketed. A lot 40 miles from Miami sold for $20,000. A beach lot sold for $75,000. Ponzi himself sold lots "near Jacksonville"—actually 65 miles west of the city; he divided each acre into 23 lots.

In the fall of 1926 the bubble burst. Two hurricanes ripped through Florida, killing more than 400 people. Property valued at $1 billion in 1925 dropped to $143 million in 1928.

A wave of similar stock swindles and business frauds took place during the 1920s. But the most striking manifestation of the decade's speculative frenzy was the stock market boom of 1928 and 1929. After rising steadily during the 1920s, stock prices began to soar in March 1928. Between March 3, 1928, and September 3, 1928, AT&T rose from $179\frac{1}{2}$ to $335\frac{5}{8}$, General Motors from $139\frac{3}{4}$ to $181\frac{7}{8}$, and Westinghouse from $91\frac{5}{8}$ to 313. By the beginning of the fall of 1929, stock prices were four times higher than five years before.

Brokerage houses lured investors into the market by selling stock on margin, requiring investors to only put down 10 or 20 percent of the stock's price in cash and borrowing the rest. By 1929, 1.5 million Americans had invested in securities.

Boosters like John Jacob Raskob, the chairman of the Democratic party, encouraged ordinary people to invest in stocks. In an article in the *Ladies' Home Journal* entitled "Everybody Ought to be Rich," he ex-

The cover image on the January 16, 1926, issue of *Judge* might have suggested the kind of land in Florida that real estate promoters were selling to investors. Still, land continued to sell until hurricanes later in the year tore through much of the state and forced the collapse of the Florida land boom.

plained that a person who invested $15 a month in the stock market for 20 years would have a nest egg of $80,000. Leading economists encouraged investors to believe that the stock market would continue to rise. At the end of October 1929, the seemingly endless surge in stock prices came to a crashing halt.

The Market Crashes

On Thursday, October 24, 1929, an unprecedented wave of sell orders shook the New York Stock Exchange. Stock prices tumbled, falling $2, $5, and even $10 between trades. As prices fell, brokers required investors who had bought stock on margin to put up money to cover their loans. To raise money, many investors dumped stocks for whatever price the stocks could fetch. During the first three hours of trading, stock values plunged by $11 billion.

At noon, a group of prominent bankers met at the offices of J. P. Morgan and Company. To stop the hemorrhaging of stock prices, the bankers' pool agreed to buy stocks well above the market. At 1:30 P.M. they put their plan into action. Within an hour, U.S. Steel was up $15 a share, AT&T up $22, General Electric up $21, Mongtomery Ward up $23.

Even though the market recovered its morning losses, public confidence was badly shaken. Rumors spread that 11 stock speculators had killed themselves and that government troops were surrounding the exchange to protect traders from an angry mob. President Hoover sought to reassure the public by declaring that the "fundamental business of the country . . . is on a sound and prosperous basis."

Prices held steady on Friday, then slipped on Saturday. Monday, however, brought fresh disaster. Eastman Kodak plunged $41 a share, AT&T went down $24, New York Central Railroad, $22. The worst was yet to come—**Black Tuesday,** October 29, the day the stock market experienced the greatest crash in its history.

As soon as the stock exchange's gong sounded, a mad rush to sell began. Trading volume soared to an unprecedented 16,410,030 shares, and the average price of a share fell 12 percent. Stocks were sold for whatever price they would bring. White Sewing Machine had reached a high of $48 a share. One purchaser—reportedly a messenger boy—bought a block of the stock for $1 a share.

The bull market of the late 1920s was over. By 1932, the index of stock prices had fallen from a 1929 high of 210 to 30. Altogether, between September 1929 and June 1932, the nation's stock exchanges lost $179 billion in value.

The great stock market crash of October 1929 brought the economic prosperity of the 1920s to a symbolic end. For the next ten years, the United States was mired in a deep economic depression. By 1933, unemployment had soared to 25 percent of the workforce, up from just 3.2 percent in 1929. Industrial production declined by 50 percent. In 1929, before the crash, investment in the U.S. economy totaled $16 billion. By 1933, the figure had fallen to $340 million, a decrease of 98 percent.

Why It Happened

Economists have been hard-pressed to explain why "prosperity's decade" ended in financial disaster. In 1929, the American economy appeared to be extraordinarily healthy. Employment was high and inflation was virtually nonexistent. Industrial production had risen 30 percent between 1919 and 1929 and per capita income had climbed from $520 to $681. The United States accounted for nearly half the world's industrial output. Still, the seeds of the depression were already present in the "boom" years of the 1920s.

For many groups of Americans, the prosperity of the 1920s was a cruel illusion. Even during the most prosperous years of the Roaring Twenties, most families lived below what contemporaries defined as the poverty line. In 1929, economists considered $2500 the income necessary to support a family. In that year, more than 60 percent of the nation's families earned less than $2000 a year, the income necessary for basic

The prosperity of the Roaring Twenties bypassed many Americans, such as this farm family posing on the front porch of their home. The gap between the rich and the poor widened in the 1920s, with the rich becoming much richer, skilled and white-collar workers making modest gains, while a majority of unskilled workers, sharecroppers and tenant farmers, African Americans, and immigrants suffered and struggled to survive.

necessities; and over 40 percent of all families earned less than $1500 annually. Although labor productivity soared during the 1920s because of electrification and more efficient management, wages stagnated or fell in mining, transportation, and manufacturing.

Prosperity bypassed specific groups of Americans entirely. A 1928 report on the condition of Native Americans found that half earned less than $500 and that 71 percent lived on less than $200 a year. Mexican Americans, too, had failed to share in the prosperity. During each year of the 1920s, 25,000 Mexicans migrated to the United States. Most lived in conditions of extreme poverty. A survey found that a substantial minority of Mexican Americans had virtually no meat or fresh vegetables in their diet; 40 percent said that they could not afford to give their children milk.

The farm sector had been mired in depression since 1921. Farm prices had been depressed ever since the end of World War I, when European agriculture revived and grain from Argentina and Australia entered the world market. Strapped with long-term debts, high taxes, and a sharp drop in crop prices, farmers lost ground throughout the 1920s. In 1910, a farmer's income was 40 percent of a city worker's. By 1930, it had sagged to just 30 percent.

The decline in farm income reverberated throughout the economy. Millions of farmers defaulted on their debts, placing tremendous pressure on the banking system. Between 1920 and 1929, more than 5000 of the country's 30,000 banks failed.

Because of the banking crisis, thousands of small businesspeople failed because they could not secure loans. Thousands more went bankrupt because they had lost their working capital in the stock market crash. A heavy burden of consumer debt also weakened the economy. Consumers built up an unmanageable amount of consumer installment and mortgage debt, taking out loans to buy cars, appliances, and homes in the suburbs. To repay these loans, consumers cut back sharply on discretionary spending. Drops in consumer spending then led inevitably to reductions in production and subsequent worker layoffs. Unemployed workers then spent less, and the cycle repeated itself.

A poor distribution of income compounded the country's economic problems. During the 1920s, there was a pronounced shift in wealth and income toward the very rich. Between 1919 and 1929, the share of income received by the wealthiest 1 percent of Americans rose from 12 percent to 19 percent, while the share received by the richest 5 percent jumped from 24 percent to 34 percent. Over the same period, the poorest 93 percent of the nonfarm population actually saw its disposable income fall. Because the rich tend to spend a high proportion of their income on luxuries—such as large cars, entertainment, and tourism—and save a disproportionately large share of their income, there was insufficient demand to keep employment and investment at a high level.

Even before the onset of the depression, business investment had begun to decline. Residential construction boomed between 1924 and 1927, but in 1929 housing starts fell to less than half the 1924 level. A major reason for the depressed housing market was the 1924 immigration law that had restricted foreign immigration. Soaring inventories also led businesses to reduce investment and production. During the mid-1920s, manufacturers expanded their productive capacity and built up excessive inventories. At the decade's end, they cut production back sharply, directing their surplus funds into stock market speculation.

The Federal Reserve, the nation's central bank, played a critical, if inadvertent, role in weakening the economy. In an effort to curb stock market speculation, the Federal Reserve slowed the growth of the money supply, then allowed that supply to fall dramatically after the stock market crash, producing a wrenching "liquidity crisis." Consumers found themselves unable to repay loans, while businesses did not have the capital to finance business operations. Instead of actively stimulating the economy by cutting interest rates and expanding the money supply—the way monetary authorities fight recessions today—the Federal Reserve allowed the country's money supply to decline by 27 percent between 1929 and 1933.

Finally, Republican tariff policies damaged the economy by depressing foreign trade. Anxious to protect American industries from foreign competitors, Congress passed the Fordney-McCumber Tariff of 1922 and the Hawley-Smoot Tariff of 1930, raising tariff rates to unprecedented levels. American tariffs stifled international trade, making it difficult for European nations to pay off their debts. As foreign economies foundered, those countries imposed trade barriers of their own, choking off U.S. exports. By 1933, international trade had plunged 30 percent.

All these factors left the economy ripe for disaster. Yet the depression did not strike instantly; it infected the country gradually, like a slow-growing cancer. Measured in human terms, the Great Depression was the worst economic catastrophe in American history. It hit urban and rural areas, blue- and white-collar families alike. In the nation's cities, unemployed men took to the streets to sell apples or shine shoes. Thousands of others hopped freight trains and wandered from town to town, looking for jobs or handouts.

Unlike most of Western Europe, the United States had no federal system of unemployment insurance. The relief burden fell on state and municipal

CHRONOLOGY OF KEY EVENTS

1914 Marcus Garvey organizes the Universal Negro Improvement Association (UNIA), in Jamaica, to promote black migration to Africa, with first U.S. UNIA branch in Harlem in 1917

1915 Ku Klux Klan is revived and claims 5 million members by 1924

1917– 1925 Some 600,000 black Americans migrate to northern industrial cities

1919 Labor unrest includes a nationwide steel strike, a coal miners' strike, a general strike in Seattle, and a police strike in Boston; race riots erupt in over 20 cities; Eighteenth Amendment bans the manufacture and sale of alcoholic beverages

1920 Palmer raids arrest suspected communists; Massachusetts trial of two Italian anarchists, Nicola Sacco and Bartolomeo Vanzetti, begins on charges of murder, and they are executed in 1927; Sinclair Lewis's *Main Street* exposes the complacency of small-town life

1921 Warren Harding's inauguration as the twenty-ninth president begins 12 years of Republican control of the presidency; Revenue Act slashes taxes on higher incomes; European immigration is restricted to a quota of 3 percent of the population of a nationality living in the United States in 1910

1922 Fordney-McCumber Tariff raises duties on imports

1923 President Harding dies; Calvin Coolidge becomes the thirtieth president

1924 Congress reduces immigration quota to 2 percent of the population of a nationality living in the United States in 1890; Senate committee begins an investigation of Teapot Dome oil-leasing scandal

1925 Scopes trial, the celebrated "Monkey Trial," attacks the teaching of evolution in public schools; F. Scott Fitzgerald's *The Great Gatsby* criticizes the American success ethic

1926 New revenue act further reduces tax rates on high incomes

1929 Herbert Hoover is inaugurated as the thirty-first president; annual quota of immigrants is reduced to about 152,000; stock market crashes

1930 Hawley-Smoot Tariff raises import duties to unprecedented levels

---

governments working in cooperation with private charities, such as the Red Cross and the Community Chest. Created to handle temporary emergencies, these groups lacked the resources to alleviate the massive suffering created by the Great Depression. Poor Southerners, whose states had virtually no relief funds, were particularly hard hit.

Urban centers in the North fared little better. Most city charters did not permit public funds to be spent on work relief. Adding insult to injury, several states disqualified relief clients from voting, while other cities forced them to surrender their automobile license plates. "Prosperity's decade" had ended in economic disaster.

CONCLUSION

In 1931, a journalist named Frederick Lewis Allen published a volume of popular history that did more to shape the popular image of the 1920s than any book ever written by a professional historian. Entitled *Only Yesterday,* it depicted the 1920s as a cynical, hedonistic interlude between the Great War and the Great Depression, a decade of dissipation, of jazz bands, raccoon coats, bathtub gin, flappers, flagpole sitters, bootleggers, and marathon dancers. Allen argued that World War I shattered Americans' faith in reform and moral crusades. The younger generation proceeded to rebel against traditional taboos while their elders engaged in an orgy of speculation.

In fact, however, the twenties present a much more complicated picture than that summed up by such catchphrases as "The Jazz Age" or "The Age of Flaming Youth." Janus, the two-faced god of antiquity, offers a more accurate symbol for America in the 1920s. The nation's image was divided, with one profile looking optimistically to the future and the other staring longingly at the past. Caught between the disillusionment of World War I and the economic malaise of the Great Depression, the 1920s witnessed a gigantic struggle between an old and a new America. Immigration, race, alcohol, evolution, gender politics, sexual morality—all became major cultural battlefields during the twenties. But what World War I started, the Great Depression interrupted. The intense cultural upheavals of the 1920s gave way to the equally intense economic debates of the 1930s and cultural politics took a back seat to the politics of survival.

CHAPTER SUMMARY AND KEY POINTS

The 1920s was both a decade of bitter cultural tensions as well as a period in which many of the features of a modern consumer society took root. In this chapter, you read about urban growth and the rise of consumerism, new trends in American popular culture, changes in traditional gender and class roles, political realignment, and the stock market crash of 1929.

- The 1920s was a decade of exciting social changes and profound cultural conflicts. For many Americans, the growth of cities, the rise of a consumer culture, and the so-called revolution in morals and manners represented liberation from the restrictions of the country's Victorian past.

- But for many others, the United States seemed to be changing in undesirable ways. The result was a thinly veiled "cultural civil war," in which a pluralistic society clashed bitterly over such issues as foreign immigration, evolution, the Ku Klux Klan, and race.

- In 1929, the American economy appeared to be healthy. Employment was high and inflation virtually nonexistent. Still, the seeds of the Great Depression were already apparent in the boom years of the 1920s.

- Prosperity bypassed many groups of Americans, income was poorly distributed, and the farm sector was mired in depression.

SUGGESTIONS FOR FURTHER READING

Kendrick A. Clements, *Hoover, Conservation, and Consumerism: Engineering the Good Life* (2000). Examines President Herbert Hoover's environmental policies and how they became incompatible with his other public goals.

Stanley Coben, *Rebellion Against Victorianism: The Impetus for Cultural Change in 1920s America* (1991). Analyzes social and intellectual changes during the 1920s.

Ann Douglas, *Terrible Honesty: Mongrel Manhattan in the 1920s* (1995). Examines the intellectual and artistic ferment in New York City.

John A. Garraty, *The Great Depression* (1986). Discusses the causes of the depression.

David J. Goldberg, *Discontented America: The United States in the 1920s.* (1999). Overall appraisal of the 1920s incorporating recent scholarship to place the 1920s in historical context. Offers a sophisticated understanding of the culture and politics of the period.

Ellis W. Hawley, *The Great War and the Search for Modern Order: A History of the American People and Their Institutions, 1917–1933,* 2nd ed. (1992). Presents an interpretive overview of the period.

John D. Hicks, *Republican Ascendancy, 1921–1933* (1960). Examines the move toward conservative politics during the 1920s.

Alan Jenkins, *The Twenties* (1974). Overview of the decade's social life and customs.

Carolyn S. Loeb, *Entrepreneurial Vernacular: Developers' Subdivisions in the 1920s* (2001). Explores home ownership and the development of the suburban landscape during the 1920s.

Roderick Nash, *The Nervous Generation: American Thought, 1917–1930* (1970). Analyzes intellectual and artistic innovation from World War I to the Great Depression.

Geoffrey Perrett, *America in the Twenties* (1982). Offers an overview of social and cultural developments of the decade.

Novels

F. Scott Fitzgerald, *The Great Gatsby* (1922).

Arnold Rampersad and David Roessel, eds., *Collected Poems of Langston Hughes* (1993).

Margaret Sanger, *Happiness in Marriage* (1926).

MEDIA RESOURCES
Web Sites

Margaret Sanger Papers Project
http://www.nyu.edu/projects/sanger
This site at New York University contains information about Margaret Sanger and digital versions of several of her works.

Automotive History at the Michigan Electronic Library
http://mel.lib.mi.us/business/autocenter/auto-history.html
This page has several links to sites about automotive history in America.

National Arts and Crafts Archives at the Arts and Crafts Society
http://arts-crafts.com/_b35c69ed/archive/archive.html
This site serves as a guide to materials on the Arts & Crafts Movement that lasted roughly from 1890 to 1929.

Harlem 1900–1940: An African-American Community
http://www.si.umich.edu/CHICO/Harlem

The New York Public Library's Schomburg Center for Research in Black Culture hosts this site that includes a database, a timeline, and an exhibit.

William P. Gottlieb Photographs of the Golden Age of Jazz
http://memory.loc.gov/ammem/wghtml/wghome.html
The Music Division of the Library of Congress has numerous images, audio, and scanned articles from the 1940s.

Negro Leagues Baseball Online Archive
http://www.negroleaguebaseball.com/
Essays about desegregation, baseball, and Jim Crow as well as images of teams and players comprise much of this site.

Popular Culture in the 1920s
http://www.louisville.edu/~kprayb01/
1920s,Society-Index.html
This site looks at how the 1920s set the stage for many aspects of modern popular culture.

The Scopes Trial
http://xroads.virginia.edu/~UG97/inherit/1925home.html
This site gives a general description of the trial and the issues surrounding it.

Temperance and Prohibition
http://www.cohums.ohio-state.edu/history/projects/prohibition/
This site looks at the temperance movement over time and contains many informative links.

The Flapper
http://www.pandorasbox.com/flapper.html
This site contains many links to information about the popular culture of the 1920s with special reference to the flapper.

The Calvin Coolidge Experience
http://www.geocities.com/CapitolHill/4921/
This site is an unusual look at one of America's less colorful presidents.

Films and Videos

The Twentieth Century: The 1920s, A Decade of Contradictions (2000). Mpi Home Video. Documentary that examines the contradicting political and social movements of the decade.

Inherit the Wind (1960). MGM/UA. Film about the Scopes Monkey Trial, starring Spencer Tracy and Frederic March.

KEY TERMS

Restrictive covenant   (p. 646)

Amos 'n Andy   (p. 649)

Jazz Age   (p. 649)

"Black Sox" scandal   (p. 651)

Existentialism   (p. 652)

Flapper   (p. 652)

Nineteenth Amendment   (p. 653)

Equal Rights Amendment   (p. 653)

Prohibition   (p. 656)

National Anti-Cigarette League   (p. 656)

Scopes "Monkey Trial"   (p. 656)

National Origins Act of 1924   (p. 657)

Sacco and Vanzetti case   (p. 657)

Ku Klux Klan   (p. 657)

National Urban League   (p. 658)

National Association for the Advancement of Colored People (NAACP)   (p. 658)

Harlem Renaissance   (p. 659)

Associationism   (p. 660)

Ohio Gang   (p. 660)

Teapot Dome scandal   (p. 660)

Ponzi scheme   (p. 662)

Black Tuesday   (p. 663)

PEOPLE YOU SHOULD KNOW

Henry Ford   (p. 647)

Alfred Sloan   (p. 647)

Charles Lindbergh   (p. 649)

George Herman ("Babe") Ruth   (p. 651)

Sigmund Freud   (p. 652)

Alfred C. Kinsey   (p. 652)

Clarence Darrow   (p. 657)

A. Philip Randolph   (p. 658)

Marcus Garvey   (p. 658)

Alfred E. Smith   (p. 661)

REVIEW QUESTIONS

1. What factors contributed to the emergence of modern American culture in the 1920s?

2. How did the appearance of new forms of art and entertainment change American society in the 1920s?

3. What were the major points of conflict within the emerging modern American culture?

4. Why did conservative politics dominate such a seemingly liberal culture as 1920s America?

5. Would government intervention have prevented the stock market crash in 1929?

24 The Age of Roosevelt

WOODY GUTHRIE: BALLADEER OF THE GREAT DEPRESSION

To fans of authentic folk music, Woodrow Wilson "Woody" Guthrie was a "Shakespeare in overalls," the finest American frontier balladeer of the twentieth century. His nasal, high-pitched singing voice was definitely an acquired taste, but Guthrie's lyrics were at once simple and penetrating. He sang of vagabonds who wandered in search of work, of union men who saw their comrades on the picket lines knocked to the ground by company goons, and of farmers who watched with horror as their land dried up and turned into a dust bowl. In short he put to music the hardships and struggles of working-class Americans trapped in the Great Depression.

Guthrie drew his material from his life. Born in 1912, Woody grew up in Oklahoma and the Texas Panhandle in a family star-crossed by disasters. When he was still a boy his older sister died from setting herself on fire; his father, once a prosperous land speculator, sank into alcoholism; and his mother slipped slowly into madness and had to be committed to the state mental hospital.

In the face of these tragedies the Guthrie household simply dissolved, leaving Woody pretty much on his own. He passed the time by learning to play the guitar and harmonica. Eventually, he dropped out of school and became a drifter, driven by an internal restlessness that kept him on the road for the rest of his life.

Guthrie spent the Great Depression riding the rails, playing his music, and visiting "his" people, in the boxcars, hobo jungles, and migrant camps from Oklahoma to California. He saw families sleeping on the ground and children with distended bellies who cried from hunger while guards hired to protect the orchards prevented them from eating fruit that lay rotting on the ground. Over time a quiet anger began to eat at him and he blamed the nation's "polli-Tish-uns" for not doing more to relieve the people's suffering.

By 1940 Guthrie had recorded several albums of Dust Bowl ballads and union protest songs. His home-grown radicalism made him an instant hit with socialist and communist intellectuals and entertainment figures who saw his music as a powerful weapon in the class struggle. They saw Guthrie as an authentic folk hero, the very embodiment of the proletarian artist. In truth, Guthrie held more

Woody Guthrie often inscribed the phrase "This machine surrounds hate and destroys it" on his guitars.

radical political views than most Americans, but he aptly fulfilled his role as the "voice of the people" by putting to music the most important themes to emerge in American life during the 1930s—the common man's defiant pride, his will to survive in the face of adversity, and the extraordinary love Americans felt for their country.

In "God Blessed America" (which later generations of Americans would recognize by its first line, "This land is your land, this land is my land"), Guthrie sang of "endless skyways," "golden valleys," "diamond deserts," and "wheat fields waving," evoking the country's grandeur with a poet's sense of beauty. What gave the song its power, however, was the idea that America belonged to the people; every verse closed with the refrain, "God blessed America for me."

Even in the depths of the Great Depression, Guthrie found much of enduring value in America. In ballad after ballad, he celebrated the fortitude and dignity of the American people. They provided the glue that held things together while President Franklin D. Roosevelt experimented with policies and programs designed to promote relief, recovery, and reform.

THE GREAT DEPRESSION IN GLOBAL PERSPECTIVE

Unlike previous economic downturns, which generally were confined to a handful of nations or specific regions, the Great Depression was a global phenome-non. Africa, Asia, Australia, Europe, and North and South America all suffered from the economic collapse. International trade fell 30 percent, as most nations tried to protect their industries by raising tariffs on imported goods. These "beggar-thy-neighbor" trade policies were a major reason why the depression persisted as long as it did.

Also, in contrast to the relatively brief economic "panics" of the past, the Great Depression dragged on with no end in sight. As it deepened, the depression had far-reaching political consequences. One response to it was military dictatorship—a response found in Argentina and many countries in Central America. Western industrialized countries cut back sharply on the purchase of raw materials and other commodities. The collapse in raw material and agricultural commodity prices led to social unrest, resulting in the rise of military dictatorships that promised to maintain order.

A second response to the depression was fascism and militarism—a response found in Germany, Italy, and Japan. In Germany, Adolf Hitler and his Nazi party promised to restore the country's economy and rebuild its military. After becoming chancellor in 1932, Hitler outlawed labor unions, restructured German industry into a series of cartels, and, after 1935, instituted a massive program of military rearmament that ended high unemployment. In Italy, fascism arose under the leadership of Italian dictator Benito Mussolini even before the depression's onset. In Japan, militarists seized control of the government during the 1930s. In an effort to relieve the depression, Japanese military officers conquered Manchuria, a region rich in raw materials, in 1931, and coastal China in 1937.

A third response to the depression was totalitarian communism. In the Soviet Union, the Great Depression helped solidify Joseph Stalin's grip on power. In 1928, Stalin instituted a planned economy. His first Five-Year Plan called for rapid industrialization and "collectivization" of small peasant farms under government control. To crush opposition to his program, which required peasant farmers to give their products to the government at low prices, Stalin exiled millions of peasants to labor camps in Siberia, instituting a program of terror called the Great Purge. Historians estimate that as many as 20 million Soviets died during the 1930s as a result of famine and deliberate killings.

A fourth and final response to the depression was welfare capitalism, which could be found in countries such as Canada, Great Britain, and France. Under welfare capitalism, the government assumed ultimate responsibility for promoting a reasonably fair distribution of wealth and power and providing security against the risks of bankruptcy, unemployment, and destitution.

The economic decline brought on by this depression was steeper and more protracted in the United States than in other industrialized countries. The unemployment rate rose higher and remained higher longer than in any other western society. While European countries significantly reduced unemployment by 1936, as late as 1939, when World War II began in Europe, the American jobless rate still exceeded 17 percent, not dropping below 14 percent until 1941.

The Great Depression transformed the American political and economic landscape. It produced a major political realignment, creating a coalition of big-city ethnics, African Americans, and Southern Democrats committed, to various degrees, to interventionist government. It strengthened the federal presence in American life, spawning such innovations as national old-age pensions, unemployment compensation, aid to dependent children, public housing, federally subsidized school lunches, insured bank deposits, the minimum wage, and stock market regulation. It fundamentally altered labor relations, producing a revived labor movement and a national labor policy protective of collective bargaining. It transformed the farm economy by introducing federal price supports and rural electrification. Above all, the Great Depression produced a fundamental shift in public attitudes. It led Americans to view the federal government as their agency of action and reform and the ultimate protector of the public's well-being.

THE HUMAN TOLL

Even after more than half a century, images of the Great Depression remain firmly etched in the American psyche—breadlines, soup kitchens, tin-can shanties and tarpaper shacks known as **"Hoovervilles,"** penniless men and women selling apples on street corners, and gray battalions of "Arkies" and "Okies" packed into Model A Fords heading out to California.

The economic collapse was staggering in its dimensions. Unemployment jumped from less than 3 million in 1929 to 4 million in 1930, 8 million in 1931, and 12½ million in 1932. By 1932, a quarter of the nation's families did not have a single employed wage earner. Only one company in ten failed to cut pay, and in 1932, three-quarters of all workers were on part-time schedules, averaging just 60 percent of the normal workweek.

Appalling in dimension, the collapse was terrifying in its scope and impact. By 1933 average family income had tumbled 40 percent, from $2300 in 1929 down to just $1500 four years later. In the Pennsylvania coalfields, three or four families crowded together in one-room shacks and lived on wild weeds. In Arkansas, families were found inhabiting caves, and in Oakland, California, whole families lived in sewer pipes.

Vagrancy shot up as many families were evicted from their homes for nonpayment of rent. The

First built by unemployed lumberjacks in the fall and winter of 1931–132, this Hooverville in Seattle was twice burned down by Seattle police when the homeless squatters living there failed to comply with the order to vacate. Built a third time, and allowed to stand, by 1934 the Hooverville was home to nearly 650 people living in 479 shanties. The scrapwood shanties were burned down for a third and final time in 1941 when the city took over the land to make way for a port.

Southern Pacific Railroad boasted that it threw 683,000 vagrants off its trains in 1931. Free public flophouses and missions in Los Angeles provided beds for 200,000 of the uprooted.

Many families sought to cope by planting gardens, canning food, buying day-old bread, and using cardboard and cotton for shoe soles. Despite a steep drop in food prices, many families did without milk or meat. To save money, families neglected medical and dental care.

President Herbert Hoover declared, "Nobody is actually starving. The hoboes are better fed than they have ever been." But in New York City in 1931 there were 20 known cases of starvation; in 1934, there were 110 deaths from hunger.

The Great Depression had a powerful impact on families. It forced couples to delay marriage and drove the birthrate below the replacement level for the first time in American history. The divorce rate fell—for the simple reason that many couples could not afford to maintain separate households or pay legal fees. But rates of desertion soared—by 1940, 1.5 million married women were living apart from their husbands. More than 200,000 vagrant children wandered the country because of the breakup of their families.

The depression inflicted a heavy psychological toll on jobless men. With no wages to reinforce their authority, many men lost power as primary decision makers. Large numbers of men lost their self-respect, became immobilized, and stopped looking for work, while others turned to alcohol or became self-destructive or abusive to their families.

In contrast to the men, many women saw their status rise during the depression. To supplement the family income, married women entered the workforce in large numbers. Although most women worked in menial occupations, the fact that they were employed and bringing home paychecks elevated their position within the family and gave them a say in family decisions.

Despite the hardships it inflicted, the Great Depression drew some families closer together. Families had to devise strategies for getting through hard times because their survival depended on it. They pooled their incomes, moved in with relatives in order to cut expenses, and did without. Many families drew comfort from their religion, sustained by the hope things would turn out well in the end, while others placed their faith in themselves, in their own dogged determination to survive that so impressed observers like Woody Guthrie. But many Americans no longer believed the problems could be solved by people acting alone or through voluntary associations. Increasingly, they looked to the federal government for help.

The Dispossessed

Economic hardship and loss visited all sections of the country. Doctors and lawyers saw their incomes fall 40 percent. But no groups suffered more from the depression than African Americans and Mexican Americans.

A year after the stock market crashed, 70 percent of Charleston's black population and 75 percent of Memphis's was unemployed. In Macon County, Alabama, home of Booker T. Washington's famous Tuskegee Institute, most black families lived in homes without wooden floors, windows, or sewage disposal and subsisted on salt pork (pork fat cured in salt), hominy grits, corn bread, and molasses. Income averaged less than a dollar a day.

Conditions were also distressed in the North. In Chicago and other large northern cities, most African Americans lived in "kitchenettes." Six-room apartments, previously rented for $50 a month, were divided into six kitchenettes renting for $8 dollars a week, assuring landlords of a windfall of an extra $142 a month.

The depression hit Mexican American families especially hard. Mexican Americans faced serious opposition from organized labor, which resented competition from Mexican workers as unemployment rose. Bowing to union pressure, federal, state, and local authorities "repatriated" more than 400,000 people of Mexican descent to prevent them from applying for relief. Because this group included many United States citizens, the deportations constituted a gross violation of civil liberties.

Private and Public Charity

The economic crisis of the 1930s overwhelmed private charities and local governments. In south Texas, the Salvation Army provided a penny per person each day. In Philadelphia, even though private and public charities distributed $1 million a month in poor relief, this provided families with only $1.50 a week for groceries. In 1932, total public and private relief expenditures amounted to $317 million—$26 for each of the nation's 12½ million jobless.

PRESIDENT HERBERT HOOVER RESPONDS

When the Great Depression struck, most political and economic leaders had regarded recessions as inevitable, a natural part of the business cycle. The prevailing economic theory held that government intervention was both unnecessary and unwise. Previous financial panics had failed to elicit much response from government; and many economists in 1929 continued to extol the virtues of inaction, arguing that the economy would recover by itself. President Herbert Hoover disagreed. Though Hoover saw the Great Crash as a temporary slump in a fundamentally healthy economy, he believed the president should try to facilitate economic recovery.

Conservative Responses

First, Hoover resorted to old-fashioned **jawboning.** Shortly after the stock market crashed, he summoned business and labor leaders to the White House. Industrial leaders promised to maintain prices and wages, and labor spokesmen pledged not to strike or demand higher wages. While Hoover remained hopeful voluntary measures would suffice, businesses struggled to survive, forcing employers to lay off workers.

Next, the president tried cheerleading. The contrast between Hoover's speeches and conditions in the country was jarring. According to Hoover, the economy in 1930 was fundamentally sound, and recovery was just around the corner. His rosy pronouncements prompted critics to accuse Hoover of being insensitive to the unemployed and the dispossessed. Cynics called the shantytown slums on the edges of cities "Hoovervilles." Newspapers became "Hoover blankets" and empty pockets turned inside out, "Hoover flags."

Neither cruel nor insensitive, Hoover was tormented by the suffering of the poor. Yet he could not bring himself to sanction large-scale federal public works programs because he honestly believed that recovery depended on the private sector, because he wanted to maintain a balanced budget, and because he feared federal relief programs would undermine individual character by making recipients dependent on the state.

Government Loans

When jawboning and cheerleading failed to revive the economy, Hoover reluctantly adopted other measures. In 1932 Congress created the **Reconstruction Finance Corporation (RFC)** and authorized it to loan $2 billion to banks, savings and loan associations, railroads, and life insurance companies. Blaming the depression on tight credit, Hoover believed federal loans would enable businesses to increase production and hire workers. The same principle applied to the Federal Home Loan Bank System (FHLBS), created by Congress in July 1932 to lend up to $500 million to savings and loan associations to revive the construction industry.

Yet by early 1933 Hoover's agencies had failed to make a dent in the Great Depression. The real prob-

Bank failures wiped out the life savings of many prudent Americans.

lem was not tight credit but the soft demand for goods, a problem that flowed both from the chronic low wages paid to the bulk of American workers and the massive layoffs following the Great Crash. It was a vicious cycle. Unemployed workers could not buy goods, so businesses cut back production and laid off additional workers. Businesspeople did not ask banks for working capital loans, which the RFC and FHLBS were created to provide, because they had no interest in increasing production.

FRANKLIN ROOSEVELT AND THE FIRST NEW DEAL

In June 1932, Franklin D. Roosevelt received the Democratic presidential nomination. At first glance he did not look like a man who could relate to other peoples' suffering, for Roosevelt had spent his entire life in the lap of luxury. A fifth cousin of Teddy Roosevelt, he was born in 1882 to one of New York's oldest and wealthiest families. He attended Groton, an exclusive private school, then went to Harvard University and Columbia Law School. After three years in the New York state senate, Roosevelt was tapped by President Wilson to serve as assistant secretary of the navy in 1913. His status as the rising star of the Democratic party was confirmed when James Cox

The Tuskegee Syphilis Study

The South in the 1930s was the section of the United States that most resembled the underdeveloped nations of the world. Its people (white and black) remained mostly rural; they were less well-educated than other Americans; and they made decidedly less money.

As a group, African Americans in the South were among the poorest of the poor—virtual paupers, chronically unemployed, without benefit of sanitation, adequate diet, or the rudiments of hygiene. They suffered from a host of diseases, including tuberculosis, syphilis, hookworm, pellagra, rickets, and rotting teeth; and their death rate far exceeded that of whites.

Despite their evident need, few blacks received proper medical care. In fact, many African Americans lived outside the world of modern medicine, going from cradle to grave without ever seeing a doctor. There was a severe shortage of black physicians, and many white physicians refused to treat black patients. In addition, there were only a handful of black hospitals in the South, and most white hospitals either denied blacks admission or assigned them to often overcrowded segregated wings.

But poverty as much as racism was to blame for the medical neglect of African Americans. Medical care in the United States was offered on a fee-for-services basis, and the simple truth was that many African Americans were too poor to be able to afford medical care.

To combat this and other problems, the federal government in 1912 united all its health-related activities under the Public Health Service (PHS). Over the next few decades, the PHS distinguished itself by launching attacks on hookworm, pellagra, and a host of other illnesses. In no field was it more active than in its efforts to fight venereal diseases.

Health reformers knew that not only was syphilis a killer, but it was also capable of inflicting blindness, deafness, and insanity on its victims. Furthermore, they saw the disease as a serious threat to the family because they associated it with prostitution and loose morals in general, thus adding a moral dimension to their medical concerns.

Taking advantage of the emergency atmosphere of World War I, progressive reformers pushed through Congress in 1918 a bill to create a special Division of Venereal Diseases within the PHS. The PHS officers who launched this new offensive against syphilis began with high motives, and their initial successes were impressive. By 1919, they had established over 200 health clinics, which treated over 64,000 patients who could not otherwise have afforded health care.

In the late 1920s, the PHS joined forces with the Rosenwald Fund (a private philanthropic foundation based in Chicago) to develop a syphilis control program for African Americans in the South. Most doctors assumed that blacks suffered a much higher infection rate than whites because blacks abandoned themselves to sexual promiscuity. And once infected, the argument went, African Americans remained infected because they were too poor and too ignorant to seek medical care.

To test these theories, the PHS selected communities in six different southern states, examined the local African American populations to ascertain the incidence of syphilis, and offered free treatment to those who were infected. This pilot program had hardly gotten underway, however, when the stock market collapse forced the Rosenwald Fund to terminate its support. The PHS was left without sufficient funds to follow up its syphilis control work among African Americans in the South.

Macon County, Alabama, was the site of one of those original pilot programs. Its county seat, Tuskegee, was the home of the famed Tuskegee Institute. It was in and around Tuskegee that the PHS had discovered an infection rate of 35 percent among those tested, the highest incidence in the six communities studied. In fact, despite the presence of the Tuskegee Institute, which boasted a well-equipped hospital that might have provided low-cost health care to African Americans in the region, Macon County was home to the worst poverty and the most sickly residents the PHS discovered anywhere in the South. It was precisely this ready-made laboratory of human suffering that prompted the PHS to return to Macon County in 1932. Since they could not afford to treat syphilis, the PHS decided to document the damage inflicted on its victims by launching a scientific study of the effects of untreated syphilis on African American males. Many white Southerners (including physicians) believed that although practically all blacks had syphilis, it did not harm them as severely as it did whites. PHS

officials knew that syphilis was a serious threat to the health of African Americans, and they intended to use the results of the study to pressure southern state legislatures into appropriating funds for syphilis control work among rural blacks.

Armed with these good motives, the PHS launched the Tuskegee Study in 1932. It involved approximately 400 African American males who tested positive for the disease and 200 nonsyphilitic black males to serve as controls. In order to secure cooperation, the PHS told the local residents that they had returned to Macon County to treat the ill men. The PHS did not inform them that they had syphilis. Instead, the men were told that they had "bad blood," a catch-all phrase rural blacks used to describe a host of ailments.

The PHS had not intended to treat the men, but state health officials demanded, as the price of their cooperation, that the men be given at least enough medication to render them noninfectious. Consequently, all of the men received a little treatment. No one worried much about the glaring contradiction of offering treatment in a study of supposedly untreated syphilis (the reasoning being that the men had not received enough treatment to cure them). Thus, the experiment was scientifically flawed from the outset.

Although the original plan called for only a one-year experiment, the Tuskegee Study continued until 1972—partly because many of the health officials became fascinated by the scientific potential of a long-range study of syphilis. No doubt others rationalized the study by telling themselves that the men were too poor to afford proper treatment, or that too much time had passed for treatment to be of any benefit. Some health officials may even have seen the men as clinical material rather than human beings.

At any rate, the Tuskegee Study killed approximately 100 African American men, who died as a direct result of syphilis; scores went blind or insane, and still others endured lives of chronic ill health from syphilis-related complications. Throughout their suffering, the PHS made no effort to treat the men, and on several occasions even took steps to prevent them from getting treatment on their own. As a result, the men did not receive penicillin when that "wonder drug" became widely available after World War II.

During those same four decades civil protests raised America's concern for the rights of African Americans, and the ethical standards of the medical profession changed dramatically. These changes had no impact on the Tuskegee Study, however. PHS officials published no fewer than 13 scientific papers on the experiment (several appearing in the nation's leading medical journals), and the PHS routinely presented sessions on it at medical conventions. The Tuskegee Study only ended in 1972 because a "whistle-blower" in the PHS named Peter Buxtun leaked the story to the press. Health officials at first tried to defend their actions, but public outrage quickly silenced them, and they agreed to end the experiment. As part of an out-of-court settlement, the survivors were finally treated for syphilis, and the men, and the families of the deceased, received small cash payments.

The 40-year deathwatch had finally ended, but its legacy can still be felt today. In the wake of its hearings, Congress enacted new legislation to protect the subjects of human experiments. The Tuskegee Study left behind a host of unanswered questions about the social and racial attitudes of the medical establishment in the United States. It served as a cruel reminder of how class distinctions and racism could negate ethical and scientific standards.

chose Roosevelt as his running mate in the presidential election of 1920.

The Election of 1932

Handsome and outgoing, Roosevelt seemed to have a bright political future. Then disaster struck. In 1921 he contracted polio, which left him paralyzed from the waist down and confined to a wheelchair for the rest of his life. Instead of retiring, however, Roosevelt labored diligently to return to public life. "If you had spent two years in bed trying to wiggle your toe," he later declared, "after that anything would seem easy."

Buoyed by an exuberant optimism and devoted political allies, Roosevelt won the governorship of New York in 1928, one of the few Democrats to survive the Republican landslide. Surrounding himself with able advisers, Roosevelt labored to convert New York into a laboratory for reform, involving conservation, old-age pensions, public works projects, and unemployment insurance.

In his acceptance speech before the 1932 Democratic convention in Chicago, Roosevelt promised "a **New Deal** for the American people." Although his speech contained few concrete proposals, Roosevelt radiated confidence, giving many desperate voters hope. He even managed during the campaign to turn his lack of a blueprint into an asset, promising to experiment.

The Republicans stuck with Hoover, but what little chance he had for reelection was dashed by his callous treatment of the **Bonus Army.** A bedraggled collection of unemployed veterans and their families, the Bonus Army marched on Washington in the spring of 1932 to ask Congress for immediate payment of their war service bonuses, which did not come due until 1945. More than 15,000 strong, they erected a shantytown, camped out in vacant lots, and occupied empty government buildings. Though the House voted to give them what they wanted, the Senate killed the bill after Hoover lobbied against it.

Most of the veterans then left Washington, D.C., but a few thousand stayed behind because they had no place to go. At Hoover's request, Congress appropriated $100,000 to help the remaining veterans return home. When police tried to evict some of the marchers in late July, a riot broke out in which two policemen and two marchers died. Hoover then ordered General Douglas MacArthur to use federal troops to remove them from government buildings. Exceeding his orders, MacArthur used tanks and tear gas to drive the veterans from the city. Newsmen captured the melee in vivid photographs, which papers carried the next day.

Although Hoover was appalled by what happened, he publicly accepted the responsibility and endorsed MacArthur's charge that the bonus marchers included dangerous radicals who wanted

Roosevelt was charming and charismatic, and many people felt he was genuinely interested in their concerns. Here Roosevelt meets with a miner during his 1932 campaign.

Army Chief of Staff Douglas MacArthur mobilized tanks, cavalry, and foot soldiers armed with tear gas to drive the Bonus Marchers and their families out of Washington, D.C., then set fire to the tent city the Marchers had erected. MacArthur's action, and President Hoover's defense of it, appalled many Americans who were horrified to see armed troops turning their weapons on the unarmed veterans who had served the country in World War I.

to overthrow the government. Most Americans were outraged by the government's harsh treatment of the Bonus Army, and Hoover encountered resentment everywhere he campaigned.

Upon learning of the Bonus Army incident, Franklin D. Roosevelt remarked: "Well, this will elect me." Roosevelt was correct—he buried Hoover in November, winning 22,809,638 votes to Hoover's 15,758,901, and 472 to 59 electoral votes. The Democrats also won commanding majorities in both houses of Congress.

Roosevelt appealed to a wide range of voters, wooing Southerners back into the Democrat fold and attracting new groups of voters, including young peo-

ple, women, and ethnic Americans. Urban Catholics, Jews, and members of the Eastern Orthodox Church voted overwhelmingly for Roosevelt. The 1932 election was the first of many in which these groups would support strongly the Democratic party.

Electoral Shift, 1928 and 1932

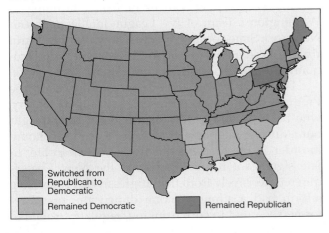

Switched from Republican to Democratic

Remained Democratic

Remained Republican

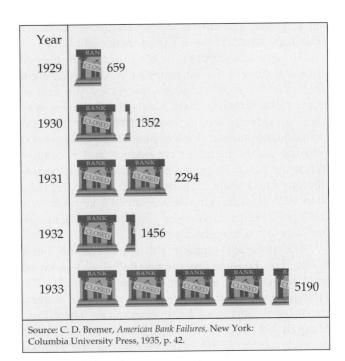

Source: C. D. Bremer, *American Bank Failures*, New York: Columbia University Press, 1935, p. 42.

FIGURE 24.1
Bank Failures, 1929–1933

The First 100 Days

The nation's plight on March 4, 1933, the day Franklin Roosevelt assumed the presidency, was desperate. A quarter of the nation's workforce was jobless. About 9000 banks, holding the savings of 27 million families, had failed since 1929—1456 in 1932 alone. Farm foreclosures were averaging 20,000 a month. The public was frantic for action. Hamilton Fish, a conservative Republican Congressman from New York, promised the president that Congress would "give you any power that you need."

In his inaugural address, Roosevelt expressed confidence that his administration could end the depression. "The only thing we have to fear," he declared, "is fear itself." The president promised decisive action. He called Congress into special session and demanded "broad executive power to wage a war against the emergency, as great as the power that would be given me if we were in fact invaded by a foreign foe." In his **First Hundred Days** in office, the president pushed 15 major bills through Congress, which would reshape every aspect of the economy, from banking and industry to agriculture and social welfare.

He attacked the bank crisis first, declaring a national bank holiday, which closed all banks. In just four days, his aides drafted the **Emergency Banking Relief Act,** which permitted solvent banks to reopen under government supervision, and allowed the RFC to buy the stock of troubled banks and keep them open until they could be reorganized. The law also gave the president broad powers over the Federal Reserve System. The law radically reshaped the nation's banking system; it passed Congress in eight hours.

To generate support for his program, Roosevelt appealed directly to the people. On March 12, eight days after he took office, he conducted the first of many radio **fireside chats.** Using the radio the way later presidents would exploit television, he explained what he had done in plain, simple terms and told the public to have "confidence and courage." When the banks reopened the following day, people demonstrated their faith by making more deposits than withdrawals. One of Roosevelt's key advisers did not exaggerate when he later boasted, "Capitalism was saved in eight days."

The president quickly pushed ahead on other fronts. The **Federal Emergency Relief Act** pumped $500 million into state-run welfare programs. The Homeowners Loan Act provided the first federal mortgage financing and loan guarantees. The **Glass-Steagall Act** provided a federal guarantee on all bank deposits under $5000 (with creation of the Federal Deposit Insurance Corporation), separated commercial and investment banking, and strengthened the Federal Reserve's ability to stabilize the economy.

TABLE 24.1	
Legislation Enacted During the First Hundred Days, March 9–June 16, 1933	
March 9	Emergency Banking Relief Act
March 20	Economy Act
March 22	Beer-Wine Revenue Act
March 31	Unemployment Relief Act
March 31	Civilian Conservation Corps Act
May 12	Agricultural Adjustment Act
May 12	Federal Emergency Relief Act
May 18	Tennessee Valley Authority Act
May 27	Securities Act of 1933
June 5	Gold Repeal Joint Resolution
June 13	Home Owners' Refinancing Act
June 16	Farm Credit Act
June 16	Banking Act of 1933
June 16	Emergency Railroad Transportation Act
June 16	National Industrial Recovery Act

In addition, Roosevelt took the nation off the gold standard, devalued the dollar, and ordered the Federal Reserve System to ease credit. Other important laws passed during the 100 days included the Agricultural Adjustment Act, the nation's first system of agricultural price and production supports; the National Industrial Recovery Act, the first major attempt to plan and regulate the economy; and the Tennessee Valley Authority Act, the first direct government involvement in energy production.

The New Dealers

Franklin Roosevelt brought a new breed of government officials to Washington. Previously, most government administrators were wealthy patricians, businessmen, or political loyalists. Roosevelt, however, looked to new sources of talent, bringing to Washington a team of Ivy League intellectuals and New York State social workers. Known as the **"brain trust,"** these advisers provided Roosevelt with economic ideas and oratorical ammunition.

The New Dealers were strongly influenced by the Progressive reformers of the early twentieth century, who believed that government had not only a right but a duty to intervene in all aspects of the economy in order to improve the quality of American life. In one significant respect, however, the New Dealers differed decisively from the Progressives. Progressive reform had a strongly moral dimension; many reformers wanted to curb drinking, regulate sexual behavior, and reshape human character. In comparison, the New Dealers were much more pragmatic—an attitude vividly illustrated by an incident that took place during World War I. One of the most intense policy debates during the war was whether to provide American troops with condoms. The secretary of the navy, Josephus Daniels, rejected the idea, fearing that it would corrupt the troops' morals. While Daniels was on vacation, however, his undersecretary, Franklin Roosevelt, authorized prophylactics for sailors. Moral reform would not drive the New Deal.

Apart from their commitment to pragmatism, the New Dealers were unified in their rejection of laissez-faire orthodoxy—the idea that the federal government's responsibilities were confined to balancing the federal budget and providing for the nation's defense. The New Dealers did, however, disagree profoundly about the best way to end the depression, offering three alternative prescriptions for rescuing the nation's economy. The "trust-busters," led by Thurman Arnold, called for vigorous enforcement of antitrust laws to break up concentrated business power. The "associationalists" wanted to encourage cooperation between business, labor, and government by establishing associations and codes supported by the three parties. The economic planners, led by Rexford Tugwell, Adolph Berle, and Gardiner Means, wanted to create a system of centralized national planning.

The Farmers' Plight

Roosevelt moved aggressively to address the crisis facing the nation's farmers. No group was harder hit by the depression than farmers and farm workers. Farm income fell a staggering two-thirds during the depression's first three years. In one day, a quarter of Mississippi's farm acreage was auctioned off to pay debts.

The farmers' problem, ironically, was that they grew too much. Worldwide crop production soared—a result of more efficient farm machinery, stronger fertilizers, and improved plant varieties—but demand fell, as people ate less bread, Europeans imposed protective tariffs, and consumers replaced cotton with rayon. The glut caused prices to fall. To meet farm debts in 1932, farmers had to grow 2.5 times as much corn as in 1929, 2.7 times as much wheat, and 2.4 times as much cotton.

As farm incomes fell, farm tenancy soared; two-fifths of all farmers worked on land that they did not own. The Gudgers, a white southern Alabama share-cropping family of six, illustrated the plight of tenants, who were slipping deeper and deeper into debt. Each year, their landlord provided them with 20 acres of land, seed, an unpainted one-room house, a shed, a mule, fertilizer, and $10 a month. In return, they owed him half their corn and cotton crop and 8 percent interest on their debts. In 1934 they were $80 in debt; by 1935, their debts had risen another $12.

Nature itself seemed to have turned against farmers. In the South, the boll weevil devoured the cotton crop, while on the Great Plains, the topsoil literally blew away, piling up in ditches like "snow drifts in winter." The **Dust Bowl** produced unparalleled human tragedy, but it had not occurred by accident. Although the Plains had always been a harsh, arid, inhospitable environment, a covering of tough grass-roots called sod allowed the land to retain moisture and support vegetation. During the 1890s, however, overgrazing by cattle severely damaged the sod. Then, during World War I, farmers driven by the demand for wheat, used gasoline-powered tractors to plow large sections of the prairie for the first time. The fragile skin protecting the prairie was stripped away. When, beginning in 1930, drought struck and temperatures soared, the wind began to blow the soil away.

Tenant farmers found themselves evicted from their land. By 1939, a million Dust Bowl refugees and other tenant farmers left the Plains to work as itinerant produce pickers in California. Whole counties were depopulated as a result.

The New Deal attacked farm problems through a variety of programs. Rural electrification programs meant that for the first time, Americans in Appalachia, the Texas hill country, and other areas would have the opportunity to share in the benefits of electric light and running water. As late as 1935 more than 6 million of America's 6.8 million farms had no electricity. Unlike their sisters in the city, farmwomen had no washing machines, refrigerators, or vacuum cleaners. Private companies insisted that it would be prohibitive to provide electrical service to rural areas.

Roosevelt disagreed. He wanted to break the private monopoly of electric power in rural areas, envisioning a future in which electric power would serve broader goals, including flood control, soil conservation, reforestation, diversification of industry, and a general improvement in the quality of life for rural Americans. Settling on the 40,000-square-mile valley of the Tennessee River as a test site, Roosevelt decided to put the government into the electric business.

Two months after he took office Congress passed a bill creating the **Tennessee Valley Authority (TVA).** The bill authorized the TVA to build 21 dams to generate electricity for tens of thousands of farm families. In 1935 Roosevelt signed an executive order creating the Rural Electrification Administration (REA) to bring electricity generated by government dams to America's hinterland.

Nor was electricity the only benefit the New Deal bestowed on farmers. The Soil Conservation

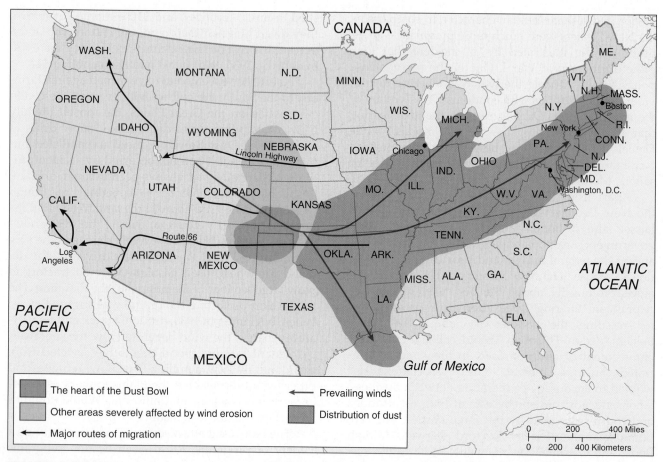

The Dust Bowl

Service helped farmers battle erosion; the Farm Credit Administration provided some relief from farm foreclosures, and the Commodity Credit Corporation permitted farmers to use stored products as collateral for loans. Roosevelt's most ambitious farm program, however, was the **Agricultural Adjustment Act (AAA).**

The AAA, led by Secretary of Agriculture **Henry Wallace,** sought a partnership between the government and major producers. Together the new allies would raise prices by reducing the supply of farm goods. Under the AAA, the large producers, acting through farm cooperatives, would agree upon a "domestic allotment" plan that would assign acreage quotas to each producer. Participation would be voluntary. Farmers who cut production to comply with the quotas would be paid for land left fallow.

Unfortunately for its backers, the AAA got off to a horrible start. Because the 1933 crops had already been planted by the time Congress established the AAA, the administration ordered farmers to plow their crops under, paying them over $100 million to destroy 10 million acres of cotton. The government also purchased and slaughtered six million pigs, salvaging only one million pounds for the needy. The

public neither understood nor forgave the agency for destroying food while jobless people went hungry.

Overall, the AAA's record was mixed. It raised farm income, but did little for sharecroppers and tenant farmers, the groups hardest hit by the agricultural crisis. Farm incomes doubled between 1933 and 1936, but those with large farms reaped most of the benefits. Many large landowners used government payments to purchase tractors and combines allowing them to mechanize farm operations, increasing crop yields and reducing the need for sharecroppers and tenants. An unintentional consequence of the New Deal farm policies was to force at least 3 million small farmers off the land. For all its inadequacies, however, the AAA established the precedent for a system of farm price supports, subsidies, and surplus purchases that continues more than half a century later.

The National Recovery Administration

To help industry and labor, Roosevelt asked for—and Congress passed—the National Industrial Recovery Act (NIRA), which authorized establishment of the **National Recovery Administration (NRA).** The NRA sought to revive industry through rational

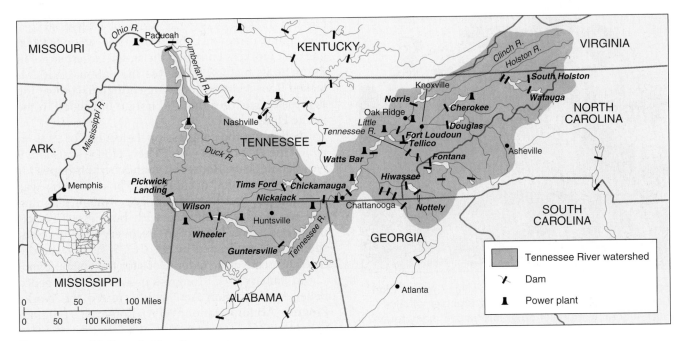

Tennessee Valley Authority

planning. Representatives of business, labor, and government would establish codes of fair practices that would set prices, production levels, minimum wages, and maximum hours within each industry. The NRA also supported workers' right to join labor unions. By ending ruinous competition, overproduction, labor conflicts, and by deflating prices, the NRA sought to stabilize the economy.

Led by General Hugh Johnson, the new agency got off to a promising start. By midsummer 1933, over 500 industries had signed codes covering 22 million workers. By the end of the summer the nation's ten largest industries had been won over, as well as hundreds of smaller businesses. All across the country businesses displayed the Blue Eagle, the insignia of the NRA, in their windows.

The NRA's success was short-lived, however. Instead of creating a smooth-running corporate state, Johnson presided over a chorus of endless squabbling. The NRA boards, dominated by representatives of big business, drafted codes that favored their interests over those of small competitors. Moreover, even though they controlled the new agency from the outset, many leaders of big business resented the NRA for interfering in the private sector. Many quipped that the NRA stood for "national run-around."

For labor the NRA was a mixed blessing. On the positive side, the codes abolished child labor and established the precedent of federal regulation of minimum wages and maximum hours. Under the National Industrial Recovery Act, union membership was expanded by the drawing of large numbers of unskilled workers into unions. On the negative side,

however, the NRA codes set wages in most industries well below what labor demanded, and large occupational groups, such as farm workers, fell outside the codes' coverage.

Jobs Programs

Harry Hopkins, one of Roosevelt's most trusted advisers, asked why the federal government could not simply hire the unemployed and put them to work. Reluctantly, Roosevelt agreed, and the first major program to attack unemployment through public works was the **Public Works Administration (PWA).** It was supposed to serve as a "pump-primer," providing people with money to spend on industrial products. In six years the PWA spent $6 billion, building such projects as Brownsville, Texas's port, the Grand Coulee Dam, and Chicago's sewer system. Unfortunately, the man who headed the program, Harold Ickes, was so concerned about potential graft and scandal that the PWA did not spend enough money to significantly reduce unemployment.

One of the New Deal's most famous jobs programs was the Civilian Conservation Corps (CCC). By mid-1933, 300,000 jobless young men between the ages of 18 and 25 went to work in the nation's parks and forests. For $30 a month, CCC workers planted saplings, built fire towers, restocked depleted streams with fish, and restored historic battlefields. Workers lived in wilderness camps, earning money that they passed along to their families. Despite its immense popularity, the CCC failed to make a serious dent in depression unemployment. It excluded

For $30 a month, workers in the Civilian Conservation Corps (CCC) planted trees and dug drainage ditches. Such federal work relief programs helped many retain their self-respect.

women, imposed rigid quotas on African Americans, and offered employment to only a small number of the young people who needed work.

Far more ambitious was the Civil Works Administration (CWA), established in November 1933. Under the energetic leadership of Harry Hopkins, the CWA put 2.6 million men to work in its first month. Within two months it employed 4 million men building 250,000 miles of road, 40,000 schools, 150,000 privies, and 3700 playgrounds. In March 1934, however, Roosevelt scrapped the CWA because he (like Hoover) did not want to run a budget deficit or create a permanent dependent class.

Roosevelt badly underestimated the severity of the crisis. As government funding slowed down and economic indicators leveled off, the depression deep-

ened in 1934, triggering a series of violent strikes. The climax came on Labor Day, 1934, when 500,000 garment workers launched the single largest strike in the nation's history. All across the nation, critics attacked Roosevelt for not doing enough to combat the depression, charges that did not go unheeded in the White House.

Following the congressional elections of 1934, in which the Democrats won 13 new House seats and 9 new Senate seats, Roosevelt abandoned his hopes for a balanced budget, deciding that bolder action was required. He had lost faith in government planning and the proposed alliance with business. This left only one other road to recovery—government spending. Encouraged by the CCC's success, he decided to create more federal jobs for the unemployed.

In January 1935 Congress passed the Emergency Relief Appropriation Act, which created the **Works Progress Administration (WPA),** Roosevelt's program to employ 3.5 million workers at a "security wage"—twice the level of welfare payments but well below union scales. To head the new agency, Roosevelt again turned to Harry Hopkins. Since the WPA's purpose was to employ men quickly, Hopkins opted for labor-intensive tasks, creating jobs that were often makeshift and inefficient. Jeering critics said the WPA stood for "We Piddle Along," but the agency built many worthwhile projects. In its first five years alone the WPA constructed or improved 2500 hospitals, 5900 schools, 1000 airport fields (including New York's La Guardia Airport), and nearly 13,000 playgrounds. By 1941 it had pumped $11 billion into the economy.

The WPA's most unusual feature was its spending on cultural programs. While folksingers like Woody Guthrie honored the nation in ballads, other artists were hired to catalog it, photograph it, paint it, record it, and write about it. In photojournalism, for example, the Farm Security Administration (FSA) employed

Murals painted by artists employed by the WPA during the Great Depression adorn post offices and other public buildings throughout the country. This mural, *Festival at Hamburg,* by WPA artist William Edward Lewis Bunn, was completed for the Hamburg, Iowa, post office.

scores of photographers to create a pictorial record of America and its people. Under the auspices of the WPA, the Federal Writers Project sponsored an impressive set of state guides and dispatched an army of folklorists into the backcountry in search of tall tales. Oral historians collected slave narratives, and musicologists compiled an amazing collection of folk music.

Valuable in their own right, the WPA's cultural programs had the added benefit of providing work for thousands of writers, artists, actors, and other creative people. In addition, these programs established the precedent of federal support to the arts and the humanities, laying the groundwork for future federal programs to promote the life of the mind in the United States.

The WPA marked the zenith of Roosevelt's influence over Congress. Following its passage, Congress dallied for several months over the remainder of his program. By 1935, opposition came from both the right and the left, as the New Deal's failure to end the depression led to growing frustration.

Roosevelt's Critics

Many conservatives regarded Roosevelt's programs as infringements on the rights of the individual, while a growing number of critics argued that they did not go far enough. Three figures stepped forward to challenge Roosevelt: **Huey Long,** a Louisiana senator; **Father Charles Coughlin,** a Catholic priest from Detroit; and **Francis Townsend,** a retired California physician.

Of the three, Huey Long attracted the widest following. Ambitious, endowed with supernatural energy, and totally devoid of scruples, Long was a fiery, spellbinding orator in the tradition of southern populism. As governor and then U.S. senator, he ruled Louisiana with an iron hand, keeping a private army equipped with submachine guns and a "deduct box," where he kept funds deducted from state employees' salaries. Yet the people of Louisiana loved him because he attacked the big oil companies, increased state spending on public works, and improved public schools. Although he backed Roosevelt in 1932, Long quickly abandoned the president and opposed the New Deal as too conservative.

Huey Long was immensely popular, especially among the poor. Part of his appeal lay in his style; he dressed in vanilla ice cream white suits and called himself "the Kingfish," after a character in the popular radio show "Amos 'n Andy." By playing up his country origins and ridiculing the rich, Long became a popular legend.

Early in 1934 Long announced his "Share Our Wealth" program. Vowing to make "Every Man a King," he promised to soak the rich by imposing a stiff tax on inheritances over $5 million and by levying a 100 percent tax on annual incomes over $1 million. The confiscated funds, in turn, would be distributed to the people, guaranteeing every American family an annual income of no less than $2000—in Long's words more than enough to buy "a radio, a car, and a home." Roosevelt had to take him seriously, for a Democratic poll revealed that Long could attract three to four million voters to an independent presidential ticket.

Like Long, Father Charles Coughlin was an early supporter who turned sour on the New Deal. Speaking on the radio to an estimated 30 million Americans from his Catholic parish in a Detroit suburb, Coughlin blamed the depression on greedy bankers and challenged Roosevelt to solve the crisis by nationalizing banks and inflating the currency. When Roosevelt refused to heed his advice, Coughlin broke with him and formed the National Union for Social Justice.

Roosevelt's least likely critic was Dr. Francis Townsend, a California public health officer who found himself unemployed at the age of 67, with only $100 in savings. Seeing many people in similar or worse straits, Townsend embraced old-age relief as the key to ending the depression. In January 1934 Townsend announced his plan, demanding a $200 monthly pension for every citizen over the age of 60. In return, recipients had to retire and spend their entire pension every month within the United States. Younger Americans would inherit the jobs vacated by senior citizens, and the economy would be stimulated by the increased purchasing power of the elderly. Although critics lambasted the Townsend plan as ludicrous, several million Americans found his plan refreshingly simple.

THE SECOND NEW DEAL

Alarmed by his critics, Roosevelt slowly abandoned his dream of building a coalition that would unite all Americans behind the New Deal. Previously, he had seen himself as an honest broker attempting to reconcile the conflicting demands of widely diverse interest groups. Now Roosevelt stopped trying to please everyone and started inching to the left. In June 1935, Roosevelt refused to dismiss Congress for summer vacation, vowing to make its members swelter in the Washington heat until they passed his new legislative agenda. The result was the "Second Hundred Days."

The Wagner Act

In 1930, only 3.4 million workers belonged to labor unions—down from 5 million in 1920. Union members were confined to a few industries, such as construction, railroads, and local truck delivery. Workers in the nation's major industries, like autos and steel, remained unorganized.

As the depression dragged on, bitter labor-management warfare erupted, with auto and steel workers and longshoremen becoming involved in violent strikes. While some of the strikes aimed at higher wages, fully a third demanded union recognition.

Labor unrest forced the federal government to step into labor relations and forge a compromise between management and labor. Under the **Wagner Act** (the National Labor Relations Act) of 1935, the federal government guaranteed the right of employees to form unions and to bargain collectively. The act also set up the National Labor Relations Board (NLRB), which had the power to prohibit unfair labor practices by employers.

During the mid-1930s, a bitter dispute broke out within labor's ranks. It involved an issue that had been simmering for half a century: Should labor focus its efforts on unionizing skilled workers; or should labor go after all workers in industry, regardless of skill level? The country's major labor federation, the American Federation of Labor (AFL), consisted of craft unions organized by occupation. In late 1935, John L. Lewis, president of the United Mine Workers since 1920, and other union leaders formed the Committee for Industrial Organization (CIO) within the AFL to organize unskilled workers in the nation's mass-production industries—particularly the auto, steel, glass, radio, and rubber industries. Within three years the AFL expelled the CIO unions. In 1938 the expelled unions established the **Congress of Industrial Organizations (CIO),** electing Lewis as president. Lewis served as CIO president for two years, but continued as UMW president until he retired in 1960.

A 44-day sit-down strike in Flint, Michigan, in 1937 forced General Motors to recognize the United Auto Workers. A few weeks later, U.S. Steel accepted unionization without a strike, but the "Little Steel" companies—Bethlehem, Inland, National, Republic, and Youngstown Sheet & Tube—vowed to resist the steelworkers union. In May 1937, police in South Chicago opened fire on marchers at the Republic mill, killing ten. Soon after, the strike was broken, but in 1941, the National Labor Relations Board ordered "Little Steel" to recognize the United Steelworkers of America and reinstate all workers fired for union activity.

Social Security

A goal of reformers since the Progressive Era, the 1935 **Social Security Act** aimed to alleviate the plight of America's visible poor—dependent children, the elderly, and the handicapped. A major political victory for Roosevelt, the Social Security Act was a triumph of social legislation. It offered workers 65 or older monthly stipends based on previous earnings, and it gave the indigent elderly small relief payments, financed by the federal government and the states. In addition, it provided assistance to blind and handicapped Americans, and to dependent children who did not have a wage-earning parent. The act also established the nation's first federally sponsored system of unemployment insurance. Mandatory payroll deductions levied equally on employees and employers financed both the retirement system and the unemployment insurance.

While conservatives argued that the Social Security Act placed the United States on the road to socialism, the legislation profoundly disappointed reformers, who demanded "cradle to grave" protection as the birthright of every American. The new system authorized pitifully small payments; its retirement system left huge groups of workers uncovered,

Despite the promise of "only a few exceptions" to eligibility for social security, the 1935 Social Security Act did not cover many groups of workers. In 1939 amendments to the act broadened its coverage and increased the amount of payments to those covered.

including migrant workers, civil servants, domestic servants, merchant seamen, and day laborers; its budget came from a regressive tax scheme that placed a disproportionate tax burden on the poor; and it did not provide health insurance.

Despite these criticisms, the Social Security Act introduced a new era in American history. It committed the government to a social welfare role by providing for elderly, disabled, dependent, and unemployed Americans. By doing so, the act greatly expanded the public's sense of entitlement and the support people expected government to give to all citizens.

The remaining "must legislation" of the Second Hundred Days included utilities regulation (Public Utility Holding Company Act), banking reform, and a new tax proposal. Yet none of these measures represented a drastic change in American politics or society. On the whole, the **Second New Deal** merely sought to make capitalism more humane. The majority of Americans did not want dramatic changes, and Roosevelt never contemplated, much less achieved, a social revolution. He made no attacks on private property; the well-to-do retained their privileges; wealth was not redistributed; and the poor remained poor.

To hear many wealthy conservatives tell it, however, Roosevelt was a wild-eyed radical who threatened the very foundation of capitalism. William Randolph Hearst ordered his newspapers to substitute the words "Raw Deal" for "New Deal." Firmly committed to a balanced budget, conservatives viewed heavy government spending as sacrilege, and they were appalled by the growth of bureaucracy in Washington, D.C. Conservatives feared government's growth would increase federal power at the expense of states' rights and individual liberties, and they believed Roosevelt would raise rich people's taxes to finance his relief programs. Viewing Roosevelt as a traitor to his class, many wealthy Americans saw the election of 1936 as their chance to save the country.

The Election of 1936

To carry its banner in 1936, the Republicans picked Alfred M. Landon of Kansas, the only Republican governor who survived the 1934 elections. Landon was far more liberal than many of his backers. He had opposed the Ku Klux Klan, backed business regulation, and supported many New Deal programs. A poor public speaker, Landon offered few alternatives to Roosevelt's programs.

To win in 1936, the Republicans needed help from a third party to splinter the Democrats, but this assistance never arrived. Huey Long's organization fell apart following his assassination in 1935; Francis Townsend's campaign, already weakened by passage of the Social Security Act in 1935, collapsed in

the spring of 1936 under charges of corruption; and by 1936 Father Coughlin had been reduced to an abusive name-caller who had been publicly rebuked by the Catholic church.

Roosevelt enjoyed the race, lashing out at "economic royalists" who opposed the New Deal. Positive economic indicators helped the Democrats. In 1936 industrial output more than doubled its 1933 figures, and the national income rose half again as much. In the election Roosevelt carried every state but Maine and Vermont. Democrats won an equally lopsided victory in the congressional races, resulting in 331 Democrats to 89 Republicans in the House and 76 Democrats to 16 Republicans in the Senate.

The 1936 Democratic victory rested on a broad base of support. Roosevelt's backers included poor people, organized labor, urban ethnics, the Democratic South, African Americans, and many intellectuals. A formidable alliance of diverse groups, Roosevelt's New Deal coalition would shape the contours of American politics for decades to come.

THE NEW DEAL, WOMEN, AND MINORITY GROUPS

Eleanor Roosevelt deserves much of the credit for the progress made by minorities. The first president's wife to stake out an independent public position, she provided the social conscience of the New Deal. The First Lady worked tirelessly to persuade her husband and the heads of government agencies to hire well-qualified women and African Americans. More courageous than her husband and less restricted politically, she did not hesitate to take a public stand on civil rights. When the Daughters of the American Revolution refused in 1939 to grant the black contralto Marian Anderson permission to sing in Washington's Constitution Hall, Mrs. Roosevelt arranged for a concert on the steps of the Lincoln Memorial on Easter Sunday.

Women

Women achieved measured progress under the New Deal. Prior to the depression, women had dominated both social work and the voluntary associations that provided charity for the poor and unemployed. Because the same skills were needed to combat the depression, women joined the throngs of professionals who rushed to Washington to work in New Deal programs.

Once there, women formed a tightly knit network of professionals who supported each other's careers. **Frances Perkins,** the secretary of labor and the first woman cabinet member in American history, brought many women into government. **Molly Dewson,** the

THE PEOPLE SPEAK

Frances Perkins, "The Social Security Act" (1935)

The Social Security Act of 1935 is one of the most significant of the New Deal programs. By providing aid to the elderly, the unemployed, and the handicapped, Social Security marked the beginning of the "welfare state," the embodiment of the idea that society should provide security for its members. Secretary of Labor Frances Perkins, one of Roosevelt's most controversial cabinet appointees, made the following radio address to announce the new program to the public.

People who work for a living in the United States of America can join with all other good citizens on this forty-eighth anniversary of Labor Day in satisfaction that the Congress has passed the Social Security Act. This act establishes unemployment insurance as a substitute for haphazard methods of assistance in periods when men and women willing and able to work are without jobs. It provides for old-age pensions which mark great progress over the measures upon which we have hitherto depended in caring for those who have been unable to provide for the years when they no longer can work. It also provides security for dependent and crippled children, mothers, the indigent disabled and the blind.

Old people who are in need, unemployables, children, mothers and the sightless, will find systematic regular provisions for needs. The Act limits the Federal aid to not more than $15 per month for the individual, provided the State in which he resides appropriates a like amount. There is nothing to prevent a State from contributing more than $15 per month in special cases, and there is no requirement to allow as much as $15 from either State or Federal funds when a particular case has some personal provision and needs less than the total allowed.

Following essentially the same procedure, the Act as passed provides for Federal assistance to the States in caring for the blind, a contribution by the States of up to $15 a month to be matched in turn by a like contribution by the Federal Government. The Act also contains provision for assistance to the States in providing payments to dependent children under sixteen years of age. There also is provision in the Act for cooperation with medical and health organizations charged with rehabilitation of physically handicapped children. The necessity for adequate service in the fields of public and maternal health and child welfare calls for the extension of these services to meet individual community needs.

Consider for a moment those portions of the Act which, while they will not be effective this present year, yet will exert a profound and far-reaching effect upon millions of citizens. I refer to the provision for a system of old-age benefits supported by the contributions of employer and employees, and to the section which sets up the initial machinery for unemployment insurance.

Old-age benefits in the form of monthly payments are to be paid to individuals who have worked and contributed to the insurance fund in direct proportion to the total wages earned by such individuals in the course of their employment subsequent to 1936. The minimum monthly payment is to be $10, the maximum $35. These payments will begin in the year 1942 and will be to those who have worked and contributed. . . .

Federal legislation was framed in the thought that the attack upon the problems of insecurity should be a cooperative venture participated in by both the Federal and State Governments, preserving the benefits of local administration and national leadership. It was thought unwise to have the Federal Government decide all questions of policy and dictate completely what the States should do. Only very necessary minimum standards are included in the Federal measure leaving wide latitude to the States. . . .

The social security measure looks primarily to the future and is only a part of the administration's plan to promote sound and stable economic life. We cannot think of it as disassociated from the Government's program to save the homes, the farms, the businesses and banks of the Nation, and especially must we consider it a companion measure to the Works Relief Act which does undertake to provide immediate increase in employment and corresponding stimulation to private industry by purchase of supplies.

Our social security program will be a vital force working against the recurrence of severe depressions in the future. We can, as the principle of sustained purchasing power in hard times makes itself felt in every shop, store and mill, grow old without being haunted by the spectre of a poverty-ridden old age or of being a burden on our children. . . .

The passage of this act, with so few dissenting votes and with so much intelligent public support is deeply significant of the progress which the American people have made in thought in the social field and awareness of methods of using cooperation through government to overcome social hazards against which the individual alone is inadequate. . . .

Source: Copyright © 1935 Vital Speeches of the Day.

director of the Women's Division of the Democratic Committee, helped place women throughout the administration. By 1939 women held one-third of all positions in the independent agencies and almost one-fifth of the jobs in the executive departments.

African Americans

Until the New Deal, African Americans had shown their traditional loyalty to the party of Lincoln by voting overwhelmingly Republican. By the end of Roosevelt's first administration, however, one of the most dramatic voter shifts in American history had occurred. In 1936, 75 percent of black voters supported the Democrats. Blacks turned to Roosevelt in part because his spending programs gave them a measure of relief from the depression and in part because the Republicans—the Grand Old Party (GOP)—had done little to repay their earlier support.

Still, Roosevelt's record on civil rights was modest at best. Instead of using New Deal programs to promote civil rights, the administration consistently bowed to the forces of discrimination. In order to pass major New Deal legislation, Roosevelt needed the support of southern Democrats. Time and time again, he backed away from equal rights to avoid antagonizing southern whites, although his wife did take a public stand in support of civil rights.

Most New Deal programs discriminated against blacks. The NRA, for example, not only offered whites the first crack at jobs but authorized separate and lower pay scales for African Americans. The Federal Housing Authority (FHA) refused to guarantee mortgages for blacks who tried to buy homes in white neighborhoods, and the CCC maintained segregated camps. Furthermore, the Social Security Act excluded those job categories traditionally filled by blacks.

The story in agriculture was particularly grim. Since 40 percent of all black workers made their living as sharecroppers and tenant farmers, the AAA acreage reduction hit blacks hard. White landlords could make more money by leaving land untilled than by putting land into production. As a result, the AAA's policies forced more than 100,000 African Americans off the land in 1933 and 1934. Even more galling to black leaders, the president failed to support an antilynching bill and a bill to abolish the poll tax. Roosevelt feared that conservative southern Democrats, who had seniority in Congress and controlled many committee chairmanships, would block his bills if he tried to fight them on the race question.

Yet the New Deal did record a few gains in civil rights. Roosevelt named **Mary McLeod Bethune,** a black educator, to the advisory committee of the National Youth Administration (NYA), and thanks to her efforts, African Americans received a fair share of

Mary McLeod Bethune, a member of the advisory committee for the National Youth Administration, meets here with Eleanor Roosevelt.

NYA funds. The WPA was color-blind, and blacks in northern cities benefited from its work relief programs. Harold Ickes, a strong supporter of civil rights who had several African Americans on his staff, poured federal funds into black schools and hospitals in the South. Most blacks appointed to New Deal posts, however, served in token positions as advisers on black affairs.

Mexican Americans

Like African Americans, most Mexican Americans reaped few benefits from the New Deal. Affected in much the same way as sharecroppers and tenant farmers, many Mexican American migrant workers lost their jobs due to AAA acreage reductions or competition in the fields from unemployed whites.

Still, the New Deal offered Mexican Americans a little help. The Farm Security Administration established camps for migrant farm workers in California, and the CCC and WPA hired unemployed Mexican Americans on relief jobs. Many, however, did not qualify for relief assistance because, as migrant workers, they did not meet residency requirements. Furthermore, agricultural workers were not eligible for benefits under workers' compensation, Social Security, and the National Labor Relations Act.

Native Americans

The so-called **Indian New Deal** was the only bright spot in the administration's treatment of minorities. In the late nineteenth century, American Indian policy had begun to place a growing emphasis on erasing a distinctive Native American identity. To weaken the authority of Native American leaders, Congress in 1871 ended the practice of treating Indian groups as sovereign nations. To undermine traditional Native American justice systems, Congress, in 1882, created a Court of Indian Offenses, to try Native Americans who violated government laws and rules. Native American schools took Native American children away from their families and sought to strip them of their heritage. Schoolchildren were required to trim their hair and speak English and were prohibited from practicing Native American religions.

The culmination of these policies was the 1887 Dawes Act, which allocated reservation lands to individual Native Americans. The purpose of the act was to encourage Native Americans to become farmers, but the plots were too small to support a family or to raise livestock. Government policies further reduced Native American–owned lands from 155 million acres to just 48 million acres in 1934.

When Roosevelt became president in 1933, he appointed John Collier, a leading reformer, as Commissioner of Indian Affairs. At Collier's request, Congress created the Indian Emergency Conservation Program (IECP), a CCC-type project for the reservations that employed more than 85,000 Native Americans. Collier also made certain that the PWA, WPA, CCC, and NYA hired Native Americans.

Collier had long been an opponent of the 50-year-old government allotment program that had broken up and distributed Native American lands. In 1934 he persuaded Congress to pass the Indian Reorganization Act, which terminated the allotment program of the Dawes Severalty Act of 1887; provided funds for Native American groups to purchase new land; offered government recognition of Native American constitutions; and repealed prohibitions on Native American languages and customs. That same year, federal grants were provided to local school districts, hospitals, and social welfare agencies to assist Native Americans.

THE NEW DEAL IN DECLINE

In his second inaugural address in early 1937, Franklin Roosevelt promised to press for new social legislation. Yet instead of pursuing new reforms, he allowed his second term to bog down in political squabbles. And he wasted his energies on an ill-conceived battle with the Supreme Court and an abortive effort to purge the Democratic party.

Court Packing

On "Black Monday," May 27, 1935, the Supreme Court struck down a basic part of Roosevelt's program of recovery and reform. A kosher chicken dealer sued the government, charging that the NRA was unconstitutional. In its famous "dead chicken" decision, *Schechter*

Poultry Corporation v. United States, the court agreed, declaring that Congress had delegated excessive authority to the president and had improperly involved the federal government in regulating interstate commerce.

In June 1936, the court ruled another of the measures enacted during the first 100 days—the Agricultural Adjustment Act—unconstitutional. Then, six months later, the high court declared invalid a New York state minimum-wage law. Roosevelt was aghast. The court, he charged, had established a "'no-man's land' where no Government—State or Federal—can function." Roosevelt feared that every New Deal reform—such as the prohibition on child labor or regulation of wages and hours—was at risk. In 1936, his supporters in Congress responded by introducing over a hundred bills to curb the judiciary's power.

After his landslide reelection in 1936, the president proposed a controversial "**court-packing** scheme." In an effort to make his opponents on the Supreme Court resign so he could replace them with justices more sympathetic to his policies, Roosevelt announced a

Fearful that the Supreme Court would invalidate the Social Security Act and other measures, Roosevelt proposed in 1937 that he be allowed to appoint an additional justice for every court member over the age of 70, up to a total of six.

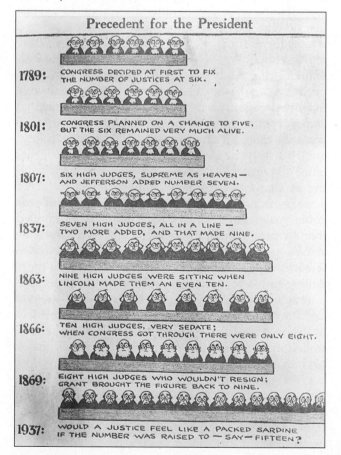

plan to add one new member to the Supreme Court for every judge who had reached the age of 70 without retiring (six justices were over 70). To offer a carrot with the stick, Roosevelt also outlined a generous new pension program for retiring federal judges.

The court-packing scheme was a political disaster. Conservatives and liberals alike denounced Roosevelt for attacking the separation of powers, and critics accused him of trying to become a dictator. Fortunately, the Court itself ended the crisis by shifting ground. In two separate cases the Court upheld the Wagner Act and approved a Washington state minimum-wage law, furnishing proof that it had softened its opposition to the New Deal.

Yet Roosevelt remained too obsessed with the battle to realize he had won the war. He lobbied for the court-packing bill for several months, squandering his strength on a struggle that had long since become a political embarrassment. In the end, the only part of the president's plan to gain congressional approval was the pension program. Once it passed, Justice Willis Van Devanter, the most obstinate New Deal opponent on the Court, resigned. By 1941 Roosevelt had named five justices to the Supreme Court. Few legacies of the president's leadership proved more important, for the new "Roosevelt Court" significantly expanded the government's role in the economy and in civil liberties.

The Depression of 1937

The sweeping Democratic electoral victory in 1936 was followed by a deep economic relapse known as the **Roosevelt recession.** In just a few months, industrial production fell by 40 percent; unemployment rose by 4 million; stock prices plunged 48 percent.

Several factors contributed to the "little depression," of which the most important was a blunder in fiscal policy. Secretary of the Treasury Henry Morgenthau urged Roosevelt to cut federal spending in an effort to balance the federal budget and restore business confidence. Reassured by good economic news in 1936, Roosevelt slashed government spending the following year. The budget cuts knocked the economy into a tailspin. Roosevelt's virulent attacks on "economic royalists" also undermined business confidence.

By the end of 1938 the reform spirit was gone. A conservative alliance of southern Democrats and northern Republicans in Congress blocked all efforts to expand the New Deal. In the congressional elections of 1938, Roosevelt campaigned against five conservative senators who opposed the New Deal; but all won reelection. The failed purge intensified the conservative-liberal split within the Democratic party by showing conservatives they could defy the president with impunity. Roosevelt may not have been able to

pass any new measures, but his opponents could not dismantle his programs. The New Deal ended in stalemate, but several reforms had been ensconced as permanent features of American politics.

POPULAR CULTURE DURING THE GREAT DEPRESSION

The popular culture of the 1930s was fraught with contradictions. It was, simultaneously, a decade of traditionalism and of modernist experimentation, of sentimentality and "hard-boiled" toughness, of longings for a simpler past and fantastic dreams of the future.

Beset by deep anxieties and insecurities, many Americans in the 1930s hungered for heroes. Popular culture offered many: superheroes like Superman and Batman, who appeared in the new comic books of the 1930s; tough, hard-boiled detectives in the fiction of Dashiell Hammett and Raymond Chandler; and radio heroes like "The Lone Ranger" or "The Shadow."

Artistic and Literary Endeavors

Seeing modern society as excessively individualistic and fragmented, many prominent intellectuals of the time looked to the past. Eleven leading white southern intellectuals, known as the **Southern Agrarians,** issued a manifesto titled *I'll Take My Stand,* urging a return to an agrarian way of life. Another group of distinguished intellectuals known as the **New Humanists,** led by Irving Babbitt and Paul Elmer More, extolled classical civilization as a bulwark against modern values. One of the decade's leading social critics was Lewis Mumford. In volumes like *Technics and Civilization* (1934), he examined how the values of a premachine culture could be blended into modern capitalist civilization.

And yet, for all the emphasis on tradition, the 1930s was also a decade in which modernism in the arts and architecture became increasingly pronounced. Martha Graham developed American modern dance. William Faulkner experimented with "stream-of-consciousness" in *As I Lay Dying* (1930) and other novels, while John Dos Passos's avant-garde trilogy, *U.S.A.,* combined newspaper headlines, capsule biographies, popular song lyrics, and fiction to document the disintegration of depression-era society. Nothing better illustrated the concern with the future than the 1939 New York World's Fair, the self-proclaimed "Fair of the Future," which promised to show fairgoers "the world of tomorrow."

The depression was, in certain respects, a powerful unifying experience. A new phrase, "the American way of life," entered the language—as did public opinion polls and statistical surveys that gave the public a better sense of what the "average American" thought, voted,

A popular attraction at the 1939 New York World's Fair was the parachute jump, which hoisted passengers to the top of a 250-foot tower, then released the chutes so that the passengers could experience the feeling of bailing out of an airplane.

and ate. The new photojournalism that appeared in new magazines like *Life* helped create a common frame of reference. Yet regional, ethnic, and class differences occupied an important place in the literature of the 1930s. The great novels of the decade successfully combined social criticism and rich detail about the facets of American life in specific social settings. In his novels of fictional Yoknapatawpha County, William Faulkner explored the traditions and history of the South. James T. Farrell's *Studs Lonigan* trilogy (1932–1935) analyzed the impact of urban industrial decay on Catholic youth, while Henry Roth's *Call It Sleep* (1934) traced the assimilation of Jewish youth into American life. John Steinbeck's *Grapes of Wrath* (1939) examined the struggle of a poor Oklahoma farming family migrating to California. Richard Wright's classic *Native Son* (1940) discussed the ways that poverty and prejudice in Chicago drove a young African American to crime.

Hollywood During the Great Depression

During the Great Depression, Hollywood played a valuable psychological role, providing reassurance to a demoralized nation. Even at the depth of the depression, 60 to 80 million Americans attended movies each week.

During the depression's earliest years, movies reflected a despairing public's mood, as Tommy-gun toting gangsters, haggard prostitutes, and sleazy backroom politicians and lawyers appeared on the screen. Screen comedies released in these years expressed an almost anarchistic disdain for traditional institutions and values. The Marx Brothers spoofed everything from patriotism to universities; W. C. Fields ridiculed families; and Mae West used sexual innuendo to poke fun at the middle-class code of sexual propriety.

A renewed sense of optimism generated by the New Deal combined with industry self-censorship to produce new kinds of films during the second half of the depression. G-men, detectives, western heroes, and other defenders of law and order replaced gangsters. Audiences enjoyed Frank Capra comedies and dramas in which little men stood up against corruption and restored America to itself. A new comic genre—the screwball comedy—presented a world in which rich heiresses wed impoverished young men, keeping alive a vision of America as a classless society.

In the face of economic disaster, the fantasy world of the movies sustained a traditional American faith in individual initiative, in government, and a common American identity transcending social class.

CONCLUSION

At the end of 1938, Harry Hopkins observed that the American people had become "bored with the poor, unemployed, and insecure." The New Deal was over. From a purely economic perspective, the New Deal barely made a dent in the Great Depression. Roosevelt's programs suffered from poor planning and moved with considerable caution. Roosevelt simply could not bring himself to support huge federal budgets. As a result, government expenditures stayed below $10 billion a year, not nearly enough to fuel economic recovery. World War II, not the New Deal, snapped America out of the depression, for then and only then did unemployment disappear.

Whatever its shortcomings, the New Deal did blunt the worst effects of the Great Depression. By means of economic reforms and public works projects Roosevelt managed to preserve the public's faith in capitalism and in democratic government at a time

CHRONOLOGY OF KEY EVENTS

1928   Herbert Hoover is elected thirty-first president

1929   Stock market crashes

1930   Hawley-Smoot Tariff raises import duties to unprecedented levels

1932   Congress creates Reconstruction Finance Corporation to lend money to banks, railroads, and insurance companies; Bonus Army, a group of veterans demanding immediate payment of World War I bonuses, is dispersed by federal troops in Washington, D.C.; to revive the construction industry, Congress creates the Federal Home Loan Bank System to lend money to savings and loan associations; Franklin Roosevelt is elected thirty-second president

1933   Emergency Banking Relief Act addresses banking crisis; Roosevelt conducts the first of many "fireside chats" over national radio; Civilian Conservation Corps puts young people to work conserving natural resources; Federal Emergency Relief Act provides relief payments to the unemployed through local and state welfare agencies; Civil Works Administration offers employment to over 4 million people; Agricultural Adjustment Act sets up a system of farm price supports and production limits; National Industrial Recovery Act authorizes industrial codes regulating production, prices, and working conditions and provides funds for public works projects; Tennessee Valley Authority constructs dams and hydroelectric plants in the Tennessee River valley; Twenty-first Amendment repeals prohibition; Glass-Steagall Act

creates the Federal Deposit Insurance Corporation to insure savings accounts against bank failure; Farm Credit Administration provides low-interest loans for farmers.

1934   Dr. Francis Townsend proposes a $200 monthly pension for every citizen over 60; former supporter, "radio priest" Father Charles Coughlin, breaks with Roosevelt and forms the National Union for Social Justice; Senator Huey Long of Louisiana announces his "Share Our Wealth" program to provide every American family with a guaranteed annual income; Indian Reorganization Act provides funds for tribes to purchase land, offers recognition of tribal constitutions, and repeals prohibitions on Native American customs

1935   *Schechter Poultry Corporation* v. *United States* declares National Industrial Recovery Act unconstitutional; Emergency Relief Appropriation Act creates Works Progress Administration and National Youth Administration; National Labor Relations Act guarantees workers' right to organize and bargain collectively; Public Utility Holding Company Act is passed to prevent monopolies in gas and electricity distribution; Social Security Act creates a federal system of old-age pensions and state-run unemployment compensation programs

1937   Roosevelt proposes his "court-packing" scheme

1938   Fair Labor Standards Act bans child labor and establishes minimum wages and maximum hours

---

when both seemed on the verge of collapse. Roosevelt accomplished this, in large measure, by reaching out to groups that Washington had largely neglected in the past. The Social Security program, while it ignored many, made the government responsible for old-age pensions and welfare payments to citizens who could not support themselves. The NIRA and the Wagner Act encouraged the growth of unions; minimum wage laws benefited many workers; and the Fair Labor Standards Act finally abolished child labor in industry (though it remained in agriculture). While the New Deal stopped far short of providing equal treatment under the law for minorities, it offered them a measure of relief from the depression.

The New Deal encouraged Americans to look to the White House for strong executive leadership. Roosevelt responded to situations with decisive action, and the public increasingly expected the other branches of government to support presidential initiatives. Roosevelt's administrative style—creating special agencies to handle specific problems and placing people in charge who answered directly to him—further enhanced presidential power. On a purely partisan level, the New Deal enabled Roosevelt to forge a Democratic coalition of diverse groups—labor, African Americans, urban ethnics, intellectuals, and southern whites—that helped shape American politics for the next several decades.

Above all, the New Deal made the federal government responsible for safeguarding the nation's economic health. Prior to the 1930s, if people were asked how the government affected them, they probably thought in terms of state or even local government. The New Deal, however, made the federal government such a daily presence in peoples' lives that they now expected Washington to involve itself in everything from farm subsidies to the sale of stocks and securities.

CHAPTER SUMMARY AND KEY POINTS

The Great Depression was steeper and more protracted in the United States than in any other industrialized country. The unemployment rate rose higher and remained higher longer than in any other western country. As it deepened, the depression had far-reaching political consequences. In this chapter you read about the depression's human toll; President Hoover's response; President Roosevelt's New Deal Programs and their impact on women and minority groups; and the response of American popular culture to the depression.

- The stock market crash of October 1929 brought the economic prosperity of the 1920s to a symbolic end. For the next ten years, the United States was mired in a deep economic depression. By 1933, unemployment had soared to 25 percent, up from 3.2 percent in 1929. Industrial production declined by 50 percent, international trade plunged 30 percent, and investment fell 98 percent.

- The Great Depression transformed the American political and economic landscape. It produced a major political realignment, creating a coalition of big-city ethnics, African Americans, and southern Democrats committed, in varying degrees, to interventionist government.

- The depression strengthened the federal presence in American life, spawning such innovations as national old-age pensions, unemployment compensation, aid to dependent children, public housing, federally subsidized school lunches, insured bank deposits, the minimum wage, and stock market regulation.

- The depression fundamentally altered labor relations, producing a revived labor movement and a national labor policy protective of collective bargaining.

- The depression transformed the farm economy by introducing federal price supports.

- Above all, the Great Depression led Americans to view the federal government as an agency of action and reform and the ultimate protector of public well-being.

SUGGESTIONS FOR FURTHER READING

Ben S. Bernanke, *Essays on the Great Depression* (2000). Series of articles examining both monetary and nonmonetary reasons for the Great Depression.

Alan Brinkley, *The End of Reform: New Deal Liberalism in Recession and War* (1995). Analyzes the reasons for the New Deal's decline.

Kenneth S. Davis, *FDR: The New York Years* (1985); *FDR: The New Deal Years* (1986); *FDR: Into the Storm* (1993). Recent biographies of the president.

Melvyn Dubovsky and Stephen Burnwood, eds., *Women and Minorities During the Great Depression* (1990). Examines issues confronting women and minority groups during the depression.

Mario T. Garcia, *Mexican-American Leadership, Ideology, and Identity* (1989). Analyzes the depression's impact on Mexican Americans and the community's responses.

Davis W. Houck, *Rhetoric As Currency: Hoover, Roosevelt, and the Great Depression* (2001). Study of the similarities of the language that both President Herbert Hoover and President Franklin D. Roosevelt used to project national confidence in the face of the Great Depression.

William E. Leuchtenburg, *The Supreme Court Reborn: The Constitutional Revolution in the Age of Roosevelt* (1995). Explores the impact of the depression on constitutional law.

Robert S. McElvaine, *The Great Depression: America, 1929–1941* (1984). Offers a thorough treatment of America during the depression.

Michael E. Parrish, *Anxious Decades: America in Prosperity and Depression* (1992). Provides insights into America during the 1930s.

Patrick D. Reagan, *Designing a New America: The Origins of New Deal Planning, 1890–1943* (1999). Detailed account of the evolution of the movement for national planning in the United States between 1890 and 1943, using a biographical approach.

Lois Scharf, *To Work and to Wed: Female Employment and Feminism in the Great Depression* (1980). Examines the impact of the depression on women.

Harvard Sitkoff, ed., *Fifty Years Later: The New Deal Evaluated* (1985). Offers recent assessments of various aspects of the New Deal.

T. H. Watkins, *The Great Depression: America in the 1930s* (1993). Offers an up-to-date account of the depression decade.

Novels

John Steinbeck, *The Grapes of Wrath* (1939).

Richard Wright, *Native Son* (1940).

James T. Farrell, *Studs Lonigan* (1932–35).

MEDIA RESOURCES

Web Sites

Voices from the Dust Bowl: The Charles L. Todd and Robert Sonkin Migrant Worker Collection, 1940–1941
http://memory.loc.gov/ammem/afctshtml/tshome.html

Farm Security Administration (FSA) studies of migrant work camps in central California in 1940 and 1941 are the bulk of this site. The collection includes audio recordings, photographs, manuscript materials, and publications.

New Deal Network
http://newdeal.feri.org/
This database includes photographs, political cartoons, and texts—including speeches, letters, and other historic documents—from the New Deal period.

Franklin Delano Roosevelt
http://www.ipl.org/ref/POTUS/fdroosevelt.html
This site provides information about FDR, the only president to serve more than two terms.

Picture Archive: Photographs of the Great Depression, 1935–1942
http://www.corbis.com/fdr/fsa/map.html
These photographs reveal the real impact of the Great Depression on American life.

Newspaper Events Not Big in History
http://www.ybi.com/brink/author/1933/index.html
This site lists dozens of events that were front-page news in 1933 but failed to make the history books.

A New Deal for the Arts
http://www.nara.gov/exhall/newdeal/newdeal.html
Artworks, documents, and photographs recount the federal government's efforts to fund artists in the 1930s in the National Archives site.

Price of Civilization: Tax in War and Depression 1933–1946
http://www.taxhistory.org/civsite/
This site is part of the Tax History Project, at Tax Analysts. It includes thousands of searchable pages of documents and analysis and is part of a larger site that contains a cartoon gallery and WWII era posters.

Films and Videos

The Grapes of Wrath (1940). Movie version of John Steinbeck's classic novel starring Henry Fonda and Jane Darwell.

The Twentieth Century: The 1930s, The Great Depression (2000). Mpi Home Video. Documentary look at political reactions to the Great Depression as well as popular culture.

Breadline: Great Depression at Home (1997). WGBH Boston Video. Documentary following the life of America's working class during the Great Depression.

KEY TERMS

Hoovervilles   (p. 671)

Jawboning   (p. 673)

Reconstruction Finance Corporation (RFC)   (p. 673)

New Deal   (p. 676)

Bonus Army   (p. 676)

First Hundred Days   (p. 678)

Emergency Banking Relief Act   (p. 678)

Fireside chats   (p. 678)

Federal Emergency Relief Act   (p. 678)

Glass-Steagall Act   (p. 678)

Brain trust   (p. 678)

Dust Bowl   (p. 679)

Tennessee Valley Authority (TVA)   (p. 679)

Agricultural Adjustment Act (AAA)   (p. 680)

National Recovery Administration (NRA)   (p. 680)

Public Works Administration (PWA)   (p. 681)

Works Progress Administration (WPA)   (p. 682)

Wagner Act   (p. 684)

Congress of Industrial Organizations (CIO)   (p. 684)

Social Security Act   (p. 684)

Second New Deal   (p. 685)

Indian New Deal   (p. 687)

Court packing   (p. 688)

Roosevelt recession   (p. 689)

Southern Agrarians   (p. 689)

New Humanists   (p. 689)

PEOPLE YOU SHOULD KNOW

Henry Wallace   (p. 680)

Harry Hopkins   (p. 681)

Huey Long   (p. 683)

Father Charles Coughlin   (p. 683)

Francis Townsend   (p. 683)

Eleanor Roosevelt   (p. 685)

Frances Perkins   (p. 685)

Molly Dewson   (p. 685)

Mary McLeod Bethune   (p. 687)

REVIEW QUESTIONS

1. How did the global economic situation compare with the depression in the United States?

2. What were the most notable effects of the depression on the general population?

3. Did President Hoover realize the magnitude of the economic crisis?

4. How did the New Deal change Americans' perception of the role of federal government?

5. What was the most significant feature of the Second New Deal? Why? Did the New Deal change the status of women and minorities in the United States?

6. What caused the decline of the New Deal?

7. How did popular culture during the depression reflect the American landscape?

25 The End of Isolation: America Faces the World, 1920–1945

THE ALLIES LIBERATE AUSCHWITZ

At 3 P.M., January 27, 1945, Russian troops of the 100th and 107th divisions entered Auschwitz, a village in southern Poland 30 miles west of Krakow. There, inside Auschwitz's concentration camps, they found 7600 inmates along with World War II's most terrible secret: the Holocaust. Two days later, the U.S. 7th Army liberated Dachau, another infamous Nazi death camp, located just outside Munich. The liberators could scarcely believe what they saw: starving prisoners, bones protruding from their skin, serial numbers tattooed on their arms; stacks of half-burned corpses, and piles of human hair.

Auschwitz was not the first Nazi concentration camp—that dubious distinction belonged to Dachau, which was set up in 1933—but it was the most infamous; 1.6 million people died there. Of the victims, 1.3 million were Jews and 300,000 were Gypsies, Polish Catholics, and Russian prisoners of war. Altogether, people from 28 nations lost their lives at Auschwitz, including the disabled, homosexuals, political prisoners, and others deemed unfit to live in Adolf Hitler's Third Reich.

Auschwitz had two main areas. "Auschwitz I" contained a gas chamber, a crematorium, housing for prisoners used in slave labor, and Dr. Josef Mengele's "medical research" station. "Auschwitz II–Birkenau" contained only gas chambers and crematoria. It was here that cattle cars dumped their exhausted passengers, who then entered through a gate inscribed with the false promise "Work Will Make You Free." SS guards directed each new arrival to the left or the right. The healthy and strong went to the right. The weak, the elderly, and the very young went up a ramp to the left—to the gas chambers, disguised as showers. Inmates were told that the showers would be used to disinfect them, but there was no plumbing and the showerheads were fake. Guards injected a poison gas, Zyklon B, through openings in the ceilings and walls; when the deadly gas had done its work, the bodies were cremated. The ashes were used as road filler and fertilizer, or simply dumped into surrounding ponds and fields.

Auschwitz was a product of Adolf Hitler's belief that Germans constituted a master race that had a right to kill those they deemed inferior. "Nature is cruel, therefore we too may be cruel," Hitler stated in 1934. "If I can send the flower of

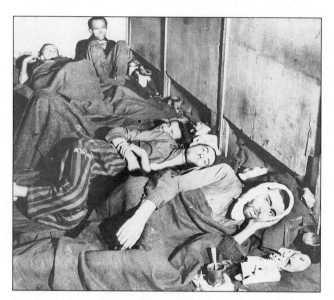

The scenes that greeted the troops who liberated Auschwitz in January 1945 almost defied belief. Perhaps as many as 12,000 people were slaughtered each day at Auschwitz.

the German nation into the hell of war . . . then surely I have a right to remove millions of an inferior race that breeds like vermin!"

In 1941 and 1942, the Nazi *Führer* (leader) initiated the "Final Solution to the Jewish Problem." The Nazis did their best to disguise their murderous scheme behind euphemisms and camouflage, but the truth sometimes slipped out. Heinrich Himmler, the official in charge of carrying out the final solution, explained to his top officers: "In public we will never speak of it. I am referring to the annihilation of the Jewish people. In our history, this is an unwritten and never-to-be written page of glory."

In the spring of 1944, four prisoners escaped from Auschwitz, carrying tangible proof of the Nazi's systematic program of mass murder. American and British leaders learned in mid-July what was happening at Auschwitz, but they rejected pleas to bomb the gas chambers or the roads and rail lines leading to the camps.

This was not the first time that western help had failed to come. During the 1930s, the U.S. State Department blocked efforts by Jewish refugees to migrate to the United States. Between 1933 and 1945, the United States allowed in only 132,000 Jewish refugees, just 10 percent of the quota allowed by law. This opposition to Jewish immigration reflected widespread anti-Semitism. As late as 1939, opinion polls indicated that 53 percent of Americans agreed with the statement "Jews are different and should be restricted." In the end, less than 500,000 Jews (out of 6.5 million) survived in Nazi-occupied Europe.

The Holocaust was an appalling and unique tragedy in human history. Never before had a sovereign state, with the co-operation of bureaucrats, industrialists, and civilians, sought to systematically exterminate an entire people. Yet many wonder whether Auschwitz's terrible lesson has been learned. Despite the establishment of the state of Israel, improved Christian-Jewish relations, and heightened sensitivity to racism, many Americans remain ignorant of the past. More than half a century after the liberation of Auschwitz, "ethnic cleansing" and the persecution of religious, racial, and ethnic groups continues in Bosnia, China, Guatemala, India, Sri Lanka, Turkey, and elsewhere.

No war in history killed more people or destroyed more property than World War II. Altogether, 70 million people served in the armed forces during the war; of these, some 7.5 million Soviet troops died in World War II, along with 3.5 million Germans, 1.25 million Japanese, and 400,000 Americans. Civilian deaths were even higher. At least 19 million Soviet civilians, 10 million Chinese, and 6 million European Jews lost their lives during the war.

More than any previous war in history, World War II was a total war. Some 70 nations took part in the war, and fighting took place on the continents of Europe, Asia, and Africa, as well as on the high seas. Entire societies participated, either as soldiers, war workers, or victims of occupation and mass murder.

Location of Nazi Concentration and Death Camps

Concentration Camps
Death Camps
Map Shows Mid-1939 Boundaries

In the United States, the war had vast repercussions: it ended unemployment, brought millions of married women into the workforce, initiated sweeping changes in the lives of the nation's minority groups, and dramatically expanded government's presence in American life. Finally, World War II marked the beginning of the nuclear age.

DIPLOMACY BETWEEN THE WARS

World War I had left the public suspicious of foreign crusades. In 1936, eight Princeton undergraduates formed the Veterans of Future Wars. The organization demanded a bonus of $1000 for every man between the ages of 18 and 36—payable immediately, so that they could enjoy it before being forced to fight the "next war." A women's auxiliary, the Future Gold Star Mothers, demanded government pensions for women, so that they could afford to visit their sons' graves in Europe.

Americans wanted to retreat from foreign affairs. "The people have had all the war, all the taxation, and all the military service they want," declared President Calvin Coolidge in 1925. During the 1920s and much of the 1930s, the United States concentrated on improving its status in the Western Hemisphere and on avoiding European entanglements.

American Diplomacy During the 1920s

During the 1920s, Republican leaders debated joining and ultimately refused to join the League of Nations or the World Court. Such commitments, they feared, might involve the United States too deeply in global politics. Yet Washington remained keenly interested in preserving international stability and tried to promote world peace through diplomatic means.

In 1921 representatives of nine Asian and European nations met in Washington to discuss ways to ease tensions in the Pacific. Secretary of State Charles Evans Hughes stunned the meeting by making specific proposals for disarmament. He called for a ten-year moratorium on the construction of battleships and an agreement that for every five naval vessels owned by the United States or Britain, Japan could have three, and France and Italy one and three-fourths. To win support for what the Japanese delegates called a ratio of "Rolls-Royce, Rolls-Royce, Ford," the United States and Great Britain agreed not to improve their fortifications in the Far East, especially in the Philippines. To appease Japanese resentment at its inferior position, the United States,

Britain, and France also agreed in the Four-Party Treaty of 1922 to consult with Japan before going to war in Asia. Neither treaty, however, contained any provision for enforcement.

In 1928 the French foreign minister, Aristide Briand, and Secretary of State Frank B. Kellogg attempted to outlaw war. The **Kellogg-Briand Pact,** which was eventually signed by 62 nations, renounced war as an instrument for resolving international disputes. If attacked, however, the signatories could defend themselves by force. While it raised hopes for peace and earned Kellogg the Nobel Peace Prize, the Kellogg-Briand Pact had no chance of preventing future bloodshed, since it, too, lacked an enforcement mechanism.

United States Policy Toward Latin America

Twenty times between 1898 and 1932, the United States intervened militarily in the Caribbean and Central America, suppressing popular uprisings in Nicaragua, seizing customs houses in Cuba, occupying Haiti (for 17 years), and supplying military and financial aid to friendly parties in the Mexican Revolution. Despite repeated American interventions, however, the region remained unstable.

During the 1920s Republican administrations inched away from gunboat diplomacy and tried to develop better relations with Latin America. Although progress was uneven and Washington's policies occasionally reverted to heavy-handed interventions, the thrust of Republican diplomacy during the 1920s clearly anticipated the shift toward improved relations with Latin America. In 1924, for example, the United States pulled the marines out of the Dominican Republic, and the following year American troops left Nicaragua, only to be sent back a few months later when a revolution broke out. But the real test of the United States' desire for improved relations came in Mexico.

Following Alvaro Obregón's election as president of Mexico in 1920, the Mexican government threatened to expropriate American-owned oil properties. The oil companies demanded government intervention, and in 1927 President Calvin Coolidge appointed Dwight Morrow, a partner in the firm of J. P. Morgan and Company, as ambassador. Mexicans expected the worst; one newspaper declared, "after Morrow come the marines." They were wrong. One of Morrow's first actions was to change the sign on the embassy to read "United States Embassy," rather than "American Embassy." It was a small gesture, but its significance was not lost on the Mexicans, who had long resented the United States' arrogance in appropriating a continental adjective. Morrow's diplomacy paid handsome dividends, and in 1927 Mexico once again recognized American-owned oil properties.

President Herbert Hoover continued the diplomacy of reconciliation. He announced plans to withdraw marines from Nicaragua and Haiti, and he resisted pressure from Congress to establish a customs receivership in El Salvador when the government there defaulted on its bonds. In 1930 Hoover approved a document written by Undersecretary of State J. Reuben Clark. The Clark Memorandum repudiated the Roosevelt Corollary to the Monroe Doctrine, which for 25 years had justified U.S. intervention in Latin America.

In his first inaugural address, President Franklin D. Roosevelt dedicated the United States "to the policy of the good neighbor." Secretary of State **Cordell Hull** stunned Latin America in December 1933 at the Seventh Pan-American Conference by declaring, "no state has the right to intervene in the international or external affairs of another." The marines left Nicaragua in 1933 and Haiti in 1934. The United States also nullified the Platt Amendment, thereby surrendering the right to intervene in the affairs of Cuba; and it gave Panama its political independence. Furthermore, when Mexico finally expropriated foreign oil properties in 1938, Roosevelt rejected calls to send in troops and let the action stand. The **Good Neighbor policy** did not solve all the problems with Latin America, but it promoted better relations just when the United States needed hemispheric solidarity to meet the threat of global war.

The Isolationist Mirage

During the Great Depression, isolationist sentiment surged. In 1935, 150,000 college students participated in a nationwide Student Strike for Peace and half a million signed pledges saying that they would refuse to serve in the event of war.

Antiwar sentiment was not confined to undergraduates. Disillusionment over World War I fed opposition to foreign entanglements. "We didn't win a thing we set out for in the last war," said Senator Gerald Nye of North Dakota. "We merely succeeded, with tremendous loss of life, to make secure the loans of private bankers to the Allies." The overwhelming majority of Americans agreed; an opinion poll in 1935 found that 70 percent of Americans believed that intervention in World War I had been a mistake.

Isolationist ideas spread through American popular culture during the mid-1930s. The Book-of-the-Month Club featured a volume entitled *Merchants of Death*. Its author contended that the United States

had been drawn into the European war by international arms manufacturers, who had deliberately fomented conflict in order to market their products. From 1934 to 1936, a congressional committee, chaired by Senator Nye, investigated charges that false Allied propaganda and unscrupulous Wall Street bankers had dragged Americans into the European war. In April 1935—the eighteenth anniversary of America's entry into World War I—50,000 veterans held a peace march in Washington, D.C.

By 1938, however, pacifist sentiment was fading. A rapidly modernizing Japan was seeking to acquire raw materials and territory on the Asian mainland; a revived Germany was rebuilding its military power and grabbing land bloodlessly on its eastern borders; and Italy was trying to restore Roman glory through military might.

THE COMING OF WORLD WAR II

The Treaty of Versailles following World War I had saddled Germany with a reparations bill of $34 billion. Unable to make the interest payments, let alone the principal, Germany staggered beneath the burden until its economy dissolved into severe unemployment and hyperinflation. Forty million marks were worth one cent.

Confronted by Germany's imminent economic collapse, the United States offered a measure of relief. In 1924 Charles Dawes, a prominent American banker, worked out a proposal (the Dawes Plan) that reduced the reparations bill and provided Germany with an American loan. With prodding from the United States, Great Britain and France cut reparations to $2 billion, but even that proved too much when the Great Depression struck. Germany entered the 1930s with its economy in shambles, providing fertile soil for Adolf Hitler.

Hitler and Germany

The modern world had never known a leader like **Adolf Hitler**. A charismatic and spellbinding orator, Hitler possessed a unique ability to articulate a nation's darkest fears and hatreds and then turn them to his own twisted purposes. Winston Churchill offered a profound truth when he described Hitler as the "monstrous product of former wrongs and shame."

Hitler exploited the psychological injuries inflicted on Germans by World War I. Rare indeed was the German who did not feel stunned by his country's sudden, unexpected defeat or who did not seethe with anger over the harsh peace imposed by the victors. Hitler's great genius (and history's great tragedy) was his ability to tap into his countrymen's anger and resentment. Exploiting the ugly strain of anti-Semitism in German culture, he claimed that the country's economic woes were the result of a conspiracy of German Jews. Hitler also attacked the Treaty of Versailles, telling his countrymen that they would regain their national honor only if they abrogated the treaty. Purged of so-called Jewish traitors, cleared of the blame for causing the war, freed from onerous reparation payments, and rescued from emasculating disarmament, Germany would rise anew and reclaim her position as a world leader.

Hitler's drive for political power began in 1919, when he joined the small National Socialist Workers' party (later known as the Nazis), which demanded that all Jews be deprived of German citizenship and that all German-speakers be united in a single country. A brilliant propagandist and organizer, Hitler gave the Nazi movement a potent symbol, the swastika; raised party membership to 15,000 by 1923; and formed a private army, the storm troopers, to attack his political opponents. In the fall of 1923, Hitler engineered a revolt, the Beer-Hall Putsch, to overthrow Germany's five-year-old Weimar Republic. It was a dismal failure; the National Socialist party was ordered dissolved and Hitler was imprisoned for nine months.

While in prison, he wrote a book titled *Mein Kampf* (My Struggle) which laid out his beliefs and vision for Germany. He called on Germans to repudiate the Versailles Treaty, rearm, conquer countries with large German populations like Austria and Czechoslovakia, and seize *lebensraum* (living space) for Germans in Russia.

Following his release from prison, Hitler persuaded the German government to lift its ban on the National Socialist party. In 1928, the Nazis polled just 810,000 votes in German elections, but by 1930, after the depression began, they polled $6\frac{1}{2}$ million votes. Two years later Hitler ran for president. He lost, but received $13\frac{1}{2}$ million votes, 37 percent of all votes cast. The Nazis had suddenly become the single largest party in the German parliament, and in January 1933, Germany's president appointed Hitler to the post of chancellor. A year and a half later Hitler was dictator of Germany.

Within months of becoming chancellor, Hitler's National Socialist government banned labor unions, imposed newspaper censorship, and outlawed all other political parties. The regime established a secret police force, the Gestapo, to suppress all opposition, and required all children ten years and older to join Nazi youth groups. By 1935, Hitler had transformed Germany into a fascist state, with the government exercising total control over all political, economic, and cultural activities.

Anti-Semitism was an integral part of Hitler's political program. The 1935 Nuremberg Laws forbade intermarriage between Jews and Germans, restricted Jewish property rights, and barred Jews from

Some of the approximately 25,000 Jews arrested on Kristallnacht—the night of broken glass when Nazis destroyed Jewish shops and stores, wrecked Jewish homes, burned synagogues, beat Jewish men, and brutalized Jewish women and children—line up for roll call at the Buchenwald concentration camp.

the civil service, the universities, and all professional and managerial occupations. On the night of November 9, 1938—a night now known as *Kristallnacht* (the night of the broken glass)—the Nazis imprisoned more than 20,000 Jews in concentration camps and destroyed more than 200 synagogues and 7500 Jewish businesses.

A reviving Germany was not the only threat to world peace. While Hitler busied himself with rearming Germany, occupying the Rhineland, annexing Austria, and seizing Czechoslovakia, Italy attacked Ethiopia, and Japan attacked China.

Italy and Mussolini

Mussolini's Italy posed another threat to world peace. **Benito Mussolini,** Italy's fascist dictator from 1922 to 1943, promised to restore his country's martial glory. Surrounded by storm troopers dressed in black shirts, Mussolini delivered impassioned speeches from balconies, while crowds chanted "Duce! Duce!"

His opponents mocked him as the "Sawdust Caesar," but for a time his admirers included Winston Churchill and humorist Will Rogers. Cole Porter, the popular songwriter, referred to the Italian leader in one of his smash hits: "You're the top," he wrote, "you're Mussolini."

Mussolini invented a political philosophy known as **fascism,** extolling it as an alternative to socialist radicalism and parliamentary inaction. By fascism, he meant one-party government, strict government control of business and labor, and severe restrictions on personal liberty. Fascism, he promised, would end political corruption and labor strife while maintaining capitalism and private property. It would make trains run on time. Like Hitler's Germany, fascist Italy adopted anti-Semitic laws banning marriages between Christian and Jewish Italians, restricting Jews' right to own property, and removing Jews from positions in government, education, and banking.

One of Mussolini's goals was to create an Italian empire in North Africa. In 1912 and 1913, Italy conquered Libya. In 1935, Mussolini provoked war with Ethiopia, conquering the country in eight months. Two years later, Mussolini sent 70,000 Italian troops to Spain to help Francisco Franco defeat the republican government in the Spanish Civil War.

Japanese Aggression in the Far East

Another major threat to international stability following World War I came in the Far East. Chronically short of raw materials, Japan was desperate to establish political and cultural hegemony in Asia. In September 1931 Japan invaded Manchuria, reducing the Chinese province to a puppet state. President Hoover, a peaceful man, rejected American military intervention. He also refused to impose economic sanctions against Japan, fearing that such reprisals might hurt American exports or, worse yet, lead to war. Instead, Hoover applied the Stimson Doctrine, which revived the Wilsonian policy of refusing to recognize governments established by force.

Expecting bolder measures, Japan ignored America's slap on the wrist and concluded that the United States would not use military might to oppose Japan's designs on the Far East. In 1934, Japan terminated the Five-Power Naval Treaty of 1922, which had limited its naval power in the Pacific, and in 1937 invaded China. In response, the League of Nations sponsored a conference that same year in Brussels. As the delegates debated whether or not to impose economic sanctions against Japan, the United States announced it would not support sanctions. The conference adjourned after passing a report that mildly criticized Japanese aggression.

Any doubts regarding United States willingness to appease Japan vanished a few weeks later. In December 1937 Japanese aircraft bombed the *Panay,* a U.S. gunboat stationed on the Yangtze River near Nanking, killing three Americans. While the attack angered the public, few called for war as they had following the sinking of the *Maine* or the *Lusitania.* Secretary of State Cordell Hull sent sharply worded protests to Tokyo, but the United States quickly accepted Japan's "profound apology," which included indemnities for the injured and the relatives of the dead, promises against future attacks, and punishment of the pilots responsible for the bloodshed. In short, by the end of 1937, as one historian has noted, "America's Far Eastern Policy had retreated to inaction."

Alliances for Expansion

Hitler had vowed to reclaim Germany's position as a world leader. True to his word, Hitler pulled Germany out of the League of Nations and secretly began to rearm. In 1935 he publicly announced that he was building an air force and a 550,000-man-strong army. He also declared that Germany would have a peacetime draft, a clear violation of the Treaty of Versailles.

In 1936, Hitler concentrated on forging alliances with nations that shared Germany's taste for expansion and aggression. First he signed the Anti-Comintern Pact (forerunner of a full-scale military alliance) with Japan. Next, he formed the Rome-Berlin Axis with Italy. Finally, he reoccupied the Rhineland,

Axis Takeovers in Europe, 1936–1939

Map legend:
- Remilitarized by Germany, 1936
- Annexed by Germany, 1938
- Protectorates established by Germany, 1939
- Annexed by Italy, 1939

Versailles. Germany's frontiers were larger than they had been in 1914, the country was rearmed, and German national pride had been restored. In addition, Germany had acquired powerful allies in Japan and Italy. All this had transpired virtually unopposed by the victors of World War I. The member states of the League of Nations had offered only feeble protests and failed to act. Everyone hoped the Germans, Italians, and Japanese would be satisfied with their acquisitions and stop their expansions. In retrospect, such hopes were clearly wrong, but at the time they did not appear unfounded. Western leaders assumed they were dealing with reasonable and responsible men; they had no way of knowing appeasement would only fuel the Axis dictators' appetites for expansion.

In late summer, Hitler took one further step. On August 24, 1939, Germany and the Soviet Union signed a nonaggression treaty. In exchange for the pact, Hitler agreed to grant the Soviet Union a sphere of influence over eastern Poland, Estonia, Latvia, Finland, and Bessarabia (northeastern Romania), while Stalin approved Germany's designs on western Poland and Lithuania. With his eastern flank protected from attack, Hitler was now prepared for war.

The American Response to Hitler

The United States responded to Europe's turmoil with caution. Preoccupied with the Great Depression, President Roosevelt had little time or energy to deal with foreign affairs. Yet America's timidity also reflected the strength of its isolationist sentiment. Congress, not the president, played the dominant role in foreign affairs for much of the 1930s, and Congress was determined to keep the United States out of another European conflict.

Roosevelt's first diplomatic initiative involved the Soviet Union. Hoping to expand foreign trade and to use the Soviet Union to balance Japan in the Far East, he formally recognized the Soviet Union in 1933, provoking the wrath of isolationists and anti-Communists alike.

Privately, Roosevelt opposed the growth of isolationist sentiment in the United States during the early and mid-1930s. In his view, the United States, like it or not, had to play an important role in world affairs because it had become a major world power. But Roosevelt's freedom to act was severely limited by isolationists in Congress. Between 1935 and 1937, Congress passed three separate neutrality laws, which, respectively, clamped an embargo on arms sales to belligerents, forbade American ships from entering war zones and prohibited them from being

the German-speaking region between the Rhine River and France. Once again, France and Great Britain did nothing to oppose Hitler's bold advance, for they believed (or wanted to believe) that the Rhineland would satisfy his expansionist ambitions.

But the Rhineland only whetted Hitler's appetite. Intent on reuniting all German-speaking peoples of Europe under the "Third Reich," Hitler annexed Austria in 1938 and imprisoned the country's chancellor. Once again, the British and the French acquiesced, hoping Austria would be Hitler's last stop. Later that year he demanded the Sudetenland, the German-speaking region of western Czechoslovakia.

This time France and Great Britain felt compelled to act. In September 1938 Edouard Daladier, the premier of France, and Neville Chamberlain, Britain's prime minister, met with Hitler in Munich, Germany, to ask whether he had further designs on Europe. Fearing that they could not count on each other to use force, British and French leaders eagerly accepted Hitler's promises not to seek additional territory in Europe. In less than a year, Munich would become synonymous with shameful appeasement and Chamberlain would be vilified for believing Hitler's lies.

By 1938, then, Hitler had kept his promise to avenge the humiliations Germans had suffered at

armed, and barred Americans from traveling on belligerent ships. Clearly, Congress was determined not to repeat what it regarded as the mistakes that had plunged the United States into World War I.

The neutrality laws troubled Roosevelt. Convinced that these laws posed a serious threat to presidential power, Roosevelt delivered a speech in October 1937 in which he spoke of the need to "quarantine the aggressors." But he immediately retreated into silence when it became clear the public did not support vigorous action. This was where matters stood when Hitler decided to take advantage of the world's indecisiveness.

War Begins

At daybreak on September 1, 1939, mechanized German forces poured across the Polish border, while German bombers and fighters attacked Polish railroads from the air. On September 17, Russia attacked Poland from the east. Poland was overrun within three weeks.

The key to Germany's success was a new military strategy known as *blitzkrieg* ("lightning war"). Blitzkrieg stressed speed, force, and surprise; by closely coordinating air power and mechanized ground forces, Germany ripped through its adversary's defenses.

Britain and France declared war on Germany on September 3, 1939, two days after the German invasion began, but they did little while Poland fell. France moved its troops to its famous Maginot line, a supposedly invincible line of defensive fortifications built to protect France's eastern border. No fighting took place in late 1939 and early 1940, leading some to call this a "phony war."

Then in April 1940, German freighters sailed secretly into Norway's major ports and the port of Copenhagen, Denmark's capital, their holds filled with German troops. The Danes, taken completely by surprise, surrendered in two hours; the Norwegians held out until June, when they, too, capitulated. British troops had tried to assist Norway, but were forced to retreat due to a lack of air support. Following the Norway debacle, British Prime Minister Neville Chamberlain was forced to resign. He was replaced by **Winston Churchill,** who, since 1932, had been warning about the danger Hitler posed. Upon becoming prime minister, Churchill told the British people that he had nothing to offer them but "blood, toil, tears, and sweat" in their fight to resist foreign aggression.

In May 1940, Hitler began his assault on western Europe. He outflanked France's Maginot line by attacking Belgium, Luxembourg, and the Netherlands before driving his forces into France. Luxembourg

Hitler's armies devastated Poland with their tremendous force and firepower. Here soldiers drive through a town battered by repeated bombings.

surrendered in one day; Holland in five. A British expeditionary force rushed across the English Channel to try to stop the German offensive. But a German tank thrust forced the British to retreat to the French seaport of Dunkirk. With the British force nearly surrounded, Hitler had a chance to crush his opponents. But Britain's Royal Air Force held off German bombers long enough to allow a flotilla of yachts, ferries, and fishing boats to evacuate 338,000 Allied troops across the English Channel.

British forces had been driven from the continent. Worse yet, they had been forced to leave their weapons and tanks behind. Britain turned to the United States for help. President Roosevelt responded to the Dunkirk disaster by ordering U.S. military arsenals to send all available war material to Britain to replace the lost equipment.

During World War I, France held out against the Germans for four years. This time, French resistance lasted two weeks. Germany began its assault on France June 5; its troops entered Paris June 14; and on June 22, a new French government, made up of pro-German sympathizers, was set up at Vichy. In just six weeks, Germany had conquered most of continental Europe.

Convinced that Britain would negotiate with him (in order to keep control of its empire), Hitler decided against an immediate invasion of Britain. But Churchill refused to bargain. Defiantly, he told his people that he would resist any German assault: "We shall fight on the beaches . . . we shall fight in the streets . . . we shall never surrender."

Hitler was furious. First, he unleashed German submarines against British shipping. Then in July he sent his air force, the Luftwaffe, to destroy Britain from the air. At the time the assault began the Royal Air Force (RAF) had just 704 serviceable planes, while Germany had 2682 bombers and fighters ready for action. Throughout July and August the Luftwaffe attacked airfields and radar stations on Britain's southern and eastern coast. Then, in September, Hitler shifted strategy and began to bomb civilian targets in London. These air raids, known collectively as the blitz, continued through the fall and winter. In May 1941, the blitz ended. The RAF, while outnumbered, had won the Battle of Britain. Churchill expressed his nation's gratitude with famous words: "Never in the field of human conflict was so much owed by so many to so few."

Having failed in his bid to destroy Britain with air power, Hitler again shifted strategy and invaded the Soviet Union. The attack, which began June 22, 1941, violated the German-Soviet nonaggression pact. Hitler's goal was to seize Soviet food, oil, and slave labor for Germany. At first, the Nazi war machine seemed invincible. By fall, Hitler's armies had overrun the grain fields of Ukraine and were approaching Moscow and Leningrad. But instead of pressing ahead toward Moscow, as his generals advised, Hitler decided to seize Leningrad and occupy the Ukraine. By the time he was ready to advance on Moscow, temperatures had plunged to 40 degrees below zero. In the frigid cold, German troops suffered frostbite and their equipment broke down.

The week between December 6 and 11, 1941, proved to be one of the most pivotal in the entire war. On December 6, Soviet forces repulsed the German attack on Moscow; it was Hitler's first military defeat. The next day, Japanese forces attacked the American naval base at Pearl Harbor, Hawaii, bringing the United States into the war. On December 11, Hitler declared war on the United States.

"The Arsenal of Democracy"

Like Wilson before him, Roosevelt responded to Europe's war by declaring America's neutrality. Unlike the idealistic Wilson, however, he did not ask his countrymen to be "neutral in thought as well as in action." After France fell, Roosevelt feared a German victory would threaten America's future security, and he resolved to save England at all costs—including war.

Before he could rescue Britain, however, Roosevelt first had to regain control of American foreign policy. Soon after Germany invaded Poland, he pushed a fourth neutrality act through Congress. It modified the earlier legislation by permitting belligerents to purchase war materials, provided they paid cash and carried the goods away in their own ships. This act was pro-British because England controlled the Atlantic. Acting on his own authority, Roosevelt then rushed thousands of planes and guns to Britain. In September 1940 he persuaded Congress to pass the first peacetime draft in American history and signed an executive agreement with Great

The crater created by a German bomb dropped on Balham in south London during the blitz was large enough to swallow a city bus.

TABLE 25.1
Road to War: World War II

1939	**Germany invades Poland**	World War II begins.
	Neutrality Act of 1939	Allows the sale of arms to belligerents.
1940	**Arms sales to Britain**	The U.S. agrees to sell Britain surplus and outmoded arms.
	Destroyers for bases	The U.S. gives 50 American destroyers to Britain in exchange for British bases in the Western Hemisphere.
	Embargo imposed	President Roosevelt imposes an embargo on the export of scrap steel and iron to Japan.
	Draft instituted	The military draft goes into effect.
	"Arsenal of Democracy"	President Roosevelt announces that the U.S. will be the "arsenal of democracy."
1941	**Lend-Lease**	President Roosevelt signs the Lend-Lease Act empowering the president to lend war materiel to countries whose freedom is vital to U.S. interests.
	Assets frozen	President Roosevelt freezes assets of Germany, Italy, and Japan in the United States and closes German and Italian consulates.
	Pearl Harbor attacked	Japanese forces attack the naval base at Pearl Harbor, Hawaii, killing 2403 Americans, sinking or disabling 19 ships, and destroying some 150 planes.
	Declaration of war	Declaring December 7 "a date that shall live in infamy," President Roosevelt asks Congress to declare war against Japan. Germany declares war on the United States on December 11, 1941.

Britain transferring 50 destroyers to England in exchange for 99-year leases on eight British bases in the Western Hemisphere. Most Americans supported the destroyers-for-bases deal.

Fearing Roosevelt was duplicating Wilson's mistakes, isolationists opposed the tilt toward Britain. Strongest in the Midwest, they represented the entire spectrum of political thought, including Republicans such as Senators Arthur Vandenberg of Michigan and Robert Taft of Ohio; Democrats such as Joseph Kennedy, ambassador to Great Britain; and progressives such as Wisconsin's Senator Robert La Follette. Their most powerful argument was that Europe's war did not threaten "fortress America." Germany had no designs on the Western Hemisphere, they insisted. The United States should therefore sit this war out.

The war dominated the election of 1940. Running for an unprecedented third term, Roosevelt handily defeated Republican challenger Wendell Willkie, 27 million votes to 22 million votes, and 449 electoral votes to 82.

During the campaign, Willkie charged Roosevelt with maneuvering the United States into the European war. On the eve of the election, Roosevelt responded, offering these reassuring words to American parents: "I have said this before, but I shall say it again and again: your boys are not going to be sent into any foreign wars." In actuality, however, events were drawing the country closer to war.

After the election, Churchill informed Roosevelt that England had run out of money and could no longer purchase war supplies. Consequently, the president replaced "cash and carry" with "lend-lease." Congress bitterly debated the bill; the **Lend-Lease Act** was signed by Roosevelt in March 1941.

To cement the Anglo-American bond, Roosevelt met with Churchill in August 1941 on board the USS *Augusta* off the coast of Newfoundland. There they negotiated the Atlantic Charter, which pledged mutual support for democracy, freedom of the seas, arms reductions, and a just peace. In everything but name the United States and Great Britain were now allies.

While the public strongly supported aid for Great Britain, many Americans balked at helping the Russians, who had been invaded by Germany in June 1941. Roosevelt, however, immediately offered lend-lease aid to the Soviet Union, and in November 1941 the United States allocated $1 billion in aid to the Soviets. While critics denounced Roosevelt, Churchill, who knew wars often made strange bedfellows, supported the decision wholeheartedly. By 1945 America's allies had received $50 billion, four times the amount loaned to the allies in World War I.

THE PEOPLE SPEAK

Election Promises Should Be Kept

As the United States came closer to entering the war in Europe, isolationists rallied against it. Isolationist interests found a voice in the America First Committee, a lobby that garnered support from prominent members of the Republican party as well as celebrated citizens, including Charles Lindbergh, who in 1928 became the first man to fly a plane solo and nonstop from New York to Paris.

WE LACK LEADERSHIP THAT PLACES AMERICA FIRST

By CHARLES A. LINDBERGH

Delivered at Madison Square Garden, New York, Rally Under the Auspices of the America First Committee, May 23, 1941

. . . On the contrary, if we go to war to preserve democracy abroad, we are likely to end by losing it at home. There are already signs of danger around us. We have been shouting against intolerance in Europe, but it has been rising in America. We deplore the fact that the German people cannot vote on the policies of their government—that Hitler led his nation into war without asking their consent. But have we been given the opportunity to vote on the policy our government has followed? No, we have been led toward war against the opposition of four-fifths of our people. We had no more chance to vote on the issue of peace and war last November than if we had been in a totalitarian state ourselves. We in America were given just about as much chance to express our beliefs at the election last fall as the Germans would have been given if Hitler had run against Goering.

The state of affairs should make every American—even the interventionists—stop and think before we plunge blindly into a second world war. There are many interventionists who actually believe that by going to war we can strengthen democracy throughout the world, and with it all the civilized virtues which we in this country support. Those people overlook our failure in the last war "to make the world safe for democracy." They overlook the persecution and the intolerance which followed that war in Europe. They do not seem to realize that the elements they dislike in Germany lie beneath the surface of every nation; that they are here in America just as they are in Europe, and that nothing is as likely to bring them out as war—especially a prolonged war.

I opposed this war before it was declared because I felt it would be disastrous for Europe. I knew that England and France were not in a position to win, and I did not want them to lose. I now oppose our entry into the war because I do not believe that our system of government in America can survive our participation or our way of life can survive our participation. . . .

Interviewing Date **8/21–26/41** — Survey #245-K Question #11b	Interviewing Date **11/15–20/41** — Survey #253-K Question #13
If Lindbergh, Wheeler, Nye, and others start a "Keep-Out-of-War" party and enter candidates in the next congressional elections, would you vote for the candidate of this party?	*Which of these things do you think is the more important—that this country keep out of the war, or that Germany be defeated?*
Yes. . . . . . . 16% No . . . . 84% (p. 298)	Keep out of the war . . . . . 32% Defeat Germany . . . . . 68% (p. 311)

Source: Dr. George H. Gallup. *The Gallup Poll: Public Opinion 1935–1971: Volume One, 1935–1948* (New York: Random House, 1972.)

In April 1941 the United States went beyond financial assistance by constructing bases in Greenland and escorting convoys as far as Iceland to protect them from German submarines. The American navy started tracking German submarines and signaling their locations to British destroyers. After a German submarine attacked an American destroyer in September, Roosevelt ordered the navy to "shoot on sight" any German ships in the waters around Iceland. Yet the president stopped short of asking Congress for a formal declaration of war; for a few more months the United States maintained the fiction of neutrality.

A Collision Course in the Pacific

Thanks to the public's preoccupation with Europe, Roosevelt had a relatively free hand in the Far East, where Japan was seeking to acquire large parts of China and the western Pacific. Yet Japan's dream of expansion clashed with the two main pillars of America's Far Eastern policy—preserving the "Open Door" for trade, and protecting China's territorial integrity.

After Japan invaded China in 1937, relations between Washington and Tokyo deteriorated rapidly. The United States pressured Japan to withdraw, but Tokyo refused. In July 1939 Secretary of State Cordell Hull, aware that American exports fueled Japan's war machine, threatened to impose economic sanctions. Roosevelt, however, held back, fearing Japan would attack the Dutch East Indies to secure the oil it needed.

Events quickly forced Roosevelt's hand. In 1940 Japan occupied northern Indochina, an obvious step toward the Dutch East Indies. Late in September, Roosevelt placed an embargo on scrap iron and steel, hoping economic sanctions would strengthen moderates in Japan who wished to avoid conflict with the United States.

When these actions failed to deter Japanese aggression, Roosevelt froze Japanese assets in the United States and cut off steel, oil, and aviation fuel exports to Japan. Hurt by these sanctions, Japan negotiated with the United States throughout 1941. Instead of compromising, however, the United States asked Japan to withdraw immediately from Indochina and China, concessions that would have ended Japan's dream of economic and military hegemony in Asia.

In a last-ditch effort to avoid war, Japan promised not to march further south, not to attack the Soviet Union, and not to declare war against the United States if Germany and America went to war. In return, Japan asked the United States to abandon China. Roosevelt refused. In October 1941 the Japanese government fell and General Hideki Tojo, the leader of the militants, seized power. War was imminent.

Most military experts expected Japan to attack the Dutch East Indies to secure oil and rubber. Before striking there, however, Japan moved to neutralize American naval power in the western Pacific.

Pearl Harbor

At 7:02 A.M., December 7, 1941, an Army mobile radar unit set up on Oahu Island in Hawaii picked up the telltale blips of approaching aircraft. The two privates operating the radar contacted the Army's General Information Center, but the duty officer there told them to remain calm; the planes were probably American B-17s flying in from California. In fact, they were Japanese aircraft that had been launched from six aircraft carriers 200 miles north of Hawaii.

At 7:55 A.M., the first Japanese bombs fell on **Pearl Harbor,** the main base of the U.S. Pacific Fleet. Moored in the harbor were more than 70 warships, including 8 of the fleet's 9 battleships. There were also 2 heavy cruisers, 29 destroyers, and 5 submarines. Four hundred airplanes were stationed nearby.

Japanese torpedo bombers, flying just 50 feet above the water, launched torpedoes at the docked American warships. Japanese dive bombers strafed the ships' decks with machine gun fire, while Japanese fighters dropped high-explosive bombs on the aircraft sitting on the ground. Within half an hour, the U.S. Pacific Fleet was virtually destroyed. The U.S. battleship *Arizona* was a burning hulk. Three other large ships—the *Oklahoma*, the *West Virginia*, and the *California*—were sinking.

A second attack took place at 9 A.M., but by then the damage had already been done. Seven of the eight battleships were sunk or severely hit. Out of 400 aircraft, 188 had been destroyed and 159 were seriously damaged. Altogether, 2403 Americans died during the Japanese attack on Pearl Harbor; another 1178 were wounded. Japan lost just 55 men.

Militarily it was not a total disaster. Japan had failed to destroy Pearl Harbor's ship-repair facilities, the base's power plant, and its fuel tanks. Even more important, three U.S. aircraft carriers, which had been on routine maneuvers, escaped destruction. But it was a devastating blow nonetheless. That same day, Japanese forces also launched other attacks throughout the Pacific, striking Guam, Hong Kong, Malaya, Midway Island, the Philippine Islands, and Wake Island.

The next day, President Roosevelt appeared before a joint session of Congress to ask for a declara-

A small boat rushes toward the USS *West Virginia* to rescue sailors aboard the burning ship, hit during the surprise Japanese attack on Pearl Harbor on December 7, 1941. The attack caused tragic and devastating loss of life and property, but it also turned U.S. public opinion against the Japanese and the Axis Powers and persuaded Congress to approve President Roosevelt's request for a declaration of war against Japan.

tion of war. He began his address with these famous words: "Yesterday, December 7, 1941—a date that will live in infamy—the United States of America was suddenly and deliberately attacked by naval and air forces of the Empire of Japan." Congress declared war on Japan, with only one dissenting vote.

AMERICA MOBILIZES FOR WAR

After Pearl Harbor, practically everyone agreed on what had to be done: jump-start the economy, raise an army, and win the war. Yet the economic challenges facing the United States were truly mind-boggling. New plants had to be built and existing ones expanded; raw materials had to be procured and distributed where needed; labor had to be kept on the job; production had to be raised; and all this had to be accomplished without producing soaring inflation.

Mobilizing the Economy

Following the declaration of war, Roosevelt easily made the switch from reformer to war leader, telling reporters that "Dr. New Deal" had to be replaced by

"Dr. Win-the-War." Like Wilson before him, Roosevelt wished to avoid government controls. He, too, would fail. World War II created a huge (and apparently permanent) federal bureaucracy. In January 1942 Roosevelt created the **War Production Board (WPB)** to "exercise general responsibility" over the economy.

Business leaders responded coolly to the call for economic conversion. With profits already high because of the war in Europe, many industrialists did not wish to jeopardize their position in the domestic market by converting factories to military production. Others worried about getting stuck with inflated capacity after the war ended.

To gain their support, the government suspended competitive bidding, offered cost-plus contracts, guaranteed low-cost loans for retooling, and paid huge subsidies for plant construction and equipment. Lured by high profits, the American auto industry began to produce war vehicles and construct new factories, like the huge Willow Run plant near Detroit, to build airplanes. In 1940, 6000 planes rolled off Detroit's assembly lines; by 1942 production had soared to 47,000, and by the end of the war it had exceeded 100,000, more than doubling Roosevelt's goal.

Consumer industries prospered, too. Robert W. Woodruff of Coca-Cola made his 5-cent drink the most widely distributed consumer product in the world by convincing the army that soldiers needed Coke to refresh their fighting spirit. Backed by government subsidies, Woodruff built an international network of plants, and then purchased them at a fraction of their cost after the war, ensuring Coca-Cola's postwar supremacy in the soft drink industry.

Most military contracts went to big businesses because large-scale production simplified buying. At Roosevelt's insistence the Justice Department stopped prosecuting antitrust violators, a policy that accelerated business consolidations. Overall, industrial profits doubled, but small industries, lacking the capital to convert to war production, got crowded away from the federal trough.

When he saw the production figures of American industry during World War II, Winston Churchill smiled broadly and exclaimed, "Nothing succeeds like excess!" Great Britain's bulldog of a prime minister was right: Allied armies won the decisive battles of World War II, but the Allied victory rested squarely on America's economic might. Within a year of the Japanese attack on Pearl Harbor, the output of the nation's war industries outstripped that of all the Axis countries combined; by 1944, it was twice as great. By the war's end, industrial production had soared an astonishing 96 percent.

Government-sponsored research became a major new industry during World War II. To counter Germany's scientific and technological superiority, Roosevelt created the Office of Scientific Research and Development (OSRD) in 1942. Federal funds supported the development of radar, flame throwers, antiaircraft guns, rockets, and even new medicines. Thanks in large part to penicillin and new blood plasma techniques, the death rate of wounded soldiers who reached medical installations was half that of World War I. Antimalarial drugs and insecticides dramatically reduced the incidence of mosquito-carried diseases among troops in the Mediterranean and in the Pacific.

No less than industry, American agriculture performed impressively during World War II. To encourage production, Roosevelt allowed farmers to make large profits by setting crop prices at high levels. Good weather, mechanization, and a dramatic increase in the use of fertilizers did the rest.

The distribution of profits in agriculture followed the same pattern as in industry: most went to large-scale operators who could afford expensive machinery and fertilizers. Many small farmers, saddled with huge debts from the depression, abandoned their farms for jobs in defense plants or the armed services.

Overall, the war brought unprecedented prosperity to Americans. Per capita income rose from $373 in 1940 to $1074 in 1945, and total personal income went from $81 billion to $182 billion during the same years. The total income of families increased dramatically as large numbers of women joined the workforce, creating millions of two-income families. In fact, World War II brought Americans more money than they could spend, for the production of consumer goods could not keep pace with the public's new buying power.

Taming Inflation

The shortages led to inflation. Prices rose 18 percent between 1941 and the end of 1942. Apples sold for ten cents apiece; the price of a watermelon soared to $2.50; and oranges reached an astonishing $1.00 a dozen.

Many goods were unavailable regardless of price. To conserve steel, glass, and rubber for war industries, the government halted production of cars in December 1941. A month later, production of vacuum cleaners, refrigerators, radios, sewing machines, and phonographs ceased. Altogether, production of nearly 300 items deemed nonessential to the war effort—including coat hangers, beer cans, and toothpaste tubes—was banned or curtailed.

Congress responded to surging prices by establishing the **Office of Price Administration (OPA)** in January 1942, with the power to freeze prices and wages, control rents, and institute rationing of scarce items. The OPA quickly rationed foodstuffs. Every month, each man, woman, and child in the country received two ration books—one for canned goods and one for meat, fish, and dairy products. Meat was limited to 28 ounces per person a week; sugar to 8 to 12 ounces; and coffee, a pound every 5 weeks. Rationing was soon extended to tires, gasoline, and shoes. Drivers were allowed a mere 3 gallons a week, while pedestrians were limited to two pairs of shoes a year.

In addition to rationing, Washington attacked inflation by reducing the public's purchasing power. The administration encouraged the sale of war bonds, which not only helped finance the war but also absorbed more than 7 percent of the real personal income of Americans. Taxation was also used to combat inflation. To cool off consumer purchasing power, Congress passed the **Revenue Act of 1942,** which raised corporate taxes, increased the excess profits tax, and levied a 5 percent withholding tax on anyone who earned more than $642 a year. Tax reforms forced citizens to pay more than 40 percent of the war's total cost as the war progressed, laying the foundation for postwar tax policies. Wage controls offered another tool for controlling inflation. The **War Labor Board (WLB),** established in 1942, had the power to set wages, hours, and working conditions.

The first head of the Office of Price Administration (OPA) during World War II was Leon Henderson. This sign, posted in an A&P grocery store, bears Henderson's warning to sugar hoarders to use up what sugar they have before trying to use their ration stamps to get more. Henderson managed to get Congress to approve punishments for those who violated OPA regulations. The maximum penalty was one year's imprisonment and a $5000 fine.

These programs, working together, brought inflation under control. After 1942 the annual inflation rate did not exceed 1.5 percent. Still, the administration's methods pleased no one. Everyone groused about taxes; manufacturers and farmers denounced price controls as an attack on their profits; and labor officials condemned wage freezes as an assault on their incomes.

Yet American workers clearly reaped a bonanza from World War II. Because the war created 17 million new jobs at the exact moment when 15 million men and women entered the armed services, unemployment virtually disappeared. After Pearl Harbor, labor soared to an absolute premium, drawing into the workforce previously unemployed and underemployed groups such as women, teenagers, African Americans, senior citizens, and the handicapped. Under the benevolent hand of government protection, unions rebounded from their sharp decline of the 1920s and early 1930s.

Despite these gains, labor unrest increased throughout the war. After Pearl Harbor union officials pledged not to strike until the war ended, but inflation and wage restrictions quickly eroded their goodwill. The number of work stoppages rose from 2960 in 1942 to 4956 in 1944, though most ended quickly and did not harm the war effort.

In contrast to the president, Congress took a hostile stand toward labor. Over Roosevelt's veto, Congress passed the Smith-Connally Act, which banned strikes in war industries, authorized the president to seize plants useful to the war effort, and limited political activity by unions. The Smith-Connally Act reflected a resurgence of conservatism, both in Congress and in the country at large. Though the Democrats continued to maintain a thin majority in both houses of Congress throughout the war, a coalition of Republicans and conservative Democrats after 1942 could defeat any measure.

Beginning in 1943 Roosevelt's opponents led a successful attack against the New Deal, refusing to fund the Civilian Conservation Corps, the Works Progress Administration, the National Youth Administration, and the National Resources and Planning Board. According to conservatives, these agencies had dangerously expanded federal power and deserved to die.

Election of 1944

With reform in retreat, the Republicans expected to win the election of 1944. Thomas E. Dewey, the dapper young governor of New York, won his party's nomination on the first ballot. While Dewey accepted the New Deal as part of American life, he opposed its expansion. No distance separated the two major candidates on foreign affairs.

Roosevelt easily captured his party's nomination for a fourth term. Because his health was deteriorating badly, his choice of a vice president was more important than ever. Roosevelt allowed the Democratic convention to select a nominee, and it picked Harry S Truman of Missouri, best known as leader of a Senate committee investigating corruption in defense spending.

The 1944 campaign revitalized Roosevelt. He unveiled plans for a "GI Bill of Rights," promising liberal unemployment benefits, educational support, medical care, and housing loans for veterans, which Congress approved overwhelmingly in 1944. Unwilling to switch leaders while at war, the public stuck with Roosevelt to see the crisis through.

Molding Public Opinion

Having witnessed the mistakes of World War I, Roosevelt did not want government propaganda to arouse or fuel false hopes. Shortly before Pearl Harbor, he created the Office of Facts and Figures under Archibald MacLeish, the Librarian of Congress. A poet, MacLeish became embroiled in bureaucratic struggles with government agencies, the armed services, and the Office of Strategic Services. By 1944 the

government had all but abandoned its efforts to shape public opinion about the war.

Private enterprise filled the void. Movies, comic strips, newspapers, books, and advertisements reduced the war to a struggle between good and evil as the Allies engaged in mortal combat with Japan and Germany. The Japanese bore the brunt of the propaganda, especially during the first two years of fighting. Caricatured with thick glasses and huge buck teeth, public portraits of the Japanese grew more ugly and vicious as deeply ingrained racism fed the stereotypes, reviving old fears of the "yellow peril."

Germans, by contrast, elicited more complex attitudes in Americans, largely because passions were not inflamed by racism. At first, Americans blamed Hitler for the war. As eyewitness accounts of German atrocities began to filter back from the front, however, the public's views shifted. Americans gradually came to blame not just the Nazis, but all Germans, for the war.

Motion pictures emerged as the most important instrument of propaganda during World War II. After Pearl Harbor, Hollywood immediately enlisted in the war cause. The studios quickly copyrighted movie titles like "Yellow Peril" and "V for Victory." Hollywood's greatest contribution to the war effort was in the area of morale. Combat films produced during the war emphasized patriotism, group effort, and the value of sacrifice for a larger cause. They portrayed World War II as a peoples' war, typically featuring a group of men from diverse ethnic backgrounds who were thrown together, tested on the battlefield, and molded into a dedicated fighting unit. Wartime films also featured women serving as combat nurses, riveters, welders, and long-suffering mothers who kept the home fires burning.

SOCIAL CHANGES DURING THE WAR

World War II produced important changes in American life, some trivial, others profound. One striking change involved fashion. To conserve wool and cotton, dresses became shorter, and vests and cuffs disappeared, as did double-breasted suits, pleats, and ruffles.

More significant was a tremendous increase in mobility. The war set families in motion, pulling them off farms and out of small towns, and packing them into large urban areas.

War industries sparked the urban growth. Detroit's population exploded as the automotive industry switched to war vehicles. Washington, D.C., became another boomtown, as tens of thousands of new workers staffed the swelling ranks of the bu-

Bill Mauldin's cartoon characters, Willie and Joe, were popular not only at home but also among soldiers abroad.

"*Joe, yestiddy ya saved my life an' I swore I'd pay ya back. Here's my last pair of dry socks.*"

reaucracy. The most dramatic growth occurred in California, however. Of the 15 million civilians who moved across state lines during the war, over 2 million went to California to work in defense industries.

Women

The war had a dramatic impact on women. Easily the most visible change involved the sudden appearance of large numbers of women in uniform. The military organized women into auxiliary units with special uniforms, their own officers, and, amazingly, equal pay. By 1945 more than 250,000 women had joined the **Women's Army Corps (WAC),** the Army Nurses Corps, the Women Accepted for Voluntary Emergency Service (WAVES), the Navy Nurses Corps, the Marines, and the Coast Guard.

Women also substituted for men on the home front. The war challenged the conventional image of female behavior, as "Rosie the Riveter" became the popular symbol of women who abandoned traditional female occupations to work in defense industries.

Women paid a price for their economic independence, though. Outside employment did not free wives from domestic duties. The same women who put in full days in offices and factories went home to cook, clean, shop, and care for children. They had not one job, but two, and the only way they could fill both was to sacrifice relaxation, recreation, and sleep. Outside employment also raised the problem of child

care. A few industries, such as Kaiser Steel, offered day-care facilities, but most women had to make their own informal arrangements.

Social critics had a field day attacking women. Social workers blamed working mothers for the rise in juvenile delinquency during the war, while other critics condemned women for their immodesty, self-indulgence, drinking, dress standards, and sexual promiscuity.

Amid this confusion, many women elected to cling to the familiar by embracing the traditional roles of housewives and mothers. Between 1941 and 1945, the marriage rate reached new heights: 105 marriages per every 1000 women between the ages of 17 and 29, well above 89.1, the rate during the "normal" years of 1925 to 1929. The birthrate increased, too, rebounding sharply from the all-time low of 18 to 19 per 1000 people during the depression. In 1943 the birthrate jumped to 22.7, and by 1946 it had reached 25, where it remained, with modest fluctuations, for the rest of the decade. Overall, the "baby boom" did not signal a return to large families; rather, the birthrate rose because women married at younger ages and had their families earlier in life.

Hasty marriages between young partners often proved brittle. Wartime separations forced newlyweds to develop new roles and become self-reliant, and many couples later found it difficult to reestablish their relationships. Rather than remain in unhappy marriages, they often opted for divorce. In

During the war, a growing number of women not only joined the armed forces but also helped out in the labor force at home by filling jobs normally held by men.

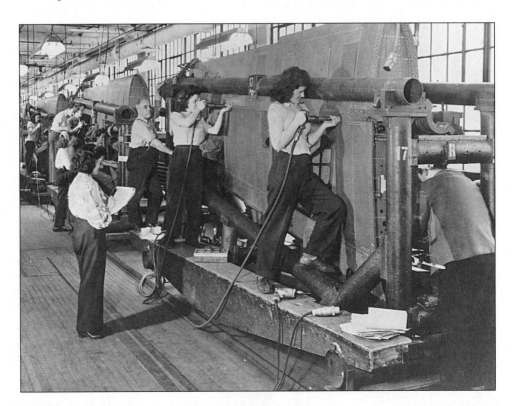

1946 the American courts granted a record 600,000 divorces. By 1950 the divorce rate stood at one quarter of the marriages, well above the prewar levels.

Yet Americans had not given up on marriage. The divorce rate had been climbing steadily (except during the depression years when many people could not afford to get married or divorced) since 1900. Furthermore, most Americans who divorced during the 1940s promptly remarried. They had rejected their mates, not marriage.

African Americans

During World War II, African Americans waged battles on two fronts. They helped the country win the war overseas and pressed for equal rights at home. African Americans called this dual struggle for victory against fascism and discrimination the **Double V campaign.** They played many critical roles in the war effort. About a million African Americans served in the armed forces during World War II, about half serving overseas. The armed forces were segregated, and many African American soldiers complained that they were treated like prisoners of war. Nevertheless, all-black units like the famous "Tuskegee Airmen" (the 99th Pursuit Squadron), which flew combat missions in Europe; the 92nd Division, which suffered 3161 casualties in campaigns in Italy; and the 761st Tank Battalion, which fought at the Battle of the Bulge, played pivotal battlefield roles.

World War II helped reshape the nation's race relations. In 1941, the overwhelming majority of the nation's African American population—10 out of 13 million—lived in the South, primarily in rural areas. During the war, more than one million African Americans migrated to the North and West—twice the number during World War I—and more than two million found work in defense industries. Yet African Americans continued to be the last hired and the first fired, and other forms of discrimination remained blatant, especially in housing and employment.

African American leaders fought discrimination vigorously. In the spring of 1941 (months before America entered the war), the president of the Brotherhood of Sleeping Car Porters, A. Philip Randolph, with strong backing from the National Association for the Advancement of Colored People (NAACP), called for 150,000 people to march on Washington to protest discrimination in defense industries. Embarrassed and concerned, Roosevelt issued an executive order prohibiting discrimination in defense industries and creating the Fair Employment Practices Commission (FEPC). But the FEPC's tiny staff lacked the power and resources to enforce its decisions. During the war the FEPC did not even process most complaints, and contractors ignored 35 of the 45 compliance orders the commission issued.

African Americans fared no better in the public sector. Most African Americans in the federal bureaucracy worked as janitors, and the armed services treated its African American soldiers as second-class citizens. The marines excluded blacks; the navy used them as servants; and the army created separate black regiments commanded mostly by white officers. The Red Cross even segregated blood plasma.

Not surprisingly, racial tensions deepened during the war. The number of African American GIs rose from 100,000 in 1941 to 700,000 in 1944. Many joined the armed services hoping to find social mobility. Instead, they encountered segregation and discrimination. They resented white officials who denounced Nazi racism but remained silent about discrimination at home. Northern African Americans stationed in the South found race relations shocking.

Conditions in the civilian sector were no better. As urban areas swelled with defense workers, housing and transportation shortages exacerbated racial tensions. In 1943 a riot broke out in Detroit in a federally sponsored housing project. Polish Americans wanted African Americans barred from the new apartments named, ironically, in honor of Sojourner Truth, a former slave who became an abolitionist and poet. White soldiers from a nearby base joined the fighting, and other federal troops had to be brought in to disperse the mobs. The violence left 35 African Americans and 9 whites dead.

Similar conflicts erupted across the nation, exposing in each instance the same jarring contradic-

Tuskegee Airfield in Alabama was the first training facility for African American pilots of the U.S. Army Air Force. Graduates of the training program were known as Tuskegee Airmen.

tion: white Americans espoused equality abroad but practiced discrimination at home. A 1942 survey showed that many African Americans sympathized with the Japanese struggle to expel white colonialists from the Far East. Significantly, the same survey revealed that a majority of white industrialists in the South preferred a German victory to racial equality in America.

Many African Americans responded to the rising tensions by joining civil rights organizations—during World War II, the NAACP, for example, intensified its legal campaigns against discrimination. Its membership grew from 50,000 to 500,000 as large numbers of African Americans and middle-class whites demanded racial equality.

Some African Americans, however, considered the NAACP too slow and too conciliatory. Rejecting legal action, the Congress of Racial Equality (CORE), founded in 1942, organized a series of "sit-ins." Civil disobedience produced a few victories in the North, but the South's response was brutal. While civil rights activists made few gains during World War II, they did forge new demands and tactics that would shape the civil rights movement after the war.

Federal officials did little to advance civil rights. Personally, Roosevelt sympathized with African Americans, but he feared losing the Solid South's support if he moved too rapidly on the race issue. Thus, while he admitted African American leaders to the White House to hear their grievances, Roosevelt seldom took action. Eleanor Roosevelt remained the conscience of the administration, voicing her sympathy for civil rights at every juncture, but the president refused to take the political risks needed to end discrimination and promote racial equality.

Mexican Americans

World War II affected Mexican Americans no less than African Americans and women. Almost 400,000 Mexican Americans served in the armed forces during the war. As soldiers, they expanded their contacts with American society, for the first time visiting new parts of the country in which large groups of people held few prejudices against them. For Mexican Americans in the civilian sector, jobs in industry provided an escape hatch from the desperate poverty of migratory farm labor. In New Mexico, for example, about one-fifth of the rural Mexican American population left for war-related jobs.

The need for farm workers rose dramatically after Pearl Harbor. To meet the demand, the United States established the *bracero* (work hands) program in 1942; by 1945 several hundred thousand Mexican workers had immigrated to the Southwest. Commer-

cial farmers welcomed them, but labor unions resented the competition, leading to animosity and discrimination against Mexicans and Mexican Americans alike.

In Los Angeles, ethnic tensions erupted into violence. White society both feared and resented newly formed Mexican American youth gangs, whose members celebrated their ethnicity by wearing flamboyant "zoot suits" and by tattooing their left hands. In June 1943 hundreds of white sailors on liberty from nearby naval bases invaded downtown Los Angeles. Eager to put down the Mexican American youths, they attacked the "zooters" and riots broke out for several nights. The local press blamed Mexican American gangs, and the riots did not end until military police ordered sailors back to their ships.

Despite outbursts of violence and discrimination, World War II benefited the poor of all races. Thanks to full employment and progressive taxation, people at the bottom had income redistributed in their favor. Before the war there were 12 families with an income under $2000 for every family with an income over $5000; after the war the ratio was almost even. Still, the gains made by poor people came from the state of the economy (the need for soldiers and workers), not from federal policies or the efforts of organized labor.

Fear of Enemy Aliens

On December 8, 1941, Roosevelt issued an executive order regarding enemy aliens. It suspended naturalization proceedings for Italian, German, and Japanese immigrants, required them to register, restricted their mobility, and prohibited them from owning items that might be used for espionage and sabotage, such as cameras and shortwave radios. In practice, however, the government did not accord enemy aliens the same treatment: Italian and German aliens received lenient treatment, while Japanese aliens suffered gross injustices.

Approximately 600,000 Italian aliens lived in the United States in 1940. In general, the government treated them well throughout the war, administering the enemy alien laws with compassion. On Columbus Day, 1942 (just before the congressional elections), Roosevelt lifted the enemy alien designation for Italians and established simplified naturalization procedures. German aliens received similar treatment. Though less numerous (264,000) and not as politically important to the Democrats, Roosevelt's administration treated them fairly throughout the war.

Jewish refugees complicated the German question. Reflecting a nasty strain of anti-Semitism, Congress in 1939 refused to raise immigration quotas to admit 20,000 Jewish children fleeing Nazi oppression.

Instead of relaxing immigration quotas, American officials worked in vain to persuade Latin American countries and Great Britain to admit Jewish refugees. Other officials, such as Assistant Secretary of State Breckinridge Long, the chief administrator for immigration policy, insisted that winning the war offered the best means for rescuing European Jews. Bitterly anti-Semitic in his private views, Long argued that any relaxation of the quota system would permit Nazi spies to slip into the country along with legitimate refugees.

While the futile debates dragged on, Hitler's death camps killed helpless victims at the rate of 2000 an hour. As late as 1944, American officials who knew the ghastly truth even publicly downplayed reports of genocide in the press.

Finally, in January 1944, Secretary of the Treasury Henry Morgenthau forced the issue. The only Jew in the Cabinet, Morgenthau presented to Roosevelt the "Report to the Secretary on the Acquiescence of this Government in the Murder of the Jews." Shamed into action, Roosevelt created the **War Refugee Board,** which, in turn, set up refugee camps in Italy, North Africa, and the United States. But America's response offered too little, too late. During the 18 months of the War Refugee Board's existence, Hitler killed far more Jews than the War Refugee Board saved.

Internment of Japanese Americans

Like Jews, Japanese Americans got a bitter taste of discrimination during World War II. Barred from migrating to the United States by the Immigration Act of 1924, they comprised only a tiny portion of the population in 1941—no more than 260,000 people; 150,000 lived in Hawaii, with the remaining 110,000 concentrated on the West Coast, where they worked mostly as small farmers or businesspeople serving the Japanese community. After Pearl Harbor, rumors spread about Japanese troops preparing to land in California, where they allegedly planned to link up with Japanese Americans and Japanese aliens poised to strike as a fifth column for the invasion.

On February 19, 1942, Roosevelt authorized the Department of War to designate military areas and to exclude any or all persons from them. Armed with this power, military authorities immediately moved against Japanese aliens. In Hawaii, where residents of Japanese ancestry formed a large portion of the population and where the local economy depended on their labor, the military did not force Japanese Americans to relocate. On the West Coast, however, military authorities ordered the Japanese to leave, making no distinction between aliens and citizens.

Forced to sell their property for pennies on the dollar, most Japanese Americans suffered severe financial losses. Relocation proved next to impossible, as no other states would take them.

When voluntary measures failed, Roosevelt created the **War Relocation Authority.** It resettled 100,000 Japanese Americans in ten camps scattered across six western states and Arkansas called relocation camps. Resembling minimum security prisons, these concentration camps locked American citizens who had committed no crimes behind barbed wire. They were crowded into ramshackle wooden barracks where they lived one family to a room furnished with nothing but cots and bare light bulbs, forced to endure bad food, inadequate medical care, and poorly equipped schools.

Nearly 18,000 Japanese American men won release from the camps to fight for the United States Army. Most served with the 100th Infantry Battalion and the 442nd Regimental Combat Team. In Italy, the 442nd sustained nearly 10,000 casualties, with 3600 Purple Hearts, 810 Bronze Stars, 342 Silver Stars, 123 divisional citations, 47 Distinguished Service Crosses, 17 Legions of Merit, 7 Presidential Unit Citations, and 1 Congressional Medal of Honor. In short, they fought heroically for the United States, emerging as the most decorated military unit in World War II. In one of the most painful scenes in American history, Japanese American parents, still locked inside

Japanese Americans of all ages, tagged like pieces of luggage, await their relocation to one of ten detention camps in seven states. This family was from Hayward, California.

Location of Internment Camps for Japanese Americans

concentration camps, received posthumous Purple Hearts for their sons.

Japanese Americans protested their treatment, claiming numerous civil rights violations. Citing national security considerations, the Supreme Court backed the government, 6 to 3, in *Korematsu* v. *United States* (1944). But in a dissenting opinion, Frank Murphy admitted federal policy had fallen "into the ugly abyss of racism." On December 18, 1944, in the *Endo* case, the Supreme Court ruled that a civilian agency, the War Relocation Authority, had no right to incarcerate law-abiding citizens. Two weeks later the federal government began closing down the camps, ending one of the most shameful chapters in American history.

THE WAR IN EUROPE

The Grand Alliance

Following Pearl Harbor, the **Axis Powers** of Germany, Japan, and Italy faced the **Grand Alliance,** composed of the United States, Great Britain, Free France, and the Soviet Union. Yet from the beginning the Grand Alliance was an uneasy coalition, born of necessity and racked with tension. Apart from the need to defeat the enemy, the Allies found it difficult to agree on anything.

Winston Churchill, Great Britain's prime minister, approached international affairs in spheres-of-

influence, balance-of-power terms. He wanted to block Soviet expansion and was determined that Britain play a major role in postwar Europe. Furthermore, he wanted Britain to emerge form the war with its colonial empire intact.

France's goals reflected the vision of one man— **General Charles de Gaulle,** who after the fall of France in 1940 had established in London a French government-in-exile. Above all, de Gaulle wanted to restore France to greatness. By nature aloof and suspicious, he fought to retain his country's empire, and as the war progressed American officials came to regard de Gaulle as a political extremist. In policy disputes, he often sided with Britain to oppose American and Soviet demands.

Joseph Stalin spoke for the Soviet Union. The son of a cobbler, Stalin rose to power by crushing all political rivals during the turbulent years following the Bolshevik revolution. Iron-willed, deeply paranoid, and bold as a thief, "Uncle Joe" enjoyed a well-deserved reputation as a formidable negotiator. Throughout World War II, he pressed for a postwar settlement that would guarantee the Soviet Union's future security and open new lands for Communism. To protect the Soviet Union from future attacks, Stalin insisted upon Germany's total destruction. As additional insurance, he demanded parts of Poland and Finland and all of the Baltic states. Eastern Europe would then form a buffer against future aggression from the West, provide colonies for rebuilding the Soviet economy, and add new territory to the Communist world map.

Roosevelt had his own ideas about how the world should look after the war. In broad terms, he opposed colonialism and the spread of Communism; and he supported open markets, democratic elections to counter spheres of influence, and a new League of Nations to promote world peace. Among these objectives, anticolonialism and support for free markets were his top priorities, and both goals reflected Roosevelt's remarkable ability to join political principle with economic advantage.

No less than his counterparts, Roosevelt's personality shaped his policies. Because he disliked the rough and tumble of hard bargaining, he tried to avoid clashes with other leaders by postponing difficult decisions and by relying too heavily on his personal charm. In addition, Roosevelt's pragmatic approach to problem solving made him seek compromises whenever possible, which meant that he often sacrificed principles in order to preserve Allied cooperation.

From the outset, then, dissent riddled the Grand Alliance. In pursuit of its own national interests, each ally had a separate agenda, its own set of demands, and its own vision of the how the world map should look when the war ended. Given these conflicts, the Allies could look forward not to harmony but to clashes over military strategy throughout the war, bitter debates over peace terms at the war's end, and decades of international strife in the postwar era.

Early Axis Victories

For six months after Pearl Harbor, Japan looked unbeatable. Japanese forces captured Guam, Wake Island, the Philippines, Hong Kong, and Malaya and slashed deep into Burma. General Douglas MacArthur was driven from the Philippines in March 1942. In a matter of months Japanese troops had conquered a vast expanse of territory extending from the Gilbert Islands through the Solomons and from New Guinea to Burma, leaving India and Australia vulnerable to attack.

Nor did the Allied cause look any brighter in Europe. During the first ten months of 1942, German submarines sank over 500 American merchant ships. On the Russian front, German troops pressed toward Stalingrad, and in North Africa, where German Field Marshal Erwin Rommel, the famous "Desert Fox," was sweeping toward the Suez Canal, the situation seemed equally bleak. In short, 1942 opened badly for the Allies. Axis victories in the Pacific, Europe, and Africa served notice the war would be long and costly.

Stemming the German Tide

Roosevelt decided to assign Germany top priority for two reasons: First, he doubted Hitler could be dislodged from Europe if Britain fell; and, second, Roosevelt wanted to placate Stalin, whose troops were bearing the brunt of the German war machine. As the Germans drove deep into Soviet territory in 1942, Stalin demanded a second front in France to force Germany to divide her armies, thereby relieving some of the pressure on the Soviet Union.

By the autumn of 1942 the tide was beginning to turn on the eastern front. In September the Red Army won a key victory at Stalingrad. Then the Soviets launched a furious counterattack, beginning the long drive to push the Germans back across the Ukraine. Despite Soviet victories and Stalin's repeated pleas for a second front, the Allies, at Churchill's insistence, decided to attack the Germans in North Africa instead of France. Stalin saw this as a betrayal and his suspicions deepened.

Allied victories in Africa seemed to confirm Churchill's wisdom. British Field Marshal Sir Bernard Montgomery drove the Germans back to Tu-

nis in October, and in November 1942 General Dwight D. Eisenhower led a force of 400,000 Allied soldiers in a full-scale invasion of North Africa. Complete victory in North Africa came on May 12, 1943, when the remnants of the Axis armies surrendered. Germany and Italy had both suffered a major defeat and Allied shipping could now cross the Mediterranean in safety.

Cheered by North African victories, Churchill and Roosevelt met in Casablanca, French Morocco, in January 1943. Stalin did not attend, explaining he could not leave the Soviet Union at this critical juncture of the war. Haunted by ghastly memories of World War I and fearing a premature invasion of France might bog down into trench-style warfare, Churchill pushed hard for an attack on Sicily and then Italy. The United States initially opposed the plan, arguing it would delay the invasion of France, but Churchill prevailed. With the promised invasion of France again put on hold, Churchill and Roosevelt moved to reassure Stalin. Vowing publicly to make peace with the Axis powers only on the basis of unconditional surrender, the two leaders also renewed their pledge to open a second front.

Sicily fell in August 1943 after a campaign of slightly more than a month. Victory in Italy, however, did not come cheaply. The terrain was mountainous, and the Germans offered savage resistance. Stalin deeply resented the commitment of Allied troops there, which further postponed the long-promised second front in France. Moreover, since Soviet troops had not fought in the Italian campaign, Roosevelt and Churchill did not allow Stalin to participate in organizing an occupation government there. The next time Stalin wanted a voice in a region he made certain to have his armies on site.

Liberating Europe

In November 1943 Roosevelt, Churchill, and Stalin held their first face-to-face conference, meeting in Teheran, the capital of Iran. Buoyed by military success, Stalin sounded conciliatory as they discussed a second front. The leaders set May 1944 as the target date for Operation OVERLORD, the code name for the invasion of France. To increase the odds for success, Stalin promised to coordinate Russia's spring offensive with the invasion.

Once the leaders turned to postwar issues, however, the conference dissolved into bitter controversy. Stalin demanded Soviet control over Eastern Europe and insisted Germany be divided into several weak states. Opposing both demands, Churchill proposed democratic governments for Eastern Europe, especially in Poland, for which England had gone to war,

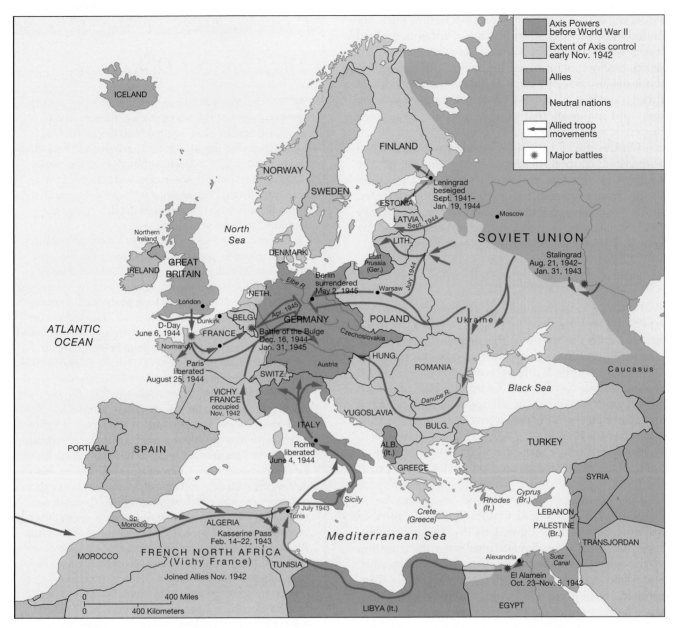

World War II, European Theater

and argued that the balance of power in postwar Europe required a united Germany. Roosevelt, on the other hand, knew Stalin had the inside track in Eastern Europe. Convinced he could handle "Uncle Joe," Roosevelt decided to leave territorial questions to a postwar international organization dominated by the victors. Apart from reaching agreement on the second front, the Teheran Conference merely aired the leaders' conflicting demands.

In preparation for the invasion, the Allies instituted saturation bombing of German territory. They dropped 2,697,473 tons of bombs, killing 305,000 civilians and damaging over 5.5 million homes. The air raids were supposed to wipe out the German war machine and break the people's will to resist, but missions such as the firebombing of Dresden, which killed 100,000 people, convinced many Germans that Hitler's ravings about the evil Allies were true, and that stiffened their will to fight.

As the bombers pounded Germany the Allies prepared for the invasion of France, massing more than 3 million soldiers in England under the command of General Dwight D. Eisenhower. **D-Day** came on June 6, 1944. After two weeks of desperate fighting on the beaches of Normandy, the Allies began to push inland. A month later Allied troops were sweeping across Europe in a race for Berlin. They liberated Paris in August, and by mid-September Allied forces had crossed the German border. True to his word, Stalin synchronized his spring offensive with the invasion. Soviet troops engaged the Germans in furious combat all across Eastern Europe, tying up men and materials that otherwise could have been hurled against the Allies.

On December 16, 1944, German troops launched a massive counteroffensive. In the **Battle of the Bulge,** German armored divisions slashed 60 miles to the Franco-Belgian border before being defeated by **General George Patton**'s Third Army. By January 1945 Soviet troops had captured Warsaw, and by February they were within 45 miles of Berlin.

The Yalta Conference

With victory in Europe at hand, Roosevelt, Churchill, and Stalin met in February 1945 at Yalta, on the Black Sea, to settle the shape of the postwar world. They concurred on the partition of Germany, but there the agreement stopped. Stalin wanted $20 billion in reparation payments from Germany, half of which would go to Russia. Churchill opposed him, rejecting any plan that would leave Germany financially prostrate after the war.

Eastern Europe was the most divisive issue at Yalta. Stalin had long insisted on Soviet control over the Baltic states (Estonia, Lithuania, and Latvia), as well as portions of Finland, Poland, and Romania. In October 1944 Stalin and Churchill met secretly in Moscow, where they agreed to divide Eastern Europe into British and Soviet spheres for the duration of the war. Consistent with these earlier demands, Stalin laid claim to eastern Poland at the **Yalta Conference,** reminding Churchill and Roosevelt that since he had not opposed their political decisions in Italy, he would not tolerate any interference in Eastern Europe. Under pressure from Roosevelt and Churchill, however, Stalin grudgingly agreed to hold free elections in Poland itself, promising that any new government formed there would include democratic elements. Yet as one of Roosevelt's chief military advisers warned the president, Stalin tacked so many amendments onto the Polish agreement that the Soviets "could stretch it all the way from Yalta to Washington without technically breaking it."

The remaining issues at Yalta proved less troublesome. Stalin pledged to enter the war against Japan within three months after Germany surrendered, and he renewed his promise to join the United Nations. Roosevelt considered both concessions to be important victories because he wanted Soviet help in defeating Japan and because he remained hopeful

LANDINGS ON D-DAY

The Longest Day

For the Allies in World War II, the D-Day landing on June 6, 1944, was the long-planned, long-anticipated blow against Nazi Germany. Originally scheduled for 1942, it had been pushed back first to 1943 and finally to 1944. Although both the Soviet Union and impatient Americans had clamored for an earlier invasion, Prime Minister Winston Churchill of Great Britain, who remembered the difficulties of Dunkirk, counseled caution.

The cross-channel invasion was a risky proposition and an immense undertaking. During early 1944, the Allies moved thousands of aircraft, tanks, trucks, jeeps, and men into southeastern England, moving soldiers to joke that if the invasion was long postponed, England would tilt and sink into the Channel. Then there were the imponderables no amount of careful planning could predict: weather, visibility, the state of the Channel.

As much as possible General Dwight D. Eisenhower, who was the overall commander of the invasion, tried to deceive the Germans into believing that the invasion would take place at the Pas de Calais, around Boulogne, Calais, and Dunkirk. It appears that Hitler did believe that the Allies would strike there. Instead, Ike centered his attack further to the west, along the French coast between Cherbourg and Le Havre. Altogether, the Allies assaulted five beaches and dropped paratroopers and airborne infantry into three sites.

Further east, British paratroopers were given the task of securing the left flank by gaining control of the Orne River. American paratroopers were given the job of securing the right flank along the Merderet River. In between these two points, the Allies landed on five beaches: Sword (British), Juno (Canadian), Gold (British), Omaha (American), and Utah (American). All totaled, 2,876,000 soldiers, sailors, and airmen; 11,000 aircraft; and over 2000 vessels played a part in the invasion.

At several beaches, especially Utah, the Allies met little opposition. At others, notably Omaha, the story was much different and losses were heavy. More than 2000 Americans were killed or wounded securing Omaha beach on June 6. But by the end of that "longest day" the Allies had accomplished their goal. They were back in France and ready to move east toward Germany.

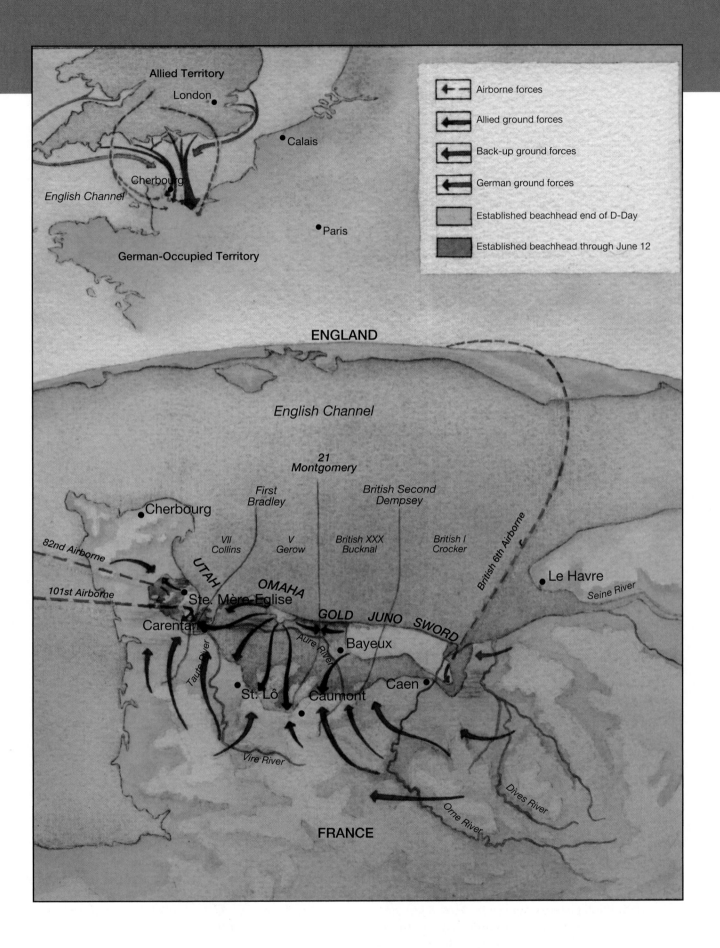

the United Nations could negotiate peaceful solutions to the disputes between the United States and the Soviet Union after the war.

Critics have denounced Roosevelt for his role at Yalta, insisting Stalin would have surrendered Eastern Europe had Roosevelt held firm. This argument seriously discounts Stalin's obsession with protecting his homeland from future attacks. The Soviet Union had paid a staggeringly high price for victory in World War II. When the war finally ended, the country had suffered approximately 18 million military and civilian deaths. Stalin's determination to maintain Soviet control of Eastern Europe was also bolstered by the fact that the Red Army occupied Eastern Europe in the spring of 1945. Stalin was not about to lose at the conference table what he had won on the battlefield.

Allied victories came rapidly after the Battle of the Bulge. On March 4, American troops reached the Rhine River, and in April they joined forces with the Soviet army 60 miles south of Berlin. After Roosevelt's death on April 12, however, Stalin immediately tested the new president, Harry S Truman. Stalin ordered the execution of democratic leaders in Eastern Europe and replaced them with Communist governments. Truman deplored Stalin's disregard for the Yalta agreements, but like Roosevelt he refused to fight the Soviets to save Eastern Europe. Instead, he followed General Eisenhower's advice about finishing off Germany. On April 22 Soviet troops reached Berlin and occupied the city after house-to-house fighting, and on April 30 Hitler committed suicide. Germany surrendered one week later. On May 8, 1945, the Allies celebrated victory in Europe—**V-E Day.**

THE WAR IN THE PACIFIC

On December 7, 1941, Japan had launched an offensive incredible in its scale. A thousand Japanese warships attacked an area comprising one-third of the earth's surface, including Guam, Hong Kong, Malaya, Midway Island, the Philippine Islands, and Wake Island. The offensive was a stunning success. Hong Kong was overrun in 18 days; Wake Island in two weeks; Singapore held out for two months. By May, the Japanese had also captured the islands of Borneo, Bali, Sumatra, and Timor. In addition, Japan had taken Rangoon, Burma's main port, and seized control of the rich tin, oil, and rubber resources of southeast Asia.

But by mid-summer of 1942, American forces had halted the Japanese advance. In May, a Japanese troop convoy was intercepted and destroyed by the U.S. Navy at Coral Sea, preventing a Japanese attack on Australia. In early June, at Midway Island in the Central Pacific, the Japanese launched an aircraft carrier offensive to cut American communications and isolate Hawaii to the east. In a three-day naval battle the Japanese lost three destroyers, a heavy cruiser, and four carriers. The Battle of Midway broke the back of Japan's navy.

Island Hopping

On August 7, 1942, the 1st Marine Division attacked Guadalcanal in the Solomon Islands; after six months of hard fighting they drove the Japanese troops into the sea, securing the Allied supply line to Australia. The victory also protected the Allies' eastern flank, enabling General Douglas MacArthur, commander of southwest Pacific forces, to seize the northern coast of nearby New Guinea in September 1943. Instead of assaulting Japanese strong points on the island, MacArthur leapfrogged up the coast. By capturing isolated positions, MacArthur cut Japanese supply lines and forced Japanese troops to abandon their fortifications. By July 1944 MacArthur's forces controlled all of New Guinea.

Meanwhile, Admiral Chester Nimitz's naval and marine forces in the Central Pacific were "island hopping" toward Japan, capturing important positions, building airstrips, and then moving on to the next island. After securing the Gilbert Islands and the Marshall Islands, Nimitz attacked Saipan, Tinian, and Guam, from which the Americans could strike the main Japanese islands with B-29 bombers. Determined to protect their homeland against air raids, Japanese commanders resolved to fight to the last man. In the battle for Saipan, 30,000 of the island's 32,000 Japanese defenders died, and 6000 of the island's 12,000 Japanese civilians committed suicide rather than surrender. Tinian and Guam fell to the Americans in early August, and B-29s began regular bombing raids over Japan in November 1944.

On October 21, 1944, General MacArthur invaded the Philippines. That same month the navy won a stunning victory at the Battle of Leyte Gulf, where the Japanese lost virtually their entire remaining battle fleet. American submarines now controlled Pacific shipping lanes, sealing the Japanese islands off from military and food supplies. In January, Allied forces invaded Luzon, the main island of the Philippines, and Allied troops claimed victory five months later.

While MacArthur was reclaiming the Philippines, the American island-hopping strategy was entering its final phase. By early March the island of Iwo Jima fell to U.S. marines. Its capture enabled fighter planes to link up with B-29s heading out of Saipan, providing escorts for their raids on Japan. On April 1, 1945, American troops attacked Okinawa, 350 miles southwest of Japan. Japanese resistance

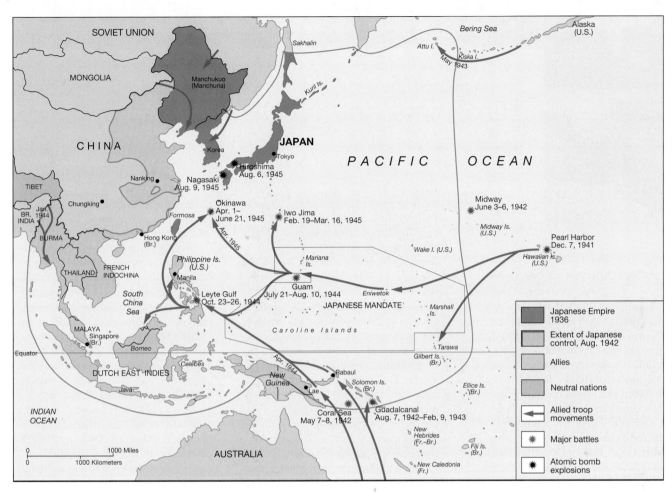

World War II, Pacific Theater

was fierce. Kamikaze attacks (suicide flights by Japanese pilots) rose dramatically. Okinawa fell in June, after 70,000 Japanese soldiers had died defending it. In the meantime, B-29s firebombed Japan, killing more than 330,000 civilians and cutting deeply into war production.

Confronted with certain defeat, many moderate leaders in Japan wanted to avoid an invasion, but strong factions within the military vowed to keep fighting. In an effort to save Japan, the Emperor switched his support to the peace party in February 1945. He then sent out peace feelers to Stalin, who in turn conveyed them to Truman at the Potsdam Conference in July 1945.

The Dawn of the Atomic Age

Few presidents have been asked to conduct diplomacy with less preparation than Harry S Truman. He had risen to power as a loyal machine politician in Kansas City. Both as vice president and former senator from Missouri he knew next to nothing about foreign affairs, especially since Roosevelt kept him in the dark, neither seeking his counsel nor confiding in him. When Roosevelt's death elevated him to the White House, Truman told reporters: "I felt like the moon, the stars, and all planets had fallen on me." Yet Truman brought certain assets to the challenge. A man who possessed the courage of his convictions, he fully intended to be a strong president and to make decisions resolutely.

Truman's first test came at Potsdam, a suburb of Berlin, where the Allied leaders convened in July 1945 for their last wartime meeting. Though new to the job, Truman had been in office long enough to believe Roosevelt had been too soft on Stalin, whom he viewed as a liar and a bully. Yet like his predecessor Truman did not wish to risk a showdown over Eastern Europe, largely because his military advisers insisted the United States still needed the Soviet Union's help against Japan. The Potsdam Declaration of July 26 demanded immediate "unconditional surrender," warning that any other action would lead to "prompt and utter destruction."

During the **Potsdam Conference,** Truman learned that American scientists had successfully

THE AMERICAN MOSAIC

Hiroshima and Nagasaki

On July 16, 1945, the Atomic Age became reality. The place was Alamogordo Air Force Base in the southern desert region of New Mexico. The occasion was the first successful detonation of an atomic bomb. Observers witnessed "a blinding flash that lighted the entire northwestern sky." Next came "a huge billow of smoke," followed by "an enormous ball of what appeared to be fire and closely resembled a rising sun." Dr. J. Robert Oppenheimer, the chief scientist in charge of the team that designed the weapon, was so astonished by the scale of the blast that he recalled the Hindu quotation: "I am become death, shatterer of worlds."

Back in 1939 two brilliant scientists, Albert Einstein and Enrico Fermi, both of whom had fled fascism and anti-Semitism in Europe, warned President Roosevelt that German nuclear physicists under Adolf Hitler's control might well be trying to develop such a bomb. Roosevelt realized the implications, and he set in motion what became the "Manhattan Project," a top-secret effort involving civilian scientists and army engineers to apply the theory of nuclear fission to a bomb. Hitler's scientists never succeeded, but in July 1945, with the war over in Europe, the United States now had a weapon with the potential to threaten civilization itself. The question was whether the bomb would be used against Japan, the last of the Axis powers still at war.

The Japanese were a formidable foe. Since 1942 U.S. troops had been rolling back their empire, all the way to the shore of Japan and the Chinese mainland by the summer of 1945. The casualty toll was horrendous. Japanese soldiers fought with a sense of personal honor that struck Americans as fanatical. They would not surrender when beaten but would fight to their death. To do otherwise would be to disgrace themselves, their families, and their emperor, whom they considered a god.

At first, in defending Pacific islands such as Guadalcanal (August 1942–February 1943), Japanese soldiers mounted suicidal *banzai* charges. They ran forward in waves at U.S. troops, inflicting massive damage before being shot down. Later, on islands such as Iwo Jima (February–March 1945), they used elaborate networks of underground bunkers to wreak havoc, so effectively that U.S. casualties started to reach the 50 percent range. By 1945 the Japanese were unleashing kamikaze raids in which pilots sacrificed themselves for the glory of the empire by dive-bombing their planes into U.S. naval vessels. In the bloody battle of Okinawa (April–June 1945), kamikaze pilots flew some 2800 planes into American ships, inflicting 10,000 casualties and sinking 28 vessels and damaging 325 others.

American soldiers, as well as the U.S. public at large, neither understood nor respected Japanese martial values. Explained a Marine Corps general, to shoot "a Jap . . . was like killing a rattlesnake." A Guadalcanal veteran stated that the Japanese soldier "possessed considerable cleverness; he could not be classified as an intellectual. He was more of an animal. He could live on a handful of rice." Almost universally, Americans used terms of racial derision to describe an enemy that had not only mounted the "sneak attack" on Pearl Harbor but now refused to surrender when beaten.

Such attitudes affected the development of a comprehensive U.S. war plan, known as Operation DOWNFALL, that was constructed on the assumption that only a full-scale invasion of Japan would bring total victory in the Pacific. The first phase of the plan, called Operation OLYMPIC, involved an assault on Kyushu, the southernmost island of Japan, to begin in November 1945. The Joint Chiefs of Staff presented OLYMPIC to President Truman in June and stated that American casualties could reach 268,000 (out of 767,000 participants). The Japanese still had 2.3 million soldiers ready to fight and another 4 million citizens trained in the use of arms. If they battled to the death, as they had so far, American casualties, the Joint Chiefs predicted, would exceed 1 million by the time U.S. troops conquered the main island of Honshu in 1946 or 1947.

Because of the bloody price everyone expected to pay, high-ranking American officials were anxious to involve Russia—attacking through Manchuria and Korea—in the final crushing of Japan. At Yalta in February 1945 President Roosevelt secured pledges of Soviet assistance. Then at Potsdam in July, President Truman seemed much less interested. Having just learned of the test results in New Mexico, Truman told Joseph Stalin of "a new weapon of unusual destructive force." Stalin, however, would not be cast aside. He still wanted the territory (the lower half of Sakhalin Island, the Kurile Islands, and certain considerations in Manchuria) promised at Yalta. The Soviet leader thus "hoped" the United States "would make good use" of the

three B-29s at 31,600 feet of altitude appeared over Hiroshima. Colonel Paul Tibbets, piloting the lead bomber, *Enola Gay,* turned the controls over to Major Thomas Ferebee, the bombardier officer, who completed the run. It took 45 seconds, as *Enola Gay* banked away quickly, for the atomic bomb to reach the ground. As the fireball erupted toward the sky, nearly 100,000 people, including thousands of soldiers at the headquarters of Japan's Second General Army just 2000 yards from ground zero, died instantly. Three days later, in the absence of a firm willingness of the Japanese to surrender, a second bomb flattened Nagasaki and killed about 35,000 people. Thousands more perished later from serious burns, radiation poisoning, and other devastating effects of the two bombings.

The dropping of the atomic bombs gave peace advocates in Japan the muscle they needed to overcome the militarists. When on August 10 Emperor Hirohito agreed to seek peace terms, the war faction reluctantly acceded, but only after General Anami Korechika, the war minister, upheld his honor on August 14 by committing suicide. He could not bear hearing Hirohito's proclamation of surrender.

When American troops training for Operation OLYMPIC heard about the surrender, they rejoiced. "We would not be obliged to run up the beaches near Tokyo assault-firing while being mortared and shelled," wrote one soldier. "We are going to live. We are going to grow up to adulthood after all." They did not realize how different the world would be with nuclear weapons in the hands of the two superpowers to emerge from World War II. For a moment, however, General Douglas MacArthur understood. After the Japanese surrender ceremony on September 2, 1945, he stated: "We have had our last chance. If we do not devise some greater and more equitable system, Armageddon will be at our door."

weapon "against the Japanese," but the Russians would not be denied their part in the invasion or the promised territory.

Meanwhile, a committee of American scientists and military officers were working at selecting possible targets. Some advocated a demonstration at a preannounced neutral site as a way of cajoling the Japanese into surrender, but others feared what might happen should the bomb prove to be a dud—all leverage would then be lost. Finally, with great reluctance, these advisers agreed that there was "no acceptable alternative to direct military use" of the bomb.

In public, Truman never admitted to any qualms about the decision to employ the new weapon, but in private, he wondered how "we as the leader of the world for common wel-

fare" could drop "this terrible bomb." Still, he accepted the responsibility for many reasons. He hoped to save thousands of American lives by avoiding a full invasion of Japan against soldiers who fought like "savages, ruthless, merciless, and fanatic." Likely, too, Truman and his advisers feared the expansionism of the Communist regime of Joseph Stalin. Using the bomb might prove a great point of leverage in dealing with the Soviets in the days ahead.

While Truman and others considered the alternatives, a select unit of the Army Air Force, flying B-29s, made a series of practice bomb runs over Japan. Since these planes did not attack, as they had so often before in firebombing cities like Tokyo, no one paid much attention. Then on August 6, 1945, at a few minutes past 8:00 A.M.,

tested the first atomic bomb. Hoping to impress Stalin, Truman told him in a conversation one evening the United States now possessed a new weapon of awesome power. Stalin blithely replied he trusted the United States would make good use of it against Japan.

The Manhattan Project

In 1939, Albert Einstein wrote a letter to President Roosevelt, warning him that the Nazis might be able to build a weapon with incredible destructive potential: an atomic bomb. The idea seemed impossible, and at first scientists worked on the project largely on their own. Then on December 2, 1942, **Enrico Fermi,** an Italian refugee, demonstrated that it was possible to produce a nuclear chain reaction. In an old squash court beneath the University of Chicago's football field, he built the world's first nuclear reactor. Fermi's reactor produced the first self-sustained, controlled nuclear chain reaction.

To ensure that the United States developed a bomb before Nazi Germany, the federal government started the **Manhattan Project,** a secret $2-billion program with 120,000 employees. At Los Alamos, New Mexico; Oak Ridge, Tennessee; and Hanford, Washington, the world's top physicists—including many Jewish refugees from Germany—worked in secrecy to develop the new weapon.

At dawn on July 16, 1945, in the New Mexico desert near Alamogordo, the Manhattan Project's scientists watched the first atomic bomb explode. There was a blinding flash of pink, blue, red, and yellow light. The heat generated by the bomb at that instant was ten thousand times hotter than the sun. The explosion broke windows 125 miles away.

President Truman had never heard of the Manhattan Project until he was sworn in. It was during the Potsdam negotiations that he learned that American scientists had tested the first atomic bomb. Many scientists who worked on the Manhattan Project, as well as several key political figures, pleaded with Truman not to use the bomb because they foresaw its implications for a postwar arms race with the Soviet Union. Others, arguing from a moral position, wanted the United States to warn the Japanese about the bomb's terrifying power, giving them a chance to surrender. Truman rejected these arguments and approved the use of the new weapon.

Hiroshima and Nagasaki

On the morning of August 6, 1945, the **Enola Gay,** a B-29 Superfortress, took off from a tiny Pacific atoll bound for Hiroshima, Japan's eighth-largest city. At 8:15 A.M., the plane released an atomic bomb nicknamed "Little Boy." The explosion when it hit began as a pinpoint of light that grew into a fireball half a mile across. A cloud of smoke rose upward, gradually assuming the shape of a giant mushroom 50,000 feet high.

On the ground, 4.7 square miles of central Hiroshima was obliterated. Buildings melted, steel bridges burned, the city's river caught fire. Peoples'

The bomb dropped on Hiroshima on August 6, 1945, marked the first use of a nuclear weapon in warfare. The bomb, carrying a destructive force equal to 20,000 tons of TNT, obliterated nearly 60 percent of the city.

shadows were photographed onto walls and sidewalks. Black rain containing radioactive dust fell on the city, leaving red splotches on the bodies it touched. Between 80,000 and 140,000 people were killed or fatally wounded.

Three days later, on August 9, another B-29, the *Bock's Car*, dropped a second bomb, this time on the city of Nagasaki. About 35,000 people were killed. The following day Japan sued for peace. On September 2, 1945, Japanese officials surrendered unconditionally to General Douglas MacArthur aboard the battleship U.S.S. *Missouri* in Tokyo Bay. World War II was over.

President Truman's decision to order the atomic bombings has been the subject of intense historical debate. Truman's defenders argue that the bombs ended the war quickly, avoiding the necessity of a costly invasion and the probable loss of tens of thousands of Americans lives and hundreds of thousands of Japanese lives. According to some intelligence estimates, an invasion might have cost 268,000 American casualties, with Japanese costs several times that figure.

Truman's defenders also argue that Hiroshima and Nagasaki were legitimate targets with both military bases and war industry, and their civilian populations had been showered with leaflets warning them to evacuate. Finally, they argue that two bombs were ultimately necessary to end the war. They note that even after the atomic bomb had fallen on Hiroshima, the Japanese war minister implored the nation's Supreme Council "for one last great battle on Japanese soil—as demanded by the national honor. . . . Would it not be wondrous for this whole nation to be destroyed like a beautiful flower."

Truman's critics argue that the war might have ended even without the atomic bombings. They maintain that the Japanese economy would have been strangled by a continued naval blockade and forced to surrender by conventional firebombing. The revisionists also contend that the president had options apart from using the bombs. They believe that it might have been possible to induce a Japanese surrender by a demonstration of the atomic bomb's power or by providing a more specific warning of the damage it could produce or by guaranteeing the emperor's position in postwar Japan.

The revisionists also believe that estimates of potential American casualties were grossly inflated after the war to justify the bombing. And finally, they argue that the bomb might have been dropped mainly to justify its cost or to scare the Soviet Union. The Soviet Union entered the Japanese war August 8, and some revisionists charge that the bombings were designed to end the war before the Red army could occupy northern China.

CONCLUSION

Fifty years after the United States brought World War II to an end by dropping two atomic bombs on Japan, a major public controversy erupted over plans to exhibit the fuselage of the *Enola Gay* at the Smithsonian Institution's Air and Space Museum. As originally conceived, the exhibit, titled "The Last Act: The Atomic Bomb and the End of World War II," was designed to provoke debate about the decision to drop atomic bombs. Museum visitors would be encouraged to reflect on the morality of the bombing and to ask whether the bombs were necessary to end the war.

The proposal generated a firestorm of controversy. The part of the script that produced the most opposition stated: "For most Americans, this . . . was a war of vengeance. For most Japanese it was a war to defend their unique culture against Western imperialism." Another controversial section addressed the question: "Would the bomb have been dropped on the Germans?" The answer began "Some have argued that the United States would never have dropped the bomb on the Germans, because Americans were more reluctant to bomb 'white people' than Asians."

Veterans groups considered the proposed exhibit too sympathetic to the Japanese, that it portrayed them as victims of racist Americans hell-bent on revenge for Pearl Harbor. They called the exhibit an insult to the U.S. soldiers who fought and died during the war and complained that it paid excessive attention to Japanese casualties and suffering and insufficient attention to Japanese aggression and atrocities. The U.S. Senate unanimously passed a resolution calling a revised version of the exhibit "unbalanced and offensive" and reminding the museum of "its obligation to portray history in the proper context of its time."

In the end, the Smithsonian decided to scale back the exhibit, displaying the *Enola Gay's* fuselage along with a small plaque. In announcing the decision, a Smithsonian official explained, "In this important anniversary year, veterans and their families were expecting, and rightly so, that the nation would honor and commemorate their valor and sacrifice. They were not looking for analysis and, frankly, we did not give enough thought to the intense feelings such an analysis would evoke."

World War II cost America one million casualties and over 400,000 deaths. In both domestic and foreign affairs, its consequences were far-reaching. It had an immediate and spectacular impact on the economy by ending the Great Depression. Fueled by government contracts, the economy expanded dramatically, soaring to full employment and astounding the world with its productivity. Labor unions

CHRONOLOGY OF KEY EVENTS

1921 Washington Naval Conference places limits on construction of large warships

1922 Mussolini seizes power in Italy

1924 Dawes Plan to help Germany pay war reparations

1928 Kellogg-Briand Pact renounces war "as an instrument of national policy"; Clark Memorandum states that the United States does not have a right to intervene militarily in the affairs of Latin American nations

1931 Japan invades Manchuria

1932 Stimson Doctrine declares that the United States would not recognize Japanese territorial gains in China

1933 Adolf Hitler is appointed chancellor of Germany; Roosevelt announces Good Neighbor Policy, withdraws marines from Haiti, and nullifies Platt Amendment

1935 Neutrality Act allows president to bar arms sales to nations at war (is extended in 1936 to bar loans to belligerents and in 1937 to bar shipments of nonmilitary goods)

1936 German troops reoccupy the Rhineland; Spanish Civil War begins

1937 Japan invades China

1938 Germany annexes Austria; Munich Pact hands over a third of Czechoslovakia to Nazi Germany

1939 Soviet Union and Germany sign a nonaggression pact; World War II begins following Germany's invasion of Poland

1940 United States transfers 50 destroyers to Britain in exchange for bases in Newfoundland and the Caribbean; United States institutes first peacetime military draft; Roosevelt is elected to third term

1941 Lend-Lease Act allows United States to lend war materials to Britain; Roosevelt issues order prohibiting discrimination in defense industries; Germany invades USSR; United States sets embargo on scrap metal, oil, and fuel to Japan; Japan attacks Pearl Harbor, killing over 2400 U.S. soldiers and sailors; United States enters World War II

1942 Congress creates the Office of Price Administration to control prices and ration scarce goods; President Roosevelt authorizes internment of 112,000 West Coast Japanese Americans; Philippine Islands surrender to Japan; U.S. Navy wins a major victory at Midway Island in the central Pacific; British and U.S. forces land in French North Africa

1943 British and U.S. forces defeat Axis forces in North Africa; U.S. marines secure control of Guadalcanal in the Solomon Islands; Soviets halt German drive into Soviet Union; Allies invade Italy; Mussolini is overthrown and new Italian government surrenders to Allies

1943–1944 U.S. marines and navy seize islands of Tarawa, Kwajelin, Wake, and Guam in central Pacific and New Guinea in South Pacific

1944 U.S. Supreme Court upholds legality of the forced relocation of Japanese Americans; D-Day—Allies launch amphibious invasion of northern France; U.S. forces begin an invasion of Philippine Islands and aerial attacks on Japan; Bretton Woods Conference draws up plans for International Monetary Fund and International Bank to finance postwar economic recovery; Dumbarton Oaks Conference makes plans for creation of United Nations; German troops launch counteroffensive in the Ardennes Forest along Belgium-Luxembourg border

1945 At Yalta, Roosevelt, Churchill, and Stalin discuss Soviet entry into the war against Japan, the postwar division of Europe, and plans for the United Nations; Roosevelt dies; Harry S Truman becomes thirty-third president; Germany surrenders; Potsdam Conference plans postwar settlement in Europe and final attack on Japan; United States drops atomic bombs on Hiroshima and Nagasaki; Japan surrenders

also grew during the war as the government adopted prounion policies, continuing the New Deal's sympathetic treatment of organized labor.

Presidential power expanded enormously during World War II, anticipating the rise of what postwar critics termed the "imperial presidency." The Democrats reaped a political windfall from the war. Roosevelt rode the wartime emergency to unprecedented third and fourth terms, preserving the New Deal coalition so effectively that many people wondered if the Republicans would ever elect another president. Despite such victories, however, the reform spirit had waned, a victim, it seemed, of the country's unmistakable swing to the right in politics.

The war's social effects varied from group to group. For most people, it had a disruptive influence—separated families, overcrowded housing, and a shortage of consumer goods. The war also accelerated the movement from the countryside to the cities, and it challenged gender and racial roles, opening new opportunities for women and minority groups. Yet sexual and racial barriers remained, highlighting reforms left unfinished at home, even as American troops fought totalitarian forces abroad.

In foreign policy, the many disagreements between the Allies on military strategy and peace terms foreshadowed the major conflicts that dominated the postwar era. Gone forever was the notion of fortress America, isolated and removed from world affairs. In its place stood a strong internationalist state, determined to exercise power on a global scale. Second only to the victory the Allies won for freedom, the war's most important legacy was the end of isolation and the rise of America's commitment to international security.

CHAPTER SUMMARY AND KEY POINTS

No war in history killed more people or destroyed more property than World War II. Altogether, 70 million people served in the armed forces; of these, 17 million combatants—including 400,000 Americans—lost their lives in the conflict. Civilian deaths were even higher. At least 19 million Soviet civilians, 10 million Chinese, and 6 million European Jews lost their lives during the war. In this chapter you read about the war's causes, military history, and consequences. You learned how the United States mobilized for war; the impact of the war on women and racial and ethnic minorities; the internment of Japanese Americans; and the dawn of the atomic age.

- On September 1, 1939, Germany invaded Poland, starting World War II. By November 1942, the Axis powers controlled territory from Norway to North Africa and from France to the Soviet Union.

- After defeating the Axis in North Africa in May 1941, the Allies invaded Sicily in July 1943 and forced Italy to surrender in September.

- The American home front was essential to success in the war. The war ended depression-era unemployment and led the federal government to create a War Production Board to oversee conversion to a wartime economy and the Office of Price Administration to set prices on many items and to supervise a rationing system.

- During the war, African Americans, women, and Mexican Americans found new opportunities in industry. But Japanese Americans living on the Pacific coast were relocated from their homes and placed in internment camps.

- On D-Day, June 6, 1944, the Allies landed in northern France. A German counteroffensive, known as the Battle of the Bulge, in December failed, and Germany surrendered in May 1945.

- After attacking the U.S. Pacific fleet at Pearl Harbor, Hawaii, on December 7, 1941, drawing the United States into the war, Japanese forces seized Burma, Hong Kong, Malaya, the Dutch East Indies (now Indonesia), the Philippines, Singapore, and Thailand.

- The Allies halted Japanese expansion at the Battle of Midway in June 1942 and in other campaigns in the South Pacific. From 1943 to August 1945, the Allies hopped from island to island across the central Pacific and also battled the Japanese in China, Burma, and India.

- Japan agreed to surrender on August 14, 1945 after the United States dropped the first atomic bombs on the Japanese cities of Hiroshima and Nagasaki.

SUGGESTIONS FOR FURTHER READING

Michael C. C. Adams, *The Best War Ever* (1994). Offers a succinct interpretation of the impact of World War II on American troops and the home front.

P. M. H. Bell, *The Origins of the Second World War in Europe*, 2d ed. (1989). Examines the conflict's causes.

Frances B. Cogan, *Captured: The Internment of American Civilians in the Philippines, 1941–1945.* (2000). Tells the story of American civilians in the Philippines who were captured and interned by the Japanese during World War II.

Justus D. Doenecke, *Storm on the Horizon: The Challenge to American Intervention, 1939–1941.* (2000). Intellectual history of the movement against U.S. entry into World War II, beginning with the German invasion of Poland and ending with the Japanese attack on Pearl Harbor.

John Ellis, *Brute Force: Allied Strategy and Tactics in the Second World War* (1990). Discusses military strategy.

Akira Iriye, *The Origins of the Second World War in Asia and the Pacific* (1987). Analyzes the roots of the war with Japan.

John W. Jeffries, *Wartime America: The World War II Home Front.* (1996). Analysis of America during World War II which notes revisionist interpretations while still maintaining traditional explanations for business-government relations, racial tensions, and partisan politics.

Brenda L. Moore, *To Serve My Country, To Serve My Race: The Story of the Only African American WACs Stationed Overseas During World War II.* (1996). Examines the issues of race and gender in World War II using the stories of African American women who served in the U.S. Army overseas.

Novels

Herman Wouk, *The Caine Mutiny* (1951).

Ben Kono, *The Last Fox: A Novel of the 100th/442nd RTC* (2001).

Beirne Lay and Sy Bartlett, *Twelve O'Clock High (Five Great Classic Stories of World War II)* (1980).

MEDIA RESOURCES

Web Sites

A People at War
http://www.nara.gov/exhall/people/people.html
This National Archives Exhibit takes a close look at the contributions millions of Americans made to the war effort.

Powers of Persuasion—Poster Art of World War II
http://www.nara.gov/education/teaching/posters/poster.html
These powerful posters at the National Archives were part of the battle for the hearts and minds of the American people.

America from the Great Depression to World War II: Photographs from the FSA and OWI, ca. 1935–1945
http://memory.loc.gov/ammem/fsowhome.html
These images in the Farm Security Administration–Office of War Information Collection show Americans from all over the nation experiencing everything from despair to triumph in the 1930s and 1940s.

A-Bomb WWW Museum
http://www.csi.ad.jp/ABOMB/
This site offers information about the impact of the first atomic bomb as well as the background and context of weapons of total destruction.

The United States Holocaust Memorial Museum
http://www.ushmm.org/index.html
This is the official Web site of the Holocaust Museum in Washington, D.C.

World War II Era Links
http://wrightmuseum.org/links.html
The Wright Museum maintains this page with its many links to information about the World War II era.

World War II Pictures
http://www.corbis.com/FDR/ww2.html
This Corbis site houses many pictures about the second world war and American involvement in the conflict.

Tuskegee Airmen
http://www.wpafb.af.mil/museum/history/prewwii/ta.htm
The Air Force Museum at Wright-Patterson Air Force Base maintains this site about the African American pilots of World War II.

Abraham Lincoln Brigade Archives
http://www.alba-valb.org
This Brandeis University site has posters and photographs from the Spanish Civil War and the unit of American volunteers who fought in it.

World War II Resources: Primary Source Materials on the Web
http://www.sunsite.unc.edu/pha/index.html
This site has a large number of searchable primary texts from all aspects of World War II.

The Enola Gay Controversy
http://www.glue.umd.edu/~enola/
This comprehensive site at the University of Maryland explores all facets of the dropping of the first atomic bomb in 1945 from the development of the bomb to controversy around the recent Smithsonian exhibit.

Manzanar Project
http://www.mvhs.srvusd.k12.ca.us/~mleck/man/Default.html
A site that explores Japanese internment in World War II.

Films and Videos

Band of Brothers (2001). HBO Video. Ten-episode series that follows a company of airborne infantry from boot camp to the end of World War II.

Saving Private Ryan. Dreamworks SKG (1998). World War II drama about a mission to bring home the last surviving son of an American family, starring Tom Hanks and Matt Damon.

The Longest Day (1962). Epic account of the 1944 invasion of Normandy, starring Richard Burton and John Wayne.

Enola Gay and the Atomic Bombing of Japan (1995). A&E Entertainment. Documentary of the atomic bombing of Japan to end World War II.

Windtalkers (2002). Story of the Navajo Indians who joined the U.S. Army and developed an unbreakable code based on their language, starring Nicolas Cage and Christian Slater.

KEY TERMS

Kellogg-Briand Pact   (p. 697)

Good Neighbor policy   (p. 698)

Fascism   (p. 700)

Lend-Lease Act   (p. 704)

Pearl Harbor   (p. 706)

War Production Board (WPB)   (p. 707)

Office of Price Administration (OPA)   (p. 708)

Revenue Act of 1942   (p. 708)

War Labor Board (WLB)   (p. 708)

Women's Army Corps (WAC)   (p. 711)

Double V campaign   (p. 712)

War Refugee Board   (p. 714)

War Relocation Authority   (p. 714)

Axis Powers   (p. 715)

Grand Alliance   (p. 715)

D-Day   (p. 717)

Battle of the Bulge   (p. 718)

Yalta Conference   (p. 718)

V-E Day   (p. 720)

Potsdam Conference   (p. 721)

Manhattan Project   (p. 724)

Enola Gay   (p. 724)

PEOPLE YOU SHOULD KNOW

Cordell Hull   (p. 698)

Adolf Hitler   (p. 698)

Benito Mussolini   (p. 700)

Winston Churchill   (p. 702)

General Charles de Gaulle   (p. 715)

Joseph Stalin   (p. 715)

General George Patton   (p. 718)

Enrico Fermi   (p. 724)

REVIEW QUESTIONS

1. What characterized U.S. diplomacy between the world wars?

2. Why did the Neutrality Acts fail to keep the United States out of World War II?

3. How did mobilization for World War II differ from that for World War I?

4. How did World War II change the roles and status of women and minorities in the United States?

5. How crucial was U.S. involvement in the European war?

6. Could the use of the atomic bombs have been avoided? How?

26 Waging Peace and War

THE HISS-CHAMBERS AFFAIR

It was Sunday, August 27, 1948. **Whittaker Chambers** appeared calm as he answered questions on "Meet the Press," a weekly radio news show. Chambers's appearance, like most of his life, was a deception. He knew he was on enemy ground and that questions were the ammunition of the war. "I sought not to let myself be crowded," he later recalled, "not to lose my temper during the baiting." Chambers was very still, waiting for the inevitable question. He didn't have to wait long. Edward T. Folliard, a reporter for the *Washington Post,* asked, "Are you willing to say now that Alger Hiss is or ever was a Communist?" Chambers paused a second before answering, for the answer could open him up to a slander or libel suit. Then came his terse, important reply: "Alger Hiss was a Communist and may be now."

The road to "Meet the Press" had begun for Chambers a generation before 1948. It was one paved with unhappiness. His father, Jay, had left his wife Laha for a time, returning after three years. He demonstrated no love or affection for his wife or children. Whittaker remembers that his father—who never allowed his children to call him "Papa"—dined alone and seldom spoke, except perhaps to say "don't." Home experiences left Chambers rebellious and feeling unwanted. After being forced to withdraw from Columbia for writing a mildly sacrilegious play, he flirted with radical political philosophies, moved through a succession of love affairs, and kicked about Europe. In 1926 his brother Richard committed suicide. It was the most painful event in Chambers's life, and for several months he was inconsolable. Almost as a form of therapy, he committed himself fully to another family—the Communist party. During his time of troubles, it gave his life a direction and a purpose.

During the late 1920s and early 1930s, as the United States sank deeper and deeper into the Great Depression, other Americans joined Chambers in the Communist party. Feeling betrayed by the capitalist order, they looked toward the Soviet Union for economic and political inspiration. The Soviet Union, under Joseph Stalin, appeared less affected by the depression than the capitalist West. Still more Americans joined the Communist party because only the Soviets seemed to be standing up against the fascist threat posed by Hitler, Mussolini, and Franco. For

Bureaucrat Alger Hiss (left), accused of being a communist spy by Whittaker Chambers (right), was convicted of perjury (in his second trial for perjury; the first ended in a hung jury). This episode helped heighten American fear of communism at home.

Chambers and his comrades, then, the Red Star represented the future and the hope of the world.

Chambers met **Alger Hiss** in 1934, when they both belonged to the same Communist "cell" in Washington, D.C. In appearance and personality they were almost perfect opposites. Chambers was sloppy; his clothes always seemed rumpled, and his face had a sleepy, slightly disinterested cast. Hiss was cut from different cloth. Handsome and aristocratic-looking, Hiss's career was marked by ambition and achievement. He was an honors student at Johns Hopkins University and Harvard Law School; he was a favorite of future Supreme Court justice Felix Frankfurter; he clerked for the legendary Oliver Wendell Holmes. Popular with influential superiors and his co-workers, Hiss obviously seemed singled out as one of the best and brightest, as one who would succeed. And he did. He acted as a counsel for the Agricultural Adjustment Administration, worked for the Senate committee investigating the munitions industry, went to the Yalta Conference with President Roosevelt, helped to organize the United Nations, and served as president of the Carnegie Endowment for International Peace.

Through these years of his impressive career, Hiss worked with Whittaker Chambers for the Com-

munist party. It was while Hiss served as a legal assistant for the Senate committee investigation of the munitions industry that he became close friends with Chambers. He allowed Chambers to use his Washington, D.C., apartment for two months, gave him an automobile, and even permitted him to stay in his home on several occasions. Although Hiss would later deny that he knew Chambers—and then admit that he knew him slightly under a different name— the evidence is clear on one point: the very different men had formed a close friendship. It was during that period of friendship in the mid-1930s, Chambers later testified, that Hiss began to give him secret government documents.

Like many of his American comrades, Chambers later, in the late 1930s, abandoned the ideology of communism and lost faith in the Soviet Union. There were sound reasons for this break. For the true believers of the early 1930s, the Soviet Union was the light that failed. By 1938 news of Stalin's purges, which would eventually lead to the deaths of millions of Soviets, had reached the West. Such gross disregard for humanity shook many American Communists. In addition, in 1939 Stalin signed a nonaggression pact with Hitler's Germany. Once seen as the bulwark against Nazi expansion, the Soviet

Union now joined Germany in dividing Poland. Although during World War II the United States and the Soviet Union were forced together as allies, communist ideology ceased to attract many American followers.

Chambers not only quit the Communist party, he turned against it with vengeful wrath. As an editor for *Time* magazine, he openly criticized communist tactics and warned about the evils of the Soviet Union. The passage of time only increased his rage. Finally in 1948 he went before the House Un-American Activities Committee (HUAC) and told his life story, carefully naming all his former Communist party friends and associates. Of all the people he named, the one who attracted the most attention was the brilliant young New Dealer Alger Hiss.

Hiss of course denied Chambers's allegations. He too appeared before HUAC. Well-dressed and relaxed despite a too-tight collar, he testified, "I am not and never have been a member of the Communist party. . . . I have never followed the Communist party line, directly or indirectly. To the best of my knowledge, none of my friends is a Communist." As he smilingly answered questions, he confidently stood on his record of public service. Unlike his nervous, rumpled accuser, Hiss was the picture of placid truthfulness. His testimony satisfied most of the committee members, even the Republicans.

Not all were satisfied, however. After listening to both Chambers and Hiss, Republican Richard Nixon, a junior congressman from California, still was not sure Hiss was as innocent as he seemed. As one psychohistorian bluntly put it, Hiss "was everything Nixon was not." Nixon's background of struggle contrasted sharply with Hiss's career, and Nixon believed Hiss treated him "like dirt." At Nixon's insistence, Hiss and Chambers were brought together face to face before HUAC. It was at that meeting that Chambers demonstrated his encyclopedic knowledge about Hiss—his family—and his life. He discussed the furniture in the other man's house and his hobbies. Chambers showed beyond any doubt that at one time he had been close to Hiss. For once Hiss's confident equanimity vanished. He challenged Chambers to make his accusations in public, where he would not be protected against a libel suit.

Chambers accepted the challenge, and on "Meet the Press" he repeated his charges. Hiss hesitated for a month and then sued Chambers for defamation. During the involved trials that followed, Chambers proved his case. He even produced a series of classified, microfilmed documents he had stored in a hollowed-out pumpkin on his Maryland farm. Experts testified that the classified documents had been written in Hiss's hand or typed on his Woodstock typewriter. Hiss was indicted for perjury by a federal grand jury. Although the first trial ended in a hung jury, the second trial was far less satisfactory for Hiss. In January 1950 he was found guilty of perjury and sentenced to five years in prison.

he **Hiss-Chambers affair** was one of the major episodes of the late 1940s. Those years were a time of momentous changes. America took an active and aggressive stand in world affairs and accepted the responsibilities and problems of world leadership. Across the globe it clashed with the Soviet Union over a series of symbolic and real issues in what was labeled the Cold War. These ideological and economic battles affected American domestic and foreign policy. During the late 1940s and early 1950s Americans attacked the communist threat inside as well as outside the United States. In an atmosphere charged with fear, anxiety, paranoia, and hatred, the United States waged peace and war with equal emotional intensity.

CONTAINING THE RUSSIAN BEAR

During World War II, when the United States and the Soviet Union were allies, **Joseph Stalin** was known as Uncle Joe. The media and Hollywood portrayed him as a stern but fair leader and pictured communism as strikingly like capitalism. Warner Brothers' 1943 film *Mission to Moscow* was particularly kind to Stalin, who appeared on screen as a gentle, pipe-smoking, sad-eyed friend of America.

In reality Joseph Stalin was a determined, ruthless leader who, over the years, had systematically eliminated his actual and suspected political rivals. Between 1933 and 1938 he violently eliminated over 850,000 members of the Communist party, and perhaps one million more died in labor camps. He was apparently suspicious of almost everyone, inside and outside of the Soviet Union. If his attitude was extreme, it was not totally irrational. Twice in his lifetime Russia had been invaded from the West. Twice Germans had pushed into his country, killing millions upon millions of Russians. Russia suffered almost 4 million military and civilian deaths in World War I, and more than 20 million in World War II. For Stalin, the West stood unalterably opposed to communism. He would take what he could from the West, but he would never trust westerners.

Stalin, however, was not the only suspicious world leader. The newest western leader, President

Harry Truman, was wary of Stalin but did not exactly regard him as the enemy, at least not in 1945—after all, the Soviet Union and America had been allies during World War II. When Truman took office on April 12, 1945, he assumed he could deal with Stalin. Advisers told him that Stalin was a tough, no-nonsense leader. These were characteristics that the tough, no-nonsense Truman could appreciate. His first meeting with Stalin at Potsdam confirmed his initial assessment of the Soviet leader. "I like Stalin," Truman wrote his wife Bess. "He is straightforward. Knows what he wants and will compromise when he can't get it."

Potsdam was the light before the long dark tunnel. Truman was overly optimistic about his ability to work with Stalin. Totally different backgrounds and philosophies separated the two leaders from the start, and the directions in which they led their countries drove them further apart. The United States and the Soviet Union emerged from World War II as the two most powerful countries in the world, even though the Soviet Union had suffered tremendous industrial, agricultural, and human losses during the war. Both countries were inexperienced as world leaders, but both knew exactly what they wanted, and what they wanted guaranteed future conflicts. The result was the **Cold War.**

Origins of the Cold War

For western leaders and their diplomats, World War II had a successful but not neat ending. Too many questions were left unanswered, too many issues unresolved. At Yalta and then at Potsdam the leaders of the Soviet Union, Great Britain, and the United States discussed the future of Poland and Germany, but no firm conclusions were reached. Afraid of further straining the already uneasy wartime alliance, they decided to leave such thorny issues to the future. When the future arrived in August 1945 after America dropped two atomic bombs on Japan, the fates of Eastern Europe and Germany were as yet undetermined, as was the relationship between the United States and the Soviet Union.

When Germany had invaded Poland in early September 1939, England and France had come to the aid of Poland. The Soviet Union had not. Instead, the Soviets had invaded Poland from the east and gobbled up a large section of the country. In 1941, however, Germany invaded the Soviet Union and forced Stalin to join the Grand Alliance against Hitler. For the remainder of World War II, the Soviets had battled heroically against Germany on the eastern front. The West contributed weapons and supplies in this theater of the war, but it was the Red

Army working alone that drove the Germans out of Eastern Europe. When the war ended, the Soviets controlled all of Eastern Europe from Stettin on the Baltic Sea to Trieste on the Adriatic Sea.

Had the Soviet Union liberated Eastern Europe or simply replaced Germany as the master of the region? That was the crucial question of 1945. The debate centered on the fate of Poland: Truman insisted that the Soviets allow free and democratic elections in Poland. Certainly, Truman conceded, the Soviets had the right to expect any Polish government to be friendly toward the Soviet Union, but he expected Stalin to give Poland its complete freedom. Poland's fate was no abstract diplomatic issue to millions of Americans of Eastern European origins who pressed Truman to take a tough stand. Truman complied. In a profanity-laced tirade, he told Soviet Foreign Minister V. M. Molotov that America would not tolerate Poland being made into a Soviet puppet state. Stalin, however, would not give away Poland or any other territory the Red Army occupied simply because of Truman's colorful phrases. Twice during the twentieth century Germany had invaded Russia through Poland. Stalin was determined it would never happen again. As he had bluntly stated at Yalta, "For the Russian people, the question of Poland is not only a question of honor but also a question of security . . . of life and death for the Soviet Union."

Confronted by an inflexible opponent, Truman played his trump card. He threatened to cut off economic aid to the Soviet Union. Devastated by World War II, the Soviet Union needed the aid, but Stalin believed Poland was more important. Rather than abandon Poland, Stalin accepted the loss of American money. In the end, Truman was powerless. Americans would certainly not accept a war with the Soviet Union to reliberate Poland, and in 1945 the Soviet Union was not about to leave Poland voluntarily. Although there was no war, there was one important casualty: relations between America and the Soviet Union were strained to the breaking point.

A World Divided

The controversy over Poland indicated the direction of postwar Soviet-American relations. The two countries were divided by substantial issues, the most important of which was the degree of control they should and did have over other nations. At the end of the war both nations occupied large areas of land. America's control was based on the strength of its economy as much as its military position. Even as the country demobilized, American leaders were confident that they could use foreign aid to exert influence on the future development of the world. They

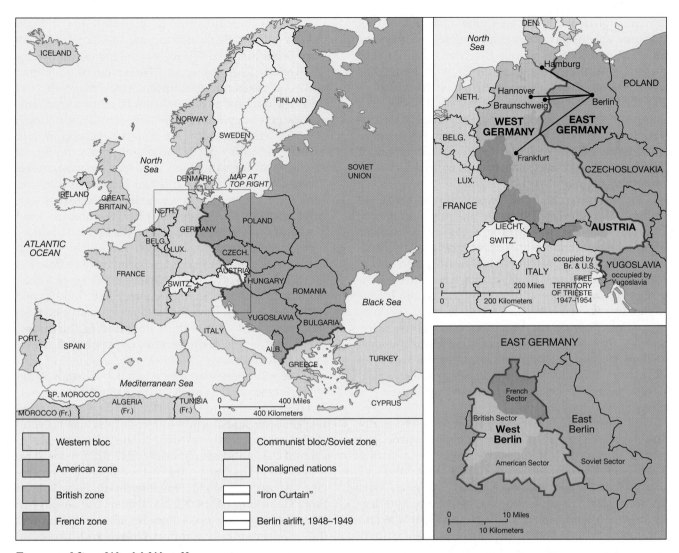

Europe After World War II

were also confident that what was good for America would be good for the world. The Soviet Union's control in all of Eastern Europe—Hungary, Romania, Bulgaria, and Czechoslovakia, as well as Poland—depended on the physical presence of the Red Army. Stalin freely granted America and England their spheres of influence, but he wanted the West to recognize his own.

Truman refused. A believer in free trade, national self-determination, and the virtues of democracy, he opposed Stalin's use of military force as a diplomatic weapon. The irony of the United States's position was clearly seen by political commentator Walter Lippmann: "While the British and the Americans held firmly . . . the whole position in Africa and the Mediterranean . . . and the whole of Western Germany . . . they undertook by negotiation and diplomatic pressure to reduce Russia's position in Eastern Europe."

Approaching the issues from different perspectives, the Soviet Union and America arrived at different conclusions. After World War II ended, they agreed on very little. The fate of Germany illustrates the basic conflict between the two powers. The Soviets wanted to punish Germany by stripping the country of its industry and imposing harsh reparation payments. Only a prostrate Germany, unarmed and unthreatening, would satisfy Stalin. As Truman lost confidence in the Soviet Union, he came to believe in the need for a strong Germany to act as a block against Soviet expansion. The result of these conflicting approaches was, literally, a divided Germany. Occupied by the Red Army, East Germany became a Soviet satellite. West Germany fell under the American, British, and French spheres of influence and soon became part of the postwar democratic alliance. Not until the early 1990s would Germany again be united.

Control over atomic weapons also divided the two powers. America developed and used the first atomic bomb—demonstrating to the world that it possessed not only the scientific knowledge to construct the bomb but also the will to use the weapon. Publicly Truman seemed favorable to international control of the world's fissionable materials. But privately he used the threat of the bomb in his negotiations with the Soviet Union. America, Secretary of War Henry L. Stimson commented, wore the "weapon rather ostentatiously on our hip."

Stalin reacted with suspicion and bitterness to this contradictory policy, distrusting any atomic control plan that originated in the United States. Rather than make Stalin more manageable, America's atomic diplomacy stiffened his resolve and made him cling even more firmly to Eastern Europe as a buffer. At a high-level meeting in the Kremlin he announced his own plan: "A single demand of you, comrades: provide us with atomic weapons in the shortest possible time. You know that Hiroshima has shaken the whole world. The equilibrium has been destroyed. Provide the bomb. It will remove a great danger from us." The result: an atomic arms race, not international cooperation.

By early 1946 U.S.-Soviet relations were badly strained. In February of that year, Stalin warned all Soviet citizens that there would never be a lasting peace with the capitalistic West; economic sacrifices and perhaps more warfare lay ahead. Supreme Court Justice William Douglas labeled the speech "the declaration of World War III." The next month Winston Churchill traveled to Fulton, Missouri, to give a lecture of his own. With Truman by his side, he announced that "from Stettin in the Baltic to Trieste in the Adriatic, an **Iron Curtain** has descended across the continent"; only a combined Anglo-American effort could lift the curtain. Fortunately, Churchill emphasized, "God has willed" the atomic bomb to America. Dramatic words, ominous warnings, threats and counterthreats—the Cold War clearly had been declared.

Tough Talk

Although real issues divided America and the Soviet Union, the emotionally charged rhetoric and the emergence of Cold War myths hardened the battle lines. Truman's public pronouncements lacked the tact and language of a diplomat. He also remembered how the British and the French had given in to Hitler at the Munich Conference of 1938. Equating Stalin's goals with Hitler's, however, was a grave mistake. Stalin was concerned more with security

than expansion; he wanted to protect his country from a future attack, not initiate World War III. As George Kennan, America's leading expert on the Soviet Union, later observed, "The image of a Stalinist Russia poised and yearning to attack the West, and deterred only by our possession of atomic weapons, was largely a creation of the Western imagination."

The Munich example and the get-tough talk turned American public opinion against the Soviet Union. Leading American diplomat Dean Acheson warned, "I think it is a mistake to believe that you can, at any time, sit down with the Russians and solve problems." Comments of this sort were aired over and over in public as the media began to build a new, more menacing image of Stalin. The pipe in hand and sad, soft eyes of Uncle Joe quickly faded in late 1945 and early 1946. News stories emphasized confrontation, conflict, and controversy. Talk turned no longer toward how to avoid an explosive conflict but rather how to win it. In the mind of the public, the Soviet Union soon became the once and future enemy of America.

The situation was exacerbated by Britain's decline. England, like much of the rest of Europe, suffered terribly during World War II. The war shattered its economy, and burned-out buildings and miles of fresh graves silently testified to the country's physical and human losses. By early 1947 Britain could no longer stand as the leader of the Western democracies. At an emergency meeting with Secretary of State George C. Marshall, the British ambassador in Washington announced that his country could no longer economically support Greece and Turkey in their fight against communist rebels. If these two countries, which were vitally important because of their position between the Soviet Union and the Mediterranean and the Middle East, were to be kept as western allies, the United States had to aid their cause.

Truman was prepared to assume the burden, but there were doubts whether the country was. Republicans had regained control of Congress in the November 1946 elections, and they were not anxious to shoulder expensive new foreign programs. In addition, rapid demobilization after World War II had drastically reduced the size and effectiveness of the American military forces. Still, something had to be done. Truman's advisers and congressional leaders recommended that he speak directly to the American people. But as Republican Senator Arthur Vandenberg warned, to win public support the president would have to "scare the hell out of the American people."

On March 12, 1947, Truman appeared before a joint session of Congress and described the Greek and Turkish situations as battles between the forces of light and the legions of darkness. "At the present moment in world history nearly every nation must choose between alternative ways of life," he said. "One way of life is based upon the will of the majority, and is distinguished by free institutions, representative government, free elections, guarantees of individual liberty, freedom of speech and religion, and freedom from political oppression. The second way of life is based upon the will of a minority forcibly imposed upon the majority. It relies upon terror and oppression." Congress sounded its approval as Truman came to his climactic sentence: "I believe that it must be the policy of the United States to support free peoples who are resisting attempted subjugation by armed minorities or outside pressures." Labeled the **Truman Doctrine,** the statement set the course U.S. foreign policy would follow during the next generation.

Specifically, Truman called for economic and financial aid to "save" Greece and Turkey. Congress responded by appropriating $400 million. By later standards it was a paltry sum, but it was a significant beginning. In the future, America would send billions of dollars in economic and military aid to countries fighting communism, even though the leaders of some of those nations were themselves dictators. In Truman's morality play, however, "anticommunists" and "free peoples" became synonymous.

Although Truman succeeded in getting aid for Greece and Turkey and in arousing the American public, a few foreign policy experts believed that his scare tactics did more harm than good. Diplomat George Kennan deplored the sweeping language of the Truman Doctrine, which placed U.S. aid to Greece "in the framework of a universal policy rather than in that of a specific decision addressed to a specific set of circumstances."

The Marshall Plan: "Saving Western Europe"

The millions of dollars sent to Greece and Turkey stabilized the pro-American governments of the two countries. But at the same time America was losing support in Western Europe, a far more vital region. The region lacked the money to rebuild its war-torn economies and scarred cities. To make matters worse, the winters of 1946 and 1947 were brutally cold. News reports from early 1947 told the sad story. Snow buried thousands of sheep in northern England; between December 1 and February 8, 40 residents of Berlin and 68 of Hamburg died from the cold; Holland was short of food; Italy was inundated

by floods; and across the continent the weather report was always the same: "cold or very cold." The winter hardships were a boon to the Communist party, which made marked gains. American leaders assumed that economic distress would continue to breed political extremism. *New York Times* correspondent Anne O'Hare McCormick told Americans: "The extent to which democratic government survives on [the] continent depends on how far this country is willing to help it survive." Truman concurred, and so did his advisers. They were upset by the emerging view in Europe of selfish, exploitative Americans. Describing the typical occupation soldier in Germany, an army chaplain wrote, "There he stands in his bulging clothes, fat, overfed, lonely, a bit wistful, seeing little, understanding less—the Conqueror, with a chocolate bar in one pocket and a package of cigarettes in the other. . . . The chocolate bar and the cigarettes are about all that he, the Conqueror, has to give the conquered."

At the Harvard University commencement on June 5, 1947, Secretary of State George C. Marshall announced a plan to give Europe more. After describing the severe problems facing Europe, Marshall suggested that America could not afford to send a Band-Aid to cover the deep European wounds. "A cure rather than a mere palliative" was in order—Europe needed massive economic blood transfusions. He told his audience that the cost might seem high. Without America's help, however, "economic, social, and political deterioration of a very grave character" would result. And from a more selfish point of view, America needed a strong, democratic Europe to provide rich markets for American goods and to act as a check against Soviet westward expansion.

In early 1948 Congress appropriated $17 billion to be spent over the next four years for the European Recovery Program (ERP), more popularly called the **Marshall Plan.** The program put food in the mouths of hungry children, coal in empty furnaces, and money in near-empty banks. More importantly, it rebuilt the economic infrastructure of Western Europe and restored economic prosperity to the region. In the process it created stable markets for American goods. Americans were proud of the Marshall Plan, and Europeans were moved by it. Winston Churchill judged it "the most unsordid act in history." All told, the Marshall Plan greatly restored America's prestige abroad.

The Marshall Plan also fostered the economic integration of Western Europe by curbing nationalistic economic policies. "A healthy Europe," John Foster Dulles remarked, could not be "divided into small compartments." Although the process toward a single economic unit in Western Europe was slow and

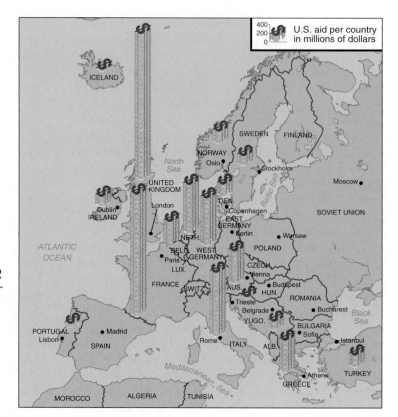

Marshall Plan Aid to Europe, 1948–1952

The Marshall Plan, also known as the European Recovery Program, provided aid totaling $13 billion to European countries following World War II. Most went to former allies Great Britain and France but former enemies Italy and West Germany also received substantial aid. To receive the grants, countries pledged to control inflation and lower tariffs.

occasionally painful, it did move forward. The European Payments Union was created in 1950, the European Coal and Steel Authority in 1951, and the European Economic Community (Common Market) in 1958. In the final analysis, the Marshall Plan served both America's Cold War strategy and plans for an economic internationalism.

THE CONTAINMENT POLICY

Money, even billions of dollars, could not substitute for a concrete foreign policy to guide U.S. actions, an explicit policy that mixed the international idealism of the Truman Doctrine and the economic realism of the Marshall Plan with the will to meet the real or perceived Soviet threat. The policy was not long in coming. In July 1947, the journal *Foreign Affairs* contained an article entitled "The Sources of Soviet Conduct" by "Mr. X." The article provided a blueprint for the policy of **containment,** which would influence American foreign policy for at least the next generation.

"Mr. X" was George Kennan, the government's foremost authority on the Soviet Union. Kennan had spent his adult life in the U.S. foreign service and was stationed in Moscow during World War II. Although he believed Russians were a "great and appealing people," he distrusted the Soviet government. In the article, Kennan argued that Soviet

communism was driven by two engines: the need for a repressive dictatorship at home and the belief that there could never be any sense of community or true accord with the capitalist West. In fact, the Kremlin used the supposed threat from capitalism to justify its continued dictatorship. But, he continued, Stalin and the leaders in the Kremlin were more interested in security than expansion. Russia would only expand when allowed to by American weakness. It could be *contained* to its present borders by a politically, economically, and militarily active United States. What was needed was "the adroit and vigilant application of counter-force at a series of constantly shifting geographical and political points, corresponding to the shifts and maneuvers of Soviet policy." Kennan even suggested that if the United States was firm in its resolve to contain Soviet expansion, "the possibility remains . . . that Soviet power . . . bears within it the seeds of its own decay." In short, Kennan held out the hope of complete victory in the Cold War.

Although Kennan later remarked that he was talking about the political containment of a political threat, in 1947 his article was read as primarily a military blueprint. As such, it satisfied hard-liners but was challenged by many other politicians and respected political commentators. Walter Lippmann challenged Kennan's policy in a series of newspaper articles later published as *The Cold War: A Study in*

U.S. Foreign Policy (1947). Containment, Lippmann commented, allowed the Soviet Union largely to decide when and where its battles against America would take place, and it promised to tie the United States to small, unstable "client" countries that would be political, economic, and military drains on America. Seeing that the plan was primarily focused on Western European problems, Lippmann suggested that if followed it might well lead America into a land war in Asia, where the idea of victory would be a cruel delusion. America, Lippmann maintained, was not in the military, economic, or strategic position to implement containment. Lippmann found it "hard to understand how Mr. X could have recommended such a strategic monstrosity."

Containment involved confronting the spread of communism across the globe and, as Americans soon learned, its price was high. It meant supporting allies around the world with billions of dollars in military and economic aid, and it meant thousands of Americans dying in foreign lands. Because containment was a defensive policy, it involved a prolonged Cold War. Unlike World War I and World War II, the Cold War emphasized the doctrine of limited wars fought for limited goals. And in this arrangement, Kennan noted, "Man would have to recognize . . . that the device of military coercion would have . . . only relative—never an absolute—value in the pursuit of political objectives." It was a policy bound to breed frustration and anxiety—certain to influence domestic as well as foreign policy.

Berlin Test

During the late 1940s containment seemed to fit American needs. American-Soviet tensions centered particularly on the future of Germany. The United States maintained that the economic revival of Western Europe depended on a reindustrialized and prosperous Germany. The Soviets believed that a reindustrialized Germany was a dangerous Germany. An early conflict over the two different viewpoints occurred in Berlin, a divided city located in the heart of East Germany, deep within the Soviet zone. Future Soviet Premier Nikita Khrushchev called democratic West Berlin a "bone in the throat" of Russia. In June 1948, Stalin decided to remove the bone by stopping all road and rail traffic between West Germany and Berlin. It was a crisis tailor-made for the containment policy. Stalin had picked the time and place. Now Truman had to decide upon a response.

He chose the sky. Stalin could close highways and railways, but he could not effectively close the skyways. For almost one year America and Britain kept West Berlin alive and democratic by a massive

During 1948 and 1949, an American and British airlift brought close to 7000 tons of food and fuel each day to Soviet-blockaded West Berlin.

airlift. Food, coal, clothing, and all other essentials were flown daily into Berlin. It was a heroic feat, a triumph of technology. Western pilots logged 277,264 flights into West Berlin; they hauled in 2,343,315 tons of food, fuel, medicine, and clothing. Finally on May 12, 1949, Stalin lifted his blockade of West Berlin. For Stalin, the success of the **Berlin airlift** had become an embarrassment for the Soviet Union. In the West, containment had passed an important test.

Troubling Times

Truman scored a series of triumphs during 1947 and 1948. The Truman Doctrine, the Marshall Plan, and the Berlin airlift strengthened his popularity at home and U.S. prestige abroad. In the election of 1948 Truman won a remarkable upset victory over Thomas E. Dewey. Then in 1949 eleven Western democracies joined the United States in signing the **North Atlantic Treaty Organization (NATO)** agreement, a mutual defense pact. NATO signified America's position as the leader of the Western Alliance, and it conformed to the containment policy. But difficult times for Truman, containment, and America lay ahead. In late August 1949, American scientists detected traces of radioactive material in the Soviet atmosphere. The cause was as clear as a mushroom-shaped cloud. The Soviets had the bomb—a full decade before American intelligence expected it.

Between 1945 and 1949 the threat of the bomb had given teeth to American policy. It was America's check on the Red Army, and U.S. policy-makers seldom allowed Soviet leaders to forget it. In 1945 Secretary of State James F. Byrnes told his Soviet counterpart V. M. Molotov, "If you don't cut out all this stalling and let us get down to work, I am going to pull an atomic bomb out of my hip pocket and let you have it." Now Molotov had one in his hip pocket. Truman responded by asking his scientists to accelerate the development of a hydrogen bomb; and Congress responded by voting appropriations for Truman's latest defense requests. Of such events and decisions are the humble origins of arms races.

On the heels of the Soviet bomb came more unwelcome news—the establishment of the communist government in China after a bitter civil war. The war between **Mao Tse-tung (Mao Zedong)** and Chou Enlai's (Zhou Enlai's) Communists and Chiang Kaishek's (Jiang Jieshi's) Nationalists had been raging since the 1930s. The United States had strongly backed Chiang during the civil war, providing him with more than $3 billion in aid between 1945 and 1949. But the aid was unable to prop up a govern-

ment that was structurally unsound, inefficient, and corrupt. In the first week of May 1949, Chiang fled across the Formosa Strait to Taiwan, and on September 21, Mao proclaimed Red China's sovereignty. With Chiang in Taiwan and Mao on the mainland, China became two countries.

The Truman administration tried to put the best face possible on the turn of events. Secretary of State Dean Acheson issued a thousand-page white paper explaining how Mao had won the civil war. It detailed the rampant corruption in the Nationalist government and Chiang's many mistakes. Assessing the role of the United States, Acheson concluded, "Nothing that this country did or could have done within the reasonable limits of its capabilities could have changed that result . . . it was the product of internal Chinese forces, forces which this country tried to influence but could not."

For the American public, however, that explanation was not good enough. The China most Americans knew, as one historian put it, was associated with novelist "Pearl Buck's peasants, rejoicing in the good earth . . . dependable, democratic, warm, and above all pro-American." Journalists supported this image during World War II. Americans were told that there were two types of Asians—the good Chinese and the evil Japanese. In 1941 *Time* magazine even ran an article entitled "How to Tell Your Friends From the Japs." It confidently reported, "the Chinese expression is likely to be more placid, kindly, open; the Japanese more positive, dogmatic, arrogant."

Republicans and supporters of Chiang in America blamed Truman for "losing" China. Led by Henry Luce, the influential publisher of *Time* and *Life* and the Chinese-born son of American missionaries, an informal group known as the **China Lobby** blasted the Truman administration. They claimed "egg-sucking phony liberals" had "sold China into atheistic slavery." The China Lobby believed that America had far more influence than it actually had, that a country that contained 6 percent of the earth's population could control the other 94 percent. They were wrong, but millions of Americans took their loud cries seriously.

"China lost itself," Acheson countered. "We picked a bad horse," Truman admitted. But given the political pressure at home, Truman was not about to change mounts in the middle of the race. Reversing America's traditional policy of recognizing de facto governments, Truman refused to recognize the Communist People's Republic of China. Instead he insisted that Chiang's Nationalist government on Taiwan was the legitimate government of China. It was an unrealistic policy, but one that future presidents

Communist Revolution in China

Legend:
- Communist base, 1945
- Areas under Communist control, 1949
- ■ Seat of Nationalist government

U.S.S.R.
MONGOLIA
Amur R.
Harbin
Baotou
Shenyang
Beijing (Capital after 1949)
NORTH KOREA
Huang He
Yan'an
Tianjin
Port Arthur (to U.S.S.R. 1945–55)
Lanzhou
Xi'an
Kaifeng
Yellow Sea
SOUTH KOREA
CHINA
Nanjing (Capital before 1949)
During 1949 Nationalist government moves to Chongqing then, Chengdu
Chengdu
Shanghai
Chongqing
Hankou
East China Sea
INDIA
Yangtze R.
Changsha
Fuzhou
Kunming
Taipei
Nanning
Guangzhou
Taiwan (End 1949, Nationalist government flees to Taiwan)
BURMA
Hong Kong (Br.)
FRENCH INDOCHINA
South China Sea
Hainan
0   250   500 Miles
0   250   500 Kilometers
THAILAND

found politically difficult to reverse. The United States and the People's Republic of China did not establish formal relations until 1979.

The Korean War

The rhetoric of the Truman administration tended to simplify complex issues, intensify the Cold War rivalry, and tie foreign policy to domestic politics. Failure abroad could have calamitous consequences for politicians at home. "If you can't stand the heat, get out of the kitchen," Truman often said. By 1950 the kitchen had become hotter. After "China fell," Truman was more determined than ever to contain communism.

The mood of the Truman administration is clearly evident in **National Security Council Paper Number 68 (NSC-68),** one of the most important documents of the Cold War. Completed in April 1950, it expressed the views of foreign-policy planners Paul Nitze and Dean Acheson that communism was a monolithic world movement directed from the Kremlin; it advocated "an immediate and large-scale build-up in our military and general strength of our allies with the intention of righting the power balance and in the hope that through means other than all-out war we could induce a change in the nature of the Soviet system." NSC-68 extended the Truman Doctrine and called for America to protect the world against the spread of communism. The cost would be great—NSC-68 estimated it at 20 percent of the gross national product, or over a 300-percent increase in military appropriations—but planners warned that without the commitment America faced the prospect of a world moving toward communism.

Truman realized that NSC-68 "meant a great military effort in time of peace. It meant doubling or tripling the budget, increasing taxes heavily, and imposing various kinds of economic controls." And he doubted whether Congress would accept such a

THE PEOPLE SPEAK

NSC-68

In 1950, at the height of the Cold War—in the wake of "lost" China and the Alger Hiss trial—President Harry Truman ordered the National Security Council to conduct "a reexamination of our objectives in peace and war and of the effect of these objectives on our strategic plans." The resulting document, NSC-68, is regarded by many as the blueprint of the Truman administration's Cold War policy. Filled with specific policies and statistics advocating a rapid military buildup, NSC-68 opens with a general description of the perceived chasm between American and Soviet values.

> The free society values the individual as an end in himself, requiring of him only that measure of self-discipline and self-restraint which make the rights of each individual compatible with the rights of every other individual. . . .
>
> From this idea of freedom with responsibility derives the marvelous diversity, the deep tolerance, the lawfulness of the free society. This is the explanation of the strength of free men. It constitutes the integrity and the vitality of a free and democratic system. . . .
>
> The idea of freedom is the most contagious idea in history, more contagious than the idea of submission to authority. For the breadth of freedom cannot be tolerated in a society which has come under the domination of an individual or group of individuals with a will to absolute power. Where the despot holds absolute power—the absolute power of the absolutely powerful will—all other wills must be subjugated in an act of willing submission, a degradation willed by the individual upon himself under the compulsion of a perverted faith. . . .
>
> The same compulsion which demands total power over all men within the Soviet state without a single exception, demands total power over all Communist Parties and all states under Soviet domination. Thus Stalin has said that the theory and tactics of Leninism as expounded by the Bolshevik party are mandatory for the proletarian parties of all countries. . . . The antipathy of slavery to freedom explains the iron curtain, the isolation, the autarchy of the society whose end is absolute power. . . .
>
> Thus unwillingly our free society finds itself mortally challenged by the Soviet system. No other value system is so wholly irreconcilable with ours, so implacable in its purpose to destroy ours, so capable of turning to its own uses the most dangerous and divisive trends in our own society, no other so skillfully and powerfully evokes the elements of irrationality in human nature everywhere, and no other has the support of a great and growing center of military power.

Source: Ernest R. May, *American Cold War Strategy: Interpreting NSC 68.* Copyright ©1993 Bedford Books of St. Martin's Press.

peacetime buildup. He never got a chance to find out, for in June 1950 America went to war in Korea.

Korea, like Germany, was a divided country. When the Japanese surrendered its forces in Korea after World War II, Soviet troops accepted the surrender north of the 38th parallel, American troops south of that line. With the deepening of the Cold War, the temporary division line became permanent. North of the 38th parallel, communist Kim Il Sung governed North Korea. Supported by the Soviet Union, Kim forged a modern, disciplined army during the late 1940s. In South Korea, 75-year-old President Syngman Rhee, who received strong aid and support from the United States, opposed any reconciliation with communist North Korea. But, as Secretary of State Acheson noted in an unfortunate speech before the National Press Club on January 12, 1950, South Korea lay outside America's primary "defense perimeter." Should an attack occur, Acheson emphasized, the "initial resistance" must come from "the people attacked."

On June 25, 1950, the attack occurred. In an orderly, coordinated offensive, North Korea sent 90,000 men across the 38th parallel into South Korea, where they faced a weak, disorderly South Korean army. It was a mismatch of epic proportions, and South Korean troops quickly mounted an all-out retreat. As the monsoon rains drenched the rice paddies and mountains, Korea moved swiftly toward unification under Kim's communist government.

Why did North Korea attack? At the time, the Truman administration believed that the Soviets directed the assault. It regarded Kim as little more than a puppet whose strings were manipulated in Moscow. There is little evidence, however, to support this contention. More likely, internal Korean politics dictated the course of events. Kim's position in North Korea was threatened by organized opposition from a rival political party. The invasion of South Korea, therefore, may have been launched to undercut that movement. Certainly Kim informed Stalin of the impending invasion, but the idea and the timing were probably his own.

Truman had just finished a Saturday dinner in Independence, Missouri, when Acheson telephoned him with news of the invasion. His reaction was as rapid and as certain as North Korea's attack. Because both Koreas were technically wards of the United Nations, the Truman administration took the matter to the Security Council. With the Soviet Union absent (it was boycotting the United Nations over the refusal of the organization to seat the People's Republic of China), the Security Council by a 9 to 0 vote condemned the North Korean assault and demanded an immediate cease-fire. Encouraged by the United Nations's prompt action and without consulting

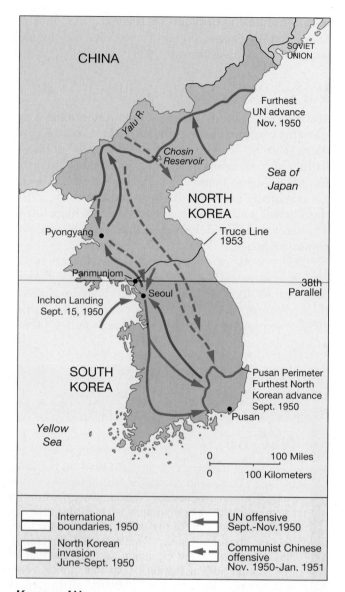

Korean War

Congress, Truman pledged American support to South Korea and strengthened the military position of the United States in Asia.

Truman termed the conflict a **UN police action** and, in fact, a number of UN members sent troops, but for all practical purposes it was a war that initially matched the United States and South Korea against North Korea. Air force advisers told Truman that they could stop the North Korean advance by bombing the communist supply line. They convinced Truman that ground forces would not be needed. Truman's advisers seemed convinced that the Asians would turn and run at the first show of western force. Although the bombs destroyed miles of roads and bridges, they did not slow the North Korean advance.

On June 30, Truman took the fateful step of ordering American occupation troops stationed in Japan to proceed to Korea. They soon joined their South Korean allies in a headlong retreat. For six weeks the allies fell steadily back until they stabilized a perimeter in southeast Korea around the port city of Pusan. With their offensive halted, North Korean troops mounted a siege. To the surprise of the world, the Pusan perimeter held firm.

For American soldiers it had been a painful and disappointing two months. They were fighting in an unfamiliar country for an unsatisfactory objective. Truman's announced goal was simply to restore the 38th parallel as the border between the two Koreas. Victory then was defined as a stalemate. Corporal Stephen Zeg of Chicago expressed the feeling of other soldiers when he commented, "I'll fight for my country, but I'll be damned if I see why I'm fighting to save this hellhole."

But fighting they were, and **General Douglas MacArthur** was determined to reverse the military situation of the war. A bold, even arrogant man, firmly fixed in his opinions and certain of his ability to command in battle, MacArthur decided to split his forces and launch a surprise attack against the North Korean rear. On the morning of September 15, 1950, American marines began an amphibious attack on Inchon, a port city, wrote one historian, "about as large as Jersey City, as ugly as Liverpool, and as dreary as Belfast." MacArthur's military advisers warned him against the move, noting that Inchon possessed every natural and geographic handicap. MacArthur, however, was confident of victory. It was a bold, risky maneuver—a bold, risky, successful maneuver.

Faced with an enemy to their front and their rear, North Korean troops retreated across the border. By the beginning of October those North Korean soldiers who were not captured or killed were above the 38th parallel. Truman had achieved his stated objective. But the warrior in MacArthur wanted more—he wanted victory on the battlefield. And he said so, loudly and publicly. In private the Truman administration was moving toward MacArthur's position. Containment was giving way to a policy of liberation. After receiving MacArthur's reassurances at a private meeting on Wake Island, Truman decided to allow U.S. forces to move across the 38th parallel and "liberate" North Korea. Like MacArthur's Inchon landing, it was a bold plan, one predicated on the widely held American belief that China would not intervene in the conflict.

This time boldness failed. North Korea was a difficult country to invade. The American army had no reliable maps and mountainous terrain rendered traditional military tactics impossible. In addition, as MacArthur's forces moved recklessly north toward Manchuria, Chinese officials sent informal warnings to the United States that unless the advance stopped, their country would enter the fray. MacArthur ignored Chinese warnings and his own intelligence reports and kept moving.

A seemingly endless file of Korean refugees trudge through the snow outside Kangnung on the east coast on January 8, 1951. Nearly a million civilians were killed in the Korean War, which ended with the country as it had been when the fighting began—divided at the 38th parallel.

Communist China struck in late November. Over 300,000 troops poured across the border and attacked unprepared American forces, radically altering the nature of the war. Victory was now out of the question. Only MacArthur continued to talk about an absolute victory. If a nation was going to fight a war, he sermonized, it should fight to win. In Washington, however, the Truman administration was shifting back to the pre-Inchon policy of containment. When MacArthur publicly criticized the administration's newest approach, an angry Truman recalled him and replaced him with General Matthew B. Ridgway. In America Truman's sacking of "Mac" raised a firestorm of protest. An April 1951 Gallup poll reported that 66 percent of Americans disapproved of Truman's firing of the general, and then in October, 56 percent indicated that they believed the Korean conflict was a "useless war."

The **Korean War** dragged on until July 10, 1951, when formal peace negotiations began, but it proved to be a long, difficult process. While diplomats talked, American soldiers fought and died. Altogether, 34,000 Americans were killed and 103,000 wounded during the Korean War. When Truman left office in early 1953 the carnage was still continuing. Finally on July 26, 1953, the war officially ended, as it began, with North Koreans above the 38th parallel and South Koreans below it. It was a victory for Truman's containment policy, but for millions of Americans it somehow tasted like defeat.

THE COLD WAR AT HOME

Commie for a day. It was a theme idea. It answered the question, "What would it be like to live under a Soviet-type, communist dictatorship?" On May Day 1950, at Mosinee, Wisconsin, American Legionnaires disguised themselves as Soviet soldiers and staged a mock communist takeover of their town. They arrested and summarily locked up the mayor and clergymen, nationalized all businesses, confiscated all firearms, and rid the library of rows of objectionable books. They even forced Mosinee residents to alter their eating habits. The local restaurants served only potato soup, dark bread, and black coffee, and only Young Communist Leaguers were permitted to eat candy. Eventually Mosinee patriots "liberated" their town, and at dusk a mass democratic rally was held amidst much patriotic music and the burning of communist literature.

For most of Mosinee's citizens it was an edifying experiment. "We really learned about what 100 percent communism would be like," one resident observed. They concluded that life under communism

was hardly worth living. Many found intolerable the lack of such basic freedoms as privacy, speech, press, religion, and decent food. One participant confessed, "I know some people who even drove to [neighboring] Wausau to get something to eat. In Russia I guess you wouldn't be able to get anything else anywhere."

Although there is an element of humor to **Mosinee's Red May Day,** behind the events was a national mood that was far from funny. As Truman waged the Cold War abroad, Cold War issues gradually came to dominate the American domestic scene. During this Second Red Scare (the first had taken place in 1919–1920 following World War I), the fear of communism disrupted American life, and the freedoms that Americans took for granted came under attack. At home as well as abroad, Americans battled real and imagined communist enemies.

Adjusting to Peace

Truman and his advisers approached the end of World War II with their eyes on the past. They were uneasy about the future: Memories of the Great Depression and the painful social and economic adjustment after World War I clouded their thinking. They knew that massive wartime spending, not the New Deal, had ended the Great Depression, and they worried that peace might bring more economic suffering. Peace with prosperity was their goal.

The solution to the problems of converting back to a peacetime economy, Truman believed, lay in the continuation, at least for a time, of wartime government economic controls. During the war, the Office of Price Administration (OPA) had controlled prices and held inflation in check. After Japan surrendered, Truman asked Congress to continue price controls and outlined a program for economic reconversion. To ensure future prosperity, Truman advocated such economic measures as a 65-cents-an-hour minimum wage, nationalization of the housing industry, and stronger fair employment practices legislation.

Congress responded half-heartedly, passing the Employment Act of 1946. Although it was less than Truman had requested, it did provide the institutional framework for more government control over the economy. The act created the Council of Economic Advisors to help "promote free competitive enterprise, to avoid economic fluctuations . . . and to maintain employment, production, and purchasing power." During the decades after 1946, the council exerted a powerful influence over economic policy.

On the other hand, Republicans and southern Democrats balked against a return to more "New

Dealism." Congress destroyed the OPA by relaxing its controls, a policy that created immediate inflation. Congress's refusal to pass Truman's economic package did not tumble America into another depression. In truth, the American economy was basically sound. Wartime employment and wartime saving had created a people whose money was burning holes in their pockets. They wanted peacetime goods—automobiles, houses, Scotch whiskey, nylon stockings, and red meat. Given the demand and the short supply, inflation was inevitable. In addition, the short supply of consumer goods increased black-market activities. Americans offered bribes for preferential treatment from car salesmen, butchers, and landlords, but as industries converted to peacetime production, consumer supplies rose to meet the new demands.

Confronting the Demands of Labor

The death of the OPA led to demands for higher wages as well as to higher prices. During the war labor unions had taken "no strike" pledges, and it was through their efforts that America became the "arsenal of democracy." Workers labored long and hard, agreeing to speedups and higher production quotas. Virtually no production time was lost to strikes.

The end of the war signaled the start of the strike season as workers demanded rewards for their wartime efforts and their loss of overtime pay. During 1946 over 4.5 million laborers struck, and 107,476,000 workdays were lost to strikes. If labor's cause was just, its timing was disastrous. After clashing repeatedly with an obstreperous Congress, Truman was in no mood to coddle labor. When two national railway brotherhoods threatened to disrupt the transportation system, Truman proposed to draft the workers. On national radio he announced, "The crisis at Pearl Harbor was the result of action by a foreign enemy. The crisis tonight is caused by a group of men within our country who place their private interests above the welfare of the nation." Confronted by hostile public opinion and an unsympathetic president, the brotherhoods went back to work.

Labor was angry. United Mine Workers leader **John L. Lewis** told reporters, "You can't mine coal with bayonets." As winter approached, Lewis took his men out on strike. The prospect of a cold winter created anxiety, and Truman reacted angrily, threatening to take over the mines. He then appealed directly to the miners, asking them to go back to work for the good and warmth of the nation. It worked. Lewis called off the strike. Truman's prestige and confidence soared.

Truman's gains were labor's losses. The congressional elections of 1946, which brought to power the conservative Republican-controlled Eightieth Congress, added to labor's problems. Led by Robert Taft, Congress pushed through the Labor-Management Relations Act of 1947 (better known as the **Taft-Hartley Act**), which was passed over Truman's veto. It outlawed the closed shop (a business or industry in which all the employees were required to join a union), gave presidents power to delay strikes by declaring a "cooling-off" period, and curtailed the political and economic power of organized labor. The act reflected the country's increasingly conservative mood.

Failure of the Fair Deal

Political experts expected America to vote Republican in the 1948 presidential elections. Truman's policies had angered liberals, labor, Southerners, and most of Congress. Moreover, Democrats had occupied the White House since 1933. Republicans reasoned that it was time for a change. They nominated Thomas E. Dewey of New York, the GOP candidate in 1944. The Democrats stayed with Truman, even though large numbers of Southerners and liberals deserted the party to follow third-party movements. Southerners, angered by Truman's support of civil rights, formed the States' Rights Democratic party—better known as the Dixiecrats—and nominated Governor J. Strom Thurmond of South Carolina for president. Liberals joined with Communists to form the Progressive party, which nominated FDR's former vice president Henry A. Wallace for president.

An underdog from the start, Truman rolled up his sleeves and took his cause to the people by train, the 17-car "Presidential Special." As it moved across the country, Truman blasted the "do-nothing" Eightieth Congress at each stop. "If you send another Republican Congressman to Washington, you're a bigger bunch of suckers than I think you are," he lectured. "Give 'em hell, Harry!" was the popular refrain. By contrast, Dewey sat tight, seemingly more concerned with his fastidious appearance than his bland speeches. His cold personality failed to move American voters. "I don't know which is the chillier experience—to have Tom ignore you or shake your hand," noted a Truman supporter. "You have to get to know Dewey to dislike him," added another.

By election day Truman had closed the gap. The old Roosevelt coalition—midwestern farmers, urban ethnic groups, organized labor, African Americans, and Southerners—remained sufficiently strong to send Truman back to the White House. Neither the Dixiecrats nor the progressives hurt Truman in any

Most pollsters predicted that Republican candidate Thomas E. Dewey would win the 1948 presidential election, but in a stunning political upset the voters reelected President Truman.

substantial way, since most Democrats chose to remain in the center of the party with Truman rather than drift toward the radical fringes. Truman's victory was a testimony to the legacy of FDR as well as Truman's scrappiness, and to the often overlooked fact that Democrats outnumbered Republicans in the nation.

"Keep America Human with Truman," read one of his campaign posters. In 1949 he announced a plan to do just that. Known as the **Fair Deal,** the legislative package included an expansion of Social Security, federal aid to education, a higher minimum wage, federal funding for public housing projects, a national plan for medical insurance, civil rights legislation for minorities, and other measures to foster social and economic justice. As Truman explained, "I expect to give every segment of our population a fair deal." At the core of the Fair Deal was his belief that government-controlled economic expansion blunts extremism from the right and left and ensures prosperity.

Congress took Truman's package, stripped off the wrapping, threw away some of the contents, and sent it back to the president for his signature. Congress did extend Social Security, raise the minimum wage to 75 cents an hour, and further developed several New Deal programs. But the more original proposals of the Fair Deal—civil rights legislation, a national health insurance program, an imaginative farm program, and federal aid to education—were rejected by a Congress that opposed anything defined as "creeping socialism."

Truman, as well as Congress, contributed to the ultimate failure of the Fair Deal to achieve its objectives. Republicans and Southerners did join forces in opposition to civil rights and government spending programs, but Truman demonstrated an almost total inability to work with Congress on domestic issues. In addition, by 1949 foreign policy dominated the president's attention and claimed an increasing share of the federal budget.

Searching for the Enemy Within

While Congress removed the heart from Truman's Fair Deal, Cold War winds were chilling the country's political landscape. The tough diplomatic rhetoric of Truman, Acheson, and other policy-makers encouraged Americans to view the rivalry between the Soviet Union and the United States in simplistic terms. America became the "defender of free people," the Soviet Union the "atheistic enslaver of millions." Every time a world event did not go America's way, it was seen as a Soviet victory. In this world of black-and-white thinking, the suspicion that "enemies within" America were secretly aiding the Soviet cause took shape. Soon, talk of American "atomic spies" giving information to the Soviets and State Department officials sabotaging U.S. foreign policy became common.

Were spies working against American interests to further the Soviet cause? Unquestionably, yes. In 1945 Igor Gouzenko, a Soviet embassy official in Ottawa, defected to the West, carrying with him documents that detailed a communist spy ring working in Canada and the United States. The evidence led to the arrests of two British physicists, Dr. Alan Munn May and Dr. Klaus Fuchs, who had worked on the Manhattan Project. Fuchs implicated a group of American radicals—Harry Gold, David Greenglass, Morton Sobell, and **Julius and Ethel Rosenberg.** Clearly these individuals had passed atomic secrets to the Soviets during the war. Whether or not this information helped the Soviet Union to develop an atomic bomb is largely conjecture.

The damage done by British spies Kim Philby, Guy Burgess, and Donald Maclean is more certain. The three men held high British diplomatic and intelligence posts and were privy to sensitive American CIA and British Secret Intelligence Service (SIS) information. In 1951 Burgess and Maclean defected to the Soviet Union, where they were joined by Philby in 1963. There is considerable circumstantial evidence that the information they passed to the Soviet Union severely compromised American Cold War intelligence and may have been influential in the Chinese intervention in the Korean War.

In 1948 and 1949, Richard M. Nixon, at that time Congressman from California, served on the House Un-American Activities Committee investigating the Alger Hiss case. Nixon is shown here leaving the Federal Courthouse in New York, NY, on May 5, 1949, after testifying before the federal grand jury examining subversive activities.

There were certainly spies, but the issue soon outgrew the question of mere espionage and became an instrument of partisan politics. Republicans accused Democrats of being "soft" on communism—in fact, of harboring spies in the State Department and other government agencies. Richard M. Nixon, who was elected to Congress in 1946, announced that Democrats were responsible for "the unimpeded growth of the communist conspiracy in the United States." As proof Republicans pointed to the "fall" of China, the atomic bomb in the Soviet Union, and Alger Hiss in the State Department.

Truman reacted to such criticism as early as 1947 by issuing **Executive Order 9835,** which established the Federal Employee Loyalty Program, authorizing the FBI to investigate all government employees. Although the search disclosed no espionage or treason, thousands of employees were forced to resign or were fired because their personal lives or past associations did not meet government inspection. Homosexuality, alcoholism, unpaid debts, contribution to left-wing causes, support of civil rights—all became grounds for dismissal.

Truman also used the anticommunism issue to drum up support for his foreign policy. At the end of World War II public opinion polls revealed that few Americans regarded communism as a serious problem. Republican charges and Truman's loyalty program, however, encouraged citizens to profess 100 percent Americanism. In 1947 the president sent a special "Freedom Train" across the country to exhibit important national documents, including the Truman Doctrine. By 1950 communism had become a more visible issue at home as well as abroad.

Ethel and Julius Rosenberg paid the supreme price for being communists. At least one may have been a spy, but the death penalty was not mandatory for their crime. But their "diabolical conspiracy to destroy a God-fearing nation," according to Judge Irving R. Kaufman, had given the Soviets the bomb "years before our best scientists predicted." He ordered the couple's execution for treason. On June 19, 1953, the Rosenbergs, parents of two young sons, died in the electric chair.

The Rise and Fall of Joseph McCarthy

More than any other person, Wisconsin Senator **Joseph McCarthy** capitalized on the anticommunism issue. Although he did not start the crusade or even join it until 1950, the entire movement bears the name "McCarthyism." His career, which was the cause of so much suffering for so many, illuminated the price the country had to pay for temporarily placing anticommunism above the Constitution.

Elected to the Senate in 1946, McCarthy spent four years in relative obscurity, all the while demonstrating his incompetence and angering his colleagues. Then on February 9, 1950, he gave a Lincoln's Birthday address in Wheeling, West Virginia. Warning his audience about the threat of communism to America, he boldly announced, "While I cannot take the time to name all of the men in the State Department who have been named as members of the Communist Party and members of a spy ring, I have in my hand a list of 205 . . . a list of names that were known to the Secretary of State and who nevertheless are still working and shaping the policy of the State Department." McCarthy had no real list; he had no names. Simply put, he was lying. But within days he became a national sensation.

McCarthy dealt in simple solutions for complex problems. He told Americans that the United States could control the outcome of world affairs if it would get the communists out of the State Department. It was those "State Department perverts," those "striped-pants diplomats" who "gave away" Poland, "lost" China, and allowed the Soviet Union to develop the bomb. It was the "bright young men who are born with silver spoons in their mouths" who were "selling the Nation out." His arguments found receptive ears among Catholics who had relatives in Eastern Europe, political outsiders who resented the power of the "Ivy League Eastern Establishment," supporters of Chiang, and pragmatic Republicans who wanted to return to the White House in 1952. McCarthy's support only grew with the outbreak of the Korean War in the early summer of 1950.

McCarthy's origins were humble; he worked his way through high school and a Catholic college and intentionally cultivated the image of a bull in a china shop. With his beetle brow, he looked the part of a movie villain. He was in all ways the opposite of Secretary of State Dean Acheson, whose Ivy League degrees, waxed mustache, and aristocratic accent were a flapping red flag to McCarthy. Throughout the early 1950s McCarthy bitterly attacked "Red Dean" and the State Department. But in the end, McCarthy ferreted out no communists, espionage agents, or traitors.

McCarthy's basic tactic was never defend. Caught in a lie, he told another; when one case dissolved, he created another. He attacked Truman and Eisenhower, Acheson and Marshall, the State Department and the U.S. Army. No authority or institution frightened him. In 1954 his campaign against the army became so bitter that the Senate arranged special hearings. Televised between April 22 and June 17, the Army-McCarthy hearings attracted a high audience rating. It was the first time that most Americans saw McCarthy in action—the bullying of witnesses,

the cruel innuendo, the tasteless humor. At one point he attempted to ruin a young lawyer's career in order to discredit the lawyer's associate, Joseph Welch, the army's chief counsel. Welch unsuccessfully tried to stop McCarthy. Appalled, the chief counsel interrupted, "Until this moment, Senator, I think I never really gauged your cruelty or your recklessness. . . . Have you no sense of decency, sir, at long last?"

He didn't, and a large television audience saw that he didn't. McCarthy's consequent downfall was as rapid as his rise. When the polls showed that his popularity had swung sharply downward, his colleagues mounted an offensive. On December 2, 1954, the Senate voted to "condemn" McCarthy for his unsenatorial behavior. Newspapers stopped printing his outlandish charges. He sank back into relative obscurity and died on May 2, 1957.

The end of the Korean War and McCarthy's downfall signaled the end of the Red Scare. The Cold War remained, but most Americans soon realized that there was no significant domestic communist threat. They learned that an occasional spy was part of the price that free societies pay for their personal freedom, and that "McCarthyism" can be the result of a curtailment of that freedom.

THE PARANOID STYLE

The Cold War mentality left its imprint on politics and culture during the late 1940s and early 1950s. A certain "paranoid style" permeated the early Cold War years. Defining the term, historian Richard Hofstadter wrote:

Senator Joseph McCarthy's downfall came about as a result of his unsubstantiated charges of communist infiltration throughout the army.

It is, above all, a way of seeing the world and of expressing oneself. . . . The distinguishing thing about the paranoid style is . . . that its exponents see . . . a "vast" or "gigantic" conspiracy as *the motive force* in historical events. . . . The paranoid spokesman sees the fate of this conspiracy in apocalyptic terms—he traffics in the birth and death of whole worlds, whole political orders, whole systems of human values. . . . Since what is at stake is always a conflict between absolute good and absolute evil, the quality needed is not a willingness to compromise but the will to fight things out to the finish.

The nature of the fight against communism contributed to the paranoid style. Politicians warned Americans that communism silently and secretly destroyed a country from within. Although allegedly directed from Moscow, its aim was subversion through the slow destruction of a country's moral fiber. No one knew which institution it would next attack, or when. It might be the State Department or the YMCA; it might be the presidency, the army, the movie industry, or the Cub Scouts. Politicians counseled vigilance. They told Americans to watch for the unexpected, to suspect everyone and everything. As a result, between 1945 and 1955 a broad spectrum of institutions, organizations, and individuals came under suspicion. Whether it was the Mafia or the fluoridation of drinking water, Americans sought the answers to complex problems in the workings of conspiracies.

HUAC Goes to Hollywood

The House of Representatives had established the **House Un-American Activities Committee (HUAC)** in the late 1930s to combat subversive right-wing and left-wing movements. Its history was less than distinguished. From the first it tended to see subversive communists everywhere at work in American society. HUAC even announced that the Boy Scouts were infiltrated by communists. During the late 1940s and the early 1950s HUAC picked up the tempo of its investigations, which it conducted in well-publicized sessions. Twice during this period HUAC "traveled" to Hollywood to investigate communist infiltration in the film industry.

HUAC first went to Hollywood in 1947. Although it didn't find the party line preached in the movies, it did call a group of radical screenwriters and producers into its sessions to testify. Asked if they were communists, a group of leftist filmmakers known as the "Hollywood Ten" refused to answer questions about their political beliefs. As Ring Lardner, Jr., one of the ten, said, "I could answer . . . but if I did, I would hate myself in the morning." They believed that the First Amendment protected them. In the politically charged late 1940s, however, their rights were not protected. Those who refused to divulge their political affiliations were tried for contempt of Congress, sent to prison, and blacklisted.

HUAC went back to Hollywood in 1951. This time it called hundreds of witnesses from both the political right and the political left. Conservatives told HUAC that Hollywood was littered with "Commies." Walt Disney even recounted attempts to have Mickey Mouse follow the party line. Of the radicals, some talked and others didn't. To cooperate with HUAC entailed "naming names"—that is, informing on one's friends and political acquaintances. Again, those who refused to name names found themselves unemployed and unemployable.

The HUAC hearings and blacklistings convinced Hollywood producers to make strongly anticommunist films. Between 1947 and 1954 they released more than 50 such films. Most were second-rate movies, starring third-rate actors. The films assured Americans that communists were thoroughly bad people—they didn't have children, they exhaled cigarette smoke too slowly, they murdered their "friends," and they went berserk when arrested. As one film historian has commented, the communists in these

Movies like *Rebel Without a Cause*, starring James Dean, depicted the futility and hopelessness of American youth in the 1950s.

The Kefauver Crime Committee

In May 1950, at the very moment that Senator Joseph McCarthy was beginning his crusade against the domestic political threat posed by communism, the U.S. Senate created a special committee to investigate another "enemy within": organized crime. The nation appeared to be in the midst of an unprecedented wave of lawlessness. A memorandum to the president reported that a serious crime was committed in the United States every 18.7 seconds. Aggravated assault was up 68.7 percent over prewar averages; rape was up 49.9 percent. Burglary, murder, robbery, prostitution, gambling, and racketeering all were on the increase. Criminologists attributed the postwar crime wave to such factors as the wartime disruption of families, shortages of goods during and after the war, and a continuing public demand for illicit gambling. But journalists, citizen crime commissions, and the Federal Bureau of Narcotics identified another villain: organized crime.

Estes Kefauver, an ambitious 47-year-old first-term Tennessee Democratic senator, originally proposed a congressional investigation of organized crime in January 1949. The Truman administration, already rocked by charges of fiscal mismanagement, financial irregularities, and favors to businessmen, feared that any inquiry might link urban Democratic political machines to criminal activities. For a time, the administration succeeded in blocking a potentially embarrassing investigation. But on April 6, 1950, the

bodies of two gangsters were found in a Kansas City, Missouri, Democratic political club under a photograph of President Truman. The Democratic-controlled Senate quickly authorized the investigation of organized crime.

For the next 15 months, the **Kefauver Crime Committee** held hearings in 14 major cities and took testimony from more than 800 witnesses. The committee immediately attracted national attention by linking individuals close to Florida's Democratic governor, Fuller Warren, to a bookmaking syndicate controlled by Al Capone's mob in Chicago. Subsequent hearings in Kansas City and Chicago revealed widespread examples of political corruption and influence peddling.

Television made the Kefauver committee's hearings among the most influential in American history. While the Kefauver committee did not hold the first televised congressional hearings (it was actually the fifth congressional committee to allow TV cameras into a hearing room), it was the first to attract a massive number of viewers. As many as 20 to 30 million Americans watched spellbound as crime bosses, bookies, pimps, and hitmen appeared on their television screens. They listened intently as the committee's chairman informed them that "there is a secret international government-within-a-government" in the United States, controlling gambling, vice, and narcotics traffic and infiltrating legitimate businesses, protected by corrupt police officers, prosecutors, judges, and politicians.

The high point of the investigation occurred in New York City, where the committee held televised hearings beginning on March 12, 1951, and last-

ing eight days. Over 50 witnesses testified before the committee, but public interest centered on the alleged boss of the New York underworld Frank Costello, alias Francisco Castaglia, alias Frank Severio. Costello was purportedly head of the organized crime family previously run by Vito Genovese and Charles Luciano.

In his initial appearance before the committee, Costello's lawyer objected to having his client's face televised. Technicians proceeded to focus the cameras on Costello's hands. The result was television at its most powerful. As committee counsel Rudolph Halley fired questions, Costello was seen nervously ripping sheets of paper to shreds, drumming his fingers on the tabletop, and clenching his fist.

During the New York hearings, daytime television audiences grew from a minuscule 1.5 percent of homes to a phenomenal 26.2 percent. In the New York metropolitan area an average of 86.2 percent of all individuals watching television watched the hearings, twice the number that had watched the World Series the previous October. The New York City electric company had to add a generator to supply power for all the television sets in use. Commented *Life* magazine: "The week of March 12, 1951, will occupy a special place in history. . . . [People] had suddenly gone indoors into living rooms, taverns and clubrooms, auditoriums and backoffices. There, in eerie half-light, looking at millions of small frosty screens, people sat as if charmed. . . . Never before had the attention of the nation been riveted so completely on a single matter."

The Kefauver committee failed to produce effective crime-fighting legis-

lation, but it did heighten public awareness of the problem of political corruption and organized crime, and generated pressure to enforce existing law. In the aftermath of the committee's investigation, more than 70 local crime commissions were established. The Special Rackets Squad of the FBI launched 46,000 investigations, and by 1957, federal prosecutors had won 874 convictions and recovered $336 million. The committee's hearings were largely responsible for the defeat of proposals to legalize gambling in Arizona, California, Massachusetts, and Montana.

The investigation was important in one other respect. The Kefauver committee played a vital role in popularizing the myth that organized crime in the United States was an alien import, brought to the United States by Italian, and especially by Sicilian, immigrants in the form of the Mafia, a highly centralized, secret organization, that used violence and deceit to prey on the weaknesses and vices of the public. In its report, the committee asserted that much of the responsibility for gambling, loan sharking, prostitution, and narcotics trafficking lay in two major syndicates.

In fact, the committee's conclusion—that organized crime was rooted in a highly centralized ethnic conspiracy—was an error. Most organized crime in the United States is organized on a municipal and regional, rather than a national, basis. And despite the image portrayed in such epics as Mario Puzo's *The Godfather,* diverse ethnic groups have participated in such sophisticated crimes as large-scale gambling, loan sharking, narcotics trafficking, and labor racketeering.

Today, the power of the nation's traditional Mafia families appears to be dwindling. Since the mid-1980s, more than 100 top Cosa Nostra leaders have been sentenced to long prison terms. In Detroit, Kansas City, Milwaukee, New England, New Jersey, Philadelphia, and St. Louis, where Mafia gangs once influenced the construction, trucking, trash collection, and garment manufacturing industries, Mafia strength has sharply declined. The decline of the mob, however, does not mean the end of organized crime; rival crime groups have stepped in and taken over such activities as illegal gambling and drug trafficking.

anticommunist films even looked alike; most were "apt to be exceptionally haggard or disgracefully pudgy," and there was certainly "something terribly wrong with a woman if her slip straps showed through her blouse."

The films may have been bad civics lessons, but they did have an impact. They seemed to confirm HUAC's position that communists were everywhere, that subversives lurked in every shadow. They reaffirmed the paranoid style and helped to justify McCarthy's harangues and Truman's Cold War rhetoric.

"What's Wrong with Our Kids Today?"

At the same time as it was turning out films about serious but bumbling communists, Hollywood was producing movies that contributed to the fear that something was terribly wrong with the youth of America. Films such as *The Wild One* (1954), *Blackboard Jungle* (1955), and *Rebel Without a Cause* (1955) portrayed adolescents as budding criminals, emerging homosexuals, potential fascists, and pathological misfits—everything but perfectly normal kids.

FBI reports and congressional investigations reinforced the theme of the moral decline of America's adolescents. J. Edgar Hoover, head of the FBI, linked the rise in juvenile delinquency to the decline in the influence of family, home, church, and local community institutions. Youths had moved away from benign authority toward the temptations of popular culture, which, Hoover said, "flout indecency and applaud lawlessness."

Frederic Wertham, a psychiatrist who studied the problem extensively, agreed, emphasizing particularly the pernicious influence of comic books. He believed that crime and horror comic books fostered racism, fascism, and sexism in their readers. In his book *Seduction of the Innocent* (1954), Wertham even linked homosexuality to the reading of comics. Describing how the comic *Batman* could lead to homosexuality, Wertham quoted one of his male patients: "I remember the first time I came across the page mentioning the 'secret bat cave.' The thought of Batman and Robin living together and possibly having sex relations came to my mind, . . . I felt I'd like to be loved by someone like Batman or Superman." Far from being an unheard voice, Wertham's attack generated congressional investigations of and local attacks against the comic book industry. In response, the industry passed several self-regulatory codes designed to restrict the violent and sexual content of comic books.

For a number of critics, sports were an antidote to the ills of wayward youths. "Organized sport is one of our best weapons against juvenile delinquency," remarked J. Edgar Hoover. Youths who competed for championship trophies felt no inclination to compete for "wrist watches, bracelets and automobiles that belong to other people." Nor would they turn to communism. As Senator Herman Welker of Idaho bluntly put it, "I never saw a ballplayer who was a Communist."

Given these widespread beliefs, the sports scandals of the early 1950s shocked the nation and raised fresh questions about the morality of American adolescents. In February 1951 New York authorities disclosed that players for the City College of New York (CCNY) basketball team had accepted money to fix games. By the time the investigations ended, Long Island University, New York University, Manhattan College, St. John's, Toledo, Bradley, and Kentucky were implicated in the scandal, which involved forging transcripts, paying players, and fixing games. In August 1951 the scandal moved to football. This one involved academic cheating, not point shaving, and was confined to one school—the United States Military Academy at West Point. Altogether, Academy officials dismissed 90 cadets, half of them football players, for violations of the school's honor code.

The West Point scandal, especially, struck at the nation's heart, for half a world away in Korea American soldiers were battling to contain communism. What of their moral fiber? They too had read comics, watched films written by left-wing screen writers, and been exposed to "subversive" influences. Did they have the "right stuff"? These questions swirled around the Korean prisoner-of-war (POW) controversy. Early reports suggested that American POWs in Korea were different from, and inferior to, those of World War II. Journalists portrayed them as undisciplined, morally weak, susceptible to "brainwashing," uncommitted to traditional American ideals, and prone to collaborate with their guards.

What was wrong? Who was corrupting the youth of America? The Republican *Chicago Tribune* blamed the New Deal. The Communist *Daily Worker* said it was the fault of Wall Street, bankers, and greedy politicians (the paranoid style, after all, had no party affiliation). Other Americans, without being too specific, simply felt that there was some ominous force working within America against America.

Adherents to the paranoid style dealt more in vague perceptions than concrete facts. They reacted more to what *seemed* to be true than to what actually was true. In fact, sociologists and historians have demonstrated that Korean POWs behaved in much the same way as POWs from earlier wars. Juvenile

CHRONOLOGY OF KEY EVENTS

1938 House Un-American Activities Committee (HUAC) is created to investigate fascist or communist subversion

1945 United Nations is founded

1947 Truman Doctrine declares that the United States will provide military and economic aid to allies faced by external aggression or internal subversion; Truman establishes a federal program to investigate the loyalty of government employees; Marshall Plan provides $17 billion over four years to Western Europe to aid in its economic recovery; Taft-Hartley Act, passed over President Truman's veto, bans the closed shop, restricts union political contributions, and allows courts to delay strikes threatening health or safety; HUAC investigates communist infiltration of the film industry

1948 State of Israel proclaimed; United States, Britain, and France merge their zones of occupation in Germany to form an independent nation, West Germany; Soviet Union blockades Berlin; excommunist Whittaker Chambers charges that former State Department official Alger Hiss gave him secret government documents

1949 NATO is founded; Berlin blockade ends; Mao Zedong's communist forces win China's civil war; Soviet Union successfully tests an atomic bomb

1950 NSC-68 argues that the United States must commit itself to whatever military steps are necessary to stop the spread of communism; Senator Joseph McCarthy claims he has the names of 205 State Department employees who were members of the Communist party; North Korean troops cross the 38th parallel, beginning the Korean War; UN forces invade North Korea; Chinese troops enter North Korea and force UN troops to retreat across the 38th parallel

1951 Negotiations to work out a cease-fire in Korea begin; HUAC conducts a second investigation of communist subversion in Hollywood; Ethel and Julius Rosenberg are sentenced to death for espionage

1953 Dwight D. Eisenhower is inaugurated as the thirty-fourth president; cease-fire signed in Korean War

1954 Army-McCarthy hearings; U.S. Senate censures McCarthy for "conduct unbecoming a member"

delinquency was not on an upswing during the late 1940s and 1950s. And alien subversive forces were not undermining American morality. In retrospect, we know this. But the rhetoric of the Cold War and McCarthyism created a political atmosphere that proved fertile for the paranoid style.

CONCLUSION

By 1953 and 1954 there were indications of a thaw in the Cold War. First came the death of Joseph Stalin, which was officially announced on March 5, 1953. Shortly thereafter Georgi Malenkov told the Supreme Soviet, the highest legislative body of the Soviet Union: "At the present time there is no disputed or unresolved question that cannot be settled peacefully by mutual agreement. . . . This applies to

our relations with all states, including the United States of America." That summer the Korean War ended in a stalemate that allowed both the United States and the communist forces to save face. In America, 1954 saw the fall of McCarthy. Certainly these events did not end the paranoid style in either America or the Soviet Union, but they did ease the tension.

In addition, by 1954 both the United States and the Soviet Union had become more comfortable in their positions as world powers. Leaders in both countries had begun to realize that neither side could readily win the Cold War. Between 1945 and 1954 each side had carved out spheres of influence. The Soviet Union and its sometime-ally China dominated most of Eastern Europe and the Asian mainland. America and its allies controlled Western Europe, North and South America, most of the Pacific, and to a lesser extent Africa, the Middle East, and Southeast Asia. Throughout much of the Third World, however, emerging nationalistic movements would challenge both U.S. and Soviet influences.

In the United States, the containment policy was seldom even debated. The Truman Doctrine and muscular internationalism governed foreign policy decisions, but economic and political questions lingered. How much would containment cost? Where would the money come from? Which Americans would pay the most? Would it mean the end of liberal reform? Over the next decade American leaders would wrestle with these and other questions.

CHAPTER SUMMARY AND KEY POINTS

Following World War II, the United States clashed with the Soviet Union over such issues as Soviet dominance over Eastern Europe, control of atomic weapons, and the Soviet blockade of Berlin. The establishment of a communist government in China in 1949 and the North Korean invasion of South Korea in 1950 helped transform the Cold War into a global conflict, in which the United States would confront the threat of communism in Iran, Guatemala, and elsewhere. In an atmosphere charged with paranoia and anxiety, there was deep fear at home about "enemies within" sabotaging U.S. foreign policy and passing atomic secrets to the Soviets. In this chapter you read about the causes of the Cold War, the containment policy and the way it was implemented; the Korean War; and the Second Red Scare.

- Following World War II the United States grew increasingly worried about the intentions of the Soviet Union. Eastern Europe fell under Soviet influence, and communist movements in Greece and Italy challenged governments in those countries.

- In China, communist forces seized power.

- By 1946 a Cold War had broken out in Europe. President Truman declared that the United States would block further communist expansion. To enforce the policy of containment, the United States sponsored the Marshall Plan, organized the Berlin airlift, and along with 11 European democracies formed the North Atlantic Treaty Organization (NATO).

- In Asia the policy of containment was tested when North Korea invaded South Korea.

- The Cold War contributed to anxieties about the threat of subversion at home. The discovery of a few cases of disloyalty fed such anxieties, and Senator Joseph McCarthy charged that many communists were active in high levels of government. McCarthy's investigations uncovered little evidence of such activities and his popularity declined after the televised Army-McCarthy hearings.

SUGGESTIONS FOR FURTHER READING

Gar Alperovitz, *Atomic Diplomacy*, rev. ed. (1985). Controversial study that ignited a serious second look at the reasons for America's use of atomic weapons.

Larry Ceplair and Steven Englund, *The Inquisition in Hollywood* (1980). Studies the impact of Washington on Hollywood and Hollywood's impact on America.

Stanley I. Kutler, *The American Inquisition: Justice and Injustice in the Cold War* (1982). A series of poignant studies of the human consequences of the domestic side of the Cold War.

Walter LeFeber, *America, Russia, and the Cold War,* 7th ed. (1993). The frequently updated story of the great rivalry of the second half of the twentieth century.

David McCullough, *Truman* (1992). Sprawling biography of Harry Truman and the world that made him.

David M. Oshinsky, *A Conspiracy So Immense: The World of Joe McCarthy* (1983). A fascinating biography of a man who gave his name to an age.

Allen Weinstein, *Perjury: The Hiss-Chambers Case* (1978). A detailed examination of Alger Hiss's guilt.

Daniel Yergin, *Shattered Peace* (1977). Well-written, balanced exploration of the origins of the Cold War.

Novels

William F. Buckley, *Who's On First* (1997).

E. L. Doctorow, *The Book of Daniel* (1966).

Norman Mailer, *The Naked and the Dead* (1948).

Gore Vidal, *Washington, D.C.* (1967).

Kurt Vonnegut, *God Bless You Mr. Rosewater* (1965).

MEDIA RESOURCES
Web Sites

Harry S Truman
http://www.ipl.org/ref/POTUS/hstruman.html
This page contains basic factual data about his election and presidency, speeches, and on-line biographies.

Harry S Truman Library
http://www.trumanlibrary.org
This presidential library has numerous photos and several important primary documents.

Senator Joe McCarthy
http://www.webcorp.com/mccarthy/

This Webcorp site includes audio clips of McCarthy's speeches.

Korean War Project
http://www.onramp.net/~hbarker
This site has information about the war and is a guide to resources on the Korean War.

Cold War
http://cnn.com/SPECIALS/cold.war/
This is the companion site to the CNN *Perspectives* series on the Cold War. It contains a lot of information including interactive time lines and a quiz.

Films and Videos

The Blackboard Jungle (1955). Richard Brooks's adaptation of the Evan Hunter novel about America's "youth problem."

Dr. Strangelove or How I Learned to Stop Worrying and Love the Bomb (1964). Stanley Kubrick's satirical look at American military policy. This film set the standard for dark comedy.

Fail-Safe (1964). Where Kubrick finds humor in the threat of a nuclear mistake, Sidney Lumet's film sees only dark foreboding.

The Front (1976). Woody Allen's take on the Hollywood blacklisting of the late 1940s and 1950s.

On the Beach (1959). Stanley Kubrick's film, based on the Nevil Shute novel, that warns Americans that nuclear destruction is only a few small mistakes away.

The Wild One (1954). Marlon Brando stars as the leader of a motorcycle gang that terrorizes a small town. The film suggests that all Brando needs is more love and more direction.

KEY TERMS

Hiss-Chambers affair   (p. 733)

Cold War   (p. 734)

Iron Curtain   (p. 736)

Truman Doctrine   (p. 737)

Marshall Plan   (p. 737)

Containment   (p. 738)

Berlin airlift   (p. 739)

North Atlantic Treaty Organization (NATO)   (p. 739)

China Lobby   (p. 740)

National Security Council Paper Number 68 (NSC-68) (p. 741)

UN police action   (p. 742)

Korean War   (p. 744)

Mosinee's Red May Day   (p. 744)

Taft-Hartley Act   (p. 745)

Fair Deal   (p. 746)

Executive Order 9835   (p. 747)

House Un-American Activities Committee (HUAC) (p. 749)

Kefauver Crime Committee   (p. 750)

PEOPLE YOU SHOULD KNOW

Whittaker Chambers   (p. 731)

Alger Hiss   (p. 732)

Joseph Stalin   (p. 733)

Mao Tse-tung (Mao Zedong)   (p. 740)

General Douglas MacArthur   (p. 743)

John L. Lewis   (p. 745)

Julius and Ethel Rosenberg   (p. 746)

Joseph McCarthy   (p. 747)

REVIEW QUESTIONS

1. During the war effort, Americans viewed the Soviet Union as an ally. How did this view so rapidly deteriorate by 1947?

2. What was the policy of containment? How did it shape America's response to the invasion of South Korea?

3. How did Joseph McCarthy become such a powerful and influential senator in the early 1950s?

4. What role did popular culture—movies, comic books, sports, etc.—play in creating a domestic mood of paranoia?

27 Ike's America

THE MURDER OF EMMETT TILL

Mose Wright stood and surveyed the courtroom. Most of the faces he saw were white. The two accused men were white. The 12 jurors were white. The armed guards were white. Slowly, Wright, a 64-year-old African American sharecropper, extended his right arm. "Thar he," Wright answered, pointing at J. W. Milam. He then pointed at Roy Bryant, the second defendant. In essence, Wright was accusing the two whites of murdering Emmett Till, his 14-year-old nephew—accusing them in a segregated courtroom in Sumner, Mississippi. Wright later recalled that he could "feel the blood boil in hundreds of white people as they sat glaring in the courtroom. It was the first time in my life I had the courage to accuse a white man of a crime, let alone something as terrible as killing a boy. I wasn't exactly brave and I wasn't scared. I just wanted to see justice done."

It was 1955, but the march of racial justice in the South had been painfully slow. In 1954 the Supreme Court of the United States, in the landmark *Brown v. Board of Education of Topeka* decision, had ruled that segregated schooling was "inherently unequal." News of the *Brown* decision drew angry comments and reactions from all corners of the Jim Crow South. Mississippi Senator James Eastland told his constituents that the decision destroyed the Constitution of the United States and counseled, "You are not obliged to obey the decisions of any court which are plainly fraudulent." Throughout Dixie, Klansmen burned crosses while other white leaders hastily organized Citizens' Councils. Self-proclaimed protectors of white America vowed "to make it difficult, if not impossible, for any Negro who advocates desegregation to find and hold a job, get credit, or renew a mortgage."

Into the racially charged atmosphere of August 1955 came Emmett Till. Taking a summer vacation from his home on the South Side of Chicago, he rode a train to visit relatives living near Money, Mississippi. Emmett had known segregation in Chicago, but nothing like what he discovered in Money, where shortly before his arrival an African American girl had been "flogged" for "crowding white people" in a store.

Emmett's mother told him what to expect and how to act: "If you have to get on your knees and bow when a white person goes past, do it willingly." But Emmett had a mind and a mouth of his own. In Chicago, he told his cousins, he was friends

Mose Wright and his three boys, seated in the "colored" section of the courtroom, attended the trial of Roy Bryant and J. W. Milam, accused of killing Emmett Till in Mississippi.

According to Milam and Bryant's account, they had only meant to scare the northern youth. But Emmett did not beg for mercy. Therefore they *had* to kill him. "What else could we do?" Milam asked. "He was hopeless. I'm no bully; I never hurt a nigger in my life. I like niggers in their place. I know how to work 'em. But I just decided it was time a few people got put on notice."

Three days later Emmett's badly beaten body was found in the Tallahatchie River. A gouged-out eye, crushed forehead, and bullet in his skull gave evidence to the beating he took. Around his neck, attached by barbed wire, was a 75-pound cotton gin fan. At the request of his mother, the local sheriff sent the decomposing body to Chicago for burial.

Mamie Bradley, Emmett's mother, grieved openly and loudly. Contrary to the wishes of Mississippi authorities, she held an open-casket funeral. Thousands of African American Chicagoans attended the viewing, and the African American press closely followed the episode. *Jet* magazine even published a picture of the mutilated corpse. In the African American community the Till murder case became a cause célèbre. In a land that valued justice, would any be found in Mississippi?

In Money, white Southerners rallied to Bryant and Milam's side. Supporters raised a $10,000 defense fund, and southern editorials labeled the entire affair a "communist plot" to destroy southern society. By the time the trial started, American interest seemed focused on Mississippi. Few people, however, expected that Bryant and Milam would be judged guilty because few expected any African Americans would testify against white men in Mississippi.

Mose Wright proved the folly of common wisdom. He dramatically testified against the white men. So did several other relatives of Emmett Till. But in his closing statement, John C. Whitten, one of the five white defense attorneys, told the all-white, all-male jury: "Your fathers will turn over in their graves if [Milam and Bryant are found guilty] and I'm sure that every last Anglo-Saxon one of you has the courage to free these men in the face of that [outside] pressure."

The jury returned a "not guilty" verdict in one hour and seven minutes. "If we hadn't stopped to drink a pop, it wouldn't have taken that long," one juror commented. On that day in 1955 there was no justice in Sumner, Mississippi. Michigan Congressman Charles Diggs, who sat with other African Americans in the rear section of the segregated courtroom, recalled, "I certainly was angered by the decision, [but] I was not surprised by it. And I was strengthened in my belief that something had to be done about the dispensation of justice in that state." Roy Wilkins of the NAACP remarked that "there is in the entire state no restraining influence of decency,

with plenty of white people. He even had a picture of a white girl, *his* white girl, he said. "Hey," challenged a listener, "there's a [white] girl in that store there. I bet you won't go in there and talk to her."

Emmett accepted the challenge. He entered Bryant's Grocery and Meat Market, browsed about, and bought some bubble gum. As he left, he said, "Bye, Baby" to Carolyn Bryant and gave a "wolf call" whistle. Outside an old black man told Emmett to scat before the woman got a pistol and blew "his brains out." The advice sounded sage enough, so Emmett beat a hasty retreat.

A few days later Roy Bryant returned to Money after hauling shrimp from Louisiana to Texas. What his wife told him is unknown, but it was enough to make him angry. After midnight that Saturday night, he and his half brother, J. W. "Big" Milam, drove to Mose Wright's unpainted cabin. They demanded the "boy who done the talkin'." Mose tried to explain that Emmett was from "up nawth," that he "ain't got good sense" and was unfamiliar with southern ways. The logic of the argument was lost on the two white men, one of whom told Mose that if he caused trouble he would never see his next birthday.

Various stories have been told about what happened during the next few hours. One thing is for certain: Emmett Till did not live much past daybreak.

not in the state capital, among the daily newspapers, the clergy, not among any segment of the so-called lettered citizens."

But if there was no justice that day, there were clear signs of change. An African American man had demanded justice in white-controlled Mississippi. Soon—very soon—other voices would join Mose Wright's. Their peaceful but insistent cries would be heard over the surface quiet of Dwight Eisenhower's America. They would force America to come to terms with its own ideology. After a heroic struggle against fascism and during a cold conflict against communism, Americans no longer could ignore racial injustice and inequality at home.

It was time for change. During the late 1940s and the 1950s the process began. Slow, painful, poignant, occasionally uplifting—the march toward justice moved forward. It was part of other significant social and economic changes taking place in America. Against the backdrop of Eisenhower's calm assurances, a new country was taking shape.

QUIET CHANGES

Most white Americans during the late 1940s and the early 1950s were unconcerned about the struggles of their African American compatriots. Perhaps some admired Jackie Robinson's efforts on the baseball field, but few made the connection between integration in sports and civil rights throughout society. Other con-

cerns seemed more urgent. In November 1952 the Korean War was dragging into its third year, and the chances for a satisfactory peace were fading. Joseph McCarthy was still warning Americans about the communist infiltration of the U.S. government. Political corruption had stained the Truman administration. At the polls Americans were ready to vote for change.

"I Like Ike"

Republicans certainly felt it was time for change. The Democrats had occupied the White House for the previous 20 years. In 1952 they ran Governor Adlai Stevenson of Illinois for the presidency. A political moderate and a vocal anticommunist, the witty, sophisticated Stevenson was burdened by Truman's unpopularity. His Republican opponent was Dwight David Eisenhower, a moderate, anticommunist war hero. The Republican campaign strategy was summarized in a formula—K_1C_2. Eisenhower promised that if elected he would first end the war in Korea then battle communism and corruption at home. The nation responded. Eisenhower was swept into office. He even carried several southern states and cut into the urban-ethnic coalition of the Democrats.

"I Like Ike" campaign buttons and posters captured the public sentiment. There was much to like. Few people had advanced so far while making so few enemies. Ike's was the classic Horatio Alger success story. Although born in Texas, he was raised in Abilene, Kansas, the northern terminus of the Chisholm Trail. An accomplished athlete and a good student, Ike earned an appointment to West Point, where he graduated in 1915 among "the class on which the

Delegates at the 1952 Republican National Convention raise banners, signs, and placards to show their enthusiastic support for "Ike," Dwight D. Eisenhower, the Republican nominee for president. Even defeated Democratic candidate Adlai Stevenson admitted that he too "liked Ike."

stars fell." (Fifty-nine of the 164 graduates of the class would rise to the rank of brigadier general or higher.)

As an army officer, Eisenhower demonstrated rare organizational abilities and a capacity for complex detail work. If by 1939 he had only risen to the rank of lieutenant colonel, he had nonetheless impressed his superiors. With the outbreak of World War II, he was promoted with startling rapidity. In fact, in 1942 General George Marshall passed over 366 more senior officers to promote Eisenhower to major general and appoint him commander of the European Theater of Operations. It was Ike who planned and oversaw America's invasions of North Africa, Sicily, and Italy and who led the combined British-American D-Day invasion of France. By the end of the war, Ike was a four-star general and an international hero.

Ike's ability to win the loyalty of others and work with people of diverse and difficult temperaments would serve him well as a politician. But during the early postwar years, he expressed no interest in holding political office. "I cannot conceive of any set of circumstances that could drag out of me permission to consider me for any political post from dog catcher to Grand High Supreme King of the Universe," he told a reporter in 1946. And indeed there is no evidence that Ike had ever voted or had any party affiliation before running for the presidency on the Republican ticket in 1952.

Eisenhower did have strong beliefs concerning America's domestic and foreign policies. His fiscal conservatism led him to the Republican party, and his internationalism convinced him to run for the presidency. He did not want to see an isolationist Republican elected in 1952, and the early front-runner was isolationist Robert Alphonso Taft, the powerful Ohio senator. Once Ike had defeated Taft for the nomination, his victory over Stevenson was almost anticlimactic.

Almost overnight the image of Eisenhower was transformed from one of a master military organizer to one of mumbling, bumbling, smiling incomprehensibility. Reporters commented on his friendly smile, engaging blue eyes, and his mangled syntax. As a young officer Eisenhower had written striking speeches for Douglas MacArthur, and as a World War II general he had impressed reporters with the precision of his thought. Commenting on Ike's speaking style, FDR's press secretary said, "He knows his facts, he speaks freely and frankly, and he has a sense of humor, he has poise, and he has command."

Had Eisenhower somehow sunk into senility on taking office? Certainly not. He sensed that the country needed a rest from 20 years of active presidents. Rather than needing an earthshaker, the country needed a "dirt smoother." The result was the "hidden-hand leadership" of Ike. In public he seemed everyone's favorite grandfather and golfing buddy, friendly, outgoing, quick to please, but only slightly interested in being president. Although he had read widely in both military history and the classics, he insisted publicly that he only read westerns, and those not too closely. But throughout his eight years in office, Eisenhower focused closely on his two major priorities: U.S.-Soviet relations and a balanced budget. These issues, not civil rights or other important social concerns, occupied most of his attention.

"Dynamic Conservativism"

Eisenhower saw himself as a forward-looking Republican. He called himself a conservative, "but an extremely liberal conservative," one who was concerned with fiscal prudence but not at the expense of human beings. Ike termed his approach **"modern Republicanism"** and "dynamic conservativism," by which he meant, "conservative when it comes to money matters and liberal when it comes to human beings." In practice this approach led the Eisenhower administration to cut spending while not rolling back New Deal social legislation.

George Humphrey, a conservative Ohio industrialist, served as Eisenhower's treasury secretary. More conservative than Eisenhower, Humphrey believed that the federal government should shift more fiscal responsibilities to the state and private sectors. He did succeed in getting Congress to abolish the Reconstruction Finance Corporation (see Chapter 24) and turn over off-shore oil rights to the seaboard states. The *New York Times* called this latter piece of legislation, the Submerged Land Act, "one of the greatest and surely the most unjustified give-away programs in all the history of the United States." On the whole, however, Eisenhower's domestic programs were hardly reactionary.

During Ike's two terms the country made steady and at times spectacular economic progress. In 1955 the minimum wage was raised from 75 cents to $1 per hour, and during the 1950s the average family income rose 15 percent and real wages went up 20 percent. And work was plentiful. During the decade, unemployment averaged only 4.5 percent per year, a figure close to the magical 4 percent economists considered "full employment." Stable prices, full employment, and steady growth were the economic hallmarks of the 1950s. "American labor has never had it so good," AFL-CIO chief George Meany told his associates in 1955. Although the population increased by 28 million people, the country was on the whole better housed and fed than ever before. The output of goods and services rose 15 percent. Especially for white Americans, "modern Republicanism" seemed a viable alternative to New Dealism.

A Country on Wheels

If Eisenhower labored to curtail the role of the federal government in some areas, he expanded it in other places. As an expert on military logistics, Ike frequently expressed concern about the sad state of the American highway system. During World War II he had been impressed by Hitler's system of *Autobahnen,* which allowed the German dictator to deploy troops to different parts of Germany with incredible speed. From his first days in office, Eisenhower worked for legislation to improve America's highway network.

The highway lobby agreed. Following the philosophy that what was good for General Motors was good for the country, the highway lobby—a loose collection of pressure groups that included representatives from the automobile, trucking, bus, oil, rubber, asphalt, and construction industries—pushed for a new federally subsidized interstate highway system. Not only would such a project provide millions of new jobs, it would contribute to a safer America by making it easier to evacuate major cities in the event of a nuclear attack.

As a result of presidential and lobby pressure, in 1956 Congress passed the **National System of Interstate and Defense Highways Act,** the most significant piece of domestic legislation enacted under Eisen-

hower. As planned, the system would cover 41,000 (later expanded to 42,500) miles, cost $26 billion, and take 13 years to construct. Although it took longer to complete and cost far more than Congress projected, it did provide the United States with the world's most extensive superhighway system. Secretary of Commerce Sinclair Weeks estimated that the act would create 150,000 new construction jobs and rank as "the greatest public works program in history."

More than any other piece of legislation, it also changed America. The commitment to internal combustion engines altered the culture and landscape of America. It accelerated the decline of the inner city and the flight to the suburbs. The downtown portions of cities, once thriving with commerce and excitement, rapidly turned into ghost towns. As downtown businesses, hotels, and theaters closed, suburban shopping malls with multiscreen cinemas and roadside motels began to dot the American highway landscape. Drive-in theaters, gasoline service stations, mobile homes, and multicar garages signified the birth of a new extended society, one without center or focus. Indeed, highway construction was simply one expression of Americans' obsession with the automobile during the 1950s and 1960s. After being deprived of new cars during the war—when the maximum speed limit was 35 miles per hour—Americans adopted the

Highway construction initiated under the 1956 National System of Interstate and Defense Highways Act spawned an abundance of enterprises geared to automobile traffic. Drivers could do their banking, take in a movie, eat a meal—even attend a church service—without ever having to leave their cars.

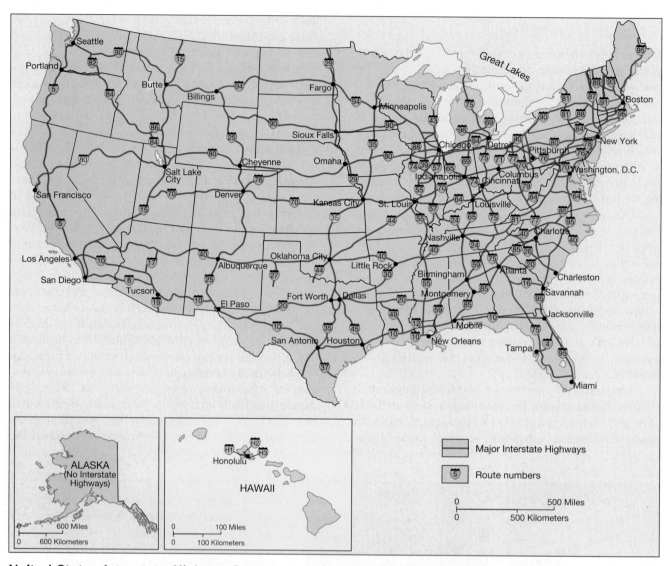

United States Interstate Highway System

The 1956 plan to create an interstate highway system drastically changed America's landscape and culture.

new automobile philosophy of bigger is better and the biggest and fastest is the best. In 1952 over 52 million cars crowded American roads, and that number doubled during the next 20 years.

New home architecture exemplified America's mobile-minded culture. The garage, once separated from and located behind the house, achieved a new position. By the 1960s the average home devoted more space to the family automobiles than to individual family members. With access to the house itself—usually through the kitchen—the garage had become an integrated part of the house and the car an important member of the family.

America's commitment to highways and cars created numerous problems. Mass transportation suffered most conspicuously. Streetcars and commuter railroads languished, as did the country's major interstate railroads. Since highway construction was financed by a nondivertible gasoline tax, government often ignored mass transit. In the years since the end of World War II, 75 percent of government expenditures for transportation have gone for highways as opposed to 1 percent for urban mass transit. As a result, those not able to use automobiles—the old, the very young, the poor, the handicapped—became victims of America's automobile obsession.

Ike, Dulles, and the World

For Eisenhower, "modern Republicanism" was more than simply a domestic economic credo. It also implied an internationalist foreign policy. As with domestic policy, Ike preferred to operate behind the scenes in foreign policy. But he did make all major foreign policy decisions.

The point man for Ike's foreign policy was Secretary of State **John Foster Dulles.** International diplomacy was in his blood. Dulles's maternal grandfather had served as Benjamin Harrison's secretary of state, and one of his uncles, Robert Lansing, had occupied the same post under Woodrow Wilson. In 1919, as a young man, Dulles had been part of the American delegation to the Versailles Peace Conference. After World War II, he helped organize the United Nations and then served as a delegate. In addition, throughout his life Dulles was a careful student of foreign affairs and international politics. Eisenhower noted, there was "only one man I know who has seen *more* of the world and talked with more people and *knows* more than [Dulles] does—and that's me."

Dulles's experience and knowledge were somewhat offset by his rigidity and excessive moralism. If Americans felt comfortable calling President Eisenhower "Ike," not even close friends called Dulles "Jack." Plain and as unpolished as granite, Dulles took himself, his Presbyterian religion, and the world seriously. "His face," commented an associate, "was permanently lined with an expression of unhappiness mingled with faint distaste—the kind of face that, on those rare occasions when it was drawn into a smile, looked as though it ached in every muscle to get back into its normal shape." Dulles tended to see opposition to communism in religious terms. A friend recalled a conversation in which China's Chiang Kai-shek and South Korea's Syngman Rhee were criticized. Offended, Dulles announced: "No matter what you say about them, those two gentlemen are modern-day equivalents of the founders of the church. They are Christian gentlemen who have suffered for their faith."

Although Eisenhower and Dulles had strikingly different public styles, they shared a common vision of the world. Both were internationalists and cold warriors who believed that the Soviet Union was the enemy and that the United States was and should be the protector of the free world. Peace was their objective—but never a peace won by appeasement. To keep honorable peace, both were willing to consider the use of nuclear weapons and go to the brink of war. As Dulles said in 1956, "You have to take some chances for peace, just as you must take chances in war."

Occasionally Dulles's impassioned anticommunist rhetoric obscured the actual policies pursued by the Eisenhower administration. In public Dulles rejected the containment doctrine as a "negative, futile and immoral policy" and advocated the "liberation" of Eastern Europe. It was time to "roll back" the Iron Curtain, he said, and if nuclear weapons were needed to achieve America's objectives—well, then, so be it. In public Dulles constantly flexed his—and America's—muscles.

In reality, Eisenhower's objectives were far more limited and his approach toward foreign policy much more cautious. Eisenhower supported containment, but not as practiced by Truman. In Eisenhower's eyes, Truman's approach was unorganized and far too expensive. Ike believed that the United States could not support every country that claimed to be fighting communism. As historian Charles C. Alexander noted, "The chief lesson Eisenhower and his associates drew from Korea was that limited wars, fought with conventional weaponry on the periphery of the Communist world, only drained the nation's resources and weakened its allies' resolve." If America continued Truman's shotgun policies, the costs would soon become higher than Americans would be willing to pay. A change, Ike maintained, was needed.

Eisenhower termed his adjustments of the containment doctrine the **"New Look."** Ike's program began with the idea of saving money. To do this he decided to emphasize nuclear weapons over conventional weapons, assuming that the next major war would be a nuclear conflict. This "more bang for the buck" program drew angry criticism. Congressional hawks claimed that Eisenhower was "putting too many eggs in the nuclear basket," and liberals suggested that the program would inevitably lead to nuclear destruction.

Whatever the criticisms, the New Look did save money. While air and missile forces were expanded, the army's budget was trimmed of all its fat and much of its bone. In fact, if Eisenhower had had his way, the army would have been completely reorganized. The results of Eisenhower's approach were dramatic. In 1953 defense cost $50.4 billion. By 1956 Eisenhower had reduced the defense budget to $35.8 billion. In addition, during the same period troop levels were reduced by almost one-third. Future presidents did not so much reverse Eisenhower's approach as enlarge it. They continued the nuclear buildup started by Eisenhower, and at the same time insisted on increased spending on conventional weapons. The result was an ever-escalating defense budget.

The New Look took an unconventional approach to conventional warfare. Ike had learned from Truman's mistakes in Korea. America could not send weapons and men to all corners of the world to contain communism. It was a costly, deadly policy. Instead, the New Look emphasized the threat of massive retaliation to keep order and reinforced America's position with a series of foreign alliances that encouraged indigenous troops and peoples to resist communist expansion. Finally, Eisenhower used the CIA as a covert foreign policy arm. Through timely assassinations and political coups engineered by the CIA, Eisenhower was able to prevent—or at least forestall—the emergence of anti-American regimes. While historians argue about the morality of the CIA's covert operations, they were very much a part of the New Look.

A New Face in Moscow

The world changed dramatically a few months after Eisenhower took office. On March 5, 1953, Joseph Stalin, the Soviet dictator whom Ike knew personally, died. Always fearful of rivals, Stalin did not groom a successor. The result was a power struggle within the Kremlin, from which **Nikita Khrushchev** emerged as the winner.

Khrushchev looked like a cross between a Russian peasant and Ike himself. Short, rotund, and bald, he had a warm smile and alert eyes. Unlike Stalin, Khrushchev enjoyed meeting people, making speeches, and traveling abroad. If occasionally he lost his temper and uttered belligerent remarks—he once even took off his shoe and pounded it on a table at the United Nations—Khrushchev did try to lessen the tensions between the Soviet Union and the United States.

Ike shared Khrushchev's dream for peaceful co-existence between the two world leaders. In fact, Eisenhower used Stalin's death as an opportunity to extend an olive branch. The Soviet Union peacefully responded. During 1955 the nations resolved several thorny issues: the Soviets repatriated German prisoners of war who had been held in the Soviet Union since World War II, established relations with Greece and Israel, and gave up claims to Turkish territory. The Soviet Union's most significant action was to withdraw from its occupation zone of Austria. Until the massive changes in Eastern Europe in 1990 and 1991, it was the only time that the Soviet Union withdrew from territory that it had seized during the war.

The cold winter of the Cold War seemed to be over. Khrushchev condemned Stalin's excesses, and Eisenhower talked guardedly about a new era of cooperation. In July 1955, the two leaders met in Geneva, Switzerland, for a summit conference. During the meeting, Eisenhower suggested that the United States and the Soviet Union allow aerial surveillance and photography of each other's nations to lessen the chance of a possible surprise attack. Khrushchev rejected this "open skies" proposal, calling it "a very transparent espionage device." Actually, although the meeting achieved few tangible results, the two leaders seemed to be working toward the same peaceful ends. Against Dulles's advice, Eisenhower even smiled when posing for pictures with the Soviets. "A new spirit of conciliation and co-operation" had been achieved, Ike announced. Un-

fortunately, "the spirit of Geneva" would not survive the confrontations ahead.

1956: The Dangerous Year

Neither Eisenhower nor Khrushchev was completely candid. While working for **"peaceful coexistence,"** both still had to satisfy critics at home. In Washington, Dulles continued to call for the "liberation" of Eastern Europe and to hint that the United States would rally behind any Soviet-dominated country that struck a blow for freedom. In reality, Eisenhower was not about to risk war with the Soviet Union to come to the defense of Poland, Hungary, or Czechoslovakia.

At the same time, Khrushchev made speeches that condemned Stalin's domestic crimes and foreign policy mistakes, endorsed "peaceful coexistence" with the West, and indicated a willingness to allow greater freedom behind the "Iron Curtain."

Poland took Khrushchev at his word and moved in a more liberal, anti-Stalinist direction. **Wladyslaw Gomulka,** who represented the nationalistic wing of the Polish Communist party, gained power in Poland and moved his country away from complete Soviet domination. Claiming that "there is more than one road to socialism," Gomulka announced that Poles would defend with their lives their new freedoms. Since Poland did not attempt to withdraw from the Soviet bloc, Khrushchev allowed Poland to move along its more liberal course.

What Poland had won, Hungary wanted—and perhaps a bit more. On October 23, 1956, students and workers took to the streets in Budapest loudly demanding changes. They knocked over a gigantic statue of Stalin and desecrated it with freedom slogans and graffiti. As in Poland, they forced a political change. Independent Communist Imre Nagy replaced a Stalinist leader. The Soviets peacefully recognized the new government. Pressing his luck, Nagy then announced that he planned to pull Hungary out of the Warsaw Pact—the Soviet-dominated defense community created in response to the signing of the NATO Pact—and allow opposition political parties.

Khrushchev sent Soviet tanks and soldiers into Budapest to crush the **Hungarian revolution,** which he now termed a "counter-revolution" and the work of "fascist reactionary elements." Students with bricks and hastily made Molotov cocktails were no match for the Red Army. The Soviets kidnapped Nagy (and later executed him), killed hundreds of demonstrators, and brutally restored their control over Hungary. All the while the Eisenhower administration just watched, demonstrating that the notion of "liberation" was mere rhetoric, not policy. Ike even refused a CIA request to parachute weapons and

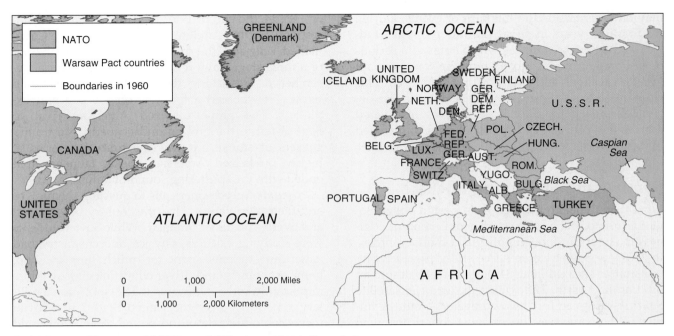

Cold War Alliances: NATO and Warsaw Pact Countries

supplies to the Hungarian freedom fighters. Hungary, said Ike, was "as inaccessible to us as Tibet."

Actually, at the time of the Soviet move into Budapest, Eisenhower was more concerned with the troubled Western alliance. The source of the problem was Egypt, whose nationalistic leader, President **Gamal Abdel Nasser,** was struggling to remain neutral in the Cold War. The United States had attempted to win Nasser's favor by promising to finance the construction of the Aswan High Dam on the Nile. But when Nasser recognized the People's Republic of China and pursued amicable relations with the Soviet Union, the Eisenhower administration withdrew the proposed loan. Neither Dulles nor Eisenhower was happy with Nasser's fence-sitting diplomacy.

Nasser struck back. On July 26, he nationalized the Suez Canal, the waterway linking the oil-rich Gulf of Suez and the Mediterranean. Half of Western Europe's oil came through the Suez Canal, which Ike believed was essential to the security of Western Europe. "And it will be run by Egyptians," Nasser added in an emotional message to the world. If Eisenhower was upset, British and French leaders were outraged, loudly claiming that the seizure threatened their Middle Eastern oil supplies. Eisenhower counseled caution, but Britain, France, and Israel resorted to "drastic actions." On October 29, Israel invaded Egypt and Britain and France used the hostilities as a pretext to seize the Suez Canal.

Eisenhower was furious. He told Dulles to inform the Israelis that "goddamn it, we're going to apply sanctions, we're going to the United Nations, we're going to do everything that there is so we can stop this thing."

Ike stood on the high ground, uncomfortably aligned with the Soviet Union. Without law there can be no peace, he claimed, adding, "and there can be no law—if we were to invoke one code of international conduct for those who oppose us—and another for our friends." Cut off from American support and faced with angry Soviet threats, Britain, France, and Israel halted their operations on November 6, the same day Eisenhower overwhelmingly defeated Adlai Stevenson and was reelected for a second term.

Taken together, the Hungarian revolution and the **Suez Canal crisis** strained America's relations with both the Soviet Union and Western Europe. "The spirit of Geneva" was being replaced by a more hostile mood. Nowhere was this better seen than in the 1956 Olympic Games, held in Melbourne, Australia, only two weeks after the November incidents. Egypt, Lebanon, and Iraq refused to take part in any games that included Britain, France, and Israel. And in the water polo competition, a match between the Soviet Union and Hungary quickly deteriorated into a form of aquatic warfare. The contest had to be halted before its official end, as the pool ran red with blood.

The Troubled Second Term

In foreign affairs, Eisenhower's second term was less successful than his first. Although he restrained military spending and shrewdly utilized information gathered by U-2 spy missions, his actions received more criticism at home and abroad. Age and health may have contributed to this turn of events. During his first four years in office, Ike suffered a heart attack and a bout with ileitis, which entailed a serious operation. During his second term, he was more apt to take vacations and play golf and bridge with his close friends. John Foster Dulles's health was also declining. During the Suez crisis doctors discovered that he had cancer. Acute physical pain punctuated his last years as secretary of state and he died in 1959.

Sputnik and Sputtering Rockets

More than ill health plagued Ike's foreign policy. Soviet technological advances created a mood of edginess in American foreign policy and military circles. In 1957 the Soviet Union successfully placed a tiny transmitter encased in a 184-pound steel ball into an orbit around earth. They called the artificial satellite *Sputnik*—Russian for "fellow traveler"—but the humor of the name was lost on most Americans, who were too concerned about Soviet rocket advances to laugh.

Less than one month later, the Soviet Union launched its second *Sputnik,* this one built on a larger and grander scale. It weighed 1120 pounds, contained instruments for scientific research, and carried a small dog named Laika who was wired with devices to gauge the effects of extragravitational flight on animal functions. If the first *Sputnik* demonstrated that the Soviets had gained the high ground, the second indicated that they intended to go higher and to place men in space.

Before the end of 1957, the United States tried to respond with a satellite launch of its own. Code-named *Vanguard,* the satellite was placed on the top of a three-stage navy rocket that was ignited on December 6. Describing the "blast off," a historian wrote, "It wobbled a few feet off the pad and exploded. The grapefruit-sized American rival to *Sputnik* fell to the ground and beeped its last amid geysers of smoke." It was the first of a series of highly publicized American rocket launches that ended with the sputtering sound of failure.

Sputnik forced Americans to question themselves and their own values. Had the country become soft and overly consumer oriented? While Soviet students were studying calculus, physics, and chemistry, had American students spent too much time in shop, home economics, and driver education classes? More importantly, did *Sputnik* give the Soviet Union a military superiority over the United States? If a Soviet rocket could put a thousand-pound ball in orbit could the same rocket armed with a nuclear warhead hit a target in the United States? Such questions disturbed ordinary Americans and U.S. policy-makers alike.

In truth, Americans overrated the importance of *Sputnik.* It was not all that it seemed. As German-born Wernher von Braun, one of America's leading rocket scientists, would later demonstrate, launching a satellite was no great accomplishment. It simply took rockets with great thrust. Delivering a warhead to a specific target was quite another matter. That entailed sophisticated guidance systems, which the Soviet Union had certainly not developed.

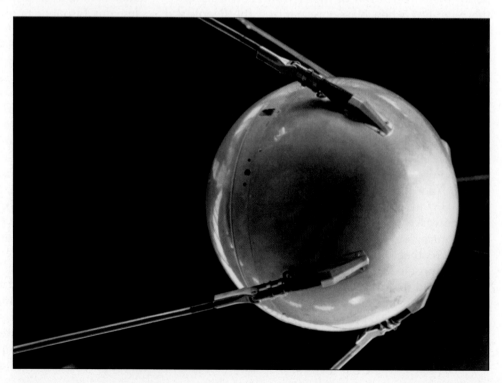

The Soviet Union's launch of *Sputnik I,* the world's first artificial satellite, on October 4, 1957, alarmed Americans who feared that the United States was falling behind the USSR in science, technology, and military preparedness. Four months after the *Sputnik I* launch, the United States successfully sent an *Explorer* satellite into space. In 1958 the U.S. Congress established the National Aeronautics and Space Administration (NASA) to supervise the nation's space program.

Sputnik then did not demonstrate Soviet technological superiority. It did, however, indicate the willingness of Soviet leaders to place military advancement ahead of the physical well-being of their citizens. As a French journalist noted, the price of *Sputnik* was "millions of pots and shoes lacking." The Soviet Union lagged behind the West in diet, health care, education, housing, clothing, and transportation.

American policy-makers reacted to the illusion of Soviet success. Congress appropriated more money for "defense-related" research and funneled more dollars into higher education in the United States. In fact, *Sputnik* was a tremendous boon for education. In an attempt to improve science and mathematics skills, Congress passed the **National Defense Education Act** (1958) to help finance the undergraduate and graduate educations of promising students. The Eisenhower administration jumped into the "space race," determined to be the swiftest. A leading historian of space measured the success of Eisenhower's effort by noting, "More new starts and technical leaps occurred in the years before 1960 than in any comparable span. Every space booster and every strategic missile in the American arsenal, prior to . . . the 1970s, date from these years."

Third World Challenges

If *Sputnik* was largely an illusionary challenge, nationalist movements in the Third World created more serious problems. Eisenhower's response to such movements varied from case to case. On the one hand, he opposed Britain and France's efforts to use naked physical aggression to whip Egypt into line. On the other hand, Ike employed covert CIA operations to achieve his foreign policy goals. In 1953 the CIA planned and executed a coup d'état which replaced a popularly elected government in Iran with a pro-American regime headed by Shah Mohammad Reza Pahlavi. One year later the CIA masterminded the overthrow of a leftist government in Guatemala and replaced it with an unpopular but strongly pro-American government. In 1958, Ike ordered marines from America's Sixth Fleet into Lebanon after Lebanese Moslems threatened a revolt against the Beirut government dominated by the Christian minority. But the short-term benefits of these CIA activities came with long-term costs. Increasingly, the United States became identified with unpopular, undemocratic, and intolerant right-wing regimes. Such actions tarnished America's image in the Third World.

The problems of Eisenhower's approach toward the Third World were clearly seen in his handling of the **Cuban Revolution.** In 1959, revolutionary **Fidel Castro** overthrew Fulgencio Batista, a right-wing dictator who had encouraged American investments in

Cuba at the expense of the Cuban people. Before the revolution, in fact, American companies owned 90 percent of Cuban mining operations, 80 percent of its utilities, and 40 percent of its sugar operations. Castro quickly set about to change the situation. He confiscated land and properties in Cuba owned by Americans, executed former Batista officials, built hospitals and schools, ended racial segregation, improved workers' wages, and moved leftward. Before long, Castro had begun to jail writers and critics, hold public executions, postpone elections, and condemn the United States as the "vulture . . . feeding on humanity."

Instead of waiting for Cuba's anti-American feelings to subside, Eisenhower decided to move against Castro. He gave the CIA permission to plan an attack on Cuba by a group of anti-Castro exiles, a plan that would culminate with the disastrous Bay of Pigs invasion (see Chapter 28). As one of his last acts as president, in 1961 Eisenhower severed diplomatic relations with Cuba. Such actions only increased Castro's anti-American resolve and further drove him into the arms of the Soviet Union.

Ultimately, the Truman and Eisenhower brands of containment were unsuccessful in dealing with nationalistic independence movements. Such movements dominated the post–World War II world. Between 1944 and 1974, for example, 78 countries won their independence. These included more than one billion people, or close to one-third of the world's population. By using a political yardstick to evaluate these movements, American presidents since Truman have made critical mistakes that have lowered the image of the United States in the Third World and given ammunition to Third World politicians who have pandered to anti-American emotions.

Not with a Bang, But a Whimper

Going into his last year in office, Eisenhower hoped to improve on the foreign policy record of his second term. Since his last meeting with Khrushchev in Geneva, the Cold War had intensified. In particular, the Soviets were once again threatening to cut off Western access to West Berlin, an action Eisenhower feared might lead to a nuclear war. To solve the problem—or at least to neutralize it—Eisenhower invited Khrushchev to visit the United States. The Soviet leader toured Iowa farms, visited Hollywood, and was generally warmly received by the American people. Turning to politics, he spent two days in private talks with Eisenhower at Camp David, where the two agreed to a formal summit meeting set for May 1960 in Paris.

The two world leaders never again had serious talks. Just before the meeting the Soviets shot down an American **U-2 spy plane** over their territory. So sophisticated was the plane's surveillance equipment, it could read a newspaper headline from 10 miles above the earth's surface or take pictures of the earth's surface 125 miles wide and 3000 miles long. During the previous few years, U-2 missions had kept Eisenhower abreast of Soviet military developments and convinced him that *Sputnik* posed no military threat to the United States. Nevertheless, the existence of such planes was a military secret, and U-2 pilots had strict orders to self-destruct their planes rather than be forced down in enemy territory. (For crash landings in neutral countries, the pilots carried a silk banner with the same statement in 14 languages: "I bear no malice toward your people. If you help me you will be rewarded.")

Assuming that the pilot had followed orders, Eisenhower responded to the Soviet charges of spying by publicly announcing that the Soviets had shot down a weather plane that had blown off course. Unfortunately for Ike, the pilot, **Francis Gary Powers,** had not followed orders, and the Soviets had him and the wreckage of his plane. Trying to save the summit, Khrushchev offered Eisenhower a way to save face. The Soviet leader indicated that he was sure that Eisenhower had not known about the flights. Eisenhower, however, accepted full personal responsibility and refused to apologize for actions he deemed were in defense of America. Rather than appear soft himself, Khrushchev refused to engage in the Paris summit.

Eisenhower's presidency ended on this note of failure—a chance to improve Soviet-American relations had been lost. But this end to his presidency should not obscure his positive accomplishments. He had ended one war, kept America out of several others, limited military spending, and presided over seven and a half years of relative peace. Like George Washington, when Eisenhower left office he issued warnings to America about possible future problems. In particular, he noted, the "military-industrial complex"—an alliance between government and business—could threaten the democratic process in the country. As Eisenhower remarked early in his presidency, "Every gun that is made, every warship launched, every rocket fired signifies, in the final sense, a theft from those who hunger and are not fed, those who are cold and are not clothed."

WE SHALL OVERCOME

When Dwight Eisenhower took office in early 1953 almost everywhere in the United States racism—often institutionalized, sometimes less formal—was the order of the day. Below the Mason-Dixon line it reached its most virulent form in the Jim Crow laws that gov-

erned the everyday existence of southern blacks. Whites framed the **Jim Crow laws** to separate the races and to demonstrate to all the superiority of whites and the inferiority of African Americans. Jim Crow dictated that whites and blacks eat in separate restaurants, drink from separate water fountains, sleep in separate hotels, and learn in separate schools.

Jim Crow subjected African Americans to daily degradation and soul-destroying humiliation. Blacks had to give way on sidewalks to whites, tip their hats, and speak respectfully. African Americans addressed whites of all ages as Mr., Mrs., or Miss; whites addressed African Americans of all ages by their first names. Although the underpinning of the Jim Crow laws was the "separate but equal" doctrine enunciated in *Plessy v. Ferguson* (1896), both blacks and whites realized that subjugation, not equality, was the object of the laws. Jim Crow even leaped over national boundaries. When a waitress at a Howard Johnson's in Dover, Delaware, refused to serve a glass of orange juice to the finance minister of Ghana, America's image abroad suffered.

North of Dixie the situation was not much better. To be sure, rigid Jim Crow laws did not exist, but, informally, blacks were excluded from the better schools, neighborhoods, and jobs. Whites argued that the development of ghettos was a natural process, not some sort of racist agreement between white realtors. Such, however, was not the case. **William Levitt,** the most famous post–World War II suburban housing developer, attempted to keep African Americans out of his developments. A passage in the New York Levittown covenant read: "No dwelling shall be used . . . by members of other than the Caucasian race, but the employment and maintenance of other than Caucasian domestic servants shall be permitted." Even after the courts struck down such restrictions, Levitt instructed his realtors not to sell to blacks. Indeed, *Shelley v. Kraemer* (1948), the court case that stated that state courts could not uphold housing restrictions, only declared such restrictions legally unenforceable; it did not outlaw such practices per se. To break a racially motivated housing restriction, a black had to take the initiative and force a court test.

When Ike left office in 1961, segregation remained largely unchanged. In that year, John Howard Griffin's book *Black Like Me* gave white America a stark look at the daily life of millions of African Americans. After shaving his head and darkening his skin chemically, Griffin traveled about the South to experience what it was like to live as a black in Jim Crow America. He described the humiliating search for hotels, restaurants, and restrooms in a land where for blacks unequal facilities were a constant and no facilities always a real possibility. He also described how blacks came to each other's aid and support. A national bestseller that sold

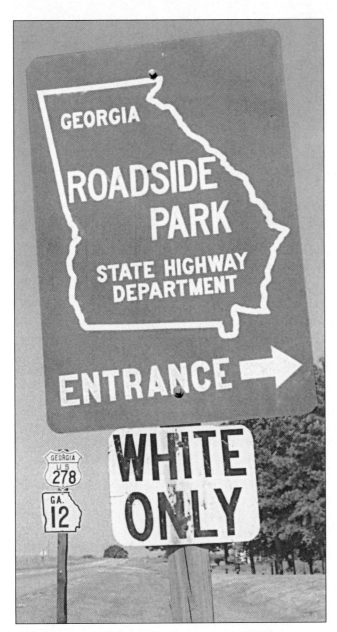

Jim Crow laws were not limited to restaurants or hotels in cities. This roadside sign shows that segregation was common in areas outside southern metropolitan locations.

over five million copies, Griffin's tale shocked and shamed many whites who never realized—or even considered—the plight of black Americans.

During Eisenhower's years in office, however, African Americans did make some significant strides in their quest for civil rights. In particular, during the decade after 1954 African Americans won a series of legal victories that in theory if not always in practice buried Jim Crow. They were years of joy and years of sadness, when the best as well as the worst aspects of the American character were clearly visible.

Taking Jim Crow to Court

World War II underscored the yawning gap between the promise and reality of life in America. Fighting against Nazi racist theories helped to draw attention to real racial problems at home. At the start of the war, defense industry managers refused to hire African Americans, and the races were segregated in the armed services. The war and a threat by African American leader A. Philip Randolph to organize a protest march on Washington led to some changes. Executive Order 8802 prohibited discrimination in the war industries. But the outbreak of the Detroit race riot during the hot summer of 1943 demonstrated that African Americans were dissatisfied with racial conditions at home. "Our war is not against Hitler and Europe," claimed one African American columnist, "but against the Hitlers in America."

After the war conditions improved at a snail's pace. With an eye on African American Democratic northern voters, Truman established the President's Committee on Civil Rights, which issued a report that most white politicians ignored. While Truman called for "fair employment throughout the federal establishment" and ordered the racial desegregation of the armed services, southern politicians proclaimed the need to return to the embrace of Jim Crow. "No Negro will vote in Georgia for the next four years," Eugene Talmadge promised after he was elected governor of Georgia. And in Congress, Southerners like Senator Theodore G. Bilbo railed against Truman's moderate racial reforms. Opposing Truman's plan for universal military training, Bilbo exhorted, "If you draft Negro boys into the army, give them three good meals a day and let them shoot craps and drink liquor around the barracks for a year, they won't be worth a tinker's dam thereafter."

By the late 1940s African Americans had realized that they would have to lead the fight against racial injustice. In the early years of the battle, the NAACP spearheaded the struggle. But the organization faced a number of problems, both within and outside the African American community. For example, many believed the NAACP was racist and elitist. The organization was staffed by educated middle-class African Americans who seemed out of touch with the majority of their race. Worse yet, many African Americans charged that the NAACP was staffed by light-skinned blacks because it accepted the theory that mulattos were more aggressive, enterprising, and ambitious than their pure-blooded counterparts.

Outside of the African American community, the NAACP encountered a hostile white society. In Congress, southern Democrats—there were few southern Republicans—opposed any assault on segregation—the prevailing form of institutionalized racism.

Integration in Sports

On April 18, 1946, the sports world focused on a baseball field in Jersey City, an industrial wasteland on the banks of the Passaic River. It was the opening day for the Jersey City Giants of the International League. Their opponents were the Montreal Royals, the Brooklyn Dodgers' leading farm team. Playing second base for the Royals was **Jackie Roosevelt Robinson,** a pigeon-toed, highly competitive, marvelously talented African American athlete. The stadium was filled with curious and excited spectators, and in the press box sportswriters from New York, Philadelphia, Baltimore, and cities further west fidgeted with their typewriters. It was not just another season-opening game. Professional baseball, America's national game, was about to be integrated.

Since the late nineteenth century professional baseball and most other professional team sports had prohibited interracial competition. White athletes played for the highest salaries, in the best stadiums, before the most spectators. During the same years black teams barnstormed the country playing where they could and accepting what was offered. For them, the pay was low, the stadiums rickety, and the playing conditions varied between bad and dangerous. The *Plessy v. Ferguson* ideal of "separate but equal" was a cruel joke.

During the period of forced segregation, whites stereotyped African American athletes. Since colonial times whites had maintained that blacks were instinctive rather than thoughtful, physical rather than intellectual, complacent rather than ambitious. As athletes, whites believed blacks were physically gifted but lazy, undisciplined, and wholly lacking in competitive drive. Disregarding the success of black athletes in individual sports whites clung to the racist theory that nature had fashioned blacks to laugh and sing and dance and play, but not to sacrifice, train, work, compete, and win.

The most successful African American athletes and teams catered to these stereotypes. The Harlem Globetrotters, for example, played the role of Sambo in sweats. Started in 1927 by white Chicago entrepreneur Abe Saperstein, the all-black Harlem Globetrotters basketball team presented African American athletes as wide-eyed, toothy, camera-mugging clowns. White audiences loved their antics—Marques Haynes dribbling circles around his hopeless white opponents while the rest of the Trotters stretched out on the floor feigning sleep; Meadowlark Lemon hiding the basketball under his jersey and sneaking down the court to make a basket; Goose Tatum slam-dunking while reading a comic book; all of them cavorting around with deflated, lopsided, or balloon balls, throwing confetti-filled water buckets on an indulgent crowd, and deviously getting away with every conceivable infraction of the rules.

Saperstein insisted that "his boys" conform off as well as on the court. As a Trotter veteran told new teammate Connie Hawkins, "Abe don't care what you do with colored, but don't let him catch you with no white broads . . . And don't let him see you with a Cadillac. He don't stand for that either." Nor did Saperstein allow his players to contradict whites. He wanted only "happy darkies," not "uppity niggers," on his team.

The Indianapolis Clowns were the Harlem Globetrotters of baseball. They played in grass skirts and body paint and engaged in comedy as much as baseball. Pregame routines included acrobatics and dancing, exaggerated black English, minstrel slapstick, and grinning, always lots of grinning. How could any reasonable person expect major league performances out of people playing baseball in grass skirts and war paint?

Jackie Robinson came to bat in the first inning. His very presence had ended segregation in "organized baseball." Now he wanted to strike a blow against the racist stereotyping. Nervous, he later recalled that his palms seemed "too moist to grip the bat." He didn't even swing at the first five pitches. On the sixth pitch he hit a bouncing ball to the shortstop who easily threw him out. It was a start of sorts.

In the third inning Robinson took his second turn at bat. With runners on first and second, he lashed out at the first pitch and hit it over the left-field fence 330 feet away. In the press box Wendell Smith and Joe Bostic, two African American reporters for the *Amsterdam News,* "laughed and smiled. . . . Our hearts beat just a little faster and the thrill ran through us like champagne bubbles." According to another account, among the white sportswriters "there were some very long faces."

Robinson wasn't through for the day. In the fifth inning he had a bunt single, stole second, advanced to third on a ground ball, and, faking an attempt to steal home, forced a balk and scored. It was a virtuoso performance. During the remainder of the game he had two more hits, another stolen base, and forced a second balk. In the field he was tough, intense, and smart, a reverse image of the stereotypical black athlete. It was a fine day for Robinson and his supporters. "Baseball took up the cudgel of democracy," Bostic wrote, "and an unassuming, but superlative Negro boy ascended the heights of excellence to prove the rightness of the experiment. And prove it in the only correct crucible for such an experiment—the crucible of white hot competition."

The success of Jackie Robinson in baseball led to the integration of the other major professional sports. In 1946 the Cleveland Rams moved their football franchise to Los Angeles, and to boost ticket sales they signed African Americans Kenny Washington and Woody Strode, both of whom

had played football with Robinson at UCLA. Professional football thus became the next to be integrated. In 1950 the Boston Celtics of the National Basketball Association signed Chuck Cooper of Duquesne to a professional contract, and the New York Knicks signed Nat "Sweetwater" Clifton away from the Harlem Globetrotters, over Abe Saperstein's bitter protests. The same year, the United States Lawn Tennis Association allowed African Americans to compete at Forest Hills. In a relatively short time integration came to American professional sports.

The process was not without individual pain. Robinson especially became the object of hate mail, death threats, and racial slurs. Opposition runners spiked him and pitchers threw at him. Off the field he faced a life of segregated restaurants, clubs, theaters, and neighborhoods. Patient, witty, and quick to forgive, he endured extraordinary humiliation. He became an American hero, but he paid dearly. Throughout the 1946 and 1947 seasons Robinson was plagued by headaches,

bouts of depression, nausea, and nightmares. Talking about the pressures on her husband, Rachel Robinson recalled, "There were the stresses of just knowing that you were pulling a big weight of a whole lot of people on your back . . . I think Jackie felt . . . that there would be serious consequences if he didn't succeed and that one of them would be that nobody would try again for a long time." Of course, other African American players also confronted trials on and off the field, but as Robinson's teammate Roy Campanella said, "nothing compared to what Jackie was going through."

Integration in sports preceded integration in society at large. But in both sports and the civil rights movement, racial gains were paid for by individuals willing to risk serious hardships. Change seldom came easily and the struggle never ended quickly. In baseball, for example, as late as 1988 many white bureaucrats still resisted the idea of African American managers, resorting to the same racial stereotyping that had plagued America for over 350 years.

Given this racial climate, the NAACP moved cautiously. Instead of attacking segregation head-on and demanding full equality, the organization chose to chip away at the legal edges of Jim Crow. The separate but equal doctrine was particularly vulnerable. In *Missouri ex rel Gaines* (1938), *Sweatt v. Painter* (1950), and *McLaurin v. Board of Regents* (1950), the NAACP lawyers demonstrated the impossibility, even the absurdity, of applying the separate but equal yardstick to graduate education and law schools. In all three cases, the Supreme Court agreed. If, the court implied, separate but equal educational systems were to be continued, then states had to pay more than lip service to equality.

In grade school and high school education, just as in graduate education, the South translated separate but equal to read "separate and highly unequal." In South Carolina's Clarendon County, for example, 75 percent of the students were African American, but the white minority received 60 percent of the educational funds. On the average, the county spent $179 per year on each white student and $43 per year on each African American student. Educational resources were separate, but highly unequal.

Intellectual and financial considerations were not the only factors that precluded equality. Psychologists argued that segregation instilled feelings of inferiority among African American children. Psychologist Kenneth Clark conducted a simple test with African American children attending segregated schools. He showed the children two dolls, one black and the other white. In one case, of the 16 children tested, 10 said they liked the white doll better, 11 added that the black doll looked "bad," and 9 remarked that the white doll looked "nice." Recalling the tests, Clark noted, "The most disturbing question—and the one that really made me, even as a scientist, upset—was the final question: 'Now show me the doll that's most like you.' Many of the children became emotionally upset when they had to identify with the doll they had rejected. These children saw themselves as inferior, and they accepted the inferiority as part of reality." When asked that question, one child even smiled and pointed to the black doll: "That's a nigger. I'm a nigger."

It was inhumane to continue such psychological damage, the NAACP concluded. In 1952 the NAACP consolidated a series of cases under the name of the first case—***Brown v. Board of Education of Topeka***—which challenged the very existence of the separate but equal doctrine. The Supreme Court listened to the arguments and began its extended deliberation. Then in September 1953 Chief Justice Fred M. Vinson, who seemed to be leaning against ending segregation, died of a heart attack.

President Eisenhower named **Earl Warren** to take Vinson's place. It was a political, not an ideological,

appointment. Formerly governor of California, Warren had helped Ike win the Republican nomination in 1952. Appointment as Chief Justice of the United States was a fine reward. On the surface, minorities had little reason to suspect that Warren would be on their side. During World War II he had been active in the relocation of 100,000 Japanese Americans into internment camps; but in the years after that action, Warren realized that his action had been a mistake. The *Brown* case offered him a second chance.

After working to achieve unanimity in the court, Warren read the Court's decision on May 17, 1954. "Does segregation of children in public schools solely on the basis of race, even though the physical facilities and other tangible factors may be equal, deprive children of the minority group of equal educational opportunities?" Warren asked. "We believe it does," he answered. "To separate them from others of similar age and qualifications solely because of their race generates a feeling of inferiority as to their status in the community that may affect their hearts and minds in a way very unlikely ever to be undone." In public education, he concluded, the "separate but equal" doctrine has no place. "Separate educational facilities are inherently unequal."

The *Chicago Defender* labeled the *Brown* decision "a second emancipation proclamation," and the *Washington Post* called it "a new birth of freedom." But such Court decisions have to be enforced. As Charles Houston, a leading NAACP lawyer, remarked, "Nobody needs to explain to a Negro the difference between the law in the books and the law in action."

A Failure of Leadership

A year after the *Brown* decision, the Supreme Court ruled that schools should desegregate "with all deliberate speed." It was a vague, cautious, legally meaningless phrase. Perhaps it was the price Warren had to pay for the previous year's unanimous verdict. In any case, the second decision placed the burden of desegregation into the hands of local, state, and national leaders. If the process was to be accomplished with the minimum amount of conflict, those leaders would have to be firm in their resolve to see justice done. Such, however, would not be the case.

On the national level, Eisenhower moved uncomfortably and cautiously on the issue of civil rights and desegregation. He did not see racism as a great moral issue, and believed that the *Brown* decision had been a mistake, for which he blamed Earl Warren. He later asserted that the appointment of Warren had been the "biggest damn fool mistake" he had ever made. When questioned about the decision in 1954, he claimed, "I don't believe you can change the hearts of men with laws or decisions."

The brand of Ike's leadership and his ambitions for the Republican party further weakened his response. His behind-the-scenes approach—the "hidden-hand" style—led him to avoid speaking out clearly and forcefully on the subject. Moral outrage was not his style. In addition, he was popular in the South and harbored hopes of bringing that section of the country into the Republican party. Finally, his commitment to integration was lukewarm at best, and he placed controlling military spending above desegregating the South. Therefore, instead of deploring the killing of Emmett Till and other atrocities by southern whites, Eisenhower kept quiet.

In the South, Eisenhower's silence was often as deadly as bullets. If Eisenhower had acted decisively in support of the *Brown v. Board of Education* decision—if he had placed the full weight of his office behind desegregation—there is some evidence that the South would have complied peacefully with the verdict. By not acting forcefully, however, Eisenhower strengthened the position of Southerners who equated desegregation with death. "Ending segregation," Governor James F. Byrnes of South Carolina said, "would mark the beginning of the end of civilization in the South as we have known it."

The **Little Rock crisis** demonstrated the failure of national and state leadership. In 1957 in Little Rock, Arkansas, school officials were ordered to desegregate. As they prepared to do so, Governor **Orval Faubus,** locked in a reelection fight, intervened.

Angry whites taunt, jeer, shout, and threaten black high school student 15-year-old Elizabeth Eckford as she attempts to enter all-white Central High School in Little Rock, Arkansas.

Announcing that any integration attempt would disrupt public order, he sent in the National Guard to prevent black children from entering Central High. While Eisenhower quietly tried to maneuver behind the scenes, a crisis was brewing. On the morning of September 23, 1957, when black children attempted to attend school, they were inhospitably greeted by an angry mob chanting, "two, four, six, eight, we ain't going to integrate."

Television turned the ugly episode into a national drama. Millions of Americans for the first time witnessed violent racism, as angry whites moved around the defenseless children like hungry sharks. Television gave a face to racism, a concept that for many white Americans was still an abstraction. It showed the reality of hate and racism in the South. For the first but not last time, television aided the cause of civil rights by conveying the human suffering caused by racism.

To restore order, Eisenhower federalized the Arkansas National Guard and sent one thousand paratroopers from the 101st Airborne Division to Little Rock. It was the first time since Reconstruction that a president had ordered troops to the South. Although their presence desegregated Central High School in 1957, the following year Faubus closed Little Rock's public schools, declaring "I stand now and always in opposition to integration by force or at bayonet point." Taken together, Faubus's short-sighted political moves and Eisenhower's refusal to take action until public order had been disrupted created a crisis that more thoughtful leadership might have avoided.

The Word from Montgomery

This failure on the part of white leaders convinced African Americans that court orders would not magically produce equal rights. The fight would be difficult, the march long. Many realized this even before the Little Rock crisis. On a cold afternoon in 1955 in Montgomery, Alabama, **Rosa Parks,** a well-respected African American seamstress who was active in the NAACP, took a significant stride toward equality. She boarded a bus and sat in the first row of the "colored" section. The white section of the bus quickly filled, and according to Jim Crow rules, African Americans were expected to give up their seats rather than force whites—male or female—to stand. The time came for Mrs. Parks to give up her seat. She stayed seated. When told by the bus driver to get up or he would call the police, she said, "You may do that." Later she recalled that the act of defiance was "just something I had to do." The bus stopped, the driver summoned the police, and Rosa Parks was arrested.

African American Montgomery rallied to Mrs. Parks's side. Like her, they were tired of riding in the back of the bus, tired of giving up their seats to whites, tired of having their lives restricted by segregation laws. Local leaders decided to organize a boycott of Montgomery's white-owned and white-operated bus system. They hoped that economic pressure would force changes that court decisions could not. For the next 381 days, more than 90 percent of Montgomery's African American citizens participated in a heroic and successful demonstration against racial segregation. Among African Americans, the common attitude toward the protest was voiced by an elderly woman when a black leader offered her a ride. "No," she replied, "my feets is tired, but my soul is rested."

To lead the boycott, Montgomery African Americans turned to the new minister of the Dexter Avenue Baptist Church, a young man named **Martin Luther King, Jr.** Reared in Atlanta, the son of a respected and financially secure minister, King had been educated at Morehouse College, Crozier Seminary, and Boston University, from which he earned a doctorate in theology. King was an intellectual, excited by ideas and deeply influenced by the philosophical writings of Henry David Thoreau and Mahatma Gandhi as well as by the teachings of Jesus, all of whom believed in the power of nonviolent, direct action.

King's words as well as his ideas stirred people's souls. At the start of the Montgomery boycott he told his followers:

> There comes a time when people get tired. We are here this evening to say to those who have mistreated us so long that we are tired—tired of being segregated and humiliated, tired of being kicked about by the brutal feet of oppression . . . We've come here tonight to be saved from the patience that makes us patient with anything less than freedom and justice . . . If you protest courageously and yet with dignity and Christian love, in the history books that are written in future generations, historians will have to pause and say "there lived a great people—a black people—who injected a new meaning and dignity into the veins of civilization."

In King, civil rights had found a genuine spokesman, one who preached a doctrine of change guided by the Christian ideal of love and not by racial hatred. "In our protest," he observed, "there will be no cross burnings. No white person will be taken from his home by a hooded Negro mob and brutally murdered. There will be no threats and no intimidation."

The success of the Montgomery boycott inspired nonviolent protests elsewhere in the South. Increasingly, young African Americans took the lead. Violence and biased law enforcement did not stop the protesters. Indeed, within a few months of the successful conclusion of the Montgomery boycott, demonstrations erupted in 54 cities in 9 states. The protesters were arrested, jailed, beaten, and even knocked off their feet by high-pressure fire hoses, but still they pressed on.

The protests were widely reported in the country's newspapers and televised nightly on the news shows. Americans everywhere were confronted with the stark reality of segregation. Ignorance of the situation became an impossibility; and as the violence continued, national pressure mounted on white politicians to take decisive action. By the early 1960s the word from Montgomery had reinforced the *Brown* decision. It was time for freedom to become a reality. (See Chapter 29 for further discussion of civil rights.)

THE SOUNDS OF CHANGE

Beginning in the 1970s, American advertisers started to market a new commodity—the fifties. They marketed it as a Golden Decade, a carefree time before the assassination of John F. Kennedy, the Vietnam War, and Watergate. According to the popular myth, kids in the 1950s thought "dope" referred to a dull-witted person, parents married for life, and major family problems revolved around whether or not sis had a date for the prom. This image of the decade has taken different forms. *Happy Days* presented it on television; *American Graffiti* detailed it on the silver screen. It was an age of innocence, tranquility, and static charm. In truth, however, that carefully packaged Golden Decade never existed. Instead, the decade was alive with dynamic, creative tensions.

Father Knows Best

The stock television situation comedy (sitcom) of the 1950s centered on a white family with a happily married husband and wife and two—or sometimes three—well-adjusted children. Most often, the family lived in a white, two-story suburban home, from which the father ventured daily to his white-collar job. Mothers stayed home to tend the children. *Father Knows Best* was the classic example of this genre. It ran from 1954 to 1962 and signaled an optimistic outlook through its title song, "Just Around the Corner There's a Rainbow in the Sky."

The picture these sitcoms presented of America was not entirely inaccurate. Starting after World War II, Americans moved steadily toward the suburbs, which during the 1950s grew six times faster than cities. Several factors contributed to this migration. The high price of urban real estate had driven industries out of the cities, and as always in American history, the population followed the jobs. By 1970 suburban areas had more manufacturing jobs than the central cities. In addition, developers were building abundant, inexpensive homes, which newly married

TABLE 27.1

Population of Metropolitan Areas, by Region, Size, and Race, 1950–1970

Year		Inner City	Suburbs	African American Population as Percent of Inner City	African American Population as Percent of Suburbs
1950	White	43,001,634	33,248,836		
	Black	6,194,948	1,736,521	12.5	4.9
	Other	216,210	102,531		
1970	White	49,430,443	71,148,286		
	Black	13,140,331	3,630,279	20.5	4.8
	Other	1,226,169	843,303		

Source: Data taken from *Historical Statistics of the United States,* Bicentennial Edition, vol. 1, p. 40.

couples, aided by VA and FHA loans, purchased. Of the 13 million homes constructed during the 1950s, 11 million were built in the suburbs.

Nor was the television image of a lily-white suburbia misleading. A far greater percentage of whites than African Americans moved to the suburbs. In 1950 African Americans were 12.5 percent of America's urban population and 4.9 percent of the country's suburban population. By 1970 the urban figure had climbed to 20.5 percent with the suburban number declining modestly to 4.8 percent. Housing and job restrictions worked to keep African Americans in the central cities while allowing whites to fill the suburban areas.

Even the image of the suburban housewife preoccupied with her husband and her family was socially sanctioned. American women in the 1950s had babies as never before. The population of the United States increased by under 10 million in the 1930s, 19 million in the 1940s, and a staggering 30 million in the 1950s. During the 1950s the nation's growth rate approached that of India. The bestsellers list indicated America's concern with children: between 1946 and 1976 the pocket edition of Dr. Benjamin Spock's *Baby and Child Care* sold over 23 million copies, ranking it behind only the Bible and the combined works of Mickey Spillane and Dr. Seuss.

During that age of remarkable fertility, popular writers glorified the role of the mother. The bestseller *Modern Woman: The Lost Sex* went as far as to say that an independent woman was "a contradiction in terms." The ideal woman, writers observed, was content being a wife and a mother or, in a word, a homemaker. "Women must boldly announce," wrote novelist Sloan Wilson, "that no job is more exacting, more necessary, or more rewarding than that of housewife and mother." In the 1950s women married younger and had children sooner than they had in the previous two decades.

The Other Side of the Coin

Father Knows Best and other shows portrayed an ideal world where serious problems seldom intrude and where life lacks complexity. In fact, the move to suburbia and the changes in family life forced Americans to reevaluate many of their beliefs. Cultural critics, for example, claimed that life in suburbia fostered mindless conformity. Lewis Mumford described suburbs as "a multitude of uniform, unidentifiable houses, lined up inflexibly, at uniform distances, on uniform roads, in a treeless communal wasteland, inhabited by people of the same class, the same income, the same age group."

Some writers feared the United States had become a country of unthinking consumers driven by

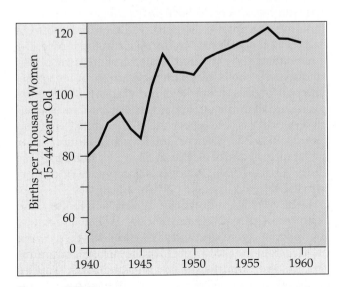

FIGURE 27.1
American Birthrate, 1940–1960

THE PEOPLE SPEAK

Images and Illusions

In 1946, a few thousand Americans owned television sets. By 1950, TVs were in 5 million households, a number that increased at a rate of around 5 million a year for the rest of the decade. To some social critics, it was the culmination of what historian Daniel Boorstin called the "graphic revolution"—an ability to quickly transmit images through print, radio, film, and now television. In his 1961 book *The Image,* Boorstin illustrated how a culture suffused in quick images and illusions had transformed American life, with some very dire consequences.

> We expect the papers to be full of news. If there is no news visible to the naked eye, or to the average citizen, we still expect it to be there for the enterprising newsman. The successful reporter is one who can find a story, even if there is no earthquake or assassination or civil war. If he cannot find a story, then he must make one—by the questions he asks of public figures, by the surprising human interest he unfolds from some commonplace event, or by "the news behind the news." If all this fails, then he must give us a "think piece"—an embroidering of well-known facts, or a speculation about startling things to come.
>
> This change in our attitude toward "news" is not merely a basic fact about the history of American newspapers. It is a symptom of a revolutionary change in our attitude toward what happens in the world, how much of it is new, and surprising, and important. Toward how life can be enlivened, toward our power and the power of those who inform and educate and guide us, to provide synthetic happenings to make up for the lack of spontaneous events. Demanding more than the world can give us, we require that something be fabricated to make up for the world's deficiency. This is only one example of our demand for illusions.
>
> Many historical forces help explain how we have come to our present immoderate hopes. But there can be no doubt about what we now expect, nor that it is immoderate. Every American knows the anticipation with which he picks up his morning newspaper at breakfast or opens his evening paper before dinner, or listens to the newscasts every hour on the hour as he drives across country, or watches his favorite commentator on television interpret the events of the day. Many enterprising Americans are now at work to help us satisfy these expectations. Many might be put out of work if we should suddenly moderate our expectations. But it is we who keep them in business and demand that they fill our consciousness with novelties, that they play God for us.

Source: Reprinted with the permission of Scribner, a Division of Simon & Schuster from *The Image* by Daniel J. Boorstin. Copyright © 1961 Daniel J. Boorstin; copyright renewed 1989.

advertisers to desire only the latest gadget. Americans bought automobiles, houses, and electrical appliances as never before. Thirty percent more Americans owned homes in 1970 than in 1940. Between 1945 and 1960 the number of cars in the country increased by 133 percent and the use of electricity tripled. This consumerism fueled the tremendous economic growth between 1945 and 1970. Clearly, buying was good for the American economy, but was it beneficial to the individuals who spent more and more of their time in their cars and watching their televisions? Cultural observers despaired.

Some women also expressed frustration about their roles as wives and mothers. One poll of the 1934 graduates of the best women's colleges reported that one out of every three women felt unfulfilled. Although many women worked, cultural stereotyping prevented most of them from rising to the higher-paying, more prestigious positions. In addition, Betty Friedan, a leader in the women's rights movement, noted that women who did place a career above marriage or family were regarded as abnormal.

The problems of suburban life were explored in numerous films, novels, articles, and advice books. The film *Invasion of the Body Snatchers* (1956) is an outstanding example of the perceived fear that suburbia had created a nation of conformists. In the movie, the inhabitants of the town of Santa Mira are turned into emotionless shells by giant pods from outer space. The pod-people utterly lack individuality; as one explains, podism means being "reborn into an untroubled world, where everyone's the same." In that world, "there is no need for love or emotion." For such cultural critics as David Riesman, author of *The Lonely Crowd* (1955), America's acceptance of conformity threatened to make podism a reality.

The critics, however, overreacted to the **"suburban threat."** If the houses looked the same, the people were individuals—even if they often banded together to try to form suburban communities. In the suburbs, white working-class families could afford for the first time to purchase homes and live middle-class lives. This was a real accomplishment. The problems that critics observed in the sub-

The classic science fiction film *Invasion of the Body Snatchers* (1956) tells the story of the struggle of one man of conscience, small-town doctor Miles Bennell (Kevin McCarthy), to overcome the deadly menace taking over the earth. Critics interpreted that menace as any one of a number of ills plaguing American society in the early Cold War era—paranoia about communism, fear of McCarthyism, the spread of some indestructible malignant disease or germ, but most often as the loss of individuality and human emotion in a world that had succumbed to conformity and replaced humanity with technology and machinery.

urbs—the tendency toward conformity, cultural homogeneity, materialism, and anxiety over sex roles—were urban problems as well.

The Meaning of Elvis

The harshest critics of "suburban values" were American youths. Their criticism took different forms. Some of it was thoughtful and formalized, the result of the best efforts of young intellectuals. At other times it took a more visceral form, a protest that came from the gut rather than the mind. Of the second type, none was more widely embraced by youths—or roundly attacked by adults—than **rock and roll.**

Rock and roll was the bastard mulatto child of a heterogeneous American culture. It combined black rhythm and blues with white country music. It was made possible by the post–World War II demographic changes. The movement of Southerners to the cities of the upper South and North threw together different musical traditions and forged an entirely new sound. Its lyrics and heavy beat challenged the accepted standards of "good taste" in music. Confronting conventional morality, rock and roll was openly vulgar. The very term—"rock 'n' roll"—had long been used in blues songs to describe lovemaking, and early black rock-and-roll singers glorified physical relationships. Little Richard sang:

I'm gonna RIP IT UP!
I'm gonna rock it up!

I'm gonna shake it up. I'm gonna ball it up!
I'm gonna RIP IT UP and ball tonight.*

From its emergence in the early 1950s, rock and roll generated anger and criticism. In the South, white church groups attacked it as part of an NAACP plot to corrupt the morals of southern youths and foster integration. In Hartford, Connecticut, Dr. Francis J. Braceland described rock and roll as "a communicable disease, with music appealing to adolescent insecurity and driving teenagers to do outlandish things . . . It's cannibalistic and tribalistic." Particularly between 1954 and 1958, there were numerous crusades to ban rock and roll from the airways.

Most of the criticism of rock and roll focused on **Elvis Presley,** who more than any other artist most fully fused country music with rhythm and blues. In his first record, he gave the rhythm-and-blues song "That's All Right Mama" a country feel and the country classic "Blue Moon over Kentucky" a rhythm-and-blues swing. It was a unique exhibition of genius. In addition, Presley exuded sexuality. When he appeared on the Ed Sullivan Show, network executives instructed cameramen to avoid shots of Elvis's suggestive physical movements. Finally, Presley

---

Rip it Up Robert A. Blackwell/John S. Marascalco. Copyright © 1956. Renewed 1984 Venice Music Inc. All Rights Controlled and Administered by SBK Blackwood Music Inc. Under License from ATV Music (Venice). All Rights Reserved. International Copyright Secured. Used by Permission.

Elvis Presley, one of the great pioneers of rock-and-roll music, was the target of much controversy throughout his life.

upset segregationists by performing "race music." Head of Sun Records Sam Phillips had once claimed, "If I could find a white man who had the Negro sound and the Negro feel, I could make a million dollars." Presley was that white man.

In the end, however, the protests implicit in Elvis Presley and rock and roll were largely co-opted by middle-class American culture. Record producers, most of whom were white, smoothed the jagged edges of rock and roll. Sexually explicit recordings were rewritten and rerecorded—a process known as "covering"—by white performers and then sold to white youths. African American singer Joe Turner, for example, recorded "Shake, Rattle and Roll" for an African American audience. Its lyrics ran:

> Get out of that bed,
> And wash your face and hands.
> Get into the kitchen,
> Make some noise with the pots and pans.
> Well you wear low dresses,
> The sun comes shinin' through.
> I can't believe my eyes,
> That all of this belongs to you.*

The white group Bill Haley and the Comets "covered" the song for a white audience. The new version stated:

Shake, Rattle and Roll, words and music by Charles Calhoun. Copyright © 1954 (Renewed) Unichappel Music. (BMI). All Rights Reserved. Warner Bros. Publications, Miami, FL 33014.

> Get out in that kitchen,
> And rattle those pots and pans.
> Roll my breakfast
> 'Cause I'm a hungry man.
> You wear those dresses,
> Your hair done up so nice.
> You look so warm,
> But your heart is cold as ice.

In the second version all references to beds and bodies have been eliminated; by 1959 rock and roll had become an accepted part of mainstream American culture.

A Different Beat

Rock-and-roll artists never rejected the idea of success in America. If they challenged conventional sexual mores and tried to create a unique sound, they accepted the rewards of success in a capitalistic society. Elvis Presley translated success into a steady stream of Cadillacs and conventional, unchallenging films. Not all youth protests, however, were so easily absorbed into middle-class culture. The Beat movement, for example, questioned the values at the heart of that culture.

The **Beat generation** extolled the very thing that conventional Americans abhorred, and they rejected what the others prized. Beats scorned materialism,

Allen Ginsberg was educated at the University of California, Berkeley, and at Columbia University. His poetry expressed the Beat generation's dissatisfaction with conventional middle-class values.

traditional family life, religion, traditional sexuality, and politics. They renounced the American Dream. Instead, they valued spontaneity and intuition, searching for truth through Eastern mysticism and drugs. Although whites formed the rank and file of the Beat generation, they glorified the supposedly "natural" life of African Americans, a life representing (at least for whites) pure instinctual drives. They adopted African American music and the jive words of the black lexicon. Terms such as *cat, solid, chick, Big Apple,* and *square,* were all absorbed into the Beat vocabulary.

Allen Ginsberg was the leading poet of the Beat generation. A graduate of Columbia University, where he was influenced by the lifestyle of New York City lowlifes and artists, Ginsberg moved to San Francisco in the mid-1950s. There, surrounded by kindred souls, Ginsberg came to accept his homosexuality and preached a life based on experimentation. He also developed an authentic poetic voice. In 1955 he wrote "Howl," the prototypical Beat poem, while he was under the influence of drugs. "Howl" is a literary kaleidoscope, a breathless succession of stark images and passionate beliefs. In a unique but soon to be widely imitated style, Ginsberg declared,

> I saw the best minds of my generation
> destroyed by madness, starving hysterically
> naked,
> dragging themselves through the negro streets
> at dawn looking for an angry fix . . .

Ginsberg and Jack Kerouac, the leading Beat novelist, outraged adults but discovered followers on college campuses and in cities across America. They tapped an underground dissatisfaction with the prevailing blandness of conventional culture. In this, their appeal was similar to that of rock and roll. Both were scattering seeds that would bear fruit during the next decade.

CONCLUSION

Ike's America was both more and less than what it seemed. In foreign and domestic affairs, Eisenhower appeared to allow his subordinates to run the country, when in reality he made the important decisions. Whether it was national highways or the Middle East, Eisenhower's vision of order helped shape American policy. He was more influential than most Americans during the 1950s realized.

CHRONOLOGY OF KEY EVENTS

1944 GI Bill of Rights grants veterans financial aid for education and government loans for building houses and starting businesses

1947 25-year-old Jackie Robinson becomes the first black player in major league baseball

1948 President Truman bans segregation in armed forces

1953 Dwight D. Eisenhower becomes thirty-fourth president; Stalin dies; Nikita Khrushchev emerges as leader of the Soviet Union; CIA helps bring Shah Mohammad Reza Pahlavi to power in Iran

1954 CIA masterminds overthrow of leftist government of Guatemala; *Brown v. Board of Education of Topeka* decision holds that "separate educational facilities are inherently unequal"

1955 Emmett Till murdered; black residents of Montgomery, Alabama, organize a bus boycott to protest segregation; Eisenhower and Khrushchev hold summit in Geneva, Switzerland

1956 Soviet troops crush Hungarian uprising; Suez crisis; United States begins interstate highway system

1957 Eisenhower sends troops to Little Rock, Arkansas, to enable black students to enroll in formerly all-white public schools; Soviet Union launches the first satellite, *Sputnik*

1958 U.S. marines intervene in Lebanon; Congress passes the National Defense Education Act to provide federal aid to schools and colleges

1959 Fidel Castro leads Cuban Revolution against the regime of Fulgencio Batista

1960 U-2 spy plane is shot down over the Soviet Union

If Eisenhower was more active than he appeared, then the country was more dynamic than it seemed on the surface. Although critics railed against the conformity of suburban America, everywhere there were signs of change. During the 1950s African Americans quickened the pace of their struggle for equality, and youths experimented with alternatives to traditional behavior. And increasingly these two rebellions merged to form a distinct subculture. During the 1960s, the war in Vietnam would give a political edge to that subculture.

CHAPTER SUMMARY AND KEY POINTS

Television's images of the 1950s were bland. The stock situation comedy centered on a white suburban family with a happily married husband and wife and two or sometimes three well-adjusted children. *Father Knows Best* was the classic example of this genre. Its theme song was entitled: "Just Around the Corner There's a Rainbow in the Sky." But television sit-coms were not documentaries. In fact, the postwar era was characterized by tension, diversity, and unsettling social changes. In this chapter you read about President Eisenhower's conception of "dynamic Republicanism" and his foreign policy; the impact of the Soviet Union's launching of *Sputnik*; the beginnings of the modern civil rights movements; and the changes taking place in the American family and in youth culture.

- As president, Dwight Eisenhower pursued a moderate course. He did not dismantle any New Deal programs. His major domestic accomplishment was the construction of the interstate highway system.

- Despite outward calm, the 1950s was a decade of profound social transformations. The Supreme Court ruled that segregation in public schools was unconstitutional and black Americans increased protests against segregation.

- Many families moved to rapidly growing suburbs.

- Young people created a new youth culture, with its own distinctive form of music, rock and roll.

- The Beat generation scorned materialism, traditional family life, and sexuality and tapped into dissatisfaction with the prevailing blandness of conventional culture.

SUGGESTIONS FOR FURTHER READING

Taylor Branch, *Parting the Waters: America in the King Years, 1954–1963* (1988). Fascinating epic study of the first decade of the civil rights movement.

Robert A. Caro, *The Power Broker: Robert Moses and the Fall of New York* (1974). A long, detailed, intriguing look at power politics in New York City.

John D'Emilio and Estelle Freedman, *Intimate Matters: A History of Sexuality in America* (1988). An open look at an important topic normally ignored by historians.

David Garrow, *Bearing the Cross: Martin Luther King, Jr., and the Southern Christian Leadership Conference* (1986). A prize-winning biography of the most important civil rights leader.

Kenneth Jackson, *The Crabgrass Frontier: The Suburbanization of the United States* (1985). The reasons for, and the impact of, the suburb.

Richard Kluger, *Simple Justice: The History of* Brown v. Board of Education *and Black America's Struggle for Equality* (1976). A detailed and humane examination of one of the most important Supreme Court cases of the twentieth century.

Melton A. McLaurin, *Separate Pasts: Growing Up White in the Segregated South* (1987). A close look at everyday relations between the races.

Greil Marcus, *The Mystery Train*, 3d ed. (1990). This group of essays gives one of the best looks at the meaning of Elvis Presley.

Novels

Saul Bellow, *The Adventures of Augie March* (1953).

William Burroughs, *Naked Lunch* (1959).

E. L. Doctorow, *The Book of Daniel* (1966).

Ralph Ellison, *Invisible Man* (1952).

Jack Kerouac, *On the Road* (1948).

Grace Metalious, *Peyton Place* (1954).

Arthur Miller, *The Crucible* (1953).

J. D. Salinger, *Catcher in the Rye* (1951).

Richard Wright, *Native Son* (1940).

MEDIA RESOURCES

Web Sites

Levittown: Documents of an Ideal American Suburb
http://www.uic.edu/~pbhales/Levittown/
The postwar boom in housing made suburban living the cultural norm in America and shaped a generation. The story of the classic suburb, Levittown, is told on this site in pictures and text.

Fifties Web
http://www.fiftiesweb.com/

This entertaining site tells about and samples music and television from the 1950s. It also includes a related links page.

1950s America
http://dept.english.upenn.edu/~afilreis/50s/home.html
This site by Professor Al Filreis of the University of Pennsylvania contains a large array of 1950s literature and images in an alphabetical index.

Eisenhower National Historic Site
http://www.nps.gov/htdocs4/eise/home.htm
This National Park Service site has photographs of Eisenhower, quotes, and lists of his best and worst actions as President.

Dwight D. Eisenhower Library
http://www.eisenhower.utexas.edu/
This site has mainly photos, but it includes an interesting collection of campaign images for all the presidents.

The History of NATO
http://www.cnn.com/SPECIALS/1999/nato/
This site from CNN Interactive has an excellent time line and images telling the history of the North Atlantic Treaty Organization.

Films and Videos

All That Heaven Allows (1955). Douglas Sirk's beautifully realized melodrama about the values of small-town America.

Black Like Me (1964). Based on a novel by the same name, the film attempts to show white America what it is like to be African American, and in the end tells more about what it is like to be white.

The Defiant Ones (1958). Stanley Kramer's exploration of race relations and the interdependency of the races.

Gentleman's Agreement (1949). Elia Kazan's film concerning anti-Semitism in late-1940s America. It is a document from an era when Hollywood was attempting to deal with important issues.

To Kill a Mockingbird (1962). A fine realization of the Harper Lee novel about race relations and life in the South as filtered through the eyes of a child. Horton Foote's screenplay captures a tme and a place beautifully.

Rebel Without a Cause (1955). In this Nicholas Ray film, actor James Dean seemingly creates the mannerisms and attitudes of the alienated teenager. A good example of how life will follow art.

KEY TERMS

Modern Republicanism (p. 760)
National System of Interstate and Defense Highways Act (p. 761)

New Look (p. 763)
Peaceful coexistence (p. 764)
Hungarian revolution (p. 764)
Suez Canal crisis (p. 765)
Sputnik (p. 766)
National Defense Education Act (p. 767)
Cuban Revolution (of 1959) (p. 767)
U-2 spy plane (p. 767)
Jim Crow laws (p. 768)
Black Like Me (p. 768)
Brown v. Board of Education of Topeka (p. 772)
Little Rock crisis (p. 773)
Suburban threat (p. 776)
Rock and roll (p. 777)
Beat generation (p. 778)

PEOPLE YOU SHOULD KNOW

John Foster Dulles (p. 763)
Nikita Khrushchev (p. 764)
Wladyslaw Gomulka (p. 764)
Gamal Abdel Nasser (p. 765)
Fidel Castro (p. 767)
Francis Gary Powers (p. 768)
William Levitt (p. 768)
Jackie Roosevelt Robinson (p. 770)
Earl Warren (p. 772)
Orval Faubus (p. 773)
Rosa Parks (p. 773)
Reverend Martin Luther King, Jr. (p. 774)
Elvis Presley (p. 777)
Allen Ginsberg (p. 779)

REVIEW QUESTIONS

1. How did the election of Dwight Eisenhower reflect the national mood of the 1950s, both in domestic and international affairs?

2. What strides did Eisenhower and Khrushchev make toward thawing the Cold War? What barriers remained?

3. What gains did African Americans make in the 1950s toward ending segregation? What tactics did they adopt?

4. In what ways are television's stereotypes of American life in the 1950s accurate? In what ways do they obscure more nonconformist aspects of American culture?

28 Vietnam and the Crisis of Authority

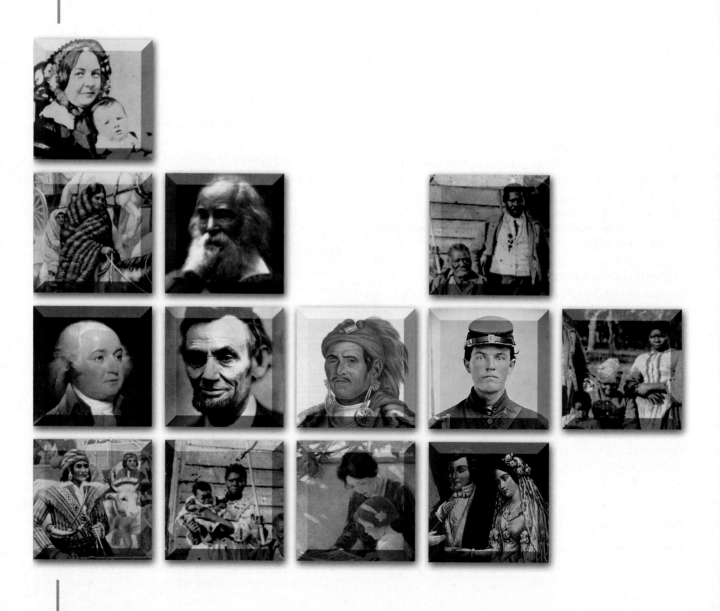

HO CHI MINH AND THE STRUGGLE FOR AN INDEPENDENT VIETNAM

Born roughly 9000 miles from America, **Ho Chi Minh** might as well have come from a different planet. He was a tiny, frail, thin splinter of a man. He was gentle, and in public always deferential. Even after he had come to sole power in North Vietnam, he steadfastly avoided all the trappings of authority. Instead of uniforms or the white sharkskin suit of the mandarin, Ho favored the simple shorts and sandals worn by the Vietnamese peasants. He was sure of who he was—certain of his place in Vietnamese history—and he had no desire to impress others with his position. To his followers, he was "Uncle Ho," the kind, bachelor relative who treated all Vietnamese citizens like the children he never had. But in the pursuit of Vietnamese independence and the realization of a Communist nation, Ho could be cold-blooded and ruthless.

Ho was born in 1890 in a village in a central province of the French colony of **Vietnam** and was originally named Nguyen Sinh Cung. In 1912 he left Vietnam and began a generation-long world odyssey. Signing on as a sailor aboard a French freighter, he moved from one port to the next. For a time he stayed in the United States, visiting Boston, New York City, and San Francisco. He was amazed not only by America's skyscrapers but also by the fact that immigrants in the United States enjoyed the same legal rights as American citizens. He was also struck by the impatience of the American people, their expectations of immediate results. (Later, during the Vietnam War, Ho would say to his military leaders, "Don't worry, Americans are an impatient people. When things begin to go wrong, they'll leave.")

After three years of almost constant travel, Ho settled in London, where he worked at the elegant Carlton Hotel. His living quarters were squalid, and he quickly learned that poverty existed even in the wealthiest, most powerful countries. Then it was on to Paris, where he came in contact with the French left. As he studied there, his nationalist ambitions became tinged with revolutionary teachings. He was still in Paris when World War I ended and the world leaders came to Versailles for the Peace Conference. Inspired by Woodrow Wilson's call for national self-determination, Ho wrote that "all subject peoples are filled with hope by

Nearly nine years after Ho Chi Minh proclaimed Vietnam independent, Vietnamese forces succeeded in driving the French out of the country. Ho is pictured here preparing to mount a pony during an offensive against the French.

the Japanese. Ho allied himself with the United States. Working alongside American Office of Strategic Services (OSS) agents, he proved his mettle. He impressed the agents with his bravery, intelligence, and unflagging devotion to his cause. On September 2, 1945, borrowing passages from the American Declaration of Independence, Ho declared Vietnamese independence.

The French, who returned to Vietnam after the war, had different plans for Vietnam, so Ho's struggle continued. In candid moments he admitted that he didn't expect to live to see Vietnam fully independent. Yet he knew that the struggle of others would eventually secure independence. Ho had patience. It was a quality that the West found difficult to understand.

That was only one of the qualities of Ho and of the Vietnamese that the West did not understand. A deep intellectual chasm divided Vietnam and the West. The latter viewed history as a straight line in which progress was the governing principle. Emphasizing technological advancements and material improvements, Westerners glorified change and prized individualism.

The Vietnamese were products of different beliefs. Notions of competition, individualism, and technological change were anathema to tradition-bound Vietnamese. For a thousand years they had survived using the same rice-cultivating methods. Often, however, the margin between survival and death was a razor's edge. Unlike the United States, Vietnam did not have fertile frontiers to settle. To make do with the land they had, the Vietnamese organized life around villages and practiced a cooperative existence. Rich people were considered selfish because their wealth *had* to be gained at the direct expense of others. As one authority explained, "the idea remains with the Vietnamese that great wealth is antisocial, not a sign of success but a sign of selfishness."

Like wealth, individualism threatened the corporate nature of village life, which was based on duties and social harmony, not individual rights and individual justice. Even their language excluded the idea of individualism. Vietnamese has no personal pronoun equivalent to the Western *I, je, ich*. A person speaks of oneself in relationship to the person being addressed—for example, as "your teacher," "your brother," "your wife."

Nor did the Vietnamese believe in intellectual freedom, which fostered debate and discord, rather than community stability. Americans considered Soviet Communism evil because it discouraged the exchange of free ideas; Ho Chi Minh was drawn to the doctrine because it provided a set of answers not subject to questioning; he was the product of that closed world. America was the prophet of an open

the prospect that an era of right and justice is opening to them." Ho wanted to meet Wilson; he wanted to plead for independence for his country. Wilson ignored his request; Vietnam remained France's colony. Ho moved on—farther east and further left.

Disillusioned with France and socialism, Ho traveled to Moscow, where Lenin had declared war against imperialism; there Ho embraced Communism. In Communist ideology he saw a road to his ultimate goal, the liberation of Vietnam. By the early 1920s he was actively organizing Vietnamese exiles into a revolutionary force. He continued to travel—to Western Europe, back to Russia, to China, back to Russia, to Thailand, back to the West. He lived a life of secrecy, moving from place to place, changing his name, renouncing anything even remotely resembling a personal life. No wife, no children, few friends—only a cause. As he advised one Vietnamese returning to the homeland, "The colonialists will be on your trail. Keep away from our friends' homes and don't hesitate to pose as a degenerate if it will help put the police off the scent."

In 1941 Ho returned to Vietnam. The time was right, he believed, to free Vietnam from colonial domination. During the early part of World War II, the Japanese had won control of the country from the French; now Ho and his followers would force out

world. Motivated by the Cold War, during the period between 1954 and 1973, U.S. officials became convinced that they had to "save" Vietnam from Ho Chi Minh and his Communist brand of nationalism. Given Vietnamese leadership, traditions, and desire for independence, the American intervention in Vietnam was almost certain to fail.

THE ILLUSION OF GREATNESS

In the 1960 presidential race Kennedy challenged his Republican opponent, Richard M. Nixon, to a series of television debates. At the time, Kennedy faced an uphill battle. Young, handsome, and wealthy, Kennedy was considered by many too young, too handsome, and too wealthy to make an effective president. His undistinguished political record stood in stark contrast to Nixon's work in Congress and his eight years as Eisenhower's vice president. In addition, Kennedy was Catholic, and Americans had never elected a Catholic president. Behind in the polls, Kennedy needed a dramatic boost. Thus the challenge. Against the advice of his campaign manager, Nixon accepted.

Television's President

John Fitzgerald Kennedy was made for television. His tall, thin body gave him the strong vertical line that cameras love, and his weather-beaten good looks appealed to women without intimidating men. He had a full head of hair, and even in the winter he maintained a tan. Complementing his appearance

was his attitude. He was always "cool" in public. This too was tailor-made for the "cool medium," television. Wit, irony, and understatement, all delivered with a studied nonchalance, translate well on television. Table-thumping, impassioned speech, and even earnest sincerity often just do not work on television.

The first debate was held in Chicago on September 26, 1960, only a little more than a month before the election. Nixon arrived looking ill and weak—during the previous six weeks he had banged his kneecap, which became infected, spent several weeks in the hospital, and then caught a bad chest cold that left him hoarse and weak. By the day of the debate he looked like a nervous corpse—pale, 20 pounds underweight, and haggard. Makeup experts offered to hide his heavy beard and soften his jowls, but Nixon accepted only a thin coat of Max Factor's "Lazy Shave," a pancake cosmetic.

Kennedy looked better, very much better. He didn't need makeup to appear healthy, nor did he need special lighting to hide a weak profile. He did, however, change suits. He believed that a dark blue rather than a gray suit would look better under the bright lights. Kennedy was right, of course, as anyone who watches a nightly news program realizes.

When the debate started, Kennedy spoke first. Although he was nervous, he intentionally slowed down his delivery. His face was controlled and cool. He smiled with his eyes and perhaps the corners of his mouth, and his laugh was a mere suggestion of a laugh. His body language was perfect. As for what he said, Kennedy disregarded the prearranged ground rules and shifted what was supposed to be a debate on domestic issues to one on foreign policy.

During the Kennedy-Nixon debates, the Democratic candidate demonstrated that for television politics, style was as important as substance. Listeners who heard the debate on the radio thought the candidates were evenly matched, but television viewers, observing Kennedy's polished and confident appearance, regarded him as the clear winner of the debate.

Nixon fought back. He perspired, scored debating points, produced memorized facts, and struggled to win; but his efforts were "hot"—bad television. Instead of hearing a knowledgeable candidate, viewers saw a nervous, uncertain man, one whose clothes did not fit and whose face looked pasty and white. In contrast, what Kennedy said sounded statesmanlike, and he *looked* right. Kennedy was the clear winner. Only later did Nixon realize that the telecast had been a production, not a debate.

When the polls on the results came out, Kennedy inched ahead of Nixon in a Gallup poll for the first time during the campaign. Republicans realized the impact of the debate—Republican Senator Barry Goldwater called it "a disaster." Most of the people who were undecided before watching the debate ended up voting for Kennedy. That proved to be the margin of victory: only one-tenth of one percent separated the two candidates. Perhaps the most important result of the election, however, was not Kennedy's victory but the demonstration of the power of television. The medium came into its own in 1960.

The "Macho" Presidency

In his inaugural address Kennedy issued threats and challenges as well as making promises. Proud to be the first American president born in the twentieth century, determined to be the torch-bearer for "a new generation," Kennedy wanted the world to know where he stood: "Let every nation know, whether it wishes us well or ill, that we shall pay any price, bear any burden, meet any hardship, support any friend, oppose any foe to assure the survival and the success of liberty." And who would pay, bear, meet, support, and oppose? On this point too Kennedy was clear: "And so, my fellow Americans: ask not what your country can do for you—ask what you can do for your country."

After listening to the blandness and mangled syntax of Eisenhower's addresses, here was a speaker of rare ability, here were speeches beautifully phrased. Only years after his death did people begin to ask if he was serious or if he was more concerned with how he said something rather than with what he said. Indeed, he and his speech writers were attracted to verbal sleight-of-hand tricks: "If a free society cannot help the many who are poor, it cannot save the few who are rich. . . . Let us never negotiate out of fear, let us never fear to negotiate." Like the television debates, such statements emphasized style over substance.

Who was this speaker? Competition and an aggressively masculine view of the world ran through the life of John F. Kennedy. He was the son of a multimillionaire who demanded excellence of all his sons and who believed that as Boston Irish Catholics they

had to try harder and be tougher than their Protestant neighbors. This was particularly difficult for John Kennedy, who suffered throughout his life from a series of illnesses and physical problems, including Addison's disease and chronic back trouble. His brother Bobby recalled, "At least one-half of the days that he spent on this earth were days of intense physical pain."

But he never used—and his father never accepted—pain as an excuse for inactivity. At Harvard University he played football, boxed, swam, and ran, and during vacations at the family home in Hyannisport he roughhoused with his brothers and sisters. Throughout his life, Kennedy maintained this physical view of life. To impress the Kennedys, one associate remembered, you had to "show raw guts, fall on your face now and then. Smash into the house once in a while going after a pass. Laugh off twisted ankles or a big hole torn in your best suit."

Kennedy's macho ethos extended to his attitude toward women. Like his father, he regarded sexual conquests as a sign of manhood. During his Washington years as a U.S. senator, he moved from one affair to the next. He did not even bother to learn the names of his one-night-stands, referring to them by such generic names as "Kiddo" or "Sweetie." Nor did Kennedy's affairs end after he was married and elected president. When he wanted companionship and conversation he turned to his male friends.

In his speeches Kennedy stressed the theme that America was entering a period of crisis: "In the long history of the world, only a few generations have been granted the role of defending freedom in its maximum danger. I do not shrink from this responsibility—I welcome it." Without crisis, Kennedy believed, no person could achieve greatness, and he desired greatness. As was expressed in his Pulitzer-Prize-winning *Profiles in Courage*, "Great crises produce great men, and great deeds of courage."

Something Short of Camelot

From the very first journalists associated the Kennedy administration with Camelot. According to the popular legend, King Arthur and his Knights of the Round Table established in the realm of Camelot a period of unparalleled peace and prosperity. Although Kennedy himself enjoyed the Camelot comparisons, the record of his administration and personal behavior fell short of the ideal.

Several factors worked to limit the success of Kennedy's domestic programs. To begin with, Kennedy lacked both political support in Congress and a firm commitment to push for liberal reforms. Ideologically, he was a centrist Democrat. In addition, although his party held a solid majority in the House, 101 of 261 Democratic representatives came from southern and border states, and they normally voted with conservative Republicans. Added to this problem was Kennedy's distaste for legislative in-fighting and his poor working relations with many senators. He limited his domestic agenda to such traditional Democratic proposals as a higher minimum wage, increased Social Security benefits, and modest housing and educational programs. In his inaugural address he did not even mention poverty or race. In the final analysis, Kennedy was so concerned with the "crises abroad" that he did not want to risk any of his political capital on unpopular domestic reforms.

There were small successes. Congress raised the minimum wage, expanded Social Security, and appropriated a few billion dollars for public housing and aid to economically depressed areas. But such legislation hardly amounted to the "new frontier" Kennedy promised. Congress defeated the president's plan for federal aid to education, a health insurance plan for the aged, and programs to help migrant workers, unemployed youths, and urban commuters.

African Americans were especially disappointed with Kennedy's performance. They had, after all, supplied Kennedy's margin of victory in the 1960 election. But once elected JFK was slow in using his office to further the cause of civil rights.

For African Americans, the early 1960s were difficult, violent years that tested their resolve. White segregationists confronted nonviolent desegregation efforts with unprovoked ferocity. Violence erupted in city after city. NAACP organizer Medgar Evers was shot down outside his home in Jackson, Mississippi. Four young African American girls were killed when a Birmingham church was bombed. Police authorities sprayed civil rights protesters, including children, with high-pressure fire hoses and unleashed attack dogs on them. (See Chapter 29 for a more detailed discussion of the fight for civil rights.)

Through his first two years in office, Kennedy remained largely silent. To win southern congressional support he even backed the nomination of a Mississippi jurist—who had once referred to African Americans as "chimpanzees"—for a seat on the federal bench. Although Attorney General Robert Kennedy aided protesters when federal laws were violated, JFK and the FBI did virtually nothing.

In 1963 Kennedy changed his position. In part this about-face was the result of Robert Kennedy's prodding; in part it was the result of television, which daily showed shocking examples of brutality in the South and accelerated the demand for change. In late May 1963, Kennedy eloquently announced his new position. It should be possible, he said, "for American students of any color to attend any public institution without having to be backed up by troops. . . . But this is not the case. . . . We preach freedom around the world . . . but are we to say to the world . . . that we have no second-class citizens except Negroes, that we have no class or caste system, no ghettos, no master race except with respect to Negroes?"

Perhaps Kennedy was convinced that the time had come for "the nation to fulfill its promise." Perhaps, as his supporters claim, in 1963 Kennedy was beginning to fulfill his own promise. His death in late 1963 left questions unanswered, potential unrealized. Judged by his accomplishments, however, Kennedy's Camelot, like King Arthur's, existed largely in the realm of myth. Although he could inspire people to follow, too often on domestic issues he chose not to lead.

Cuba Libre Revisited

Foreign affairs consumed Kennedy's interest. Unlike domestic politics, international conflicts were more clear-cut, and the divisions between "us" and "them" more certain. Foreign affairs also allowed Kennedy to express his masculine view of the world. He could employ the Kennedy approach to difficult decisions, which he once described as: calculate the odds, make your choice, and "grab [your] balls and go."

In his approach to the world, Kennedy generally continued the essentially Cold War policies of Truman and Eisenhower. He accepted the strategy of containment and the notion that the Soviet Union would take advantage of any sign of weakness by the United States. He was also suspicious of conventional diplomatic channels, preferring to listen to his young advisers rather than seasoned State Department officials.

Kennedy's handling of Cuban relations revealed his bellicose tendencies. Like Eisenhower, Kennedy was dismayed by the success of Fidel Castro. Just as Americans during the 1890s had cried *"Cuba Libre,"* on taking office Kennedy began to search for a way to "free" Cuba, this time from Castro's communism rather than Spain's colonialism. His desire to strike a blow against communism led him to embrace a CIA plan to overthrow Castro. If the CIA had successfully planned coups in Guatemala, Iran, and Laos, Kennedy reasoned, then perhaps it could do the job in Cuba.

The CIA plan, hatched during the Eisenhower administration, entailed both the assassination of Castro and the training and transporting of a force of Cuban exiles to Cuba, where they would launch a counterrevolution. It was a plan that even the joint chiefs of staff believed would probably fail. Even worse, the plan was one of the worst-kept secrets in the Western Hemisphere. As one historian noted, "Washington knew because the CIA had to drum up broad support in the government for it. Miami knew because the CIA had done everything but take out classified ads to get volunteers. Guatemala knew because the exile brigade was training there, as a local newspaper pointed out. And Castro knew because everyone else did—except the American people." Pierre Salinger, Kennedy's press secretary, later called the plan "the least covert military operation in history."

The invasion on April 17, 1961 at the Bay of Pigs was an unmitigated disaster. Several attempts to assassinate Castro failed, and the Cuban people did not rise up to join the invaders, who were trapped on the beaches. Nor would Kennedy authorize U.S. air support for the exile forces. As a result, all but 300 of the 1500 invaders were killed or captured. If anything, the **Bay of Pigs fiasco** strengthened Castro's position in Cuba.

The Bay of Pigs invasion, however, did not end Kennedy's problems with Cuba. In the fall of 1962 a more serious crisis arose when the Soviet Union began to install intermediate-range ballistic missiles (IRBMs) in Cuba. Instead of trying to work through proper diplomatic avenues—a process that would have taken time and might have hurt the Democrats in the upcoming election—Kennedy announced the alarming news to an anxious television audience. After showing the public the American cities that the missiles could destroy, Kennedy said he would not permit Soviet ships transporting the weapons to enter Cuban waters. "The people were assured," a scholar commented, "that he would run any risk, including thermonuclear war, on their behalf." Such assurances created a genuine mood of crisis in the country.

Behind the scenes, President Kennedy and Soviet Premier Nikita Khrushchev searched for a way to defuse the crisis. During the entire affair Robert Kennedy counseled level-headed restraint and Khrushchev eschewed any shoe-pounding antics. In the end, the world leaders achieved a solution. Khrushchev agreed to remove the missiles under United Nations inspection in return for an American pledge not to invade Cuba. The Kennedy administration interpreted the result as a victory. "We're eyeball to eyeball and I think the other fellow just blinked," Secretary of State Dean Rusk observed during the episode. And, indeed, the Soviet Union could hardly disagree. The **Cuban missile crisis** provided the ammunition to force Khrushchev out of power.

The two "superpowers" had stood at the brink, gazed into the abyss, and stepped back. And for what? "When all is said and done," observed one historian, "it seems that President Kennedy had risked ultimate disaster in service to a crisis that was more illusory than real, at least in military terms."

Again, the unsatisfactory "perhaps" reappeared. Perhaps Kennedy learned more from the Cuban missile crisis than he had from the Bay of Pigs invasion. Friends of Kennedy claimed that he reached maturity during the crisis and that it motivated him to move toward détente—an easing of tensions—with the Soviet Union. In several 1963 speeches he called for "not merely peace in our time but peace for all time" and a "world safe for diversity." And he did support a treaty banning all atmospheric testing of nuclear weapons. Perhaps Kennedy had come to a new maturity.

The tragedy is that nobody can ever know. On November 22, 1963, Lee Harvey Oswald assassinated President Kennedy in Dallas, Texas. (Later investigations questioned whether Oswald acted alone, although the most thorough study of the assassination concluded that he did.) The event moved the nation. Newsman Walter Cronkite cried on television, and millions of Americans cried in their homes. Once again, television gave the event a mythical quality—showing his grieving wife, his barely understanding children, his solemn funeral. Americans mourned together, eyes fixed on their television sets. And immediately commentators began to evaluate Kennedy's presidency in terms of not what had been but what might have been.

VIETNAM: AMERICA'S LONGEST WAR

How did it start? And when? Even while the war in Vietnam tore at the heart of America in the 1960s most Americans, including some foreign policy experts, were not exactly sure of the answers to such basic questions. Johnson said he was continuing Kennedy's policy, who had continued Eisenhower's, who had continued Truman's, who had acted as he believed Roosevelt would have acted. The answers stretch back into time.

A Small Corner of a Bigger Picture

Struggle, like a mighty river, runs through the history of the small country of Vietnam. For almost 2000 years agriculturally fertile Vietnam battled against the invading Chinese for its independence. Next came the French. During the seventeenth, eighteenth, and nineteenth centuries, French traders and missionaries penetrated Vietnam, establishing their control over the country in the name of *la mission civilisatrice*. This "civilizing mission," however, robbed the Vietnamese of the wealth of their land and their independence. France's rules of governing Vietnam—described as "a lot of subjugation, very little autonomy, a dash of assimilation"—created discontent among the Vietnamese, some of whom welcomed the next invader, Japan, who took over the country during World War II.

The Vietnamese declared their independence in 1945, but that same year the French returned, bent on the resubjugation of the country. The struggle continued, with the communist **Vietminh** under Ho Chi Minh controlling the north of the country and the French in the south. Between 1945 and 1954 both sides suffered terrible losses in the bitter guerrilla struggle.

The United States faced a difficult decision over this struggle. During World War II, Franklin Roosevelt had favored Vietnamese independence and had aided Ho's fight against the Japanese. He recognized that the age of colonialism was doomed, and he wanted the United States identified with anticolonialism. At the same time, however, Roosevelt believed that a strong postwar Western Europe was essential to American security, and he did not want to alienate Britain or France by pressing too hard for an end to empires.

On Roosevelt's death, Harry Truman inherited FDR's problems. Even more than his former boss, he advocated a strong Western Europe, even if that strength had to be based on the continuation of empires. It was a Cold War decision. The United States, Truman maintained, "had no interest" in "championing schemes of international trusteeship" that would weaken the "European states whose help we need to balance Soviet power in Europe."

Vietnam became a pawn in the game of Cold War politics. Truman wanted French support against the Soviet Union. France wanted Vietnam. Truman willingly agreed to aid France's ambitions in exchange for that country's support. The success of Mao Zedong's communist revolution in China strengthened America's support of the French in Vietnam. Obsessed with the idea of an international communist conspiracy, Truman and his advisers contended that Stalin, Mao, and Ho were united by the single ambition of world domination. They overlooked the historical rivalries that pulled Russia, China, and Vietnam apart. As Ho Chi Minh once told his people, "It is better to sniff French dung for a while than eat China's all our life."

By the late 1940s, the United States had assumed a large part of the cost of France's effort to regain its control over Vietnam, and the price escalated during the early 1950s. By 1952 the United States was shouldering roughly one-third of the cost of the war, and between 1950 and 1954 America contributed $2.6 billion to France's war effort. But it was not enough—France could not defeat Ho's Vietminh.

In 1954 the war reached a crisis stage. In an effort to lure the Vietminh into a major engagement, the leading French commander moved more than 13,000 soldiers to **Dien Bien Phu,** a remote outpost in a river valley in northwest Vietnam. The Vietminh surrounded the fort and moved artillery pieces to the hills above the French airstrip. From there they mounted a siege of the outpost. As the months

passed, French manpower and prestige suffered punishing blows. Inside Dien Bien Phu, latrines overflowed, food supplies ran out, water spoiled, and unburied bodies fouled the air. Finally, on May 7, 1954, the last French commander surrendered.

During the siege the French continually asked President Eisenhower for military support, but he refused to act without the consent of Congress and Britain. Neither favored American military intervention. Senator Lyndon Johnson of Texas expressed the majority view in Congress when he opposed "sending American G.I.s into the mud and muck of Indochina on a blood-letting spree to perpetuate colonialism and white man's exploitation in Asia." As a result, France gave up its attempt to recolonize Vietnam. At the peace talks in Geneva, the countries involved agreed to temporarily divide Vietnam at the 17th parallel into two countries and hold elections in the summer of 1956 to reunify Vietnam.

Eisenhower would not militarily aid France, but he quickly supported the independent government established in South Vietnam under the leadership of **Ngo Dinh Diem.** In America, where he spent several years in a Catholic seminary, Diem was known as an anticommunist and a nationalist. In Vietnam, where he had not been for 20 years, he was hardly known at all. As a popular leader, he had no appeal. Imperious, often paranoid, overly reliant on his own family, Diem, a Catholic in an overwhelmingly Buddhist nation, successfully alienated almost everyone who came into contact with him. Even United States intelligence sources rated his chances of establishing order in South Vietnam as "poor."

Diem, nevertheless, was America's man. Why? Because he was an anticommunist and a nationalist, and, as John Foster Dulles said, "because we know of no one better." Lyndon Johnson put it more bluntly in 1961: "Diem's the only boy we got out there." Even Eisenhower supported Diem militarily and politically. Vietnam became a test case, an opportunity for the United States to battle communism in Asia with dollars instead of Americans. When the time came to hold the unification election, Diem, with American backing, refused. Instead, to show his popularity he held "free" elections in South Vietnam, where he received an improbable 98.2 percent of the popular vote. The dishonesty of the elections was underscored by the Saigon returns where Diem received 605,000 votes, although there were only 405,000 registered voters.

Diem's absolutist policies created problems. By the end of 1957, Vietminh guerrillas in South Vietnam—often called the **Vietcong**—were in open revolt. Two years later, North and South Vietnam resumed hostilities. The United States increased its aid, most of which went to improving the South Vietnamese military or into the pockets of corrupt officials. The United States spent little money on improving the quality of life of the peasants. Nor did the United States object strongly to Diem's dictatorial methods. Diem once said that the sovereign was "the mediator between the people and heaven," and he demanded absolute obedience.

By the end of Eisenhower's second term America had become fully committed to Diem and South Vietnam. To be sure, problems in Vietnam were not America's major concern. In fact, most Americans were unaware of their country's involvement there. More than anything, Vietnam was a small corner of a bigger picture. U.S. policy there was determined by larger Cold War concerns. America's presence in Vietnam, however, would soon be expanded.

Kennedy's Testing Ground

On taking office, John Kennedy reaffirmed his country's commitment to Diem and South Vietnam. He announced his intention to be even more aggressive than Truman or Eisenhower. In Vietnam Kennedy saw an opportunity to "prove" his nation's resolve and strength. Ultimately, however, South Vietnam as a country was less important to Kennedy than the challenge it presented.

Kennedy believed that the United States needed a fresh military approach. Eisenhower's "massive retaliation" was too limited. It was of no use in a guerrilla war like Vietnam. Kennedy labeled his approach **"flexible response,"** and it entailed the development

of conventional and counterinsurgency (antiguerrilla) forces as well as a nuclear response. Vietnam rapidly became the laboratory for counterinsurgency activities, a place for Special Forces (Green Berets) units to develop their own tactics. To achieve this end, Kennedy expanded the Special Forces from 2500 to 10,000 men.

To "win" in Vietnam, Kennedy realized that he would have to strengthen America's presence there. In November of 1961 he decided to deploy American troops to South Vietnam. By the end of 1961, 3205 American "advisers" were in Vietnam. Kennedy increased this force to 11,300 in 1962 and 16,300 in 1963. Although several of his advisers questioned this military escalation, arguing that once the United States committed troops it would be more difficult to pull out of the conflict, Kennedy remained firm in his desire to "save" South Vietnam.

As American involvement deepened, Diem's control over South Vietnam declined. He alienated peasants by refusing to enact meaningful land reforms and Buddhists by passing laws to restrict their activities. Responding to Diem's pro-Catholic policies, Buddhists began organized protests. They conducted hunger strikes and nonviolent protests. Several Buddhist monks engaged in self-immolation. In full view of American reporters and cameras, one burned himself to death on a busy, downtown Saigon intersection. Although the gruesome sight shocked Americans, Diem's sister-in-law, Madame Nhu, laughed at the "barbecues," offering gasoline and matches for more fiery deaths.

A Vietnamese policeman attempts to extinguish the flames engulfing a Buddhist monk who set himself on fire in front of Saigon's Roman Catholic Cathedral to protest the South Vietnamese government's pro-Catholic policies and persecution and ill treatment of Buddhists.

More deaths followed, and protests mounted. Diem exerted little influence outside of Saigon. Insightful American reporters such as David Halberstam, Neil Sheehan, Peter Arnett, and Stanley Karnow argued that the Diem regime was isolated and paranoid, that a stable democracy would never develop as long as Diem held power. Rather than talk with reporters, Diem would deliver bizarre five-, six-, even ten-hour monologues.

The Kennedy administration soon reached the conclusion that without Diem South Vietnam had serious problems, with Diem the country was doomed. In sum, Diem had to go. Behind the scenes, Kennedy encouraged Vietnamese generals to overthrow Diem. On November 1, 1963, Vietnamese army officers arrested and murdered Diem and his brother. Although Kennedy did not approve of the assassination, the United States quickly aided the new government.

Three weeks later Kennedy was assassinated in Dallas. Several of his friends have suggested that he had begun to reevaluate his Vietnam policy and that after the 1964 election he would have started the process of American disengagement. In a moment of insight, Kennedy himself had observed, "The troops will march in; the bands will play; the crowds will cheer; and in four days everyone will have forgotten. Then we will be told we have to send more troops. It's like taking a drink. The effect wears off, and you have to take another." But whatever Kennedy's future plans or insights, he still had increased U.S. involvement in Vietnam.

Unfortunately for Kennedy's successor, the prospects for South Vietnam's survival were less than they had been in 1961. By 1963 South Vietnam had lost the fertile Mekong Delta to the Vietcong and with it most of the country's rural population. From the peasants' perspective, the Saigon government stood for heavy taxes, no services, and military destruction; and increasingly they identified the United States with Saigon. Such was the situation Lyndon Johnson inherited.

Texas Tough in the Gulf of Tonkin

Lyndon Baines Johnson (LBJ) was a complex man—shrewd, arrogant, intelligent, sensitive, vulgar, vain, and occasionally cruel. He loved power, and he knew where it was, how to get it, and how to use it. "I'm a powerful sonofabitch," he told two Texas congressmen in 1958 when he was the most powerful legislator on Capitol Hill. Everything about Johnson seemed to emphasize or enhance his power. He was physically large and seemed even bigger, and he used his size to persuade people. The "Johnson treatment" involved "pressing the flesh"—a backslapping, hugging sort of camaraderie. He also used symbols of power adroitly, especially the telephone, which had replaced the sword and pen as the symbol of power. "No gunman," remarked one historian, "ever held a Colt .44 so easily" as Johnson handled a telephone.

A legislative genius, Johnson had little experience in foreign affairs. Reared in the poverty of the Texas hill country, educated at a small teachers' college, and concerned politically with domestic issues, before becoming president LBJ had expressed little interest in foreign affairs. "Foreigners are not like the folks I am used to," he often said, and whether it was a joke or not he meant it. He was particularly uncomfortable around foreign dignitaries and ambassadors, often receiving them in groups and scarcely paying attention to them. "Why do I have to see them?" he once asked. "They're [Secretary of State] Dean Rusk's clients, not mine."

Yet to say Johnson had little experience in foreign affairs is not to suggest that he did not have strong opinions on the subject. Like most politicians of the period, Johnson was an unquestioning Cold Warrior. In addition, along with accepting the **domino theory**—the idea that if Vietnam fell, other nations would also fall to communism—and a monolithic view of communism, Johnson cherished a traditionally southern notion of honor and masculinity. It was his duty, he maintained, to honor commitments made by earlier presidents. "We are [in Vietnam] because . . . we remain fixed on the pursuit of freedom, a deep and moral obligation *that will not let us go*." Leaving Vietnam, Johnson believed, would be a dishonorable act, dangerous for the nation's future. Raised in an area where the frontier was still visible, Johnson approached foreign policy like a Texas Ranger. To show weakness and back down was worse than cowardly—it was unmanly. As he often said, "If you let a bully come into your front yard one day, the next day he will be up on your porch and the day after that he will rape your wife in your own bed."

Furthermore, Johnson believed that any retreat from Vietnam would destroy him politically. Soon after becoming president, he told America's ambassador to Vietnam, "I am not going to be the President who saw Southeast Asia go the way China went." No, he would not "lose" Vietnam and allow Republican critics to attack him as they had Truman. "I knew," LBJ later noted, "that Harry Truman and Dean Acheson had lost their effectiveness from the day the communists took over China." Johnson was determined to win the war, to "nail the coonskin to the wall."

Before winning in Vietnam, however, he had to win in the United States. The presidential election in 1964 was his top priority. He was pitted against Barry Goldwater, the powerful Arizona senator from the Republican Right. "Extremism in the defense of liberty is no vice," Goldwater said, and if elected he promised to defend South Vietnam at any cost. He also preached against the welfare state, Social Security, the Nuclear Test Ban Treaty of 1963, and any rapprochement with the Soviet Union or China. Democrats transformed his campaign slogan "In Your Heart, You Know He's Right," to "In Your Heart, You Know He Might," by which they meant that Goldwater might start a nuclear war. Goldwater did little to discourage such thinking. In his campaign he labored to make "nukes" socially acceptable, even coining the uncomfortably comforting phrase "conventional nuclear weapon."

Johnson's campaign strategy was to appear as the thoughtful, strong moderate. He would not lose Vietnam, he told voters, but neither would he use nuclear weapons or "send American boys nine or ten thousand miles from home to do what Asian boys ought to be doing themselves." Johnson promised that if elected he would create a "Great Society" at home and honor American commitments abroad. As usual, he knew what the voters wanted to hear, and they rewarded him with a landslide victory in the November election.

Behind the scenes, however, the Johnson administration was maneuvering to obtain a free hand for conducting a more aggressive war in Vietnam. He did not want a formal declaration of war, which might frighten voters. Rather he desired a quietly passed resolution giving him the authority to deploy American forces. Such a resolution would allow him to act without the consent of Congress. Johnson and his advisers were planning to escalate American involvement in the Vietnam War, but they hoped it would go unnoticed.

Johnson used two reported North Vietnamese attacks on the American destroyer *Maddox* as a pretext for going before Congress to ask for the resolution. Actually, he was less than truthful about the circumstances of the attack. The first incident occurred in the Gulf of Tonkin in early August 1964 when the North Vietnamese suspected the *Maddox* of aiding a South Vietnamese commando raid into North Vietnam, a violation of that country's sovereignty. When North Vietnamese patrol boats approached the *Maddox,* the American ship and supporting navy jets opened fire, sinking one of the North Vietnamese ships and crippling two others. Although the North Vietnamese ships had launched several torpedoes, the *Maddox* was not hit and suffered only superficial machine-gun damage and a loss of ammunition. The second of the Gulf of Tonkin incidents probably never occurred. Assaulted by high waves, thunderstorms, and freak atmospheric conditions, the *Maddox's* sonar equipment apparently malfunctioned, registering 22 invisible enemy torpedoes. No enemy ships were visually sighted, and none of the electronically sighted torpedoes hit the *Maddox* or its accompanying ship the *C. Turner Joy.* Soon after the incident the commander of the *Maddox* reached the conclusion that no attack had ever taken place.

Johnson realized the dubious nature of the second attack. He told an aide, "Hell, those dumb stupid soldiers were just shooting at flying fish." Nevertheless, he went on national television and announced, "Aggression by terror against peaceful villages of South Vietnam has now been joined by open aggression on the high seas against the United States of America." Reassuring the country, he continued, "We know, although others appear to forget, the risks of spreading conflict. We seek no wider war." A few days later he pressed Congress for a resolution. American ships, he emphasized, had been repeatedly attacked, and he wanted authorization to "take all necessary measures" to repel attacks, prevent aggression, and protect American security. It was a broad resolution; Johnson said that it was "like Grandma's nightshirt—it covered everything." Almost without debate, the Senate passed the resolution on August 7 with only two dissenting votes, and the House of Representatives endorsed it unanimously. You "will live to regret it," Wayne Morse, who voted against it in the Senate, told the resolution's supporters. In the years that followed, as Johnson used his new powers to escalate the war, Morse's vote and prediction were vindicated, for the **Gulf of Tonkin Resolution** allowed Johnson to act in an imperial fashion.

Lyndon's War

Lyndon Johnson liked to personalize things. He did not start the Vietnam War, but once reelected he quickly made it "his war." One authority described **Lyndon's war:**

> He made appointments, approved promotions, reviewed troop requests, determined deployments, selected bombing targets, and restricted aircraft sorties. Night after night, wearing a dressing gown and carrying a flashlight, he would descend into the White House basement "situation room" to monitor the conduct of the conflict . . . often, too, he would doze by his bedside telephone, waiting to hear the outcome of a mission to rescue one of "my pilots" shot down over Haiphong or Vinh or Thai Nguyen. It was his war.

When he became president it was still a relatively obscure conflict for most Americans. Public opinion polls showed that 70 percent of the American public paid little attention to U.S. activities in Vietnam. At the end of 1963 only 16,300 U.S. military personnel were in Vietnam, with the number rising to 23,300 by the end of 1964. Most of the soldiers there, however, were volunteers. Only a few people strongly opposed America's involvement. All this would change dramatically over the next four years.

With the election behind him, Johnson started in early 1965 to reevaluate the position of the United States. In Saigon crisis followed crisis as one unpopular government gave way to the next. Something had to be done, and Johnson's advisers suggested two courses. The military and most of LBJ's foreign policy experts called for a more aggressive military presence in Vietnam, including bombing raids into North Vietnam and more ground troops. Other advisers, notably Under Secretary of State George Ball, believed the United States was making the same mistakes as the French. Ball believed that a land war in Indochina was not in America's best strategic interests and that bombing North Vietnam would only stiffen the resolve of the communists. "Once on the tiger's back," Ball warned, "we cannot be sure of picking the place to dismount."

Johnson chose the first course, claiming it would be dishonorable not to come to South Vietnam's aid. In February 1965 Vietcong troops attacked the American base in Pleiku, killing several soldiers. Johnson used the assault as a pretext to commence air raids into the North. Code-named ROLLING THUNDER, the operation was designed to use American technological superiority to defeat North Vietnam. At first, Johnson limited U.S. air strikes to enemy radar and bridges below the 20th parallel. But as the war dragged on, he ordered "his pilots" to hit military targets in metropolitan areas. Between 1965 and 1973, American pilots flew more than 526,000 sorties and dropped 6,162,000 tons of bombs on enemy targets. (As a point of contrast, the total tonnage of explosives dropped in World War II by *all* belligerent countries was 2,150,000 tons.) Some of the landscape of South and North Vietnam began taking on a lunar look.

But the bombs did not lead to victory. Ironically, as Ball had predicted, the bombing missions actually strengthened the communist government in North Vietnam. As a U.S. intelligence report noted, the bombing of North Vietnam "had no significantly harmful effects on popular morale. In fact, the regime has apparently been able to increase its control of the populace and perhaps even to break through the political apathy and indifference which have characterized the outlook of the average North Vietnamese in recent years."

The massive use of air power also undermined U.S. counterinsurgency efforts. Colonel John Paul Vann, an American expert on counterinsurgency warfare noted, "The best weapon 'for this type of war' . . . would be a knife. . . . The worst is an airplane. The next worst is artillery. Barring a knife, the best is a rifle—you know who you're killing." By us-

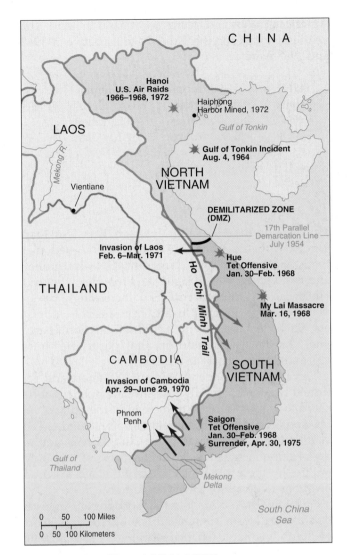

Vietnam Conflict, 1964–1975

ing bombing raids against the enemy in both the North and South, U.S. forces inevitably killed large numbers of civilians, the very people they were there to help. For peasants everywhere in Vietnam, U.S. jets, helicopters, and artillery "meant more bombing, more death, and more suffering."

A larger air war also led to more ground troops. As Johnson informed Ambassador Maxwell Taylor, "I have never felt that this war will be won from the air, and it seems to me what is much more needed and will be more effective is a larger and stronger use of rangers and special forces and marines." Between 1965 and 1968 the escalation of American forces was dramatic. When George Ball warned in 1965 that 500,000 American troops in Vietnam might not be able to win the war, other members of the Johnson administration laughed. By 1968 no one was laughing. Ball's prediction was painfully accurate. Escalation of

American troops and deaths went hand in hand. The year-end totals for the United States between 1965 and 1968 were:

1965:	184,300 troops	636 killed.
1966:	385,300 troops	6644 killed.
1967:	485,600 troops	16,021 killed.
1968:	536,000 troops	30,610 killed.

But still there was no victory.

To Tet and Beyond

Throughout the escalation Johnson was less than candid with the American people. He argued that there had been no real change in American policy and that victory was in sight. Any reporter who said otherwise was roundly criticized. Increasingly he demanded unquestioning loyalty from his close advisers. Such demands led to an administration "party line." As the war ground on, the "party line" bore less and less similarity to reality.

In late 1967, General William Westmoreland returned to America briefly to assure the public that he could now see the "light at the end of the tunnel." In his annual report Westmoreland commented, "The year ended with the enemy increasingly resorting to desperation tactics; . . . and he has experienced only failure in these attempts." Westmoreland assured everyone that victory there was certain.

Then with a suddenness that caught all America by surprise, North Vietnam struck into the very heart of South Vietnam. On the morning of January 30, 1968, North Vietnam launched the **Tet offensive.** "Tet," the Vietnamese holiday that celebrates the lunar new year, traditionally is supposed to determine family fortunes for the rest of the year. Certainly the Tet offensive boded well for North Vietnam. A Vietcong suicide squad broke into the U.S. embassy in Saigon, and Vietnamese communists mounted offensives against every major target in South Vietnam, including 5 cities, 64 district capitals, 36 provincial capitals, and 50 hamlets.

For what it was worth, the United States repelled the Tet offensive. For a few days the fighting was ferocious and bloody, as the rivals fought in highly populated cities and almost evacuated hamlets. In order to retake Hue, the ancient cultural center close to the border between North and South Vietnam where the fighting lasted for several weeks, allied U.S. and South Vietnamese troops had to destroy part of the city. One observer recorded that the city was left a "shattered, stinking hulk, its streets choked with rubble and rotting bodies." When the allied troops finally recaptured Hue, they discovered that North Vietnamese and Vietcong soldiers had killed several thousand political leaders, teachers, and other civilians, many of whom had been buried alive in one mass grave. Both sides suffered terribly. But after the allies cleared the cities of enemy troops, General Westmoreland judged the episode a great allied victory. In the end, American and South Vietnamese troops recaptured lost areas and South Vietnamese civilians did not rally to the Vietcong cause. Indeed the Vietcong was so decimated by the Tet offensive that it never regained its full fighting strength.

This photo, from April 1968, shows U.S. soldiers, under attack by the Vietcong, attempting to take cover in a trench on Hill Timothy. The level of U.S. troops in Vietnam and the number of U.S. casualties reached their highest totals for a single year in 1968, but the fighting—and the casualties—continued for five more years.

If, technically speaking, the Tet offensive was a military defeat for North Vietnam, it was also a profound psychological victory. Johnson, his advisers, and his generals had been proclaiming that the enemy was on the run, almost defeated, tired of war, ready to quit. Tet demonstrated that the contrary was true. Upset and confused, CBS anchorman Walter Cronkite, the national voice of reason, expressed that attitude on his nightly newscast: "What the hell is going on? I thought we were winning the war?" The Tet offensive, more than any other single event, turned the media against the war and exposed the widening "credibility gap" between official pronouncements and public beliefs. NBC anchorman Frank McGee reported that the time had come "when we must decide whether it is futile to destroy Vietnam in the effort to save it."

After Tet, Americans stopped thinking about victory and turned toward thoughts of how best to get out of Vietnam. "Lyndon's planes" and "Lyndon's boys" had been unable to achieve Lyndon's objectives. For Johnson this fact was politically disastrous. His popularity plummeted, and in the New Hampshire primary Democratic peace candidate Eugene McCarthy received surprisingly solid support. On CBS's the *Smothers Brothers Comedy Hour* folk singer Pete Seeger openly criticized Johnson in the song "Waist Deep in the Big Muddy" about a "Big Fool [who] Says To Push On." Too intelligent a politician not to realize what was happening, on the night of March 31, 1968, LBJ went on television and made two important announcements. First, he said that the United States would limit its bombing of North Vietnam and would enter into peace talks any time and at any place. And second, Johnson surprised the nation by saying, "I will not seek, and I will not accept, the nomination of my party for another term as your President." A major turning point had been reached. The gradual escalation of the war was over. The period of deescalation had started. Even in official government circles, peace had replaced victory as America's objective in Vietnam.

The Politics of a Divided Nation

If Johnson's fall seemed remarkably swift, and if it seemed as if he were surrendering power without a fight, it was because he knew that his policies had badly divided the nation. LBJ honestly believed he had pursued the only honorable course in Vietnam, that he had had America's best interests at heart. His problem, however, was *not* that his intentions were dishonorable but that his *modus operandi*—the style of his leadership—involved great duplicity. Instead of fully committing the United States by calling up the reserves and National Guardsmen and by pushing

for higher taxes to pay for the war, Johnson gambled that a slow, steady escalation would be enough to force North Vietnam to accept a negotiated peace. All during the buildup, LBJ assured the American people that he was not drastically changing policy and, besides, victory was in sight. But he could not fool all the people, and after the Tet offensive he knew that he could not even fool most of the people any more.

Dissatisfaction with Johnson's policy surfaced first among the young, the very people who were being asked to fight and die for the cause. Most of the young men who were drafted did serve, and most served bravely. In the early years of "Lyndon's war," many soldiers sincerely believed that they were fighting—and dying—to preserve freedom and nourish democracy in Southeast Asia. One career soldier, who did his first tour in Vietnam in 1966, recalled the idealism of his experience. He talked enthusiastically about American contributions to the improvements in South Vietnamese village life. But by his last tour, in 1970, his idealism had died. As he told a friend, "I'm still ready to serve—any time. But as a killing machine, not a humanitarian."

As the war lengthened, an ever-growing number of soldiers shared in this disillusionment, which took different forms. Journalist Michael Herr has written eloquently about the horrors of the war: "Satchel charges and grenades blew up jeeps and movie houses, the VC (Vietcong) got work inside all the camps as shoeshine boys and laundresses, . . . they'd starch your fatigues . . . then go home and mortar your area. Saigon and Cholan and Danang held such hostile vibes that you felt that you were being dry sniped every time someone looked at you." Drugs and sex helped some soldiers—many just boys away from home for the first time—to cope with the nature of a guerrilla war. One GI recalled that R&R—the traditional rest and recreation leave—was really I&I— "intoxication and intercourse." A 1969 Pentagon study estimated that nearly two of every three American soldiers in Vietnam were using marijuana and that one of every three or four had tried heroin. In 1970 CBS News televised a "smoke-in," in which GIs smoked marijuana through the barrel of a combat rifle. In such an atmosphere boys became men, fast. "How do you feel," Herr asked, "when a nineteen-year-old kid tells you from the bottom of his heart that he has gotten too old for this kind of shit?"

Other soldiers reacted by viewing *all* Vietnamese as the enemy. The nature of the war against the Vietcong caused this attitude in part. In a village of "civilians" any man, woman, or child *might* be the enemy. "Vietnam was a dark room full of deadly objects," wrote Herr, "and the VC were everywhere all at once like spider cancer." Tension and anxiety were as ever-present as olive drab.

Empty government phrases, however, also contributed to the problem. How could soldiers win the "hearts and minds" of villagers one day and rain napalm on them the next? Reacting to the surface idealism of U.S. policy, one experienced soldier commented, "All that is just a *load*, man. We're here to kill gooks, period." The My Lai massacre, in which American soldiers killed more than 100 (the official figure was 122 but it was probably many more) South Vietnamese civilians, was the sad extension of this attitude.

The morale of American soldiers plummeted. Desertion and absent-without-leave (AWOL) rates skyrocketed. The army desertion rate in 1966 had been 14.9 men per thousand; by 1971 it had risen to 73.5. In 1966 there were 57.2 AWOL incidents per thousand; that figure leaped to 176.9 in 1971. Even worse, "fragging"—the assassination of overzealous officers and noncommissioned officers (NCOs) by their own troops—increased at an alarming rate. The army claimed that at least 1011 officers and NCOs were killed or wounded by their own men during the Vietnam War.

At home, university students, most of whom were draft-exempt, also reacted to the war and Johnson's policies. The earliest and most vocal critics of the Vietnam War, they may have lacked a coherent ideology, but they were strong in numbers and energy. Between 1946 and 1970 enrollments in institutions of higher education had climbed from 2 to 8 million. Although not all students protested against the war, the most politically active ones did. As politicians they formed a curious breed—segregated from society as a whole, freed from adult responsibilities, bound to no real constituency, and encouraged by their teachers to think critically. Most student protesters were from upper middle-class families and could afford the intellectual luxury of being political idealists.

Led by such leftist groups as **Students for a Democratic Society (SDS),** university students called for a more just society in which political life was governed by morality, not greed. During the early 1960s they focused on the civil rights movement, participating in freedom rides and voter registration drives. By the mid-1960s, however, they were increasingly shifting their attention to America's "unjust and immoral" war in Southeast Asia. With the shift their numbers swelled—only ten universities had SDS chapters in 1962, and each chapter had only a handful of members. By 1968 the organization could boast more than 100,000 members. By then, too, older voices had joined the student chorus of condemnation.

It was the older voices, energized by the idealism of youth, that led to Johnson's decision not to seek reelection in 1968. For many, it seemed as if the future

LOGISTICS IN A GUERRILLA WAR

The Longest War

The Vietnam War, fought 9000 miles from America's shores, was a logistical nightmare for the United States. It had to ship hundreds of tons of supplies daily from the United States to bases in the Pacific and finally to fortified positions along the coast of Vietnam. Once the supplies were in Vietnam, they had to be protected from Vietcong guerrillas, who blended into the civilian population and often obtained jobs on U.S. bases. As a result, although American forces established defense perimeters around their bases, the areas were never totally secure. Bombs in U.S. movie theaters or even mess halls were haunting reminders of the unpredictability of guerrilla warfare.

North Vietnam sent much of its supplies south along the Ho Chi Minh Trail. Following a traditional series of trails through mountains and jungles from North Vietnam into Laos and Cambodia, finally emptying into South Vietnam, the Ho Chi Minh Trail was widened into a road capable of handling heavy trucks and thousands of troops. Along the Trail, support facilities, often built underground to escape American detection and air strikes, included operating rooms, fuel storage tanks, and supply caches. Throughout the war, United States forces tried, but failed, to effectively disrupt the flow of supplies and soldiers south.

The Vietcong tunnel complex, another example of the unconventional war in Vietnam, created even more problems for American troops. The tunnels allowed Vietcong troops to appear and disappear almost by magic. The most famous tunnel complex was under Cu Chi, approximately 25 miles northeast of Saigon. It contained conference rooms, sleeping chambers, storage halls, and kitchens. U.S. forces bombed, gassed, and defoliated the Cu Chi area but failed to destroy the tunnels. "Tunnel rats"—South Vietnamese soldiers and short, wiry GI combat engineer SWAT teams—fought heroically in the tunnels, but they too were unable to destroy the complexes. In the end, it was the unconventional nature of the Vietnam War that guaranteed frustration and made it America's longest war.

Source: From *The Tunnels of Cu Chi* by Tom Mangold and John Penycate. Copyright © 1985 by Tom Mangold and John Penycate. Reprinted by permission of Random House, Inc. Map: Harold Ober Associates.

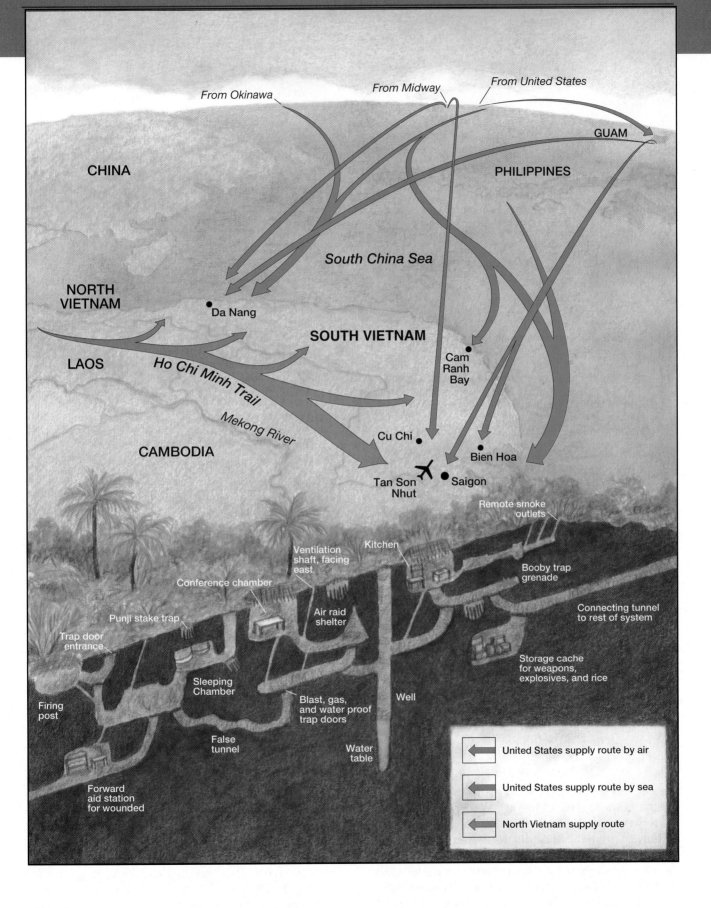

THE PEOPLE SPEAK

Bloods

Arthur E. Woodley "went to Vietnam as a basic naive young man of eighteen." By his nineteenth birthday, he described himself as an "animal." A proud black man from a poor, "hard-core" neighborhood in Baltimore, Woodley volunteered to serve as a Special Forces Ranger. He chose this difficult and dangerous path partly out of patriotism, and partly out of his own individual pride. His experience, however, hardly matched his ideals. Perhaps his most difficult experience came in the second week of February 1969, on a reconnaissance mission for a downed helicopter.

> We recon this area, and we came across this fella, a white guy, who was staked to the ground. His arms and legs tied down to stakes. And he had a leather band around his neck that's staked to the ground so he couldn't move his head to the left or right.
>
> He had numerous scars on his face where he might have been beaten and mutilated. And he had been peeled from his upper part of chest to down to his waist. Skinned. Like they slit your skin with a knife. And they take a pair of pliers or a instrument similar, and they just peel the skin off your body and expose it to the elements. . . .
>
> And he start to cryin', beggin' to die.
>
> He said, "I can't go back like this. I can't live like this. I'm dying. You can't leave me here like this dying."

It was a situation where it had to be remove him from his bondage or remove him from his suffering. Movin' him from this bondage was unfeasible. It would have put him in more pain than he had ever endured. There was no use talkin' 'bout tryin' and takin' him back, because there was nothing left of him. It was that or kill the brother, and I use the term "brother" because in a war circumstance, we all brothers. . .

It took me somewhere close to 20 minutes to get my mind together. Not because I was squeamish about killing someone, because I had at that time numerous body counts. Killing someone wasn't the issue. It was killing another American citizen, another GI. . . .

The only thing that I could see that had to be done is that the man's sufferin' had to be ended.

I put my M-16 next to his head. Next to his temple.

I said, "You sure you want me to do this?"

He said, "Man, kill me. Thank you."

I stopped thinking. I just pulled the trigger. I cancelled his suffering.

When the team came back, we talked nothing about it.

We buried him. We buried him. Very deep.

Then I cried.

Source: Wallace Terry, *Bloods: An Oral History of the Vietnam War by Black Veterans* (New York: Ballantine, 1984), pp. 241–243. Copyright © 1984 by Wallace Terry. Reprinted by permission of Random House.

of American politics belonged to the proponents of peace and morality. Students flocked to presidential candidate Gene McCarthy's peace cause. They cut their long hair, shaved their beards ("be clean for Gene"), put on coats and ties, and worked for McCarthy's campaign. McCarthy's success encouraged **Robert F. Kennedy** (RFK) to throw his hat into the ring. Although McCarthy supporters saw him as a political opportunist, Kennedy spoke eloquently for the cause of humanity and peace. When students at a Catholic university called for more bombings, RFK asked, "Do you understand what that means? It means you are voting to send people, Americans and Vietnamese, to die. . . . Don't you understand that what we are doing to the Vietnamese is not very different than what Hitler did to the Jews?" Kennedy, who enjoyed midnight bull sessions on the meaning of existence and looked at ease with his tie loosened and his shirt sleeves rolled above his elbows, spoke a language that radical students understood. He exhibited the passion and commitment that McCarthy

lacked. By the conclusion of the campaign, Kennedy had become the foremost peace candidate, and representative of young liberals.

At the celebration party after his narrow victory in the California primary, Kennedy said, "We are a great country, an unselfish country, and a compassionate country. I intend to make that my basis for running." Moments later a fanatic Palestinian shot him in the head. Along with Kennedy died the dreams of many Americans for a moral society. Columnist Murray Kempton spoke for many people: "I have liked many public men immensely, but I guess [RFK] is the only one I have ever loved." Although RFK had started in political life as a committed, aggressive anticommunist and Cold Warrior, by the time of his death he had radically reevaluated his earlier beliefs.

The Democratic party went to the Chicago convention without a candidate. There they battled among themselves—young and old; radical, liberal, and conservative. In the streets, outside the convention hall, police beat protesters in full view of televi-

At the Democratic convention in Chicago, police attacked thousands of unarmed, middle-class, antiwar college students in what was later termed a "police riot."

sion cameras. An official commission later termed it a "police riot." Inside the convention hall the fighting was largely verbal, but it was just as intense and bitter. Abraham Ribicoff, a senator from Connecticut, accused Chicago's mayor Richard Daley of allowing the police to use "Gestapo tactics" in the street; Daley accused Ribicoff of having unnatural relations with his mother. In the end, the Democratic party chose **Hubert Humphrey,** Johnson's liberal vice president, as their presidential candidate. Instead of change, the Democratic party chose a representative of the "old politics."

In a more tranquil convention in Miami, the Republican party endorsed Richard M. Nixon, who promised when elected to honorably end the Vietnam War, move against forced busing of black children to white schools, and restore "law and order." Calmer and more relaxed than ever before, the "new Nixon" claimed to speak for the great majority of Americans who obeyed the nation's laws, paid their taxes, regularly attended church, and loved their country. It was the same message Alabama's Governor **George Wallace** used as the foundation of his third-party candidacy. Running on the American Independent ticket, Wallace spoke for millions of working-class white Americans, young and old alike, who opposed forced integration of schools and neighborhoods, the activities of radical college students, and what they believed was the country's drift toward the left. Although Humphrey's finish in the campaign was strong, Nixon's and Wallace's appeal to traditional values had an undeniable attraction. And on election day, Nixon received 43.4 percent of the popular vote, Humphrey 42.7 percent, and Wal-

lace 13.5 percent. Given the combined votes for Nixon and Wallace—57 percent—it was clear that the country was moving right rather than left.

THE TORTUOUS PATH TOWARD PEACE

During the presidential campaign of 1968, Richard Nixon expected the American voter to accept certain things on faith. First, he asked them to believe that he had a plan to honorably end the war in Vietnam. Second, he hoped that they would "buy" his new public image—the "new Nixon," experienced, statesmanlike, mature, secure, and ever so well adjusted. Most Americans probably did not believe either in the "new Nixon" or his pledge to "bring us together." On election day only 27 percent of eligible voters cast their ballot for him, but in 1968 that proved enough votes to win the election.

Outsiders on the Inside

If Nixon had developed "new" characteristics, those qualities had not forced out the "old." Richard Nixon still considered himself something of an outsider, a battler against an entrenched political establishment. Reared on the West Coast in humble circumstances, he had to overcome considerable obstacles in his rise to power. In the process certain character traits emerged. He was a hard worker—careful, studious, with a tendency toward perfectionism; no detail was too small for his consideration. He also did not shy away from an unpopular task. During his years as Eisenhower's vice president, Nixon had proved particularly adept as a political hatchet man. He was also a loner—shy, introverted, humorless, uncomfortable in social situations. He was essentially a man of action, one who for most of his career carried a list of things to do in the inside pocket of his suit coat. Journalist Tom Wicker noted that the new Nixon was not very different from the old. Wicker observed: "He is, if anything, more reserved and inward, as difficult as ever to know, driven still by deep inner compulsion toward power and personal vindication, painfully conscious of slights and failures, a man who had imposed upon himself a self-control so rigid as to be all but visible."

As a restless outsider, Nixon harbored a heightened suspicion of political insiders. Throughout his career he had been an outspoken critic of State Department officials and other establishment bureaucrats. On taking office he, therefore, surrounded himself with close advisers who held noncabinet titles. Cabinet appointees, and particularly his secretary of state, William Rogers, had almost no voice in key decisions. Personal aides H. R. Haldeman and John

Ehrlichman—called the "Germans" by the White House press corps—advised Nixon on domestic political issues. Vice President Spiro Agnew assumed the role of the administration's hatchet man so well that he became known as "Nixon's Nixon." He attacked the establishment with the ferocity of a professional wrestler verbally abusing an archrival. The "sniveling, hand-wringing power structure," he said, "deserves the violent rebellion it encourages." As for foreign affairs, Nixon relied on his national security advisor, **Henry Kissinger.**

Most commentators regarded Kissinger as a strange ally for Nixon. Kissinger, after all, taught at Harvard, was a close associate of Nelson Rockefeller—Nixon's longtime Republican opponent—and had even offered to work for Nixon's Democratic opponent Hubert Humphrey. "Look," Kissinger said in 1968, "I've hated Nixon for years." Yet even while Kissinger was courting Humphrey, he was secretly working for Nixon's election. No matter who won in 1968, Kissinger would be on the victorious side. It was a piece of Machiavellian maneuvering that Nixon might have appreciated.

Beneath Kissinger's sophisticated exterior, he shared with Nixon fundamental characteristics and beliefs. Like Nixon, Kissinger's path to power was not a traditional one. A German Jew, he had lived for five years (between the ages of 10 and 15) in Nazi Germany; he had been verbally and physically abused by his Aryan classmates. He fled with the rest of his family to the United States during the late 1930s. After serving as an army translator-interrogator during World War II, he enrolled as a scholarship student at Harvard, from where he graduated *summa cum laude* in 1950 and earned his Ph.D. in 1954. During the late 1950s and 1960s, Kissinger wrote, taught, and emerged as a leading expert on foreign affairs. Kissinger viewed himself as a political realist, and he resisted rigid ideological or moral stands. Successful diplomacy, he believed, demanded flexible and creative leaders.

Vain, irreverent, articulate, and intellectual, Kissinger shared Nixon's desire to alter the very nature of the country's foreign relations and to make history. Neither particularly enjoyed being part of a committee process, and the diplomacy of secrecy and intrigue attracted both. For all their surface differences, the shy politician and the flamboyant scholar were kindred spirits who combined to form an impressive team. As one historian observed, "each filled a vital gap in the other's abilities. Kissinger had no gift for American politics; he needed to serve a president who could manipulate the electorate into supporting his policies. Nixon benefited from Kissinger's good press contacts since his own were disastrous."

Vietnamization: The Idea and the Process

During his campaign Nixon had promised "peace with honor." He suggested that he had a secret plan to achieve those ends, but controversy surrounded just what that plan entailed. Several historians have suggested that Nixon's plan was an updated version of Eisenhower's plan to end the Korean War: threatening to use nuclear weapons. Nixon told his White House aide H. R. Haldeman that his plan was similar to Eisenhower's. He wanted North Vietnam to believe that he was a "madman." "I want the North Vietnamese to believe I've reached the point where I might do anything to stop the war," Nixon told Haldeman. "We'll just slip the word to them that 'for God's sakes, you know Nixon is obsessed about communists. We can't restrain him when he's angry—and he has his hand on the nuclear button'—and Ho Chi Minh himself will be in Paris in two days begging for peace." The "madman theory" helps to explain Nixon's dramatic shifts during his first four years in office as he moved between the poles of peacefully concluding the war and violently expanding the conflict.

One thing was certain, however. Nixon knew that he could not continue Johnson's policy. "I'm not going to end up like LBJ," he remarked, "holed up in the White House afraid to show my face on the street." The country needed something new. Whatever else he did, Nixon realized that to ensure some semblance of domestic tranquility he would have to begin to remove American troops from Vietnam. In May 1969 he announced, "The time is approaching when the South Vietnamese forces will be able to take over some of the fighting fronts now being manned by Americans." That summer he drummed harder on the idea of the South Vietnamese fighting their own war. In what has become known as the **Nixon Doctrine,** the president insisted that Asian soldiers must carry more of the combat burden. Certainly the United States would continue to materially aid any anticommunist struggle, but the aid would not include the wholesale use of American troops.

The Nixon Doctrine formed the foundation of Nixon's Vietnamization policy. Working from the questionable premise that the government of Nguyen Van Thieu was stable and prepared to assume greater responsibility for fighting the war, Nixon announced that he planned to gradually deescalate American military involvement. Increasingly, U.S. aid would be limited to war materiel, military advice, and air support. He coupled Vietnamization with a more strenuous effort to move along the peace talks.

Actually, the idea of Vietnamization was hardly new. In 1951 the French had called it *jaunissement,* or "yellowing." Advisers for Eisenhower, Kennedy, and

Johnson had suggested one variation or another of the plan as the solution to the war. The major problem was that the South Vietnamese could not successfully fight the war—not in 1951, or 1961, or 1971. But faced with angry criticism at home, Nixon had no choice but to implement the policy.

At the same time as he extended the olive branch, he expanded the nature of the conflict. Hoping to slow down the flow of North Vietnamese supplies and soldiers into South Vietnam, Nixon ordered American B-52 pilots to bomb the Ho Chi Minh Trail both in Vietnam and in Cambodia. He kept this violation of Cambodian neutrality secret from the American public. It was a bold move, but not very productive. The bombs only reduced the flow of men and supplies by approximately 10 percent.

When both the increased bombing of North Vietnam and Kissinger's peace talks with North Vietnamese officials failed to end the war, Nixon resorted to harsher military efforts. After watching *Patton*, his favorite movie, on board the presidential yacht *Sequoia*, he decided to "go for all the marbles" and send American ground forces to Cambodia to destroy Communist supply bases. On the night of April 30, 1970, he went on television and told the American people of his plan. Ignoring previous American violations of Cambodian neutrality, he said that U.S. policy had been "to scrupulously respect the neutrality of the Cambodian people," while North Vietnam had used the border areas for "major base camps, training sites, logistics facilities, weapons and ammunition factories, airstrips and prisoner-of-war compounds," as well as their chief military head-quarters. As a result, Nixon announced a joint American and South Vietnamese "incursion" into Cambodia's border regions, to be limited to 60 days.

Militarily the invasion fell far short of success. Although American forces captured large stockpiles of weapons and supplies, the operation did not force North Vietnam to end the war. But the "incursion" had dangerously enlarged the battlefield. More importantly, the invasion of Cambodia reignited the fires of the peace movement at home. Throughout the country, colleges and universities shut down in protest. Students raged at what they believed was an "immoral, imperialist policy." At Kent State University in Ohio a volley of gunshots fired by Ohio National Guardsmen broke up a peaceful demonstration. The shots killed 4 students and wounded 9 others. Less than two weeks later, policemen shot 2 more innocent students at Jackson State University in Mississippi. Instead of victory or even peace, Nixon's efforts had further divided America.

As an effective policy for ending the war, Vietnamization was a failure. To be sure, the policy allowed Nixon to bring home American combat troops. When Nixon took office 540,000 American troops were in Vietnam; four years later only 70,000 remained. But American reductions were not accompanied by a marked improvement in the South Vietnamese army. This was clearly illustrated by the unsuccessful 1971 South Vietnamese invasion into Laos. If anything, South Vietnam became more dependent on the United States during the years of Vietnamization. By 1972 South Vietnam's only product and export was war, and even this commodity was of inferior quality.

In the spring of 1970, Ohio National Guardsmen fired into a group of protesting students at Kent State University, killing four students.

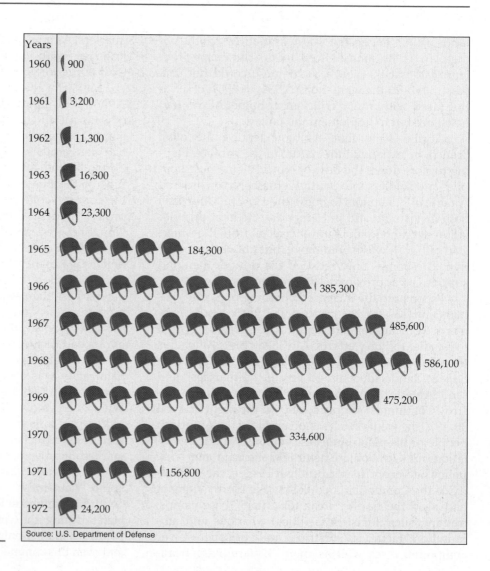

FIGURE 28.1
U.S. Troop Levels in Vietnam, 1960–1972

A "Decent Interval"

By 1972 Nixon simply wanted to end the war with as little embarrassment as possible. As a viable country, South Vietnam was hopeless. Without an active U.S. military presence, the country's demise was a foregone conclusion. Negotiations presented the only way out. Nixon and Kissinger hoped to arrange for a peace that would permit the United States and South Vietnam to save face and allow a "decent interval" of time to ensue between the American departure and the collapse of the government in Saigon. In the pursuit of the goal, Nixon changed the character of American foreign policy.

The Soviet Union and the People's Republic of China aided and advised North Vietnam. Yet the two large communist nations were hardly allies themselves. In fact, the Sino-Soviet split demonstrated to American leaders the fallacy of the old Cold War theme of a monolithic communist movement. Nixon and Kissinger were astute enough to use the Sino-Soviet rift to improve U.S. relations with both countries. Improved relations, they believed, would move

the United States several steps closer to an "honorable" peace in Vietnam. Unfortunately, Nixon and Kissinger greatly overestimated the influence of the Soviet Union and China on North Vietnam.

From his first days in office, Nixon had his eyes on the People's Republic of China, a nation that the United States had refused to recognize. One Nixon aide reported in 1969, "You're not going to believe this, but Nixon wants to recognize China." It seemed remarkable, since Nixon's Cold War record—his opposition to any concession to the communists—was well known. But Nixon understood that his very record would protect him from public cries of being soft on communism; Nixon knew that unlike Truman, Kennedy, and Johnson, he did not have a Nixon to worry about.

Nixon approached China like a man holding a vase from the Ming dynasty, mixing caution with slow careful movements. In fact, both China and the United States walked on eggshells. Mao Tse-tung (Zedong) told reporter Edgar Snow that he "would be happy to talk with [Nixon] either as a tourist or as President."

In 1972 Richard Nixon visited China in an attempt to improve relations with that country. It was the first step toward achieving détente with the Soviet Union.

And Mao ended China's athletic isolation in 1971 by sending a table tennis team to the world championships in Nagoya, Japan, and then inviting an American team to compete in Beijing. Capitalizing on the success of **ping-pong diplomacy,** in the summer of 1971 Kissinger made a very secret trip to China. Kissinger's mission paved the way for Nixon's own very public trip to China in February 1972. American television cameras recorded Nixon's every move as he toured the Great Wall, the Imperial Palace, and the other sites of historic China. For the White House, one reporter noted, "It was the social event of the year." Constantly smiling and bubbling with excitement, Nixon thoroughly enjoyed the event, going so far as quoting Chairman Mao at an official toast and learning to eat with chopsticks. Although full diplomatic relations would not be established until 1979 under Jimmy Carter, Nixon's trip to China was the single most important event in the history of the relations between the United States and the People's Republic of China. It bridged, as Chinese foreign minister Chou En-lai remarked, "the vastest ocean in the world, twenty-five years of no communication."

Concerned about the growing rapprochement between China and America, the Soviet Union sought to move closer to the United States. Once again, Nixon and Kissinger were pleased to oblige. In late May 1972, after many months of preparatory talks, Nixon traveled to Moscow to sign an arms control treaty with Soviet leader Leonid Brezhnev. The **Strategic Arms Limitation Treaty of 1972 (SALT I)** certainly did not preclude a future nuclear war between the superpowers. Although it froze intercontinental ballistic missile (ICBM) deployment, it did not alter the buildup of the more dangerous multiple independent reentry vehicles (MIRVs), which, according to one historian "was about as meaningful as freezing the cavalry of the European nations in 1938 but not the tanks." As so often has been the case during the Cold War, SALT I provided more of a warm breeze than the real heat wave necessary for a complete thaw of the Cold War.

Although Nixon had not been able to end the Vietnam War, his 1972 triumphs in the Soviet Union and China gave him more influence with North Vietnam's major allies. His visits to Beijing and Moscow also dazzled American voters. In 1972 Nixon easily defeated Democratic candidate George McGovern, capturing 61 percent of the popular vote and 521 of the 538 votes of the electoral college. Nixon's success with blue-collar workers, conservative Catholics, and Southerners signified the end of the New Deal coalition.

Once reelected, Nixon again focused on Vietnam. A month before the election, Kissinger had announced, "Peace is at hand," but no sooner was Nixon safely reelected than the peace talks broke down once again. Nixon's response was more and heavier bombing of North Vietnam. Starting on December 18 and continuing for the next ten days, the Christmas bombings—code-named Operation LINEBACKER II—attacked military targets in Hanoi and Haiphong and killed more than 1500 civilians, leveled a hospital, and destroyed large parts of Hanoi. Critics charged that Nixon was attempting to "wage war by tantrum" and that the bombings served no military purpose. Some even suggested that Nixon had become mentally unbalanced. Military authorities, however, maintained that the bombings quickened the pace of the peace process. When the bombings concluded, the warring nations resumed peace talks.

In a week North Vietnam and the United States had hammered out a peace, one that was strikingly similar to the October proposal. On January 27, 1973, America ended its active participation in the Vietnam War. The peace treaty provided for the release of all prisoners of war and America's military withdrawal from Vietnam. It also established a monitored cease-fire between North and South Vietnam and set up procedures aimed at solving the differences between the two countries. Nixon quickly claimed that he had won an honorable peace, that his "secret plan" had worked, even if it had taken four years and claimed the lives of 21,000 Americans, 107,000 South Vietnamese, and more than 500,000 North Vietnamese soldiers. And, of course, the lives of many thousands of Vietnamese civilians. Informing the American people of the peace, Nixon claimed, "South Vietnam has gained the right to determine its own future. . . . Let us be proud that America did not settle for a peace that would have betrayed our ally . . . that would have ended the war for us but continued the war for the fifty million people of Indochina." But as one historian commented, "In all likelihood, the peace accords that were finally signed in January 1973 could have been negotiated four years earlier. In the name of credibility, honor, and patriotism, hundreds of thousands of lives had been lost."

America left the war in 1973, but the war did not end then. All the peace provided for was a "decent interval" between America's withdrawal and North Vietnam's complete victory. When the South Vietnamese leader Nguyen Cao Ky heard Nixon's peace speech, he commented, "I could not stomach [it], so nauseating was its hypocrisy and self-delusion . . . there is no reason why they [the Communists] should stop now. . . . I give them a couple of years before they invade the South." He was right. Almost as soon as the ink on the "peace treaty" was dry, both North Vietnam and South Vietnam began to violate the treaty. Finally, in the spring of 1975 South Vietnamese forces collapsed. In March North Vietnam forces took Hue and Da Nang; by late April they were close to Saigon. On April 21 President Nguyen Van Thieu publicly lambasted the United States, resigned, and beat a hasty retreat from his country. On April 30 South Vietnam formally announced its unconditional surrender. Vietnam was finally unified. Free elections in 1956 might have accomplished the same results.

The Legacy of the War

Although America's active military participation in the Vietnam War ended in 1973, the controversy engendered by the war raged on long after the firing of the last shot. Much of the controversy centered on the returning veterans. Reports of drug use and fragging frightened many Americans who had come no closer to the war than their television sets. And veterans—most of whom had served their country faithfully and to the best of their abilities—were shocked by the cold, hostile reception they received when they returned to the United States. In *First Blood* (1982), John Rambo, played by Sylvester Stallone, captured the pain of the returning veterans: "Nothing is over. Nothing! You just don't turn it off. It wasn't my war—you asked me, I didn't ask you . . . and I did what I had to do to win . . . . Then I came back to the world and I see all those maggots at the airport, protesting me, spitting on me, calling me a baby-killer and all kinds of vile crap. . . . Back there I could fly a gunship, I could drive a tank, I was in charge of million-dollar equipment. Back here I can't even hold down a job parking cars. . . . Back here there's nothing!"

During the 1970s and 1980s the returning Vietnam War veteran loomed large in American popular culture. He was first portrayed as a dangerous killer, a deranged ticking time bomb that could explode at any time and in any place. He was Travis Bickle in *Taxi Driver* (1976), a veteran wound so tight that he seemed perpetually on the verge of snapping. Travis Bickle, wrote one film historian, "is the prototypical movie vet: in ways we can only imagine, the horror of the war unhinged him. He's lost contact with other human beings. . . . He's edgy: he can't sleep at night." He waits to explode. Or he was Colonel Kurtz in *Apocalypse Now* (1979), who adjusted to a mad war by going mad himself.

Not until the late 1970s did popular culture begin to treat the Vietnam War veteran as a victim of the war rather than a madman produced by the war. *Coming Home* (1978) and *The Deer Hunter* (1978) began the popular rehabilitation of the veteran, and such films as *First Blood* (1982), *Rambo: First Blood II* (1985), and *Missing in Action* (1984) transformed the veteran into a hero. On television, "Magnum, P.I.," "The A-Team," and "Air Wolf" also presented the veteran as a misunderstood hero.

The transformation of the veteran that took place in the late 1970s and 1980s indicated a fundamental shift in America's attitude toward the war. Millions of Americans began once again to see the war in terms of a noble crusade that could have been won. As John

The Vietnam War inspired a number of movies dealing with the effects of the conflict on those who fought there. Some movies, like Oliver Stone's *Born on the Fourth of July*, starring Tom Cruise in the role of Vietnam veteran Ron Kovic, portrayed the veterans as victimized though not defeated by the tragic and senseless war. Other films, like *Rambo: First Blood II*, starring Sylvester Stallone, made the veteran a hero and transformed the war into a noble crusade. In *Apocalypse Now*, directed by Francis Ford Coppola, the terrible horrors of the war completely destroy the veteran's humanity, as illustrated by the character of Colonel Kurtz (Marlon Brando), the former Green Beret who becomes a deranged killer and godlike leader/dictator of a renegade band of fighters.

Rambo said in *Rambo: First Blood II*, "Do we get to win this time?" His former commander replied: "This time it's up to you." This message fit well with the political message of Ronald Reagan's America.

As American filmmakers "Ramboized" the conflict, Vietnam labored to reconstruct a viable nation out of the rubble of war. It was a difficult struggle. Roads and bridges, power plants and factories lay in ruins. Ports suffered from damage and neglect. Raw materials and investment capital were in short supply. If peace brought hope, it also brought the specter of economic ruin.

The recovery of the Socialist Republic of Vietnam was slow. One of the poorest countries in the world, it suffered from high inflation and unemployment, food shortages and starvation, and government inefficiency and corruption. In addition, military campaigns—such as the 1978 war against the Khmer Rouge in Kampuchea (formerly Cambodia)—siphoned off money needed to rebuild the country. Finally, the Soviet Union, Vietnam's closest ally, did not solve Vietnam's economic problems. "Americans without dollars," the Vietnamese have called the Soviets. One Vietnamese joke reflected the new relationship with the Soviet Union. After appealing to the Soviets for loans, Vietnam receives the cable: "Tighten your belts." Vietnam replies: "Send belts."

My Lai and the Question of War Ethics

That terrible day began early on the morning of March 16, 1968, with the *whop-whop-whop-whop* sound of helicopters carrying the men of Charlie Company to their designated battle stations for the Pinkville operation. Their goal, along with the rest of Task Force Barker, was to utterly destroy the 48th Local Force Battalion of the National Liberation Front, the elusive and deadly Vietcong unit operating in Quang Ngai Province. Slightly more than 100 men comprised Charlie Company of the United States Army's 1st Battalion, 20th Infantry. Most were young, between 18 and 22 years old, and most were nervous. Each hoped that he would live though the day, but nobody had any guarantees and they all expected that some members of their company would not see the sun set.

There were sound reasons for the gloomier expectations. Although they had been in Vietnam for less than three months and had yet to have a major confrontation with a Vietcong unit, the company had been bloodied on several occasions. Trudging through Quang Ngai, a beautiful stretch of land between the Annamese mountains and the white sandy beaches of the South China Sea—a quiltwork province of rice paddies dotted with bamboo and banana trees—soldiers in Charlie Company had lost legs, arms, and lives to Vietcong boobytraps. February 25, 1968, had been a particularly bad day. Part of the unit had wandered into the

middle of a minefield. Although the officer in charge screamed "Freeze!", a few men panicked, moved, and detonated more mines. "Anyone who moved to try to help someone just got blown up themselves," recalled one GI. One soldier was split open from his crotch to his chest cavity "as if someone had taken a cleaver" to him. Three GIs were killed, another 12 badly injured, and everyone was shaken. One GI remembered thinking, "This is war, this is what it is all about, this is what happens to you."

The men of Charlie Company regarded the Pinkville operation as a chance for revenge—revenge for their friends who had died or been wounded, revenge for their uncomfortable patrols though hostile country, revenge for the fear they felt and a land they hated and a people they did not understand. One sergeant recalled that the central message at the briefing on the eve of the operation was: "This was a time for us to get even. A time for us to settle the score. . . . The order we were given was to kill and destroy everything that was in the village. It was to kill the pigs, drop them in the wells; pollute the water supply; kill, cut down the banana trees; burn the village; burn the hootches as we went through it. It was clearly explained that there were to be no prisoners. The order that was given was to kill everything in the village. Someone asked if that meant women and children. And the order was: everyone in the village. Because those people that were in the village—the women, the kids, the old men—were VC. . . . It was quite clear that no one was to be spared in that village."

Thus when the men of Charlie Company climbed out of their helicopter transports near the tiny village designated **My Lai** 4, they expected to engage the enemy, and they expected to kill. The enemy, as so often had been the case, was gone. If they had been in Quang Ngai—and even that was doubtful—they had left. When the men moved into My Lai 4 and several subhamlets in the same general area, they encountered no enemy fire. The only people they met were villagers, mostly women, children, and old men. Unquestionably some were Vietcong supporters; Quang Ngai had long been regarded as VC country. But according to the rules of military engagement, the villagers were noncombatants, and U.S. soldiers were required to treat them accordingly.

On this day the rules of "civilized" warfare were not observed. From the very beginning, soldiers shot anything that moved, including unarmed villagers. Once the shooting began there was a chain reaction, as more and more soldiers discharged their weapons. They shot pigs, chickens, cows, ducks, and water buffalo in the fields. They shot old men sitting outside their homes, women holding babies, children searching for places to hide. A few soldiers raped women before they killed them. One group of children were shot as they reached their hands out toward a GI in the hope of receiving food or candy. At several points, scores of villagers were gathered into groups and executed. Altogether, the soldiers killed about 400 villagers.

Not every member of Charlie Company participated in the slaugh-

ter. Some only fired when they were given direct orders to fire, others simply refused to fire at all. Each man was presented with a difficult moral choice—follow what he believed were his orders or do what his conscience told him was right. At one point helicopter pilot Hugh Thompson, Jr., shocked by what he saw from his Plexiglass "bubble ship," landed his chopper to protect a group of defenseless villagers. He told the American soldiers—his own countrymen— that if they shot the villagers he would turn his machine gun on them. He simply could not abide what he saw happening. And when he returned to base he reported what he had seen.

What had happened in those four hours the morning of March 16, 1968, was a spontaneous tragedy. Soldiers following orders, men out of control, the logical end result of a policy of free-fire zones and search and destroy missions and systematic body counts—all these explanations would later be employed to explain the massacre. There is no doubt that the GIs were given orders to shoot. Lieutenant William Calley, the ranking of-

ficer in My Lai, both ordered and participated in the worst executions, and he certainly believed that he was following the orders of his commander, Captain Ernest Medina. At one point, Calley told Medina that civilians were slowing the progress of Charlie Company; Medina "told Calley simply to get rid of them." In the mass confusion of the morning—in what one military strategist has called "the fog of war"—things happened that probably no one could have predicted.

But what happened after that morning was coldly calculated. A massacre, not a battle, had taken place—the signs of indiscriminate killing of civilians were apparent. Battles mean that your own men get killed and wounded; the only casualty in Charlie Company was one accidental, self-inflicted wound. Battles successfully waged mean the capture of enemy soldiers and weapons; the official account of the "battle" of My Lai listed 128 enemies killed but only 3 weapons recovered. Just looking at the numbers, any experienced officer could have guessed what had taken place. Thompson had reported the truth. But there was no serious inves-

tigation, only an unspoken coverup that reached up the chain of command from Captain Medina to Lieutenant Colonel Frank Barker to Colonel Oran Henderson to Major General Samuel Koster. As far as they were concerned, no infractions of the military code of engagement had occurred.

Later the world learned differently. On April 2, 1969, Ronald Ridenhour, a former soldier who had heard of the massacre while serving with several former members of Charlie Company, wrote letters to 31 leading United States senators and government officials, including President Richard Nixon and Secretary of Defense Melvin Laird, reporting what he had learned of the massacre. The letters led to several in-depth investigations, which ultimately resulted in charges against two generals, four full colonels, four lieutenant colonels, four majors, six captains, and eight lieutenants. Lieutenant General William Peers, head of the official military investigation, listed 224 serious violations of the military code. In the end, however, only one man, William Calley, was convicted of any wrongdoing, and he was pardoned three years after his conviction.

CHRONOLOGY OF KEY EVENTS

1954 The French garrison at Dien Bien Phu falls to Vietnamese nationalists led by Ho Chi Minh; Geneva conference divides Vietnam into two regions with the promise to hold elections to reunify the country in 1956; North Vietnam is led by the communist government of Ho Chi Minh and South Vietnam by the government of Ngo Dinh Diem

1956 South Vietnam refuses to participate in elections to unify the two Vietnams

1961 John F. Kennedy is inaugurated thirty-fifth president; Alliance for Progress pledges $20 billion in U.S. aid to Latin America over a ten-year period; Cuban exiles stage abortive invasion of Cuba at Bay of Pigs; East Germans erect Berlin Wall; Soviet Union breaks a three-year moratorium on nuclear tests

1962 Cuban missile crisis: In response to Khrushchev's decision to build missile bases in Cuba, President Kennedy imposes a naval blockade of Cuba, and Khrushchev orders the bases dismantled; President Kennedy increases the number of American advisers in South Vietnam to approximately 16,000

1963 United States and Soviet Union agree to ban nuclear tests in atmosphere; South Vietnamese army officers arrest and murder President Diem; President Kennedy is assassinated; Lyndon Johnson becomes thirty-sixth president

1964 North Vietnamese torpedo boats attack the U.S. destroyers *Maddox* and *C. Turner Joy* in the Gulf of Tonkin off the North Vietnamese coast; Congress passes Gulf of Tonkin Resolution, which gives the president authority to retaliate against North Vietnamese aggression

1965 United States begins regular bombing missions over North Vietnam and sends first American ground combat troops into South Vietnam

1968 Tet offensive: During Tet, the Vietnamese lunar new year, the Vietcong stage attacks on major South Vietnamese cities; President Johnson suspends the bombing of North Vietnam and announces that he will not run for reelection; Democratic presidential candidate Robert F. Kennedy is assassinated; Richard M. Nixon is elected thirty-seventh president

1969 Nixon announces "Vietnamization" policy; South Vietnam to take increased responsibility for fighting the war

1970 32,000 U.S. troops join the South Vietnamese army in invading Cambodia; in antiwar protests, 4 students are killed and 9 injured at Kent State University in Ohio; and 2 students die and 12 are injured at Jackson State University in Mississippi; Congress repeals Gulf of Tonkin Resolution

1972 Nixon travels to China, ending 25 years of nonrecognition of the People's Republic of China; Strategic Arms Limitation Treaty with the Soviet Union freezes intercontinental ballistic missile deployment

1973 United States ends active participation in the Vietnam War

1975 North Vietnamese forces enter Saigon; North and South Vietnam are reunited; the former South Vietnamese capital is renamed Ho Chi Minh City

In 1986 Vietnam committed itself to radical change. A new generation of leaders turned to increased democracy and capitalism to solve their country's problems. They also turned to the West, and particularly the United States, for help. American leaders during the late 1980s and early 1990s, however, rejected Vietnam's pleas for aid. Although Vietnam had weakened its ties to the Soviet Union, withdrawn from Kampuchea, and tried to resolve the prisoners of war–missing in action (POW-MIA) issue, official American policy continued to regard the Socialist Republic of Vietnam as a country untouchable. Vietnam may have won the war, but it had not won peace. Finally, however, in the summer of 1995, President Bill Clinton's administration extended diplomatic recognition to Vietnam. Ironically, Clinton's decision was based partially on his belief that recognition would finally resolve the MIA issue.

CONCLUSION

The Vietnam War confused and divided the nation. Tim O'Brien captured something of this confusion in his acclaimed novel *Going After Cacciato* (1978). After fighting in the war, his protagonist "didn't know who was right, or what was right; he didn't know if it was a war of self-determination or self-destruction, outright aggression or national liberation; he didn't know which speeches to believe, which books, which politicians; he didn't know if nations would topple like dominos or stand separate like trees; he didn't know who started the war, or why, or when, or with what motives; he didn't know if it mattered."

Richard Nixon promised in 1968 that if he were elected president, he would end the war honorably and bring Americans together again. Instead, he enlarged the scope of the war before ending it and further divided the country. So, too, Johnson had divided the nation. His vision of a better, more just society—the Great Society (see Chapter 29)—was dashed on the rocks of Vietnam. There was in Johnson's position the essence of tragedy. As he later explained to biographer Doris Kearns, "I knew from the start that I was bound to be crucified either way I moved. If I left the woman I really loved—the Great Society—in order to get involved with the bitch of a war on the other side of the world, then I would lose everything at home . . . but if I left that war and let the communists take over South Vietnam, then I would be seen as a coward and my nation would be seen as an appeaser and we would both find it impossible to accomplish anything for anybody anywhere on the entire globe." In Johnson's view he was like a Puritan wrestling with the question of his own salvation:

Damned if you do,
Damned if you don't.
Damned if you will
Damned if you won't.

Of course, both Nixon and LBJ further injured their cause by being consciously deceptive in their dealings with the American people.

Vietnam, then, destroyed Johnson's presidency and it helped to undermine Nixon's. It was a war that left scars—on the people who fought in it and on the people who opposed and supported it; on Americans and on Vietnamese; and on U.S. foreign policy and its position in the world. For almost 35 years the United States had been actively involved in Indochina, but its influence in the region effectively ended in 1975. The Vietnam War, like the communist victory in China in 1949, undercut America's position in Asia.

The most constructive outcome of the war was the lessons it taught. Congress learned that it had to take a more active role in foreign affairs. The War Powers Act (1973), which requires the president to account for his actions within 48 hours of committing troops in a foreign war, demonstrated that the Gulf of Tonkin Resolution had taught Congress a painful lesson. Ho Chi Minh's nationalism taught policy-makers that communism was not a monolithic movement and that not all small nations are dominoes. Perhaps politicians, policy-makers, and citizens alike even learned that national policy should be based on the realities of individual situations and not Cold War stereotypes.

CHAPTER SUMMARY AND KEY POINTS

It was the longest war in American history and the most unpopular American war of the twentieth century. It resulted in nearly 60,000 American deaths and an estimated 2 million Vietnamese deaths. Even today, many Americans still ask whether the American effort in Vietnam was a blunder, a pawn in the game of Cold War politics, or an idealistic, if failed, effort to protect the South Vietnamese people from totalitarian government. In this chapter, you read about the war's origins, military history, and consequences.

- Between 1945 and 1954, the Vietnamese waged an anticolonial war against France, which received $2.6 billion in financial support from the United States.

- The French defeat at Dien Bien Phu was followed by a peace conference in Geneva, in which Laos, Cambodia, and Vietnam received their independence and Vietnam was temporarily divided between an anticommunist South and a communist North.

- In 1956, South Vietnam, with American backing, refused to hold unification elections. By 1958, communist-led guerrillas known as the Vietcong had begun to battle the South Vietnamese government.

- To support the South's government, the United States sent in 2000 military advisors, a number that grew to 16,300 in 1963.

- The military condition deteriorated, and by 1963 South Vietnam had lost the fertile Mekong Delta to the Vietcong.

- In 1965, Johnson escalated the war, commencing air strikes on North Vietnam and committing American ground forces, which numbered 536,000 in 1968. The 1968 Tet offensive by the North Vietnamese turned many Americans against the war.

- The next president, Richard Nixon, advocated Vietnamization, withdrawing American troops and giving South Vietnam greater responsibility for fighting the war. His attempt to slow the flow of North Vietnamese soldiers and supplies into South Vietnam by sending American forces to destroy communist supply bases in Cambodia in 1970 in violation of Cambodian neutrality provoked antiwar protests on the nation's college campuses.

- From 1968 to 1973 efforts were made to end the conflict through diplomacy. In January 1973, an agreement was reached and U.S. forces were withdrawn from Vietnam and U.S. prisoners of war were released. In April 1975, South Vietnam surrendered to the North and Vietnam was reunited.

Suggestions for Further Reading

Carl Bernstein and Robert Woodward, *All the President's Men* (1974). The study of how two men, following a story, helped bring down a presidency.

Michael Beschloss, *The Crisis Years, Kennedy and Krushchev, 1960–1963* (1992). A readable popular narrative that presents a case study in misunderstanding.

Robert Caro, *The Years of Lyndon Johnson* and *The Path to Power* (1982), and *Means of Ascent* (1990). The first two volumes read like an indictment of Lyndon Johnson but are fascinating nonetheless.

David Halberstam, *The Making of a Quagmire: America and Vietnam During the Kennedy Era*, rev. ed. (1988). Sprawling study of the reasons for America's failure in Vietnam.

Robert S. McNamara, *In Retrospect: The Tragedy and Lessons of Vietnam* (1995). A recent attempt by one of Kennedy's advisers to explain why and how America became mired in Vietnam.

Allen Matusow, *The Unraveling of America: A History of Liberalism in the 1960's* (1984). A hard look at the few successes and many failures of the 1960s.

Neil Sheehan, *A Bright Shining Lie: John Paul Vann and America in Vietnam* (1988). Uses the career of John Paul Vann to provide an in-depth look at the war in Vietnam.

Novels

Philip Caputo, *A Rumor of War* (1977).

John Del Vecchio, *The 13th Valley* (1982).

Graham Greene, *The Quiet American* (1956).

David Halberstam, *One Very Hot Day* (1967).

William J. Lederer and Eugene Burdick, *The Ugly American* (1958).

Tim O'Brien, *Going After Cacciato* (1978).

James Webb, *A Sense of Honor* (1981).

Media Resources
Web Sites

May 4, 1970: 25 Years of Remembrance
http://www.library.kent.edu/exhibits/4may95/index.html
This site commemorates the 25th anniversary of the shootings at Kent State University with a detailed chronology and other information.

14 Days in October: The Cuban Missile Crisis
http://library.advanced.org/11046/
This clever site allows the viewer to interactively explore the Cuban missile crisis.

Investigating the Vietnam War
http://www.spartacus.schoolnet.co.uk/vietintro.htm
This site from Spartacus Educational Publishing, U.K. has an excellent list of annotated links to the best Vietnam-related sites.

Vietnam War Bibliography
http://hubcap.clemson.edu/~eemoise/bibliography.html
Edwin Moise of Clemson University maintains this extensive bibliography of print works about Vietnam and the Vietnam War.

Vietnam Online
http://www.pbs.org/wgbh/pages/amex/vietnam/index.html
From PBS and the *American Experience*, this site contains a detailed, interactive time line of the war, interpretive essays, and autobiographical reflections.

My Lai Courts Martial (1970)
http://www.law.umkc.edu/faculty/projects/ftrials/mylai/mylai.htm
This site contains images, chronology, court and official documents maintained by Dr. Doug Linder at University of Missouri—Kansas City Law School.

John F. Kennedy
http://www.ipl.org/ref/POTUS/jfkennedy.html
This page contains basic factual data about his election and presidency, speeches, and on-line biographies.

John F. Kennedy Library and Museum
http://www.cs.umb.edu/jfklibrary/
This site features exhibits about Robert Kennedy and Jacqueline Kennedy.

The Kennedy Assassination
http://mcadams.posc.mu.edu/home.htm
This well-organized site has images, essay, and photos.

JFK Assassination Web Page
http://ourworld.compuserve.com/homepages/
MGriffith_2/jfk.htm
This is a personal but a very thorough page, which is a
guide to the best Internet resources for the assassination.

Films and Videos

Apocalypse Now (1979). Francis Ford Coppola's search for
the deeper meaning of the war. It is the *Huckleberry Finn* of
the Vietnam War.

Coming Home (1978). This film examines the impact of the
war on the home front and the returning soldiers.

The Deer Hunter (1978). Michael Cimino's powerful interpretation of the suicidal nature of the war and the profound impact it had on everyone involved in it.

The Green Berets (1968). John Wayne's attempt to justify and
glorify America's fight in Vietnam. It came out at the
height of the antiwar movement.

Hearts and Minds (1974). The most important documentary
on the war. Its impact on the viewer is beyond question,
but its interpretation and presentation of the war remain
controversial.

Platoon (1986). Oliver Stone's first commercial film about
the Vietnam War. More than any other director, he explored the multiple meanings of the war. His Vietnam War
films also include *Born on the Fourth of July* (1991) and
Heaven and Earth (1994)

The Quiet American (2002). A recent and successful attempt
to do justice to Graham Greene's insightful novel.

KEY TERMS

Vietnam   (p. 783)

Bay of Pigs fiasco   (p. 788)

Cuban missile crisis   (p. 788)

Vietminh   (p. 789)

Dien Bien Phu   (p. 789)

Vietcong   (p. 789)

Flexible response   (p. 790)

Domino theory   (p. 791)

Gulf of Tonkin Resolution   (p. 792)

Lyndon's war   (p. 792)

Tet offensive   (p. 794)

Students for a Democratic Society (SDS)   (p. 796)

Nixon Doctrine   (p. 800)

Ping-pong diplomacy   (p. 803)

Strategic Arms Limitation Treaty of 1972 (SALT I)
(p. 803)

My Lai   (p. 806)

PEOPLE YOU SHOULD KNOW

Ho Chi Minh   (p. 783)

Ngo Dinh Diem   (p. 789)

Robert F. Kennedy   (p. 798)

Hubert Humphrey   (p. 799)

George Wallace   (p. 799)

Henry Kissinger   (p. 800)

REVIEW QUESTIONS

1. Why do Americans continue to revere John F.
   Kennedy? What were his actual accomplishments as
   president?

2. How had America become involved in Vietnam before
   the presidency of Lyndon B. Johnson?

3. Why did Lyndon B. Johnson escalate American involvement in Vietnam? What effect did it have in Vietnam? In America?

4. What were Richard Nixon's strategies for ending the
   war in Vietnam? To what extent was he successful?

5. How has the American understanding of the Vietnam
   War changed in more recent times? Why?

29 The Struggle for a Just Society

FROM CASSIUS CLAY TO MUHAMMAD ALI

It was meant to be touching, but for many Americans it was painful to watch. It was supposed to signify the healing of a wound, but for many Americans it only suggested how much their country had changed and how little their once shining idealism had really achieved. It was 1996 and **Muhammad Ali** was once again on center stage. The world, almost literally, was watching. Many years before Ali had aroused controversy with his fists and his mouth. In the ring he pounded and occasionally humiliated his opponents, stinging them with cutting jabs and bruising right-hand leads. Outside of the ring his verbal jabs and leads were just as cutting and even more bruising to an older generation of men—mostly white but some black—who held positions of power in America. He took controversial positions on the most heated topics of his day: race, war, men, women, America itself.

Now, standing on a platform in Atlanta, Georgia, he prepared to light the Olympic flame. Dressed in some sort of running suit, he seemed naked. His once powerful hands shook from tremors brought on from Parkinson's syndrome to such an extent that when he raised the torch above his head the flames threatened to ignite his arm. The same disease had robbed him of the ability to fully articulate his beliefs. He had become a fighter who couldn't punch and a spokesman who couldn't talk. For many commentators, even worse, he had become a symbol for a nation he had once challenged. It made many reporters ask the simple questions: Who was Muhammad Ali? What did he mean?

Muhammad Ali was born Cassius Marcellus Clay, Jr., in Louisville, Kentucky, on a cold afternoon in January 1942. He and his father both bore the name of a famous, white Kentucky abolitionist, and, like the abolitionist, both in their own way rebelled against the southern status quo. Cassius Clay, Sr., was a billboard and sign painter, a man of some talent but few opportunities. He was a good father, but at times he was an unsettled man, subject to disorderly moods and domestic violence. The frustrations of a life lived in the thorny confines of the Jim Crow South led him to drink a little too much and complain about the inequities of America.

His son inherited his sense of the country's injustice, and he had a strong faith that he would do something about it. "I always felt I was born to do something for my people," he said years later. "Some people have special resources inside, and when God blesses you to have more than others, you have a responsibility to use it right."

Ali's special gifts included a strong body, lightning reflexes, a quick mind, and an indomitable spirit. Even as a youth he had an odd detachment in the ring, almost as if he were watching the action rather than participating in the fight. He learned the basics of boxing at the age of 12 and soon became a prodigy. He fought his way to the top of the amateurs, representing the United States in the light-heavyweight class at the 1960 Olympic Games in Rome. Not only did he win a gold medal, but he also entranced nearly everyone who met him with his over-the-top personality and winning smile.

A spokesman for the United States Olympic team said that the young boxer was "putting on an amazing performance." "In the ring he murders 'em with his fists. Outside the ring he kills them with kindness and his solid Americanism." When a reporter from the Soviet Union questioned the boxer about America's race problem, Clay shot a reply as quick as a jab: "Tell your readers we got qualified people working on that, and I'm not worried about the outcome. To me the U.S.A. is still the best country in the world, counting yours. It may be hard to get something to eat sometimes, but anyhow I ain't fighting alligators and living in a mud hut."

After the Olympics he turned professional, rising quickly to the top of the heavyweight division. He was an oddity in the world of boxing: an engaging, fresh, talkative fighter. During the 1950s and early 1960s the sport was dominated by organized crime, and it sometimes seemed that a stint in a federal penitentiary was a prerequisite for a career in the fight game. At the top of the heavyweight division sat Sonny Liston, a tough, mean, sullen ex-con who frightened nearly everyone who came into contact with him. There was talk that even the brash Louisville fighter was afraid of him. But in February 1964 at the Miami Beach convention center Cassius Clay—not yet known as Muhammad Ali—shocked the boxing world. A seven-to-one underdog, he boldly predicted a victory and promptly made good on his prediction, punishing Liston into submission. The fight ended with Liston slumped on his stool, refusing to come out for round seven. While Liston sat, the new champion took center stage, announcing, "I am the greatest! . . . I shook up the world! I'm the king of the world! I'm pretty! I'm a bad man! I shook up the world! I shook up the world! I shook up the world!"

In an offbeat symbolic way the 1960s began at that moment. In his inaugural address in 1961, President John F. Kennedy talked about the torch of leadership being "passed to a new generation of Americans." In athletics Cassius Clay represented that new generation—individuals who refused to conform to the stereotype of dumb jocks, spoke their minds on a wide range of social and political topics, and refused

Muhammad Ali dominated headlines in the 1960s and 1970s for his brashness and outspokenness outside the boxing ring as much as for his talent, style, and speed in the ring.

to mouth the tired platitudes of previous generations. In time, reporters spoke to him as though he were a congressman or a senator, seeking his views on race and poverty rather than boxing. Even his nickname "The Louisville Lip" suggested that talking was just as important to his fame as fighting. Perhaps nothing said more about the direction of American culture, the new links being forged between a fresh popular culture and an older political culture, than the meeting shortly before the Liston fight between Clay and the British rock and roll group the Beatles. In their own way Ali and the Beatles would erase the lines between popular culture and politics.

No sooner was Cassius Clay champion than he began his assault on that very distinction. The day after winning the heavyweight title he announced that he had joined the Nation of Islam—or the Black Muslims, as the Nation was popularly known—and renounced his "slave name" of Cassius Clay. He became Cassius X, and then a few weeks later Muhammad Ali. When he joined the Nation of Islam he effectively distanced himself from the older sports world. The Nation was then seen as controversial and violent. Its leader Elijah Muhammad and its most famous spokesman Malcolm X renounced the integrationist goals of Martin Luther King, Jr., and the mainstream civil rights movement. The Black Muslims preached the notion that whites were "white devils" and the idea of racial separation. They also renounced King's belief in nonviolent civil disobedience in favor of a more confrontational philosophy of self-defense. In other words, strike me and I'll strike you back.

At the press conference Ali expounded on his new separatist beliefs. "In the jungle, lions are with lions and tigers with tigers, redbirds stay with redbirds and bluebirds with bluebirds. That's human nature, too, to be with your own kind. I don't want to go where I'm not wanted." Reporters, most of whom were liberal and supported the civil rights platform that endorsed the goal of an integrated country, challenged Ali and questioned his beliefs. Why couldn't Ali be like Joe Louis, Jackie Robinson, or Floyd Patterson, black athletes who supported the liberal, integrationist agenda, athletes who never went too strongly against the grain? In his most profound statement, Ali answered them: "I don't have to be what you want me to be, I'm free to be who I want." It was all about choice. His choice. Not theirs. His press conference was his declaration of independence, his emancipation proclamation.

During the 1960s Ali continued to exercise his right to be who he wanted to be and say what he chose to say. Like other young Americans, he continued to speak out on political and social issues that confronted America. As an African American he talked most often about race. But he also spoke out and took a stand on the United States' war in Vietnam. When a draft reclassification made him eligible for military service he announced that he would refuse induction on the basis that he was a conscientious objector. The war in Vietnam was not his war, he said. "I ain't got no quarrel with them Vietcong." When Ali made the statement in 1966 millions of other Americans had arrived at or were beginning to arrive at the same conclusion; however, he went on record with the statement, and he paid the price.

On April 28, 1967, Ali officially refused to step forward when his name was called at an induction proceeding in Houston, Texas. A federal officer told him that his refusal was a violation of the Universal Military Training and Service Act, punishable by up to five years in prison and a $5000 fine. Again Ali refused to step forward, claiming he was exempt as a minister of the religion of Islam. Within an hour of his refusal—before he was charged with any crime, let alone convicted—the New York State Athletic Commission stripped Ali of his title and suspended his boxing license, an action that other jurisdictions soon followed. For the next three years, while his case wound its way to the Supreme Court, Ali was a fighter who couldn't fight, a champion without a title, and one of the most loved and hated men in America. Finally the Supreme Court overturned his draft conviction, and he was once again free to resume his career.

Eventually he would regain his championship. And inevitably he would lose it, this time in the ring. During the next several decades the hard edge that had made him so controversial softened, just as the bitter debates that tore the country apart in the 1960s lost some of their sense of immediacy. During Ali's prime, however, between 1963 and 1973, he came to symbolize the deep divisions in the United States between black and white, young and old, doves and hawks, and, ultimately, the future of the nation.

uhammad Ali would became a defining symbol of the tumultuous 1960s—a decade when hundreds of thousands of ordinary Americans also challenged the status quo. These struggles against inequality gave new life to the nation's democratic ideals. African Americans used sit-ins, freedom rides, and protest marches to fight segregation, poverty, and unemployment. Feminists demanded equal employment opportunities and an end to sexual discrimination. Mexican Americans protested discrimination in voting, education, and employment. Native Americans demanded that the government recognize their land rights and the right of tribes to govern themselves. Gays and lesbians fought for the end of discrimination according to sexual preference. Environmentalists demanded legislation that controlled the amount of pollution released into the atmosphere.

Although consumerists, environmentalists, civil rights workers, feminists, and other activists seemed to fade from public view during the 1980s and 1990s, they never abandoned their causes. Today they remain a powerful force in American life. Indeed, the very success of liberal activists led to a conservative reaction, one in which equally committed Americans protested busing, affirmative action, quotas, and abortion.

The Struggle for Racial Justice

For African Americans in 1960 statistics were grim. Their average life span was seven years less than that of white Americans. Their children had only half the chance of completing high school, only a third the chance of completing college, and a third the chance of entering a profession, when they grew up. On average, African Americans earned half as much as white Americans and were twice as likely to be unemployed.

Despite a string of court victories during the late 1950s, many African Americans remained second-class citizens. Six years after the landmark *Brown v. Board of Education* decision, just 1 percent of black schoolchildren in the 11 states of the former Confederacy attended public school with white classmates. Less than a quarter of the South's African American voting-age population could vote, and in certain Southern counties African Americans could not vote, serve on grand juries and trial juries, or frequent all-white beaches, restaurants, and hotels.

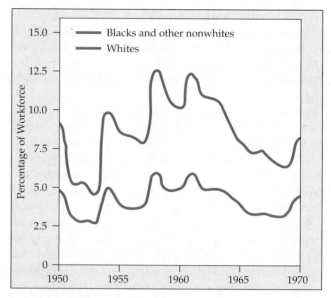

Figure 29.1
Unemployment, 1950–1970

In the North, too, African Americans suffered humiliation, insult, embarrassment, and discrimination. Many neighborhoods, businesses, and unions totally excluded them. Unemployment soared as laborsaving technology eliminated many semiskilled and unskilled jobs that historically provided many African Americans with work. "If you're white, you're right," a black folk saying went; "if you're brown, stick around; if you're black, stay back."

During the 1960s, however, a growing hunger arose among African Americans for full equality. The Rev. Dr. **Martin Luther King, Jr.,** gave voice to the new mood: "We're through with tokenism and gradualism and see-how-far-you've-comeism. We're through with we've-done-more-for-your-people-than-anyone-elseism. We can't wait any longer. Now is the time."

Freedom Now

"Now is the time." These words became the credo and rallying cry for a generation. On Monday, February 1, 1960, Ezell Blair, Jr., Franklin McClain, Joseph McNeill, and David Richmond—four African American freshmen at North Carolina Agricultural and Technical College—walked into the F. W. Woolworth store in Greensboro, North Carolina, and sat down at the lunch counter. They asked for a cup of coffee. A waitress told them that she would only serve them if they stood.

Instead of walking away, the four college freshmen stayed in their seats until the lunch counter closed—giving birth to the **"sit-in."** The next morn-

TABLE 29.1 High School Graduates (Percentage of Population Ages 25–29)			
	1960	**1966**	**1970**
African Americans			
Male	36	49	54
Female	41	47	58
Whites			
Male	63	73	79
Female	65	79	76

TABLE 29.2

Income Distribution of African Americans, Other Nonwhites, and Whites 1960, 1969

	African Americans and Other Nonwhites (Percentage)		Whites (Percentage)	
	1960	1969	1960	1969
Under $3000	38	20	14	~8
$3000–4999	22	19	14	10
$5000–6999	16	17	19	12
$7000–9999	14	20	26	22
$10,000 and over	~9	24	27	49

ing, the four college students reappeared at Woolworth's, accompanied by 25 fellow students. By the end of the week protesters filled Woolworth's and other lunch counters in town. Although the student protesters subscribed to King's doctrine of nonviolence, their opponents did not—assaulting the students both verbally and physically. When the police finally arrived, they arrested African American protesters but not the whites who tormented them.

By the end of February, lunch counter sit-ins had spread to 30 cities in 7 southern states. In Charlotte, North Carolina, a storekeeper unscrewed the seats from his lunch counter. Alabama, Georgia, Mississippi, and Virginia hastily passed antitrespassing laws to stem the outbreak of sit-ins. Despite these efforts, the nonviolent student actions spread across the South as students protested segregated libraries, swimming pools, and other "public" facilities.

In April, 142 student sit-in leaders from 11 states met in Raleigh, North Carolina, and voted to set up a new group to coordinate the sit-ins, the **Student Nonviolent Coordinating Committee (SNCC).** Martin Luther King, Jr., told the students that their willingness to go to jail would "be the thing to awaken the dozing conscience of many of our white brothers."

In the summer of 1960, sit-ins gave way to "wade-ins" at segregated public beaches. In Atlanta, Charlotte, Greensboro, and Nashville, African Amer-

Sit-ins were one example of the nonviolent direct action that characterized the civil rights movement in the early 1960s. Demonstrators endured the taunts and abuse of opponents, only to be arrested for "disturbing the peace" or "inciting a riot."

ican students lined up at white-only box offices of segregated movie theaters. Other students staged pray-ins (at all-white churches), study-ins (at segregated libraries), and apply-ins (at all-white businesses). By the end of the year, 70,000 people had taken part in sit-ins in over 100 cities in 20 states. Police arrested and jailed more than 3600 protesters. But the new tactic worked. By August 1 lunch counters in 15 states had been integrated and by year's end protesters had succeeded in integrating eating establishments in 108 cities.

The Greensboro sit-in initiated a new, activist phase in black America's struggle for equal rights. Fed up with the slow, legalistic approach that had characterized the civil rights movement in the past, African American college students in the South began to attack Jim Crow directly. In the upper South, federal court orders and student sit-ins successfully desegregated lunch counters, theaters, hotels, public parks, churches, libraries, and beaches. In three states, however,—Alabama, Mississippi, and South Carolina—segregation in restaurants, hotels, and bus, train, and airplane terminals remained intact. In those states, young civil rights activists launched new assaults against segregation.

To the Heart of Dixie

In early May 1961 two busloads of men and women, African American and white, set out from Washington, D.C. They called themselves **"freedom riders,"** and they wanted to demonstrate that, despite a federal ban on segregated travel on interstate buses, segregation prevailed throughout much of the South. The freedom riders' trip was sponsored by the **Congress of Racial Equality (CORE),** a civil rights group dedicated to breaking down racial barriers through nonviolent protest.

In Virginia and North Carolina, the freedom riders met little trouble. But outside Anniston, Alabama, a white hurled a bomb through one of the bus's windows, setting the vehicle on fire. Waiting white thugs beat the freedom riders as they tried to escape the smoke and flames. Eight other whites boarded the second bus and assaulted the freedom riders before police restrained the attackers.

In Birmingham and Montgomery, Alabama, mobs attacked the freedom riders with clubs, blackjacks, and lengths of pipe. President **John F. Kennedy** was appalled by the violence. He hastily deputized 400 federal marshals and Treasury agents and flew them to Alabama to protect the freedom riders' rights. The president publicly called for a "cooling-off period," but conflict continued. When freedom riders arrived in Jackson, Mississippi, 27 were ar-

In a violent confrontation in Anniston, Alabama, angry whites set the Freedom Riders bus on fire, then beat the riders with blackjacks, iron bars, clubs, and tire chains as they tried to escape the smoke and flames. Local hospital workers refused to treat the injured riders.

rested for entering a "white-only" washroom and were sentenced to 60 days on the state prison farm.

The threat of racial violence in the South led the Kennedy administration to pressure the Interstate Commerce Commission to desegregate air, bus, and train terminals. In more than 300 southern terminals, signs saying "white" and "colored" were taken down from waiting room entrances and lavatory doors.

Civil rights activists next aimed to open state universities to African American students. Many Southern states integrated their universities without incident. Other states were stiff-backed in their opposition to integration, including Mississippi. In September 1962, a federal court ordered the state of Mississippi to admit **James Meredith**—a nine-year veteran of the Air Force—to the University of Mississippi (Ole Miss) in Oxford. Governor Ross Barnett vowed that he would "not surrender to the evil and illegal forces of tyranny" and would go to jail rather than permit Meredith to register for classes. Barnett flew into Oxford, named himself special registrar of the university, and ordered the arrest of federal officials who tried to enforce the court order.

James Meredith refused to back down. A "man with a mission and a nervous stomach," Meredith was determined to get a higher education. "I want to go to the university," he said. "This is the life I want. Just to live and breathe—that isn't life to me. There's got to be something more." He arrived at the Ole Miss campus in the company of police officers, federal marshals, and lawyers. Angry white students waited, chanting, "Two, four, six, eight—we don't want to integrate."

Four times James Meredith tried to register at Ole Miss. He finally succeeded on the fifth try, escorted by several hundred federal marshals. The ensuing riot left 2 people dead and 375 injured, including 166 marshals. Ultimately, President Kennedy sent 16,000 troops to put down the violence.

"Bombingham"

By the end of 1961, protests against segregation, job discrimination, and police brutality had erupted from Georgia to Mississippi and Tennessee to Alabama. Staunch segregationists responded by vowing to defend segregation. The symbol of unyielding resistance to integration was Alabama governor **George C. Wallace.** Elected on an extreme segregationist platform, Wallace declared at his inauguration in January 1963: "I draw the line in the dust and toss the gauntlet before the feet of tyranny, and I say segregation now, segregation tomorrow, segregation forever."

It was in Birmingham, Alabama, that civil rights activists faced the most determined resistance. A sprawling steel town of 340,000, Birmingham had a long history of racial acrimony. In open defiance of Supreme Court rulings, Birmingham had closed its 38 public playgrounds, 8 swimming pools, and 4 golf courses rather than integrate them. Calling Birmingham "the most thoroughly segregated city in the United States," Martin Luther King, Jr., announced in early 1963 that he would lead demonstrations in the city until demands for fair hiring practices and desegregation were met.

Day after day, well-dressed and carefully groomed men, women, and children marched against segregation—only to be jailed for demonstrating without a permit. On April 12 King himself was arrested. While in jail he wrote his now-famous "Letter from Birmingham City Jail," a scathing response to a group of white clergymen who in a newspaper article had asked African Americans to wait patiently for equal rights. On pieces of toilet paper and newspaper margins, King wrote, "I am convinced that if your white brothers dismiss us as 'rabble rousers' and 'outside agitators'—those of us who are working through the channels of nonviolent direct action—and refuse to support our nonviolent efforts, millions of Negroes, out of frustration and despair, will seek solace and security in black nationalist ideologies, a development that will lead inevitably to a frightening racial nightmare."

For two weeks all was quiet, but in early May demonstrations resumed with renewed vigor. On May 2 and again on May 3, more than a thousand of Birmingham's African American youth marched for equal rights. In response, Birmingham's police chief, Theophilus Eugene "Bull" Connor, unleashed police dogs on the protesters and sprayed them with high-pressure fire hoses. Watching the willful brutality on television, millions of Americans, white and African American, were shocked by this violent face of segregation.

Tension mounted as police arrested 2543 African Americans and whites between May 2 and May 7, 1963. Under intense pressure, the Birmingham

Police used dogs, clubs, bludgeons, electric cattle prods, and high-pressure water hoses to break up the nonviolent civil rights demonstration in Birmingham, Alabama, in May 1963. Scenes like this, televised to millions of viewers, aroused public indignation and sympathy for the civil rights movement.

THE PEOPLE SPEAK

Rev. Martin Luther King, Jr. Letter from Birmingham City Jail

In 1963, the Rev. Martin Luther King, Jr., came to Birmingham, Alabama to lead protests against segregation, job discrimination, and police brutality. After he was arrested for demonstrating without a permit, he wrote his "Letter from a Birmingham Jail," a scathing response to eight white Alabama clergymen who denounced King's protests and claimed that they were designed to provoke violence. Writing on scraps of toilet paper and newspaper margins, King defended his strategy of nonviolent direct as he explained why African Americans were unwilling to wait patiently for equal rights.

> We know through painful experience that freedom is never voluntarily given by the oppressor, it must be demanded by the oppressed. Frankly I have never yet engaged in a direct action movement that was "well timed," according to the timetable of those who have not suffered unduly from the disease of segregation. For years now I have heard the word "Wait!" It rings in the ear of every Negro with a piercing familiarity. This "wait" has almost always meant "never." . . . We have waited for more than 340 years for our constitutional and God-given rights. The nations of Asia and Africa are moving with jetlike speed toward the goal of political independence, and we still creep at horse and buggy pace toward the gaining of a cup of coffee at a lunch counter.
>
> I guess it is easy for those who have never felt the stinging darts of segregation to say wait. But when you have seen the vicious mobs lynch your mothers and fathers at will and drown your sisters and brothers at whim; when you have seen hate-filled policemen curse, kick, brutalize, and even kill your black brothers and sisters with impunity; when you see the vast majority of your 20 million Negro brothers smothering in an airtight cage of poverty in the midst of an affluent society; when you suddenly find your tongue twisted and your speech stammering as you seek to explain to your six-year-old daughter why she can't go to the public amusement park that has just been advertised on television, and see the tears welling up in her little eyes when she is told that Funtown is closed to colored children, and see the depressing clouds of inferiority begin to form in her little mental sky, and see her begin to distort her little personality by developing a bitterness toward white people; . . . when you are humiliated day in and day out by nagging signs reading "white" and "colored"; when your first name becomes "nigger," your middle name becomes "boy" (however old you are) and your last name becomes "John," and your wife and mother are never given the respected title "Mrs." . . . — then you will understand why we find it difficult to wait. There comes a time when the cup of endurance runs over, and men are no longer willing to be plunged into the abyss of despair. I hope, sirs, you can understand our legitimate and unavoidable impatience.
>
> You express a great deal of anxiety over our willingness to break laws. This is a legitimate concern. . . . I would be the first to advocate obeying just laws. . . . Conversely, one has a moral responsibility to disobey unjust laws. . . .
>
> One who breaks an unjust law must do so openly, lovingly, and with a willingness to accept the penalty. I submit that an individual who breaks a law that conscience tells him is unjust, and who willingly accepts the penalty of imprisonment in order to arouse the conscience of the community over its injustice, is in reality expressing the highest respect for law.

Source: "Letter from Birmingham Jail" and "Dr. King's Message to White Clergymen." Reprinted by arrangement with The Heirs to the Estate of Martin Luther King, Jr., c/o Writers House, Inc. as agent for the proprietor. Copyright © 1963 by Martin Luther King, Jr., copyright renewed 1991 by Coretta Scott King.

Chamber of Commerce reached an agreement on May 9 with African American leaders to desegregate public facilities, hire African Americans as clerks and salespersons, and release demonstrators without bail in return for an end to the protests.

The violence unleashed against civil rights activists and demonstrators in Birmingham gave the city its nickname **"Bombingham."** On May 11, white extremists firebombed an integrated motel. That same night, a bomb destroyed the home of King's brother.

Shooting incidents and racial confrontations quickly spread across the South. In June, a gunman killed 37-year-old **Medgar Evers,** the NAACP field representative in Mississippi. In September, an explosion destroyed Birmingham's 50-year-old Sixteenth Street Baptist Church, killing 4 young African American girls and injuring 14 others. All told, 10 people died during civil rights protests in 1963, 35 African American homes and churches were firebombed, and 20,000 people were arrested during civil rights protests.

Kennedy Finally Acts

The eruption of violence forced the Kennedy administration to introduce legislation guaranteeing civil rights. Twice before, in 1957 and 1960, the federal government had adopted weak civil rights acts designed to provide federal protection guaranteeing voting rights for African Americans. Now Kennedy responded to the racial violence by proposing a new, stronger civil rights bill that required the desegregation of public facilities, outlawed discrimination in employment and voting, and allowed the attorney general to initiate school desegregation suits.

Kennedy's record on civil rights inspired little confidence. As a senator, he had voted against the 1957 Civil Rights Act, and in the 1960 presidential campaign many African American leaders, including former athlete and businessman Jackie Robinson, backed Republican candidate Richard Nixon even though Kennedy worked hard to court the African American vote by promising new civil rights legislation and declaring that he would end housing discrimination with a "stroke of the pen." A few weeks before the 1960 election, Kennedy broadened his African American support by helping to secure the release of Martin Luther King from an Atlanta jail, where he had been imprisoned for leading an antisegregation demonstration.

Once in office, however, Kennedy moved slowly on civil rights issues—both because he feared alienating white Southern Democrats and because he had no real commitment to the cause. Although Kennedy's administration filed 28 suits to protect African American voting rights (compared to 10 suits filed during the Eisenhower years), it was not until November 1963 that Kennedy took steps to fulfill his campaign promise to end housing discrimination with a "stroke of the pen"—after he had received hundreds of pens from frustrated civil rights leaders.

The March on Washington

The violence that erupted in Birmingham and elsewhere alarmed many veteran civil rights leaders. In December 1962 two veteran fighters for civil rights— A. Philip Randolph and Bayard Rustin—met at the office of the Brotherhood of Sleeping Car Porters in Harlem. Both men were pacifists, eager to rededicate the civil rights movement to the principle of nonviolence. Both men decided that a massive march for civil rights and jobs might provide the necessary pressure to prompt Kennedy and Congress to act.

The **1963 March on Washington** occurred on August 28, when over 200,000 people gathered around the Washington Monument and marched to the Lin-

coln Memorial. The marchers carried placards reading: "Effective Civil Rights Laws—Now! Integrated Schools—Now! Decent Housing—Now!" and sang the civil rights anthem, "We Shall Overcome." Ten speakers addressed the crowd, but the event's highlight was Martin Luther King, Jr.'s legendary "I have a dream" speech, which combined passion with an insistence on equal citizenship. "I have a dream," King declared, "that one day on the red hills of Georgia the sons of former slaves and the sons of former slaveowners will be able to sit down together at the table of brotherhood. . . . I have a dream that one day even the state of Mississippi, a state sweltering with people's injustices, sweltering with the heat of oppression, will be transformed into an oasis of freedom and justice." As his audience roared its approval, King continued: "I have a dream that one day

On August 28, 1963, over 200,000 African Americans and whites gathered for a day-long rally at the Lincoln Memorial to demand an end to racial discrimination. The highlight of the event was Martin Luther King, Jr.'s inspiring "I Have a Dream" speech.

this nation will rise up and live out the true meaning of its creed: 'We hold these truths to be self-evident; that all men are created equal.'"

The Civil Rights Act of 1964 and the Voting Rights Act of 1965

For seven months, debate raged in the halls of Congress. In a futile effort to delay the Civil Rights Bill's passage, opponents proposed over 500 amendments and staged a protracted filibuster in the Senate. On July 2, 1964—a little over a year after President Kennedy had sent it to Congress—the Civil Rights Bill was enacted into law. President Lyndon Johnson, who had succeeded to the presidency after Kennedy's assassination in November 1963, had skillfully pushed it through Congress. The act prohibited discrimination in voting, employment, and public facilities such as hotels and restaurants, and it established the Equal Employment Opportunity Commission to prevent discrimination in employment on the basis of race, religion, or gender.

In the first weeks after the act's passage, segregated restaurants and hotels across the South opened their doors to African American patrons. Over the next 10 years, the Justice Department brought legal suits against hundreds of school districts, hotels, restaurants, taverns, gas stations, and truck stops charged with racial discrimination.

The **Civil Rights Act of 1964** prohibited discrimination in employment and public accommodations, but many African Americans were denied an equally fundamental constitutional right, the right to vote. The most effective barriers to voting were state laws requiring prospective voters to read and interpret sections of the state constitution. In Alabama, voters had to provide written answers to a 20-page test on the Constitution and state and local government. Questions included: "Where do presidential electors cast ballots for president?" "Name the rights a person has after he has been indicted by a grand jury."

In early 1965, in an effort to bring the issue of voting rights to national attention, Martin Luther King, Jr., launched a voter-registration drive in Selma, Alabama. Even though African Americans slightly outnumbered whites in the city of 29,500 people, Selma's voting rolls were 99 percent white and 1 percent African American. For seven weeks, King led hundreds of Selma's African American residents to the county courthouse to register to vote. County Sheriff James Clark jailed nearly 2000 African American demonstrators, including King, for contempt of court, juvenile delinquency, and parading without a permit. After a federal court ordered Clark not to interfere with orderly registration, the sheriff forced African American applicants to stand in line for up to five hours before being permitted to take a "literacy" test. Not a single African American was added to the registration rolls.

When a young African American man was shot and killed by an Alabama state trooper during a voting rights demonstration, King called for a march from Selma to the state capitol of Montgomery, 50 miles away. On March 7, 1965, voting-rights demonstrators began their march but were attacked as they crossed a bridge spanning the Alabama River. The march was temporarily halted. It resumed on March 21 with federal protection. The demonstrators chanted: "Segregation's got to fall . . . you never can jail us all." On March 25, a crowd of 25,000 gathered at the state capitol to celebrate the march's completion. King addressed the crowd and called for an end to segregated schools, poverty, and voting discrimination. "I know you are asking today, 'How long will it take?' . . . How long? Not long, because no lie can live forever."

Two measures helped safeguard the voting rights of all Americans. On January 23, 1964, the required three-fourths of the states completed ratification of the **Twenty-fourth Amendment** to the Constitution, which barred use of a poll tax to deny voters the right to vote in federal elections. At the time, five Southern states still had a poll tax. On August 6, 1965, President Johnson signed the **Voting Rights Act of 1965,** which prohibited literacy tests and sent federal examiners to seven Southern states to register voters. Within a year, 450,000 Southern African Americans had registered to vote.

Black Nationalism and Black Power

At the same time that such civil rights leaders as Martin Luther King, Jr., fought for racial integration, other African American leaders emphasized separatism and identification with Africa. One of the most important expressions of the separatist impulse during the 1960s was the rise of the **Nation of Islam,** founded in 1931. The organization drew over 100,000 members, appealing to the growing numbers of urban African Americans living in poverty. The **Black Muslims,** as members of the Nation were known, emphasized racial separatism. "The white devil's day is over," cried Black Muslim leader Elijah Muhammad. "He was given six thousand years to rule. . . . He's already used up most trapping and murdering the black nations by the hundreds of thousands. Now he's worried, worried about the black man getting his revenge." Unless whites acceded to the Black Muslims' demand for a separate territory for themselves, Muhammad said, "Your entire race will be destroyed and removed from this earth by Almighty God. And those black men who

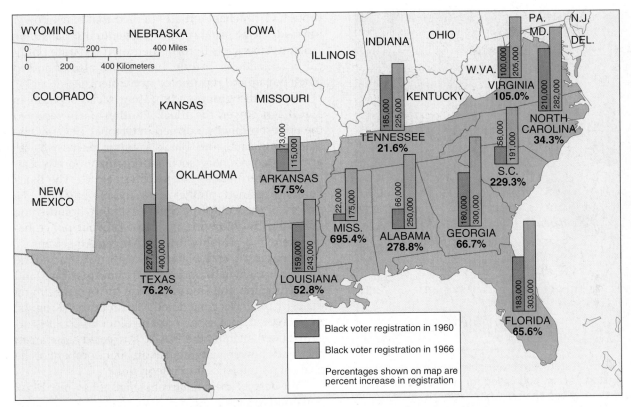

Black Voter Registration Before and After the Voting Rights Act of 1965

are still trying to integrate will inevitably be destroyed along with the whites."

The Black Muslims did more than vent anger and frustration. The organization was also a vehicle of African American uplift and self-help. It called upon African Americans to "wake up, clean up, and stand up" to achieve true freedom and independence. To root out any behavior that conformed to racist stereotypes, the Black Muslims forbade eating pork and cornbread, drinking alcohol, and smoking cigarettes. Black Muslims also emphasized the creation of African American businesses.

The most controversial exponent of black nationalism was **Malcolm X.** The son of a Baptist minister who had been an organizer for Marcus Garvey's Universal Negro Improvement Association, he was born Malcolm Little in Omaha, Nebraska. A reformed drug addict and criminal, Malcolm X learned about the Black Muslims in a maximum-security prison. After his release in 1952, he adopted the name Malcolm X to replace "the white slave-master name which had been imposed upon my paternal forebears by some blue-eyed devil." He quickly became one of the Black Muslims' most eloquent speakers, preaching a message of black nationalism and black pride.

His main message was that discrimination led many African Americans to despise themselves. Self-hatred, claimed Malcolm X, had caused many African Americans to lose their identity and become involved in crime, drug addiction, and alcoholism. Condemned by some whites as a demagogue for such statements as "If ballots won't work, bullets will," Malcolm X gained widespread public notoriety by attacking Martin Luther King, Jr., as a "chump" and an Uncle Tom, by advocating self-defense against white violence, and by emphasizing black political power.

In 1963, the Nation of Islam suspended Malcolm X after he responded to the assassination of President John F. Kennedy with the words: "The chickens have come home to roost." After making a pilgrimage to Mecca and Africa, he formed his own Organization of Afro-American Unity, which sought to bring all peoples of African descent together regardless of religion or nationality. Less than a year later, his life ended in bloodshed. On February 21, 1965, in front of 400 followers, he was shot and killed, apparently by followers of Black Muslim leader Elijah Muhammad.

Inspired by Malcolm X's example, young black activists increasingly challenged the traditional leadership of the civil rights movement and its philosophy of nonviolence. The single greatest contributor to the growth of militancy was the violence perpetrated by white racists. One of the most publicized incidents

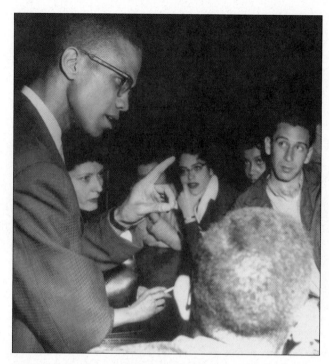

Malcolm X, frustrated with civil rights moderates, spoke sharply against racism and called for African Americans to defend themselves against white violence. In 1964, he founded the Organization of Afro-American Unity, which was socialist in its philosophy.

took place in June 1964 when three young civil rights workers—two whites, Andrew Goodman and Michael Schwerner, and one African American, James Chaney—disappeared near Philadelphia, Mississippi. Six weeks after they were reported missing, their bodies were found buried under a dam; all three had been beaten, then shot. In December, the sheriff and deputy sheriff of Neshoba County, Mississippi, along with 19 others, were arrested on charges of violating the three men's civil rights, but just six days later the charges were dropped. David Dennis, a black civil rights worker, spoke at James Chaney's funeral. He angrily declared, "I'm sick and tired of going to the funerals of black men who have been murdered by white men. . . . I've got vengeance in my heart."

In 1966 two key civil rights organizations— SNCC and CORE—embraced black nationalism. **Stokely Carmichael** was elected chairman of SNCC in May and proceeded to transform SNCC from an interracial organization committed to nonviolence and integration into an all-black organization committed to **"black power."** Black power meant pride in one's African heritage and one's blackness; it also entailed blacks exercising control over their own communities and institutions. "Integration is irrelevant," declared Carmichael. "Political and economic power is what the black people have to have." Al-

though Carmichael initially denied that black power implied racial separatism, he eventually called on African Americans to form their own separate political organizations. In July 1966 CORE also endorsed black power and repudiated nonviolence.

Of all the groups advocating racial separatism and black power, the **Black Panther party** received the widest publicity. Formed in October 1966 in Oakland, California, the Black Panther party was an armed revolutionary socialist organization advocating self-determination for urban ghettoes. The Black Panthers gained public notoriety by entering the gallery of the California State Assembly brandishing guns and by following police to prevent police harassment and brutality toward African Americans.

Separatism and black nationalism attracted no more than a small minority of African Americans, and public opinion polls indicated that the overwhelming majority of blacks considered Martin Luther King, Jr., their favored spokesperson. The older civil rights organizations such as the NAACP rejected separatism and black power, viewing it as an abandonment of the goals of nonviolence and integration.

Yet despite their relatively small following, black power advocates exerted a powerful and positive influence upon the civil rights movement. In addition to giving birth to a host of community self-help organizations, supporters of black power spurred the creation of black studies programs in universities and encouraged African Americans to take pride in their racial background. A growing number of African Americans began to wear "Afro" hairstyles and take African or Islamic surnames. Singer James Brown captured the new spirit: "Say it loud—I'm black and I'm proud."

In an effort to maintain support among more militant African Americans, civil rights leaders began to address the problems of the lower classes who lived in the nation's cities. By the mid-1960s King had begun to move toward the political left. He said it did no good to be allowed to eat in a restaurant if you had no money to pay for a hamburger. King denounced the Vietnam War as "an enemy of the poor" and urged a radical redistribution of wealth and political power in the United States to provide medical care, jobs, and education for all of the country's people.

The Civil Rights Movement Moves North

On August 11, 1965, five days after President Lyndon Johnson signed the Voting Rights Act, accusations of police brutality following the arrest of a 21-year-old for drunk driving ignited a riot in Watts, a predominantly black section of Los Angeles. The **Watts riot of 1965** lasted five days and resulted in 34 deaths, 3900 arrests, and the destruction of over 744 buildings and

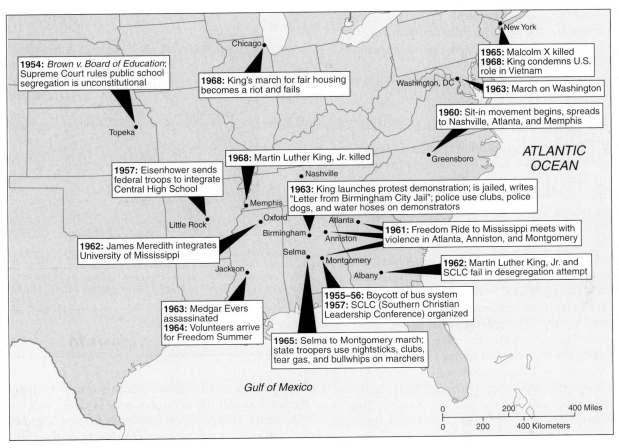

1954: *Brown v. Board of Education*; Supreme Court rules public school segregation is unconstitutional

Topeka

Chicago

1968: King's march for fair housing becomes a riot and fails

New York

1965: Malcolm X killed
1968: King condemns U.S. role in Vietnam

Washington, DC

1963: March on Washington

1960: Sit-in movement begins, spreads to Nashville, Atlanta, and Memphis

ATLANTIC OCEAN

Greensboro

1968: Martin Luther King, Jr. killed

1957: Eisenhower sends federal troops to integrate Central High School

Nashville

1963: King launches protest demonstration; is jailed, writes "Letter from Birmingham City Jail"; police use clubs, police dogs, and water hoses on demonstrators

Memphis

Oxford

Little Rock

Birmingham

Atlanta

Anniston

1961: Freedom Ride to Mississippi meets with violence in Atlanta, Anniston, and Montgomery

1962: James Meredith integrates University of Mississippi

Selma

Montgomery

1962: Martin Luther King, Jr. and SCLC fail in desegregation attempt

Albany

Jackson

1955–56: Boycott of bus system
1957: SCLC (Southern Christian Leadership Conference) organized

1963: Medgar Evers assassinated
1964: Volunteers arrive for Freedom Summer

1965: Selma to Montgomery march; state troopers use nightsticks, clubs, tear gas, and bullwhips on marchers

Gulf of Mexico

0   200   400 Miles
0   200   400 Kilometers

Milestones in the Civil Rights Movement

200 businesses in a 20-square-mile area. Rioters smashed windows, hurled bricks and bottles from rooftops, and stripped store shelves.

Over the next four summers, the nation's inner cities experienced a wave of violence and rioting. The worst violence occurred during the summer of 1967, when riots occurred in 127 cities. In Newark 26 persons lost their lives, over 1500 were injured, and 1397 were arrested. In Detroit 43 people died, $500 million in property was destroyed, and 14 square miles were gutted by fire. The last major wave occurred following the assassination of the Rev. Dr. Martin Luther King, Jr., in Memphis, Tennessee, on April 4, 1968. Violence erupted in 168 cities, leaving 46 dead, 3500 injured, and $40 million worth of damage. In Washington, D.C., fires burned within three blocks of the White House. Joblessness, poverty, a lack of political power, decaying and dilapidated housing, police brutality, and poor schools bred a sense of frustration and rage that had exploded into violence.

In 1968 President **Lyndon B. Johnson** appointed a commission to examine the causes of the race riots of the preceding three summers. The commission attributed racial violence to "white racism" and its heritage of discrimination and exclusion. The commis-

sion warned that unless major steps were taken, the United States would inevitably become "two societies, one black, one white—separate and unequal."

Until 1964 most white Northerners regarded race as a peculiarly Southern problem that could be solved by extending political and civil rights to Southern African Americans. Beginning in 1964 thousands of African Americans in the North staged demonstrations to protest segregation in the schools and discrimination in housing and employment. The nation learned that discrimination and racial prejudice were nationwide problems.

In the North, African Americans suffered from de facto discrimination in housing, schooling, and employment—discrimination that lacked the overt sanction of law. "De facto segregation," wrote James Baldwin, "means that Negroes are segregated but nobody did it." The most obvious example of de facto segregation was the fact that the overwhelming majority of northern black schoolchildren attended predominantly black inner-city schools while most white children attended schools with a majority of whites. In 1968—14 years after the *Brown v. Board of Education* decision—federal courts began to order busing as a way to deal with de facto segregation brought about by housing patterns. In April 1971 in the case of *Swann v. Charlotte-Mecklenburg Board of Education,* the Supreme Court upheld "bus transportation as a tool of school desegregation."

The Great Society and the Drive for Equality

Lyndon B. Johnson had a vision for America. Believing that problems of housing, income, employment, and health were ultimately a federal responsibility, Johnson used the weight of the presidency and his formidable political skills to enact the most impressive array of reform legislation since the days of Franklin Roosevelt. He envisioned a society without poverty or discrimination, in which all Americans enjoyed equal educational and job opportunities. He called his vision the **"Great Society."**

A major feature of Johnson's Great Society was the "War on Poverty." The federal government raised the minimum wage and enacted programs to train poorer Americans for new and better jobs, including the 1964 Manpower Development and Training Act and the Economic Opportunity Act, which established such programs as the Job Corps and the Neighborhood Youth Corps. To assure adequate housing, in 1966 Congress adopted the Model Cities Act to attack urban decay, set up a cabinet-level Department of Housing and Urban Development, and began a program of rent supplements.

To promote education, Congress passed the Higher Education Act in 1965 providing student loans and scholarships, the Elementary and Secondary Schools Act of 1965 to pay for textbooks, and the Educational Opportunity Act of 1968 to help the poor finance college educations. To address the nation's health needs, the Child Health Improvement and Protection Act of 1968 provided for prenatal and postnatal care, the Medicaid Act of 1968 paid for the medical expenses of the poor, and Medicare, estab-

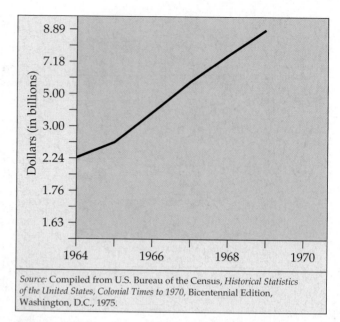

Source: Compiled from U.S. Bureau of the Census, *Historical Statistics of the United States, Colonial Times to 1970,* Bicentennial Edition, Washington, D.C., 1975.

FIGURE 29.3
Federal Aid to Education, 1964–1970

lished in 1965, extended medical insurance to older Americans under the Social Security system.

Johnson also prodded Congress to pass a broad spectrum of civil rights laws, ranging from the Civil Rights Act of 1964 and the Voting Rights Act of 1965 to the 1968 Fair Housing Act, which barred discrimination in the sale or rental of housing. In 1965, LBJ issued an executive order requiring government contractors to ensure that job applicants and employees were not discriminated against. The order required all contractors to prepare an "affirmative action plan" to achieve these goals.

Johnson broke many other color barriers. In 1966, he named the first black cabinet member—Robert Weaver as Secretary of Housing and Urban Development. He also appointed the first black woman to the federal bench, naming Constance Baker Motley to serve as a federal district court judge in southern New York. In 1967 he appointed Thurgood Marshall to become the first African American to serve on the Supreme Court. The first Southerner to reside in the White House in half a century, Johnson showed a stronger commitment to improving the position of African Americans than any previous president.

During the 1960s, the Supreme Court greatly increased the ability of accused criminals to defend themselves. In *Mapp v. Ohio* (1961), the high Court ruled that evidence secured by the police through unreasonable searches must be excluded from trial. In *Gideon v. Wainwright* (1963), it declared that indigent defendants have a right to a court-appointed attorney. In *Escobedo v. Illinois* (1964), it ruled that suspects being interrogated by police have a right to legal counsel.

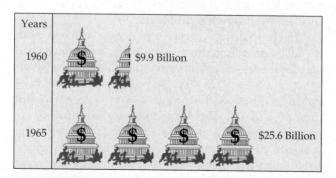

FIGURE 29.2
Federal Spending on Social Programs, Excluding Social Security

Before being named the first black Supreme Court justice in 1967, Thurgood Marshall had presented the legal arguments against school segregation before the Supreme Court that resulted in the 1954 *Brown v. Board of Education of Topeka* decision.

When President Johnson announced his Great Society program in 1964, he promised substantial reductions in the number of Americans living in poverty. By the time he left office in 1969, he could legitimately argue that he had delivered on his promise. In 1960, 40 million Americans, 20 percent of the population, were classified as poor. By 1969, the number of poor had fallen to 24 million, 12 percent of the population. Johnson also pledged to qualify the poor for new and better jobs, to extend health insurance to the poor and elderly to cover hospital and doctor costs, and to provide better housing for low-income families. Here, too, Johnson delivered. Infant mortality among the poor, which had barely declined between 1950 and 1965, fell by one-third in the decade after 1965 as a result of expanded federal medical and nutritional programs. Before 1965, 20 percent of the poor had never seen a doctor; by 1970 the figure had been cut to 8 percent. The proportion of families living in houses lacking indoor plumbing also declined steeply, from 20 percent in 1960 to 11 percent a decade later.

Although critics argued that Johnson took a shotgun approach to reform and pushed poorly thought-out bills through Congress, supporters responded that at least Johnson tried to move toward a more compassionate society. For African Americans during the 1960s median family income rose 53 percent; employment in professional, technical, and clerical occupations doubled; and average educational attainment increased by four years. The proportion of African Americans below the poverty line fell from 55 percent in 1960 to 27 percent in 1968. The country had taken major strides toward extending equality of opportunity to both African Americans and whites below the poverty line.

White Backlash

Ghetto rioting, the rise of black militancy, and resentment over Great Society social legislation combined to produce a backlash among many whites. Commitment to granting African Americans full equality declined. In the wake of the riots, many whites fled the nation's cities. The Census Bureau estimated that 900,000 whites moved each year from central cities to the suburbs between 1965 and 1970.

The 1968 Republican candidate **Richard Nixon** promised to eliminate "wasteful" federal antipoverty programs and to name "strict constructionists" to the Supreme Court. As president, Nixon moved quickly to keep his commitments. In an effort to curb Great Society social programs, Nixon did away with the Model Cities program and the Office of Economic Opportunity. The administration urged Congress not to extend the Voting Rights Act of 1965 and to end a fair housing enforcement program.

President Nixon made a series of Supreme Court appointments that brought to an end the liberal activist era of the Court. To succeed Earl Warren who resigned in June 1969, Nixon selected Warren Burger, a moderate conservative, as chief justice of the Supreme Court. Eventually Nixon named four justices to the high court: Burger, Harry Blackmun, Lewis Powell, and William Rehnquist.

Under Chief Justice Burger and his successor William Rehnquist, the Supreme Court clarified the remedies that can be used to correct past racial discrimination. In 1974 the Court limited the use of school busing for purposes of racial desegregation by declaring that busing could not take place across school district lines. In the landmark 1978 case, *Bakke v. Regents of the University of California,* the Court held that educational institutions could take race into account when screening applicants but could not use rigid racial quotas.

The Struggle Continues

Over the past quarter-century, African Americans have made impressive social and economic gains, yet full equality remains an unrealized dream. State-sanctioned segregation in restaurants, hotels, courtrooms, libraries, drinking fountains, and public washrooms has been eliminated and many barriers to equal opportunity have been shattered. In political representation, educational attainment, and representation in white collar and professional occupations, African Americans have made striking gains. African American mayors have governed many of the nation's largest cities, including Chicago, Detroit, Los Angeles, New York, Philadelphia, and Washington, D.C.

Respect for African American culture has also grown. The number of African American performers on television and in film has increased, though most still appear in comedies and crime films. African Americans also compose and perform much of the country's popular music, but one particular form of musical expression—rap—provoked calls for censorship from those who believed that its lyrics espoused violence.

Nevertheless, millions of African Americans still do not share fully in the promise of American life. African Americans still suffer twice the unemployment rate of whites and earn only about half as much. The proportion of families headed by women increased from 8 percent in 1950 to 21 percent in 1960 and to 33.6 percent by 1970. The poverty rate among black families is three times that of whites, the same ratio as in the 1950s, and almost half of all African American children are born into families whose incomes fall below the poverty level. Although the United States has eliminated many obstacles to progress in civil rights, reformers maintain that much remains to be done before the country attains the equality that Martin Luther King and Lyndon Johnson envisioned.

THE YOUTH REVOLT

During the 1960s, one age group—young people in their teens and early twenties—loomed larger than any other. As a result of depressed birthrates during the 1930s and the postwar baby boom, there was a sudden explosion in the number of teenagers and young adults. Unlike their parents, whose values had been shaped by the Depression and World War II, young people of the 1960s grew up during a period of prosperity. Growing up in good times allowed them to dismiss the success-oriented lives of their parents' generation in favor of seeking personal fulfillment.

At no earlier time in American history had the gulf between generations seemed so wide. Blue jeans, long hair, psychedelic drugs, casual sex, hippie communes, campus demonstrations, and rock music all became symbols of the distance separating youth from the world of conventional adulthood.

The New Left

Late in the spring of 1962, five dozen college students gathered at a lakeside camp near Port Huron, Michigan, to discuss politics. For four days and nights the members of an obscure student group known as **Students for a Democratic Society (SDS)** talked passionately about such topics as civil rights, foreign policy, and the quality of American life. The gathering ended when the participants agreed on a political platform that expressed their sentiments. This manifesto, one of the pivotal political documents of the 1960s, became known as the **Port Huron Statement.**

The goal set forward in the Port Huron Statement was the creation of a radically democratic political movement in the United States that rejected hierarchy and bureaucracy. In its most important paragraphs, the document called for "participatory democracy"—direct individual involvement in the decisions that affected their lives. This notion would become the battle cry of the student movement of the 1960s—a movement that came to be known as the **New Left.**

During the 1960s, thousands of young college students became politically active. The first issue to spark student radicalism was the modern university, which many students criticized for being too bureaucratic and impersonal. Students questioned university requirements, restrictions on student political activities, and dormitory rules limiting the hours that male and female students could socialize with each other. Restrictions on students handing out political pamphlets on university property led to the first campus demonstrations that broke out at the University of California at Berkeley and soon spread to other campuses.

Involvement in the civil rights movement in the South initiated many students into radical politics. In the early 1960s, many white students from northern universities began to participate in voter registration drives, freedom schools, sit-ins, and freedom rides to help desegregate the South.

In late summer 1964 the first major student demonstrations took place at the University of California at Berkeley. Student protests against war, racism, and poverty continued throughout the country into the 1970s.

Student radicalism also drew inspiration from a literature of social criticism that had flourished in the 1950s. During that decade, many of the most popular films, novels, and writings aimed at young people criticized conventional middle-class life. Popular films, like *Rebel Without a Cause*, and popular novels, like J. D. Salinger's *Catcher in the Rye*, celebrated sensitive, directionless, alienated youths unable to conform to the conventional adult values of suburban and corporate America. Sophisticated works of social criticism by such maverick sociologists, psychologists, and economists as Herbert Marcuse, Norman O. Brown, Paul Goodman, Michael Harrington, and C. Wright Mills, documented the growing concentration of power in the hands of social elites, the persistence of poverty in a land of plenty, and the stresses and injustices in America's social order.

Above all, student radicalism owed its support to student opposition to the Vietnam War. In 1965 an SDS antiwar march attracted at least 15,000 protesters to Washington and commanded wide press attention. Over the next three years, opposition to the war brought thousands of new members to SDS. SDS also tried to organize a democratic "interracial movement of the poor" in northern city neighborhoods.

Many members of SDS quickly grew frustrated by the slow pace of social change and began to embrace violence as a tool to transform society. After 1968 SDS rapidly tore itself apart as an effective political force, and its final convention in 1969 degenerated into a shouting match between radicals and moderates. That same year the Weathermen, a surviving faction of SDS, attempted to launch a guerrilla war in the streets of Chicago—an incident known as the "Days of Rage"—to "tear pig city apart." Finally, in 1970 three members of the Weathermen blew themselves up in a Greenwich Village brownstone trying to make a bomb out of a stick of dynamite and an alarm clock.

Throughout the 1960s, the SDS and other radical student organizations claimed to speak for the na-

tion's youth, and in thousands of editorials and magazine articles, journalists accepted this claim. In fact, the SDS represented only a small minority of college students, who themselves composed a minority of the country's youth. Far more young Americans voted for George Wallace in 1968 than joined SDS, and most college students during the decade spent far more time studying and enjoying the college experience than protesting. Nevertheless, radical students did help to draw the nation's attention to the problem of racism in American society and the moral issues involved in the Vietnam War. In that sense, their impact far exceeded their numbers.

The Making and Unmaking of a Counterculture

The New Left had a series of heroes—ranging from Marx, Lenin, Ho, and Mao to Fidel, Che, and other revolutionaries. It also had its own uniforms, rituals, and music. Faded blue work shirts and jeans, wire-rimmed glasses, and work shoes were de rigueur—so was the political protest music of Phil Ochs, Bob Dylan, and their ilk.

The New Left, however, was only one part of youth protest during the 1960s. While the New Left labored to change the world and remake American society, other youths attempted to alter themselves and reorder consciousness. Variously labeled the counterculture, hippies, or flower children, they had their own heroes, music, dress, and approach to life.

In theory, supporters of the counterculture rejected individualism, competition, and capitalism. Adopting rather unsystematically ideas from oriental religions, they sought to become one with the universe. Rejection of monogamy and the traditional nuclear family gave way to the tribal or communal ideal, where members renounced individualism and private property and shared food, work, and sex. In

Counterculture protest of the 1960s challenged mainstream society in many ways. The bus and attire of these young people reflected "psychedelic" design, inspired by the hallucinatory highs of LSD and other drugs.

such a community, love was a general abstract ideal rather than a focused emotion.

The quest for oneness with the universe led many youths to experiment with hallucinogenic drugs. **LSD** had a particularly powerful allure. Under its influence, poets, musicians, politicians, and thousands of other Americans claimed to have tapped into an all-powerful spiritual force.

Although LSD was outlawed in 1966, use of the drug continued to spread. Perhaps some takers discovered profound truths, but by the late 1960s drugs had done more harm than good. The history of the Haight-Ashbury section of San Francisco illustrated the problems caused by drugs. In 1967 Haight was the center of the "counterculture," the home of the "flower children." In the "city of love" hippies ingested LSD, smoked pot, listened to "acid rock," and proclaimed the dawning of a new age. Yet the area was suffering from severe problems. High levels of racial violence, venereal disease, rape, drug overdoses, and poverty ensured more bad trips than good.

Even music, which along with drugs and sex formed the counterculture trinity, failed to alter human behavior. In 1969 the Woodstock Music Festival in upstate New York billed itself as "three days of peace and music." A few months later, however, a group of Hell's Angels violently interrupted a concert at the Altamont Raceway near San Francisco. As Mick Jagger of the Rolling Stones sang "Sympathy for the Devil" an Angel stabbed an African American man to death.

Like the New Left, the counterculture fell victim to its own excesses. Sex, drugs, and rock and roll did not solve the problems facing the United States. By the early 1970s the counterculture had lost its force.

LIBERATION MOVEMENTS

The struggle of African Americans for racial justice inspired a host of other groups to seek full equality. Women, Mexican Americans, Native Americans, and many other deprived groups protested against discrimination and organized to promote social change.

Women's Liberation

One of the most popular daytime television shows of the 1950s was "Queen for a Day." Five times a week, three women, each with a hard-luck story, recited their tales of woe—diseases, difficult children, poverty—and the studio audience, with the aid of an applause meter, decided which woman was the most miserable. She became "Queen for a Day." Gifts for the queen included a year's supply of Helena Rubinstein cosmetics; a Clairol permanent and makeover by a Hollywood makeup artist; and the electric appliances thought to be necessary for female happiness—a toaster oven, automatic washer, automatic dryer, and an iron. Altogether, everything a woman needed to be a prettier and better housewife.

One woman in the television audience was **Betty Friedan.** A 1942 honors graduate of Smith College and former psychology Ph.D. candidate at the University of California at Berkeley, Friedan had quit graduate school, married, moved to the New York suburbs, and bore three children in rapid succession. American culture told her that a husband, a house, children, and electric appliances were all she needed to attain true happiness. Friedan, however, was not happy, and she was not alone.

In 1957 Friedan sent out a questionnaire to fellow members of her college graduating class. The replies amazed her. Again and again, she found women suffering from "a sense of dissatisfaction." Over the next five years, Friedan interviewed hundreds of other women, and she repeatedly found many of them reporting an unexplainable sense of melancholy and incompleteness.

Friedan was not the only observer to detect a widespread sense of discontent among American women. Doctors identified a new female malady, housewife's syndrome, characterized by a mixture of frustration and exhaustion. When *Redbook* magazine ran an article entitled "Why Young Mothers Feel Trapped," it received 24,000 letters about the story.

Why, Friedan asked, were American women so discontented? In 1963 she published her answer in a book entitled *The Feminine Mystique*. Friedan analyzed and criticized the role of educators, psychologists, sociologists, and the mass media in conditioning women to believe that they could find fulfillment only as housewives and mothers. By requiring women to subordinate their own aspirations to the welfare of their husbands and children, the "feminine mystique" prevented women from achieving self-fulfillment and inevitably left women unhappy. One of the most influential books ever written by an American, *The Feminine Mystique* helped launch a new movement for women's liberation. The book touched a nerve, but the origins of the movement lay deeper, in the role of females in American society.

Sources of Discontent

During the 1950s, many American women reacted against the poverty of the Depression and the upheavals of World War II by placing renewed emphasis on family life. Young women married earlier than had their mothers, had more children, and bore them faster—producing a population growth rate approaching that of India. Growing numbers of women decided to forsake higher education or a career outside the home and achieve emotional fulfillment as wives and mothers.

Politicians, educators, psychologists, and the mass media all echoed the view that women would

Betty Friedan articulated in *The Feminine Mystique* (1963) a message to which many women responded: The restricted roles to which many American women found themselves relegated made it difficult for women to achieve self-fulfillment. Her book helped to spark the women's liberation movement of the 1960s and 1970s.

find their highest fulfillment managing a house and caring for children. Women's magazines pictured housewives as happy with their tasks and depicted career women as neurotic, unhappy, and dissatisfied.

Already underway, however, were dramatic social changes that would contribute to a rebirth of feminism. A dramatic upsurge took place during the 1950s in women's employment and education, as more and more married women entered the labor force. The number of women receiving college degrees also rose. Meanwhile, beginning in 1957 the birthrate began to drop as women elected to have fewer children. A growing discrepancy had begun to appear between the popular image of women as full-time housewives and mothers and the actual realities of many women's lives.

Feminism Reborn

In 1960 women played a limited role in American government. Although women constituted about half of the nation's voters, there were no female Supreme Court justices, federal appeals court justices, governors, cabinet officers, or ambassadors.

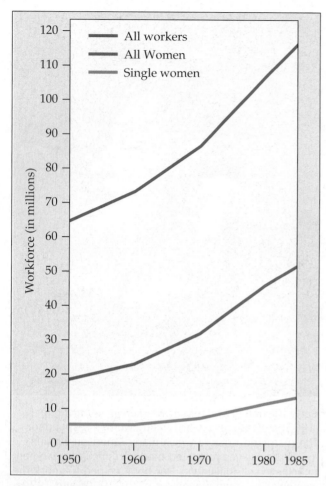

FIGURE 29.4
Women in the Workforce, 1950–1985

In December 1961 President John F. Kennedy placed the issue of women's rights on the national political agenda by establishing a President's Commission on the Status of Women. Chaired by Eleanor Roosevelt, the commission issued its report in 1963, the year that Betty Friedan published *The Feminine Mystique.* The report's recommendations included a call for an end to all legal restrictions on married women's right to own property, to enter into business, and to make contracts; equal opportunity in employment; and greater availability of child-care services.

The most important reform to grow out of the commission's investigations was the 1963 Equal Pay Act, which required equal pay for men and women who performed the same jobs under equal conditions. The Equal Pay Act was the first federal law to prohibit discrimination on the basis of gender.

The next year, Congress enacted a new weapon in the fight against gender discrimination. Title VII of the 1964 Civil Rights Act prohibited discrimination in hiring or promotion based on race, color, religion, national origin, or gender by private employers and unions. This act made it illegal for employers to discriminate against women in hiring and promotion unless the employer could show that gender was a "bona fide occupational qualification" (for example, hiring a man as an attendant for a men's restroom). To investigate complaints of employment discrimination, the act set up the **Equal Employment Opportunity Commission (EEOC).**

At first, the EEOC focused its enforcement efforts on racial discrimination and largely ignored gender

Only 2 of 100 U.S. senators and 15 of 435 representatives were women.

Economically, women workers were concentrated in low-paying service and factory jobs. The overwhelming majority worked as secretaries, waitresses, beauticians, teachers, nurses, and librarians. Lower pay for women doing the same work as men was commonplace. One out of every three companies had separate pay scales for male and female workers. A female bank teller typically made $15 a week less than a man with the same amount of experience, and a female laundry worker made 49 cents an hour less than her male counterpart. Altogether, the earnings of women working full-time averaged only about 60 percent of those of men.

In many parts of the country, the law discriminated against women. In three states—Alabama, Mississippi, and South Carolina—women could not sit on juries. Many states restricted married women's right to make contracts, sell property, engage in business, control their own earnings, and make wills. In practically every state, men had a legal right to have intercourse with their wives whenever they chose to do so.

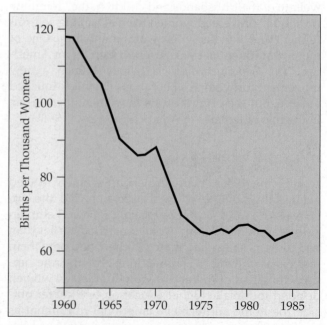

FIGURE 29.5
American Birthrate, 1960–1985

Women have been involved in protest movements throughout the years. Here women march in support of the Equal Rights Amendment. Failure to achieve ratification by the required three-fourths of states sent the amendment to its final defeat in 1982.

discrimination. To pressure the EEOC to enforce the law prohibiting sex discrimination, Betty Friedan and 300 other women formed the **National Organization for Women (NOW)** in 1966. With Friedan as president, the organization filed suit against the EEOC "to force it to comply with its own government rules." It also sued the country's 1300 largest corporations for sex discrimination and lobbied President Johnson to issue an executive order that would include women within federal affirmative action requirements.

At its second national conference in November 1967, NOW drew up an eight-point bill of rights for women. It called for adoption of an **Equal Rights Amendment (ERA)** to the Constitution, prohibition of sex discrimination; provision for equal educational, job training, and housing opportunities for women; and repeal of laws limiting access to contraceptive devices and abortion.

Two proposals produced fierce dissension within the new organization. One source of disagreement was the Equal Rights Amendment, which stated "Equality of rights under the law shall not be denied or abridged by the United States or by any state on account of sex." The other issue that generated controversy was the call for reform of abortion laws.

Despite internal disagreements, NOW's membership grew rapidly. The group broadened its attention to include such issues as the plight of poor and minority women, domestic violence, rape, sexual harassment, the role of women in sport, and the rights of lesbians. The organization claimed a number of achievements. Two victories were particularly important. In 1967, NOW persuaded President Lyndon Johnson to issue Executive Order 11375, which prohibited government contractors from discriminating on the basis of sex and required them to take "affirmative ac-

tion" to ensure that women are properly represented in their workforce. The next year, the EEOC ruled that separate want ads for men and women were a violation of Title VII of the 1964 Civil Rights Act.

Alongside NOW, other more radical feminist groups emerged during the 1960s. In cities across the country, independent women's groups sprouted up, establishing the first feminist bookstores, shelters for battered women, rape crisis centers, and abortion counseling centers. In 1971 Gloria Steinem and others published *Ms.,* the first national feminist magazine. The first 300,000 copies sold out in eight days.

Meanwhile, radical new ideas began to fill the air and a host of new words and phrases entered the language, such as "consciousness raising," "bra burning," "sexism," "male chauvinist pig."

The Growth of Feminist Ideology

In the years following the publication of *The Feminine Mystique,* feminists developed a large body of literature analyzing the economic, psychological, and social roots of female subordination. It was not until 1970, however, that the more radical feminist writings reached the broader reading public with the publication of Shulamith Firestone's *The Dialectic of Sex,* Germaine Greer's *The Female Eunuch,* and Kate Millett's *Sexual Politics.* These books argued that gender distinctions structure virtually every aspect of individual lives, not only in such areas as law and employment but also in personal relationships, language, literature, religion, and individual's self-perceptions. Even more controversially, these works attributed female oppression to men and an ideology of male supremacy. "Women have very little idea how much men hate them," declared Greer. As examples of this hatred, these authors cited pornography, grotesque portrayals of women in literature, sexual harassment, wife abuse, and rape.

Since 1970 **feminist theory** has exploded in many different directions. Today, there are more than 30 national feminist news and opinion magazines along with an additional 20 academic journals dealing with women's issues. Historians, feminist literary and film critics, and physical and social scientists have begun to take insights derived from feminism and ask new questions about women's historical experience, gender role socialization, economic and legal discrimination, and the depiction of women in literature.

The Supreme Court and Sex Discrimination

Despite its conservative image, the Supreme Court under chief justices Warren Burger and William Rehnquist has been active in the area of sex discrimination and women's rights. The Burger Court issued its first important discrimination decision in 1971. In its landmark decision, *Griggs v. Duke Power Company*, the Court established the principle that regardless of an employer's intentions, any employment practice is illegal if it has a "disparate" impact on women or minorities and "if it cannot be shown to be related to job performance."

In 1975 the Burger Court reversed the Warren Court by striking down a Louisiana statute calling for all-male juries. In subsequent decisions, the Court ruled against a Utah law setting different ages at which men and women became adults and overturned an Alabama law setting minimum height and weight requirements for prison guards, standards that disqualified almost all women.

The Court's most controversial decision involving women's rights was delivered in 1973 in the case of *Roe v. Wade.* A single, pregnant Texas waitress, assigned the pseudonym Jane Roe to protect her privacy, brought suit against Dallas district attorney Henry Wade, to prevent him from enforcing a nineteenth-century Texas statute prohibiting abortion. The Court ruled on the woman's behalf and struck down the Texas law and all similar laws in other states. In its ruling, the Court declared that the decision to have an abortion is a private matter of concern only to a woman and her physician and that only in the last three months of pregnancy could the government limit the right to abortion.

Many Americans—including many Catholic lay and clerical organizations—bitterly opposed the Supreme Court's *Roe v. Wade* decision and banded together to form the "right-to-life" movement. The major legislative success of the right-to-life movement was adoption by Congress of the so-called Hyde Amendment, which permitted states to refuse to fund abortions for indigent women.

The Equal Rights Amendment

In March 1972 Congress passed an Equal Rights Amendment (ERA) to the U.S. Constitution, prohibiting gender discrimination. Before the year was over, 22 state legislatures ratified the ERA. Ratification by 38 states (a three-fourths majority) was required before the amendment could be added to the Constitution. Over the next five years, only 13 more states ratified the amendment—and 5 states rescinded their ratification. In 1978 Congress gave proponents of the amendment 39 more months to complete ratification, but no other state gave its approval.

The ERA had been defeated in part by organized labor, which feared that the amendment would eliminate state "protective legislation" that established

Right-to-life groups, backed by Protestant fundamentalists, conservatives, and the Catholic Church, scored a victory with the Hyde Amendment, which prohibited the use of federal funds to pay for abortions. Pro-choice groups, however, helped organize privately funded agencies and clinics to finance abortions for poor women.

minimum wages and maximum hours for women workers. Increasingly, however, resistance to the amendment came from conservative activists such as Phyllis Schlafly, a Radcliffe-educated mother of six from Alton, Illinois. Schlafly argued that the ERA was unnecessary because women were already protected by the Equal Pay Act of 1963 and the Civil Rights Act of 1964, which barred sex discrimination, and that the ERA would outlaw separate public restrooms for men and women and deny wives the right to financial support. She also raised the "women in combat" issue by suggesting that the passage of the ERA would mean that women would have to fight alongside men during war.

Impact of the Women's Liberation Movement

Since 1960 women have made impressive social gains. Gains in employment have been particularly noteworthy. During the 1970s, the number of women working outside the home climbed 42 percent and much of the increase was in what traditionally was considered "men's" work and professional occupations—lawyers, professors, doctors, and administrators.

Striking gains have been made in undergraduate and graduate education. Today, for the first time in American history, women constitute a majority of the nation's college students and nearly as many women as men receive master's degrees. In addition, the number of women students receiving degrees from professional schools has shot upward. Between the early 1970s and the mid-1990s, the proportion of women receiving law degrees rose from 7 percent to 43 percent and the proportion obtaining medical degrees from 9 percent to 38 percent.

Women have also made noteworthy political gains. As of 2002, women made up 14 percent of Congress and 27 percent of all state and local elected officials. In 1981 Sandra Day O'Connor became the first woman to sit on the U.S. Supreme Court, and in 1984 a major political party nominated a woman, Geraldine Ferraro, for the vice presidency.

In spite of all that has been achieved, however, problems remain. Most women today continue to work in a relatively small number of traditional "women's" jobs, and a full-time female worker earns only 68 cents for every $1 paid to men. Even more troubling is the fact that large numbers of women live in poverty. Today, nearly half of all marriages end in divorce and many others end in legal separation and desertion—and the economic plight of these women is often grave. Although female-headed families constitute only 15 percent of the U.S. population, they account for over 50 percent of the poor population.

¡Viva La Raza!

During the 1960s, "Viva la Raza"—"Long Live the People"—was the rallying cry of Mexican-American activists. The United Farm Workers used the slogan in its successful efforts to organize Latino workers in California's agricultural fields. Political organizers in Texas's Rio Grande Valley used the slogan to register voters. Students across the Southwest chanted the slogan in their struggle to promote equal educational opportunity.

On election day in 1963, hundreds of Mexican Americans in Crystal City, Texas, the "spinach capital of the world," gathered near a statue of Popeye the Sailor to do something that most had never done before: vote. Although Mexican Americans outnumbered Anglos two to one, Anglos controlled all five seats on the Crystal City council. For three years, organizers struggled to register Mexican American voters. When the election was over, Mexican Americans had won control of the city council. "We have done the impossible," declared Albert Fuentes, who led the voter-registration campaign. "If we can do it in Crystal City, we can do it all over Texas. We can awaken the sleeping giant."

As the 1960s began, Mexican Americans shared problems of poverty and discrimination with other minority groups. The median income of a Mexican American family was just 62 percent of the median income of the general population, and over a third of Mexican American families lived on less than $3000 a year. Unemployment was twice the rate among non-Hispanic whites, and four-fifths of employed Mexican Americans were concentrated in semiskilled and unskilled jobs, a third in agriculture.

Educational attainment lagged behind other groups (Mexican Americans averaged less than nine years of schooling in 1970), and Mexican American pupils were concentrated in predominantly Mexican American schools, less well staffed and supplied than non–Mexican American schools, with few Hispanic or Spanish-speaking teachers. Gerrymandered election districts and restrictive voting legislation resulted in the political underrepresentation of Mexican Americans. In addition, they were underrepresented or excluded from juries by requirements that jurors be able to speak and understand English.

During the 1960s, a new Mexican American militancy arose. In 1962 **César Chávez** formed the National Farm Workers Association (later the **United Farm Workers**), a union for agricultural workers. Three years later, in Delano, California, he led his first strike. He called for a nationwide boycott of table grapes to win recognition for the union. At the same time that Chávez led the struggle for higher

TABLE 29.3

Percentage of Females in Selected Occupations

Occupation	1972 (Percentage)	1980 (Percentage)	1989 (Percentage)
Professional/technical	39.3	44.3	45.2
Accountants	21.7	36.2	48.6
Computer specialists	16.8	25.7	35.7
Engineers	0.8	4.0	7.6
Lawyers and judges	3.8	12.8	22.3
Life/physical scientists	10.0	20.3	26.9
Physicians/dentists	9.3	12.9	16.5
Professors	28.0	33.9	38.7
Engineering/science technicians	9.1	17.8	19.2
Writers/artists/entertainers	31.7	39.3	46.0
Sales	41.6	45.3	49.3
Real estate agents/brokers	36.7	50.7	51.0
Clerks, retail	68.9	71.1	81.8
Clerical	75.6	80.1	80.0
Bookkeepers	97.9	90.5	91.7
Clerical supervisors	57.8	70.5	58.2
Office machine operators	71.4	72.6	62.6
Secretaries	99.1	99.1	98.3
Crafts workers	3.6	6.0	8.6
Blue-collar supervisors	6.9	10.8	n/a[*]
Machinists and jobsetters	0.6	4.0	n/a[*]
Tool and die makers	0.5	2.8	n/a[*]
Mechanics (except automobile)	1.0	2.6	3.1

Source: U.S. Bureau of the Census, *Statistical Abstract of the United States: 1982–83* (103d edition), *1991* (111th edition), Washington, D.C., 1982, 1991.

[*]n/a = not available.

wages, enforcement of state labor laws, and recognition of the farm workers' union, Reies Lopez Tijerina fought to restore the legal rights of heirs to Spanish and Mexican land grants that had been guaranteed under the treaty ending the Mexican-American War.

In Denver, Rodolfo ("Corky") Gonzales formed the Crusade for Justice in 1965 to protest school discrimination; provide legal, medical, and financial services and jobs for Chicanos; and foster the Mexican American culture. In South Texas, La Raza Unida, an independent political party, fielded candidates for mayor, city council, and school boards and spread in the early 1970s to other Southwestern states. On college campuses across the Southwest, Mexican Americans formed political organizations.

In 1968 Congress responded to the demand among Mexican Americans for equal educational opportunity by enacting legislation encouraging school districts to adopt bilingual education programs to instruct non–English speakers in both English and their native language. In 1986, Congress moved to legalize the status of many immigrants, including many Mexicans, who entered the United States illegally. The Immigration Reform and Control Act of 1986 provided permanent legal residency to undocumented workers who had lived in the United States since before 1982 and prohibited employment of illegal aliens.

Since 1960 Mexican Americans have made important political gains. During the 1960s four Mexican Americans—Senator Joseph Montoya of New Mexico and Representatives Eligio de la Garza and Henry B. Gonzales of Texas and Edward R. Roybal of California—were elected to Congress. In 1974 two Mexican Americans were elected governors—Jerry Apodaca in New Mexico and Raul Castro in Arizona—becoming the first Mexican American governors since early in the twentieth century. In 1981 Henry Cisneros of San Antonio, Texas, became the first Mexican American mayor of a large city. Today, 20 million Mexican Americans continue to struggle to expand their political influence, improve their economic condition, and preserve their distinctive culture.

Mexican Americans celebrate their heritage even as they continue to struggle for political and economic gains in the United States. Here, children perform traditional dances at a Cinco de Mayo (or "Fifth of May") gathering in Denver, Colorado. The holiday, which commemorates the victory of Mexican soldiers over an invading French army in 1862, celebrates Mexican patriotism and culture.

The Native American Power Movement

In November 1969, 200 Native Americans seized the abandoned federal penitentiary on Alcatraz Island in San Francisco Bay. For 19 months Indian activists occupied the island to draw attention to conditions on the nation's Indian reservations. Alcatraz, the Native Americans said, symbolized conditions on reservations: "It has no running water; it has inadequate sanitation facilities; there is no industry, and so unemployment is very great; there are no health care facilities; the soil is rocky and unproductive."

On Thanksgiving Day, 1970, 350 years after the Pilgrims' arrival, Wampanoag Indians, who had taken part at the first Thanksgiving, held a National Day of Mourning at Plymouth, Massachusetts. A tribal representative declared, "We forfeited our country. Our lands have fallen into the hands of the aggressor. We have allowed the white man to keep us on our knees." Meanwhile, another group of Native Americans established a settlement at Mount Rushmore, to demonstrate Indian claims to the Black Hills.

During the late 1960s and early 1970s, a new spirit of political militancy arose among the first Americans, just as it had among African Americans, women, and Mexican Americans. No other group, however, faced problems more severe than Native Americans. Throughout the 1960s, Native Americans were the nation's poorest minority group, worse off than any other group by virtually every socioeco-

nomic measure. In 1970 the Indian unemployment rate was 10 times the national average, and 40 percent of the Native American population lived below the poverty line. In that year, Native American life expectancy was just 44 years, a third less than that of the average American. Half a million Indian families lived in unsanitary dilapidated dwellings, many in shanties, huts, or even abandoned automobiles.

Native Americans had started to revolt against such conditions during World War II. In 1944 they formed the National Congress of American Indians (NCAI), the first major intertribal association. Among the group's primary concerns were protection of Native American land rights and improved educational opportunities for Native Americans. When Congress voted in 1953 to allow states to assert legal jurisdiction over Native American reservations without tribal consent, and the federal government sought to transfer federal responsibilities for a dozen tribes to the states (a policy known as "termination") and to relocate Native Americans into urban areas, the NCAI led opposition to these measures.

By the late 1950s a new spirit of Native American nationalism had arisen. In 1961 a militant new Native American organization appeared, the National Indian Youth Council, which called for "Red Power." The council sponsored demonstrations, marches, and "fish-ins" to protest state efforts to abolish Native American fishing rights guaranteed by federal treaties. Native Americans in the San Francisco Bay area in 1964 established the Indian

César Chávez and *La Causa*

In early April 1962, a 35-year-old community organizer named César Estrada Chávez set out to single-handedly organize impoverished migrant farm laborers in the California grape fields. He, his wife, and their eight children packed their belongings into a dilapidated nine-year-old station wagon, and moved to Delano, California, a town of 12,000 that was the center of the nation's table-grape industry. Over the next two years, Chávez spent his entire lifetime savings of $1200 creating a small social service organization for Delano's field laborers; it offered immigration counseling, citizenship classes, funeral benefits, credit to buy cars and homes, assistance with voter registration, and a cooperative to buy tires and gasoline. As the emblem of his new organization, the National Farm Workers Association, Chávez chose a black Aztec eagle inside a white circle on a red background.

Chávez's sympathy for the plight of migrant farm workers came naturally. He was born in Yuma, Arizona, in 1927, one of five children of Mexican immigrants. When he was 10 years old, his parents lost their small farm; he, his brothers and sisters, and his parents hoed beets, picked grapes, and harvested peaches and figs in Arizona and California. There were times when the family had to sleep in its car or camp under bridges. When young César was able to attend school (he attended more than 30 schools as a child), he was often shunted into special classrooms set aside for Mexican-American children.

In 1944, when he was 17, Chávez joined the navy and served for two years on a destroyer escort in the Pacific. After World War II ended, he married and spent two and a half years as a sharecropper raising strawberries. That was followed by work in apricot and prune orchards and in a lumber camp. Then in 1952 his life took a fateful turn. He joined the Community Service Organization (CSO), which wanted to educate and organize the poor so that they could solve their own social and economic problems. After founding CSO chapters in Madera, Bakersfield, and Hanford, California, Chávez became the organization's general director in 1958. Four years later, he broke with the organization when it rejected his proposal to establish a farm workers' union.

Most labor leaders considered Chávez's goal of creating the first successful union of farm workers in U.S. history an impossible dream. Not only did farm laborers suffer from high rates of illiteracy and poverty (average family earnings were just $2000 in 1965), they also experienced persistently high rates of unemployment (traditionally around 19 percent) and were divided into a variety of ethnic groups (Mexican, Arab, Filipino, and Puerto Rican). Making unionization even more difficult were the facts that farm workers rarely remained in one locality for very long, and they were easily replaced by inexpensive Mexican day laborers, known as *braceros,* who were trucked into California and the Southwest at harvest time.

Moreover, the National Labor Relations Act of 1935 specifically excluded farm workers. Unlike other American workers, farm workers were not guaranteed the right to organize, had no guarantee of a minimum wage, and had no federally guaranteed standards of work in the fields. State laws requiring toilets, rest periods, and drinking water in the fields were largely ignored.

In September 1965, Chávez was drawn into his first important labor controversy. The Filipino grape pickers went on strike. "All right, Chávez," said one of the Filipino grape pickers' leaders, "are you going to stand beside us, or are you going to scab against us?" Despite his fear that the National Farm Workers Association was not sufficiently well organized to support a strike (it had less than $100 in its strike fund), he assured the Filipino workers that members of his association would not go into the field as strikebreakers. *¡Huelga!*—the Spanish word for strike—became the grape pickers' battle cry.

Within weeks, the labor strike began to attract national attention. Unions, church groups, and civil rights organizations offered financial support for *La Causa,* as the farm workers' movement became known. In March 1966, Chávez led a 250-mile Easter march from Delano to Sacramento to dramatize the plight of migrant farm laborers. That same year, Chávez's National Farm Workers Association merged with an AFL-CIO affiliate to form the United Farm Workers Organizing Committee.

A staunch apostle of nonviolence, Chávez was deeply troubled by violent incidents that marred the strike. Some growers raced tractors along the roadside, covering the strikers with dirt and dust. Others drove spraying machines along the edges of their fields, spraying insecticide and

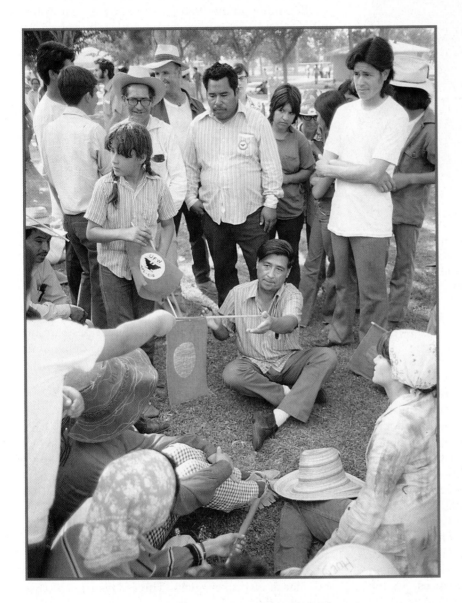

fertilizer on the picketers. Local police officers arrested a minister for reading Jack London's definition of a scab ("a two-legged animal with a corkscrew soul, a water-logged brain, and a combination backbone made of jelly and glue"). Some strikers, in turn, intimidated strikebreakers by pelting them with marbles fired from slingshots and by setting fire to packing crates. One striker tried to drive a car into a group of growers.

In an effort to quell the escalating violence and to atone for the mili-

tancy of some union members, Chávez began to fast on February 14, 1968. For five days he kept the fast a secret. Then, in an hour-long speech to striking workers, he explained that continued violence would destroy everything the union stood for. He said that the "truest act of courage, the strongest act of manliness, is to sacrifice ourselves for others in a totally nonviolent struggle for justice." For 21 days he fasted; he lost 35 pounds and his doctor began to fear for his health. He finally agreed to

take a small amount of bouillon and grapefruit juice and medication. On March 11, he ended his fast by taking communion and breaking bread with Senator Robert F. Kennedy.

The strike dragged on for three years. To heighten public awareness of the farm workers' cause, Chávez in 1968 initiated a boycott of table grapes. It was the boycott that pressured many of the growers into settling the strike. An estimated 17 million American consumers went without grapes in support of the farm workers' bargaining position. By mid-1970, two-thirds of California grapes were grown under contract with Chávez's union.

In the years following its 1970 victory, Chávez's union has been beset by problems from within and without. Union membership dwindled from a high of more than 60,000 in 1972 to a low of 5000 in 1974. (It has since climbed back to around 30,000). Meanwhile, public concern for the plight of migrant farm workers declined.

Chávez died in 1993, at age 66. To commemorate his legacy, 25,000 people marched for more than two and a half hours to the spot where he had founded the United Farm Workers Union. As a result of Chávez's efforts, the most backbreaking tool used by farm workers, the short hoe, was eliminated, and the use of many dangerous pesticides in the grape fields was prohibited. His efforts also brought about a 70 percent increase in real wages from 1964 to 1980 and establishment of health-care benefits, disability insurance, pension plans, and standardized grievance procedures for farm workers. He helped secure passage of the nation's first agricultural labor relations act in California in 1975, which prohibited growers from firing striking workers or engaging in bad-faith bargaining. Thanks to his efforts, migrant farm laborers won a right held by all other American workers: the right to bargain collectively.

In 1972 members of the American Indian Movement (AIM) occupied the Bureau of Indian Affairs—the federal government bureau charged with managing Indian reservations in the United States—building in Washington, D.C., to draw attention to the plight of Native Americans and to protest government policies toward them.

Historical Society to present history from the Indian point of view, while the Native American Rights Fund brought legal suits against states that had taken Indian land and abolished Indian hunting, fishing, and water rights in violation of federal treaties. Many Indian peoples also took legal action to prevent strip mining or spraying of pesticides on Native American lands.

The best known of all Indian Power groups was the **American Indian Movement (AIM),** formed by a group of Chippewa in Minneapolis in 1966 to protest police brutality against Native Americans. In the fall of 1972, AIM seized the offices of the Bureau of Indian Affairs in Washington, D.C., and occupied them for a week to dramatize their grievances. In the spring of 1973, 200 heavily armed Native Americans took over the town of Wounded Knee, South Dakota, site of an 1890 massacre of 300 Sioux by the U.S. army cavalry. They occupied the town for 71 days.

Militant protests paid off. The 1972 Indian Education Act gave Indian parents greater control over their children's schools. The 1976 Indian Health Care Act sought to address deficiencies in health care, while the 1978 Indian Child Welfare Act gave tribes control over custody decisions involving Native American children. A series of landmark Supreme Court decisions aided the cause of Native American sovereignty and national self-government. The 1959 *Williams v. Lee* case upheld the authority of Native American courts to make decisions involving

non–Native Americans. The 1968 case of *Menominee Tribe v. United States* declared that states could not invalidate fishing and hunting rights Native Americans had acquired through treaty agreements.

Beginning in the 1970s, a number of Indian tribes initiated lawsuits to recover land illegally seized by whites. In 1980, the federal government agreed to pay $81.5 million to the Passamaquoddy and Penobscot of Maine, and $105 million to the Sioux in South Dakota. Court decisions also permitted tribal authorities to sell cigarettes, run gambling casinos, and levy taxes.

Native Americans are no longer a vanishing group of Americans. The 1990 census recorded a Native American population of over 2 million, five times the number recorded in 1950. About half of these people live on reservations. The largest Native American populations are located in Alaska, Arizona, California, New Mexico, and Oklahoma. As the Native American population has grown in size, individual Indians have claimed many accomplishments, including receipt of the Pulitzer Prize for fiction by N. Scott Momaday, a Kiowa. Although Native Americans continue to face severe problems of employment, income, and education, they have decisively demonstrated that they will not abandon their identity and culture or be treated as dependent wards of the federal government.

Gay and Lesbian Liberation

On June 27, 1969, New York City police staged an early morning raid on the Stonewall Inn, a Greenwich Village bar catering primarily to transvestites, gay men, and lesbians. Raids on gay or crossdressers' bars were common at the time. State law threatened bars with the loss of their liquor licenses if they tolerated same-sex dancing or employed or served men who wore women's clothing. Instead of acquiescing passively in the raid, the bar's patrons fought back, battling the police with bricks, bottles, and shards of broken glass. Three days of civil disobedience followed.

This incident ushered in a new era for gays and lesbians in the United States: an era of pride, openness, and activism. It led many gays and lesbians to "come out of the closet" and publicly assert their sexual identity and organize politically. In Stonewall's wake, activist organizations like the Gay Liberation Front transformed sexual orientation into a political issue, attacking customs and laws that defined homosexuality as a sin, a crime, or a mental illness.

Hostility toward homosexuality had deep roots in American society. State sodomy laws criminalized homosexual acts. Federal immigration laws excluded homosexual aliens. The 1873 Comstock Act permitted postal authorities to exclude homosexual publications from the mail, while Hollywood's "Production Code," adopted in 1934, prohibited the depiction of gay characters or open discussion of homosexuality in film. The American Psychiatric Association's diagnostic manual defined homosexuality as a psychopathology. During the McCarthy era, the charge that homosexuals were "moral perverts" and security risks led the government to adopt rules explicitly excluding them from federal jobs or military service.

Although the emergence of the **gay and lesbian liberation** movement caught the general public by surprise, it did not emerge overnight. During the 1950s, a handful of advocacy groups, including the Mattachine Society and the Daughters of Bilitis, arose, opposing laws that prohibited and punished homosexuality. By the late 1960s, gay and lesbian subcultures and communities had grown in many of the nation's cities, complete with bars, cabarets, magazines, and restaurants.

At the same time, challenges to earlier legal and medical opinions about homosexuality appeared. Alfred Kinsey's studies of sexual behavior, published in 1948 and 1953, suggested that homosexual and lesbian behavior was far more prevalent than most Americans previously suspected. Kinsey estimated about 10 percent of men and 5 percent of women were sexually attracted primarily to members of their own sex. In 1961, Illinois became the first state to repeal its sodomy statutes. The next year the Supreme Court ruled that a magazine featuring photographs of male nudes was not obscene and, therefore, not subject to censorship. In 1973, the American Psychiatric Association removed homosexuality from its list of psychopathologies.

In recent years, gay rights has become one of the most highly charged issues in American politics. In 1986 the Supreme Court upheld state sodomy laws, ruling that private acts of homosexuality were not protected by the Constitution. Gay advocacy groups responded to the decision by lobbying for passage of state and city civil rights acts that would ban discrimination on the basis of sexual orientation in employment and housing. Twelve states passed laws barring workplace discrimination based on sexual orientation, and 8 states, some 130 local governments, and about 4,500 companies offer health benefits to domestic partners, including same-sex partners.

A number of municipalities and states, including Colorado, responded to these initiatives by passing referenda prohibiting government from extending special rights to homosexuals. State courts, however, found these to be unconstitutional infringements on the right of gay and lesbian citizens to petition government. In 1993, a major controversy erupted after President Bill Clinton proposed allowing gays and lesbians to serve openly in the military. Widespread opposition forced him to back down and compromise on a policy that permitted gays to serve in the military as long as they did not reveal their sexual orientation and refrained from homosexual conduct. Nicknamed "don't ask, don't tell," the compromise policy satisfied few, and federal courts refused to permit the expulsion of gays from the military.

A major landmark in the history of gay rights took place in 1999, when the Vermont Supreme Court ruled that gay and lesbian couples have a right to the same benefits and protections as heterosexual married couples. The next year, Vermont's legislature authorized gay and lesbian couples to form civil unions carrying the same benefits, protections, and responsibilities granted to spouses in a marriage.

The Earth First

In 1962, **Rachel Carson,** a marine biologist, published a book that would do more to awaken environmental consciousness than any other single work.

A gay couple walk with their toddler at a gay rights march in New York City. As legal and societal restrictions ease, more gays and lesbians are raising children.

Entitled *Silent Spring*, it described how DDT and other chemical pesticides contaminated nature's food chain, killing large numbers of birds and fish and causing human illnesses.

Modern environmentalism began at the end of the nineteenth century. In 1872, Congress created the first national park, Yellowstone. In 1891, the Forest Reserve Act gave the president the power to set up national forests. The next year saw the founding of the Sierra Club, the nation's first organization committed to protecting wilderness areas.

During the Progressive era of the early twentieth century, conflicting visions of the environment struggled for dominance. Some figures, including Gifford Pinchot, the head of the U.S. Forest Service under Theodore Roosevelt, were primarily interested in using scarce natural resources more rationally and efficiently. Others, including the naturalist John Muir, who was the Sierra Club's first president, were eager to preserve wilderness and wildlife for their own sake and prevent industrial development from spoiling nature's beauty.

Franklin Roosevelt's New Deal initiated a number of important conservation projects. The Civilian Conservation Corps put three million young men to work restoring national parks and forests. The Tennessee Valley Authority restored the region's forests by planting trees and controlling flooding and provided cheap electricity by building dams. The Soil Conservation Service combated the poor farming and ranching practices that contributed to the loss of topsoil during the Dust Bowl of the early 1930s.

It was during the 1960s, however, that environmentalism became a mass movement. A series of environmental horror stories broadened the environmentalist constituency from naturalists to include a majority of Americans. Cleveland's Cuyahoga River caught fire; toxic residues were discovered in mothers' breast milk; acid rain destroyed lakes and streams.

The establishment of new organizations, like the Environmental Defense Fund, which was founded in 1967, and the heightened interest in "organic farming" and "natural foods"—foods produced without using synthetic chemicals—testified to the growing public interest in environmental protection. The National Environmental Policy Act, passed in 1969, required preparation of environmental impact statements for all federally funded highways, dams, pipelines, and power plants. The celebration of the first "Earth Day," however, underscored public concern for the environment. On April 22, 1970, 20 million Americans gathered in parks, planted trees, and staged demonstrations to observe Earth Day.

In Earth Day's wake, Congress combined 15 federal pollution programs to create the Environmental Protection Agency to set and enforce pollution standards, passed the Clean Air and Clean Water Acts, and enacted the Endangered Species Act in 1973, protecting threatened species of wildlife. Since these initial measures were adopted, environmental concern has surged and ebbed. During the mid-1970s, when the United States experienced severe oil shortages and economic productivity dipped, fewer Americans were willing to sacrifice economic growth or a high standard of living for environmental protection. Whenever news reports of environmental degradation appeared, however, public concern quickly resurfaced. In 1978 reports that dangerous chemicals had been buried beneath Love Canal in New York led Congress to create the "Superfund" to finance the clean-up of the nation's most dangerous toxic waste sites. Publicity over the dangers of "ozone depletion" led the United States and most other nations to negotiate a 1989 treaty cutting production of chlorofluorocarbons that destroy the atmosphere's protective ozone shield.

The report card on the nation's environmental record offers a mixed picture. Contamination levels of DDT, lead, and cancer-causing polychlorinated biphenyls have declined sharply. By 1995, environmental regulations had reduced sulfur dioxide emissions by 53 percent; carbon monoxide by 57 percent; smoke and soot by 59 percent; and smog by 39 percent; and had made America's water supply the cleanest in the industrial world. Strict federal rules curbed automobile and industrial emissions, while increasing automobile mileage and the efficiency of appliances. As a result, while the American economy grew by 50 percent between 1970 and 1995, energy usage increased by only 10 percent.

Yet in spite of the regulation of power-plant smokestacks, aquatic life in 4000 lakes remains threatened by acid rain. While automobile tailpipe emissions have been sharply curtailed, half the population lives in counties that violate federal clean air standards. Despite efforts to clean the nation's rivers and lakes, many freshwater fish contain dangerous levels of toxic chemicals. As some older environmental hazards have been addressed, new concerns have arisen, such as global warming—the greenhouse effect caused by the buildup of carbon dioxide and other gases in the stratosphere—and the depletion of the earth's protective ozone shield.

Public opinion polls indicate that Americans overwhelmingly support environmental protection, and over three-quarters consider themselves environmentalists. Whether or not a fundamental change has taken place in America's relationship to nature remains uncertain. Despite limited efforts at recycling, the United States remains a "throwaway" nation that produces twice as much garbage as all of Europe. With just 2 percent of the world's population, the

Among the threats to the fragile ecosystem of the Mojave Desert is its use as a garbage dump in some areas. Despite decades of environmental activism in the United States, environmental protection remains an unachieved goal.

United States uses 24 percent of the world's energy—twice as much as Japan and Western Europe. And the United States remains a growth-oriented society that continues to absorb millions of acres of cropland each year for highways, tract housing, and office buildings. Each year the federal government continues to add 35 to 50 species to the list of endangered species.

CONCLUSION

It was the country's greatest technological achievement—even greater than the construction of the Panama Canal and the transcontinental railroad. At 10:56 P.M. Eastern Daylight Time on July 20, 1969, Neil Armstrong took "one small step" off the Lunar Lander Eagle and became the first human being to set foot on the moon. His boots sank a couple of inches into the moon's powdery surface, but, given the moon's weak gravity, his weight was the equivalent of 60 pounds.

This triumph did not come easily. Several times during Lunar Lander's descent, the onboard computer had flashed alarms. Then, as the astronauts approached the surface—with less than five minutes of fuel left—they discovered that the landing site was a field of boulders and craters. If the landing struts hit a large rock, the lander might suffer severe structural damage or even tip over. The astronauts decided to fly 1100 feet west and hope for the best. By then, no more than 45 seconds of fuel remained.

In 1961, President John F. Kennedy had challenged the nation to land astronauts on the moon by the end of the decade. To accomplish this task, the National Aeronautics and Space Administration (NASA), the federal government's space agency, spent nearly 6 percent of the entire federal budget. After the success of Apollo 11, public interest in space exploration faded. On December 11, 1972, Harrison H. Schmitt and Eugene Cernan became the last astronauts to land on the moon. Three more Apollo missions were scheduled to fly to the moon, but all were cancelled due to budgetary restraints. Today, the unused Saturn V rocket that was to carry Apollo 18 to the moon lies on the ground at the Johnson Space Center in Houston. Not a mock-up, it is a fully functional rocket.

The 1960s was a decade of heady idealism when anything seemed possible. President John F. Kennedy held up a bold vision of America embarking on a "New Frontier" and President Lyndon Johnson called on Americans to build a "Great Society" and to wage a "War on Poverty." The 1960s did witness far-reaching societal changes, including a sexual revolution, women's liberation, and a civil rights revolution. The 1960s, however, was also a decade of increasing political polarization. Racial tensions mounted, culminating in race riots. The war in Vietnam produced division within families, on campuses, and in Congress.

Decades later, the nation's politics and culture still bear the imprint of the 1960s. During this crucial decade the foundations were laid for many of the social movements that flourish today, including the women's movement, the environmental movement, and the gay and lesbian rights movement. Societal changes that began in the 1960s also persist, such as a massive influx of married women into the workforce. The social movements of the decade also produced a

CHRONOLOGY OF KEY EVENTS

1960   Four freshmen at North Carolina Agricultural and Technical College in Greensboro, North Carolina, stage the first sit-in to protest segregation; Student Nonviolent Coordinating Committee (SNCC) is founded

1961   Congress of Racial Equality (CORE) stages freedom rides to expose segregation in transportation; *Mapp v. Ohio* holds that evidence obtained by unreasonable searches must be excluded at trial

1962   James Meredith enrolls at the University of Mississippi; Students for a Democratic Society (SDS) issue Port Huron Statement; César Chávez begins to organize California farm workers

1963   George C. Wallace is inaugurated Alabama governor; Martin Luther King, Jr., leads demonstrations against segregation in Birmingham, Alabama; racial violence in the South leaves 10 people dead, 35 black homes and churches firebombed; Betty Friedan publishes *The Feminine Mystique,* helping launch a new feminist movement; Equal Pay Act, first federal law to prohibit sex discrimination, requires equal pay for identical work; *Gideon v. Wainwright* holds that indigent defendants have a right to a court-appointed attorney; March on Washington, D.C., for civil rights and jobs; John F. Kennedy is assassinated; Lyndon Johnson becomes thirty-sixth president

1964   President Johnson announces War on Poverty; Manpower Development and Training Act and Economic Opportunity Act establish the Job Corps and Neighborhood Youth Corps; in *Escobedo v. Illinois,* Supreme Court rules that suspects being interrogated by police have a right to legal counsel; Civil Rights Act prohibits discrimination in employment and public facilities; Twenty-fourth Amendment prohibits poll taxes in federal elections

1965   Malcolm X is assassinated; Martin Luther King, Jr., leads demonstrations in Selma, Alabama, to bring issue of voting rights to national attention; Voting Rights Act prohibits literacy tests and sends federal examiners to seven southern states to register black voters; riot in Watts, predominantly black section of Los Angeles, results in 34 deaths; Medicare extends medical insurance to older Americans; Executive Order 11246 requires government contractors to prepare affirmative action plans; Ralph Nader publishes *Unsafe at Any Speed*

1966   SNCC and CORE embrace black nationalism; Black Panther party is organized; National Organization for Women (NOW) is formed; Congress passes Model Cities Act to attack urban blight

1967   Riots take place in 127 cities

1968   Medicaid expanded to cover the medical expenses of the poor; assassination of Martin Luther King, Jr., in Memphis, Tennessee, is followed by riots in 168 cities

1969   Three days of civil disobedience follow a police raid on the Stonewall Inn in New York City, a gay and lesbian bar

1970   Twenty million Americans celebrate the first Earth Day; Congress creates the Environmental Protection Agency and passes the Clean Air and Clean Water Acts

1971   In *Swann v. Charlotte-Mecklenburg Board of Education,* U.S. Supreme Court upholds school busing as a tool of racial integration

1973   *Roe v. Wade* decision legalizes abortion; the American Psychiatric Association removes homosexuality from its list of psychopathologies; Congress enacts the Endangered Species Act

1986   Immigration Reform and Control Act provides permanent legal residency to undocumented workers who have lived in United States since 1982

1993   Gays and lesbians are permitted to serve in the military

backlash among those who associated the decade with illicit drugs, sexual immorality, declining patriotism, and family breakdown. But if some of the sense of promise and possibilities that characterized the 1960s has faded, still the decade brought our nation closer to achieving its ideals of liberty and equality.

CHAPTER SUMMARY AND KEY POINTS

The 1960s was a decade when hundreds of thousands of ordinary Americans gave new life to the nation's democratic ideals. African Americans used sit-ins, freedom rides, and protest marches to fight segregation, poverty, and unemployment. Feminists called for equal job opportunities and an end to sexual discrimination. Mexican Americans protested discrimination in voting, education, and jobs. Native Americans demanded that the government recognize their land claims and the right of tribes to govern themselves. Gays and lesbians struggled to end discrimination based on sexual orientation. Environmentalists demanded legislation to control the amount of pollution released into the environment.

- Early in the decade, African American college students, impatient with the slow pace of legal change, staged sit-ins, freedom rides, and protest marches to challenge segregation in the South. Their efforts led the federal government to pass the Civil Rights Act of 1964, prohibiting discrimination in public facilities and employment, and the Twenty-Fourth Amendment and the Voting Rights Act of 1965, guaranteeing voting rights.

- The example of the civil rights movement inspired other groups to press for equal rights. The women's movement fought for equal educational and employment opportunities and a transformation of traditional views about women's place in society.

- Mexican Americans battled for bilingual education programs in schools, unionization of farm workers, improved job opportunities, and increased political power.

- Native Americans pressed for control over their lands and resources, the preservation of native cultures, and tribal self-government.

- Gays and lesbians organized to end legal discrimination based on sexual orientation.

- In a far-reaching effort to reduce poverty, alleviate malnutrition, extend medical care, provide adequate housing, and enhance employment opportunities for the poor, President Lyndon Johnson launched his Great Society Program in 1964. But the Vietnam War, ghetto rioting, and the rise of a militant antiwar movement and the counterculture contributed to a political backlash that would lead the Republican party to control the presidency for 20 of the next 24 years.

SUGGESTIONS FOR FURTHER READING

Rodolfo Acuña, *Occupied America*, 4th ed. (2000). Discusses the Mexican American struggle for equality.

Clayborne Carson et al., *The Eyes on the Prize Civil Rights Reader* (1991). Documents, speeches, and first hand accounts of the civil rights struggle.

John D'Emilio, *Sexual Politics, Sexual Communities: The Making of a Homosexual Minority in the United States, 1940–1970* (1983). Traces the roots of the struggle for gay and lesbian liberation.

John Dittmer, *Local People: The Struggle for Civil Rights in Mississippi* (1994). Examines the civil rights movement in a specific state.

Sara Evans, *Personal Politics: The Roots of Women's Liberation in the Civil Rights Movement and the New Left* (1980). Examines how women active in civil rights and the New Left struggles developed a feminist consciousness and struggled to promote gender equality.

Jo Freeman, *The Politics of Women's Liberation: A Case Study of an Emerging Social Movement and Its Relation to the Policy Process* (2000). An analysis of the history of different branches of the feminist movement from the mid-1960s to the mid-1970s and the campaigns for equal pay and job opportunities and legalized abortion.

David G. Gutierrez, *Walls and Mirrors: Mexican Americans, Mexican Immigrants, and the Politics of Ethnicity* (1995). Analyzes the quest of Mexican Americans for equal rights.

Daniel Horowitz, *Betty Friedan and the Making of the Feminine Mystique: The American Left, the Cold War, and Modern Feminism* (1998). This biography traces the evolution of Friedan's feminist outlook.

Donald L. Parman, *Indians and the American West in the Twentieth Century* (1994). Examines the Native American struggle to preserve tribal self-government and reassert control over resources.

James T. Patterson, *Brown v. Board of Education: A Civil Rights Milestone and Its Troubled Legacy* (2000). A thorough examination of the landmark case and its fifty-year aftermath.

Philip Shabecoff, *A Fierce Green Fire: The American Environmental Movement* (1993). Chronicles the growth of the American environmental movement.

Robert Weisbrot, *Freedom Bound: A History of America's Civil Rights Movement* (1991). A succinct single volume history of the civil rights movement by a leading authority on the topic.

Juan Williams, *Eyes on the Prize: America's Civil Rights Years, 1954–1965* (1987). The companion volume to the six-part PBS series offers a highly readable history of the civil rights movement.

Novels

Sandra Cisneros, *House on Mango Street* (1984).

Don DeDillo, *Libra* (1988).

Louise Erdrich, *Love Medicine* (1984).

Richard Farina, *Been Down So Long It Looks Like Up To Me* (1962).

Maxine Hong Kingston, *The Woman Warrior* (1976).

Leslie Marmon Sikko, *Ceremony* (1977).

Amy Tan, *Joy Luck Club* (1989).

Tom Wolfe, *The Electric Kool-Aid Acid Test* (1967).

MEDIA RESOURCES

Web Sites

American Socrates: The Life of Bayard Rustin
http://www.rustin.org/
The companion site to a film about Bayard Rustin contains biographical information and a variety of online resources.

Chicano! History of the Mexican American Civil Rights Movement
http://chicano.nlcc.com/
The companion site to the PBS series contains a time line, biographies, and episode summaries.

Civil Rights Documentation Project
http://www-dept.usm.edu/~mcrohb/
A collection of oral histories documenting the Civil Rights movement in Mississippi.

CLNet Research Center
http://latino.sscnet.ucla.edu/research/
This site includes an extensive set of Mexican American history links.

Environmental History Timeline
http://www.radford.edu/~wkovarik/histl/timeline.new.html
A detailed illustrated chronology by a leading environmental historian.

The Feminist Movement
http://www.jofreeman.com/feminism/feminist.htm
Essays by a leading authority on the history of the women's movement.

Free Speech Movement
http://www.lib.berkeley.edu/BANC/FSM/
Oral histories and other materials documenting the history of student protests at the University of California, Berkeley, in the early and mid-1960s.

LBJ Library Oral History HomePage
http://www.lbjlib.utexas.edu/johnson/archives.hom/biopage.asp
In addition to oral histories, other online resources available from the LBJ Library include presidential speeches and messages, National Security, Action Memoranda, photographs, and audio and video resources.

MLK Online
http://www.mlkonline.com/
This site contains speech transcripts, links, and audio and video files.

Native Voices
http://www.gliah.uh.edu/native_voices/native_voices.cfm
Primary sources document the Native American struggle for political, cultural, and economic sovereignty.

Out of the Past: 400 Years of Lesbian and Gay History in America
http://www.pbs.org/outofthepast/
The companion site to the PBS documentary.

People With a History
http://www.fordham.edu/halsall/pwh/
Primary sources document the history of gays and lesbians in the United States and elsewhere.

The Sixties Project
http://lists.village.virginia.edu/sixties/
An extensive collection of documents and personal narratives from the 1960s.

SNCC, 1960–1966
http://www.ibiblio.org/sncc/index.html
Information about the Student Nonviolent Coordinating Committee's first years.

United States v. Cecil Price et al.
http://www.law.umkc.edu/faculty/porojects/ftrials/price&bowers/price&bowers.htm
This site contains documents, a chronology, and images relating to the trial on which the film *Mississippi Burning* was based.

We Shall Overcome: Historic Places of the Civil Rights Movement
http://www.cr.nps.gov/nr/travel/civilrights/
The national register of historic places of the Civil Rights movement.

Films and Videos

Before Stonewall: The Making of a Gay and Lesbian Community. A social history of homosexuality in America from the 1920s to 1969.

Berkeley in the Sixties. The Free Speech, antiwar, and counterculture movements.

Chicago 1968. This documentary from public television's *American Experience* series explores the atmosphere surrounding the 1968 Democratic National Convention in Chicago.

Chicano!: The History of the Mexican American Civil Rights Movement. A four-part series chronicling the struggles for equal rights by Mexican Americans.

Eyes on the Prize: America's Civil Rights Years. A history of the people, the stories, the events, and the issues of the civil rights struggle, which presents behind-the-scenes insights into such major events as the Montgomery bus boycott, the March on Washington, and the march from Selma to Montgomery.

Four Little Girls. Spike Lee's documentary about the fatal bombing of a black church in Birmingham, Alabama, in 1963, and the girls, ages 11 through 14, who were killed.

Ghosts of Mississippi. An account of the efforts to bring to justice the man who murdered Medgar Evers of the NAACP in Mississippi.

LBJ. An episode from public television's *American Experience* series, covering Lyndon B. Johnson's political life from his early political career through his years of the presidency.

The Long Walk Home. A dramatization of the Montgomery bus boycott and its impact on a black maid and her white employers.

Making Sense of the Sixties. A documentary that examines the roots of the social movements of the 1960s, including the youth rebellion and the antiwar, environmental, and women's movements, and their legacy.

Malcolm X. Spike Lee chronicles the life and evolving thought of Malcolm X.

Mississippi Burning. Based on the murder of Andrew Goodman and Michael Schwerner.

Once Upon a Time . . . When We Were Colored. The rise of the Civil Rights movement in Glen Allan, Mississippi, through the eyes of a child.

To Kill a Mockingbird. Adaptation of the Pulitzer–winning novel by Harper Lee.

KEY TERMS

Sit-in   (p. 816)

Student Nonviolent Coordinating Committee (SNCC) (p. 817)

Freedom riders   (p. 818)

Congress of Racial Equality (CORE)   (p. 818)

Bombingham   (p. 820)

1963 March on Washington   (p. 821)

Civil Rights Act of 1964   (p. 822)

Twenty-fourth Amendment   (p. 822)

Voting Rights Act of 1965   (p. 822)

Nation of Islam   (p. 822)

Black Muslims   (p. 822)

Black power   (p. 824)

Black Panther party   (p. 824)

Watts Riot of 1965   (p. 824)

Great Society   (p. 826)

Students for a Democratic Society (SDS)   (p. 828)

Port Huron Statement   (p. 828)

The New Left   (p. 828)

LSD (Lysergic Acid Diethylamide)   (p. 830)

Equal Employment Opportunity Commission (EEOC) (p. 832)

National Organization for Women (NOW)   (p. 833)

Equal Rights Amendment (ERA)   (p. 833)

Feminist theory   (p. 833)

Roe v. Wade   (p. 834)

United Farm Workers   (p. 835)

American Indian Movement (AIM)   (p. 840)

Gay and lesbian liberation   (p. 841)

PEOPLE YOU SHOULD KNOW

Muhammad Ali   (p. 813)

Martin Luther King, Jr.   (p. 816)

John F. Kennedy   (p. 818)

James Meredith   (p. 818)

George C. Wallace   (p. 819)

Medgar Evers   (p. 820)

Malcolm X   (p. 823)

Stokely Carmichael   (p. 824)

Lyndon B. Johnson   (p. 825)

Richard Nixon   (p. 827)

Betty Friedan   (p. 831)

César Chávez   (p. 835)

Rachel Carson   (p. 841)

REVIEW QUESTIONS

1. To what extent was the civil rights movement a grassroots movement shaped by ordinary Americans?

2. How did the political message of major civil rights leaders change by the late 1960s?

3. Was the New Left an important force in American politics? How did their ideas disseminate into the popular culture?

4. What does it mean to be a feminist? How did the feminist movement evolve in the 1960s and 1970s?

5. Why did so many social protest movements—including Mexican American activism, Native American Power, gay liberation, and environmentalism—begin to flourish in the late 1960s and early 1970s?

30 Power Shifts: The Emergence of the South and West

JOHN WAYNE: WESTERN ICON, POLITICAL CONSERVATIVE

There was something about actor John Wayne that simply intrigued other people. He was like his country—oversized, powerful, and dramatic; part Daniel Boone, part Mike Fink, and all American. He was the Ringo Kid framed against a Monument Valley butte, holding a gun in one hand and a saddle in the other; he was Sergeant John M. Stryker telling his men to "Saddle up" before assaulting Iwo Jima; he was Thomas Dunston parting a sea of longhorns to get to Montgomery Clift; he was Captain Nathan Brittles reading the inscription on his "brand-new silver watch"; he was all those men on horseback or performing a service for their country or taking matters into their own hands.

Over the years he lost the smooth, fresh handsomeness of his youth. His hair fell out, his waist thickened, his face became lined and weathered. But the changes seemed to have made him even more appealing. His face seemed to take on a chiseled, Mount Rushmore quality, as if it had existed forever. Perhaps it was that quality, his granite sense of permanence, that attracted such awe. As much as any man of his century, he had become a symbol of America. As cultural critic Eric Bentley wrote, John Wayne was "the most important American of our time. . . . In the age when the image is the most important thing, Wayne is the principal image."

Yet during the late 1960s and 1970s no American seemed more out of step with the social and cultural changes in America than John Wayne. His critics charged that he was a political Neanderthal, a monument to such outmoded concepts as rugged individualism and sentimental patriotism. Since the 1920s he had starred in over 150 films in which he played varieties of the same character: the independent man of action who rode tall in the saddle, confronted evil on deserted streets at high noon, and protected innocent men and women. About his character—and indeed himself—there was a certain surliness, a roughness about the edges that manifested itself in his coarse, blunt language and bull-in-a-china-closet behavior, yet no one who watched his films doubted what he stood for or where he would be when the trouble began.

During the years of Lyndon Johnson's Great Society and protests against the war in Vietnam, John Wayne's simplistic attitudes and patriotism seemed naive. He preached individuality in an age of bureaucracy and *laissez-faire* in an era of

Born Marion Michael Morrison in Winterset, Iowa, in 1907, John "Duke" Wayne came to symbolize the man of the West—honest, brave, upright, and true—in his movie roles. As cattleman Thomas Dunston in *Red River* (1948), he led his Texas longhorns on the 1000-mile long drive along the Chisholm Trail from San Antonio, Texas, to the railroad center at Abilene, Kansas.

social engineering. Liberal critics asserted that he was a dangerous superpatriot and attacked his 1968 film *The Green Berets*, which defended America's role in Vietnam. *New York Times* reviewer Renata Adler wrote that the film was "unspeakable, . . . stupid, . . . rotten and false"; another critic called it "immoral, in the deepest sense." The attacks confused Wayne. "I am an . . . honest-to-goodness, flag-waving patriot," he told reporters. "It's kind of a sad thing when a normal love of country makes you a superpatriot."

Wayne responded to his critics with his own scathing denunciation of liberalism. He could not abide freeloaders and reserved his sharpest barbs for what he felt were the weakest links in liberalism's chain of being—crime, welfare, and affirmative action. Perhaps his views on evil and justice had been shaped by his own Western movies, but he believed that some people were just badly flawed and incapable of even minimally acceptable social behavior except when the threat of swift punishment hung permanently over their heads. "I don't go along with . . . this new thing of genuflecting to the downtrodden," he told a reporter

in 1969. "We ought to go back to praising the kids who get good grades, instead of making excuses for the ones who shoot the neighborhood groceryman." And he insisted that society had not only the right but the absolute duty to punish criminal behavior.

Just as he deplored coddling criminals, he opposed most welfare programs, which he claimed robbed clients of self-respect and personal responsibility. A firm believer in individual charity, he scoffed at the idea of government charity, especially when it was financed by his and his friends' money. "I don't want any handouts from a benevolent government," he explained in 1970. "I do not want the government to take away my human dignity and ensure me of anything more than normal security." To his way of thinking, entitlement programs were addictions, monkeys on the back of America, and a terrible disservice to recipients. "You never do anybody a favor giving them something for nothing," he said. "You take away their survival instincts, their ambition, and their self-respect."

If liberals condemned Wayne's views, conservatives in the 1980s and 1990s embraced them. For millions of Americans John Wayne—tall, rugged, forthright, and independent—became the embodiment of the American ethos. President Jimmy Carter, against whom Wayne campaigned in 1976, said John Wayne was "bigger than life. In an age of few heroes, he was the genuine article. But he was more than a hero; he was the symbol of many of the qualities that make America great. . . ." And Irish actress Maureen O'Hara remarked, "To the people of the world, John Wayne is not just an actor. . . . John Wayne is the United States of America. He is what they believe it to be. He is what they hope it to be. And he is what they hope it will always be."

To America and to the world John Wayne was the embodiment of another ethos as well: the American West. Not only did he play western roles and live in Southern California, in so many ways he spoke for the West. In his films, Easterners were often portrayed as corrupt and effete, men who controlled power to the detriment of "the people"; Westerners were portrayed as freedom-loving, independent sorts who wanted only to escape the domination of eastern bankers and land agents. This resentment of the political and economic power of the East helped to shape twentieth-century western—as well as southern and southwestern—history. It helped explain Richard Nixon's sense that he was an outsider and the conservative political revolts led by Barry Goldwater and Ronald Reagan. Indeed, by the 1980s and 1990s the beliefs John Wayne espoused underlay a great power shift in the United States.

THE EMERGENCE OF THE SOUTHERN RIM

The central political, social, economic, and cultural fact of the second half of the twentieth century has been the gradual shift in power from the older industrial states and cities of the Northeast and upper Midwest to the southern and western rim of the United States. This rim—circling half the country from the Chesapeake region to Raleigh and Charlotte; south to Atlanta, Jacksonville, Miami, and Tampa; west to Birmingham, New Orleans, Houston, Dallas, San Antonio, Albuquerque, Phoenix, San Diego, and Los Angeles; then north up the coast of California to San Francisco Bay, to Oregon, and on to Seattle—has experienced the country's greatest growth and economic success. It has been and continues to be the destination for millions of immigrants from Asia, Mexico, and Central America, the spawning ground of new political ideas, and the most fertile area for cultural expression. Since 1964, all of the country's elected presidents—Lyndon Johnson, Richard Nixon, Jimmy Carter, Ronald Reagan, George Bush, Bill Clinton, and George W. Bush—have either been born or claim residence in the South and West.

It is a region that defies hasty attempts at labeling. Is it the home of Ronald Reagan's conservatism or Jimmy Carter's liberalism? Merle Haggard's redneck revolt or San Francisco's Summer of Love? John Wayne's go-for-your-gun philosophy or Robert Redford's passion for the wilderness? It is all of these and more. But above anything else, this southern and western rim has defined itself by two measures: first, by its antithesis to the East; and second, by its concern for individual liberty. Like a John Wayne movie, the two go together. Running through much of southern and western political and cultural rhetoric is the idea that the East—especially the economic power of Wall Street and the political power of Washington—threatens individualism.

From the Long Hot Summer to the Sunbelt

When World War II ended, the South was the poorest, most economically backward section of the United States. Per capita income was barely one-half that of the national average, and income distribution was badly skewed. Pockets of the South in South Carolina, Georgia, Mississippi, and Louisiana seemed never to have recovered from the Civil War, and other regions in Appalachia had *never* had a prosperous time. Altogether, the South was the "Nation's No. 1" economic problem.

Changes since 1945 have been remarkable, though not uniform. Poverty still plagues much of the inner South, especially the rural sections of Alabama, Arkansas, Kentucky, Mississippi, and Tennessee. The South as a whole continues to lag behind the nation in funding for public education, high school graduation rates, health standards, working conditions, and hourly wages. But along the rim of the South—from the Chesapeake Bay down to Florida and over to Texas—and in the cities and suburbs of the Carolinas, Georgia, and Louisiana, prosperity has replaced poverty.

No one factor accounts for the changes. Technology, politics, and social and cultural shifts have aided the rise of the "New South." Perhaps it all began with the end of the long hot summer. If the Northeast and Midwest had cold winters, the South had uncomfortably hot, long summers, normally accompanied by high humidity, mosquitoes, and disease. In the areas closest to the Gulf of Mexico, summer conditions often began in April and lasted well into October. It was not a climate that encouraged immigration or industrial relocation.

Wealthy Southerners tried to escape the oppressive heat and humidity by building houses with high ceilings, long breezeways, large windows, bedroom transoms, and broad awnings. With the invention in 1882 of the electric fan—or "whirligig" as it was called in the South—the urban middle class also found some relief from the heat if not the humidity. But the urban poor and rural dwellers lacking electric power found little comfort. During the first half of the twentieth century, however, engineers developed and refined the technology of "air-conditioning," an electrical system that simultaneously cooled, circulated, dehumidified, and cleansed air. First used in southern textile and tobacco industries, by the 1920s and 1930s air-conditioning had spread into the better hotels, first-run movie theaters, Pullman railroad cars, and some public buildings. By the end of the 1930s theater owners knew that they could vastly increase ticket sales by installing air-conditioning and putting up frost-covered signs advertising "20 DEGREES COOLER INSIDE."

But it was not until after World War II that most Southerners felt the impact of air-conditioning. Air-conditioning spread to department stores, banks, government buildings, hospitals, schools, and, finally, homes and automobiles. Home air-conditioning soared after the introduction in 1951 of an inexpensive, efficient window unit. By 1960, 18 percent of all southern homes had either window units or central air-conditioning. That number topped 50 percent in 1970 and almost 75 percent by 1980. Still, there were limitations. In 1980, for example, 79.9 percent of urban houses had air-conditioning, compared to 59.2 percent of rural houses.

"The South of the 1970s could claim air-conditioned shopping malls, domed stadiums, dugouts, green-houses, grain elevators, chicken coops, aircraft hangers, crane cabs, off-shore oil rigs, cattle barns, steel mills, and drive-in movies and restaurants," wrote one historian. In Texas, the South's most air-conditioned state, even the Alamo has central air, and the annual cost for air-conditioning in Houston exceeded the gross national product of some Third World countries. The victory over heat also had great significance. It has helped to promote "the Americanization of Dixie" by removing one obstacle to the movement of people to the region. During the first half of the twentieth century more Americans moved out of the South than moved into the region. The exodus began to slow in the 1950s, and during the 1960s the trend reversed: more people moved into the South than left. The *New York Times* called the 1970 census "The Air-Conditioned Census." "The humble air-conditioner," a *Times* editorialist wrote, "has been a powerful influence in circulating people as well as air in this country."

The innovation also encouraged industries to relocate to the South, the history of which had been dominated by agriculture. At the time of Pearl Harbor, more than 40 percent of all Southerners were farmers. Forty years later only 3 to 4 percent of Southerners were farmers. The spread of industry southward has provided new sources of income and jobs. With the decline of heavy industry in the 1960s and 1970s, many manufacturers have relocated to the South where they could buy less expensive land, pay fewer taxes and lower wages, and avoid union difficulties.

If air-conditioning eased this industrial transition, it also opened the South to tourism. The reality of the long, hot summer gave way to the ideal of the Sunbelt—a vision of year-round golf, Christmas barbecues, and life without snow tires. Vacationers flocked to southern resorts, from Hilton Head, South Carolina, in the Southeast to Scottsdale, Arizona, in the Southwest. Older Americans moved to the South and West when they retired. Without air-conditioning such demographic shifts would have been difficult to imagine. "Can you conceive a Walt Disney World . . . in the 95-degree summers of central Florida without air-conditioned hotels, attractions and shops?" a newspapers editorialist asked. "Can you see a Honeywell or Sperry or anyone else opening a big plant where their workers would have to spend much of their time mopping brows and cursing mosquitoes?"

A Shift in Race Relations

More than air-conditioning, however, accounted for the change in the South. Race relations, long the defining characteristic of the region, also underwent profound changes. Institutional racism, as characterized by a series of Jim Crow laws (see Chapter 19), died a slow death in Dixie. Throughout the 1940s white Southerners ignored the stirring of racial progress taking place in the North, and even after the 1954 *Brown v. Board of Education of Topeka* decision, which delivered the most decisive blow to the

The widespread availability of air conditioning following World War II made the Sunbelt a much more desirable place to live and contributed significantly to its population growth. Air conditioning in the Houston Astrodome means that even sports events and concerts can take place during the withering Texas heat.

concept of separate but equal, many white Southerners refused to accept racial change. During the 1950s and early 1960s such southern politicians as Governor Lester Maddox of Georgia, Governor Ross Barnett of Mississippi, and Governor George Wallace of Alabama fought rear-guard actions against any change in the racial status quo. (See Chapters 27 and 29 for more detail on the quest for civil rights.)

But change did come. Civil rights acts in 1957, 1960, and 1964 struck down the legal basis of Jim Crow, and the Voting Rights Act of 1965 gave African Americans in the South (and elsewhere) the instrument to win even more changes. Such organizations as the Southern Christian Leadership Conference, the Congress of Racial Equality, and the Student Nonviolent Coordinating Committee struggled to ensure the reality of change. The end result was a new South—certainly not one where all racial problems had been solved or the distinction between black and white had been eliminated, but one that was at least confronting the question of race.

Perhaps **Jimmy Carter** from Plains, Georgia, best demonstrated the changes in the South. Carter grew up in a segregated South, in a county that resisted civil rights laws and all attempts to eradicate racial distinctions. Martin Luther King, Jr., had spent time in one of the county's jails, and in the 1960s white officials attempted to enforce illegal segregation statutes. But when Carter won the state's governorship in 1970, he announced that the South had entered a new age: "I say to you quite frankly that the time for racial discrimination is over. . . . No poor, rural, weak, or black person should ever have to bear the burden of being deprived of the opportunity of an education, a job, or simple justice." As a symbol of his fresh approach, he ordered a portrait of Martin Luther King, Jr., hung in the state capitol.

Advances against racism opened a new age of prosperity in the South. Attitudes expressed by Jimmy Carter and other politicians like him announced that the desire for progress in the South had finally overcome the desire for white supremacy. Since the 1870s proponents of the New South had called for Southerners to stop living in the past, to renounce overt racism, and to accept industrialism. Only then, they argued, would the South enjoy the same material progress as the North. Though it took almost a century for the new ethos to emerge—aided by Supreme Court decisions and congressional legislation—by the 1970s it had gained a firm foothold, especially in southern cities. It was no coincidence that urban business leaders became some of the most influential advocates of desegregation.

The Business of the South Is Business

Although talk of a New South—an economically diversified South—had begun almost as soon as the Civil War ended, it took almost one hundred years to make the transition from a fine idea to a reality. Before World War II, most of the talk about southern industrialism and prosperity was mere boosterism, and the profits from what little industry had developed usually flowed north. Thanks largely to the federal government, the southern economy did grow during the 1940s. During the war, Uncle Sam invested almost $9 billion in the South, mostly in defense-related activities. Although the government spent even more in other regions, the war provided the greatest infusion of cash and jobs in the South's history. At Oak Ridge, Tennessee, for example, where uranium was processed for atomic bombs, over 100,000 new jobs were created.

Throughout the region the story was much the same. Government shipyards in Newport News, Norfolk, Charleston, Tampa, Mobile, Pascagoula, New Orleans, and Houston provided hundreds of thousands of jobs. Aircraft, oil refinery, chemical, aluminum, and tin milling plants created many more. The South's industrial capacity increased by 40 percent, and per capita income tripled.

After the war the government closed some but not all of the bases and production facilities. As late as 1980, 24 of the Army's major American posts were located in the South, and almost half the soldiers in uniform were stationed below the Mason-Dixon line. In 1980 alone, the Department of Defense spent more than $50 billion in the South, or 39.5 percent of its budget. Together, the bases and plants gave the South a start from which to grow.

In the late 1960s and 1970s the South enjoyed spectacular growth. For investors, businesspeople, and industrialists, the region had certain natural advantages. Labor was cheaper and labor unions were weaker in the South than in the North. In addition, the South offered industry cheaper land, lower taxes, and fewer regulations. As industry in the Midwest declined—the result of high taxes, labor strife, technological obsolescence, and government interference—the South became an attractive place for industrial resettlement. The Midwest became known as the Rustbelt, the South as the Sunbelt. Rust and Sun, decay and growth—Americans quickly responded to the images. By the 1960s the South had reversed its century-old problem of outmigration—more people were moving into the region than out.

The 1970s were boom years in the southern Sunbelt. Young, well-educated Northerners moved into

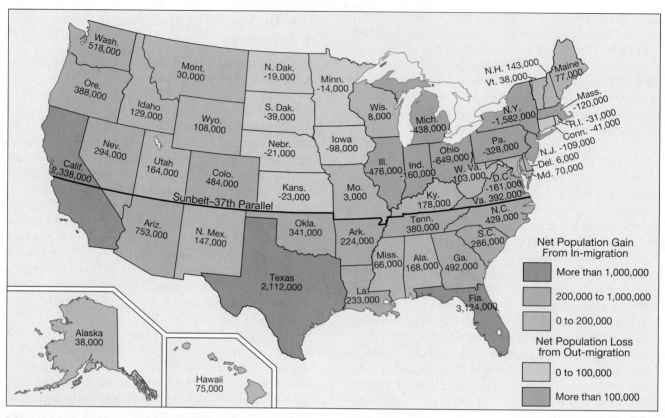

Migration to the Sunbelt, 1970–1981

the region looking for economic opportunity, and middle-class retirees relocated to the Carolinas and Florida to take advantage of the sun and lower cost of living. At the same time, northern and foreign capital poured into the South for industrial expansion. In the years immediately following World War II, Ford and General Motors built plants in Georgia; in the last third of the twentieth century Nissan and Saturn set up shop in Tennessee, Toyota in Kentucky, BMW in South Carolina, and Mercedes-Benz in Alabama. Critics of the southern automobile plants charged that state officials paid too high a price, that the subsidies and incentives offered the companies—including tax-free municipal bonds to subsidize construction and millions of dollars to train workers—negated the creation of new jobs. But the new plants *did* mean jobs; they *did* mean economic growth. While the wages and benefits in the new factories were below national averages, they were usually well above local averages.

Urbanization accompanied industrialization, and the South's traditional dependency on agriculture declined. As the percentage of Southerners engaged in farming fell from 40 to 3 or 4 percent during the period from 1941 to 1981, the number of farms shrank from 2.9 million to 949,000. The transition from rural to urban, from farm to industry, brought with it a human toll of pain and suffering. Thousands

of country music and blues songs lament the agony of transition. Songs like "Detroit City" and "Cotton Mill Colic" emphasize the coldness of factory towns and the numbing boredom of industrial work.

Progress, desegregation, and increasing industrialism have not cost the South its distinctiveness. Throughout the second half of the twentieth century, regional and sectional pride remained stronger below the Mason-Dixon line than above it. For example, in one sociological study about 90 percent of people living in North Carolina responded that they believed they lived in the "best state." In Massachusetts only about 40 percent of the residents so answered. Similarly, regional identifications—such as "southern" or "northern," "Dixie" or "Yankee"—in businesses remained much stronger in the South than the North. The popular magazine *Southern Living,* aimed at the southern middle class, illustrated the continued appeal of regional identity in its stories about southern football and tailgate parties, bourbon advertisements, and recipes for wild game.

While many lament the passing of the traditional South, many more celebrate the new levels of prosperity. The South has become more like the rest of the country, a land where rich suburbs and pockets of poverty coexist, and strip-mall and fast-food restaurants compete with older, family-run operations.

Companies like General Motors, which opened this Saturn automobile assembly plant in Tennessee, provided more opportunities for lucrative employment in the South and contributed to the economic expansion of the South in the late twentieth century.

THE MYTH AND REALITY OF THE WEST

The West is an image and a bundle of myths firmly ingrained in the American imagination. It is a tactile image. It can be touched as well as seen, smelled as well as read. It has been portrayed in thousands of Westerns on movie and television screens, and in even more novels and short stories. And unlike tales about Puritan settlers or cotton planters, its appeal has not diminished with the end of the twentieth century.

Packaging the West

Advertisers understand the appeal of the West; they package the West to sell products. Consider the Marlboro Man and Marlboro Country. This figure of rugged independence, riding alone across a snow-covered high plateau or a dried-out range, his face tanned and weathered by work in the sun and exposure to the elements, became a fixture in American and world popular culture in the mid-twentieth century. In the minds of many consumers, the Marlboro Man was the essence of masculinity, and the advertising image itself became an icon. The history of the Marlboro Man, however, suggests just how potent images of the West are. In 1954, Marlboro was the name brand of a filtered cigarette produced by Philip Morris and sold primarily to women. The cigarettes came in a white soft pack, had a red "beauty tip" filter to camouflage lipstick, and sold under the slogan, "Mild as May." Considered effeminate cigarettes, Marlboros had less than one-quarter of one percent

market share. "Men will never smoke cigarettes with filters," was the common advertising wisdom.

One of the most widespread of the Western images in advertising was the Marlboro Man, who invited smokers to "Come to Marlboro Country."

Come to Marlboro Country.

Then Chicago advertiser Leo Burnett took over the Marlboro account. He changed the woman's cigarette into a man's cigarette, in fact a man's man's cigarette. The white soft pack became a strong red and white hard, flip-top pack. The "beauty tip" bit the dust, as did the "Mild as May" slogan, replaced by the image of a cowboy with a tattoo on the back of one hand. The original photographer of the series later recalled, however, that he used pilots, not cowboys, for models "because pilots seem to have little wrinkles around the eyes." The combination of rustic masculinity and a western setting—Marlboro Man and Marlboro Country—had an immediate appeal, and Burnett's campaign became the most financially successful in advertising history.

The West had always been America's great romance. In the nineteenth century, wealthy Americans bought the western paintings of Frederic Remington and Charles Russell, while their poorer countrymen purchased dime novels featuring the exploits of Billy the Kid, Doc Holliday, or the James Brothers. They went to see William "Buffalo Bill" Cody's Wild West Show and thrilled at the Indian attacks and narrow escapes. By the end of the century, the West was a key element in American popular culture, and it seemed in the blood of the people.

The popular nineteenth-century, western formulas carried over into the twentieth century. In the pulp fiction, short stories, and novels of Zane Grey, Max Brand, Ernest Haycox, Alan Le May, and Louis L'Amour, Americans received a steady supply of guns, guts, and grit. Grey's preachy western tales proved endlessly popular in the first half of the century, and no writer has had more films made of his works. L'Amour has been one of the biggest selling writers in the second half of the century. By the 1980s, his western novels had sold over 200 million copies.

If the West translated well to the printed page, it found its true medium on the silver screen. The marriage between Hollywood and the West has been a long one. Although it was filmed in New Jersey, *The Great Train Robbery* (1903) portrayed a train hold-up, the formation of a posse, a horseback chase, and dance hall scene; it was the earliest fiction western film. Thousands more followed. In the 1920s Broncho Billy Anderson, Tom Mix, and Hoot Gibson portrayed the western hero in scores of silent films. In the 1930s, during Hollywood's first decade of sound production, the "B" westerns of such actors as John Wayne, Buck Jones, and Gene Autry were popular attractions in small theaters in the South, Midwest, and West. After the success of *Stagecoach* in 1939, "A" westerns began to dominate the biggest theaters in the nation's largest cities. The great western boom carried through World War II into the early decades of television in the 1950s and 1960s.

The millions of Americans who watched westerns every year received civic instruction along with their entertainment. The message of many of the westerns was that Washington and Wall Street, the seats of national political and economic power, could not be trusted. John Wayne's westerns, for example, told the story of a West besieged by evil—ruthless merchants, monopolistic land and water agents, greedy bankers, and corrupt government officials. Innocent people are shot at, beaten up, and left for dead; they are cheated, robbed, and chased off their land. Order is restored only by a tough, independent man with a gun. Although some films deal with the threat of Native Americans, the vast majority center on the dangers inherent in Washington bureaucrats and big-city bankers.

Washington and the West

For many real-life Westerners, John Wayne's message and the circumstances of his films were not that far from the truth. By the late nineteenth century the battles between U.S. settlers in the West and their Hispanic and Native American opponents had ended and the West had been conquered. But the new western leaders soon grew to resent the economic and political power of the East. Throughout the late nineteenth century and the twentieth century there were revolts against the entrenched power of the East. Populists fought against discriminatory railroad freight rates, a banking industry centralized east of the Mississippi, corporate greed, and high protective tariffs. Talk of the "financial dictatorship" of Wall Street and the "Eastern corporate aristocracy" came easily to hard-pressed farmers and ranchers living in the West.

Yet at the same time that Westerners were complaining about federal power, they received more than their share of federal dollars. The prosperity of the post–World War II West was largely financed and constructed by Washington, D.C. Although the federal government had always pumped money into the West, the investment steeply increased in the 1930s. Disappointed by fellow Westerner President Herbert Hoover's agricultural and cattle programs, conservation policies, and opposition to federally funded public power, Westerners, like most other Americans, turned against him in 1932 and supported Franklin D. Roosevelt. FDR did not disappoint them. His New Deal provided relief in the form of jobs, agricultural price supports, farm loans, and rural electrification.

But more importantly, Roosevelt enthusiastically supported western dam, power, and irrigation projects. In particular, he promoted the Central Valley Project on the Sacramento River to divert water from northern California to provide water, irrigation, and electric power for the rest of the state; the completion of the Hoover (Boulder) Dam on the Colorado River to provide water and electric power for southern California, the Imperial Valley, and the Southwest; the Grand Coulee Dam on the Columbia River to provide electric power, irrigation, flood control, and navigational improvements in the Northwest; and Colorado-Big Thompson Project to provide electric power in eastern Colorado.

The various dam projects helped to turn the West, in the words of historian Donald Worster, into "a modern **hydraulic society,** which is to say, a social order based on the intensive manipulation of water and its products in an arid setting." By 1978 the Census of Agriculture reported that the West had one-tenth of the world's irrigated land—43,668,834 acres—and nine of the top ten agriculturally productive counties in the United States. California, with eight of those counties, was the most agriculturally productive state in the country.

World War II accelerated the growth of the West at the same time that it created new bonds between Washington and the region. "Never in western history," wrote historian Richard White, "did changes come so quickly or have such far-reaching consequences as between 1941 and 1945. It was as if someone had tilted the country: people, money, and soldiers all spilled west. That tilt came from the federal bureaucracies, which devoted a disproportionate share of their enlarged resources to western development." During the war the federal government spent $70 billion in the western states and poured $40 billion more into factories, military bases, and capital improvements, over half of which was spent in California. The money provided more jobs, and the jobs lured newcomers to the region. In southern California alone, government orders created more than 250,000 new jobs in the aircraft and shipbuilding industries. More than one million people moved to California, and most settled in the southern part of the state. Before the war, San Diego was a small city of 60,000 people; during the war, it grew to more than 250,000.

Defense industries spurred the growth and industrial expansion of the West. Probably more than any other person, industrialist **Henry J. Kaiser** epitomized the driving concern for defense and dollars. A central player in the development of the western infrastructure of roads, dams, bridges, and pipelines, Kaiser went into the shipbuilding business at the outbreak of war. He built steelworks in Fontana, California, and shipyards in Richmond, Oakland, Sausalito, Vallejo, and San Pedro, California. Altogether, his industries employed close to 300,000 people, to whom they paid high wages and offered attractive medical and retirement benefits.

Others followed the trail Kaiser blazed. The Boeing plant in Seattle and the Douglas, Lockheed,

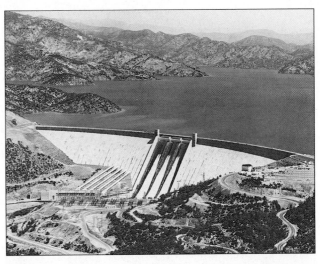

Water regulation projects often helped foster the tourist industry in the West. This view of the Shasta Dam and Reservoir, part of the Central Valley Project on the Sacramento River in California, is from a high point above the tourists' vista overlooking the dam.

North American, Northrop, and Hughes plants in southern California dominated the aircraft industry and provided several hundred thousand good-paying jobs. The growth of the aircraft industry even threatened to overshadow the motion picture industry in southern California. Almost as a symbol of the emergence of the new industry, Warner Brothers Studios, located near Lockheed and fearing an enemy attack, painted a 20-foot arrow on the roof of a sound stage with the message: LOCKHEED—THATAWAY. And Hollywood film stars complained that all the good chauffeurs, butlers, cooks, and maids had either enlisted or taken better-paying jobs in aircraft factories. One advertisement announced: "Maid wanted; will pay Lockheed wages."

The end result was the transformation of the West, and especially California, from a virtual colony of the East into the fastest growing, most economically booming section of the country. Once Westerners had complained about the East's near monopoly over banks and financial institutions. By the end of the war, the largest bank in the world was the Bank of America, the San Francisco–based bank run by the Giannini family which had financed not only much of the growth of the film industry but the expansion of Bendix, Chrysler, Westinghouse, North American Aviation, and Northrop Aircraft Corporation. As G. P. Giannini observed in 1945: "The West has all the money to finance whatever it wants to; we no longer have to go New York for financing, and we're not at its mercy. Wall Street used to give a western enterprise plenty of rope, and when it broke, it took over." Now the West owned the rope.

Henry Kaiser epitomized the close relationship between government and industry in the West. Government loans financed Kaiser's shipyards and cost-plus government contracts guaranteed his profits.

From Extraction to Diversification

Walter O'Malley was once described as having "a face even Dale Carnegie would want to punch." In the mid-1950s, O'Malley, the owner of the Brooklyn Dodgers, was known for his penny-pinching concern for profits and his lack of humor. But in late 1957, many residents of Brooklyn added "traitor" to O'Malley's list of character flaws. In that year he announced his decision to move his Dodgers the following year from Brooklyn to Los Angeles, and for good measure, he convinced Horace Stoneham, owner of the New York Giants, to relocate his team to San Francisco. Dodger and Giant fans sent up a howl of betrayal. Journalist Arthur Daley wrote that some "teams were forced to move by apathy, or incompetence. The only word that fits the Dodgers is greed. . . . Baseball is a sport, eh? . . . the crass materialism of O'Malley and Horace Stoneham of the Giants presents the disillusioning fact that it's big business, just another way to make a buck."

Actually, the Dodgers' move west was more complicated than the "disillusioning fact" suggests. O'Malley was concerned about the deterioration of the Brooklyn neighborhood that was the home of Ebbets Field. The quaint structure was located in an increasingly unsafe section of the city, and it lacked parking facilities. O'Malley wanted to move to a new Brooklyn stadium, but his plans were blocked by New York power broker Robert Moses. In the end, O'Malley fled the labyrinthine politics and regulations of New York for the more generous political and cultural climate of Los Angeles.

The Dodgers' move west symbolized the new westward tilt of the country. Professional baseball teams were businesses, subject to the same market forces as other businesses. Chambers of Commerce throughout the country actively competed to bring new businesses to their communities. New businesses translated into more jobs and more money. Eager state and local governments used promises of low-interest loans, free land, cheap leases on city-built facilities, low property taxes or even property tax exemptions, and the building of county access roads to factory sites to attract new businesses. Certainly by the end of World War II, the West could boast that it was the land of sunshine and jobs.

In the half-century after World War II, the West completed the transition from being a land of extractive industries—mining, agriculture, ranching, oil, and logging—to being a region of vast economic diversification. By the 1970s, the newer electronic, aerospace, high-technology, and service industries had surpassed in financial importance the older economic staples of farming and ranching, coal and copper mining, and oil drilling and lumber operations. This economic leap led directly to millions of new jobs and accelerated the flow of emigrants into the West. Between 1945 and 1960, population west of the Mississippi River increased from 32 to 45 million people. The population of Arizona, one of the fastest growing states, grew by 163 percent. In 1960, California, which led the rest of the West in growth and prosperity, passed New York as the most populous American state. By the 1980s, the combined population of the West and the South for the first time exceeded the combined population of the Northeast and Midwest.

As it had during World War II, the federal government aided the growth of the West. Part of the reason lies in the fact that the federal government owned so much of the arid land of the West: more than 85 percent of Nevada, 63 percent of Idaho, 61 percent of Utah, and 50 percent of Wyoming. By 1960, close to one-third of all workers in the Los Angeles area worked for the defense industry, and that figure was well over two-thirds in San Diego. Up and down the West Coast it was more of the same. From the marine base at Camp Pendleton and the ship-yards in San Diego to the nuclear complex at Hanford, Washington, and the shipyards in Seattle, the federal government's military spending helped to subsidize the boom in the West.

In the process, the West became the nuclear heartland of America, a development that rested uneasily on the minds of many people in the region. Offutt Air Force Base near Omaha, Nebraska, headquartered the country's Strategic Air Command; Colorado's Cheyenne Mountain housed the Combat Operations Center of the North American Air Defense Command; and New Mexico, where the first atomic bomb was tested, provided a home for various missile sites, military bases, and Sandia Laboratories, the Atomic Energy Commission's primary research facility. In addition, the federal government assembled nuclear bombs in plants at Rocky Flats, Colorado, and Pantex, Texas; conducted extensive nuclear testing in Utah and Nevada; and dumped—or hoped to dump—nuclear waste in unoccupied western desert land.

Defense activity bred new industries and new jobs. Billions of dollars in federal and state grants went to researchers in western universities, enlarging the reputations of such schools as California Institute of Technology, the University of California at Berkeley, and the University of Washington. Private companies such as Martin-Marietta and General Dynamics contributed to western economies in the form of skilled, high-paying jobs. The aerospace industry, which blossomed in the West during World War II, remained largely in the West after the war. From Wichita, Kansas's line of smaller aircraft such as Learjet, Beach, and Cessna; to Los Angeles's and Fort Worth's line of larger jets such as Lockheed, Douglas, and North American; to Houston's Johnson Space Center—the skies belonged to the West.

The Problems and Benefits of Growth

Such development was not without troubles. As the West discovered, government money and government waste went hand-in-hand. Few people complained when the government paid too much for a lug nut or toilet seat, but waste and sloppiness in nuclear development had more dire consequences. Under the pressures of the Cold War, the government proceeded recklessly in the development of its nuclear capabilities. Test blasts probably showered many Westerners with deadly radioactive fallout. In 1953, for instance, the Atomic Energy Commission detonated 11 atomic bombs in the dry lake bed of Yucca Flats, Nevada. Two of the bombs were especially "dirty" with strontium 90 and cesium 137 isotopes. The surrounding desert was covered with a

fine gray ash, and an aberrant wind carried some of the fallout more than 150 miles to the east, blanketing St. George, Utah, and the Escalante Valley. In 1954, when the John Wayne movie *The Conqueror* was filmed in the area, the levels of radioactivity were still high. Over the next thirty-five years, 91 of the cast and crew of 220 people would develop cancer, a number three times higher than actuarial tables would predict. Similarly, cancer rates in and around St. George would be among the highest in the nation.

Dealing with the hundreds of thousands of gallons of nuclear waste compounded the problem. The simple truth was that the government gave far too little thought to the by-products of nuclear development, and it wasn't until the end of the Cold War that more attention was focused on the problem. While some nuclear waste experts suggested a Yucca Flats dumping ground, others argued that there was no safe way to bury "hot" material with isotopes that might remain active for a hundred thousand years. To a large degree, it is still a debate that is being conducted in the West by Westerners.

Nuclear waste was not the only problem created by the rapid growth of the West. Led by the Bureau of Reclamation and the Corps of Engineers, who often worked at cross-purposes, government planners and wealthy Westerners continued their helter-skelter dam building. "Every major river of the West came, to a greater or lesser extent, under the control of the dam builders and water pumpers," commented two authorities on the twentieth-century West. Never had any country created a more elaborate "hydraulic society." Water from the great western rivers—from the Columbia, the Snake, the Colorado, the South Platte, and the Rio Grande to the Red, the Missouri, and the Arkansas—was dammed, drained, and diverted to provide irrigation, electricity, shipping channels, and leisure activities.

The benefits of the damming of the West were many, though they were not equally distributed throughout western society. With the help of irrigation, the West became the new American breadbasket, and the billions of kilowatt-hours of electric power supported the needs of the region. But there were costs as well. Flood control was often illusionary; water accumulated salt and selenium; land suffered from siltation, erosion, and salt residues; dams threatened to collapse. Most of all, water supplies dwindled. By the 1980s, many Americans grew alarmed by the declining levels of the Ogallala Aquifer, which provided water for irrigation in Texas and the Great Plains states.

A final problem created by the economic growth of and emigration to the West was its dependence on the automobile. Unlike many eastern cities that developed before the advent of the internal combustion

Damming Western Waters

engine—indeed, before the development of any useful form of mass transportation—the West matured with automobiles. This mobility, coupled with the availability of inexpensive land for individual homes, resulted in the emergence of an extended society of suburbs, connected by miles of highways woven together by underpasses and overpasses. If Boston, New York, and Philadelphia were "walking cities," Los Angeles, Phoenix, Denver, Dallas, and Houston became "driving cities." This condition was made worse by the decline in railroads and urban mass transit. By the 1970s it became clear that western cities had developed twin dependencies: diverted water and gasoline.

The gasoline addiction had predictable, but long-ignored, results. In the 1930s the word **smog** had been coined to describe the chemical-laden fogs that fell like a blanket over Pittsburgh. By the 1940s smog had become a problem—albeit a small, acceptable one—in the land of sunshine. The winds—or, more precisely, the lack of winds—in the Los Angeles basin contributed to the problem. The smog was the residue of unburned hydrocarbons, the by-product of running automobile engines. To make matters even worse, smog was not just an aesthetic eyesore; it was an actual eyesore and a serious health problem, capable of killing crops and trees and endangering the lives of humans and animals.

For most of the second half of the twentieth century, however, the benefits of western growth overshadowed the question of nuclear waste, the shrinking water supply, and the spread of smog. From 1945 to the early 1970s, almost every sector of the western economy leaped forward. With the development of the interstate highway system and less expensive commercial air travel, western tourism flourished. Millions of tourists visited the Badlands, the Grand Canyon, Monument Valley, Yellowstone National Park, or the other natural sites in the West. Millions more invaded the ski resorts at Vail, Aspen, Snowbird, Sundance, and Sun Valley. Las Vegas and Reno attracted tourists determined to have fun and make money. Disneyland and the beaches of southern California acted like a magnet for young people—and their parents—from all over the world. Increasingly, when Europeans and South Americans thought of the United States, their minds conjured visions of deep canyons and Mickey Mouse.

For a while, even the traditional western extractive industries—agriculture, ranching, mining, lumber, and petroleum—boomed. More than even before the war, farming and ranching became big businesses. Highly capitalized, heavily mechanized, often dependent on federal price supports, both were fabulously productive. The same was true for mining, lumbering, and petroleum industries. Western

Progress comes with a price. Extensive logging in public forests has resulted in clashes among the government, environmentalists, and the lumber industry over how to balance economic growth with environmental protection.

copper, uranium, wood, and oil were in constant demand. But in the late 1960s and early 1970s those industries began to face difficult times. Foreign competition plagued all of them. Chilean copper, Canadian lumber, and Arab oil often undersold Americans even in their own markets. In addition, environmentalists and government regulatory agencies made it more difficult, and more expensive, for lumber interests, miners, and oil drillers to practice business as usual. By the 1990s, there were signs that the oil industry might regain some of its former profitability, but the outlook for agriculture, lumber operations, and mining was less optimistic.

The post–World War II West was too diversified, however, for the decline in the extractive industries to mean a collapse of the western economy. Manufacturing, tourism, service, and high-tech industries ensured that the West would continue to grow economically. The emergence of high-tech manufacturing in California's Silicon Valley, Austin, Texas, and Seattle, Washington; the shipyards of Oakland and Long Beach in California; the banking and medical complex in Houston, Texas; and the defense-aerospace industries throughout the West prospered even while the national economy sagged. The age of the cowboy, the romantic man on horseback, had ended. Increasingly, Bill Gates, founder of Microsoft Corporation and America's wealthiest individual, sitting in front of his home computer screen in Seattle, Washington, symbolized the new West.

POLITICS WESTERN STYLE

In the early 1960s, Arizona Senator **Barry Goldwater** seemed out of step with most of his colleagues in Washington. In both parties eastern liberalism and style seemed the order of the day. Democratic President John F. Kennedy talked confidently and eloquently about a more active role for government in the quest for social justice. Republican politicians such as Nelson Rockefeller of New York, Henry Cabot Lodge of Massachusetts, William Scranton of Pennsylvania, and George Romney of Michigan also advocated a more liberal domestic agenda, one more in accordance with Franklin D. Roosevelt's New Deal and Dwight Eisenhower's Modern Republicanism than the more conservative ideas of such former Republican leaders as Senator Robert Taft of Ohio. But Goldwater seemed unaffected by the charge toward liberalism.

Goldwater believed that the country's problem was not too little government activity but too much. In his 1960 book *The Conscience of a Conservative* Goldwater wrote that he was dedicated to "achieving the maximum amount of freedom for individuals that is consistent with the maintenance of social order." The enemy of individual freedom, he argued, was the federal government, which had become "a Leviathan, a vast national authority out of touch with the people, and out of control." He wanted to rein in the government, reduce its size, and restrict

In his campaign appearances during the 1964 presidential race, Barry Goldwater drew crowds of well-wishers as well as detractors, who were often concerned that his aggressive stance against communists might lead to nuclear war.

its activities to establishing order, maintaining defense, and administering justice.

In terms of concrete measures, Goldwater called for the end of all subsidies and price supports for farmers, the passage of right-to-work laws and the abolition of the closed shop, a new form of taxation (he called the federal income tax "confiscatory"), and a reduction of federal bureaucracy and spending. He opposed most forms of welfare and government spending on social, educational, public housing, and urban renewal programs. "I have little interest in streamlining government or making it more efficient, for I mean to reduce its size," he wrote. "I do not undertake to promote welfare, for I propose to extend freedom. My aim is not to pass laws, but to repeal them." As for foreign affairs, he called for a vigorous fight against communism and the defense of freedom throughout the world.

An Aberration or an Omen?

Who was this new conservative marksman? Barry Goldwater was a product of the twentieth-century West. "My life," he wrote, "parallels that of twentieth-century America—raw energy amid boundless land and unlimited horizons." He was born in Arizona when it was still a territory and raised on tales of the men and women who settled in the West. "My mother spoke a lot about our country when we were kids—our heritage of freedom, the history of Arizona, how individual initiative had made the desert bloom." But, as a Westerner, he was quite aware that the federal government restricted his freedom. Only

17 percent of his home state, he noted, was "in private hands," and often the capital needed for western development was in the hands of eastern bankers. In his successful 1952 race for the U.S. Senate, he attacked "America's new super state—burgeoning federal spending and a bloated bureaucracy."

Once in the Senate, Goldwater continued his attack on eastern power bases and leaders. "For a century, the West had been a colony of big Eastern money—a boom when they had invested and a bust when they had pulled out of various mining and other operations," he noted. "We had been left with ghost towns and holes in the ground where gold, silver, and mineral deposits had been discovered." Goldwater saw himself as an outsider and had no desire to become part of the inner circle of the Republican party. Instead, he articulated a political credo that aimed at taking power away from Washington and Wall Street and returning it to individual states. What he called for was a radical change in the Republican party that reflected the new realities of America, an "effort to move the party from the dominance of less than a dozen families and others in the East to hundred of thousands of small businessmen and others in the South, West, and elsewhere."

In 1964 Goldwater saw an opportunity. Attacking big government, deficit spending, high taxes, and social programs, he campaigned for the Republican nomination for president. "I will not change my beliefs to win a vote," he promised. "I will offer a choice, not an echo." Although the delivery of his speeches was often flat and his personal style wooden, his words were charged with outrage over a

THE PEOPLE SPEAK

The Conscience of a Conservative

Barry Goldwater's 1960 book *The Conscience of a Conservative* was small (only 123 pages, with large print) and ghostwritten (it was mostly culled from his past speeches and notes), but it sold 3.5 million copies in just four years. It also inspired a new generation of conservative thinkers. Patrick Buchanan called the volume "our new testament; it contained the core beliefs of our political faith, it told us why we had failed, what we must do. We read it, memorized it, quoted it. . . . For those of us wandering around in the arid desert of Eisenhower Republicanism, it hit like a rifle shot." Here Goldwater uses the notion of individual freedom to outline the theoretical foundations behind Conservatism.

Surely the first obligation of a political thinker is to understand the nature of man. The Conservative does not claim special powers of perception on this point, but he does claim a familiarity with the accumulated wisdom and experience of history, and he is not too proud to learn from the great minds of the past.

The first thing about man is that each member of the species is a unique creature. Man's most sacred possession is his individual soul—which has an immortal side, but also a mortal one. The mortal side establishes his absolute differentness from every other human being. *Only a philosophy that takes into account the essential differences between men, and, accordingly, makes provision for developing the different potentialities of each man can claim to be in accord with Nature.* We have heard much in our time about the "common man." It is a concept that pays little attention to the history of a nation that grew great through the initiative and ambition of uncommon men. The Conservative knows that to regard man as part of an undifferentiated mass is to consign him to slavery.

Secondly, the Conservative has learned that the economic and spiritual aspects of man's nature are inextricably intertwined. He cannot be economically free, or even economically efficient, if he is enslaved politically; conversely, man's political freedom is illusory if he is dependent for his economic needs on the State.

The Conservative realizes, thirdly, that man's development, in both its spiritual and material aspects, is not something that can be directed by outside forces. Every man, for his individual good and for the good of his society, is responsible for his *own* development. The choices that govern his life are choices that *he* must make: they cannot be made by any other human being, or by a collectivity of human beings. If the Conservative is less anxious than his Liberal brethren to increase Social Security "benefits," it is because he is more anxious than his Liberal brethren that people be free throughout their lives to spend their earnings when and as they see fit.

Source: Barry Goldwater, *The Conscience of a Conservative.* Copyright © 1960 Chariot-Victor Books.

government that he believed had become too big, too fat, and too complacent. Throughout the winter and spring of 1964, he stumbled toward the nomination, eliminating one Republican rival after another. At times, the political struggles became bitter. Rockefeller branded Goldwater as a wild-eyed radical who might lead the country into a nuclear war. "WHO DO YOU WANT IN THE ROOM WITH THE H-BOMB BUTTON?" asked a Rockefeller campaign flyer. Other opponents also accused him of being trigger-happy and harboring racist beliefs; they even compared him to Adolph Hitler. But Goldwater won the battle. Reflecting the beliefs of their new candidate, the Republican platform called for spending cuts, reduced taxes, and a balanced budget; advocated stopping the flow of pornography through the mail and restoring school prayers; and demanded a foreign policy that aggressively confronted communists.

In the 1964 presidential election Goldwater faced Lyndon Johnson and his well-oiled Democratic machine. Johnson promised more government and more federal activity. Summarizing the Democratic agenda, Johnson said, "I just want to tell you this—we're in favor of a lot of things and we're against mighty few." On Johnson's side were prosperity and a substantial legislative record, which included the Civil Rights Act, the Wildlife Preservation Act, and the War on Poverty's Economic Opportunity Act. Looking toward the future, the Texas politician promised a **Great Society,** where want and suffering were eliminated. Medicare, Medicaid, regional redevelopment, urban renewal, and support for education—all were on Johnson's ambitious agenda. As several politicians suggested, criticizing Lyndon Johnson was like taking a shot at Santa Claus.

Not content just to say what they were for, Johnson and his campaign organizers made it clear what they were against. In two words: Barry Goldwater. In their public statements, television advertisements, and bumper stickers, they implied that if Goldwater was

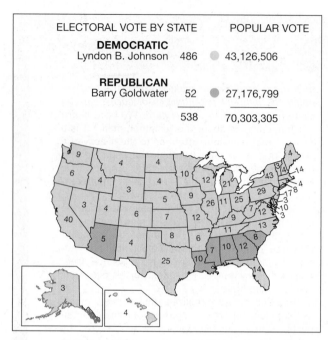

ELECTORAL VOTE BY STATE		POPULAR VOTE
DEMOCRATIC		
Lyndon B. Johnson	486	43,126,506
REPUBLICAN		
Barry Goldwater	52	27,176,799
	538	70,303,305

Election of 1964

elected he might lead the nation into a nuclear war. "In your heart, you know he might" and "In your guts, you know he's nuts" were their constant refrains. In one television commercial, a young girl was shown picking the petals of a daisy in a sun-drenched field. As she plucked she counted, until her voice was drowned out by a stronger, military voice that commenced a military countdown, ending with the sight of a nuclear blast. The commercial ended with the voice of Lyndon Johnson: "These are the stakes. To make a world in which all of God's children can live, or go into the dark. We must either love each other, or we must die." To the end, the Democrats waged a bitter, effective campaign. Later in his life, Goldwater said, "I've often said that if I hadn't known Barry Goldwater in 1964 and I had to depend on the press and the cartoons, I'd have voted against the son of the bitch."

That is exactly what most Americans did. Goldwater lost big in 1964—43 million votes to 27 million votes. Johnson carried over 60 percent of the popular vote, something that few other presidential candidates had ever done. Newspaper and television commentators were quick to write off Goldwater and his conservative supporters as a political aberration. A *Time* magazine writer prophesied, "The conservative cause whose championship Goldwater assumed suffered a crippling setback. . . . The humiliation of their defeat was so complete that they will not have another shot at party domination for some time to come." Yet when conservatives began to study the returns, the defeat did not seem so absolute. Goldwater had run well in the Deep South,

long considered sacred ground for the Democratic party. He had also attracted considerable support in the Southwest, the mountain states, southern California, and northeastern urban, ethnic-Catholic neighborhoods.

Taken as a whole, Republican strategist Kevin Phillips believed that the 1964 returns contained good news for the future of the Republican party and the Conservative movement. In his book *The Emerging Republican Party* (1969), Phillips argued that an important shift in power was taking place in American politics. New Deal liberalism and the northeastern intellectual and media elite no longer expressed the needs and met the demands of most Americans, especially Westerners and Southerners. Deep in the South, out on the range, on the Sunbelt golf courses, and in working-class Catholic neighborhoods, a new ethos was taking shape. The political revolt, Phillips noted, would be led by people like Goldwater, men and women who wanted less government, less special-interest reforms, and more of their own paychecks. As one conservative Texan later said, "The '64 campaign was the Alamo before San Jacinto. . . . 1964 would prove a pivotal election, a beginning rather than an end."

Shifting Party Loyalties

Ultimately, Phillips was right. There was a political earthquake taking place in the United States, and its rumblings would be felt for the rest of the century. In 1968 and 1972, presidential candidate Californian Richard Nixon, though more moderate than Goldwater on social issues, attacked liberal rulings by the Supreme Court, called for a return to "law and order," and appealed to the traditional values of hard work, religious faith, patriotism, and family. The South and West responded. In 1968, Nixon carried almost the entire West and most of the upper South (the Deep South went to American Independent candidate George Wallace). In his 1972 landslide victory, Nixon won every southern and western state. Eight years later, Ronald Reagan captured the presidency running on a platform that could have been written by Barry Goldwater. Reagan called upon American politicians to get tough on the Soviet Union, balance the federal budget, reduce the size of government, and support legislation to strengthen family values. Americans responded, sending him into office in 1980 and then overwhelmingly endorsing his first term in 1984. Texas Republican George Bush served two terms as vice president and then won the presidency in 1988, uniting the same coalition that Goldwater and Nixon had built and Reagan had satisfied.

The reasons for the shift in the center of political power from Northeast and Midwest to South and

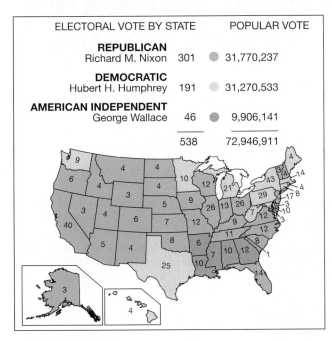

ELECTORAL VOTE BY STATE | POPULAR VOTE

REPUBLICAN
Richard M. Nixon 301 ● 31,770,237

DEMOCRATIC
Hubert H. Humphrey 191 ● 31,270,533

AMERICAN INDEPENDENT
George Wallace 46 ● 9,906,141

538 | 72,946,911

Election of 1968

Republicans made their largest gains, millions of Americans relocated and immigrants moved to the South and West: the population of Florida increased by 3,124,000, California by 2,338,000, and Texas by 2,112,000; while New York's population declined by 1,582,000, Ohio by 649,000, and Illinois by 476,000. The same pattern was true for other states. Traditional industrial states—Massachusetts, Pennsylvania, Michigan, and Indiana—suffered sharp declines. Southern and western states—Virginia, North Carolina, Georgia, Arizona, Colorado, Oregon, and Washington—enjoyed equally sharp increases. By 1980, for the first time in American history, the majority of the population lived in the South and West. Such population shifts bolstered the political power of the South and West and reduced the political clout of the Northeast and the Midwest.

The same decade saw a shift in party loyalties in the South. For nearly a century white Southerners had voted Democrat, or, more precisely, non-Republican. For them, the Republican party was the party of Lincoln, the Civil War, and military Reconstruction. Their Democratic party stood for limiting the size and power of the federal government and for allowing the states to take care of their own problems and exploit their own resources. Barry Goldwater, and then Richard Nixon, appealed directly to these issues. In

West and party alliances from Democrat to Republican had become clear by the 1990s. The power shift was largely the result of the movements of peoples. In the 1970s, for example, the decade in which the

Population Shifts, 1980–1986

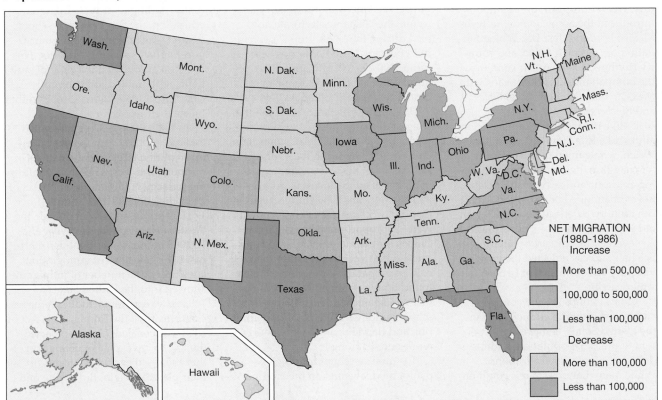

NET MIGRATION
(1980-1986)
Increase

■ More than 500,000

■ 100,000 to 500,000

□ Less than 100,000

Decrease

■ More than 100,000

■ Less than 100,000

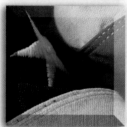

The New Immigration

She was the undisputed queen of Tejano, the music of the Texas-Mexico border. There had been many earlier Latina popular singers, including Edie Gorme, Vicki Carr, Linda Ronstadt, and Gloria Estafan. But Selena was different. With her dark brown skin, long jet-black hair, and prominent Indian features, she became a validating symbol of Mexican American identity, an entertainer who never abandoned her cultural roots.

Her music epitomized the complexity of border culture. Tejano music originated in the nineteenth century, when European immigrants introduced the accordion to the Texas-Mexico border. A fast-paced blend of Latin pop, German polka, and country rhythms, Tejano music combined the oompah music of Europeans with Mexican ballads known as *cumbias* and *rancheras*.

Unlike many earlier Latina personalities, like Rita Hayworth and Raquel Welch, who gained their fame only after changing their names and projecting an exotic and sexy image, Selena never abandoned her Mexican American identity. Selena, who was 23 years old when she was slain, nevertheless achieved extraordinary popularity. Selena's success reflected the growing visibility and influence of Latinos in American life.

Today, Latinos are the youngest and fastest growing ethnic group in the United States, comprising 13 percent of the U.S. population. Latinos defy any simple generalizations. While many Latinos share a common bond of culture and language, many trace their origins to disparate places, including Central America, Cuba, Mexico, and Puerto Rico. Hispanics include liberals and conservatives, recent immigrants and Americans who can trace their ancestry back to the sixteenth century. Hispanics, who can be of any race, are changing American life irreversibly. More than any other ethnic group, they are transforming a biracial society into a multiracial society. They are also transforming a monolingual society into an increasingly bilingual society. Today, roughly 10 percent of the American population speaks Spanish at home.

Concentrated in the nine states that have the largest number of votes in the electoral college, Latinos and Latinas are poised to have a significant impact on American politics. In California, the Hispanic electorate doubled during the 1990s, from 7 percent to 14 percent. In 2001, Latinos held some 5000 elective and appointive political offices, including about 4 percent of the seats in Congress.

Still, many Hispanics have felt the sting of discrimination. A six-volume report issued by the U.S. Commission on Civil Rights during the 1970s documented a pattern of unequal treatment in the education of many Hispanic Americans. The study showed that many Spanish-speaking students were disproportionately assigned to classes for the mentally retarded and tracked into vocational rather than college preparatory programs. It also found that less money was spent on many Hispanic students, that their school buildings were physically inferior, and that Hispanics were poorly represented among teachers.

To equalize school funding Hispanics filed lawsuits. In the landmark case of *Serrano v. Priest* (1998), the California Supreme Court ruled that financing education through local property taxes violated the state constitution. Since then, courts ordered many states to equalize funding of public schools.

Another strategy to promote equal educational opportunity has been bilingual education. In 1968, Congress passed Title VII of the Elementary and Secondary Education Act, mandating that children from diverse language backgrounds be instructed in two languages and that teachers be trained, materials developed, and research conducted to help these children move as rapidly as possible from bilingual education to classrooms using English. In 1974, in the case of *Lau v. Nichols,* the Supreme Court ruled that by failing to provide bilingual education, the San Francisco school district was discriminating against non-English-speaking students. This decision guaranteed the right of students with limited English proficiency to an educational program that meets their needs.

In 1965, the U.S. Congress voted to end the quota system that restricted immigration largely to the nations of northern and western Europe. Following passage of the Immigration Act of 1965, the United States admitted 170,000 immigrants from outside the Western Hemisphere each year and 120,000 immigrants from the Americas. Later revisions of immigration laws raised the number of immigrants allowed into the United States to 700,000 a year, not including refugees.

At the time the Immigration Act of 1965 was enacted, no one expected the law to have a major change on either the number of immigrants or their place of origin. But by the mid-

1980s, the number of legal immigrants to the United States was averaging 600,000 a year. Undocumented immigrants probably increased this figure by a third. Most of the immigrants came from Latin America, the Caribbean, and Asia. It is estimated that their descendants will make up almost half the total population by 2050.

Some of the new immigrants were refugees from troubled lands. After Fidel Castro nationalized many Cuban businesses and aligned his country with the Soviet Union, thousands of Cubans migrated to the United States. Many viewed their stay in the United States as temporary, and some participated in the failed Bay of Pigs invasion in 1961.

Between 1965 and 1971, another 300,000 Cubans arrived from Cuba by boat or on "Freedom Flights." In 1980, an additional 120,000 Cubans fled to the United States. In the summer of 1994, more than 35,000 Cubans set sail in rafts and homemade boats toward the United States.

During the 1960s and 1970s, with the exception of Mexicans, political refugees from Cuba comprised the largest number of migrants from the Americas. Since 1980, increasing numbers of immigrants have also ar-

rived from Dominican Republic, Haiti, Jamaica, El Salvador, Guatemala, Nicaragua, and Costa Rica. Many of these migrants are refugees, fleeing war, political violence, and oppressive governments.

Immigration policy has been strongly influenced by foreign policy and domestic political considerations. In general, those migrants who were perceived as seeking to escape communist rule, such as Cubans and Nicaraguans during the period of Sandinista rule during the 1980s, received a warmer welcome than those who arrived from countries with anti-communist governments and who were treated as economic migrants.

The single largest contributor to American immigration is Mexico. Today, one out of five immigrants living in the United States is Mexican-born. Immigration has been propelled by the rapid growth of Mexico's population, which tripled in the past fifty years, as well as by the wages paid in the United States, which are six times higher than those in Mexico.

Work has been the great magnet pulling Mexican and other Hispanic migrants to the United States. Today, the United States has a ravenous appetite for service workers, nonunionized manufacturing workers, farm

workers, and skilled artisans. Hispanic immigrant workers have met many of those needs.

Hispanic immigrants were not alone in streaming toward America. After the fall of Saigon in 1975, hundreds of thousands of Vietnamese began to flee the country. Some escaped across the border into Thailand on foot. Others fled their country in small wooden boats in typhoon- and pirate-infested waters. Over a million Vietnamese left their country between 1975 and 1981. Following their perilous flight, thousands were placed in detention camps across Southeast Asia. Eventually, 823,000 were resettled in the United States and over 200,000 in Australia and Canada.

Between 1820 and 1965, about 1.3 million Asian immigrants had arrived in the United States, making up less than 4 percent of all immigrants. Since 1965, Asians—mainly from the Philippines, China, Taiwan, Hong Kong, Vietnam, Korea, and India—have comprised about 25 percent of legal immigration. In 1965, Asian Americans numbered barely a million. Today, there are more than 8 million.

As a result of massive immigration, the United States is becoming the first advanced industrial nation in which every resident will be a member of a minority group. Although most Americans consider the United States a haven for oppressed people the world over, hostility toward immigrants has often flourished in times of economic uncertainty. Nativists have worried that immigrants pose a threat to the nation's culture, depress wages, and take away jobs from native-born Americans.

During the economic recession of the early 1990s, anti-immigrant sentiment was especially pronounced. In 1994, California voters approved Proposition 187, which would have cut off health and social services, including access to public education, to illegal aliens and their children. The initiative was later declared unconstitutional by the federal courts.

The Conscience of a Conservative, Goldwater's condemnation of the growth in federal power was a defense of the constitutional principle of states' rights. He particularly attacked the idea that the federal government could demand the integration of southern public schools. Goldwater wrote, "I am firmly convinced—not only that integrated schools are not required—but that the Constitution does not permit any interference whatsoever by the federal government in the field of education." Although Nixon did not go quite as far as Goldwater, he did succeed in limiting the role of the federal government in forcing desegregation of southern public schools. In addition, he argued that the Supreme Court had enlarged the power of the federal government; he appointed justices who were committed to reversing that trend. By the time Reagan ran for the presidency in 1980, the Republican party had become "the new Grand Old Party" for much of the white South.

Unlike the South, the West had never had a strong tradition of party loyalties. The seats of both parties, they argued, were in the East, and both parties were dominated by eastern interests. As a result the West never developed the machine politics of the East and was more sensitive to democratic political innovations. Initiative, referendum and recall, and woman suffrage, for instance, were more quickly accepted in the West than in other sections of the country. Similarly, the West was more receptive to left-wing and right-wing third-party movements. From the Populist movement in the 1890s and the Wobblies in the early part of the twentieth century to Francis Townsend's campaign in the 1930s and Barry Goldwater's revolt in the 1960s, the West had been more apt to swing toward political extremes.

The Politics of Liberation

The idea of individual freedom, as measured by less government and fewer restrictions, has characterized much of the political thinking of the post–1945 West. To be sure, individual freedom provided the core of the Goldwater and Reagan movements. It helps explain Goldwater's attack on the federal government and defense of a version of states' rights and Reagan's demands for deregulation. But the idea of individual freedom has also energized movements outside of Republican politics.

On the political left, the West Coast counterculture movement and such African American liberation movements as the Black Panthers proclaimed a profound distrust of "government" solutions and federal bureaucracies. **Ken Kesey,** the novelist whose fictional heroes seemed to speak for many alienated youths, rejected the politics of party organizations and mass solutions. The heroes of his novels *One Flew*

Over the Cuckoo's Nest (1962) and *Sometimes a Great Notion* (1964) are first and foremost individualists who battle more for individual dignity—the right to make individual decisions—than any sort of collective ideal. Similarly, Black Panther leaders struggled to gain control of their own communities and steered clear of traditional party politics.

Yet it was on the political right where individualism and antifederal sentiment made their most important political impact. Often the battle was over the control of land and natural resources. With the downturn in the economy in the 1970s, Western developers and businesspeople began to complain about federal environmental legislation. The debate over "beneficial use" became the flash point. Environmentalist groups such as the Sierra Club and the Friends of the Earth charged that developers were willing to destroy the land and the ecosystem in their pursuit of profits. Loggers, ranchers, miners, and other Westerners who depended on inexpensive access to government lands argued that the mass of federal regulations made it impossible for them to hold their own in competitive world markets.

The **Sagebrush rebellion** was the most dramatic example of the battle between state and federal governments over control of state land. In the late 1970s and early 1980s, some conservative western politicians began to clamor for the federal government to cede its control of western land to the individual states. The idea was to develop some of the land, sell much of the rest, and promote western growth and prosperity. (Other Westerners, liberal and conservative, saw the rebellion as an attempted land grab by miners, ranchers, and loggers, a sort of return to the most exploitive methods of the nineteenth century.) Utah Senator Orrin Hatch introduced in 1979 legislation to return 544 million acres in 13 Western states from federal to state control; then-presidential-hopeful Ronald Reagan endorsed the proposal. But the rebellion failed. Arizona governor Bruce Babbitt summed it up as an attempt to "sell off the land into private ownership, lock the gates, post the no-trespassing sign, and proceed to use and abuse the land." In truth, though many Westerners had little faith in the wisdom of the federal government and resented federal regulation, they had even less faith in and more fear of their own developers. In the battle between developers and preservationists, most Westerners found themselves seeking middle ground.

The fight over western lands, however, did not slow down the West's steady political drift to the right. Tax revolts were more successful than the Sagebrush rebellion. If Westerners were content to allow the government to control a vast portion of their land, they steadfastly maintained that they should be able to control more of their own incomes.

The tax rebellion was waged on state and federal fronts. In 1978 California passed Proposition 13, which demanded a 57 percent cut in state property taxes. The bill drained the state's treasury surplus and resulted in less services. In other states the rebellion was less extreme, but most western state politicians had to move toward rigid fiscal conservatism to win election or to stay in office. In several cases, politicians—most notably Phil Gramm of Texas—even left the Democratic party and became Republicans.

CONCLUSION

The November 21, 1994, cover of *Time* magazine said it all without a word. A stampeding elephant, eyes fixed straight ahead in a pitiless stare, has trampled and killed a tiny donkey. The donkey is utterly flattened, its eyes and tongue forced out of its head. The off-year elections, the cartoon indicated, had resulted in a complete and total Republican victory. Before the election the Democratic party had controlled the Senate 56 to 44, the House of Representatives 256 to 178, and state governors' mansions 29 to 20. After the election, the Republican party controlled the Senate 53 to 47, the House 227 to 199, and governorships 30 to 17. It was a landslide rejection of President Bill Clinton's first two years in office and, according to many commentators, a generation of Democratic policy-making. Putting the election into perspective, a *Newsweek* magazine writer noted, "Seventy-seven years ago, almost to the day, Bolsheviks in Petrograd raced into the Winter Palace in the name of communism. Last week in one of the most profound electoral routs in American history, Republicans won the right to occupy the Capitol and to mount what their more hyperbolic commanders think of as a counterrevolution: a full-scale attack on the notion that a central government should play a central role in the life of a nation."

The importance of the election seemed to transcend party politics. It was not so much which party had won the election but which Republicans controlled the agenda that was crucial. The new Speaker of the House, and Republican lightning rod, was Newt Gingrich, a southern congressman who spoke the language of Barry Goldwater. Gingrich's "Contract With America" called for major budget cuts, tax cuts, and federal bureaucratic cuts. He promised to make the federal government cheaper and smaller, to return power to the states, and to reform government benefit programs. Sounding every bit a revolutionary, Gingrich said, "I will cooperate, but I won't compromise. . . . I may fail, we may fail. But this is real. I am who I seem to be."

Gingrich and his message underscored an important shift in American history. No longer were leaders from the biggest eastern and midwestern

CHRONOLOGY OF KEY EVENTS

1951   Inexpensive, efficient window air-conditioning unit introduced

1958   Dodgers and Giants professional baseball teams move from New York to California

1960   The *Conscience of a Conservative*, in which politician Barry Goldwater outlines his beliefs, is published; sells 3.5 million copies in four years; California surpasses New York as the nation's most populous state

1964   Barry Goldwater wins the Republican nomination for president; Democrat Lyndon Johnson defeats Goldwater in landslide victory

1966   Braves professional baseball team moves from Milwaukee to Atlanta

1968   Richard Nixon is elected nation's thirty-seventh president

1972   Nixon is elected to second term, winning every southern and western state

1978   California voters approve Proposition 13, which calls for a 57 percent reduction in state property taxes

1980   Ronald Reagan is elected fortieth president

1984   Reagan is reelected to second term

1988   George Bush, Reagan's vice president, is elected forty-first president

1992   Democrat Bill Clinton defeats Bush to become nation's forty-second president

1994   Democrats suffer overwhelming defeats in congressional and gubernatorial elections

states. The new leaders in Washington came from the South and the West. Gingrich represented Georgia, Senate Majority Leader Robert Dole, Kansas; Phil Gramm, Texas. Their battle call was freedom. Criticizing President Clinton's comment that the election represented the wish by Americans for a government that "empowers" them, Gramm remarked, "He just doesn't get it. Government doesn't empower you. Freedom empowers you." It was a western credo he proclaimed, a doctrine that runs through a hundred John Wayne films.

The Gingrich revolution—like Goldwater's bid for the presidency—ended in failure. Gingrich's allies from the South, Southwest, and West were better at winning elections than convincing Congress to pass their legislative package that included drastic budget cuts and welfare reform coupled with added military spending, term limits, tax cuts, a tougher stand on crime, and a line-item veto power for the president. Their rhetoric was strident, their actions often bullish, and their ability to project compassion for all Americans almost totally absent. In addition, President Bill Clinton was able to move toward the center and co-opt such traditionally Republican proposals as budget cuts and welfare reform. By January 1996 the Gingrich revolution was over, but many of the movement's proposals would soon be passed into law. In an odd way, the ideas of Goldwater, Reagan, and Gingrich, of conservatives in the South and West, were still very much alive. In fact, Clinton moved those ideas to the political center. The question unanswered was: Is it a credo for the twenty-first century?

CHAPTER SUMMARY AND KEY POINTS

The central political, social, economic, and cultural fact of the second half of the twentieth century was the shift in power from the older industrial states and cities of the Northeast and upper Midwest to the South and West. In this chapter you read about the reasons for the rise of the Sunbelt; myths and realities about the history of the West; and the distinctive politics of the western United States.

- Since 1945, the South and West have experienced the country's greatest growth and have dominated the presidency.

- Growing prosperity in the South is the result of technology, a shift in race relations, and the movement of industry into the South, which was accelerated by World War II.

- In contrast to the myth that the West has been exploited by the East and by the federal govern-

ment, much of the region's growth has depended on federal financing and construction. Especially important are water projects, including dams, power, and irrigation projects.

- Since World War II, the western economy has shifted away from extractive industries such as mining, agriculture, ranging, oil, and logging and has developed a more diversified economy.

- Rapid western growth has produced many environmental problems.

- Western politics has tended to emphasize individual liberty.

SUGGESTIONS FOR FURTHER READING

Carl Abbott, *New Urban America: Growth and Politics in the Sunbelt Cities of the South* (1981). A perceptive and knowledgeable analysis of regional demographics and politics.

Raymond Arsenault, *The End of the Long Hot Summer: The Air Conditioner and Southern Culture* (1984). Explores the social impact of air-conditioning in the South—a neglected but important aspect of the region's history.

William Cronon, George Miles, and Jay Gitlin, eds., *Under An Open Sky: Rethinking America's Western Past* (1992). Seeks to dislodge western history from its old moorings and point it in new directions.

Patricia Nelson Limerick, Clyde Millner II, and Charles Rankin, eds., *Trails: Toward a New Western History* (1991). Essays on the cutting edge of new historical interpretations of the West.

Randy Roberts and James S. Olson, *John Wayne: American* (1995). Explores the life of an important Western icon, and examines his influence on national identity.

Richard Slotkin, *Gunfighter Nation: The Myth of the Frontier in Twentieth-Century America* (1992). Surveys the intersection between popular culture and the mythic American West.

Richard White, *"It's Your Misfortune and None of My Own": A New History of the American West* (1991). A fresh perspective on the history of a region.

Donald Worster, *Rivers of Empire: Water, Aridity, and the Growth of the American West* (1985). How the West's most precious resource shaped regional identity.

Novels

Max Brand, *Destry Rides Again* (1930).

E. L. Doctorow, *Welcome to Hard Times* (1960).

Zane Grey, *Riders of the Purple Sage* (1913).

Louis L'Amour, *Hondo* (1953).

Larry McMurtry, *Lonesome Dove* (1985).

Larry McMurtry, *Horseman, Pass By* (1961).

Jack Schaefer, *Shane* (1949).

Wallace Stegner, *The Big Rock Candy Mountain* (1943).

Nathanael West, *The Day of the Locust* (1939).

Owen Wister, *The Virginian* (1902).

MEDIA RESOURCES

Web Sites

Virtual Museum of Computing
http://www.cs.reading.ac.uk/museum/vlmp/computing.html
This University of Reading site says it is "an eclectic Collection of World Wide Web hyperlinks connected with the history of computing and on-line computer-based exhibits."

Lyndon B. Johnson
http://www.ipl.org/ref/POTUS/lbjohnson.html
This page contains basic factual data about his election and presidency, speeches, and on-line biographies.

Lyndon B. Johnson Library and Museum
http://www.lbjlib.utexas.edu/
This presidential library contains images and on-line exhibits.

A Giant Leap—America and Space
http://cnn.com/TECH/specials/apollo/
This CNN site commemorates the thirtieth anniversary of the 1969 moonwalk and tells the story of NASA and the ongoing space program.

National Aeronautics and Space Administration
http://www.hq.nasa.gov/office/pao/History/histsub.htm
NASA's Office of Policy and Plans History Office maintains this site about NASA and its history.

Information Age: People, Information and Technology Exhibit
http://photo2.si.edu/infoage.html
National Museum of American History hosts this site about how technology, particularly information technology, has shaped American's lives.

History of the Computer
http://www.tcm.org/html/history/index.html
Included are a time line of the history of computers and computing as well as information about the people and inventions who made it possible.

Films and Videos

The Great Train Robbery (1903). This early, important film did for Western film what *The Virginian* did for Western literature. It established the basic themes of horses, gun, violence, and white hats.

High Noon (1952). Fred Zinnemann Cold War film had masqueraded as a Western. Gary Cooper plays the hunted sheriff.

The Last Picture Show (1972). Based on a Larry McMurtry novel, this film reflects on the passing of the mythic West.

The Searchers (1956). Perhaps John Ford's greatest film, it centered on the obsession and racism that was always present in the West.

Stagecoach (1939). John Ford's masterpiece that revived the mythic Western just as the United States was moving toward World War II. The film virtually made John Wayne's persona.

The Unforgiven (1992). Clint Eastwood's anti-Western Western. The film subverts all the stock Western conventions.

KEY TERMS

Hydraulic society   (p. 857)

Smog   (p. 860)

Great Society   (p. 863)

Sagebrush rebellion   (p. 868)

PEOPLE YOU SHOULD KNOW

Jimmy Carter   (p. 853)

Henry J. Kaiser   (p. 857)

Walter O'Malley   (p. 858)

Barry Goldwater   (p. 861)

Ken Kesey   (p. 868)

REVIEW QUESTIONS

1. What factors turned the idea of the "New South" into a reality in the post–World War II era?

2. How has the West developed such a booming, diverse economy?

3. What qualities define "Politics—western style"? How have these values influenced modern American politics?

31 Crises and Resurgence, 1970–1990

THE WATERGATE BREAK-IN

Shortly after 1 A.M. on the morning of June 17, 1972, a security guard at the Washington, D.C., Watergate office complex, spotted a strip of masking tape covering the lock of a basement door. He removed it. A short while later, he found the door taped open again. He called the police, who found two more taped locks, and a jammed door leading into the offices of the Democratic National Committee. Inside they discovered five men with cameras and electronic eavesdropping equipment.

At first, the **Watergate break-in** seemed like a minor incident. The identities of the burglars, however, suggested something more serious. One, James McCord, was chief security coordinator and electronics expert of the Committee for the Reelection of the President (CREEP). Others had links to the CIA.

Over the course of the next year, it became clear that the break-in was only one of a series of secret operations coordinated by the White House. Financed by illegal campaign contributions, these operations posed a threat to America's constitutional system of government and eventually forced **Richard Nixon** to resign the presidency.

The Watergate break-in had its roots in Richard Nixon's obsession with secrecy and political intelligence. To stop leaks of information to the press, in 1971 the Nixon White House assembled a team of "plumbers," consisting of former CIA operatives. This private police force, paid for, in part, by illegal campaign contributions, engaged in a wide range of criminal acts, including phone tapping and burglary, against those on its "enemies list."

In 1972 when President Nixon was running for reelection, his campaign committee authorized another series of illegal activities. It hired Donald Segretti to stage "dirty tricks" against potential Democratic candidates, which included mailing letters that falsely accused one candidate of homosexuality and fathering an illegitimate child. It considered a plan to use prostitutes to blackmail Democrats at their national convention and to kidnap anti-Nixon radical leaders. The committee also authorized $250,000 for intelligence-gathering operations. Four times the committee sent burglars to break into Democratic headquarters.

Precisely what the campaign committee hoped to learn from these intelligence-gathering activities remains a mystery. It seems likely that it was seeking information

873

about the Democratic party's campaign strategies and any information the Democrats had about illegal campaign contributions to the Republican party.

On June 23—six days after the botched break-in—President Nixon ordered aides to block an FBI investigation into White House involvement in the break-in on grounds that an investigation would endanger national security. He also counseled his aides to lie, under oath if necessary: "I don't give a [expletive deleted] what happens," he told his former attorney general, John Mitchell, who was then his campaign manager, "I want you all to stonewall it, let them plead the Fifth Amendment, cover-up, or anything else."

The Watergate break-in did not hurt Nixon's re-election campaign, since between the activities of the burglars and the president were layers of deception that had to be carefully peeled away. *Washington Post* reporters Bob Woodward and Carl Bernstein, sensing that the break-in was only part of a larger scandal, slowly pieced together part of the story. Facing long jail terms, some of the burglars began to tell the truth, and the truth illuminated a path leading to the White House.

If Nixon had few political friends, he had legions of enemies. Over the years he had offended or attacked many Democrats—and a number of prominent Republicans. His detractors latched onto the Watergate issue with the tenacity of bulldogs.

The Senate appointed a special committee to investigate the Watergate scandal. Most of Nixon's top aides continued the cover-up. **John Dean,** the president's counsel, did not. Throughout the episode he had kept careful notes, and in a quiet, precise voice he told the Senate Watergate Committee that the president was deeply involved in the cover-up. The matter was still not solved. All the committee had was Dean's word against the other White House aides.

On July 16, 1973, a former White House employee dropped a bombshell by testifying that Nixon had recorded all Oval Office conversations. Whatever Nixon and his aides had said about Watergate in the Oval Office, therefore, was faithfully recorded on tape.

Nixon tried to keep the tapes from the committee by invoking executive privilege, insisting that a president had a right to keep confidential any White House communication, whether or not it involved sensitive diplomatic or national security matters. When Archibald Cox, a special prosecutor investigating the Watergate affair, persisted in demanding the tapes, Nixon ordered his attorney general, Elliot Richardson, to fire him; Richardson refused and resigned; Richardson's assistant, William Ruckelshaus, also resigned. Ruckelshaus's assistant, Robert Bork, finally fired Cox, but Congress forced Nixon to name a new special prosecutor, Houston attorney Leon Jaworski.

In the midst of the Watergate investigations, another scandal broke. Federal prosecutors accused Vice President **Spiro Agnew** of extorting payoffs from engineers and road building contractors while

The Senate Watergate Committee, chaired by Senator Sam Ervin of North Carolina, investigated the secret operations and "dirty tricks" of the Nixon White House. The revelation by a witness before the committee that all conversations in the Oval Office had been secretly recorded—and President Nixon's reaction to that revelation—eventually forced him to resign the presidency.

THE PEOPLE SPEAK

The Watergate Tapes

In July of 1973, Fred Thompson, a Republican attorney for the Senate Watergate committee, (and later a Republican senator from Tennessee), called on a surprise witness, Alexander Butterfield, a former aide to White House chief of staff H. R. (Bob) Haldeman.

> THOMPSON: "Mr. Butterfield, are you aware of the installation of any listening devices in the Oval Office of the President?"
>
> BUTTERFIELD: "I was aware of listening devices, yes sir."

The Secret Service had installed recording devices in the White House, the Executive Office Building, and the presidential retreat at Camp David early in 1971. Five microphones were placed in the president's desk and two others were installed in wall lamps by the Oval Office fireplace. Line taps were also placed in telephones. Altogether, the Nixon White House made 3,700 hours of recordings containing about 2,800 hours of conversations.

From the moment that Alexander Butterfield disclosed the existence of a White House taping system, the investigation into the break-in at Democratic Party headquarters in the Watergate office complex became a battle over access to the tapes.

In an April 1974 televised address, Nixon released heavily edited transcripts of the tapes. The public was surprised by the repeated use of the phrase "Expletive Deleted." An 18½-minute section of a June 20, 1972 meeting was inexplicably missing. In July 1974 the Supreme Court, voting 8 to 0, ruled that President Nixon must hand over tapes to Federal District Judge John Sirica.

In a March 1971 tape Nixon proposed asking the milk industry for large campaign contributions in exchange for price supports. In a June 1971 conversation with his chief of staff the president proposed a break-in at the Brookings Institution to find classified documents that might embarrass the Democrats: "I want it implemented. . . . (Expletive), get in and get those files. Blow the safe and get it." In a September 1971 tape the president ordered the Internal Revenue Service to investigate Jews who made large contributions to the Democratic Party. In another tape he talks about placing a price tag on ambassadorships: "My point is that anybody that wants to be an ambassador, wants to pay at least $250,000."

June 23, 1972

The Watergate break-in occurred June 17, 1972. Six days later—June 23, 1972—in a conversation with Chief of Staff H. R. ("Bob") Haldeman, President Nixon discussed the progress of the FBI's investigation. Haldeman expressed special concern about the FBI's efforts to trace the source of money found on the burglars:

> HALDEMAN: ". . . The FBI is not under control. . . . Their investigation is leading into some productive areas, because they've been able to trace the money. . . ."
>
> HALDEMAN: "The way to handle this now is for us to . . . call [FBI Director] Pat Gray and just say, "Stay the hell out of this . . . this is ah, business here we don't want you to go any further on it."

Told that the FBI's investigation was leading to Nixon's reelection campaign, the president instructed his chief of staff to derail the investigation. He should tell the FBI, "Don't go any further into this case, period."

August 1, 1972

President Nixon and his chief of staff Bob Haldeman talk about using illegally diverted campaign money to buy silence from the Watergate burglars.

> NIXON: Let's be fatalistic about the goddamned thing.
>
> HALDEMAN: If it blows it blows.
>
> NIXON: If it blows it blows and so on. I'm not that worried about it, to be really candid with you. . . .
>
> HALDEMAN: But if it blows, we'll survive it. [Former CIA operative and the organizer of the Watergate break-in E. Howard] Hunt's happy.
>
> NIXON: At considerable cost, I guess.
>
> HALDEMAN: Yes.
>
> NIXON: It's worth it.
>
> HALDEMAN: It's very expensive. It's that costly.
>
> NIXON: That's what the money is for. . . . Well, well, they have to be paid.

he was Maryland's governor and Baltimore County executive. In a plea bargain, Agnew pleaded no contest to a relatively minor charge—that he had falsified his income tax in 1967—in exchange for a $10,000 fine. Agnew resigned and Nixon appointed **Gerald Ford** to succeed Agnew as vice president.

The Watergate scandal gradually came to encompass not just the cover-up but a wide range of presidential wrongdoings, including political favors to business groups in exchange for campaign contributions; misuse of public funds; deceiving Congress and the public about the secret bombing of Cambodia in 1969 and 1970; authorization of illegal domestic political surveillance and espionage against dissidents, political opponents, and journalists; and attempts to use FBI investigations and income tax audits by the Internal Revenue Service to harass political enemies.

On July 24, 1974, the House Judiciary Committee recommended that the House of Representatives impeach Nixon for obstruction of justice, abuse of power, and refusal to relinquish the tapes. On August 5 Nixon obeyed the Supreme Court ruling to release the tapes, which confirmed Dean's detailed testi-

Faced with the release of his secret tapes and impending impeachment proceedings, Richard Nixon resigned the office of president on August 9, 1974. Here he signals his farewell as he prepares to leave the White House for the last time. The Watergate scandal and Nixon's role in it undermined public trust in and respect for the presidency.

mony. Nixon had indeed been involved in a cover-up. On August 9, in a tearful farewell, Nixon became the first American president to resign from office. The following day, Gerald Ford became the new president. "Our long national nightmare," he said, "is over."

CRISIS OF POLITICAL LEADERSHIP

The Vietnam War and the Watergate scandal had a profound effect on the presidency. The office suffered a dramatic decline in public respect, and Congress became increasingly unwilling to defer to presidential leadership. Congress enacted a series of reforms that would make future Watergate-type abuses of presidential authority less likely. In the process Congress recaptured constitutional powers that had been ceded to an increasingly dominant executive branch.

Restraining the Imperial Presidency

Over the course of the twentieth century, the presidency gradually supplanted Congress as the center of federal power. Presidential powers increased, presidential staffs grew in size, and the executive branch gradually acquired a dominant relationship over Congress.

Beginning with Theodore Roosevelt, the president, and not Congress, established the nation's legislative agenda. Increasingly, Congress ceded its budget-making authority to the president. Presidents even found a way to make agreements with foreign nations without congressional approval. After World War II, presidents substituted executive agreements for treaties requiring Senate approval. Even more important, presidents gained the power to wage undeclared war, despite the fact that Congress is the sole branch of government empowered by the Constitution to declare war.

No president went further than Richard Nixon in concentrating powers in the presidency. He refused to spend funds that Congress had appropriated; he claimed executive privilege against disclosure of information on administration decisions; he refused to allow key decision makers to be questioned before congressional committees; he reorganized the executive branch and broadened the authority of new cabinet positions without congressional approval. During the Vietnam War, he ordered harbors mined and bombing raids launched without consulting Congress.

Watergate brought an end to the "imperial presidency" and the growth of presidential power. Over the president's veto, Congress enacted the **War Powers Act** (1973), which required future presidents to win specific authorization from Congress to engage

U.S. forces in foreign combat for more than 90 days. Under the law, a president who orders troops into action abroad must report the reason for this action to Congress within 48 hours.

In the wake of Watergate, Congress enacted a series of laws designed to reform the political process. Disclosures during the Watergate investigations of money laundering led Congress to provide for public financing of presidential elections, public disclosure of sources of funding, limits on private campaign contributions and spending, and enforcement of campaign finance laws by an independent Federal Election Commission.

To make it easier to investigate crimes in the executive branch, Congress required the attorney general to appoint a special prosecutor to investigate accusations of illegal activities. To reassert its budget-making authority, Congress created a Congressional Budget Office and specifically forbade a president to impound funds without its approval. To open government to public scrutiny, Congress opened more committee deliberations and enacted the **Freedom of Information Act,** which allows the public and press to request declassification of government documents.

The post-Watergate reforms have not been as effective as reformers anticipated. The War Powers Act has never been invoked and while various administrations have attempted to comply with the spirit of the law, no president has accepted its constitutional validity.

Campaign financing reform did not curb the power of special interests to curry favor with politicians or the ability of the very rich to outspend opponents. The Supreme Court struck down laws that forbade candidates from giving more than $50,000 to their own presidential campaign and, more importantly, barred any limitations on unauthorized "independent expenditures" by individuals on behalf of a candidate.

On the other hand, Congress had somewhat more success in reining in the Federal Bureau of Investigation (FBI) and the Central Intelligence Agency (CIA). During the 1970s, congressional investigators discovered that both organizations had, in defiance of their charters and federal law, broken into the homes, tapped the phones, and opened the mail of American citizens; illegally infiltrated antiwar groups and black radical organizations; and accumulated dossiers on dissidents. Investigators also found that the CIA had been involved in assassination plots against foreign leaders, among them Fidel Castro, and had tested the effects of radiation, electric shock, and drugs (such as LSD) on unsuspecting citizens.

In the wake of these investigations, the government severely limited CIA operations in the United States and laid down strict guidelines for FBI activities. To tighten congressional control over the CIA, Congress established a joint committee to supervise CIA operations.

New-Style Presidents

In contrast to Nixon and his abuses of presidential powers, the next two presidents, Gerald Ford and **Jimmy Carter,** cultivated reputations as modest, honest, forthright leaders. Both were men of decency and integrity, but neither established reputations as strong, dynamic leaders. Although many Americans admired their honesty and sincerity, neither succeeded in winning the confidence of the American people. Moreover, neither administration had a clear sense of direction. Both Ford and Carter seemed to waffle on major issues of public policy. As a result, both came to be regarded as unsure, vacillating presidents.

A 13-term congressman from Grand Rapids, Michigan, Gerald Ford dismissed the possibility of pardoning Richard Nixon for his Watergate misdeeds, then changed his mind. In the realm of economic policy, he began by urging tax increases but later called for a large tax cut. Similar indecision crippled his energy policy. At first, he tried to raise prices by imposing import fees on imported oil and ending domestic price controls; then he abandoned that position in the face of severe political pressure.

Carter, too, suffered from the charge that he modified his stances in the face of political pressure. A two-term Democratic governor of Georgia who defeated Ford in the 1976 presidential election, Carter came to office determined to cut military spending, calling for the abolition of nuclear weapons and the withdrawal of American troops from South Korea. By the end of his term, however, Carter spoke of the need for sustained growth in defense spending, upgrading nuclear forces in Europe, and developing a new strategic bomber.

Both Ford and Carter were described as "passionless presidents" who failed to project a clear vision of where they wanted to lead the country. In their defense, however both faced serious problems, ranging from dealing with soaring oil prices to confronting third-world terrorists.

WRENCHING ECONOMIC TRANSFORMATIONS

At one time, the carmakers in Detroit produced automobiles that mirrored America's strength and power. They were big, heavy, powerful cars, with such expensive options as power windows, power brakes, and power steering. So what if they weren't energy efficient. So what if they only traveled 10 to 13 miles on a gallon of gas. Until 1973, gas was cheap; just 37 cents a gallon that year.

By the late 1970s, the rising costs of Middle Eastern oil forced the American automotive industry to rethink its strategy. Emerging Arab nationalism and the solidarity of the Organization of Petroleum Exporting Countries (OPEC) drove the price of a gallon of gasoline up toward the dollar mark. American drivers started purchasing smaller, better engineered, fuel-efficient cars manufactured by Japanese and European automakers. By 1982, Japanese-made cars had captured 30 percent of the U.S. market.

After 1973, the American economy underwent a series of wrenching economic transformations. Economic growth slowed, productivity flagged, inflation rose, and major industries faltered in the face of foreign competition. Despite a massive influx of women into the workforce, family wages stagnated. A quarter century of rapid post–World War II economic growth ended.

The Age of Inflation

In 1967 the average price of a three-bedroom house was $17,000. A brand-new Cadillac convertible went for $6700 and a new Volkswagen for $1497. A Hershey chocolate bar sold for a nickel, a pound of sirloin for 89 cents. Two decades later, the prices of these products had quadrupled.

The upsurge in inflation started when Lyndon Johnson decided to fight the Vietnam War without raising taxes enough to pay for it. By 1968 the war was costing the United States $3 billion dollars a month, and the federal budget skyrocketed to $179 billion. With hundreds of thousands of Americans in the military service and even more working in defense-related industries, unemployment fell, wages rose, demand mushroomed, and government deficits increased. A series of crop failures and sharp rises in price of commodities, especially oil, also fueled inflation.

High inflation had many negative effects on the American economy. It wiped out many families' savings. It encouraged speculation in tangible assets—like art, antiques, precious metals, and real estate—rather than productive investment in new factories and technology. Above all, while certain organized interest groups were able to keep up with inflation, other less powerful groups, such as welfare recipients, saw the value of their benefits decline significantly.

Inflation reduced the purchasing power of most Americans. For over a decade, family wages remained flat. Yet inflation raised the prices of virtually all goods and services. Health care and housing, in particular, experienced price rises far above the inflation rate. The consequences were a sharp increase in the number of Americans unable to afford health insurance and a dramatic increase in homelessness.

Oil Embargo

Political unrest in the oil-rich Middle East contributed significantly to America's economic troubles. After suffering a humiliating defeat at the hands of Israel in the 1973 "Yom Kippur" war, Arab leaders unsheathed a new political weapon: oil. To pressure Israel out of territory conquered in the 1967 and 1973 wars, Arab nations cut oil production 25 percent and

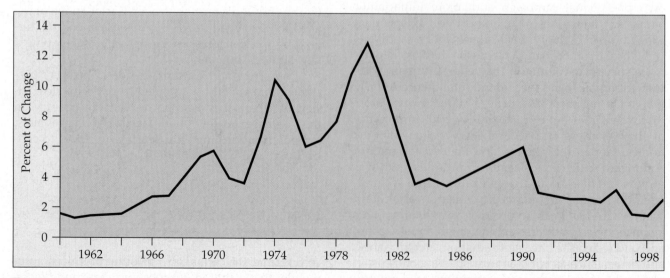

FIGURE 31.1
Consumer Price Index, 1960–1990

The 1973 oil embargo by OPEC resulted in long lines at gas stations, and a form of rationing was imposed under a system in which drivers could buy a limited amount of gasoline only on alternate days, depending on whether their license plates ended in odd or even numbers. Other efforts to conserve energy included a reduction in the national speed limit and an extension of Daylight Savings Time.

embargoed all oil exports to the United States. Leading the way was the Organization of Petroleum Exporting Countries (OPEC), which had been formed by Iran, Saudi Arabia, and Venezuela in 1960 to fight a reduction in prices by oil companies.

Because Arab nations controlled 60 percent of the proven oil reserves in the non-Communist world, they had the western nations over a barrel. Production cutbacks produced an immediate global shortage. The United States imported a third of its oil from Arab nations; western Europe imported 72 percent of its oil from the Middle East; Japan, 82 percent. Gasoline prices rose, long lines formed at gas pumps, some factories shortened the workweek, and some shopping centers restricted business hours.

The **oil crisis** brought to an end an era of cheap and ample energy. Americans had to learn to live with smaller cars and less heating and air-conditioning. The crisis, however, did have a positive side effect: It increased public consciousness about the environment and stimulated awareness of the importance of conservation. But for millions of Americans the lessons were painful.

Foreign Competition and Deindustrialization

In 1947, the United States was truly the world's factory. Half of all the world's manufacturing took place in the United States. Americans made 57 percent of the world's steel and 80 percent of the world's cars. It was inevitable that other countries would eventually challenge the dominance that American manufactur-

ers had enjoyed in the aftermath of World War II. During the early 1960s, foreign manufacturers produced 6 percent of the cars purchased by Americans. That figure climbed to 20 percent in the late 1970s.

Foreign penetration extended far beyond the market for compact cars. Foreign countries began to dominate highly profitable, technologically advanced fields, such as consumer electronics, luxury automobiles, and machine tools. Americans discovered that technologies their country had pioneered—such as semiconductors, color televisions, and videocassette recorders—were now produced almost exclusively by foreign manufacturers. The decline in the American share of the market meant fewer jobs in the American automobile, steel, rubber, and electronics industries. In addition, American and even Japanese companies shifted low-skill production work to such places as Hong Kong, Indonesia, Singapore, South Korea, and Taiwan, where goods could be produced more cheaply because of lower wage scales.

Few economic developments aroused as much public concern during the 1970s as the loss of American jobs in basic industry. According to one estimate, 30 million jobs disappeared during the 1970s as the direct result of factory, store, and office shutdowns. Displaced workers saw their savings depleted, mortgages foreclosed, and health and pension benefits lost. Even when they found new jobs, they typically had to settle for wages substantially below what they had earned before. Plant shutdowns and closings had profound effects on entire communities, which lost their tax bases just when they needed to fund health and welfare services.

Whipping Stagflation

During the 1960s, the primary goal of economic policy was to encourage growth and keep unemployment low. Inflationary pressures were successfully tamed through "jawboning" industry leaders and unions to keep prices and wages stable. By the early 1970s, however, the economy started to suffer from **stagflation**—high unemployment and inflation coupled with stagnant economic growth. This presented economic policymakers with a new and perplexing problem since unemployment and inflation do not usually coexist.

The problem with stagflation was the pain of its options. To attack inflation by reducing consumer purchasing power only made unemployment worse. The other choice was no better. Stimulating purchasing power and creating jobs drove prices higher. Not surprisingly, economic policy during the 1970s was a nightmare of confusion and contradiction.

By 1971 pressures produced by the Vietnam War and federal social spending pushed the inflation rate to 5 percent and unemployment to 6 percent. President Richard Nixon responded by increasing federal budget deficits and devaluing the dollar in an attempt to stimulate the economy and to make American goods more competitive overseas. He also imposed a 90-day wage and price freeze, followed by a mandatory set of wage-price guidelines, and then by voluntary controls. Inflation stayed at about 4 percent during the freeze, but once controls were lifted, inflation resumed its upward climb.

In 1974 during the first oil embargo, inflation hit 12 percent. Gerald Ford, the new president, initially attacked the problem in a traditional Republican fashion, tightening the money supply by raising interest rates and limiting government spending. In the end his economic policy proved to be no more than a series of ineffectual wage and price guidelines monitored by the federal government. In the subsequent recession, unemployment reached 9 percent.

When Jimmy Carter took office in January 1977 7.4 percent of the workforce was unemployed. Carter responded with an ambitious spending program and called for the Federal Reserve Board to expand the money supply. Within two years, inflation had accelerated to 13.3 percent.

With inflation getting out of hand, the Federal Reserve Board announced in 1979 that it would fight inflation by restraining the growth of the money supply. Unemployment increased and interest rates moved to their highest levels in the nation's history. By November 1982, unemployment hit 10.8 percent, the highest since 1940. One out of every five American workers went some time without a job.

Along with high interest rates, the Carter administration adopted another weapon in the battle against stagflation: **deregulation.** Convinced that regulators too often protected the industries they were supposed to oversee, the Carter administration deregulated air and surface transportation and the savings and loan industry.

The effects of deregulation are hotly contested. Rural towns suffered cutbacks of bus, rail, and air service. Truckers and rail workers lost the economic benefits of regulation. Travelers complained about rising airfares and congested airports. Cable TV viewers resented rising rates. Champions of deregulation argued that the policy increased competition, stimulated new investment, and forced inefficient firms either to become more efficient or shut down.

A NEW AMERICAN ROLE IN THE WORLD

In his inaugural address in 1961 John Kennedy stated that America would "pay any price, bear any burden, meet any hardship, support any friend or oppose any foe to assure the survival and the success of liberty." By 1973, however, in the wake of the Vietnam War, American foreign policymakers regarded Kennedy's stirring pledge as unrealistic.

The Vietnam War offered a lesson about the limits of American power. It underscored the need to distinguish between vital national interests and peripheral interests and the need to balance America's military commitments with its available resources. Above all, the Vietnam War appeared to illustrate the dangers of obsessive anti-Communism. Such a policy failed to recognize the fact that the world was becoming more complex, that power blocs were shifting, and that the interests of Communist countries and the United States could sometimes overlap. Too often, American policy seemed to have driven nationalists and reformers into Communist hands and to have led the United States to support corrupt, unpopular authoritarian regimes. The great challenge facing American foreign policymakers was how to preserve the nation's international prestige and influence in the face of declining defense budgets and mounting congressional opposition to direct overseas intervention.

Détente

As president, Richard Nixon radically redefined America's relationship with its two foremost adversaries, China and the Soviet Union. In a remarkable turnabout from his record of staunch anti-Communism, he opened relations with China and began strategic arms limitation talks with the Soviet Union. The goal of **détente** (the easing of tensions between nations) was to continue to resist and deter Soviet adventurism while striving for "more constructive relations" with the Communist world.

Nixon believed that it was necessary to curb the arms race, improve great power relationships, and learn to coexist with Communist regimes. The Nixon administration sought to use the Chinese and Soviet need for western trade and technology as a way to extract foreign policy concessions.

In 1972 Nixon took part in a summit meeting in Beijing, walked the Great Wall, and slowly expanded American trade with China. Less dramatic, but no less important, was the reduction of tensions with the Soviet Union, culminating in a massive trade pact and strategic arms limitation talks. In a 1972 summit meeting in Moscow, the United States and Soviet Union vowed not to seek "unilateral advantages" against each other.

Recognizing that one of the legacies of Vietnam was a reluctance on the part of the American public to risk overseas interventions, Nixon also sought to build up regional powers that shared American strategic interests, most notably China, Iran, and Saudi Arabia.

Jimmy Carter's greatest triumph as president came with the signing of the Camp David Accords between Egypt and Israel.

At the beginning of his historic visit to China in 1972, Nixon shook hands with the Chinese leader Chou En-Lai, and then he inspected the honor guard that greeted him at Beijing Airport.

By the late 1970s, an increasing number of Americans believed that Soviet hard-liners viewed détente as a mere tactic to lull the West into relaxing its vigilance. Soviet Communist party chief Leonid Brezhnev reinforced this view when he boasted of gains that his country had made at the United States' expense—in Vietnam, Angola, Cambodia, Ethiopia, and Laos.

An alarming Soviet arms build-up contributed to the sense that détente was not working. By 1975 the Soviet Union had 50 percent more intercontinental ballistic missiles (ICBMs) than the United States, three times as many army personnel, three times as many attack submarines, and four times as many tanks. The United States continued to have a powerful strategic deterrent, however, holding a 9000 to 3200 advantage in deliverable nuclear bombs and warheads; however, the arms gap between the countries was narrowing.

Foreign Policy Triumphs

In the Middle East Jimmy Carter achieved a tremendous diplomatic success by negotiating peace between Egypt and Israel. Since the founding of Israel in 1948, Egypt's foreign policy had been built around destroying the Jewish state. In 1977, **Anwar el-Sadat,** the practical and farsighted leader of Egypt, decided to seek peace with Israel. It was an act of rare political courage, for Sadat risked alienating Egypt from the rest of the Arab world without a firm commitment for a peace treaty with Israel.

Jimmy Carter convinced Israel to return the Sinai to Egypt. In return, Egypt promised to recognize

Israel, and as a result became a staunch American ally. For Carter it was a proud moment. Unfortunately, the **Camp David Accords** were denounced by the rest of the Arab Middle East, and in 1981 Sadat paid for his vision with his life when anti-Israeli Egyptian soldiers assassinated him.

In 1978 Carter also pushed the **Panama Canal Treaty** through the Senate, which provided for the return of the Canal Zone to Panama and improved the image of the United States in Latin America. One year later, he extended diplomatic recognition to the People's Republic of China. Carter's successes in the international arena, however, would soon be overshadowed by the greatest challenge of his presidency—the Iranian hostage crisis.

No Island of Stability

During Jimmy Carter's presidency, the United States began to show a growing regard for the human rights practices of its allies. Carter was convinced that American foreign policy should embody the country's basic moral beliefs. In 1977 Congress began to require reports on human rights conditions in countries receiving American aid.

Of the nations accused of practicing torture, one of the most frequently cited was Iran. Estimates of the number of political prisoners in Iran ranged from 25,000 to 100,000. It was widely believed that most of them had been tortured by SAVAK, the secret police. Tortures included electric shock, beatings, insertions of bottles in the rectum, hanging weights from the testicles, and rape. Writers, artists, and intellectuals were often targets of torture.

Since the end of World War II, Iran had been a valuable friend of the United States in the troubled Middle East. In 1953 the CIA had worked to ensure the power of the young Shah, **Mohammad Reza Pahlavi.** During the next 25 years, the Shah had often repaid the debt. He allowed the United States to establish electronic listening posts in northern Iran along the border of the Soviet Union, and during the 1973 to 1974 Arab oil embargo the Shah continued to sell oil to the United States. The Shah also bought arms from the United States, which helped ease the American balance-of-payments problem. Few world leaders were more loyal to the United States.

The Shah was popular among wealthy Iranians and Americans. In the slums of the southern section of Teheran and in the poverty-stricken villages of Iran, however, there was little respect, admiration, or love for his regime. Led by a fundamentalist Islamic clergy and emboldened by want, the masses of Iranians turned against the Shah and his westernization policy.

In the early fall of 1978 the revolutionary surge in Iran gained force. The Shah, who had once seemed

so powerful and secure, was paralyzed by indecision, alternating between ruthless suppression and attempts to liberalize his regime. In Washington, Carter also vacillated, uncertain whether to stand firmly behind the Shah or to cut losses and prepare to deal with a new government in Iran.

In January 1979, the Shah fled to Egypt. Exiled religious leader **Ayatollah Ruhollah Khomeini** returned to Iran, preaching the doctrine that the United States was the "Great Satan" behind the Shah. Relations between the United States and the new Iranian government were terrible, but Iranian officials warned that they would become infinitely worse if the Shah were granted asylum. Nevertheless, Carter permitted the Shah to come to the United States for treatment of lymphoma. The reaction in Iran was severe.

On November 4, 1979, Iranian supporters of Khomeini invaded the American embassy in Teheran and captured 66 Americans, 13 of whom were freed several weeks later and one was released in July 1980. The rest were held hostage for 444 days and were the objects of intense political interest and media coverage.

Carter was helpless. Because Iran was not a stable country in any recognizable sense, pressure was not possible. Iran's demands—the return of the Shah to Iran and admission of U.S. guilt in supporting the Shah—were unacceptable. Carter devoted far too much attention to the almost insoluble problem. The hostages stayed in the public spotlight in part because Carter kept them there.

Carter's foreign policy problems mounted in December 1979 when the Soviet Union sent tanks into Afghanistan. In response, the Carter administration imposed an embargo on grain and high-technology exports to the USSR and boycotted the 1980 Olympics

After 444 days the Iranian hostage crisis ended, but not before it had virtually paralyzed Carter's administration and destroyed his chances for reelection.

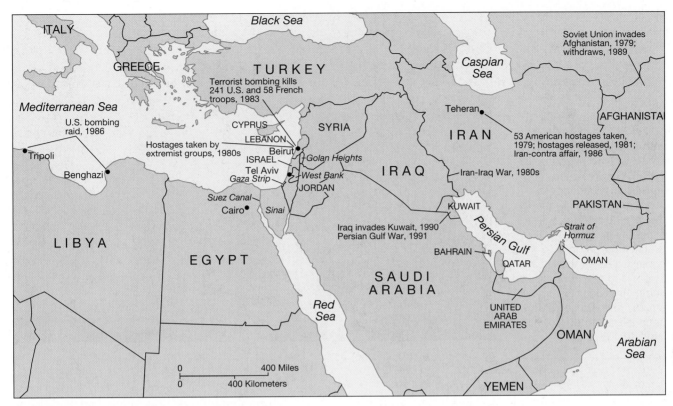

Conflict in the Middle East and Europe

in Moscow. The Soviet Union gradually withdrew its troops from Afghanistan a decade later.

As public disapproval of the president's handling of the Iran crisis increased, some Carter advisors advocated the use of force to free the hostages in Teheran. At first, Carter disagreed, but eventually he authorized a rescue attempt. It failed and his position became even worse. Negotiations finally brought the hostages' release, but in a final humiliation for Carter, the hostages were held until minutes after Ronald Reagan, Carter's successor, had taken the oath of office as president.

When Carter left office in January 1981 many Americans judged his presidency a failure. Instead of being remembered for the good he accomplished for the Middle East at Camp David, he was remembered for what he failed to accomplish. **The Iranian hostage crisis** had become emblematic of a perception that America's role in the world had declined.

THE REAGAN REVOLUTION

The traumatic events of the 1970s—Watergate, stagflation, the energy crisis, the defeat of South Vietnam, and the Iranian hostage crisis—produced a severe loss of confidence among the American people. Americans were deeply troubled by the relative de-

cline of American strength in the world; the decline of the productivity and innovation in American industry; and the dramatic growth of lobbies and special-interest groups that seemed to have paralyzed the legislative process. Many worried that too much power had been stripped from the presidency and that political parties were so weakened and Congress so splintered that it was impossible to enact a coherent legislative program.

Republican **Ronald Reagan** capitalized on this frustration. In 1980 he won a landslide victory, carrying 43 states. A former movie actor and radio and television announcer, Reagan was catapulted into the national spotlight in 1964 when he gave an emotional television speech in support of Republican presidential nominee Barry Goldwater, denouncing big government, foreign aid, welfare, urban renewal, and high taxes. Two years later, Reagan successfully ran for governor of California, promising to cut state spending and crack down on student protesters.

In the 1980 presidential campaign, Reagan drew strong support from white Southerners, suburban Roman Catholics, evangelical Christians, and particularly the New Right, a confederation of disparate political and religious groups bound together by their concern over what they considered the erosion of values in America. In March 1981 when an assassin's bullet nearly killed Reagan, he captured the nation's

Ronald Reagan was an occasional churchgoer who won strong support among conservative Christians. In 1982 Reagan signed legislation mandating a permanent annual national day of prayer on the first Thursday in May. The practice dated back to the earliest days of the United States and was formalized under President Eisenhower, but the specific day had been left up to the individual president.

imagination by responding to the shooting with remarkable courage. From his hospital bed, he sent a message to his wife Nancy, "Honey, I forgot to duck."

Reaganomics

When President Reagan took office he promised to rebuild the nation's defenses, cut inflation, restore economic growth, and trim the size of the federal government. He pledged to end exorbitant union contracts to make American goods competitive again, to cut taxes drastically to stimulate investment and purchasing power, and to decontrol business strangled by federal regulation to restore competition.

To strengthen the nation's defenses, the Reagan administration doubled the defense budget to more than $330 billion in 1987. Reagan believed that a militarily strong United States would not have been humiliated by Iran and would have discouraged Soviet adventurism.

Reagan blamed the country's economic ills on declining capital investment and a tax structure biased against work and productive investment. To stimulate the economy, he persuaded Congress to slash tax rates. In August 1981, Reagan dealt a devastating blow to organized labor by dismissing 15,000 striking air traffic controllers.

Reagan expanded the Carter administration's efforts to decontrol and deregulate the economy. Congress deregulated the banking and natural gas industries and lifted ceilings on interest rates. Federal price controls on airfares were lifted as well.

The Environmental Protection Agency relaxed its interpretation of the Clean Air Act, and the Department of the Interior opened up large areas of the federal domain, including offshore oil fields, to private development.

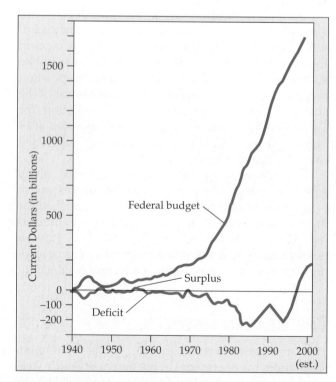

FIGURE 31.2
Budget Deficits, 1940–2000

Reagan left office with the economy in the midst of its longest post–World War II expansion. The economy was growing faster, with less inflation, than at any time since the mid-1960s. Adjusted for inflation, disposable personal income per person rose 20 percent after 1980. Inflation fell to less than 4 percent. Unemployment was down to around 5 percent. These figures compared favorably to January 1981, the month Reagan became president, when inflation was running at 13 percent a year and unemployment stood at 7.4 percent.

Reagan's critics, however, charged that Reagan had created only the illusion of prosperity. They denounced the massive federal debt, which increased $1.5 trillion during the Reagan presidency, three times the debt accumulated by all 39 of Reagan's presidential predecessors. They decried the growing income gap between rich and poor, as well as the expensive consequences of reduced government regulation, such as cleaning up federal nuclear weapons facilities, and, especially, bailing out the nation's savings and loans industry.

The Reagan Doctrine

During the early years of the Reagan presidency, Cold War tensions between the Soviet Union and the United States intensified. Reagan entered office deeply suspi-cious of the Soviet Union, describing it as "an evil empire." He called for a space-based missile defense system, derided by critics who labeled it "Star Wars."

In his 1985 state of the union address, President Reagan pledged his support for anti-Communist revolutions in what would become known as the **"Reagan Doctrine."** In Afghanistan, the United States was already providing aid to anti-Soviet freedom fighters, ultimately forcing Soviet troops to withdraw. In Nicaragua, however, the Reagan doctrine received its most controversial application.

In 1979 Nicaraguans revolted against a corrupt Somoza regime, and a new junta took power, dominated by young Marxists known as Sandinistas. The Sandinistas insisted that they favored free elections, nonalignment, and a mixed economy, but once in power they postponed elections, forced opposition leaders into exile, and turned to the Soviet bloc for arms and advisers.

In his first months in office, President Reagan approved covert training of anti-Sandinista rebels (called "contras"). While the contras waged war on the Sandinistas from camps in Honduras, the CIA provided assistance, mining Nicaraguan harbors and issuing a manual describing ways to assassinate Sandinistas. In 1984 Congress ordered an end to all covert aid to the contras. The Reagan administration circumvented Congress by soliciting contributions for the contras

U.S. Involvement in Central America and the Caribbean

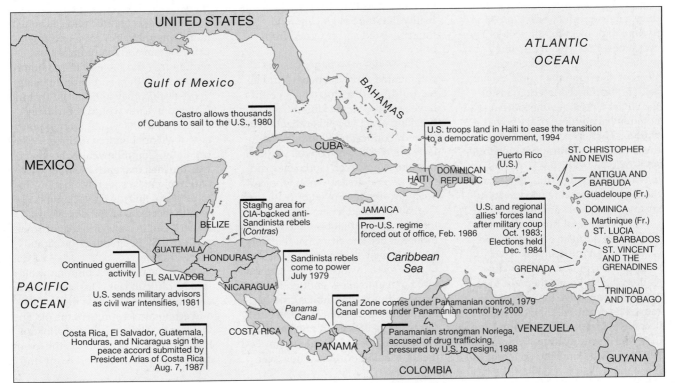

The End of Two Eras

The dates on the obituary read 1922 to 1991. When the death was duly recorded in newspapers and magazines throughout the world, only a handful of bureaucrats mourned the corpse. That body—the Union of Soviet Socialist Republics (USSR)—was the light that failed. Born in the cold and ice of a late Russian December, the USSR promised equality and justice. Driven by the belief in communism, Vladimir Lenin, the leader of the Bolsheviks who came to power in Russia in 1917 and founded the USSR five years later, announced that Russia was only the first step. Eventually, he said, communism would free the entire world and introduce a new epoch of peace, prosperity, and happiness for all people. The epoch never arrived. It remained only in the minds of the true believers. Instead of liberating the world, Soviet leaders suppressed freedom inside the Soviet Union. As one journalist noted in his obituary of the Soviet Union, "There is no reason to mourn the death of a country that killed millions of its own citizens in the collectivization campaign, the purges and the famines that were used as an instrument of government policy."

Born in a brutal Russian winter, the USSR died in an equally severe winter. About the death there was a singular note of irony. The Soviet leader who had done the most to reform and humanize the country caused its death. Mikhail Gorbachev became the leader of the Soviet Union in 1985. He was relatively young—in 1980 he had become the youngest full member of the Politburo, the ruling body in the USSR—and very well educated. He knew that every year his country was falling further and further behind the West in every material sense. Determined to correct the slide, he introduced measures to restructure the Soviet economy (*perestroika*) and to create a new political openness (*glasnost*). His economic measures never worked, but his political initiatives worked all too well.

First, Eastern Europe used the new openness to break away from the Soviet orbit. Then, the USSR's Baltic republics of Lithuania, Latvia, and Estonia demanded and received independence. Finally, the remaining 12 republics of the Soviet Union decided that the union was unworkable and undesirable. Gorbachev attempted to hold the republics together but failed. On Christmas Day, 1991, he faced the reality that the Soviet Union no longer existed and resigned from office.

The Soviet newspaper *Izvestia* commented that Gorbachev "did all he could." Perhaps no leader could have kept the Soviet Union from breaking apart once liberalization had started. Political freedom was singularly out of step with Soviet political traditions; however, Gorbachev did fail in several areas. A man who had risen through the Soviet bureaucracy, Gorbachev failed to significantly reform or abolish that bureaucracy even though it became clear that that very bureaucracy was the primary obstacle to *perestroika*. In addition, he never devised a plan to allow enough freedom in the individual republics, and he even tacitly permitted Soviet security forces to use tanks and guns to suppress the Baltic independence movements. Most importantly, however, Gorbachev's *perestroika* did not work because it did not bring a new era of prosperity to the Soviet Union. Gorbachev admitted that "the old system fell apart even before the new system began to work," but as one authority commented, "there was no new system." Like every Soviet leader since Lenin, Gorbachev had promised far more than he delivered.

The death of the Soviet Union posed immense problems both for the newly independent republics and the United States. Even before Gorbachev's resignation, 11 of the 12 remaining republics—only the republic of Georgia was excluded—joined together into a new confederation called the Commonwealth of Independent States. Led by the republics of Russia, Byelorussia, and Ukraine, the new entity was more an alliance than a state. The republics agreed to cooperate in economic reforms aimed at moving them toward a free enterprise system and maintain at least temporarily the ruble as the common currency. Further, and without being very specific, they announced that the Commonwealth would coordinate economic, military, and foreign policies of its independent members. Central to the Commonwealth, however, was the idea that each member was and remained a sovereign nation. To underscore this idea, the Commonwealth located its capital in Minsk rather than Moscow, the seat of Soviet power, or St. Petersburg, the capital of czarist Russia.

From the first, the Commonwealth faced a difficult task. Disputes quickly arose over how to divide the military and economic resources of the old Soviet Union. The sovereign republics had to decide how to divide the forces and equipment of the Red Army and

the Soviet Navy as well as the Soviet state treasury, central television network, space infrastructure, and the hundreds of other assets once controlled by the Soviet Union. As a symbol of the great change, in February 1992 the Commonwealth Olympic team competed in the Albertville Winter Games under the Olympic flag and their victories were marked by the playing of the Olympic anthem.

Even more pressing than the decision on how to divide Soviet property was the conversion to a limited free-market system. In early 1992 the Commonwealth lifted most price controls and the cost of goods shot upward. The prices of such basic commodities as bread and gasoline, over which some controls still existed, tripled or quadrupled literally overnight. The prices of noncontrolled items increased much more. A kilo of kielbasa sausages was 2.20 rubles in January 1991; the price rose to 43.75 rubles (and as high as 200 rubles in particularly hard-pressed St. Petersburg) in January 1992. The ruble itself experienced the shock. The official exchange used to be 1.8 per

dollar; in January 1992 the exchange rate rose to well over 100 rubles per dollar. The economic changes created severe hardships for people whose monthly income averaged 400 rubles. Many citizens of the Commonwealth considered the winter of 1992 as the worst in their lives.

The death of the Soviet Union also had a profound effect on the United States. On one level the United States had to redirect its foreign policy. The era of the Cold War was over. The Soviet Union, America's Cold War rival, no longer existed. President George Bush responded to the changes by announcing victory in the Cold War, recognizing the new independent republics, and sending aid to the beleaguered members of the Commonwealth. Although Americans continued to worry about who controlled the Commonwealth's nuclear weapons, there was no longer the fear of war between the Soviet Union and the United States.

On another level, the end of the Cold War undermined one of the organizing principles of American culture. American mass culture in partic-

ular revolved around the idea of "us" and "them." Throughout the Cold War era Hollywood made successful movies that played on this theme. From such movies as *I Was a Communist for the FBI, My Son John, Dr. Strangelove, Fail Safe, Red Alert,* and *On the Beach* to the James Bond action pictures and John Wayne westerns, Cold War issues provided the explicit or implicit basis for the films. Not to be outdone, popular writers capitalized on Cold War themes. John Le Carré, William F. Buckley, Jr., and Tom Clancy wrote best-sellers that centered on Cold War plots. Television also pitted "us" against "them" on numerous programs. During the 1960s *The Man from U.N.C.L.E., Mission Impossible,* and *I Spy* were popular programs that featured Cold War storylines. Even sports were influenced by the Cold War. In particular, the Olympic Games reflected Cold War tension and anxieties. American cheers of "USA, USA" at Olympic events became ritualistic Cold War chants.

American education and science similarly were partial hostages to the Cold War. After the success of the Soviet *Sputnik* in 1957, Congress appropriated funds for the establishment of the National Aeronautics and Space Administration (NASA) and passed the National Defense Education Act. In the Cold War the space race and education became highly political issues. President John F. Kennedy's decision to push America's space program toward putting a person on the moon—a decision that many of America's leading scientists opposed—was more a response to the Cold War than the needs of science. Neil Armstrong's July 21, 1969, moon walk was confirmation of America's victory in the space race.

The death of the Soviet Union, then, ended two eras. How citizens of both the United States and the Commonwealth of Independent States will respond to that death will be one of the most important issues in the twenty-first century.

from private individuals and from foreign governments seeking U.S. favor. The president also permitted the sale of arms to Iran, with profits diverted to the contras. Exposure of the **Iran-Contra Affair** in late 1986 provoked a major congressional investigation. The scandal seriously weakened the influence of the president. In national elections in 1990, the Nicaraguan opposition routed the Sandinistas, bringing an end to 10 turbulent years of Sandinista rule.

A Remarkable Ideological Turnaround

In 1985, **Mikhail Gorbachev,** a 54-year-old agricultural specialist with little formal experience in foreign affairs, became leader of the Soviet Union. Within weeks, Gorbachev called for sweeping political liberalization—*glasnost*—and economic reform—*perestroika.* He allowed wider freedom of the press, assembly, travel, and religion. He persuaded the Communist party leadership to end its monopoly on power, created the Soviet Union's first working legislature, allowed the first nationwide competitive elections in 1989, and freed hundreds of political prisoners. In an effort to boost the sagging Soviet economy, he legalized small private business cooperatives, won parliamentary approval for the leasing of lands to individuals with the right of inheritance, and approved foreign investment within the Soviet Union.

In foreign affairs Gorbachev completely reshaped world politics. He cut the Soviet defense budget, withdrew Soviet troops from Afghanistan and eastern Europe, allowed a unified Germany to become a member of NATO, and agreed with the United States to destroy short-range and medium-range nuclear weapons. Most dramatically, Gorbachev actively promoted the democratization of former Soviet satellite nations in Eastern Europe. For his accomplishments in defusing Cold War tensions, he was awarded the 1990 Nobel Peace Prize.

The Reagan Revolution in Perspective

In the presidential election of 1984, Ronald Reagan and Vice President George Bush won in a landslide over Walter Mondale and Geraldine Ferraro, the first woman nominated for vice president on a major party ticket. Although Reagan's second term was plagued by the Iran-contra scandal, he left office after eight years more popular than he arrived. He could claim the distinction of being the first president to serve two full terms since Dwight Eisenhower.

Ronald Reagan could also point to an extraordinary string of accomplishments. He had dampened inflation, restored public confidence in government, and presided over the beginning of the end of the Cold War. He doubled the defense budget; named the first woman, Sandra Day O'Connor, to the Supreme Court; launched a strong economic boom; and created a heightened sense of national unity. He restored vigor to the national economy and psyche, rebuilt America's military might, regained the nation's place as the world's preeminent power, restored American patriotism, and championed traditional family values.

On the other hand, his detractors criticized him for a reckless use of military power and for circumventing Congress in foreign affairs. They accused Reagan of fostering greed and intolerance, and charged that his administration, in its zeal to cut waste from government, ripped the social safety net and skimped on the government's regulatory functions. The administration, they further charged, was insensitive on racial issues.

Reagan's detractors were particularly concerned about his economic legacy. During the Reagan years the national debt tripled, from $909 billion to almost $2.9 trillion (the interest alone amounted to 14 percent of the federal budget), soaking up savings, causing interest rates to rise, depressing local economies, and forcing the federal government to shift more and more responsibilities onto the states. Corporate and individual debt also soared. During the early 1990s, the American people consumed $1 trillion more goods and services than they produced. The combined effects of a weak dollar, a low level of exports, and the need to borrow abroad to finance budget deficits made the United States the world's biggest debtor nation.

Collapse of Communism

For 40 years Communist party leaders in Eastern Europe had ruled confidently. Although each year their countries fell further behind the West, they remained secure in the knowledge that the Soviet Union, backed by the Red Army, would always send in the tanks when the forces for change became too great. But they had not bargained on a liberal Soviet leader like Mikhail Gorbachev.

As Gorbachev moved toward reform within the Soviet Union and détente with the West, he pushed the conservative regimes of Eastern Europe outside his protective umbrella. By the end of 1989 the Berlin Wall had been smashed and across Eastern Europe citizens took to the streets, overthrowing 40 years of Communist rule. Like a series of falling dominos, Communist regimes in Poland, East Germany, Hungary, Czechoslovakia, and Bulgaria fell from power.

Gorbachev, who had wanted to reform communism, had not anticipated the swift swing toward democracy in Eastern Europe. Nor had he fully fore-

For nearly three decades the Berlin Wall was the most visible symbol of the Cold War and of the division between East and West. The most dramatic incident marking the end of the Cold War was the destruction of the Wall in November 1989.

seen the impact that democracy in Eastern Europe would have on the Soviet Union. By 1990 leaders of several Soviet republics began to demand independence or greater autonomy within the Soviet Union.

In 1990, following the example of Eastern Europe, the three Baltic states of Lithuania, Latvia, and Estonia announced their independence, and other Soviet republics demanded greater sovereignty. Nine of the 15 Soviet Republics agreed to sign a new union treaty, granting far greater freedom and autonomy to individual republics. In August 1991, however, before the treaty could be signed, conservative communists tried to oust Gorbachev in a coup d'état. **Boris Yeltsin,** president of the Republic of Russia, and his supporters defeated the coup, which undermined support for the Communist party. Despite the failure of the coup, Gorbachev fell from power. The Soviet Union ended its existence in December 1991 when Russia and most other republics formed the Commonwealth of Independent States.

In 1993 a new power struggle broke out, pitting Yeltsin against communists and nationalists in the Russian Parliament. In August, Yeltsin dissolved the Parliament, charging an "irreconcilable opposition"

with blocking his reforms. Yeltsin ordered opposition legislators, holed up in the Parliament building, to evacuate. Fierce street battles erupted between troops loyal to Yeltsin and thousands of armed communists and nationalists before the army crushed the uprising, attacked the building, and forced Yeltsin's opponents to surrender.

The struggles between reformers, nationalists, and communists persisted. The former Soviet Union remained beset by deep economic problems and severe ethnic and regional conflicts that showed little sign of abating.

CONCLUSION

In the late 1970s many academic authorities suggested that the United States was in decline, that such societies as Japan and West Germany were growing faster and were beginning to dominate cutting-edge industries such as consumer electronics and luxury automobiles. Many Americans were cynical about their government, anxious about the future of their economy, and uneasy about America's proper role in the world.

As the twenty-first century began, however, the United States had reasserted its economic, military, and cultural preeminence. It became the world's sole superpower. It dominated not only the Internet and computer software and hardware but also film and television production. Still, the United States was also faced by new threats, especially from terrorist organizations.

CHAPTER SUMMARY AND KEY TERMS

Three fundamental challenges that arose during the 1970s and 1980s shaped the politics of the last quarter of the twentieth century. These were a crisis of political leadership, wrenching economic transformations, and growing uncertainty over the proper role of the United States in world affairs.

- As a result of the Vietnam War and the Watergate scandal, public cynicism toward politicians intensified and political party discipline declined. Meanwhile, lobbies and special interests grew more powerful.

- Economic growth slowed, productivity flagged, and inflation soared. Family income stagnated and major industries faltered in the face of foreign competition.

- Policymakers debated how to preserve the nation's international prestige and influence in the face of mounting public opposition to direct overseas interventions.

CHRONOLOGY OF KEY EVENTS

1971 A secret tape-recording system is installed in the White House; Nixon authorizes establishment of a "plumbers" unit to "stop security leaks and investigate other sensitive matters"

1972 Five burglars arrested breaking into Democratic national headquarters at Washington's Watergate office complex; President Nixon takes part in summit in China; President Nixon is reelected with 61 percent of the vote

1973 Televised Senate hearings on Watergate begin; Spiro Agnew pleads no contest to a charge of income tax evasion and resigns as vice president

1974 Federal grand jury indicts Nixon aides for perjury and obstruction of justice and names the president as an unindicted co-conspirator; House Judiciary Committee adopts three articles of impeachment against President Nixon; Nixon becomes the first president to resign from office; Ford becomes thirty-eighth president; Federal Campaign Reform Act sets limits on private campaign contributions and provides tax funds to presidential candidates

1976 Jimmy Carter is elected thirty-ninth president

1978 President Carter mediates Egyptian-Israeli peace settlement; Iranian revolution begins

1979 United States formally recognizes China; Iranian militants seize American hostages; Soviet Union invades Afghanistan; Somoza regime in Nicaragua is overthrown, Sandinistas take power

1980 Ronald Reagan is elected fortieth president

1981 American hostages are released from Iran; Reagan is shot in assassination attempt; Reagan approves covert training of anti-Sandinista contras; Reagan tax cuts are approved

1982 Congress deregulates banking industry and lifts controls on airfares

1983 Reagan proposes "Star Wars" missile defense system; United States topples Communist government on the Caribbean island of Grenada

1984 Congress orders an end to all covert aid to Nicaraguan contras

1985 United States begins secret arms-for-hostages negotiations with Iran; Mikhail Gorbachev becomes leader of the Soviet Union

1986 Profits from Iranian arms sales are diverted to Nicaraguan contras

1987 Iran-Contra hearings; stock market plunges 508 points in a single session

1988 George Bush is elected forty-first president

1989 Opposition defeats Sandinistas in Nicaraguan elections; Communist regimes collapse in Eastern Europe

---

- Presidents Nixon, Ford, and Carter sought to address America's changing role in the world through détente and arms control negotiations. President Ronald Reagan's strategy emphasized increased military spending and a more assertive foreign policy. On the domestic front, he addressed stagflation through deregulation, tax cuts, and cutbacks in government spending on social programs.

- The collapse of communism in Eastern Europe and the breakup of the Soviet Union brought the Cold War to an end and made the United States the world's sole superpower.

SUGGESTIONS FOR FURTHER READING

William C. Berman, *America's Right Turn: From Nixon to Bush* (1998). An incisive interpretation of recent American political history that examines the way that the American political system responded to the Vietnam War, the inflation of the 1970s, the rights revolution, and the globalization of the economy.

William H. Chafe, *The Unfinished Journey: America Since World War II*, 4th ed. (1998). A concise synthesis of recent scholarship that examines politics, civil rights, foreign policy, and issues of gender.

Paul Gottfried, *The Conservative Movement*, rev. ed. (1993). A history of conservatism in politics, publishing, and the academy that carefully distinguishes among the Old Right, the Neo-Conservatives, and the New Right.

Stanley I. Kutler, *The Wars of Watergate: The Last Crisis of Richard Nixon* (1990). The definitive history of the Watergate Affair.

Michael Schudson, *Watergate in American Memory* (1992). Dissects the changing ways that Americans have remembered the Watergate Affair .

Bruce J. Schulman, *The Seventies: The Great Shift in American Culture, Society, and Politics* (2002). Rebutting the claim that the 1970s was a decade when nothing happened, this book argues that it was a period of political, cultural, social, and religious upheavals that transformed American life.

Novels

Le Ly Hayslip, *When Heaven and Earth Changed Places* (1989).

Alice Walker, *The Color Purple* (1982).

Tom Wolfe, *The Bonfire of the Vanities* (1987).

MEDIA RESOURCES
Web Sites

The Watergate Tapes Online
http://www.hpol.org/master
.asp?t=browse&s=speaker&id=19
Transcripts and sound files of the White House tapes.

Revisiting Watergate
http://www.washingtonpost.com/wp-srv/onpolitics/
watergate/splash.html
Newspaper coverage, editorial cartoons, and documents from the *Washington Post*.

American Presidents: Life Portraits
http://www.americanpresidents.org/
The companion site to the C-SPAN series includes profiles of Presidents Nixon, Ford, Carter, and Reagan.

Constitutional Issues: Watergate and the Constitution
http://www.archives.gov/digital_classroom/lessons/
watergate_and_constitution/watergate_and_constitution
.html
This National Archives site provides an overview of the legal and constitutional issues raised by the Watergate Affair.

Films and Videos

All the President's Men (1976). Dramatization of *Washington Post* reporters Carl Bernstein and Bob Woodward, whose investigation into the Watergate Affair helped to bring about the resignation of President Richard Nixon.

Coming Home (1977). Examines the impact of the Vietnam war on the men who fought it and the women in their lives.

Kramer v. Kramer (1979). A dramatization of the problems of divorce and shifting gender roles.

Network (1976). A critique of network television and its quest for higher ratings.

The Godfather (1972). This multigenerational study of an organized crime family questions the American cult of success and upward mobility.

Wall Street (1987). Director Oliver Stone's critique of business culture during the Reagan era is best remembered for the ironic line: "Greed is good."

KEY TERMS

Watergate break-in   (p. 873)

War Powers Act   (p. 876)

Freedom of Information Act   (p. 877)

Oil crisis   (p. 879)

Stagflation   (p. 880)

Deregulation   (p. 880)

Détente   (p. 881)

Camp David Accords   (p. 882)

Panama Canal Treaty   (p. 882)

Iranian Hostage Crisis   (p. 883)

"Reagan Doctrine"   (p. 885)

Iran-Contra Affair   (p. 888)

PEOPLE YOU SHOULD KNOW

Richard Nixon   (p. 873)

John Dean   (p. 874)

Spiro Agnew   (p. 874)

Gerald Ford   (p. 876)

Jimmy Carter   (p. 877)

Anwar el-Sadat   (p. 881)

Mohammad Reza Pahlavi   (p. 882)

Ayatollah Ruhollah Khomeini   (p. 882)

Ronald Reagan   (p. 883)

Mikhail Gorbachev   (p. 888)

Boris Yeltsin   (p. 889)

REVIEW QUESTIONS

1. What was the "imperial presidency"? How did it come to an end?

2. What problems did the American economy face in the 1970s? How did the federal government respond?

3. How did the "Reagan revolution" signal a change in domestic policies? In international relations? In American culture?

4. Was the Bush presidency an active and successful force in international affairs? In domestic affairs?

32 America in Our Time

THE TERRORIST ATTACKS OF SEPTEMBER 11, 2001

At 9:08 A.M., Tuesday, September 11, 2001, two fire trucks carrying 13 fire fighters rushed to New York's World Trade Center after the first of two hijacked planes struck the buildings. Twelve never returned. They were among 343 fire fighters who died in the collapse of the World Trade Center towers.

While employees struggled to exit the World Trade Center, fire fighters rushed in, to try to rescue those who were injured or trapped. Engine 40 and Hook and Ladder 35 were based on Manhattan's Upper West Side, six miles north of Ground Zero, the site of the terrorist attacks. Video footage would show these brave men entering the World Trade Center's South Tower just before it collapsed at 9:50 A.M.

The lone survivor, Kevin Shea, the son and the brother of fire fighters, had joined this fire company just two months before the attacks. His shift over, he was getting into his car when the first bulletins arrived that an airliner had struck the World Trade Center's North Tower. Rescue workers had to dig him out from under mounds of debris. He had suffered a broken neck, a severe concussion, amnesia, severed fingers, and other serious injuries.

On September 11 hijackers turned commercial airlines into missiles and attacked key symbols of American economic and military might. These attacks leveled the World Trade Center towers in New York, destroyed part of the Pentagon in Washington, D.C., and left Americans in a mood similar to that which the country experienced after the devastating Japanese attack on the American fleet at Pearl Harbor in 1941. A fourth hijacked plane, apparently destined to destroy another target in the nation's capital—possibly the White House or the Capitol building—crashed in Pennsylvania when passengers aboard the plane wrested control of the aircraft from the hijackers but could not prevent the plane from crashing.

The succession of horrors began at 8:45 A.M., when American Airlines Flight 11, carrying 92 people from Boston to Los Angeles, crashed into the World Trade Center's north tower. Eighteen minutes later, United Airlines Flight 175, carrying 65 people, also bound for Los Angeles from Boston, struck the World Trade Center's south tower. At 9:40 A.M., American Airlines Flight 77, flying from Washington,

Fire fighters wade through the debris of the collapsed World Trade Center towers.

D.C., to Los Angeles and carrying 64 people aboard, crashed into the Pentagon. At 10 A.M., United Airlines Flight 93, flying from Newark, N.J., to San Francisco, crashed 80 miles southeast of Pittsburgh. Passengers on board the airliner, having heard about the attacks on New York and Washington, D.C., apparently stormed the airplane's cockpit and prevented the hijackers from reaching their target.

As millions of television viewers watched in utter horror, at 9:50 A.M., the World Trade Center's south tower collapsed. At 10:29 A.M., the World Trade Center's north tower fell.

More than three thousand innocent civilians and rescue workers perished as a result of these acts of terror. This was about the same number of Americans who died on June 6, 1944, during the D-Day invasion of Nazi-occupied France, and nearly as many as the 3620 Americans who died at the Civil War battle of Antietam on September 17, 1862, the largest number of Americans to die in combat on a single day. More Americans died in two hours on Septem-

ber 11th than died in the War of 1812, the Spanish American War, or the Gulf War.

Authorities quickly discovered that a Middle Eastern terrorist network known as **al-Qaeda,** led by a Saudi Arabian dissident named Osama bin-Laden, had masterminded the attacks. Al-Qaeda had been responsible for earlier attacks against American interests, including a truck bombing at the World Trade Center in 1993, which left six dead, and truck bombings at U.S. embassies in Africa in 1998, which had killed 224 civilians. Based in Afghanistan, Al-Qaeda attributed its hatred of the United States to the presence of American troops in Saudi Arabia, the U.S. embargo against the government of Saddam Hussein in Iraq, and U.S. support for Israel.

The September 11 attacks were followed by apparently unrelated acts of bioterrorism. Letters containing billions of deadly anthrax spores, which could be fatal if touched or inhaled, contaminated post offices and Congressional office buildings and left five people dead. The result was to intensify Americans' sense of vulnerability.

In the aftermath of the September 11 attacks, many Americans asked why the terrorist network Al-Qaeda would target innocent American civilians. The underlying explanation lies in the organization's hatred of American values and culture and the military and economic power of the United States.

As the twenty-first century began, the United States had achieved a degree of economic, cultural, and military preeminence unmatched since the period immediately following World War II. The United States was the world's lone superpower, its spending on the military greater than that of the next 10 largest countries combined. Its economy, by far the world's most productive, dominated the fields of entertainment, finance, and high technology. Its movies, music, and television programs spread American culture around the globe. For millions of people the world over, the United States symbolized freedom, opportunity, and prosperity. Among some people, however, it provoked hatred, envy, and resentment.

THE GLOBALIZATION OF THE AMERICAN ECONOMY

"His Airness" is the world's most idolized athlete. The former Chicago Bulls basketball star has been the subject of at least eight videos and DVDs and 48 books. But unlike Joe Louis, Jackie Robinson, or Muhammad Ali, **Michael Jordan** has remained almost totally apolitical. He is known as a superstar

THE PEOPLE SPEAK

International Reaction to the September 11, 2001, Attacks on New York City and the Pentagon in Washington

Citizens from across the United States and the world reacted to the September 11 attacks with prayer sessions and rallies. Nearly 500 foreigners from 91 countries died in the attacks, including dozens of Bangladeshis, Britons, Chinese, Filipinos, Germans, Irish, Israelis, Italians, Japanese, Mexicans, South Koreans, Taiwanese, Thais, and Zimbabweans. Britain suffered the most deaths with 67. World leaders reacted with revulsion to the terrorist attacks.

President George W. Bush

September 11, 2001

Today, our fellow citizens, our way of life, our very freedom came under attack in a series of deliberate and deadly terrorist acts. The victims were in airplanes or in their offices: secretaries, business men and women, military and federal workers, moms and dads, friends and neighbors. Thousands of lives were suddenly ended by evil, despicable acts of terror.

The pictures of airplanes flying into buildings, fires burning, huge structures collapsing have filled us with disbelief, terrible sadness and a quiet, unyielding anger. These acts of mass murder were intended to frighten our nation into chaos and retreat. But they have failed. . . .

Terrorist attacks can shake the foundations of our biggest buildings, but they cannot touch the foundation of America. These acts shatter steel, but they cannot dent the steel of American resolve. . . . Today, our nation saw evil, the very worst of human nature, and we responded with the best of America, with the daring of our rescue workers, with the caring for strangers and neighbors who came to give blood and help in any way they could.

British Prime Minister Tony Blair

September 11, 2001

This mass terrorism is the new evil in our world. The people who perpetrate it have no regard whatever for the sanctity or value of human life, and we the democracies of the world, must come together to defeat it and eradicate it. This is not a battle between the United States of America and terrorism, but between the free and democratic world and terrorism. We, therefore, here in Britain stand shoulder to shoulder with our American friends in this hour of tragedy, and we, like them, will not rest until this evil is driven from our world.

French President Jacques Chirac

September 11, 2001

The attacks that struck the United States today are a terrible tragedy. Never has any country in the world been the target of terrorist attacks of such scope or of such violence. I want to convey to the American people once again the solidarity of the entire French people during this tragic ordeal.

Russian President Vladimir Putin

September 12, 2001

The event that occurred in the U.S. today goes beyond national borders. It is a brazen challenge to the whole humanity, at least to civilized humanity. And what happened today is added proof of the relevance of the Russian proposal to pool the efforts of the international community in the struggle against terrorism, that plague of the 21st century.

Russia knows at first hand what terrorism is. So, we understand as well as anyone the feelings of the American people. Addressing the people of the United States on behalf of Russia I would like to say that we are with you, we entirely and fully share and experience your pain. We support you.

Saudia Arabian Ambassador to the United States, Prince Bandar bin Sultan bin Abdulaziz

September 13, 2001

Whoever committed these criminal acts, which violate all divine religions and all religious, moral and human values, is not Muslim. . . . Islam specifically refutes terrorists and terrorism. . . . If it turns out, beyond reasonable doubt, that those who carried out these acts were people who claim to belong to Islam, they are Muslim in name only. . . . The Saudis, like all Arabs and Muslims, are standing firm behind efforts to unveil the identity of those who committed these acts.

Yasir Arafat, Chairman of the Palestine Liberation Organization (PLO)

September 11, 2001

We are completely shocked. It's unbelievable. We completely condemn this very dangerous attack, and I convey my condolences to the American people, to the American President, and to the American administration, not only in my name but on behalf of the Palestinian people.

Sheik Ahmed Yassin, leader of the militant Middle Eastern group Hamas

September 11, 2001

No doubt this is a result of injustice the U.S practices against the weak in the world. The U.S. has been sowing the seed of injustice and racial discrimination against the weak, and therefore the U.S. is collecting now the harvest of what it did.

athlete and as an advertising symbol for Nike footwear and many other products. He has been, however, largely silent on his political views and opinions.

At the 1992 Olympics, Jordan draped himself in the American flag to cover the Reebok (a Nike competitor) logo on the official team warm-up suit. In 1993, after scoring 55 points in the Bulls' victory over the Phoenix Suns, he delayed joining his teammates in celebration so that he could film a McDonald's ad on the court.

As a pitchman for Nike, Gatorade, and Wheaties, Michael Jordan has helped bring American consumer capitalism and American popular culture to all corners of the world. As Jordan was transforming the sport of basketball with his breathtaking slam dunks, many leading American corporations were experimenting with new ways of selling their products in a global marketplace. The **globalization** of the American economy has also involved both the greater use of foreign labor and overseas production facilities as well as global advertising campaigns using international television networks pioneered by such media giants as Ted Turner and Rupert Murdock.

Since 1980 the number of television sets in the world has doubled. Using powerful communication satellites, American-based multinational corporations reach consumers in all parts of the world. In international television ads for Wheaties, Hanes underwear, Coca-Cola, Gatorade, and Nike, Michael Jordan appeared before hundreds of millions of watchers. A recent poll reported that Chinese schoolchildren ranked him second only to former Chinese leader Zhou Enlai as the greatest figure of the twentieth century.

Today American brand names and celebrities are known around the world. McDonald's, one of the companies endorsed by Michael Jordan, operates in 121 countries and feeds 1 percent of the world's population each day. American culture influences the language, eating preferences, clothes, and television viewing habits of people worldwide. The spread of American culture, however, has also bred resentment and fueled anti-Americanism.

The Resurgence of the American Economy

In the late 1960s and 1970s, the American economy was beset by severe problems. These included sluggish growth, rapidly rising prices and interest rates, relatively high rates of unemployment, mounting foreign competition, and a stagnant stock market. The jobless rate averaged 6.7 percent between 1970 and 1982, compared to 4.8 percent between 1950 and 1962. The inflation rate, which stood at 1.4 percent in 1960, rose to 6.2 percent by 1969, to 12.3 percent by

No bird soars too high
If he soars with his own wi
—William Blake

Michael Jordan was both a superstar athlete and superstar pitchman.

1974, finally reaching a peak of 13.3 percent in 1979. This prolonged period of inflation was unprecedented in the American experience.

Especially worrisome was a slowdown in productivity. The growth in productivity, which measures the amount of goods and services that each worker produces for every hour worked, declined sharply. Between 1947 and 1965, the productivity rate was 3.6 percent; it fell to 1.7 percent between 1980 and 1990.

In the mid-1990s, however, the United States entered an economic boom. In 1997, unemployment fell below 5 percent and down to 3.9 percent early in 2000. Inflation rose just 2.9 percent in 1992 and 2.7 percent in 1999. A sharply rising stock market encouraged many Americans, including those of relatively modest means, to increase their stake in stocks, bonds, and mutual funds. By 1998, almost half of all Americans owned stocks, up from just 13 percent in 1980.

Economists attributed the economic boom to a sharp decline in the price of basic commodities such as oil and the restructuring of American businesses

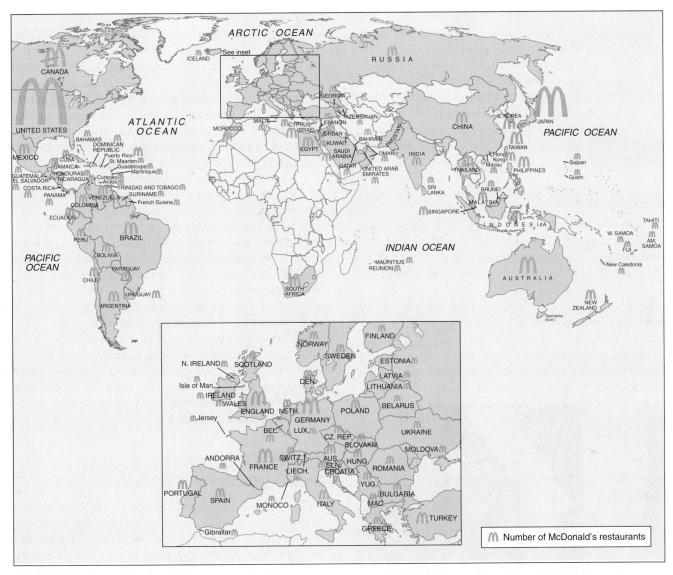

McDonald's Around the World

The relative size of the logo suggests the number of McDonald's franchises operating in each country in 2001. The largest logo represents the 13,099 McDonald's in the United States. The smallest logo stands for the single McDonald's in such countries as Azerbaijan, Brunei, and Liechtenstein.

in the 1980s and early 1990s, which made them more efficient. America's leading competitors, Germany and Japan, became less competitive as their labor costs rose and their domestic economies slowed. In the United States, rising real incomes and declining interest rates made houses, cars, and other goods more affordable for more Americans.

Perhaps the most important factor spurring America's economic resurgence was the growth of new computer and communication technologies dominated by American firms such as Microsoft and Intel. Global demand for information and entertainment soared during the 1990s, and American-owned companies dominated the information superhighway.

The New Economy

In 1995 Netscape, which produces a web "browser," announced that it would sell 3.5 million shares of its stock at $12 to $14 a share. So great was public enthusiasm for Netscape stock that the company eventually offered five million shares at $28 a share. On the first day of trading the stock closed at over $58 a share.

During the mid- and late 1990s, the stock market underwent a spectacular boom as the stock prices of many high technology companies rose to astounding heights. Contributing to America's economic resurgence was a series of dazzling new technologies, including personal computers, the Internet, and wireless telecommunications. Between 1989 and 2000, the share of households with personal computers rose from 15 percent to 51 percent.

High technology contributed to improvements in productivity. Computers replaced secretaries; computerized supply systems allowed companies to better manage their inventories. From 1995 to 2001 productivity grew at an annual rate of 2.6 percent, more than 50 percent higher than during the previous two decades.

The Aftermath

It was the nation's seventh largest corporation. *Fortune* magazine named Enron, a global electricity and national gas company, the top corporation for "Quality of Management" and the second best company for "Employee Talent." For five straight years, *Fortune* ranked Enron as the "Most Innovative Company" in America. Enron's stock price stood at $90 a share. Late in 2001, however, the company went bankrupt. At the time, it was the largest corporate bankruptcy in American history. Other corporate bankruptcies followed, including telecommunications giants WorldCom, Global Crossing, and Adelphia Communications. Investors lost billions of dollars as a result of alleged accounting fraud.

Like the boom of the 1920s, soaring stock prices and a "get-rich-quick" mentality allowed certain economic problems to accumulate with little public comment. Some companies manipulated their earning reports to increase stock prices, while some accountants rationalized dubious accounting procedures. Some Internet stocks were valued far beyond their real worth. The stock of an online toy store, eToys, had reached $78 a share before the company went bankrupt. Yet for all the troubles that the American economy experienced in the aftermath of the boom, its economic system continued to be the world's most prosperous and productive. Its success fueled the global economy, allowing the world economic system to overcome severe economic problems in Asia and in Russia.

THE POLITICS OF THE POST–COLD WAR ERA

Mudslinging and personal invective are nothing new in American politics, but the election campaigns of the late 1980s and 1990s were unusually vicious and cynical. Real differences over health care, housing policy, foreign policy, and defense spending were submerged in battles over character, family values, and patriotism. The politics of the late 1980s and 1990s dramatized developments that had been reshaping American politics since the late 1960s: the growing power of media consultants and pollsters who marketed candidates by emphasizing imagery, symbolism, and negative campaigning.

Politics during the post–Cold War era was marked by intense partisanship and extremely close presidential elections. In three straight elections—1992, 1996, and 2000—presidents came to office without winning a majority of the popular vote. In the 2000 election the victor received fewer popular votes than the loser.

A Kinder, Gentler Nation

The presidential election of 1988 was the first since 1836 in which a two-term president succeeded in passing on the presidency to his handpicked successor. **George Herbert Walker Bush,** who had been vice president throughout Reagan's administration,

Laid-off Enron employees with their belongings in front of the Enron building in Houston. Enron's staggeringly large bankruptcy symbolized corporate corruption and greed for many people around the world.

was said to have the best resume in Washington. After winning the Distinguished Service Cross during World War II, he made a fortune in the Texas oil business. He then went to Washington, where he served as a member of Congress, ambassador to the United Nations, envoy to China, and director of the CIA. He was elected president in 1988, defeating the Democratic candidate, Massachusetts governor Michael Dukakis, with 56 percent of the popular vote.

In his inaugural address, Bush promised to be a more hands-on administrator than his predecessor and he committed his presidency to creating a "kinder, gentler" nation, more sensitive and caring to the poor and disadvantaged.

During his one term in office, he and the Democratic-controlled Congress addressed many issues ignored during the Reagan years. For the first time in eight years, the federal government raised the minimum wage. For the first time in 13 years, Congress amended federal air pollution laws to reduce noxious emissions from smokestacks and tailpipes. For the first time since 1971, Congress considered childcare legislation and ultimately voted to provide subsidies to low-income families to defray the costs of childcare. In other actions, Congress prohibited job discrimination against the disabled, required nutrition labeling on processed foods, and expanded immigration into the United States.

The most difficult domestic issue that Bush faced was a mounting federal budget deficit. Soon after Bush took office, Americans learned that substantial federal revenues would have to be spent to bail out the nation's troubled savings and loan industry. The roots of this crisis had been planted during the presidency of Jimmy Carter, when high inflation and high interest rates threatened to bankrupt savings and loan institutions, which could not compete effectively with other financial institutions. A 1980 law lifted limits on the interest rates savings and loan institutions could pay and allowed them to make a limited amount of investments in commercial real estate. In 1982 and 1983, Congress broadened the savings and loans' capacity to make unsecured commercial loans and investments in commercial real estate.

In the mid-1980s, falling oil prices led to a collapse of land values, especially in the Southwest. Facing losses reaching billions of dollars, savings and loan institutions began to fail in large numbers. The mounting bills for the savings and loan bailout, which eventually reached between $500 and $700 billion, propelled President Bush in 1990 to violate his campaign pledge for "no new taxes" and helped elect a Democrat to the presidency in 1992.

The central issue in the 1992 election was the nation's sluggish economy. During the Bush presidency fewer new jobs were created than in any other

presidential term since World War II. Indeed, fewer Americans were on private payrolls at the end of Bush's term than when he took office. Unemployment reached the highest level in eight years, personal income stagnated, businesses failed in record numbers, the federal debt surpassed $4 trillion, and medical care absorbed 15 percent of the nation's output, while a quarter of the population lacked health insurance. Poverty rose to the highest rate in over two decades—a fact dramatically underscored by the outbreak of a riot in Los Angeles in April 1992.

Shortly after midnight on March 3, 1991, Rodney King, a 25-year-old employed black construction worker, was stopped for speeding after a 15-minute high-speed chase. The police ordered King from his car and forced him to lie prone on the ground. An onlooker videotaped four police officers beating and kicking the motorist, who was never charged in connection with the traffic stop.

The acquittal of four white police officers, charged with beating black motorist Rodney King, touched off five days of deadly rioting in Los Angeles in 1992. In this most deadly and costly incidence of urban violence in the twentieth century, 50 people died and property damage exceeded $1 billion.

Four officers were indicted for assault with a deadly weapon and the use of excessive force. A seven-week-long trial was held in 1992 in a mostly white county 45 miles northwest of Los Angeles. The jury, which included no African Americans, concluded that the officers had not broken any laws when they had beaten King and acquitted them.

Protestors, outraged that an apparently clear-cut act of police brutality had gone unpunished, took to the streets. The rioting left 54 people dead and 2000 injured and caused property damage exceeding $1 billion. The violence sparked by the officers' acquittal revealed deep racial and ethnic tensions in Los Angeles, especially between recent immigrants from Central America, African Americans, and Korean Americans. The rioting was also fueled by joblessness and economic distress. At the time of the riot, Los Angeles was suffering through its worst economic downturn since the Great Depression of the 1930s, brought on by the collapse of the aerospace industry after the end of the Cold War.

In a bitter three-way contest, marked by intense assaults on the candidates' records and character, Arkansas Governor Bill Clinton defeated George Bush and Texas businessman Ross Perot to become the first Democratic president in 12 years. President Bush, whose popularity had soared to 90 percent after the Persian Gulf War, received 38 percent of the vote, to Clinton's 43 percent and Perot's 19 percent.

Enter Bill Clinton

The youngest person elected to the presidency since John F. Kennedy, **Bill Clinton,** who was 46 years old when he took office, had served nearly 12 years as governor of Arkansas before entering the White House. A self-described "new Democrat," Clinton promised a new approach to government between the unfettered free market championed by the Republicans and the welfare state economics that the Democratic Party had represented in the past.

As president, Clinton committed his administration to ending 12 years of social neglect. During his first two years in office, he enjoyed a string of legislative successes. To reduce the federal budget deficit, he persuaded Congress to raise taxes on the wealthiest Americans and on gasoline and to cut government spending. To create jobs, he convinced the Senate to ratify the **North American Free Trade Agreement (NAFTA),** eliminating tariffs barriers between Canada, Mexico, and the United States. He completed negotiations that established the World Trade Organization to reduce barriers to international trade. To aid working parents, he signed parental leave legislation, allowing parents to take unpaid leave during family emergencies. To combat violent crime, he convinced

Congress to enact a waiting period for handgun purchases and a ban on the sale of assault weapons.

Two of his proposals, however, alienated many voters. In the face of vocal opposition, Clinton backed away from a promise to let gays serve in the military and instead instituted a compromise "don't-ask, don't-tell" policy, which allowed gays to serve as long as they kept silent about their sexual orientation and refrained from homosexual conduct. The compromise satisfied no one. Meanwhile, the centerpiece of Clinton's legislative agenda—a program of universal health care coverage—had to be withdrawn. His plan to guarantee lifelong care to Americans through local networks of insurers, hospitals, and doctors was criticized for its complexity and for excessive government involvement in the healthcare system.

Clinton also suffered from allegations of financial and sexual misconduct before he became president. One controversy stemmed from investments he and his wife had made in the Whitewater Development Corporation, an Arkansas real estate development firm. Another concerned charges of sexual harassment made by a former Arkansas government employee. Clinton eventually settled the sexual misconduct lawsuit for $850,000 and was ordered by a judge to pay an additional $90,000 for lying under oath. In 2000 an independent counsel ended a six-year inquiry into the Whitewater case by clearing President and First Lady Hillary Rodham Clinton of any criminal wrongdoing in the real estate deal.

In the midterm elections of 1994, Republicans won control of both houses of Congress. Campaigning on a 10-point **Contract With America** drawn up by House Speaker **Newt Gingrich,** Congressional Republicans called for welfare reform; term limits for political office holders; a moratorium on environmental, health, and safety regulations; and a Constitutional Amendment requiring a balanced budget. Public support for President Clinton rebounded, however, after the Congressional Republicans temporarily shut down the federal government in an effort to force budget cuts and tax reductions, and antigovernment extremists blew up the Alfred P. Murrah Federal Office Building in Oklahoma City, killing 168 people—including 19 children—and injuring 624.

In 1996 Bill Clinton became the first Democrat since Franklin Roosevelt to be elected to two full terms in office. He successfully portrayed the Republicans as extremists and received about 50 percent of the popular vote to 42 percent for his Republican opponent, Senate Majority Leader Robert Dole, and 8 percent for Ross Perot. By the time his second term was over, Clinton could legitimately argue that he had fulfilled his promise to cut the federal deficit in half, create millions of new jobs, and "end welfare as

In his second term, Clinton was impeached by the House of Representatives on charges of perjury and obstruction of justice in connection with his sexual liaison with White House intern Monica Lewinsky, who is shown here embracing the president.

we know it." Over Republican opposition in Congress, the Clinton administration raised the minimum wage and the Earned Income Tax Credit, which provides financial assistance to the working poor. His administration also started AmeriCorp, a national service program; allowed workers up to 12 weeks of unpaid leave to deal with family emergencies; and blocked efforts to restrict abortions. Working with Congressional Republicans, the administration reduced the size of the government workforce, expanded international trade, and eliminated the federal budget deficit. Clinton and the Congressional Republicans also reformed the 60-year-old welfare system. The welfare reform measures limited the time that people can spend on welfare rolls and required welfare recipients to work or receive training.

The low point in Clinton's presidency began in 1998 when he was accused of encouraging Monica Lewinsky, a 24-year-old White House intern, to lie to lawyers in a sexual harassment lawsuit about whether she had had an affair with the president. For seven months the President denied any inappropriate relationship with Lewinsky, but ultimately in a televised address on August 17, 1998, Clinton acknowledged the relationship and admitted that he had misled the American people about it. In December 1998 the House Judiciary Committee, voting along straight party lines, approved four articles of impeachment, asserting that Clinton had twice committed perjury before grand juries, obstructed justice, and abused his power. Later that month, the House of Representatives approved two articles of impeachment—perjury and obstruction of justice—making Clinton only the

second American president to face an impeachment trial in the Senate. A two-thirds vote was required for conviction and removal from office. On the article charging the President with committing perjury before a grand jury, Senators voted 45 guilty and 55 not guilty. On the charge of obstruction of justice, 50 Senators voted guilty and 50 not guilty. While a majority of the American people told pollsters that they did not approve of President Clinton's behavior, they continued to support his policies, in part because of his success in handling the economy. With the stock market soaring to record highs and inflation and unemployment at their lowest levels in decades, it seemed likely that President Clinton would pass on the presidency to his vice president, Al Gore, in 2000.

The Disputed Election of 2000

The presidential election of 2000 hinged on the outcome in Florida. First the television networks said that Vice President Al Gore had carried the state. Then they reversed their decision and said that Texas Governor George W. Bush had won the state. Finally, they reported that the count in Florida was "too close to call."

It was a presidential election that was so close that it took five weeks to determine the winner. Gore carried the East and West coasts and inland industrial cities, while Bush won much of the Midwest and

Election of 2000

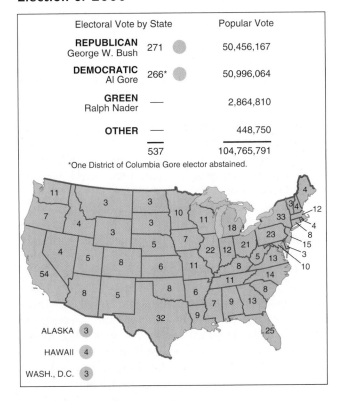

	Electoral Vote by State		Popular Vote
REPUBLICAN George W. Bush	271		50,456,167
DEMOCRATIC Al Gore	266*		50,996,064
GREEN Ralph Nader	—		2,864,810
OTHER	—		448,750
	537		104,765,791

*One District of Columbia Gore elector abstained.

ALASKA 3

HAWAII 4

WASH., D.C. 3

Plains as well as the South. Gore piled up a half-million more votes than Bush, but he lost the Electoral College when he lost Florida. On November 26, 19 days after the election, Florida's Secretary of State declared Bush the winner in the state with a margin of 537 votes.

With the presidency hanging on a few hundred votes in a single state, there were lawsuits and requests for recounts. Bitter disputes centered on confusing ballots, names missing from voting rolls, and minority voters subjected to multiple requests for identification. One major problem was punch card ballots, which are vulnerable to voter error, such as not punching a hole all the way through. Democrats appealed the decision to award the state's electoral votes to Bush to the Florida Supreme Court, which in a 4-3 decision, ordered a recount of the disputed ballots. Bush's lawyers appealed to the U.S. Supreme Court to stop the recount. Finally on December 12, 2000, five weeks after the election, in an extraordinary late-night decision and by a narrow 5-4 majority, the U.S. Supreme Court halted the recount, ruling that the recount ordered by the Florida Supreme Court violated the principle that all votes must be treated equally and that there was not enough time to conduct a new manual recount that would meet constitutional muster. The next day Gore conceded. The 2000 presidential election was the first in 112 years in which a president lost the popular vote but captured enough states to win the electoral vote.

Compassionate Conservatism

The son of President George Herbert Walker Bush, **George W. Bush** received his college degree from Yale University and a Master of Business Administration from Harvard Business School. He served as an F-102 pilot for the Texas Air National Guard during the Vietnam War, before beginning his career in the oil and gas business in Midland in the Texas panhandle. He later served as managing general partner of the Texas Rangers baseball team until he was elected Governor of Texas in 1994.

During the 2000 presidential campaign, George W. Bush described himself as a "compassionate conservative" committed to the principles of limited government, personal responsibility, strong families, and local control. He proposed to improve public schools by insisting on competency testing. Under his proposed "faith-based initiative," religious institutions would be able to compete for government funds to provide social services. A major legislative success involved cutting taxes. The events that took place on September 11, 2001, however, would reshape the whole direction of his presidency.

THE UNITED STATES AND THE POST–COLD WAR WORLD

In an article widely published in 1989, **Francis Fukuyama**, a senior State Department official, announced the "end of history." With the collapse of authoritarian regimes of the right and the left, Fukuyama argued, the clash of political ideologies that had shaped the history of the twentieth century was over. Liberal democracy and free market capitalism, he proclaimed, had emerged triumphant.

Many Americans hoped that the end of the Cold War would usher in a new era of peace and international stability. To be sure, many encouraging developments in international affairs occurred following the end of the Cold War, among them the end of apartheid and the replacement of white rule with a multiracial democracy in South Africa.

Discord and instability failed to disappear, however. In fact, the end of the Cold War unleashed violent ethnic, religious, national conflicts, especially in the Balkans, the Middle East, and Africa. The Cold War, which had pitted superpower against superpower, had tended to suppress ethnic tensions in many multi-ethnic states. With the Cold War over, however, many ethnic animosities surfaced. In recent years, bitter and brutal conflicts have erupted in Africa, in Angola, Eritrea, Liberia, Sierra Leone, and Somalia; in Europe and the former Soviet Union, in the Balkans, Chechnya, and Northern Ireland; and in the Middle East, in Iraq, Israel, Kuwait, and Palestine, and Turkey.

Panama and the Persian Gulf

America's first significant foreign policy crisis of the post–Cold War era involved Panama. In 1989, General **Manuel Noriega,** the strongman who ruled Panama, had voided the results of the country's presidential elections and sent paramilitary forces into the streets of Panama City where they beat up opposition candidates. After Panamanian troops fired on four unarmed American military personnel, killing one, President George H. W. Bush dispatched a force of 10,000 U.S. troops to invade Panama to safeguard the lives of Americans there, to protect the Panama Canal Zone, and to force Noriega from power. An estimated 300 to 500 Panamanians were killed in the invasion, named **Operation Just Cause**. There were 23 American casualties. In the end, Noriega was forced out of office and deported to the United States, where he was convicted on charges of drug trafficking.

A much larger military crisis occurred in the Middle East. At 2 A.M., on August 2, 1990, Iraqi troops invaded and occupied Kuwait, a small, oil-rich emirate on the Persian Gulf. Iraq's leader,

United States troops patrol the streets of Panama City during the U.S. invasion of Panama in December 1989.

Saddam Hussein, justified the invasion on the grounds that Kuwait, which he accused of intentionally depressing world oil prices, was historically a part of Iraq.

Iraq's invasion of Kuwait caught the United States off-guard. Hussein's regime was a brutal military dictatorship that ruled by secret police and used poison gas against Iranians, Kurds, and Shiite Muslims. During the 1970s and 1980s, the United States, Britain, France, the Soviet Union, and West Germany had sold Iraq an awesome arsenal of weapons, including equipment used in the production of biological, chemical, and nuclear weapons, in an attempt to encourage Hussein to moderate his rule. The West hoped that Iraq would counter the power of its neighbor Iran. During the eight-year war between Iraq and Iran, the United States, which opposed the Islamic fundamentalist extremism of Iran's government, tilted toward Iraq.

President Bush, reassessing American national interest, decided to oppose Iraq's aggression against Kuwait. The Iraqi invasion had given Hussein direct control over a significant portion of the world's oil supply. It also disrupted the balance of power in the Middle East and placed Saudi Arabia and the Persian Gulf emirates in jeopardy. Iraq's battle-hardened war machine—consisting of 545,000 troops, 5000 tanks, and 500 fighter aircraft—also threatened the security of such valuable U.S. allies as Egypt and Israel.

In a sharp departure from American foreign policy during the Reagan presidency, Bush organized an international coalition against Iraq, convincing Turkey and Syria to close Iraqi pipelines, winning Soviet support for an arms embargo, and establishing a multinational army with contingents from Western and Arab nations. The administration also persuaded the Security Council of the United Na-

tions to adopt a series of resolutions condemning the Iraqi invasion, demanding restoration of the Kuwaiti government, and imposing an economic blockade.

The victory of the multinational forces in the Persian Gulf War did not mean an end of hostilities. Saddam Hussein remained in power and in the war's aftermath he brutally suppressed independence movements by two minority groups—the Kurds and the Shiite Muslims—in his own country. Still, his ability to control events in the region was dramatically curtailed.

Humanitarian Intervention

As a Rhodes scholar at Oxford University in England, Bill Clinton had avoided the military draft and demonstrated against the Vietnam War. During his two terms in office, President Clinton had to repeatedly wrestle with a question that had arisen during the Vietnam War: should the United States intervene to suppress conflict within sovereign nations?

As president, Clinton quickly withdrew American forces from Somalia in East Africa after 18 American peacekeepers were killed there in 1993. The next year, when one of the most terrible massacres of the postwar years occurred in the African nation of **Rwanda,** where the ruling Hutus killed more than 800,000 Tutsis in three months, he declined to intervene. In 1994, he did send American forces to Haiti to oversee that country's transition from military to civilian rule.

Arguments over U.S. intervention became most heated over the former Yugoslavia in the Balkan peninsula of southeastern Europe. After bitter fighting in 1991 and 1992, Croatia, a former constituent republic of Yugoslavia, broke away and declared its independence. A bloody three-year war ended with **Bosnia-Herzegovina** gaining independence from Yugoslavia, but ethnic and religious conflict and civil war continued to consume the newly independent country. In 1995, the United States helped negotiate a settlement that divided the country into areas dominated by Croats, Muslims, and Serbs.

To prevent the province of **Kosovo** from achieving independence, Yugoslav authorities carried out a campaign of repression and abuse against the ethnic Albanians who made up 90 percent of the Kosovar population. When Yugoslavia rejected international pressure to grant autonomy to Kosovo, the United States and NATO launched a bombing campaign in 1999. In response, Yugoslavia's dictator, **Slobodan Milosevic,** used his military and police forces to evict Kosovo's Albanian population from their homeland. Ultimately, a casualty-free, two-month

NATO air campaign forced Yugoslav forces to leave Kosovo. Nearly a million ethnic Albanians returned to their homes under international protection.

September 11, 2001

Born in 1957 to a Yemeni bricklayer, one of the youngest of nearly fifty children, **Osama bin-Laden** grew up in Saudi Arabia, where his father founded a construction firm that would become the largest in the desert kingdom. He inherited millions of dollars after his father's death and graduated from a leading Saudi university with a degree in civil engineering.

In 1979, he left Saudi Arabia for Afghanistan, raising money and recruits to help Muslims there expel the Soviet army, which was trying to prop up a Communist government in the country. During the mid-1980s, he built roads, tunnels, and bunkers in Afghanistan.

Although the United States had helped him and his fellow warriors expel the Soviets from Afghanistan, bin-Laden turned against the United States. He was furious about the deployment of American troops in Saudi Arabia, the birthplace of the Prophet Muhammad and home to the two holiest Muslim shrines, who had been sent to protect the oil-rich kingdom from an Iraqi invasion. U.S. support for Israel and the American role in enforcing an economic embargo against Iraq further fueled his rage. His goal was to remove American forces from his Saudi homeland, destroy the Jewish state in Israel, and defeat pro-Western dictatorships throughout the Middle East.

By 1998, he had formed a terrorist network called al-Qaeda, which in Arabic means "The Base," and provided training camps, financing, planning, recruitment, and other support services for fighters seeking to strike at the United States. American officials believe bin-Laden's associates operate in over 40 countries—in Europe and North America, as well as in the Middle East and Asia. U.S. government officials also believe that bin-Laden was involved in at least four major terrorist attacks against U.S. interests before September 11, 2001: the 1993 bombing of the World Trade Center in New York City, a 1996 bombing in Saudi Arabia that killed 19 U.S. soldiers, the 1998 bombings of U.S. embassies in Kenya and Tanzania, and the 2000 attack on the USS *Cole* at a port in Yemen, in which 17 U.S. sailors were killed. Al-Qaeda viewed the U.S. responses to these attacks as half-hearted. In 1998, American cruise missiles struck against a network of terrorist compounds in Afghanistan and a pharmaceutical plant in Sudan, which was mistakenly believed to be producing chemicals for use in nerve gas, in retaliation for the bombings of the U.S. embassies in Africa.

THE FIRST CRISIS OF THE POST–COLD WAR ERA

The Persian Gulf War

In August 1990, with Iraqi forces poised near the Saudi Arabian border, the Bush administration dispatched 180,000 troops to protect the Saudi kingdom. The crisis took a dramatic turn in November 1990 when Bush doubled the number of American troops deployed in the Persian Gulf. Iraqi forces in Kuwait had climbed to 430,000 and coalition forces had to increase if Iraq was to be ejected from Kuwait by force. The president went to the United Nations for a resolution permitting the use of force against Iraq if it did not withdraw by January 15, 1991. After a heated debate, Congress also gave the president authority to wage war.

The 545,000-strong Iraqi army, the world's fourth largest, was equipped with antiship Exocet missiles, top-of-the-line Soviet T-72 tanks, and long-range artillery capable of firing nerve gas. Hussein tried to bring Israel into the war by launching Scud missiles at Israeli cities, a strategy thwarted when the United States sent Patriot antimissile missiles to Israel. A month of allied bombing gave the coalition forces air supremacy and destroyed thousands of Iraqi tanks and artillery pieces, supply routes and communications lines, command-and-control bunkers, and limited Iraq's ability to produce nuclear, chemical, and biological weapons. Iraqi troop morale suffered so badly during the bombing that an estimated 30 percent of Baghdad's forces deserted before the ground campaign even started.

The allied ground campaign relied on deception, mobility, and overwhelming air superiority to defeat a larger Iraqi army. The allied strategy was to mislead the Iraqis into believing that the allied attack would occur along the Kuwaiti coastline and Kuwait's border with Saudi Arabia. Meanwhile, General H. Norman Schwarzkopf, U.S. commander of the coalition forces, shifted more than 300,000 U.S., British, and French troops into western Saudi Arabia, allowing them to strike deeply into Iraq and trap Iraqi forces deep in southern Iraq and Kuwait. Only 100 hours after the ground war started, the war ended.

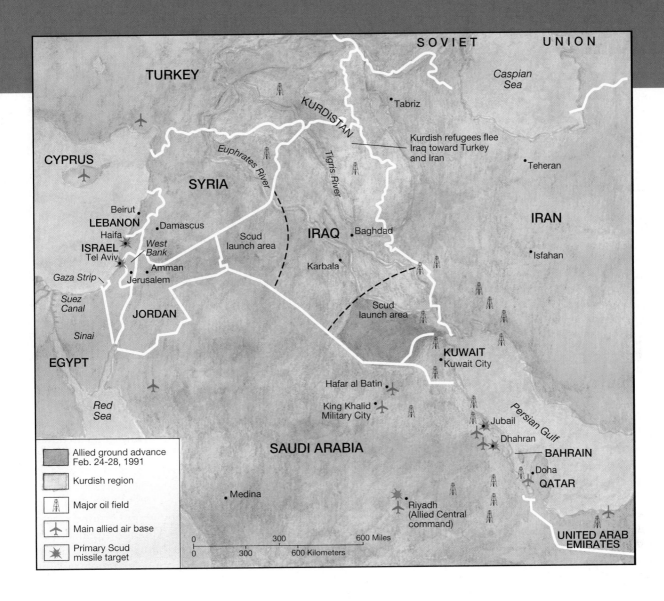

SOVIET UNION

TURKEY

Caspian Sea

•Tabriz

KURDISTAN

Kurdish refugees flee
Iraq toward Turkey
and Iran

CYPRUS

•Teheran

Euphrates River

SYRIA

Tigris River

IRAN

Beirut•
LEBANON
Haifa
•Damascus

ISRAEL
*West
Bank*
Tel Aviv•
Scud
launch
area

IRAQ
•Baghdad

•Isfahan

Gaza Strip
•Amman
•Jerusalem
Karbala•

Scud
launch
area

*Suez
Canal*

JORDAN

Sinai

EGYPT

KUWAIT
•Kuwait City

Hafar al Batin•

*Red
Sea*

King Khalid
Military City

Persian Gulf

•Jubail
•Dhahran
BAHRAIN

SAUDI ARABIA

•Doha
QATAR

	Allied ground advance Feb. 24-28, 1991
	Kurdish region
⛏	Major oil field
✈	Main allied air base
✸	Primary Scud missile target

•Medina

✸Riyadh
(Allied Central
command)

UNITED ARAB
EMIRATES

| 0 | | 300 | | 600 Miles |
| 0 | 300 | | 600 Kilometers | |

The Serbian campaign of "ethnic cleansing" forced the evacuation of many ethnic Albanians from the province of Kosovo. By the end of April 1999 nearly half of the two million residents of Kosovo had become refugees. The NATO bombing campaign, launched to halt Serbian aggression against the Kosovars, instead led to increased Serbian attacks.

In contrast, the U.S. response to the September 11 attacks was immediate and forceful. Over a period of just three days, Congress voted to spend $40 billion for recovery. Then, like his father in the period before the Persian Gulf War, George W. Bush organized an international coalition against al-Qaeda and the **Taliban** government in Afghanistan that supported it. He persuaded Pakistan, which had been the main sponsor of Afghanistan's Taliban government, to support the United States diplomatically and logistically.

On October 7, 2001, in retaliation for the September 11 attacks, a U.S.-led coalition launched an attack against targets in Afghanistan in the beginning of what President Bush promised to be a long campaign against terrorist groups and the states that support them. The American strategy in Afghanistan involved using American air power and ground targeting to support the Northern Alliance, the major indigenous force opposing the Taliban. Later, U.S. and British forces coordinated ground operations against al-Qaeda and the Taliban.

Americans and people around the world watched on television as the U.S.-led coalition launched attacks in Afghanistan in the fall of 2001 to topple the Taliban regime. Following the initial bombings of key targets, much of the action took place in Afghanistan's rugged mountains and caves, to which Taliban members and supporters fled. Here, members of the 82nd Airborne division prepare for a dawn raid.

Afghanistan's rugged terrain, weather extremes, and veteran guerrilla-style fighters presented a serious challenge to the American military. The effective use of laser-guided missiles and cluster bombs and 2000-pound Daisy Cutter bombs, unmanned drones, and U.S. and British special forces, in conjunction with indigenous Afghani forces, succeeded in overthrowing the Taliban government, though some members of al-Qaeda and Taliban apparently escaped into isolated regions along the Afghanistan-Pakistan border. Between 1000 and 1300 Afghani civilians were killed.

Civil Liberties and National Security: Trying to Strike a Balance

The war on terrorism has forced the nation to toughen its national security. Following the events of September 11, the federal government detained more than a thousand people, mainly Arab and Muslim men who were suspected of having information about terrorism. They were held without charges, and their names and whereabouts largely kept secret.

In the wake of the September 11 attacks, Congress enacted legislation giving law enforcement agencies broader authority to wiretap suspects and monitor online communication. Congress also expanded the government's authority to detain or deport aliens who associate with members of terrorist organizations and authorized greater intelligence sharing among the FBI, the CIA, the Immigration and Naturalization Service, and local law enforcement agencies.

President Bush responded to the attacks by proposing a cabinet-level **Department of Homeland Security** to prevent terrorist attacks within the United States, reduce the country's vulnerability to terrorism, and minimize the damage and hasten the recovery from attacks that do occur. The new department would be responsible for border security; responding to chemical, biological, and radiological attacks; and information analysis.

Arab Americans and Muslim Americans

In the immediate aftermath of the September 11 attacks, some Americans directed their anger at Arab Americans, Muslims, and South Asians. In a suburb of Phoenix, Arizona, an Indian immigrant who practiced the Sikh faith was murdered, apparently just because of his religious affiliation. So too was a Pakistani grocer in Dallas, Texas. In Irving, Texas, bullets were fired into an Islamic community center. Some 300 protestors tried to storm a Chicago-area mosque.

Near Detroit, an Islamic school had to close down because of daily bomb threats.

Those who directed their anger against Arab Americans and Muslims should be ashamed, President Bush declared. "Muslim Americans make an incredibly valuable contribution to our country," he said. "They need to be treated with respect."

Today, there are approximately three million Arab Americans in the United States. About a third live in California, Michigan, and New York. Arab Americans belong to many different religions. While most are Muslims, many are Catholics, Orthodox Christians, Jews, or Druze. Prominent political figures of Arab descent include consumer advocate Ralph Nader, former Senate Majority leader George Mitchell, and former Secretary of Health and Human Services Donna Shalala.

According to a poll conducted by the Pew Memorial Trusts, approximately two-fifths of the nation's nearly seven million Muslim Americans were born in the United States, with the rest coming from 80 other countries. About 32 percent are South Asian, 26 percent are Arab, 20 percent are African American, and 7 percent are African; 14 percent report some other background. About a fifth are converts to Islam.

CONCLUSION: THE MEANING OF SEPTEMBER 11

The September 11 attacks dramatically altered the way the United States looked at itself and the world. The attacks produced a surge of patriotism and national unity and pride; however, the terrorist strikes also fostered a new sense of vulnerability.

As the twenty-first century began, the United States was without a doubt the strongest, wealthiest, most powerful nation on earth. It possessed the world's most productive economy and mightiest armed forces. It dominated global manufacturing and trade and held an unchallenged lead in invention, science, and technology. Its popular culture was dominant around much of the globe. The United States seemed to be leading the way to a new economy built around the Internet and the global distribution of finance, manufacturing, and entertainment. It stood as a model of freedom and pluralism that people throughout the world strive to emulate. Then, seemingly out of nowhere, the United States was struck by the most deadly terrorist attack in history.

In 1859, when Abraham Lincoln could not have imagined that he would soon become president of the United States and would hold office during a great civil war that would lead to the abolition of

Terrorism in Historical Perspective

The attacks on the World Trade Center and the Pentagon came as an utter shock to the American public. In fact, however, terrorist acts had been increasing in frequency and deadliness even before the September 11 attacks. In 1993, a truck bomb exploded in a parking garage below the World Trade Center in New York, killing six people and injuring more than 1000. In 1995, Timothy McVeigh, an army veteran with extreme antigovernment views, killed 168 people at the Alfred P. Murrah Federal Building in Oklahoma City in 1995. That same year, a car bomb at U.S. military headquarters in Riyadh, Saudi Arabia, killed five American service personnel. In 1996, a truck bomb exploded outside Khobar Towers military barracks in Dhahran, Saudi Arabia, killing 19 American servicemen and wounding hundreds of others. In 1998, truck bombs destroyed the U.S. embassies in Kenya and Tanzania in Africa, killing 224 civilians and injuring over 5000.

On September 11, 2001, three other acts that can be described as terrorism took place. In Colombia, paramilitaries killed 15 villagers they accused of collaborating with Marxist guerrillas. In Londonderry, Northern Ireland, a roadside bomb, targeting three police officers, exploded. Meanwhile, a suicide bomber in Istanbul detonated a bomb to protest conditions in Turkish prisons.

Terrorism is not a new phenomenon. Our vocabulary makes this abundantly clear. Such words as *zealot*, *assassin*, and *thug* reveal that the use of terror as a political weapon has a long history. Our word *zealot* comes from the first-century Hebrew Zealots who assassinated Roman officials in a failed attempt to end Roman rule in biblical Palestine. The Zealots committed mass suicide in 73 A.D.

Our word *assassin* comes from imaginative accounts of a Muslim sect by such writers as the explorer Marco Polo. According to these accounts, members of the sect engaged in acts of political murder in Persia and the Middle East from the eleventh through the thirteenth centuries after using the drug hashish. Our word *thug* comes from the name given to social bandits in India who were followers of the Indian goddess Kali and were accused of committing murders from the thirteenth to the nineteenth centuries.

The word *terrorism* arose during the French Revolution, when terror was used as an instrument of state policy. Terror was employed to eliminate counterrevolutionary elements in the population, to save France from anarchy and military defeat, and to suppress hoarding and profiteering. Unapologetic about the use of terror to eliminate political enemies, the French revolutionist Robespierre said, "Terror is nothing but justice, prompt, severe and inflexible." An estimated 40,000 people were sentenced to death during the Reign of Terror in France.

Modern terrorism first appeared in Tsarist Russia in the 1870s, and terrorist tactics were subsequently adopted by some dissident groups in the Ottoman and British empires and by some anarchists in the United States and Western Europe. Late nineteenth- and early-twentieth-century terrorism typically took the form of assassination attempts on heads of state and bomb attacks on public buildings. Between 1880 and 1901, the president of France, a Spanish prime minister, an Austrian empress, an Italian king, and two U.S. presidents were assassinated. Attempts were also made on the life of a German chancellor and emperor. The terrorists' objectives were threefold: to publicize grievances through the "propaganda of the deed"; to destabilize governments and divide the population; and to provoke authorities to overreact and generate international sympathy for the perpetrators' cause.

During the 1920s and 1930s a new form of terrorism emerged, fascist terror. In Germany and Italy, supporters of Adolf Hitler and Benito Mussolini used murder and violent intimidation to achieve political power and attack specific elements in the population. Meanwhile, government authorities in the Soviet Union began to dispatch assassins and saboteurs to eliminate their enemies.

Terrorist acts aimed at overthrowing colonial rule were widespread following World War II. Societies as diverse as Algeria, Kenya, and Israel achieved independence in part as a result of terrorist tactics. Terrorism was later adopted by other nationalist and separatist groups, including some Basque separatists in Spain and France, some Irish nationalists in Northern Ireland, some Quebec separatists in Canada, and some African and Latin American revolutionaries. In the cases of Northern Ireland,

South Africa, and Latin America, terrorist tactics were also utilized by the nationalists' and the revolutionaries' militant opponents.

The late 1960s and 1970s saw the rise of new forms of revolutionary terror in the affluent West. Such groups such as the Red Army Faction in Germany, the Red Brigades in Italy, and the Weather Underground and the Symbionese Liberation Army in the United States kidnapped and assassinated people whom they blamed for economic exploitation and political repression. Terrorism emerged on the world stage with the 1972 murder of 11 Israeli athletes at the 1972 Munich Olympics by Palestinian militants in an effort to end Israeli occupation of their territories and establish a Palestinian homeland.

In recent years, the nature of terrorism has apparently changed. The most striking developments have been the increase in the number of terrorist acts committed in the name of religion. In 1980, just two of 64 international terrorist groups were considered to be religiously motivated. In 1995, the figure was 26 out of 56 organizations.

CHRONOLOGY OF KEY EVENTS

1988   Republican George H. W. Bush is elected forty-first president

1989   Opposition defeats Sandinistas in Nicaraguan elections; Communist regimes collapse in Eastern Europe

1990   Iraqi troops invade and occupy Kuwait

1991   U.S., Western, and Arab forces eject Iraq from Kuwait by force; failed coup in Soviet Union results in a shift in power to the Soviet republics and independence for Lithuania, Latvia, and Estonia

1992   Democrat Bill Clinton is elected forty-second president

1993   Congress passes North American Free Trade Agreement (NAFTA), eliminating trade barriers between Canada, Mexico, and the United States; General Agreement on Trade and Tariffs (GATT) is passed, reducing global trading barriers

1994   Congress defeats Clinton's health-care plan; Republicans win control of both the House and the Senate in the 1994 mid-term elections

1996   Clinton is reelected president

1998   The House of Representatives votes to impeach Clinton for perjury and obstruction of justice

1999   The Senate fails to convict Clinton; the United States leads the NATO bombing campaign of Yugoslavia

2000   Republican candidate George W. Bush is named winner of the 2000 presidential election when Florida's 25 electoral votes are awarded to him, giving him a total of 271 electoral votes to Democratic candidate Al Gore's 266 (one District of Columbia Gore elector abstained)

2001   British and American biologists decode the human DNA

Terrorist attacks kill thousands of civilians and destroy the World Trade Center towers in New York City and part of the Pentagon in Washington, D.C; a fourth plane, hijacked by terrorists, crashes in Pennsylvania, near Pittsburgh

The United States retaliates for the September 11 attacks by conducting a bombing campaign in Afghanistan against the al-Qaeda terrorist organization and the country's Taliban government and installs a new provisional government in Afghanistan; 22 cases of anthrax infection are detected in the United States, resulting in five deaths

---

slavery, he told a story in which he reminded his listeners about history's utter unpredictability.

It is said an Eastern monarch once charged his wise men to invent him a sentence to be ever in view and appropriate in all times and situations. They presented him the words, "And this, too, shall pass away." How much it expresses! How chastening in the hour of pride! How consoling in the depths of affliction.

The study of history cannot help us foresee the future, but it can help us understand the forces and trends that are transforming our lives. It can help us remember the sacrifices of those who came before us and the debts that we owe them. It can help us recognize not only how far we have come but also how far we have yet to go. A knowledge of history helps us

recognize that change is an inevitable part of life and that the future is determined not by abstract historical forces but the choices, actions, and struggles of living human beings.

CHAPTER SUMMARY AND KEY POINTS

The end of the Cold War, marked by the collapse of communist governments in Eastern Europe and the breakup of the Soviet Union, had profound foreign policy, economic, and political consequences for the United States. At the end of the twentieth century, the United States enjoyed virtually unrivaled global influence. Its adversary for four decades, the Soviet Union, had disintegrated, and its strongest economic competitors faced problems of their own. Japan was mired in a decade-long economic recession, while Germany was preoccupied with the stresses of reunification. The end of the Cold War also unleashed violent ethnic, religious, national conflicts, especially in the Balkans, the Middle East, and Africa, which resulted in U.S. interventions in Bosnia and Kosovo and the Persian Gulf.

The United States enjoyed a sustained economic boom following the end of the Cold War. Unemployment fell to near-record lows while the stock market reached record highs. The post–Cold War period also witnessed the expansion of the global economy, the rapid rise of high technology industries, and bitter political divisions, which were evident in the impeachment of Bill Clinton and the contested presidential election of 2000.

The terrorist attacks of September 11, 2001, brought renewed unity and a resurgence of professed patriotism to the United States. In response to the attacks, the United States launched a war on terrorism, targeting al-Qaeda, the organization that orchestrated the attacks, and the Taliban government in Afghanistan that had provided bases for terrorists.

- Following the Cold War, the U.S. economy globalized, as American corporations made greater use of foreign labor and factories and sold their products all over the world.

- During the mid-1990s, the U.S. economy boomed as a result of declining energy prices, improvements in productivity, falling interest rates, and the growth of computer and communication technologies.

- Intense partisanship and extremely close presidential elections characterized politics in the post–Cold War era.

- The end of the Cold War unleashed violent ethnic, religious, and national conflicts in the Balkans, the Middle East, and Africa.

- U.S. forces intervened in Panama in 1989; led an international coalition in 1991 that reversed Iraq's occupation of Kuwait; and participated in 1999 in a NATO air campaign that forced the Yugoslav military to leave Kosovo.

- Al-Qaeda staged attacks on American interests, culminating on September 11, 2001, in strikes on the World Trade Center in New York City and the Pentagon in Washington, D.C., which killed over 3000 people and prompted the United States to attack the terrorist network and the Afghani government that supported it.

SUGGESTIONS FOR FURTHER READING

William C. Berman, *From the Center to the Edge: The Politics and Policies of the Clinton Presidency* (2001). A political historian's balanced appraisal of the major domestic and foreign policy issues of the Clinton presidency, including welfare reform, deficit reduction, impeachment, American relations with Russia and China, and conflicts in Bosnia and Kosovo.

E. J. Dionne and William Kristol, *Bush v. Gore: The Court Cases and the Commentary* (2001). A compilation of the U.S. Supreme Court and Florida court decisions in the contested presidential election of 2000, supplemented with commentary by leading political journalists and scholars.

John Robert Green, *The Presidency of George Bush* (1999). A concise and balanced account of the Bush presidency based on documents from the Bush presidential library and extensive interviews with former administration officials.

David Halberstam, *Firehouse* (2002). Presents the story of the 26 firefighters of New York City Engine 40, Ladder 35, 12 of whom lost their lives while responding to the terrorist attacks on the World Trade Center on September 11, 2001.

_____, *War in a Time of Peace: Bush, Clinton and the Generals* (2001). Examines how Presidents George H. W. Bush and Bill Clinton handled foreign policy during their terms of office, including conflicts in Africa, the Balkans, the Middle East, and Persian Gulf.

Bruce Hoffman, *Inside Terrorism* (1999). A succinct history of terrorism that examines terrorists' changing methods and motivations.

David Marannis, *First in His Class: The Biography of Bill Clinton* (1995). A vivid portrait of the 42nd president covering his life up to the 1991 announcement of his candidacy for the presidency.

Novels

Jen Gish, *Mona in the Promised Land* (1996).

Esmeralda Santiago, *When I Was Puerto Rican* (1993).

Tom Wolfe, *A Man in Full* (1998).

MEDIA RESOURCES

Web Sites

George Bush
http://www.americanpresident.org/KoTrain/Courses/GB/GB_In_Brief.htm
Extensive information on George H. W. Bush's presidency from "The American President" series presented on PBS.

The Clinton Years
http://www.pbs.org/wgbh/pages/frontline/shows/clinton/
From ABC News's Nightline and PBS's Frontline, this site chronicles the Clinton era.

Perspectives from the Social Sciences
http://www.ssrc.org/sept11/
This site features essays by leading social scientists discussing the events and aftermath of the September 11 terrorist attacks.

The September 11 Digital Archive
http://www.911digitalarchive.org/
A collection of resources created by the Smithsonian Institution and other organizations detailing the public response to the September 11, 2001, attacks in New York, Virginia, and Pennsylvania.

Films and Videos

Behind Enemy Lines (2001). Loosely based on the true-life story of Scott O'Grady, a U.S. naval aviator shot down over Bosnia during the conflict between Bosnian Muslims, Croatians, and Serbs.

Black Hawk Down (2001). Dramatization of the abortive 1993 U.S. military operation in Somalia in Africa, which resulted in the deaths of 18 Americans and hundreds of Somalis.

Courage Under Fire (1996). This fictional account of the Persian Gulf War examines the difficulty of reconstructing events during the fog of war.

The Siege (1998). This fictional film depicts the unjust internment of Arab Americans following terrorist incidents in New York City.

KEY TERMS

Al-Qaeda   (p. 894)

Globalization (p. 896)

North American Free Trade Agreement (NAFTA)   (p. 900)

Contract With America   (p. 900)

Operation Just Cause (p. 902)

Rwanda (p. 903)

Bosnia-Herzegovina (p. 903)

Kosovo (p. 903)

Taliban   (p. 906)

Department of Homeland Security   (p. 907)

PEOPLE YOU SHOULD KNOW

Michael Jordan   (p. 894)

George Herbert Walker Bush   (p. 898)

Bill Clinton   (p. 900)

Newt Gingrich   (p. 900)

George W. Bush   (p. 902)

Francis Fukuyama   (p. 902)

Manuel Noriega   (p. 902)

Saddam Hussein   (p. 903)

Slobodan Milosevic   (p. 903)

Osama bin Laden   (p. 904)

REVIEW QUESTIONS

1. What factors contributed to the resurgence of the American economy in the 1990s?

2. Why were politics in the late 1980s and 1990s characterized by especially intense partisanship?

3. In what parts of the world were violent ethnic, religious, and national conflicts unleashed after the end of the Cold War? How did the United States respond to these conflicts?

4. How did the September 11, 2001, terrorist attacks alter the way the United States looked at itself and the world?

APPENDIX

The Declaration of Independence

The Constitution of the United States of America

Amendments to the Constitution

Presidential Elections

Present Day United States

Present Day World

For additional reference material, go to **www.ablongman.com/martin5e/appendix**
The online appendix includes the following:

The Declaration of Independence
The Articles of Confederation
The Constitution of the United States of America
Amendments to the Constitution
Presidential Elections
Vice Presidents and Cabinet Members by Administration
Supreme Court Justices
Presidents, Congresses, and Chief Justices, 1789–2001
Territorial Expansion of the United States (map)
Admission of States to the Union
U.S. Population, 1790–2000
Ten Largest Cities by Population, 1700–1990
Birthrate, 1820–2000 (chart)
Death Rate, 1900–2000 (chart)
Life Expectancy, 1900–2000 (chart)
Urban/Rural Population, 1750–1900 (chart)
Women in the Labor Force, 1890–1990 (chart)
United States Physical Features (map)
United States Native Vegetation (map)
Ancient Native American Communities (map)
Native American Peoples, c. 1500 (map)
Present Day United States (map)

The Declaration of Independence

In Congress, July 4, 1776

The Unanimous Declaration of the Thirteen United States of America

When, in the course of human events, it becomes necessary for one people to dissolve the political bonds which have connected them with another, and to assume, among the powers of the earth, the separate and equal station to which the laws of nature and of nature's God entitle them, a decent respect to the opinions of mankind requires that they should declare the causes which impel them to the separation.

We hold these truths to be self-evident: That all men are created equal; that they are endowed by their Creator with certain unalienable rights; that among these are life, liberty, and the pursuit of happiness; that, to secure these rights, governments are instituted among men, deriving their just powers from the consent of the governed; that whenever any form of government becomes destructive of these ends, it is the right of the people to alter or to abolish it, and to institute new government, laying its foundation on such principles, and organizing its powers in such form, as to them shall seem most likely to effect their safety and happiness. Prudence, indeed, will dictate that governments long established should not be changed for light and transient causes; and accordingly all experience hath shown that mankind are more disposed to suffer, while evils are sufferable, than to right themselves by abolishing the forms to which they are accustomed. But when a long train of abuses and usurpations, pursuing invariably the same object, evinces a design to reduce them under absolute despotism, it is their right, it is their duty, to throw off such government, and to provide new guards for their future security. Such has been the patient sufferance of these colonies; and such is now the necessity which constrains them to alter their former systems of government. The history of the present King of Great Britain is a history of repeated injuries and usurpations, all having in direct object the establishment of an absolute tyranny over these states. To prove this, let facts be submitted to a candid world.

He has refused his assent to laws, the most wholesome and necessary for the public good.

He has forbidden his governors to pass laws of immediate and pressing importance, unless suspended in their operation till his assent should be obtained; and, when so suspended, he has utterly neglected to attend to them.

He has refused to pass other laws for the accommodation of large districts of people, unless those people would relinquish the right of representation in the legislature, a right inestimable to them, and formidable to tyrants only.

He has called together legislative bodies at places unusual, uncomfortable, and distant from the depository of their public records, for the sole purpose of fatiguing them into compliance with his measures.

He has dissolved representative houses repeatedly, for opposing, with manly firmness, his invasions on the rights of the people.

He has refused for a long time, after such dissolutions, to cause others to be elected; whereby the legislative powers, incapable of annihilation, have returned to the people at large for their exercise; the state remaining, in the mean time, exposed to all the dangers of invasions from without and convulsions within.

He has endeavored to prevent the population of these states; for that purpose obstructing the laws for naturalization of foreigners; refusing to pass others to encourage their migration hither, and raising the conditions of new appropriations of lands.

He has obstructed the administration of justice, by refusing his assent to laws for establishing judiciary powers.

He has made judges dependent on his will alone, for the tenure of their offices, and the amount and payment of their salaries.

He has erected a multitude of new offices, and sent hither swarms of officers to harass our people and eat out their substance.

He has kept among us, in times of peace, standing armies, without the consent of our legislatures.

He has affected to render the military independent of, and superior to, the civil power.

He has combined with others to subject us to a jurisdiction foreign to our constitution, and unacknowledged by our laws, giving his assent to their acts of pretended legislation:

For quartering large bodies of armed troops among us;

For protecting them, by a mock trial, from punishment for any murder which they should commit on the inhabitants of these states;

For cutting off our trade with all parts of the world;

For imposing taxes on us without our consent;

For depriving us, in many cases, of the benefits of trial by jury;

For transporting us beyond seas, to be tried for pretended offenses;

For abolishing the free system of English laws in a neighboring province, establishing therein an arbitrary government, and enlarging its boundaries, so as to render it at once an example and fit instrument for introducing the same absolute rule into these colonies;

For taking away our charters abolishing our most valuable laws, and altering fundamentally the forms of our governments;

For suspending our own legislatures, and declaring themselves invested with power to legislate for us in all cases whatsoever.

He has abdicated government here, by declaring us out of his protection and waging war against us.

He has plundered our seas, ravaged our coasts, burned our towns, and destroyed the lives of our people.

He is at this time transporting large armies of foreign mercenaries to complete the works of death, desolation, and tyranny already begun with circumstances of cruelty and perfidy scarcely paralleled in the most barbarous ages, and totally unworthy the head of a civilized nation.

He has constrained our fellow-citizens, taken captive on the high seas, to bear arms against their country, to become the executioners of their friends and brethren, or to fall themselves by their hands.

He has excited domestic insurrection among us, and has endeavored to bring on the inhabitants of our frontiers the merciless Indian savages, whose known rule of warfare is an undistinguished destruction of all ages, sexes, and conditions.

In every stage of these oppressions we have petitioned for redress in the most humble terms; our repeated petitions have been answered only by repeated injury. A prince, whose character is thus marked by every act which may define a tyrant, is unfit to be the ruler of a free people.

Nor have we been wanting in our attentions to our British brethren. We have warned them, from time to time, of attempts by their legislature to extend an unwarrantable jurisdiction over us. We have reminded them of the circumstances of our emigration and settlement here. We have appealed to their native justice and magnanimity; and we have conjured them, by the ties of our common kindred, to disavow these usurpations, which would inevitably interrupt our connections and correspondence. They, too, have been deaf to the voice of justice and of consanguinity. We must, therefore, acquiesce in the necessity which denounces our separation, and hold them, as we hold the rest of mankind, enemies in war, in peace friends.

We, therefore, the representatives of the United States of America, in General Congress assembled, appealing to the Supreme Judge of the world for the rectitude of our intentions, do, in the name and by the authority of the good people of these colonies, solemnly publish and declare, that these United Colonies are, and of right ought to be, FREE AND INDEPENDENT STATES; that they are absolved from all allegiance to the British crown, and that all political connection between them and the state of Great Britain is, and ought to be, totally dissolved; and that, as free and independent states, they have full power to levy war, conclude peace, contract alliances, establish commerce, and do all other acts and things which independent states may of right do. And for the support of this declaration, with a firm reliance on the protection of Divine Providence, we mutually pledge to each other our lives, our fortunes, and our sacred honor.

JOHN HANCOCK

BUTTON GWENNETT
LYMAN HALL
GEO. WALTON
WM. HOOPER
JOSEPH HEWES
JOHN PENN
EDWARD RUTLEDGE
THOS. HEYWARD, JUNR.
THOMAS LYNCH, JUNR.
ARTHUR MIDDLETON
SAMUEL CHASE
WM. PACA
THOS. STONE
CHARLES CARROLL OF CARROLLTON
GEORGE WYTHE
RICHARD HENRY LEE
TH. JEFFERSON
BENJA. HARRISON

THS. NELSON, JR.
FRANCIS LIGHTFOOT LEE
CARTER BRAXTON
ROBT. MORRIS
BENJAMIN RUSH
BENJA. FRANKLIN
JOHN MORTON
GEO. CLYMER
JAS. SMITH
GEO. TAYLOR
JAMES WILSON
GEO. ROSS
CAESAR RODNEY
GEO. READ
THO. M'KEAN
WM. FLOYD
PHIL. LIVINGSTON
FRANS. LEWIS
LEWIS MORRIS

RICHD. STOCKTON
JNO. WITHERSPOON
FRAS. HOPKINSON
JOHN HART
ABRA. CLARK
JOSIAH BARTLETT
WM. WHIPPLE
SAML. ADAMS
JOHN ADAMS
ROBT. TREAT PAINE
ELBRIDGE GERRY
STEP. HOPKINS
WILLIAM ELLERY
ROGER SHERMAN
SAM'EL. HUNTINGTON
WM. WILLIAMS
OLIVER WOLCOTT
MATTHEW THORNTON

The Constitution of the United States of America

PREAMBLE

We the People of the United States, in Order to form a more perfect Union, establish Justice, insure domestic Tranquility, provide for the common defence, promote the general Welfare, and secure the Blessings of Liberty to ourselves and our Posterity, do ordain and establish this Constitution for the United States of America.

ARTICLE I.

Section 1 All legislative Powers herein granted shall be vested in a Congress of the United States, which shall consist of a Senate and House of Representatives.

Section 2 The House of Representatives shall be composed of Members chosen every second Year by the People of the several States, and the Electors in each State shall have the Qualifications requisite for Electors of the most numerous Branch of the State Legislature.

No Person shall be a Representative who shall not have attained to the Age of twenty five Years, and been seven Years a Citizen of the United States, and who shall not, when elected, be an inhabitant of that State in which he shall be chosen.

Representatives and direct Taxes shall be apportioned among the several States which may be included within this Union, according to their respective Numbers, *which shall be determined by adding to the whole Number of free Persons, including those bound to Service for a Term of Years, and excluding Indians not taxed, three fifths of all other Persons.** The actual Enumeration shall be made within three Years after the first Meeting of the Congress of the United States, and within every subsequent Term of ten Years, in such Manner as they shall by Law direct. The Number of Representatives shall not exceed one for every thirty Thousand, but each State shall have at Least one Representative; *and until such enumeration shall be made, the State of New Hampshire shall be entitled to chuse three, Massachusetts eight, Rhode-Island and Providence Plantations one, Connecticut five, New York six, New Jersey four, Pennsylvania eight, Delaware one, Maryland six, Virginia ten, North Carolina five, South Carolina five, and Georgia three.*

When vacancies happen in the Representation from any State, the Executive Authority thereof shall issue Writs of Election to fill such Vacancies.

*Passages no longer in effect are printed in italic type.

The House of Representatives shall choose their Speaker and other Officers; and shall have the sole Power of Impeachment.

Section 3 The Senate of the United States shall be composed of two Senators from each State, *chosen by the Legislature thereof,* for six Years; and each Senator shall have one Vote.

Immediately after they shall be assembled in Consequence of the first Election, they shall be divided as equally as may be into three Classes. The Seats of the Senators of the first Class shall be vacated at the Expiration of the second Year, of the second Class at the Expiration of the fourth Year, and of the third Class at the Expiration of the sixth Year so that one third may be chosen every second Year; *and if Vacancies happen by Resignation, or otherwise, during the Recess of the Legislature of any state, the Executive thereof may make temporary Appointments until the next Meeting of the Legislature, which shall then fill such Vacancies.*

No Person shall be a Senator who shall not have attained to the Age of thirty Years, and been nine Years a Citizen of the United States, and who shall not, when elected, be an Inhabitant of that State for which he shall be chosen.

The Vice President of the United States shall be President of the Senate, but shall have no Vote, unless they be equally divided.

The Senate shall choose their other Officers, and also a President *pro tempore,* in the Absence of the Vice President, or when he shall exercise the Office of President of the United States.

The Senate shall have the sole Power to try all Impeachments. When sitting for that Purpose, they shall be on Oath or Affirmation. When the President of the United States is tried the Chief Justice shall preside: And no Person shall be convicted without the Concurrence of two thirds of the Members present.

Judgment in Cases of Impeachment shall not extend further than to removal from Office, and disqualification to hold and enjoy any Office of honor, Trust or Profit under the United States: but the Party convicted shall nevertheless be liable and subject to Indictment, Trial, Judgment and Punishment, according to Law.

Section 4 The Times, Places and Manner of holding Elections for Senators and Representatives, shall be prescribed in each State by the Legislature thereof; but the Congress may at any time by Law make or alter such Regulations, except as to the Places of choosing Senators.

The Congress shall assemble at least once in every Year, and such Meeting shall be on the first Monday in December, unless they shall by Law appoint a different Day.

Section 5 Each House shall be the Judge of the Elections, Returns and Qualifications of its own Members, and a Majority of each shall constitute a Quorum to do Business; but a smaller Number may adjourn from day to day, and may be authorized to compel the Attendance of absent Members, in such Manner, and under such Penalties as each House may provide.

Each House may determine the Rules of its Proceedings, punish its Members for disorderly Behaviour, and, with the Concurrence of two thirds, expel a Member.

Each House shall keep a Journal of its Proceedings, and from time to time publish the same, excepting such Parts as may in their Judgment require Secrecy; and the Yeas and Nays of the Members of either House on any question shall, at the Desire of one fifth of those Present, be entered on the Journal.

Neither House, during the Session of Congress, shall, without the Consent of the other, adjourn for more than three days, nor to any other Place than that in which the two Houses shall be sitting.

Section 6 The Senators and Representatives shall receive a Compensation for their Services, to be ascertained by Law, and paid out of the Treasury of the United States. They shall in all Cases, except Treason, Felony and Breach of the Peace, be privileged from Arrest during their Attendance at the Session of their respective Houses, and in going to and returning from the same; and for any Speech or Debate in either House, they shall not be questioned in any other Place.

No Senator or Representative shall, during the Time for which he was elected, be appointed to any civil Office under the Authority of the United States, which shall have been created, or the Emoluments whereof shall have been encreased during such time, and no Person holding any Office under the United States, shall be a Member of either House during his Continuance in Office.

Section 7 All Bills for raising Revenue shall originate in the House of Representatives; but the Senate may propose or concur with Amendments as on other Bills.

Every Bill which shall have passed the House of Representatives and the Senate, shall, before it become a Law, be presented to the President of the United States; If he approve he shall sign it, but if not he shall return it, with his Objections to the House in which it shall have originated, who shall enter the Objections at large on their Journal, and proceed to reconsider it. If after such Reconsideration two thirds of that House shall agree to pass the Bill, it shall be sent, together with the Objections, to the other House, by which it shall likewise be reconsidered, and if approved by two thirds of that House, it shall become a Law. But in all such Cases the Votes of both Houses shall be determined by Yeas and Nays, and the Names of the Persons voting for and against the Bill shall be entered on the Journal of each House respectively. If any Bill shall not be returned by the President within ten Days (Sundays excepted) after it shall have been presented to him, the Same shall be a Law, in like Manner as if he had signed it, unless the Congress by their Adjournment prevent its Return, in which Case it shall not be a Law.

Every Order, Resolution, or Vote to which the Concurrence of the Senate and House of Representatives may be necessary (except on a question of Adjournment) shall be presented to the President of the United States; and before the Same shall take Effect, shall be approved by him, or being disapproved by him, shall be repassed by two thirds of the Senate and House of Representatives, according to the Rules and Limitations prescribed in the Case of a Bill.

Section 8 The Congress shall have Power To lay and collect Taxes, Duties, Imposts and Excises, to pay the Debts and provide for the common Defence and general Welfare of the United States; but all Duties, Imposts and Excises shall be uniform throughout the United States;

To borrow Money on the credit of the United States;

To regulate Commerce with foreign Nations, and among the several States, and with the Indian Tribes;

To establish an uniform Rule of Naturalization, and uniform Laws on the subject of Bankruptcies throughout the United States;

To coin Money, regulate the Value thereof, and of foreign Coin, and fix the Standard of Weights and Measures;

To provide for the Punishment of counterfeiting the Securities and current Coin of the United States;

To establish Post Offices and post Roads;

To promote the Progress of Science and useful Arts, by securing for limited Times to Authors and Inventors the exclusive Right to their respective Writings and Discoveries;

To constitute Tribunals inferior to the supreme Court;

To define and punish Piracies and Felonies committed on the high Seas, and Offences against the Law of Nations;

To declare War, grant Letters of Marque and Reprisal, and make Rules concerning Captures on Land and Water;

To raise and support Armies, but no Appropriation of Money to that Use shall be for a longer Term than two Years;

To provide and maintain a Navy;

To make Rules for the Government and Regulation of the land and naval Forces;

To provide for calling forth the Militia to execute the Laws of the Union, suppress Insurrections and repel Invasions;

To provide for organizing, arming, and disciplining the Militia, and for governing such Part of them as may be employed in the Service of the United States, reserving to the States respectively, the Appointment of the Officers, and the Authority of training the Militia according to the discipline prescribed by Congress;

To exercise exclusive Legislation in all Cases whatsoever, over such District (not exceeding ten Miles square) as may, by Cession of particular States, and the Acceptance of Congress, become the Seat of the Government of the United States, and to exercise like Authority over all Places purchased by the Consent of the Legislature of the State in which the Same shall be, for the Erection of Forts,

Magazines, Arsenals, dock-Yards, and other needful Buildings;—And

To make all Laws which shall be necessary and proper for carrying into Execution the foregoing Powers, and all other Powers vested by this Constitution in the Government of the United States, or in any Department of Officer thereof.

Section 9 The Migration or Importation of such Persons as any of the States now existing shall think proper to admit, shall not be prohibited by the Congress prior to the Year one thousand eight hundred and eight, but a Tax or duty may be imposed on such Importation, not exceeding ten dollars for each Person.

The Privilege of the Writ of Habeas Corpus shall not be suspended, unless when in Cases of Rebellion or Invasion the public Safety may require it.

No Bill of Attainder or ex post facto Law shall be passed.

No Capitation, or other direct, Tax shall be laid, unless in Proportion to the Census or Enumeration herein before directed to be taken.

No Tax or Duty shall be laid on Articles exported from any State.

No Preference shall be given by any Regulation of Commerce or Revenue to the Ports of one State over those of another: nor shall Vessels bound to, or from, one State, be obliged to enter, clear, or pay Duties in another.

No Money shall be drawn from the Treasury, but in Consequence of Appropriations made by Law; and a regular Statement and Account of the Receipts and Expenditures of all public Money shall be published from time to time.

No Title of Nobility shall be granted by the United States: And no Person holding any Office of Profit or Trust under them, shall, without the Consent of the Congress, accept of any present, Emolument, Office, or Title, of any kind whatever, from any King, Prince, or foreign State.

Section 10 No State shall enter into any Treaty, Alliance, or Confederation; grant Letters of Marque and Reprisal; coin Money; emit Bills of Credit; make any Thing but gold and silver Coin a Tender in Payment of Debts; pass any Bill of Attainder, ex post facto Law, or Law impairing the obligation of Contracts, or grant any Title of Nobility.

No State shall, without the Consent of the Congress, lay any Imposts or Duties on Imports or Exports, except what may be absolutely necessary for executing its inspection Laws: and the net Produce of all Duties and Imposts, laid by any State on Imports or Exports, shall be for the Use of the Treasury of the United States; and all such Laws shall be subject to the Revision and Control of the Congress.

No State shall, without the Consent of Congress, lay any Duty of Tonnage, keep Troops, or Ships of War in time of Peace, enter into any Agreement or Compact with another State, or with a foreign Power, or engage in War, unless actually invaded, or in such imminent Danger as will not admit of delay.

ARTICLE II.

Section 1 The executive Power shall be vested in a President of the United States of America. He shall hold his Office during the Term of four Years, and, together with the Vice President, chosen for the same Term, be elected, as follows:

Each State shall appoint, in such Manner as the Legislature thereof may direct, a Number of Electors, equal to the whole Number of Senators and Representatives to which the State may be entitled in the Congress: but no Senator or Representative, or Person holding an Office of Trust or Profit under the United States, shall be appointed an Elector.

The Electors shall meet in their respective States, and vote by Ballot for two Persons, of whom one at least shall not be an Inhabitant of the same State with themselves. And they shall make a List of all the Persons voted for, and of the Number of Votes for each; which List they shall sign and certify, and transmit sealed to the Seat of the Government of the United States, directed to the President of the Senate. The President of the Senate shall, in the Presence of the Senate and House of Representatives, open all the Certificates, and the Votes shall then be counted. The Person having the greatest Number of Votes shall be the President, if such Number be a Majority of the whole number of Electors appointed; and if there be more than one who have such Majority, and have an equal Number of Votes, then the House of Representative shall immediately choose by Ballot one of them for President; and if no Person have a Majority, then from the five highest on the List the said House shall in like Manner choose the President. But in choosing the President, the Votes shall be taken by States, the Representation from each State having one Vote; A quorum for this Purpose shall consist of a Member or Members from two thirds of the States, and a Majority of all the States shall be necessary to a Choice. In every Case, after the Choice of the President, the Person having the greatest Number of Votes of the Electors shall be the Vice President. But if there should remain two or more who have equal Votes, the Senate shall choose from them by Ballot the Vice President.

The Congress may determine the time of choosing the Electors, and the Day on which they shall give their Votes; which Day shall be the same throughout the United States.

No person except a natural born Citizen, *or a Citizen of the United States, at the time of the Adoption of this Constitution,* shall be eligible to the Office of President; neither shall any Person be eligible to that Office who shall not have attained to the Age of thirty five Years, and been fourteen Years a Resident within the United States.

In Case of the Removal of the President from Office, or of his Death, Resignation, or Inability to discharge the Powers and Duties of the said Office, the Same shall devolve on the Vice President, and the Congress may by Law provide for the Case of Removal, Death, Resignation or Inability, both of the President and Vice President, declaring what Officer shall then act as President, and such Officer shall act accordingly, until the Disability be removed, or a President shall be elected.

The President shall, at stated Times, receive for his Services, a Compensation, which shall neither be encreased nor diminished during the Period for which he shall have been elected, and he shall not receive within that period any other Emolument from the United States, or any of them.

Before he enter on the Execution of his Office, he shall take the following Oath or Affirmation:—"I do solemnly swear (or affirm) that I will faithfully execute the Office of President of the United States, and will to the best of my Ability, preserve, protect and defend the Constitution of the United States."

Section 2 The President shall be Commander in Chief of the Army and Navy of the United States, and of the Militia of the several States, when called into the actual Service of the United States; he may require the Opinion, in writing, of the principal Officer in each of the executive Departments, upon any Subject relating to the Duties of their respective Offices, and he shall have Power to grant Reprieves and Pardons for Offences against the United States, except in Cases of Impeachment.

He shall have Power, by and with the Advice and Consent of the Senate, to make Treaties, provided two thirds of the Senators present concur; and he shall nominate, and by and with the Advice and Consent of the Senate, shall appoint Ambassadors, other public Ministers and Consuls, Judges of the supreme Court, and all other Officers of the United States, whose Appointments are not herein otherwise provided for, and which shall be established by Law: but the Congress may by Law vest the Appointment of such inferior Officers, as they think proper in the President alone, in the Courts of Law, or in the Heads of Departments.

The President shall have Power to fill up all Vacancies that may happen during the Recess of the Senate, by granting Commissions which shall expire at the End of their next Session.

Section 3 He shall from time to time give to the Congress Information of the State of the Union, and recommend to their Consideration such Measures as he shall judge necessary and expedient; he may, on extraordinary Occasions, convene both Houses, or either of them, and in Case of disagreement between them, with Respect to the Time of Adjournment, he may adjourn them to such Time as he shall think proper; he shall receive Ambassadors and other public Ministers; he shall take Care that the Laws be faithfully executed, and shall Commission all the officers of the United States.

Section 4 The President, Vice President and all civil Officers of the United States, shall be removed from Office on Impeachment for, and Conviction of, Treason, Bribery or other high Crimes and Misdemeanors.

ARTICLE III.

Section 1 The judicial Power of the United States, shall be vested in one supreme Court, and in such inferior Courts as the Congress may from time to time ordain and establish. The Judges, both of the supreme and inferior Courts, shall hold their offices during good Behaviour, and shall, at stated Times, receive for their Services, a Compensation, which shall not be diminished during their Continuance in Office.

Section 2 The judicial Power shall extend to all Cases, in Law and Equity, arising under this Constitution, the Laws of the United States, and Treaties made, or which shall be made, under their Authority;—to all Cases affecting Ambassadors, other public Ministers and Consuls;—to all Cases of admiralty and maritime Jurisdiction;—to Controversies to which the United States shall be a Party;—to Controversies between two or more States;—between a State and Citizens of another State;—between Citizens of different States,—between Citizens of the same State claiming Lands under Grants of different States, and between a State, or the Citizens thereof, and foreign States, Citizens or Subjects.

In all Cases affecting Ambassadors, other public Ministers and Consuls, and those in which a State shall be Party, the supreme Court shall have original Jurisdiction. In all the other Cases before mentioned, the supreme Court shall have appellate Jurisdiction, both as to Law and Fact, with such Exceptions, and under such Regulations as the Congress shall make.

The Trial of all Crimes, except in Cases of Impeachment, shall be by Jury; and such Trial shall be held in the State where the said Crimes shall have been committed, but when not committed within any State, the Trial shall be at such Place or Places as the Congress may by Law have directed.

Section 3 Treason against the United States, shall consist only in levying War against them, or in adhering to their Enemies, giving them Aid and Comfort. No person shall be convicted of Treason unless on the Testimony of two Witnesses to the same overt Act, or on Confession in open Court.

The Congress shall have Power to declare the Punishment of Treason, but no Attainder of Treason shall work Corruption of Blood, or Forfeiture except during the Life of the Person attainted.

ARTICLE IV.

Section 1 Full Faith and Credit shall be given in each State to the public Acts, Records, and judicial Proceedings of every other State. And the Congress may be general Laws prescribe the Manner in which such Acts, Records and Proceedings shall be proved, and the Effect thereof.

Section 2 The Citizens of each State shall be entitled to all Privileges and Immunities of Citizens in the several States.

A Person charged in any State with Treason, Felony, or other Crime, who shall flee from Justice, and be found in another State, shall on Demand of the executive Authority of the State from which he fled, be delivered up, to be removed to the State having Jurisdiction of the Crime.

No Person held to Service or Labour in one State, under the Laws thereof, escaping into another, shall, in Consequence of any Law or Regulation therein, be discharged from such Service or Labour, but shall be delivered up on Claim of the Party to whom such Service or Labour may be due.

Section 3 New States may be admitted by the Congress into this Union; but no new State shall be formed or erected within the Jurisdiction of any other State; nor any

State be formed by the Junction of two or more States, or Parts of States, without the Consent of the Legislatures of the States concerned as well as of the Congress.

The Congress shall have Power to dispose of and make all needful Rules and Regulations respecting the Territory or other Property belonging to the United States; and nothing in this Constitution shall be so construed as to Prejudice any Claims of the United States, or of any particular States.

Section 4 The United States shall guarantee to every State in this Union a Republican Form of Government, and shall protect each of them against Invasion; and on Application of the Legislature, or of the Executive (when the Legislature cannot be convened) against domestic violence.

ARTICLE V.

The Congress, whenever two thirds of both Houses shall deem it necessary, shall propose Amendments to this Constitution, or, on the Application of the Legislatures of two thirds of the several States, shall call a Convention for proposing Amendments, which, in either Case, shall be valid to all Intents and Purposes, as Part of this Constitution, when ratified by the Legislatures of three fourths of the several States, or by Conventions in three fourths thereof, as the one or the other Mode of Ratification may be proposed by the Congress; Provided *that no Amendment which may be made prior to the Year One thousand eight hundred and eight shall in any Manner affect the first and fourth Clauses in the Ninth Section of the first Article;* and that no State without its Consent, shall be deprived of its equal Suffrage in the Senate.

ARTICLE VI.

All Debts contracted and Engagements entered into, before the Adoption of this Constitution, shall be as valid against the United States under this Constitution, as under the Confederation.

This Constitution, and Laws of the United States which shall be made in Pursuance thereof; and all Treaties made, or which shall be made, under the Authority of the United States, shall be the supreme Law of the Land; and the Judges in every State shall be bound thereby, any Thing in the Constitution or Laws of any State to the Contrary notwithstanding.

The Senators and Representatives before mentioned, and the Members of the several State Legislatures, and all executive and Judicial Officers, both of the United States and of the several States, shall be bound by Oath or Affirmation, to support this Constitution; but no religious Test shall ever be required as a Qualification to any Office of public Trust under the United States.

ARTICLE VII.

The Ratification of the Conventions of nine States, shall be sufficient for the Establishment of this Constitution—between the States so ratifying the Same.

Done in Convention by the Unanimous Consent of the States present the Seventeenth Day of September in the Year of our Lord one thousand seven hundred and Eighty seven and of the Independence of the United States of America the Twelfth IN WITNESS whereof We have hereunto subscribed our Names,

GEORGE WASHINGTON,
President and Deputy from Virginia

New Hampshire
JOHN LANGDON
NICHOLAS GILMAN

Massachusetts
NATHANIEL GORHAM
RUFUS KING

Connecticut
WILLIAM S. JOHNSON
ROGER SHERMAN

New York
ALEXANDER HAMILTON

New Jersey
WILLIAM LIVINGSTON
DAVID BREARLEY
WILLIAM PATERSON
JONATHAN DAYTON

Pennsylvania
BENJAMIN FRANKLIN
THOMAS MIFFLIN
ROBERT MORRIS
GEORGE CLYMER
THOMAS FITZSIMONS
JARED INGERSOLL
JAMES WILSON
GOUVERNEUR MORRIS

Delaware
GEORGE READ
GUNNING BEDFORD, JR.
JOHN DICKINSON
RICHARD BASSETT
JACOB BROOM

Maryland
JAMES MCHENRY
DANIEL OF ST. THOMAS JENIFER
DANIEL CARROLL

Virginia
JOHN BLAIR
JAMES MADISON, JR.

North Carolina
WILLIAM BLOUNT
RICHARD DOBBS SPRAIGHT
HU WILLIAMSON

South Carolina
J. RUTLEDGE
CHARLES C. PINCKNEY
PIERCE BUTLER

Georgia
WILLIAM FEW
ABRAHAM BALDWIN

Amendments to the Constitution

The first ten amendments (the Bill of Rights) were adopted in 1791.

AMENDMENT I

Congress shall make no law respecting an establishment of religion, or prohibiting the free exercise thereof; or abridging the freedom of speech, or of the press; or the right of the people peaceably to assemble, and to petition the Government for a redress of grievances.

AMENDMENT II

A well regulated Militia being necessary to the security of a free State, the right of the people to keep and bear Arms, shall not be infringed.

AMENDMENT III

No Soldier shall, in time of peace be quartered in any house, without the consent of the Owner, nor in time of war, but in a manner to be prescribed by law.

AMENDMENT IV

The right of the people to be secure in their persons, houses, papers, and effects, against unreasonable searches and seizures, shall not be violated, and no Warrants shall issue, but upon probable cause, supported by Oath or affirmation, and particularly describing the place to be searched, and the persons or things to be seized.

AMENDMENT V

No person shall be held to answer for a capital, or otherwise infamous crime, unless on a presentment or indictment of a Grand Jury, except in cases arising in the land or naval forces, or in the Militia, when in actual service in time of War or public danger; nor shall any person be subject for the same offense to be twice put in jeopardy of life or limb; nor shall be compelled in any criminal case to be a witness against himself, nor be deprived of life, liberty, or property, without due process of law; nor shall private property be taken for public use, without just compensation.

AMENDMENT VI

In all criminal prosecutions, the accused shall enjoy the right to a speedy and public trial, by an impartial jury of the State and district wherein the crime shall have been committed, which district shall have been previously ascertained by law, and to be informed of the nature and cause of the accusation; to be confronted with the witnesses against him; to have compulsory process for obtaining witnesses in his favor, and to have the Assistance of Counsel for his defence.

AMENDMENT VII

In Suits at common law, where the value in controversy shall exceed twenty dollars, the right of trial by jury shall be preserved, and no fact trial by a jury, shall be otherwise re-examined in any Court of the United States, than according to the rules of the common law.

AMENDMENT VIII

Excessive bail shall not be required, nor excessive fines imposed, nor cruel and unusual punishments inflicted.

AMENDMENT IX

The enumeration in the Constitution, of certain rights, shall not be construed to deny or disparage others retained by the people.

AMENDMENT X

The powers not delegated to the United States by the Constitution, nor prohibited by it to the States, are reserved to the States respectively, or to the people.

AMENDMENT XI

[Adopted 1798]

The Judicial power of the United States shall not be construed to extend to any suit in law or equity, commenced or prosecuted against one of the United States by Citizens of another State, or by Citizens or Subjects of any Foreign State.

Amendment XII

[Adopted 1804]

The Electors shall meet in their respective states, and vote by ballot for President and Vice-President, one of whom, at least, shall not be an inhabitant of the same state with themselves; they shall name in their ballots the person voted for as President, and in distinct ballots the person voted for as Vice-President, and they shall make distinct lists of all persons voted for as President, and of all persons voted for as Vice-President, and of the number of votes for each, which lists they shall sign and certify, and transmit sealed to the seat of the government of the United States, directed to the President of the Senate;—The President of the Senate shall, in the presence of the Senate and House of Representatives, open all the certificates and the votes shall then be counted;—The person having the greatest number of votes for President, shall be the President, if such number be a majority of the whole number of Electors appointed; and if no person have such majority, then from the persons having the highest numbers not exceeding three on the list of those voted for as President, the House of Representatives shall choose immediately, by ballot, the President. But in choosing the President, the votes shall be taken by states, the representation from each state having one vote; a quorum for this purpose shall consist of a member or members from two-thirds of the states, and a majority of all the states shall be necessary to a choice. And if the House of Representatives shall not choose a President whenever the right of choice shall devolve upon them, before *the fourth day of March* next following, then the Vice-President shall act as President, as in the case of the death or other constitutional disability of the President.—The person having the greatest number of votes as Vice-President, shall be the Vice-President, if such number be a majority of the whole number of Electors appointed, and if no person have a majority, then from the two highest numbers on the list, the Senate shall choose the Vice-President; a quorum for the purpose shall consist of two-thirds of the whole number of Senators, and a majority of the whole number shall be necessary to a choice. But no person constitutionally ineligible to the office of President shall be eligible to that of Vice President of the United States.

Amendment XIII

[Adopted 1865]

Section 1   Neither slavery nor involuntary servitude, except as a punishment for crime whereof the party shall have been duly convicted, shall exist within the United States, or any place subject to their jurisdiction.

Section 2   Congress shall have power to enforce this article by appropriate legislation.

Amendment XIV

[Adopted 1868]

Section 1   All persons born or naturalized in the United States, and subject to the jurisdiction thereof, are citizens of the United States and of the State wherein they reside. No State shall make or enforce any law which shall abridge the privileges or immunities of citizens of the United States; nor shall any State deprive any person of life, liberty, or property, without due process of law; nor deny to any person within its jurisdiction the equal protection of the laws.

Section 2   Representatives shall be apportioned among the several States according to their respective numbers, counting the whole number of persons in each State, excluding Indians not taxed. But when the right to vote at any election for the choice of electors for President and Vice-President of the United States, Representatives in Congress, the Executive and Judicial officers of a State, or the members of the Legislature thereof, is denied to any of the male inhabitants of such State, being twenty-one years of age, and citizens of the United States, or in any way abridged, except for participation in rebellion, or other crime, the basis of representation therein shall be reduced in the proportion which the number of such male citizens shall bear to the whole number of male citizens twenty-one years of age in such State.

Section 3   No person shall be a Senator or Representative in Congress, or elector of President and Vice-President, or hold any office, civil or military, under the United States, or under any State, who, having previously taken an oath, as a member of Congress, or as an officer of the United States, or as a member of any State legislature, or as an executive or judicial officer of any State, to support the Constitution of the United States, shall have engaged in insurrection or rebellion against the same, or given aid or comfort to the enemies thereof. But Congress may by a vote of two-thirds of each House, remove such disability.

Section 4   The validity of the public debt of the United States, authorized by law, including debts incurred for payment of pensions and bounties for services in suppressing insurrection or rebellion, shall not be questioned. But neither the United States nor any State shall assume or pay any debt or obligation incurred in aid of insurrection or rebellion against the United States, or any claim for the loss or emancipation of any slave; but all such debts, obligations and claims shall be held illegal and void.

Section 5   The Congress shall have power to enforce, by appropriate legislation, the provisions of this article.

Amendment XV

[Adopted 1870]

Section 1   The right of citizens of the United States to vote shall not be denied or abridged by the United States or by any State on account of race, color, or previous condition of servitude.

Section 2 The Congress shall have power to enforce this article by appropriate legislation.

AMENDMENT XVI

[Adopted 1913]

The Congress shall have power to lay and collect taxes on incomes, from whatever source derived, without apportionment among the several States, and without regard to any census or enumeration.

AMENDMENT XVII

[Adopted 1913]

The Senate of the United States shall be composed of two Senators from each State, elected by the people thereof, for six years; and each Senator shall have one vote. The electors in each State shall have the qualifications requisite for electors of the most numerous branch of the State legislatures.

When vacancies happen in the representation of any State in the Senate, the executive authority of such State shall issue writs of election to fill such vacancies: *Provided,* That the legislature of any State may empower the executive thereof to make temporary appointments until the people fill the vacancies by election as the legislature may direct.

This amendment shall not be so construed as to affect the election or term of any Senator chosen before it becomes valid as part of the Constitution.

AMENDMENT XVIII

[Adopted 1919, Repealed 1933]

Section 1 After one year from the ratification of this article the manufacture, sale, or transportation of intoxicating liquors within, the importation thereof into, or the exportation thereof from the United States and all territory subject to the jurisdiction thereof for beverage purposes is hereby prohibited.

Section 2 The Congress and the several States shall have concurrent power to enforce this article by appropriate legislation.

Section 3 This article shall be inoperative unless it shall have been ratified as an amendment to the Constitution by the legislatures of the several States, as provided in the Constitution, within seven years from the date of the submission hereof to the States by the Congress.

AMENDMENT XIX

[Adopted 1920]

Section 1 The right of citizens of the United States to vote shall not be denied or abridged by the United States or by any State on account of sex.

Section 2 Congress shall have power to enforce this article by appropriate legislation.

AMENDMENT XX

[Adopted 1933]

Section 1 The terms of the President and Vice-President shall end at noon on the 20th day of January, and the terms of Senators and Representatives at noon on the 3d day of January, of the years in which such terms would have ended if this article had not been ratified and the terms of their successors shall then begin.

Section 2 The Congress shall assemble at least once in every year, and such meeting shall begin at noon on the 3d day of January, unless they shall by law appoint a different day.

Section 3 If, at the time fixed for the beginning of the term of the President, the President elect shall have died, the Vice-President elect shall become President. If a President shall not have been chosen before the time fixed for the beginning of his term, or if the President elect shall have failed to qualify, then the Vice-President elect shall act as President until a President shall have qualified; and the Congress may by law provide for the case wherein neither a President elect nor a Vice-President elect shall have qualified, declaring who shall then act as President, or the manner in which one who is to act shall be selected, and such person shall act accordingly until a President or Vice-President shall have qualified.

Section 4 The Congress may by law provide for the case of the death of any of the persons from whom the House of Representatives may choose a President whenever the right of choice shall have devolved upon them, and for the case of the death of any of the persons from whom the Senate may choose a Vice-President whenever the right of choice shall have devolved upon them.

Section 5 Sections 1 and 2 shall take effect on the 15th day of October following the ratification of this article.

Section 6 This article shall be inoperative unless it shall have been ratified as an amendment to the Constitution by the legislatures of three fourths of the several States within seven years from the date of its submission.

AMENDMENT XXI

[Adopted 1933]

Section 1 The eighteenth article of amendment to the Constitution of the United States is hereby repealed.

Section 2 The transportation or importation into any State, Territory, or possession of the United States for delivery or use therein of intoxicating liquors in violation of the laws thereof, is hereby prohibited.

Section 3 This article shall be inoperative unless it shall have been ratified as an amendment to the Constitution by conventions in the several States, as provided in the Constitution, within seven years from the date of the submission hereof to the States by the Congress.

AMENDMENT XXII

[Adopted 1951]

Section 1 No person shall be elected to the office of the President more than twice, and no person who has held the office of President, or acted as President, for more than two years of a term to which some other person was elected President shall be elected to the office of the President more than once. But this Article shall not apply to any person holding the office of President when this Article was proposed by the Congress, and shall not prevent any person who may be holding the office of President, or acting as President, during the term within which this Article becomes operative from holding the office of President or acting as President during the remainder of such term.

Section 2 This article shall be inoperative unless it shall have been ratified as an amendment to the Constitution by the legislatures of three-fourths of the several States within several years from the date of its submission to the States within seven years from the date of its submission to the States by the Congress.

AMENDMENT XXIII

[Adopted 1961]

Section 1 The District constituting the seat of Government of the United States shall appoint in such manner as the Congress shall direct:

A number of electors of President and Vice-President equal to the whole number of Senators and Representatives in Congress to which the District would be entitled if it were a State, but in no event more than the least populous State; they shall be in addition to those appointed by the States, but they shall be considered, for the purposes of the election of President and Vice-President, to be electors appointed by a State; and they shall meet in the District and perform such duties as provided by the twelfth article of amendment.

Section 2 The Congress shall have power to enforce this article by appropriate legislation.

AMENDMENT XXIV

[Adopted 1964]

Section 1 The right of citizens of the United States to vote in any primary or other election for President or Vice-President, for electors for President or Vice-President, or for Senator or Representative in Congress, shall not be denied or abridged by the United States or any state by reason of failure to pay any poll tax or other tax.

Section 2 The Congress shall have the power to enforce this article by appropriate legislation.

AMENDMENT XXV

[Adopted 1967]

Section 1 In case of the removal of the President from office or his death or resignation, the Vice-President shall become President.

Section 2 Whenever there is a vacancy in the office of the Vice-President, the President shall nominate a Vice-President who shall take the office upon confirmation by a majority vote of both houses of Congress.

Section 3 Whenever the President transmits to the President pro tempore of the Senate and the Speaker of the House of Representatives his written declaration that he is unable to discharge the powers and duties of his office, and until he transmits to them a written declaration to the contrary, such powers and duties shall be discharged by the Vice-President as Acting President.

Section 4 Whenever the Vice-President and a majority of either the principal officers of the executive departments or of such other body as Congress may by law provide, transmit to the President pro tempore of the Senate and the Speaker of the House of Representatives their written declaration that the President is unable to discharge the powers and duties of his office, the Vice-President shall immediately assume the powers and duties of the office as Acting President.

Thereafter, when the President transmits to the President pro tempore of the Senate and the Speaker of the House of Representatives his written declaration that no inability exists, he shall resume the powers and duties of his office unless the Vice-President and a majority of either the principal officers of the executive department or of such other body as Congress may by law provide, transmit within four days to the President pro tempore of the Senate and the Speaker of the House of Representatives their written declaration that the President is unable to discharge the powers and duties of his office. Thereupon Congress shall decide the issue, assembling within 48 hours for that purpose if not in session. If the Congress, within 21 days after receipt of the latter written declaration, or, if Congress is not in session, within 21 days after Congress is required to assemble, determines by two-thirds vote of both houses that the President is unable to discharge the powers and duties of his office, the Vice-President shall continue to discharge the same as Acting President; otherwise, the President shall resume the powers and duties of his office.

AMENDMENT **XXVI**

[Adopted 1971]

Section 1   The right of citizens of the United States, who are 18 years of age or older, to vote shall not be denied or abridged by the United States or any state on account of age.

Section 2   The Congress shall have the power to enforce this article by appropriate legislation.

AMENDMENT **XXVII**

[Adopted 1992]

No law varying the compensation for the services of the Senators and Representatives shall take effect, until an election of Representatives shall have intervened.

Presidential Elections

Year	Candidates	Parties	Popular Vote	Electoral Vote	Voter Participation
1789	**GEORGE WASHINGTON**		*	69	
	John Adams			34	
	Others			35	
1792	**GEORGE WASHINGTON**		*	132	
	John Adams			77	
	George Clinton			50	
	Others			5	
1796	**JOHN ADAMS**	Federalist	*	71	
	Thomas Jefferson	Democratic-Republican		68	
	Thomas Pinckney	Federalist		59	
	Aaron Burr	Dem.-Rep.		30	
	Others			48	
1800	**THOMAS JEFFERSON**	Dem.-Rep.	*	73	
	Aaron Burr	Dem.-Rep.		73	
	John Adams	Federalist		65	
	C. C. Pinckney	Federalist		64	
	John Jay	Federalist		1	
1804	**THOMAS JEFFERSON**	Dem.-Rep.	*	162	
	C. C. Pinckney	Federalist		14	
1808	**JAMES MADISON**	Dem.-Rep.	*	122	
	C. C. Pinckney	Federalist		47	
	George Clinton	Dem.-Rep.		6	
1812	**JAMES MADISON**	Dem.-Rep.	*	128	
	De Witt Clinton	Federalist		89	
1816	**JAMES MONROE**	Dem.-Rep.	*	183	
	Rufus King	Federalist		34	
1820	**JAMES MONROE**	Dem.-Rep.	*	231	
	John Quincy Adams	Dem.-Rep.		1	
1824	**JOHN Q. ADAMS**	Dem.-Rep.	108,740 (30.5%)	84	26.9%
	Andrew Jackson	Dem.-Rep.	153,544 (43.1%)	99	
	William H. Crawford	Dem.-Rep.	46,618 (13.1%)	41	
	Henry Clay	Dem.-Rep.	47,136 (13.2%)	37	
1828	**ANDREW JACKSON**	Democratic	647,286 (56.0%)	178	57.6%
	John Quincy Adams	National Republican	508,064 (44.0%)	83	
1832	**ANDREW JACKSON**	Democratic	687,502 (55.0%)	219	55.4%
	Henry Clay	National Republican	530,189 (42.4%)	49	
	John Floyd	Independent		11	
	William Wirt	Anti-Mason	33,108 (2.6%)	7	
1836	**MARTIN VAN BUREN**	Democratic	765,483 (50.9%)	170	57.8%
	W. H. Harrison	Whig		73	
	Hugh L. White	Whig	739,795 (49.1%)	26	
	Daniel Webster	Whig		14	
	W. P. Magnum	Independent		11	
1840	**WILLIAM H. HARRISON**	Whig	1,274,624 (53.1%)	234	80.2%
	Martin Van Buren	Democratic	1,127,781 (46.9%)	60	
	J. G. Birney	Liberty	7069	—	

*Electors selected by state legislatures

Year	Candidates	Parties	Popular Vote	Electoral Vote	Voter Participation
1844	**JAMES K. POLK**	Democratic	1,338,464 (49.6%)	170	78.9%
	Henry Clay	Whig	1,300,097 (48.1%)	105	
	J. G. Birney	Liberty	62,300 (2.3%)	—	
1848	**ZACHARY TAYLOR**	Whig	1,360,967 (47.4%)	163	72.7%
	Lewis Cass	Democratic	1,222,342 (42.5%)	127	
	Martin Van Buren	Free-Soil	291,263 (10.1%)	—	
1852	**FRANKLIN PIERCE**	Democratic	1,601,117 (50.9%)	254	69.6%
	Winfield Scott	Whig	1,385,453 (44.1%)	42	
	John P. Hale	Free-Soil	155,825 (5.0%)	—	
1856	**JAMES BUCHANAN**	Democratic	1,832,955 (45.3%)	174	78.9%
	John C. Frémont	Republican	1,339,932 (33.1%)	114	
	Millard Fillmore	American	871,731 (21.6%)	8	
1860	**ABRAHAM LINCOLN**	Republican	1,865,593 (39.8%)	180	81.2%
	Stephen A. Douglas	Democratic	1,382,713 (29.5%)	12	
	John C. Breckinridge	Democratic	848,356 (18.1%)	72	
	John Bell	Union	592,906 (12.6%)	39	
1864	**ABRAHAM LINCOLN**	Republican	2,213,655 (55.0%)	212	73.8%
	George B. McClellan	Democratic	1,805,237 (45.0%)	21	
1868	**ULYSSES S. GRANT**	Republican	3,012,833 (52.7%)	214	78.1%
	Horatio Seymour	Democratic	2,703,249 (47.3%)	80	
1872	**ULYSSES S. GRANT**	Republican	3,597,132 (55.6%)	286	71.3%
	Horace Greeley	Democratic	2,834,125 (43.9%)	66	
1876	**RUTHERFORD B. HAYES**	Republican	4,034,311 (48.0%)	185	81.8%
	Samuel J. Tilden	Democratic	4,288,546 (51.0%)	184	
1880	**JAMES A. GARFIELD**	Republican	4,454,416 (48.5%)	214	79.4%
	Winfield S. Hancock	Democratic	4,444,952 (48.1%)	155	
1884	**GROVER CLEVELAND**	Democratic	4,874,986 (48.5%)	219	77.5%
	James G. Blaine	Republican	4,851,981 (48.2%)	182	
1888	**BENJAMIN HARRISON**	Republican	5,439,853 (47.9%)	233	79.3%
	Grover Cleveland	Democratic	5,540,309 (48.6%)	168	
1892	**GROVER CLEVELAND**	Democratic	5,556,918 (46.1%)	277	74.7%
	Benjamin Harrison	Republican	5,176,108 (43.0%)	145	
	James B. Weaver	People's	1,041,028 (8.5%)	22	
1896	**WILLIAM McKINLEY**	Republican	7,104,779 (51.1%)	271	79.3%
	William J. Bryan	Democratic People's	6,502,925 (47.7%)	176	
1900	**WILLIAM McKINLEY**	Republican	7,207,923 (51.7%)	292	73.2%
	William J. Bryan	Dem.-Populist	6,358,133 (45.5%)	155	
1904	**THEODORE ROOSEVELT**	Republican	7,623,486 (57.9%)	336	65.2%
	Alton B. Parker	Democratic	5,077,911 (37.6%)	140	
	Eugene V. Debs	Socialist	402,283 (3.0%)	—	
1908	**WILLIAM H. TAFT**	Republican	7,678,908 (51.6%)	321	65.4%
	William J. Bryan	Democratic	6,409,104 (43.1%)	162	
	Eugene V. Debs	Socialist	420,793 (2.8%)	—	
1912	**WOODROW WILSON**	Democratic	6,293,454 (41.9%)	435	58.8%
	Theodore Roosevelt	Progressive	4,119,538 (27.4%)	88	
	William H. Taft	Republican	3,484,980 (23.2%)	8	
	Eugene V. Debs	Socialist	900,672 (6.0%)	—	
1916	**WOODROW WILSON**	Democratic	9,129,606 (49.4%)	277	61.6%
	Charles E. Hughes	Republican	8,538,221 (46.2%)	254	
	A. L. Benson	Socialist	585,113 (3.2%)	—	
1920	**WARREN G. HARDING**	Republican	16,152,200 (60.4%)	404	49.2%
	James M. Cox	Democratic	9,147,353 (34.2%)	127	
	Eugene V. Debs	Socialist	919,799 (3.4%)	—	
1924	**CALVIN COOLIDGE**	Republican	15,725,016 (54.0%)	382	48.9%
	John W. Davis	Democratic	8,386,503 (28.8%)	136	
	Robert M. La Follette	Progressive	4,822,856 (16.6%)	13	

Year	Candidates	Parties	Popular Vote	Electoral Vote	Voter Participation
1928	HERBERT HOOVER	Republican	21,391,381 (58.2%)	444	56.9%
	Alfred E. Smith	Democratic	15,016,443 (40.9%)	87	
	Norman Thomas	Socialist	267,835 (0.7%)	—	
1932	FRANKLIN D. ROOSEVELT	Democratic	22,821,857 (57.4%)	472	56.9%
	Herbert Hoover	Republican	15,761,841 (39.7%)	59	
	Norman Thomas	Socialist	881,951 (2.2%)	—	
1936	FRANKLIN D. ROOSEVELT	Democratic	27,751,597 (60.8%)	523	61.0%
	Alfred M. Landon	Republican	16,679,583 (36.5%)	8	
	William Lemke	Union	882,479 (1.9%)	—	
1940	FRANKLIN D. ROOSEVELT	Democratic	27,244,160 (54.8%)	449	62.5%
	Wendell L. Willkie	Republican	22,305,198 (44.8%)	82	
1944	FRANKLIN D. ROOSEVELT	Democratic	25,602,504 (53.5%)	432	55.9%
	Thomas E. Dewey	Republican	22,006,285 (46.0%)	99	
1948	HARRY S TRUMAN	Democratic	24,105,695 (49.5%)	304	53.0%
	Thomas E. Dewey	Republican	21,969,170 (45.1%)	189	
	J. Strom Thurmond	State-Rights Democratic	1,169,021 (2.4%)	38	
	Henry A. Wallace	Progressive	1,156,103 (2.4%)	—	
1952	DWIGHT D. EISENHOWER	Republican	33,936,252 (55.1%)	442	63.3%
	Adlai E. Stevenson	Democratic	27,314,992 (44.4%)	89	
1956	DWIGHT D. EISENHOWER	Republican	35,575,420 (57.6%)	457	60.6%
	Adlai E. Stevenson	Democratic	26,033,066 (42.1%)	73	
	Other	—	—	1	
1960	JOHN F. KENNEDY	Democratic	34,227,096 (49.9%)	303	62.8%
	Richard M. Nixon	Republican	34,108,546 (49.6%)	219	
	Other	—	—	15	
1964	LYNDON B. JOHNSON	Democratic	43,126,506 (61.1%)	486	61.7%
	Barry M. Goldwater	Republican	27,176,799 (38.5%)	52	
1968	RICHARD M. NIXON	Republican	31,770,237 (43.4%)	301	60.6%
	Hubert H. Humphrey	Democratic	31,270,533 (42.7%)	191	
	George Wallace	American Indep.	9,906,141 (13.5%)	46	
1972	RICHARD M. NIXON	Republican	47,169,911 (60.7%)	520	55.2%
	George S. McGovern	Democratic	29,170,383 (37.5%)	17	
	Other	—	—	1	
1976	JIMMY CARTER	Democratic	40,828,587 (50.0%)	297	53.5%
	Gerald R. Ford	Republican	39,147,613 (47.9%)	241	
	Other	—	1,575,459 (2.1%)	—	
1980	RONALD REAGAN	Republican	43,901,812 (50.7%)	489	52.6%
	Jimmy Carter	Democratic	35,483,820 (41.0%)	49	
	John B. Anderson	Independent	5,719,722 (6.6%)	—	
	Ed Clark	Libertarian	921,188 (1.1%)	—	
1984	RONALD REAGAN	Republican	54,455,075 (59.0%)	525	53.3%
	Walter Mondale	Democratic	37,577,185 (41.0%)	13	
1988	GEORGE H. W. BUSH	Republican	48,886,000 (53.4%)	426	57.4%
	Michael S. Dukakis	Democratic	41,809,000 (45.6%)	111	
1992	BILL CLINTON	Democratic	43,728,375 (43%)	370	55.0%
	George H. W. Bush	Republican	38,167,416 (38%)	168	
	H. Ross Perot	Independent	19,237,247 (19%)	—	
1996	BILL CLINTON	Democratic	47,402,357 (49%)	379	49.0%
	Robert Dole	Republican	39,198,755 (41%)	159	
	H. Ross Perot	Reform	8,085,402 (8%)	—	
2000	GEORGE W. BUSH	Republican	50,456,167 (47.88%)	271	51.2%
	Al Gore	Democratic	50,996,064 (48.39%)	266*	
	Ralph Nader	Green	2,864,810 (2.72%)	—	
	Other	—	834,774 (< 1%)	—	

*One District of Columbia Gore elector abstained.

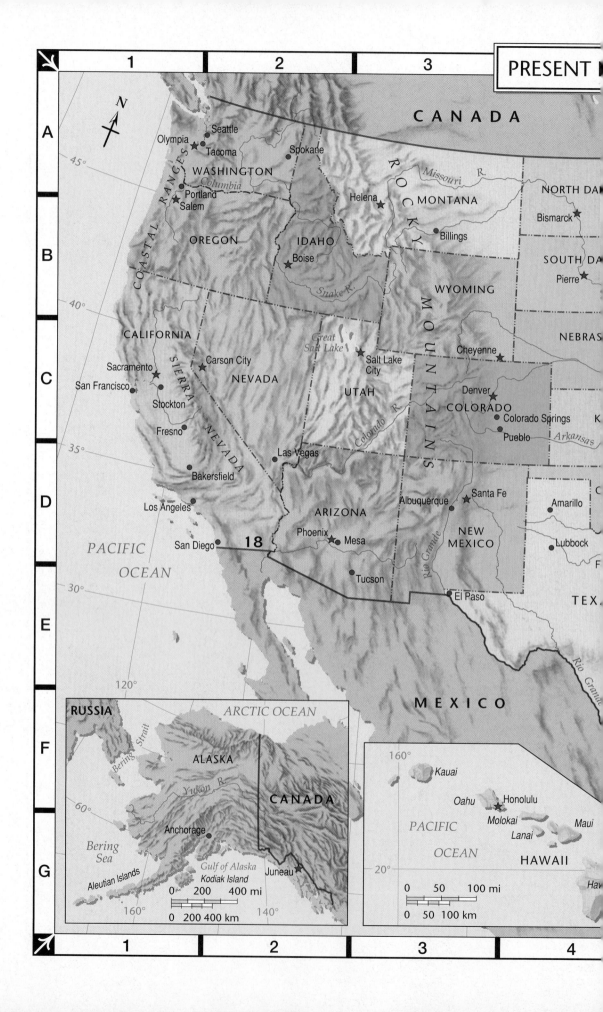

CANADA

	1	2	3

A

Seattle
Olympia ★
Tacoma
Spokane ●
WASHINGTON
Columbia
Portland ★
Salem ★
OREGON
Helena ★ MONTANA
Billings ●
Missouri R.
NORTH DA
Bismarck ★

B

IDAHO
Boise ★
Snake R.
WYOMING
SOUTH DA
Pierre ★
NEBRAS

C

CALIFORNIA
Great Salt Lake
Sacramento ★
Carson City ★
SIERRA NEVADA
NEVADA
Salt Lake City ★
UTAH
Cheyenne ★
Denver ★
COLORADO
Colorado Springs ●
Pueblo ●
Arkansas
San Francisco ●
Stockton ●
Fresno ●
Colorado R.

D

35°
Las Vegas ●
Bakersfield ●
Los Angeles ●
ARIZONA
Albuquerque ●
Santa Fe ★
NEW MEXICO
Amarillo ●
Lubbock ●

18
San Diego ●
Phoenix ★ Mesa ●
Rio Grande

PACIFIC OCEAN

Tucson ●
30°
El Paso ●
TEXA

120°

E

MEXICO

Rio Grande

RUSSIA
ARCTIC OCEAN
Bering Strait
ALASKA
Yukon R.
CANADA
Bering Sea
Anchorage ●
60°
Aleutian Islands
Kodiak Island
Gulf of Alaska
Juneau ★

0   200   400 mi
0 200 400 km

160°

160°
Kauai
Oahu
Honolulu ★
Molokai
Maui
PACIFIC
Lanai
OCEAN
HAWAII
20°

0   50   100 mi
0 50 100 km
Haw

F

G

	1	2	3	4

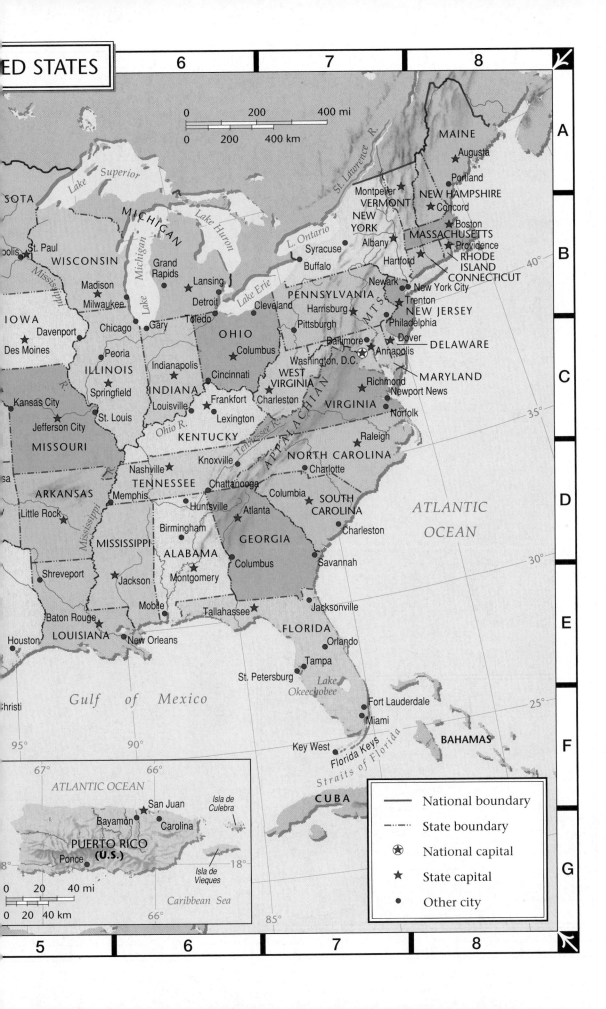

A

0   200   400 mi

0   200   400 km

MAINE

★ Augusta

● Portland

Lake Superior

SOTA

MICHIGAN

Lake Huron

St. Lawrence R.

Montpelier ★

VERMONT

NEW HAMPSHIRE

★ Concord

B

olis ● St. Paul

WISCONSIN

● Grand Rapids

Lake Michigan

● Lansing ★

NEW YORK

L. Ontario

● Syracuse

● Albany

Hartford ★

★ Boston

★ Providence

MASSACHUSETTS

RHODE ISLAND

CONNECTICUT

40°

● Madison

● Milwaukee

Lake Erie

● Detroit

Newark ●

● New York City

IOWA

● Davenport

● Chicago ● Gary

● Toledo

● Cleveland

PENNSYLVANIA

Harrisburg ★

★ Trenton

NEW JERSEY

● Pittsburgh

Philadelphia ●

★ Dover

DELAWARE

C

★ Des Moines

ILLINOIS

● Peoria

OHIO

★ Columbus

Baltimore ●

Washington, D.C. ⊛

Annapolis ★

● Indianapolis ★

● Cincinnati

WEST VIRGINIA

● Richmond ★

● Newport News

MARYLAND

Kansas City ●

● Springfield

INDIANA

Louisville ●

Frankfort ★

● Charleston

VIRGINIA

● Norfolk

35°

St. Louis ● ★

● Lexington

Ohio R.

Jefferson City ★

KENTUCKY

Tennessee R.

★ Raleigh

MISSOURI

● Knoxville

APPALACHIAN

NORTH CAROLINA

Nashville ★

● Charlotte

D

ARKANSAS

TENNESSEE

● Chattanooga

Columbia ●

SOUTH CAROLINA

ATLANTIC OCEAN

Memphis ●

● Huntsville

Little Rock ★

● Atlanta ★

● Charleston

● Birmingham

MISSISSIPPI

ALABAMA

GEORGIA

● Savannah

30°

Shreveport ●

Jackson ★

● Columbus

● Montgomery

● Mobile

Tallahassee ★

● Jacksonville

E

Baton Rouge ★

LOUISIANA

● New Orleans

FLORIDA

● Orlando

Houston ●

● Tampa

Gulf of Mexico

St. Petersburg ●

Lake Okeechobee

hristi

● Fort Lauderdale

25°

● Miami

Straits of Florida

BAHAMAS

F

Key West ●

Florida Keys

67°   66°

ATLANTIC OCEAN

San Juan ★

Isla de Culebra

CUBA

—— National boundary

Bayamón ●

● Carolina

-·-·- State boundary

⊛ National capital

PUERTO RICO (U.S.)

Ponce ●

8°

Isla de Vieques

–18°

★ State capital

● Other city

0   20   40 mi

Caribbean Sea

0   20   40 km

66°

G

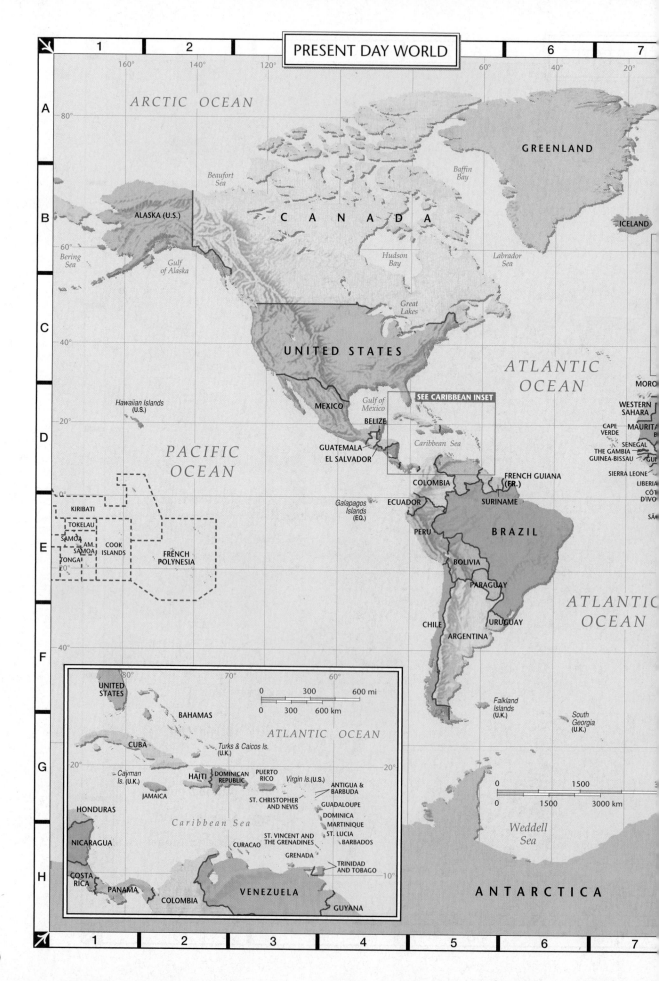

ARCTIC OCEAN

GREENLAND

Beaufort Sea

Baffin Bay

ALASKA (U.S.)

C A N A D A

ICELAND

Bering Sea

60°

Gulf of Alaska

Hudson Bay

Labrador Sea

Great Lakes

UNITED STATES

ATLANTIC OCEAN

40°

MORO

Hawaiian Islands (U.S.)

PACIFIC OCEAN

MEXICO

Gulf of Mexico

SEE CARIBBEAN INSET

WESTERN SAHARA MAURITA

CAPE VERDE

BELIZE

Caribbean Sea

SENEGAL
THE GAMBIA
GUINEA-BISSAU GUI

GUATEMALA
EL SALVADOR

SIERRA LEONE

LIBERIA
CÔT
D'IVO

COLOMBIA

FRENCH GUIANA (FR.)

0°

KIRIBATI

Galapagos Islands (EQ.)

ECUADOR

SURINAME

SÃO

TOKELAU

PERU

B R A Z I L

SAMOA
AM.
SAMOA
TONGA

COOK ISLANDS

FRENCH POLYNESIA

20°

BOLIVIA

PARAGUAY

ATLANTIC OCEAN

40°

CHILE

URUGUAY

ARGENTINA

Falkland Islands (U.K.)

South Georgia (U.K.)

0		1500	
0	1500		3000 km

Weddell Sea

ANTARCTICA

UNITED STATES

80°

70°

60°

0		300		600 mi
0	300		600 km	

BAHAMAS

ATLANTIC OCEAN

CUBA

Turks & Caicos Is. (U.K.)

20°

Cayman Is. (U.K.)

HAITI

DOMINICAN REPUBLIC

PUERTO RICO

Virgin Is.(U.S.)

20°

ANTIGUA & BARBUDA

JAMAICA

ST. CHRISTOPHER AND NEVIS

GUADALOUPE

HONDURAS

DOMINICA

Caribbean Sea

MARTINIQUE

ST. LUCIA

NICARAGUA

ST. VINCENT AND THE GRENADINES

CURACAO

BARBADOS

GRENADA

COSTA RICA

TRINIDAD AND TOBAGO

10°

PANAMA

COLOMBIA

VENEZUELA

GUYANA

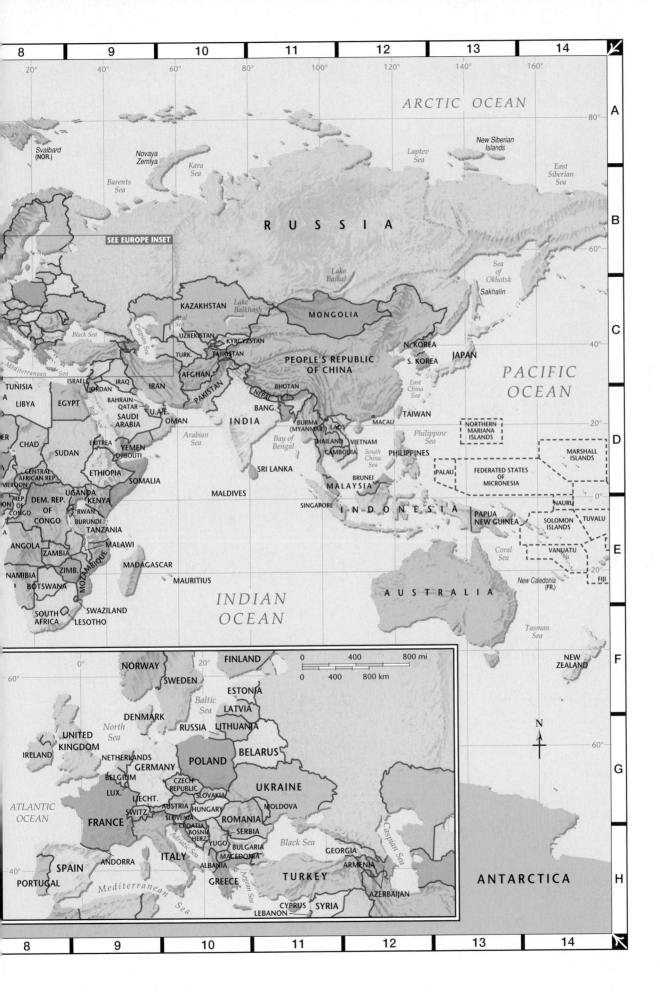

20° 40° 60° 80° 100° 120° 140° 160°

ARCTIC OCEAN

80°   A

Svalbard
(NOR.)   Novaya
              Zemlya   Kara
                            Sea   Laptev
                                                       Sea   New Siberian
                                                                  Islands
      Barents   East
      Sea   Siberian
                                                                                 Sea   B

R U S S I A

SEE EUROPE INSET   60°
                                                         Sea
                                                         of
                                              Lake   Okhotsk
                                              Baikal   Sakhalin

KAZAKHSTAN   Lake
              Balkhash   MONGOLIA   C
Aral
Sea   40°
Black Sea   UZBEKISTAN   N. KOREA
Caspian Sea KYRGYZSTAN   S. KOREA   JAPAN
TURK.   TAJIKISTAN   PACIFIC
            AFGHAN.   PEOPLE'S REPUBLIC   East   OCEAN
                          OF CHINA   China
TUNISIA   ISRAEL IRAQ   Sea
         JORDAN   IRAN   PAKISTAN   BHUTAN
LIBYA   BAHRAIN   NEPAL   TAIWAN
EGYPT   QATAR   BANG.   20°
         U.A.E. OMAN   INDIA   BURMA   MACAU   D
SAUDI   (MYANMAR) LAOS
ARABIA   Arabian   THAILAND VIETNAM   Philippine   NORTHERN
CHAD   Sea   Bay of   CAMBODIA South   Sea   MARIANA   MARSHALL
SUDAN   ERITREA   Bengal   China   ISLANDS   ISLANDS
       YEMEN DJIBOUTI SRI LANKA   Sea   PHILIPPINES
ETHIOPIA   BRUNEI   PALAU FEDERATED STATES
CENTRAL   SOMALIA MALDIVES   MALAYSIA   OF
AFRICAN REP.   MICRONESIA   0°
UGANDA KENYA   SINGAPORE   I N D O N E S I A   NAURU   E
DEM. REP.   PAPUA   SOLOMON TUVALU
OF   RWAN.   NEW GUINEA   ISLANDS
CONGO BURUNDI   VANUATU
       TANZANIA   Coral   20°
ANGOLA   MALAWI   Sea   FIJI
ZAMBIA MOZAMBIQUE   MADAGASCAR   New Caledonia
NAMIBIA ZIMB.   AUSTRALIA (FR.)
BOTSWANA   MAURITIUS   F
              INDIAN
SOUTH SWAZILAND OCEAN   Tasman
AFRICA LESOTHO   Sea   NEW
                                                                       ZEALAND

Europe Inset:

0°   NORWAY   20°   FINLAND   0   400   800 mi
60°   SWEDEN   0   400   800 km
      DENMARK ESTONIA
      North   Baltic LATVIA
UNITED Sea   Sea   LITHUANIA
KINGDOM NETHERLANDS RUSSIA
IRELAND   GERMANY POLAND BELARUS   N
         BELGIUM CZECH
         LUX.   REPUBLIC SLOVAKIA UKRAINE
ATLANTIC LIECHT. AUSTRIA HUNGARY MOLDOVA   60°
OCEAN   SWITZ. SLOVENIA ROMANIA
FRANCE   CROATIA BOSNIA SERBIA
         SLOVENIA HERZ. YUGO. BULGARIA Black Sea Caspian Sea
SPAIN   ANDORRA ITALY   MACEDONIA GEORGIA
                  ALBANIA SERBIA   ARMENIA
PORTUGAL 40°   GREECE   TURKEY   AZERBAIJAN   ANTARCTICA
         Mediterranean Aegean CYPRUS SYRIA
         Sea   Sea   LEBANON

GLOSSARY

Agricultural Adjustment Act (AAA) (p. 680) New Deal program of 1933 led by Secretary of Agriculture Henry Wallace; it was an effort to develop a partnership between the government and major agricultural producers that would raise prices by reducing the supply of farm goods. Large producers in farm cooperatives would agree upon a "domestic allotment" plan that would assign acreage quotas to each producer, and those who cut production to comply with the quotas would be paid for land left fallow.

Alamo (p. 344) A former Spanish mission in San Antonio, Texas, where, in 1836, a Texan force of about 180 was besieged by the Mexican army during Texas's war for independence.

Alien and Sedition acts (p. 195) Four acts passed in 1798 designed to curb criticism of the federal government. Adopted during a time of conflict with France, the acts lengthened the period before an immigrant could obtain citizenship, gave the president power to deport dangerous aliens, and provided for the prosecution of those who wrote "false, scandalous, and malicious" writings against the U.S. government.

Alliance movement (p. 535) Started in 1877 as a farmers' club in Texas, the group expanded into a network of organizations devoted to improving the plight of farmers, eventually through political action

Allies (p. 617) In World War I, the United States, Great Britain, France, and Russia, the alliance that opposed and defeated the Central Powers of Germany and Austria-Hungary and their allies; in World War II, primarily the United States, Great Britain, (free) France, and the Soviet Union that opposed and defeated the Axis powers of Germany, Italy, and Japan.

Al-Qaeda (p. 894) An international terrorist network led by Osama bin Laden that staged the plane hijackings and attacks on the Pentagon and New York's World Trade Center of September 11, 2001.

Amateurism (p. 512) A belief that nonprofessional athletes are the pure embodiment of sports. The concept is noble in its outlook that "the game" should be played for the joy of participation and competition. It was somewhat marred in that elitist elements could manipulate the playing field to exclude people without access to expensive equipment or facilities.

American exceptionalism (p. 554) Notion that the United States houses biologically superior people and can spread democracy to the rest of the world. An intellectual foundation of expansion and racism in the late nineteenth and early twentieth centuries.

American Federation of Labor (p. 482) A confederation of labor unions founded in 1886, it was composed mainly of skilled craft unions and was the first na-

tional labor organization to survive and experience a degree of success, largely because of its conservative leadership that accepted industrial capitalism.

American Indian Movement (AIM) (p. 840) An activist organization founded in 1968 to protect the civil rights of Native Americans and to pressure state and federal governments to strictly observe treaty obligations. To dramatize its demands, AIM occupied the Bureau of Indian Affairs Building in Washington, D.C., in 1972 and Wounded Knee, South Dakota, in 1973.

American System (of Henry Clay) (pp. 228, 256) Henry Clay's program for the national economy, which included a protective tariff to stimulate industry, a national bank to provide credit, and federally funded internal improvements to expand the market for farm products.

American system of production (p. 236) The high cost of labor led to the establishment of a system of mass production through the manufacture of interchangeable parts and the standardization of the tasks performed by workers.

Amos 'n Andy (p. 649) Popular radio show first aired in 1926 from Chicago station WMAQ; it spread vicious racial stereotypes about African Americans.

Anaconda Plan (p. 396) General Winfield Scott designed this strategic plan in the early days of the Civil War to give direction to the Union war effort against the South. The plan advocated a full naval blockade of the South's coastline, a military campaign to gain control of the Mississippi River, and the placement of armies at key points in the South to squeeze—like the anaconda snake—the life out of the Confederacy. In various ways, this plan helped inform overall Union strategy in militarily defeating the South.

Antifederalists (p. 174) These were opponents of the Constitution of 1787 who sought to continue the confederation of sovereign states and to keep power as close as possible to the people. In actuality, the Antifederalists were true federalists in seeking to balance powers among the states and the national government. Their confused identity may have cost them support in attempting to prevent ratification of the Constitution. See *Federalists*.

Anti-Masonic party (p. 251) A political organization that emerged following the alleged kidnapping and murder in 1826 of William Morgan, who had threatened to expose the secrets of the Masonic order. In 1831, the Anti-Masons held the first political nominating convention and issued the first written party platform. In 1834, Anti-Masons helped form the Whig party.

Antinomian (p. 45) Literally meaning against the laws of human governance. Antinomians believed that once they had earned saving grace, God would offer them direct revelation by which to order the steps of their lives. As such, human institutions, such as churches and government, were no longer necessary. Mainline Puritans believed Antinomianism would produce only social chaos and destroy the Bay Colony's mission, so they repudiated and even exiled prominent persons like Anne Hutchinson, who advocated such doctrines.

Artisan system of labor (p. 309)   A system of manufacturing that preceded the rise of the factory system, under which apprentices and skilled journeymen worked for self-employed master craftsmen in the master's home or a small shop nearby.

Ashcan School (p. 506)   Originating in the first decade of the twentieth century, a school of art centered on the experiences of urban life. An impressionistic offshoot, it is characterized by use of unmixed primary colors and quick brushstrokes while being concerned with content over technique.

Asiento (p. 84)   A trade agreement growing out of the War of the Spanish Succession (1702–1713) that allowed the English to sell 4800 slaves annually in New Spain. The English regularly cheated and traded much more extensively in the Spanish empire than provided for in the *Asiento,* which resulted in further warfare between Britain and Spain, beginning in 1739 with the start of the War of Jenkins's Ear.

Associationism (p. 660)   Concept proposed by Herbert Hoover as Secretary of Commerce under President Warren G. Harding, that called for voluntary trade associations to foster cooperation in industry and agriculture through commissions, trade practice controls, and ethical standards.

Atlanta Compromise (p. 473)   A term used to describe an 1895 speech by Booker T. Washington, who called upon African Americans to defer agitation in return for white Southerners' support for black educational and economic advancement.

Axis Powers (p. 715)   In World War II, the alliance of German and Italy, and later Japan.

Baltimore (p. 559)   U.S. warship that, on October 16, 1891, arrived at Valparaiso, Chile. A liberty party from the ship was involved in a riot and 2 sailors were killed and 16 injured. Aggressive and jingoistic parties used the incident to call for war against Chile.

Bank of the United States (pp. 186, 207)   A central bank, chartered by the federal government in 1791. Proposed by Alexander Hamilton, the bank collected taxes, held government funds, and regulated state banks. The bank's charter expired in 1811. A second Bank of the United States was created in 1816. See *Second Bank of the United States.*

Barbary pirates (pp. 208, 232)   During the late eighteenth and early nineteenth centuries, pirates from the North African states of Tripoli, Tunis, Morocco, and Algiers captured merchant ships and held their crews for ransom.

Bare-knuckle boxing (p. 518)   Precursor to more legitimate forms of professional boxing, bare-knuckles competitors did not use gloves and would fight until one man could not continue. The brutality of the matches brought about demands for rules and a general cleanup of the sport.

Battle of the Bulge (p. 718)   Last major Axis counteroffensive of World War II, December 16–26, 1944, when German armored divisions, driving toward Antwerp, slashed 60 miles to the Franco-Belgium border before being delayed and finally defeated by Allied forces at Bastogne.

Bay of Pigs fiasco (p. 788)   A plan to assassinate Cuban leader Fidel Castro and liberate Cuba with a trained military force of political exiles. The limited 1961 invasion was an unmitigated military failure and actually strengthened Castro's position in Cuba.

Beat generation (p. 778)   A cultural style and artistic movement of the 1950s that rejected traditional American family life and material values and celebrated African American culture. The Beats tapped an underground dissatisfaction with mainstream American culture.

Berlin airlift (p. 739)   During 1948 and 1949 the Soviet Union cut off all ground communication between the western sectors of Berlin (occupied by Britain, France, and the United States) and West Germany. The apparent purpose was to starve the three countries out of Berlin and allow the Soviets to have complete control of the city. In response to this challenge a massive airlift was conducted, supplying the city's basic needs by air for over a year. When the Soviets saw that there was no sign of capitulation and that the airlift was making great political capital for their opponents, the land blockade was abruptly and quietly lifted.

Big Stick Diplomacy (p. 599)   The proclaimed foreign policy of Theodore Roosevelt, it was based on the proverb, "Speak softly and carry a big stick," and advocated the threat of force to achieve the United States' goals, especially in the Western Hemisphere.

Bill of Rights (p. 184)   The first 10 amendments to the U.S. Constitution, which protect the rights of individuals from the powers of the national government. Congress and the states ratified the 10 amendments in 1791.

Billy Yank (p. 396)   This term referred to common soldiers serving in Union armies during the Civil War. See *Johnny Reb.*

Birds of passage (p. 491)   Immigrants who never intended to make the United States their home. Unable to make a living in their native countries, they came to America, worked and saved, and returned home. About 20 to 30 percent of immigrants returned home.

Black Codes (p. 428)   Laws passed by southern state legislatures during Reconstruction, while Congress was out of session. These laws limited the rights of former slaves and led Congress to ratify the Fourteenth Amendment.

Black Hawk War (p. 259)   In 1832, the Sauk and Fox Indians, who had lost their land in northern Illinois as a result of a disputed treaty, attempted to reclaim their lands but were defeated by state militia and army regulars.

Black Like Me (p. 768)   Novel by John Howard Griffin recounting his experiences as a white man disguised as an African American. His book told of the dreadful conditions that were permitted under the Jim Crow laws in the American South. This book was a first look into the situation for many white Americans.

Black Muslims (p. 822)   Founded in 1930, a group led by Elijah Muhammad that emphasized racial separation and worked to improve African American living conditions and root out activities that were exploited by racists.

Black Panther party (p. 824)   A militant black nationalist organization formed in 1966 in Oakland, California, by Huey Newton and Bobby Seale. The group advocated racial separation and black power.

Black power (p. 824)   A rallying cry for more militant blacks advocated by younger leaders like Stokely Carmichael and H. Rap Brown, beginning in the mid-1960s. It called for African Americans to form their own economic, political, and cultural institutions.

Black Sox scandal (p. 651)   Scandal in which eight Chicago White Sox baseball players threw the 1919 World Series and were ultimately banned from the sport.

Black Tuesday (p. 663)   October 29, 1929, the day of the stock market crash that helped to initiate the Great Depression.

Bombingham (p. 819)   Name given to Birmingham, Alabama, due to the number of bombs that were used against civil rights activists during the 1960s. In one explosion four young girls preparing for choir practice were killed in the basement of the Sixteenth Street Baptist Church.

Bonus Army (p. 676)   Group of unemployed World War I veterans who marched on Washington, D.C., in June 1932 to ask for immediate payment of their war pensions.

Bosnia-Herzegovina (p. 903)   A former Yugoslav republic that was the site of ethnic conflict between Serbs, Croats, and Muslims during the 1990s.

Brain trust (p. 678)   Close advisers to President Franklin Delano Roosevelt during the early days of his first term whose policy suggestions influenced much New Deal legislation.

Brown v. Board of Education of Topeka (p. 772)   Supreme Court decision of 1954 that overturned the "separate but equal doctrine" that justified Jim Crow laws. Chief Justice Earl Warren argued that "separate educational facilities are inherently unequal."

Cabinet (p. 184)   This term refers to the heads of the executive departments in the federal government.

Calvinism (p. 20)   Broadly influential Protestant theology emanating from the French theologian John Calvin, who fled to Switzerland, where he reordered life in the community of Geneva according to his conception of the Bible. Calvinism emphasized the power and omnipotence of God and the importance of seeking to earn saving grace and salvation, even though God had already determined (the concept of predestination) who would be eternally saved or damned.

Camp David Accords (p. 882)   Historic 1979 peace agreement negotiated between Egypt and Israel at the U.S. presidential retreat at Camp David, Maryland, with the help of U.S. President Jimmy Carter. Under the pact, Israel agreed to return captured territory to Egypt and to negotiate Palestinian autonomy in the West Bank and Gaza Strip. The pact normalized relations between the two nations and provided a framework for peace in the Middle East.

Capital punishment (p. 277)   During the early nineteenth century, a reform movement arose to end the death penalty.

Carpetbaggers (p. 435)   People who moved to the South during or following the Civil War and became active in politics, they helped to bring Republican control of southern state governments during Reconstruction and were bitterly resented by most white Southerners.

Cautious revolutionaries (p. 154)   Sometimes called reluctant revolutionaries, these leaders lacked a strong trust in the people to rise above their own self-interest and provide for enlightened legislative policies (see *Public virtue*). At the time of the American Revolution, they argued in favor of forms of government that could easily check the popular will. To assure political stability, they believed that political decision making should be in the hands of society's proven social and economic elite. John Dickinson, John Adams (very much an eager revolutionary), and Robert Morris might be described as cautious revolutionaries. See *Radical revolutionaries.*

Central Powers (p. 618)   In World War I, Germany and Austria-Hungary and their allies.

Charles River Bridge v. Warren Bridge (p. 265)   Landmark 1837 Supreme Court case which held that any ambiguities in contracts should be interpreted in the public interest.

China Lobby (p. 740)   An informal group of media leaders and political pundits who criticized the communist takeover of China, claiming the United States could have prevented it.

Chinese Exclusion Act (p. 496)   The success of the immigrants from China during the third quarter of the nineteenth century caused concern among "native-born" Americans in the West as the century closed. In order to prevent a greater influx of competitors, the Chinese Exclusion Act was passed in 1882 to suspend immigration from China for ten years. In 1892 a ten-year extension was passed and in 1902 the act was extended indefinitely.

Cincinnati Red Stockings (p. 509)   An early baseball team that helped to establish the requirements for "steady, temperate habits, and constant training" in professional sports.

Citizen Genêt Affair (p. 188)   When French envoy Charles Genêt attempted in 1794 to encourage Americans to launch naval attacks against the British, the U.S. government demanded his recall. This incident aggravated tensions between the United States and France.

City upon a Hill (p. 41)   Phrase from John Winthrop's sermon, "A Model of Christian Charity," in which he challenged his fellow Puritans to build a model, ideal community in America that would serve as an example of how the rest of the world should order its existence. Here was the beginning of the idea of America as a special, indeed exceptional society, therefore worthy of emulation by others. The concept of American exceptionalism has helped to define American history and culture down to the present.

Civil Rights Act of 1875 (p. 447)   An act that spelled out more specifically the rights guaranteed by the Fourteenth Amendment. It was meant to prohibit segregation of public accommodations but was greatly undermined by Supreme Court decisions.

Civil Rights Act of 1964 (p. 822) Landmark legislation that prohibited discrimination on the basis of race, sex, religion, or national origin in employment and public facilities such as hotels, restaurants, and playgrounds. It established the Equal Employment Opportunity Commission.

Civil Service Commission (p. 530) Established by the Pendleton Act in 1883, this body oversees the granting of federal jobs and administers tests given to applicants.

Coercive Acts (p. 114) Also known as the Intolerable Acts, they consisted of four pieces of punitive legislation from King and Parliament in the spring of 1774 to punish colonists in Massachusetts who had dumped £10,000 worth of tea into Boston harbor in December 1773.

Coinage Act of 1873 (p. 529) Called the "Crime of 73" by farmers and others who wanted to inflate the currency, this act halted the minting of silver dollars.

Cold War (p. 734) The period between the end of World War II (1945) and the final dissolution of the Soviet Union (1991) in which the Western powers, led by the United States and comprised mainly of the NATO countries (with Japan), and the Soviet bloc (including the USSR and the Warsaw Pact nations of Eastern Europe) maintained a "short-of-war" condition. Any confrontation directly between the USSR and the United States could get out of hand and result in nuclear war. Thus the two superpowers found it useful to compete via third parties, such as Israel and the Arab nations or North and South Korea. The period could be characterized by "limited war fought for limited goals."

Colonization (p. 279) The effort to encourage masters to emancipate their slaves voluntarily and to resettle free blacks in Africa.

Columbian Exchange (p. 27) The process of transferring plants, animals, foods, diseases, wealth, and culture between Europe and the Americas, beginning at the time of Christopher Columbus and continuing throughout the era of exploration and expansion. The exchange often resulted in the devastation of Native American peoples and cultures, so much so that the process is sometimes referred to as the "Columbian collision."

Committee on Public Information (p. 627) U.S. propaganda agency during World War I.

Committees of correspondence (p. 112) As American leaders became increasingly anxious about a perceived British imperial conspiracy to deprive them of their liberties, they set up networks of communication among the colonies. Beginning in 1773 colonial assemblies began to appoint committees of correspondence to warn each other about possible abuses. In some colonies, such as Massachusetts, local communities also organized such committees, all with the intention of being vigilant against arbitrary acts from British officials.

Common Sense (p. 131) This best-selling pamphlet by Thomas Paine, first published in January 1776, denounced the British monarchy, called for American independence, and encouraged the adoption of republican forms of government. Paine's bold words helped crack the power of reconciliationist leaders in the Second Continental Congress who did not believe the colonies could stand up to British arms and survive as an independent nation.

Compromise of 1850 (p. 369) A series of measures passed by Congress to resolve sectional tensions. Congress admitted California to the Union as a free state; organized the territories of New Mexico, Nevada, Arizona, and Utah without mention of slavery; paid Texas $10 million to relinquish land claims in New Mexico; abolished the slave trade in the District of Columbia (but not slavery); and enacted a law requiring the return of fugitive slaves.

Compromise of 1877 (p. 448) A bargain made between southern Democrats and Republican candidate Rutherford B. Hayes after the disputed presidential election of 1876. The southern Democrats pledged to let Hayes take office in return for his promise to withdraw the remaining federal troops from the southern states. The removal of the last troops in 1877 marked the end of Reconstruction.

Coney Island (p. 514) Popular site of New York amusement parks opening in 1890s, attracting working-class Americans with rides and games celebrating abandon and instant gratification.

Congress of Industrial Organization (CIO) (p. 684) Group formed in 1935 by union leaders of unskilled workers in mass-production industries, including auto, glass, radio, rubber, and steelworkers.

Congress of Racial Equality (CORE) (p. 818) Formed in 1942, this group was instrumental in organizing the sit-ins of the 1960s. CORE promoted nonviolent protest as a means to social change. In July 1966 CORE shifted to an endorsement of black power and repudiated the nonviolent aspect of their protests.

Conscription (p. 631) Compulsory draft of enrollees to serve in the military; put into effect in World War I by the Selective Service Act in May 1917.

Containment (p. 738) George Kennan's paper, "The Sources of Soviet Conduct," suggested that the Soviets would expand only when the United States allowed them to do so. By containing them within their current borders and not allowing any other nations to convert to communism, the Soviets could be controlled and would decay from within. The policy of containment was to be enforced by economic, political, and military means. This defensive policy may have prolonged the Cold War.

Continental System (p. 212) As part of France's conflict with Britain, Napoleon in 1806 and 1807 issued decrees that sought to prevent neutral nations, including the United States, from trading with Britain.

Contract With America (p. 900) A 1994 campaign document in which Republican congressional candidates committed themselves to a constitutional amendment requiring a balanced federal budget, stiff work requirements for welfare recipients, and term limits for elected officials.

Copperheads (p. 405) Not every person living in the North during the Civil War favored making war against the Confederacy. Such persons came to be identified as Copperheads. Often affiliated with the Democratic party and residing in the Midwest, Copperheads favored a negotiated peace settlement that would allow the South to leave the Union. Some of them were arbitrarily thrown into jail without proper *habeas corpus* proceedings after publicly advocating their views.

Court packing (p. 688)   President Franklin Roosevelt's controversial plan to make the Supreme Court more sympathetic to his views and less likely to reject his legislative proposals as unconstitutional. FDR proposed to reorganize the Supreme Court by appointing up to six new members, one new justice for each sitting member over the age of 70 who did not retire, thus increasing the size of the Court from 9 to 16 members, and offering generous pension benefits for justices who did retire. FDR's plan was denounced on all sides as an attempt to circumvent the constitutional systems of checks and balances and the separation of powers.

Coverture (p. 48)   The concept which contends that the legal identity of women is subordinated first to their fathers and then to their husbands, as the sanctioned heads of households. See *Patriarchal.*

Coxey's Army (p. 542)   A movement founded by Jacob S. Coxey to help the unemployed during the depression of the 1890s, it brought out-of-work people to Washington, D.C., to demand that the federal government provide jobs and inflate the currency.

Credit Mobilier (p. 441)   A financial scandal during Ulysses S. Grant's administration in 1872 involving his vice president, which tarnished the Republican party's image.

Cuban missile crisis (p. 788)   The conflict in 1962 prompted by Soviet installation of missiles on Cuba. After days of genuine fear on both sides, the two sides negotiated an agreement whereby the Soviet Union removed the missiles and the United States pledged not to invade Cuba.

Cuban Revolution (of 1895) (p. 575)   A revolt by local Cubans against the Spanish rulers of the island, starting in 1895. The ruthless suppression of this revolt by the Spanish would provide fuel for the coming Spanish-American War.

Cuban Revolution (of 1959) (p. 767)   A revolt against the corrupt regime of Fulgencio Batista led by Fidel Castro. Castro, a medical doctor by training, called for local ownership of national industries and resources. As most of these were owned by American interests, the U.S. government did not support the revolution. When Castro declared himself a communist after the revolution was successful, U.S.-Cuba relations became even more strained.

Cult of domesticity (p. 513)   Adherents held that women should be mothers, wives, and caregivers. Not only did this limit them in the world at large, it also prevented women from participating in most competitive sports.

Dartmouth v. Woodward (p. 231)   A landmark 1819 Supreme Court decision protecting contracts. In the case, Chief Justice John Marshall ruled that the charters of business corporations are contracts and thus protected under the U.S. Constitution.

Dawes Severalty Act (p. 446)   Legislation passed in 1887 to authorize the president to divide tribal land and distribute it to individual Native Americans; it gave 160 acres to each head of the household in an attempt to assimilate Indians into citizenship.

D-Day (p. 717)   June 6, 1944, the day Allied forces landed on the beaches of Normandy, in France, leading to the defeat of Germany in World War II.

Declension (p. 52)   A term associated with the Massachusetts Bay Colony, referring to the declining zeal of later generations or movement away from the utopian ideals of those Puritan leaders, such as John Winthrop, who founded the colony. As an example of declension, see *Half-way covenant.*

Deism (p. 274)   A form of Christianity that rejects miracles, revelation, and the literal truth of the Bible.

Democratic-Republican Party (pp. 187, 204)   One of the United States's first two political parties, it was founded by Thomas Jefferson and James Madison in opposition to the economic and foreign policies of Alexander Hamilton.

Department of Homeland Security (p. 907)   A cabinet department set up in 2002 to prevent, protect against, and respond to acts of terrorism. Its responsibilities include controlling the nation's borders, analyzing intelligence, and coordinating emergency responses to terrorist attacks.

Deregulation (p. 880)   An economic policy, begun during the administration of Jimmy Carter, which freed air and surface transportation, the savings and loan industry, natural gas, and other industries from many government economic controls.

Détente (p. 881)   A relaxation of tensions between the United States and the Soviet Union that was begun by President Richard M. Nixon.

Dien Bien Phu (p. 789)   Vietminh siege of 13,000 French soldiers in 1954 at a remote military outpost. The French surrender led to the 1956 elections designed to reunify Vietnam.

Direct taxes (p. 98)   Also called "internal" taxes, such as visibly placed taxes on newspapers, pamphlets, and a host of other items such as those listed in the Stamp Act of 1765. Direct taxes are those that people know they are paying, such as state sales taxes or federal income taxes today. See *Indirect taxes.*

Divine Right (p. 37)   Long-held belief that monarchs were God's political stewards on earth. Because their authority to rule supposedly came directly from God, the decision making of monarchs was held to be infallible and thus could not be questioned. Some of England's Stuart kings in the seventeenth century viewed themselves as ruling by divine right, a position that numerous subjects rejected, even to the point of a civil war in the 1640s and the beheading of Charles I in 1649.

Dollar diplomacy (p. 601)   The diplomatic policy of President William Howard Taft; it called for increasing American influence in the world through economic investment rather than military force.

Dominican Republic (p. 551)   Country which forms the eastern two-thirds of the island of Santo Domingo (the balance is the country of Haiti). President Ulysses S. Grant wanted the Dominican Republic not only as an asset to the U.S. economy but also as a haven for African Americans suffering from the depredations of the Ku Klux Klan.

Domino theory (p. 791)   The U.S. belief that if one country in a region were to fall under communist control then other countries, like a row of dominoes, would fall one after the other. The U.S. resolve was that the communists would not gain a "toehold" in any of the areas friendly to the United States.

Donner party (p. 339)   A party of pioneers who were stranded on their way to California in late 1846. Of the original 87 emigrants, 39 died.

Double V campaign (p. 712)   African American term for their dual struggle to combat fascism abroad and discrimination at home during and after World War II.

Doughface (p. 372)   A Northerner with sympathies toward the slave-holding South.

Dred Scott decision (p. 426)   Supreme Court ruling in the 1857 case of *Dred Scott v. Sanford* that slaves were not citizens of the United States and thus were not eligible to bring suit in a federal court, and that Congress had no power to exclude slavery from any part of U.S. territory.

Dumbbell tenements (p. 501)   Apartment buildings built to minimal codes and designed to cram the largest number of people into the smallest amount of space. The dumbbell indentation in the middle of the building, although unsightly, conformed to the Tenement Reform Law of 1879, which required all rooms to have access to light and air.

Dunmore's Ethiopian regiment (p. 130)   In November 1775 John Murray, Lord Dunmore (Virginia's last royal governor), issued an emancipation proclamation that freed all slaves and indentured servants living in Virginia who were willing to bear arms against their rebellious masters. As many as 2000 slaves fled to the British banner, and some became members of Dunmore's Ethiopian regiment. With little training in arms, this regiment fared poorly in a battle with Virginia militia in December 1775. An outbreak of smallpox later killed many of the exslaves who responded to Dunmore's proclamation.

Dust Bowl (p. 679)   Area from northern Texas to the Dakotas that suffered from severe drought and dust storms during the 1930s, with the damage compounded by previous overgrazing and overfarming.

Eighteenth Amendment (p. 629)   Amendment that established prohibition by banning the manufacture, sale, or transportation of alcohol in the United States and its territories, ratified in 1919.

Electric trolley (p. 498)   Public transportation for urban neighborhoods, using electric current from overhead wires. Between 1888 and 1902, 97 percent of urban transit mileage was electrified.

Emancipation Proclamation (p. 405)   President Abraham Lincoln issued a preliminary proclamation in September 1862 that all slaves would be declared free in those states that were still in rebellion against the Union at the beginning of 1863. Receiving no official response from the Confederacy, Lincoln announced the Emancipation Proclamation on January 1, 1863. All slaves in the rebellious Confederate states were to be forever free. However, slavery could continue to exist in border states that were not at war against the Union. Lincoln's Emancipation Proclamation represented the beginning of the end of chattel slavery in the United States.

Embargo of 1807 (p. 212)   An attempt to stop British and French interference with American shipping by prohibiting foreign trade.

Emergency Banking Relief Act (p. 678)   First New Deal program, March 9, 1933, which allowed solvent banks to stay open under government supervision and permitted the Reconstruction Finance Corporation to buy the stock of troubled banks and keep them open for reorganization.

Emergency Quota Act (p. 497)   Prelude to the National Origins Act, this 1921 law limited to 3 percent annually the number of new immigrants of any nationality, based on the number of the group counted in the 1910 census.

Enclosure Movement (p. 22)   As the demand for wool heightened in England during the sixteenth century because of the emerging textile industry, Parliament passed laws that allowed profit-seeking landowners to fence in their open fields to raise more sheep. Thousands of peasants who, as renters, had been farming these lands for generations were evicted and thrown into poverty. Many moved to the cities, where as "sturdy beggars" they too often found little work. In time, some migrated to English colonies in America, where work opportunities were far more abundant.

***Encomienda* System** (p. 17)   The government in Spain gave away large tracts of conquered land in Spanish America, including whole villages of indigenous peoples, to court favorites, including many *conquistadores*. These new landlords, or *encomenderos*, were supposed to educate the natives and teach them the Roman Catholic faith. The system, however, was rife with abuse. Landlords rarely offered much education, preferring instead to exploit the labor of the local inhabitants, whom they treated like slaves.

Enlightenment (pp. 78, 273)   A broadly influential philosophical and intellectual movement that began in Europe during the eighteenth century. The Enlightenment unleashed a tidal wave of new learning, especially in the sciences and mathematics, that helped promote the notion that human beings, through the use of their reason, could solve society's problems. The Enlightenment era, as such, has also been called the Age of Reason. Benjamin Franklin and Thomas Jefferson were leading proponents of Enlightenment thinking in America.

Enola Gay (p. 724)   B-29 Superfortress plane that dropped the atomic bomb, "Little Boy," on Hiroshima, Japan, August 6, 1945. The *Bock's Car* dropped the second bomb on Nagasaki on August 9.

Enumerated goods (p. 63)   Products grown or extracted from England's North American colonies that could be shipped only to England or other colonies within the empire. Goods on the first enumeration list included tobacco, indigo, and sugar. Later on furs, molasses, and rice would be added to a growing list of products that the English colonies could not sell directly to foreign nations.

Equal Employment Opportunity Commission (EEOC) (p. 832)   A commission set up to investigate complaints of employment discrimination by Title VII of the 1964 Civil Rights Act.

Equal Rights Amendment (p. 833)   Proposed constitutional amendment that would prohibit discrimination on the basis of gender.

Era of Good Feelings (pp. 226, 653)   Phrase used to describe the years following the War of 1812, when one party, the Jeffersonian Republicans, dominated politics, and a spirit of nationalism characterized public policy.

Erie Canal (p. 234)   Built between 1817 and 1825, the Erie Canal linked the Hudson River with the Great Lakes, cutting travel time from Buffalo to New York from 20 to 6 days and freight charges from $100 to $5 a ton.

Espionage Act (p. 627)   Law passed in June 1917 to combat spying, sabotage, or obstruction of the war effort by giving postal officials authority to ban newspapers and magazines from the mails and threatening individuals convicted of obstructing the draft with $10,000 fines and 20 years in jail.

Europeanizing (p. 76)   As the British North American colonies matured during the eighteenth century, many prospering colonists sought to ape the latest fashions and lifestyles of wealthy persons in England and on the European continent. This imitative trend has been described as the "Europeanizing" of American society in the years before the American Revolution.

Evangelical Revivalism (Revivals) (p. 274)   A current of Protestant Christianity emphasizing personal conversion, repentance of sin, and the authority of Scripture.

Executive Order 9835 (p. 747)   This order established the Federal Loyalty Program, which authorized the FBI to investigate all government employees in an attempt to root out communists. Thousands of federal workers lost their jobs but not one charge was ever filed under this order.

Executive Privilege (p. 192)   The doctrine, first asserted by President George Washington, that the constitutional principle of separation of powers allows the Executive Branch the right to withhold certain requests for information from Congress and the Judiciary.

Existentialism (p. 652)   Philosophy which maintains that life has no transcendent purpose and that each individual must salvage personal meaning from the void. Novelists of the 1920s such as F. Scott Fitzgerald and Ernest Hemingway foreshadowed this philosophy in their works.

Factory system (p. 310)   During the industrial revolution of the nineteenth century, large numbers of workers were concentrated under one roof, where they were subjected to strict supervision and close discipline.

Fair Deal (p. 746)   Failed 1948 legislative package proposed by President Truman; it included an expansion of Social Security, federal aid to education, a higher minimum wage, a national plan for medical insurance, and civil rights legislation for minorities.

Fallen Timbers, Battle of (p. 189)   General Anthony Wayne's victory over an Indian confederation near present-day Toledo, Ohio, in 1794, opened the Ohio country to white settlement.

Farewell Address (p. 193)   In this 1796 statement, in which he expressed his intention not to run for a third term as president, George Washington warned of the dangers of party divisions, sectionalism, and permanent alliances with foreign nations.

Fascism (p. 700)   Political philosophy that emerged just prior to World War II; it espoused one-party government, strict government control of business and labor, and severe restrictions on personal liberty.

Federal Emergency Relief Act (p. 678)   New Deal program enacted May 12, 1933, which gave $500 million to state-run welfare agencies.

Federal Reserve System (p. 598)   The central banking system of the United States, established with passage of the Federal Reserve Act of 1913, charged with the responsibility of managing the country's money supply through such means as lowering or raising interest rates. A board of seven members (the Federal Reserve Board), appointed by the U.S. president, oversees the 12 regional banks of the Federal Reserve System.

Federalist Papers (p. 174)   These 85 newspaper essays, written in support of ratification of the Constitution of 1787 in New York by James Madison, Alexander Hamilton, and John Jay, described the proposed plan of national government as a sure foundation for long-term political stability and enlightened legislation. Although having little effect on the ratification debate in New York, the papers soon became classics of political philosophy about the Constitution as the framework of federal government for the American republic.

Federalist Party (pp. 187, 204)   One of the United States's first two political parties, it was founded by Alexander Hamilton to promote his policies, which included a national bank and friendly relations with Britain. It advocated a strong central government.

Federalists (p. 174)   In the campaign to ratify the Constitution of 1787, nationalists started referring to themselves as federalists, which conveyed the meaning that they were in favor of splitting authority between their proposed strong national government and the states. The confusion in terminology may have helped win some support among citizens worried about a powerful—and potentially tyrannical—national government. Some leading nationalists of the 1780s became Federalists in the 1790s. See *Antifederalists*. The term also refers to a political party founded by Alexander Hamilton in the 1790s to support his economic program.

Femes sole (p. 49)   A legal concept that allowed single, adult women to own and manage their own property and households, as distinct from legal subordination to fathers or husbands. See *Coverture* and *Patriarchal*.

Feminist theory (p. 833)   Theory that analyzes the economic, psychological, and social roots of female subordination and argues that gender distinctions structure virtually every aspect of individual lives.

Fifteenth Amendment (p. 433)   Passed by Congress in February 1869 and ratified by the required three-quarters of the states in March 1870, this amendment prohibited the denial of the right to vote on the basis of race, color, or past servitude. It did not specifically grant the vote to anyone and was successfully circumvented by southern states following Reconstruction.

Fire-eaters (p. 389)   Radical leaders in the South during the years leading up to the Civil War, the fire-eaters were persons who took an extreme proslavery position. They repeatedly expressed their desire to see slavery spread throughout the United States, and they used states' rights arguments to support their uncompromising position.

Fireside chats (p. 678)   Weekly radio addresses by President Franklin Roosevelt in which he explained his actions directly to the American people.

First Continental Congress (p. 115)   This body was the most important expression of intercolonial protest activity up to 1774. Called in response to Parliament's Coercive Acts, the delegates met in Philadelphia for nearly two months. More radical delegates dominated the deliberations. Before dissolving itself, the Congress called for ongoing resistance, even military preparations to defend American communities, and a second congress, should King and Parliament not redress American grievances.

First Hundred Days (p. 678)   President Franklin Roosevelt's first 100 days in office, when he proposed and Congress passed 15 major bills that reshaped the U.S. economy.

Flapper (p. 652)   Term for a liberated woman who flaunted conventional ideas of propriety in dress and manners during the 1920s.

Flexible response (p. 790)   Approach to foreign policy of the Kennedy administration based on developing and maintaining conventional, counterinsurgency (antiguerrilla), and nuclear forces so that the United States would be able to choose from among these options in response to a communist threat anywhere in the world.

Fourteen Points (p. 634)   President Woodrow Wilson's formula for peace after World War I.

Fourteenth Amendment (p. 430)   Ratified in June 1868, this amendment defined citizenship and the rights of citizenship and specified changes required of the former Confederate states.

Free silver (p. 521)   A slogan of the 1890s, its advocates called for the inflation of the currency by minting more silver.

Free Soil party (p. 281)   An antislavery political party founded in 1848.

Freedmen's Bureau (Bureau of Refugees, Freedmen, and Abandoned Lands) (p. 423)   An organization established by Congress on March 3, 1865, to deal with the dislocations of the Civil War. It provided relief, helped settle disputes, and founded schools and hospitals.

Freedom of Information Act (p. 877)   This law allows the public and press to request declassification of government documents.

Freedom riders (p. 818)   Civil rights activists who in 1961 demonstrated that despite a federal ban on segregated travel on interstate buses, segregation prevailed in parts of the South.

French Revolution (p. 187)   A social and political revolution that took place in France between 1789 and 1799 and resulted in the overthrow of the French monarchy and the social system over which it ruled.

Fugitive Slave Law (p. 369)   The most controversial element of the Compromise of 1850, the Fugitive Slave Law provided for the return of runaway slaves to their masters.

Gadsden Purchase (p. 372)   The purchase of 30,000 square miles of land from Mexico in 1854 for a southern railroad fixed the southern boundary of the continental United States.

Gang system (p. 325)   A system of plantation labor under which field hands were divided into plow gangs and hoe gangs under the command of a driver. See *Task system.*

Gay and lesbian liberation (p. 841)   A movement among homosexuals to free themselves from the social stigma long associated with same-sex relations.

Ghost Dance (p. 445)   A movement among the Sioux in the 1890s that promised the disappearance of the white man and the return of their lands.

Gilded Age (p. 523)   A term used to describe the late nineteenth century, it highlighted the superficiality of the culture, wealth, and politics of the era.

Glass-Steagall Act (p. 678)   New Deal program that provided a federal guarantee on all bank deposits under $5000 (with creation of the Federal Deposit Insurance Corporation), separated commercial and investment banking, and strengthened the Federal Reserve's ability to stabilize the economy.

Globalization (p. 896)   Emerging patterns of trade, finance, manufacturing, and entertainment that cross international boundaries.

Gold Rush (p. 357)   Some 80,000 gold seekers moved to California in 1849 after the announcement that gold had been discovered in the Sacramento Valley.

Golden door (p. 496)   Nineteenth-century Chinese term for the United States, perhaps derived from the "Golden Gate" through which many arrived in this country from China.

Good Neighbor policy (p. 698)   During the administration of President Franklin D. Roosevelt, the U.S. policy of not interfering in the internal affairs of hemispheric neighbors.

Gospel of wealth (p. 458)   The belief that God ordains certain people to amass money and use it to further God's purposes; it justified the concentration of wealth as long as the rich used their money responsibly.

Grand Alliance (p. 715)   In World War II, the alliance between the United States, Great Britain, and France.

Great American Desert (p. 340)   A term applied to the arid, treeless land west of the Missouri River and east of the Rocky Mountains, which helped impede settlement of the Great Plains until after the Civil War.

Great Awakening (p. 79)   Spilling over into the colonies from a wave of revivals in Europe, the Awakening placed renewed emphasis on vital religious faith, partially in reaction to more secular, rationalist thinking characterizing the Enlightenment. Beginning as scattered revivals in the 1720s, the Awakening grew into a fully developed outpouring of rejuvenated faith by the 1740s. Key figures included Jonathan Edwards and George Whitefield. The Awakening's legacy included more emphasis on personal choice, as opposed to state mandates about worship, in matters of religious faith.

Great Migration (p. 630)   The mass movement of African Americans from the South to the North during World War I.

Great Society (pp. 826, 863)   The liberal reform program of President Lyndon Johnson. The program included civil rights legislation, increased public spending to help the poor, Medicare and Medicaid programs, educational legislation, and liberalized immigration policies.

Great Strike of 1877 (p. 480)   A spontaneous strike of the railroads that paralyzed two thirds of the nation's tracks for two weeks, it eventually failed after President Rutherford Hayes sent federal troops to restore control.

Greenback party (p. 529)   A political party founded in 1874 to promote the issuance of legal tender paper currency not backed by precious metals in order to inflate the money supply and relieve the suffering of people hurt by the era's deflation; most of its members merged with the Populist party.

Greenbacks (p. 403) To help fund the military forces used against the Confederacy during the Civil War, the federal Congress issued a paper currency known as greenbacks. Even though greenbacks had no backing in specie (hard currency), this currency held its value fairly well because of mounting confidence the Union would prevail in the war. See also *Specie.*

Gulf of Tonkin Resolution (p. 792) Following two reported attacks on the *U.S.S. Maddox* in 1964, American president Lyndon B. Johnson asked for and received this authorization from Congress to "take all necessary measures" to repel attacks, prevent aggression, and protect American security. It allowed Johnson to act without Congressional authorization on military matters in Vietnam.

Haciendas (p. 17) Vast landed estates awarded to full-blooded Spaniards. The native populace on these estates existed in a state of peonage and had to share their crops and labor with the *hacienda* owners. The *hacienda* system replaced the somewhat harsher *encomienda* system. See *Encomienda* System.

Half-Way Covenant (p. 52) Realizing that many children of the Massachusetts Bay Colony's first generation were not actively seeking God's saving grace and full church membership, the question was how to keep the next generation of children active in church affairs. The solution, agreed to in 1662, was to permit the baptism of children and grandchildren of professing saints, thereby according them half-way membership. Full church membership still would come only after individuals testified to a conversion experience. This compromise on standards of membership was seen as a sign of declension. See *Declension.*

Harlem Renaissance (p. 659) Self-conscious African American cultural, literary, and artistic movement centered in Harlem in New York City during the 1920s.

Harpers Ferry, Virginia (p. 381) The site of abolitionist John Brown's raid on the federal arsenal in 1859, which heightened sectional tensions and brought the nation closer to Civil War.

Hartford Convention (p. 220) Convention held in late 1814 and early 1815 by New Englanders opposed to the War of 1812, which recommended constitutional amendments to weaken the power of the South and to restrict Congress's power to impose embargoes or declare war.

Hatch Act of 1887 (p. 472) Aimed at increasing agricultural production, it provided federal support to the states for agricultural research.

Hay-Bunau-Varilla Treaty (p. 600) The treaty with the new nation of Panama in 1903 that granted the United States the right to use the Panama Canal for payment of $10 million and an annual rental fee of $250,000.

Haymarket Square riot (p. 481) A violent encounter between police and protestors in 1886 in Chicago, which led to the execution of four protest leaders, it scared the public with the specter of labor violence and demonstrated government's support of industrialists over workers.

Headright (p. 36) As an economic incentive to encourage English settlement in Virginia and other English colonies during the seventeenth century, sponsoring parties would offer 50 acres of land per person to those who migrated or who paid for the passage of others willing to migrate to America. Because of Virginia's high death rate and difficult living conditions, headrights functioned as an inducement to help bolster the colony's low settlement rate.

Hessians (p. 133) Six German principalities provided 30,000 soldiers to Great Britain to fight against the American rebels during the War for Independence. More than half of these troops-for-hire came from Hesse-Cassel. Hessian thus would serve as the generic term for all German mercenaries fighting in the war, whether or not they came from Hesse-Cassel.

Hiss-Chambers affair (p. 733) An early event in the anti-communist Red Scare. Whittaker Chambers accused Alger Hiss of being a communist and passing national security secrets to the Soviets. Hiss denied Chambers's allegations. This was an important milestone in Richard Nixon's political career.

Holy experiment (p. 66) Tolerance of religious diversity was at the core of William Penn's vision for a colony in America. As such, the colony of Pennsylvania represented a "holy experiment" for Penn. He encouraged people of all faiths to live together in harmony and to maintain peaceful relations with Native Americans in the region. The residents of early Pennsylvania never fully embraced Penn's vision, but the colony was open to religious dissenters and became a model for the diversity that later characterized America.

Homestead strike (p. 540) An unsuccessful strike at Carnegie Steel's Homestead plant in 1892, that led to violence, including the stabbing of plant manager Henry Frick by anarchist Alexander Berkman.

Hooverizing (p. 652) Herbert Hoover's program as director of the Food Administration to conserve food during World War I.

Hoovervilles (p. 671) Shantytowns of the Great Depression, named after President Herbert Hoover.

Horseshoe Bend, Battle of (p. 218) This 1814 battle in which an American army of 2600 under Andrew Jackson, combined with 600 Indians, defeated a Creek army of 1000, was the decisive battle of the Creek War (1813–1814).

House Un-American Activities Committee (HUAC) (p. 749) Committee that investigated subversive right- and left-wing movements. During the Cold War, it was best known for its two investigations of the American film industry.

Hudson Highlands strategy (p. 140) The British tried to execute this strategy early in the War for American Independence but never successfully implemented it. The idea was to gain control of the Hudson River–Lake Champlain corridor running north from New York City and south from Montreal, Canada. Had the British done so, the effect would have been to cut off New England, the initial center of rebellion, from the rest of the colonies. New England could then have been reconquered in detail. The failure to coordinate the movements of British forces in 1776 and 1777 resulted in the capture of John Burgoyne's army at Saratoga, New York, in October 1777, which ended any attempt to snuff out the rebellion by retaking New England.

Hungarian revolution (p. 764) Revolt against Soviet domination of the Hungarian government in 1956. The Soviet army was at first expelled from the country, but Khrushchev soon crushed the popular uprising with overwhelming military force.

Hydraulic society (p. 857) Defined by historian Donald Worster as "a social order based on the intensive manipulation of water and its products in an arid setting," it characterized the irrigated societies of the modern West, allowing for agricultural productivity and a massive demographic shift westward.

Immediate emancipation (p. 279) The doctrine advanced by the abolitionist William Lloyd Garrison that slaves should be immediately freed without compensation to their masters.

Immigration (p. 314) The movement of people from one country to another.

Implied powers (p. 185) The view that the national government's powers are not limited to those stated explicitly in the U.S. Constitution.

Impressment (p. 212) The British practice of seizing seamen from American merchant ships and forcing them to serve in the British navy. Impressment was one of the causes of the War of 1812.

Imprisonment for debt (p. 277) During the early nineteenth century, reformers succeeded in restricting imprisonment of debtors.

Indentured servitude (p. 35) In an effort to entice English subjects to the colonies, parties would offer legal bonded contracts that would exchange the cost of passage across the Atlantic for up to seven years of labor in America. Indenture contracts also required masters to provide food, clothing, farm tools, and sometimes land when the term of bonded service had expired, thus allowing former servants the opportunity to gain full economic independence in America.

Indian New Deal (p. 687) New Deal programs aimed specifically at Native Americans. The Indian Emergency Conservation Program provided work relief on Indian reservations; the Indian Reorganization Act of 1934 terminated the allotment program of the Dawes Severalty Act of 1887, provided funds for Native American groups to purchase new land, offered government recognition of Native American constitutions, and repealed prohibitions on Native American languages and customs.

Indian Peace Commission (p. 444) Established by Congress in 1867, the commission sought to negotiate settlements with the Plains Indians, asking them to restrict their tribes to reservations in order to promote western settlement.

Indian removal (p. 258) President Andrew Jackson's Indian policies resulted in the removal of some 46,000 Indians east of the Mississippi to Oklahoma and Arkansas, opening 25 million acres of land to white settlement.

Indirect taxes (p. 98) Also called "external" taxes, such as hidden trade duties placed on goods like those embodied in the Townshend Duties of 1767. Indirect taxes are those that people may not realize they are paying when they make purchases, such as the Townshend trade duty on tea or excise taxes placed on items like alcohol and smoking products today. See *Direct taxes.*

Indulgences (p. 19) Redemption certificates pardoning persons from punishment in the afterlife that were being sold by the Roman Catholic church. Martin Luther particularly condemned this practice in his Ninety-five Theses, bringing on the Protestant Reformation.

Industrial Workers of the World (p. 626) Organized in 1905, the IWW, or "Wobblies," were a militant socialist labor union that advocated one union for all workers and frequently employed the language of class warfare to dramatize demands.

Influence of Sea Power upon History (p. 558) An 1890 book by Alfred Thayer Mahan that argued nations expand their world power through foreign commerce and a strong navy. Strongly influenced American politicians who advocated expansion.

Initiative and Referendum (p. 537) Procedures that allow citizens to propose legislation through petitions, adopted by numerous states at the turn of the century but rarely used until the 1970s.

Insanity defense (p. 277) The legal principle that a criminal act should only be punished if the offender was fully capable of distinguishing right from wrong.

Institutional economists (p. 581) Progressive-era economists who rejected static economic theories and conducted field research to determine how the economy actually worked.

Interstate Commerce Commission (p. 531) The first federal regulatory agency, established by passage of the Interstate Commerce Act in 1887 to regulate the railroads. The ICC's powers were expanded to oversee other forms of transportation and communication.

Iran-Contra Affair (p. 888) A political scandal of the mid-1980s in which the Reagan administration attempted to secure release of U.S. hostages held in Lebanon by authorizing the sale of arms to Iran. Some of the proceeds were then channeled to opponents of the government of Nicaragua.

Iranian Hostage Crisis (p. 883) In November 1979 Iranian students seized the U.S. embassy compound in Tehran and held 52 Americans inside hostage for 444 days.

Iron Curtain (p. 736) A term coined by Winston Churchill to describe the psychological and political boundary between Western and Eastern Europe. The image was amplified when the Soviets started fortifying and sealing the western frontiers of Warsaw Pact states that bordered Western European nations. The Iron Curtain was meant as much to keep the current resident in as it was to keep Western nations out.

Jacksonian Democrats (p. 255) Made up of opponents of the administration of John Quincy Adams, Jacksonian Democrats favored strong presidential power, states' rights, Indian removal, the sale of federal land in the West at low prices, and territorial expansion. They opposed government assistance for banks and other "privileged" corporations, subsidies for internal improvements, and protective tariffs.

Jawboning (p. 673) President Herbert Hoover's initial response to the Great Depression, persuading business leaders to maintain prices and wages and labor spokesmen not to strike or demand higher wages.

Jay's Treaty (p. 192) This controversial 1794 treaty averted war between the United States and Britain by removing British forts on American soil, providing compensation for seizures from American ships, and permitting limited U.S. trade with the British West Indies.

Jazz (p. 507)   Musical style based on improvisation within a band format, combining African traditions of repetition, call and response, and strong beat with European structure.

Jazz Age (p. 649)   Catch phrase coined by author F. Scott Fitzgerald to denote the 1920s, which gave rise to popular jazz artists such as Duke Ellington, Louis Armstrong, Fletcher Henderson, and Benny Goodman as Americans' attention shifted from politics and world events to popular culture.

Jim Crow laws (p. 768)   Laws enacted by states to promote the theory of "separate but equal" facilities for whites and nonwhites. The actual purpose of these laws was to segregate the population and, implicitly, demonstrate that whites were superior.

Johnny Reb (p. 396)   This term referred to common soldiers serving in Confederate armies during the Civil War. See *Billy Yank.*

Joint Committee on Reconstruction (p. 429)   A congressional committee made up of both senators and representatives established in 1866 to investigate conditions in the southern states that were readmitted to the Union by President Andrew Johnson.

Joint Stock Trading Companies (p. 24)   These companies were given the right to develop trade between England and certain geographic regions, such as Russia or India. Investors would pool their capital, in return for shares of stock, to underwrite trading ventures. One such company, the Virginia Company, failed to secure profits for its investors but laid the basis for the first major English colony in the Americas.

Judicial review (p. 208)   The power of the courts to determine the constitutionality of acts of other branches of government and to declare unconstitutional acts null and void.

Judiciary Act of 1789 (p. 184)   The first Congress established a federal court system, including federal district and appeals courts.

Judiciary Act of 1801 (p. 207)   Passed by the Federalists after they had lost control of Congress in the election of 1800, the act reduced the size of the Supreme Court, created a new set of circuit courts, and increased the number of district court judges. The Jeffersonian Republicans repealed the act in 1801.

Kansas-Nebraska Act of 1854 (p. 374)   Controversial legislation that opened Kansas and Nebraska to white settlement, repealed the Compromise of 1820, and led opponents to form the Republican party.

Kefauver Crime Committee (p. 750)   Communists were not the only group targeted by congressional investigative committees in the 1950. Senator Estes Kefauver chaired a probe into organized crime in the United States during this time. The committee was a hit on television and helped popularize the U.S. interest in eavesdropping on governmental procedures.

Kellogg-Briand Pact (p. 697)   Pact signed by 62 nations in 1928 that renounced war and allowed countries to defend themselves with force only if attacked. The pact lacked enforcement measures and so was unsuccessful in preventing war.

Kentucky and Virginia resolutions (p. 196)   Resolutions passed by the legislatures of Kentucky and Virginia in opposition to the Alien and Sedition Acts of 1789; they represented the first statement of states' rights principles and provided a basis for the doctrine of nullification and secession.

Knights of Labor (p. 482)   A labor organization founded in 1869, that called for the unity of all workers, rejected industrial capitalism, and favored cooperatively owned businesses but was discredited by such labor violence as the Haymarket Square riot and did not survive the depression of the 1890s.

Know-Nothing Party (p. 371)   A nativist, antiforeign, anti-Catholic political party that arose in the early and mid-1850s following massive Irish and Catholic immigration during the late 1840s. Know-Nothings drew support from native-born workingmen who felt threatened by immigration and from white Southerners in the border states troubled by agitation over the slavery issue. Between 1853 and 1856, the Know-Nothing party replaced the Whigs as the second largest party in New England and some other states.

Korean War (p. 744)   Perceiving that the draw-down of U.S. forces after World War II had weakened American military power to a tremendous extent, the government of North Korea launched an invasion aimed at overthrowing the South Korean government and unifying the country. The United States managed to hold onto the southwestern corner of South Korea long enough to move forces into the country and counterattack into North Korea. The approach of U.S. forces to the Yalu River brought the Chinese communists into the war and the United States was thrown back to near the original dividing line between the two countries. At that point a stalemate developed which continues into the twenty-first century.

Kosovo (p. 903)   A predominantly Albanian part of Yugoslavia that was the site of a NATO air campaign in 1999, which reversed Serbian efforts to expel Albanian Kosovars from their homes.

Ku Klux Klan (pp. 439, 657)   A secret organization founded in the southern states during Reconstruction to terrorize and intimidate former slaves and prevent them from voting or holding public office. Officially disbanded in 1869, a second antiblack, anti-Catholic, and anti-Semitic Klan emerged in 1915 that aimed to preserve "Americanism."

Laissez-faire (p. 460)   An economic theory based on the ideas of Adam Smith; it contended that in a free economy self-interest would lead individuals to act in ways that benefited society as a whole and therefore government should not intervene.

Landed states (p. 156)   In its final form the Articles of Confederation did not provide for a national domain but allowed so-called landed states, or those states that had title claim to western lands based on English colonial charters, to maintain control of these areas. The landed states included New Hampshire, Massachusetts, Connecticut, New York, Virginia, North Carolina, South Carolina, and Georgia. The landless states objected to their exclusion from western territory, so much so that the landed states, with Virginia in the lead, began in 1781 to release their claims to the national government, thereby establishing a national domain for future development. See also *Landless states* and *National domain*.

Landless states (p. 156)   Five states, including Rhode Island, New Jersey, Pennsylvania, Delaware, and Maryland, had no claim to western lands based on colonial charters. At the time of the ratification of the Articles of Confederation, Maryland demanded full access to western lands as its price for approval of the Articles. Virginia, a landed state, agreed to turn over its claim under specified conditions, which not only helped bring about ratification but also facilitated the formation of a national domain of western lands that would be developed on behalf of the whole republic. See also *Landed states* and *National domain*.

Large policy (p. 558)   Bold foreign policy put forth by Henry Cabot Lodge and others, advocating a canal through the Central American isthmus and a strong American naval presence in the Caribbean and Pacific.

League of Nations (p. 634)   Point Fourteen of Wilson's Fourteen Points, the proposal to establish an international organization to guarantee the territorial integrity of independent nations.

Lecompton Constitution (p. 379)   In an election in 1857 in which Free Soil voters abstained, Kansas adopted a proslavery constitution. When President Buchanan urged Congress to admit Kansas as a slave state under the Lecompton Constitution, Stephen Douglas broke with the administration. In 1858, Kansas voters decisively defeated the Lecompton Constitution.

Lend-Lease Act (p. 704)   The program by which the United States provided arms and supplies to the Allies in World War II before joining the fighting.

Lewis and Clark Expedition (p. 210)   The first overland expedition to the Pacific coast and back, led by Meriwether Lewis and William Clark and initiated by President Thomas Jefferson, took place between 1804 and 1806.

Liberty party (p. 281)   An antislavery political party founded in 1839.

Lincoln-Douglas debates (p. 380)   A series of seven debates between Republican Abraham Lincoln and Democratic senator Stephen Douglas in the 1858 Illinois Senate campaign that dramatized the issues of slavery in the western territory and popular sovereignty.

Literacy testing (p. 496)   Politicians' idea to restrict immigration from southern and eastern Europe and China in the 1890s. Such bills were killed by presidential veto. Superseded by the quota system of restricting undesirable immigration.

Little Rock crisis (p. 773)   Conflict in 1957 in which Arkansas Governor Orval Faubus sent the Arkansas National Guard to prevent the racial integration of Little Rock's Central High School. After a crucial delay, President Eisenhower federalized the National Guard troops and sent in 1000 paratroopers to foster the school's integration.

Loose interpretation (p. 186)   The view that the national government has the power to create agencies or enact statutes to fulfill the powers granted by the U.S. Constitution.

Louisiana Purchase (p. 210)   Territory purchased from France in 1803 for $15 million that extended from the Mississippi River to the Rocky Mountains and that doubled the size of the country.

Loyal Nine (p. 100)   This informal group of pro-colonial rights leaders in Boston helped organize resistance against unwanted British policies, such as the Stamp Act. Working with more visible popular leaders like Samuel Adams and street leaders like Ebenezer Mackintosh, the Loyal Nine both planned and gave overall direction to controlled violent protests in defying the imperial will and protecting the community's interests in Boston during the 1760s.

LSD (Lysergic Acid Diethylamide) (p. 830)   A psychoactive drug developed originally to help in research on mental illness. The strong hallucinogenic character of the drug made it a favorite of the counterculture in the 1960s.

Lusitania (p. 619)   British ship carrying American passengers sunk by a German submarine on May 15, 1915.

Lyndon's war (p. 792)   Another name for the war in Vietnam, used by antiwar activists to indicate who they felt was responsible for continuing U.S. involvement in Vietnam.

Macon's Bill No. 2 (p. 213)   An attempt to stop British and French interference with American trade.

Manhattan Project (p. 724)   The secret government program to develop an atomic bomb during World War II.

Manifest destiny (p. 343)   A concept that justified American expansion westward and southward across North America.

Manila Bay, Battle of (p. 565)   A decisive victory against the Spanish navy in the Philippine Islands. Commodore Dewey's Asiatic Fleet sailed from China and destroyed the Spanish on May 1, 1898. This was the first fleet action between "modern" warships.

Manitou (p. 12)   Native Americans considered everything on the planet—trees, plants, and animals—to be spiritually alive or filled with spirits. Manitou is the term for spirits.

Manumission (p. 167)   The freeing or emancipation of chattel slaves by their owners, which became more common in the upper South in the wake of so much talk during the American Revolution about human liberty. George Washington was among those planters who provided for the manumission of his slaves after the death of his wife Martha.

Marbury v. Madison (pp. 208, 231)   This landmark 1803 Supreme Court decision, which established the principle of judicial review, marked the first time that the Court declared an act of Congress unconstitutional.

Maroons (p. 329)   Escaped slaves who formed communities of runaways.

Marquis of Queensberry Rules (p. 509)   Standardized boxing rules of the late nineteenth century, creating structured three-minute rounds with one-minute rest periods, outlawing wrestling throws and holds, and specifying the number of rounds.

Marshall Plan (p. 737)   A massive foreign aid program to Western Europe of $17 billion over four years, beginning in 1948. Named after Secretary of State George Marshall, the program restored economic prosperity to the region and stabilized its system of democracy and capitalism.

Matrilineal (p. 8)   Unlike European nations that were male based, or patrilineal, in organization, many Native American societies structured tribal and family power and authority through women. Quite often, use rights to land and personal property passed from mother to daughter, and the eldest women chose male chiefs. Matrilineal societies thus placed great importance on the capacities of women to provide for the long-term welfare of their tribes.

McCullouch v. Maryland (p. 231) A landmark 1819 Supreme Court decision establishing Congress's power to charter a national bank and declaring unconstitutional a tax imposed by Maryland on the bank's Baltimore branch.

McKinley Tariff Act (p. 560) An act passed to remove all tariffs on foreign sugar and placing a two-cent per pound bounty on American-produced sugar. The negative effect on Hawaiian sugar production helped Queen Liliuokalani in her drive to purge American influences in Hawaii.

Mercantilism (p. 63) An economic system built on the assumption that the world's supply of wealth is fixed and that nations must export more goods than they import to assure a steady supply of gold and silver into national coffers. Mercantile thinkers saw the inflow of such wealth as the key to maintaining and enhancing national power and self-sufficiency. Within this context, the accumulation and development of colonies was of great importance, since colonies could supply scarce raw materials to parent nations and serve as markets for finished goods.

Mexican struggle for independence (p. 337) Mexico's struggle against Spanish rule began in 1810 and independence was achieved in 1821.

Mexican-American War (p. 350) A war between the United States and Mexico that took place between 1846 and 1848.

Military Reconstruction Act (p. 431) A law passed after the South's refusal to accept the Fourteenth Amendment in 1867, it nullified existing state governments and divided the South into five military districts headed by military governors.

Mill towns (p. 474) Established by factory owners to supply necessary goods and services for their workers, these towns often caused employees to become very dependent on the mills.

Millennium (p. 274) In the biblical Book of Revelation, the millennium is a period of a thousand years during which Christ is to rule on Earth.

Mission system (p. 337) A system used by the Spanish for colonial settlement, the mission system sought to convert the native population to Christianity and use its labor in farming, ranching, and handicrafts.

Missionary diplomacy (p. 601) Name given to the diplomatic policy of Woodrow Wilson; it called for the United States to use its influence to promote democracy around the world.

Mississippi Plan (p. 542) Provisions in the 1890 Mississippi constitution designed to disfranchise African Americans through poll taxes, literacy tests, and residency requirements. These provisions were widely copied by other southern states.

Missouri Compromise (pp. 242, 365) An act passed by Congress in 1820 that admitted Missouri to the Union as a slave state and Maine as a free state, and prohib-

ited slavery in the portion of the Louisiana Purchase north of Missouri's border.

Missouri crisis (p. 254) The political debate that followed the 1819 proposal of Representative James Tallmadge of New York that Missouri be admitted to the Union only if it prohibited further slaves from entering the state and freed its slaves when they reached the age of 25.

Modern Republicanism (p. 760) Also called *dynamic conservatism*, President Eisenhower's domestic agenda advocated conservative spending approaches without drastically cutting back New Deal social programs.

Molly Maguires (p. 479) Leaders of a secret fraternal society of Irish immigrants, they waged guerilla warfare in the coalfields during 1877, disrupting the operation of several mines and attacking a few mining officials.

Monroe Doctrine (p. 233) In this 1823 statement of American foreign policy, President James Monroe declared that the United States would not allow European powers to establish new colonies in the Western Hemisphere or to expand the boundaries of existing colonies.

Mormon church (p. 348) The Church of Jesus Christ of Latter-Day Saints is a religious group organized by Joseph Smith, Jr., in 1830.

Mosinee's Red May Day (p. 744) Mosinee, Wisconsin, became a communist puppet state for a day in 1950. The local American Legionnaires dressed up as Soviets and took over the town to try to illustrate what (according to them) life would be like in the United States under a Soviet-style government. This was one symptom of the Red Scare that would soon make communist-hunting also a sport in the United States.

Motion pictures (p. 514) A revolutionary form of entertainment that came into being at the close of the nineteenth century. Using a series of still pictures projected fast enough onto a screen to produce the illusion of continuous action, they brought scenes and events that previously had been experienced only through still photography to life.

Mountain men (p. 340) The name given to the buckskin-clad trappers, explorers, and traders who engaged in the fur trade in the early nineteenth century.

Muckrakers (p. 583) Investigative journalists during the Progressive era, they wrote sensational exposés of social and political problems that helped spark the reform movements of their day.

Mugwumps (p. 525) A reform faction of the Republican party in the 1870s and 1880s that crusaded for honest and effective government and sometimes supported Democratic reform candidates.

Muller v. Oregon (p. 582) Case through which the Supreme Court in 1908, using social science research, upheld governments' rights to set limits to the working hours of women.

My Lai (p. 806) A village in South Vietnam, scene of a massacre of unarmed civilians on February 25, 1968. The only person convicted of this crime was Lt. William Calley.

Nation of Islam (p. 822) Founded by Wallace D. Fard during the Great Depression of the 1930s, the Nation of Islam emphasized black economic self-sufficiency and black nationalism under the leadership of Elijah Muhammad.

National American Woman Suffrage Association (p. 527) An organization formed in 1890 from two factions of the suffrage movement, NAWSA sought a constitutional amendment to grant women the right to vote throughout the nation, eventually leading to the Nineteenth Amendment.

National Anti-Cigarette League (p. 656) Organization formed in 1903, the embodiment of the movement to end cigarette smoking in the United States, closely allied with Prohibition. The group won success in many states but never nationally, and the movement dissipated by the end of the 1920s.

National Association for the Advancement of Colored People (NAACP) (pp. 590, 658) Organization established in 1909 to fight for African American civil rights through legal action.

National Child Labor Committee (p. 592) Founded in 1904 by Edgar Gardner Murphy and Florence Kelley, this organization fought to bring an end to child labor.

National Defense Education Act (p. 767) A reaction to the apparent lead in education held by the Soviets in light of their *Sputnik* space program. The aim of the act was to improve science and mathematical skills in the American school system.

National domain (p. 156) All territory west of the original thirteen states that was to be developed on behalf of the new American republic and, ultimately, made into new states. The national domain came into existence in the 1780s when the so-called landed states started to cede their sea-to-sea charter claims to the national government. See also *Landed states* and *Landless states*.

National Labor Union (p. 482) Founded in 1866, it was the first union to attempt to organize all workers, supported a variety of reform causes, but failed during the depression of the mid-1870s.

National Organization for Women (NOW) (p. 833) A feminist advocacy group, founded in 1966, that promotes equity for women in the workplace and reproductive rights, and opposes sexual harassment and violence against women.

National Origins Act of 1924 (pp. 497, 657) Law that restricted immigration to 2 percent for any given nationality, based on the total amounts from the 1890 census. Use of the 1890 census effectively restricted immigrants from eastern and southern Europe. Combined with the Emergency Quota Act, this law effectively stifled immigration from southern and eastern Europe and stopped Asian immigration completely.

National Recovery Administration (NRA) (p. 680) The federal government's plan to revive industry during the Great Depression through rational planning.

National Republicans (p. 255) The name that supporters of John Quincy Adams took following his defeat in the presidential election of 1828. National Republicans were committed to using the federal government to promote economic and social development.

National Security Council Paper Number 68 (NSC-68) (p. 741) Influential National Security Council document arguing communism was a monolithic world movement directed from the Kremlin and advocating a massive military buildup to counteract the encroachment of communism.

National System of Interstate and Defense Highways Act (p. 761) Legislation adapted in 1956 that created the national highway system of 41,000 miles, costing $26 billion and taking 13 years to construct. It solidified the central role of the automobile in American culture.

National Urban League (p. 658) Organization founded in 1911 by social workers, white philanthropists, and conservative African Americans on the basis of Booker T. Washington's conciliatory approach to race relations; that league concentrated on finding jobs for urban African Americans.

Nationalists (p. 156) Revolutionary leaders who favored a stronger national government than the one provided for in the Articles of Confederation. They believed that only a powerful national government, rather than self-serving states, could deal effectively with the many vexing problems besetting the new nation. George Washington, Alexander Hamilton, and James Madison were prominent nationalists.

Nativism (p. 494) A backlash against immigration by white native-born Protestants. Nativism could be based on racial prejudice (professors and scientists sometimes classified eastern Europeans as innately inferior), religion (Protestants distrusted Catholics and Jews), politics (immigrants were often associated with radical political philosophies), and economics (labor leaders resented competition).

Nativists (p. 371) People who are strongly hostile toward immigrants.

Naturalism (p. 505) Literary style of the late nineteenth and early twentieth century in which the individual was seen as a helpless victim in a world in which biological, social, and psychological forces determined his or her fate.

Navigation System (p. 63) To effect mercantilist goals, King and Parliament legislated a series of Navigation Acts (1651, 1660, 1663, 1673, 1696) that established England as the central hub of trade in its emerging empire. Various rules of trade, as embodied in the Navigation Acts, made it clear that England's colonies in the Americas existed first and foremost to serve the parent nation's economic interests, regardless of what might be best for the colonists.

Neutrality (p. 618) U.S. policy of impartiality during World Wars I and II.

New Deal (p. 676) President Franklin Delano Roosevelt's program designed to bring about economic recovery and reform during the Great Depression.

New Freedom (p. 597) A phrase used in the 1912 presidential election campaign to describe Woodrow Wilson's plan for restoring economic freedom by busting the trusts.

New Humanists (p. 689) Depression-era intellectuals who extolled classical civilization as a bulwark against modern values, exemplified by Lewis Mumford's 1934 work, *Technics and Civilization*.

New Left (p. 828) Collective term for the various political action youth groups that developed during the 1960s. Most of these groups were interested in ending the war in Vietnam and bringing about political change in the United States.

New Lights (p. 82) As the Great Awakening spread during the 1730s and 1740s, various religious groups fractured into two camps, sometimes known as the New Lights and Old Lights. The New Lights placed emphasis on a "new birth" conversion experience—gaining God's saving grace. They also demanded ministers who had clearly experienced conversions themselves. See *Old Lights.*

New Look (p. 763)   President Eisenhower's adjustment to the doctrine of containment. He advocated saving money by emphasizing nuclear over conventional weapons, on the premise that the next major world conflict would be nuclear.

New Nationalism (p. 597)   Slogan used by Theodore Roosevelt in the 1912 presidential election campaign to describe his plan for combating the power of big corporations through government regulation rather than trust busting.

New Navy (p. 557)   After the Civil War the United States Navy dwindled from first to near last among the industrialized nations. In the 1880s and 1890s a movement was undertaken to build new warships to be used to extend U.S. influence around the world. The debate over the building of these ships echoed the debate over U.S. involvement in the world at large.

New Orleans, Battle of (p. 220)   In January 1815, a ragtag army consisting of frontier fighters, pirates, and freed slaves under the command of Andrew Jackson decisively defeated a British force trying to capture New Orleans. The battle took place after the signing of the Treaty of Ghent, which ended the War of 1812.

New South (p. 473)   The ideology following Reconstruction that the South could be restored to its previous glory through a diversified economy; it was used to rally Southerners and convince outside investors to underwrite regional industrialization by extolling the resources, labor supply, and racial harmony of the South.

Niagara movement (p. 589)   Begun in 1905 by W. E. B. Du Bois and William Monroe Trotter, this group sought to counteract the accommodationist program of Booker T. Washington, helping to set the stage for the organization of the National Association for the Advancement of Colored People (NAACP).

1963 March on Washington (p. 821)   In 1963, some 250,000 demonstrators marched on Washington to demand passage of meaningful civil rights legislation, an end to school segregation and police brutality, a federal law ending discrimination in the workplace, self-government for the District of Columbia, and an increase in the minimum wage and public works programs for the unemployed. This landmark civil rights protest ended with hundreds of thousands of people congregated on Capitol Mall in Washington, D.C., to hear, among others, Dr. Martin Luther King, Jr., deliver his "I have a dream" speech.

Nineteenth Amendment (p. 653)   Passed in 1920, the Constitutional guarantee of women's right to vote.

Nixon Doctrine (p. 800)   President Richard Nixon's argument in favor of "Vietnamization," the notion that the South Vietnamese would carry more of the war's combat burden. This plan never reached full realization because of the South Vietnamese inability to carry on the war effort without American troops.

Non-Intercourse Act (p. 213)   An 1809 statute that replaced the Embargo of 1807. It forbade trade with Britain, France, and their possessions, but reopened trade with other countries.

Nonseparatists (p. 39)   Religious dissenters from England who wanted to purify, rather than separate from, what they viewed as the corrupted, state-supported Anglican church, or Church of England. By and large, the Puritans were nonseparatists, and some of them banded together to form a utopian community of believers in America. The Massachusetts Bay Colony was to be a model society that would show how godly societies and churches were to be properly organized. See *Separatists.*

North American Free Trade Agreement (NAFTA) (p. 900)   A 1994 agreement that reduced trade barriers between the United States, Canada, and Mexico.

North Atlantic Treaty Organization (NATO) (p. 739)   An organization founded in 1949 whose members signed a mutual defense pact to protect those countries bordering the North Atlantic, or having need to traverse it frequently. As these countries were the United States and its allies and the main threat to those countries was the Soviet Union, the purpose of NATO, defense against a Soviet attack on Western Europe, was clear. In response to the creation of NATO, the Soviet Union invited its communist allies in Europe to join the Warsaw Pact.

Northern Confederacy (p. 211)   Fearful that the Louisiana Purchase of 1803 would reduce their region's political influence, a number of Federalists plotted to establish an independent confederacy that would include New Jersey, New York, and New England. The scheme was repudiated by Alexander Hamilton.

Northwest Passage (p. 19)   During the Age of Exploration, adventurers from England, France, and the Netherlands sought an all-water route across North America. The goal was to gain access to Oriental material goods and riches while avoiding contact with the developing Spanish empire farther to the south in Central and South America.

Nullification (p. 256)   The doctrine, devised by John C. Calhoun, that a state has the power to "nullify" federal legislation within its borders.

Office of Price Administration (OPA) (p. 708)   Office formed in 1942 that had the authority to freeze prices and wages, control rents, and institute rationing of scarce items during World War II.

Ohio Gang (p. 660)   Friends and cronies of President Warren G. Harding who received governmental jobs during his term and subsequently plunged his administration into disgrace.

Oil crisis (p. 879)   Oil supply disruptions and soaring oil prices that the United States experienced in 1973 and 1979. In 1973, Middle Eastern nations imposed an embargo on oil shipments to punish the West for supporting Israel in that year's Arab-Israeli war. A second oil shock occurred when the Iranian Revolution disrupted oil shipments to the western nations.

Old Lights (p. 82)   As the Great Awakening spread during the 1730s and 1740s, various religious groups fractured into two camps, sometimes known as the Old Lights and the New Lights. The Old Lights were not very enthusiastic about the Awakening, particularly in terms of what they viewed as popular excesses in seeking after God's grace. Old Light ministers emphasized formal schooling in theology as a source of their religious authority, and they emphasized good order in their churches. See *New Lights.*

Open Door note (p. 572)   Policy set forth in 1899 by Secretary of State John Hay preventing further partitioning of China by European powers, and protecting the principle of free trade.

Operation Just Cause (p. 902)   Name given to an American military intervention in Panama in December 1989, which was launched after Panama's leader, Manuel Noriega, who was indicted on drug-related charges, invalidated civilian elections and declared a state of war with the United States.

Opium and cocaine (p. 515)   Two drugs that were beginning to have an impact on the social structure of the United States as early as the 1890s. The unrestricted and uncontrolled sale of these drugs caused concern that they were linked to crime and racial unrest.

Orders in Council (p. 212)   British government policies that imposed an economic blockade on European ports during the Napoleonic wars.

Oregon country (p. 345)   The United States and Britain both claimed territory in the Pacific Northwest. In 1846 they agreed to divide the territory along the 49th parallel.

Oregon Trail (p. 342)   Westward pioneer route stretching 2,000 miles from Missouri to the mouth of the Columbia River on the Pacific Coast.

Ostend Manifesto (p. 373)   A plan devised in 1854 by three U.S. diplomats, including future president James Buchanan to purchase or seize Cuba and its 300,000 slaves.

Pale of Settlement (p. 493)   Area of settlement for Polish Jews after Russia conquered Poland in the eighteenth century. This area was a ghetto for over 90 percent of Russian Jews and was the only area where they were allowed to live without special permit. Increasing repression of their religion in Russia caused large numbers of Russian Jews to emigrate to the United States and other countries "beyond the Pale."

Paleo-Indians (p. 5)   Those nomadic people who first came to the Americas via the land bridge from Asia and traveled in small bands while constantly searching for food.

Panama Canal Treaty (p. 882)   A 1977 treaty providing for transfer of control of the Panama Canal to Panamanians by 2000.

Panic of 1819 (pp. 239, 254)   A financial panic that brought the economic expansion that followed the War of 1812 to a close and resulted in bank failures, mortgage foreclosures, and widespread unemployment.

Panic of 1837 (p. 264)   A financial depression that lasted until the early 1840s.

Panic of 1873 (p. 442)   A financial collapse caused by overinvestment in railroads that ushered in a six-year economic depression.

Panic of 1893 (p. 538)   Caused primarily by a European depression, coupled with overexpansion of the American economy, this stock market crash ushered in one of the nation's worse depressions.

Paternalism (p. 323)   The belief held by many slaveowners in the pre–Civil War South that slaveholding was a duty and a burden and that they had to care for and discipline slaves as parents do children.

Patriarchal (p. 48)   Patriarchal social and political systems are denoted by power and authority residing in males, such as the father of the family. Such authority then passes from father to son through the generations, and males, in general, control decision making. See *coverture.*

Patrons of Husbandry (p. 535)   An organization founded in 1867 to aid farmers through its local granges; it was responsible for state laws regulating railroads, established cooperatives to help with marketing problems, and provided a social outlet for rural areas. Officially entitled the National Grange of the Patrons of Husbandry, the organization was also known as the *Granger movement*, and its local branches were called *granges.*

Peace without victory (p. 623)   President Woodrow Wilson's plan for a peaceful postwar world order, to be maintained by a League of Nations.

Peaceful coexistence (p. 764)   An attempt to warm the Cold War, in which Eisenhower and Khrushchev sought to improve relations between their countries. Incidents such as the U-2 shoot-down over the USSR and the Cuban missile crisis strained this policy.

Pearl Harbor (p. 706)   The main base of the U.S. Pacific fleet, which Japan attacked on December 7, 1941. Following that attack, the United States entered World War II.

Pendleton Act (p. 530)   A law passed in 1883 to eliminate political corruption in the federal government, it outlawed political contributions by appointed officeholders and established the Civil Service Commission to administer competitive examinations for coveted government jobs.

Permanent immigrants (p. 493)   Immigrants coming to America to settle permanently, often due to ethnic and religious persecution at home.

Perpetual servitude (p. 53)   Indentured servitude represented temporary service for a specified period, usually from four to seven years, to a legally designated owner. Perpetual servitude meant being owned by some other person for life—and ultimately, even through the generations. In the early days of Virginia, both English subjects and African Americans were indentured servants, but over time blacks would be subjected to perpetual servitude as chattel, defined as the movable property of their all-powerful masters and without legal rights of any kind.

Philippine Islands (p. 565)   A group of over 4,000 islands in the western Pacific, owned by Spain prior to the Spanish-American War. The Filipino struggle for independence from Spain shifted to resistance against U.S. occupation of the islands after the war.

Ping-pong diplomacy (p. 803)   Communist China's chairman Mao Tse-tung sent a table tennis team to the world championships in Nagoya, Japan, and then invited an American team to compete in Japan in 1971. This small gesture paved the way for President Nixon's visit to China in February 1972.

Planned urban growth (p. 503)   Ultimately this was a proposal that the city should serve the public (the public city), differing from earlier views that the city should cater to the wealthy and ambitious (the private city). City planners looked at the city as a place where ordinary people, with families and lives to live, resided. Such a place would have to include plans for a healthy environment for those people. Inclusion of parks, schools, and public services were part of the public city ideal, but much work would be needed to recover from the private city concept.

Plantation legend (p. 318)   A stereotype, created by popular pre–Civil War writers, that depicted the South as a region of aristocratic planters, beautiful Southern belles, poor white trash, and faithful household slaves.

Platt Amendment (p. 567)   An amendment to the Army Appropriation Bill in 1901, limiting Cuban independence by giving the United States two naval bases on Cuba and the right to intervene in Cuban affairs if the American government felt Cuban independence was threatened.

Plessy v. Ferguson (pp. 475, 593)   A Supreme Court decision in 1896 that ruled "separate but equal" facilities for African Americans were constitutional under the Fourteenth Amendment; it had the effect of legalizing segregation and led to the passage of much discriminatory legislation known as Jim Crow laws.

Political slavery (p. 111)   During the 1760s and 1770s many colonial leaders believed that if they did not keep resisting unwanted British policies, they would fall into a state of political slavery in which they had no liberties. As such, they would be akin to chattel slaves in their midst. Comprehending how potentially tyrannical chattel slavery was spurred on many colonists to defend American liberties, even to the point of open rebellion.

Ponzi scheme (p. 662)   Scheme in which Charles Ponzi promised to return $15 to anyone who lent him $10 for 90 days in order to buy foreign currencies at low prices and sell them for higher prices. Ponzi received $15 million in eight months and returned less than $200,000 to investors.

Pools (p. 462)   Agreements among railroad administrators to divide the total volume of freight among their lines, usually to be able to raise prices.

Popular sovereignty (p. 365)   The principle, incorporated into the Compromise of 1850 and the Kansas-Nebraska Act of 1854, that the people living in the western territories should decide whether or not to permit slavery.

Populist (People's) party (p. 537)   A political party established in 1892 primarily by remnants of the Farmers' Alliance and Greenback party, it sought to inflate the currency with silver dollars and to establish an income tax; some of its platform was adopted by the Democrats in 1896, and it died out after the defeat of joint candidate William Jennings Bryan.

Port Huron Statement (p. 828)   The founding document of the Students for a Democratic Society (SDS), adopted in June 1962, it attacked racial discrimination, alienating work, and uncontrolled exploitation of natural resources. The statement also called for participatory democracy and the active involvement of citizens in decisions that might affect their lives.

Potsdam Conference (p. 721)   Suburb of Berlin where Allied leaders convened in July 1945 for their last wartime meeting of World War II, the first test for President Truman. The Potsdam Declaration de-

manded that Japan immediately surrender and that any other action would lead to "prompt and utter destruction."

Pragmatism (p. 582)   A distinctly American philosophy proposed by William James, it contends that any concept should be tested and its validity determined by its outcome and that the truth of an idea is found in the conduct it dictates or inspires.

Price Revolution (p. 22)   The large influx of gold and silver into Europe from Spanish America during the sixteenth century, along with increased demand for limited supplies of goods, set off a threefold rise in prices (the "great inflation") that caused profound economic turmoil, social disruption, and political instability among European peoples and nations.

Progressive (Bull Moose) party (p. 597)   A political party established in 1912 by supporters of Theodore Roosevelt after William H. Taft won the Republican presidential nomination. The party proposed a broad program of reform but Bull Moose candidate Roosevelt and Republican nominee Taft lost to the Democratic candidate, Woodrow Wilson.

Prohibition (p. 656)   The ban of the production, sale, and consumption of alcoholic beverages. The Eighteenth Amendment to the U.S. Constitution, adopted in 1919, established prohibition. The amendment was repealed in 1933, with adoption of the Twenty-first Amendment.

Protestant Reformation (p. 19)   A religious reform movement formally begun in 1517 when the German friar Martin Luther openly attacked abuses of Roman Catholic doctrine. Luther contended that the people could read scripture for themselves in seeking God's grace and that the Bible, not church doctrine, was the ultimate authority in human relationships. Luther's complaints helped foster a variety of dissenting religious groups, some of which would settle in America to get away from various forms of oppression in Europe.

Public virtue (p. 133)   A cornerstone of good citizenship in republican states, public virtue involved the subordination of individual self-interest to serving the greater good of the whole community. Revolutionary leaders believed that public virtue was essential for a republic to survive and thrive. If absent, governments would be torn apart by competing private interests and succumb to anarchy, at which point tyrants would emerge to offer political stability but with the loss of dearly won political liberties.

Public Works Administration (PWA) (p. 681)   One of many works programs under the Federal Emergency Relief Act of the New Deal, which hired unemployed workers for various public projects, thus providing people with money to spend on industrial products.

Pullman strike (p. 541)   Called by the American Railway Union in 1894, this strike at the Pullman plant at Chicago was defeated by the use of federal troops.

Purity crusaders (p. 586)   Beginning in the 1890s, these people sought the prohibition of alcohol and prostitution and supported censorship and the regulation of narcotics.

Quasi War with France (p. 195)   An undeclared naval war fought entirely at sea by the United States and France between 1798 and 1801.

Radical Republicans (p. 426)   A faction of the Republican Party during Reconstruction, the Radicals favored forcing the former Confederate states to make fundamental changes before they could be readmitted to the Union. Eventually the Radicals won control of the Republican party because of Southerners' refusal to accept more lenient plans for Reconstruction.

Radical revolutionaries (p. 154)   At the time of the American Revolution, this group argued in favor of establishing more democratic forms of government. Radical revolutionaries had a strong trust in the people, viewed them as inherently virtuous (see *Public virtue*), and believed that citizens could govern themselves. Samuel Adams, Thomas Jefferson, and Thomas Paine might be described as radical revolutionaries. See *Cautious revolutionaries.*

Rage militaire (p. 122)   A term meaning a passion for arms, the rage militaire characterized the attitudes of American colonists as the war with Great Britain began in 1775. When the ravages and deprivations of warfare became more self-evident, however, this early enthusiasm gave out. In 1776 Thomas Paine criticized the "summer soldiers and sunshine patriots" among the colonists who seemed so eager to fight at the beginning of the War for Independence but who so quickly dropped out as the dangers of engaging in warfare increased.

Rationalism (p. 78)   A main tenet of the Enlightenment era, meaning a firm trust in the ability of the human mind to solve earthly problems, thereby lessening the role of—and reliance on—God as an active force in the ordering of human affairs.

Reagan Doctrine (p. 885)   President Ronald Reagan's 1985 pledge of American aid to insurgent movements attempting to overthrow Soviet-backed regimes in the Third World.

Rebates (p. 462)   Discounts from the normal shipping rate, they were given by the railroads to attract business in the middle of the 19th century.

Reconstruction Finance Corporation (RFC) (p. 673)   Corporation created by Congress in 1932 and authorized to loan $2 billion to banks, savings and loan associations, railroads, and life insurance companies in the hopes of spurring production and hiring in the private sector.

Red Scare (p. 633)   Fear of radicalism and Communism following World War I, triggered by labor strikes and bombings which resulted in widespread vigilantism as well as extreme measures by government.

Redeemer governments (p. 441)   A popular name for the Democratic state governments in the South that replaced the Republican-dominated ones established during Reconstruction.

Redemptioners (p. 74)   The redemptioner labor system was similar to that of indentured servitude in providing a way for persons without financial means to get to America. Normally, the family had to locate someone to pay for its passage in return for a set number of years of labor. If no buyer could be found, then ships captains could sell the family's labor, most likely on less desirable terms for the family, to recoup the costs of passage. Thousands of Germans migrated to America as redemptioners in the eighteenth century.

Referendum   See *Initiative and Referendum.*

Reform Darwinists (p. 581)   Sociologists who rejected the determinism of the Social Darwinists, they accepted evolutionary theory but held that people could shape their environment rather than only be shaped by it and accepted human intervention in society.

Religious liberalism (p. 273)   A religious viewpoint that rejected the Calvinist doctrines of original sin and predestination and stressed the basic goodness of human nature.

Remember the *Maine!* (p. 564)   A national catch phrase following the mysterious 1898 explosion of the U.S. battleship *Maine* in Havana harbor that inflamed public opinion, leading to the Spanish-American War.

Removal (Indian Removal Policy) (p. 258)   A policy of resettling eastern Indian tribes on lands west of the Mississippi River.

Renaissance (p. 10)   Beginning in the 1400s, the European Renaissance represented an intellectual and cultural flowering in the arts, literature, philosophy, and the sciences. One of the most important tenets of the Renaissance was the belief in human progress, or the betterment of society.

Rendezvous system (p. 340)   Between 1825 and 1840, fur companies held gatherings where fur trappers could trade their skins for supplies.

Republican motherhood (p. 165)   This definition of motherhood, emanating from the American Revolution, assigned mothers the task of raising dutiful children, especially sons, who would be prepared to serve the nation in disinterested fashion (see *Public virtue*). Mothers thus acquired the special charge of assuring that future generations could uphold the tenets of republicanism. This expanded role for mothers meant that women, not men, would be responsible for the domestic sphere of life.

Republican party (p. 374)   A political party established following enactment of the Kansas-Nebraska Act of 1854 that was opposed to the extension of slavery into the western territories.

Republican values (p. 205)   A set of values widely held during the Revolutionary and post-Revolutionary eras that the new nation's survival depended upon nurturing virtue and goodness of character among its citizens.

Republicanism (p. 153)   At the time of the American Revolution, republicanism referred to the concept that sovereignty, or ultimate political authority, is vested in the people—the citizens of the nation. As such, republican governments not only derive their authority from the consent of the governed but also predicate themselves on the principles of rule by law and legislation by elected representatives.

Restrictive covenant (p. 646)   A formal deed restriction that bound white property owners in a given neighborhood to sell only to whites.

Resumption Act of 1875 (p. 529)   This act required that all paper money of the United States be backed by either gold or silver.

Revenue Act of 1942 (p. 708)   World War II measure that raised corporate taxes, increased the excess profits tax, and levied a 5 percent withholding tax on anyone earning over $642 a year; it attempted to slow inflation by reducing consumer purchasing power.

Rock and roll (p. 777) Musical style new to the 1950s, combining black rhythm and blues with white country music. Listened to mostly by young Americans and embodied by Elvis Presley, the music challenged notions of sexual propriety and racial division.

Roderigue Hortalez & Cie. (p. 139) Prior to its formal involvement in the War for Independence, the French government supplied the American rebels with critically needed war goods through a bogus private trading firm known as Roderigue Hortalez & Cie. French officials did so because they hoped to see the power of Great Britain reduced but without becoming directly engaged in the war itself. Once the Franco-American alliance came into being in 1778, the French could abandon such ruses in favor of open support of their rebel allies.

Roe v. Wade (p. 834) A case from Texas that was heard before the Supreme Court in 1973 and considered whether a woman had the right to an abortion. The Court decision was that the decision to have an abortion was a private matter of concern only to the woman and her physician, and that only in the last three months of pregnancy could the government limit the right to abortion.

Roosevelt recession (p. 689) Economic relapse following the 1936 elections when industrial production fell by 40 percent and unemployment rose by 4 million.

Rough Riders (p. 568) A group of volunteer cavalry led by Theodore Roosevelt during the Cuban campaign of the Spanish-American War.

Rwanda (p. 903) A central African nation that was the site of the killing of approximately 800,000 Tutsis and moderate Hutus in 1994.

Sacco and Vanzetti case (p. 657) Italian immigrants, anarchists Nicola Sacco and Bartolomeo Vanzetti were arrested and tried for the robbery and murders of two men in Braintree, Massachusetts. The state did not prove its case but won by exploiting the men's radical views. They were put to death on July 14, 1921.

Sagebrush rebellion (p. 868) Failed movement led by conservative western politicians to cede federal control of western land to individual states, promoting private ownership and commercial development.

Salutary neglect (p. 73) This term signifies England's relatively benign neglect of its American colonies from about 1690 to 1760. During these years King and Parliament rarely legislated constraints of any kind and allowed the colonists much autonomy in provincial and local matters. In turn, the colonists supported the parent nation's economic and political objectives. This harmonious period came to an end after the Seven Year's War when King and Parliament began asserting more control over the American colonists through taxes and trade regulations.

Samoa (p. 559) Pacific island where the United States and Germany gathered warships in 1889. Both sides wanted control of the island as a coaling station, but a typhoon blew both fleets about badly and the Germans withdrew.

Santa Fe Trail (p. 341) Westward trading route stretching southward from Missouri to Santa Fe, New Mexico, which William Becknell started in 1821.

Scalawags (p. 435) Southern white Republicans during Reconstruction, they came from every class and had a variety of motives but were pictured by their opponents as ignorant and degraded.

Scopes "Monkey Trial" (p. 656) Trial against John Scopes in 1925 for teaching Charles Darwin's theory of evolution in a Tennessee public school.

Second Bank of the United States (pp. 229, 264) A national bank chartered in 1816 to hold government funds, ease the transfer of money across state lines, and regulate private banks. Its federal charter expired in 1836.

Second Continental Congress (p. 125) This body gathered in Philadelphia during May 1775 after the shooting war with Great Britain had started. The second Congress functioned as a coordinating government for the colonies and states in providing overall direction to the patriot war effort. It continued as a central legislative body under the Articles of Confederation until 1789 when a new national legislature, the federal Congress as established under the Constitution of 1787, first convened.

Second Great Awakening (p. 274) A wave of religious fervor and revivalism that swept the United States from the early nineteenth century through the Civil War.

Second New Deal (p. 685) The second stage of President Franklin Delano Roosevelt's economic recovery and reform program, launched January 4, 1935.

Second party system (p. 254) A new two-party system, pitting the Democrats against the Whigs, had appeared by 1834. The two parties began to split over the issue of slavery during the 1840s and the second party system came to an end in the early 1850s.

Sedition Act (p. 627) Law passed in 1918 which expanded the Espionage Act of 1917 and made a federal offense of using "disloyal, profane, scurrilous, or abusive language" about the Constitution, the government, the American uniform, or the flag.

Separatists (p. 39) Religious dissenters from England who believed that the state-supported Anglican church, or Church of England, was too corrupt to be reformed. Thus, like the Pilgrims, they often migrated elsewhere to form their own religious communities. See *Nonseparatists.*

Settlement house movement (p. 587) A reform movement growing out of Jane Addams's Hull House in the late nineteenth century, it led to the formation of community centers in which mainly middle-class women sought to meet the needs of recent immigrants to urban centers.

Shakers (p. 286) A religious group that called itself the United Society of Believers and originated in England in the mid-eighteenth century, the Shakers emphasized celibacy, sexual equality, and communal living.

Shamans (p. 8) Shamans were medicine men in Native American cultures. Sometimes called "powwows," shamans kept the lore of taboos to help guard against the overexploitation of nature, and they prescribed various rituals and medicines to help preserve and restore good health.

Sharecropping (pp. 438, 472) A system of labor to replace slavery that allowed landless farmers to work the land of others for a share of the crops they produced. It was favored by freedpeople over gang labor but sometimes led to virtual peonage.

Shaysites (p. 161)   Beset by a hard-hitting economic depression after the War for American Independence, these farmers from western Massachusetts finally rose up in rebellion against their state government in 1786 because they had failed to obtain tax relief. One leader of the uprising was Daniel Shays, from whom the Shaysites derived their name.

Sherman Antitrust Act (p. 532)   A law passed in 1890 to break up trusts and monopolies, it was rarely enforced except against labor unions and most of its power was stripped away by the Supreme Court, but it began federal attempts to prevent unfair, anticompetitive business practices.

Sherman Silver Purchase Act (p. 532)   Passed in 1890 in response to popular pressure, this act required the government to purchase 4.5 million ounces of silver each month at the ratio of 16 to 1.

Sit-in (p. 816)   A tactic of nonviolent direct action originally used by labor unions during the Great Depression; civil rights activists adopted this method of resistance to protest segregation in whites-only facilities.

Sixteen to one (16 to 1) (p. 529)   Referring to the mint ratio between silver and gold, this became a rallying cry for those who favored the expansion of the currency.

Skyscraper (p. 499)   Buildings with steel frameworks that exceeded the previous limitations of brick buildings. The lighter and stronger steel skeletons allowed structures to climb above the seven-story maximum. Architect William LeBaron Jenny's first skyscraper was ten stories tall. Cities could now build up instead of out, concentrating people and business in small areas.

Slave codes (p. 324)   Legal codes that defined the slaveholders' power and the slaves' status as property.

Smog (p. 860)   The chemical-laden fog caused by automobile engines, a serious problem in southern California. Like nuclear waste and the shrinking water supply, it reflects the problems associated with the rapid population shift to the West in modern times.

Social bandit (p. 335)   A Robin Hood–like figure who defends poor people against exploitation.

Social Darwinism (pp. 458, 554)   The application of Charles Darwin's evolutionary theories of natural selection and "survival of the fittest" to racial and social groups; it justified the concentration of wealth and lack of governmental protection of the weak. In the late 19th and early 20th centuries Social Darwinism was used to justify racism.

Social Gospel (p. 582)   A movement among Christian theologians, it applied Christian doctrines to social problems and advocated creating living conditions conducive to saving souls by tackling the problems of the poor.

Social Security Act (p. 684)   New Deal legislation enacted in 1935 to provide monthly stipends for workers aged 65 or older and to provide assistance to the indigent elderly, blind and handicapped persons, and dependent children who did not have a wage-earning parent. The act also established the nation's first federally funded system of unemployment insurance.

Southern Agrarians (p. 689)   Eleven white southern intellectuals who issued "I'll Take My Stand," a manifesto that urged a return to the agrarian way of life in light of the Great Depression.

Southern strategy (p. 142)   Once France formally entered the War for Independence in 1778 on the American side, the British had to concern themselves with protecting such vital holdings as their sugar islands in the Caribbean region. Needing to disperse their troop strength, the idea of the Southern strategy was to tap into a perceived reservoir of loyalist numbers in the southern colonies. Reduced British forces could employ these loyalists as troops in subduing the rebels and as civil officials in reestablishing royal governments. The plan failed for many reasons, including a shortfall of loyalist support and an inability to hold ground once conquered in places like South Carolina.

Spanish-American War (p. 565)   The 1898 war between Spain and the United States regarding the fate of Cuba. As a result of the war, Cuba gained independence and America acquired the Philippines and Puerto Rico.

Special Field Order 15 (p. 426)   An 1865 order issued by Union General William T. Sherman that set aside a strip of abandoned lands from Charleston, South Carolina, to Jacksonville, Florida, to be divided up into 40-acre lots for the use of the exslaves.

Specie (p. 93)   A term for hard coin, such as gold or silver, that can also back and give a fixed point of valuation to paper currencies.

Spirituals (p. 328)   Religious songs composed by enslaved African Americans.

Spoils system (pp. 257, 530)   The policy of awarding political or financial help with a government job. Abuses of the spoils system led to the passage in 1883 of the Pendleton Act, which created the Civil Service Commission to award government jobs on the basis of merit.

Sputnik (p. 766)   Russian satellite that successfully orbited the earth in 1957, prompting Americans to question their own values and educational system. The hysteria over Soviet technological superiority led to the 1958 National Defense Education Act.

Stagflation (p. 880)   The economic conditions of slow economic growth, rising inflation, and flagging productivity that characterized the American economy during the 1970s.

Stalwarts and Half-breeds (p. 525)   Two factions of the Republican party in the late nineteenth century, they were primarily focused on which group would get government jobs.

Stamp Act Congress (p. 102)   This intercolonial body of political leaders from nine colonies met for a few days in October 1765 to consider ways to protest the Stamp Act. The delegates drafted a petition declaring that Parliament should not tax Americans, since they were not represented in that legislative body. The Congress showed that the colonies, when aggrieved, could act in unity, an important precedent for further intercolonial resistance efforts in years to come.

States' rights (p. 263)   The doctrine that the states possess certain rights and powers that supersede those of the federal government.

Storyville (p. 507)   The red-light district of New Orleans, Louisiana, a major area of development for jazz music.

Strategic Arms Limitation Treaty of 1972 (SALT I) (p. 803) Arms control treaty signed by President Richard

Nixon and Soviet premier Leonid Brezhnev. Although it froze the deployment only of relatively inconsequential intercontinental ballistic missiles, this first treaty would lead to more comprehensive arms reduction treaties in the future.

Streetcar suburbs (p. 499)   Residential areas outside the urban center that were made accessible by mass transit. In the last part of the nineteenth century the people who could afford suburban real estate, the upper and middle classes, fled the ever more crowded cities and left the poorer classes behind. This economic division exacerbated the social and political divisions developing at the time.

Strict construction (p. 185)   The view that the powers of the national government are limited to those described in the U.S. Constitution.

Student Nonviolent Coordinating Committee (SNCC) (p. 817)   A civil rights organization formed in 1960 to coordinate nonviolent direct-action, such as sit-ins and voter-registration and desegregation campaigns in the South.

Students for a Democratic Society (SDS) (pp. 796, 828)   Founded in Port Huron, Michigan, in 1962, this radical organization aimed to rid American society of poverty, racism, and violence through an individually oriented approach called participatory democracy. By 1968, the organization had over 100,000 followers and was responsible for demonstrations at nearly 1000 colleges.

Submarine warfare (p. 619)   War waged by submarines, silent underground vessels that Germany introduced during World War I. Submarine tactics violated international law since they attacked from under water and depended on the element of surprise.

Suburban threat (p. 776)   A growing fear in the 1950s that the sameness of the suburban landscape would cause the residents to become homogeneous to the point of losing their individuality. Critics pointed out that people in the cities had very similar problems and that the phenomenon was overstated.

Suez Canal Crisis (p. 765)   Egyptian President Gamal Abdel Nasser nationalized the Suez Canal in 1956 after the United States withdrew a promised loan when Nasser appeared to be making friends with the Soviets. England and France responded by occupying the canal, and Israel invaded Egypt. The United States refused to support the Europeans and the invading parties withdrew.

***Sussex* pledge** (p. 622)   Agreement between Germany and the United States during World War I in which Germany promised not to launch surprise submarine attacks on passenger and merchant ships. The pledge was the result of the U.S. threat to sever diplomatic ties with Germany following the March 24, 1916, attack on the *Sussex*, an unarmed French passenger ship that was carrying several Americans.

Taft-Hartley Act (p. 745)   Legislation in 1947 that reflected the conservative postwar mood. It outlawed the closed shop, gave presidential power to delay strikes with a "cooling-off" period, and curtailed the political and economic power of organized labor.

Taliban (p. 906)   An Islamic fundamentalist political and military movement, intensely hostile to both Communism and Western (including U.S.) interests, that seized control of Afghanistan during the 1990's. Following the terrorist attacks of September 11, 2001, U. S. armed forces entered Afghanistan and overthrew the Taliban in retaliation for their having allowed the terrorist network al-Qaeda to use Afghan territory for military purposes.

Tariff of Abominations (p. 256)   An 1828 protective tariff opposed by many Southerners.

Task system (p. 325)   A system of plantation labor found mainly on rice plantations in which each field hand was given a specific daily work assignment. See *Gang system.*

Teapot Dome scandal (p. 660)   Scandal in which President Warren G. Harding's Secretary of the Interior Albert B. Fall was convicted of accepting large bribes in exchange for leasing drilling rights on federal naval oil reserves. This was the first conviction of a cabinet member for crimes in office.

Temperance (p. 276)   The pre-Civil War reform movement that sought to curb the drinking of hard liquor.

Ten percent plan (p. 427)   Lincoln's plan for Reconstruction in December 1863 that provided for the readmission to the Union of the former Confederate states. It stated that when 10 percent of a state's 1860 voters took an oath of loyalty, a civilian government could be formed.

Tennessee Valley Authority (TVA) (p. 679)   Organization established by Congress in May 1933 to build 21 dams to generate electricity for tens of thousands of farm families and to develop the region in other ways. In 1935 President Franklin D. Roosevelt signed an executive order to create the Rural Electrification Administration to bring the electricity generated by government dams to America's hinterland.

Tenure of Office Act (p. 431)   Enacted in 1867, the law required the president to get the consent of the Senate before removing certain appointed officers. The goal was to prevent President Andrew Johnson from removing Secretary of War Edwin Stanton and became a basis for Johnson's impeachment by the House of Representatives.

Tet offensive (p. 794)   As American military and political leaders suggested victory in Vietnam was in sight, North Vietnam launched an offensive in January 1968 against major South Vietnamese targets. Although the United States repelled the Tet offensive, it prompted waves of criticism from those who felt the government had been misleading the American people.

Texas annexation (p. 345)   Following the Texas Revolution, a treaty that would have annexed Texas to the United States failed to pass. Texas remained an independent republic until 1845, when a convention voted to accept a joint congressional resolution admitting Texas to the Union.

Tippecanoe, Battle of (p. 214)   An 1811 battle in which an American force under William Henry Harrison defeated an Indian confederacy led by the Shawnee Prophet Tenskwatawa.

Tory (p. 131)   In England during the eighteenth century the Tory party was closely identified with the king's interests and monarchism, or in the minds of many American patriots, with tyrannical government. As the Revolution dawned, tory became a term of derision applied to those colonists who sought to maintain their allegiance to the British crown. They preferred to think of themselves as loyalists, since they were not rebelling against but were still supporting British imperial authority in America.

Total War (p. 403)   As opposed to limited war, total war usually denotes a military conflict in which warfare ultimately affects the entire population, civilian as well as military. The American Civil War, at least in its latter stages, might serve as an example of total war because of the destruction of both military and civilian resources in the South by Union armies operating under General Grant and especially General Sherman during 1864 and 1865.

Trail of Tears (p. 259)   The forced migration of the Cherokee Indians in 1838 and 1839 from western Georgia to Oklahoma resulted in the deaths of some 4,000 people.

Transcendentalists (p. 288)   A group of New England intellectuals who glorified nature and believed that each person contains godlike potentialities.

Treaty of Ghent (p. 220)   This 1814 treaty ended the War of 1812.

Treaty of Guadalupe Hidalgo (p. 353)   The peace agreement that ended the Mexican-American War, under which Mexico recognized the Rio Grande as the boundary with Texas and ceded to the United States California, Nevada, New Mexico, Utah, and parts of Arizona, Colorado, Kansas, and Wyoming in exchange for $15 million and the assumption of $3.25 million in debts owed to Americans by Mexico.

Treaty of Versailles (p. 637)   The treaty that ended World War I.

Triangle Shirtwaist Company (p. 592)   A fire at this company on March 25, 1911, which killed 147 workers—most of them women—opened the eyes of many Americans to workplace dangers, leading to pressure for reform.

Truman Doctrine (p. 737)   President Truman made a speech in March 1947 and set the course of U.S. foreign policy for the next generation, painting international affairs as a struggle between free democratic governments and tyrannical communist governments, and advocating American intervention to protect democratic governments.

Trust (p. 463)   A form of business organization that allowed a single board of trustees to oversee competing firms; the term came to apply when any single entity had the power to control competition within a given industry, such as oil production.

Twenty-Fourth Amendment (p. 822)   This amendment, adopted in 1964, barred a poll tax in federal elections.

U-2 spy planes (p. 781)   Ultra-high flying surveillance aircraft used by the United States to take reconnaissance photos. The U.S. government denied that the planes were flying over Russia until one was shot down and the pilot captured. The incident caused a downturn in U.S.-Soviet relations.

UN police action (p. 742)   President Truman's term for the war in Korea. As the Soviet member of the UN Security Council was absent when the vote was taken to send troops to aid South Korea, the United Nations was officially against the North Korean aggression. Many UN members sent at least token forces to assist

in the war, and the UN resolution gave legitimacy to the U.S.-led resistance to the spread of communism in this theater.

Underground Railroad (p. 370)   The routes used by enslaved African Americans to escape from slavery. Some escapes were made by individuals or small groups who fled on their own; other escapes were highly organized.

United Farm Workers (p. 835)   This union of agricultural workers came into being in 1966 as a result of a merger between the Agricultural Workers Organizing Committee, established in 1959 by the AFL-CIO, and the National Farm Workers Association, started by César Chávez and Dolores Huerta in 1962. It established credit unions, health plans, and community centers for farm laborers.

Universal white manhood suffrage (p. 249)   The elimination of property, tax-paying, and religious qualification for voting in the early nineteenth century extended the vote to all native-born white men.

Utopian communities (p. 286)   Hundreds of experimental communities were established in America during the eighteenth and nineteenth centuries inspired by religious and secular ideals. Despite their differences, all shared a vision of extending the intimacy of the family to a broader range of social relationships.

V-E Day (p. 720)   May 8, 1945, Victory in Europe Day, the day Germany surrendered to the Allies in World War II.

Vertical integration (p. 464)   The practice of controlling every phase of production by owning the sources of raw materials and often the transportation facilities needed to distribute the product; it was a means of gaining a competitive edge over rival companies.

Vice-admiralty courts (p. 97)   The English government established these courts in its North American colonies to deal with issues of maritime law, including smuggling. If judges condemned vessels for smuggling, they would share in profits from the sale of such craft and their cargoes. Judges made all rulings without juries and thus could clearly benefit from their own decisions, which caused many colonists to view these courts as centers of despotic imperial power. The Stamp Act of 1765 stated that colonists who did not pay stamp duties could be tried in vice-admiralty courts, which became another colonial grievance—in this case the prospect of being convicted and sent to jail without a jury trial, a violation of fundamental English liberties.

Vietcong (p. 789)   An offshoot of the Vietminh in South Vietnam. Their political goal was the reunification of the two Vietnams under the rule of the communist North.

Vietminh (p. 789)   Communist guerrilla force ("Viet" for Vietnam and "Minh" for their leader, Ho Chi Minh) who fought the French colonial forces after World War II.

Vietnam (p. 783)   Country in Southeast Asia, part of French Indochina until after World War II. Ho Chi Minh led guerrilla fighters (the Vietminh) in a war for independence when the French refused to grant independence despite promises made during the war. This refusal initiated a conflict of long duration that eventually involved the U.S. military in a war to prevent the divided North and South Vietnams from being re-unified under Ho's communist government. When the United States withdrew, North Vietnam overran South Vietnam and united the country.

Virtual representation (p. 98)   King George III's chief minister, George Grenville, employed this concept in 1765 in relation to the Stamp Act. He insisted that all colonists were represented in Parliament by virtue of being English subjects, regardless of where they lived. Grenville was attempting to counter the colonists' position that King and Parliament had no authority to tax them, since the Americans had no elected representatives serving in Parliament.

Voting Rights Act of 1965 (p. 822)   This law prohibited literacy tests and sent federal examiners to the South to register voters.

Wade-Davis Bill (p. 427)   Congress's answer to Lincoln's plan for Reconstruction that required a majority of a state's voters to express their loyalty to the Union. It also limited participation in the forming of a new government to those who took an "iron clad" oath of past loyalty to the Union. It was pocket-vetoed by Lincoln.

Wagner Act (National Labor Relations Act) (p. 684)   New Deal legislation enacted in 1935 guaranteeing the right of workers to form unions and bargain collectively. The act established the National Labor Relations Board (NLRB) to settle union-management disputes over unfair labor practices.

War cabinet (p. 624)   Six boards established by President Woodrow Wilson to unify the nation's efforts toward World War I that conferred broad powers on the federal government. Included in the effort were the War Industries Board, the Fuel Administration, the War Trade Board, the Shipping Administration, and the U.S. Railroad Administration. The War Industries Board was the central unit, designed to coordinate government purchases of military supplies.

War Hawks (p. 214)   Nickname applied to young Republicans in Congress who pushed for war against Britain in 1812.

War Labor Board (WLB) (p. 708)   Board established in 1942 that had power to set wages, hours, and working conditions for the duration of World War II.

War of 1812 (p. 218)   War between Britain and the United States. Causes included British interference with American shipping, impressment of seamen, a desire to end British aid to Indians, and an American desire for expansion.

War Powers Act (p. 876)   This 1973 law required presidents to win specific authorization from Congress to engage U.S. forces in foreign combat for more than 90 days.

War Production Board (WPB) (p. 707)   The board was established in January 1942 to help mobilize the U.S. economy for war production.

War Refugee Board (p. 714)   World War II authority that set up refugee camps in Italy, North Africa, and the United States to help save Jewish refugees.

War Relocation Authority (p. 714)   Program of forcible relocation of Japanese Americans to internment camps during World War II. In December 1944, the Supreme Court ruled that as a civilian authority the War Relocation Authority had no right to incarcerate law-abiding citizens, and the camps closed.

Watergate break-in (p. 873)   During the 1972 presidential campaign, burglars, tied to the Nixon White House, were caught installing eavesdropping devices in Democratic party headquarters in the Watergate Complex in Washington, D.C. Revelations of White House efforts to obstruct the investigation of the break-in, of financial irregularities, and the use of government agencies for partisan purposes led President Nixon to resign in 1974.

Watts Riot of 1965 (p. 824)   A riot in Los Angeles's South Central neighborhood in 1965 left 34 people dead and marked the beginning of four "long, hot" summers of riots.

Webster-Ashburton Treaty (p. 345)   An 1842 treaty that fixed the present-day border between Maine and Canada.

Whig party (Whigs) (pp. 111, 266)   During the eighteenth century in England the Whig party was a loosely organized coalition of political leaders opposed to any hint of arbitrary authority that might emanate from the monarchy and royally appointed officials in government. Like the radical whig pamphleteers, they also viewed themselves as defenders of liberty, which is one reason why many American leaders, even though not organized as a political party, called themselves whigs. During the 1830s and 1840s in the United States, there was a Whig party that opposed the policies of Andrew Jackson, Martin Van Buren, and other members of the Democratic party.

Whiskey Rebellion (p. 188)   Popular protests against a federal tax on liquor in western Pennsylvania in 1794 were quickly dissolved when President Washington sent 15,000 troops to the area to demonstrate the central government's willingness to enforce federal law.

White man's burden (p. 555)   The belief that the white race was naturally superior and should take on the task of "civilizing" the rest of the races. This required them to spread their cultures and religions around the world.

Wilmot Proviso (p. 355)   An amendment attached to an appropriations bill during the Mexican-American War that would have forbade slavery in any territory acquired from Mexico. The amendment passed the House in 1846 and 1847 but was defeated in the Senate.

Woman's Christian Temperance Union (WCTU) (p. 586)   An organization led by Frances Willard to stop the abuse of alcohol; it joined forces with other groups in the movement for the prohibition of alcohol to reduce such problems as wife abuse. Founded in 1874, the WCTU proved instrumental in the passage of the Eighteenth Amendment to the Constitution.

Women's Army Corps (WAC) (p. 711)   The auxiliary women's unit to the U.S. army.

Workmen's compensation laws (p. 592)   Legislation establishing mandatory insurance to be carried by employers to cover on-the-job injuries to their workers; it was a reform that provided protection to workers while also lowering the financial risk to employers.

Works Progress Administration (WPA) (p. 682)   Works program of the Second New Deal that established a much larger system of work relief for the unemployed than earlier efforts.

Wounded Knee, Battle of (p. 445)   The massacre of more than 300 Native Americans in 1890 by federal troops. It became a symbol of white oppression of Indians.

Writs of assistance (p. 100)   Blanket search warrants used by English customs collectors in the colonies to try to catch suspected smugglers. These writs did not require any form of prior evidence to justify searches, which the colonies viewed as yet another imperial violation of fundamental English liberties.

XYZ Affair (p. 195)   A diplomatic incident in 1797 and 1798 that occurred when three agents of French foreign minister Charles Talleyrand demanded a $250,000 bribe and a $10 million loan as a precondition for negotiations.

Yalta Conference (p. 729)   The meeting between President Franklin Roosevelt, British prime minister Winston Churchill, and Soviet premier Joseph Stalin at Yalta in the Russian Crimea in February 1945 to determine the post–World War II world order.

Yellow journalism (p. 563)   Sensationalistic press accounts of the volatile Cuban situation in the 1890s, printed by William Randolph Hearst's *New York Journal* and Joseph Pulitzer's *New York World*. These stories helped mobilize prointerventionist public opinion prior to the Spanish-American war.

Zimmermann telegram (p. 623)   Telegram from German Foreign Minister Arnold Zimmermann to the German ambassador to Mexico pledging a Mexican-German alliance against the United States, which helped bring the United States into World War I.

CREDITS

Page abbreviations are as follows: (T)top, (C)center, (B)bottom, (L)left, (R)right.

Title page and chapter openers: *First row:* Picture Collection, The Branch Libraries, New York Public Library, Astor, Lenox, and Tilden Foundations. *Second row:* Robert Lindneux, *Trail of Tears,* Woolaroc Museum, Bartlesville, Oklahoma; Library of Congress; and Library of Congress. *Third row:* John Adams by John Trumbull, White House Historical Association (White House Collection); Library of Congress; Library of Congress; Library of Congress and Library of Congress. *Fourth row:* Robert Lindneux, *Trail of Tears,* Woolaroc Museum, Bartlesville, Oklahoma; Library of Congress; ©PhotoDisc; and Library of Congress.

CHAPTER 16

422 Library of Congress **425** The Granger Collection, New York **428** Library of Congress **429** Library of Congress **432** Library of Congress **433** Library of Congress **434** Valentine Richmond History Center **436** Library of Congress **437** Culver Pictures, Inc. **439** Library of Congress **442** Library of Congress **445(T)** Courtesy of the Southwest Museum, Los Angeles **445(B)** Nebraska State Historical Society, Photographic Collections **447** Culver Pictures, Inc.

CHAPTER 17

454 Chicago Historical Society **456** The Science Museum, London. Photo by Dave King/Dorling Kindersley Media Library **457** National Park Service, Edison National Historic Site **458** Picture History **460(L)** Culver Pictures, Inc. **460(B)** Culver Pictures, Inc. **463** Culver Pictures, Inc. **466** © Collection of The New York Historical Society, (Neg. No. 71880t) **467** Library of Congress **468** Nebraska State Historical Society, Photographic Collections **469** Nebraska State Historical Society, Photographic Collections **471** Stock Montage, Inc. **473** Fred Hulstrand History in Pictures Collection, NDIRS-NDSU Archives, Fargo **474** © CORBIS **476(B)** Courtesy George Eastman House **478** Library of Congress **479** Brown Brothers **481** The Granger Collection, New York

CHAPTER 18

490 © Bettmann/CORBIS **493** Library of Congress **495** Culver Pictures, Inc. **499** W. Louis Sonntag Jr. "The Bowery at Night," 1895. Museum of the City of New York **504** © CORBIS **506** John Sloan, "Sunday, Women Drying Their Hair," 1912. Addison Gallery of American Art, MA. Photo © Addison Gallery of American Art, Phillips Academy, Andover, MA. All Rights Reserved **507** Courtesy of the Hogan Jazz Archive, Tulane University **511** The Granger Collection, New York **514** Stock Montage, Inc.

CHAPTER 19

522(L) © CORBIS **522(R)** The Granger Collection, NY **526** Smithsonian Institution, Washington, DC, Harry P. Lepman Collection **527** Culver Pictures, Inc. **528** Culver Pictures, Inc. **530** Library of Congress **534** The Granger Collection, New York **536(T)** Library of Congress **536(B)** Wisconsin Historical Society, (WHi-3397) **540** Courtesy of the Carnegie Library, Pittsburgh **541** Picture History **542** Department of Special Collections, The University of Chicago Library **543** Library of Congress **545** Library of Congress

CHAPTER 20

552 Library of Congress **554** © Jean Miele/CORBIS **557** © Bettmann/CORBIS **560** © CORBIS **563** Culver Pictures, Inc. **564** Chicago Historical Society **569** Courtesy Frederic Remington Art Museum, Ogdensburg, New York **572** Library of Congress

CHAPTER 21

578(L) Library of Congress **578(R)** Culver Pictures, Inc **580(L)** Courtesy George Eastman House **580(R)** Picture History **581** © CORBIS **582** Sophia Smith Collection, Smith College, Northampton, MA **583** The Ida M. Tarbell Collection, Pelletier Library, Allegheny College, Meadville, PA **585(L)** The Granger Collection, New York **585(R)** Centers for Disease Control and Prevention **587** Chicago Historical Society, (DN64, 920) **588(T)** © CORBIS **588(B)** Library of Congress **590** Library of Congress **591** State Historical Society of Wisconsin **592** Martin P. Catherwood Library, School of Industrial and Labor Relations, Cornell University **595(B)** Brown Brothers **595(T, L)** Library of Congress **595(T, R)** Photo by Clifford Kennedy Berryman/Picture History **596** © Bettmann/CORBIS **598** Brown Brothers **600** Picture History **603** National Archives **607** Picture History

CHAPTER 22

614 Columbia University Archives- Columbiana Library **615** © Bettmann/CORBIS **621** Imperial War Museum, London **626** Wayne State University Press **627** Library of Congress **628** National Archives **630** Jacob Lawrence, Panel 32 from "The Migration Series". The Museum of Modern Art, New York, Gift of Mrs. David M. Levy. Digital Image (c) The Museum of Modern Art/Licensed by SCALA/Art Resource, NY. © Gwendolyn Knight Lawrence, Courtesy of Jacob and Gwendolyn Lawrence Foundation **635** Culver Pictures **638** The Chicago Tribune

CHAPTER 23

644 Culver Pictures, Inc. **648** The Granger Collection, New York **650** Hulton|Archive/Getty Images **652** Charles Demuth, "The Figure 5 in Gold," 1928. The Metropolitan Museum of Art, Alfred Stieglitz Collection, 1949 (49.59.1). Photograph © 1986 The Metropolitan Museum of Art **655** Culver Pictures, Inc. **657** Ben Shahn, "Bartolomeo Vanzetti and Nicola Sacco," 1931–32. The Museum of Modern Art, NY, Gift of Abby Aldrich Rockefeller. Digital Image © The Museum of Modern Art/Licensed by SCALA/Art Resource, NY. © Estate of Ben Shahn/Licensed by VAGA, New York, NY **658** Brown Brothers **659** Archibald J. Motley "Black Belt", 1935. Hampton University Museum, VA **662** The Granger Collection, New York **663** Picture History

CHAPTER 24

670 Culver Pictures, Inc. **671** © Seattle Post-Intelligencer Collection; Museum of History & Industry/CORBIS **673** © CORBIS **675** Library of Congress **676** AP/Wide World Photos **677** Culver Pictures, Inc. **682(T)** AP/Wide World Photos **682(B)** William Edward Lewis Bunn, "Festival at Hamburg" (mural study for the Hamburg, Iowa Post Office), 1941. Smithsonian American Art Museum. Photo © Smithsonian American Art Museum, Washington, DC/Art Resource, NY **684** The Granger Collection, New York **687** © CORBIS **688** Library of Congress **690** © Rykoff Collection/CORBIS

CHAPTER 25

696 Hulton|Archive/Getty Images **699** American Jewish Joint Distribution Committee, Courtesy of the United States Holocaust Memorial Museum Photo Archives **702** © CORBIS **703** Hulton|Archive/Getty Images **707** Hulton|Archive/Getty Images **709** Hulton|Archive/Getty Images **710** "Upfront" by Bill Mauldin,

INDEX

Page abbreviations are as follows: (t)tables, (f)figures, (m)maps, (i)illustrations.

CHAPTER 16 • THE NATION RECONSTRUCTED: NORTH, SOUTH, AND THE WEST, 1865–1877

SUMMARY

The twelve years following the Civil War carried vast consequences for the nation's future. They helped set the pattern for future race relations and defined the federal government's role in promoting racial equality.

KEY POINTS

- Immediately following the war, all-white Southern legislatures passed black codes which denied blacks the right to purchase or rent land.

- These efforts to force former slaves to work on plantations led Congressional Republicans to seize control of Reconstruction from President Andrew Johnson, deny representatives from the former Confederate states their Congressional seats, and pass the Civil Rights Act of 1866 and draft the 14th Amendment, extending citizenship rights to African Americans and guaranteeing equal protection of the laws.

- In 1870, the 15th Amendment gave voting rights to black men

- The freedmen, in alliance with carpetbaggers and southern white Republicans known as scalawags, temporarily gained power in every former Confederate state except Virginia. The Reconstruction governments drew up democratic state constitutions, expanded women's rights, provided debt relief, and established the South's first state-funded schools.

- Internal divisions within the southern Republican party, white terror, and northern apathy allowed white southern Democrats known as Redeemers to return to power.

- During Reconstruction former slaves and many small white farmers became trapped in a new system of economic exploitation known as sharecropping.

CHAPTER SYNOPSIS

The Civil War left the former Confederacy's economy in shambles. The large number of homeless and hungry led the government to establish the Bureau of Refugees, Freedmen and Abandoned Lands to provide relief and to settle land and labor disputes. The Freedmen's Bureau also founded schools to which African Americans, young and old, flocked. It also forced former slaves to sign labor contracts that tied them to the land and paid substandard wages. Former slaves viewed literacy, land, and the vote as the keys to securing freedom, but planters largely retained their land holdings.

Lincoln's plan for Reconstruction—the 10 percent plan, devised during the war—granted rebels a presidential pardon after they swore allegiance to the Union and accepted the end of slavery. Certain Confederate officials were excluded, particularly former U. S. officials who had resigned to serve the Confederacy, and rebels accused of mistreating captured black Union soldiers. When 10 percent of those who voted in 1860 took the oath, the state could form a civilian government to draft a constitution that outlawed slavery. Once reconstructed, Lincoln promised to recognize the states. Lincoln's plan did not address the status of the ex-slaves. Although Tennessee, Arkansas, and Louisiana met these requirements, many Republicans considered Lincoln's plan too lenient. They also believed Reconstruction was a congressional matter, and so refused to recognize these states.

Congress presented its own plan in the Wade-Davis Bill. It required an oath from a majority of the states' voters to form a government and permanently barred a small number of high Confederate officials from participating in politics. It mandated a repudiation of the Confederate debt to forestall profiteering from treason. Congress would decide when these requirements were met by each state. Lincoln threatened to veto the bill, but his assassination ended this threat.

Andrew Johnson was considered a less formidable opponent to Congressional plans, but he pursued a plan similar to Lincoln's. He issued an amnesty proclamation that applied to all rebels except those owning more than $20,000 worth of property, who had to apply for a presidential pardon that was readily given. Johnson restored all property rights to southern whites. His reconstruction plan allowed a native Unionist to call for a constitutional convention without Lincoln's 10 percent requirement. Readmission, however, required ratifying the Thirteenth Amendment, repudiating the Confederate debt, abolishing slavery, renouncing secession, and providing limited black suffrage.

Southerners, however, angered many Northerners with their actions. New state governments enacted black codes that greatly circumscribed black freedom and rights, attempting to force the ex-slaves into a labor system similar to slavery. There was also violence perpetrated against African-Americans. Congress refused to seat the new Southern representatives and conducted an inquiry into prevailing conditions in the South.

The investigation by the congressional Joint Committee on Reconstruction documented the brutality of whites against blacks. When Congress extended the life of the Freedmen's Bureau and expanded its power, Johnson vetoed the bill. His attack on the committee angered Congress, which passed the Civil Rights Act and then overrode Johnson's veto. It then passed a revised Freedmen's Bureau Bill over Johnson's veto. Next, Congress drafted the Fourteenth Amendment that reversed the Dred Scott decision and extended citizenship rights and guaranteed due process and equal protection under the laws. The overwhelming victory by the Republicans in the 1866 elections, in the face of Johnson's campaign to oust the Radicals, was seen as a mandate for congressional reconstruction.

Congress passed the Military Reconstruction Act that divided the South into five military districts and provided for new constitutional conventions that included black participation and excluded former rebel leaders. Each state had to provide for black suffrage and ratify the Fourteenth Amendment. Only after the amendment was ratified were states granted representation in Congress. Johnson's veto was overridden. Congress also passed bills that limited presidential military power and required Senate consent for the removal of any official confirmed by that body. Any opposition from the Supreme Court was eliminated by bills that limited the court's power to review cases. Johnson's attempt to block Reconstruction and remove Secretary of War Stanton led the House to impeach him. After the Senate failed by one vote to convict the president, Johnson's opposition to Congressional Reconstruction ended.

The election of Grant in 1868 led Congress to debate the issue of black suffrage, raising the question of the vote for women. The controversy over the Fifteenth Amendment split the women's movement. The Fifteenth Amendment declared that the right to vote shall not be abridged on account of race, color, or previous condition of servitude.

Congressional reconstruction did not harshly punish most Confederates; nor did it lead to major reforms in land ownership. But it did allow coalitions of blacks, northern white migrants, and some southern whites, to head state government that implemented many reforms. Meanwhile, many southern whites, committed to white supremacy, opposed these governments.

Many officeholders were northern carpetbaggers, typically veterans who saw opportunity in the South. Scalawags (white southern Republicans) included former Whigs and yeoman farmers and poor whites. Many of the latter two groups had resented planter domination and had opposed secession. The Republicans appealed to these classes by voicing opposition to the slave aristocracy, but most southern whites returned to Democratic ranks in the late 1870s.

The Republican reconstruction governments were the most democratic the South had ever experienced. Any remaining property requirements for voting or running for office were removed. Reapportionment was largely fair, and salaries for public officials increased so that the non-wealthy could serve, too. Women enjoyed expanded rights and taxation was made more equitable. The greatest success was establishing public education. The devastated state of the South and the scarcity of money hindered progress. Recovery created a large tax burden and a rising debt that was partially due to corruption.

Landholdings became even more concentrated into fewer hands. Although some blacks succeeded in acquiring land, most blacks and an increasing number of whites worked as paid laborers. Sharecropping arose from the desire for black autonomy and the lack of cash among white landowners. The system seemed to offer opportunity, but tenants were often reduced to debt peonage.

Racial violence was directed against blacks by organizations such as the Ku Klux Klan. The federal government suppressed the Klan, but violence against blacks persisted, "Redeemer" governments to emerge.

Events transpiring in the North and West contributed to Reconstruction's failure. By the mid-1870s, Northerners had grown weary of Reconstruction. Scandals haunted the Grant administration, splitting the Republican party in 1872. Though Grant won reelection, by 1874, the Democrats signaled their return to power by capturing the House of Representatives and increasing their numbers in the Senate. Growing public disenchantment was fueled by the Panic of 1873, caused by overspeculation, which thrust the nation into its most serious economic depression up until that time.

The panic highlighted the tremendous changes occurring in the North during this period. The completion of the transcontinental railroad eclipsed reports of violations of African Americans' civil rights. The Republicans were committed to economic modernization and western expansion of the United States. In the process, the Republicans abandoned reform and became the party of conservatism that protected vested interests.

The major reason for Reconstruction's decline was white supremacy, which was also evident in western expansion and the treatment of the Plains Indians. A major obstacle to white settlement was the massive herds of buffalo that provided many Native Americans with food, clothing, and other necessities of life. In addition, cultural differences created problems between white settlers and the Native Americans, particularly the divergent concepts of land use and land ownership. Indian resistance led to outbreaks of violence, but proved futile. The rise of the Ghost Dance in the late 1880s fueled white fears of Native American uprisings that ended with the Wounded Knee massacre in 1890. Wounded Knee closed the era of violence between whites and Indians, but solutions to Native American problems remained illusive.

The government and reformers launched several efforts to assimilate Native Americans into American society by destroying their traditional culture. The Dawes Severalty Act of 1887 distributed tribal lands to individual Native American families. Subsequent acts also sought to weaken tribal culture. In addition, boarding schools arose to educate Native American children in the ways of mainstream American

The disputed presidential election of 1876 ended with a compromise that allowed the victory of Republican Rutherford B. Hayes. The removal of troops from the South and the demise of the few remaining Republican governments symbolically ended the Reconstruction era, though the battle for African American rights had been lost years earlier.

OBJECTIVES

After reading this chapter, you should be able to:

1. Describe Presidents Lincoln's and Johnson's plans to readmit the Confederate states to the Union as well as the more stringent Congressional plan.

2. Trace the contributions made to civil rights during Reconstruction.

3. Describe the power struggle between President Andrew Johnson and Congress, including the vote over the president's impeachment.

4. Identify the groups that ruled the southern state governments from 1866 to 1877.

5. Explain why Reconstruction ended in 1877.

KEY TERMS
Freedmen's Bureau
Radical Republicans
Black Codes
Military Reconstruction Act
Carpetbaggers
Scalawags
Sharecropping
Ku Klux Klan
Wounded Knee
Dawes Severalty Act
Compromise of 1877

KEY FIGURES
Andrew Johnson
Thaddeus Stevens
Edwin M. Stanton
Charles Sumner
Colonel J.M. Chivington
George A. Custer
Rutherford Hayes

CHAPTER 16 • THE NATION RECONSTRUCTED: NORTH, SOUTH, AND THE WEST, 1865–1877

_____ 1. Slavery was abolished in the United States by
   a. the Emancipation Proclamation
   b. the 13th Amendment
   c. the surrender of Robert E. Lee's army at Appomattox

_____ 2. Originally, the Freedmen's Bureau main function was to provide _____ for the freedmen.
   a. protection from the violence perpetrated by former Confederates
   b. food and clothing
   c. transportation to the North and West

_____ 3. The Freedmen's Bureau was most successful in providing freedmen with
   a. land
   b. schools
   c. economic independence

_____ 4. After the Civil War, most southern freedmen wanted to
   a. own their own land
   b. work for wages
   c. move to the North

_____ 5. The Black Codes
   a. sought to fashion a labor system as close to slavery as possible
   b. guaranteed the civil rights of African Americans
   c. were abolished by the 13th Amendment

_____ 6. As Reconstruction began, the _____ clause of the Constitution seemed to work to an unfair advantage for the South and the Democratic party.
   a. necessary and proper
   b. Three-Fifths
   c. due process

_____ 7. President Johnson's plan for Reconstruction required all of the following EXCEPT
   a. That the former Confederate states abolish slavery
   b. That Confederate officials apply to the President for a pardon
   c. That the former Confederate states give freedmen the vote

_____ 8. The main purpose of the Black Codes was to
   a. open economic opportunities to blacks
   b. put blacks in an economically dependent position
   c. build up the Republican party in the South

_____ 9. The 14th Amendment guaranteed _____ to freedmen.
   a. land ownership
   b. the right to vote
   c. citizenship

_____ 10. The governments of the South during the Reconstruction era are best characterized as
   a. corrupt and inefficient
   b. progressive and beneficial to the South, though run by people who had generally not held power in the South prior to the war
   c. worse than the governments that ruled the South prior to Reconstruction, and run by Northerners who had no real interest in the region

_____ 11. The Reconstruction governments in the South
   a. stripped plantation owners of their land
   b. implemented needed reforms in education and tax structure
   c. were directed, in every southern state, by African American legislators

_____ 12. President Johnson's impeachment was provoked by his
   a. dismissal of Secretary of War Edwin Stanton
   b. hostility toward black freedmen
   c. pardoning of ex-Confederate planter aristocrats

_____ 13. During Reconstruction, Congress
   a. redistributed Confederate lands to the freedmen
   b. imprisoned the civilian and military leaders of the Confederacy
   c. insisted that former slaves become full citizens of the United States

_____ 14. The Ku Klux Klan and _____ shared the goal of restoring white Democrats to political office in the South.
   a. redeemers
   b. carpetbaggers
   c. scalawags

_____ 15. The decline of Congressional Reconstruction resulted from all the following EXCEPT
   a. intimidation and violence by the Ku Klux Klan
   b. the waning of reforming idealism in the North and corruption in the Grant administration
   c. the return of economic prosperity in the 1870s

_____ 16. The Credit Mobilier scandal involved
   a. illegal post office contracts
   b. fraudulent railroad investments
   c. exploitation of Indians

_____ 17. Resistance by the Plains Indians was unsuccessful for all of the following reasons EXCEPT
   a. a viral infection killed most of the Indians' horses
   b. the buffalo was hunted to near extinction
   c. railroads allowed U.S. troops to be deployed rapidly and brought large numbers of settlers to the Plains

_____ 18. The Dawes Act of 1887 undermined Indian cultures by
   a. breaking up reservations into individual landholdings
   b. forbidding Indian religious practices
   c. ordering the education of Indian children in white-run boarding schools

_____ 19. The candidate who received the largest popular vote in the election of 1876 was
   a. Ulysses S. Grant
   b. Rutherford Hayes
   c. Samuel J. Tilden

_____ 20. The dispute over contested electoral votes in the 1876 election was decided by
   a. the House of Representatives
   b. the Supreme Court
   c. an electoral commission

_____ 21. In the Compromise of 1877, Republican candidate Rutherford B. Hayes promised the South all but one of the following. Select the EXCEPTION.
   a. federal aid for southern railroads
   b. to revoke the Civil Rights Act of 1875
   c. appointment of a Southern Democrat to his cabinet

CHAPTER 17 • EMERGENCE AS AN ECONOMIC POWER

SUMMARY

Between 1865 and 1900 the United States was transformed from a largely rural nation to one of the world's leading industrial powers. In this chapter you read about the technological transformations of the era; the legal, financial, and cultural factors that encouraged rapid industrialization; business consolidation; the growth of new management techniques; and the impact of and response to these changes on the part of American workers.

KEY POINTS

• The late 19th century saw the creation of a modern industrial economy.

• A national transportation and communication network was created, the corporation became the dominant form of business organization, and a managerial revolution transformed business operations.

• Long hours and hazardous working conditions led many workers to attempt to form labor unions despite strong opposition from industrialists and the courts.

CHAPTER SYNOPSIS

During the late 19th century, the United States emerged as an economic powerhouse. Across the Far West, the mining industry extracted coal, copper, lead, and oil, fueling such industries as steel, petroleum, and electric power. Dazzling late 19th century technological innovations included the typewriter, the hand-held camera, and the electric light. The most famous inventor was Thomas Edison who set up the first research and development laboratory in Menlo Park, New Jersey, producing such wonders as the mimeograph machine, the dynamo, and motion pictures. Underlying economic growth was the railroad. The rapid growth of railroads changed the United States from a nation of isolated communities into a unified market, thereby accelerating economic development.

A set of ideas known as Social Darwinism helped rationalize the survival-of-the-fittest mentality of business leaders and posited the inevitability of poverty and slums. Some business magnates even suggested divine intervention lay behind their riches. This Gospel of Wealth equated poverty with sin. The idea that wealth came to the hard-working righteous was propagated in popular literature by the McGuffey Readers and the Horatio Alger novels.

Favorable governmental policies created a fertile environment in which industry grew. The late 19th century was an era of "laissez-faire," a phrase that refers to noninterference by government in the economy. In practice, laissez-faire meant that the government aided business but did not regulate it. Building on antebellum precedents, land grants, financing of education, and tariffs all helped businesses develop. The biggest aid was the granting of 180 million acres of state and federal land to various railroads. Labor and financial legislation also favored business, while non-regulation allowed for rapid growth and immoral practices.

The central feature of business organization was the rise of the corporation, aided by new incorporation laws and the privileged status accorded corporations by the courts. The doctrine of limited liability made investment safer and more appealing, thus facilitating the raising of huge amounts of capital from domestic and foreign sources. The growing competitiveness of the economy, however, created a chaotic situation.

Most business leaders sought to eliminate competition and achieve order. The first industry to confront excessive competition was the railroads. Overbuilding had created too much competition in some areas, leading to lower rates and rebates to large customers. Rate wars gave way to cooperative action through the formation of regional "pools" in the 1870s. But attempts to divide traffic equitably and raise rates lacked legal sanctions and greed doomed many pacts. Backed by ruthless tactics to drive out competitors, consolidation provided a solution to controlling competition.

John D. Rockefeller employed a different strategy in the petroleum industry, underselling and eventually buying out competitors. His Standard Oil Company controlled 90 percent of the oil business. Legal problems led him to found the trust, which brought major companies together under a single board of trustees and provided for profit-sharing from all operations. This innovation was quickly adopted by almost all major industries.

Andrew Carnegie, however, disliked trusts and pools, favoring vertical integration to overwhelm competition. His success was based upon controlling all aspects of business from the sources of raw materials to the transportation facilities needed to distribute his manufactured products. Carnegie also lowered wages and increased hours for labor, explored new methods of productivity, and focused on the long term growth rather than short run profits. Not only did he drive many other companies into bankruptcy by undercutting their prices, but he often purchased his competitors during economic downturns when prices were low. The ultimate result was better steel at cheaper prices, which aided the growth of railroads and the rise of subsidiary industries. During hard times bankers reorganized failing companies into large corporations. The price paid for the more orderly economy was centralized control in the hands of an unelected elite.

Accompanying business consolidation was the development of new management techniques. Railroads pioneered this process. In the 1850s, Erie Railroad employee Daniel McCallum devised the first organizational table for an administrative structure that established a chain of command and divorced top management from daily operations. Improved accounting procedures followed as did the evolution of such new divisions as the controller and the treasurer. Other large businesses adopted accounting methods, hierarchical administrative structures, and divisional organization, creating a middle management who coordinated operations and reported to top executives. The emergence of white-collar bureaucracies meant that the middle class expanded.

Economic transformation was also evident in meat-packing. The interplay of new technology and new organization brought forth new marketing techniques, with railroads playing a key role tying the Great Plains cattle ranches to urban markets. Because it was a railroad hub, Chicago became the center of the meat-packing business. Cattle from its stock yards were shipped to abbatoirs located on the outskirts of eastern cities for slaughtering and then distributed by local butchers to consumers. A major problem was deterioration of the stock during long rail journeys. Gustavus Swift recognized the solution refrigeration offered He also noticed that centralized slaughtering allowed waste products to be made into buttons, glue, fertilizer, soap, and glycerin. Swift improved production by instituting assembly lines that subdivided the slaughtering and packing process into a number of separate jobs.

By the early 1900s, in at least 50 different industries, one company accounted for 60 percent or more of the total output. Competition was not entirely eliminated, and bigness did lower prices and raise standards of living. But the transition in the economy transformed work and life while initiating a fearful cycle of boom and bust. Periodic depressions convulsed the nation, causing widespread unemployment and business failures. The rise of big business also created a class of millionaires who flaunted their wealth through ostentatious homes and lavish life styles. The rich were the most blatant symbols of an increasingly unequal distribution of wealth that bred envy and resentment.

Although industrialization was concentrated in the Northeast, all regions underwent profound changes as a national, interdependent economy evolved. Growing industrial needs and expansion onto new western lands contributed to the growth of agriculture. The urban demand for food stimulated an agricultural revolution based upon scientific farming supported by increasing mechanization in every farm region except the South. The various efforts to construct a "New South" failed to keep up with the economic pace of change in the rest of the nation.

The problems of getting cattle to market prompted the growth of "cowtowns" like Abilene, Kansas, from which the cattle were shipped east. The extension of rail lines into Texas led to scientific breeding of livestock on huge ranches. The competition for grazing land produced bloody confrontations that animated much of the folklore of the "Wild West." But by the 1890s, ranching had become much more a business than a western adventure. Ranching followed the pattern of consolidation evident in industry and was often helped by government policies that offered vast expanses of land for sale for low prices to large cattle barons. Mining and timber interests also profited from friendly federal land policies. Farmers were the last to arrive on the Great Plains. Motivated by the Homestead Act and railroad promotions, many farmers eked out a subsistence living as "sodbusters" on the worst western lands.

Farming itself changed after the Civil War. Unable to compete with newer western corn and wheat growers, established farmers in the Old Northeast produced vegetables, dairy products, poultry, and pigs for growing urban markets. The expansion of cities also provided a lucrative market for land sold to developers. Western farmers developed new "dry farming" techniques to adapt to an arid environment. But economic and climatic forces created boom and bust cycles that doomed many farms on the Great Plains. The South had to rebuild its agricultural system after the Civil War. The demise of the slave plantation required developing a new system to take its place. In contrast to the consolidation evident in much of the economy, southern agriculture was characterized by tenancy, sharecropping, and a shortage of capital.

The dominant trend in agriculture was toward commercial farming, which involved crop specialization, technological innovation, mechanization, market expansion, greater investment of capital, and use of interstate transportation. Farmers' attempts to commercialize their farms often trapped their families in debt.

Many Southerners sought to participate in the new economic order. The "New South" doctrine promoted by editor Henry Grady regarded diversified farming, industrialization, and racial accommodation and cooperation as the keystones of regional development. Black leader Booker T. Washington seconded Grady's optimistic outlook for a new South. Increased railroad construction and industrial development in textiles, tobacco, lumber, and steel combined with the recovery of cotton production forecasted a rosy future. But the region remained tied to an inefficient monoculture based upon cotton, which experienced the same boom and bust cycles of many other crops. Similarly, the stress on white supremacy thwarted black advancement, eventually resulting in the rise of legal segregation. Southern development was dependent upon outside capital, resulting in an outflow of profits to pay off debts. The upshot was that the South remained at the bottom of the economic ladder.

While wages rose and prices fell during the late nineteenth and early twentieth centuries, workers fought a constant battle to escape poverty. A family's well-being depended upon how many members worked. Ethnicity and birthplace also affected income levels. The highly skilled laborers were mostly English-speaking, Protestant, and white. They enjoyed job security and good wages. Semi-skilled and unskilled workers were mostly foreign immigrants from southern and eastern Europe who spoke little if any English. They had no job security and received low wages. African Americans, Asians, and Mexicans worked under the most oppressive conditions.

Industrialization altered attitudes toward time. Pre-industrial labor was governed by the sun and seasons and often mixed socializing with work. Industrial time was rigid and fixed, determined by the time clock or work bell. The number of hours worked varied by industry but usually were higher than the 40-hour week desired by workers. Women found their domestic duties increased as industrial America placed more emphasis on cleanliness; access to different types of food allowed for a more varied diet but also required more time for preparation.

Many aspects of industrial work and life stimulated worker discontent. The structured, mechanized, output-driven nature of the factory led to a decline in traditional skilled trades and greater impersonality. Questions of safety, monotony, and inhumanity figured in worker complaints, as did the uncaring attitude of employers who seemed unconcerned about the welfare of their employee. Scientific management ideas, including the ideas of Frederick Taylor, proved dehumanizing.

Absenteeism and frequent job changes plagued employers. Collective action through strikes also became common in the late 19th century, and sometimes turned violent. Violence in the Pennsylvania coal fields in the mid-1870s was followed by a massive and violent railroad strike in 1877. In both cases, the worker's efforts failed. The Haymarket Square riot on Chicago in 1884 heightened public suspicion of unions. Of eight men arrested for throwing a bomb at police patrolling a labor demonstration, three were executed despite the lack of any evidence connecting them to the bomb.

During the late nineteenth century, workers' efforts to form unions that could negotiate successfully with employers frequently failed. Divisions among the workers and outdated organizational techniques hampered unions. Early attempts to organize all workers in one union, such as the National Labor Union and the Knights of Columbus, failed due to financial and administrative difficulties. These two efforts sought to remake American society. The American Federation of Labor founded by Samuel Gompers stressed practical goals, such as higher wages and shorter hours. The AFL also accepted industrial society. But the AFL also made few gains before 1900.

OBJECTIVES

After reading this chapter, you should be able to:

1. Describe the factors that aided the rapid expansion of American industry in the late 19th century.

2. Identify the Gospel of Wealth and Social Darwinism and indicate the effect of these ideas in discouraging interest in reform.

3. Explain why business consolidated in the late 19th century.

4. Discuss how the nature of work changed in the late 19th century and how workers responded to these changes.

KEY TERMS
Social Darwinism
Gospel of Wealth
Laissez-Faire
Pool or cartel
Trust
Vertical Integration
New South
Plessy v. Ferguson
Haymarket Square Riot
Knights of Labor
American Federation of Labor

KEY FIGURES
Andrew Carnegie
John D. Rockefeller
Herbert Spencer
Samuel Gompers

CHAPTER 17 • EMERGENCE AS AN ECONOMIC POWER

_____ 1. Which of the following statements about the World's Columbian Exposition of 1893 is FALSE?
   a. It displayed the United States' economic growth and technology progress
   b. It commemorated the 400th anniversary of Columbus' first voyage to the New World
   c. It attracted such a small number of people that the United States would not host another world's fair until 1964

_____ 2. The policy of laissez faire following in the quarter century after Reconstruction refers to
   a. letting government solve economic and social problems
   b. regulating trade between sections to benefit all equally
   c. surrendering control over public policy to private interests

_____ 3. What was the primary cause for the growth of the urban industrial labor force in the late 19th century?
   a. the high birthrate of the urban population
   b. migration from America's rural areas
   c. immigration from Europe

_____ 4. The Gospel of Wealth asserted that business success was the outgrowth of
   a. a process of natural selection
   b. free competition
   c. God's blessing

_____ 5. In the late 19th century, the U.S. government did NOT provide
   a. protective tariffs for industry
   b. consumer protection laws for the public
   c. land grants for railroads

_____ 6. In _Santa Clara County v. The Southern Pacific Railroad_, the Supreme Court ruled that
   a. corporations were entitled to the protection of the 14th Amendment
   b. government land grants to railroads were illegal
   c. the principle of "limited liability" was unconstitutional

_____ 7. Through consolidation, 19th century business leaders like John D. Rockefeller and J.P. Morgan intended to bring more _____ to the national economy.
   a. competition
   b. order
   c. opportunity

_____ 8. Which industry pioneered modern management styles in the 19th century?
   a. steel
   b. meat-packing
   c. railroads

_____ 9. The founder of scientific management methods was
   a. Horatio Alger
   b. Frederick W. Taylor
   c. J.P. Morgan

_____ 10. The primary cause of the farmers' economic woes in the South and West in the late 19th century was
   a. overproduction
   b. high land prices
   c. high taxes

_____ 11. The doctrine of the New South called for
   a. adoption of the northern model of industrial growth, coupled with the legend of the graceful Old South
   b. an emphasis on diversified agricultural growth
   c. the reestablishment of the pre-Civil War social and economic order

_____ 12. A leading advocate of the doctrine of the New South was
   a. William Howard Taft
   b. Alexander Crummell
   c. Henry W. Grady

_____ 13. Booker T. Washington encouraged southern blacks to
   a. agitate for full political and economic rights
   b. make themselves economically indispensable to southern whites
   c. move to the North to seek greater economic opportunity

_____ 14. The post-Civil War South's economy remained backward because of all but one of the following. Select the EXCEPTION.
   a. the failure to develop a textile industry
   b. reliance on single-crop agriculture
   c. a chronic shortage of investment capital

_____ 15. The Haymarket incident (1886) was significant to the labor movement because it
   a. aroused public opposition against labor and contributed to the decline of the Knights of Labor
   b. resulted in the first federal intervention on behalf of labor
   c. opened the way for the peaceful settlement of labor disputes by collective bargaining

_____ 16. Samuel Gompers and the American Federation of Labor, founded in 1881, worked for all of the following EXCEPT
   a. economic goals such as higher pay and shorter work hours
   b. organizing unskilled and minority group members
   c. rejecting utopian and political goals in order to further immediate economic objectives

CHAPTER 18 • THE RISE OF AN URBAN SOCIETY AND CITY PEOPLE

SUMMARY

In this chapter you read about the changing nature of the American city. You learned about the new immigrants who arrived from eastern and southern Europe; the anti-immigrant reaction; the expansion of cities horizontally and vertically; the problems caused by urban growth; the depiction of cities in art and literature; and the changing nature of urban life, including the emergence of new forms of urban entertainment.

KEY POINTS

- Cities expanded rapidly in the late 19th century. Immigration and the growth of industry were factors that contributed to urban growth.
- The emergence of large cities transformed American life. Large cities produced a vibrant, heterogeneous culture. They also were the source of new social and political problems.
- Cities provided new forms of entertainment and excitement.

CHAPTER SYNOPSIS

The Statue of Liberty symbolized the promise of America to many immigrants. Over 25 million immigrants arrived in the United States between 1860 and 1920. European immigrants came not only to the United States; millions also went to Australia, New Zealand, Canada, and Latin America, indicating the push out of Europe exerted more influence than the pull of the United States.

Historians have divided the immigration into two phases. The old immigration came from northern and western Europe, and, save for the Irish, assimilated rather easily into American society. The new immigration beginning in the 1880s was from eastern and southern Europe. These people arrived in great numbers, but their backgrounds made assimilation more difficult. Their respective motivations for leaving Europe, varying images of America; settlement patterns, and occupations differentiated these two immigrant groups.

Another distinction involved the two kinds of immigrants who came to the United States. On the one hand, some people came to settle permanently. On the other hand, many came as migrant workers—birds of passage—who sought better work opportunities but always planned on returning home. The birds of passage were largely young men, particularly from Greece and Italy, though others came from eastern Europe, China, and Mexico.

Often members of religious or ethnic minorities migrated to escape persecution and abuse. The Jewish situation deteriorated when Russia, Prussia, and Austria divided up Poland in the 1700s. Russian authorities segregated the Jews, restricted their employment opportunities, conducted pogroms, and conscripted Jewish youth. Conditions worsened after the assassination of Tsar Alexander II in 1881, stimulating migration to America, primarily by families headed by skilled workers.

The Hennessy case waged against Italians in New Orleans in 1891 showed the strong resentments harbored by native-born Americans against foreign immigrants. Known as nativism, the anti-immigrant backlash was expressed in many ways. Racial nativism propounded the biological inferiority of the immigrants. The supposed radicalism of immigrants generated political fears. But the strongest arguments were economic. American workers complained that not only did immigrants bring wages down by working cheaper, they also blocked union efforts to improve working conditions. The onset of depression in 1893 unleashed a virulent wave of anti-immigrant sentiment.

Earlier, Chinese immigrants, numbering 160,000, had suffered from nativism. Subjected to discrimination, the Chinese became the target of nativistic attacks from the Irish during the 1870s depression. Public pressure grew, resulting in passage of the Chinese Exclusion Act of 1882, which was extended in 1892, and made indefinite in 1902. Other measures aimed at limiting all immigration, such as requiring a literacy test, which eventually passed over President Wilson's veto in 1917. The culmination of nativism came with passage of the National Origins Act of 1924, which established an immigrant quota system.

Urbanization, like mass immigration, altered the country's face. In the mid-nineteenth century, the absence of mass transportation influenced urban design as the walking city emerged encompassing a patchwork of residences and businesses. The stress on walking thrust people of all classes together in a compact area. This urban model was shattered by industrialization that accelerated growth of cities both in size and complexity. The foreign immigration fueled the urban population explosion and was supplemented by migrants from rural areas in America, particularly African Americans after 1900.

Walking cities could not meet the demands the huge influx created, leading to technological advances in transportation and building construction. The horse railway allowed city limits to expand, as did cable cars that proved useful in hillier cities like San Francisco. Electricity provided the best solution as trolley lines proliferated. Clogged surface streets led to the construction of subways and elevated train lines. The rise of mass transportation allowed for city expansion way beyond the core of the walking city, and was paralleled by advances in construction. Developments in steel helped revolutionize construction as iron, masonry, glass, and steel replaced the traditional brick and masonry materials that had limited the vertical height of buildings. The result was the skyscraper innovated by architect William LeBaron Jenney.

Horizontal and vertical growth transformed residential patterns as the middle and upper classes moved further from the city's core to the "streetcar suburbs." Their former homes were often subdivided into small apartments for the working class. In addition, black migration produced racially segregated ghettos in many cities, while the immigrant flood created Old World-styled ethnic neighborhoods. The working class tended to settle close to their work to save transportation costs. In addition, the central business district boomed as real estate values rose, transforming these areas into centers of business and commerce exclusively.

The growth of cities was largely uncontrolled, creating problems of aesthetics and public services. This was especially true regarding police, as crime rates soared, and health, as diseases ran rampant. But the biggest problem was housing, the lack of which created a boom in the building industry. Opulent mansions filled Gold Coast neighborhoods, while tenements housed the masses. Designed to maximize vertical space, poorly lit and badly ventilated dumbbell tenements packed enormous numbers of people into small apartments. Another pressing problem concerned the city streets that became repositories for trash and animal waste. Waste disposal plagued cities as rivers frequently served as dumping grounds, polluting water supplies and spreading disease.

The result was an unhealthy urban environment that led to periodic epidemics of diphtheria, smallpox, typhoid, and yellow fever. The efforts to improve health conditions were thwarted by political machines who valued party loyalty over knowledge of public health in filling city jobs. Still, improvements came with the construction of sewer systems and the use of large filtration and chlorination plants to provide clean water.

In the quest for better cities, public need often conflicted with private interest. The development of transportation, the construction of buildings, and the provision of water were usually undertaken by private entrepreneurs hoping to earn large profits. As such, they catered to those who could pay for housing and services, leading to the emergence of what historians call the "private city," where the profit motive determined urban development. The profit motive contributed to the ugliness of many cities and exacerbated existing problems. By 1900, "public city" advocates, largely urban engineers and other experts, pressed alternative plans, bringing knowledge, administrative expertise, and aesthetic taste to city government.

Electric lighting transformed the city. The evening hours became a time of labor for the working class and leisure for the wealthy. Entertainment venues proliferated as did restaurants, thus transforming the eating habits of urban dwellers. Not only did city residents consume different types of food, the middle and upper classes consumed more of it. The rise in consumption was encouraged by a fear of overproduction and stimulated by advertisers who worked to change Americans from savers to spenders, which required overturning long-instilled traditional values. Evidence of the new consumer ethic was seen in the rise of department stores and luxury hotels. All these things contributed to the emergence of a new, vibrant, and diverse urban culture that inspired a response from writers, artists, and musicians.

During this period, literature moved from the genteel tradition that focused on reinforcing morality toward realism. Among the first proponents of the new school were Frank Norris, who used gritty realism to portray what he considered the truth, and local colorists like Bret Harte, who employed humor and innocence to capture the flavor of American life, though their characters were largely stylized. Mark Twain transcended this genre and influenced other writers to show the harsh and often sordid reality of life. Eventually, realism gave rise to another school called naturalism that depicted the individual as a helpless pawn subject to natural forces beyond a person's control. Influenced by Karl Marx, Charles Darwin, and later Sigmund Freud, writers such as Theodore Dreiser explored how the impersonal forces of industrialism and urbanization determined the course of peoples' lives. Dreiser depicted the tragic decline of the main character in Sister Carrie. Stephen Crane explored the influence of poverty in *Maggie: A Girl of the Street*. Both realism and naturalism challenged prevailing beliefs that individuals could control their own destinies.

American artists had largely eschewed the city as a subject preferring to focus upon America's natural wonders. By the end of the 1800s, the "ash can" school arose in New York City, headed by Robert Henri, which used the city as inspiration, painting gritty, realistic portraits of urban life. At the same time, the modernist school headed by Alfred Steiglitz was inspired by the urban landscape. The dynamism of the modern city was evident in their nonrepresentational abstract paintings. Both groups, along with leaders of European postimpressionism, participated in the 1913 Armory Show that was the most important art exhibition in American history.

Music, too, developed new forms influenced by city life. New Orleans gave rise to jazz. The red-light district of the city, Storyville, provided employment to jazz musicians and to ragtime players who performed in bordellos and cafes. Rural migrants also brought the emerging sounds of blues to the city. When Storyville was closed, black musicians scattered to other cities, bringing their music to new audiences.

The growing mass character of the cities gave rise to various forms of mass entertainment and sports. Commercial entertainment arose in response to transportation and communication advances that made promotion and travel easier. There was also a growing recognition that entertainment was not necessarily bad. Victorian values that condemned play, gratification, and revelry were opposed first by immigrants and later by Americans generally, promoting new attitudes toward sport and leisure.

Baseball was an urban game. Professional teams were located in cities and most paid players came from urban backgrounds. But the mythology of the sport symbolized America's rural past, as did the open, grassy fields where it was played. The team concept and the virtues of hard work and punctuality reflected the urban, industrial environment. Like business, baseball went through a period of consolidation and organization that increased its appeal to the middle classes. By 1909, baseball had become the national pastime, a status recognized by the tradition of having the president throw out the first ball of the season.

The only sport to rival baseball in popularity in the late 1800s was boxing. It was dominated by poor immigrants who used the sport to climb the economic and social ladders. Champions, like John L. Sullivan who won the world heavyweight title in 1882, emerged as national heroes. In the 1880s the sport sought greater respectability as the Marquis of Queensbury's rules were adopted, gloves replaced bare knuckles, and a specified number of rounds regulated the length of the fight.

Though professional sports were somewhat open to immigrants and their sons, the world of sports generally excluded many Americans. The wealthy established exclusive sports and athletics clubs, engaging in rather expensive pastimes like yachting or polo, and golf. To further distance themselves from the masses, the wealthy embraced a code of amateurism, thereby separating their efforts from the professionals of lesser backgrounds. More blatant discrimination excluded blacks, though this developed largely in the 1890s as segregation became the rule. Women also faced restriction due in part to popular stereotypes and cultural expectations of their roles. Sports for women stressed developing qualities that would attract men.

Parks evolved to satisfy other urban demands. Designers like Frederick Law Olmstead saw parks as an antidote for urban anxieties and tensions by providing a rural retreat in the midst of the city. For those seeking more excitement, amusement parks were developed, offering rides and promoting the new values of the good life.

Another form of entertainment that emerged in the early 1900s was the motion picture. Developed at Edison's research laboratory, movies eventually offered immigrant masses cheap, escapist entertainment, but were criticized for promoting idleness and immorality. Movies became the business of immigrant entrepreneurs, many of whom were Jewish, who expanded the appeal of film to middle class audiences. Critics of movies and amusement parks suggested these venues served as opiates for the masses. In reality, drugs like opium and cocaine had few restrictions and so were readily available, often upon prescription by doctors. As the harmful effects of drugs became evident, movements arose to combat addiction that culminated with the Harrison Anti-Narcotic Act of 1914.

OBJECTIVES

After reading this chapter, you should be able to:

1. Discuss how the "new immigrants" of the late 19th century differed from previous immigrants.

2. Describe the forms that nativism took in late 19th century America.

3. Discuss the problems plaguing growing American cities, and how literature, art, and music reflected the social tensions and possibilities of the new American city.

KEY TERMS
Birds of Passage
Permanent Immigrants
Nativism
National Origins Act
Electric Trolley
Dumbbell Tenements
Naturalism
Jazz
Marquis of Queensberry Rules
Coney Island

KEY FIGURES
Lizzie Borden
Grover Cleveland
Leo Frank
Jacob Riis
Mark Twain
Theodore Dreiser
John L. Sullivan
Marshall Field

CHAPTER 18 • THE RISE OF AN URBAN SOCIETY AND CITY PEOPLE

_____ 1. Chinese immigrants, for the most part, came to America to
   a. accumulate money for their families in China
   b. found communities for the permanent settlement of their families
   c. flee from religious persecution

_____ 2. Most old immigrants came from
   a. Italy
   b. England, Ireland and Germany
   c. Russia

_____ 3. The new immigrants differed from their predecessors mainly in their
   a. reasons for coming to this country
   b. ethnic and religious backgrounds and countries of origin
   c. inability to adapt their skills to the needs of a factory-oriented economy

_____ 4. The new immigrants came mainly from
   a. southern and eastern Europe
   b. Scandinavia
   c. China and Japan

_____ 5. Which of the following statements about nativism is FALSE?
   a. Nativists opposed the influence of Roman Catholics in America
   b. Nativists favored immigration
   c. Nativists argued that southern and eastern Europeans were inferior

_____ 6. Who determined the pattern of urban growth and development in the "private city" of the late 19th century?
   a. government planners
   b. profit-seeking businessmen
   c. zoning boards

_____ 7. The 19th century genteel tradition in American literature dwelt on all the following themes EXCEPT
   a. moral ideals
   b. sentimentality
   c. reality

_____ 8. Novelist Theodore Dreiser wrote in the literary genre known as
   a. realism
   b. the genteel tradition
   c. local color

_____ 9. Literary naturalists in late 19th century American pursued the theme of
   a. America's natural beauty and grandeur
   b. the effect of modern urban society on the helpless individual
   c. regional differences and regional dialects in rural America

_____ 10. Scott Joplin wrote popular music in the syncopated style called
   a. ragtime
   b. the blues
   c. jazz

_____ 11. By the end of the 19th century, the sport of _____ was governed by the Marquis of Queensberry rules.
   a. baseball
   b. boxing
   c. tennis

_____ 12. Coney Island became famous
    a. as a rural retreat for the harried urban middle class
    b. a weekend retreat for the urban upper class
    c. an escapist adventureland for working-class Americans

CHAPTER 19 • END-OF-THE-CENTURY CRISIS

SUMMARY

The 1880s and 1890s were years of turbulence. In this chapter you read about Gilded Age politics; disputes over currency, tariffs, patronage, and railroads; the problems facing the nation's farmers; farmers' efforts to organize; and the critical election of 1896.

KEY POINTS

- An era of intense political partisanship, the Gilded Age was also an era of reform. The Civil Service Act sought to curb government corruption by requiring applicants for certain governmental jobs to take a competitive examination. The Interstate Commerce Act sought to end discrimination by railroads against small shippers and the Sherman Antitrust Act outlawed business monopolies.

- These were turbulent years that saw labor violence, rising racial tension, militancy among farmers, and discontent among the unemployed.

- These years also saw the rise of the Populist crusade. Burdened by heavy debts and falling farm prices, many farmers joined the Populist party, which called for an increase in the amount of money in circulation, government assistance to help farmers repay loans, tariff reductions, and a graduated income tax.

CHAPTER SYNOPSIS

In the closing decades of the nineteenth century, the nation's political parties were more interested in gaining office and maintaining patronage than in enacting policies to address the problems accompanying industrialization and urbanization. Between 1876 and 1896, Democrats and Republicans enjoyed almost equal support. Presidential races were extremely close. The Democrats typically ruled the House while the Republicans dominated in the Senate. No president was elected to consecutive terms and the locus of power was centered in Congress, making presidents more administrators than leaders. But rules and power often stalemated Congress, resulting in little substantive legislation. Government inaction reflected a popular consensus that the role of government should be limited. At the same time, court decisions stymied reform by striking down laws regulating business.

Headed by men of wealth, neither party risked taking forceful positions on public issues. Both the Democratic and Republican parties supported tariffs and sound currency while rejecting radicalism and aid to workers. Their constituencies were extremely loyal and heterogeneous, creating the need for weak positions to avoid alienating voters. Region, religion, and ethnic origin often determined party loyalty, but the mixed constituencies, such as the combination of white, racist southerners with northern, ethnic immigrants in the Democratic party, created internal party divisions.

The Gilded Age stress on party management and electioneering to sustain political careers resulted in record voter turnouts. A major difference between the two parties was the Republican reliance on state organizations and the Democratic focus on urban political machines. These machines enhanced Democratic efforts by providing services that strained urban governments proved unable to supply. Widespread graft and corruption were prevalent nationwide.

The pageantry of the political process provided exciting entertainment for the public. Politics also promoted private interests and provided some ethnic and lower-class groups upward mobility. Women, however, found access to the political arena largely closed to them. Susan B. Anthony introduced the constitutional amendment on voting rights for women in 1878. The suffrage amendment was introduced in Congress annually for the next 18 years, but never passed. State suffrage proved easier to attain but was often limited.

Inertia on the federal level meant that governmental action took place largely at the local and state levels. The first major national political issue to arise after Reconstruction was the "currency" question. President Hayes assumed office in the midst of a severe depression that was complicated by long-term deflation that reduced the buying power of the farmer's dollar but provided a tremendous bonus to creditors. This growing discrepancy prompted several proposed solutions. One aimed to increase the circulation of paper "greenback" dollars, but was defeated during Grant's presidency. Another was bimetallism, but it was affected by market conditions and government actions and did not alleviate the currency problems.

Patronage became a major issue in the 1880 election, raised in large part by President Garfield's assassination by a deranged office seeker. The reformist Mugwumps and others increasingly focused on government corruption, seeking reform of the "spoils" system." After Garfield's assassination, Congress established the Civil Service Commission, but patronage prevailed as every president manipulated the act to his own advantage.

The question of the growing power of the railroads arose during Grover Cleveland's presidency. Many states had established railroad commissions to regulate rates and charges. The strongest advocates for regulation were farmers whose efforts produced strong legislation in several states. State regulation proved difficult because of limited jurisdiction and negative court rulings, creating pressure for national regulation. In 1887, the Interstate Commerce Act was passed, but the limited power of the Interstate Commerce Commission hampered regulation and its powers were weakened by hostile court decisions.

The tariff was one of the few issues dividing the parties. Both parties supported taxes on imports, but Republicans typically favored higher rates. Tariff revenues created budget surpluses that led to congressional proposals President Cleveland considered dangerous expansions of federal authority. He made tariff reduction the foremost issue in his 1888 reelection bid. Harrison defeated Cleveland, after which Congress enacted the protectionist McKinley Tariff, but it proved to be unpopular.

Trusts also raised public ire. State legislation was ineffective and failed to withstand court scrutiny. Congress responded with the Sherman Antitrust Act of 1890, but it was seldom enforced during the following decade and was later weakened by the courts. That same year, currency became an issue and led to the passage of the Sherman Silver Purchase Act, but it did little to inflate currency values.

Social legislation was sparse and often failed to fulfill its goals. The declining political status of southern blacks prompted the Lodge Bill of 1890 to protect voter registration and guarantee fair congressional elections. Opposed by white Southerners, it became a casualty in the dealing that led to the passage of the McKinley Tariff. That same year, the Blair Bill to provide federal aid to primarily black schools failed. Most legislation, particularly at state and local levels, enhanced racial discrimination against blacks. Chinese and Native Americans also suffered from national legislation. Social issues that did receive some attention at state and local levels typically achieved few results. Republicans proved unsuccessful in pursuing expansion of public education and prohibition of the manufacture and sale of liquor.

The farmers were perhaps the biggest losers in the changing economy of the United States. The Populist movement achieved few successes but mounted the first mass movement against Social Darwinism and laissez-faire while promoting greater government involvement in society. Falling crop prices caused largely by overproduction were the basic causes of the farmers' economic problems. But the farmers refused to accept this explanation; instead, they blamed high freight and credit rates, taxation, exploitative middlemen, and a deflated currency.

To address their problems, farmers established a variety of organizations. Founded in 1867, the Patrons of Husbandry was organized around local granges that planned social gatherings. Membership hit one million by 1874 and the Grange began focusing upon economic concerns, developing railroad regulation legislation and cooperatives. These successes proved short-lived as the courts nullified the laws and the cooperatives failed due to lack of capital and administrative expertise.

The Farmers Alliance movement arose in the late 1870s in Texas. The movement spread rapidly across the South in the late 1880s. By 1890, there were 2.5 million black and white Alliance members. Activities centered around cooperatives and expanded social and educational programs as well as an extensive network of newspapers. A self-help philosophy soon gave way to political activism. Southern Alliance members tried to capture state Democratic parties from within. Northwestern and Great Plains farmers organized independent parties. Their demands were influenced by the idea that the nation had divided into the "haves" and "have-rots." Workers were considered to be members of the exploited classes, too.

The Alliance demands proved radical for the age even though most have become part of 20th-century life. They called for government ownership of the railroad, telegraph, and telephone networks. They proposed a flexible currency and a subtreasury crop marketing plan to ease the credit crisis. A graduated income tax would help fund government programs. Behind these ideas stood the belief in a more active and responsive government that worked for the people rather than for the industrialists. To achieve greater accountability, the Populists supported the initiative and referendum, direct primaries, direct election of U. S. Senators, and the secret ballot.

In 1890, the Alliance successfully entered politics in the West and the South. Third parties in the West elected a governor, two senators, and captured four state legislatures. In the South, the Alliance elected four governors; 44 congressmen and several senators on the Democratic slate. This triumph led to the founding of the People's or Populist Party in 1892. The majority of the members were small farmers whose single cash crop operations were barely mechanized. Few had good access to credit and most lived in isolated locations. To broaden their appeal to urban workers, the Populists expanded their platform to include the eight-hour day and immigration restriction. Populist presidential candidate James B. Weaver garnered one million votes, carrying four states. In mining areas, the party's espousal of free silver proved popular. In the South, however, the Populists did not carry a single state.

Bank failures, a stock market crash, and high unemployment intensified the problems of farmers and workers. The violent defeat of workers in the 1892 Homestead and 1894 Pullman strikes drove some into the radical camp. The depression prompted hundreds of unemployed workers led by Jacob Coxey to march to Washington, D. C. to demand jobs.

At the same time, race relations were deteriorating. Violence against blacks, including lynching, was prevalent. Legal attempts to reduce the numbers of black voters led to a steady erosion of all black rights that ended with legal segregation.

The growing divisions in American society served as the backdrop to the election of 1896. When Bryan endorsed the silver issue, the Populists lost a major campaign issue. They also faced a dilemma: They could nominate a candidate to oppose Bryan, thus splitting the silver vote and ensuring Republican William McKinley's election, or they could nominate Bryan, which meant losing their distinctive identity. Most Populists endorsed the latter strategy.

McKinley's victory shattered the parity of the previous decades, enabling the Republicans to become the majority party. In the aftermath of the election, the Populists collapsed. As prosperity returned, the farmers' plight eased temporarily, while the spread of the telephone and rural free delivery that brought mail-order catalogs into farm homes alleviated their isolation.

OBJECTIVES

After reading this chapter, you should be able to:

1. Identify the basic sources of electoral support for the Democratic and Republican Parties, and explain the high level of popular participation in politics.

2. Discuss the major political issues of the late 19th century, including those involving currency, tariffs, patronage, and railroads.

3. Discuss the problems confronting late 19th century American farmers.

4. Trace the rise of the Populist party and the reasons for its decline after 1896.

5. Evaluate the contributions of the Populist movement to social and economic reform.

KEY TERMS
Gilded Age
Mugwumps
National American Woman Suffrage Association
Greenback Party
Spoils System
Pendleton Act
Interstate Commerce Commission
Sherman Act
Patrons of Husbandry
Alliance Movement
Populists
Initiative and Recall
Homestead
Pullman
Coxey's Army

KEY FIGURES
William Jennings Bryan
Lord James Bryce
James A. Garfield
Chester A. Arthur
Grover Cleveland
Eugene V. Debs
Ida B. Wells
William McKinley

CHAPTER 19 • END-OF-THE-CENTURY CRISIS

_____ 1. The phrase "you shall not crucify mankind on a cross of gold" referred to
   a. the anti-religious movement of secularists during the late 1890s
   b. William Jennings Bryan's opposition to the gold standard in the presidential campaign of 1896
   c. President William McKinley's rebuttal to gold-standard advocates in Congress

_____ 2. The term "free silver" refers to
   a. putting more money into circulation
   b. removing silver from the list of metals used to back U.S. currency
   c. reducing farm prices

_____ 3. The phrase Mark Twain used to describe the political and cultural climate that existed in American between 1877 and 1900 was the
   a. Progressive era
   b. Gilded Age
   c. Age of mediocrity

_____ 4. Lord Bryce, in his _The American Commonwealth_,
   a. praised the American political system
   b. called on Britain to adopt American political institutions and practices
   c. warned that patronage rather than substantive issues characterizes politics in America

_____ 5. Between 1877 and 1896
   a. presidential elections were usually close contests
   b. voter turnout was usually low by modern standards
   c. Democratic candidates usually won the presidency

_____ 6. Party loyalty among voters during the post-Reconstruction era was
   a. low, because voters were more interested in a candidate's appeal than in issues
   b. low for both the Democrats and Republicans, but high for various third parties
   c. high for both major parties, because party attachments reflected voters' religious and cultural values

_____ 7. By 1890, women had full political equality with men only in _____ .
   a. Massachusetts
   b. Wyoming Territory
   c. Alaska Territory

_____ 8. The Pendleton Act, providing for a federal civil service, was passed largely as a result of the popular outcry over
   a. the assassination of James Garfield
   b. abuse of the patronage by every President since Grant
   c. the Credit Mobilier scandal

_____ 9. The Granger laws were enacted in an attempt to
   a. regulate railroad rates
   b. reduce the tariff
   c. lower the price of public lands

_____ 10. The nation's first federal regulatory agency was created by
   a. the Supreme Court's ruling in _Munn v. Illinois_
   b. the Interstate Commerce Act
   c. the Sherman Anti-Trust Act

_____ 11. The key issue dividing the two major parties in the late 1880s was _____ policy.
   a. Indian
   b. foreign
   c. tariff

_____ 12. President Grover Cleveland opposed the current tariff because he thought
  a. the tariff was too low
  b. the tariff was producing a treasury surplus and tempting Congress to dangerously expand federal activities
  c. the tariff reduced American industrial productivity and impeded technological innovation

_____ 13. The basic problem of farmers in the last half of the 19th century was caused by
  a. excessive government regulation
  b. overproduction
  c. foreign restrictions on the import of American crops

_____ 14. In the late 19th century, farmers in the West and South suffered from all of these problems EXCEPT
  a. low agricultural prices
  b. high freight rates
  c. high taxes

_____ 15. The first national farmers' organization devoted to economic self-help and political agitation for farmers' goals was the
  a. Southern Farmers Alliance
  b. Populist Party
  c. the Grange (the Patrons of Husbandry)

_____ 16. To alleviate their problems, farmers tried all of the following EXCEPT
  a. forming cooperatives
  b. organizing a third political party and passing laws to regulate railroads
  c. reducing agricultural production

_____ 17. The farmers' agenda included all the following EXCEPT
  a. an income tax
  b. inflation of the currency
  c. government ownership of industry

_____ 18. Coxey's Army marched on Washington to demand
  a. jobs for the unemployed
  b. pensions for Civil War veterans
  c. civil service reform

_____ 19. The widespread enactment of Jim Crow laws that disfranchised and segregated blacks began
  a. during the 1850s
  b. in the 1890s
  c. during World War I

_____ 20. The Mississippi Plan was a scheme to
  a. deprive blacks of the vote
  b. segregate southern schools
  c. lease black prison labor to private interests

_____ 21. The Supreme Court in _Plessy v. Ferguson_ asserted that
  a. separate facilities for blacks were inherently unequal and therefore unconstitutional
  b. separate but equal facilities were constitutional
  c. the 14th Amendment was unconstitutional

CHAPTER 20 • IMPERIAL AMERICA, 1870–1900

SUMMARY

At the end of the 19th century, the United States emerged as a world power. In this chapter you read about the country's lack of concern with foreign affairs prior to the 1880s; the reasons why the United States adopted a more aggressive foreign policy; the growing willingness of the United States to threaten force to resolve international disputes; and the causes, military history, and consequences of the Spanish American War.

KEY POINTS

- In 1898 and 1899, the United States annexed Hawaii and acquired the Philippines, Puerto Rico, parts of the Samoan islands, and other Pacific islands.

- Expansion raised the fateful question of whether the newly annexed peoples would receive the rights of American citizens.

- The Spanish-American War and the acquisition of the Philippines represented both an extension of earlier expansionist impulses and a sharp departure from assumptions that had guided American foreign policy in the past. For the first time, the United States made a major strategic commitment in the Far East, acquired territory never intended for statehood, and committed itself to police actions and intervention in the Caribbean and Central America.

CHAPTER SYNOPSIS

In 1869, the State Department commanded little respect. The Secretary of State was a reward for party loyalists or a refuge for failed presidential candidates. Until the 1890s, domestic concerns overshadowed diplomatic affairs. Before the 1890s, Congress dictated foreign policy, following in the isolationist spirit of Washington and Monroe. Both the State Department and the military budgets were trimmed.

The navy, in particular, felt the budget-cutting knife. It was reduced from the world's largest in 1865 with 971 vessels to one of the smallest with 29 within nine months of the Confederate surrender. Its effectiveness declined as other countries converted to steel and steam, while the United States maintained a wood and sails fleet. The army was similarly cut, reducing its number from over 1 million in May 1865 to just over 11,000 in November 1866. The absence of enemies and geography protected the United States from attack but also inhibited the nation's ability to extend its influence beyond its borders.

Following the Civil War, presidents and secretaries of state called for a more aggressive foreign policy. Secretary of State William Seward attempted to expand U.S. interests in the Caribbean and the Pacific, crowned by the purchase of Alaska from the Russians. But when he sought further expansion, Congress blocked his moves, protesting against the acquisition of Alaska.

During the closing decades of the nineteenth century, sentiment grew for a more aggressive foreign policy grew. Several factors contributed to this shift in sentiment. Businesses wanted access to overseas resources and markets. Foreign markets offered the promise of prosperity to help relieve dissent at home. Others believed that a more aggressive policy was necessary to protect the nation's strategic interests. Other factors included a belief that nation's were engaged in a struggle for survival. Some believed that the United States had a special mission was to uplift the less fortunate people of the world by assuming the "white man's burden."

William Seward and Hamilton Fish, Grant's secretary of state, pursued aggressive foreign policies. Seward proposed acquiring Pacific islands as stepping stones to Asia. Fish acted on this idea by establishing relations with Hawaii and Samoa. Other secretaries under Garfield and Arthur focused on opening up Latin American markets, signing bilateral reciprocity agreements with a number of nations. Eventually, Congress reevaluated its isolationist stance, but neither the merchant marine nor the navy were up to meeting the challenge of expansion.

During the last two decades of the nineteenth century, a naval modernization program was implemented. These efforts were aided by the 1890 publication of *The Influence of Sea Power Upon History* by Captain Alfred Thayer Mahan, which declared no nation could enjoy full prosperity and security without a strong navy. Mahan's ideas were supported by American business and government leaders who came to dominate the nation's foreign policy. Their proposals included constructing a canal through Central America and acquiring fueling stations and naval bases in the Pacific to penetrate the Chinese market. Protecting these efforts would be a powerful navy.

Behind the movement to create a powerful navy and a more active world presence was a growing acceptance of the notion that force could be a final arbiter of international disputes. This attitude led to the Spanish-American War of 1898. It also brought the United States close to war several times between 1885 and 1897. The first confrontation was over Samoa with whom a treaty had been signed in 1878. Germany and Britain vied with the United States for influence in the Pacific island nation, but eventually the United States was pitted against both nations. A conference in Washington in 1887 failed to produce a compromise. After a typhoon sank both German and United States warships, a conference in Berlin partitioned the islands among the powers without consulting Samoa.

In 1891, troubles with Chile erupted after a riot in Valparaiso, Chile, and the subsequent jailing of some American sailors. After demanding an official apology, which was refused, President Harrison threatened to break off diplomatic relations, but Chile backed down. The next target was Hawaii, tied economically to the United States through the sugar trade In 1890, the McKinley Tariff Act caused prices of Hawaiian sugar to plummet as it lost its favored status. The ascension of Queen Liliuokalani to the throne in 1891 led to anti-American policies. Supported by the American minister, white islanders overthrew the queen and proclaimed the islands an American protectorate. Hawaii was annexed by the United States during the Spanish-American War.

The most dangerous conflict was with the British in 1895 and involved a dispute between British Guiana and Venezuela over their common border after gold was discovered in an area claimed by both nations. Diplomatic maneuvering between the United States and Britain raised the threat of war, but the British agreed to arbitration and won their claim. The United States also felt it had triumphed. The resolution enhanced the powers of the president in foreign affairs.

During the 1890s, Americans were frustrated by economic problems at home. The country suffered from the ravages of a severe depression, and was plagued by internal strife. Violent strikes and Populist protests threatened to split an already divided nation. This violent thrust was reflected in such popular heroes as boxer John L. Sullivan and the popularity of the military marches of John Philip Sousa. Weakness and cowardice were considered crimes and sins, giving rise to a spirit of war and jingoistic nationalism, in part fueled by fading memories of the horrors of the Civil War and its glorification by the younger generation.

The outbreak of a rebellion for independence in Cuba in 1895 drew American attention. Partially, this was due to American investments in the island, but also important were humanitarian reasons and the cheering for an underdog engaged in a struggle that seemed similar to the American Revolution. Cuban rebels played on American opinion, offering stories of Spanish atrocities. The guerrilla war waged by the Cubans was met by repression and the relocation of over a half million Cubans into relocation camps where approximately 200,000 died. The American press used the lurid and inflammatory stories of Cuban hardship as part of a circulation war between Hearst and Pulitzer. The resulting "yellow journalism" was exaggerated but convinced many Americans that the United States should intervene. At first, President McKinley pursued diplomatic efforts to end the conflict. In 1898, the de Lome letter followed by the explosion that sank the Maine led to war with Spain. In the Teller Amendment, Congress stated that the United States would not annex Cuba.

The United States military was unprepared for war. The training of troops was plagued by supply shortages and unsanitary conditions, which caused more deaths than combat. As the army struggled to mobilize, the navy attacked Manila Bay, destroying Spain's Asiatic fleet. Achieving victory in Cuba proved difficult as the hostile climate and geography combined with stiff Spanish opposition slowed American advances. But a combined army-naval force captured Santiago Bay, leading to the Spanish surrender.

This short, triumphant war led the nation into a period of imperialism, as Hawaii and part of Samoa, Guam, Puerto Rico, and the Philippines were annexed. American troops remained in Cuba until 1903 when that country was granted independence though the Platt Amendment provided for U. S. intervention in Cuba. The annexation of the Philippines, however, aroused strong opposition from powerful anti-imperialists, including William Jennings Bryan, Andrew Carnegie, and Mark Twain. The issue was decided in 1899 when the Senate ratified the Treaty of Paris that ended the Spanish-American War. Led by Emilio Aguinaldo, Filipino rebels battled for independence, waging a three-year guerrilla war against American troops that was characterized by brutality and atrocities on both sides. The warfare ended in 1902 with the capture of Aguinaldo. The victory had cost $400 million and shocked many Americans with its brutal nature.

Still the United States had gained a gateway to China. The problem was stopping other countries from carving up the teetering Manchu empire. Secretary of State John Hay issued a note in 1899 that set the policy of the United States. He called for an Open Door that stopped the partition of China among several European powers and also demanded the establishment of open trade that respected the rights of all nations. Hay announced European support for the policy, though few European nations had shown any interest. The Boxer Rebellion revealed strong anti-foreign sentiment existed in China. Another note by Hay advanced the idea that the United States was China's protector, signifying the increasing world role being assumed by the United States.

OBJECTIVES

After reading this chapter, you should be able to:

1. Discuss the changing social and economic trends that encouraged an expansionistic foreign policy by the end of the 19th century.

2. Identify the causes and consequences of the Spanish-American War.

3. Identify the groups opposed to this country's acquisition of an empire, outline their arguments, and assess their impact on American public opinion.

KEY TERMS
American Exceptionalism
The Influence of Sea Power upon History
Large Policy
Yellow Journalism
"Remember the Maine!"
Platt Amendment
Open Door Note

KEY FIGURES
William Henry Seward
Queen Liliuokali
Lord Salisbury

CHAPTER 20 • IMPERIAL AMERICA, 1870–1900

_____ 1. President Ulysses Grant wanted to annex the Dominican Republic for all but one of the following reasons. Select the EXCEPTION.
   a. Because the Dominican Republic had an important natural harbor and rich mineral resources
   b. Because it could serve as a haven for African Americans
   c. Because annexation had strong support in Congress

_____ 2. During the 1860s, 1870s, and 1880s, public interest in overseas expansion was
   a. intense
   b. non-existent
   c. limited largely to missionary organizations, Social Darwinists, and a limited number of business interests

_____ 3. Which of the following statements about the foreign service in 1869 is FALSE?
   a. The State department had just 31 clerks
   b. The State Department was located in a former orphan asylum
   c. The post of Secretary of State was regarded as a stepping-stone to the presidency

_____ 4. All of the following factors retarded interest in expansion EXCEPT
   a. preoccupation with Reconstruction, the tariff, Indian warfare, and railroad building
   b. fear of war with European powers
   c. opposition from a strongly anti-imperialist press

_____ 5. In the years immediately following the Civil War, the United States
   a. sharply increased the size of its army and navy
   b. acquired Alaska from Russia
   c. purchased bases in Haiti, Cuba, Iceland, Greenland, and Honduras

_____ 6. Those who favored American expansion in the late 19th century argued that
   a. increasing industrial and agricultural production meant that the United States needed new markets
   b. it was our duty to extend our government and culture to less privileged people
   c. if the United States failed to expand, other nations would acquire foreign markets and sources of raw materials
   d. all of the above
   e. none of the above

_____ 7. Periodic depressions in the late 19th century fostered a belief that expansion would benefit the economy by providing
   a. new investors for the stock market
   b. higher government expenditures on the military
   c. new markets to buy up surplus American production

_____ 8. Who was the author of the influential book _The Influence of Sea Power upon History_?
   a. Henry Cabot Lodge
   b. Alfred Thayer Mahan
   c. William H. Seward

_____ 9. The basic argument of _The Influence of Sea Power upon History_ was that
   a. naval power was the key to national greatness
   b. the military needed to become more influential in shaping foreign policy
   c. the United States should solve problems at home rather than worry about foreign policy

_____ 10. The "Large Policy" called for
   a. the acquisition of Cuba, Hawaii, Puerto Rico, and the Philippines
   b. construction of a canal through Central America, a powerful navy, and coaling stations in the Pacific
   c. an expanded army capable of waging wars overseas

_____ 11. Between 1885 and 1897, American foreign policy
  a. remained isolationist
  b. became increasingly belligerent
  c. emphasized negotiations and alliances with foreign nations

_____ 12. The key event that precipitated the overthrow of Queen Liliuokalani of Hawaii was
  a. fear that Germany was about to annex the Hawaiian Islands
  b. a popular revolt among the Hawaiian people
  c. a change in American tariff policies that would have cost Hawaiian sugar producers $12 million

_____ 13. The term "jingoism" describes
  a. those Americans who were opposed to overseas expansion
  b. the spirit of warlike patriotism advocated by many Americans in the late 19th century
  c. a nationalist movement for Chinese independence that emerged at the end of the 19th century

_____ 14. The main reason the United States declared war on Spain in 1898 was to
  a. annex the Philippines
  b. protect U.S. business interests in Cuba
  c. establish an American empire
  d. liberate Cuba from Spain

_____ 15. Causes of the war with Spain in 1898 include all of the following EXCEPT
  a. the explosion that ripped apart the American battleship Maine
  b. sympathy for Cubans rebelling against Spanish rule
  c. Spain's total refusal to negotiate the Cuban issue

_____ 16. Those who pressed hard for war with Spain prior to 1898 included all of the following EXCEPT
  a. yellow journalists such as William Randolph Hearst
  b. Leading members of Congress
  c. President William McKinley

_____ 17. As a result of the Spanish-American War, the United States acquired
  a. the Philippines, Puerto Rico and Guam
  b. Alaska
  c. Cuba

_____ 18. The Platt Amendment
  a. made Cuba an American colony
  b. authorized the United States to intervene in Cuba's internal and external affairs
  c. required the United States to pay $20 million to end the Spanish American War

_____ 19. As a direct result of the Spanish-American War the United States had to fight another war to
  a. suppress a revolt against American rule in the Philippines
  b. put down a revolt by Cuban rebels
  c. fend off German encroachments in the South Pacific

_____ 20. Which of the following statements about the Open Door Note of 1899 is FALSE?
  a. It sought to prevent the further partitioning of China by the European powers
  b. It was intended to guarantee Americans' right to trade in China
  c. It was warmly accepted by the Chinese people

CHAPTER 21 • THE PROGRESSIVE STRUGGLE, 1900–1917

SUMMARY

In this chapter you read about the sources of the Progressive movement; Progressivism at the municipal, state, and national levels; and the influence of Progressive ideas upon foreign policy.

KEY POINTS

- Progressivism is an umbrella label for a wide range of economic, political, social, and moral reforms.
- Drawing support from the urban, college-educated middle class, Progressive reformers sought to eliminate corruption in government, regulate business practices, address health hazards, improve working conditions, and give the public more direct control over government through direct primaries to nominate candidates for public office, direct election of Senators, the initiative, referendum, and recall, and women's suffrage.
- At the local level, many Progressives sought to suppress red-light districts, expand high schools, construct playgrounds, and replace corrupt urban political machines with more efficient system of municipal government.
- At the state level, Progressives enacted minimum wage laws for women workers, instituted industrial accident insurance, restricted child labor, and improved factory regulation.
- At the national level, Congress passed laws establishing federal regulation of the meat-packing, drug, and railroad industries, and strengthened anti-trust laws. It also lowered the tariff, established federal control over the banking system, and enacted legislation to improve working condition.
- Four constitutional amendments were adopted during the Progressive era, which authorized an income tax, provided for the direct election of senators, extended the vote to women, and prohibited the manufacture and sale of alcoholic beverages.

CHAPTER SYNOPSIS

Around the turn of the 20th century, glaring social problems came to light. In 1901, one percent of American families owned nearly seven-eighths of the nation's wealth, while four-fifths lived at a subsistence level. Working conditions in many industries were horrifying, as were housing conditions in poor neighborhoods. The rapid expansion in business trusts after 1898 seemed to threaten economic opportunity. A growing number of Americans worried about political corruption.

A revolution in social thought provided the basis for reform. During the late 19th century, Social Darwinism, laissez-faire economics, and the gospel of wealth began to be challenged. Earlier challengers, such as Henry George and Edward Bellamy, had offered simplistic or radical alternatives to doctrines that had justified the concentration of wealth and a lack of government regulation of business and assistance to the poor. Increasingly, however, respectable artistic, literary, and religious voices spoke out. The ashcan school painted scenes revealing urban problems. Realist writers described the world as it was. Naturalists portrayed the powerlessness of the individual against the forces of urbanization and industrialization. Meanwhile, scholars in the social sciences began to collect concrete data and used the information to challenge the status quo, while lawyers and jurists constitutional interpretations that reflected laissez-faire doctrines. Especially influential was the urban clergy and the Social Gospel, which sought to apply Christian principles to society's problems. The rapid expansion of higher education created an audience receptive to these arguments for reform.

The popular press aroused public outrage and lit the fire of reform. Muckraking writers exposed the evils of some aspect of society, like child labor, race relations, or even the U. S. Senate, in articles serialized in such magazines as McClure's.

The movement for reform touched all classes, as many Americans from diverse backgrounds called themselves "Progressives." They sought to reform whatever evil had caught their interest, often focusing on legislation. They also espoused cooperation, forming organizations to improve society. The organizational impulse became prominent at the turn of the century. Doctors and historians, for example, formed professional organizations, reflecting the rise of professionalism that enabled a number of experts to achieve reform. Not surprisingly, church-related organizations emerged, too, like the interdenominational Federal Council of Churches of Christ of America, which focused upon labor reform. The impulse toward organization was also evident in such diverse groups as the Boy Scouts of America and the National Collegiate Athletic Association.

Many leading proponents of reform were middle-class women. They concentrated not only on issues relating to morality and the family, such as prohibition and prostitution, but on poverty and social justice. The National Consumers League lobbied for better working and living conditions, child labor laws, and protection of women in the workplace. Settlement house workers, like Jane Addams of Hull House, offered education and social services to the poor. African Americans actively pressed for reform. Ida B. Wells led the anti-lynching crusade. Backed by white progressives, W.E.B. Du Bois disavowed Booker T. Washington's strategy of accommodation and formed the National Association for the Advancement of Colored People to fight for civil rights. Some progressives also formed groups to protect the rights of immigrants.

To combat corrupt political machines, urban reformers devised the commission form of government and the practice of hiring a city manager, but efficiency was often achieved at the cost of reducing democracy. In some instances, immigrants and the working classes rejected reform efforts as they seemed to work against their interests. In others, as was true with Mayor Samuel "Golden Rule" Jones in Toledo, working class support formed his power base. An aspect of urban reform involved the move toward public ownership of utilities, advocated by Socialists.

Four goals animating reformers at the state level were direct democracy, economic regulation, increasing state services, and social control. The initiative, referendum, recall, direct primary, and secret ballot expanded democracy, but the culmination was the Seventeenth Amendment, providing for the direct election of U.S. Senators. Several states gave women the right to vote and hold office. In the West, Progressives, building upon the Populist program, sought to regulate utilities and railroads. In industrial states, Progressives fought for workers' compensation. Child labor and workplace protection for women and children were state issues, as was pensions to allow widows to keep their children at home. Another area of concern was education where the goal of expanding compulsory education to the high school level required greater funding.

Social justice represented one side of the reform coin. Social control was the other, with prohibition being the top issue. In the South, segregation was defended as a Progressive reform. Often segregation laws were enacted under progressive governors who pursued such measures as school funding and railroad regulation. Although reforms at the state level achieved some success, it became evident that many problems were national in scope and required federal government action.

Theodore Roosevelt's assumption of the presidency inaugurated a national reform movement that altered the role of government in society. Roosevelt considered himself a conservative but accepted progressive notions that government should be administered by competent people and that industrialization had created the need for expanded governmental action. He reorganized the executive branch, modernized the army and consular service, pursued federal government economic regulation, and initiated the conservation movement. He also showed that business could not assume the government would automatically take its side in labor disputes, and became known as a trust-buster. In pursuit of the "Square Deal," Roosevelt tightened railroad regulation and, in the wake of the scandal caused by Upton Sinclair's *The Jungle*, pushed for passage of the Pure Food and Drug Act.

William Howard Taft succeeded Roosevelt and he proved sympathetic to reform. Taft supported the eight-hour day, sought to improve mine safety, and pushed for legislation to increase the power of the ICC. But Taft's style could not heal the growing divisions in the Republican party between conservatives and Progressives. Taft eventually alienated the progressive wing, which threatened to bolt the party if Taft were renominated. Roosevelt declared his candidacy but lost the nomination to his successor and left the Republicans to form the Progressive, or Bull Moose Party. The Progressive party attracted many reformers, and its platform was a litany of progressive reforms.

The split in the Republican ranks opened the door for Democrats who supported Woodrow Wilson and his "New Freedom" program. Wilson's goal was to restore competition through trust-busting. Roosevelt countered with the "New Nationalism," which focused on federal regulation of business. Wilson won the election. He brought a strong moral tone to the presidency and actively pursued reform. In his first term, the Sixteenth Amendment providing for an income tax was ratified, the Federal Reserve System was set up, and prohibition gained ground. The Federal Trade Commission was founded to regulate business, and the Clayton Antitrust Act was passed. Farmers gained from the Federal Farm Loan Act. Labor reform led to the passage of several bills that attacked child labor, established the eight-hour day for railroads, and provided Workman's Compensation for federal employees.

Progressives were activists in foreign policy. Roosevelt followed the idea of big stick diplomacy. He successfully arbitrated the peace in the Russo-Japanese War. In the Americas, he sent Marines to Cuba when protests against the Platt Amendment broke out. The Roosevelt Corollary to the Monroe Doctrine placed the United

States in the role of assuring that Latin American nations would pay their foreign debts. His biggest initiative was the Panama Canal.

Taft followed a different approach to foreign policy. He tried to use America's economic might to ensure stability and order in Latin America through "dollar diplomacy." Although Wilson's foreign policy, like that of his predecessors, stressed the importance of maintaining stability in the Americas, it also had a moral dimension. He wanted Latin Americans to elect good men. Wilson sent troops to the Dominican Republic, Haiti, and maintained them in Nicaragua. His biggest problem arose when the Mexican Revolution broke out, but the rise of an acceptable Mexican government and the outbreak of World War I eased rising tensions.

Progressive reformers believed that reform could make government more honest, efficient, and democratic. Anti-trust, government regulation, workers' compensation, child labor laws, and other reforms were supposed to increase social justice, restore fair competition, and improve the quality of American life. In practice, Progressivism left a mixed legacy. Direct election of senators did not seem to alter the kinds of people elected. The initiative, referendum, and recall were rarely used. Political bosses were still able to dominate primaries and elections. Voter participation actually declined. Attempts to regulate railroad rates or trusts did not seem to have the effects that reformers anticipated. Morality legislation created new opportunities for organized crime. Nevertheless, the doctrine of laissez faire had suffered an irreversible blow. Beneficiaries of progressive reform included engineers, health professionals, and trained managers. African Americans in the South were among the biggest losers as segregation and disfranchisement prevailed.

OBJECTIVES

After reading this chapter, you should be able to:

1. Define Progressivism, identify the sources of the progressive impulse, and provide examples of Progressivism in action.

2. Describe the goals of Progressive reformers at the municipal, state, and national levels.

3. Discuss the influence of Progressivism on American foreign policy.

4. Assess the Progressive reformers' successes and failures.

KEY TERMS

Reform Darwinists
Pragmatism
Social Gospel
Muckrakers
Women's Christian Temperance Union
Settlement House Movement
National Association for the Advancement of Colored People
Workmen's Compensation Laws
Progressive (Bull Moose) Party
Federal Reserve System
"Big Stick" Diplomacy

KEY FIGURES

Theodore Roosevelt
William Howard Taft
Woodrow Wilson
Carrie Chapman Catt
Alice Paul
W.E.B. DuBois

CHAPTER 21 • THE PROGRESSIVE STRUGGLE, 1900–1917

_____ 1. The 1902 anthracite coal strike
   a. marked the first time that a president intervened on the side of workers in a labor dispute
   b. resulted in lower wages and longer hours for the coal workers
   c. led many middle class citizens to support management in its battles with labor

_____ 2. Henry George and Edward Bellamy
   a. offered practical and pragmatic proposals to solve the problems of late 19th century society that were quickly instituted into law
   b. argued that any government interference in society would have negative consequences
   c. were two early challengers of Social Darwinism and laissez-faire

_____ 3. The Social Gospel movement
   a. argued that the only way to solve the problem of poverty was to first convert Americans to Christianity
   b. maintained that the Bible should be taught in public schools
   c. maintained that people should apply Christianity to address social problems

_____ 4. The journalists who exposed social evils in American society during the Progressive era were called
   a. Know Nothings
   b. abolitionists
   c. muckrakers

_____ 5. A pioneer in the settlement house movement was
   a. Florence Kelly
   b. Carrie Chapman Catt
   c. Jane Addams

_____ 6. The Niagara movement, organized in 1905 by W.E.B. DuBois and others, sought
   a. unionization of the unskilled
   b. political and economic equality for African Americans
   c. voting rights for women

_____ 7. The Progressives
   a. believed that experts should manage public affairs
   b. drew their support mainly from the lower classes
   c. embraced laissez-faire

_____ 8. At the state level, which of the following was NOT a proposal progressives made to achieve "direct democracy"?
   a. The poll tax
   b. Women's suffrage and direct election of Senators
   c. The initiative, referendum and recall

_____ 9. President Theodore Roosevelt's handling of trusts suggests that he believed
   a. bigness is the equivalent of badness
   b. the federal government should break up large corporations only in cases of monopoly or flagrant abuses
   c. regulation of large corporations should be left to state and local authorities

_____ 10. Upton Sinclair's The Jungle was instrumental in gaining congressional legislation for the regulation of
   a. railroads
   b. trusts
   c. food and drugs

_____ 11. As a result of the passage of a federal meat inspection law in 1906
   a. the working conditions of exploited meatpackers were improved
   b. federal standards for meat were established
   c. the meatpacking trust was broken up

_____ 12. President Theodore Roosevelt was ahead of his time in his views on
   a. the limits of American police power in the world
   b. the need for free trade
   c. the need for protection of natural resources

_____ 13. Roosevelt's foreign policy in the Western Hemisphere is best characterized by his
   a. repudiation of the Monroe Doctrine
   b. belief that the United States should intervene in the internal affairs of nations in the Americas when political stability or American interests are threatened
   c. belief that each nation within the hemisphere has independent sovereign rights

_____ 14. In order to secure rights to build a canal through Central American, the United States
   a. purchased the right of way through Panama from England
   b. aided a revolution in Panama against Columbia
   c. supported Columbia's claim to ownership of Panama

_____ 15. Dollar diplomacy refers to the policy of
   a. Theodore Roosevelt, who urged greater American investment in China
   b. William Howard Taft, who favored economic penetration of foreign markets by American banks and corporations
   c. Woodrow Wilson, who believed that an American economic blockade against Mexico would force the Mexicans to select a president acceptable to the United States

_____ 16. Who was the President known for a highly moralistic approach to diplomacy?
   a. Theodore Roosevelt
   b. William Howard Taft
   c. Woodrow Wilson

_____ 17. Which of the following was NOT among the groups that gained the most from Progressive reform?
   a. middle-class professionals
   b. women
   c. racial and ethnic minorities

_____ 18. The event that caused the decline of the Progressive movement was
   a. the split in the Republican party in 1912
   b. the Supreme Court ruling in Baker v. Carr
   c. World War I

CHAPTER 22 • THE UNITED STATES AND WORLD WAR I

SUMMARY

World War I killed more people—9 million combatants and 5 million civilians—and cost more money—$186 billion in direct costs and another $151 billion in indirect costs—than any previous war in history. In this chapter, you read about the war's causes; the reasons why the United States intervened in the conflict; how American industry and the military were mobilized for war; wartime propaganda and political repression; and the social changes and social unrest produced by the war.

KEY POINTS

- Triggered by the assassination of Archduke Franz Ferdinand, the heir to the throne of the Austro-Hungarian Empire, World War I began in August 1914 when Germany invaded Belgium and France

- Politically, World War I resulted in the downfall of four empires and contributed to the Bolshevik rise to power in Russia in 1917 and the triumph of fascism in Italy in 1922.

- The war allowed the United States to become the world's leading creditor and industrial power.

- Its consequences included the mass murder of Armenians in Turkey and an influenza epidemic that killed over 25 million people worldwide.

- Several events led to U.S. intervention: the sinking of the Lusitania, a British passenger liner; unrestricted German submarine warfare; and the Zimmerman note, which revealed a German plot to provoke Mexico to war against the United States.

- Millions of American men were drafted and Congress created a War Industries Board to coordinate production and a National War Labor Board to unify labor policy.

- The Treaty of Versailles deprived Germany of territory and forced it to pay reparations. President Wilson agreed to the treaty because it provided for establishment of a League of Nations, but he was unable to persuade the Senate to ratify the treaty.

CHAPTER SYNOPSIS

World War I killed more people, involved more nations, and had more far-reaching consequences than previous war. Entrapped within a tangled web of alliances, Europe erupted into war following the assassination of Archduke Franz Ferdinand. After Germany, allied with Austro-Hungary, Italy, and Turkey, invaded Belgium, Britain entered the war on the side of France and Russia. Though both sides expected a short war followed by victory, the conflict bogged down into a deadly stalemate fostered by trench warfare. The deadlock in Europe spread military action to other areas. T. E. Lawrence organized revolts against the Ottoman Empire in the Middle East while Japanese and British forces seized German islands in the Pacific and British forces captured German colonies in Africa. The military stalemate also led to an Irish rebellion to secure independence and in Russia, the effects of the war prompted the Russian Revolution.

In the United States, the outbreak of war came as a surprise. Wilson's neutrality statement was widely praised, though the president and most of his advisors favored Britain. Given the ethnic diversity of the nation and the recent arrival of many immigrants, Wilson recognized that favoring one side or the other would further split an already divided people. In addition, he feared that his domestic reform program would fail if the nation joined the conflict.

Recognizing German superiority on land, Britain launched a naval blockade of Europe. In the process, American vessels bound for neutral ports were seized. These actions combined with their ruthless suppression of a revolt in Ireland angered Wilson and led to firm protests from the State Department. The huge trade initiated by the war, however, had lifted the nation out of a recession, and persuaded Wilson to provide loans to belligerents, a move that favored Britain and France. As both nations became major creditors to the United States, Americans gained an economic interest in the Allied victory.

Germany attempted to wreck the British naval blockade by using the submarine. When Germany began unrestricted submarine warfare in 1915, Wilson sent a strong note holding it accountable for the loss of American lives. The sinking of the Lusitania outraged Americans but a compromise sustained American neutrality. After tensions rose again following the sinking of the Sussex, Wilson threatened to sever relations with Germany, but again negotiations maintained the peace. The recurring crises, however, heightened the debate among Americans over the war. Theodore Roosevelt pushed for entry into the conflict. Socialists, radicals, and others argued for peace. Wilson began a moderate preparedness campaign in early 1916, calling this a defensive move.

The election of 1916 pitted Wilson against the Progressive Republican, Charles Evans Hughes. Running on his record, Wilson made peace the key campaign issue. He won a close race by fusing Progressivism with peace, and sought to fulfill the voters' mandate by calling for a peace without victory through negotiation. The renewal of unrestricted submarine warfare in 1917, the discovery of the Zimmermann telegram, and the Russian Revolution brought the United States into the conflict. On April 2, 1917, Wilson asked Congress to declare war. One reason for fighting was to guarantee that the United States participated in negotiating the peace settlement.

The United States was unprepared to fight the war. Beyond the small military forces available, there were problems regarding mobilization that touched upon the still unresolved debate over the role of government in society. Wilson decided to use economic incentives to encourage American voluntarism in support of the war. It took almost a year to develop an effective war administration. The War Industries Board under Bernard Baruch managed the economy by fixing prices, setting priorities, and reducing waste. The profit motive boosted production, as the WIB set prices artificially high, trebling profits.

The Fuel Administration, the War Trade Board, the Shipping Board, and the U.S. Railroad Administration employed similar policies that increased production while conserving supplies. The Food Administration headed by Herbert Hoover organized agricultural production. Hoover raised farm prices and guaranteed a minimum price for crops, stabilizing the market. He also promoted food conservation among the public.

To gain labor support, important concessions were made. The right to organize and engage in collective bargaining was recognized. The eight-hour day was mandated, and the National War Labor Board was established to settle any disputes. But, where Wilson backed the American Federation of Labor which thrived during the war, he opposed unions like the IWW that often engaged in strikes.

The question of how to finance the war, which cost $33.5 billion by 1920, led Wilson to pursue a middle ground between conservatives and Progressives. Because taxes on income, corporate profits, and estates rose, the heaviest tax burdens fell on the wealthy. In the process, the revenue policy of the government changed from taxing consumption to income.

By substituting voluntarism for state controls, Wilson made patriotism and the profit motive the major supports of the war. This policy had profound social consequences, particularly in regards to civil liberties. Through George Creel's Committee on Public Information, public support was mobilized, eventually deteriorating into violent and repressive hysteria. The Espionage and Sedition Acts curtailed freedom of the press and expression, with radicals suffering the most. The Supreme Court gave legal approval to the attacks on civil liberties.

The wartime repression intensified existing fears and led to a strange alliance between reformers and superpatriots which allowed prohibitionists to gain passage of the Eighteenth Amendment. As women came to play increasingly important roles in the war effort, the suffrage movement gained momentum, resulting in passage of the Nineteenth Amendment. But the vote was the only real gain women experienced. Economic opportunities opened by the war largely closed with the return of peace. African Americans tried to use the war to improve their plight. Black troops served with distinction on the battlefield when given the chance, but most served in support capacities. At home, black migration northward became a mass exodus. While many found jobs in northern factories, they faced discrimination that kept them at the lowest-paying positions. In addition, both southern and northern whites reacted against the migration, leading to race riots in a number of cities.

Wilson had hoped that by providing supplies, financial credits, and moral support, the Allies would triumph. But the Allied military effort was on the verge of collapse, and Germany's submarine warfare had left Britain with only a six weeks' food supply. To ease the situation, the Navy helped relieve British patrols and joined the fight against submarines. The U. S. idea of employing the convoy system to protect merchant ships with warships cut shipping losses in half.

General John J. Pershing, commander of the American Expeditionary Force, refused Allied pleas to use raw American troops to fill gaps in their lines. In America, the debate over mobilizing troops led to the draft. As part of the training process, psychological tests were administered to recruits that discriminated in favor of native born, the eastern front. Italian troops suffered stinging defeats while mutinies broke out among the French. A German offensive reached 50 miles from Paris, at which time Marshal Ferdinand Foch assumed the Allied command. Aided by U. S. troops, the Allies stopped the German offensive, launching their own attack that pushed the Germans back to the Belgian border. By September 1918, 1.2 million American soldiers had joined the Allied forces. This tipped the manpower balance in their favor, and also provided fresh troops. Facing certain defeat,

Austria-Hungary sued for peace while Turkey and Bulgaria ceased military actions, and Germany asked for an armistice. Wilson refused, saying he would only negotiate with a democratic German government. A revolution led to the abdication of the Kaiser and an Armistice on November 11, 1918.

The jubilation that greeted the return of peace quickly degenerated into fear, resulting in vicious attacks on blacks, organized labor, and political dissidents. In the South, lynchings increased, reaching 70 in the first year of peace. Twenty-five cities experienced race riots, with the worst being in Chicago. The wartime inflation and worsening labor-management relations led to a spate of strikes that resulted in a sharply reduced labor movement, particularly among unskilled workers. The strikes combined with fears of communism fueled by the Bolshevik revolution and a bomb scare created America's first Red Scare. Vigilantism spread throughout the nation leading to the persecution of IWW members, Socialists, and other radicals. This public response was supported by government actions begun by Attorney General A. Mitchell Palmer, who led lightning raids against radicals in 12 cities that were widely denounced. By 1920, the Red Scare had exhausted itself.

President Wilson felt a punitive treaty would lead to future wars, but Britain and France were more interested in gaining revenge on Germany. Reflecting his own interests, Wilson announced his Fourteen Points. His liberal capitalist views were reflected in the free market that would result from his call for freedom of the seas and free trade that would open the world's markets to American goods. By proposing self-determination that would bring independence to many European minorities, he hoped to attract millions of immigrants into the Democratic party. The core of the plan was the League of Nations that would guarantee the peace, thus relieving the United States of that burden.

Wilson's prestige peaked with the Armistice. But his partisanship and other actions doomed his peace plans. As the elections of 1918 approached, Wilson called for support of Democratic candidates to gain a mandate, which offended Republicans who had loyally supported his war policies. When voters gave Republicans a slim majority in Congress, Wilson faced problems passing the peace treaty. Another mistake was personally heading the American Peace Commission and then not naming any prominent Republican as a member.

At the Versailles Conference, the Allies disagreed on three primary issues: territory, reparations, and future security. France wanted to exact a heavy toll on Germany including breaking up the German Empire. Britain often allied with Wilson but would not yield on issues of reparations and colonies. Italy desired to expand its territory into the Tyrol and on the Adriatic. Premier Orlando left the conference when this request was refused. Japan sought Germany's Asian interests. Another factor was the absence of the Bolsheviks, whose communist state prompted the Allies to send troops to help fight against the regime. Given these conditions, Wilson had to compromise to succeed. In terms of territory, results were mixed. Japan gained much of Germany's East Asian interests but Germany's colonies were governed by the Allies through a mandate under the League of Nations supervision. Nation states were carved out of Eastern Europe that sketchily accorded with the continent's language and cultural map. The League of Nations was the primary bulwark of security, but it was supplemented by security treaties among the Allies and the French occupation of Alsace-Lorraine. In addition, Germany dismantled its military forces. Reparations ended all hopes of a just peace as Germany was forced to accept blame for the war and pay $34 billion in reparations.

Wilson accepted this compromise to guarantee the formation of the League of Nations, but opposition arose in Congress among three groups. Irreconcilables totally rejected the treaty. Strong reservationists headed by Senator Henry Cabot Lodge of Massachusetts desired to modify the treaty. Limited reservationists sought a middle ground between isolation and the commitment Wilson proposed. The president, however, refused to compromise, and though his health was failing, he launched a national tour to rally public support for the treaty. Upon returning to Washington, Wilson suffered a stroke. In the end, the Senate refused to ratify the treaty. Wilson tried to use the 1920 election as a referendum on the treaty, but the Democrats refused to nominate him for a third term and Warren Harding rode the Republican standard to easy victory. The United States never did join the League.

OBJECTIVES

After reading this chapter, you should be able to:

1. Describe the causes and consequences of World War I.

2. Discuss the steps taken by President Woodrow Wilson to mobilize the nation for war.

3. Examine the relationship between the effort to mobilize public opinion during World War I and the violation of the civil liberties of radicals and aliens that occurred during and after the war.

4. Identify the major provisions of President Wilson's Fourteen Points.

5. Identify the major provisions of the Treaty of Versailles, the compromises with Wilson's original peace objectives that the treaty represented, and the reasons why the Senate failed to ratify the treaty.

6. Discuss the war's impact on labor and ethnic and on racial minorities.

KEY TERMS
Allies
Neutrality
Central Powers
Lusitania
Zimmerman Telegram
Hooverizing
Committee on Public Information
Great Migration
Fourteen Points
League of Nation
Treaty of Versailles

KEY FIGURES
Randolph Bourne
Franz Ferdinand
Gavrilo Princip
Woodrow Wilson
Herbert Hoover
George W. Creel
Oliver Wendell Holmes
A. Mitchell Palmer
David Lloyd George
George Clemenceau
Henry Cabot Lodge
James M. Cox

CHAPTER 22 • THE UNITED STATES AND WORLD WAR I

_____ 1. Randolph Bourne believed that World War I
   a. was a struggle to make the world safe for democracy
   b. would lead to the suppression of civil liberties, kill reform, and increase the power of government
   c. was a necessary struggle against German militarism

_____ 2. Which of the following statements about World War I is FALSE?
   a. The war ended in stalemate.
   b. It resulted in the deaths of 9 million combatants and 5 million civilians—more than any previous war
   c. It resulted in the collapse of four empires—in Russia, Austria-Hungary, Germany, and Turkey—and the triumph of Communism in Russia and fascism in Italy

_____ 3. The event that set off the train of events leading to the outbreak of World War I in 1914 was
   a. the sinking of the Lusitania
   b. the Zimmermann Note
   c. the assassination of the Austro-Hungarian Archduke Franz Ferdinand

_____ 4. World War I was the result of
   a. the greed of financiers, munitions manufacturers and others eager for wartime profits
   b. the failure of international diplomacy and a web of entangling alliances
   c. the fear of communist revolutions throughout Europe

_____ 5. At the beginning of the war in Europe, President Wilson
   a. favored entering the war on the side of Britain and France
   b. believed that the United States should be neutral in thought and deed
   c. blamed Germany for the war because it had invaded Belgium, a neutral country

_____ 6. The German policy that was most directly responsible for bringing the United States into the war was
   a. unrestricted submarine warfare
   b. the sinking of the Lusitania
   c. German use of poison gas

_____ 7. Why did the publication of the Zimmermann telegram convince many Americans that Germany threatened to their national security?
   a. Because it urged Mexico to launch a surprise attack on the United States
   b. Because it revealed Germany's plans to resume unrestricted submarine warfare
   c. Because it proposed an alliance between Germany and Mexico

_____ 8. When he asked Congress for a declaration of war in 1917, President Wilson's ultimate goal was to put the United States in a position to
   a. influence the terms of the postwar peace settlement
   b. suppress Russia's Communist Revolution
   c. liberate Europe's African and Asian colonies

_____ 9. What was the central agency for mobilizing and managing the American economy during World War I?
   a. The Office of Price Administration
   b. The Office of Management and Budget
   c. The War Industries Board

_____ 10. To mobilize public support for World War I, President Wilson established the _____, America's first propaganda agency.
   a. Central Intelligence Agency
   b. U.S. Information Agency
   c. Committee on Public Information

_____ 11. Which of the following does NOT describe the experience of African Americans during World War I?
   a. Most opposed U.S. involvement in the war
   b. Many moved north seeking wartime jobs
   c. They were frequently victims of racial discrimination and violence

_____ 12. The emergency atmosphere in World War I resulted in important benefits for all but one of the following groups. Select the EXCEPTION.
   a. prohibitionists
   b. the women's suffrage movement
   c. the IWW and the Socialist Party

_____ 13. For the first time in American history, during World War I the United States
   a. enlisted black troops in its armed forces
   b. used a draft to raise military manpower
   c. administered intelligence tests to military recruits

_____ 14. The United States's entry into World War I in 1917 was
   a. opposed by a majority of the American public
   b. decisive to an Allied victory
   c. unexpected by Germany

_____ 15. In Schenck v. the United States, the Supreme Court ruled that in time of war, the government could limit the right to
   a. due process
   b. keep and bear arms
   c. free speech

_____ 16. The immediate post-World War I environment in America was characterized by all of the following EXCEPT
   a. race riots
   b. declining prices
   c. labor strikes

_____ 17. The attorney general who led the attack on postwar radicalism in 1919 and 1920 was
   a. George Creel
   b. Bernard Baruch
   c. A. Mitchell Palmer

_____ 18. Wilson's Fourteen Points provided for all the following EXCEPT
   a. national self-determination
   b. freedom of the seas
   c. creation of a post-war alliance between Britain, France, and the United States to ensure world peace

_____ 19. All of the following provisions of the Treaty of Versailles helped to set the stage for World War II EXCEPT
   a. the massive financial reparations Germany was forced to pay
   b. the requirement that Germany accept blame for World War I
   c. the establishment of the League of Nations

_____ 20. In the United States Senate, the most controversial part of the Treaty of Versailles was its provision for
   a. a League of Nations
   b. war reparations
   c. a system of colonial "mandates"

_____ 21. It is likely that the Senate would have ratified the Treaty of Versailles if
   a. President Wilson had taken his case directly to the American people
   b. the President had won over recalcitrant Democrats with promises of patronage
   c. President had compromised with moderate Republicans on some of the treaty's provisions

CHAPTER 23 • MODERN TIMES, 1920–1929

SUMMARY

The 1920s was both a decade of bitter cultural tensions as well as a period in which many of the features of a modern consumer society took root.

KEY POINTS

- The 1920s was a decade of exciting social changes and profound cultural conflicts. For many Americans, the growth of cities, the rise of a consumer culture, and the so-called "revolution in morals and manners" represented a liberation from the restrictions of the country's Victorian past.

- But for many others, the United States seemed to be changing in undesirable ways. The result was a thinly veiled "cultural civil war," in which a pluralistic society clashed bitterly over such issues as foreign immigration, evolution, the Ku Klux Klan, and race.

- In 1929, the American economy appeared to be healthy. Employment was high and inflation virtually nonexistent. Still the seeds of the Great Depression were already apparent in the boom years of the '20s.

- Prosperity bypassed many groups of Americans; income was poorly distributed; and the farm sector was mired in depression.

CHAPTER SYNOPSIS

In the 1920s, for the first time, more Americans lived in cities than in rural areas. Urban growth was due largely to foreign immigration, but it also reflected the massive movement of southern African Americans into northern cities. Racial tensions and the emergence of ghettos accompanied the influx of African Americans into the nation's cities. Simultaneously, middle-class whites began moving to the suburbs as new roads and automobiles created new residential opportunities.

During the 1920s as the United States became a modern consumer society. Advertising helped increase consumer demand, and modern merchandising strategies such as installment buying made purchasing goods easier. The automobile industry symbolized the rise of consumerism, pioneering new production and merchandising techniques. The rapid integration of the car into American life stimulated road-building and had a ripple effect on other industries supplying materials or services for autos. Electrification had a similar effect on household appliances. Other innovations included ready-to-wear clothes, processed foods, and chain stores. Consumerism shifted the emphasis on business from production of capital goods to consumption of consumer goods. Americans spent less on necessities such as food, clothing, and utilities, and more on appliances, consumer products, and recreation.

The radio and the phonograph were two of the most influential appliances to enter the American home. The phonograph played a pivotal part in popularizing three basic forms of popular music: blues, jazz, and "hillbilly." The most significant mass entertainment medium was the movies. Along with radio, the movies helped create a new, homogeneous popular culture.

Spectator sports also became increasingly popular. Boxing, football, and especially baseball created cultural heroes such as Jack Dempsey, "Red" Grange, and Babe Ruth. In addition, a variety of fads and crazes flourished. Crossword puzzles, Mah Jong, contract bridge, arid photography attracted enthusiasts. Americans also embraced golf, tennis, and bowling, and several dance crazes. Pulp fiction pandered to various reading tastes.

The 1920s also marked a flowering of American literature, music, and art. The greatest plays of Eugene O'Neill, the first novels of Ernest Hemingway and William Faulkner, and the poetry of Langston Hughes and e.e. cummings, among many others, transformed American literature. The decade also saw the founding of 50 symphony orchestras and the emergence of such noted composers as Aaron Copland, Charles Ives, and George Gershwin. Underlying this cultural renaissance lay the disillusionment with World War I and a distaste for the shallow, narrow-minded aspects of American life. Other aspects of cultural change included a revolution in morals, fueled, in part, by the ideas of Sigmund Freud. One symbol of cultural change the appearance of the "flapper," the newly liberated woman, who cut her hair, raised her hemline, and smoked in public.

The 1920s featured intense cultural conflicts over such matters as gender, immigration, prohibition, the teaching of evolution, and race. Sexuality and women's roles provoked controversy. After winning the vote in 1920, the women's movement split over the proposed Equal Rights Amendment.

Meanwhile, class, ethnicity, and religion were factors in the conflict over prohibition. With legal means of getting alcohol closed off, the public taste for liquor was filled by smugglers and illegal producers. Supplying alcohol to the public transformed organized crime into a national enterprise. The inability to enforce prohibition contributed to its repeal by states and ultimately by constitutional amendment.

The conflict between religious fundamentalists and liberals reached a peak with the Scopes trial over the teaching of evolution. The high profile case pitted Clarence Darrow against William Jennings Bryan. While the defendant John Scopes was found guilty, the issue of teaching creation remained unresolved.

Immigration was another source of cultural conflict. The National Origins Act of 1924 changed immigration policy, favoring old stock, white, Protestant groups. In the Sacco and Vanzetti case, two Italian anarchist immigrants were tried and convicted on flimsy evidence and highly questionable procedures. The guilty verdicts prompted a wave of protests from many Americans who claimed that the men had been convicted for their political views rather than on the merits of the case. But these protests failed and both men were executed in 1927.

Race was another point of tension. A series of race riots wracked the country in 1919. Due to the Ku Klux Klan's adoptions of modern advertising techniques, the racist organization achieved a purported membership of 5 million in 1925. Though strongest in the South, the Klan became a power in the Midwest, Southeast, and Far West, too. Most members came from the old stock, lower middle class.

At the same time, however, African Americans challenged racial prejudice. Through the United Negro Improvement Association, Marcus Garvey advocated racial pride and black separatism as well as migration to Africa. An emphasis upon racial pride was also evident in the Harlem Renaissance in literature, music, and art.

Promising to support business, restore prosperity, and follow a conservative path, the Republican party dominated the American political scene in the 1920s. Herbert Hoover epitomized the 1920s Republican vision, stressing "associationalism," the founding of voluntary trade association to eliminate destructive economic competition and waste.

The Harding administration was run largely by conservative managers in the cabinet who pursued policies friendly to big business. But cronyism plagued Handing, leading to major scandals that broke just before he died in 1923. The biggest, Teapot Dome, involved the bribery of Secretary of Interior Albert B. Fall in return for leasing drilling rights on federal naval oil reserves. Harding's successor, Calvin Coolidge, believed his main task was to promote business and was a passive leader. The election of 1928 pitted Herbert Hoover against Alfred E. Smith, governor of New York. A Catholic, Smith was regarded as a representative of urban culture, while Hoover was viewed as the candidate of rural America. Hoover won an easy victory.

A variety of get-rich schemes appeared during the 1920s. Stockbrokers sold stock on margin, requiring only 10 percent down in cash. But when the market crashed in 1929, investors had to make full payment for their stock purchases, often selling issues far below the prices paid. The stock market crash signaled the start of the Great Depression.

In seeking to explain the stock market crash and the onset of the Depression, economists point to a number of factors. The prosperity of the twenties bypassed millions of American living in poverty and minorities. Industrial wages either fell or remained stagnant during the twenties. Debts and defaults caused one-sixth of the nation's banks to fail. The bank failures, in turn, led many small businesses to fail. Other factors that contributed to a decade-long depression included a decline in business investment, large manufacturing inventories, and flawed government policies, including a decision to raise tariffs.

OBJECTIVES

After reading this chapter, you should be able to:

1. Discuss the social changes that transformed American society during the 1920s, including the growth of cities, the rise of a consumer-oriented economy, the changing roles of women and ethnic and racial minorities, and the spread of mass entertainment.

2. Examine the deep cultural conflicts of the decade, in which an increasingly pluralistic society clashed over such issues as foreign immigration, prohibition, evolution, and race.

3. Identify the underlying causes of the Great Depression.

KEY TERMS

Flapper
19th Amendment
Equal Rights Amendment
Prohibition
Scopes "Monkey Trial"
National Origins Act of 1924
Ku Klux Klan
Harlem Renaissance
Black Tuesday

KEY FIGURES

Margaret Sanger
Henry Ford
Alfred Sloan
Nicolo Sacco and Bartelomeo Vanzetti
John Scopes
William Jennings Bryan
Clarence Darrow
Marcus Garvey
Warren Harding
Calvin Coolidge
Herbert Hoover
Al Smith
Charles Ponzi

CHAPTER 23 • MODERN TIMES, 1920–1929

_____ 1. Margaret Sanger
   a. was a leader in the suffrage movement
   b. promoted birth control
   c. headed the Women's Christian Temperance Union

_____ 2. The most important economic development of the 1920s was the
   a. growth of heavy industry
   b. expansion of labor unions
   c. rise of a consumer-oriented economy

_____ 3. According to the 1920 census, for the first time in American history most
   a. Americans were non-Protestants
   b. Americans lived in cities or towns
   c. African Americans lived in the North

_____ 4. Henry Ford
   a. made cars affordable for the average family
   b. introduced an annual model changeover for his cars
   c. encouraged buyers to purchase cars on credit

_____ 5. Alfred Sloan, the president of General Motors from 1923 to 1941,
   a. revolutionized American manufacturing by introducing the automated assembly line
   b. emphasized marketing and prestige and introduced the yearly model change and set up the nation's first national consumer credit agency
   c. introduced a minimum daily wage of $5

_____ 6. Innovations of the 1920s included
   a. buying on the installment plan
   b. chain stores revolutionizing retailing
   c. the appearance of the first commercial radio stations and first national radio networks
   d. all of the above

_____ 7. Young women of the 1920s who adopted an original style of dress and challenged traditional societal values were called
   a. Gibson girls
   b. Flappers
   c. Suffragettes

_____ 8. Following the ratification of the 19th Amendment, guaranteeing women the right to vote, the women's movement divided over
   a. the issue of abortion rights
   b. contraception
   c. the Equal Rights Amendment to the Constitution

_____ 9. Prohibition failed because
   a. many Americans believed the law interfered with their personal freedom
   b. rural America failed to support it
   c. it adversely affected the American economy

_____ 10. He became the national symbol for organized crime in the 1920s.
   a. Rudolph Valentino
   b. Al Capone
   c. Billy Sunday

_____ 11. Prohibition's strongest supporters were
   a. urban residents
   b. rural residents and religious fundamentalists
   c. immigrants

_____ 12. The conclusion of the Sacco and Vanzetti case suggested that
   a. the two men were clearly guilty
   b. many Americans had an unreasonable fear of radicals and foreigners
   c. African Americans could not get a fair trial in most southern states

_____ 13. This 1925 case involved a Tennessee law against the teaching of Charles Darwin's theory of evolution in public schools.
   a. The Lindbergh Trial
   b. The Scopes Trial
   c. Leopold and Loeb

_____ 14. The immigration legislation of the 1920s regulated immigration on the basis of
   a. national quotas
   b. labor needs
   c. literacy in the English language

_____ 15. The effect of the immigration quotas set by the National Origins Act of 1924 was to
   a. reduce immigration to a trickle from eastern and southern Europe and exclude Asians altogether
   b. open up new opportunities to racial minority groups that had been discriminated against during the early 20th century
   c. cause the American population to decline in size during the late 1920s and 1930s

_____ 16. During the 1920s, the Ku Klux Klan
   a. was strong in the South, but took root in no other section of the country
   b. opposed Jews and Catholics as well as blacks
   c. was outlawed by the federal government

_____ 17. The leader of the first mass movement in African American history was
   a. A. Philip Randolph
   b. W.E.B. DuBois
   c. Marcus Garvey

_____ 18. Which of the following statements is most consistent with the philosophy of Marcus Garvey's Universal Negro Improvement Association?
   a. blacks should demand integration in all areas of American society
   b. blacks should separate themselves from corrupt white American society
   c. blacks must elect their own candidates to state and national offices in order to become an integral part of American society

_____ 19. The Harlem Renaissance refers to
   a. the movement of African-American artists, poets, and writers who expressed their pride in being black
   b. the "Lost Generation" of writers who moved to Europe during the 1920s
   c. the name of the shipping company owned by the United Negro Improvement Association, promoting a "Back-To-Africa" movement

_____ 20. All of the following characterized the writing of the "Lost Generation" EXCEPT
   a. disillusionment with materialism and consumerism.
   b. a sense of lost values and purpose.
   c. anxiety about a decline in religious faith

_____ 21. When Warren Harding called for a return to normalcy, he meant
   a. a return to the Jeffersonian ideal of an agrarian republic
   b. strict government regulation of business.
   c. turning away from Europe and away from the programs of the Progressive Era

_____ 22. This political scandal involved a cabinet member in President Harding's administration.
   a. Teapot Dome
   b. Credit Mobilier
   c. Abscam

_____ 23. Which of the following best describes the administrations of Warren Harding and Calvin Coolidge
    a. The trusts must be broken
    b. The business of America is business
    c. The world must be made safe for democracy

_____ 24. Republican leaders in the 1920s believed that the government should _____ big business.
    a. regulate
    b. cooperate with
    c. break up

_____ 25. The most important problem faced by the Democratic party in the 1920s was
    a. a serious split between urban and rural wings of the party.
    b. the fact that recent immigrants no longer supported the party.
    c. the restriction of immigration reduced the number of recruits to the party.

_____ 26. In 1928, Al Smith was the first presidential candidate of a major party who was
    a. a bachelor
    b. an immigrant
    c. a Catholic

_____ 27. Serious problems in the American economy by 1929 included all of the following EXCEPT
    a. depressed farm incomes
    b. a poor distribution of income
    c. high unemployment

_____ 28. Part of the reason for the stock market crash was
    a. the low tariff, which allowed imports to corner several important American markets
    b. the tax policies of the 1920s, which especially hurt the wealthy who might otherwise have brought more stocks
    c. the buying of great amounts of stock "on margin"

_____ 29. A major cause of the Great Depression was
    a. the inability of wages to keep pace with production increases
    b. reliance upon a single metallic base for currency
    c. the inability of production to keep pace with wage increases

CHAPTER 24 • THE AGE OF ROOSEVELT

SUMMARY

The Great Depression was steeper and more protracted in the United States than in other industrialized countries. The unemployment rate rose higher and remained higher longer than in any other western country. As it deepened, the Depression had far-reaching political consequences. In this chapter you read about the Depression's human toll; President Hoover's response; President Roosevelt's New Deal Programs and their impact on women and minority groups; and the response of American popular culture to the Depression.

KEY POINTS

- The stock market crash of October 1929 brought the economic prosperity of the 1920s to a symbolic end. For the next ten years, the United States was mired in a deep economic depression. By 1933, unemployment had soared to 25 percent, up from 3.2 percent in 1929. Industrial production declined by 50 percent, international trade plunged 30 percent, and investment fell 98 percent.

- The Great Depression transformed the American political and economic landscape. It produced a major political realignment, creating a coalition of big-city ethnics, African Americans, and Southern Democrats committed, to varying degrees, to interventionist government.

- It strengthened the federal presence in American life, spawning such innovations as national old-age pensions, unemployment compensation, aid to dependent children, public housing, federally-subsidized school lunches, insured bank depositions, the minimum wage, and stock market regulation.

- It fundamentally altered labor relations, producing a revived labor movement and a national labor policy protective of collective bargaining.

- It transformed the farm economy by introducing federal price supports.

- Above all, it led Americans to view the federal government as an agency of action and reform and the ultimate protector of public well-being.

CHAPTER SYNOPSIS

The Great Depression was a global tragedy that elicited various responses from the world's nations, including military dictatorship, fascism and militarism, totalitarian communism, and welfare capitalism. In the United States, the disaster profoundly altered public attitudes and helped create a political coalition committed to interventionist government. The federal government came to be viewed as the protector of public welfare and an active agency of reform.

During the Depression, millions of Americans suffered a severe decline in pay or lost their jobs. Marriages were delayed and the birth rate fell. The divorce rate declined, but separations increased. Family roles were altered as unemployed fathers lost status and self-respect, sometimes leading to alcoholism, abuse, and desertion. Hardship often drew families closer together. Wives and children as well as husbands and fathers worked and pooled their resources to sustain their families. Economic hardship was particularly intense among African-Americans and Mexican-Americans.

At the beginning of the Depression, most economic leaders believed the downturn was a normal part of the economic cycle and would eventually correct itself. President Hoover considered the Depression a temporary aberration in a fundamentally healthy economy and believed recovery could be facilitated by government action. He tried to reassure the public, but his speeches rang hollow in the face of the disaster. His administration established the Reconstruction Finance Corporation and the Federal Home Loan Bank in 1932 to provide loans to businesses, but these initiatives did not have much impact on the economic decline.

Franklin Delano Roosevelt soundly defeated Hoover in the 1932 election. As governor of New York, Roosevelt had created an able team of advisors who made the state a laboratory for testing a variety of reforms that would become integral parts of his recovery program. A charismatic leader who exuded optimism, Roosevelt calmed public fears and gave hope to the American people. He defeated Hoover, whose fortunes plummeted after the "Bonus Army" episode.

In Roosevelt's first 100 days in office, Congress passed 15 major bills that addressed problems in banking, welfare, agriculture, and energy production. To sell his programs, Roosevelt broadcast "fireside chats" on the radio, appealing directly to the people. Behind Roosevelt was a "brain trust" of Ivy League intellectuals and New York social workers, strongly influenced by Progressivism. But the New Dealers were more pragmatic and less moralistic than progressive reformers. They were also more committed to an activist federal government.

To address the problems faced by the nation's farmers, the New Deal established the Tennessee Valley Authority and the Rural Electrification Administration to bring electric power to rural areas; the Soil Conservation Service to combat erosion; and the Farm Credit Administration to forestall farm foreclosures. The most important initiative, the Agricultural Adjustment Act, sought to raise crop prices by reducing supply. Large farmers benefited, but tenants received little aid.

The National Recovery Administration sought to revive the economy through labor-management partnerships in diverse industries. The NRA's goal was to end destructive competition, overproduction, and labor conflict. To provide jobs, the government put many jobless to work on large public works projects run by the Civil Works Administration and the Works Progress Administration. In addition to construction projects, the WPA sponsored cultural programs that employed millions of Americans. The Civilian Conservation Corps (CCC) offered jobs to youths primarily in the national parks, but it only employed a small number of the young men needing work.

The New Deal programs attracted criticism from both the right and the left. Three critics were particularly influential The charismatic Louisiana Senator Huey Long had initially backed Roosevelt but then opposed the New Deal as too conservative. Long's "Share Our Wealth" program was based on stiff inheritance and income taxes which would be redistributed to guarantee an annual income of $2,000 per family. The radio priest Charles Coughlin was an early New Deal supporter turned critic. Retired California physician Francis Townsend promoted $200 monthly pensions for every citizen over 60.

Criticisms of the New Deal's inadequacies led to a second wave of legislation. The National Labor Relations Act (Wagner Act) guaranteed the right of labor to organize and bargain collectively. The Social Security act not only offered old-age pensions, but also established a system of workman's compensation, assistance to the handicapped, and aid to dependent children without a working parent.

In the 1936 election, Roosevelt defeated Republican Alf Landon, winning a landslide victory. But the New Deal was already in decline. Roosevelt responded to a series of adverse Supreme Court decisions by proposing a court-packing scheme that alienated many Americans. A reduction in government spending in 1937 to help balance the budget caused a precipitous economic decline. By 1938, election results showed the reform spirit had dissipated, making it difficult to expand the New Deal. Although the New Deal did not solve the problem of depression era unemployment, the government's efforts blunted the depression's worst effects and preserved the public's faith in capitalism and democracy.

Popular culture followed contradictory paths, embracing tradition on one hand and espousing modern views on the other. In comic books, fiction, and on radio, American discovered new heroes. Modernism in the arts and architecture was evident in the works of Martha Graham in dance and William Faulkner in literature. The Depression also unified Americans imparting a sense of an American way of life but race, class, ethnic, and regional differences were major literary themes. Hollywood played a vital role by reassuring demoralized Americans. The fantasy world of the movies helped sustain the faith of Americans in individual initiative and their country.

OBJECTIVES

After reading this chapter, you should be able to:

1. Compare and contrast the economic situation and the government response in the United States during the Great Depression to that of other major countries.

2. Discuss the impact of the Great Depression on the general population.

3. Explain how Presidents Herbert Hoover and Franklin Roosevelt responded to the economic crisis.

4. Examine how the New Deal changed Americans' perception of the federal government's role in American life.

5. Describe the major features of the New Deal, examine how it altered the status of women and minorities in the United States, and explain why the New Deal declined.

6. Discuss how popular culture in the 1930s responded to the Great Depression.

KEY TERMS
Hoovervilles
New Deal
Bonus Army
First 100 Days
Fireside Chats
Brain Trust
National Recover Administration
Wagner Act
Social Security Act
Second New Deal
Court Packing

KEY FIGURES
Woody Gurthrie
Herbert Hoover
Franklin Roosevelt
Hugh Johnson
Harry Hopkins
Huey Long
Father Charles Coughlin
Francis Townsend
Alfred M. Landon

CHAPTER 24 • THE AGE OF ROOSEVELT

_____ 1. Woody Guthrie
   a. was the leader of the Bonus army
   b. led the National Recovery Agency
   c. was one of the finest American balladeers of the 20th century

_____ 2. Woody Guthrie regarded music as
   a. a weapon in the class struggle
   b. "bread and circuses" for the masses and a diversion from politics
   c. a way to make lots of money

_____ 3. Compared to other industrialized countries,
   a. the response of the U.S.-government to the Depression was more effective, basically ending Depression unemployment by 1935
   b. American government policies were far more radical, as the federal government began to plan the economy and nationalize businesses
   c. Depression-era unemployment was higher and lasted longer in the United States

_____ 4. By 1932 _____ percent of the nation's families did not have a single employed wage earner?
   a. 5 percent
   b. 10 percent
   c. 25 percent

_____ 5. The Great Depression
   a. delayed marriages
   b. lowered the divorce rate
   c. caused the birthrate to drop below the replacement level for the first time in American history
   d. all of the above

_____ 6. President Hoover responded to the Depression in all of the following ways EXCEPT
   a. by getting business and labor leaders to promise to maintain prices and wages
   b. by assuring the public that recovery was just around the corner
   c. by instituting large-scale public works programs

_____ 7. The Reconstruction Finance Corporation reflected President Hoover's mistaken assumption that the Depression was caused by
   a. the chronic low wages paid to the bulk of American workers
   b. tight credit
   c. the lack of consumer demand for manufactured goods

_____ 8. What was the event in 1932 that ensured President Hoover's defeat in his reelection bid?
   a. the callous treatment of the Bonus Army
   b. the failure of the Reconstruction Finance Corporation
   c. a speech in which President Hoover extolled the virtues of "rugged individualism"

_____ 9. Just prior to his election as president, Franklin D. Roosevelt had been
   a. a U.S. Senator
   b. Governor of New York
   c. Secretary of the Treasury

_____ 10. When he became president in 1933, Franklin D. Roosevelt offered the American people all of the following EXCEPT
   a. a concrete plan for solving the Depression
   b. a willingness to experiment
   c. confidence and optimism

_____ 11. What was President Roosevelt's first action against the Depression?
   a. raising tariff rates to protect American jobs
   b. convincing Congress to create public works programs
   c. closing the nation's banks

_____ 12. The Federal Deposit Insurance Corporation
   a. was a government agency in which Americans could deposit their savings
   b. purchased the stock of troubled banks to keep them operating until they could be reorganized
   c. guaranteed individual bank deposits up to $2,500

_____ 13. The 100 Days refers to
   a. the time between President Roosevelt's election and his inauguration
   b. Roosevelt's first hundred days in office when he pushed 15 major bills through Congress
   c. the 100 days that banks remained closed

_____ 14. Leading government administrators and advisors during the New Deal were mainly
   a. wealthy patricians like Roosevelt himself
   b. businessmen and party loyalists
   c. Ivy League intellectuals and New York State social workers

_____ 15. The Agricultural Adjustment Act proposed to solve the farm problem by
   a. raising crop prices by reducing production
   b. subsidizing farm exports
   c. mechanizing agriculture

_____ 16. The main beneficiaries of the New Deal's agricultural policies were
   a. sharecroppers and tenant farmers
   b. farm workers
   c. large landowners

_____ 17. The National Recovery Administration sought to
   a. introduce rational planning to industry by establishing codes of conduct for businesses in different industries
   b. reduce prices and increase production
   c. raise wages

_____ 18. Which New Deal jobs program put young men to work in the nation's parks and forests?
   a. the PWA
   b. the CCC
   c. the WPA

_____ 19. This colorful Louisiana Senator started the "share the wealth" movement.
   a. Charles Coughlin
   b. Huey Long
   c. Francis Townsend

_____ 20. This doctor proposed that Americans 60 years of age or older should get $200 a month as long as they spent it within 30 days.
   a. Charles Coughlin
   b. Huey Long
   c. Francis Townsend

_____ 21. This law guaranteed unions workers' right to form unions and bargain collectively.
   a. The Wagner Act
   b. The Securities Exchange Act
   c. The Labor Dispute Joint Resolution

_____ 22. In addition to providing the elderly with monthly pensions, the Social Security Act of 1935 also established
   a. federally-financed health insurance for the poor
   b. a federally sponsored system of unemployment insurance
   c. insured individual retirement accounts, which allowed individuals to save for their retirement

_____ 23. A new national labor union that arose during the 1930s to organized workers regardless of their skill level was the
   a. American Federal of Labor
   b. Industrial Workers of the World
   c. Congress of Industrial Organizations

_____ 24. Which of the following statements about African Americans and the New Deal is FALSE?
    a. By the end of Roosevelt's first administration, most black voters had shifted their support to the Democratic party
    b. Most New Deal programs discriminated against African Americans
    c. During the New Deal, lynching was outlawed and the poll tax was abolished

_____ 25. The New Deal
    a. ended Depression-era unemployment
    b. produced a major political realignment, creating a coalition of big city ethnics, African Americans and Southern Democrats committed to government intervention
    c. significantly redistributed the nation's wealth

CHAPTER 25 • THE END OF ISOLATION: AMERICA FACES THE WORLD, 1920–1945

SUMMARY

No war in history killed more people or destroyed more property than World War II. Altogether, 70 million people served in the armed forces; of these, 17 million combatants—including 400,000 Americans—lost their lives in the conflict. Civilian deaths were even higher. At least 19 million Soviet civilians, 10 million Chinese, and 6 million European Jews lost their lives during the war. In this chapter you read about the war's causes, military history, and consequences. You learned about how American mobilized for war; the impact of the war on women and racial and ethnic minorities; the internment of Japanese Americans; and the dawn of the atomic age.

KEY POINTS

- On September 1, 1939, Germany invaded Poland, starting World War II. By November 1942, the Axis powers controlled territory from Norway to North Africa and from France to the Soviet Union.

- After defeating the Axis in north Africa in May 1941, the Allies invaded Sicily in July 1943 and forced Italy to surrender in September.

- The American home front was essential to success in the war. The war ended depression unemployment, and led the federal government to create a War Production Board to oversee conversion to a wartime economy and the Office of Price Administration to set prices on many items and to supervise a rationing system.

- During the war, African Americans, women, and Mexican Americans founded new opportunities in industry. But Japanese Americans living on the Pacific coast were relocated from their homes and placed in internment camps.

- On D-Day, June 6, 1944, the Allies landed in Northern France. A German counteroffensive, known as the Battle of the Bulge, in December failed, and Germany surrendered in May 1945.

- After attacking the U.S. Pacific fleet at Pearl Harbor, Hawaii, on December 7, 1941, drawing the United States into the war, Japanese forces seized Burma, Hong Kong, Malaya, the Dutch East Indies (now Indonesia), the Philippines, Singapore, and Thailand.

- The Allies halted Japanese expansion at the Battle of Midway in June 1942 and in other campaigns in the South Pacific. From 1943 to August 1945, the Allies hopped from island to island across the Central Pacific and also battled the Japanese in China, Burma, and India.

- Japan agreed to surrender on August 14, 1945 after the United States dropped the first atomic bombs on the Japanese cities of Hiroshima and Nagasaki.

CHAPTER SYNOPSIS

United States diplomacy after World War I vacillated between isolationism and involvement, including adoption of a less domineering policy toward Latin America. Although the United States refused to join the League of Nations, the United States used diplomacy to promote international stability and world peace. Treaties in 1921 and 1922 reduced naval fleets while establishing policies regarding Far Eastern affairs and declarations of war. In 1928, the Kellogg-Briand Pact prompted 62 nations to renounce war as a means of resolving international disputes, but these were largely paper promises that contained no enforcement mechanism.

The Republican administrations worked to improve relations with Latin American nations. The slow abandonment of gunboat diplomacy paved the way for the "Good Neighbor Policy" of the 1930s, which included a declaration against the right of any state to interfere in the affairs of another.

In the 1930s, antiwar sentiment fueled isolationist ideas, but the actions of Japan, Germany, and Italy led to a decline of pacifism. Adolf Hitler's rise of power in Germany was aided by German anger over their defeat in World War I and the harsh peace conditions. In addition, Hitler provided a convenient scapegoat for Germany's problems, the Jews. In the 1930s, Hitler's Nazi party established a brutal dictatorship in Germany.

Japanese aggression posed another threat to international stability. Lacking natural resources, the Japanese invaded Manchuria in 1931 and set up a puppet state. Though this action violated a number of agreements, neither the United States nor the League of Nations responded strongly. Japan later terminated naval treaties and invaded China.

In Italy, Benito Mussolini created the first fascist state. Mussolini pursued his vision of an Italian empire by conquering Ethiopia in 1935. He also aided Francisco Franco's forces in Spain.

Upon coming to power in 1933, Hitler repudiated the Treaty of Versailles, withdrew from the League of Nations, and, in 1935, began rebuilding the German military. The Italian invasion of Ethiopia led to an alliance between Hitler and Mussolini. Beginning with the takeover of the Rhineland in 1935, Hitler pursued his vision of uniting all Germans in a third reich, meeting little resistance from France or Great Britain. In 1939, Hitler signed a Non-Aggression Pact with Stalin.

Isolationist sentiment and the Depression kept the Roosevelt administration focused on domestic policy. Roosevelt's first European diplomatic move involved recognizing the Soviet Union in 1933. Isolationist forces in Congress usually dominated foreign policy. Though Roosevelt did not advocate isolationism, he could not stop Congress from passing three separate neutrality laws between 1935 and 1937.

The 1939 attack on Poland by Germany and the Soviet Union opened World War II. In 1940, Germany unleashed several offensives that led to the takeover of Denmark, Norway, Belgium, the Netherlands, and France. When Britain refused negotiation, Hitler began submarine warfare and bombing raids on British airfields and cities. The bombing blitz continued until May 1941, when the British won the air war in the Battle of Britain.

The failure in Britain prompted Hitler to invade the Soviet Union. Despite rapid gains, the coming of winter hampered German efforts and contributed to the Soviet victory at Moscow on December 6, 1941. The next day, Japan attacked the U. S. Naval base at Pearl Harbor, Bringing America into the war.

Roosevelt feared a German victory but could not act aggressively until he gained control over foreign affairs. He pushed a fourth Neutrality Act through Congress that allowed the sale of war materials if paid in cash and transported on the buyer's ships. He convinced Congress to set up a peacetime draft and then allowed the transfer of naval destroyers to Britain in exchange for leases on British bases in the Americas. Isolationists opposed Roosevelt's tilt toward Britain, and the war dominated the 1940 election. Seeking an unprecedented third term, Roosevelt defeated Republican Wendell Wilkie.

Shortly after the election, Churchill notified the president that Britain had no money to buy war materials. Roosevelt set up a lend-lease system that passed Congress. In August 1941, Churchill and Roosevelt met, negotiating the Atlantic Charter. During this time, Germany invaded the Soviet Union. Stalin joined with the Gland Alliance against Germany, and Roosevelt offered Lend-Lease aid to the Soviet Union.

Meanwhile, relations with Japan deteriorated steadily. The 1937 Japanese invasion of China led to protests. After Japan invaded Indochina, the U.S. issued an embargo on iron, steel, and aviation fuel. Still, negotiations continued, but when militarists seized control of the Japanese government in October 1941, war seemed imminent. On December 7, 1941, the Japanese attack on Pearl Harbor decimated the U.S. Pacific fleet. That same day, Japan launched offensives throughout the Pacific.

To mobilize the economy, Roosevelt created the War Production Board. The government to offered profit incentives to facilitate the switch to war production. By the end of 1942, American industrial production exceeded that of all the Axis power combined. U. S. economic might determined victory.

Research emerged as a new industry, supported by government grants typically administered by the Office of Scientific Research and Development. Radar, a large range of weaponry, and new medicines were developed using federal monies. Agriculture also performed superbly during the war, aided by large profit margins provided farmers. As was true in industry, large farms prospered at the expense of small operations. This precipitated a huge wartime migration of rural residents to urban areas and jobs in defense plants.

For most Americans, the war signaled a return to prosperity. Per capita income almost trebled in part because of the increasing number of women employed. Consumer good production could not keep pace with buying power, leading to shortages that caused inflation. Swift price rises in 1942 led the government to establish the Office of Price Administration to institute rationing programs and set price ceilings for many items. Another strategy used to attack inflation was to promote war bond sales. Tax reform led to increased corporate taxes and personal withholding taxes on income.

The war eliminated unemployment, but not labor unrest. Temporary work stoppages led Congress to pass the Smith-Connally Act that outlawed strikes in defense plants. The trend was toward conservatism as Republicans and conservative Democrats formed a coalition that began attacking New Deal programs. Optimistic about the 1944 election, the Republicans nominated New York Governor Thomas Dewey. But the Democrats won as Roosevelt unveiled his "GI Bill of Rights," and the public seemed unwilling to change presidents in wartime.

Roosevelt created the Office of Facts and Figures to disseminate war information, but bureaucratic snafus meant that most Americans relied on popular culture for war imagery. Books, magazines, cartoons, and the like reduced the conflict to a struggle between good and evil. Movies proved to be the most potent propaganda medium.

World War II stimulated urban growth, in part due to heavy migration, particularly to California. The war also led to a rapid influx of women into the wage workforce. In addition, the war also witnessed a rise in the marriage, birth, and divorce rates.

African-Americans fought two wars. A million African Americans served in segregated units in the military, where they frequently suffered from racial discrimination. On the home front, African American leaders protested against discrimination. The influx of black migrants from the South also created housing and transportation shortages that led to a riot in Detroit in 1943, and similar conflicts elsewhere.

Mexican-Americans also faced discrimination. The growing need for farm labor led to the bracero program in 1942 that stimulated migration to the United States. The zoot suit riots of 1943 in Los Angeles indicated that anti-Mexican-American feelings ran high.

Yet for all the violence and discrimination, most minorities benefited from the war, particularly economically. The poor experienced higher incomes due to the booming economy.

The treatment of aliens from enemy countries was mixed. Germans and Italians fared much better than Japanese. The government refused to ease Jewish immigration quotas. Japanese Americans suffered under government policies. In 1942, Roosevelt authorized what became the relocation program under which over 100,000 Japanese-Americans were forced into internment camps. Ironically, 18,000 Japanese American men enlisted in the armed forces, sustaining heavy casualties and emerging as the most decorated military outfit in World War II.

The Grand Alliance of the United States, Britain, Free France, and the Soviet Union was an uneasy coalition; each member had different war aims and visions of the future. Roosevelt made Europe the top priority because of the need to defeat Hitler and to placate Stalin. The tide began to turn in late 1942 as the Germans faltered at Stalingrad and the Russians launched a counterattack. Allied victories followed in North Africa and Italy.

In November 1943, at Teheran, Iran, the Big Three met for the first time to discuss the second front and the postwar world. The latter topic aroused bitter controversy, with Roosevelt playing the conciliator. Massive bombing paved the way for the invasion of France. Two weeks after landing on Normandy beaches, the Allied forces pushed east toward Germany while Soviet forces moved west. A German counteroffensive in the Battle of the Bulge failed.

With victory near, Stalin, Roosevelt, and Churchill met at Yalta to discuss the postwar world. They agreed to partition Germany, that the Soviet Union would declare war on Japan, and that the Soviets would join the planned United Nations. But disagreement continued over Eastern Europe. Soon after Yalta, Hitler committed suicide and Germany surrendered.

The United States halted Japanese advances in summer of 1942 by winning the Battle of Midway. The United States then launched an attack on Guadalcanal in the Solomon Islands which was followed by advances in New Guinea, and other island-hopping victories in the South Pacific. MacArthur invaded the Philippines in October 1944. The capture of Iwo Jima facilitated the bombing of Japan. Faced with defeat, the Emperor sent out peace feelers.

Kept largely in the dark by Roosevelt, Truman faced a difficult task upon assuming the presidency. His first test came at Potsdam where the deadlock on Eastern Europe continued, but agreement was reached on the Potsdam Declaration calling for Japan's unconditional surrender. Truman learned of the atomic bomb while at Potsdam and adopted a hard line with Stalin.

The Manhattan Project had begun in response to fears Germany was building an atomic bomb. Truman decided to drop atomic bombs on Hiroshima on August 6, 1945, and Nagasaki on August 9. The following day, Japan surrendered. World War II had ended.

OBJECTIVES

After reading this chapter, you should be able to:

1 Discuss the characteristics of U.S. diplomacy between the world wars.

2. Explain how the mobilization for World War II differed from that of World War I.

3. Describe the changes that World War II made in the roles and status of women and minorities.

4. Cite the political and military factors leading to President Truman's decision to drop atomic bombs on Japan in 1945.

KEY TERMS

Good Neighbor Policy
Lend-Lease Act
Pearl Harbor
War Production Board
Women's Army Corps
Axis Powers
Grand Alliance
D-Day
Yalta Conference
Manhattan Project

KEY FIGURES

Adolf Hitler
Benito Mussolini
Franklin Roosevelt
Winston Churchill
Joseph Stalin
Harry Truman

PRACTICE TEST

CHAPTER 25 • THE END OF ISOLATION: AMERICA FACES THE WORLD, 1920–1945

_____ 1. Auschwitz
   a. was a forced labor camp established by the Nazis in Poland where large numbers of prisoners died primarily because of malnutrition and disease
   b. was a death camp where prisoners were murdered with poison gas and then their bodies were cremated
   c. was mainly intended to serve as a prison for Soviet prisoners of war

_____ 2. In the 1930s, isolationism was a policy favored by
   a. most Americans
   b. left and right wing extremists exclusively
   c. few Americans

_____ 3. The 1921 Washington naval conference
   a. guaranteed freedom of the seas
   b. imposed a 10-year moratorium on the construction of battleships and restricted the number of battle ships each country could have
   c. outlawed war

_____ 4. Which of the following statements about the Kellogg-Briand Pact of 1927 is FALSE?
   a. It renounced war as an instrument for resolving international disputes
   b. It failed to gain the support of more than a dozen nations
   c. It contained no enforcement mechanism

_____ 5. Between 1898 and 1932, the United States intervened militarily in the Caribbean and Central America
   a. five times
   b. ten times
   c. twenty times

_____ 6. It repudiated the Roosevelt Corollary to the Monroe Doctrine.
   a. the Clark Memorandum
   b. the Good Neighbor Policy
   c. the Alliance for Progress

_____ 7. The Nye Commission
   a. blamed U.S. intervention in World War I on false Allied propaganda and unscrupulous Wall Street bankers
   b. called for improved U.S. relations with Latin America
   c. recommended a preparedness program to ready the United States for possible conflict with Germany, Italy, and Japan

_____ 8. Adolf Hitler
   a. blamed Germany's defeat in World War I and its economic problems on Jews
   b. hated the United States because it refused to assist Germany in paying reparations after World War I
   c. kept his plans to conquer countries with large German populations and seize land in Russia secret until he attained power in Germany in 1933

_____ 9. The United States responded to Japan's expansionist policies in East Asia by
   a. establishing an alliance with countries bordering Japan
   b. dispatching the U.S. fleet to the Far East
   c. imposing economic sanctions on trade with the Japanese

_____ 10. Franklin Roosevelt responded to the outbreak of war in Europe in all but one of the following ways. Select the EXCEPTION.
   a. He called on Americans to be neutral in thought as well as action
   b. He allowed Britain to purchase war materials and transferred 50 destroyers to England in

exchange for leases on British bases

   c. He persuaded Congress to pass a peacetime military draft

_____ 11. One of the most important domestic results of the war effort was to

   a. encourage the growth of small businesses

   b. end discrimination against African Americans.

   c. swiftly end of Depression-era unemployment and raise wages

_____ 12. During the Second World War, African Americans

   a. moved from the North to the South to fill vacated agricultural jobs.

   b. fought in a segregated military.

   c. were not allowed to fight in the military.

_____ 13. The victims of the Zoot Suit riots were mainly

   a. Japanese Americans

   b. African Americans

   c. Mexican Americans

_____ 14. Which of the following statements about the internment of Japanese-Americans during World War II is FALSE?

   a. The Supreme Court upheld their evacuation from the West Coast as constitutional.

   b. Reparations were finally paid to evacuees about forty years after the end of the war.

   c. Outside California, there was strong public opposition to the internment policy.

_____ 15. Attitudes in the United States toward Jews fleeing persecution in Europe during World War II were reflected in the

   a. refusal to relax immigration restrictions for Jews

   b. emotional welcome given to Jewish refugees who arrived in the United States

   c. monetary and legal assistance given to Jews for immigration

_____ 16. In World War II, the Allied strategy, agreed upon by the U. S. and Britain, was to

   a. concentrate on defeating Japan first before turning to Germany

   b. divide all resources equally between the war against Japan and that against Germany

   c. concentrate on defeating Germany first before turning on Japan

_____ 17. On June 6, 1944, the United States opened a second front with the invasion of

   a. France

   b. Sicily

   c. Spain

_____ 18. The top secret Manhattan Project

   a. deciphered German and Japanese diplomatic dispatches

   b. constructed long-range missiles

   c. created the atomic bomb

_____ 19. Which of the following was the MAJOR reason President Truman used to justify his decision to drop the atomic bomb on Hiroshima in August 1945?

   a. He felt it would shorten the war and eliminate the need for an invasion of Japan

   b. He wanted to send a strong warning message to the Russians to watch their step in the Pacific after Japan was defeated

   c. Once the bomb was completed, Truman felt he had to use it in order to justify the huge investments in time, resources, scientific expertise, and expense involved in developing it

CHAPTER 26 • WAGING PEACE AND WAR

SUMMARY

Across the globe, the United States clashed with the Soviet Union over such issues as the Soviet dominance over eastern Europe, control of atomic weapons, and the Soviet blockade of Berlin. The establishment of a Communist government in China in 1949 and the North Korean invasion of South Korea in 1950 helped transform the Cold War into a global conflict, in which United States would confront the threat of Communism in Iran, Guatemala, and elsewhere. In an atmosphere charged with paranoia and anxiety, there was deep fear at home about "enemies within" sabotaging U.S. foreign policy and passing atomic secrets to the Soviets. In this chapter you read about the causes of the Cold War, the Containment policy and the way it was implemented; the Korean War; and the Second Red Scare.

KEY POINTS

- Following World War II the United States grew increasingly worried about the intentions of the Soviet Union. Eastern Europe fell under Soviet influence, and communist movements in Greece and Italy challenged governments in those countries.

- In China, communist forces seized power.

- By 1946 a Cold War had broken out in Europe. President Truman declared that the United States would block further communist expansion. To enforce the policy of Containment, the United States sponsored the Marshall Plan, organized the Berlin airlift, and joined NATO.

- In Asia the policy of Containment was tested when North Korea invaded South Korea.

- The Cold War contributed to anxieties about the threat of subversion at home. The discovery of a few cases of disloyalty fed such anxieties, and Senator Joseph McCarthy charged that many communists were active in high levels of government. McCarthy's investigations uncovered little evidence of such activities and his popularity declined after the televised Army-McCarthy hearings.

CHAPTER SYNOPSIS

The end of World War II was followed by a four decade long Cold War between the United States and the Soviet Union. The conflict's origins involved such issues as the fate of eastern Europe and Germany, control over nuclear weapons, and postwar reconstruction aid to the Soviet Union. A key source of tension was whether Poland would be free and independent or a satellite of the Soviets. Seeking security, Stalin kept Soviet troops in Poland. Truman responded by cutting off economic aid. The Polish controversy showed the deep divisions existing between the two major powers who approached issues from different perspectives. Other divisive issues included the fate of Germany and control over atomic weapons. By early 1946, relations were strained to the point where Stalin warned Soviet citizens that a lasting peace with the West was impossible and Churchill delivered his famous iron curtain speech. The Cold War had begun.

The split between the United States and the Soviet Union was hardened by emotionally-charged rhetoric and misperceptions. Truman and his advisers equated Stalin with Hitler, but the Soviet leader's goal was security, not expansion. Contributing to the deteriorating situation was the decline of Britain as a world power, indicated by Britain's ending aid to Greece and Turkey in their fight against communist rebels and requesting that the United States carry the load. The resulting Truman Doctrine promised American aid to governments resisting subjugation by internal or external forces. Greece and Turkey were the first recipients, opening the door to the expenditure of billions of dollars to countries fighting communism. The next goal was to save war-ravaged Western Europe by providing help for rebuilding. The Marshall Plan supplied $17 billion for relief and for rebuilding Western Europe's economic infrastructure. The resulting economic stability helped restore America's prestige abroad, and fostered economic integration in Western Europe, leading to the European Economic Community (Common Market) in 1958.

George Kennan's influential article in the July 1947 Foreign Affairs expressed the need to contain Soviet expansion. The containment policy sought to halt the spread of communism throughout the world by providing military and economic aid as well as fighting limited wars. The first test occurred in 1949 when the Soviets closed Berlin to access by rail and highways. In response, the United States conducted the Berlin airlift to furnish the city with needed supplies. In addition, the North Atlantic Treaty Organization (NATO) was created in

1949. The explosion of a nuclear device by the Soviets removed the advantage the United States had enjoyed over Stalin. That same year, the Chinese civil war was won by the Communists.

The fall of China hardened Truman's determination to fight communism. He issued National Security Council Paper Number 68 (NSC68). The United States went to war in Korea in June 1950, following an invasion of South Korea by North Korea. The United Nations Security Council condemned the invasion and ordered a cease-fire. The Soviets were boycotting the proceedings because of the refusal to seat the People's Republic of China. Truman ordered U.S. troops to Korea in what he called a UN police action. Eventually, the North Koreans retreated across the border, but MacArthur secured approval from Truman to liberate North Korea The Chinese protested but their warnings went unnoticed until they joined the war on the side of North Korea. Although negotiations for peace began in July 1951, it was not until 1953 that the war ended.

The end of wartime economic control led to demands for higher wages in the fate of rising prices. Strikes broke out in many industries, but the public proved unsympathetic and the president hostile to labor demands. The 1946 elections gave conservative Republicans control of Congress and they passed the Labor-Management Relations Act (Taft-Hartley Act) that outlawed the closed shop. Though Truman was the underdog in the 1948 election, he won a surprise victory. Although Congress extended Social Security and raised the minimum wage, it balked at passing legislation aimed at civil rights, national health insurance, or farm and school aid.

The onset of the Cold War had led to the uncovering of several spy rings operated by the Soviets. The issue of espionage, however, soon became political as Republicans portrayed the Democrats as being soft on communism and harboring spies in government. Truman reacted to such charges with the Federal Employee Loyalty Program, which found no evidence of widespread espionage but led to the resignation or firing of thousands of government employees anyway. Truman also used anticommunism to gain support for his foreign policy. Paying a heavy price were Ethel and Julius Rosenberg who were convicted of espionage and executed, though the death penalty was not mandatory.

The politician who most successfully capitalized on anticommunism was Wisconsin Senator Joseph McCarthy. In 1954, he launched a tirade against the army that resulted in televised congressional hearings where McCarthy was shown as the charlatan he was. He sank back into obscurity. McCarthy's downfall, combined with end of the Korean War, ended the Red Scare.

The Cold War contributed to a distinctive mentality, emphasizing paranoia and fear of subversion, that pervaded popular culture. Suspicion fell on a broad spectrum of institutions, organizations, and individuals. The House Un-American Activities Committee accused the Boy Scouts of subversion, but concentrated its investigations on the motion picture industry. Its first investigation in 1947 focused on the "Hollywood Ten," who refused to cooperate and were punished with blacklisting or prison sentences. In 1951, HUAC returned to Hollywood and called hundreds of witnesses who testified to communist influences in the industry. The result was blacklisting and a spate of anticommunist films. There was also deepening concern about juvenile delinquency. Sports were considered an antidote for many youth problems, but gambling and cheating scandals tainted them, too.

OBJECTIVES

After reading this chapter, you should be able to:

1. Explain why U.S.-Soviet relations deteriorated rapidly after World War II.

2. Identify the containment policy and explain how it was implemented.

3. Discuss why Joseph McCarthy became such a powerful and influential Senator in the early 1950s.

4. Describe the role of popular culture in contributing to a domestic mood of paranoia.

KEY TERMS
Containment
Truman Doctrine
Berlin Blockade
Marshall Plan
NATO
China Lobby
National Security Council Paper 68
Taft-Hartley Act
Fair Deal
House Un-American Activities Committee

KEY FIGURES
Joseph Stalin
General Douglas MacArthur
Alger Hiss
Julius and Ethel Rosenberg
Joseph McCarthy

CHAPTER 26 • WAGING PEACE AND WAR

_____ 1. The former State Department official who was convicted of perjury in the celebrated "pumpkin papers" trial during the Second Red Scare was
   a. Joseph McCarthy
   b. Whittaker Chambers
   c. Alger Hiss

_____ 2. Which of the following did NOT make the Soviet Union suspicious of the motives of the United States?
   a. The terms of the German and Japanese surrender after World War II
   b. The U.S. refusal to recognize a Soviet sphere of influence in eastern Europe
   c. The American monopoly on atomic bomb technology

_____ 3. Which of the following did NOT make the United States suspicious of the motives of the Soviet Union?
   a. The Soviet refusal to allow free elections in Poland
   b. The organization of the United Nations
   c. The Soviet demand for a sphere of influence in eastern Europe

_____ 4. The Truman Doctrine was announced in response to a British plea to have the United States provide aid to anticommunist forces in
   a. Iran and Iraq
   b. Afghanistan and Pakistan
   c. Greece and Turkey

_____ 5. The Containment policy, proposed by George Kennan,
   a. sought to roll-back Communism
   b. attempted to prevent Soviet power and Communism from expanding into non-Communist nations
   c. entailed a commitment to working with the Soviet Union

_____ 6. President Truman's response to the Berlin Blockade was to
   a. evacuate the Western-occupied portions of Berlin
   b. use military force to break the blockade of land routes into Berlin
   c. airlift all necessary supplies into Berlin for almost a year

_____ 7. The Marshall Plan could be understood as part of an American desire to
   a. make communism less appealing to Europeans by creating economic prosperity
   b. maintain Western Europe in a state of permanent economic dependence on the United States
   c. prevent a future depression by creating viable economic markets for American goods in Europe

_____ 8. During the struggle in China between nationalists and communists after World War II, the United States
   a. continued to support nationalists with money and weapons even when it became clear their cause was lost
   b. supported the communist leader Mao Zedong hoping that a communist China friendly to the United States would help stop Soviet aggression
   c. intervened militarily to put an end to the struggle

_____ 9. The critical Cold War document titled National Security Council Paper Number 68
   a. criticized the Containment policy
   b. advocated a massive build-up of America's military strength
   c. warned President Truman of North Korea's plan to invade South Korea

_____ 10. The Korean War
   a. was a clear example of Communist aggression
   b. resulted in a clear victory for the South Koreans
   c. was authorized by Congress

_____ 11. President Truman contributed to the anti-Communist fear after the Second World War by
   a. recommending that "pro-Communist" books be removed from the nation's libraries and bookstores.
   b. ordering investigations into the loyalty of federal employees.
   c. releasing classified information revealing an international Communist conspiracy.

_____ 12. He was executed along with his wife for transferring atomic secrets to a Soviet spy.
   a. Alger Hiss
   b. Whittaker Chambers
   c. Julius Rosenberg

_____ 13. Joseph McCarthy
   a. symbolized America's concern over communist subversion
   b. provided proof of dozens of cases of communist espionage
   c. proved that Hollywood filmmakers were inserting pro-Communist messages in their films

_____ 14. Which of the following statements about the Taft-Harley Act of 1947 is FALSE?
   a. It gave the president the power to delay strikes by declaring a cooling-off period
   b. It outlawed the closed-shop in which all employees were required to join unions
   c. It gave a major boost to labor unionization

_____ 15. The House Un-American Activities Committee was
   a. responsible for a series of highly publicized hearings designed to expose communist influence in American life
   b. the name that Senator Joseph McCarthy gave to the House Armed Services Committee
   c. declared by the Supreme Court to be in violation of basic civil liberties and therefore unconstitutional

_____ 16. Those who are drawn to the paranoid style see the shaping of world events as the work of
   a. menacing conspiracies
   b. powerful leaders
   c. complex international relationships

_____ 17. Following World War II, the United States did NOT
   a. join a multinational organization aimed at preserving world peace
   b. form military alliances with its allies to guard against invasion by mutual enemies
   c. enter a prolonged period of economic stagnation
   d. enter a period of extreme anti-communism that led to the persecution of suspected radicals

_____ 18. Evidence of a thaw in the Cold War in the 1950s included all these events EXCEPT
   a. the death of Stalin
   b. the end of the Korean War
   c. the demise of McCarthyism
   d. America's abandonment of the Containment doctrine

CHAPTER 27 • IKE'S AMERICA

SUMMARY

Television's images of the 1950s were bland. The stock situation comedy centered on a white suburban family with a happily married husband and wife and two or sometimes three well-adjusted children. *Father Knows Best* was the classic example of this genre. Its theme song was entitled: "Just Around the Corner There's a Rainbow in the Sky." Television sit-coms were not documentaries. In fact, the postwar era was characterized by tension, diversity, and unsettling social changes. In this chapter you read about President Eisenhower's conception of "dynamic Republicanism" and his foreign policy; the impact of the Soviet Union's launching of Sputnik; the beginnings of the modern civil rights movements; and the changes taking place in the American family and in youth culture.

KEY POINTS

- As president, Dwight Eisenhower pursued a moderate course. He did not dismantle any New Deal programs. His major domestic accomplishment was the construction of the interstate highway system.
- Despite outward calm, the 1950s was a decade of important change. The Supreme Court ruled that segregation in public schools was unconstitutional and black Americans increased protests against segregation.
- Many families moved to rapidly growing suburbs.
- Young people created a new youth culture, with its own distinctive form of music, rock and roll.
- The Beat Generation scorned materialism, traditional family life and sexuality and tapped into dissatisfaction with the prevailing blandness of conventional culture.

CHAPTER SYNOPSIS

After 30 years of Democratic control of the presidency, the 1952 election indicated that Americans were ready for a change, as Dwight Eisenhower was swept into the oval office. The reality of the Eisenhower presidency frequently diverged from the prevailing imagery. The seeming hands-off policy of the president masked a tight control behind the scenes. Eisenhower assumed a public pose of affability and inaction that contrasted with his strong, behind the scenes leadership in pursuit of his top priorities. Eisenhower called his philosophy dynamic conservatism, which meant cutting spending without rolling back New Deal social legislation. During his two terms of office, the nation's economy experienced sustained prosperity, achieving stable prices, full employment, and steady growth.

As a military logician, Eisenhower had been impressed with Germany's road system and expressed concern over the sorry condition of America's highways. Working with the highway lobby, in 1956, he persuaded Congress to pass the National System of Interstate and Defense Highways Act to construct over 40,000 miles of roads over 13 years at a projected cost of $26 billion, though it took longer to complete and cost more. This legislation profoundly impacted on the nation's development. It contributed to the decline of inner cities while providing impetus to the flight to the suburbs. Central business cores were robbed of their status as centers of commerce and excitement as shopping malls and motels arose along the highway system.

The American infatuation with the automobile was also intensified, achieving symbolic recognition in multi-car garages, gas stations, and drive-in movie theaters. Mobility became a defining characteristic of American life. The emerging automobile culture created a variety of problems. Mass transit systems declined as did the major interstate railroads, meaning the elderly, the very young, the poor, and the disabled who may not have been able to use cars found their movements restricted.

Eisenhower's vision of "modern Republicanism" extended beyond the domestic sector to include an internationalist foreign policy. Here, too, he operated behind the scenes making all major decisions, while Secretary of State John Foster Dulles acted as point man. The goal of both men was peace, but not through appeasement. Their beliefs were based on internationalism and the vigorous prosecution of the Cold War. Eisenhower practiced a more calculated brand of Truman's containment policy called the "New Look." It involved cutting costs by stressing nuclear weapons over conventional ones. His foreign policy implied not becoming involved in wars like Korea but using the threat of massive retaliation to maintain order. Foreign alliances were pursued to encourage anticommunist resistance, and the CIA was employed as a covert branch of foreign policy engaging in assassinations and coups.

Relations with the Soviet Union were altered by the death of Stalin and the rise of Nikita Khrushchev to power. Like Eisenhower, the new Soviet leader sought peaceful coexistence. Eisenhower responded to Stalin's death with words of peace to which the Soviets responded, allowing several issues to be resolved. German prisoners of war were repatriated from Russia. The Soviet Union established relations with Greece and Israel, and surrendered claims on Turkish territory. It also withdrew from its Austrian occupation zone. In addition, Khrushchev condemned the excesses of Stalin. Eisenhower and Khrushchev leaders met at a 1955 summit conference in Geneva, Switzerland. The meeting produced few results as the Soviet leader rejected Eisenhower's plan for aerial surveillance of each other's nation to reduce the risk of a surprise attack.

Khrushchev's speeches promised greater freedom for Soviet satellites in Eastern Europe. Greater Polish autonomy was allowed because it implied no break in the Soviet Bloc. When the new Hungarian leader, Imre Nagy, tried to pull out of the Warsaw Pact, Khrushchev crushed the revolt with Russian tanks and troops.

In the Middle East, Egypt accepted U.S. aid to build the Aswan High Dam. It then recognized the People's Republic of China and pursued friendly relations with the Soviets, leading the United States to cancel a loan. Nasser responded by nationalizing the Suez Canal, through which half of Europe's oil supply traveled. Britain and France seized the Canal, while Israel invaded Egypt. An angry Eisenhower found himself allied with the Soviets in support of international law that led to the cessation of the attack.

The Hungarian and Suez crises removed hopes of peace and intensified hostile moods, presaging the foreign policy problems of Ike's second term. Advancing age and declining health, including a heart attack, may have affected Eisenhower during his second term. In addition, Secretary of State Dulles contracted cancer in 1956 and died in 1959. Meanwhile, Russia launched Sputnik and a dog into space in 1957. U.S. space efforts initially failed, precipitating discussion in America over values and education as well as raising fears over defense. Congress responded with increases in defense-related research and higher education funding.

Nationalist movements in the Third World were the source of many foreign policy issues during the Eisenhower presidency. Eisenhower opposed the French and British moves in Egypt but supported covert action by the CIA in Iran and Guatemala. He also sent troops into Lebanon. The United States became identified with oppressive and totalitarian governments in the Third World. The flaws in Eisenhower's approach were most evident in his response to the Cuban Revolution of 1959. American firms had controlled much of the Cuban economy. Rebel leader Fidel Castro confiscated American holdings and launched social programs, but also instituted repressive measures. Eisenhower gave the CIA permission to launch a counterattack that became the disastrous Bay of Pigs invasion. One of his last acts as president was to sever diplomatic ties with Cuba, fueling the anti-American sentiment that he had helped to generate.

A blow to Eisenhower's foreign policy came after a summit meeting with Khrushchev at Camp David. The shooting down of an American U2 spy plane created a diplomatic crisis that led to the cancellation of another summit planned for Paris. Eisenhower left office having missed a chance to improve American-Soviet relations. He issued warnings of a growing military-industrial complex that threatened democracy.

When Eisenhower left office, important legal advances had been made in the black quest for civil rights. World War II's fight against Nazi oppression highlighted the large gap between the promise of democracy and its reality. The threat of a march on Washington led Franklin Roosevelt to issue Executive Order 8802, outlawing discrimination in war industries. President Harry Truman established the President's Commission on Civil Rights and desegregated the armed forces. In the meantime, beginning in the late 1930s, the NAACP won a series of stunning court victories that chipped away at legal segregation based on the separate but equal doctrine. The pivotal case was Brown v. Board of Education of Topeka filed in 1952. Earl Warren, who was appointed Chief Justice of the Supreme Court, had been active in the Japanese relocation program but now considered that a mistake that he helped rectify by gaining unanimous support for declaring segregation unconstitutional. Eisenhower's behind-the-scenes style coupled with his ambivalence regarding the decision may have intensified resistance to desegregation by white Southerners. In 1957, attempts to desegregate Central High School in Little Rock, Arkansas, led to violence; the president ordered National Guard troops to the high school to ensure the court order was enforced. In Montgomery, Alabama, in 1955, Rosa Parks refused to move her seat on a bus. Her arrest led to an extended and successful boycott of the city's bus system and thrust Rev. Martin Luther King, Jr. into the forefront of the civil rights leadership. It also precipitated demonstrations throughout the nation and launched the civil rights movement in earnest.

The image of the 1950s as a golden, carefree decade of innocence contrasted sharply with reality. This image evolved out of television shows, particularly situation comedies like Father Knows Best, which offered a vision of American life based on a happy and prosperous white family living in the suburbs. There was tremendous suburban growth during the decade. Critics deplored the static uniformity of the suburban landscape and the increasing stress on materialism. There were signs of frustration among women who felt unfulfilled in their roles as wives and mothers. The suburban stress on conformity was attacked in movies like *Invasion of the Body Snatchers* (1956). But these criticisms overlooked the accomplishment signified by working-class families owning their own homes and living middle-class lives.

A rebellion against suburban culture came from American youths who embraced rock and roll, a synthesis of blues, rhythm and blues, and country music. Another protest movement came from the writers of the Beat movement, which rejected conventional American norms. Led by writers like poet Allen Ginsberg and Jack Kerouac, the Beats sowed seeds that would mature in the 1960s.

OBJECTIVES

After reading this chapter, you should be able to:

1. Discuss foreign and domestic policy under President Dwight Eisenhower

2. Describe the gains that African Americans made in the 1950s toward ending segregation and the tactics they adopted.

3. Identify the significant social and economic changes that occurred during the 1950s in transportation, housing, family life, and the experiences of youth.

KEY TERMS

Modern Republicanism
National System of Interstate and Defense Highways Act
The New Look
Sputnik
Brown v. Board of Education of Topeka
Little Rock Crisis
Rock and Roll
Covering
Beat Generation

KEY FIGURES

Emmett Till
Dwight D. Eisenhower
John Foster Dulles
Nikita Khrushchev
Fidel Castro
Rosa Parks
Elvis Presley
Allen Ginsberg
Jack Kerouac

CHAPTER 27 • IKE'S AMERICA

_____ 1. Emmett Till
   a. was murdered for speaking to a white woman in Money, Alabama
   b. led the Montgomery, Alabama, bus boycott
   c. integrated major league baseball

_____ 2. President Dwight Eisenhower's domestic strategy of modern Republicanism advocated
   a. acceptance of existing New Deal programs
   b. increasing military spending
   c. strong and vocal support for McCarthyism

_____ 3. The largest public works project during Eisenhower's presidency was
   a. the space program
   b. the building of Grand Coulee Dam
   c. construction of the interstate highway system

_____ 4. During Dwight Eisenhower's terms in office
   a. Americans left cities for suburbs in record numbers
   b. inner cities experienced a revival in construction and renewal
   c. the federal government created mass transit systems in many of the nation's big cities

_____ 5. During the 1950s
   a. real wages rose by about 20 percent
   b. the influence of organized labor declined
   c. unemployment averaged over 8 percent

_____ 6. Dwight Eisenhower's New Look policy
   a. emphasized nuclear weapons over conventional weapons
   b. stressed the development of special forces to fight guerrilla wars
   c. involved active steps to roll-back communism in eastern Europe

_____ 7. During the 1950s, President Eisenhower used the Central Intelligence Agency (CIA) to overthrow anti-American governments in _____.
   a. Cuba and Laos
   b. Iran and Guatemala
   c. Nicaragua and Lebanon

_____ 8. The Eisenhower administration's foreign policy in the Middle East included all of the following EXCEPT
   a. the landing of Marines at Beirut to protect the existing regime from a possible coup
   b. the use of the CIA to help stage a coup to overthrow the nationalist prime minister of Iran and replace his with a pro-American leader
   c. support for the British and French invasion of the Suez

_____ 9. In his farewell address in January 1961, President Eisenhower warned the American people against
   a. the tendency to hysterical anti-communism
   b. the risk of creeping socialism
   c. the influence of the military-industrial complex

_____ 10. The 1956 boycott of the Montgomery bus system
   a. began because the city doubled bus fares
   b. was instigated by the arrest of Rosa Parks
   c. lasted for three weeks and failed to achieve its goal

_____ 11. The case of *Brown vs. Board of Education of Topeka, Kansas* (1954) concerned the
   a. constitutionality of federal aid to education
   b. closing of public schools by the governor of Kansas
   c. constitutionality of racial segregation in public schools

_____ 12. When the effort to desegregate Little Rock's Central High School became violent, President Eisenhower

a. stood by and allowed state and local authorities to restore order
b. nationalized the Arkansas National Guard and sent federal paratroopers to maintain order
c. appealed to the Supreme Court to delay enforcement of its school desegregation decisions

_____ 13. Early rock and roll was largely the product of combining
a. gospel music with country music
b. folk music with jazz
c. rhythm and blues with country music

_____ 14. During the 1950s, in the recording industry, "covering" referred to
a. designing appealing album covers to help sell records
b. rewriting songs that were originally recorded by black artists, then having them re-recorded by white performers
c. substituting relatively unknown performers when big-name acts failed to appear

_____ 15. Of the following, the Beat Generation most admired
a. political activism
b. the acquisition of material possessions
c. spontaneity and intuition

_____ 16. The Beat Generation's leading poet was _____, while _____ was the Beats' leading novelist.
a. Allen Ginsberg; Jack Kerouac
b. Betty Friedan; James Baldwin
c. Kurt Vonnegut; Ken Kesey

CHAPTER 28 • VIETNAM AND THE CRISIS OF AUTHORITY

SUMMARY

It was the longest war in American history and the most unpopular American war of the twentieth century. It resulted in nearly 60,000 American deaths and an estimated 2 million Vietnamese deaths. Even today, many Americans still ask whether the American effort in Vietnam was a blunder, a pawn in the game of Cold War politics, or an idealistic, if failed, effort to protect the South Vietnamese people from totalitarian government. In this chapter, you read about the war's origins, military history, and consequences.

KEY POINTS

- Between 1945 and 1954, the Vietnamese waged an anti-colonial war against France, which received $2.6 billion in financial support from the United States.

- The French defeat at the Dien Bien Phu was followed by a peace conference in Geneva, in which Laos, Cambodia, and Vietnam received their independence and Vietnam was temporarily divided between an anti-Communist South and a Communist North.

- In 1956, South Vietnam, with American backing, refused to hold the unification elections. By 1958, Communist-led guerrillas known as the Viet Cong had begun to battle the South Vietnamese government.

- To support the South's government, the United States sent in 2,000 military advisors, a number that grew to 16,300 in 1963.

- The military condition deteriorated, and by 1963 South Vietnam had lost the fertile Mekong Delta to the Vietcong.

- In 1965, Johnson escalated the war, commencing air strikes on North Vietnam and committing ground forces, which numbered 536,000 in 1968. The 1968 Tet Offensive by the North Vietnamese turned many Americans against the war.

- The next president, Richard Nixon, advocated Vietnamization, withdrawing American troops and giving South Vietnam greater responsibility for fighting the war. His attempt to slow the flow of North Vietnamese soldiers and supplies into South Vietnam by sending American forces to destroy Communist supply bases in Cambodia in 1970 in violation of Cambodian neutrality provoked antiwar protests on the nation's college campuses.

- From 1968 to 1973 efforts were made to end the conflict through diplomacy. In January 1973, an agreement reached and U.S. forces were withdrawn from Vietnam and U.S. prisoners of war were released. In April 1975, South Vietnam surrendered to the North and Vietnam was reunited

CHAPTER SYNOPSIS

John F. Kennedy's election to the presidency in 1960 demonstrated the increasing power of the media. Kennedy's vibrant oratory and skillfully written speeches provided a sharp contrast to the bland Richard Nixon, creating a feeling of energy and activism in tune with his macho ethos. Surrounding himself with equally energetic advisers, Kennedy established an image of his presidency that journalists equated with Camelot. But his record and personal behavior fell far short of the ideal vision he presented.

Kennedy's domestic program was hampered by his poor relations with Congress and distaste for legislative in-fighting. He passed legislation that raised the minimum wage, expanded Social Security, and provided aid for public housing and depressed areas, but Congress turned down his plan for federal aid to education, a health insurance plan for the elderly, and programs aimed at migrant workers, unemployed youths, and commuters. African-Americans also were disappointed with Kennedy's civil rights efforts, particularly because they had provided his narrow margin of victory.

The Civil Rights movement often met with violence in the early 1960s as leaders were murdered and churches were bombed. Protesters sometimes were hit with high-pressure fire hoses and attacked by police dogs. Kennedy did not speak out against this treatment during his first two years in office. In 1963, influenced by the upcoming election, Kennedy adopted a much more active pose, explicitly expressing his support for racial equality.

But domestic policy was less Kennedy's interest than foreign affairs, where the battle lines were clearly drawn. He largely continued the Cold War policies of his predecessors, and supported the failed Bay of Pigs invasion, even though his military advisers predicted it would fail. A more serious crisis arose over Cuba when the Soviet Union began installing missiles there. Instead of trying to solve the situation through secret diplomacy, Kennedy made it public, creating a war-threatening crisis that led to an agreement by Khrushchev to remove the missiles in return for a U.S. pledge not to invade Cuba. In the aftermath of the missile crisis, it appears that Kennedy was moving toward a policy of détente, but his assassination in Dallas, Texas, on November 22, 1963, makes this impossible to know. The sorrowing nation assessed the slain president not so much by what he did as by what might have occurred.

America's involvement in Vietnam represented one phase of virtually millennia of fighting by that nation for its freedom, first against China, then France, and finally the United States. The modern phase began with the Vietnamese declaration of independence in 1945 and was followed by a successful war against the French that ended in 1954 with the partition of the country into the North and South. American leaders saw Vietnam as a pawn in the Cold War, misrepresenting the struggle as an example of communist expansion rather than the decolonization movement it was. Eisenhower would not support the French militarily, but he recognized the government of South Vietnam that became a test case of containment through economic aid. But the autocratic and corrupt rule of Ngo Dinh Diem led to open revolt by guerrillas known as the Vietcong.

Kennedy reaffirmed the American commitment to Diem. He opposed Eisenhower's massive retaliation doctrine, preferring a "flexible response" based on supporting conventional and counterinsurgency movements as well as nuclear weapons. Vietnam became the laboratory for this policy. Kennedy sent American troops to Vietnam as "advisers." By 1963, 16,300 American troops were stationed there. Internally, the Vietnamese responded to Diem's refusal to initiate land reform and his restriction of Buddhism with organized protests and self-immolation on the streets by Buddhist priests. Outside Saigon, the government had little power. Diem's mounting problems led Kennedy to encourage his overthrow, which occurred in November 1963. Again Kennedy's assassination made this an unfinished chapter in his legacy.

Lyndon Johnson inherited a deteriorating situation as the Vietcong captured the Mekong Delta. He also lacked interest in foreign affairs, but continued the U.S. commitment to Vietnam after defeating Barry Goldwater in the 1964 election. Domestically, he promised a "Great Society" at home. In Vietnam, he used reports of North Vietnamese naval attacks to gain passage of the Tonkin Gulf Resolution that provided expanded presidential powers to fight in Vietnam. His advisers provided opposing opinions. Some called for a more aggressive military presence, while other suggested no escalation. Johnson chose the first option and began launching massive air strikes that stiffened resistance as adviser George Ball had prophesied. The next move was to expand the ground troop commitment, reaching over half a million troops by 1968, that resulted in over 30,000 American deaths.

After military experts declared the end of the war was in sight, the Tet Offensive of 1968 occurred. U.S troops repelled the offensive, so decimating the Vietcong that it never regained its total fighting strength. The offensive showed that the war was far from over and the media began criticizing government actions, thus widening the credibility gap. In the process, Johnson's popularity plummeted and when peace candidate Eugene McCarthy received surprisingly strong support in the New Hampshire primary, Johnson announced that he would not seek re-election. The war had reached a turning point, with victory being replaced by peace as the objective.

Johnson's failure was probably due to an error in tactics and his duplicitous leadership style. He had speculated that a slow build-up instead of full commitment of troops would force negotiations and he kept assuring the American people that victory was in sight when it became very apparent to the public that this was not true. The young were the first to oppose Johnson's war effort. This was evident in the changing attitudes of the soldiers who became disillusioned and turned to drugs and sex for relief, and began considering all Vietnamese as the enemy. Desertion and AWOL rates soared.

In the United States, many college students, most of whom were draft exempt, became vocal critics of the war. A large number had participated in the civil rights movement. They shifted their attention to the war, leading to the rise of radical organizations like the SDS (Students for a Democratic Society.) But older people joined the antiwar movement, too.

The 1968 election saw the rise of Eugene McCarthy and Robert Kennedy as peace candidates. After winning the California primary, Kennedy was assassinated. In Chicago, where the city streets were filled with violence later termed a police riot, Hubert Humphrey won the Democratic nomination. The Republicans nominated Richard Nixon who won a narrow vote, with third party candidate George Wallace capturing 13 percent of the vote.

As president, Richard Nixon insisted that South Vietnamese soldiers carry more of the military burden. At the same time, he sought to slow the flow of North Vietnamese supplies and soldiers into South Vietnam by bombing the Ho Chi Minh Trail in Vietnam and Cambodia. The bombing only reduced the flow of men and supplies by 10 percent. On April 30, 1970, the president sent American ground forces into Cambodia to destroy communist supply bases, violating Cambodian neutrality. The invasion reignited the peace movement and many colleges and universities shut down in protest, particularly after the shooting of innocent students at Kent State University in Ohio and Jackson State University in Mississippi.

Nixon reduced American troop strength in Vietnam from 540,000 to 70,000, but without an active U.S. military presence, South Vietnam's demise was inevitable. President Nixon hoped to negotiate a peace treaty that would allow a decent interval between the American departure from Vietnam and the collapse of the government Saigon. In attempting to reach this goal, Nixon transformed the character of American foreign policy. Nixon realized that long-standing enmities between the Soviet Union and the People's Republic of China made the old image of monolithic communism a fallacy. He hoped improving relations with both nations would aid the peace process but overestimated the Chinese and Soviet influence on North Vietnam.

With his anticommunist background, Nixon knew he could deal with the Chinese. When Mao agreed to a meeting, Nixon visited China in 1972, opening a dialogue that ended with diplomatic relations being established in 1979. Concerned about these developments, the Soviet Union eased its stance, leading to a Nixon trip to Moscow, where talks with Leonid Brezhnev ended with signing of the Strategic Arms Limitations Treaty of 1972. Nixon's successes helped him win a landslide victory over George McGovern in 1972.

After peace talks broke down late in 1972, Nixon ordered heavier bombing of North Vietnam, killing more than 1,500 civilians. When the bombings concluded, the nations resumed peace talks and on January 27, 1973, the United States ended its active involvement in Vietnam. The war did not end until April 30, 1975, when South Vietnam announced its unconditional surrender and Vietnam was unified.

The controversies engendered by the war persisted long after the conflict was over. The legacy of the war was most evident among returning veterans, many of whom received a cold, hostile reception upon their return to the United States. Their frustration and anger was the subject of several films in which they were often shown in a negative context. Not until the late seventies did the popular culture view change to one where the veteran was considered a victim rather than a madman. Vietnam, meanwhile, has experienced a rocky road to recovery. The country suffered from government inefficiency and corruption, unemployment, food shortages, and high inflation, as well as a war against Cambodia. Although Vietnam turned to increased democracy and capitalism to solve the country's problems in 1986, it was not until 1995 that the United States extended diplomatic recognition to Vietnam.

OBJECTIVES

After reading this chapter, you should be able to:

1. Explain why many Americans revere John F. Kennedy and describe his accomplishments as president.

2. Discuss how America became involved in Vietnam before the presidency of Lyndon Johnson.

3. Describe how President Johnson escalated American involvement in Vietnam and the effects of the war on Vietnam and the United States.

4. Identify President Richard Nixon's strategies for ending the war in Vietnam

5. Explain how American understanding of the Vietnam War has changed in recent times.

KEY TERMS
Bay of Pigs
Cuban Missile Crisis
Dien Bien Phu
Flexible Response
Gulf of Tonkin Resolution
Tet Offensive
Vietnamization
The Nixon Doctrine
Ping Pong Diplomacy
Strategic Arms Limitation Treaty of 1972

KEY FIGURES
Ho Chi Minh
John F. Kennedy
Lyndon B. Johnson
Ngo Dinh Diem
Richard Nixon
Robert Kennedy
George Wallace
Henry Kissinger

CHAPTER 28 • VIETNAM AND THE CRISIS OF AUTHORITY

_____ 1. Ho Chi Minh modeled the Democratic Republic of (North) Vietnam's 1946 statement of national independence after which country's?
   a. France's
   b. The United States's
   c. The Soviet Union's

_____ 2. What may have provided John F. Kennedy's margin of victory over Richard Nixon in the 1960 presidential election was Kennedy's
   a. strong anticommunist position
   b. skillful performance in the campaign's televised debates
   c. greater experience in the conduct of foreign policy

_____ 3. The Bay of Pigs invasion
   a. involved the training and transporting of a force of Cuban exiles to Cuba
   b. was a well-kept secret
   c. undermined support for Fidel Castro in Cuba

_____ 4. President Kennedy's main goal in the United States' 1962 decision to blockade Cuba was to
   a. use the CIA to overthrow the Castro government forcibly.
   b. encourage the Soviet Union to stop sending soldiers and aid to Castro.
   c. force the Soviet Union to remove its missiles from Cuba.

_____ 5. President Harry Truman
   a. favored Vietnamese independence
   b. recognized that the age of colonialism was doomed
   c. viewed Vietnam through the lens of Cold War politics

_____ 6. Which country provided $2.6 billion to pay for France's military effort to restore its colonial rule in 1946-54?
   a. Britain
   b. Australia
   c. The United States

_____ 7. During the siege of the French outpost at Dien Bien Phu in 1954, Senator Lyndon Johnson
   a. recommended American military intervention
   b. opposed intervention, calling it an effort to perpetuate "white man's exploitation"
   c. called for the United Nations to send peacekeepers to Vietnam

_____ 8. The countries involved in the 1954 Geneva Conference agreed that
   a. North and South Vietnam should be reunified by popular elections
   b. North and South Vietnam should be two permanently independent countries
   c. the United States should provide military aid to South Vietnam

_____ 9. Following the French defeat in Vietnam, President Eisenhower
   a. provided large sums of money to improve the quality of life of South Vietnamese peasants
   b. strongly objected to President Diem's dictatorial methods
   c. supported President Diem's decision to cancel elections in 1956 to reunify Vietnam

_____ 10. President Kennedy's military policy placed much more stress on _____ than had President Eisenhower's military policy, and was labeled _____.
   a. counterinsurgency; flexible response
   b. nuclear weapons; massive retaliation
   c. naval strength; search and destroy

_____ 11. President Kennedy
   a. opposed American involvement in Vietnam
   b. deployed American ground troops in Vietnam
   c. sent thousands of American advisors to Vietnam

_____ 12. President Kennedy favored the removal of Ngo Dinh Diem from the presidency of South Vietnam after
   a. Diem massacred a large number of Viet Cong
   b. Diem launched attacks on the country's Buddhists
   c. Diem refused to allow American soldiers to engage in combat

_____ 13. President Lyndon Johnson received authorization for the use of force in Vietnam through
   a. the Southeast Asia Treaty Organization
   b. the Gulf of Tonkin Resolution
   c. a declaration of war by Congress

_____ 14. Which of the following was not part of Johnson's strategy for fighting the war in Vietnam?
   a. A bombing campaign against the north, called Operation Rolling Thunder
   b. Dispatching of 500,000 ground troops to Vietnam
   c. Attempting to assassinate North Vietnamese leaders, including Ho Chi Minh

_____ 15. The 1968 Tet Offensive
   a. was depicted in the American news media as a major victory for U. S. forces
   b. brought an immediate end to the Vietnam War
   c. led to the belief in the United States that the Vietnam War was unwinnable

_____ 16. What did President Nixon call his policy to replace U.S. ground troops with South Vietnamese?
   a. Flexible response
   b. Vietnamization
   c. Incursion

_____ 17. From 1969 to 1972, President Nixon's strategy in Vietnam involved
   a. withdrawing all American forces from Vietnam, but supplying South Vietnam with economic aid
   b. decreasing the commitment of American ground troops, but intensifying bombing missions
   c. increasing the American commitment of ground troops

_____ 18. The invasion of Cambodia by U. S. and South Vietnamese forces in the spring of 1970
   a. resulted in a crushing defeat of the U. S. forces
   b. revived the domestic antiwar movement in the United States and led to large demonstrations
   c. led to Chinese intervention on the side of the North Vietnamese

_____ 19. American soldiers were involved in a massacre of South Vietnamese men, women and children in what village?
   a. Hue
   b. My Lai
   c. Da Nang

_____ 20. Which university in 1970 witnessed the first killing of U.S. student protesters?
   a. Kent State University
   b. Harvard University
   c. The University of California at Berkeley

_____ 21. After the final withdrawal of American forces from Southeast Asia
   a. the pro-Western government of South Vietnam fell and was replaced by a communist government
   b. a neutral coalition government was established in South Vietnam
   c. the United States provided reconstruction assistance to North Vietnam

CHAPTER 29 • THE STRUGGLE FOR A JUST SOCIETY

SUMMARY

The 1960s was a decade when hundreds of thousands of ordinary Americans gave new life to the nation's democratic ideals. In this chapter, you read about these efforts. African Americans used sit-ins, freedom rides, and protest marches to fight segregation, poverty, and unemployment. Feminists demanded equal job opportunities and an end to sexual discrimination. Mexican Americans protested discrimination in voting, education, and jobs. Native Americans demanded that the government recognize their land claims and the right of tribes to govern themselves. Gays and lesbians struggled to end discrimination based on sexual orientation. Environmentalists demanded legislation to control the amount of pollution released into the environment.

KEY POINTS

- Early in the decade, African American college students, impatient with the slow pace of legal change, staged sit-ins, freedom rides, and protest marches to challenge segregation in the South. Their efforts led the federal government to pass the Civil Rights Act of 1964, prohibiting discrimination in public facilities and employment, and the 24th Amendment and the Voting Rights Act of 1965, guaranteeing voting rights.

- The example of the civil rights movement inspired other groups to press for equal rights. The women's movement fought equal educational and employment opportunities and a transformation of traditional views about women's place in society.

- Mexican Americans battled for bilingual education programs in schools, unionization of farm workers, improved job opportunities, and increased political power.

- Native Americans pressed for control over their lands and resources, the preservation of native cultures, and tribal self-government.

- Gays and lesbians organized to end legal discrimination based on sexual orientation.

- In a far-reaching effort to reduce poverty, alleviate malnutrition, extend medical care, provide adequate housing, and enhance the employability of the poor, President Lyndon Johnson launched his Great Society Program in 1964. But the Vietnam War, ghetto rioting, and the rise of a militant antiwar movement and the counterculture contributed to a political backlash that would lead the Republican party to control the presidency for twenty of the next 24 years.

CHAPTER SYNOPSIS

During the early 1960s, the civil rights movement entered an activist phase, using sit-ins to obtain equal access to public accommodations, while freedom riders sought to desegregate transportation facilities. In 1962, James Meredith desegregated the University of Mississippi. In 1963, Martin Luther King, Jr. led a campaign to end segregation in Birmingham Alabama.

Violence directed against civil rights activists led President Kennedy to introduce legislation to guarantee equal access to jobs and public accommodations. A. Phillip Randolph and Bayard Rustin organized a march on Washington that brought over 200,000 people to the nation's capital to promote civil rights legislation. The high point was King's "I Have a Dream" speech. The 1964 Civil Rights Act barred discrimination on the basis of race, sex, and national origin and established the Equal Employment Opportunity Commission.

To guarantee black voting rights, King opened a voter registration drive in Selma, Alabama. In 1965, Congress enacted the Voting Rights Act and the states ratified the 27th Amendment, which outlawed poll taxes.

The fight for racial integration was accompanied by a growing movement for black political and economic power. Largely in response to the violence perpetrated by white racists, SNCC and CORE moved away from their earlier emphasis on integration and non-violence. The most highly publicized black power group was the Black Panther party. Partly in response to the growth of black nationalism, the mainstream civil rights movement focus more of its energies on the needs of the poor.

President Lyndon John pushed for passage of civil rights, voting rights, and fair housing legislation. He also supported affirmative action. He named the first black cabinet officer, the first black woman to the federal bench, and the first black Supreme Court justice. He also launched the Great Society program to combat poverty.

Many whites responded to ghetto rioting, black militancy, and civil rights legislation by fleeing from the nation's cities and supporting conservative political candidates such as George Wallace and Richard Nixon. As president, Nixon replaced liberal Supreme Court justices with conservative ones.

During the 1960s, youth was the most influential age group. As a result of the post-war baby boom, one in five Americans was between the age of 14 and 25 and their influence was felt in politics, culture, and fashion.

In 1962, 60 college students formed the Students for a Democratic Society and wrote the Port Huron Statement that express their commitment to participatory democracy. One of the first issues to arouse interest among the young was the impersonality of the modern university. Free speech demonstrations were held at the University of California at Berkeley and quickly spread to other institutions. The Vietnam War was the biggest force in the radicalization of the nation's youth.

The civil rights movement inspired other groups to fight for their rights. In 1966, Betty Friedan and others formed the National Organization of Women to force the Equal Employment Opportunity Commission to address sex discrimination. NOW's major achievements were the issuing of Executive Order 11375 by President Johnson prohibiting government contractors from discriminating on the basis of sex and requiring affirmative action procedures to be instituted; and a ruling against separate want ads for men and women. In rulings that attacked employment discrimination and restrictions on women's service on juries the Supreme Court contributed to the movement for women's rights. In Roe v. Wade, the court affirmed the right to abortion. The women's movement's major defeat was failure to ratify the Equal Rights Amendment to the Constitution.

A new activism against discrimination and poverty emerged among Mexican Americans. Cesar Chavez organized California farmworkers and led a campaign to improve working conditions. Reies Lopez Tijerina focused on recovering lands illegally seized from holders of Spanish and Mexican land grants. Political movements led to bilingual education programs and to efforts to assist undocumented immigrants. The election of state and local officials underscored Mexican Americans' political gains.

Native Americans, the nation's poorest minority, sought to improve conditions on reservation, protect Indians' land rights, and expand educational and employment opportunities. The Native American movement produced gains in health and Indian sovereignty.

A police raid on a gay bar in New York helped spark the gay rights movement. Many gays confronted longstanding public hostility and repressive laws, and openly expressed their sexual preference and organized politically.

In 1962, Rachel Carson awakened environmental consciousness by publishing Silent Spring on the effects of pesticides on the food chain. During the 1960s, environmentalism became a mass movement. While the 1970s saw Congress enact several environment laws, economic stagnation and mounting conservativism in politics eroded some of those gains.

OBJECTIVES

After reading this chapter, you should be able to:

1. Discuss the history of the Civil Rights movement during the 1960s, including the tactics that activists used to fight segregation and racial inequality.

2. Describe the feminist struggle for equal opportunities and an end to sexual discrimination; the Mexican American struggle against discrimination in voting, education, and employment; the Native American struggle for tribal sovereignty and land rights; the gay and lesbian struggle for an end to discrimination based on sexual preference; and the efforts of environmentalists to reduce pollution.

3. Identify the major achievements of Lyndon Johnson's Great Society program and explain why it produced a political backlash against liberalism.

KEY TERMS
Sit-In
Freedom Riders
Civil Rights Act of 1964
24th Amendment
Voting Rights Act of 1965
Black Power
Great Society
Students for a Democratic Society
Counterculture
Equal Rights Amendment
American Indian Movement
Stonewall

KEY FIGURES
Ralph Nader
James Meredith
Martin Luther King, Jr.
Malcolm X
Betty Friedan
Cesar Chavez
Rachel Carson

CHAPTER 29 • THE STRUGGLE FOR A JUST SOCIETY

_____ 1. Which of the following statements about Muhammad Ali is FALSE?
   a. He was born Cassius Marcellus Clay, Jr.
   b. He spoke out openly about social and political topics and joined the Nation of Islam
   c. Following his conviction for refusing induction into the military, he spent the next two decades in prison

_____ 2. By 1961, a new phase in the civil rights movement began that depended on _____ to attack segregation
   a. court decisions
   b. federal intervention
   c. non-violent direct action

_____ 3. Where was the tactic of the sit-in protest first used?
   a. At a Woolworth's lunch counter in Greensboro, North Carolina
   b. At a high school in Little Rock, Arkansas
   c. On a bus in Birmingham, Alabama

_____ 4. The freedom rides were trying to end segregation of
   a. schools
   b. bus terminals
   c. restaurants

_____ 5. Who was the author of "Letter from Birmingham Jail" that warned that frustrated African Americans might turn to violence?
   a. Stokely Carmichael
   b. Martin Luther King, Jr.
   c. Malcolm X

_____ 6. For nearly two years, John Kennedy did little on behalf of the civil rights movement because he
   a. personally disliked Martin Luther King, Jr.
   b. needed congressional voting support from white southern Democrats
   c. had not promised any civil rights legislation in his election campaign

_____ 7. In his 1963 "I Have a Dream" speech during the March on Washington, Martin Luther King, Jr., expressed his desire for
   a. black nationalism
   b. racial amalgamation
   c. racial integration

_____ 8. Which was NOT a major achievement of the Civil Rights movement during the 1960s?
   a. The desegregation of the armed forces
   b. Enactment of legislation prohibiting discrimination in housing and employment
   c. Prohibition against literacy tests and poll taxes

_____ 9. Who was known as the Nation of Islam's most effective minister until he broke from the group in 1964 and formed his own group, the Organization of Afro-American Unity?
   a. Louis Farrakhan
   b. Thurgood Marshall
   c. Malcolm X

_____ 10. The Black Muslim's advocacy of black separatism drew most of its support from
   a. poor urban African Americans
   b. middle class African Americans
   c. white liberals

_____ 11. Malcolm X believed that _____ was the severest damage to African Americans caused by white discrimination.
   a. poverty
   b. self-hate
   c. political impotence

_____ 12. The growing militancy of the civil rights movement in the mid-1960s was the result of all of the following EXCEPT
  a. white racist violence
  b. the failure of the first phases of the civil rights movement to address the problem of urban poverty
  c. outside agitation by Communists

_____ 13. By 1967, black power was endorsed by all of the following organizations EXCEPT
  a. SNCC (the Student Non-Violent Coordinating Committee)
  b. CORE (the Congress of Racial Equality)
  c. the NAACP (the National Association for the Advancement of Colored People)
  d. the Black Panthers

_____ 14. The Watts riot, the first of several summertime race riots between 1965 and 1968, occurred in
  a. Detroit
  b. Los Angeles
  c. Washington, D.C.

_____ 15. _____ established the legal basis for busing school students as a tool for desegregating schools.
  a. Swann v. Charlotte-Mechlenburg Board of Education
  b. President Johnson's Executive Order 11246
  c. The Civil Rights Act of 1964

_____ 16. Which of the following was NOT an achievement of Lyndon Johnson's Great Society program?
  a. Medicare and Medicaid, providing medical care for the elderly and the poor
  b. The Voting Rights Act, authorizing federal officials to register voters
  c. The Peace Corps, sending Americans to work on projects for economic and social betterment in underdeveloped countries

_____ 17. The Supreme Court decisions in _Mapp v. Ohio, Gideon v. Wainwright,_ and _Escobedo v. Illinois_ protected the rights of
  a. women seeking abortions
  b. criminal defendants
  c. aliens residing in the United States

_____ 18. The women's movement was able to achieve all but one of the following goals. Select the EXCEPTION.
  a. An executive order requiring affirmative action in employment by government contractors
  b. Ratification of an Equal Rights Amendment to the Constitution prohibiting discrimination on the basis of sex.
  c. Legislation prohibiting sexual harassment in schools and mandating equality in school activities, including athletics

_____ 19. What concept did Betty Friedan's _The Feminine Mystique_ contribute to feminist ideology?
  a. Men oppress women because they fear them
  b. Women are conditioned to believe they can only find fulfillment as wives and mothers
  c. Girls lose self-esteem as they enter adolescence

_____ 20. Cesar Chavez succeeded in
  a. halting the Bracero Plan, a special program for Mexican workers.
  b. organizing migratory farm workers
  c. forming a Hispanic political party in the Southwest, calling for improved public services and an end to job discrimination

_____ 21. America's poorest minority group in the 1960s was
  a. African Americans
  b. Mexican Americans
  c. Native Americans

CHAPTER 30 • POWER SHIFTS: THE EMERGENCE OF THE SOUTH AND WEST

SUMMARY

The central political, social, economic, and cultural fact of the second half of the 20th century was the shift in power from the older industrial states and cities of the Northeast and upper Midwest to the South and West. In this chapter you read about the reasons for the rise of the Sunbelt; myths and realities about the history of the West; and the distinctive politics of the western United States.

KEY POINTS

- Since 1945, the South and West have experienced the country's greatest growth and have dominated the presidency.

- Growing prosperity in the South is the result of technology, a shift in race relations, and the movement of industry into the South, which was accelerated by World War II.

- In contrast to the myth that the West has been exploited by the East and by the federal government, much of the region's growth has depended on federal financing and construction. Especially important are water projects, including dams, power, and irrigation projects.

- Since World War II, the western economy has shifted away from extractive industries such as mining, agriculture, ranging, oil, and logging and has developed a more diversified economy.

- Rapid western growth has produced many environmental problems.

- Western politics has tended to emphasize individual liberty.

CHAPTER SYNOPSIS

A central fact of the second half of the 20th century was a shift in power from the older industrial cities of the Northeast and Midwest to the South and West. Long the nation's poorest region, the South experienced increasing prosperity, partly as a result of the spread of air conditioning and the growth of tourism. The weakening of racial discrimination also helped prosperity develop.

Government investment during and after World War II, especially in defense industries, nurtured industrialization in the South. Less expensive land, lower wages and taxes, and less unionization also lured new industries to the South. Rapid economic growth increased urbanization and led to declining dependence on agriculture.

The image of the West as a region of strong masculinity, of independence and strength was touted in advertising, art, popular fiction, and the movies. A popular theme in western movies was antagonism toward the East and the federal government that often found expression in real life.

Ironically, the post-World War II prosperity of the region was largely the result of federal programs. The New Deal financed western dams, power, and irrigation projects. Particularly in California, the federal government financed factories, military bases and capital improvements that stimulated heavy migration into the region.

The move of the Dodgers baseball team from Brooklyn to Los Angeles symbolized the westward slant of the nation. The western economy was transformed from a focus on extractive industries to increasing diversification. The rise of electronics, aerospace, high technology and service industries created millions of new jobs that fueled immigration and spurred population growth.

The West developed as an automobile culture, influencing the rise of expansive urban areas and an extensive road system. But auto exhausts created a smog problem. The West also suffered from problems of disposing of nuclear wastes, soil erosion, and from depleted water supplies.

Barry Goldwater's conservative politics reflected his western upbringing. Goldwater railed against big government and eastern interests. Despite his defeat by Lyndon Johnson in 1964, the returns showed a growing conservative ascendancy in the West. Population growth in the South and West contributed to a political power shift and the increasing strength of the Republican party. The Sagebrush rebellion failed to loosen the federal grip on open lands, but the conservative drift continued.

OBJECTIVES

After reading this chapter, you should be able to:

1. Describe the reasons for the shift in power from the Northeast and upper Midwest to the South and West

2. Explain why the South became more prosperous and industrial after World War II.

3. Discuss the ways that the West has been depicted in American popular culture, and the way that these images diverge from historical realities.

4. Explain the shift from a western economy based on extractive industries to a more diversified economy.

5. Identify the distinctive features of politics in the West.

KEY TERMS
Sunbelt
Hydraulic Society
Great Society
Sagebrush Rebellion
Contract with America

KEY FIGURES
John Wayne
Henry J. Kaiser
Walter O'Malley
Barry Goldwater
Ken Kesey
Newt Gingrich

PRACTICE TEST

CHAPTER 30 • POWER SHIFTS: THE EMERGENCE OF THE SOUTH AND WEST

_____ 1. John Wayne
   a. embodied the image of the rugged Western hero
   b. opposed the Vietnam War and supported affirmative action
   c. was warmly embraced by liberals during the 1960s

_____ 2. Which was the poorest and most economically backward region of the United States at the end of World War II?
   a. the Midwest
   b. the Northeast
   c. the South

_____ 3. The central political, social, economic, and cultural fact of the second half of the 20th century was:
   a. the steady and unbroken expansion of the role of the federal government
   b. the steady rise in American standard of living
   c. the shift in power from the Northeast and upper Midwest to the South and West

_____ 4. Between 1964 and 2000, every elected American president
   a. was educated at an Ivy League college
   b. came from the South or West
   c. served only one term in office

_____ 5. Which technology was most critical to the rise of industrialization in the South after World War II?
   a. the mechanical cotton picker
   b. air conditioning
   c. railroads

_____ 6. Which of the following developments has NOT transformed the South since World War II?
   a. Much of the gap between the South and the rest of the country in education, health standards, and wages disappeared
   b. Unionization became a strong in the South as in the rest of the United States
   c. The South renounced overt racism and accepted industrialization

_____ 7. Northern manufacturers became more attracted to relocating in the South because of all but one of the following. Select the EXCEPTION.
   a. lower taxes
   b. cheaper land
   c. more extensive social services

_____ 8. Which of the following statements about the West's economy is TRUE?
   a. The federal government significantly hindered the region's economic development
   b. Westerners received substantial amounts of federal dollars which have contributed to the region's economic growth
   c. The East has had a near monopoly over banks and financial institutions in the West

_____ 9. A hydraulic society
   a. is a society that emphasizes dam, power, and irrigation projects
   b. is a society with a plentiful water supply
   c. is a society that relies on shipping rather than trucking and railroads

_____ 10. Henry Kaiser
   a. moved the Brooklyn Dodgers to Los Angeles
   b. depended on government loans to finance his shipyards
   c. transformed Las Vegas into a center of legalized gambling

_____ 11. Prior to World War II, the Western economy was best characterized as
   a. an extractive economy
   b. a diversified economy
   c. an urban and industrial economy

_____ 12. In contrast to the eastern United States, the West
   a. was less dependent on the automobile
   b. had a larger supply of water
   c. was more dependent on tourism

_____ 13. Political thinking in the West has tended to emphasize
   a. government planning
   b. individual freedom
   c. states' rights

_____ 14. Barry Goldwater
   a. wanted to restrict the activities of the federal government
   b. believed that a strong government was necessary to protect individual freedom and economic opportunity
   c. called for subsidies and price supports for farmers

_____ 15. The Sagebrush Rebellion
   a. was a revolt against taxes
   b. demanded that the federal government cede control of western lands to the individual states
   c. called on the government to end construction of western dams

CHAPTER 31 • CRISES AND RESURGENCE, 1970–1990

SUMMARY

In the late 1970s, many academic authorities suggested that the United States was in decline, and that Japan and West Germany were growing faster and were beginning to dominate cutting-edge industries such as consumer electronics and luxury automobiles. Americans were cynical about their government, anxious about the future of their economy, and uneasy about America's proper role in the world.

Presidents Nixon, Ford, and Carter sought to address America's changing role in the world through détente and arms control negotiations. President Ronald Reagan's strategy emphasized increased military spending and a more assertive foreign policy. On the domestic front, President Reagan addressed stagflation addressed through deregulation, tax cuts, and cutbacks in government spending on social programs.

The collapse of East European Communism and the breakup of the Soviet Union brought the Cold War to a sudden and unexpected end. It also made the United States the world's sole superpower.

KEY POINTS

- The last quarter of the 20th century was shaped by three fundamental challenges that arose in the late 1960s and early 1970s. The first was a crisis of political leadership. Public cynicism toward politicians intensified, political party discipline declined, and lobbies and special interest groups grew in power.

- The second challenge involved wrenching economic transformations. Economic growth slowed, productivity flagged, inflation and oil prices soared, family income stagnated, and major industries faltered in the face of foreign competition.

- The third challenge involved growing uncertainty over America's proper role in the world. A major challenge facing policymakers was how to preserve the nation's international prestige and influence in the face of mounting public opposition to direct overseas interventions.

- Presidents Nixon, Ford, and Carter attempted to strengthen the United States' influence in foreign affairs through détente and arms control negotiations. President Reagan emphasized sharply increased military spending and an assertive foreign policy.

- President Reagan addressed economic stagnation and inflation through deregulation, tax cuts, reductions in government budget deficits, and the development of new computer and communication technologies.

- The collapse of the Soviet Union made the United States the only superpower.

CHAPTER SYNOPSIS

The Vietnam War and the Watergate Affair contributed to a decline in the prestige and power of the presidency. To prevent future Watergate-like scandals and to regain constitutional powers relinquished to the executive branch, Congress enacted a series of reforms, including the War Powers Act, the Freedom of Information Act, and Campaign Finance Reform.

After 1973, the American economy was characterized by sluggish growth, rising inflation, and a failure to compete with foreign companies. Wages and family income remained static even though the number of working women increased.

Inflation became a major problem when President Johnson prosecuted the Vietnam war without raising taxes to pay for it. Unemployed dropped as wages rose and demand grew. Government deficits also rose. In the early 1970s, crop failures coupled with sharply rising prices in such products as oil fueled inflation. This wiped out savings while stimulating speculation in precious metals and real estate, causing a decline in investment in new physical plants and technology. Dramatic increases occurred in the number of the homeless and of Americans who could not afford health insurance.

Foreign competition chipped away at the United States' economic preeminence. Foreign companies began to dominate such industries as consumer electronics, luxury automobiles, and machine tools. Pioneering American technology was exported overseas and manufactured by foreign firms. During the 1970s, there was a loss of an estimated 30 million jobs in basic industry. The displaced workers lost their savings and had to settle for lower-paying jobs that reduced their communities' tax bases. In 1982, unemployment hit 10.8 percent and inflation reached double digits.

The Vietnam War caused a reevaluation of America's role in the world. President Nixon redefined the American relationship with China and the Soviet Union by developing a policy of détente. Nixon wanted to curb the arms race and improve relations by shifting the emphasis from anticommunism to national interest. The first step was to normalize relations with China. The United States also sought to built up regional powers such as Iran and Saudi Arabia to eliminate the need for military interventions. By the late 1970s, many Americans regarded the policy of détente as a failure, as the Soviets continued their arms buildup and boasted of their gains made at America's expense. The establishment of an anti-American Islamic state in Iran and the seizure of the American embassy and diplomats as hostages symbolized the declining American influence in the world.

The traumas of the 1970s created a loss of confidence among Americans. Ronald Reagan capitalized on this frustration to win a landslide victory in the 1980 presidential election. Reagan blamed the nation's economic woes on a decline in capital investment and a tax structure that worked against productivity. He achieved a tax cut, broke an air traffic controllers' strike, doubled the defense budget, and deregulated the banking, airline, and natural gas industries. His administration also eased environmental controls and opened up federal lands to private development. But while the economy was enjoying its longest period of expansion since World War II, and while inflation and unemployment were down, the federal budget deficit and national debt were both rapidly rising.

In the early 1980s, Reagan pursued an aggressive policy that intensified tensions with the Soviet Union. In 1985, he issued the Reagan doctrine that declared American support for anti-communist revolutions. U.S. aid and military assistance was provided to Afghans and to Nicaraguan contra rebels. The president authorized arms sales to Iran, diverting the profits to the Nicaraguan rebels. The exposure of the Iran-Contra affair and the resulting congressional investigation weakened the president's influence.

The rise of Mikhail Gorbachev led to an easing of tensions with the Soviets. Gorbachev instituted policies of liberalization (*glastnost*) and economic reform (*perestroika*). The most important development of the late 1980s was the collapse of east European communism. East and West German were unified and the Soviet Union itself broke into a number of republics.

OBJECTIVES

After reading this chapter, you should be able to:

1. Identify the "imperial presidency" and explain why it came to an end in the 1970s.

2. Describe the problems the American economy faced during the 1970s and the ways that the federal government responded.

3. Identify the policy of détente and explain why many Americans at the end of the 1970s believed that the policy had been a failure.

4. Discuss how the Reagan revolution altered domestic and foreign policy.

KEY TERMS
Watergate Affair
War Powers Act
Freedom of Information Act
Oil Crisis
Stagflations
Deregulation
Détente
Camp David Accords
Iranian Hostage Crisis
"Reagan Doctrine"
Glastnost
Perestroika

KEY FIGURES
Richard Nixon
Henry Kissinger
Gerald Ford
Jimmy Carter
Mikhail Gorbachev
George H.W. Bush

PRACTICE TEST

CHAPTER 31 • CRISES AND RESURGENCE, 1970–1990

_____ 1. The Watergate incident that started the chain of events leading to President Nixon's downfall involved
   a. the wiretapping of the Democratic party's national headquarters
   b. political sabotage of the campaign of Democratic Senator Edmund Muskie
   c. illegal use of the FBI to harass political opponents

_____ 2. The tapes that President Nixon kept of his Oval Office conversations indicate that the president
   a. was involved in the planning of the Watergate break-in
   b. stole the election of 1972
   c. was involved in a conspiracy to obstruct justice in the Watergate affair

_____ 3. The investigation of the Watergate affair revealed that the Nixon White House had done all of the following EXCEPT
   a. done political favors for business groups in exchange for campaign contributions
   b. deceived Congress about the secret bombing of Cambodia in 1969 and 1970
   c. kidnapped anti-Nixon radical leaders who planned to disrupt the 1972 Republican National Convention

_____ 4. For his role in the Watergate affair, Richard Nixon was
   a. impeached and removed from office
   b. forced to resign the presidency
   c. sent to prison

_____ 5. Public respect for the office of the presidency eroded in the late 1960s and early 1970s for all but one of the following reasons. Select the EXCEPTION.
   a. The disclosure that Vice President Spiro T. Agnew had accepted bribes while he was serving as governor of Maryland.
   b. The revelation that the Nixon White House had planted electronic eavesdropping equipment in the Democratic Party's national headquarters
   c. The discovery that President Richard Nixon had had an affair with a White House intern

_____ 6. To curb the powers of the president and eliminate corruption in presidential campaigns, Congress enacted all but one of the following measures in the early 1970s EXCEPT
   a. Requiring presidents to receive explicit Congressional authorization in order to send American forces into combat
   b. Imposing limits on campaign contributions and providing funds for presidential candidates who met certain qualifications
   c. Restricting a president to two terms in office

_____ 7. The War Powers Act of 1973 was passed mainly in response to concern that Presidents Johnson and Nixon
   a. involved the nation's armed forces in combat without congressional approval
   b. made treaties without informing the Senate
   c. spent funds that Congress had failed to appropriate

_____ 8. The policy of détente was intended to
   a. rebuild the strength of the American military following the Vietnam war
   b. strengthen American relations with Latin America
   c. used the lure of American trade to extract foreign policy concessions from the Soviet Union and China

_____ 9. Richard Nixon's approach to China was to
   a. isolate the mainland government because of its support for North Vietnam in the Vietnam War
   b. visit mainland China and begin diplomatic relations
   c. try to stir Soviet-Chinese border conflict so that both nations would be preoccupied with each other and reduce tensions with the United States

_____ 10. Which was NOT a major economic problem during the 1970s?
   a. rising oil prices and climbing rates of inflation
   b. mounting foreign competition displacing American jobs and stagnating real wages
   c. a sharply falling stock market

_____ 11. All but one of the following suggested that the United States was losing influence in world affairs during the 1970s. Select the EXCEPTION.
   a. The fall of South Vietnam to communist North Vietnam
   b. The seizure of American hostages in Iran
   c. Iraq's invasion of Kuwait

_____ 12. Which was NOT part of Richard Nixon's efforts to restore American influence in foreign affairs?
   a. He began trade and diplomatic talks with China
   b. He initiated détente with the Soviet Union
   c. He helped establish NATO, a military alliance combining the United States, Canada, and nations in Western Europe

_____ 13. President Ronald Reagan combated stagflation by all of the following EXCEPT
   a. deregulation
   b. cutting taxes and attempting to reduce the scale of government
   c. wage and price controls

_____ 14. In the Reagan Doctrine, the Reagan administration declared that it would
   a. allow all nations to determine their own political and economic future.
   b. openly support anti-Communist forces fighting the Soviets or Soviet-backed governments.
   c. push for free trade

_____ 15. The so-called Iran-Contra Scandal involved the Reagan administration in
   a. a secret CIA effort to arm Iranian exiles and stage an invasion.
   b. selling weapons to the anti-American government in Iran and using the profit to aid the pro-American Contras in Nicaragua.
   c. planting misleading intelligence information with the governments of Iran and Iraq in order to stir up a war between them.

_____ 16. Mikhail Gorbachev attempted to reform Soviet society in all but one of the following ways. Select the EXCEPTION.
   a. He wanted to move from a one party to a multiparty political system
   b. He wanted to shift from a command economy to an increasingly market-oriented economy
   c. He wanted his country to totally abandon Communism

CHAPTER 32 • AMERICA IN OUR TIME

SUMMARY

On September 11, 2001, in the deadliest terrorist attack on American soil, hijackers crashed passenger planes into the Pentagon and the World Trade Center towers in New York, toppling the 110-story twin towers, killing all aboard the jets and nearly 3,000 people on the ground.

Authorities quickly discovered that the attacks had been masterminded by a Middle Eastern terrorist network known as Al-Qaeda, led by a Saudi Arabian dissident named Osama Bin-Laden. Al-Qaeda claimed that its hatred of the United States was fueled by the presence of American troops in Saudi Arabia, the U.S. embargo against the government of Saddam Hussein in Iraq, and U.S. support for Israel.

During the last years of the twentieth century, the United States became the world's sole superpower. It possessed the world's most productive economy and most mighty military. It dominated global trade and banking and its popular culture was influential across much of the globe.

The end of the Cold War unleashed violent ethnic, religious, national conflicts, especially in the Balkans, the Middle East, and Africa. The first important foreign policy crisis of the post-Cold War era involved Panama, which the United States invaded in 1989 to safeguard American lives and protect the Canal Zone. This was followed in 1990 by Iraq's invasion and occupation of Kuwait, which was reversed by the Gulf War. The breakup of the former Yugoslavia resulted in U.S. intervention in Bosnia and Kosovo. The September 11, 2001, led the United States to overthrow the Taliban government in Afghanistan that had provided a haven to al-Quaeda, and, in 2003, toppling the government of Saddam Hussein in Iraq.

KEY POINTS

- On September 11, 2001 hijackers who were members of a terrorist network known as al-Qaeda turned commercial airlines into missiles and attacked key symbols of American economic and military might.

- The terrorists' motivation lay in their rabid hatred of American values and culture, U.S. policies in the Middle East, and our country's military and economic power.

- The September 11th attacks were followed by apparently unrelated acts of bioterrorism, as anthrax-laden letters contaminated post offices and Congressional office buildings.

- During the 1990s, the U.S. economy grew rapidly due to a sharp fall in interest rates and the price of oil, the growth of new computer and communication technologies, and globalization: the expansion of international trade, finance, and entertainment.

- With the Cold War over, bitter ethnic conflicts have erupted in Angola, the Balkans, Burundi, Chechnya, Iraq, Israel and Palestine, Kashmir, Liberia, Northern Ireland, Rwanda, Sierra Leone, Somalia, Sri Lanka, and Turkey.

- The United States intervened in Panama, the Persian Gulf, Somalia, Haiti, and the former Yugoslavia, and responded to the September 11, 2001, terrorist strikes by defeating Afghanistan's Taliban government and, in 2003, toppling the government of Saddam Hussein in Iraq.

CHAPTER SYNOPSIS

As the 21st century began, the United States had achieved a degree of economic, cultural, and military preeminence unmatched since the period immediately following World War II. Among some people, American preeminence provoked hatred, envy, and resentment.

In the 1970s, the American economy suffered from sluggish growth, rapidly rising prices and interest rates, high rates of unemployment, and a stagnant stock market. Especially worrisome was a slowdown in productivity growth. In the mid-1990s, the United States entered an economic boom resulting from a decline in the price of oil, the restructuring of American businesses, and the growth of new computer and communications technologies, which contributed to productivity improvements.

Intense partisanship and extremely close presidential elections characterized politics during the Post-Cold War era. During President George H.W. Bush's term in office, Congress provided subsidies to low income families to defray childcare costs; and prohibited job discrimination against the disabled. A sluggish economy and mounting budget deficits helped to elect Bill Clinton president in 1992.

A self-described "New Democrat," Clinton persuaded Congress to raise taxes on the wealthiest Americans and on gasoline; and negotiated the North American Free Trade Agreement (NAFTA) and establishment of the

World Trade Organization (WTO), to reduce trade barriers. He also convinced Congress to enact a waiting period for handgun purchases and a ban on the sale of assault weapons; to raise the minimum wage and the Earned Income Tax Credit; and to pass welfare reform, limiting the time that people could spend on welfare rolls and requiring welfare recipients to work or receive training. In December 1998, the House of Representatives impeached President Clinton for committing perjury before grand juries, obstructing justice, and abusing his power in connection with a sexual liaison with a White House intern. The Senate, however, failed to muster the two-thirds vote required for conviction and removal from office.

The end of the Cold War unleashed violent ethnic, religious, and national conflicts, especially in the Balkans, the Middle East, and Africa. America's first significant post-Cold War foreign policy crisis involved Panama in 1989. President George H.W. Bush dispatched 10,000 U.S. troops to force General Manuel Noriega from power. Following Iraq's invasion of Kuwait in 1990, President Bush organized an international coalition that restored Kuwaiti independence.

A major foreign policy issue of the Clinton presidency was when the United States should intervene to suppress conflict within sovereign nations. After 18 American peacekeepers were killed in Somalia in 1993, President Clinton quickly withdrew American forces from the African nation. Based partly on that experience, he refused to send American forces to Rwanda, where the ruling Hutu ethnic group killed more than 800,000 Tutsis in 1994. That year, the president did send American forces into Haiti to oversee that country's transition from military to civilian rule.

The most heated debates over American overseas intervention involved the former Yugoslavia. After Yugoslavia refused to grant autonomy to the province of Kosovo, the United States and its NATO allies launched a bombing campaign in 1999, forcing Yugoslav forces to leave the province.

The 2000 election was the first in 112 years in which a president lost the popular vote but captured enough states to win the electoral vote. It took five weeks to determine the election's outcome, which hinged on a few hundred votes in Florida. By a 5-4 majority, the U.S. Supreme Court halted a recount ordered by the Florida Supreme Court on the ground that it violated the principle that all votes must be treated equally and that there was not enough time to conduct a new manual recount that would meet constitutional muster.

Terrorist attacks on New York's World Trade Center and the Pentagon in Washington, D.C., on September 11, 2001, shaped the presidency of George W. Bush, the son of former president George H.W. Bush. In retaliation for the attacks, a U.S.-led coalition overthrew the Taliban government of Afghanistan, which harbored al-Qaeda, the terrorist networks that had staged the assaults. Congress enacted legislation giving law enforcement agencies broader authority to detain or deport aliens and to conduct wiretaps. It also created a cabinet-level Department of Homeland Security to reduce the country's vulnerability to terrorism. In 2003, the United States overthrew the government of Saddam Hussein in Iraq, one of the countries that President Bush regarded (along with Iran and North Korea) as part of an "axis of evil."

OBJECTIVES

1. Describe the events of September 11, 2001; identify the perpetrators of the terrorist attacks and their motivations; and explain the American response.

2. Explain why the United States entered an economic boom during the mid-1990s after many years of slow economic growth and slowly growing rates of productivity.

3. Describe the impact of the end of the Cold War on international stability.

4. Explain the resurgence of the American economy in the mid and late 1990s.

5. Explain why the House of Representatives voted to impeach President Clinton and why the Senate failed to convict him.

6. Identify the countries that United States intervened in during the late 1980s and 1990s and explain why.

KEY TERMS
Al-Qaeda
Bosnia
Contact With America
Globalization
Kosovo
North American Free Trade Agreement
Rwanda
Taliban

KEY FIGURES
George H.W. Bush
George W. Bush
Bill Clinton
Francis Fukuyama
Saddam Hussein
Michael Jordan
Osama bin Laden
Manuel Noriega

CHAPTER 32 • AMERICA IN OUR TIME

_____ 1. On September 11, 2001, terrorists attacked all but one of the following buildings. Select the EXCEPTION.
   a. The Pentagon
   b. The U.S. Capitol
   c. The World Trade Center

_____ 2. How many airliners were hijacked on September 11, 2001?
   a. three
   b. four
   c. five

_____ 3. The mastermind behind the terrorist attack was
   a. Timothy McVeigh
   b. Saddam Hussein
   c. Osama Bin Laden

_____ 4. The terrorist network behind the attack is known as
   a. Al Quaeda
   b. the NLF
   c. the KGB

_____ 5. The United States responded to the terrorist strikes by attacking the Taliban government, which harbored the terrorists, in:
   a. Afghanistan
   b. Iraq
   c. Yemen

_____ 6. Several weeks after the September 11th terrorist strike, the United States suffered a number of deaths produced by
   a. smallpox
   b. sarin gas
   c. anthrax

_____ 7. The term globalization refers to:
   a. the movement of labor, capital, natural resources, entertainment, and trade across international borders
   b. support for policies that promote a sustainable natural environment
   c. the acquisition of overseas territories

_____ 8. As President, the first President George Bush did all but one of the following. Select the EXCEPTION.
   a. He sent American forces into Panama to force that country's strongman from power
   b. He dispatched the American forces to the Persian Gulf to expel the Iraqi military from Kuwait
   c. He ordered the U.S. military to force Serbia to remove its forces from Kosovo

_____ 9. The major reason the first President Bush was defeated for reelection in 1992 was
   a. his failure to remove Saddam Hussein from power in Iraq
   b. a deadly race riot in Los Angeles
   c. the nation's sluggish economy which was mired in recession

_____ 10. Bill Clinton's major political success was
   a. cutting taxes
   b. enacting a system of national health care
   c. reforming the nation's welfare system

_____ 11. The economic boom of the late 1990s was due to all of the following factors EXCEPT
   a. sharply falling prices of commodities such as oil
   b. the growth of new computer and communication technologies
   c. sharply rising military spending

_____ 12. The major foreign policy crisis of the Clinton presidency involved
   a. Iraq's invasion of Kuwait
   b. the breakup of Yugoslavia
   c. terrorist attacks on the World Trade Center and Pentagon